WORLD MAP: PHYSICAL

ARCTIC OCEAN

Svalbard

Norwegian
Sea

N. Cape

North
Sea

Baltic Sea

L. Ladoga

Scandinavia

Ural Mts.

Ob

West
Siberian
Plain

Irtysh

Novaya
Zemlya

Severnaya
Zemlya

Yenisey

Lr. Tunguska

New Siberian Is.

Lena

Aldan

Angara

A s i a

S i b e r i a

Sayan Mts.

Altai

Stanovoy Ra.

Baikal

Amur

Kamchatka

Sea of
Okhotsk

Sakhalin

Hokkaido

Europe

Mont
Blanc
4808

Apennines

Carpathian

Alps

Balkans

Danube

Pic d'Aneto
404

Black Sea

Elbrus
5642

Caucasus

Caspian Sea

Aral
Sea

Syrdarya

Amudarya

L. Balkhash

Tian Shan

Tarim
Basin

Pamirs

Hindu Kush

K2
8611

Karakoram

Kunlun Shan

Qilian Shan

Hwang-Ho

North China Plain

Gobi
Desert

Korea

Yellow
Sea

Sea of
Japan

Japan

Honshu

Mt. Fuji
3776

Don

Volga

Mediterranean Sea

Anatolia

Mt. Ararat
5165

Elburz Mts.

Zagros

Tigris

Euphrates

Dead
Sea
-403

Isthmus
of Suez

Libyan
Desert

Sulaiman Ra.

Thar Desert

Plateau of Tibet

Himalaya

Mt. Everest
8848

Gongga Shan
7556

Yangtze

China

Si

East
China
Sea

Taiwan

PACIFIC

Wake

Hoggar

Tibesti

Sahara

Africa

Sahel

Guinea

Red Sea

Arabia

Rub' al Khali

The Gulf

Nile

White Nile

Blue Nile

L. Chad

Mt. Cameroon
4095

Congo

Congo
Basin

Kasai

Ethiopian
Highlands

L.
Turkana

Somali
Peninsula

Socotra

C. Guardafui

Arabian
Sea

W. Ghats

Deccan

E. Ghats

India

Ganges

Indus

Salween

Mekong

Indo-
China

Hainan

Bay of
Bengal

C. Comorin

Ceylon

Str. of Malacca

Sumatra

South China Sea

Philippine
Is.

Mariana Is.

Guam

Mariana Trench
11022

Marshall
Is.

Kinabalu
4101

Celebes
Sea

Caroline Is.

OCEAN

Borneo

Celebes

Moluccas

Gilbert
Is.

Nauru

Mt. Kenya
5199

Lake
Victoria

Kilimanjaro
5895

L.
Tanganyika

Seychelles

INDIAN

OCEAN

Java
Sea

Java

Banda
Sea

Timor

Puncak Jaya
5029

New Guinea

Bismarck
Arch.

Solomon
Is.

Ellice
Is.

L. Malawi

Zambezi

Comoros

Madagascar

Mozambique Chan.

Pic Boby
2658

Mauritius

Réunion

7450
Java Trench

Sunda Is.

Cocos

Torres Str.

C. York

Coral
Sea

New
Hebrides

Fiji
Is.

Cubango

Orange

Drakensberg

Kalahari
Desert

Cape of
Good Hope

Hamersley
Ra.

MacDonnell
Ra.

Great Divide

Australia

Great Victoria
Desert

New
Caledonia

Crozet Is.

Kerguelen

C. Leeuwin

Great
Australian
Bight

Murray

Darling

Great Divide

Mt.
Kosciuszko
2237

Bass Str.

Tasman
Sea

North I.

New
Zealand

Aoraki-
Mt. Cook
3753

South I.

Tasmania

SOUTHERN OCEAN

Queen Maud Land

Enderby Land

Queen Mary
Coast

Wilkes Land

South Magnetic
Pole

Antarctica

Victoria
Land

Ross Sea

EAST FROM GREENWICH

PROJECTION: HAMMER EQUAL AREA

COPYRIGHT: GEORGE PHILIP LTD.

PHILIP'S
GREAT WORLD ATLAS

PHILIP'S
GREAT WORLD ATLAS

Specialist Geography Consultants

Philip's is grateful to the following people for acting as specialist geography consultants on the 'Introduction to World Geography' front section:

Professor D. Brunsden, Kings College, University of London, UK

Dr C. Clarke, Oxford University, UK

Professor P. Haggett, University of Bristol, UK

Professor M-L. Hsu, University of Minnesota, Minnesota, USA

Professor K. McLachlan, Geopolitical and International Boundaries Research Centre, School of Oriental and African Studies, University of London, UK

Professor M. Monmonier, Syracuse University, New York, USA

Professor M. J. Tooley, University of St Andrews, UK

Dr T. Unwin, Royal Holloway, University of London, UK

Philip's would also like to thank:

Keith Lye

Robin Scagell

Dr I. S. Evans, Durham University, UK

Dr Andrew Tatham, The Royal Geographical Society

Images of Earth (pages xvii–xxxii)
All satellite images in this section courtesy of NPA Group Limited, Edenbridge, Kent (www.satmaps.com)

Introduction to World Geography
Picture Acknowledgements
Courtesy of NPA Group, Edenbridge, UK 9, 48
Science Photo Library /Earth Satellite Corporation 20, /NOAA 22
bottom left and bottom right

Illustrations
Stefan Chabluk
William Donohoe
Bernard Thornton Artists /Steve Seymour

Star charts
John Cox and Richard Monkhouse

Cartography by Philip's

Published in Great Britain in 2001
by Philip's,
a division of Octopus Publishing Group Ltd,
2–4 Heron Quays, London E14 4JP

This edition produced for Borders, 2002

Copyright © 2001 Philip's

ISBN 0–681–62753–0

Printed in Slovenia

Details of other Philip's titles and services can be found on our website at:
www.philips-maps.co.uk

Philip's World Maps

The reference maps which form the main body of this atlas have been prepared in accordance with the highest standards of international cartography to provide an accurate and detailed representation of the Earth. The scales and projections used have been carefully chosen to give balanced coverage of the world, while emphasizing the most densely populated and economically significant regions. A hallmark of Philip's mapping is the use of hill shading and relief colouring to create a graphic impression of landforms: this makes the maps exceptionally easy to read. However, knowledge of the key features employed in the construction and presentation of the maps will enable the reader to derive the fullest benefit from the atlas.

Map Sequence

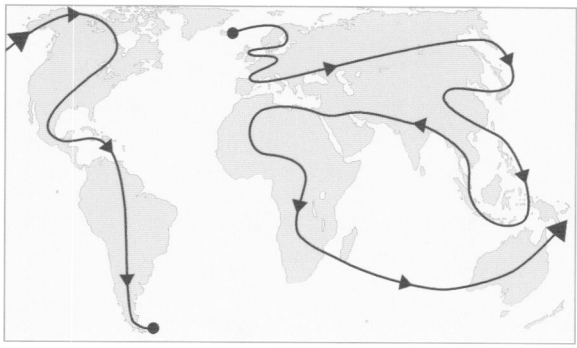

The atlas covers the Earth continent by continent: first Europe; then its land neighbour Asia (mapped north before south, in a clockwise sequence), then Africa, Australia and Oceania, North America and South America. This is the classic arrangement adopted by most cartographers since the 16th century. For each continent, there are maps at a variety of scales. First, physical relief and political maps of the whole continent; then a series of larger-scale maps of the regions within the con-tinent, are followed, where required, by still larger-scale maps of the most important or densely populated areas. The governing principle is that by turning the pages of the atlas, the reader moves steadily from north to south through each continent, with each map overlapping its neighbours.

Map Presentation

With very few exceptions (for example, for the Arctic and Antarctic), the maps are drawn with north at the top, regardless of whether they are presented upright or sideways on the page. In the borders will be found the map title; a locator diagram showing the area covered and the page numbers for maps of adjacent areas; the scale; the projection used; the degrees of latitude and longitude; and the letters and figures used in the index for locating place names and geographical features. Physical relief maps also have a height reference panel identifying the colours used for each layer of contouring.

Map Symbols

Each map contains a vast amount of detail which can only be conveyed clearly and accurately by the use of symbols. Points and circles of varying sizes locate and identify the relative importance of towns and cities; different styles of type are employed for administrative, geographical and regional place names to aid identification. A variety of pictorial symbols denote landforms such as glaciers, marshes and coral reefs, and man-made structures including roads, railways, airports and canals. International borders are shown by red lines. Where neighbouring countries are in dispute, for example in parts of the Middle East, the maps show the *de facto* boundary between nations, regardless of the legal or historical situation. The

symbols are explained on the first page of the World Maps section of the atlas.

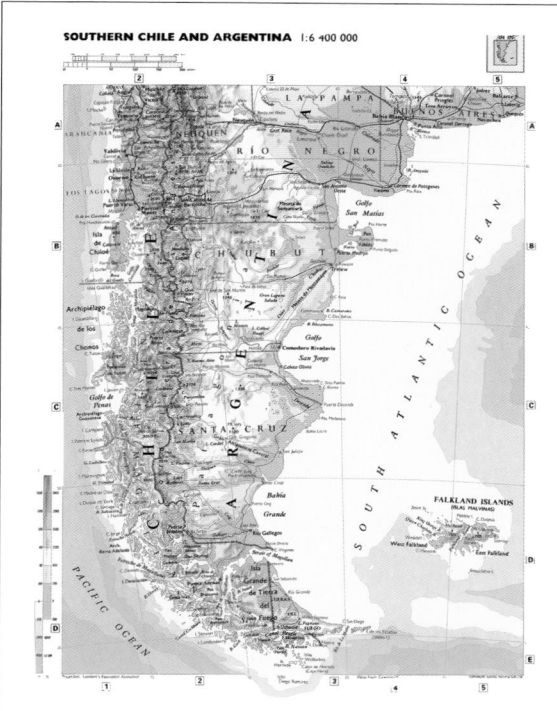

Map Scales

1:16 000 000
1 inch = 252 statute miles

The scale of each map is given in the numerical form known as the 'representative fraction'. The first figure is always one, signifying one unit of distance on the map; the second figure, usually in millions, is the number by which the map unit must be multiplied to give the equivalent distance on the Earth's surface. Calculations can easily be made in centimetres and kilometres, by dividing the Earth units figure by 100 000 (i.e. deleting the last five 0s). Thus 1:1 000 000 means 1 cm = 10 km. The calculation for inches and miles is more laborious, but 1 000 000 divided by 63 360 (the number of inches in a mile) shows that 1:1 000 000 means approximately 1 inch = 16 miles. The table below provides distance equivalents for scales down to 1:50 000 000.

LARGE SCALE		
1:1 000 000	1 cm = 10 km	1 inch = 16 miles
1:2 500 000	1 cm = 25 km	1 inch = 39.5 miles
1:5 000 000	1 cm = 50 km	1 inch = 79 miles
1:6 000 000	1 cm = 60 km	1 inch = 95 miles
1:8 000 000	1 cm = 80 km	1 inch = 126 miles
1:10 000 000	1 cm = 100 km	1 inch = 158 miles
1:15 000 000	1 cm = 150 km	1 inch = 237 miles
1:20 000 000	1 cm = 200 km	1 inch = 316 miles
1:50 000 000	1 cm = 500 km	1 inch = 790 miles
SMALL SCALE		

Measuring Distances

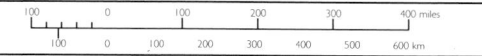

Although each map is accompanied by a scale bar, distances cannot always be measured with confidence because of the distortions involved in portraying the curved surface of the Earth on a flat page. As a general rule, the larger the map scale, the more accurate and reliable will be the distance measured. On small-scale maps such as those of the world and of entire continents, measurement may only be accurate along the 'standard parallels', or central axes, and should not be attempted without considering the map projection.

Map Projections

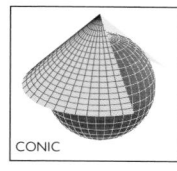  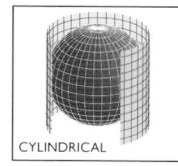

Unlike a globe, no flat map can give a true scale representation of the world in terms of area, shape and position of every region. Each of the numerous systems that have been devised for projecting the curved surface of the Earth on to a flat page involves the sacrifice of accuracy in one or more of these elements. The variations in shape and position of landmasses such as Alaska, Greenland and Australia, for example, can be quite dramatic when different projections are compared.

For this atlas, the guiding principle has been to select projections that involve the least distortion of size and distance. The projection used for each map is noted in the border. Most fall into one of three categories – conic, cylindrical or azimuthal – whose basic concepts are shown above. Each involves plotting the forms of the Earth's surface on a grid of latitude and longitude lines, which may be shown as parallels, curves or radiating spokes.

Latitude and Longitude

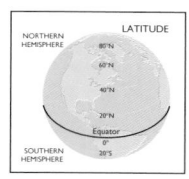 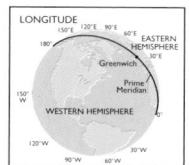 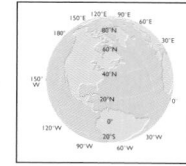

Accurate positioning of individual points on the Earth's surface is made possible by reference to the geometrical system of latitude and longitude. Latitude parallels are drawn west–east around the Earth and numbered by degrees north and south of the Equator, which is designated 0° of latitude. Longitude meridians are drawn north–south and numbered by degrees east and west of the prime meridian, 0° of longitude, which passes through Greenwich in England. By referring to these co-ordinates and their subdivisions of minutes (1/60th of a degree) and seconds (1/60th of a minute), any place on Earth can be located to within a few hundred metres. Latitude and longitude are indicated by blue lines on the maps; they are straight or curved according to the projection employed. Reference to these lines is the easiest way of determining the relative positions of places on different maps, and for plotting compass directions.

Name Forms

For ease of reference, both English and local name forms appear in the atlas. Oceans, seas and countries are shown in English throughout the atlas; country names may be abbreviated to their commonly accepted form (e.g. Germany, not The Federal Republic of Germany). Conventional English forms are also used for place names on the smaller-scale maps of the continents. However, local name forms are used on all large-scale and regional maps, with the English given in brackets only for important cities – the large-scale map of Russia and Central Asia thus shows Moskva (Moscow). For countries which do not use a Roman script, place names have been transcribed according to the systems adopted by the British and US Geographic Names Authorities. For China, the Pin Yin system has been used, with some more widely known forms appearing in brackets, as with Beijing (Peking). Both the English and local names appear in the index, the English form being cross-referenced to the local form.

Contents

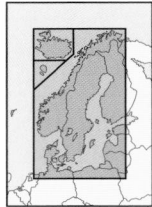
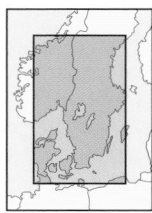
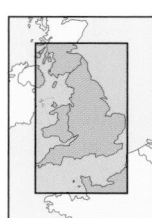
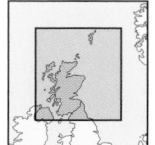

Asia

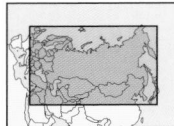

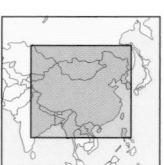

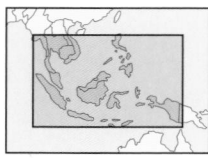
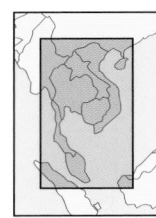
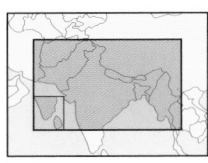
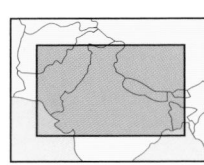
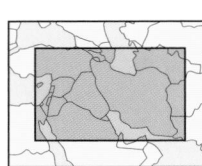
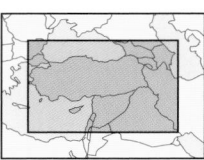
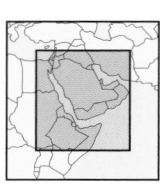
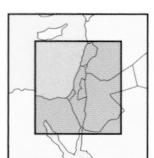
Africa

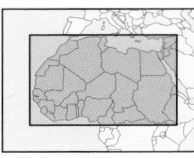
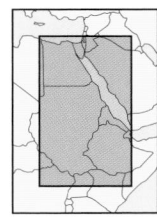
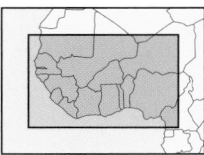
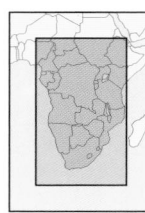

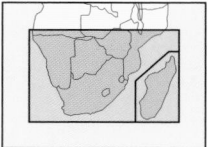

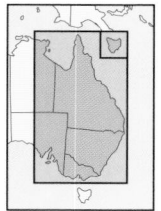
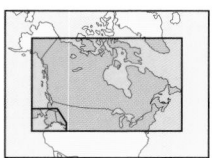
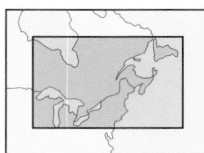
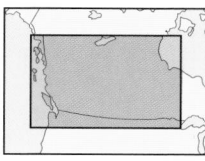
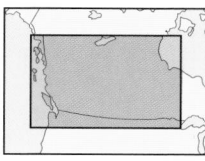
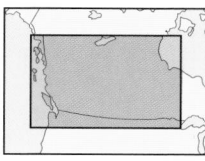
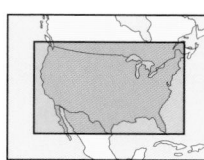

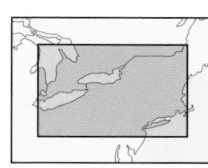
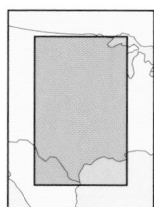
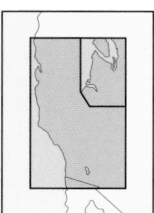
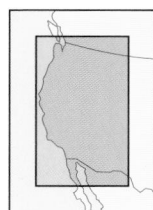
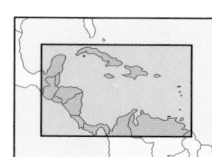

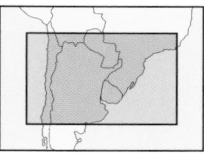

World Statistics: Countries

This alphabetical list includes all the countries and territories of the world. If a territory is not completely independent, then the country it is associated with is named. The area figures give the total area of land, inland water and ice. Units for areas and populations are thousands. The population figures are 2000 estimates. The annual income is the Gross National Product per capita in US dollars. The figures are the latest available, usually 1999 estimates.

Country/Territory	Area km² Thousands	Area miles² Thousands	Population Thousands	Capital	Annual Income US $
Afghanistan	652	252	26,511	Kabul	800
Albania	28.8	11.1	3,795	Tirana	870
Algeria	2,382	920	32,904	Algiers	1,550
American Samoa (US)	0.20	0.08	39	Pago Pago	2,600
Andorra	0.45	0.17	49	Andorra La Vella	18,000
Angola	1,247	481	13,295	Luanda	220
Anguilla (UK)	0.1	0.04	8	The Valley	6,800
Antigua & Barbuda	0.44	0.17	79	St John's	8,520
Argentina	2,767	1,068	36,238	Buenos Aires	7,600
Armenia	29.8	11.5	3,968	Yerevan	490
Aruba (Netherlands)	0.19	0.07	58	Oranjestad	22,000
Australia	7,687	2,968	18,855	Canberra	20,050
Austria	83.9	32.4	7,613	Vienna	25,970
Azerbaijan	86.6	33.4	8,324	Baku	550
Azores (Portugal)	2.2	0.87	238	Ponta Delgada	–
Bahamas	13.9	5.4	295	Nassau	20,100
Bahrain	0.68	0.26	683	Manama	7,640
Bangladesh	144	56	150,589	Dhaka	370
Barbados	0.43	0.17	265	Bridgetown	7,890
Belarus	207.6	80.1	10,697	Minsk	2,630
Belgium	30.5	11.8	9,832	Brussels	24,510
Belize	23	8.9	230	Belmopan	2,730
Benin	113	43	6,369	Porto-Novo	380
Bermuda (UK)	0.05	0.02	62	Hamilton	35,590
Bhutan	47	18.1	1,906	Thimphu	510
Bolivia	1,099	424	9,724	La Paz/Sucre	1,010
Bosnia-Herzegovina	51	20	4,601	Sarajevo	1,720
Botswana	582	225	1,822	Gaborone	3,240
Brazil	8,512	3,286	179,487	Brasília	4,420
Brunei	5.8	2.2	333	Bandar Seri Begawan	24,630
Bulgaria	111	43	9,071	Sofia	1,380
Burkina Faso	274	106	12,092	Ouagadougou	240
Burma (= Myanmar)	677	261	51,129	Rangoon	1,200
Burundi	27.8	10.7	7,358	Bujumbura	120
Cambodia	181	70	10,046	Phnom Penh	260
Cameroon	475	184	16,701	Yaoundé	580
Canada	9,976	3,852	28,488	Ottawa	19,320
Canary Is. (Spain)	7.3	2.8	1,494	Las Palmas/Santa Cruz	–
Cape Verde Is.	4	1.6	515	Praia	1,330
Cayman Is. (UK)	0.26	0.10	35	George Town	20,000
Central African Republic	623	241	4,074	Bangui	290
Chad	1,284	496	7,337	Ndjaména	200
Chile	757	292	15,272	Santiago	4,740
China	9,597	3,705	1,299,180	Beijing	780
Colombia	1,139	440	39,397	Bogotá	2,250
Comoros	2.2	0.86	670	Moroni	350
Congo	342	132	3,167	Brazzaville	670
Congo (Dem. Rep. of the)	2,345	905	49,190	Kinshasa	110
Cook Is. (NZ)	0.24	0.09	17	Avarua	900
Costa Rica	51.1	19.7	3,711	San José	2,740
Croatia	56.5	21.8	4,960	Zagreb	4,580
Cuba	111	43	11,504	Havana	1,560
Cyprus	9.3	3.6	762	Nicosia	11,960
Czech Republic	78.9	30.4	10,500	Prague	5,060
Denmark	43.1	16.6	5,153	Copenhagen	32,030
Djibouti	23.2	9	552	Djibouti	790
Dominica	0.75	0.29	87	Roseau	3,170
Dominican Republic	48.7	18.8	8,621	Santo Domingo	1,910
Ecuador	284	109	13,319	Quito	1,310
Egypt	1,001	387	64,210	Cairo	1,400
El Salvador	21	8.1	6,739	San Salvador	1,900
Equatorial Guinea	28.1	10.8	455	Malabo	1,170
Eritrea	94	36	4,523	Asmara	200
Estonia	44.7	17.3	1,647	Tallinn	3,480
Ethiopia	1,128	436	61,841	Addis Ababa	100
Faroe Is. (Denmark)	1.4	0.54	49	Tórshavn	16,000
Fiji	18.3	7.1	883	Suva	2,210
Finland	338	131	5,077	Helsinki	23,780
France	552	213	58,145	Paris	23,480
French Guiana (France)	90	34.7	130	Cayenne	6,000
French Polynesia (France)	4	1.5	268	Papeete	18,050
Gabon	268	103	1,612	Libreville	3,350
Gambia, The	11.3	4.4	1,119	Banjul	340
Georgia	69.7	26.9	5,777	Tbilisi	620
Germany	357	138	76,962	Berlin	25,350
Ghana	239	92	20,564	Accra	390
Gibraltar (UK)	0.007	0.003	32	Gibraltar Town	5,000
Greece	132	51	10,193	Athens	11,770
Greenland (Denmark)	2,176	840	60	Nuuk (Godthåb)	16,100
Grenada	0.34	0.13	83	St George's	3,450
Guadeloupe (France)	1.7	0.66	365	Basse-Terre	9,200
Guam (US)	0.55	0.21	128	Agana	19,000
Guatemala	109	42	12,222	Guatemala City	1,660
Guinea	246	95	7,830	Conakry	510
Guinea-Bissau	36.1	13.9	1,197	Bissau	160
Guyana	215	83	891	Georgetown	760
Haiti	27.8	10.7	8,003	Port-au-Prince	460
Honduras	112	43	6,846	Tegucigalpa	760
Hong Kong (China)	1.1	0.40	6,336	–	23,520
Hungary	93	35.9	10,531	Budapest	4,650
Iceland	103	40	274	Reykjavik	29,280
India	3,288	1,269	1,041,543	New Delhi	450
Indonesia	1,905	735	218,661	Jakarta	580
Iran	1,648	636	68,759	Tehran	1,760
Iraq	438	169	26,339	Baghdad	2,400
Ireland	70.3	27.1	4,086	Dublin	19,160
Israel	27	10.3	5,321	Jerusalem	17,450
Italy	301	116	57,195	Rome	19,710
Ivory Coast (Côte d'Ivoire)	322	125	17,600	Yamoussoukro	710
Jamaica	11	4.2	2,735	Kingston	2,330
Japan	378	146	128,470	Tokyo	32,230
Jordan	89.2	34.4	5,558	Amman	1,500
Kazakstan	2,717	1,049	19,006	Astana	1,230
Kenya	580	224	35,060	Nairobi	360
Kiribati	0.72	0.28	72	Tarawa	910
Korea, North	121	47	26,117	Pyŏngyang	1,000
Korea, South	99	38.2	46,403	Seoul	8,490
Kuwait	17.8	6.9	2,639	Kuwait City	22,700
Kyrgyzstan	198.5	76.6	5,403	Bishkek	300
Laos	237	91	5,463	Vientiane	280
Latvia	65	25	2,768	Riga	2,470
Lebanon	10.4	4	3,327	Beirut	3,700
Lesotho	30.4	11.7	2,370	Maseru	550
Liberia	111	43	3,575	Monrovia	1,000
Libya	1,760	679	6,500	Tripoli	6,700
Liechtenstein	0.16	0.06	28	Vaduz	50,000
Lithuania	65.2	25.2	3,935	Vilnius	2,620
Luxembourg	2.6	1	377	Luxembourg	44,640
Macau (China)	0.02	0.006	656	Macau	16,000
Macedonia	25.7	9.9	2,157	Skopje	1,690
Madagascar	587	227	16,627	Antananarivo	250
Madeira (Portugal)	0.81	0.31	253	Funchal	–
Malawi	118	46	12,458	Lilongwe	190
Malaysia	330	127	21,983	Kuala Lumpur	3,400
Maldives	0.30	0.12	283	Malé	1,160
Mali	1,240	479	12,685	Bamako	240
Malta	0.32	0.12	366	Valletta	9,210
Marshall Is.	0.18	0.07	70	Dalap-Uliga-Darrit	1,560
Martinique (France)	1.1	0.42	362	Fort-de-France	10,700
Mauritania	1,030	412	2,702	Nouakchott	380
Mauritius	2.0	0.72	1,201	Port Louis	3,590
Mayotte (France)	0.37	0.14	141	Mamoundzou	1,430
Mexico	1,958	756	107,233	Mexico City	4,400
Micronesia, Fed. States of	0.70	0.27	110	Palikir	1,810
Moldova	33.7	13	4,707	Chişinău	370
Monaco	0.002	0.0001	30	Monaco	25,000
Mongolia	1,567	605	2,847	Ulan Bator	350
Montserrat (UK)	0.10	0.04	13	Plymouth	4,500
Morocco	447	172	31,559	Rabat	1,200
Mozambique	802	309	20,493	Maputo	230
Namibia	825	318	2,437	Windhoek	1,890
Nauru	0.02	0.008	10	Yaren District	10,000
Nepal	141	54	24,084	Katmandu	220
Netherlands	41.5	16	15,829	Amsterdam/The Hague	24,320
Netherlands Antilles (Neths)	0.99	0.38	203	Willemstad	11,500
New Caledonia (France)	18.6	7.2	195	Nouméa	11,400
New Zealand	269	104	3,662	Wellington	13,780
Nicaragua	130	50	5,261	Managua	430
Niger	1,267	489	10,752	Niamey	190
Nigeria	924	357	105,000	Abuja	310
Northern Mariana Is. (US)	0.48	0.18	50	Saipan	11,500
Norway	324	125	4,331	Oslo	32,880
Oman	212	82	2,176	Muscat	7,900
Pakistan	796	307	162,409	Islamabad	470
Palau	0.46	0.18	18	Koror	5,000
Panama	77.1	29.8	2,893	Panama City	3,070
Papua New Guinea	463	179	4,845	Port Moresby	800
Paraguay	407	157	5,538	Asunción	1,580
Peru	1,285	496	26,276	Lima	2,390
Philippines	300	116	77,473	Manila	1,020
Poland	313	121	40,366	Warsaw	3,960
Portugal	92.4	35.7	10,587	Lisbon	10,600
Puerto Rico (US)	9	3.5	3,836	San Juan	8,200
Qatar	11	4.2	499	Doha	17,100
Réunion (France)	2.5	0.97	692	Saint-Denis	4,800
Romania	238	92	24,000	Bucharest	1,520
Russia	17,075	6,592	155,096	Moscow	2,270
Rwanda	26.3	10.2	10,200	Kigali	250
St Kitts & Nevis	0.36	0.14	44	Basseterre	6,420
St Lucia	0.62	0.24	177	Castries	3,770
St Vincent & Grenadines	0.39	0.15	128	Kingstown	2,700
Samoa	2.8	1.1	171	Apia	1,020
San Marino	0.06	0.02	25	San Marino	20,000
São Tomé & Príncipe	0.96	0.37	151	São Tomé	270
Saudi Arabia	2,150	830	20,697	Riyadh	6,910
Senegal	197	76	8,716	Dakar	510
Seychelles	0.46	0.18	75	Victoria	6,540
Sierra Leone	71.7	27.7	5,437	Freetown	130
Singapore	0.62	0.24	3,000	Singapore	29,610
Slovak Republic	49	18.9	5,500	Bratislava	3,590
Slovenia	20.3	7.8	2,055	Ljubljana	9,890
Solomon Is.	28.9	11.2	429	Honiara	750
Somalia	638	246	9,736	Mogadishu	600
South Africa	1,220	471	43,666	C. Town/Pretoria/Bloem.	3,160
Spain	505	195	40,667	Madrid	14,000
Sri Lanka	65.6	25.3	19,416	Colombo	820
Sudan	2,506	967	33,625	Khartoum	330
Surinam	163	63	497	Paramaribo	1,660
Swaziland	17.4	6.7	1,121	Mbabane	1,360
Sweden	450	174	8,560	Stockholm	25,040
Switzerland	41.3	15.9	6,762	Bern	38,350
Syria	185	71	17,826	Damascus	970
Taiwan	36	13.9	22,000	Taipei	12,400
Tajikistan	143.1	55.2	7,041	Dushanbe	290
Tanzania	945	365	39,639	Dodoma	240
Thailand	513	198	63,670	Bangkok	1,960
Togo	56.8	21.9	4,861	Lomé	320
Tonga	0.75	0.29	92	Nuku'alofa	1,720
Trinidad & Tobago	5.1	2	1,484	Port of Spain	4,390
Tunisia	164	63	9,924	Tunis	2,100
Turkey	779	301	66,789	Ankara	2,900
Turkmenistan	488.1	188.5	4,585	Ashkhabad	660
Turks & Caicos Is. (UK)	0.43	0.17	12	Cockburn Town	5,000
Tuvalu	0.03	0.01	11	Fongafale	600
Uganda	236	91	26,958	Kampala	320
Ukraine	603.7	233.1	52,558	Kiev	750
United Arab Emirates	83.6	32.3	1,951	Abu Dhabi	17,870
United Kingdom	243.3	94	58,393	London	22,640
United States of America	9,373	3,619	266,096	Washington, DC	30,600
Uruguay	177	68	3,274	Montevideo	5,900
Uzbekistan	447.4	172.7	26,044	Tashkent	720
Vanuatu	12.2	4.7	206	Port-Vila	1,170
Venezuela	912	352	24,715	Caracas	3,670
Vietnam	332	127	82,427	Hanoi	370
Virgin Is. (UK)	0.15	0.06	15	Road Town	–
Virgin Is. (US)	0.34	0.13	135	Charlotte Amalie	12,500
Wallis & Futuna Is. (France)	0.20	0.08	26	Mata-Utu	–
Western Sahara	266	103	228	El Aaiún	300
Yemen	528	204	13,219	Sana	350
Yugoslavia	102.3	39.5	10,761	Belgrade	2,300
Zambia	753	291	12,267	Lusaka	320
Zimbabwe	391	151	13,123	Harare	520

World Statistics: Cities

T his list shows the principal cities with more than 500,000 inhabitants (for Brazil, China and India only cities with more than 1 million inhabitants are included). The figures are taken from the most recent census or population estimate available, and as far as possible are the population of the metropolitan area, e.g. greater New York, Mexico or Paris. All the figures are in thousands. Local name forms have been used for the smaller cities (e.g. Kraków).

AFGHANISTAN
Kabul 1,565
ALGERIA
Algiers 2,168
Oran 916
ANGOLA
Luanda 2,418
ARGENTINA
Buenos Aires 11,256
Córdoba 1,208
Rosario 1,118
Mendoza 773
La Plata 642
San Miguel de Tucumán 622
Mar del Plata 512
ARMENIA
Yerevan 1,248
AUSTRALIA
Sydney 3,770
Melbourne 3,217
Brisbane 1,489
Perth 1,262
Adelaide 1,080
AUSTRIA
Vienna 1,595
AZERBAIJAN
Baku 1,720
BANGLADESH
Dhaka 6,105
Chittagong 2,041
Khulna 877
Rajshahi 517
BELARUS
Minsk 1,700
Homyel 512
BELGIUM
Brussels 948
BENIN
Cotonou 537
BOLIVIA
La Paz 1,126
Santa Cruz 767
BOSNIA-HERZEGOVINA
Sarajevo 526
BRAZIL
São Paulo 16,417
Rio de Janeiro 9,888
Salvador 2,211
Belo Horizonte 2,091
Fortaleza 1,965
Brasília 1,821
Curitiba 1,476
Recife 1,346
Pôrto Alegre 1,288
Manaus 1,157
Belém 1,144
Goiânia 1,004
BULGARIA
Sofia 1,116
BURKINA FASO
Ouagadougou 690
BURMA (MYANMAR)
Rangoon 2,513
Mandalay 533
CAMBODIA
Phnom Penh 920
CAMEROON
Douala 1,200
Yaoundé 800
CANADA
Toronto 4,344
Montréal 3,337
Vancouver 1,831
Ottawa–Hull 1,022
Edmonton 885
Calgary 831
Québec 693
Winnipeg 677
Hamilton 643
CENTRAL AFRICAN REP.
Bangui 553
CHAD
Ndjaména 530
CHILE
Santiago 5,067
CHINA
Shanghai 15,082
Beijing 12,362
Tianjin 10,687
Hong Kong (SAR)* 6,502
Chongqing 3,870

Shenyang 3,860
Wuhan 3,520
Guangzhou 3,114
Harbin 2,505
Nanjing 2,211
Xi'an 2,115
Chengdu 1,933
Dalian 1,855
Changchun 1,810
Jinan 1,660
Taiyuan 1,642
Qingdao 1,584
Fuzhou, Fujian 1,380
Zibo 1,346
Zhengzhou 1,324
Lanzhou 1,296
Anshan 1,252
Fushun 1,246
Kunming 1,242
Changsha 1,198
Hangzhou 1,185
Nanchang 1,169
Shijiazhuang 1,159
Guiyang 1,131
Ürümqi 1,130
Jilin 1,118
Tangshan 1,110
Qiqihar 1,104
Baotou 1,033
Hefei 1,000
COLOMBIA
Bogotá 6,004
Cali 1,985
Medellin 1,970
Barranquilla 1,157
Cartagena 812
CONGO
Brazzaville 937
Pointe-Noire 576
CONGO (DEM. REP.)
Kinshasa 1,655
Lubumbashi 851
Mbuji-Mayi 806
COSTA RICA
San José 1,220
CROATIA
Zagreb 931
CUBA
Havana 2,241
CZECH REPUBLIC
Prague 1,209
DENMARK
Copenhagen 1,362
DOMINICAN REPUBLIC
Santo Domingo 2,135
Santiago 691
ECUADOR
Guayaquil 1,973
Quito 1,487
EGYPT
Cairo 9,900
Alexandria 3,431
El Gîza 2,144
Shubra el Kheima 834
EL SALVADOR
San Salvador 1,522
ETHIOPIA
Addis Ababa 2,112
FINLAND
Helsinki 532
FRANCE
Paris 9,319
Lyon 1,262
Marseille 1,087
Lille 959
Bordeaux 696
Toulouse 650
Nice 516
GEORGIA
Tbilisi 1,300
GERMANY
Berlin 3,470
Hamburg 1,706
Munich 1,240
Cologne 964
Frankfurt 651
Essen 616
Dortmund 600
Stuttgart 587
Düsseldorf 571
Bremen 549
Duisburg 535
Hanover 524

GHANA
Accra 949
GREECE
Athens 3,097
GUATEMALA
Guatemala 1,167
GUINEA
Conakry 1,508
HAITI
Port-au-Prince 1,255
HONDURAS
Tegucigalpa 813
HUNGARY
Budapest 1,885
INDIA
Bombay (Mumbai) 12,572
Calcutta (Kolkata) 10,916
Delhi 7,207
Madras (Chennai) 5,361
Hyderabad 4,280
Bangalore 4,087
Ahmadabad 3,298
Pune 2,485
Kanpur 2,111
Nagpur 1,661
Lucknow 1,642
Surat 1,517
Jaipur 1,514
Coimbatore 1,136
Vadodara 1,115
Indore 1,104
Patna 1,099
Madurai 1,094
Bhopal 1,064
Vishakhapatnam 1,052
Varanasi 1,026
Ludhiana 1,012
INDONESIA
Jakarta 11,500
Surabaya 2,701
Bandung 2,368
Medan 1,910
Semarang 1,366
Palembang 1,352
Tangerang 1,198
Ujung Pandang 1,092
Bandar Lampung 832
Malang 763
Padang 721
Pakanbaru 558
Samarinda 536
Banjarmasin 535
Surakarta 516
IRAN
Tehran 6,750
Mashhad 1,964
Esfahan 1,221
Tabriz 1,166
Shiraz 1,043
Ahvaz 828
Qom 780
Bakhtaran 666
Karaj 588
IRAQ
Baghdad 3,841
Diyala 961
As Sulaymaniyah 952
Arbil 770
Al Mawsil 664
Kadhimain 521
IRELAND
Dublin 952
ISRAEL
Tel Aviv-Yafo 1,502
Jerusalem 591
ITALY
Rome 2,775
Milan 1,369
Naples 1,067
Turin 962
Palermo 698
Genoa 678
IVORY COAST
Abidjan 2,500
JAMAICA
Kingston 644
JAPAN
Tokyo–Yokohama 26,836

Osaka 10,601
Nagoya 2,152
Sapporo 1,757
Kyoto 1,464
Kobe 1,424
Fukuoka 1,285
Kawasaki 1,203
Hiroshima 1,109
Kitakyushu 1,020
Sendai 971
Chiba 857
Sakai 803
Kumamoto 650
Okayama 616
Sagamihara 571
Hamamatsu 562
Kagoshima 546
Funabashi 541
Higashiosaka 517
Hachioji 503
JORDAN
Amman 1,300
Az-Zarqā 609
KAZAKSTAN
Almaty 1,150
Qaraghandy 573
KENYA
Nairobi 2,000
Mombasa 600
KOREA, NORTH
Pyŏngyang 2,639
Hamhung 775
Chŏngjin 754
Chinnampo 691
Sinŭiju 500
KOREA, SOUTH
Seoul 11,641
Pusan 3,814
Taegu 2,449
Inchon 2,308
Taejŏn 1,272
Kwangju 1,258
Ulsan 967
Sŏngnam 869
Puch'on 779
Suwŏn 756
Anyang 590
Chŏnju 563
Chŏngju 531
Ansan 510
P'ohang 509
KYRGYZSTAN
Bishkek 584
LATVIA
Riga 846
LEBANON
Beirut 1,900
Tripoli 500
LIBYA
Tripoli 1,083
LITHUANIA
Vilnius 580
MACEDONIA
Skopje 541
MADAGASCAR
Antananarivo 1,053
MALAYSIA
Kuala Lumpur 1,145
MALI
Bamako 800
MAURITANIA
Nouakchott 735
MEXICO
Mexico City 15,048
Guadalajara 2,847
Monterrey 2,522
Puebla 1,055
León 872
Ciudad Juárez 798
Tijuana 743
Culiacán Rosales 602
Mexicali 602
Acapulco de Juárez 592
Mérida 557
Chihuahua 530
San Luis Potosí 526
Aguascalientés 506
MOLDOVA
Chişinău 700
MONGOLIA
Ulan Bator 627

MOROCCO
Casablanca 3,079
Rabat-Salé 1,344
Fès 735
Marrakesh 621
MOZAMBIQUE
Maputo 2,000
NEPAL
Katmandu 535
NETHERLANDS
Amsterdam 1,101
Rotterdam 1,076
The Hague 694
Utrecht 548
NEW ZEALAND
Auckland 997
NICARAGUA
Managua 864
NIGERIA
Lagos 10,287
Ibadan 1,365
Ogbomosho 712
Kano 657
NORWAY
Oslo 714
PAKISTAN
Karachi 9,863
Lahore 5,085
Faisalabad 1,875
Peshawar 1,676
Gujranwala 1,663
Rawalpindi 1,290
Multan 1,257
Hyderabad 1,107
PARAGUAY
Asunción 945
PERU
Lima–Callao 6,601
Callao 638
Arequipa 620
Trujillo 509
PHILIPPINES
Manila 9,280
Quezon City 1,989
Davao 1,191
Caloocan 1,023
Cebu 662
Zamboanga 511
POLAND
Warsaw 1,638
Lódz 825
Kraków 745
Wroclaw 642
Poznań 581
PORTUGAL
Lisbon 2,561
Oporto 1,174
ROMANIA
Bucharest 2,060
RUSSIA
Moscow 9,233
St Petersburg 4,883
Nizhniy Novgorod 1,425
Novosibirsk 1,400
Yekaterinburg 1,300
Samara 1,200
Omsk 1,200
Chelyabinsk 1,100
Kazan 1,100
Ufa 1,100
Volgograd 1,003
Perm 1,000
Rostov 1,000
Voronezh 908
Saratov 895
Krasnoyarsk 869
Togliatti 689
Simbirsk 678
Izhevsk 654
Krasnodar 645
Vladivostok 632
Yaroslavl 629
Khabarovsk 618
Barnaul 596
Irkutsk 585
Novokuznetsk 572
Ryazan 536
Penza 534
Orenburg 532
Tula 532
Naberezhnyye-Chelny 526

Kemerovo 503
SAUDI ARABIA
Riyadh 1,800
Jedda 1,500
Mecca 630
SENEGAL
Dakar 1,571
SIERRA LEONE
Freetown 505
SINGAPORE
Singapore 3,104
SOMALIA
Mogadishu 1,000
SOUTH AFRICA
Cape Town 2,350
East Rand 1,379
Johannesburg 1,196
Durban 1,137
Pretoria 1,080
West Rand 870
Port Elizabeth 853
Vanderbijlpark–Vereeniging 774
Soweto 597
Sasolburg 540
SPAIN
Madrid 3,029
Barcelona 1,614
Valencia 763
Sevilla 719
Zaragoza 607
Málaga 532
SRI LANKA
Colombo 1,863
SUDAN
Omdurman 1,267
Khartoum 925
Khartoum North 879
SWEDEN
Stockholm 1,744·
Göteborg 775
SWITZERLAND
Zürich 1,175
Bern 942
SYRIA
Aleppo 1,591
Damascus 1,549
Homs 644
TAIWAN
Taipei 2,653
Kaohsiung 1,405
Taichung 817
Tainan 700
Panchiao 544
TAJIKISTAN
Dushanbe 524
TANZANIA
Dar-es-Salaam 1,361
THAILAND
Bangkok 5,572
TOGO
Lomé 590
TUNISIA
Tunis 1,827
TURKEY
Istanbul 7,490
Ankara 3,028
Izmir 2,333
Adana 1,472
Bursa 1,317
Konya 1,040
Gaziantep 930
Icel 908
Antalya 734
Diyarbakir 677
Kocaeli 661
Urfa 649
Kayseri 648
Manisa 641
Hatay 561
Samsun 557
Eskisehir 508
Balikesir 501
TURKMENISTAN
Ashkhabad 536
UGANDA
Kampala 773
UKRAINE
Kiev 2,630
Kharkiv 1,555
Dnipropetrovsk 1,147
Donetsk 1,088
Odesa 1,046

Zaporizhzhya 887
Lviv 802
Kryvyy Rih 720
Mariupol 510
Mykolayiv 508
UNITED KINGDOM
London 8,089
Birmingham 2,373
Manchester 2,353
Liverpool 852
Glasgow 832
Sheffield 661
Nottingham 649
Newcastle 617
Bristol 552
Leeds 529
UNITED STATES
New York 16,329
Los Angeles 12,410
Chicago 7,668
Philadelphia 4,949
Washington, DC 4,466
Detroit 4,307
Houston 3,653
Atlanta 3,331
Boston 3,240
Dallas 2,898
Minneapolis–St Paul 2,688
San Diego 2,632
St Louis 2,536
Phoenix 2,473
Baltimore 2,458
Pittsburgh 2,402
Cleveland 2,222
San Francisco 2,182
Seattle 2,180
Tampa 2,157
Miami 2,025
Newark 1,934
Denver 1,796
Portland (Or.) 1,676
Kansas City (Mo.) 1,647
Cincinnati 1,581
San Jose 1,557
Norfolk 1,529
Indianapolis 1,462
Milwaukee 1,456
Sacramento 1,441
San Antonio 1,437
Columbus (Oh.) 1,423
New Orleans 1,309
Charlotte 1,260
Buffalo 1,189
Salt Lake City 1,178
Hartford 1,151
Oklahoma 1,007
Jacksonville (Fl.) 665
Omaha 663
Memphis 614
El Paso 579
Austin 514
Nashville 505
URUGUAY
Montevideo 1,378
UZBEKISTAN
Tashkent 2,107
VENEZUELA
Caracas 2,784
Maracaibo 1,364
Valencia 1,032
Maracay 800
Barquisimeto 745
Ciudad Guayana 524
VIETNAM
Ho Chi Minh City 4,322
Hanoi 3,056
Haiphong 783
YEMEN
Sana 972
Aden 562
YUGOSLAVIA
Belgrade 1,137
ZAMBIA
Lusaka 982
ZIMBABWE
Harare 1,189
Bulawayo 622

* SAR = Special Administrative Region of China

World Statistics: Distances

The table shows air distances in miles and kilometres between 30 major cities. Known as 'Great Circle' distances, these measure the shortest routes between the cities, which aircraft use wherever possible. The maps show the world centred on six cities, and illustrate, for example, why direct flights from Japan to northern America and Europe are across the Arctic regions. The maps have been constructed on an Azimuthal Equidistant projection, on which all distances measured through the centre point are true to scale. The red lines are drawn at 5,000, 10,000 and 15,000 km from the central city.

*Distance table — upper-right (above the city-name diagonal) values are in **km**; lower-left values are in **miles**. The diagonal holds the city names.*

	Beijing	Bombay	Buenos Aires	Cairo	Calcutta	Caracas	Chicago	Hong Kong	Honolulu	Johannesburg	Lagos	London	Los Angeles	Mexico City	Moscow	Nairobi	New York	Paris	Rio de Janeiro	Rome	Singapore	Sydney	Tokyo	Wellington
Beijing	—	2956	11972	4688	2031	8947	6588	1220	5070	7276	7119	5057	6251	7742	3600	5727	6828	5106	10773	5049	2783	5561	1304	6700
Bombay	4757	—	9275	2706	1034	9024	8048	2683	8024	4334	4730	4467	8700	9728	3126	2816	7793	4356	8332	3837	2432	6313	4189	7686
Buenos Aires	19268	14925	—	7341	10268	3167	5599	11481	7558	5025	4919	6917	6122	4591	8374	6463	5298	6867	1214	6929	9867	7332	11410	6202
Cairo	7544	4355	11814	—	3541	6340	6127	5064	8838	3894	2432	2180	7580	7687	1803	2197	5605	1994	6149	1325	5137	8959	5947	10268
Calcutta	3269	1664	16524	5699	—	9609	7978	1653	7048	5256	5727	4946	8152	9494	3438	3839	7921	4883	9366	4486	1800	5678	3195	7055
Caracas	14399	14522	5096	10203	15464	—	2502	10166	6009	6847	4810	4664	3612	2228	6175	7173	2131	4738	2825	5196	11407	9534	8801	8154
Chicago	10603	12953	9011	3206	12839	4027	—	7783	4247	8689	5973	3949	1742	1694	4971	8005	711	4132	5311	4809	9369	9243	6299	8358
Hong Kong	1963	4317	18478	8150	2659	16360	12526	—	5543	6669	7360	5980	7232	8775	4439	5453	8047	5984	11001	5769	1615	4582	1786	5857
Honolulu	8160	12914	12164	14223	11343	9670	6836	8921	—	11934	10133	7228	2558	3781	7036	10739	4958	7437	8290	8026	6721	5075	3854	4669
Johannesburg	11710	6974	8088	6267	8459	11019	13984	10732	19206	—	2799	5637	10362	9063	5692	1818	7979	5426	4420	4811	5381	6860	8418	7308
Lagos	11457	7612	7916	3915	9216	7741	9612	11845	16308	4505	—	3118	7713	6879	3886	2366	5268	2929	3750	2510	6925	9643	8376	9973
London	8138	7190	11131	3508	7961	7507	6356	9623	11632	9071	5017	—	5442	5552	1552	4237	3463	212	5778	889	6743	10558	5942	11691
Los Angeles	10060	14000	9852	12200	13120	5812	2804	11639	4117	16676	12414	8758	—	1549	6070	9659	2446	5645	6310	6331	8776	7502	5475	6719
Mexico City	12460	15656	7389	12372	15280	3586	2726	14122	6085	14585	11071	8936	2493	—	6664	9207	2090	5717	4780	6365	10321	8058	7024	6897
Moscow	5794	5031	13477	2902	5534	9938	8000	7144	11323	9161	6254	2498	9769	10724	—	3942	4666	1545	7184	1477	5237	9008	4651	10283
Nairobi	9216	4532	10402	3536	6179	11544	12883	8776	17282	2927	3807	6819	15544	14818	6344	—	7358	4029	5548	3350	4635	7552	6996	8490
New York	10988	12541	8526	9020	12747	3430	1145	12950	7980	12841	8477	5572	3936	3264	7510	11842	—	3626	4832	4280	9531	9935	6741	8951
Paris	8217	7010	11051	3210	7858	7625	6650	9630	11968	8732	4714	342	9085	9200	2486	6485	5836	—	5708	687	6671	10539	6038	11798
Rio de Janeiro	17338	13409	1953	9896	15073	4546	8547	17704	13342	7113	6035	9299	10155	7693	11562	8928	7777	9187	—	5725	9763	8389	11551	7367
Rome	8126	6175	11151	2133	7219	8363	7739	9284	12916	7743	4039	1431	10188	10243	2376	5391	6888	1105	9214	—	6229	10143	6127	11523
Singapore	4478	3914	15879	8267	2897	18359	15078	2599	10816	8660	11145	10852	14123	16610	8428	7460	15339	10737	15712	10025	—	3915	3306	5298
Sydney	8949	10160	11800	14418	9138	15343	14875	7374	8168	11040	15519	16992	12073	12969	14497	12153	15989	16962	13501	16324	6300	—	4861	1383
Tokyo	2099	6742	18362	9571	5141	14164	10137	2874	6202	13547	13480	9562	8811	11304	7485	11260	10849	9718	18589	9861	5321	7823	—	5762
Wellington	10782	12370	9981	16524	11354	13122	13451	9427	7513	11761	16050	18814	10814	11100	16549	13664	14405	18987	11855	18545	8526	2226	9273	—

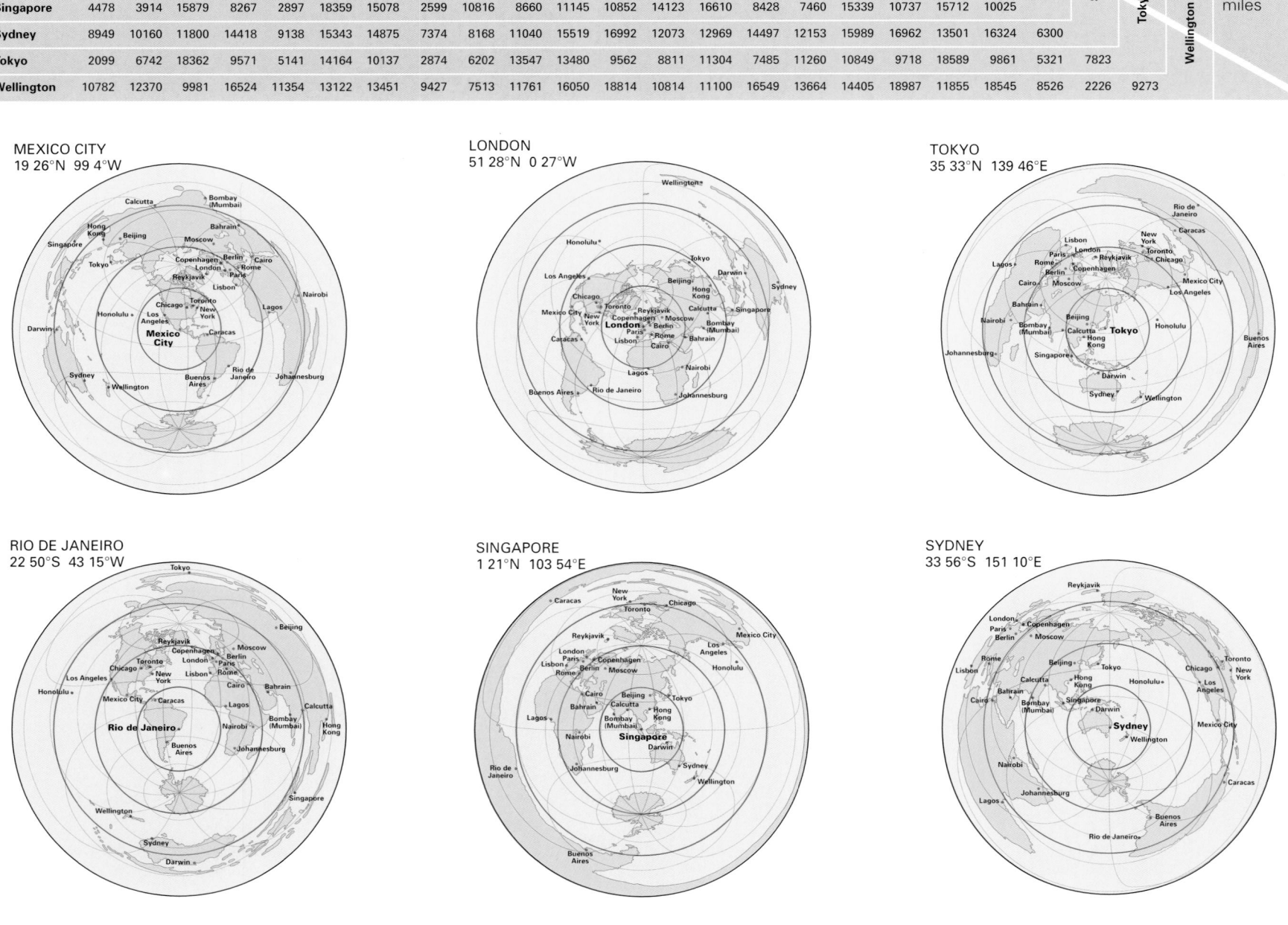

MEXICO CITY
19 26°N 99 4°W

LONDON
51 28°N 0 27°W

TOKYO
35 33°N 139 46°E

RIO DE JANEIRO
22 50°S 43 15°W

SINGAPORE
1 21°N 103 54°E

SYDNEY
33 56°S 151 10°E

World Statistics: Climate

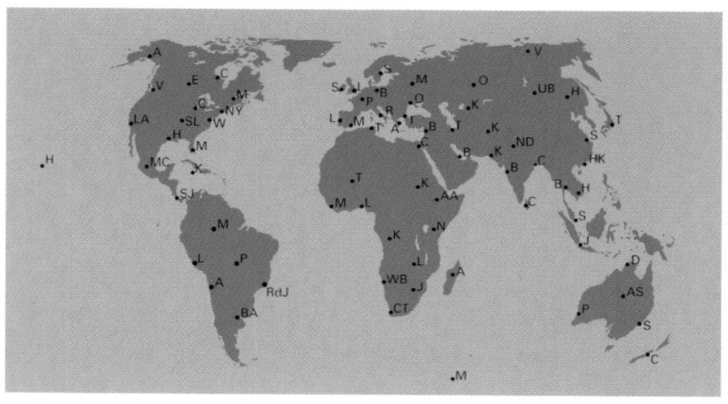

Rainfall and temperature figures are provided for more than 70 cities around the world. As climate is affected by altitude, the height of each city is shown in metres beneath its name. For each month, the figures in blue show the total rainfall or snow in millimetres, and in red the average temperature in degrees Celsius; the total annual rainfall and average annual temperature are at the end of the rows.

EUROPE	Jan.	Feb.	Mar.	Apr.	May	June	July	Aug.	Sept.	Oct.	Nov.	Dec.	Year
Athens, Greece	62	37	37	23	23	14	6	7	15	51	56	71	402
107 m	10	10	12	16	20	25	28	28	24	20	15	11	18
Berlin, Germany	46	40	33	42	49	65	73	69	48	49	46	43	603
55 m	–1	0	4	9	14	17	19	18	15	9	5	1	9
Istanbul, Turkey	109	92	72	46	38	34	34	30	58	81	103	119	816
14 m	5	6	7	11	16	20	23	23	20	16	12	8	14
Lisbon, Portugal	111	76	109	54	44	16	3	4	33	62	93	103	708
77 m	11	12	14	16	17	20	22	23	21	18	14	12	17
London, UK	54	40	37	37	46	45	57	59	49	57	64	48	593
5 m	4	5	7	9	12	16	18	17	15	11	8	5	11
Málaga, Spain	61	51	62	46	26	5	1	3	29	64	64	62	474
33 m	12	13	16	17	19	29	25	26	23	20	16	13	18
Moscow, Russia	39	38	36	37	53	58	88	71	58	45	47	54	624
156 m	–13	–10	–4	6	13	16	18	17	12	6	–1	–7	4
Odesa, Ukraine	57	62	30	21	34	34	42	37	37	13	35	71	473
64 m	–3	–1	2	9	15	20	22	22	18	12	9	1	10
Paris, France	56	46	35	42	57	54	59	64	55	50	51	50	619
75 m	3	4	8	11	15	18	20	19	17	12	7	4	12
Rome, Italy	71	62	57	51	46	37	15	21	63	99	129	93	744
17 m	8	9	11	14	18	22	25	25	22	17	13	10	16
Shannon, Irish Republic	94	67	56	53	61	57	77	79	86	86	96	117	929
2 m	5	5	7	9	12	14	16	16	14	11	8	6	10
Stockholm, Sweden	43	30	25	31	34	45	61	76	60	48	53	48	554
44 m	–3	–3	–1	5	10	15	18	17	12	7	3	0	7
ASIA													
Bahrain	8	18	13	8	<3	0	0	0	0	0	18	18	81
5 m	17	18	21	25	29	32	33	34	31	28	24	19	26
Bangkok, Thailand	8	20	36	58	198	160	160	175	305	206	66	5	1,397
2 m	26	28	29	30	29	29	28	28	28	28	26	25	28
Beirut, Lebanon	191	158	94	53	18	3	<3	<3	5	51	132	185	892
34 m	14	14	16	18	22	24	27	28	26	24	19	16	21
Bombay (Mumbai), India	3	3	3	<3	18	485	617	340	264	64	13	3	1,809
11 m	24	24	26	28	30	29	27	27	27	28	27	26	27
Calcutta, India	10	31	36	43	140	297	325	328	252	114	20	5	1,600
6 m	20	22	27	30	30	30	29	29	29	28	23	19	26
Colombo, Sri Lanka	89	69	147	231	371	224	135	109	160	348	315	147	2,365
7 m	26	26	27	28	28	27	27	27	27	27	26	26	27
Harbin, China	6	5	10	23	43	94	112	104	46	33	8	5	488
160 m	–18	–15	–5	6	13	19	22	21	14	4	–6	–16	3
Ho Chi Minh, Vietnam	15	3	13	43	221	330	315	269	335	269	114	56	1,984
9 m	26	27	29	30	29	28	28	28	27	27	27	26	28
Hong Kong, China	33	46	74	137	292	394	381	361	257	114	43	31	2,162
33 m	16	15	18	22	26	28	28	28	27	25	21	18	23
Jakarta, Indonesia	300	300	211	147	114	97	64	43	66	112	142	203	1,798
8 m	26	26	27	27	27	27	27	27	27	27	27	26	27
Kabul, Afghanistan	31	36	94	102	20	5	3	3	<3	15	20	10	338
1,815 m	–3	–1	6	13	18	22	25	24	20	14	7	3	12
Karachi, Pakistan	13	10	8	3	3	18	81	41	13	<3	3	5	196
4 m	19	20	24	28	30	31	30	29	28	28	24	20	26
Kazalinsk, Kazakstan	10	10	13	13	15	5	5	8	8	10	13	15	125
63 m	–12	–11	–3	6	18	23	25	23	16	8	–1	–7	7
New Delhi, India	23	18	13	8	13	74	180	172	117	10	3	10	640
218 m	14	17	23	28	33	34	31	30	29	26	20	15	25
Omsk, Russia	15	8	8	13	31	51	51	51	28	25	18	20	318
85 m	–22	–19	–12	–1	10	16	18	16	10	1	–11	–18	–1
Shanghai, China	48	58	84	94	94	180	147	142	130	71	51	36	1,135
7 m	4	5	9	14	20	24	28	28	23	19	12	7	16
Singapore	252	173	193	188	173	173	170	196	178	208	254	257	2,413
10 m	26	27	28	28	28	28	28	27	27	27	27	27	27
Tehran, Iran	46	38	46	36	13	3	3	3	3	8	20	31	246
1,220 m	2	5	9	16	21	26	30	29	25	18	12	6	17
Tokyo, Japan	48	74	107	135	147	165	142	152	234	208	97	56	1,565
6 m	3	4	7	13	17	21	25	26	23	17	11	6	14
Ulan Bator, Mongolia	<3	<3	3	5	10	28	76	51	23	5	5	3	208
1,325 m	–26	–21	–13	–1	6	14	16	14	8	–1	–13	–22	–3
Verkhoyansk, Russia	5	5	3	5	8	23	28	25	13	8	8	5	134
100 m	–50	–45	–32	–15	0	12	14	9	2	–15	–38	–48	–17
AFRICA													
Addis Ababa, Ethiopia	<3	3	25	135	213	201	206	239	102	28	<3	0	1,151
2,450 m	19	20	20	20	19	18	18	19	21	22	21	20	20
Antananarivo, Madagas.	300	279	178	53	18	8	8	10	18	61	135	287	1,356
1,372 m	21	21	21	19	18	15	14	15	17	19	21	21	19
Cairo, Egypt	5	5	5	3	3	<3	0	0	<3	<3	3	5	28
116 m	13	15	18	21	25	28	28	28	26	24	20	15	22
Cape Town, S. Africa	15	8	18	48	79	84	89	66	43	31	18	10	508
17 m	21	21	20	17	14	13	12	13	14	16	18	19	17
Johannesburg, S. Africa	114	109	89	38	25	8	8	8	23	56	107	125	709
1,665 m	20	20	18	16	13	10	11	13	16	18	19	20	16

	Jan.	Feb.	Mar.	Apr.	May	June	July	Aug.	Sept.	Oct.	Nov.	Dec.	Year
Khartoum, Sudan	<3	<3	<3	<3	3	8	53	71	18	5	<3	0	158
390 m	24	25	28	31	33	34	32	31	32	32	28	25	29
Kinshasa, Congo (D.R.)	135	145	196	196	158	8	3	3	31	119	221	142	1,354
325 m	26	26	27	27	26	24	23	24	25	26	26	26	25
Lagos, Nigeria	28	46	102	150	269	460	279	64	140	206	69	25	1,836
3 m	27	28	29	28	28	26	26	25	26	26	28	28	27
Lusaka, Zambia	231	191	142	18	3	<3	<3	0	<3	10	91	150	836
1,277 m	21	22	21	21	19	16	16	18	22	24	23	22	21
Monrovia, Liberia	31	56	97	216	516	973	996	373	744	772	236	130	5,138
23 m	26	26	27	27	26	25	24	25	25	25	26	26	26
Nairobi, Kenya	38	64	125	211	158	46	15	23	31	53	109	86	958
1,820 m	19	19	19	19	18	16	16	16	18	19	18	18	18
Timbuktu, Mali	<3	<3	3	<3	5	23	79	81	38	3	<3	<3	231
301 m	22	24	28	32	34	35	32	30	32	31	28	23	29
Tunis, Tunisia	64	51	41	36	18	8	3	8	33	51	48	61	419
66 m	10	11	13	16	19	23	26	27	25	20	16	11	18
Walvis Bay, Namibia	<3	5	8	3	3	<3	<3	3	<3	<3	<3	<3	23
7 m	19	19	19	18	17	16	15	14	14	15	17	18	18
AUSTRALIA, NEW ZEALAND AND ANTARCTICA													
Alice Springs, Australia	43	33	28	10	15	13	8	8	8	18	31	38	252
579 m	29	28	25	20	15	12	12	14	18	23	26	28	21
Christchurch, N. Zealand	56	43	48	48	66	66	69	48	46	43	48	56	638
10 m	16	16	14	12	9	6	6	7	9	12	14	16	11
Darwin, Australia	386	312	254	97	15	3	<3	3	13	51	119	239	1,491
30 m	29	29	29	29	28	26	25	26	28	29	30	29	28
Mawson, Antarctica	11	30	20	10	44	180	4	40	3	20	0	0	362
14 m	0	–5	–10	–14	–15	–16	–18	–18	–19	–13	–5	–1	–11
Perth, Australia	8	10	20	43	130	180	170	149	86	56	20	13	881
60 m	23	23	22	19	16	14	13	13	15	16	19	22	18
Sydney, Australia	89	102	127	135	127	117	117	76	73	71	73	73	1,181
42 m	22	22	21	18	15	13	12	13	15	18	19	21	17
NORTH AMERICA													
Anchorage, Alaska, USA	20	18	15	10	13	18	41	66	66	56	25	23	371
40 m	–11	–8	–5	2	7	12	14	13	9	2	–5	–11	2
Chicago, Illinois, USA	51	51	66	71	86	89	84	81	79	66	61	51	836
251 m	–4	–3	2	9	14	20	23	22	19	12	5	–1	10
Churchill, Man., Canada	15	13	18	23	32	44	46	58	51	43	39	21	402
13 m	–28	–26	–20	–10	–2	6	12	11	5	–2	–12	–22	–7
Edmonton, Alta., Canada	25	19	19	22	43	77	89	78	39	17	16	25	466
676 m	–15	–10	–5	4	11	15	17	16	11	6	–4	–10	3
Honolulu, Hawaii, USA	104	66	79	48	25	18	23	28	36	48	64	104	643
12 m	23	18	19	20	22	24	25	26	26	24	22	19	22
Houston, Texas, USA	89	76	84	91	119	117	99	99	104	94	89	109	1,171
12 m	12	13	17	21	24	27	28	29	26	22	16	12	21
Kingston, Jamaica	23	15	23	31	102	89	38	91	99	180	74	36	800
34 m	25	25	25	26	26	28	28	28	27	27	26	26	26
Los Angeles, Calif., USA	79	76	71	25	10	3	<3	<3	5	15	31	66	381
95 m	13	14	14	16	17	19	21	22	21	18	16	14	17
Mexico City, Mexico	13	5	10	20	53	119	170	152	130	51	18	8	747
2,309 m	12	13	16	18	19	19	17	18	18	16	14	13	16
Miami, Florida, USA	71	53	64	81	173	178	155	160	203	234	71	51	1,516
8 m	20	20	22	23	25	27	28	28	27	25	22	21	24
Montréal, Que., Canada	72	65	74	74	66	82	90	92	88	76	81	87	946
57 m	–10	–9	–3	–6	13	18	21	20	15	9	2	–7	6
New York City, NY, USA	94	97	91	81	81	84	107	109	86	89	76	91	1,092
96 m	–1	–1	3	10	16	20	23	23	21	15	7	2	11
St Louis, Mo., USA	58	64	89	97	114	114	89	86	81	74	71	64	1,001
173 m	0	1	7	13	19	24	26	26	22	15	8	2	14
San José, Costa Rica	15	5	20	46	229	241	211	241	305	300	145	41	1,798
1,146 m	19	19	21	21	22	21	21	21	21	20	20	19	20
Vancouver, BC, Canada	154	115	101	60	52	45	32	41	67	114	150	182	1,113
14 m	3	5	6	9	12	15	17	17	14	10	6	4	10
Washington, DC, USA	86	76	91	84	94	99	112	109	94	74	66	79	1,064
22 m	1	2	7	12	18	23	25	24	20	14	8	3	13
SOUTH AMERICA													
Antofagasta, Chile	0	0	0	<3	<3	3	5	3	<3	3	<3	0	13
94 m	21	21	20	18	16	15	14	14	15	16	18	19	17
Buenos Aires, Argentina	79	71	109	89	76	61	56	61	79	86	84	99	950
27 m	23	23	21	17	13	9	10	11	13	15	19	22	16
Lima, Peru	3	<3	<3	<3	5	5	8	8	8	3	3	<3	41
120 m	23	24	24	22	19	17	17	16	17	18	19	21	20
Manaus, Brazil	249	231	262	221	170	84	58	38	46	107	142	203	1,811
44 m	28	28	28	27	28	28	28	28	29	29	29	28	28
Paraná, Brazil	287	236	239	102	13	<3	3	5	28	127	231	310	1,582
260 m	23	23	23	23	23	21	21	22	24	24	24	23	23
Rio de Janeiro, Brazil	125	122	130	107	79	53	41	43	66	79	104	137	1,082
61 m	26	26	25	24	22	21	21	21	21	22	23	25	23

World Statistics: Physical Dimensions

Each topic list is divided into continents and within a continent the items are listed in order of size. The order of the continents is the same as in the atlas, beginning with Europe and ending with South America. The bottom part of many of the lists is selective in order to give examples from as many different countries as possible. The world top ten are shown in square brackets; in the case of mountains this has not been done because the world top 30 are all in Asia. The figures are rounded as appropriate.

WORLD, CONTINENTS, OCEANS

THE WORLD

	km²	miles²	%
The World	509,450,000	196,672,000	–
Land	149,450,000	57,688,000	29.3
Water	360,000,000	138,984,000	70.7
Asia	44,500,000	17,177,000	29.8
Africa	30,302,000	11,697,000	20.3
North America	24,241,000	9,357,000	16.2
South America	17,793,000	6,868,000	11.9
Antarctica	14,100,000	5,443,000	9.4
Europe	9,957,000	3,843,000	6.7
Australia and Oceania	8,557,000	3,303,000	5.7
Pacific Ocean	179,679,000	69,356,000	49.9
Atlantic Ocean	92,373,000	35,657,000	25.7
Indian Ocean	73,917,000	28,532,000	20.5
Arctic Ocean	14,090,000	5,439,000	3.9

SEAS

PACIFIC

	km²	miles²
South China Sea	2,974,600	1,148,500
Bering Sea	2,268,000	875,000
Sea of Okhotsk	1,528,000	590,000
East China and Yellow	1,249,000	482,000
Sea of Japan	1,008,000	389,000
Gulf of California	162,000	62,500
Bass Strait	75,000	29,000

ATLANTIC

	km²	miles²
Caribbean Sea	2,766,000	1,068,000
Mediterranean Sea	2,516,000	971,000
Gulf of Mexico	1,543,000	596,000
Hudson Bay	1,232,000	476,000
North Sea	575,000	223,000
Black Sea	462,000	178,000
Baltic Sea	422,170	163,000
Gulf of St Lawrence	238,000	92,000

INDIAN

	km²	miles²
Red Sea	438,000	169,000
The Gulf	239,000	92,000

MOUNTAINS

EUROPE

		m	ft
Elbrus	Russia	5,642	18,510
Mont Blanc	France/Italy	4,807	15,771
Monte Rosa	Italy/Switzerland	4,634	15,203
Dom	Switzerland	4,545	14,911
Liskamm	Switzerland	4,527	14,852
Weisshorn	Switzerland	4,505	14,780
Taschorn	Switzerland	4,490	14,730
Matterhorn/Cervino	Italy/Switz.	4,478	14,691
Mont Maudit	France/Italy	4,465	14,649
Dent Blanche	Switzerland	4,356	14,291
Nadelhorn	Switzerland	4,327	14,196
Grandes Jorasses	France/Italy	4,208	13,806
Jungfrau	Switzerland	4,158	13,642
Barre des Ecrins	France	4,103	13,461
Gran Paradiso	Italy	4,061	13,323
Piz Bernina	Italy/Switzerland	4,049	13,284
Eiger	Switzerland	3,970	13,025
Monte Viso	Italy	3,841	12,602
Grossglockner	Austria	3,797	12,457
Wildspitze	Austria	3,772	12,382
Monte Disgrazia	Italy	3,678	12,066
Mulhacén	Spain	3,478	11,411
Pico de Aneto	Spain	3,404	11,168
Marmolada	Italy	3,342	10,964
Etna	Italy	3,340	10,958
Punta del'Argentera	Italy	3,297	10,817
Zugspitze	Germany	2,962	9,718
Musala	Bulgaria	2,925	9,596
Olympus	Greece	2,917	9,570
Triglav	Slovenia	2,863	9,393
Monte Cinto	France (Corsica)	2,710	8,891
Gerlachovka	Slovak Republic	2,655	8,711
Torre de Cerredo	Spain	2,648	8,688
Galdhøpiggen	Norway	2,468	8,100
Hvannadalshnúkur	Iceland	2,119	6,952
Kebnekaise	Sweden	2,117	6,946
Ben Nevis	UK	1,343	4,406

ASIA

		m	ft
Everest	China/Nepal	8,850	29,035
K2 (Godwin Austen)	China/Kashmir	8,611	28,251
Kanchenjunga	India/Nepal	8,598	28,208
Lhotse	China/Nepal	8,516	27,939
Makalu	China/Nepal	8,481	27,824
Cho Oyu	China/Nepal	8,201	26,906
Dhaulagiri	Nepal	8,172	26,811
Manaslu	Nepal	8,156	26,758
Nanga Parbat	Kashmir	8,126	26,660
Annapurna	Nepal	8,078	26,502
Gasherbrum	China/Kashmir	8,068	26,469
Broad Peak	China/Kashmir	8,051	26,414
Xixabangma	China	8,012	26,286
Kangbachen	India/Nepal	7,902	25,925
Jannu	India/Nepal	7,902	25,925
Gayachung Kang	Nepal	7,897	25,909
Himalchuli	Nepal	7,893	25,896
Disteghil Sar	Kashmir	7,885	25,869
Nuptse	Nepal	7,879	25,849
Khunyang Chhish	Kashmir	7,852	25,761
Masherbrum	Kashmir	7,821	25,659
Nanda Devi	India	7,817	25,646
Rakaposhi	Kashmir	7,788	25,551
Batura	Kashmir	7,785	25,541
Namche Barwa	China	7,756	25,446
Kamet	India	7,756	25,446
Soltoro Kangri	Kashmir	7,742	25,400
Gurla Mandhata	China	7,728	25,354
Trivor	Pakistan	7,720	25,328
Kongur Shan	China	7,719	25,324
Tirich Mir	Pakistan	7,690	25,229
K'ula Shan	Bhutan/China	7,543	24,747
Pik Kommunizma	Tajikistan	7,495	24,590
Demavend	Iran	5,604	18,386
Ararat	Turkey	5,165	16,945
Gunong Kinabalu	Malaysia (Borneo)	4,101	13,455
Yu Shan	Taiwan	3,997	13,113
Fuji-San	Japan	3,776	12,388

AFRICA

		m	ft
Kilimanjaro	Tanzania	5,895	19,340
Mt Kenya	Kenya	5,199	17,057
Ruwenzori (Margherita)	Uganda/Congo (D.R.)	5,109	16,762
Ras Dashan	Ethiopia	4,620	15,157
Meru	Tanzania	4,565	14,977
Karisimbi	Rwanda/Congo (D.R.)	4,507	14,787
Mt Elgon	Kenya/Uganda	4,321	14,176
Batu	Ethiopia	4,307	14,130
Guna	Ethiopia	4,231	13,882
Toubkal	Morocco	4,165	13,665
Irhil Mgoun	Morocco	4,071	13,356
Mt Cameroon	Cameroon	4,070	13,353
Amba Ferit	Ethiopia	3,875	13,042
Pico del Teide	Spain (Tenerife)	3,718	12,198
Thabana Ntlenyana	Lesotho	3,482	11,424
Emi Koussi	Chad	3,415	11,204
Mt aux Sources	Lesotho/S. Africa	3,282	10,768
Mt Piton	Réunion	3,069	10,069

OCEANIA

		m	ft
Puncak Jaya	Indonesia	5,029	16,499
Puncak Trikora	Indonesia	4,750	15,584
Puncak Mandala	Indonesia	4,702	15,427
Mt Wilhelm	Papua NG	4,508	14,790
Mauna Kea	USA (Hawaii)	4,205	13,796
Mauna Loa	USA (Hawaii)	4,169	13,681
Mt Cook (Aoraki)	New Zealand	3,753	12,313
Mt Balbi	Solomon Is.	2,439	8,002
Orohena	Tahiti	2,241	7,352
Mt Kosciuszko	Australia	2,237	7,339

NORTH AMERICA

		m	ft
Mt McKinley (Denali)	USA (Alaska)	6,194	20,321
Mt Logan	Canada	5,959	19,551
Citlaltepetl	Mexico	5,700	18,701
Mt St Elias	USA/Canada	5,489	18,008
Popocatepetl	Mexico	5,452	17,887
Mt Foraker	USA (Alaska)	5,304	17,401
Ixtaccihuatl	Mexico	5,286	17,342
Lucania	Canada	5,227	17,149
Mt Steele	Canada	5,073	16,644
Mt Bona	USA (Alaska)	5,005	16,420
Mt Blackburn	USA (Alaska)	4,996	16,391
Mt Sanford	USA (Alaska)	4,940	16,207
Mt Wood	Canada	4,848	15,905
Nevado de Toluca	Mexico	4,670	15,321

NORTH AMERICA (contined)

		m	ft
Mt Fairweather	USA (Alaska)	4,663	15,298
Mt Hunter	USA (Alaska)	4,442	14,573
Mt Whitney	USA	4,418	14,495
Mt Elbert	USA	4,399	14,432
Mt Harvard	USA	4,395	14,419
Mt Rainier	USA	4,392	14,409
Blanca Peak	USA	4,372	14,344
Longs Peak	USA	4,345	14,255
Tajumulco	Guatemala	4,220	13,845
Grand Teton	USA	4,197	13,770
Mt Waddington	Canada	3,994	13,104
Mt Robson	Canada	3,954	12,972
Chirripó Grande	Costa Rica	3,837	12,589
Pico Duarte	Dominican Rep.	3,175	10,417

SOUTH AMERICA

		m	ft
Aconcagua	Argentina	6,960	22,834
Bonete	Argentina	6,872	22,546
Ojos del Salado	Argentina/Chile	6,863	22,516
Pissis	Argentina	6,779	22,241
Mercedario	Argentina/Chile	6,770	22,211
Huascaran	Peru	6,768	22,204
Llullaillaco	Argentina/Chile	6,723	22,057
Nudo de Cachi	Argentina	6,720	22,047
Yerupaja	Peru	6,632	21,758
N. de Tres Cruces	Argentina/Chile	6,620	21,719
Incahuasi	Argentina/Chile	6,601	21,654
Cerro Galan	Argentina	6,600	21,654
Tupungato	Argentina/Chile	6,570	21,555
Sajama	Bolivia	6,542	21,463
Illimani	Bolivia	6,485	21,276
Coropuna	Peru	6,425	21,079
Ausangate	Peru	6,384	20,945
Cerro del Toro	Argentina	6,380	20,932
Siula Grande	Peru	6,356	20,853
Chimborazo	Ecuador	6,267	20,561
Alpamayo	Peru	5,947	19,511
Cotapaxi	Ecuador	5,896	19,344
Pico Colon	Colombia	5,800	19,029
Pico Bolivar	Venezuela	5,007	16,427

ANTARCTICA

	m	ft
Vinson Massif	4,897	16,066
Mt Kirkpatrick	4,528	14,855
Mt Markham	4,349	14,268

OCEAN DEPTHS

ATLANTIC OCEAN

	m	ft	
Puerto Rico (Milwaukee) Deep	9,220	30,249	[7]
Cayman Trench	7,680	25,197	[10]
Gulf of Mexico	5,203	17,070	
Mediterranean Sea	5,121	16,801	
Black Sea	2,211	7,254	
North Sea	660	2,165	
Baltic Sea	463	1,519	
Hudson Bay	258	846	

INDIAN OCEAN

	m	ft
Java Trench	7,450	24,442
Red Sea	2,635	8,454
Persian Gulf	73	239

PACIFIC OCEAN

	m	ft	
Mariana Trench	11,022	36,161	[1]
Tonga Trench	10,882	35,702	[2]
Japan Trench	10,554	34,626	[3]
Kuril Trench	10,542	34,587	[4]
Mindanao Trench	10,497	34,439	[5]
Kermadec Trench	10,047	32,962	[6]
Peru–Chile Trench	8,050	26,410	[8]
Aleutian Trench	7,822	25,662	[9]

ARCTIC OCEAN

	m	ft
Molloy Deep	5,608	18,399

LAND LOWS

THE WORLD

		m	ft
Dead Sea	Asia	−411	−1,348
Lake Assal	Africa	−156	−512
Death Valley	N. America	−86	−282
Valdés Peninsula	S. America	−40	−131
Caspian Sea	Europe	−28	−92
Lake Eyre North	Oceania	−16	−52

RIVERS

EUROPE

		km	miles	
Volga	Caspian Sea	3,700	2,300	
Danube	Black Sea	2,850	1,770	
Ural	Caspian Sea	2,535	1,575	
Dnepr (Dnipro)	Black Sea	2,285	1,420	
Kama	Volga	2,030	1,260	
Don	Black Sea	1,990	1,240	
Petchora	Arctic Ocean	1,790	1,110	
Oka	Volga	1,480	920	
Belaya	Kama	1,420	880	
Dnister (Dniester)	Black Sea	1,400	870	
Vyatka	Kama	1,370	850	
Rhine	North Sea	1,320	820	
N. Dvina	Arctic Ocean	1,290	800	
Desna	Dnepr (Dnipro)	1,190	740	
Elbe	North Sea	1,145	710	
Wisla	Baltic Sea	1,090	675	
Loire	Atlantic Ocean	1,020	635	

ASIA

		km	miles	
Yangtze	Pacific Ocean	6,380	3,960	[3]
Yenisey–Angara	Arctic Ocean	5,550	3,445	[5]
Huang He	Pacific Ocean	5,464	3,395	[6]
Ob–Irtysh	Arctic Ocean	5,410	3,360	[7]
Mekong	Pacific Ocean	4,500	2,795	[9]
Amur	Pacific Ocean	4,400	2,730	[10]
Lena	Arctic Ocean	4,400	2,730	
Irtysh	Ob	4,250	2,640	
Yenisey	Arctic Ocean	4,090	2,540	
Ob	Arctic Ocean	3,680	2,285	
Indus	Indian Ocean	3,100	1,925	
Brahmaputra	Indian Ocean	2,900	1,800	
Syrdarya	Aral Sea	2,860	1,775	
Salween	Indian Ocean	2,800	1,740	
Euphrates	Indian Ocean	2,700	1,675	
Vilyuy	Lena	2,650	1,645	
Kolyma	Arctic Ocean	2,600	1,615	
Amudarya	Aral Sea	2,540	1,575	
Ural	Caspian Sea	2,535	1,575	
Ganges	Indian Ocean	2,510	1,560	
Si Kiang	Pacific Ocean	2,100	1,305	
Irrawaddy	Indian Ocean	2,010	1,250	
Tarim–Yarkand	Lop Nor	2,000	1,240	
Tigris	Indian Ocean	1,900	1,180	

AFRICA

		km	miles	
Nile	Mediterranean	6,670	4,140	[1]
Congo	Atlantic Ocean	4,670	2,900	[8]
Niger	Atlantic Ocean	4,180	2,595	
Zambezi	Indian Ocean	3,540	2,200	
Oubangi/Uele	Congo (D.R.)	2,250	1,400	
Kasai	Congo (D.R.)	1,950	1,210	
Shaballe	Indian Ocean	1,930	1,200	
Orange	Atlantic Ocean	1,860	1,155	
Cubango	Okavango Delta	1,800	1,120	
Limpopo	Indian Ocean	1,600	995	
Senegal	Atlantic Ocean	1,600	995	
Volta	Atlantic Ocean	1,500	930	

AUSTRALIA

		km	miles	
Murray–Darling	Indian Ocean	3,750	2,330	
Darling	Murray	3,070	1,905	
Murray	Indian Ocean	2,575	1,600	
Murrumbidgee	Murray	1,690	1,050	

NORTH AMERICA

		km	miles	
Mississippi–Missouri	Gulf of Mexico	6,020	3,740	[4]
Mackenzie	Arctic Ocean	4,240	2,630	
Mississippi	Gulf of Mexico	3,780	2,350	
Missouri	Mississippi	3,780	2,350	
Yukon	Pacific Ocean	3,185	1,980	
Rio Grande	Gulf of Mexico	3,030	1,880	
Arkansas	Mississippi	2,340	1,450	
Colorado	Pacific Ocean	2,330	1,445	
Red	Mississippi	2,040	1,270	
Columbia	Pacific Ocean	1,950	1,210	
Saskatchewan	Lake Winnipeg	1,940	1,205	
Snake	Columbia	1,670	1,040	
Churchill	Hudson Bay	1,600	990	
Ohio	Mississippi	1,580	980	
Brazos	Gulf of Mexico	1,400	870	
St Lawrence	Atlantic Ocean	1,170	730	

SOUTH AMERICA

		km	miles	
Amazon	Atlantic Ocean	6,450	4,010	[2]
Paraná–Plate	Atlantic Ocean	4,500	2,800	
Purus	Amazon	3,350	2,080	
Madeira	Amazon	3,200	1,990	
São Francisco	Atlantic Ocean	2,900	1,800	
Paraná	Plate	2,800	1,740	

SOUTH AMERICA (continued)

		km	miles	
Tocantins	Atlantic Ocean	2,750	1,710	
Paraguay	Paraná	2,550	1,580	
Orinoco	Atlantic Ocean	2,500	1,550	
Pilcomayo	Paraná	2,500	1,550	
Araguaia	Tocantins	2,250	1,400	
Juruá	Amazon	2,000	1,240	
Xingu	Amazon	1,980	1,230	
Ucayali	Amazon	1,900	1,180	
Marañón	Amazon	1,600	990	
Uruguay	Plate	1,600	990	

LAKES

EUROPE

		km²	miles²	
Lake Ladoga	Russia	17,700	6,800	
Lake Onega	Russia	9,700	3,700	
Saimaa system	Finland	8,000	3,100	
Vänern	Sweden	5,500	2,100	
Rybinskoye Res.	Russia	4,700	1,800	

ASIA

		km²	miles²	
Caspian Sea	Asia	371,800	143,550	[1]
Lake Baykal	Russia	30,500	11,780	[8]
Aral Sea	Kazak./Uzbekistan	28,687	11,086	[10]
Tonlé Sap	Cambodia	20,000	7,700	
Lake Balqash	Kazakstan	18,500	7,100	
Lake Dongting	China	12,000	4,600	
Lake Ysyk	Kyrgyzstan	6,200	2,400	
Lake Orumiyeh	Iran	5,900	2,300	
Lake Koko	China	5,700	2,200	
Lake Poyang	China	5,000	1,900	
Lake Khanka	China/Russia	4,400	1,700	
Lake Van	Turkey	3,500	1,400	

AFRICA

		km²	miles²	
Lake Victoria	E. Africa	68,000	26,000	[3]
Lake Tanganyika	C. Africa	33,000	13,000	[6]
Lake Malawi/Nyasa	E. Africa	29,600	11,430	[9]
Lake Chad	C. Africa	25,000	9,700	
Lake Turkana	Ethiopia/Kenya	8,500	3,300	
Lake Volta	Ghana	8,500	3,300	
Lake Bangweulu	Zambia	8,000	3,100	
Lake Rukwa	Tanzania	7,000	2,700	
Lake Mai-Ndombe	Congo (D.R.)	6,500	2,500	
Lake Kariba	Zam./Zimbabwe	5,300	2,000	
Lake Albert	Ug./Congo (D.R.)	5,300	2,000	
Lake Nasser	Egypt/Sudan	5,200	2,000	
Lake Mweru	Zam./Congo (D.R.)	4,900	1,900	
Lake Cabora Bassa	Mozambique	4,500	1,700	
Lake Kyoga	Uganda	4,400	1,700	
Lake Tana	Ethiopia	3,630	1,400	

AUSTRALIA

		km²	miles²	
Lake Eyre	Australia	8,900	3,400	
Lake Torrens	Australia	5,800	2,200	
Lake Gairdner	Australia	4,800	1,900	

NORTH AMERICA

		km²	miles²	
Lake Superior	Canada/USA	82,350	31,800	[2]
Lake Huron	Canada/USA	59,600	23,010	[4]
Lake Michigan	USA	58,000	22,400	[5]
Great Bear Lake	Canada	31,800	12,280	[7]
Great Slave Lake	Canada	28,500	11,000	
Lake Erie	Canada/USA	25,700	9,900	
Lake Winnipeg	Canada	24,400	9,400	
Lake Ontario	Canada/USA	19,500	7,500	
Lake Nicaragua	Nicaragua	8,200	3,200	
Lake Athabasca	Canada	8,100	3,100	
Smallwood Reservoir	Canada	6,530	2,520	
Reindeer Lake	Canada	6,400	2,500	
Nettilling Lake	Canada	5,500	2,100	
Lake Winnipegosis	Canada	5,400	2,100	

SOUTH AMERICA

		km²	miles²	
Lake Titicaca	Bolivia/Peru	8,300	3,200	
Lake Poopo	Bolivia	2,800	1,100	

ISLANDS

EUROPE

		km²	miles²	
Great Britain	UK	229,880	88,700	[8]
Iceland	Atlantic Ocean	103,000	39,800	
Ireland	Ireland/UK	84,400	32,600	
Novaya Zemlya (N.)	Russia	48,200	18,600	
W. Spitzbergen	Norway	39,000	15,100	
Novaya Zemlya (S.)	Russia	33,200	12,800	
Sicily	Italy	25,500	9,800	
Sardinia	Italy	24,000	9,300	
N. E. Spitzbergen	Norway	15,000	5,600	

EUROPE (continued)

		km²	miles²	
Corsica	France	8,700	3,400	
Crete	Greece	8,350	3,200	
Zealand	Denmark	6,850	2,600	

ASIA

		km²	miles²	
Borneo	S. E. Asia	744,360	287,400	[3]
Sumatra	Indonesia	473,600	182,860	[6]
Honshu	Japan	230,500	88,980	[7]
Sulawesi (Celebes)	Indonesia	189,000	73,000	
Java	Indonesia	126,700	48,900	
Luzon	Philippines	104,700	40,400	
Mindanao	Philippines	101,500	39,200	
Hokkaido	Japan	78,400	30,300	
Sakhalin	Russia	74,060	28,600	
Sri Lanka	Indian Ocean	65,600	25,300	
Taiwan	Pacific Ocean	36,000	13,900	
Kyushu	Japan	35,700	13,800	
Hainan	China	34,000	13,100	
Timor	Indonesia	33,600	13,000	
Shikoku	Japan	18,800	7,300	
Halmahera	Indonesia	18,000	6,900	
Ceram	Indonesia	17,150	6,600	
Sumbawa	Indonesia	15,450	6,000	
Flores	Indonesia	15,200	5,900	
Samar	Philippines	13,100	5,100	
Negros	Philippines	12,700	4,900	
Bangka	Indonesia	12,000	4,600	
Palawan	Philippines	12,000	4,600	
Panay	Philippines	11,500	4,400	
Sumba	Indonesia	11,100	4,300	
Mindoro	Philippines	9,750	3,800	

AFRICA

		km²	miles²	
Madagascar	Indian Ocean	587,040	226,660	[4]
Socotra	Indian Ocean	3,600	1,400	
Réunion	Indian Ocean	2,500	965	
Tenerife	Atlantic Ocean	2,350	900	
Mauritius	Indian Ocean	1,865	720	

OCEANIA

		km²	miles²	
New Guinea	Indon./Papua NG	821,030	317,000	[2]
New Zealand (S.)	Pacific Ocean	150,500	58,100	
New Zealand (N.)	Pacific Ocean	114,700	44,300	
Tasmania	Australia	67,800	26,200	
New Britain	Papua NG	37,800	14,600	
New Caledonia	Pacific Ocean	19,100	7,400	
Viti Levu	Fiji	10,500	4,100	
Hawaii	Pacific Ocean	10,450	4,000	
Bougainville	Papua NG	9,600	3,700	
Guadalcanal	Solomon Is.	6,500	2,500	
Vanua Levu	Fiji	5,550	2,100	
New Ireland	Papua NG	3,200	1,200	

NORTH AMERICA

		km²	miles²	
Greenland	Atlantic Ocean	2,175,600	839,800	[1]
Baffin Is.	Canada	508,000	196,100	[5]
Victoria Is.	Canada	212,200	81,900	[9]
Ellesmere Is.	Canada	212,000	81,800	[10]
Cuba	Caribbean Sea	110,860	42,800	
Newfoundland	Canada	110,680	42,700	
Hispaniola	Dom. Rep./Haiti	76,200	29,400	
Banks Is.	Canada	67,000	25,900	
Devon Is.	Canada	54,500	21,000	
Melville Is.	Canada	42,400	16,400	
Vancouver Is.	Canada	32,150	12,400	
Somerset Is.	Canada	24,300	9,400	
Jamaica	Caribbean Sea	11,400	4,400	
Puerto Rico	Atlantic Ocean	8,900	3,400	
Cape Breton Is.	Canada	4,000	1,500	

SOUTH AMERICA

		km²	miles²	
Tierra del Fuego	Arg./Chile	47,000	18,100	
Falkland Is. (East)	Atlantic Ocean	6,800	2,600	
South Georgia	Atlantic Ocean	4,200	1,600	
Galapagos (Isabela)	Pacific Ocean	2,250	870	

World: Regions in the News

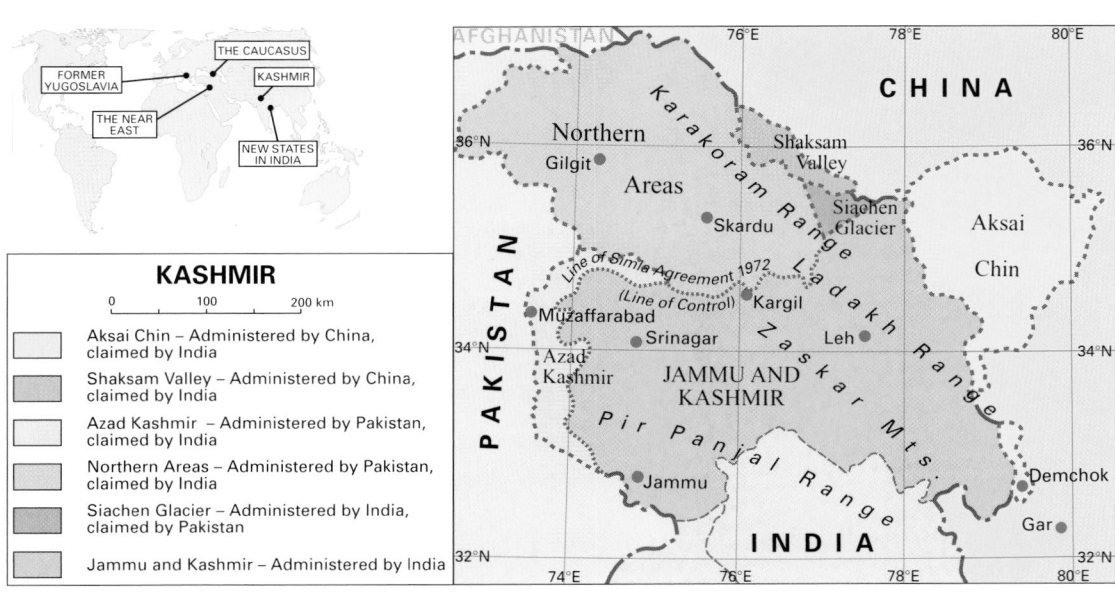

KASHMIR

Scale: 0 — 100 — 200 km

- Aksai Chin – Administered by China, claimed by India
- Shaksam Valley – Administered by China, claimed by India
- Azad Kashmir – Administered by Pakistan, claimed by India
- Northern Areas – Administered by Pakistan, claimed by India
- Siachen Glacier – Administered by India, claimed by Pakistan
- Jammu and Kashmir – Administered by India

THREE NEW STATES IN INDIA

Scale: 0 — 100 — 200 km

- Chhattisgarh: Created 01/11/00 (formerly part of Madhya Pradesh) Population: 17.6 million Capital: Raipur
- Uttaranchal: Created 09/11/00 (formerly part of Uttar Pradesh) Population: 7.0 million Provisional capital: Dehra Dun
- Jharkhand: Created 15/11/00 (formerly part of Bihar) Population: 26.9 million Capital: Ranchi

FORMER YUGOSLAVIA

YUGOSLAVIA
Population 10,761,000
(Serb 62.6%, Albanian 16.5%, Montenegrin 5%, Hungarian 3.3%, Muslim 3.2%)
Serbia Population: 5,799,800
(Serb 87.7%, excluding the provinces of Kosovo and Vojvodina)
Kosovo Population: 2,084,4000
(Albanian 81.6%, Serb 9.9%)
Vojvodena Population: 1,980,800
(Serb 56.8%, Hungarian 16.9%)
Montenegro Population: 635,000
(Montenegrin 61.9%, Muslim 14.6%, Albanian 7%)

CROATIA
Population: 4,960,000
(Croat 78.1%, Serb 12.2%)

SLOVENIA
Population: 2,055,000
(Slovene 88%, Croat 3%, Serb 2%)

MACEDONIA (F. Y. R. O. M.)
Population: 2,157,000
(Macedonian 64%, Albanian 21.7%, Turkish 5%, Romanian 3%, Serb 2%)

BOSNIA-HERZEGOVINA
Population: 4,601,000
(Muslim 49%, Serb 31.2%, Croat 17.2%)

Scale: 0 — 100 — 200 km

- ⋅–⋅– International boundaries
- –⋅– Republic boundaries
- – – Province boundaries
- ■ Capital cities
- — Dayton Peace Agreement Boundary
- Muslim–Croat Federation
- Bosnian Serb Republic

COUNTRIES AND REPUBLICS OF THE CAUCASUS REGION

RUSSIAN REPUBLICS
North Ossetia (Alania)
Population: 695,000
(Ossetian 53%, Russian 29%, Chechen 5.2%, Armenian 1.9%)

Chechenia Population: 1,308,000
(Chechen and Ingush 70.7%, Russian 23.1%, Armenian 1.2%)

Ingushetia (Split from Chechenia in June 1993)
Population: 250,000

GEORGIA
Population: 5,777,000
(Georgian 70.1%, Armenian 8.1%, Russian 6.3%, Azerbaijani 5.7%, Ossetian 3%, Greek 2%, Abkhazian 2%)

Abkhazia Population: 537,500
(Georgian 45.7%, Abkhazian 17.8%, Armenian 14.6%, Russian 14.3%)

Ajaria Population: 382,000
(Georgian 82.8%, Russian 7.7%, Armenian 4%)

ARMENIA
Population: 3,968,000
(Armenian 93%, Azerbaijani 3%)

Nagorno-Karabakh
Population: 192,400 (Armenian 76.9%, Azerbaijani 21.5%)

AZERBAIJAN
Population: 8,324,000
(Azerbaijani 83%, Russian 6%, Armenian 6%, Lezgin 2%)

Naxçivan Population: 300,400

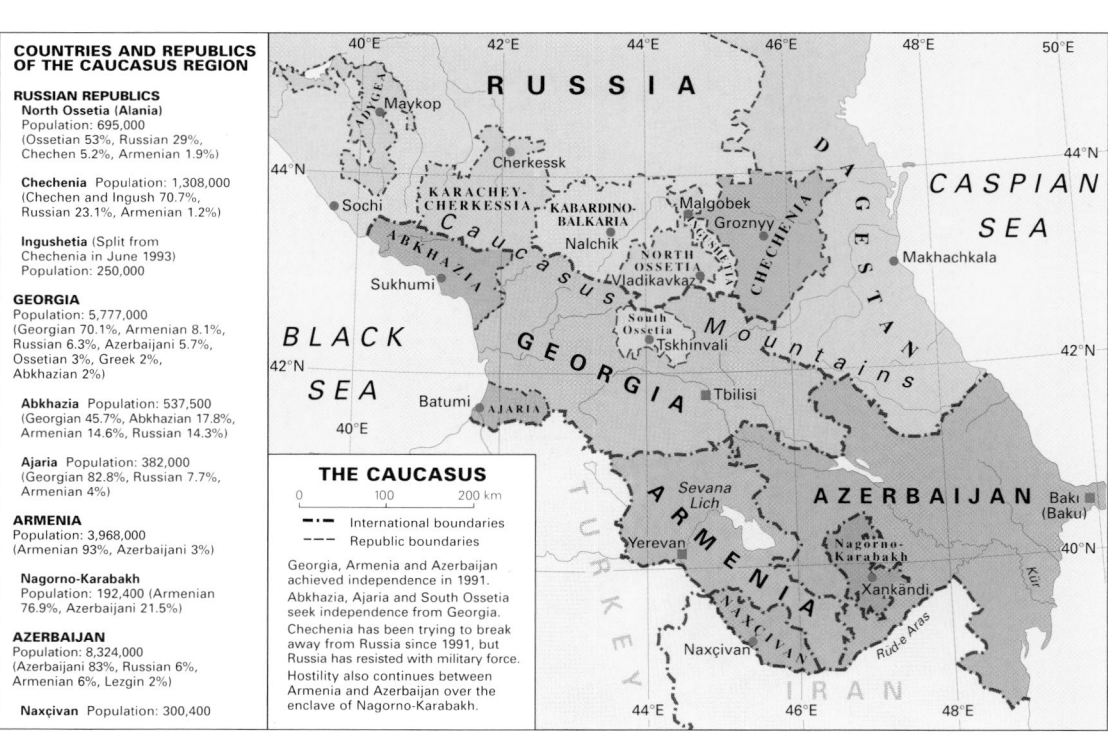

THE CAUCASUS

Scale: 0 — 100 — 200 km

- ⋅–⋅– International boundaries
- –⋅– Republic boundaries

Georgia, Armenia and Azerbaijan achieved independence in 1991. Abkhazia, Ajaria and South Ossetia seek independence from Georgia. Chechenia has been trying to break away from Russia since 1991, but Russia has resisted with military force. Hostility also continues between Armenia and Azerbaijan over the enclave of Nagorno-Karabakh.

THE NEAR EAST

Scale: 0 — 25 — 50 km

- ⋅–⋅– 1949 Armistice Line
- – – 1974 Cease–fire Line
- Palestinian control
- Joint Israeli/ Palestinian control
- ● *Efrata* Main Jewish settlements in the West Bank and Gaza Strip
- □ *Halhul* Main Palestinian Arab towns in the West Bank and Gaza Strip
- — Road corridor linking Gaza and West Bank

ISRAEL
Population: 5,321,000 (inc. East Jerusalem and Jewish settlers in the areas under Israeli administration. Jewish 82%, Arab Muslim 13.8%, Arab Christian 2.5%, Druze 1.7%)

West Bank
Population: 1,122,900 (Palestinian Arabs 97% [of whom Arab Muslim 85%, Jewish 7%, Christian 8%])

Gaza Strip
Population: 748,400 (Arab 98%)

JORDAN
Population: 5,558,000 (Arab 99% [of whom about 50% are Palestinian Arab])

LEBANON
Population: 3,327,000 (Arab 93% [of whom 83% are Lebanese Arab and 10% Palestinian Arab])

Images of Earth

– CHICAGO, ILLINOIS, USA –

This image shows the entire urban area of greater Chicago, which is situated on the south-western shore of Lake Michigan. The runway pattern of the second busiest airport in the world, O'Hare International, can be clearly seen towards the top of the image.

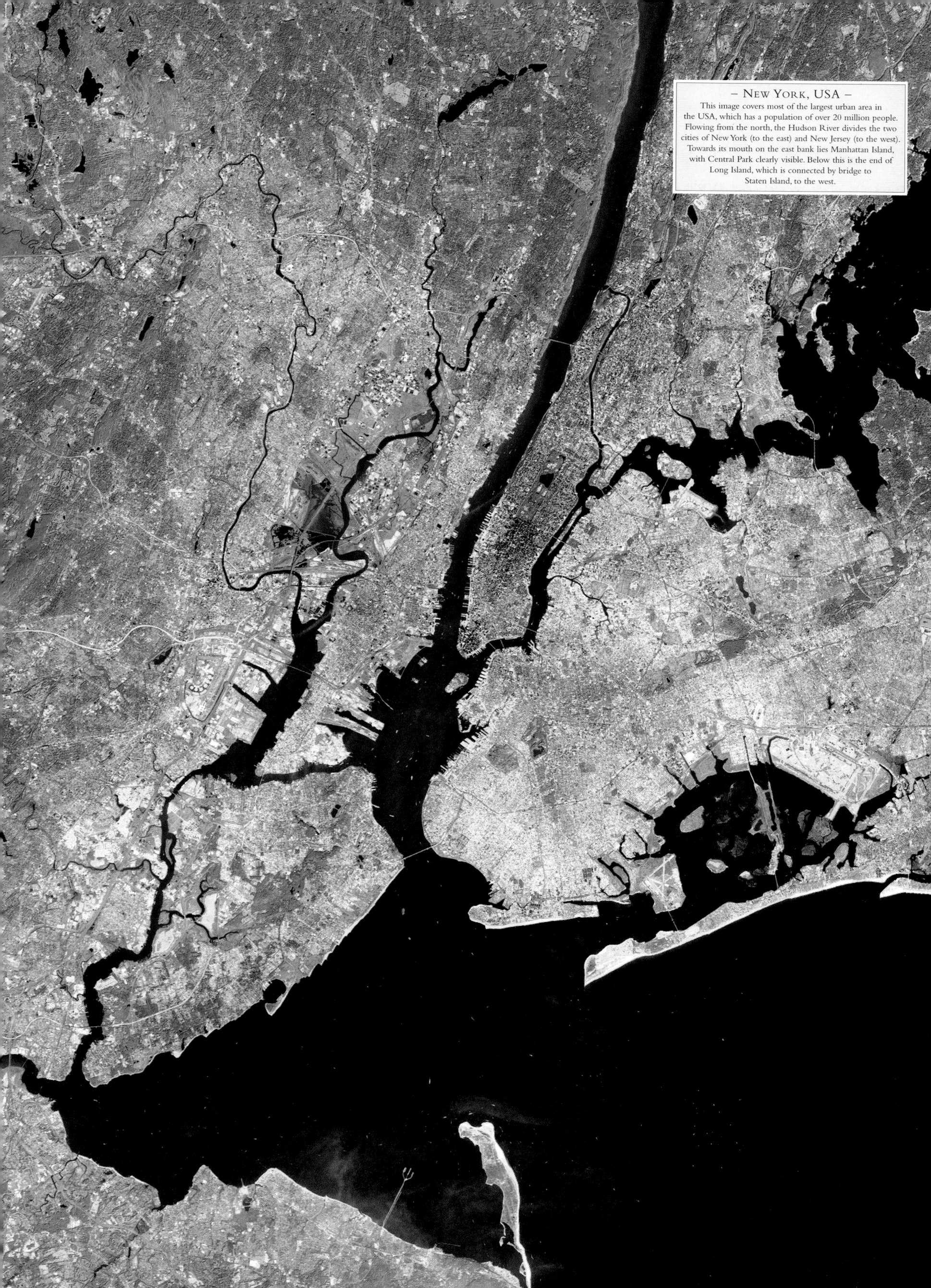

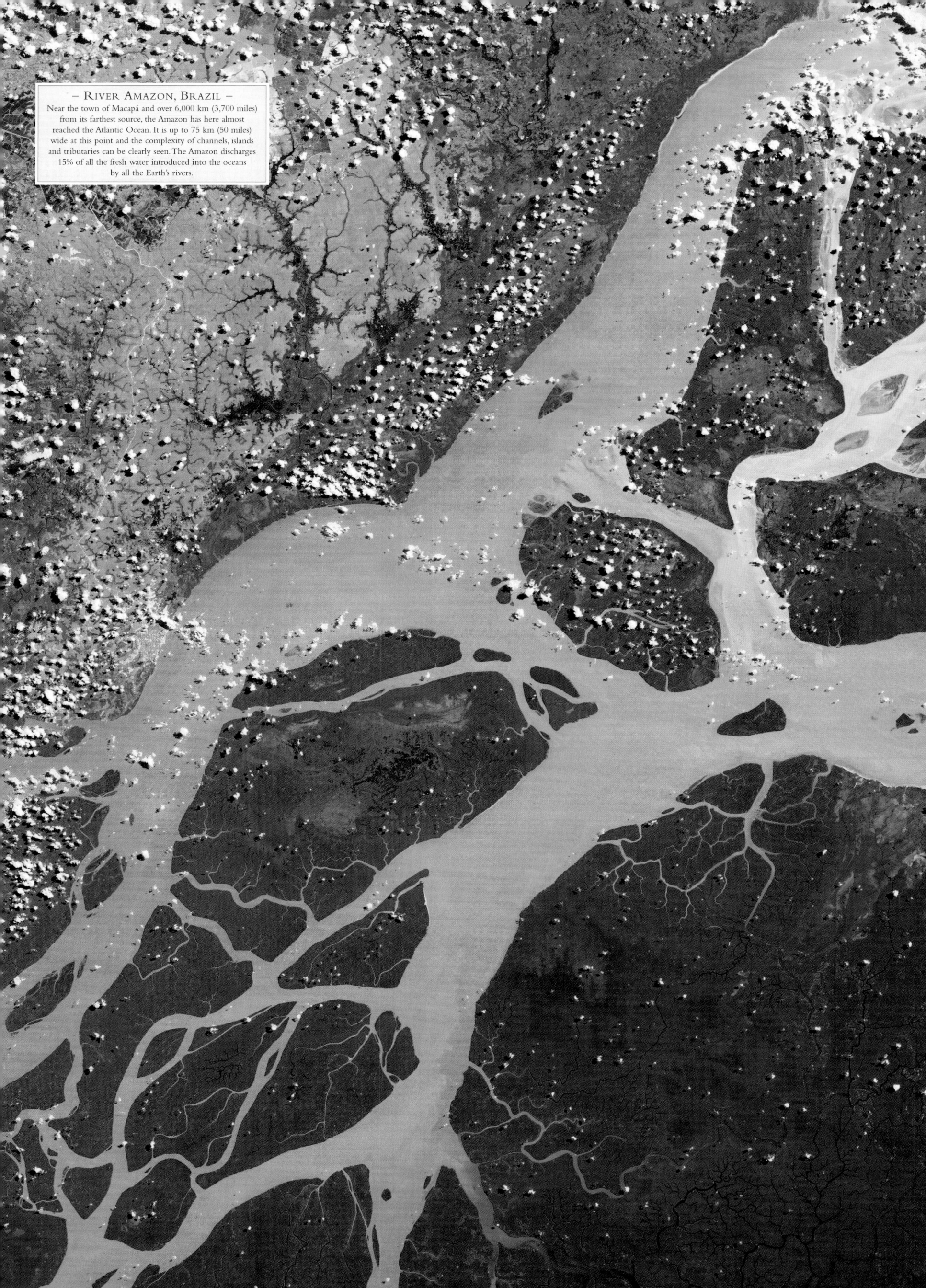

— RIVER AMAZON, BRAZIL —

Near the town of Macapá and over 6,000 km (3,700 miles)
from its farthest source, the Amazon has here almost
reached the Atlantic Ocean. It is up to 75 km (50 miles)
wide at this point and the complexity of channels, islands
and tributaries can be clearly seen. The Amazon discharges
15% of all the fresh water introduced into the oceans
by all the Earth's rivers.

— BUENOS AIRES, ARGENTINA —
Buenos Aires is situated where the continent's second
largest river system, the Paraná–Paraguay–Uruguay, flows into
the flooded river valley that forms its estuary, the Río de la
Plata (River Plate). The River Paraná flows in at top left of
the image. To the city's south and west is grazing land for
livestock, while in the top right-hand corner, in Uruguay,
wheat is the predominant crop locally.

– LONDON, UNITED KINGDOM –

The whole area of Greater London is shown here, including Heathrow Airport at far left. The River Thames stands out, as do the former London docks and the reservoirs in the River Lea valley to the north-east. Despite having a population in excess of 8 million people, there are still many open spaces and parks around the city centre.

— IJSSELMEER, NETHERLANDS —
This unique feature was created in the 13th century when the sea breached a protective sand bar, flooding all the low-lying land. The remnants of the bar can still be seen as the chain of Frisian Islands at the top of the image. Reclamation on a large scale started in 1932 with the completion of the causeway in the north. Since then four 'polders' have been drained and reclaimed. The city of Amsterdam is situated at bottom left.

— CAIRO, EGYPT —

The largest city in Africa with almost 10 million inhabitants,
Cairo evolved on the eastern bank of the River Nile, near
its delta. This image clearly shows the differences between the
arid desert areas to the south-east and south-west, the fertile
lands of the Nile flood plain, and the urban area itself.
The shadows of the Pyramids on the Giza Plateau can be
seen on the left-hand edge of the cultivated area, below
where the road crosses it.

— WESTERN CAPE, SOUTH AFRICA —
Cape Town sits to the bottom left of this image, with
the Cape Peninsula running south-east to the Cape of
Good Hope. Inland from the fertile coastal plain, where most
of South Africa's wine is produced, is the rugged interior
of the Great Karoo where parallel mountain ranges are
dissected by river valleys.

– SHANGHAI, CHINA –

This image shows Shanghai (at bottom centre) in its setting on the south bank of the mouth of the Chang Jiang (Yangtse). It is the natural focus for much of China's sea trade, sitting at the gateway to one of China's richest regions and with the river navigable for ocean-going vessels up to Hankou, 1,000 km (600 miles) inland. As such it has grown to a town of over 15 million people and is China's major commercial and financial centre.

— TOKYO, JAPAN —

At the head of Tokyo Bay, the city, with its satellites of
Kawasaki and Yokohama, forms one of the world's most
densely populated areas with over 26 million people. Owing
to the shortage of space, much development has taken place
on areas reclaimed from the sea. One of these is Haneda
International Airport, whose runway pattern is clearly
visible at the mouth of the Tama River. The Tokyo Bay
bridge/tunnel projects into the Bay from the eastern shore.

Introduction to

WORLD GEOGRAPHY

The Universe

About 15 billion years ago, time and space began with the most colossal explosion in cosmic history: the so-called 'Big Bang' that is believed to have initiated the universe. According to current theory, in the first millionth of a second of its existence it expanded from a dimensionless point of infinite mass and density into a fireball about 30 billion kilometres across; and it has been expanding ever since.

It took almost a million years for the primal fireball to cool enough for atoms to form. They were mostly hydrogen, still the most abundant material in the universe. But the new matter was not evenly distributed around the young universe, and a few billion years later atoms in relatively dense regions began to cling together under the influence of gravity, forming distinct masses of gas separated by vast expanses of empty space. To begin with, these first proto-galaxies were dark places: the universe had cooled. But gravitational attraction continued, condensing matter into coherent lumps inside the galactic gas clouds. About three billion years later, some of these masses had contracted so much that internal pressure produced the high temperatures necessary to bring about nuclear fusion: the first stars were born.

There were several generations of stars, each feeding on the wreckage of its extinct predecessors as well as the original galactic gas swirls. With each new generation, progressively larger atoms were forged in stellar furnaces and the galaxy's range of elements, once restricted to hydrogen, grew larger. About 10 billion years after the Big Bang, a star formed on the outskirts of our galaxy with enough matter left over to create a retinue of planets. Nearly five billion years after that human beings evolved.

The Sun is one of more than 100 billion stars in the home galaxy alone. Our galaxy, in turn, forms part of a local group of approximately 30 similar structures, some much larger than our own; there are at least 100 billion other galaxies in the universe as a whole. The most distant ever observed, a highly energetic galactic core known only as quasar PC 1247 +3406, lies about 12 billion light-years away.

Life of a Star

For most of its existence, a star produces energy by the nuclear fusion of hydrogen into helium at its core. The duration of this hydrogen-burning period – known as the main sequence – depends on the star's mass; the greater the mass, the higher the core temperatures and the sooner the star's supply of hydrogen is exhausted. Dim, dwarf stars consume their hydrogen slowly, eking it out over 1,000 billion years or more. The Sun, like other stars of its mass, should spend about 10 billion years on the main sequence; since it was formed less than five billion years ago, it still has half its life left.

Once all a star's core hydrogen has been fused into helium, nuclear activity moves outwards into layers of unconsumed hydrogen. For a time, energy production sharply increases: the star grows hotter and expands enormously, turning into a so-called red giant. Its energy output will increase a thousandfold, and it will swell to a hundred times its present diameter.

After a few hundred million years, helium in the core will become sufficiently compressed to initiate a new cycle of nuclear fusion: from helium to carbon. The star will contract somewhat, before beginning its last expansion, in the Sun's case engulfing the Earth and perhaps Mars. In this bloated condition, the Sun's outer layers will break off into space, leaving a tiny inner core, mainly of carbon, that shrinks progressively under the force of its own gravity: dwarf stars can attain a density more than 10,000 times that of normal matter, with crushing surface gravities to match. Gradually, the nuclear fires will die down, and the Sun will reach its terminal stage: a black dwarf, emitting insignificant amounts of energy.

However, stars more massive than the Sun may undergo another transformation. The additional mass allows gravitational collapse to continue indefinitely: eventually, all the star's remaining matter shrinks to a point, and its density approaches infinity – a state that will not permit even subatomic structures to survive.

The star has become a black hole: an anomalous 'singularity' in the fabric of space and time. Although vast coruscations of radiation will be emitted by any matter falling into its grasp, the singularity itself has an escape velocity that exceeds the speed of light, and nothing can ever be released from it. Within the boundaries of the black hole, the laws of physics are suspended, but no physicist can ever observe the extraordinary events that may occur.

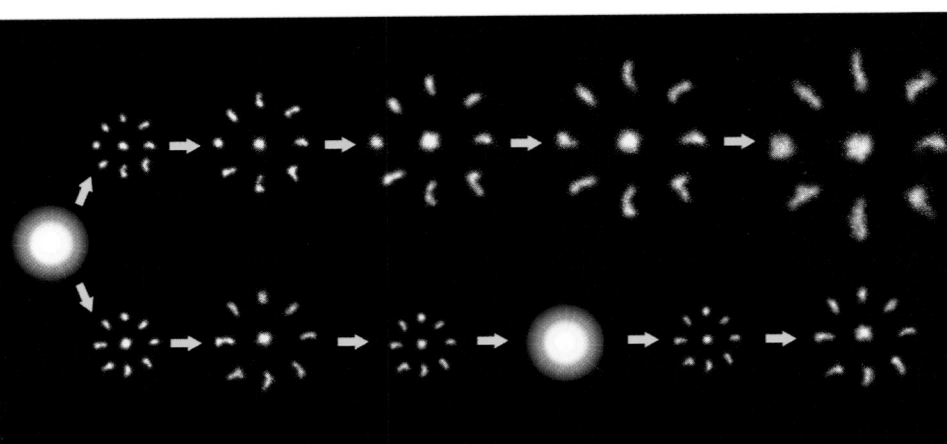

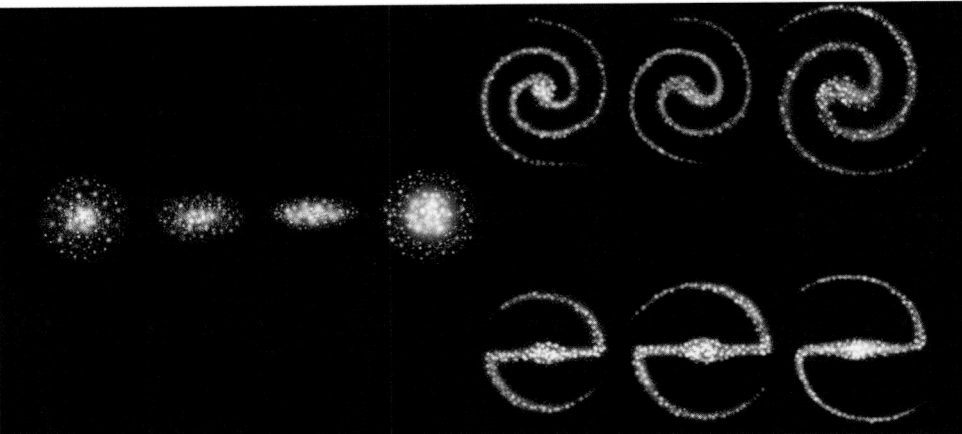

The End of the Universe

The likely fate of the universe is disputed. One theory (shown top left) dictates that the expansion begun at the time of the Big Bang will continue 'indefinitely', with ageing galaxies moving further and further apart in an immense, dark graveyard.

Alternatively, gravity may overcome the expansion (bottom left). Galaxies will fall back together until everything is again concentrated at a single point, followed by a new Big Bang and a new expansion, in an endlessly repeated cycle.

The first of these theories is supported by the amount of visible matter in the universe; the second theory assumes that there is enough dark material to bring about the gravitational collapse.

Galactic Structures

Many of the universe's 100 billion galaxies show clear structural patterns, originally classified by the American astronomer Edwin Hubble in 1925. Spiral galaxies like our own (top row) have a central, almost spherical bulge and a surrounding disk composed of spiral arms. Barred spirals (bottom row) have a central bar of stars across the nucleus, with spiral arms trailing from the ends of the bar. Elliptical galaxies (far left) have a uniform appearance, ranging from a flattened disk to a near sphere. So-called SO galaxies (left row, right) have a central bulge, but no spiral arms. Most galaxies, however, have no obvious structure at all.

Galaxies also vary enormously in size, from dwarfs only 2,000 light-years across to great assemblies of stars 80 or more times larger.

The Home Galaxy

The Sun and its planets are located in one of the spiral arms, a little less than 28,000 light-years from the galactic centre and orbiting around it in a period of 200 million years. The centre is invisible from the Earth, masked by vast, light-absorbing clouds of interstellar dust. The galaxy is probably around 12 billion years old and, like other spiral galaxies, has three distinct regions. The central bulge is about 30,000 light-years in diameter. The disk in which the Sun is located is not much more than 1,000 light-years thick but 100,000 light-years from end to end. Around the galaxy is the halo, a spherical zone 300,000 light-years across, studded with globular star-clusters and sprinkled with individual suns.

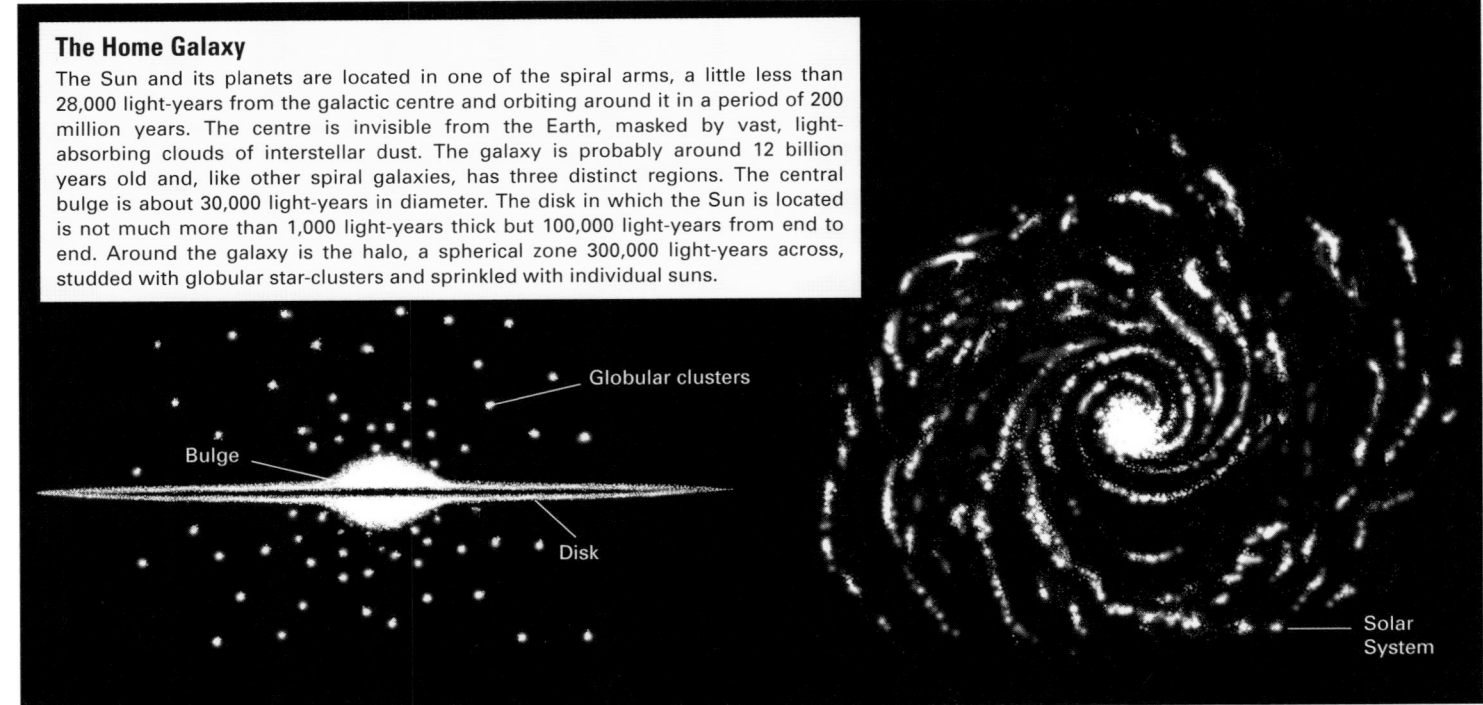

Globular clusters

Bulge

Disk

Solar System

Star Charts

Star charts are drawn as projections of a vast, hollow sphere with the observer in the middle. Each circle below represents slightly more than one hemisphere, centred on the north and south celestial poles respectively – projections of the Earth's poles in the heavens. At the present era, the north pole is marked by the star Polaris; the south pole has no such convenient reference point.

Astronomical co-ordinates are normally given in terms of 'Right Ascension' for longitude and 'Declination' for latitude or altitude. Since the stars appear to rotate around the Earth once every 24 hours, Right Ascension is measured eastwards – anticlockwise – in hours and minutes and is marked around the edge of the map. One hour is equivalent to 15 angular degrees; zero on the scale is the point at which the Sun crosses the celestial equator at the spring equinox, known to astronomers as the First Point in Aries. Unlike the Sun, stars always rise and set at the same point on the horizon. Declination measures (in degrees) a star's angular distance above or below the celestial equator and is marked on the vertical line.

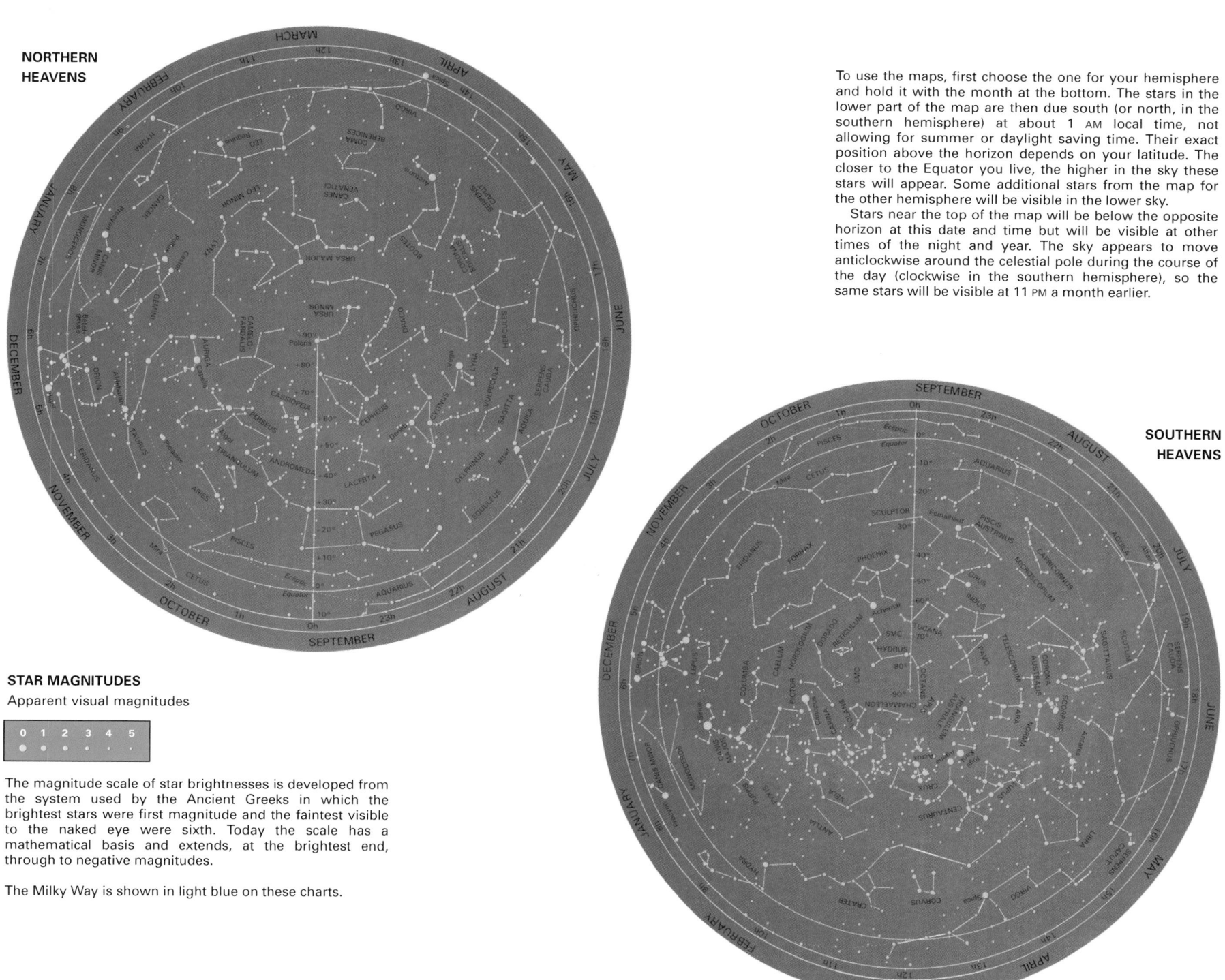

NORTHERN HEAVENS

SOUTHERN HEAVENS

To use the maps, first choose the one for your hemisphere and hold it with the month at the bottom. The stars in the lower part of the map are then due south (or north, in the southern hemisphere) at about 1 AM local time, not allowing for summer or daylight saving time. Their exact position above the horizon depends on your latitude. The closer to the Equator you live, the higher in the sky these stars will appear. Some additional stars from the map for the other hemisphere will be visible in the lower sky.

Stars near the top of the map will be below the opposite horizon at this date and time but will be visible at other times of the night and year. The sky appears to move anticlockwise around the celestial pole during the course of the day (clockwise in the southern hemisphere), so the same stars will be visible at 11 PM a month earlier.

STAR MAGNITUDES

Apparent visual magnitudes

0	1	2	3	4	5

The magnitude scale of star brightnesses is developed from the system used by the Ancient Greeks in which the brightest stars were first magnitude and the faintest visible to the naked eye were sixth. Today the scale has a mathematical basis and extends, at the brightest end, through to negative magnitudes.

The Milky Way is shown in light blue on these charts.

THE NEAREST STARS

The 20 nearest stars, excluding the Sun, with their distance from Earth in light-years*

Proxima Centauri	4.25	Many of the nearest stars, like
Alpha Centauri A	4.3	Alpha Centauri A and B, are
Alpha Centauri B	4.3	doubles, orbiting about the
Barnard's Star	6.0	common centre of gravity
Wolf 359	7.8	and to all intents and
Lalande 21185	8.3	purposes equidistant from
Sirius A	8.7	Earth. Many of them are dim
Sirius B	8.7	objects, with no name other
UV Ceti A	8.7	than the designation given
UV Ceti B	8.7	by the astronomers who
Ross 154	9.4	investigated them. However,
Ross 248	10.3	they include Sirius, the
Epsilon Eridani	10.7	brightest star in the sky,
Ross 128	10.9	and Procyon, the seventh
61 Cygni A	11.1	brightest. Both are far larger
61 Cygni B	11.1	than the Sun; of the nearest
Epsilon Indi	11.2	stars, only Epsilon Eridani is
Groombridge 34A	11.2	similar in size and luminosity.
Groombridge 34B	11.2	
L789-6	11.2	* A light-year equals approx.
Procyon A	11.4	9,500,000,000,000 kilometres
Procyon B	11.4	

THE CONSTELLATIONS

The constellations and their English names

Andromeda	Andromeda	Circinus	Compasses	Lacerta	Lizard	Piscis Austrinus	Southern Fish
Antlia	Air Pump	Columba	Dove	Leo	Lion	Puppis	Ship's Stern
Apus	Bird of Paradise	Coma Berenices	Berenice's Hair	Leo Minor	Little Lion	Pyxis	Mariner's Compass
Aquarius	Water Carrier	Corona Australis	Southern Crown	Lepus	Hare	Reticulum	Net
Aquila	Eagle	Corona Borealis	Northern Crown	Libra	Scales	Sagitta	Arrow
Ara	Altar	Corvus	Crow	Lupus	Wolf	Sagittarius	Archer
Aries	Ram	Crater	Cup	Lynx	Lynx	Scorpius	Scorpion
Auriga	Charioteer	Crux	Southern Cross	Lyra	Lyre	Sculptor	Sculptor
Boötes	Herdsman	Cygnus	Swan	Mensa	Table	Scutum	Shield
Caelum	Chisel	Delphinus	Dolphin	Microscopium	Microscope	Serpens	Serpent
Camelopardalis	Giraffe	Dorado	Swordfish	Monoceros	Unicorn	Sextans	Sextant
Cancer	Crab	Draco	Dragon	Musca	Fly	Taurus	Bull
Canes Venatici	Hunting Dogs	Equuleus	Little Horse	Norma	Level	Telescopium	Telescope
Canis Major	Great Dog	Eridanus	Eridanus	Octans	Octant	Triangulum	Triangle
Canis Minor	Little Dog	Fornax	Furnace	Ophiuchus	Serpent Bearer	Triangulum Australe	Southern Triangle
Capricornus	Goat	Gemini	Twins	Orion	Orion	Tucana	Toucan
Carina	Keel	Grus	Crane	Pavo	Peacock	Ursa Major	Great Bear
Cassiopeia	Cassiopeia	Hercules	Hercules	Pegasus	Winged Horse	Ursa Minor	Little Bear
Centaurus	Centaur	Horologium	Clock	Perseus	Perseus	Vela	Sails
Cepheus	Cepheus	Hydra	Water Snake	Phoenix	Phoenix	Virgo	Virgin
Cetus	Whale	Hydrus	Sea Serpent	Pictor	Easel	Volans	Flying Fish
Chamaeleon	Chameleon	Indus	Indian	Pisces	Fishes	Vulpecula	Fox

The Solar System

Lying 28,000 light-years from the centre of one of billions of galaxies that comprise the observable universe, our Solar System contains nine planets and their moons, innumerable asteroids and comets, and a miscellany of dust and gas, all tethered by the immense gravitational field of the Sun, the middling-sized star whose thermonuclear furnaces provide them all with heat and light. The Solar System was formed about 4,600 million years ago, when a spinning cloud of gas, mostly hydrogen but seeded with other, heavier elements, condensed enough to ignite a nuclear reaction and create a star. The Sun still accounts for almost 99.9% of the system's total mass; one planet, Jupiter, contains most of the remainder.

By composition as well as distance, the planetary array divides neatly in two: an inner system of four small, solid planets, including the Earth, and an outer system, from Jupiter to Neptune, of four much larger planets composed of lighter materials, such as gas, liquid and ice. Between the two groups lies a scattering of rocky asteroids, perhaps as many as 400,000. They may be debris left over from the inner solar system's formation. The outermost planet, Pluto, may simply be the largest of a number of bodies composed of rock and ice orbiting beyond Neptune, similarly left over from the formation of the outer solar system.

By the 1990s, however, the Solar System also included some newer anomalies: several thousand spacecraft. Most were in orbit around the Earth, but some had probed far and wide around the system. The valuable information beamed back by these robotic investigators has transformed our knowledge of our celestial environment.

Much of the early history of science is the story of people trying to make sense of the errant points of light that were all they knew of the planets. Now, men have stood on the Earth's Moon; probes have landed on Mars and Venus, and orbiting radars have mapped far distant landscapes with astonishing accuracy. In the 1980s, the US *Voyagers* skimmed all four major planets of the outer system, bringing new revelations with each close approach. Only Pluto, inscrutably distant in an orbit that takes it 50 times the Earth's distance from the Sun, remains unvisited by our messengers.

Orbits of the Planets

The solar planets and their orbits, showing the relative position of each planet at the vernal equinox of 1992.

Orbits are drawn to exact scale, but with the Sun and planets greatly enlarged for clarity. The Solar System is shown from the viewpoint of an observer a few light-hours distant in the direction of the constellation Hercules. Seen from such a position, above the plane of the ecliptic, all the planets revolve about the Sun in an anti-clockwise direction. The perspective view exaggerates the elliptical form of all the planetary orbits: only Pluto and Mercury follow paths that deviate noticeably from circularity. Near perihelion – its closest approach to the Sun – Pluto actually passes inside the orbit of Neptune, an event that last occurred in 1983. Pluto did not regain its station as the Sun's outer-most planet until February 1999.

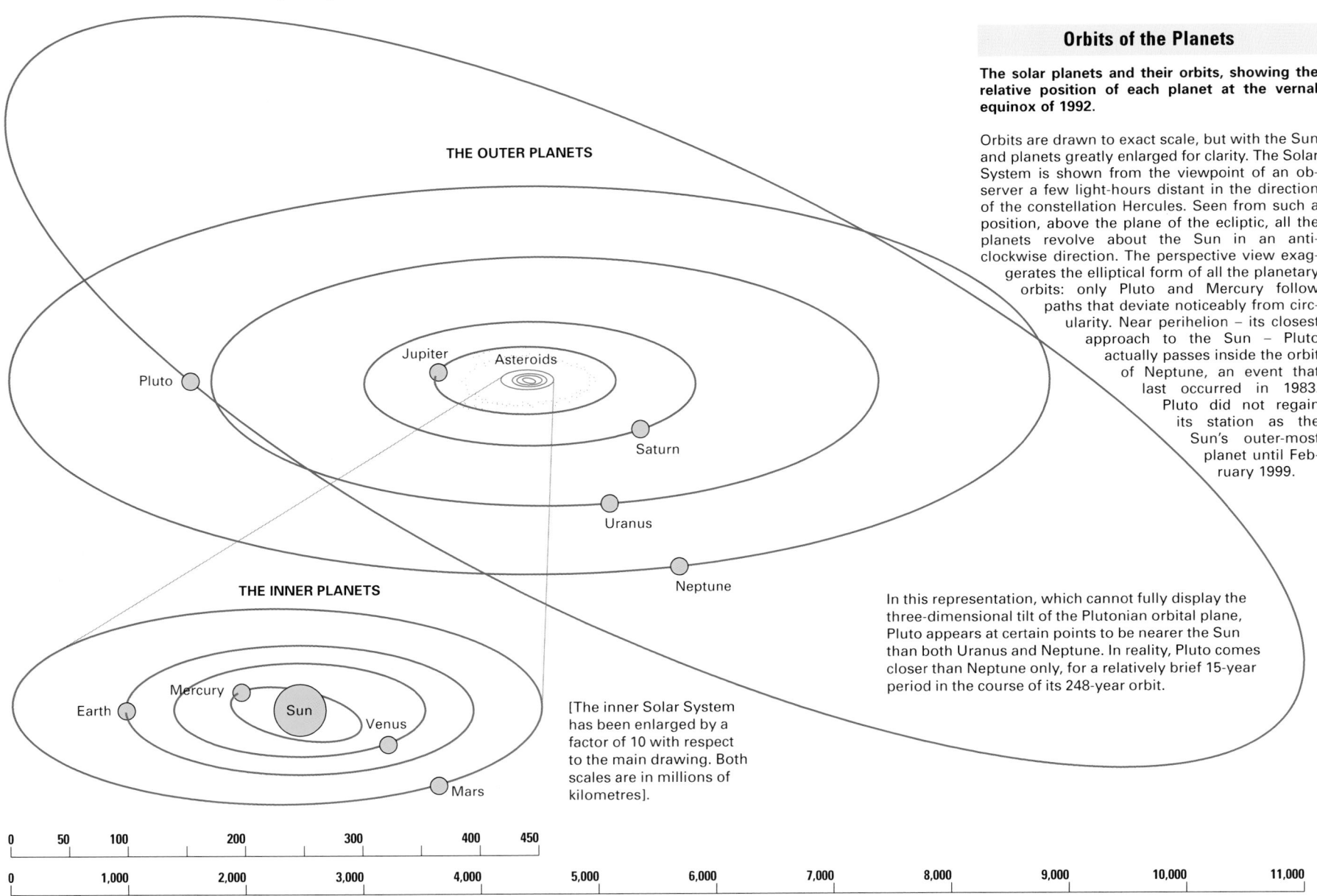

THE OUTER PLANETS

Pluto
Jupiter   Asteroids
Saturn
Uranus
Neptune

THE INNER PLANETS

Mercury
Earth   Sun   Venus
Mars

[The inner Solar System has been enlarged by a factor of 10 with respect to the main drawing. Both scales are in millions of kilometres].

In this representation, which cannot fully display the three-dimensional tilt of the Plutonian orbital plane, Pluto appears at certain points to be nearer the Sun than both Uranus and Neptune. In reality, Pluto comes closer than Neptune only, for a relatively brief 15-year period in the course of its 248-year orbit.

| 0 | 50 | 100 | 200 | 300 | 400 | 450 |

| 0 | 1,000 | 2,000 | 3,000 | 4,000 | 5,000 | 6,000 | 7,000 | 8,000 | 9,000 | 10,000 | 11,000 |

Planetary Data

	Mean distance from Sun (million km)	Mass (Earth = 1)	Period of orbit (Earth years)	Period of rotation (Earth days)	Equatorial diameter (km)	Average density (water = 1)	Surface gravity (Earth = 1)	Escape velocity (km/sec)	Number of known satellites
Sun	–	332,946	–	25.38	1,392,000	1.41	27.9	617.5	–
Mercury	57.9	0.06	0.241	58.67	4,878	5.43	0.38	4.25	0
Venus	108.2	0.8	0.615	243.00	12,100	5.24	0.90	10.36	0
Earth	149.6	1.0	1.00	1.00	12,756	5.52	1.00	11.18	1
Mars	227.9	0.1	1.88	1.02	6,794	3.93	0.38	5.03	2
Jupiter	778.3	317.8	11.86	0.41	142,800	1.33	2.69	59.60	16
Saturn	1,426.8	95.2	29.46	0.42	120,000	0.706	1.16	35.60	18
Uranus	2,869.4	14.5	84.01	0.45	52,400	1.25	0.93	21.10	15
Neptune	4,496.3	17.1	164.79	0.71	48,400	1.77	1.21	24.60	8
Pluto	5,900.1	0.002	247.7	6.39	2,445	1.40	0.05	1.20	1

Planetary days are given in sidereal time – that is, with respect to the stars rather than the Sun. Most of the information in the table was confirmed by spacecraft and often obtained from photographs and other data transmitted back to the Earth. In the case of Pluto, however, only earthbound observations have been made, and no spacecraft will encounter it until well into the 21st century. Given the planet's small size and great distance, figures for its diameter and rotation period have only recently been confirmed.

Pluto is not massive enough to account for the perturbations in the orbits of Uranus and Neptune that led to its 1930 discovery, but it is now widely believed that these perturbations can be explained away as observational errors made by the earlier observers.

The Planets

Mercury is the closest planet to the Sun and hence the fastest-moving. It is very hot with a cratered, wrinkled surface very similar to that of Earth's Moon. It is small and has no gravity, hence there is no significant atmosphere.

Venus has much the same physical dimensions as Earth. Its dense atmosphere is composed of 97% CO_2 resulting in a runaway greenhouse effect that makes the Venusian surface, at 475°C, the hottest of all the planets in the Solar System. Radar mapping shows relatively level land with volcanic regions whose sulphurous discharges explain the sulphuric acid rains reported by soft-landing space probes before they succumbed to Venus' fierce climate.

Earth seen from space is easily the most beautiful of the inner planets; it is also, and more objectively, the largest, as well as the only home of known life. Living things are the main reason why the Earth is able to retain a substantial proportion of corrosive and highly reactive oxygen in its atmosphere, a state of affairs that contradicts the laws of chemical equilibrium; the oxygen in turn supports the life that constantly regenerates it.

Mars, smaller and cooler than the Earth, is nevertheless the most likely planet other than Earth where life may have formed. Vast water channels show that it was once warmer and wetter; there may still be traces of former simple life forms, though whether life could thrive in its current cold, dry and thin atmosphere is doubtful. The ice caps are mainly frozen carbon dioxide, and whatever oxygen the planet once possessed is now locked up in the iron-bearing rock that covers its cratered surface and gives it its characteristic red hue. Mars is a dustbowl with occasional storms whirling the dust high into the air.

Jupiter masses almost three times as much as all the other planets combined; had it scooped up rather more matter during its formation, it might have evolved into a small companion star for the Sun. The planet is mostly gas, under intense pressure in the lower atmosphere above a core of fiercely compressed hydrogen and helium. The upper layers form strikingly-coloured rotating belts, the outward sign of the intense storms created by Jupiter's rapid diurnal rotation. Close approaches by spacecraft have shown an orbiting ring system and discovered several previously unknown moons: Jupiter has at least 16 moons.

Saturn is structurally similar to Jupiter, rotating fast enough to produce an obvious bulge at its equator. It is composed of 89% hydrogen and 11% helium, and has wind velocities in the outer atmosphere of 500 metres per second. Ever since the invention of the telescope, however, Saturn's rings have been the feature that has attracted most observers. *Voyager* probes in 1980 and 1981 sent back detailed pictures that showed them to be composed of thousands of separate ringlets, each in turn made up of tiny icy particles.

Uranus was unknown to the ancients. Although it is faintly visible to the naked eye, it was not discovered until 1781. Its interior is largely water, with an atmosphere of hydrogen, helium and some methane, which gives the planet its blue-green colour. Observations in 1977 suggested the presence of a faint ring system, amply confirmed when *Voyager 2* swung past the planet in 1986.

Neptune is always more than 4,000 million km from Earth, and despite its diameter of almost 50,000 km, it can only be seen by telescope. Its 1846 discovery was the result of mathematical predictions by astronomers seeking to explain irregularities in the orbit of Uranus, but until *Voyager 2* closed with the planet in 1989, little was known of it. Like Uranus, it has a ring system; *Voyager's* photographs revealed a total of eight moons.

Pluto is the most mysterious of the solar planets, if only because even the most powerful telescopes can scarcely resolve it from a point of light to a disk. It was discovered as recently as 1930, like Neptune as the result of perturbations in the orbits of the two then outermost planets. Its small size, as well as its eccentric and highly tilted orbit, has led to suggestions that it is a former satellite of Neptune, somehow liberated from its primary. In 1978 Pluto was found to have a moon of its own, Charon, apparently half the size of Pluto itself.

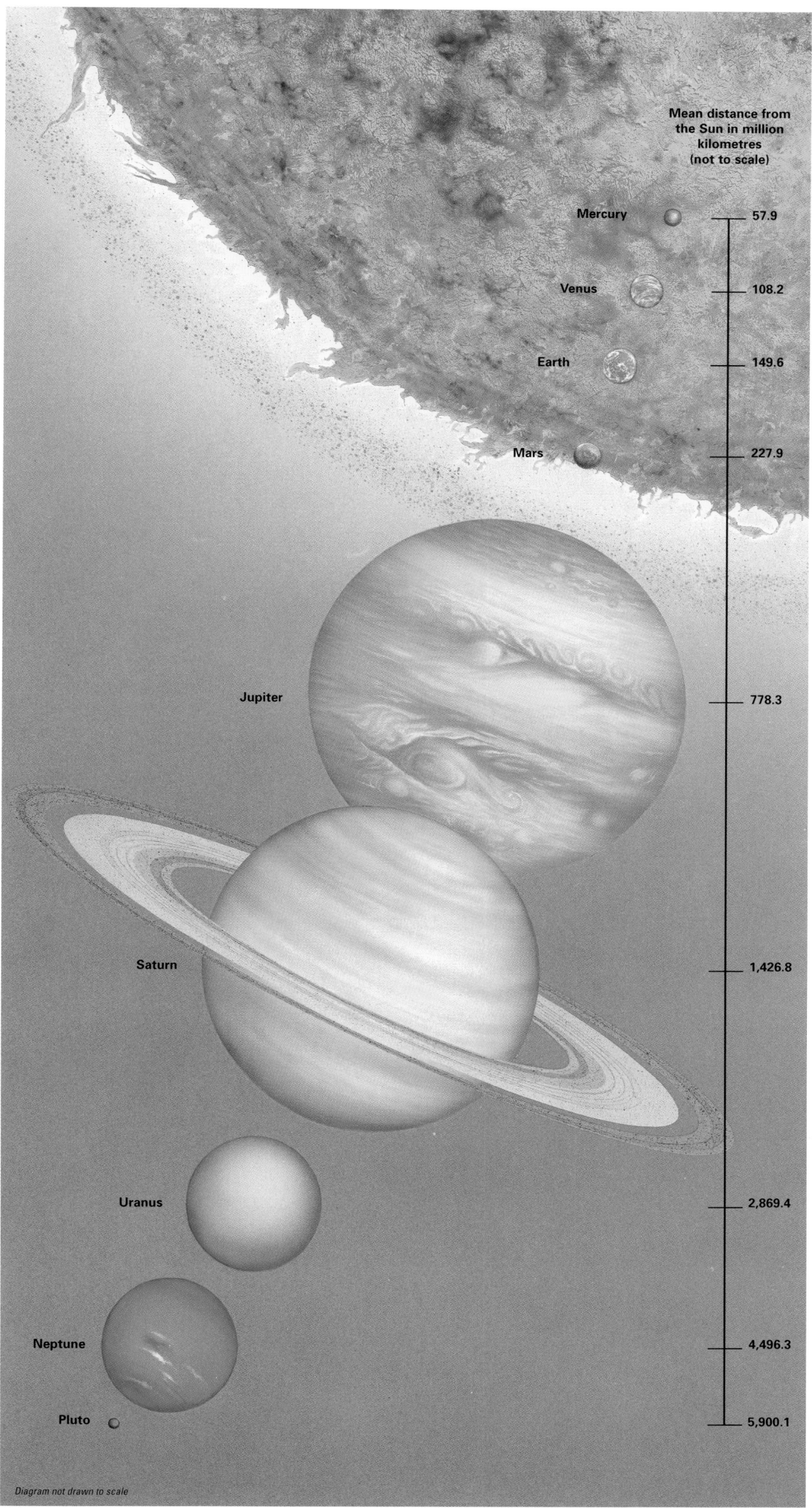

Mean distance from the Sun in million kilometres (not to scale)

Mercury	57.9
Venus	108.2
Earth	149.6
Mars	227.9
Jupiter	778.3
Saturn	1,426.8
Uranus	2,869.4
Neptune	4,496.3
Pluto	5,900.1

Diagram not drawn to scale

CARTOGRAPHY BY PHILIP'S. COPYRIGHT GEORGE PHILIP LTD

Time and Motion

The basic unit of time measurement is the day, that is, one rotation of the Earth on its axis. Our present calendar is based on the solar year of 365.24 days, the time taken by the Earth to orbit the Sun.

Calendars based on the movements of the Sun and Moon have been used since ancient times. The average length of the year, according to the Julian Calendar introduced by Julius Caesar, was about 11 minutes too long. The cumulative error was rectified in 1582 by the Gregorian Calendar, when Pope Gregory XIII decreed that the day following 4 October was 15 October, and in that century years did not count as leap years unless they were divisible by 400. England finally adopted the reformed calendar in 1752, when it was 11 days behind the European mainland.

The rotation of the Earth on its axis causes day and night. Because the Earth rotates through 360° every 24 hours, the world is divided into 24 time zones centred on lines of longitude at 15° longitude.

The tilt of the Earth's axis, also called the obliquity of the ecliptic, accounts for the seasons which are so familiar in the middle latitudes. But geological evidence shows that, over long periods of time, climates change and the advances and retreats of the ice during the Pleistocene Ice Age may have been caused by regular variations in the Earth's tilt, its orbit around the Sun, and changes in the season when it is closest to the Sun (perihelion).

Earth Data

Aphelion (maximum distance from Sun): 152,007,016 km

Perihelion (minimum distance from Sun): 147,000,830 km

Angle of tilt (obliquity of the ecliptic): 23° 27' 08"

Length of year – solar tropical (equinox to equinox): 365.24 days

Length of year: 365 days, 5 hours, 48 minutes, 46 seconds of mean solar time

Superficial area: 510,000,000 sq km

Land surface: 149,000,000 sq km (29.2%)

Water surface: 361,000,000 sq km (70.8%)

Equatorial circumference: 40,077 km

Polar circumference: 40,009 km

Equatorial diameter: 12,756.8 km

Polar diameter: 12,713.8 km

Equatorial radius: 6,378.4 km

Polar radius: 6,356.9 km

Volume of the Earth: 1,083,230 x 10^6 cu km

Mass of the Earth: 5.9 x 10^21 tonnes

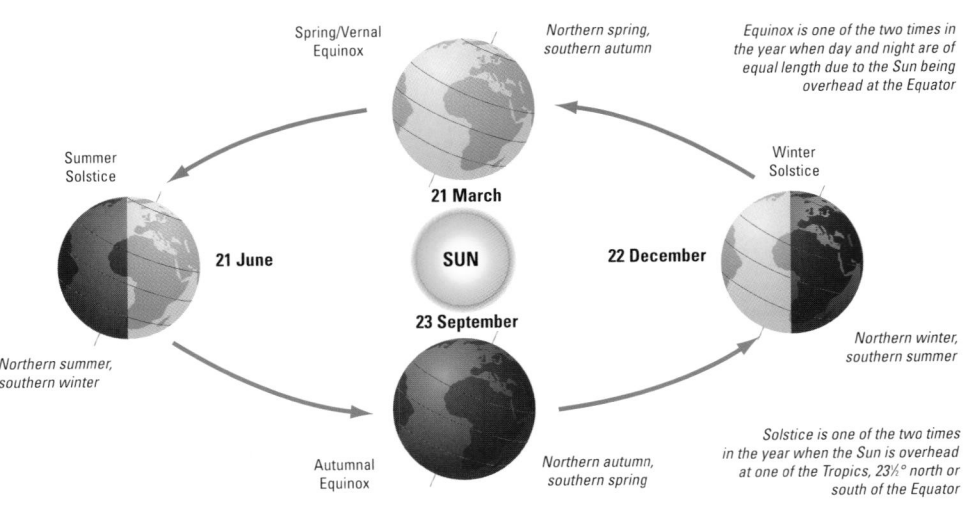

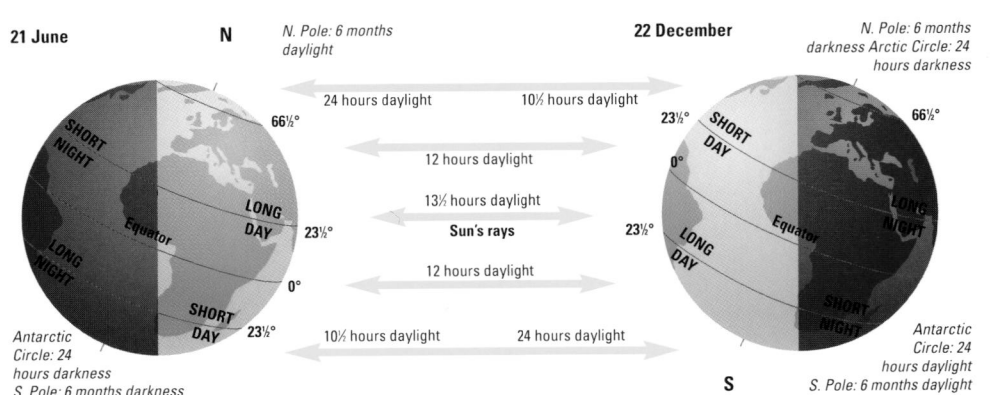

The Seasons

Seasons occur because the Earth's axis is tilted at a constant angle of 23½°. When the northern hemisphere is tilted to a maximum extent towards the Sun, on 21 June, the Sun is overhead at the Tropic of Cancer (latitude 23½° North). This is midsummer, or the summer solstice, in the northern hemisphere.

On 22 or 23 September, the Sun is overhead at the Equator, and day and night are of equal length throughout the world. This is the autumn equinox in the northern hemisphere. On 21 or 22 December, the Sun is overhead at the Tropic of Capricorn (23½° South), the winter solstice in the northern hemisphere. The overhead Sun then tracks north until, on 21 March, it is overhead at the Equator. This is the spring (vernal) equinox in the northern hemisphere.

In the southern hemisphere, the seasons are the reverse of those in the north.

Day and Night

The Sun appears to rise in the east, reach its highest point at noon, and then set in the west, to be followed by night. In reality, it is not the Sun that is moving but the Earth rotating from west to east. The moment when the Sun's upper limb first appears above the horizon is termed sunrise; the moment when the Sun's upper limb disappears below the horizon is sunset.

At the summer solstice in the northern hemisphere (21 June), the Arctic has total daylight and the Antarctic total darkness. The opposite occurs at the winter solstice (21 or 22 December). At the Equator, the length of day and night are almost equal all year.

The Sun's Path

The diagrams on the right illustrate the apparent path of the Sun at (A) the Equator, (B) in mid-latitude (45°), (C) at the Arctic Circle (66½°), and (D) at the North Pole, where there are six months of continuous daylight and six months of continuous night.

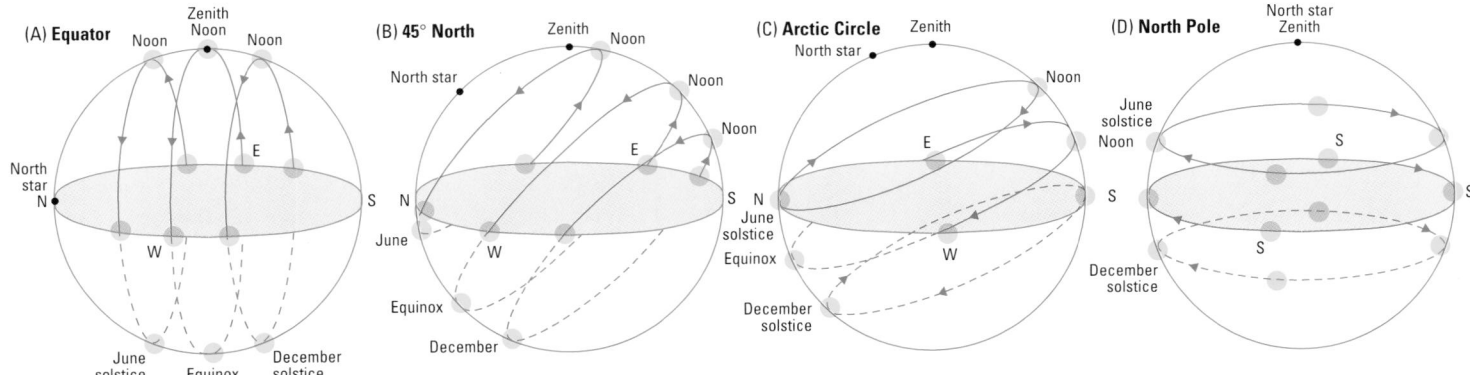

Sunrise and Sunset

The term equinox comes from two Latin words meaning 'equal night'. At the spring and autumn equinoxes, the Sun is vertically overhead at the Equator and all places on Earth have 12 hours of darkness and 12 of daylight. The graphs showing sunrise and sunset show that these occasions occur on 21 March and on 22 or 23 September. The graphs also show that, because the Sun remains high in the sky throughout the year, the length of the day and night at the Equator remain roughly the same throughout the year, with sunrise occurring around 6 AM and sunset at around 6 PM. The further north or south one travels, the greater the difference between the number of hours of daylight and darkness. For example, the graph, right, shows that at latitude 60°N, sunrise varies from just after 9 AM in midwinter (on 22 or 23 December) to about 2.30 AM in midsummer (around the summer solstice on 21 June). By contrast, the second graph, far right, shows that sunset at latitude 60°N occurs at about 2.45 PM in midwinter and 9.20 PM in midsummer.

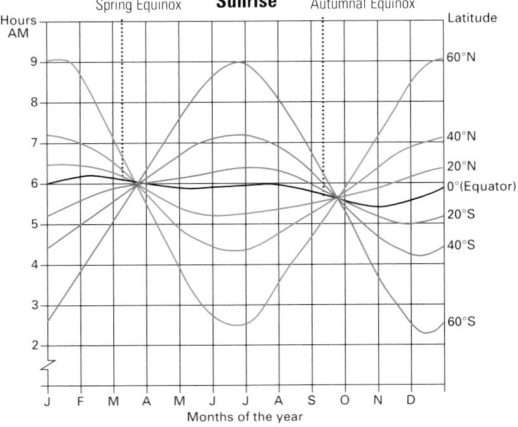

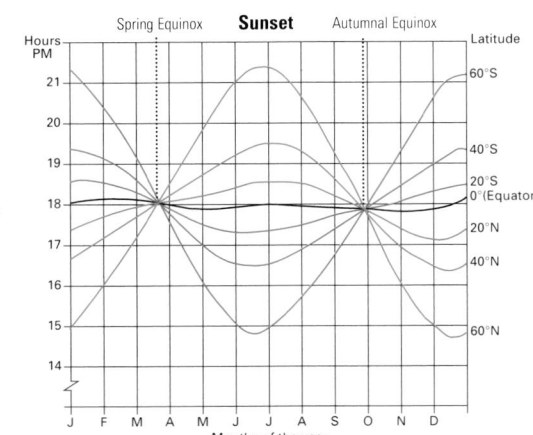

The Moon

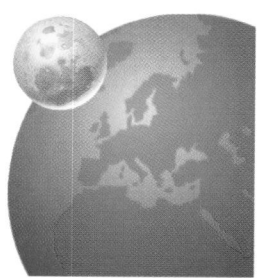

The Moon rotates more slowly than the Earth, making one complete turn on its axis in just over 27 days. Since this corresponds to its period of revolution around the Earth, the Moon always presents the same hemisphere or face to us, and we never see 'the dark side'. The interval between one full Moon and the next (and between new Moons) is about 29½ days – a lunar month. The apparent changes in the shape of the Moon are caused by its changing position in relation to the Earth; like the planets, it produces no light of its own and shines by reflecting the rays of the Sun.

Phases of the Moon

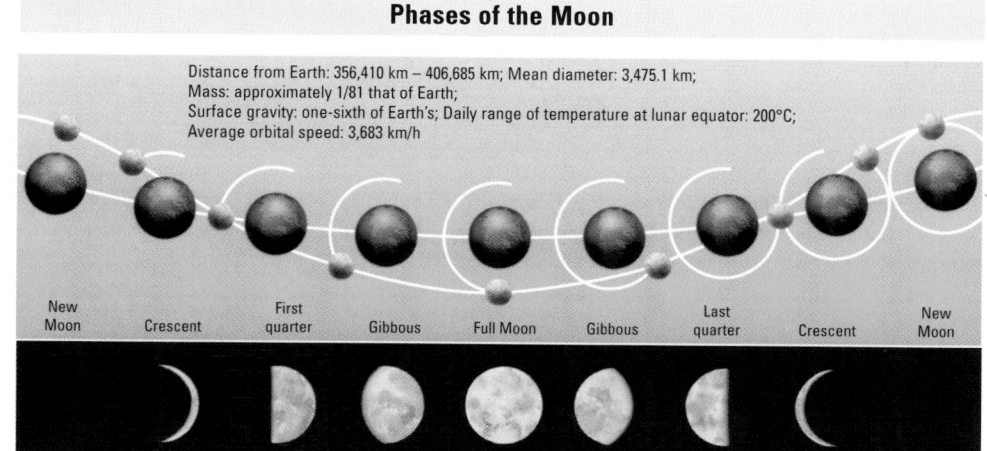

Distance from Earth: 356,410 km – 406,685 km; Mean diameter: 3,475.1 km;
Mass: approximately 1/81 that of Earth;
Surface gravity: one-sixth of Earth's; Daily range of temperature at lunar equator: 200°C;
Average orbital speed: 3,683 km/h

New Moon · Crescent · First quarter · Gibbous · Full Moon · Gibbous · Last quarter · Crescent · New Moon

Moon Data

Distance from Earth
The Moon orbits at a mean distance of 384,199.1 km, at an average speed of 3,683 km/h in relation to the Earth.

Size and mass
The average diameter of the Moon is 3,475.1 km. It is 400 times smaller than the Sun but is about 400 times closer to the Earth, so we see them as the same size. The Moon has a mass of 7,348 x 10^{19} tonnes, with a density 3.344 times that of water.

Visibility
Only 59% of the Moon's surface is directly visible from Earth. Reflected light takes 1.25 seconds to reach Earth – compared to 8 minutes 27.3 seconds for light to reach us from the Sun.

Temperature
With the Sun overhead, the temperature on the lunar equator can reach 117.2°C [243°F]. At night it can sink to –162.7°C [–261°F].

Eclipses

When the Moon passes between the Sun and the Earth it causes a partial eclipse of the Sun (1) if the Earth passes through the Moon's outer shadow (P), or a total eclipse (2) if the inner cone shadow crosses the Earth's surface. In a lunar eclipse, the Earth's shadow crosses the Moon and, again, provides either a partial or total eclipse.

Eclipses of the Sun and the Moon do not occur every month because of the 5° difference between the plane of the Moon's orbit and the plane in which the Earth moves. In the 1990s only 14 lunar eclipses were possible, for example, seven partial and seven total; each was visible only from certain, and variable, parts of the world. The same period witnessed 13 solar eclipses – six partial (or annular) and seven total.

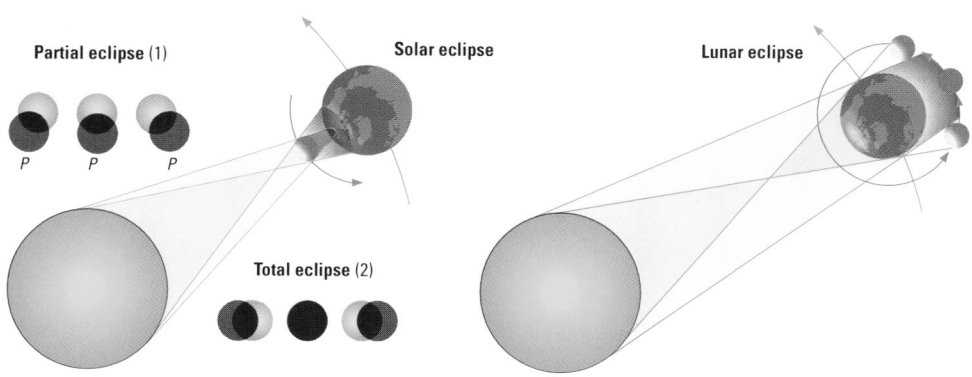

Partial eclipse (1)
P   P   P

Solar eclipse

Lunar eclipse

Total eclipse (2)

Tides

The daily rise and fall of the ocean's tides are the result of the gravitational pull of the Moon and that of the Sun, though the effect of the latter is only 46.6% as strong as that of the Moon. This effect is greatest on the hemisphere facing the Moon and causes a tidal 'bulge'. When the Sun, Earth and Moon are in line, tide-raising forces are at a maximum and Spring tides occur: high tide reaches the highest values, and low tide falls to low levels. When lunar and solar forces are least coincidental with the Sun and Moon at an angle (near the Moon's first and third quarters), Neap tides occur, which have a small tidal range.

Spring tide

Neap tide

Spring tide

Last quarter

New Moon

Full Moon

Neap tide

Gravitational pull by the Sun

First quarter

Time Zones

The Earth rotates through 360° in 24 hours, and so moves 15° every hour. The world is divided into 24 standard time zones, each centred on lines of longitude at 15° intervals. At the centre of the first zone is the Prime meridian or Greenwich meridian. All places to the west of Greenwich are one hour behind for every 15° of longitude; places to the east are ahead by one hour for every 15°. When it is 12 noon at the Greenwich meridian, 180° east it is midnight of the same day – while 180° west the day is just beginning. To overcome this, the International Date Line was established, approximately following the 180° meridian. Thus, if you travelled eastwards from Japan (140° East) to Samoa (170° West), you would pass from Sunday night into Sunday morning.

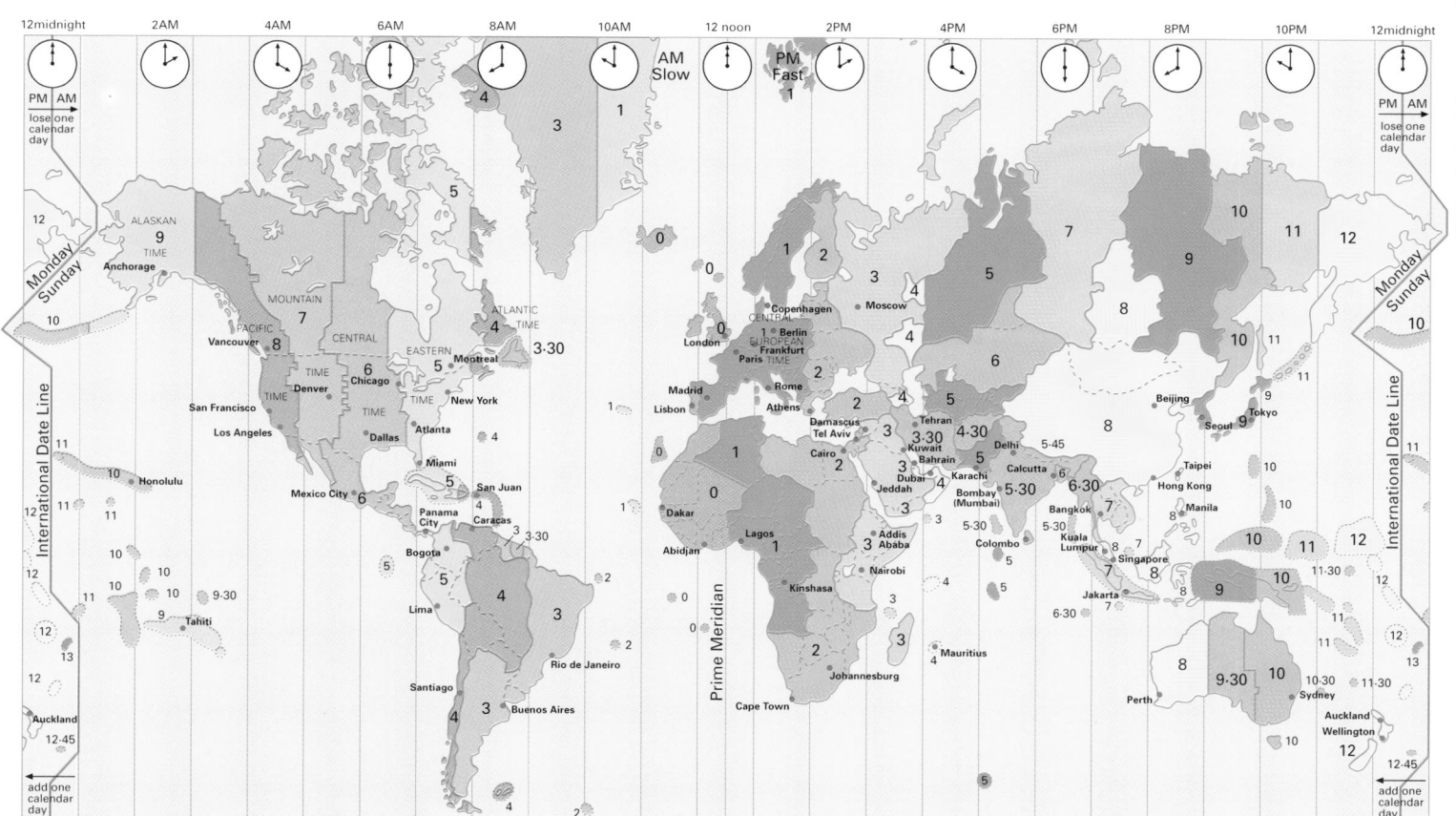

Projection: Mercator

Zones using GMT

Zones slow of GMT

International boundaries

10   Hours slow or fast of GMT or Greenwich Mean Time

Zones fast of GMT

Half-hour zones

Time zone boundaries

International Date Line

Oceans

Seawater

The chemical composition of the sea, by percentage, excluding the elements of water itself

Chloride (Cl)	55.04%
Sodium (Na)	30.61%
Sulphate (SO₄)	7.69%
Magnesium (Mg)	3.69%
Calcium (Ca)	1.16%
Potassium (K)	1.10%
Bicarbonate (HCO₃)	0.41%
Bromide (Br)	0.19%
Boric Acid (H₃BO₃)	0.07%
Strontium (Sr)	0.04%
Fluoride (Fl)	0.003%
Lithium (Li)	trace
Rubidium (Rb)	trace
Phosphorus (P)	trace
Iodine (I)	trace
Barium (Ba)	trace
Arsenic (As)	trace
Cesium (Cs)	trace

The chemical composition of the sea, by percentage, excluding the elements of water itself: Chloride (Cl) 55.04%, Sodium (Na) 30.61%, Sulphate (SO_4) 7.69%, Magnesium (Mg) 3.69%, Calcium (Ca) 1.16%, Potassium (K) 1.10%, Bicarbonate (HCO_3) 0.41%, Bromide (Br) 0.19%, Boric Acid (H_3BO_3) 0.07%, Strontium (Sr) 0.04%, Fluoride (Fl) 0.003%, Lithium (Li) trace, Rubidium (Rb) trace, Phosphorus (P) trace, Iodine (I) trace, Barium (Ba) trace, Arsenic (As) trace, Cesium (Cs) trace.

Eleven constituents account for over 99% of the salt content of seawater, but seawater also contains virtually every other element. In natural conditions, its composition is broadly consistent across the world's seas and oceans; but in coastal areas especially, variations are sometimes substantial. The oceans are about 35 parts water to one part salt.

The last 40 years have been described as the 'Space Age', but another exciting and perhaps even more important area of discovery, proceeding at the same time, has been the exploration of 'inner space', namely the oceans which cover more than 70% of our planet. The study of the ocean floor and oceanic islands has revealed features that help to explain how continents move, and how the movements are related to earthquakes and volcanic activity.

Manned submersibles have established that life exists even in the deepest trenches, where the pressure reaches 1,000 atmospheres, the equivalent of the force of one tonne bearing down on every square centimetre. Further exploration in the pitch-black environment of the ocean ridges has revealed strange forms of marine life around scalding hot vents. The creatures include giant tube-worms, blind shrimps, and bacteria, some of which are genetically very different from any other known life forms. In 1996, an analysis of one micro-organism revealed that at least half of its 1,700 or so genes were hitherto unknown. This environment, which is based on chemicals, not sunlight, may resemble the places where life on Earth first began.

Another vital area of contemporary research concerns the interactions between the oceans and the atmosphere, as exemplified in the El Niño–Southern Oscillation (ENSO), and the bearing that these have on climatic change.

Most geographers divide the world's ocean waters into four areas: the Pacific, Atlantic, Indian and Arctic oceans. The most active zone in the oceans is the sunlit upper layer, where the water is moved around by wind-blown currents. It is the home of most

Life in the Oceans

An imaginary profile of the typical coastal and oceanic zones is shown, with a selection of the life forms that might occur in the water off the Pacific Coast of Central America. The animals illustrated are not drawn to scale as the range of sizes is too great. Most marine life is confined to the first 200 metres, the upper sunlit (photic) zone, where sunlight can still penetrate. Plant and animal plankton, the basis of life in the ocean, occur in great quantities in all zones.

In the pelagic environment (open sea), vertical gradients, including those of light, temperature and salinity, determine the distribution of organisms. From the tidal zone at the coastline, the continental shelf, geologically still part of the continental landmass, drops gently to about 200 metres – the sunlit zone. At the end of the shelf, the seabed falls away in the steeper angle of the continental slope. The subsequent descent to the deep ocean floor, known as the continental rise, is more gentle, with gradients between 1 in 100 and 1 in 700 until the abyssal plains and hills between 2,500 and 6,000 metres below the surface.

The deep sea floor contains seamounts, some of which are capped by coral reefs, ocean ridges, the longest mountain chains on Earth, and deep ocean trenches, especially in the Pacific Ocean where six trenches reach depths of more than 10,000 metres, including the 11,022-metre deep Mariana Trench.

Each of these zones contains a distinctive community of species adapted to the different conditions of salinity, temperature and light intensity. Indeed, a few organisms have been found even in the abyssal darkness of the great ocean trenches.

sea life and acts as a membrane through which the ocean breathes, absorbing great quantities of carbon dioxide and partly exchanging it for oxygen.

As the depth increases, so light fades and temperatures fall until just before 1,000 metres where there is a marked temperature change at the thermocline, the boundary between the warm surface zone and the cold deep zone. Below the thermocline, slow currents are caused by density differences between bodies of water with varying temperatures and salinity.

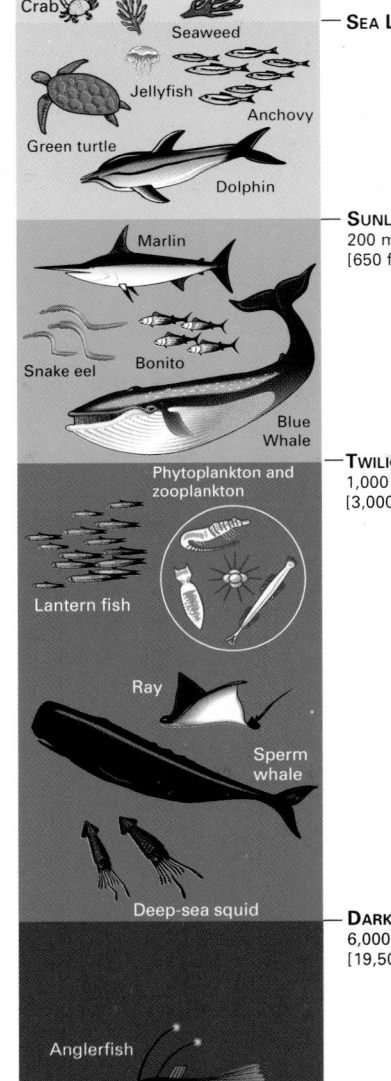

- Crab
- Seaweed
- **SEA LEVEL**
- Jellyfish
- Green turtle
- Anchovy
- Dolphin
- **SUNLIT ZONE** 200 metres [650 feet]
- Marlin
- Snake eel
- Bonito
- Blue Whale
- **TWILIGHT ZONE** 1,000 metres [3,000 feet]
- Phytoplankton and zooplankton
- Lantern fish
- Ray
- Sperm whale
- Deep-sea squid
- **DARK ZONE** 6,000 metres [19,500 feet]
- Anglerfish
- Halosaur
- Sea cucumber
- Sponge
- **TRENCH ZONE** 10,000 metres [33,000 feet]
- Isopod

Atoll Building

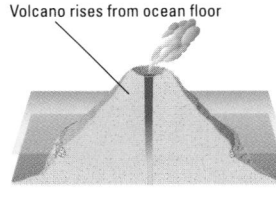

Volcano rises from ocean floor

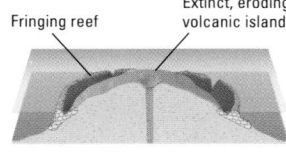

Fringing reef

Extinct, eroding volcanic island

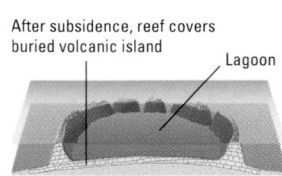

After subsidence, reef covers buried volcanic island

Lagoon

A coral atoll usually begins existence as a bare volcanic peak, thrusting above the surface of the ocean. A colony of coral – organisms with calcium carbonate skeletons – forms itself in the shallow water around the peak. The volcano is eroded and slowly sinks, leaving the coral forming a ring of hard limestone around its remnant. In time, the barrier reef of an atoll is all that remains.

The El Niño Phenomenon

The importance of the ocean–atmosphere interaction is nowhere more dramatically demonstrated than the El Niño phenomenon in the southern Pacific Ocean.

Under normal conditions, shown in the diagram, top right, surface water flows eastwards from South America under the influence of trade winds while, near the coast, cold, nutrient-rich water (dark blue) rises to the surface and spreads westwards. In the western Pacific, sea surface temperatures reach 28°C or more and warm air rises, creating a low pressure air system and causing heavy rains. The rising warm air spreads out and some of it descends over South America and the eastern Pacific creating a high pressure air system from which winds blow westwards. This rotating system is called a Walker Circulation Cell.

An El Niño event, also called an El Niño–Southern Oscillation cycle, or ENSO cycle, is characterized by a reversal of currents whereby the eastward-moving South Equatorial Current extends much further eastwards and the trade winds weaken. The upwelling of cold water off South America is greatly reduced and surface water temperatures rise, causing a drastic reduction in fish life. The heaviest rainfall is over the eastern Pacific, while South-east Asia is much drier than usual. Warm air rises in the east and spreads out, descending in the western Pacific, which then becomes a high pressure area, as shown on the second diagram, below right.

During an intense El Niño, such as in 1982–83 when sea temperatures in the eastern Pacific rose by 6°C, the effects of the current and wind reversals affect the weather around the world. In Australia and South-east Asia, the monsoon rainfall is reduced, while, in 1983–84, a severe drought occurred in the Sahel, south of the Sahara, and also in southern Africa. The south-east coast of the United States also suffered storms and heavy rainfall, and even Europe experienced changes in weather patterns, possibly as a result of consequent changes in the course of the jet stream.

Scientists have found evidence that the frequency

of the El Niño event, which normally occurs every two to seven years, may have increased in recent years with warm conditions persisting in the eastern Pacific from 1990 until mid-1995, an unprecedented length of time during the 114 years for which data exist. Another intense El Niño occurred in 1997–98, with resultant freak weather conditions across the entire Pacific region. Scientists do not know the causes of the El Niño event, though some researchers are investigating possible connections between major volcanic eruptions in the tropical Pacific region, the ENSO cycle and atmospheric circulation.

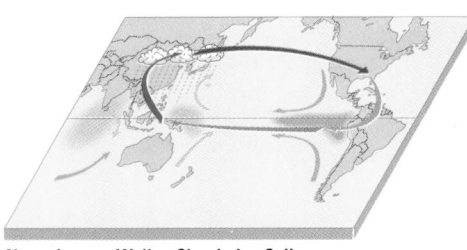

Normal year – Walker Circulation Cell

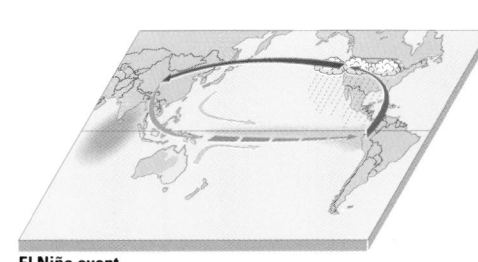

El Niño event

Ocean Currents

JANUARY CURRENTS AND TEMPERATURES
(Northern Hemisphere: winter)

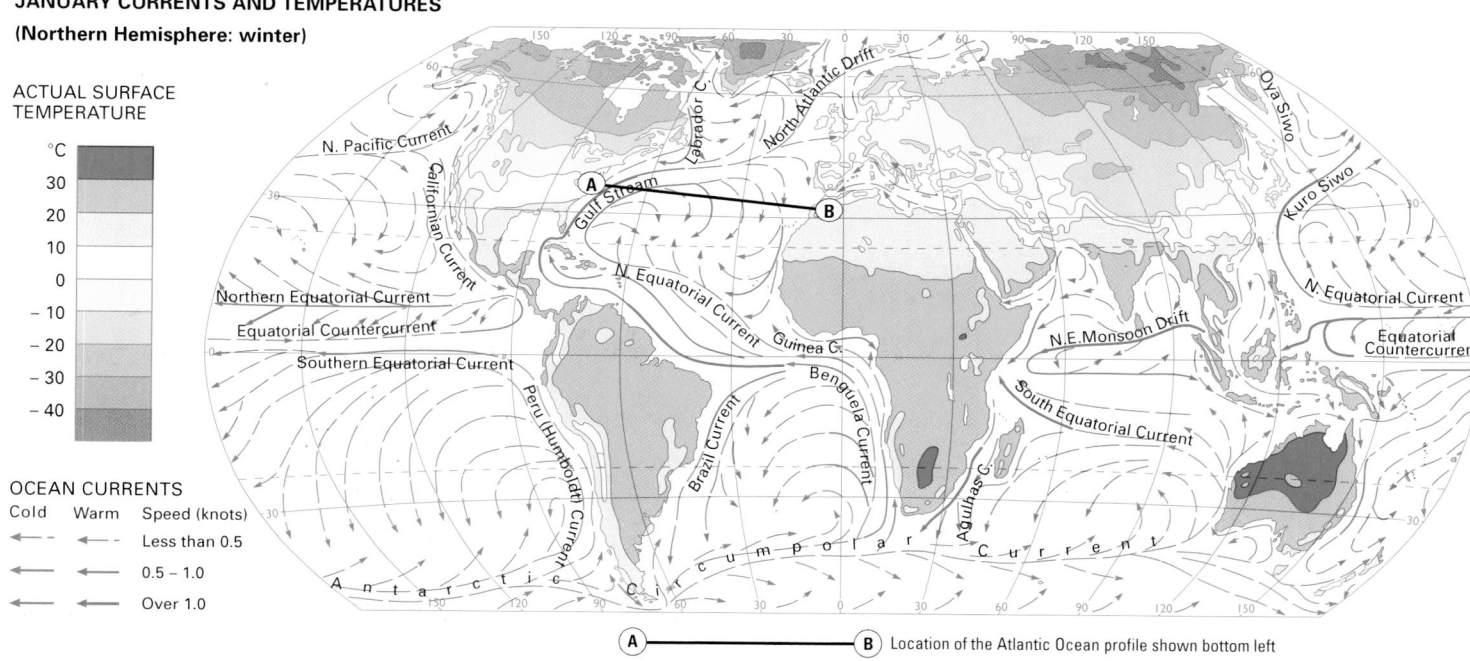

ACTUAL SURFACE TEMPERATURE

°C
30
20
10
0
-10
-20
-30
-40

OCEAN CURRENTS

Cold	Warm	Speed (knots)
← - -	← - -	Less than 0.5
←	←	0.5 – 1.0
←	←	Over 1.0

A ———— B Location of the Atlantic Ocean profile shown bottom left

JULY CURRENTS AND TEMPERATURES
(Northern Hemisphere: summer)

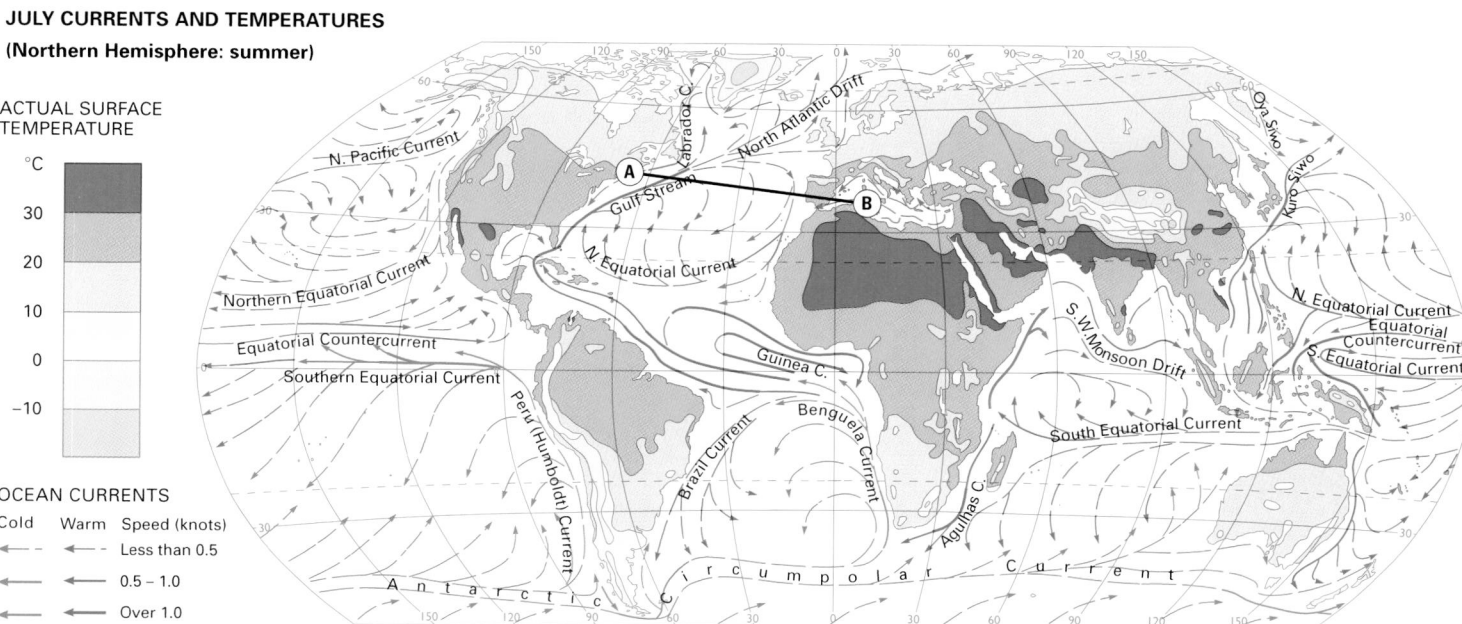

ACTUAL SURFACE TEMPERATURE

°C
30
20
10
0
-10

OCEAN CURRENTS

Cold	Warm	Speed (knots)
← - -	← - -	Less than 0.5
←	←	0.5 – 1.0
←	←	Over 1.0

Moving immense quantities of energy as well as billions of tonnes of water every hour, the ocean currents are a vital part of the great heat engine that drives the Earth's climate. They themselves are produced by a twofold mechanism. At the surface, winds push huge masses of water before them; in the deep ocean, below an abrupt temperature gradient that separates the churning surface waters from the still depths, density variations cause slow vertical movements.

The pattern of circulation of the great surface currents is determined by the displacement known as the Coriolis effect. As the Earth turns beneath a moving object – whether it is a tennis ball or a vast mass of water – it appears to be deflected to one side. The deflection is most obvious near the Equator, where the Earth's surface is spinning eastwards at 1,700 km/h; currents moving polewards are curved clockwise in the northern hemisphere and anti-clockwise in the southern.

The result is a system of spinning circles known as gyres. Warm currents move constantly from the Equator towards the poles, while cold water moves in the reverse direction. In this way, ocean currents act like a thermostat, helping to regulate temperatures around the world.

Depending on the annual movements of the prevailing wind belts, some currents on or near the Equator may reverse their direction in the course of the year, a variation on which Asia's monsoon rains depend and whose occasional failure has brought disaster to millions of people.

Topography of the Ocean Floor

Profile of the Atlantic Ocean

The deep ocean floor was once believed to be flat, but maps compiled from readings made by sonar equipment show that it is no more uniform than the surface of the continents. The profile, below, shows some of the features on the Atlantic Ocean floor between Massachusetts in North America and Gibraltar (for location of profile, see maps above). Around the continents are shallow continental shelves composed of rocks which are less dense than the underlying oceanic crust. The continents end at the top of the steep continental slope, which descends to the abyss via the continental rise, made up of sediments washed down from the continental shelves. The abyss contains large plains overlain by oozes but the plains are broken by volcanic seamounts and guyots (flat-topped seamounts), a few of which reach the surface as islands. The other main feature is the Mid-Atlantic Ridge, through which runs a rift valley where new crustal rock is being formed as the plates on either side move apart.

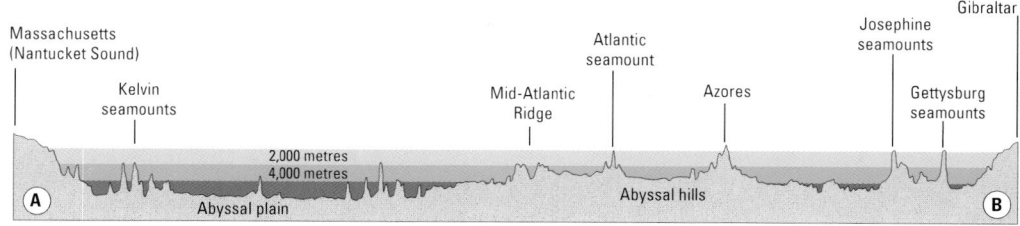

Topography of the ocean floor around Australia

In the image on the right, land areas are shown in grey, with shaded relief. The colours represent sea depth, with red representing the shallowest areas, through yellow and green to dark blue (the deepest). The data for the sea topography are from the Seasat radar satellite. The deep blue area in the upper left is the Java Trench which forms the boundary between the Indo-Australian plate and the Eurasian plate. In the top right, the New Guinea trench, which has a maximum depth of 9,103 metres, forms the border of the Indo-Australian and Pacific plates. Alongside the trenches are volcanic islands formed from magma, created as the edge of the Indo-Australian plate is subducted and melted.

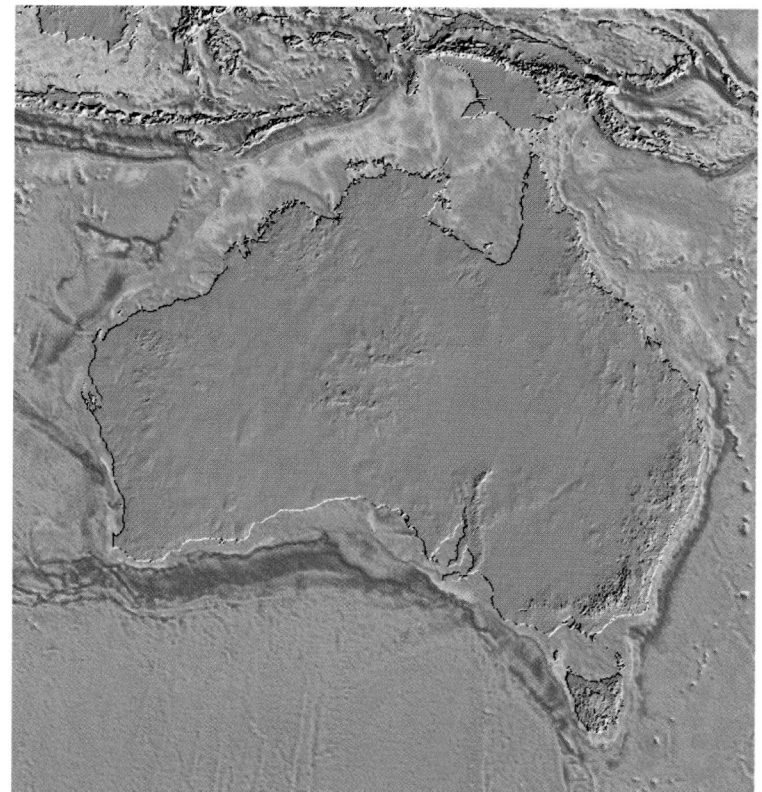

Geology of the Earth

Every year, earthquakes and volcanic eruptions cause much destruction throughout the world. Such phenomena were once thought to be unconnected but since the late 1960s, scientists have understood that these events are surface manifestations of the tremendous forces operating in the Earth's interior that are slowly but constantly changing the face of our planet.

The Earth is divided into three zones. The crust, a brittle, low-density zone, overlies the dense mantle. Separating the crust from the mantle is a distinct boundary called the Mohorovičić (or Moho) discontinuity. Enclosed by the mantle is the Earth's core, which consists mainly of iron and nickel.

Temperatures inside the Earth range from about 870°C in the upper mantle to perhaps 5,000°C in the core. Heat creates convection currents in a semi-molten part of the mantle called the asthenosphere. Above the asthenosphere is the lithosphere, a solid layer about 70 km thick, consisting of the crust and part of the mantle. The lithosphere is divided into rigid plates, moved around by the currents in the asthenosphere, a process named plate tectonics.

The Earth was formed around 4.6 billion years ago. Lighter elements floated towards the surface, where they formed crustal rocks. The oldest rocks so far discovered are nearly 4 billion years old, while the oldest fossils occur in rocks formed around 3.5 billion years ago. An explosion of life occurred at the start of the Cambrian period, 570 million years ago. The fossil record since the start of the Cambrian has enabled scientists to piece together the story of life on Earth.

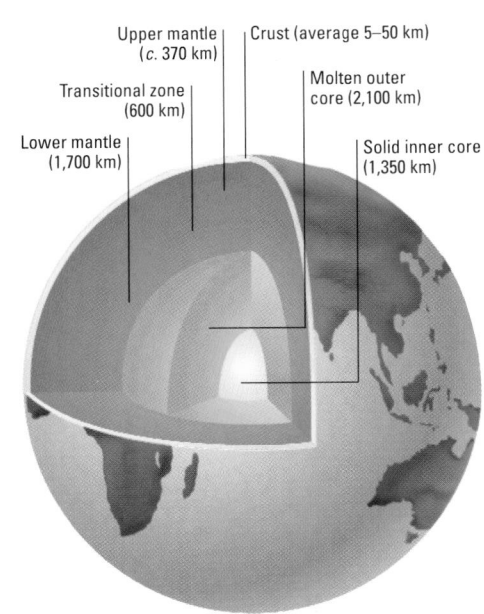

Upper mantle (c. 370 km)
Crust (average 5–50 km)
Transitional zone (600 km)
Molten outer core (2,100 km)
Lower mantle (1,700 km)
Solid inner core (1,350 km)

Plate Tectonics

In the early 20th century, the German scientist Alfred Wegener and others noticed similarities between the shapes of the continents. From a study of rocks and fossils in widely separated continents, they suggested that the continents had once been joined together and that somehow they had drifted apart. But no one knew of a mechanism that might cause continents to drift. However, in the 1950s and 1960s, evidence from studies of the ocean floor suggested that the low-density continents rest on huge slow-moving plates.

Sea-floor spreading in the Indian Ocean and continental plate collision

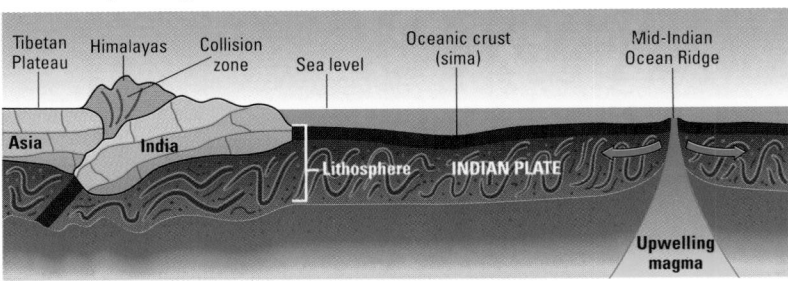

Tibetan Plateau · Himalayas · Collision zone · Sea level · Oceanic crust (sima) · Mid-Indian Ocean Ridge · Asia · India · Lithosphere · INDIAN PLATE · Upwelling magma

Sea-floor spreading in the Atlantic Ocean and plate collision

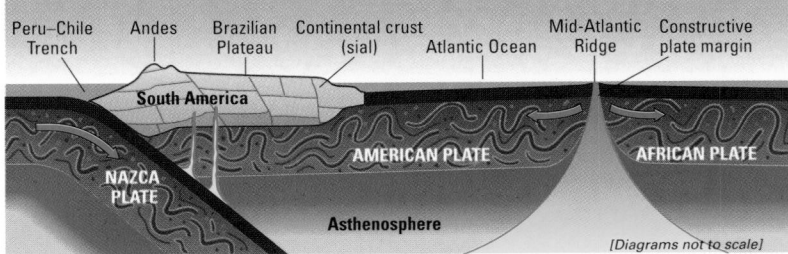

Peru–Chile Trench · Andes · Brazilian Plateau · Continental crust (sial) · Atlantic Ocean · Mid-Atlantic Ridge · Constructive plate margin · South America · AMERICAN PLATE · AFRICAN PLATE · NAZCA PLATE · Asthenosphere · [Diagrams not to scale]

The huge ridges that run through the oceans represent boundaries between plates. Here plates are diverging at rates of 20–41 mm a year. Molten magma from the mantle rises along a central rift valley to form new crustal rock. These ocean ridges, which are active zones where earthquakes and volcanic eruptions are common, are called constructive plate margins. Destructive plate margins, which occur when two plates converge, are marked by deep ocean trenches as one plate is forced under the other. The descending plate is melted to produce the magma that fuels volcanoes alongside the trenches. Movements of descending plates are often sudden and violent, triggering earthquakes in overlying continental areas. Where two continents collide, their margins are buckled up to form fold mountain ranges. A third type of plate margin, the transform fault, is not illustrated above. Along these plate margins, such as California's San Andreas fault, plates are moving parallel to each other.

The debate about plate tectonics is not over. Questions still arise as to why some active volcanoes lie far from plate margins, and why major earthquakes occur in mid-plate areas.

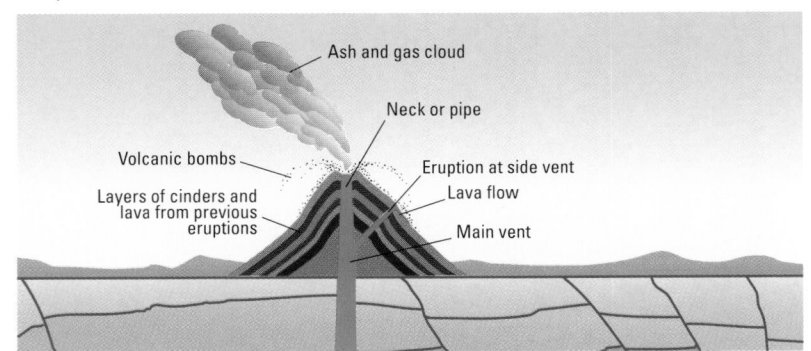

Ash and gas cloud · Neck or pipe · Volcanic bombs · Eruption at side vent · Layers of cinders and lava from previous eruptions · Lava flow · Main vent

Continental Drift

In 1915, Alfred Wegener produced a series of world maps proposing that, around 200 million years ago, the continents had been joined together in a super-continent which he called Pangaea. This landmass started to break up about 180 million years ago and the parts drifted to their present positions. The arrows on the present day world map shows that the continents are still on the move.

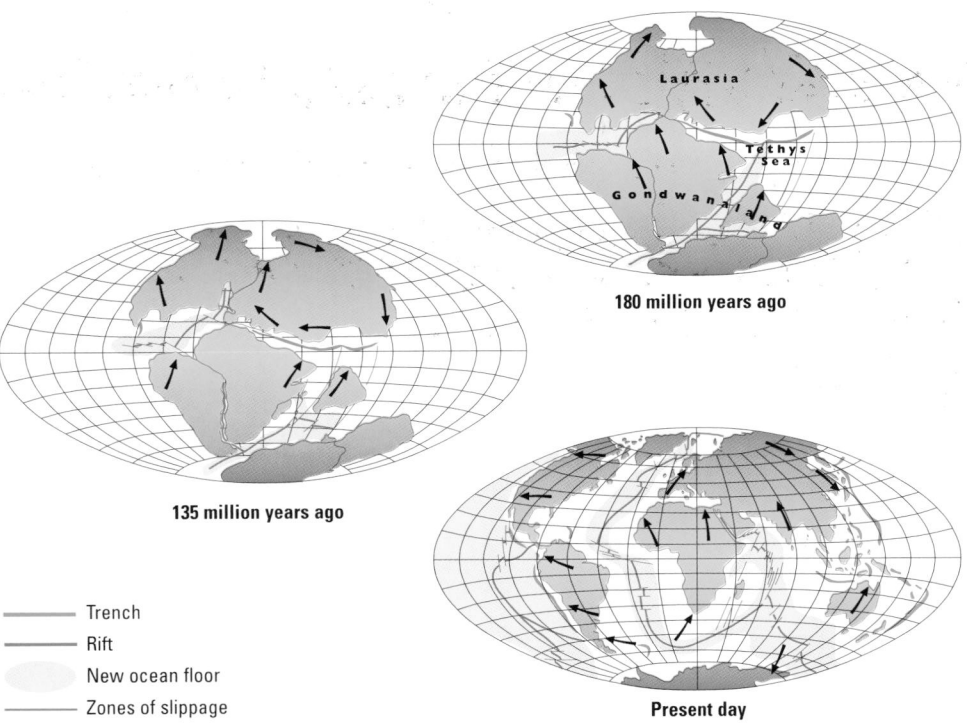

Laurasia · Tethys Sea · Gondwanaland
180 million years ago

135 million years ago

— Trench
— Rift
New ocean floor
— Zones of slippage

Present day

Distribution of Volcanoes

Volcanoes occur when hot liquefied rock beneath the Earth's crust is pushed up by pressure to the surface as molten lava. There are some 550 known active volcanoes, around 20 of which are erupting at any one time.

▲ Land volcanoes active since 1700
• Submarine volcanoes
5.5 Direction of movement (cm/year)
♦ Geysers
～ Boundaries of tectonic plates

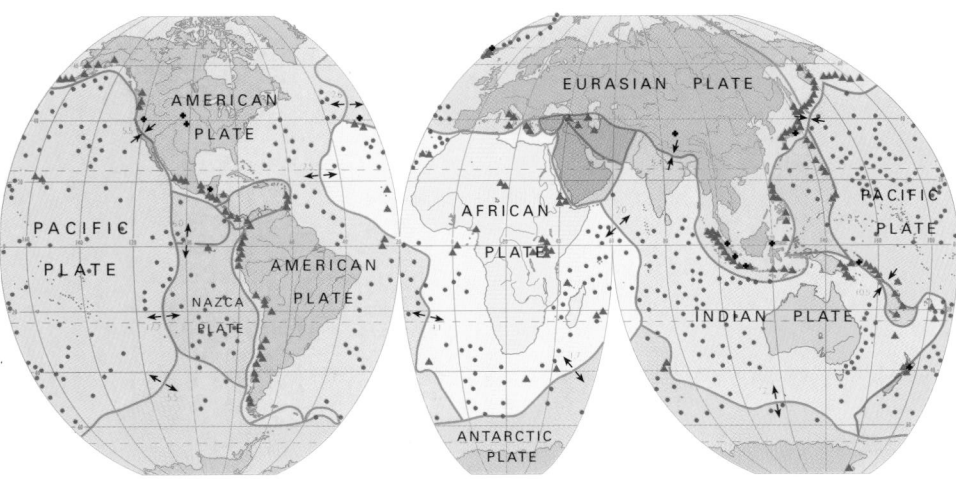

AMERICAN PLATE · PACIFIC PLATE · NAZCA PLATE · AMERICAN PLATE · EURASIAN PLATE · AFRICAN PLATE · PACIFIC PLATE · INDIAN PLATE · ANTARCTIC PLATE

Geological Time

Time, in millions of years before the present, is shown on a sliding scale, greatly compressed in the distant past.

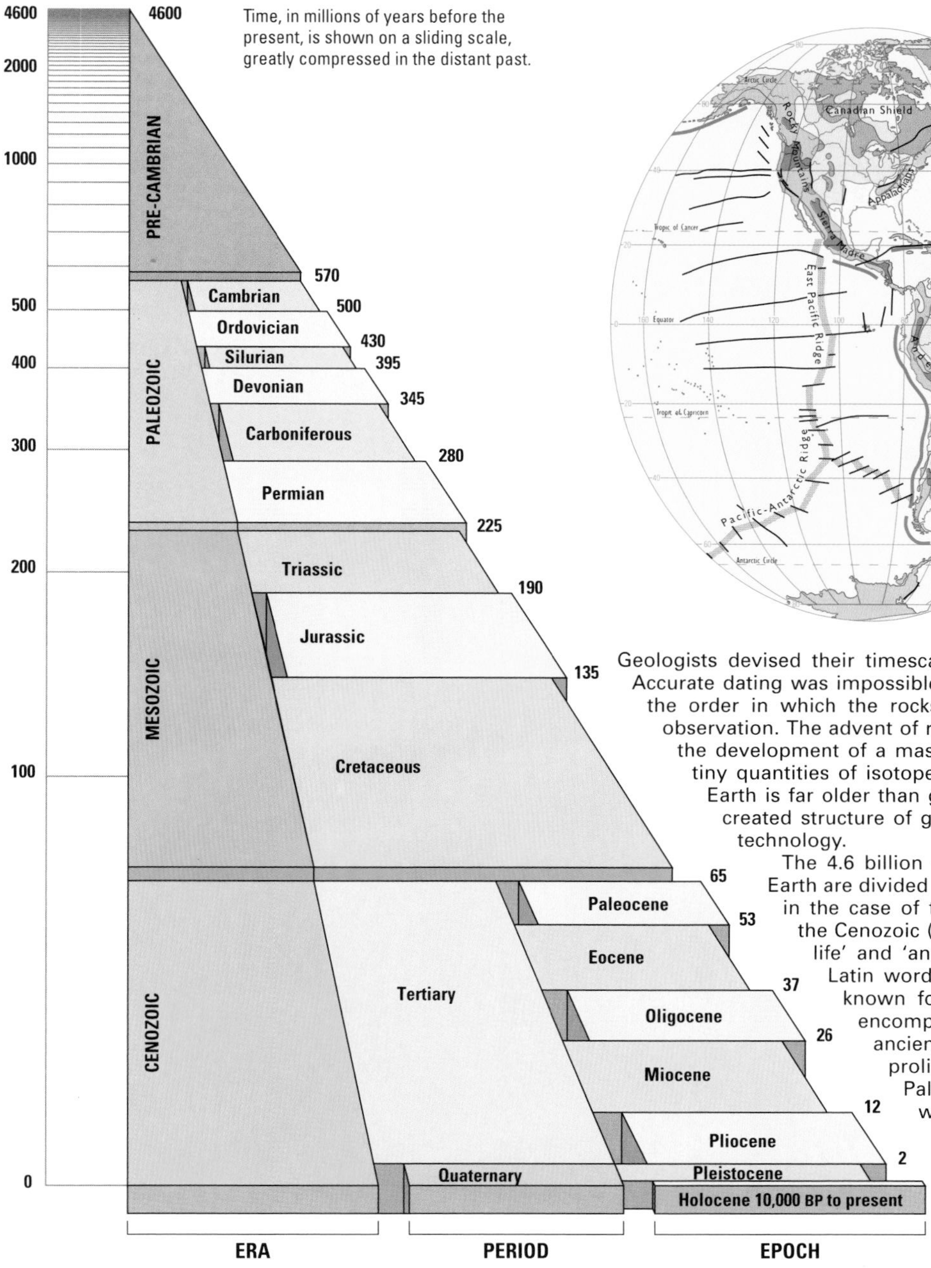

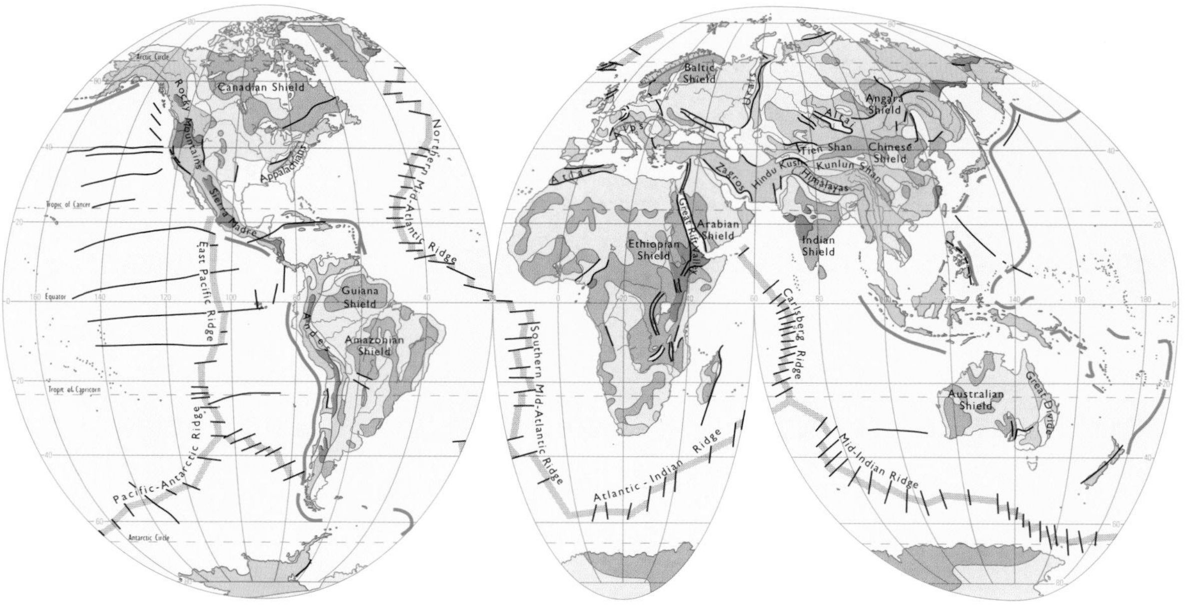

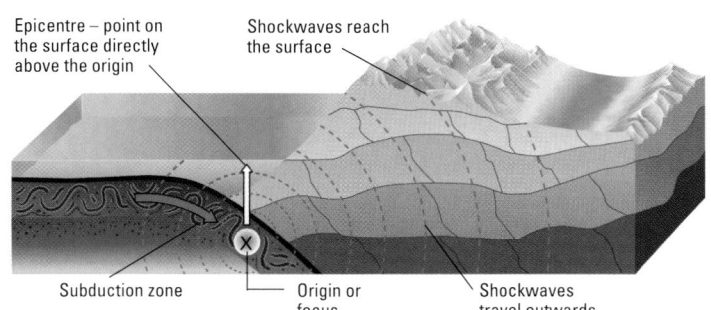

Geologists devised their timescale on the basis of relative, not calendar, ages. Accurate dating was impossible and estimates were often bitterly disputed, but the order in which the rocks were formed could be deduced from careful observation. The advent of radioactive dating – culminating in the 1950s with the development of a mass spectrometer capable of accurately measuring tiny quantities of isotopes – appears to have settled the arguments. The Earth is far older than geologists first imagined, but their painstakingly-created structure of geological time has withstood the advent of high technology.

The 4.6 billion (4,600 million) years since the formation of the Earth are divided into four great eras, further split into periods and, in the case of the most recent era, epochs. The present era is the Cenozoic ('new life'), extending backwards through 'middle life' and 'ancient life' to the Pre-Cambrian, named after the Latin word for Wales, the location of some of the earliest known fossils. Most of the Earth's geological history is encompassed by the Pre-Cambrian: though traces of ancient life have since been found, it was largely the proliferation of fossils from the beginning of the Paleozoic era onwards, some 570 million years ago, which first allowed precise subdivisions to be made.

Like the Cambrian, most are named after regions exemplifying a period's geology. Others – such as the Carboniferous ('coal-bearing') or the Cretaceous ('chalk-bearing') – are more directly descriptive.

- Pre-Cambrian shields
- Sedimentary cover on Pre-Cambrian shields
- Paleozoic (Caledonian and Hercynian) folding
- Sedimentary cover on Paleozoic folding
- Mesozoic folding
- Sedimentary cover on Mesozoic folding
- Cenozoic (Alpine) folding
- Sedimentary cover on Cenozoic folding
- Intensive Mesozoic and Cenozoic vulcanism
- Principal faults
- Oceanic marginal troughs
- Mid-oceanic ridges
- Overthrust faults

ERA — PERIOD — EPOCH

PRE-CAMBRIAN 4600

PALEOZOIC: Cambrian 570, Ordovician 500, Silurian 430, Devonian 395, Carboniferous 345, Permian 280

MESOZOIC: Triassic 225, Jurassic 190, Cretaceous 135

CENOZOIC: Tertiary 65 — Paleocene 65, Eocene 53, Oligocene 37, Miocene 26, Pliocene 12; Quaternary 2 — Pleistocene 2, Holocene 10,000 BP to present

---

Earthquakes

Earthquake magnitude is usually rated according to either the Richter or the Modified Mercalli scale, both devised by seismologists in the 1930s. The Richter scale measures absolute earthquake power with mathematical precision: each step upwards represents a ten-fold increase in the amplitude of the shockwave. Theoretically, there is no upper limit, but the largest earthquakes measured have been rated at between 8.8 and 8.9. The 12-point Mercalli scale, based on observed effects, is often more meaningful, ranging from I (earthquakes noticed only by seismographs) to XII (total destruction); intermediate points include V (people awakened at night; unstable objects overturned), VII (collapse of ordinary buildings; chimneys and monuments fall) and IX (conspicuous cracks in ground; serious damage to reservoirs).

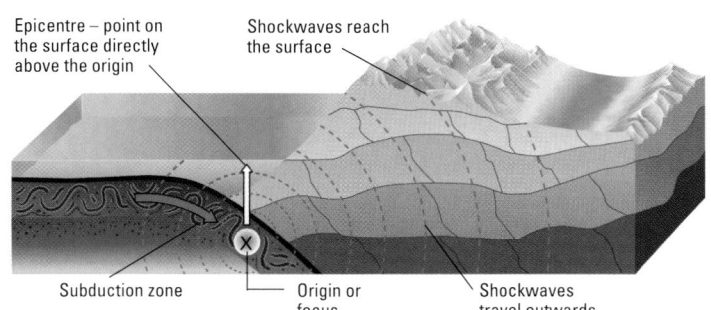

Epicentre – point on the surface directly above the origin

Shockwaves reach the surface

Subduction zone

Origin or focus

Shockwaves travel outwards

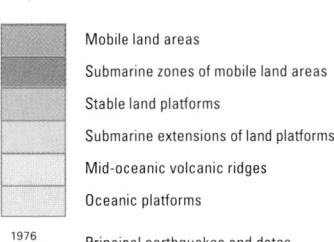

- Mobile land areas
- Submarine zones of mobile land areas
- Stable land platforms
- Submarine extensions of land platforms
- Mid-oceanic volcanic ridges
- Oceanic platforms

1976 ○ Principal earthquakes and dates

Earthquakes are a series of rapid vibrations originating from the slipping or faulting of parts of the Earth's crust when stresses within build up to breaking point. They usually happen at depths varying from 8 km to 30 km. Severe earthquakes cause extensive damage when they take place in populated areas, destroying structures and severing communications. Most initial loss of life occurs due to secondary causes such as falling masonry, fires and flooding.

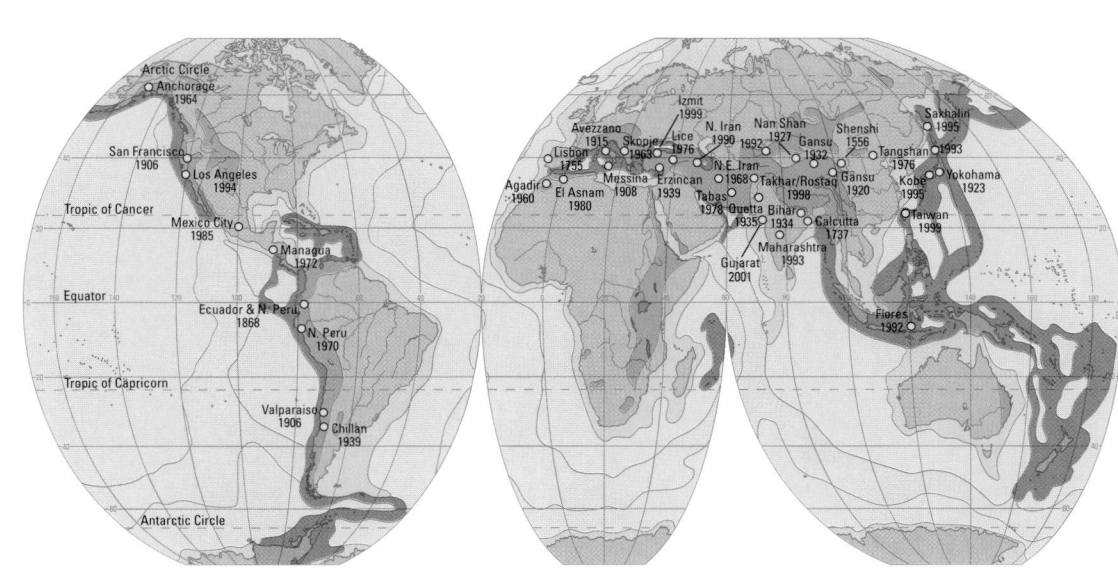

Notable Earthquakes Since 1900

Year	Location	Mag.	Deaths
1906	San Francisco, USA	8.3	503
1906	Valparaiso, Chile	8.6	22,000
1908	Messina, Italy	7.5	83,000
1915	Avezzano, Italy	7.5	30,000
1920	Gansu (Kansu), China	8.6	180,000
1923	Yokohama, Japan	8.3	143,000
1927	Nan Shan, China	8.3	200,000
1932	Gansu (Kansu), China	7.6	70,000
1933	Sanriku, Japan	8.9	2,990
1934	Bihar, India/Nepal	8.4	10,700
1935	Quetta, India*	7.5	60,000
1939	Chillan, Chile	8.3	28,000
1939	Erzincan, Turkey	7.9	30,000
1960	Agadir, Morocco	5.8	12,000
1962	Khorasan, Iran	7.1	12,230
1968	N.E. Iran	7.4	12,000
1970	N. Peru	7.7	66,794
1972	Managua, Nicaragua	6.2	5,000
1974	N. Pakistan	6.3	5,200
1976	Guatemala	7.5	22,778
1976	Tangshan, China	8.2	255,000
1978	Tabas, Iran	7.7	25,000
1980	El Asnam, Algeria	7.3	20,000
1980	S. Italy	7.2	4,800
1985	Mexico City, Mexico	8.1	4,200
1988	N.W. Armenia	6.8	55,000
1990	N. Iran	7.7	36,000
1992	Flores, Indonesia	6.8	1,895
1993	Maharashtra, India	6.4	30,000
1994	Los Angeles, USA	6.6	51
1995	Kobe, Japan	7.2	5,000
1995	Sakhalin Is., Russia	7.5	2,000
1996	Yunnan, China	7.0	240
1997	N.E. Iran	7.1	2,400
1998	Takhar, Afghanistan	6.1	4,200
1998	Rostaq, Afghanistan	7.0	5,000
1999	Izmit, Turkey	7.4	15,000
1999	Tapei, Taiwan	7.6	1,700
2001	Gujarat, India	7.7	18,600

The most devastating quake ever was at Shaanxi (Shenshi) province, central China, on 3 January 1556, when an estimated 830,000 people were killed.

* now Pakistan

Landforms

The theory of plate tectonics has offered new insights as to how the Earth works, elucidating mysteries concerning continental drift, volcanic eruptions and earthquakes. It has also contributed to our understanding of how plate collisions can squeeze up layers of sediments on seabeds into fold mountain ranges, such as the Himalayas.

Yet even as mountains rise, natural forces are wearing them away. In hot, dry climates, mechanical weathering, a result of rapid temperature changes, causes the outer layers of rocks to peel away, while, in cold mountain regions, boulders are prised apart when water freezes in cracks in rocks. Chemical weathering is responsible for hollowing out limestone caves and decomposing granites.

Climatic conditions have a great bearing on the principle agent of erosion in any area. Running water is most important in moist temperate regions. In cold regions, ice is the major agent of erosion, and in many mountain ranges, U-shaped valleys are evidence of the erosive power of valley glaciers. Ice sheets moulded much of the Earth's surface during the Ice Ages, the most recent of which, in the northern hemisphere, ended 10,000 years ago. Polar climates also shape the scenery of periglacial areas that border bodies of ice. Such areas are subject to constant freeze-thaw action, which creates such features as pingos (domed mounds).

Climatic change has also affected many of the landforms in hot deserts, which were shaped by running water at a time when the deserts enjoyed much wetter climates. However, the major agent of erosion in deserts today is wind-blown sand which erodes rock strata to form mushroom-shaped rocks and caves.

The surface of the Earth is under constant assault from tectonic processes and the agents of erosion. The products of erosion, fragments of rock such as sand, are deposited to form sedimentary rocks. Metamorphic rocks are created when igneous or sedimentary rocks are buried and metamorphosed by heat and pressure. Eventually the rocks are recycled to form magma, which rises upwards to start the rock cycle all over again.

The Rock Cycle

James Hutton first proposed the rock cycle in the late 1700s after he observed the slow but steady effects of erosion.

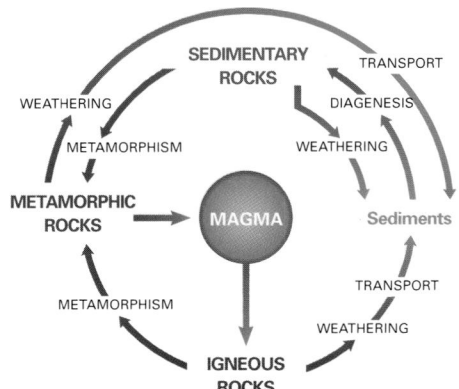

Rocks are divided into three types, according to the way in which they are formed:

Igneous rocks, including granite and basalt, are formed by the cooling of magma from within the Earth's crust.

Metamorphic rocks, such as slate, marble and quartzite, are formed below the Earth's surface by the compression or baking of existing rocks.

Sedimentary rocks, like sandstone and limestone, are formed on the surface of the Earth from the remains of living organisms and eroded fragments of older rocks.

Mountain Building

Mountains are formed when pressures on the Earth's crust caused by continental drift become so intense that the surface buckles or cracks. This happens where oceanic crust is subducted by continental crust or, more dramatically, where two tectonic plates collide: the Rockies, Andes, Alps, Urals and Himalayas resulted from such impacts. These are all known as fold mountains because they were formed by the compression of the rocks, forcing the surface to bend and fold like a crumpled rug. The Himalayas are formed from the folded former sediments of the Tethys Sea which was trapped in the collision zone between the Indian and Eurasian plates.

The other main mountain-building process occurs when the crust fractures to create faults, allowing rock to be forced upwards in large blocks; or when the pressure of magma within the crust forces the surface to bulge into a dome, or erupts to form a volcano. Large mountain ranges may reveal a combination of those features; the Alps, for example, have been compressed so violently that the folds are fragmented by numerous faults and intrusions of molten igneous rock.

Over millions of years, even the greatest mountain ranges can be reduced by the agents of erosion (especially rivers) to a low rugged landscape known as a peneplain.

Types of faults: Faults occur where the crust is being stretched or compressed so violently that the rock strata break in a horizontal or vertical movement. They are classified by the direction in which the blocks of rock have moved. A normal fault results when a vertical movement causes the surface to break apart; compression causes a reverse fault. Horizontal movement causes shearing, known as a strike-slip fault. When the rock breaks in two places, the central block may be pushed up in a horst fault, or sink (creating a rift valley) in a graben fault.

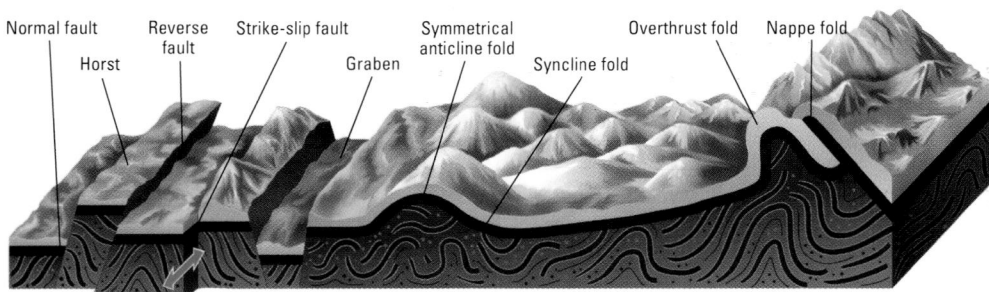

Normal fault — Horst — Reverse fault — Strike-slip fault — Graben — Symmetrical anticline fold — Syncline fold — Overthrust fold — Nappe fold

Types of fold: Folds occur when rock strata are squeezed and compressed. They are common, therefore, at destructive plate margins and where plates have collided, forcing the rocks to buckle into mountain ranges. Geographers give different names to the degrees of fold that result from continuing pressure on the rock. A simple fold may be symmetric, with even slopes on either side, but as the pressure builds up, one slope becomes steeper and the fold becomes asymmetric. Later, the ridge or 'anticline' at the top of the fold may slide over the lower ground or 'syncline' to form a recumbent fold. Eventually, the rock strata may break under the pressure to form an overthrust and finally a nappe fold.

Continental Glaciation

Many landforms in the northern hemisphere were shaped by ice sheets and meltwater during the Pleistocene Ice Age, which began about two million years ago. During the Ice Age, the ice sheets periodically advanced and retreated. The first map shows the ice cover at its greatest extent about 200,000 years BP (before the present), when it covered about 30% of the land surface, as compared with 10% today. About 18,000 years BP, the ice covered most of Canada and as far south as the Bristol Channel in England. Around the ice sheets, land areas experienced periglacial conditions.

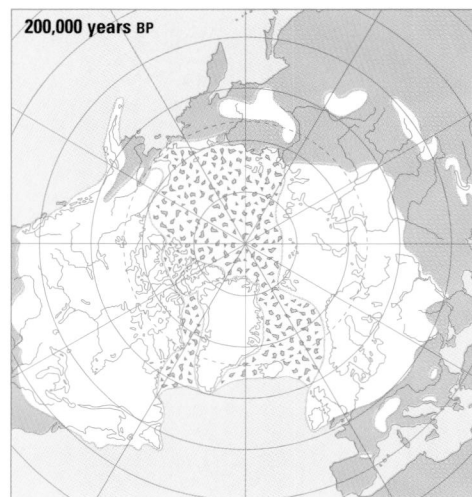

200,000 years BP

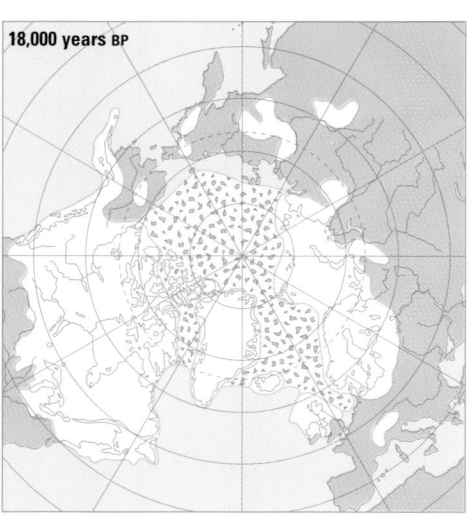

18,000 years BP

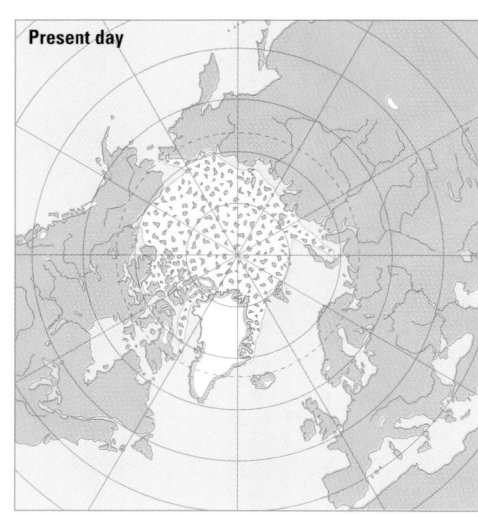

Present day

Natural Landforms

Natural landforms reflect the influence of plate tectonics through mountain-building and the generation of new rocks from the interior, together with the agents of erosion: running water, ice, winds and coastal waves. Over millions of years, mountains are gradually eroded, producing landforms that reflect the major forces that have been at work, as well as the underlying geology, the climatic conditions, which often vary over time, and the vegetation cover. The stylized diagram, below, shows some major natural landforms found in the mid-latitudes.

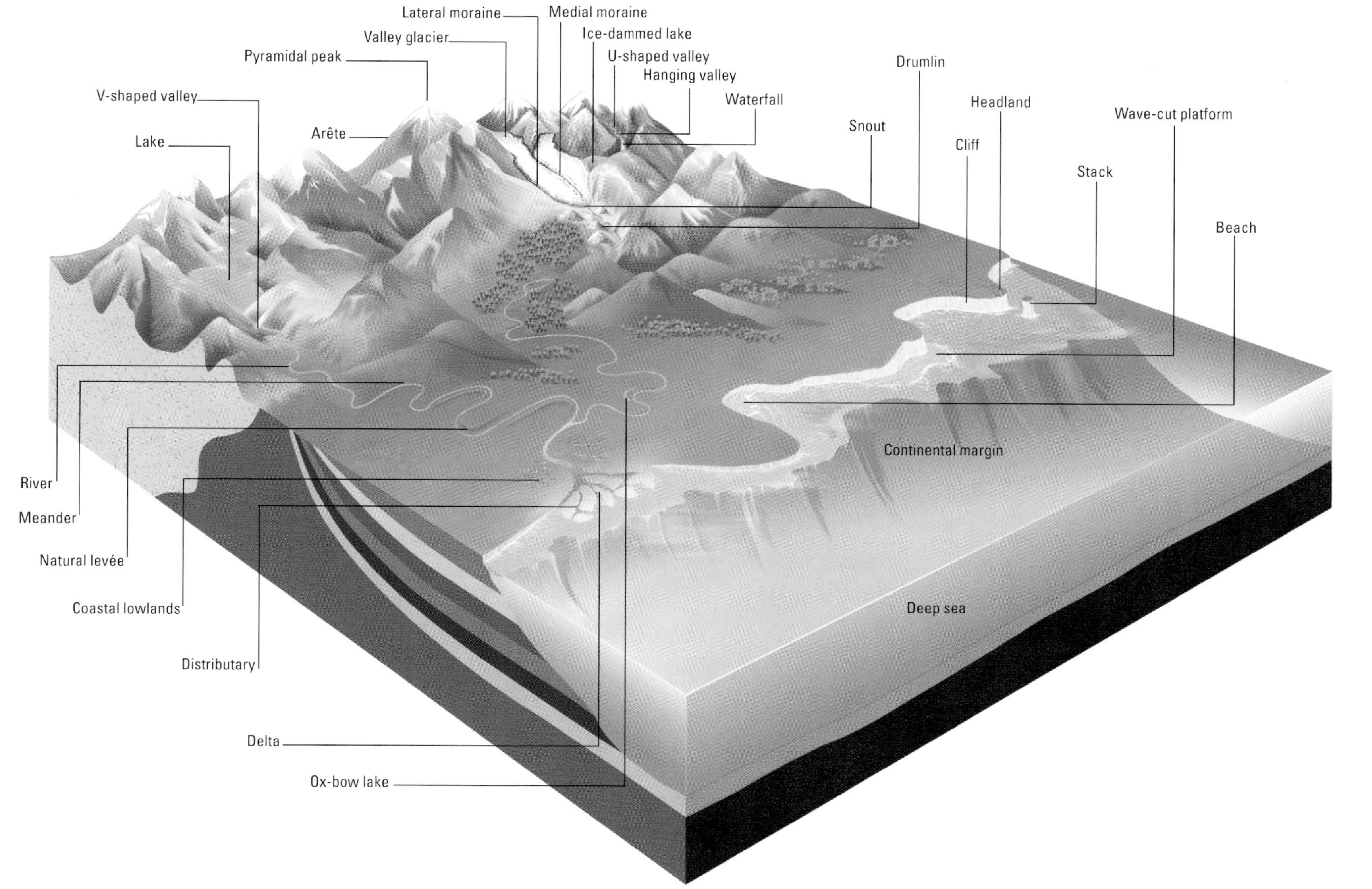

V-shaped valley
Lateral moraine
Medial moraine
Valley glacier
Ice-dammed lake
Pyramidal peak
U-shaped valley
Hanging valley
Drumlin
Waterfall
Headland
Wave-cut platform
Lake
Arête
Snout
Cliff
Stack
Beach
River
Meander
Natural levée
Coastal lowlands
Continental margin
Distributary
Deep sea
Delta
Ox-bow lake

Desert Landforms

Deserts are defined as places with an average annual precipitation of 250 mm per year, though places with a higher rainfall and a high evaporation rate may also qualify as deserts. The three types of desert landforms are known by their Arabic names, a reflection of the fact that the Sahara in North Africa is the world's largest desert. Sand desert, called erg, covers about one-fifth of the world's deserts. The rest is divided between hammada (areas of bare rock) and reg (broad plains covered by loose gravel or pebbles).

The shapes of dunes in sand deserts reflect the character of local winds. Where winds are constant in direction, the sand often piles up in crescent-shaped dunes, called barchans. Barchans are constantly on the move and their forward march, unless halted by vegetation, may overwhelm settlements at oases. Seif dunes, named after the Arabic word for sword, are long ridges of sand which lie parallel to the direction of the wind, but where winds are variable, the sand sheets are often featureless.

Wind-blown sand is an effective agent of erosion but because of the weight of sand grains, this type of erosion is confined to within two metres of the land surface, creating caves and mushroom-shaped rocks.

In assessing desert landforms, it is important to remember that other processes were at work in the past when the climate was very different from today. For example, cave paintings suggest that the Sahara had a much wetter climate after the end of the Ice Age and only began to dry up after about 5000 BC. However, human action, including overgrazing and the cutting down of trees for firewood, can turn a grassland region into desert – a process known as desertification.

Erg

Hammada

Reg

Surface Processes

Catastrophic changes to landforms are periodically caused by such phenomena as avalanches, landslides and volcanic eruptions, but most of the processes that shape the Earth's surface operate extremely slowly in human terms. One estimate, based on a study of landforms in the United States, suggests that, on average, one metre of land is removed from the entire surface of the country every 29,500 years. However, the terrain and the climate have a great effect on the erosion rate. For example, on cold plains, such as the Hudson Bay lowlands, the rate drops to around one metre for every 154,200 years, while in wet, tropical mountain areas, the rate may reach one metre for every 1,300 years.

Chemical weathering is at its greatest in warm, humid regions, while mechanical weathering, or the physical break-up of rocks, predominates in cold mountain or hot desert regions. The most familiar type of chemical weathering is caused by the reaction of rainwater containing dissolved carbon dioxide on limestone. This leads to the creation of labyrinthine cave networks dissolved by groundwater. Mechanical weathering includes frost action, while in hot deserts, rapid temperature changes cause the outer layers of rocks to expand and contract until they crack and peel away, a process called exfoliation.

The most important product of weathering is soil, which consists of rock fragments and humus, the decayed remains of plants and animals, together with living organisms, including vast numbers of micro-organisms. Soils vary in character according to the climate, ranging from the heavily leached, red laterite soils of wet tropical areas to the fertile, brown soils of dry grasslands. Soils are important because they support plants, which in turn anchor the soil and act as a protection against erosion. Soil erosion is greatest on sloping land because the steeper the slope, the greater the tendency for the soil to creep or flow downhill. The degree of movement of soil and rock downhill under the influence of gravity, called mass wasting, depends on a slope's stability. The stability may be disturbed by earthquakes or by heavy rain (water acts as a lubricant and increases the weight of the overlying material) which may trigger flows, slides or large falls of rock.

Running water is probably the world's leading agent of erosion and transportation. The energy of a river depends on several factors, including its velocity and volume, and its erosive power is at its peak when it is in full flood, sweeping soil, pebbles and even boulders along its course, cutting downwards into the bedrock or widening its valley. Sea waves also exert tremendous erosive power during storms when they hurl pebbles and large rocks against the shore, undercutting cliffs and hollowing out caves. Headlands are often attacked on both sides, forming caves, then a natural arch and eventually an isolated stack.

Glacier ice forms in mountain hollows, called cirques, and spills out to form valley glaciers, which transport rocks shattered by frost action. As a glacier moves, rocks embedded in the base and sides scrape away bedrock, eroding steep-sided, flat-bottomed, U-shaped valleys. Evidence of past glaciation in mountain regions includes cirques, knife-edged ridges, or arêtes, and pyramidal peaks, or horns.

Geologists once considered that landforms evolved from 'young', newly uplifted mountainous areas, through a 'mature' hilly stage, to an 'old age' stage when the land was reduced to an almost flat plain, or peneplain. This theory, called the 'cycle of erosion', fell into disuse when it became evident that so many factors, including the effects of plate tectonics and climatic change, constantly interrupt the cycle, which takes no account of the highly complex interactions that shape the surface of our planet.

The Atmosphere

The atmosphere is a meteor shield, a radiation deflector, a thermal blanket and a source of chemical energy for the Earth's diverse life forms. Five-sixths of its mass is in the lowest layer, the troposphere which ranges in thickness from 18 to 10 km between the Equator and the poles. Powered by the Sun, the air is always on the move, flowing generally from high- to low-pressure areas. The troposphere is the layer where nearly all weather phenomena, including clouds, precipitation and winds, occur. Above the troposphere is the stratosphere, which contains the ozone layer and extends to 50 km above the Earth's surface. Beyond 100 km, the density is lower than most laboratory vacuums.

Circulation of the Air

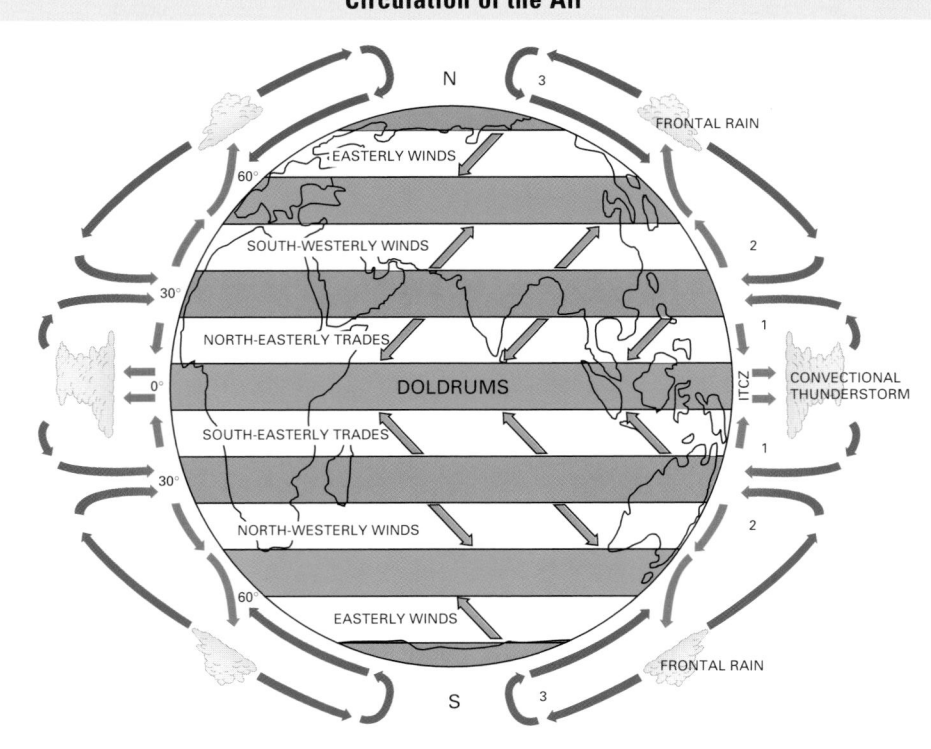

High pressure
Low pressure
Warm air
Cold air
Surface winds
Clouds

1 Hadley Cell
2 Ferrel Cell
3 Polar Cell

ITCZ Intertropical convergence zone

Structure of the Atmosphere

HUBBLE SPACE TELESCOPE
600 km [370 miles]   600 KM   Pressure 10^{-35} mb

EXOSPHERE 10^{-22} mb

350 KM

MIR SPACE STATION
325 km [200 miles]

300 KM 10^{-16} mb

SPACE SHUTTLE
275 km [170 miles]

250 KM

THERMOSPHERE 10^{-10} mb

200 KM

VOSTOCK MANNED CAPSULE
(first manned space flight, 1961)
175 km [110 miles]

150 KM

AURORAE

METEOR TRAILS   100 KM 10^{-3} mb

MESOSPHERE

50 KM

OZONE LAYER

STRATOSPHERE

CONCORDE
MOUNT EVEREST
8,848 m [29,029 ft]   10 KM   TROPOSPHERE 10^{3} mb

Chemical Composition

Gaseous composition of the principal atmospheric layers

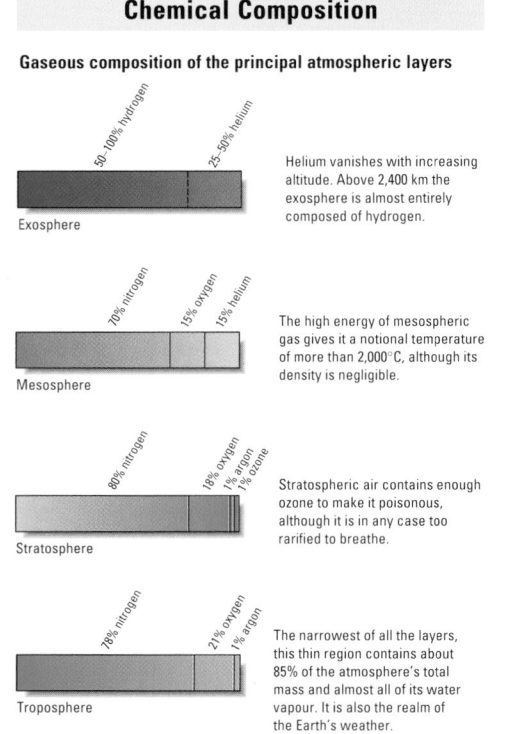

50–100% hydrogen   25–50% helium
Exosphere

Helium vanishes with increasing altitude. Above 2,400 km the exosphere is almost entirely composed of hydrogen.

70% nitrogen   15% oxygen   15% helium
Mesosphere

The high energy of mesospheric gas gives it a notional temperature of more than 2,000°C, although its density is negligible.

80% nitrogen   18% oxygen   1% argon   1% ozone
Stratosphere

Stratospheric air contains enough ozone to make it poisonous, although it is in any case too rarified to breathe.

78% nitrogen   21% oxygen   1% argon
Troposphere

The narrowest of all the layers, this thin region contains about 85% of the atmosphere's total mass and almost all of its water vapour. It is also the realm of the Earth's weather.

Frontal Systems

Depressions, or cyclones, form along the polar front where dense polar easterlies meet warm subtropical westerlies. Depressions occur when warm air flows into waves in the polar front, while cold air flows in behind it, creating rotating air systems that bring changeable weather. Along the warm front (the boundary on the ground between the warm and cold air), the warm air flows upwards over the cold air, producing a sequence of clouds which help forecasters to predict a depression's advance. Along the cold front, the advancing cold air forces warm air to rise steeply. Towering cumulonimbus clouds form in the rising air. When the cold front overtakes the warm front, the warm air is pushed above ground level to form an occluded front. Cloud and rain persist along occlusions until temperatures equalize, the air mixes, and the depression dies out.

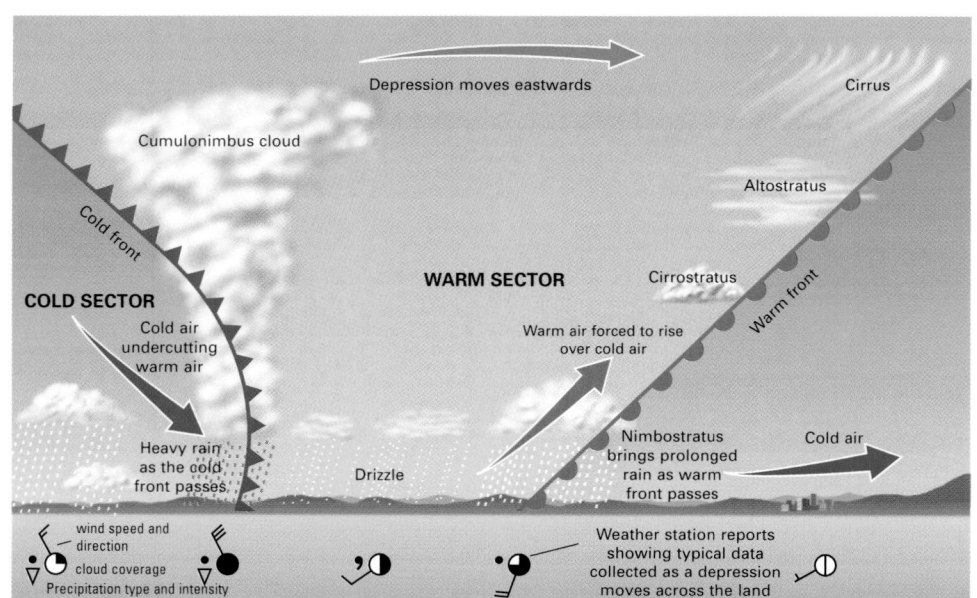

Depression moves eastwards   Cirrus

Cumulonimbus cloud   Altostratus

Cold front   Cirrostratus

WARM SECTOR   Warm front

COLD SECTOR
Cold air undercutting warm air   Warm air forced to rise over cold air

Heavy rain as the cold front passes   Drizzle   Nimbostratus brings prolonged rain as warm front passes   Cold air

wind speed and direction
cloud coverage
Precipitation type and intensity

Weather station reports showing typical data collected as a depression moves across the land

Air Masses

Air masses are bodies of air whose characteristics are broadly the same over a large area. Around the Equator, where the Sun's heat creates relatively high surface temperatures, warm air rises to create a zone of low pressure called the doldrums. The air cools and finally spreads out towards the poles. Around latitudes 30° north and south, the air sinks back to the surface, becoming warmer as it descends and creating zones of high pressure called the horse latitudes.

The high- and low-pressure zones are both areas of comparative calm, but between them lie the prevailing trade wind belts. Air also flows north and south from the high-pressure horse latitudes and these air flows meet up with cold, dense air flowing from the poles along the polar front. This basic circulatory system is complicated by the Coriolis effect, brought about by the spinning Earth. Because of the Coriolis effect, the prevailing winds do not flow directly north–south but are deflected to the right in the northern hemisphere and to the left in the southern. Along the polar front, depressions form where the polar easterlies meet the westerlies.

The first classification of clouds was developed by a London chemist, Luke Howard, in 1803, and it was later modified by the World Meteorological Organization. The main types are divided into three groups according to their altitude, and into subgroups according to their shape, which vary from hairlike filaments (cirrus), heaps or piles (cumulus), and layers (stratus). Each cloud carries some kind of message, though not always a clear one, to weather forecasters.

Classification of Clouds

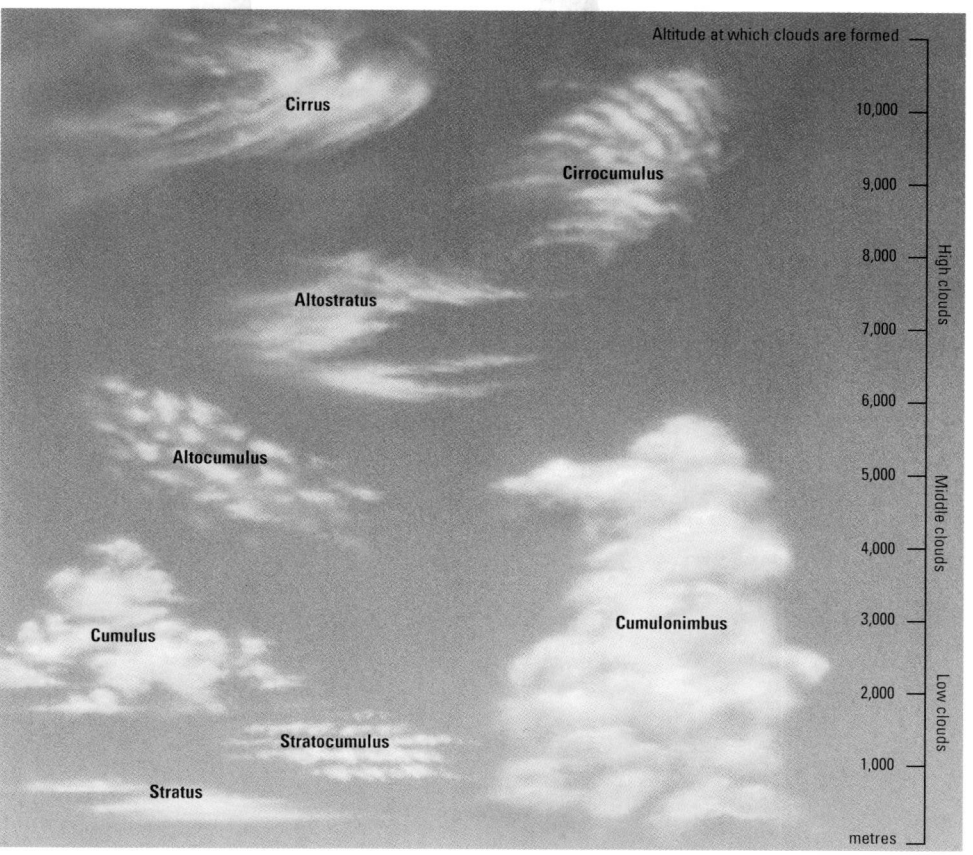

Clouds form when damp, usually rising, air is cooled. Thus they form when a wind rises to cross hills or mountains; when a mass of air rises over, or is pushed up by, another mass of denser air; or when local heating of the ground causes convection currents.

The types of clouds are classified according to altitude as high, middle or low. The high ones, composed of ice crystals, are cirrus, cirrostratus and cirrocumulus. The middle clouds are altostratus, a grey or bluish striated, fibrous or uniform sheet producing light drizzle, and altocumulus, a thicker and fluffier version of cirrocumulus.

Low clouds include nimbostratus, a dark grey layer that brings rain or snow; cumulus, a detached heap, dark at the base; stratus, which forms dull, overcast skies at low levels; and stratocumulus, which consists of fluffy greyish-white layers.

Cumulonimbus, associated with storms and rains, heavy and dense with a flat base and a high, fluffy outline, can be tall enough to occupy middle as well as low altitudes.

Pressure and Surface Winds

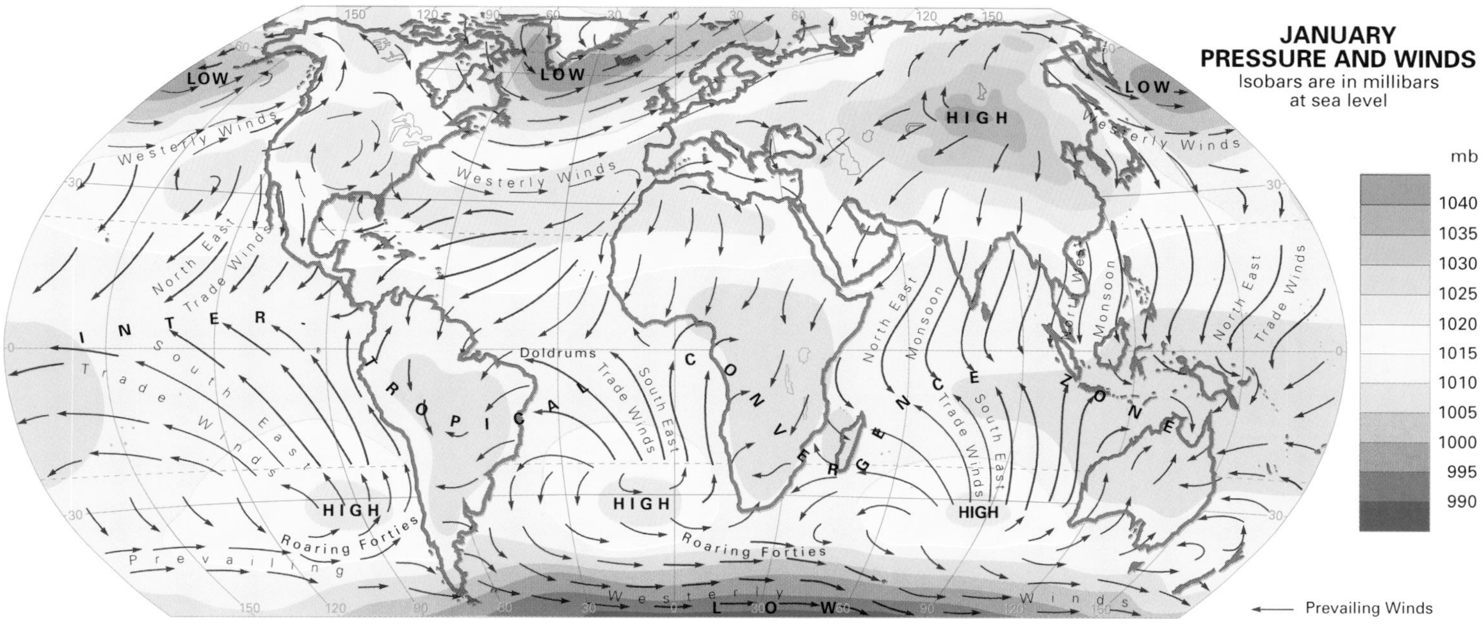

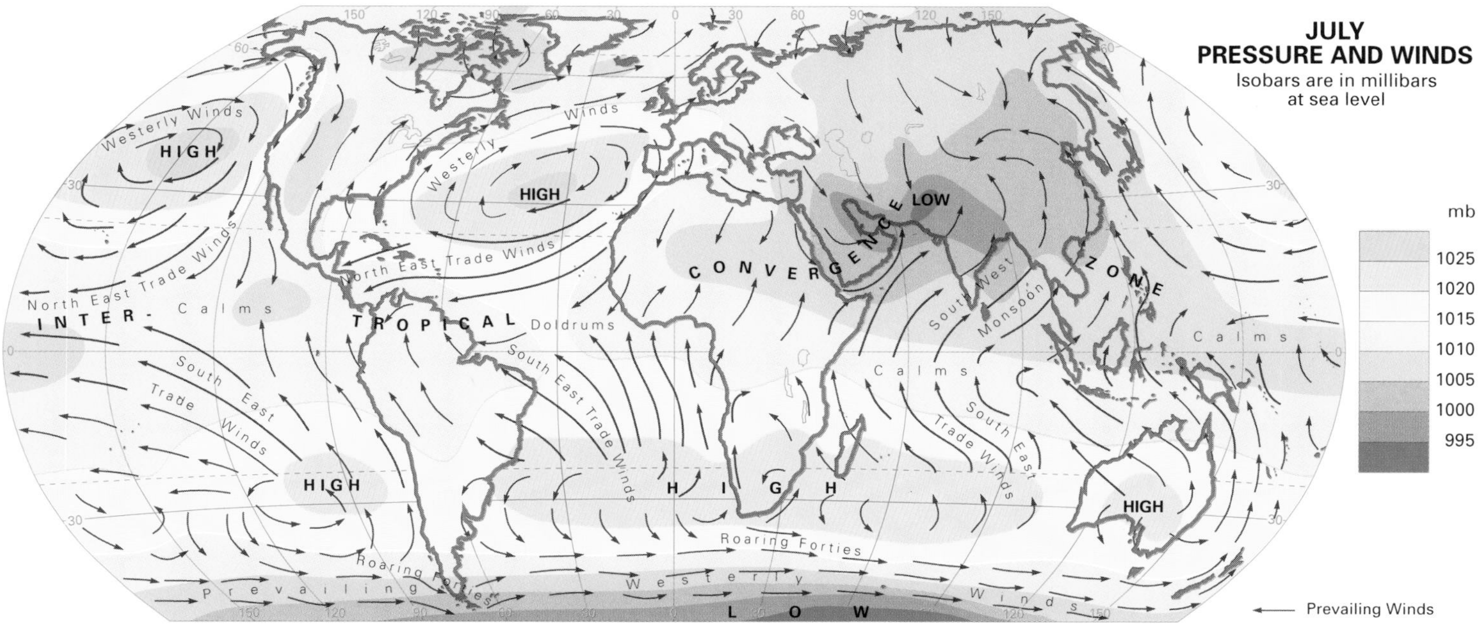

JANUARY PRESSURE AND WINDS
Isobars are in millibars at sea level

mb
1040
1035
1030
1025
1020
1015
1010
1005
1000
995
990

← Prevailing Winds

JULY PRESSURE AND WINDS
Isobars are in millibars at sea level

mb
1025
1020
1015
1010
1005
1000
995

← Prevailing Winds

Climate Records

Pressure and winds

Highest barometric pressure: Agata, Siberia, 1,083.8 mb at altitude 262 m [862 ft], 31 December 1968.

Lowest barometric pressure: Typhoon Tip, 480 km [300 mls] west of Guam, Pacific Ocean, 870 mb, 12 October 1979.

Highest recorded wind speed: Mt Washington, New Hampshire, USA, 371 km/h [231 mph], 12 April 1934. This is three times as strong as hurricane force on the Beaufort Scale.

Windiest place: Commonwealth Bay, George V Coast, Antarctica, where gales frequently reach over 320 km/h [200 mph].

Worst recorded storm: Bangladesh (then East Pakistan) cyclone*, 13 November 1970 – over 300,000 dead or missing. The 1991 cyclone, Bangladesh's and the world's second worst in terms of loss of life, killed an estimated 138,000 people.

Worst recorded tornado: Missouri/Illinois/Indiana, USA, 18 March 1925 – 792 deaths. The tornado was only 275 m [300 yds] wide.

* Tropical cyclones are known as hurricanes in Central and North America, as typhoons in the Far East, and as willy-willies in northern Australia.

Climate

For more information:

- 9 Ocean currents
- 14 Circulation of the air
- 15 Classification of clouds
- Pressure and winds
- 18 Hydrological cycle
- 19 Natural vegetation
- 21 Greenhouse effect
- 22 Global warming

Weather is the day-to-day or hour-to-hour condition of the air, while climate is weather in the long term, the seasonal pattern of hot and cold, wet and dry, averaged over a long period. Most classifications of climate are based on a system developed by a Russian meteorologist, Vladimir Köppen, in the early 19th century. Using a code based on letters and a classification centred on two main features, temperature and precipitation, he identified five main climatic types: tropical (A), dry (B), warm temperate (C), cold temperate (D), and polar (E). A highland mountain climate (H), was added later to account for the variety of altitudinal climatic zones on high mountains. Each region was then further subdivided.

Latitude is a major factor in determining climate, but other factors add to the complexity. They include the differential heating of land and sea, the distance from the sea, the effect of mountains on winds, and the influence of ocean currents. For example, New York City, Naples and the Gobi Desert share almost the same latitude, but their climates are very different.

Climates are not indefinitely stable. During the last Ice Age, the Earth underwent alternating cold periods, called glacials, separated by warm interglacials. The Milankovich theory suggests such cycles may be caused by variations in the Earth's path around the Sun, changing from almost circular to elliptical every 95,000 years, and variations in the Earth's tilt from 21.5° to 24.5° every 42,000 years. Another factor is that the Earth is now closest to the Sun in the middle of winter in the northern hemisphere and furthest away in summer. But 12,000 years ago, at the height of the last glacial period, the northern winter fell with the Sun at its most distant.

Studies of these cycles suggest we are in an interglacial with a glacial period on the way. But, many scientists believe global warming, largely a result of burning fossil fuels and deforestation, is occurring faster than the slow cycles of the Solar System.

Tropical rainy climates
All mean monthly temperatures above 18°C.

- Af — Rainforest climate
- Am — Monsoon climate
- Aw — Savanna climate

Dry climates
Low rainfall combined with a wide range of temperatures

- BS — Steppe climate
- BW — Desert climate

Warm temperate rainy climates
The mean temperature is below 18°C but above −3°C and that of the warmest month is over 10°C.

- Cw — Dry winter climate
- Cs — Dry summer climate
- Cf — Climate with no dry season

Cold temperate rainy climates
The mean temperature of the coldest month is below −3°C but that of the warmest month is still over 10°C.

- Dw — Dry winter climate
- Df — Climate with no dry season

Polar climates
The mean temperature of the warmest month is below 10°C, giving permanently frozen subsoil.

- ET — Tundra climate

The mean temperature of the warmest month is below 0°C, giving permanent ice and snow.

- EF — Polar climate

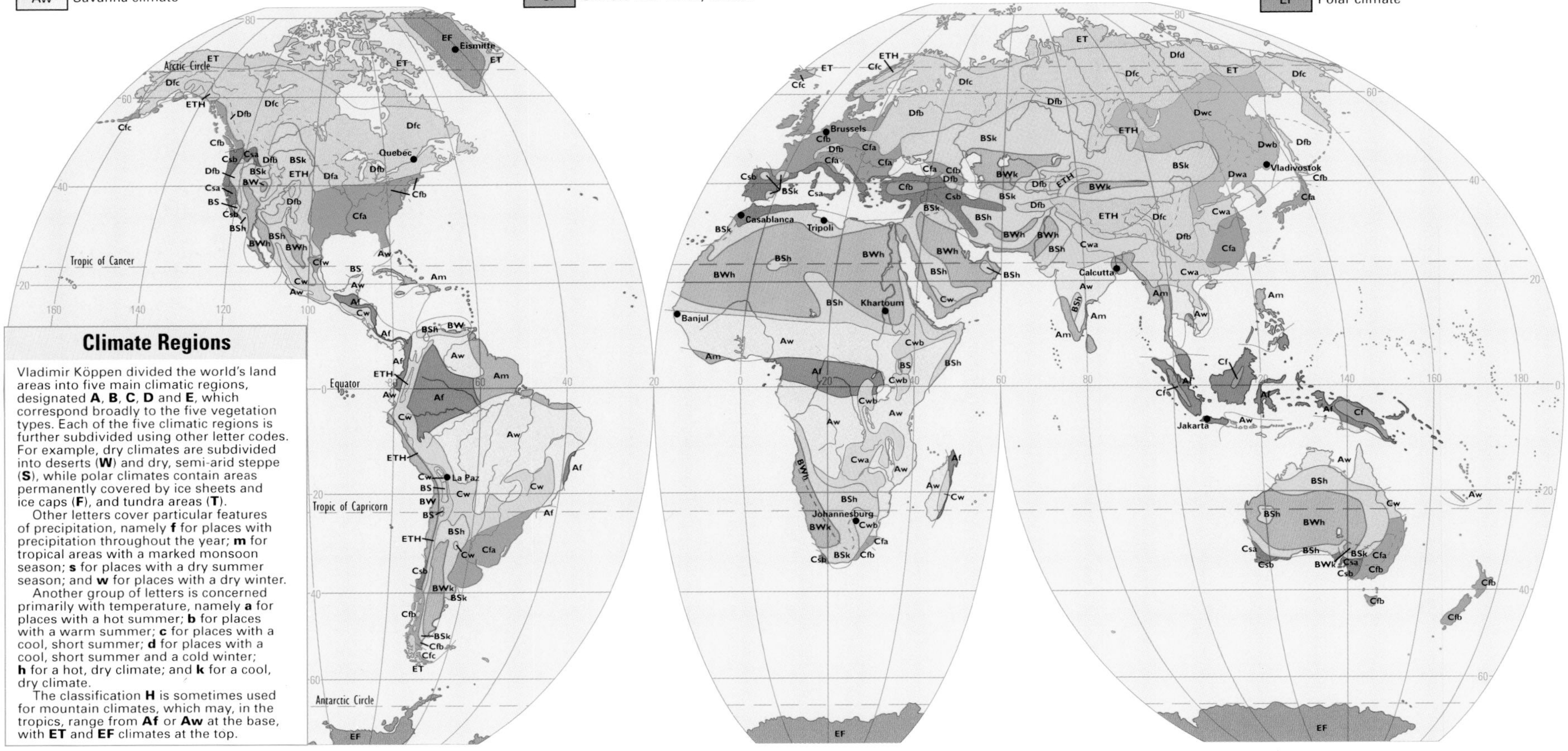

Climate Regions

Vladimir Köppen divided the world's land areas into five main climatic regions, designated **A**, **B**, **C**, **D** and **E**, which correspond broadly to the five vegetation types. Each of the five climatic regions is further subdivided using other letter codes. For example, dry climates are subdivided into deserts (**W**) and dry, semi-arid steppe (**S**), while polar climates contain areas permanently covered by ice sheets and ice caps (**F**), and tundra areas (**T**).

Other letters cover particular features of precipitation, namely **f** for places with precipitation throughout the year; **m** for tropical areas with a marked monsoon season; **s** for places with a dry summer season; and **w** for places with a dry winter.

Another group of letters is concerned primarily with temperature, namely **a** for places with a hot summer; **b** for places with a warm summer; **c** for places with a cool, short summer; **d** for places with a cool, short summer and a cold winter; **h** for a hot, dry climate; and **k** for a cool, dry climate.

The classification **H** is sometimes used for mountain climates, which may, in the tropics, range from **Af** or **Aw** at the base, with **ET** and **EF** climates at the top.

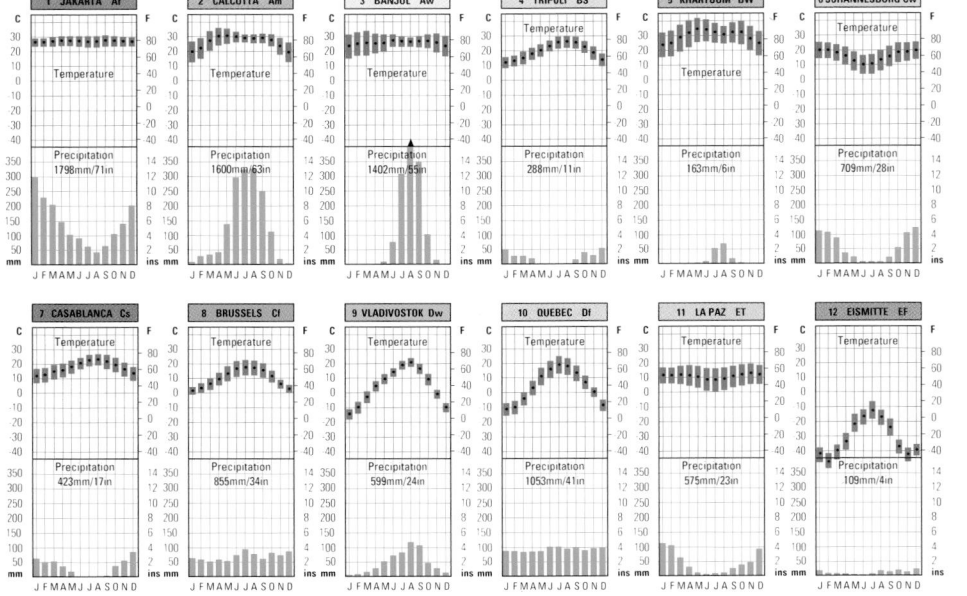

Climate and Weather Terms

Anticyclone: area of high pressure with light winds and generally quiet weather.
Absolute humidity: amount of water vapour contained in a given volume of air.
Cloud cover: amount of cloud in the sky; measured in oktas (from 1 – 8), with 0 clear, and 8 total cover.
Condensation: the conversion of water vapour, or moisture in the air, into liquid.
Cyclone: violent storm resulting from anticlockwise rotation of winds in the northern hemisphere and clockwise in the southern: called hurricane in N. America, typhoon in the Far East.
Depression: area of low pressure. The pressure gradient is towards the centre.
Dew: water droplets condensed out of the air after the ground has cooled at night.
Dew point: temperature at which air becomes saturated (reaches a relative humidity of 100%) at a constant pressure.
Drizzle: precipitation where drops are less than 0.5 mm (0.02 in) in diameter.
Evaporation: conversion of water from liquid into vapour, or moisture in the air.
Front: the dividing line between two air masses.
Frost: dew that has frozen when the air temperature falls below freezing point.
Hail: frozen rain; small balls of ice, often falling during thunderstorms.
Hoar frost: formed on objects when the dew point is below freezing point.
Humidity: amount of moisture in the air.
Isobar: cartographic line connecting places of equal atmospheric pressure.
Isotherm: cartographic line connecting places of equal temperature.
Lightning: massive electrical discharge released in thunderstorm from cloud to cloud or cloud to ground, the result of the tip becoming positively charged and the bottom negatively charged.
Precipitation: measurable rain, snow, sleet or hail.
Prevailing wind: most common direction of wind at a given location.
Rain: precipitation of liquid particles with diameter larger than 0.5 mm (0.02 in).
Relative humidity: amount of water vapour contained in a given volume of air at a given temperature.
Snow: formed when water vapour condenses below freezing point.
Thunder: sound produced by the rapid expansion of air heated by lightning.
Tornado: severe funnel-shaped storm that twists as hot air spins vertically (waterspout at sea).
Whirlwind: rapidly rotating column of air, only a few metres across, made visible by dust.

Climate Change

Human factors, such as the emission of greenhouse gases through the burning of fossil fuels and defor-estation, have contributed to global warming. The histogram, below, shows in blue the average global temperatures from 1860 (when sufficient observ-ations became available for global averages to be calculated) to 1996. The red line is a 10-year running average. Overall, there is an upward trend, particu-larly so since the 1970s, when global warming became a matter of concern in scientific circles. The large year-to-year changes indicate the Earth's natural climatic variability and the influence of such factors as major volcanic eruptions.

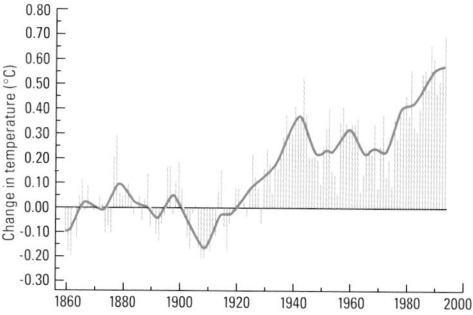

Data from the Hadley Centre for Climate Research and Prediction

Beaufort Wind Scale

Named after the 19th-century British naval officer who devised it, Admiral Beaufort, the Beaufort Scale assesses wind speed according to its effects. It was originally designed as an aid for sailors, but has since been adapted for use on the land. It is used internationally.

Scale	Wind speed km/h	mph	Effect
0	0–1	0–1	**Calm** Smoke rises vertically
1	1–5	1–3	**Light air** Wind direction shown only by smoke drift
2	6–11	4–7	**Light breeze** Wind felt on face; leaves rustle; vanes moved by wind
3	12–19	8–12	**Gentle breeze** Leaves and small twigs in constant motion; wind extends small flag
4	20–28	13–18	**Moderate** Raises dust and loose paper; small branches move
5	29–38	19–24	**Fresh** Small trees in leaf sway; crested wavelets on inland waters
6	39–49	25–31	**Strong** Large branches move; difficult to use umbrellas; overhead wires whistle
7	50–61	32–38	**Near gale** Whole trees in motion; difficult to walk against wind
8	62–74	39–46	**Gale** Twigs break from trees; walking very difficult
9	75–88	47–54	**Strong gale** Slight structural damage
10	89–102	55–63	**Storm** Trees uprooted; serious structural damage
11	103–117	64–72	**Violent storm** Widespread damage
12	118+	73+	**Hurricane**

The Monsoon

Monsoon is the term given to the seasonal reversal of wind direction, most noticeably in South-east Asia. It results from a combination of factors: the extreme heating and cooling of large landmasses in relation to the less marked changes in temperature of the adjacent seas; the northwards movement of the Intertropical Convergence Zone (ITCZ); and the effect of the Himalayas on the circulation of the air.

In early March, which normally marks the end of the sub-continent's cool season and the start of the hot season, winds blow outwards from the main-land. But as the overhead Sun and the ITCZ move northwards, the land is intensely heated, and a low-pressure system develops. The south-east trade winds, which are drawn across the Equator, change direction and are sucked into the interior to become south-westerly winds, bringing heavy rain. By November, the overhead Sun and the ITCZ have again moved southwards and the wind directions are again reversed. Cool winds blow from the Asian interior to the sea, losing any moisture on the Himalayas before descending to the coast.

Temperature

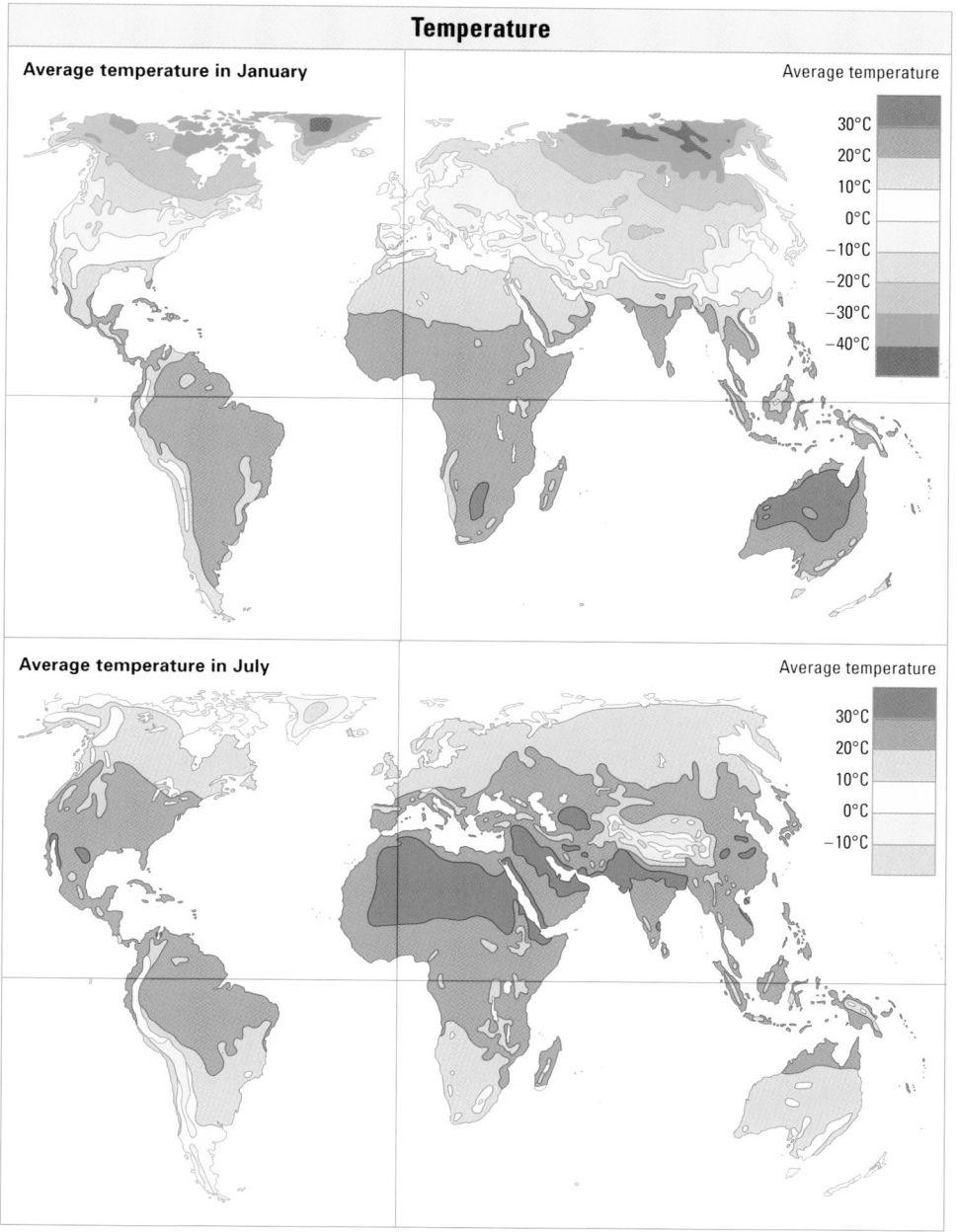

Average temperature in January

Average temperature

30°C / 20°C / 10°C / 0°C / −10°C / −20°C / −30°C / −40°C

Average temperature in July

Average temperature

30°C / 20°C / 10°C / 0°C / −10°C

Precipitation

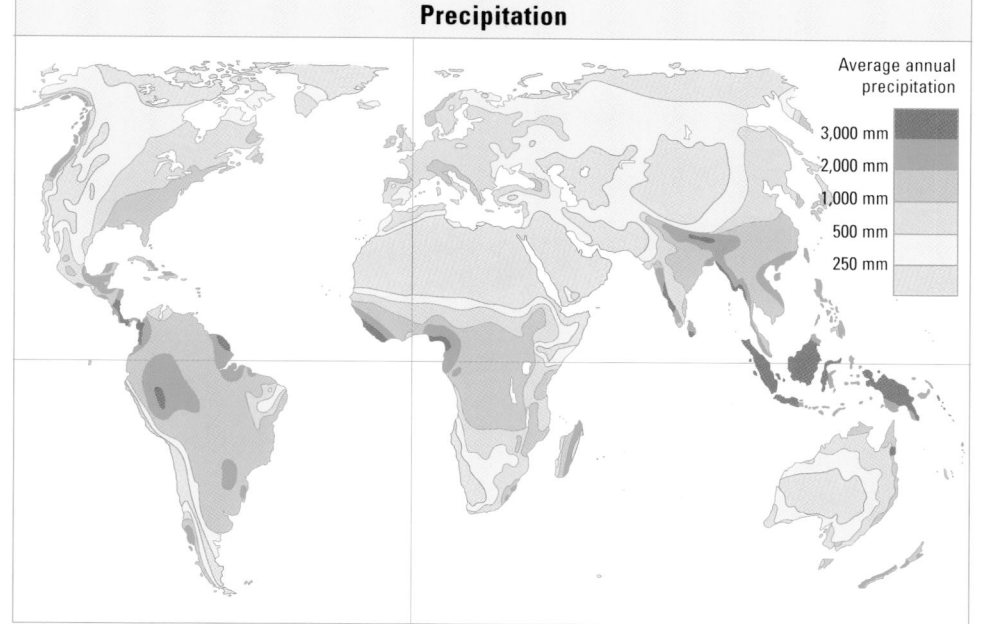

Average annual precipitation

3,000 mm / 2,000 mm / 1,000 mm / 500 mm / 250 mm

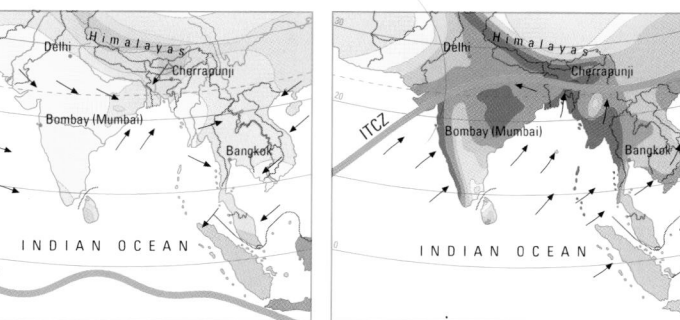

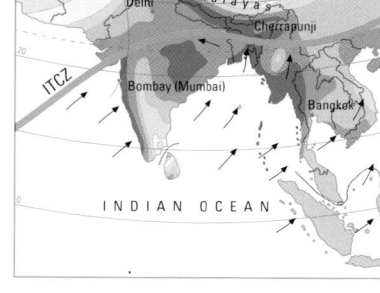

March – Start of the hot, dry season. The ITCZ is over the southern Indian Ocean.

July – The rainy season. The ITCZ has migrated northwards; winds blow onshore.

November – The ITCZ has returned south. The offshore winds are cool and dry.

Monthly rainfall (mm)

>400 / 200–400 / 100–200 / 50–100 / 25–50 / <25

→ wind direction
— ITCZ

Climate Records

Temperature

Highest recorded temperature: Al Aziziyah, Libya, 58°C [136.4°F], 13 September 1922.

Highest mean annual temperature: Dallol, Ethiopia, 34.4°C [94°F], 1960–66.

Longest heatwave: Marble Bar, W. Australia, 162 days over 38°C [100°F], 23 October 1923 to 7 April 1924.

Lowest recorded temperature (outside poles): Verkhoyansk, Siberia, −68°C [−90°F], 6 February 1933. Verkhoyansk also registered the greatest annual range of temperature: −70°C to 37°C [−94°F to 98°F].

Lowest mean annual temperature: Polus Nedostupnosti, Pole of Cold, Antarctica, −57.8°C [−72°F].

Precipitation

Driest place: Calama, N. Chile: no recorded rainfall in 400 years to 1971.

Wettest place (average): Tututendo, Colombia: mean annual rainfall 11,770 mm [463.4 in].

Wettest place (12 months): Cherrapunji, Meghalaya, N.E. India, 26,470 mm [1,040 in], August 1860 to August 1861. Cherrapunji also holds the record for rainfall in one month: 2,930 mm [115 in], July 1861. (See maps below.)

Wettest place (24 hours): Cilaos, Réunion, Indian Ocean, 1,870 mm [73.6 in], 15–16 March 1952.

Heaviest hailstones: Gopalganj, Bangladesh, up to 1.02 kg [2.25 lb], 14 April 1986 (killed 92 people).

Heaviest snowfall (continuous): Bessans, Savoie, France, 1,730 mm [68 in] in 19 hours, 5–6 April 1969.

Heaviest snowfall (season/year): Paradise Ranger Station, Mt Rainier, Washington, USA, 31,102 mm [1,224.5 in], 19 February 1971 to 18 February 1972.

Water and Vegetation

Without the hydrological cycle, whereby water is constantly recycled between the oceans, the atmosphere and the land, the continents would be barren. Precipitation enables plants to grow and soils to form, creating the world's natural vegetation regions and the ecosystems that support animal life. Running water also plays a major role in shaping landforms. Yet in many parts of the world, people do not have safe water to drink and suffer from diseases caused by water-borne organisms or pollution. In addition, the limited water supplies have to be shared with agriculture and industry.

In 1996, UN experts argued that the demand for water is increasing at about twice the rate of population growth. They predict that, by 2025, two-thirds of the world's population will face water shortages. This could lead to conflict and even boundary wars, especially because 300 major rivers cross national frontiers and access to their water is likely to be disputed.

The Hydrological Cycle

The world's water balance is regulated by the constant recycling of water between the oceans, atmosphere and land. The movement of water between these three reservoirs is known as the hydrological cycle. The oceans play a vital role in the hydrological cycle: 74% of the total precipitation falls over the oceans and 84% of the total evaporation comes from the oceans. Water vapour in the atmosphere circulates around the planet, transporting energy as well as the water itself. When the vapour cools, it falls as rain or snow. The whole cycle is driven by the Sun.

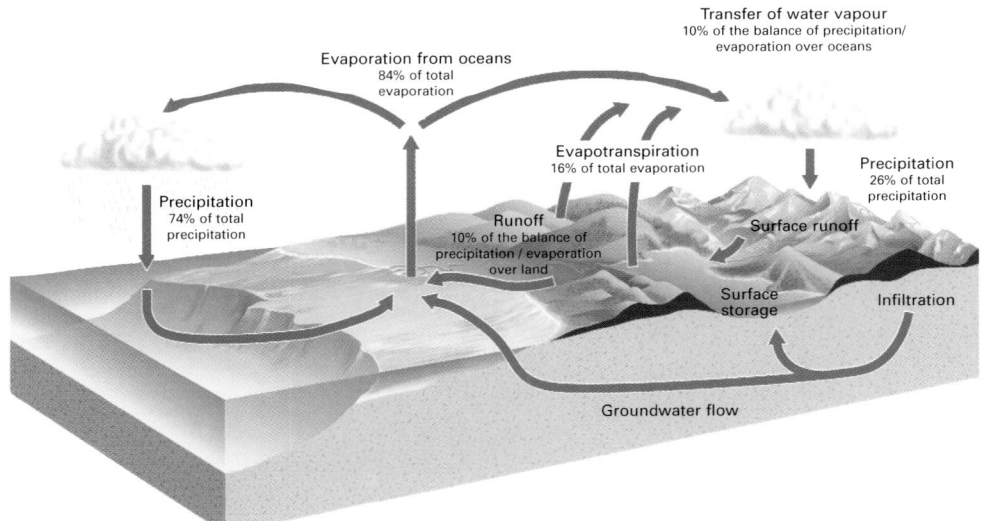

Water Distribution

The distribution of planetary water, by percentage. Oceans and ice caps together account for more than 99% of the total; the breakdown of the remainder is estimated.

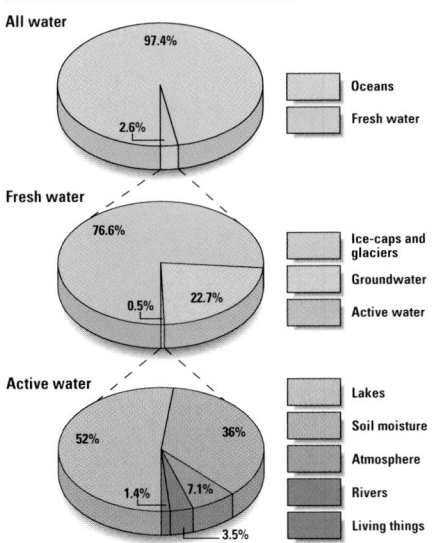

All water
- 97.4% Oceans
- 2.6% Fresh water

Fresh water
- 76.6% Ice-caps and glaciers
- 0.5% Groundwater
- 22.7% Active water

Active water
- 52% Lakes
- 36% Soil moisture
- 1.4% Atmosphere
- 7.1% Rivers
- 3.5% Living things

Almost all the world's water is 3,000 million years old, and all of it cycles endlessly through the hydrosphere, though at different rates. Water vapour circulates over days, even hours; deep ocean water circulates over millennia; and ice-cap water remains solid for millions of years.

Water Utilization

The percentage breakdown of water usage by sector, selected countries (1996)

Domestic
Industrial
Agriculture

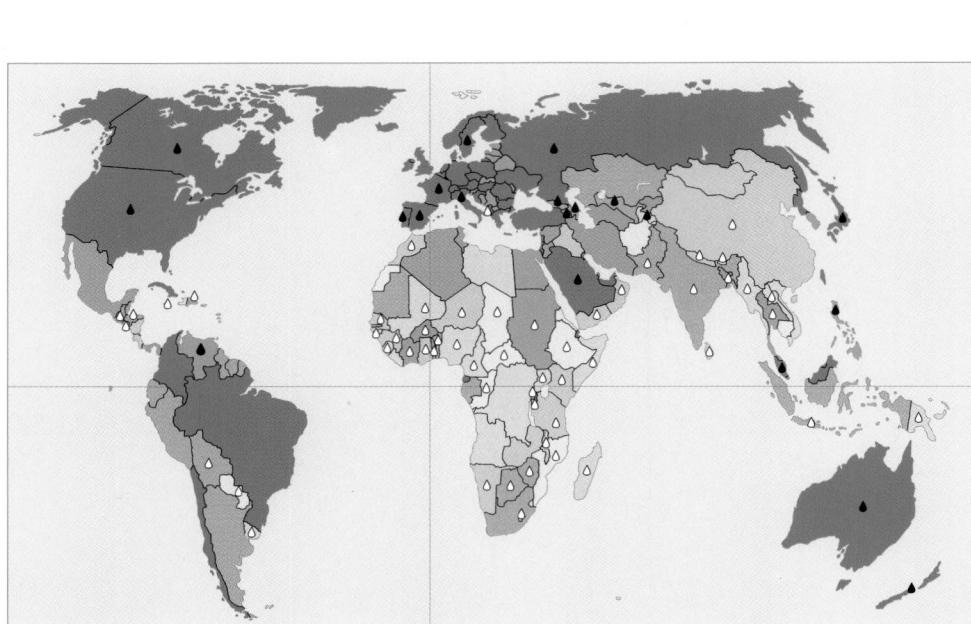

Countries: Algeria, Australia, Egypt, France, Ghana, India, Mexico, Poland, Russian Fed., Saudi Arabia, UK, USA

Water Runoff

Annual freshwater runoff by continent in cubic kilometres

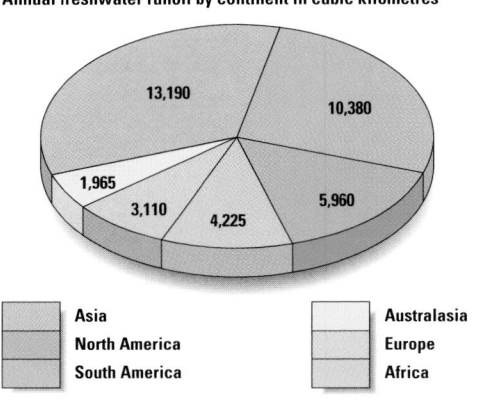

- Asia 13,190
- North America 5,960
- South America 10,380
- Australasia 1,965
- Europe 3,110
- Africa 4,225

Water Supply

Percentage of total population with access to safe drinking water (1995)

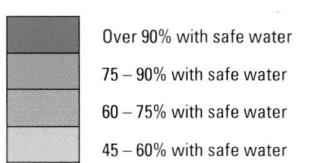

- Over 90% with safe water
- 75 – 90% with safe water
- 60 – 75% with safe water
- 45 – 60% with safe water
- 30 – 45% with safe water
- Under 30% with safe water

△ Under 80 litres average per capita daily water consumption

▲ Over 320 litres average per capita daily water consumption

Least well-provided countries

Paraguay	8%	Central Afr. Rep.	18%
Afghanistan	10%	Bhutan	21%
Cambodia	13%	Congo (D. Rep.)	25%

Watersheds

The world's major rivers; the rank of the world's 20 longest is shown in square brackets, led by the Nile and the Amazon.

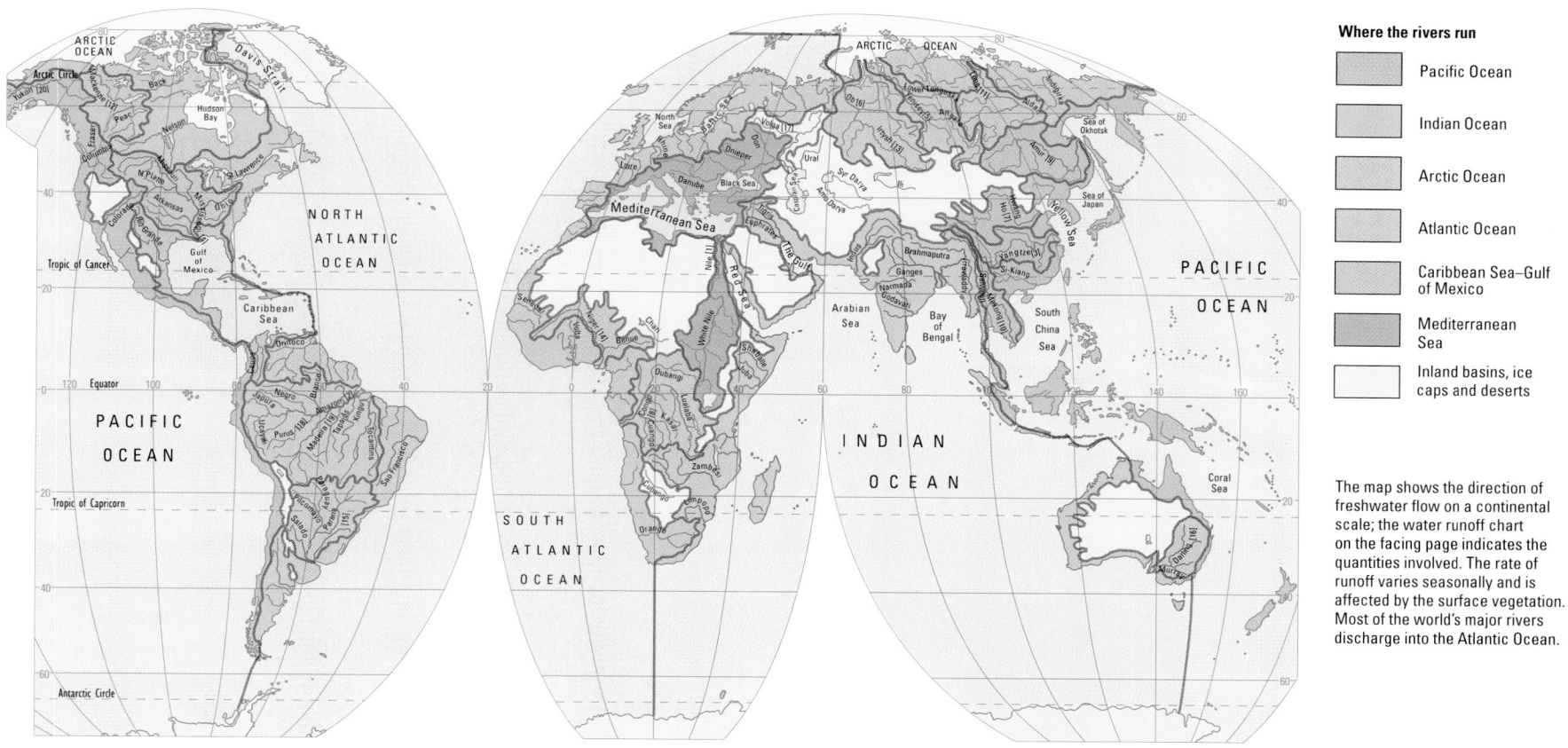

Where the rivers run

- Pacific Ocean
- Indian Ocean
- Arctic Ocean
- Atlantic Ocean
- Caribbean Sea–Gulf of Mexico
- Mediterranean Sea
- Inland basins, ice caps and deserts

The map shows the direction of freshwater flow on a continental scale; the water runoff chart on the facing page indicates the quantities involved. The rate of runoff varies seasonally and is affected by the surface vegetation. Most of the world's major rivers discharge into the Atlantic Ocean.

Annual Sediment Yield

Around 20% of all land-derived sediment is carried by three Asian rivers: the Brahmaputra, Huang He (Yellow River) and Ganges. Together these three rivers carry 3,206 million tonnes of sediment per year into the oceans. Sediment yield is affected by runoff and vegetation cover and is steadily increasing due to large-scale deforestation, most notably in South-east Asia and the Amazon basin. In these regions, deforesting the slopes allows the heavy tropical rains to wash away whatever thin and fragile soil there is, leading to severe erosion of the land.

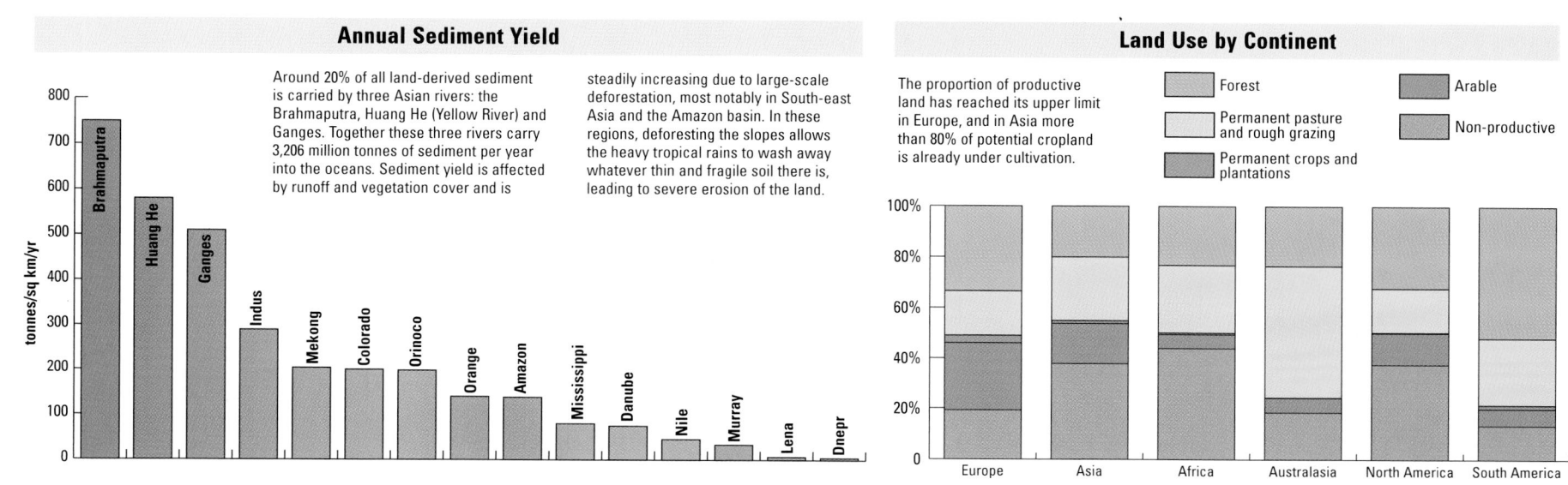

Land Use by Continent

The proportion of productive land has reached its upper limit in Europe, and in Asia more than 80% of potential cropland is already under cultivation.

- Forest
- Permanent pasture and rough grazing
- Permanent crops and plantations
- Arable
- Non-productive

Natural Vegetation

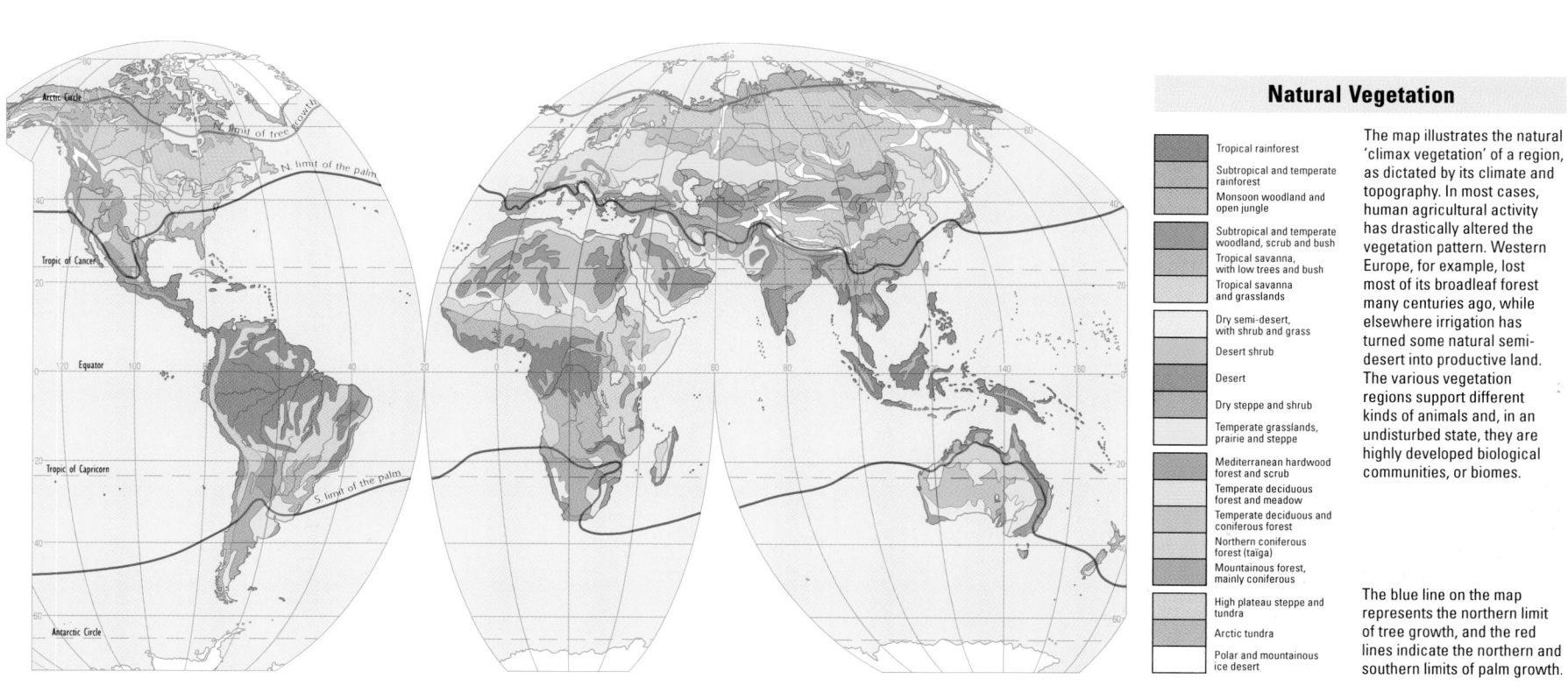

- Tropical rainforest
- Subtropical and temperate rainforest
- Monsoon woodland and open jungle
- Subtropical and temperate woodland, scrub and bush
- Tropical savanna, with low trees and bush
- Tropical savanna and grasslands
- Dry semi-desert, with shrub and grass
- Desert shrub
- Desert
- Dry steppe and shrub
- Temperate grasslands, prairie and steppe
- Mediterranean hardwood forest and scrub
- Temperate deciduous forest and meadow
- Temperate deciduous and coniferous forest
- Northern coniferous forest (taiga)
- Mountainous forest, mainly coniferous
- High plateau steppe and tundra
- Arctic tundra
- Polar and mountainous ice desert

The map illustrates the natural 'climax vegetation' of a region, as dictated by its climate and topography. In most cases, human agricultural activity has drastically altered the vegetation pattern. Western Europe, for example, lost most of its broadleaf forest many centuries ago, while elsewhere irrigation has turned some natural semi-desert into productive land. The various vegetation regions support different kinds of animals and, in an undisturbed state, they are highly developed biological communities, or biomes.

The blue line on the map represents the northern limit of tree growth, and the red lines indicate the northern and southern limits of palm growth.

The Natural Environment

Recent discoveries of life forms in some of the world's most hostile environments, such as around the black smokers along the ocean ridges, prepared the way for the announcement by NASA scientists in 1996 that they had found microfossils in a Martian meteorite. But other scientists were sceptical, believing them to be natural mineral structures and not evidence of extraterrestrial life.

Until further evidence is available, the Earth remains the only planet where we know for sure that life exists. According to the fossil record, life on Earth appeared at least 3,500 million years ago. Since then, it has evolved from its primitive beginnings to its modern biodiversity, including millions of plants, animals and micro-organisms. Living organisms have not only adapted to the environment but they have also changed their environment to suit themselves. For example, the Earth's early atmosphere contained little oxygen but the emergence of multi-celled, oxygen-producing algae, around 2,000 million years ago, led to the creation of an oxygen-rich atmosphere. This enabled land animals to populate the ancient continents.

The amount of the greenhouse gas carbon dioxide in the atmosphere would steadily increase from its present 0.03% were it not for plants. Without them, the Earth's atmosphere would, in a few million years, be similar to that of Venus, where surface temperatures reach 475°C. The Earth has evolved into a complex control system, sensing and reacting to changes and tending always to maintain the balance it has achieved.

Much discussion has centred on how that balance changes. Only recently, scientists were suggesting that we may be living in an inter-glacial stage of the Pleistocene Ice Age. From the 1980s, however, predictions of future climates have concentrated more on global warming, caused by pollution which has led to an increase in greenhouse gases in the atmosphere. Interference in the natural cycles that control the environment may have consequences that are hard to predict.

Furthermore, we are currently experiencing a period of mass extinction of species, causing a rapid reduction in our planet's biodiversity. A report by the World Conservation Union in 1996 stated that, of the 4,327 known mammal species, 1,096 were at risk and 169 'critically endangered'.

Biodiversity in California

The photograph, left, is a false-colour satellite image of central California in the south-western United States. The large inlet of the Pacific Ocean is San Francisco Bay. San Francisco lies just below the entrance to the bay, with Oakland on the far side and San Jose to the south-east. California, nicknamed the Golden State, is the third largest state in the United States and the most populous.

Because of its varied terrain and climate, California has a wide range of diverse habitats within a relatively small area. East of the forested Coast Ranges (the grey and red areas just inland from the bay) lies the fertile Central Valley, which appears as a red and blue chequerboard. The Sierra Nevada is the red area in the top right corner. In the north-west and south-west of the state, not shown here, lie parts of the Basin and Range region, much of which is desert. It includes Death Valley, which contains the country's lowest point on land at 86 m below sea level.

Forests cover about 40% of California and they include bristlecone pines, thought to be the oldest living things on Earth, together with coastal red-woods, the world's tallest trees. Wildlife is still abundant, though some species, such as the rare California condor, are on the endangered list.

The state has achieved much to protect its biodiversity. It contains eight of the 54 national parks in the United States. Two of them, Death Valley and Joshua Tree, were designated national parks as recently as 1994, as part of a conservation measure, including the protection of large areas of wilderness in the deserts.

California has vast resources and, were it a separate nation, it would rank among the world's ten most productive in terms of the total value of its goods and services. This means that, like the United States as a whole, it has resources, which many developing countries lack, to finance conservation measures. For example, the World Conservation Union reported in 1996 that 8% of mammals were threatened in the United States, as compared with 32% in the Philippines and 44% in Madagascar, two countries where habitat destruction has been on a large scale.

Endangered Species

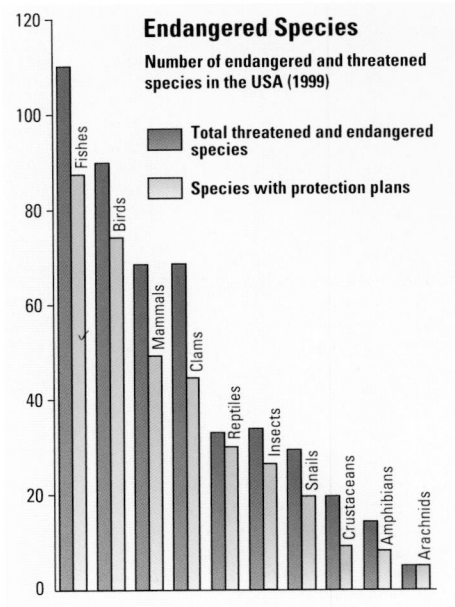

Number of endangered and threatened species in the USA (1999)

■ Total threatened and endangered species

□ Species with protection plans

Threatened Mammals

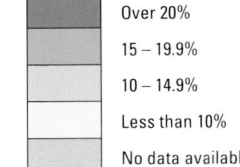

Percentage of mammal species classified as threatened (1996). Many scientists believe we are currently experiencing a period of mass extinction of species rivalling five other periods in the past half a billion years. Among the most threatened mammals are elephants, primates and rhinoceroses.

Over 20%
15 – 19.9%
10 – 14.9%
Less than 10%
No data available

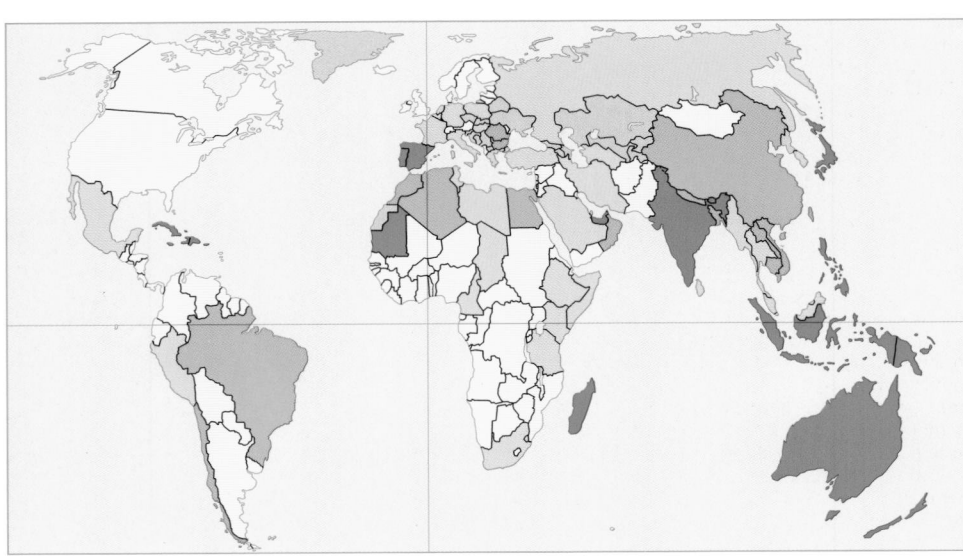

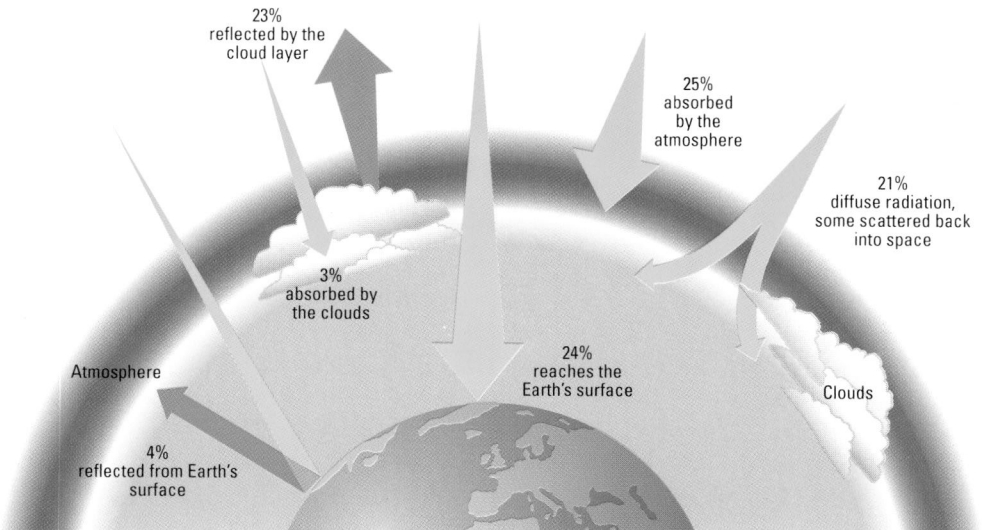

The Earth's Energy Balance

Apart from a modest quantity of internal heat from its molten core, the Earth receives all of its energy from the Sun. If the planet is to remain at a constant temperature, it must reradiate exactly as much energy as it receives. Even a minute surplus would lead to a warmer Earth, a deficit to a cooler one. The temperature at which thermal equilibrium is reached depends on a multitude of interconnected factors. Two of the most important are the relative brightness of the Earth – its index of reflectivity, called the 'albedo' – and the heat-trapping capacity of the atmosphere – the celebrated 'greenhouse effect' (see below).

Because the Sun is very hot, most of its energy arrives in the form of relatively short-wave radiation: the shorter the waves, the more energy they carry. Some of the incoming energy is reflected straight back into space, exactly as it arrived; some is absorbed by the atmosphere on its way towards the surface; some is absorbed by the Earth itself. Absorbed energy heats the Earth and its atmosphere alike. But since its temperature is very much lower than that of the Sun, the outgoing energy is emitted at much longer infra-red wavelengths. Some of the outgoing radiation escapes directly into outer space; some of it is reabsorbed by the atmosphere. Atmospheric energy eventually finds its way back into space, too, after a complex series of interactions. These include the air movements we call the weather and, almost incidentally, the maintenance of life on Earth.

This diagram does not attempt to illustrate the actual mechanisms of heat exchange, but gives a reasonable account (in percentages) of what happens to 100 energy 'units'. Short-wave radiation is shown in yellow, long-wave in orange.

The Carbon Cycle

Most of the constituents of the atmosphere are kept in constant balance by complex cycles in which life plays an essential and indeed a dominant part. The control of carbon dioxide, which if left to its own devices would be the dominant atmospheric gas, is possibly the most important, although since all the Earth's biological and geophysical cycles interact and interlock, it is hard to separate them even in theory and quite impossible in practice.

The Earth has a huge supply of carbon, only a small quantity of which is in the form of carbon dioxide. Of that, around 98% is dissolved in the sea; the fraction circulating in the air amounts to only 340 parts per million of the atmosphere, where its capacity as a greenhouse gas is the key regulator of the planetary temperature. In turn, life regulates the regulator, keeping carbon dioxide concentrations below danger level.

If all life were to vanish from the Earth tomorrow, the atmosphere would begin the process of change immediately, although it might take several million years to achieve a new, inorganic stability. First, the oxygen content would begin to fall away; with no more assistance than a little solar radiation, a few electrical storms and its own high chemical potential, oxygen would steadily combine with atmospheric nitrogen and volcanic outgassing. In doing so, it would yield sufficient acid to react with carbonaceous rocks such as limestone, releasing carbon dioxide. Once carbon dioxide levels exceeded about 1%, its greenhouse power would increase disproportionately. Rising temperatures – well above the boiling point of water – would speed chemical reactions; in time, the Earth's atmosphere would consist of little more than carbon dioxide and superheated water vapour.

Living things, however, circulate carbon. They do so first by simply existing: after all, the carbon atom is the basic building block of living matter. During life, plants absorb carbon dioxide from the atmosphere and, along with various chemicals, as soluble salts from the soil, incorporating the carbon into their structure – leaves and trunks in the case of land plants, shells in the case of plankton and the tiny creatures that feed on it. The oxygen thereby freed is added to the atmosphere, at least for a time. The carbon is returned to circulation when the plants die or is passed up the food chain to the herbivores and then the carnivores that feed on them. As organisms at each of these trophic levels die, they decay, releasing the carbon which then combines once more with the oxygen released during life.

However, a small proportion of carbon, about one part in 1,000, is removed almost permanently, buried beneath mud on land or at sea, sinking as dead matter to the ocean floor. In time, it is slowly compressed into sedimentary rocks such as limestone and chalk.

But in the evolution of the Earth, nothing is quite permanent. On an even longer timescale, the planet's crustal movements force new rock upwards in mid-ocean ridges. Limestone deposits are moved, and sea levels change; ancient carboniferous rocks are exposed to weathering, and a little of their carbon is released to be fixed in turn by the current generation of plants.

The carbon cycle has continued quietly for an immensely long time, and without gross disturbance there is no reason why it would not continue almost indefinitely in the future. However, human beings have found a way to release fixed carbon at a rate far faster than existing global systems can recirculate it. The fossil fuels, coal, oil, gas and peat deposits, represent the work of millions of years of carbon accumulation; but it has taken only a few human generations of high-energy scavenging to endanger the entire complex regulatory cycle.

The Greenhouse Effect

Constituting less than 1% of the atmosphere, the natural greenhouse gases (water vapour, carbon dioxide, methane, nitrous oxide and ozone) have a hugely disproportionate effect on the Earth's climate and even its habitability. Like the glass panes in a greenhouse, the gases are transparent to most incoming short-wave radiation, which passes freely to heat the planet beneath. But when the warmed Earth retransmits that energy, in the form of longer-wave infra-red radiation, the gases function as an opaque shield preventing some of it from escaping, so that the planetary surface (like the interior of a greenhouse) stays relatively hot.

Over the last 150 years, there has been a gradual increase in the levels of greenhouse gases (with the exception of water vapour which remains a constant in the system). These increases are causing alarm – global warming associated with a runaway greenhouse effect could bring disaster – and what is more, predictions suggest that there could be a further rise of 1.5–4.5°C by the year 2100. A serious reduction in the greenhouse gases would be just as damaging; a total absence of CO_2, for example, would leave the planet with a temperature roughly 33°C colder than at present.

N.B. The thickness of the Earth's atmosphere is proportionately much thinner than the peel of an apple.

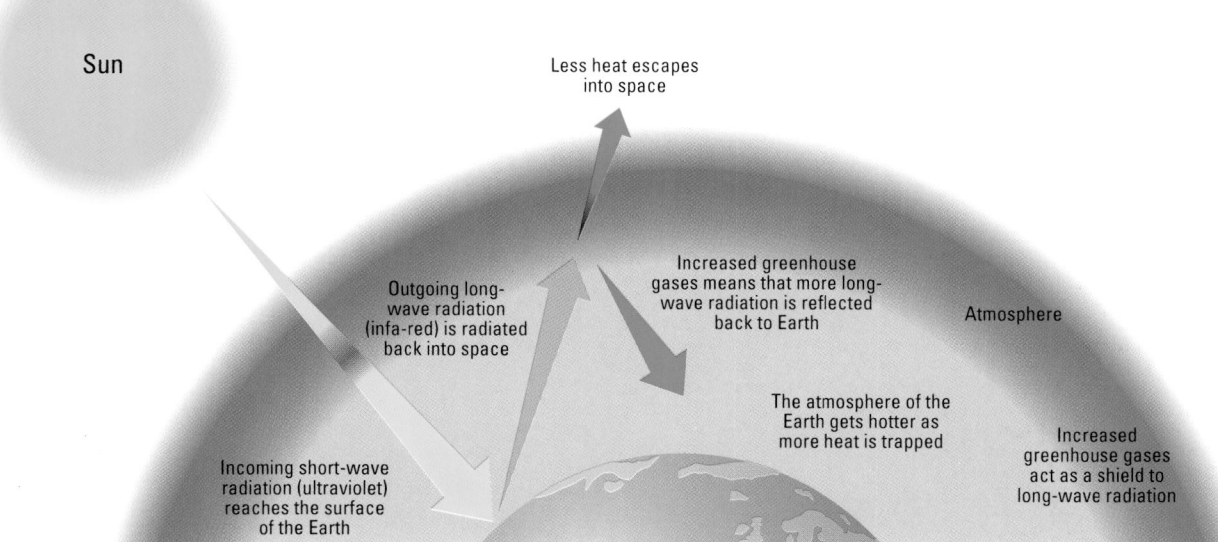

People and the Environment

In 1996, the Intergovernmental Panel on Climate Change issued a report stating that 'The balance of evidence suggests a discernible human influence on global climate through emissions of carbon dioxide and other greenhouse gases.' The report acknowledged that average global temperatures have risen by about 0.5°C since the mid-19th century, but there were still reasons for caution, such as discrepancies between measurements of temperatures around the world. Furthermore, our knowledge about how climates change of their own accord is incomplete, as is our understanding of human interference, how this varies in different parts of the world and how it differs from natural climatic variability.

Human interference with nature is nothing new, at least since people turned to agriculture over 10,000 years ago. At first, human actions seemed to have no ill effects because the systems that regulate the global environment absorbed the damage. But from the late 18th century, the Industrial Revolution and population explosion have caused pollution on a scale that threatens to overwhelm the Earth's ability to cope.

The 20th century experienced many disasters, including the dumping of industrial wastes in rivers and seas, accidents at nuclear power stations, and the creation of acid rain through the release of sulphur dioxides and nitrous oxides by the burning of fossil fuels. The release of greenhouse gases are held to be the main reason for global warming, while CFCs (chlorofluorocarbons) have damaged the ozone layer in the stratosphere, the planet's screen against ultraviolet radiation.

Global warming will lead to melting ice sheets and the flooding of fertile coastal plains. Computer models suggest that it might affect ocean currents so that north-western Europe, which owes its mild climate to the Gulf Stream, could expect bitterly cold winters. Some models have suggested that cloud cover could increase, reflecting more solar energy back into space and so start a new Ice Age.

In many tropical areas, deforestation is making productive land barren, while in the dry grasslands bordering deserts, the removal of plant cover is causing desertification. But human ingenuity can respond to this crisis in planet management.

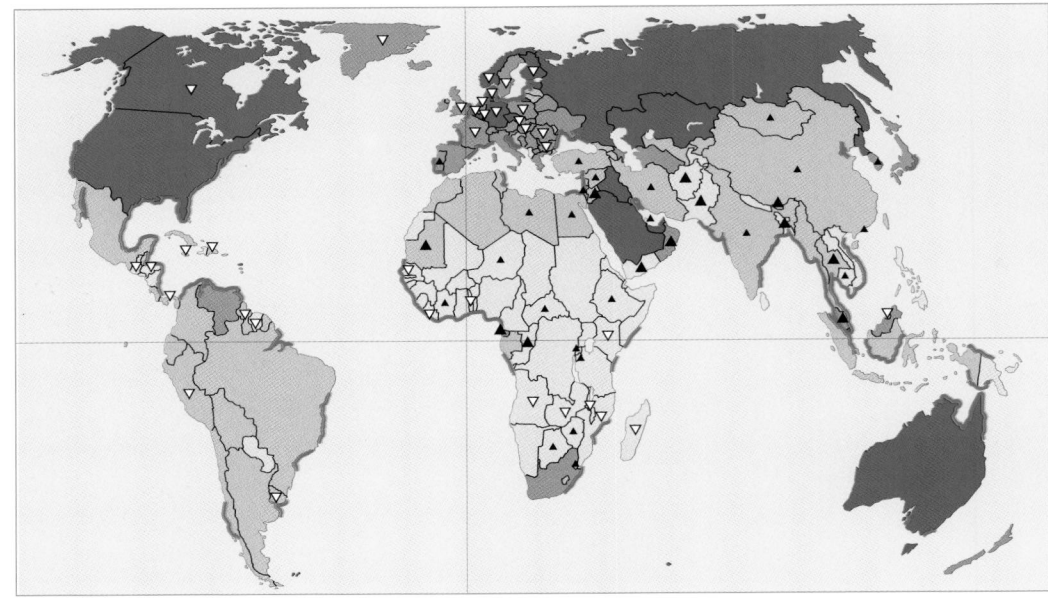

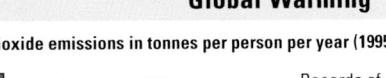

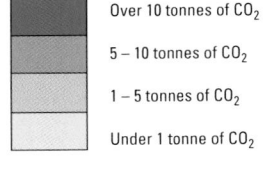

Global Warming

Carbon dioxide emissions in tonnes per person per year (1995)

- Over 10 tonnes of CO_2
- 5 – 10 tonnes of CO_2
- 1 – 5 tonnes of CO_2
- Under 1 tonne of CO_2

Changes in CO_2 emissions 1980–90

- ▲ Over 100% increase
- ▲ 50–100% increase
- ▽ Reduction
- — Coasts in danger of flooding from rising sea levels

Records of global mean surface temperatures from 1860 to the present show that 1995 was the warmest year and that nine of the ten warmest years have occurred since 1983.
This evidence of global warming is attributed mainly to the Greenhouse Effect, caused by the emission of certain gases, notably carbon dioxide (CO_2), into the atmosphere since the start of the Industrial Revolution. At first, much of the CO_2 was absorbed by the oceans. However, the vast increase in fuel combustion since 1950 has led CO_2 content in the atmosphere to increase gradually from 280 parts per million to more than 350 parts per million. Despite international action to control the emissions of some greenhouse gases, CO_2 levels are still rising.

Greenhouse Power

Relative contributions to the Greenhouse Effect by the major heat-absorbing gases in the atmosphere

The chart combines greenhouse potency and volume. Carbon dioxide has a greenhouse potential of only 1, but its concentration of 350 parts per million makes it predominate. CFC 12, with 25,000 times the absorption capacity of CO_2, is present only as 0.00044 ppm.

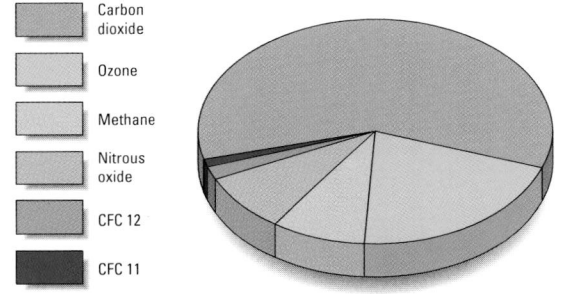

- Carbon dioxide
- Ozone
- Methane
- Nitrous oxide
- CFC 12
- CFC 11

Carbon Dioxide

Carbon dioxide released in millions of tonnes (latest available year)

USA 4,932
Former USSR 3,581
China 2,543
Japan
Germany
India
UK
Iraq
Canada
Italy
France
Mexico

Temperature Rise

The rise in average temperatures caused by carbon dioxide and other greenhouse gases (1960–2020)

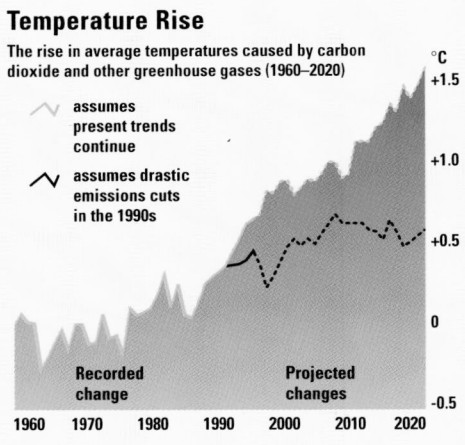

- ⌇ assumes present trends continue
- ⌇ assumes drastic emissions cuts in the 1990s

Recorded change

Projected changes

°C
+1.5
+1.0
+0.5
0
-0.5

1960 1970 1980 1990 2000 2010 2020

The Thinning Ozone Layer

Total atmospheric ozone concentration in the southern and northern hemispheres (Dobson units, 1995)

In 1985, scientists working in Antarctica discovered a thinning of the ozone layer, commonly known as an 'ozone hole'. This caused immediate alarm because the ozone layer absorbs most of the Sun's dangerous ultraviolet radiation, which is believed to cause an increase in skin cancer, cataracts and damage to the immune system. Since 1985, ozone depletion has increased and, by 1996, the ozone hole over the South Pole was estimated to be as large as North America. The false colour images, right, show the total atmospheric ozone concentration in the southern hemisphere (in October 1995) and the northern hemisphere (in March 1995) with the ozone hole clearly identifiable at the centre. The data are from the Tiros Ozone Vertical Sounder, an instrument on the American TIROS weather satellite. The colours represent the ozone concentration in Dobson Units (DU). Normal healthy values are around 280 DU but the lowest value in the northern hemisphere reached 98 DU. Scientists agree that ozone depletion is caused by CFCs, a group of manufactured chemicals used in air conditioning systems and refrigerators. In a 1987 treaty most industrial nations agreed to phase out CFCs and a complete ban on most CFCs was agreed after the end of 1995. However, scientists believe that the chemicals will remain in the atmosphere for 50 to 100 years. As a result, ozone depletion will continue for many years.

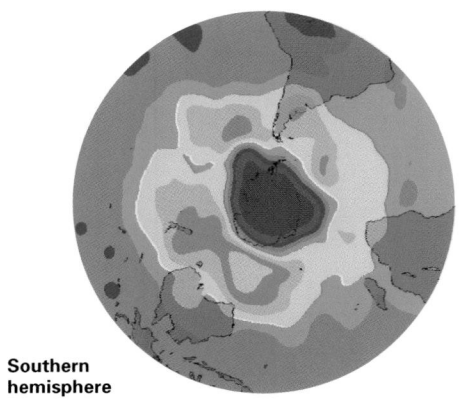

Southern hemisphere

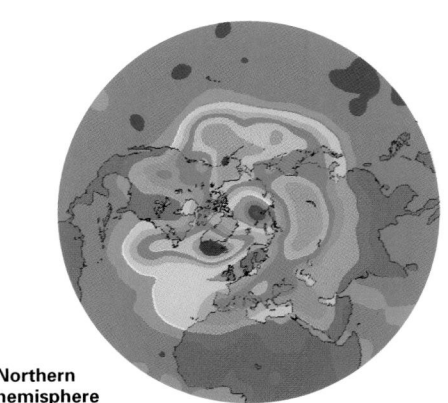

Northern hemisphere

World Pollution

Acid rain and sources of acidic emissions (latest available year)

Acid rain is caused by high levels of sulphur and nitrogen in the atmosphere. They combine with water vapour and oxygen to form acids (H_2SO_4 and HNO_3) which fall as precipitation.

 Regions where sulphur and nitrogen oxides are released in high concentrations, mainly from fossil fuel combustion

• Major cities with high levels of air pollution (including nitrogen and sulphur emissions)

Areas of heavy acid deposition

pH numbers indicate acidity, decreasing from a neutral 7. Normal rain, slightly acid from dissolved carbon dioxide, never exceeds a pH of 5.6.

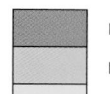

pH less than 4.0 (most acidic)

pH 4.0 to 4.5

pH 4.5 to 5.0

Areas where acid rain is a potential problem

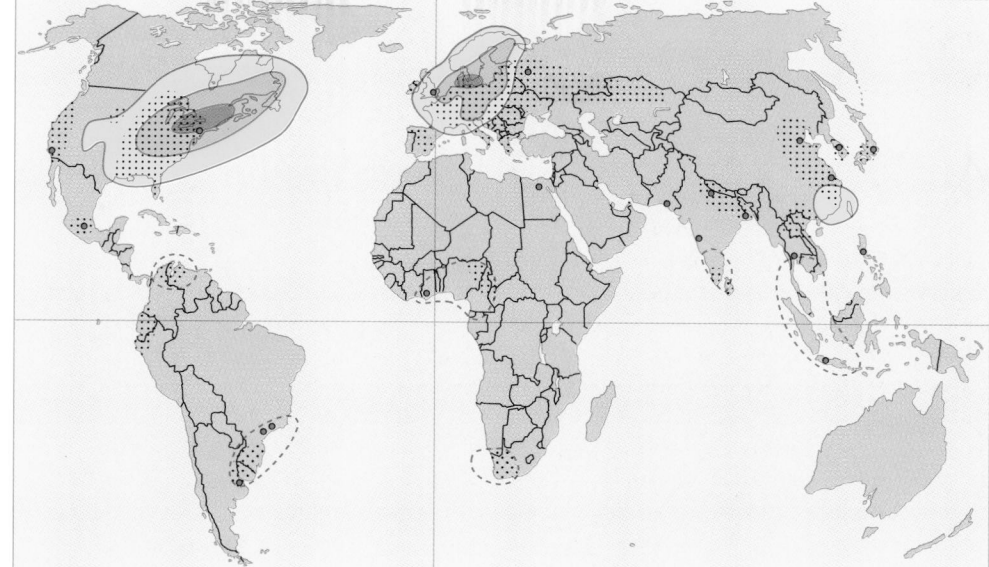

Desertification

 Existing deserts

Areas with a high risk of desertification

Areas with a moderate risk of desertification

Former areas of rainforest

Existing rainforest

Deforestation

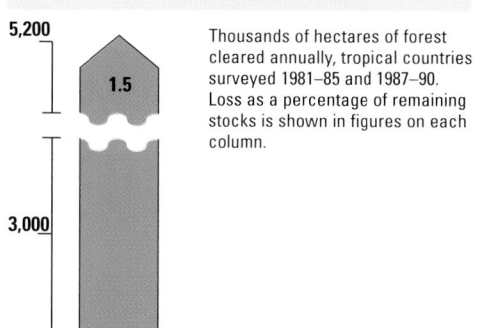
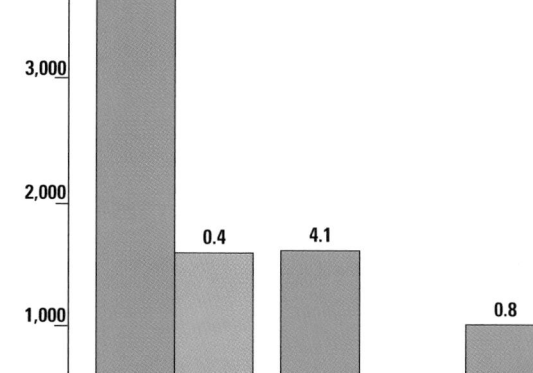
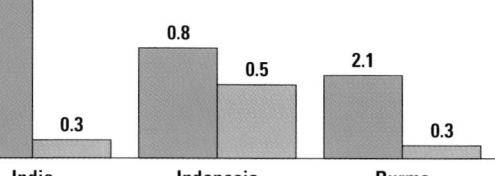

Thousands of hectares of forest cleared annually, tropical countries surveyed 1981–85 and 1987–90. Loss as a percentage of remaining stocks is shown in figures on each column.

5,200

1.5

3,000

2,000

1,000

0

Brazil	India	Indonesia	Burma	Thailand	Vietnam	Philippines	Costa Rica	Cameroon
1.5 / 0.4	4.1 / 0.3	0.8 / 0.5	2.1 / 0.3	2.5 / 2.4	2.0 / 0.7	1.5 / 1.0	7.6 / 4.0	0.6 / 0.4

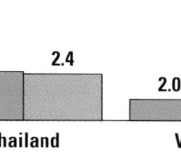 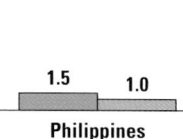 1987–90 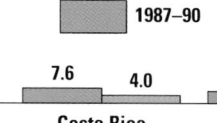 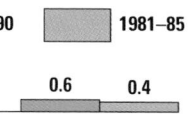 1981–85

Water Pollution

 Severely polluted sea areas and lakes

Polluted sea areas and lakes

Areas of frequent oil pollution by shipping

↘ Major oil tanker spills

▲ Major oil rig blow-outs

▼ Offshore dumpsites for industrial and municipal waste

——— Severely polluted rivers and estuaries

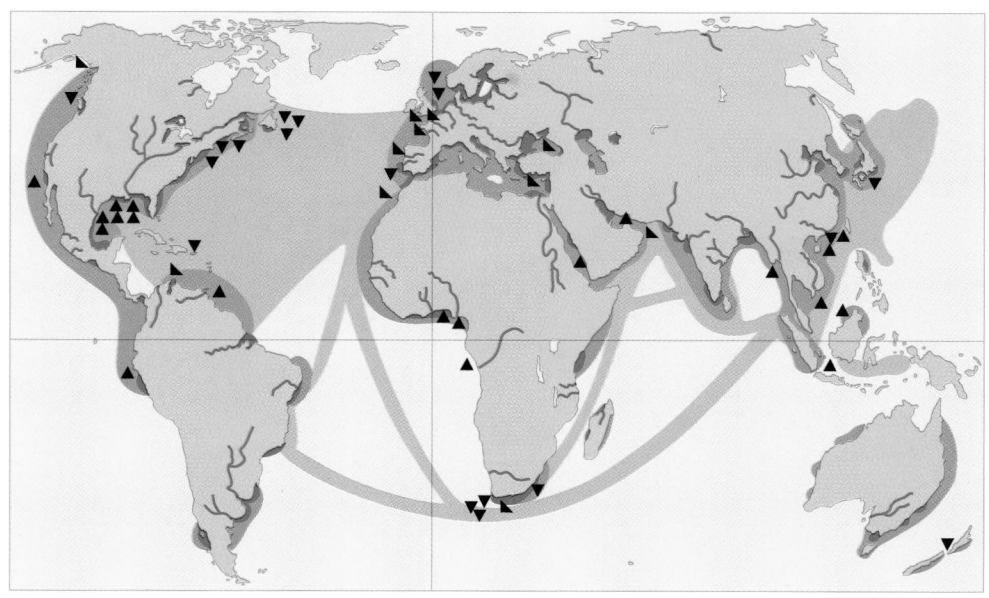

Antarctica

The vast Antarctic ice sheet, containing some 70% of the Earth's fresh water, plays a crucial role in the circulation of the atmosphere and oceans, and hence in determining the planetary climate. The frozen southern continent is also the last remaining wilderness – the largest area to remain free from human colonization.

Ever since Amundsen and Scott raced for the South Pole in 1911, various countries have pressed territorial claims over sections of Antarctica, spurred in recent years by its known and suspected mineral wealth: enough iron ore to supply the world at present levels for 200 years, large oil reserves and, probably, the biggest coal deposits on Earth.

However, the 1961 Antarctic Treaty set aside the area for peaceful uses only, guaranteeing freedom of scientific investigation, banning waste disposal and nuclear testing, and suspending the issue of territorial rights. By 1990, the original 12 signatories had grown to 25, with a further 15 nations granted observer status in subsequent deliberations. However, the Treaty itself was threatened by wrangles between different countries, government agencies and international pressure groups.

Finally, in July 1991, the belated agreement of the UK and the USA assured unanimity on a new accord to ban all mineral exploration for a further 50 years. The ban can only be rescinded if all the present signatories, plus a majority of any future adherents, agree. While the treaty has always lacked a formal mechanism for enforcement, it is firmly underwritten by public concern generated by the efforts of environmental pressure groups such as Greenpeace, which has been foremost in the campaign to have Antarctica declared a 'World Park'.

However, from the mid-1990s, the continent appeared to be under threat from global warming, which some scientists believe was the cause of the break-up of ice shelves along the Antarctic peninsula. Rising temperatures have also disturbed the breeding patterns of Adelie penguins.

Poisoned rivers, domestic sewage and oil spillage have combined in recent years to reduce the world's oceans to a sorry state of contamination, notably near the crowded coasts of industrialized nations. Shipping routes, too, are constantly affected by tanker discharges. Oil spills of all kinds, however, declined significantly during the 1980s, from a peak of 750,000 tonnes in 1979 to under 50,000 tonnes in 1990. The most notorious tanker spill of that period – when the *Exxon Valdez* (94,999 grt) ran aground in Prince William Sound, Alaska, in March 1989 – released only 267,000 barrels, a relatively small amount compared to the results of blow-outs and war damage. Over 2,500,000 barrels were spilled during the Gulf War of 1991. The worst tanker accident in history occurred in July 1979, when the *Atlantic Empress* and the Aegean Captain collided off Trinidad, polluting the Caribbean with 1,890,000 barrels of crude oil.

Population

In 8000 BC, following the development of agriculture, the world had an estimated population of 8 million and by AD 1000 it was about 300 million. The onset of the Industrial Revolution in the late 18th century led to a population explosion. The 1,000 million mark was passed by 1850, it doubled by the 1920s and doubled again to 4,000 million by 1975.

Most demographers agree that the world's population, which passed the 6 billion mark in October 1999, will reach 8.9 billion by 2050. It is not expected to level out until 2200, when it will peak at around 11 billion. After 2200, it is expected to level out or even decline a little. Rapid population growth is concentrated in the developing world; the populations of some developed countries, such as Belgium and Germany, are static or have started to decline.

The developing world includes what the World Bank describes as low-income economies, with an average per capita GNP of US $380, and middle-income economies, with a per capita GNP of $2,520. Most developing countries are in Africa, Asia and Latin America. The developed world, made up of high-income, industrialized economies with an average per capita GNP of $23,420, contains Australasia, most of Europe and North America, and Japan in Asia.

In poorer developing countries, a high proportion of the population is young. They face high levels of expenditure on education and health until population growth rates start to decline. In developed countries, where the population pyramids are becoming increasingly top-heavy, expenditure on pensions and healthcare for the elderly is becoming a social problem.

Crowded Nations

Population per square kilometre (1998), excluding nations of less than 1 million

1.	Monaco	32,894
2.	Macau	25,501
3.	Hong Kong	6,373
4.	Singapore	5,624
5.	Gibraltar	4,239
6.	Bermuda	1,199
7.	Malta	1,214
8.	Vatican City	1,090
9.	Maldives	909
10.	Bahrain	877
11.	Bangladesh	866
12.	Barbados	624
13.	Mauritius	559
14.	Nauru	529
15.	Armenia	487
16.	South Korea	466
17.	Puerto Rico	428
18.	Tuvalu	428
19.	San Marino	424
20.	Netherlands	384

Largest Nations

The world's most populous nations, in millions (2000 est.)

1.	China	1,299
2.	India	1,041
3.	USA	266
4.	Indonesia	218
5.	Brazil	179
6.	Pakistan	162
7.	Russia	155
8.	Bangladesh	150
9.	Japan	128
10.	Mexico	107
11.	Nigeria	105
12.	Vietnam	82
13.	Philippines	77
14.	Germany	76
15.	Iran	68
16.	Turkey	66
17.	Egypt	64
18.	Thailand	63
19.	Ethiopia	61
20.	France	58
21.	UK	58
22.	Italy	57
23.	Ukraine	52
24.	Burma (Myanmar)	51

Population Density

Inhabitants per square kilometre

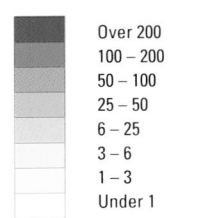

- Over 200
- 100 – 200
- 50 – 100
- 25 – 50
- 6 – 25
- 3 – 6
- 1 – 3
- Under 1

Urban population

- ■ Over 10,000,000
- ◉ 5,000,000 – 10,000,000
- • 1,000,000 – 5,000,000

Places marked are conurbations, not city limits; San Francisco itself, for example, has an official population of less than a million.

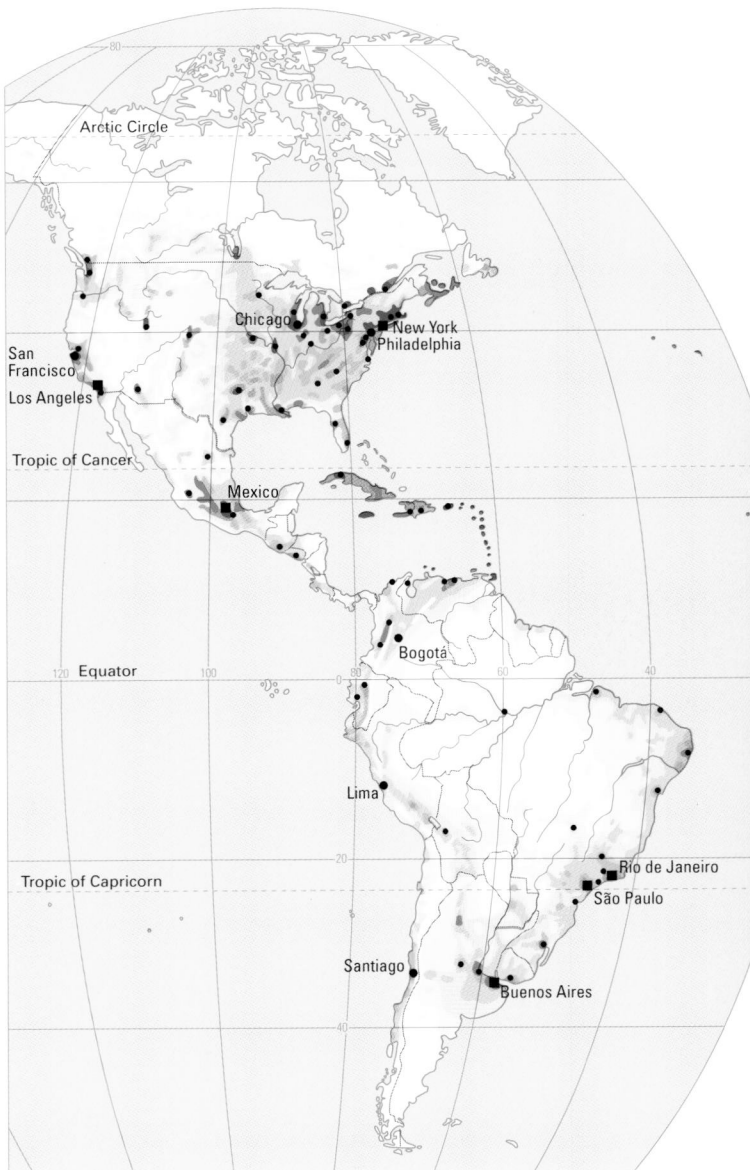

Population pyramids

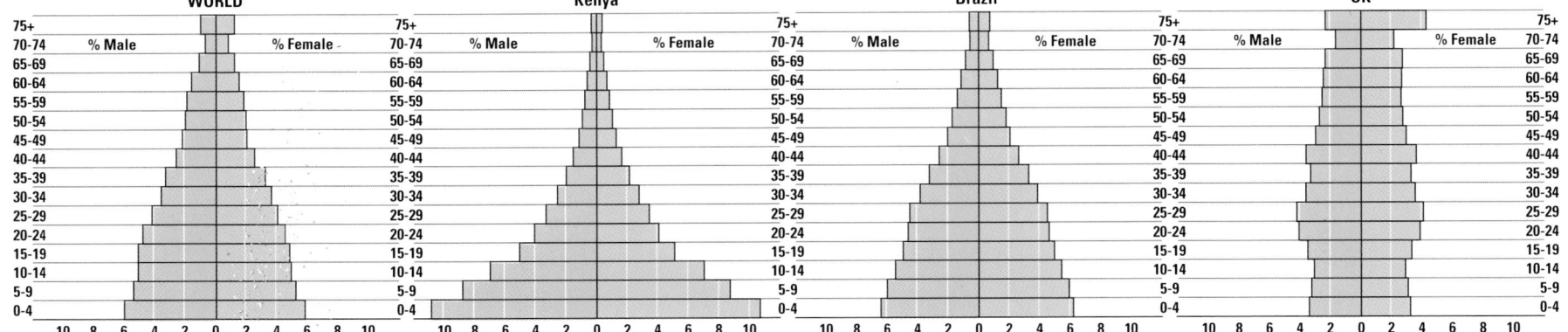

WORLD — Kenya — Brazil — UK

Rates of Growth

The world population doubled between 1950 and 1990. Small rates of population growth led to dramatic increases over two or three generations. The table below translates annual percentage growth into the number of years required to double a population.

% change	Doubling time
0.5	139.0
1.0	69.7
1.5	46.6
2.0	35.0
2.5	28.1
3.0	23.4
3.5	20.1
4.0	17.7

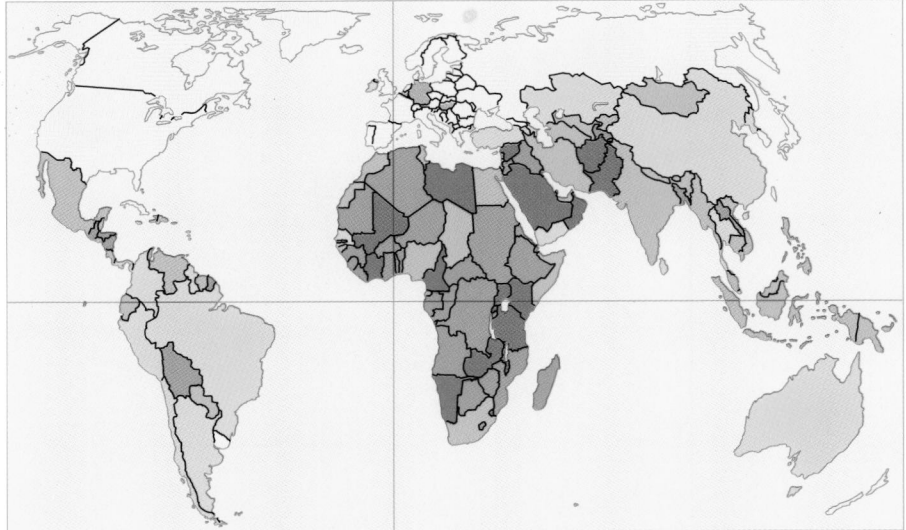

Population Change 1990–2000

The predicted population change for the years 1990–2000

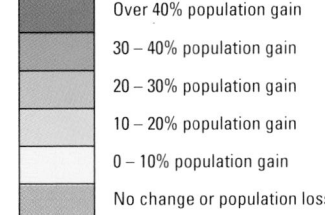

- Over 40% population gain
- 30 – 40% population gain
- 20 – 30% population gain
- 10 – 20% population gain
- 0 – 10% population gain
- No change or population loss

Top 5 countries		Bottom 5 countries	
Kuwait	+75.9%	Belgium	−0.1%
Namibia	+62.5%	Hungary	−0.2%
Afghanistan	+60.1%	Grenada	−2.4%
Mali	+55.5%	Germany	−3.2%
Tanzania	+54.6%	Tonga	−3.2%

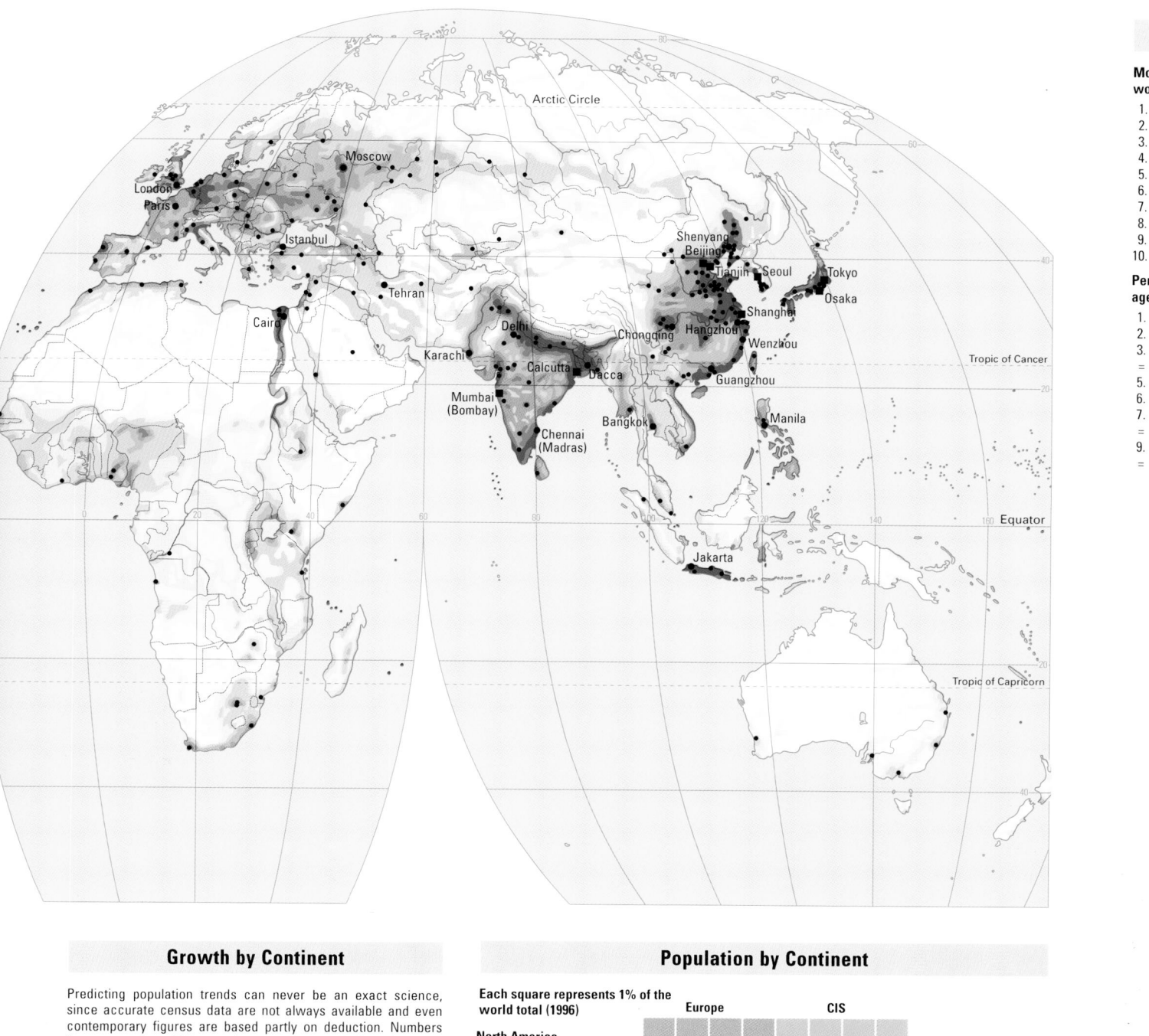

Arctic Circle

London
Paris
Moscow
Istanbul
Tehran
Cairo
Karachi
Delhi
Calcutta
Mumbai (Bombay)
Chennai (Madras)
Dacca
Bangkok
Shenyang
Beijing
Tianjin
Seoul
Tokyo
Osaka
Shanghai
Hangzhou
Wenzhou
Chongqing
Guangzhou
Manila
Jakarta

Tropic of Cancer
Equator
Tropic of Capricorn

Demographic Extremes

Most men per 100 women (1997)		Fewest men per 100 women (1997)	
1. Qatar	193.3	1. Latvia	84.3
2. U. Arab Em.	176.4	2. Ukraine	86.8
3. Bahrain	133.7	3. Russia	88.0
4. Saudi Arabia	125.1	4. Estonia	88.7
5. Oman	113.4	5. Belarus	88.8
6. Trin. & Tob.	111.3	6. Lithuania	89.7
7. Brunei	110.3	7. Georgia	91.4
8. Tunisia	109.8	8. Hungary	91.6
9. Libya	108.2	= Moldova	91.6
10. Hong Kong	107.6	10. Swaziland	92.4

Percentage of people aged under 15 (1996)		Percentage of people aged over 65 (1996)	
1. W. Bank/Gaza	51.7	1. Sweden	17.3
2. Uganda	48.6	2. Italy	16.1
3. Benin	48.4	3. Greece	15.9
= Niger	48.4	= Norway	15.9
5. Zambia	48.2	5. Belgium	15.8
6. Angola	47.7	= UK	15.8
7. Somalia	47.5	7. France	15.2
= Yemen	47.5	= Germany	15.2
9. Burkina F.	47.4	9. Denmark	15.1
= Mali	47.4	10. Spain	15.0

Growth by Continent

Predicting population trends can never be an exact science, since accurate census data are not always available and even contemporary figures are based partly on deduction. Numbers for years after 2000 are long-term extrapolations involving projections of current growth rates, and become increasingly speculative as they advance into the future.

Population by continent in millions, 1990–2025, with estimated annual growth rates.

	1990	2000	2025	% growth, 1990–2000	% growth, 2000–2025
Africa	641	860	1,589	2.97	2.50
South America	437	523	709	1.82	1.23
Asia	3,080	3,650	4,923	1.71	1.20
Australasia	24	28	34	1.44	0.64
North America	277	300	339	0.81	0.50
Europe	787	825	882	0.47	0.27
World	**5,246**	**6,185**	**8,476**	**1.66**	**1.27**

The graph, below, shows the extraordinary explosion of the world's population which has occurred in the last 250 years, with projections showing the predicted rate of growth in the 21st century. According to 1996 UN figures, the annual rate of world population growth between 1990 and 1995 fell to 1.48%, as compared with 1.57% predicted in a UN report in 1994. As a result of such data, future projections have to be constantly revised. In 1996, the most likely scenario is that population growth will continue until around 2080 and then start to decline. But very different predictions can be made. For example, high birth rates and fast declining death rates could give the world a population of 23,000 million by 2100. Another scenario, based on such assumptions as rampant disease and falling birth rates, would indicate a fall in world population of 4 million. Demographers give each of these predictions a probability of less than 1%.

Population by Continent

Each square represents 1% of the world total (1996)

North America
Europe
CIS
Africa
Asia
South America
Australasia

10,000 million
9,000
8,000
7,000
South Asia
6,000
5,000
East Asia
4,000
Australasia
Africa
3,000
South America
2,000
North America
1,000
USSR
CIS
Europe

1750 1775 1800 1825 1850 1875 1900 1925 1950 1975 2000 2025 2050

Cities

Following the development of agriculture more than 10,000 years ago, people began to live in farming villages. Around 5,500 years ago, the world's first cities appeared in the lower Tigris and Euphrates valleys in Mesopotamia. Cities were founded in Ancient Egypt around 5,000 years ago and in China around 3,600 years ago. By contrast with the villages, most people in the early cities were not engaged in farming. Instead, they worked in craft industries, in government services, in religion and trade. Cities became centres of early civilizations and, through trade, their influence spread far and wide. However, they were dependent on the surrounding farming communities for their food and other materials.

In 1750, prior to the start of the Industrial Revolution, barely 3% of the world's population lived in urban areas. By 1850, London and Paris had more than a million people, and, by 1900, 14% of the world's population lived in cities. By 1950, the world had 83 cities with over a million people, and by 1996, there were 280. By 2015, experts predict that there will be more than 500. New York City was the only city with a population of over 10 million in 1950; by 2015 experts predict 27 such cities worldwide, the majority located in the developing world.

By the end of the 20th century, more than half of the world's population was living in urban areas. Despite the rapid growth of cities in developing countries, urbanization is highest in industrialized countries. For example, 78% of the people in the United States live in urban areas, with the European Union not far behind with 77%. But in countries with low-income economies, which contained nearly 60% of the world's total population in 1996, only 28% lived in urban areas.

The rapid rate of urbanization has created problems, especially in cities which have not been able to provide enough jobs and services for the expanding population. Most new city dwellers are people from rural areas and since many of them are young there is a consequent acceleration in the rate of city population growth. In developed countries, with highly mechanized agriculture, it is population pressure that drives many people into urban areas. In developing countries, the grinding poverty of rural life and the lack of services leads to migration to urban areas.

A typical city in a developing country contains millions of people living in shanty towns (or 'informal settlements' in politically correct parlance), while thousands live on the streets. Yet many shanty towns are healthier than the industrial cities of 19th-century Europe and North America. Indeed, surveys have shown that the migrants to the cities in developing countries are less likely to face poverty than they are in rural areas, while benefiting from greater access to healthcare services and education.

Modern cities face many problems, including pollution, crime and unemployment. Yet, given competent central and local government, they are capable of generating the wealth they need to solve them, as well as making a major contribution to the economy.

The Urbanization of the Earth

City-building, 1850–2000; each white spot represents a city of at least 1 million inhabitants.

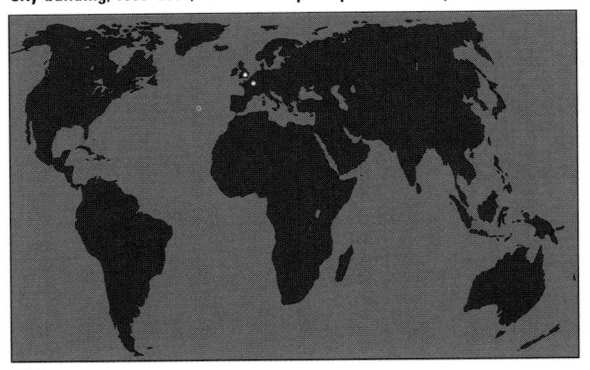

1850

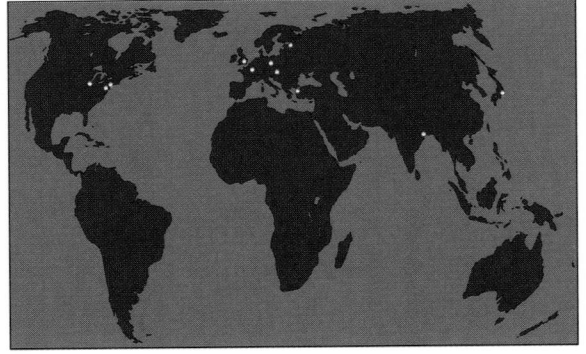

1900

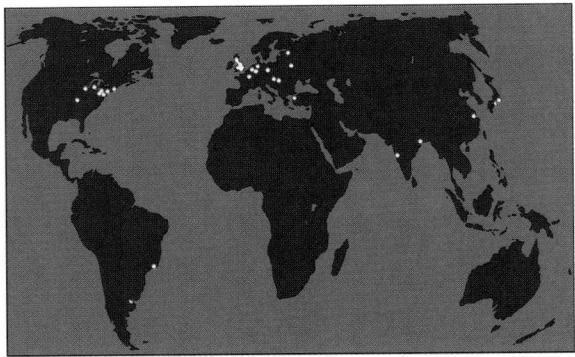

1925

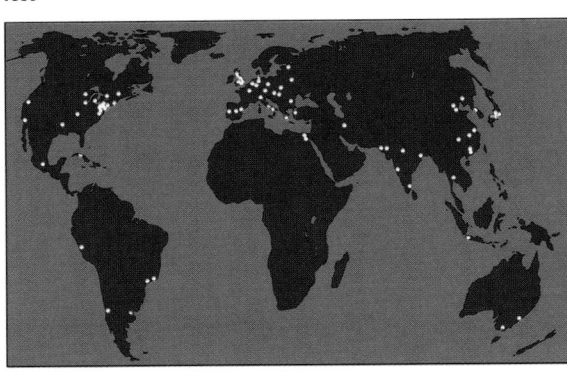

1950

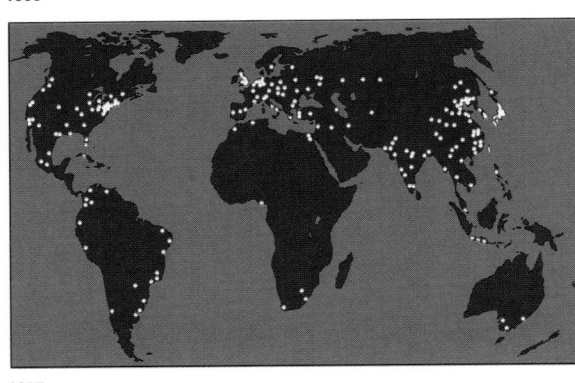

1975

2000

Urban Population

Percentage of total population living in towns and cities (1997)

Most urbanized

Singapore	100%
Belgium	97%
Israel	91%
Uruguay	91%
Netherlands	89%

[UK 89%]

Least urbanized

Rwanda	6%
Bhutan	8%
Burundi	8%
Nepal	11%
Swaziland	12%

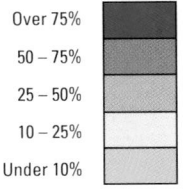

Over 75%
50 – 75%
25 – 50%
10 – 25%
Under 10%

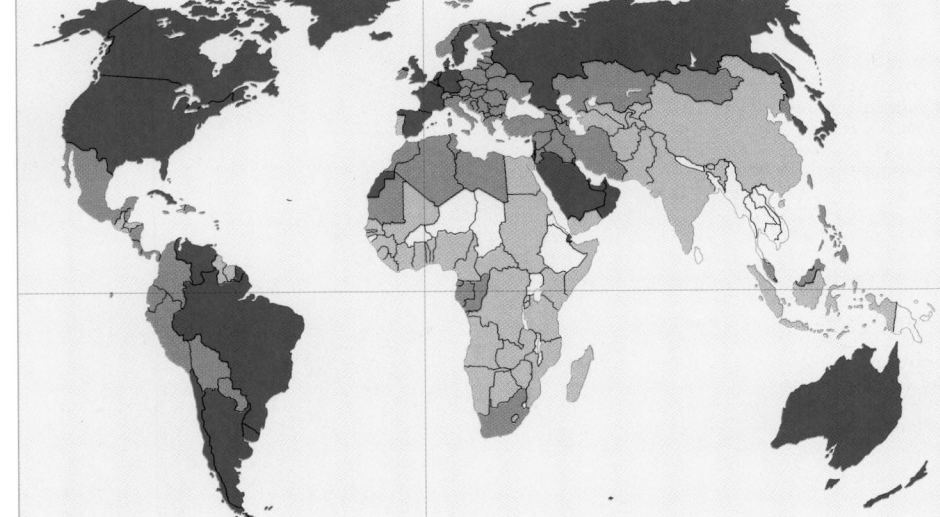

Expanding Cities

The growth of some of the world's largest cities in millions, 1950–2015.
Comparisons of city populations over time are problematic due to changes in the definition of the city limits. These figures attempt to take such changes into consideration. The figure for London is the metropolitan region.

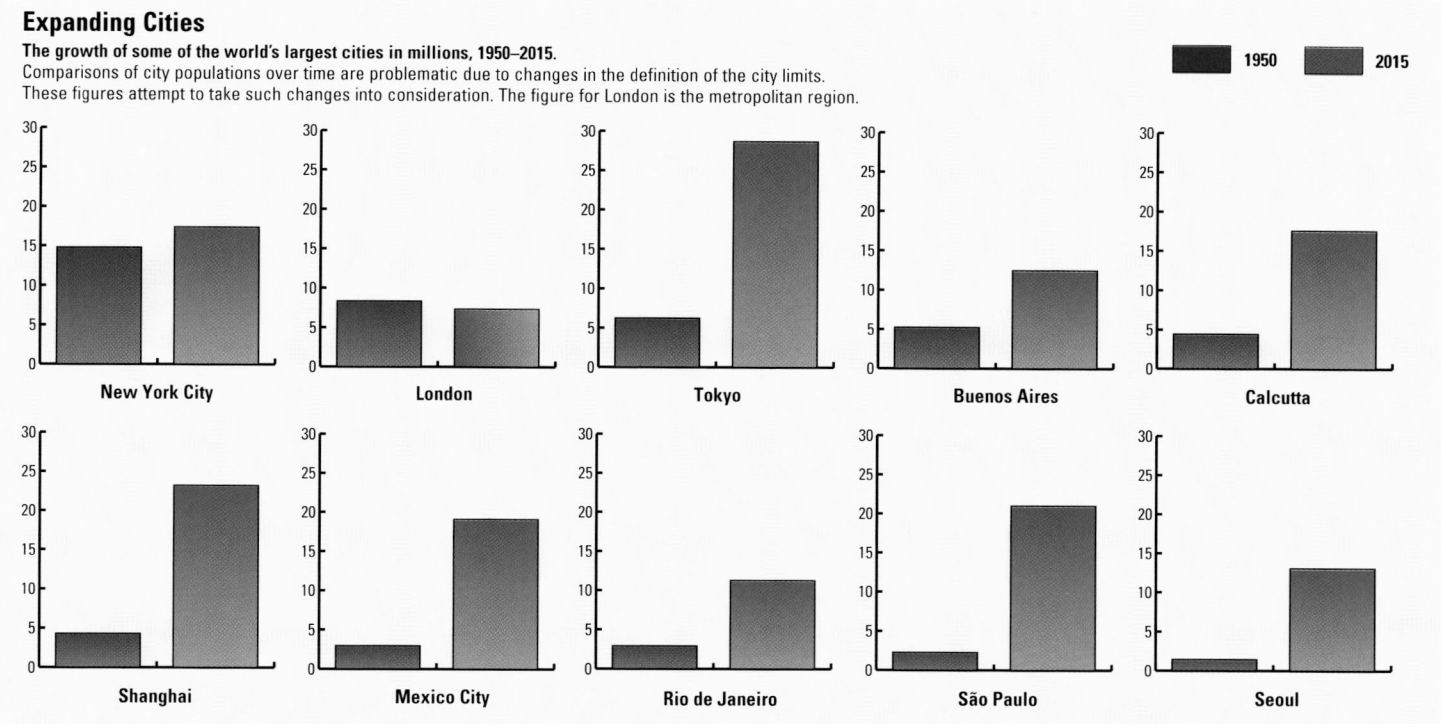

■ 1950 ■ 2015

New York City · London · Tokyo · Buenos Aires · Calcutta
Shanghai · Mexico City · Rio de Janeiro · São Paulo · Seoul

The graphs show the projected growth of megacities between 1950 and 2015. New York City, the world's largest city in 1950, reached a peak in 1970, but it has experienced periods of negative growth. London's population also declined between 1970 and 1985, before resuming a modest rate of increase. In both cases, the divergence from world trends is explained in part by counting methods. Each lies at the centre of a great agglomeration, and definitions of the 'city limits' may vary over time. Also, in developing countries, many areas around the megacities which are counted as urban, are rural in character. The rates of city population growth in developing countries have also often been over-estimated. For example, it was once predicted that Calcutta would have a population of 40 million by the late 1990s. The reason why many estimates have proven incorrect is partly explained by a new trend, namely that rapid urban growth is now greatest, in some regions, in the smaller cities. For example, the main expansion in West Bengal is no longer in Calcutta, but in a rash of small cities across the state.

Cities in Danger

As the decade of the 1980s advanced, most industrial countries, alarmed by acid rain and urban smog, took significant steps to limit air pollution. Well into the 1990s, however, these controls proved expensive to install and difficult to enforce, and clean air remains a luxury most developed as well as developing cities must live without.

Those taking part in the United Nations' Global Environment Monitoring System (see right) frequently show dangerous levels of pollutants ranging from soot to sulphur dioxide and photo-chemical smog; air in the majority of cities without such sampling equipment is likely to be at least as bad. Traffic, a major source of air pollution world-wide, loses Thailand's workforce 44 working days each year.

Urban Air Pollution

The world's most polluted cities: number of days each year when sulphur dioxide levels exceeded the WHO threshold of 150 micrograms per cubic metre (averaged over 4 to 15 years, 1970s – 1980s)

Sulphur dioxide is the main pollutant associated with industrial cities. According to the World Health Organization, more than seven days in a year above 150 µg per cubic metre bring a serious risk of respiratory disease: at least 600 million people live in urban areas where SO₂ concentrations regularly reach damaging levels.

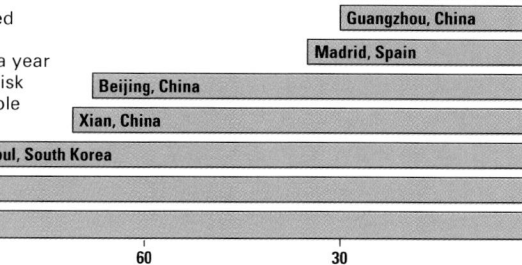

Calcutta, India
Milan, Italy
Zagreb, Croatia
Guangzhou, China
Madrid, Spain
Beijing, China
Xian, China
Seoul, South Korea
Tehran, Iran
Shenyang, China

120 · 90 · 60 · 30

Urban Housing Needs

Proportion of the population living in squatter settlements and the number of homeless per thousand, for selected cities (1993)

Urbanization in most developing countries has been proceeding so rapidly that local governments have been unable to provide the necessary services and housing. In some cities, many people find their homes in squatter settlements, frequently without power, water and sanitation. Yet these communities are often a dynamic part of the city's economy, while their inhabitants sometimes take all kinds of initiatives, including the setting up of their own local government and self-help associations. Some of the world's richest cities also have a homeless underclass, although calculating the numbers of people involved is problematic. Yet it is the case that homelessness and unemployment are currently affecting an increasing number of people in the developed world.

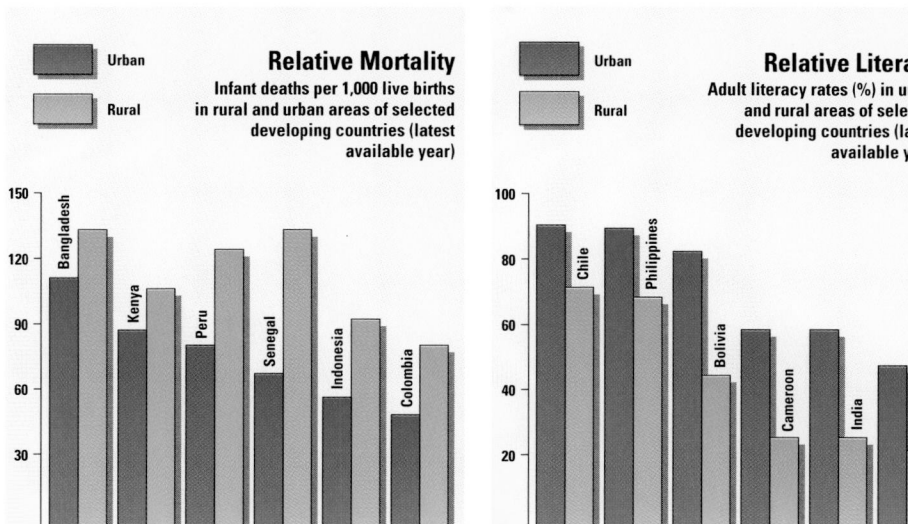

(11.5)

Dar es Salaam, Tanzania
Istanbul, Turkey
Quito, Ecuador
Kingston, Jamaica
Delhi, India
Dhaka, Bangladesh
Bogotá, Colombia
Cairo, Egypt
Helsinki, Finland
Paris, France
Washington DC, USA
Madrid, Spain
Tokyo, Japan

Homelessness per 1,000
Percentage of squatters

8 · 6 · 4 · 2 · 0 · 20 · 40 · 60

Largest Cities

Early in the 21st century, for the first time in history, the majority of the world's population will live in cities. Below is a list of all the cities with more than 10 million inhabitants, based on estimates for the year 2015.*

1.	Tokyo–Yokohama	28.7
2.	Bombay	27.4
3.	Lagos	24.1
4.	Shanghai	23.2
5.	Jakarta	21.5
6.	São Paulo	21.0
7.	Karachi	20.6
8.	Beijing	19.6
9.	Dhaka	19.2
10.	Mexico City	19.1
11.	Calcutta	17.6
12.	Delhi	17.5
13.	New York City	17.4
14.	Tianjin	17.1
15.	Manila	14.9
16.	Cairo	14.7
17.	Los Angeles	14.5
18.	Seoul	13.1
19.	Buenos Aires	12.5
20.	Istanbul	12.1
21.	Rio de Janeiro	11.3
22.	Lahore	10.9
23.	Hyderabad	10.6
24.	Bangkok	10.4
25.	Osaka	10.2
26.	Lima	10.1
27.	Tehran	10.0

City populations are based on urban agglomerations rather than legal city limits. In some cases where two adjacent cities have merged into one concentration, such as Tokyo–Yokohama, they have been regarded as a single unit.

* For a list of current city estimates, see page XI.

Urban Advantages

Despite overcrowding and poor housing, living standards in the developing world's cities are almost invariably better than in the surrounding countryside. Resources – financial, material and administrative – are concentrated in the towns, which are usually also the centres of political activity and pressure. Governments – frequently unstable, and rarely established on a solid democratic base – are usually more responsive to urban discontent than rural misery.

In many countries, especially in Africa, food prices are kept artificially low, appeasing underemployed urban masses at the expense of agricultural development. The imbalance encourages further cityward migration, helping to account for the astonishing rate of post-1950 urbanization and putting great strain on the ability of many nations to provide even modest improvements for their people.

■ Urban ■ Rural

Relative Mortality
Infant deaths per 1,000 live births in rural and urban areas of selected developing countries (latest available year)

150 · 120 · 90 · 60 · 30

Bangladesh · Kenya · Peru · Senegal · Indonesia · Colombia

■ Urban ■ Rural

Relative Literacy
Adult literacy rates (%) in urban and rural areas of selected developing countries (latest available year)

100 · 80 · 60 · 40 · 20

Chile · Philippines · Bolivia · Cameroon · India · Tunisia

The Human Family

For more information:
24 Population density
30 The world's refugees
   War since 1945
31 United Nations
   International
   organizations

Racial, language and religious differences have led to appalling acts of inhumanity throughout history. Yet strictly speaking, all human beings belong to one species, *Homo sapiens*, which has no subspecies. The differences between the three racial types which most people identify – namely Caucasoid, Mongoloid and Negroid – reflect not so much evolutionary differences as long periods of separation.

Migration has recently mingled the various groups to an unprecedented extent, and most nations now have some degree of racial mixing. For example, the United States has often been called a melting pot, because of the large numbers of people from various geographical locations which make up the population. The country has no official language but, until recently, English was spoken by the vast majority of the people. But in recent years, some of the immigrants from Mexico, Cuba and other parts of Latin America have not learned English and speak only Spanish. This development disturbs those Americans who believe that the use of English binds the nation together, and several states have passed laws stating that English is their only official language.

Language is fundamental to human culture and any particular language is almost the definition of that particular culture. Because definitions of languages vary, estimates of the total number range from 3,000 to 6,000, although most are spoken by only a few people. The world's languages are grouped into families, the largest of which are the Indo-European and Sino-Tibetan. Chinese, a Sino-Tibetan language, is spoken by more people as a first language than any other. English, an Indo-European tongue, ranks second, but it is the leading international language, because so many people speak it as their second tongue.

Like language, religion encourages cohesion in single human groups and it satisfies a deep human need by assigning people a place in a divinely ordered world. Religion is a way in which a culture can express its individuality. For example, the rise of Islamic fundamentalism in the late 20th century was partly an expression of resentment that secular Western values are being imposed on Muslims.

World Migration

The greatest voluntary migration was the colonization of North America by 30–35 million European settlers during the 19th century. The greatest forced migration involved 9–11 million Africans taken as slaves to America between 1550 and 1860. The migrations shown on the map below are mostly international, as population movements within borders are not usually recorded. Many of the statistics are necessarily estimates as so many refugees and migrant workers enter countries illegally and unrecorded. Emigrants may have a variety of motives for leaving, thus making it difficult to distinguish between voluntary and involuntary migrations.

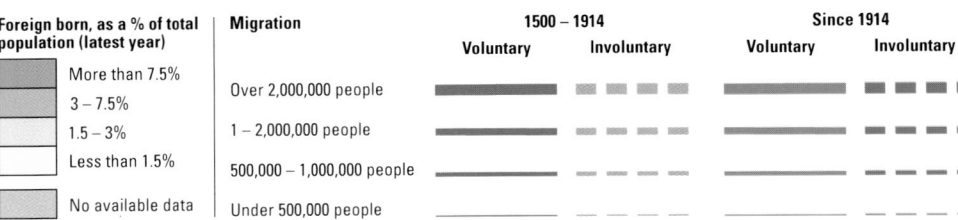

Foreign born, as a % of total population (latest year)
- More than 7.5%
- 3 – 7.5%
- 1.5 – 3%
- Less than 1.5%
- No available data

Migration
- Over 2,000,000 people
- 1 – 2,000,000 people
- 500,000 – 1,000,000 people
- Under 500,000 people

	1500 – 1914		Since 1914	
	Voluntary	Involuntary	Voluntary	Involuntary

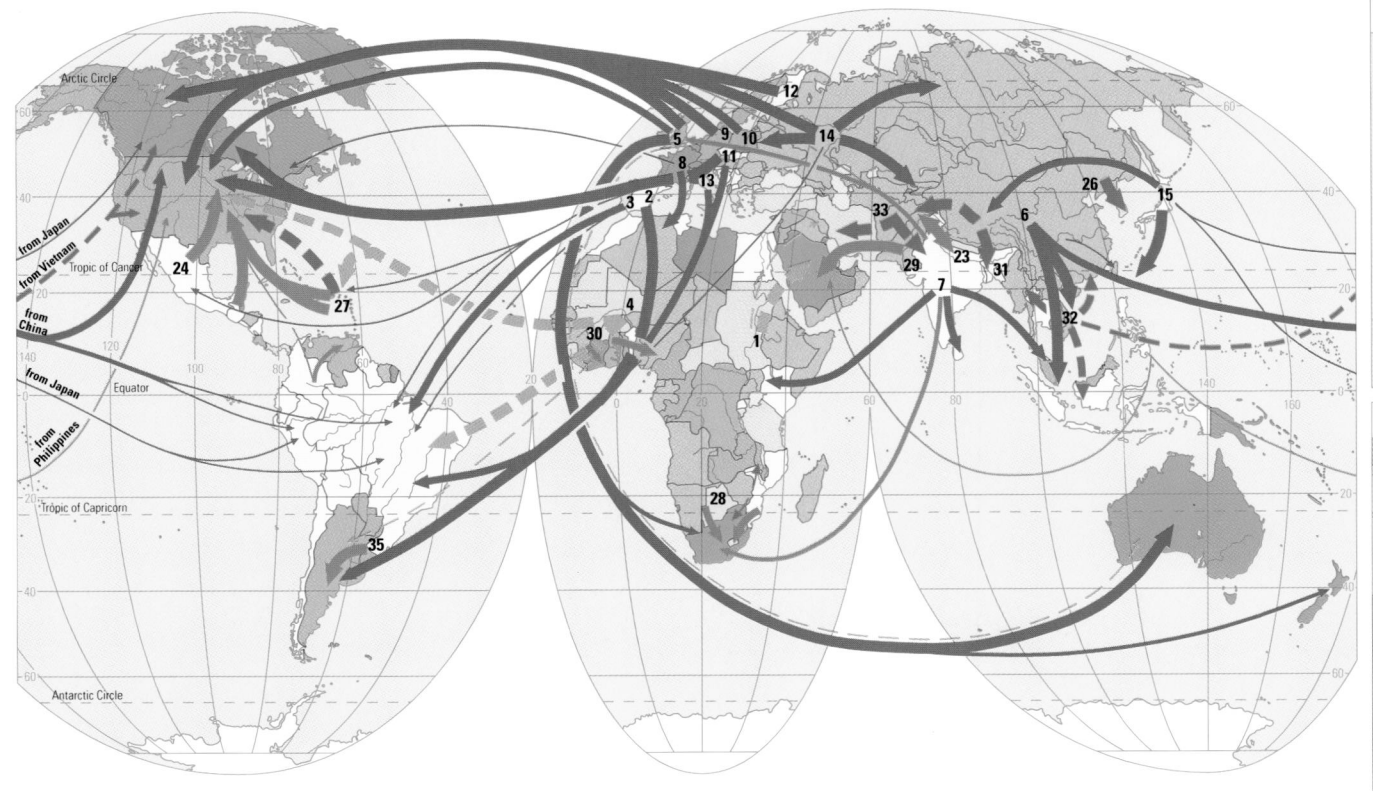

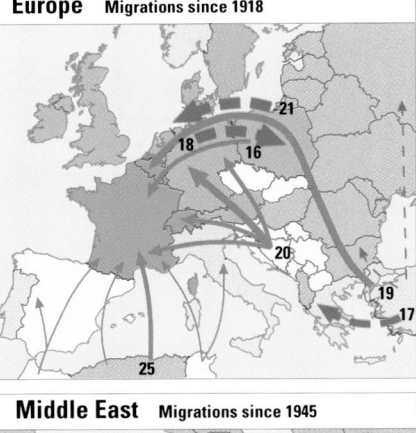

Europe Migrations since 1918

Middle East Migrations since 1945

Building the USA

US Immigration 1820–1990
'Give me your tired, your poor / Your huddled masses yearning to breathe free....'
So starts Emma Lazarus's poem 'The New Colossus', inscribed on the Statue of Liberty. For decades the USA was the magnet that attracted millions of immigrants, notably from Central and Eastern Europe, the flow peaking in the early years of the 20th century. By the mid-1990s the proportion of immigrants had increased again to pre-World War II rates. In 1993/4, net immigration accounted for 30% of US population growth. Of the 904,000 immigrants, 40% were from Asia and 31% from Central America and the Caribbean.

Germany 7,047,000
Italy 5,333,000
UK 5,064,000
Austria/Hungary 4,322,000
Canada 4,290,000
Ireland 4,077,000
Russia 3,433,000
Mexico 2,802,000
West Indies 2,520,000
Sweden 1,281,000
Others 14,259,000

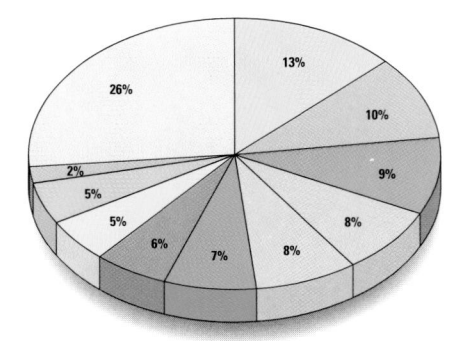

Major world migrations since 1500 (over 1,000,000 people)
1.	North and East African slaves to Arabia (4.3m)	1500–1900
2.	Spanish to South and Central America (2.3m)	1530–1914
3.	Portuguese to Brazil (1.4m)	1530–1914
4.	West African slaves... to South America (4.6m)	1550–1860
	to Caribbean (4m)	1580–1860
	to North/Central America (1m)	1650–1820
5.	British and Irish... to North America (13.5m)	1620–1914
	to Australasia and South Africa (3m)	1790–1914
6.	Chinese... to South-east Asia (22m)	1820–1914
	to North America (1m)	1880–1914
7.	Indian migrant workers (3m)	1850–1914
8.	French to North Africa (1.5m)	1850–1914
9.	Germans to North America (5m)	1850–1914
10.	Poles to North America (3.6m)	1850–1914
11.	Austro-Hungarians.... to North America (3.2m)	1850–1914
	to Western Europe (3.4m)	1850–1914
	to South America (1.8m)	1850–1914
12.	Scandinavians to North America (2.7m)	1850–1914
13.	Italians... to North America (7.5m)	1860–1914
	to South America (3.7m)	1860–1914
14.	Russians... to North America (2.2m)	1880–1914
	to Western Europe (2.2m)	1880–1914
	to Siberia (6m)	1880–1914
	to Central Asia (4m)	1880–1914

15.	Japanese to Eastern Asia, South-east Asia and America (8m)	1900–1914
16.	Poles to Western Europe (1m)	1920–1940
17.	Greeks and Armenians from Turkey (1.6m)	1922–1923
18.	European Jews to extermination camps (5m)	1940–1944
19.	Turks to Western Europe (1.9m)	1940–
20.	Yugoslavs to Western Europe (2m)	1940–
21.	Germans to Western Europe (9.8m)	1945–1947
22.	Palestinian refugees (2m)	1947–
23.	Indian and Pakistani refugees (15m)	1947
24.	Mexicans to North America (9m)	1950–
25.	North Africans to Western Europe (1.1m)	1950–
26.	Korean refugees (5m)	1950–1954
27.	Latin Americans and West Indians to North America (4.7m)	1960–
28.	Migrant workers to South Africa (1.5m)	1960–
29.	Indians and Pakistanis to The Gulf (2.4m)	1970–
30.	Migrant workers to Nigeria and Ivory Coast (3m)	1970–
31.	Bangladeshi and Pakistani refugees (2m)	1972
32.	Vietnamese and Cambodian refugees (1.5m)	1975–
33.	Afghan refugees (6.1m)	1979–
34.	Egyptians to The Gulf and Libya (2.9m)	1980–
35.	Migrant workers to Argentina (2m)	1980–
36.	Mozambique refugees (1.7m)	1985–
37.	Yugoslav/Balkan refugees (1.7m)	1992–
38.	Rwanda/Burundi refugees (2.6m)	1994–

Predominant Languages

INDO-EUROPEAN FAMILY			
1	Balto-Slavic group (incl. Russian, Ukrainian)		
2	Germanic group (incl. English, German)		
3	Celtic group		
4	Greek		
5	Albanian		
6	Iranian group		
7	Armenian		
8	Romance group (incl. Spanish, Portuguese, French, Italian)		
9	Indo-Aryan group (incl. Hindi, Bengali, Urdu, Punjabi, Marathi)		
10	**CAUCASIAN FAMILY**		

AFRO-ASIATIC FAMILY	
11	Semitic group (incl. Arabic)
12	Kushitic group
13	Berber group
14	**KHOISAN FAMILY**
15	**NIGER-CONGO FAMILY**
16	**NILO-SAHARAN FAMILY**
17	**URALIC FAMILY**

ALTAIC FAMILY	
18	Turkic group
19	Mongolian group
20	Tungus-Manchu group
21	Japanese and Korean
SINO-TIBETAN FAMILY	
22	Sinitic (Chinese) languages
23	Tibetan-Burmic languages
24	**TAI FAMILY**

AUSTRO-ASIATIC FAMILY	
25	Mon-Khmer group
26	Munda group
27	Vietnamese
28	**DRAVIDIAN FAMILY** (incl. Telugu, Tamil)
29	**AUSTRONESIAN FAMILY** (incl. Malay-Indonesian)
30	**OTHER LANGUAGES**

Official Languages

Language	Total population	World %
English	1,400m	27.0%
Chinese	1,070m	19.1%
Hindi	700m	13.5%
Spanish	280m	5.4%
Russian	270m	5.2%
French	220m	4.2%
Arabic	170m	3.3%
Portuguese	160m	3.0%
Malay	160m	3.0%
Bengali	150m	2.9%
Japanese	120m	2.3%

Languages form a kind of tree of development, splitting from a few ancient proto-tongues into branches that have grown apart and further divided with the passage of time. English and Hindi, for example, both belong to the great Indo-European family, although the relationship is only apparent after much analysis and comparison with non-Indo-European languages such as Chinese or Arabic; Hindi is part of the Indo-Aryan subgroup, whereas English is a member of Indo-European's Germanic branch; French, another Indo-European tongue, traces its descent through the Latin, or Romance, branch. A few languages – Basque is one example – have no apparent links with any other, living or dead. Most modern languages, of course, have acquired enormous quantities of vocabulary from each other.

Distribution of Living Languages

The figures refer to the number of languages currently in use in the regions shown.

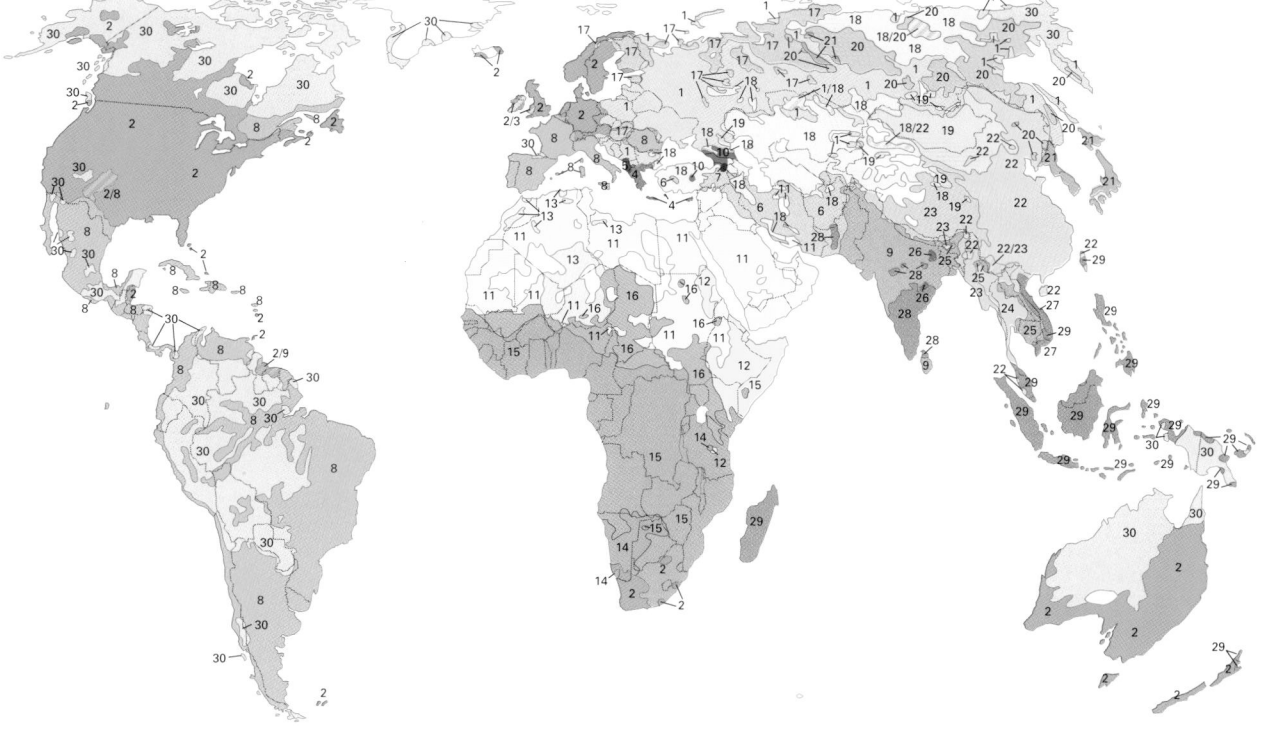

Predominant Religions

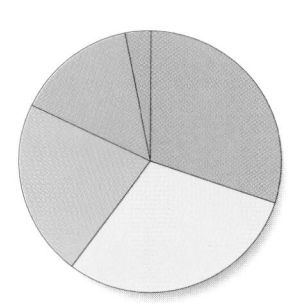

▲	Roman Catholicism
	Orthodox and other Eastern Churches
•	Protestantism
	Sunni Islam
	Shia Islam
	Buddhism
	Hinduism
	Confucianism
✶	Judaism
	Shintoism
	Tribal Religions

Religions are not as easily mapped as the physical contours of the land. Divisions are often blurred and frequently overlapping: most nations include people of many different faiths – or no faith at all. Some religions, like Islam and Christianity, have proselytes worldwide; others, like Hinduism and Confucianism, are restricted to a particular area, though modern migrations have taken some Indians and Chinese very far from their cultural origins. It is also difficult to show the degree to which religion controls daily life: Christian Western Europe, for example, is now far less dominated by its religion than are the Islamic nations of the Middle East. Similarly, figures for the major faiths' adherents make no distinction between nominal believers enrolled at birth and those for whom religion is a vital part of existence.

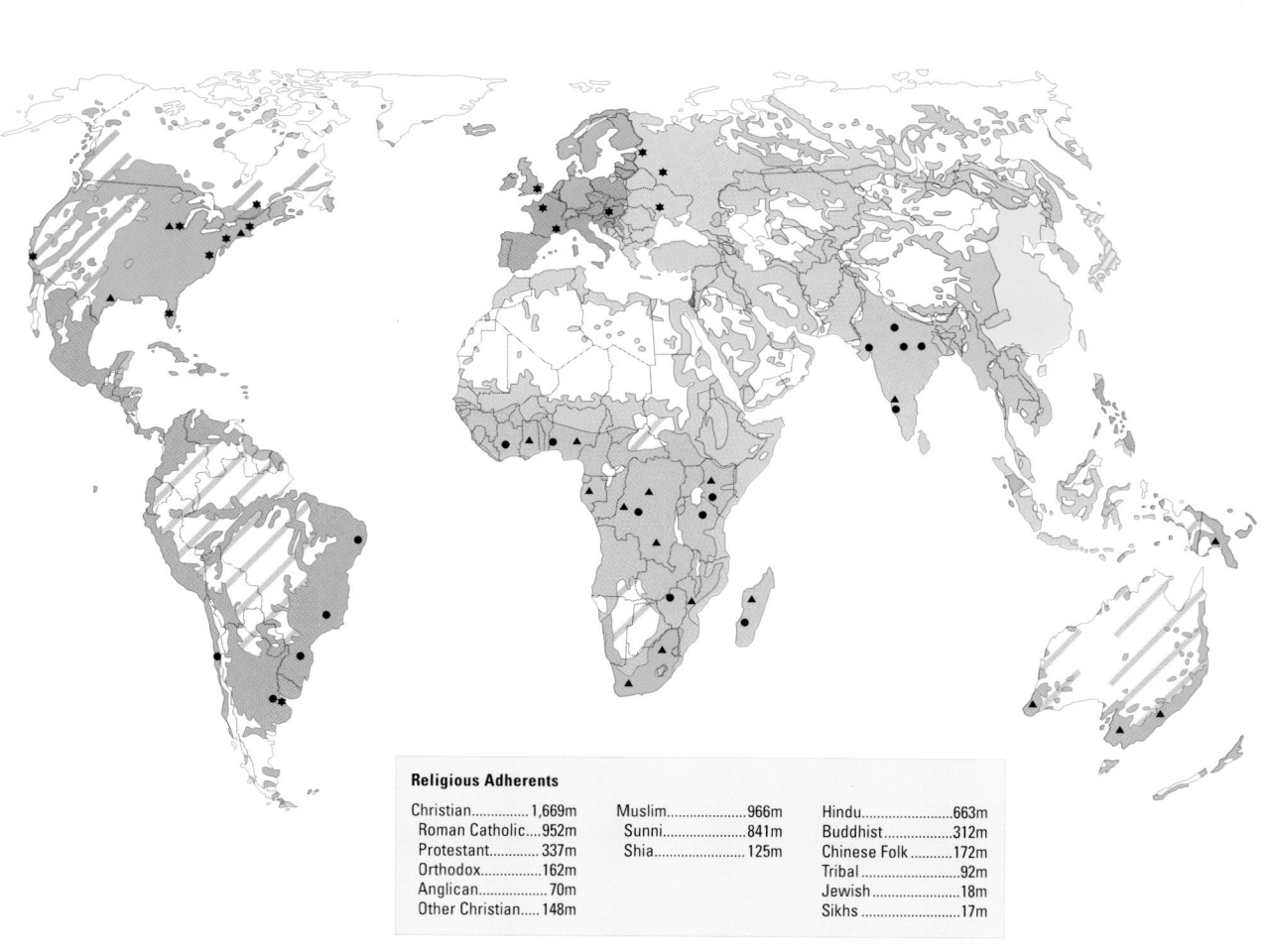

Religious Adherents

Christian..............1,669m	Muslim..............966m	Hindu..............663m
Roman Catholic....952m	Sunni..............841m	Buddhist..............312m
Protestant............337m	Shia..............125m	Chinese Folk..........172m
Orthodox..............162m		Tribal..............92m
Anglican............70m		Jewish..............18m
Other Christian.....148m		Sikhs..............17m

CARTOGRAPHY BY PHILIP'S. COPYRIGHT GEORGE PHILIP LTD

Conflict and Co-operation

For more information:
28 Migration
29 Religion

The 20th century witnessed two world wars, followed by a Cold War which several times threatened to erupt into a third world war, fought with nuclear weapons. The Cold War was marked by a great number of conflicts. Some were colonial wars, as the empires of the first half of the century fell apart, some were border wars, and some were civil wars. All wars have caused great suffering among civilians, many of whom were forced to become refugees.

In the late 1980s, many people hoped that the end of the Cold War, following the collapse of Communist regimes in the former Soviet Union and Eastern Europe, would herald a new era of international stability. Instead, old ethnic and religious antagonisms surfaced in many areas, leading to civil war in such places as Chechenia, in Russia, and the former Yugoslavia. Nationalist rivalries, suppressed under Communist rule, replaced ideological factors as the major cause of conflict.

War is a very human activity, with no real equivalent in other species. Yet humans also function well when they co-operate. Evolution has made this so. Hunter-gatherers in co-operative bands were more effective than animals that prowled. Agriculture, urbanization and industrialization all depend on the ability of humans to co-operate.

The creation of the United Nations in 1945 held out hope that the world's nations, tired of war, would have the means to control humanity's aggressive instincts. Though the UN lacks the power to halt conflicts, it has often helped to achieve negotiation. Economic pressures have led to another kind of co-operation, the creation of common markets and economic unions, such as ASEAN in South-east Asia, the European Union and NAFTA in North America.

The World's Refugees

Refugees by host nation (bar-chart, left) and by nation of origin (pie-chart, left) (1995). The source is the United Nations High Commission for Refugees (UNHCR). The 3.2 million Palestinian refugees living in Jordan, Syria, Lebanon, Gaza and the West Bank fall under the mandate of United Nations Relief and Works Agency (UNRWA) and are not included on the bar-chart.

The pie-chart shows the origins of the world's refugees, while the bar-chart below shows their destinations. According to the United Nations High Commission for Refugees (UNHCR) in 1995 there were 14.5 million refugees. However, the UNHCR definition of a refugee, 'a person who has left or remains outside their own country because they have a well-founded fear of persecution, or because their safety is threatened by events seriously disturbing public order', does not include people who are in a refugee-like situation but who have not been formally recognized. In 1995, there were a further 3.5 million of these people worldwide and a further 4.5 million people who were internally displaced.

All but a few who cross international boundaries seek asylum in neighbouring countries, which are often the least equipped to deal with them. Lacking any rights or power, they frequently become an unwelcome burden to their hosts. Usually, the best any refugee can hope for is rudimentary food and shelter in temporary camps. Many Palestinians have been forced to live in camps since 1948.

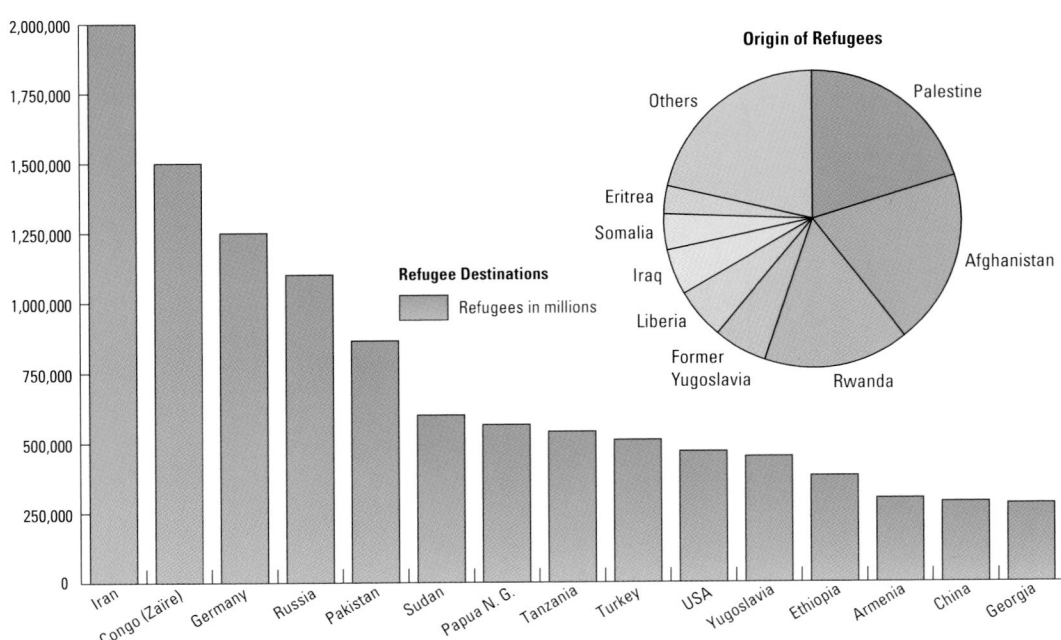

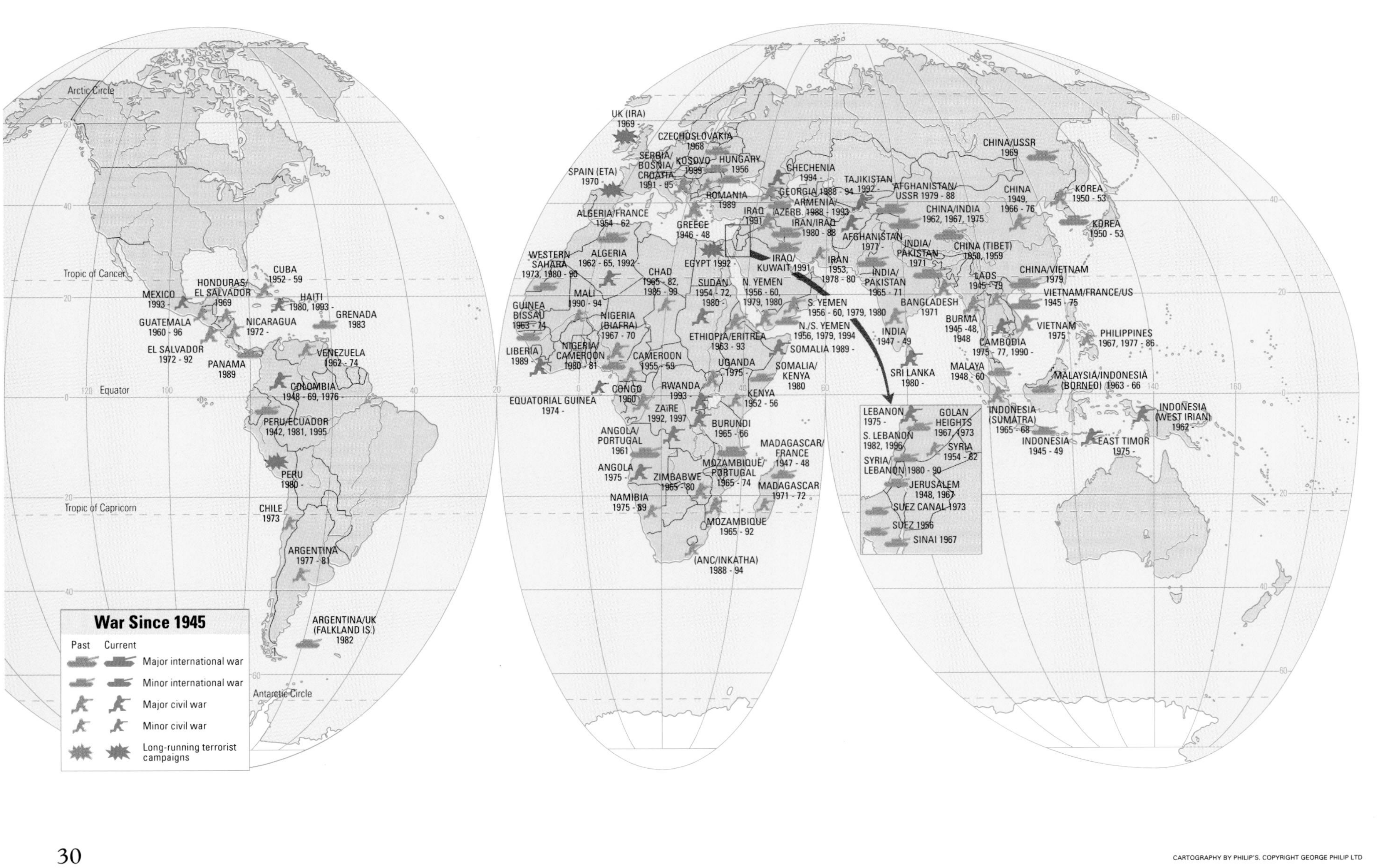

Origin of Refugees (pie-chart): Others, Palestine, Eritrea, Somalia, Iraq, Liberia, Former Yugoslavia, Rwanda, Afghanistan

Refugee Destinations — Refugees in millions

Bar-chart host nations: Iran, Congo (Zaire), Germany, Russia, Pakistan, Sudan, Papua N.G., Tanzania, Turkey, USA, Yugoslavia, Ethiopia, Armenia, China, Georgia

War Since 1945

Past	Current	
		Major international war
		Minor international war
		Major civil war
		Minor civil war
		Long-running terrorist campaigns

United Nations

The United Nations Organization was born as World War II drew to its conclusion. Six years of strife had strengthened the world's desire for peace, but an effective international organization was needed to help achieve it. That body would replace the League of Nations which, since its inception in 1920, had failed to curb the aggression of at least some of its member nations. At the United Nations Conference on International Organization held in San Francisco, the United Nations Charter was drawn up. Ratified by the Security Council and signed by the 51 original members, it came into effect on 24 October 1945.

The Charter set out the aims of the organization: to maintain peace and security, and develop friendly relations between nations; to achieve international co-operation in solving economic, social, cultural and humanitarian problems; to promote respect for human rights and fundamental freedoms; and to harmonize the activities of nations in order to achieve these common goals.

The United Nations has five principal organs:

The General Assembly
The forum at which member nations discuss moral and political issues affecting world development, peace and security meets annually in September, under a newly-elected President whose tenure lasts one year. Any member can bring business to the agenda, and each member nation has one vote.

The Security Council
A legislative and executive body, the Security Council is the primary instrument for establishing and maintaining international peace by attempting to settle disputes between nations. It has the power to dispatch UN forces, and member nations undertake to provide armed forces, assistance and facilities. The Security Council has ten temporary members elected by the General Assembly for two-year terms, and five permanent members – China, France, Russia, UK and USA.

The Economic and Social Council
By far the largest United Nations executive, the Council operates as a conduit between the General Assembly and the many United Nations agencies it instructs to implement Assembly decisions, and whose work it co-ordinates. The Council also commissions studies on economic conditions, collects data and makes recommendations to the Assembly.

The Secretariat
This is the staff of the United Nations, and its task is to administer the policies and programmes of the UN and its organs, and assist and advise the Head of the Secretariat, the Secretary-General – a full-time, non-political appointment made by the General Assembly.

The Trusteeship Council
This no longer administers any of the original 11 trust territories as they are all now independent.

The International Court of Justice (the World Court)
The World Court is the judicial organ of the United Nations. It deals only with United Nations disputes and all members are subject to its jurisdiction. There are 15 judges, elected for nine-year terms by the General Assembly and the Security Council.

The social and humanitarian operations of the UN include:
United Nations Development Programme (UNDP) Plans and funds projects to help developing countries make better use of their resources.
United Nations International Childrens' Fund (UNICEF) Created at the General Assembly's first session in 1945 to help children in the aftermath of World War II, it now provides basic health care and aid worldwide.
Food and Agriculture Organization (FAO) Aims to raise living standards and nutrition levels in rural areas by improving food production and distribution.
United Nations Educational, Scientific and Cultural Organization (UNESCO) Promotes international co-operation through broader and better education.
World Health Organization (WHO) Promotes and provides for better health care, public and environmental health and medical research.

United Nations agencies are involved in many aspects of international trade, safety and security:
International Maritime Organization (IMO) Promotes unity amongst merchant shipping, especially in regard to safety, marine pollution and standardization.
International Labour Organization (ILO) Seeks to improve labour conditions and promote productive employment to raise living standards.
World Meteorological Organization (WMO) Promotes co-operation in weather observation, reporting and forecasting.
World Trade Organization (WTO) On 1 January 1995 the WTO replaced GATT. It advocates a common code of conduct and its aim is the liberalization of world trade.
Disarmament Commission Considers and makes recommendations to the General Assembly on disarmament issues.
International Atomic Energy Agency (IAEA) Fosters development of peaceful uses for nuclear energy and establishes safety standards.

The World Bank comprises three United Nations agencies:
International Monetary Fund (IMF) Cultivates international monetary co-operation and expansion of trade.
International Bank for Reconstruction and Development (IBRD) Provides funds and technical assistance to developing countries.
International Finance Corporation (IFC) Encourages the growth of productive private enterprise in less developed countries.

Membership There are four independent states which are not members of the UN – Switzerland, Taiwan, Tuvalu and Vatican City. Official languages are Chinese, English, French, Russian, Spanish and Arabic.
Funding The UN budget for 1996–97 was US $2.6 billion. Contributions are assessed by the members' ability to pay, with the maximum 25% of the total, the minimum 0.01%.
Peacekeeping The UN has been involved in 43 peacekeeping operations worldwide since 1948. At the end of 1996 there were 16 areas of UN patrol and 25,649 'blue berets'.

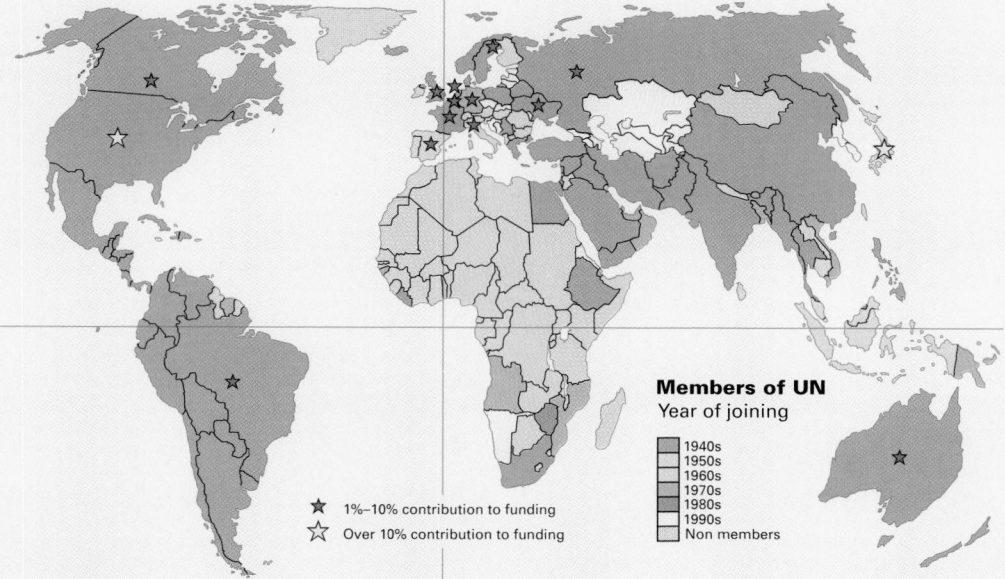

Members of UN
Year of joining
- 1940s
- 1950s
- 1960s
- 1970s
- 1980s
- 1990s
- Non members

☆ 1%–10% contribution to funding
☆ Over 10% contribution to funding

Military Spending

Military expenditure as a % of GNP or GDP, ranked selection of countries (1994)

1. Iraq	74.9%	14. Jordan	7.5%
2. North Korea	26.3%	15. Laos	7.4%
3. Angola	23.9%	16. Pakistan	6.0%
4. Oman	18.1%	17. UAE	5.7%
5. Syria	17.9%	18. Seychelles	5.6%
6. Sudan	17.1%	19. Sierra Leone	4.9%
7. Saudi Arabia	14.2%	20. Taiwan	4.8%
8. Yemen	14.1%	21. Liberia	4.8%
9. Russia	12.4%	22. Singapore	4.5%
10. Kuwait	11.1%	23. Sri Lanka	4.5%
11. Mozambique	8.7%	24. USA	4.3%
12. Israel	8.6%	25. Malaysia	4.2%
13. Rwanda	7.6%		

It is worth noting that the total amount of expenditure varies considerably depending on the size of the economy, so that although the percentages show the importance given to military spending within each country, they give no idea as to the total expenditure. In 1997, for example, the USA spent a total of US $271 billion, Russia US $70 billion, and the UK US $36 billion. In 1993, the USA also provided the most military assistance worldwide, providing US $3.4 billion, compared to a total of US $0.9 billion from Western Europe.

The period 1987–94 saw a decline in global military spending which generated what the United Nations Development Programme term a 'peace dividend' of US $935 billion. Unfortunately, there is no clear link between reduced military spending and enhanced expenditure on human development. Moreover, the poorest regions of the world (notably sub-Saharan Africa) failed to contain their military spending and, in some cases, it increased.

International Organizations

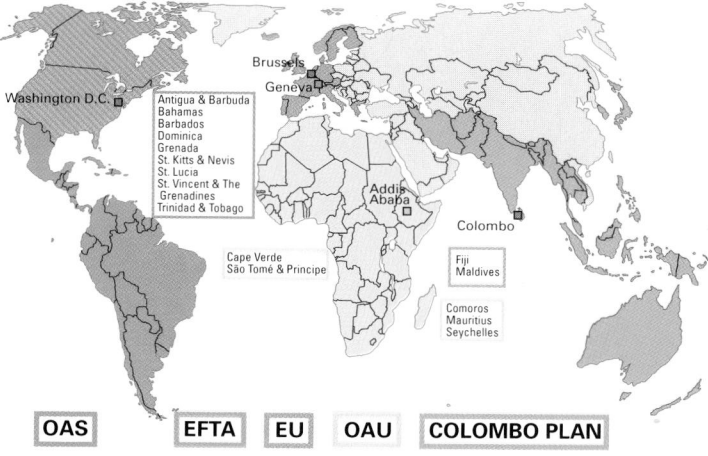

OAS EFTA EU OAU COLOMBO PLAN

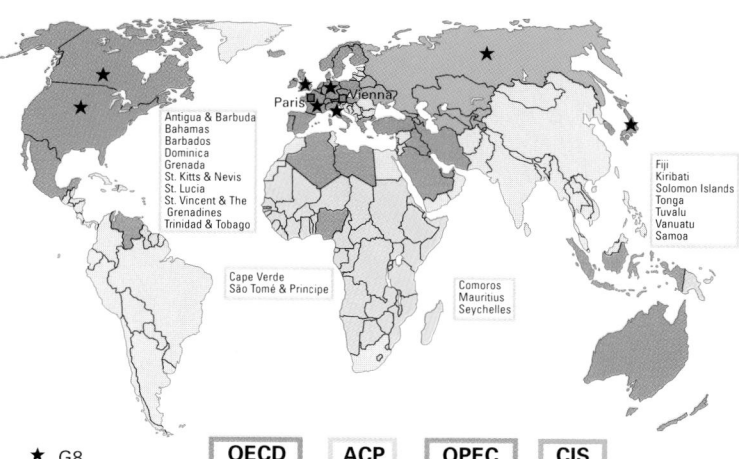

★ G8   OECD ACP OPEC CIS

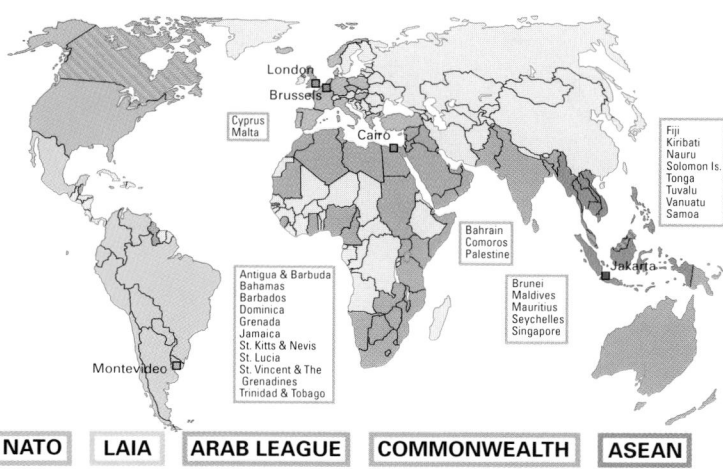

NATO LAIA ARAB LEAGUE COMMONWEALTH ASEAN

EU The European Union evolved from the European Community (EC) in 1993. The original body, the European Coal and Steel Community (ECSC), was created in 1951 following the signing of the Treaty of Paris. The 15 members of the EU – Austria, Belgium, Denmark, Finland, France, Germany, Greece, Ireland, Italy, Luxembourg, Netherlands, Portugal, Spain, Sweden and the UK – aim to integrate economies, co-ordinate social developments and bring about political union. These members, of what is now the world's biggest market, share agricultural and industrial policies and tariffs on trade.
EFTA European Free Trade Association (formed in 1960). Portugal left the original 'Seven' in 1989 to join what was then the EC, followed by Austria, Finland and Sweden in 1995. There are now only four members: Iceland, Liechtenstein, Norway and Switzerland.
ACP African-Caribbean-Pacific (formed in 1963). Members enjoy economic ties with the EU.
NATO North Atlantic Treaty Organization (formed in 1949). It continues despite the winding up of the Warsaw Pact in 1991. The Czech Rep., Hungary and Poland were the latest to join in 1999.
OAS Organization of American States (formed in 1948). It aims to promote social and economic co-operation between countries in the developed North America and developing Latin America.
ASEAN Association of South-east Asian Nations (formed in 1967). Cambodia joined in 1999.
OAU Organization of African Unity (1963). Its 53 members represent over 94% of Africa's population. Arabic, English, French and Portuguese are recognized as working languages.
LAIA The Latin American Integration Association (formed in 1980) superceded the Latin American Free Trade Association formed in 1961. Its aim is to promote freer regional trade.
OECD Organization for Economic Co-operation and Development (formed in 1961). It comprises 29 major free-market economies. The 'G8' is its 'inner group' of leading industrial nations, comprising Canada, France, Germany, Italy, Japan, Russia, UK and the USA.
COMMONWEALTH The Commonwealth of Nations evolved from the British Empire; it comprises 16 nations recognizing the British monarch as head of state, 32 republics and 5 indigenous monarchies, giving a total of 53. Nigeria was suspended in 1995.
CIS The Commonwealth of Independent States (formed in 1991) comprises the countries of the former Soviet Union except for Estonia, Latvia and Lithuania.
OPEC Organization of Petroleum Exporting Countries (formed in 1960). It controls about three-quarters of the world's oil supply. Gabon formally withdrew from OPEC in August 1996.
ARAB LEAGUE (1945) Aims to promote economic, social, political and military co-operation.
COLOMBO PLAN (formed in 1951) Its 26 members aim to promote economic and social development in Asia and the Pacific.

Agriculture

Bad harvests in 1995 caused a drop in world grain reserves to a 20-year low. This revived the ongoing debate as to whether the population explosion will cause major food crises in the 21st century.

Experts estimate that 3 billion tonnes of cereals will be needed to feed the world's population in 25 years' time, as compared with 1.9 billion tonnes at present. To expand food production to this extent, some argue, will place a strain on the environment. One suggestion to alleviate the situation is that people in developed countries should eat less meat. This would release more grain, which is used as cattle fodder, to feed people.

Other experts argue that there should be no food crises. World grain production tripled between 1950 and 1990, largely as a result of the Green Revolution, during which genetically improved, high-yield varieties of maize, rice and wheat, the world's three leading staple crops, were developed. These new varieties have helped many developing countries to achieve food surpluses and prevent widespread starvation.

The only region of the world which seems likely to suffer food shortages in the 21st century is sub-Saharan Africa, where in the late 1990s the average daily calorie intake was 6% less than what was needed and where the population is expected to double in 20 years. Improved land management and a huge increase in global trade, especially in food distribution, is necessary if sub-Saharan Africans are not to go hungry.

The development of agriculture more than 10,000 years ago transformed human existence more than any other major advance. By supporting larger populations, it led to the growth of early civilizations and later it sustained people in the industrial cities which sprang up in the 19th century.

Today, agricultural production greatly varies between the developed world, where it is highly mechanized and employs few people, such as 3% of the workforce in the United States, and the developing world, such as sub-Saharan Africa, where it employs 66% of the workforce. Many Africans are engaged in subsistence farming, providing the basic needs of their families but not contributing to the economy. Much of Africa also suffers from economic mismanagement, as well as civil war.

Political problems have also affected food production in other parts of the world. The former USSR had much excellent farmland, but the failure of the collectives and state farms to maintain sufficiently high levels of production helped to bring about the collapse of Communism.

Farmers are under great pressure not only to maintain high levels of production but to increase them. However, the cultivation of marginal areas is one of the prime causes of soil erosion and desertification.

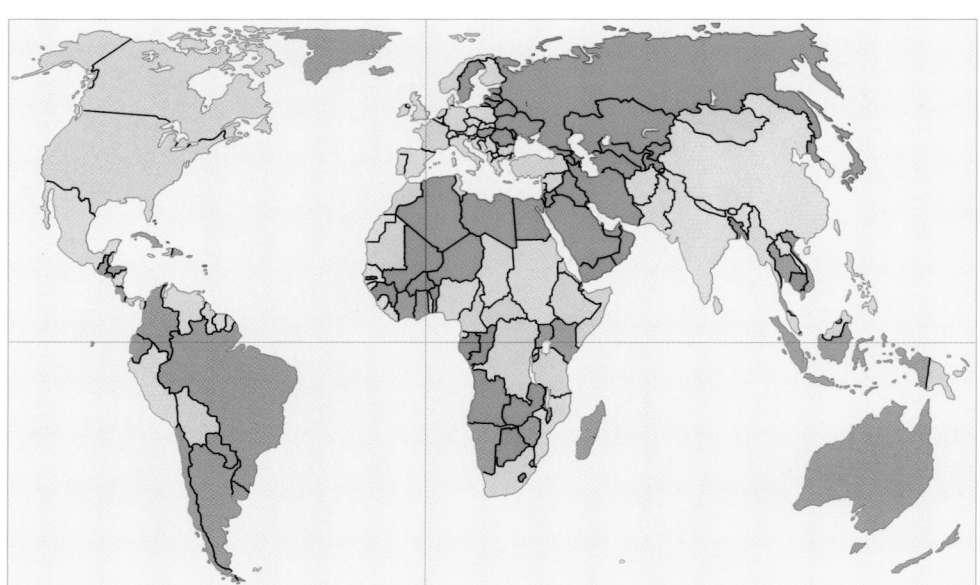

Self-sufficiency in Food

Balance of trade in food products as a percentage of total trade in food products – S.I.T.C. Classes 0, 1 and 4 (latest available year)

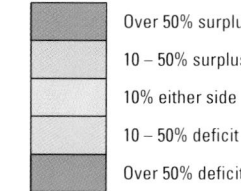

- Over 50% surplus
- 10 – 50% surplus
- 10% either side
- 10 – 50% deficit
- Over 50% deficit

Most self-sufficient		Least self-sufficient	
Argentina	95%	Algeria	–98%
Zimbabwe	87%	Djibouti	–97%
Honduras	81%	Yemen	–95%
Malawi	81%	Zambia	–95%
Costa Rica	79%	Japan	–91%
Iceland	78%	Gabon	–90%
Chile	75%	Kuwait	–90%
Uruguay	75%	Brunei	–89%
Ecuador	74%	Burkina Faso	–82%

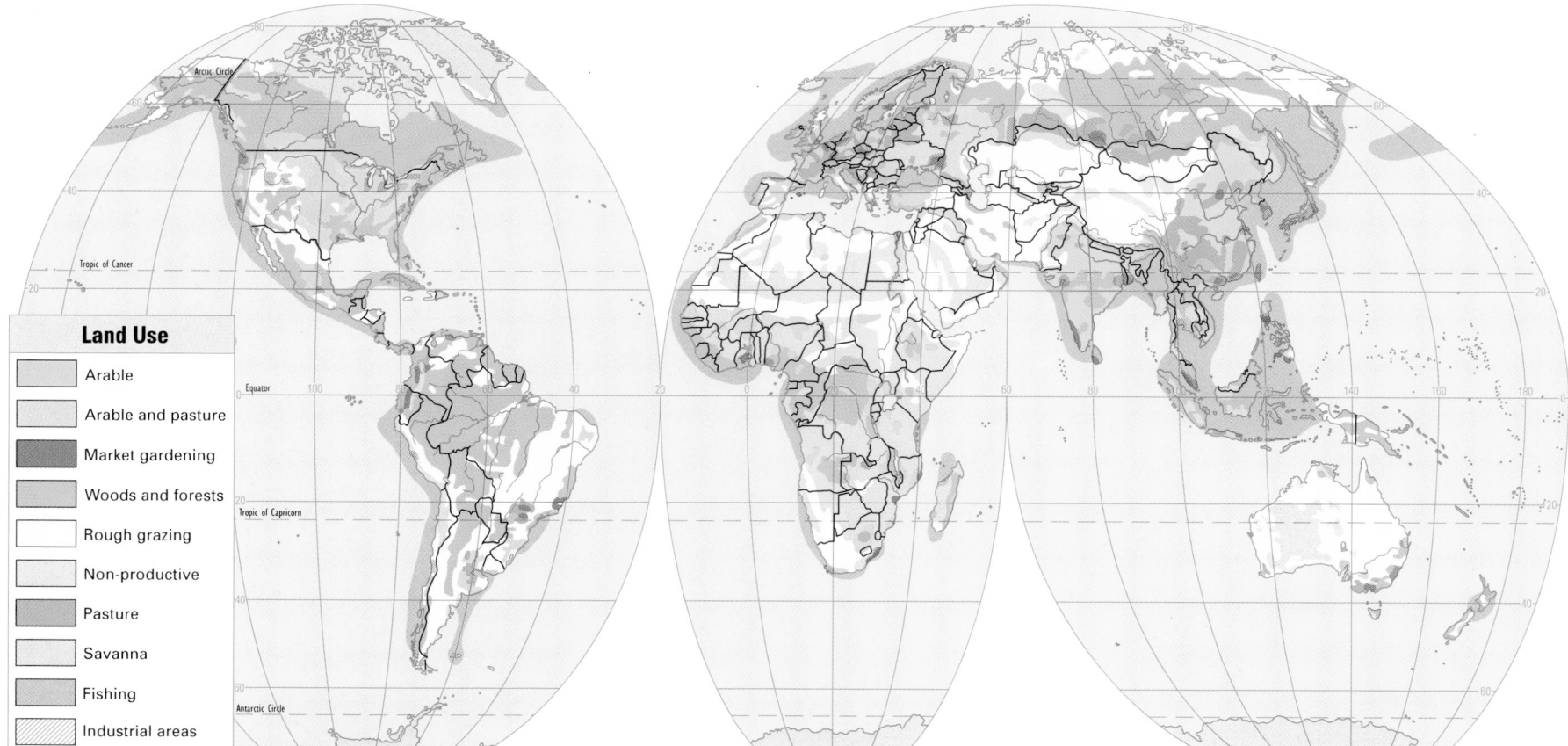

Land Use

- Arable
- Arable and pasture
- Market gardening
- Woods and forests
- Rough grazing
- Non-productive
- Pasture
- Savanna
- Fishing
- Industrial areas

Staple Crops

Wheat: Grown in a range of climates, with most varieties – including the highest-quality bread wheats – requiring temperate conditions. Mainly used in baking, it is also used for pasta and breakfast cereals.

World total (1996): 584,874,000 tonnes

Maize: Originating in the New World and still an important human food in Africa and Latin America, in the developed world it is processed into breakfast cereals, oil, starches and adhesives. It is also used for animal feed.

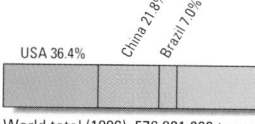

World total (1996): 576,821,000 tonnes

Oats: Most widely used to feed livestock, but eaten by humans as oatmeal or porridge. Oats have a beneficial effect on the cardiovascular system, and human consumption is likely to increase.

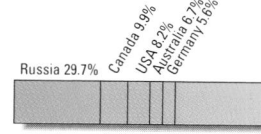

World total (1996): 28,794,000 tonnes

Millet: The name covers a number of small-grained cereals, members of the grass family with a short growing season. Used to produce flour, meal and animal feed, and fermented to make beer, especially in Africa.

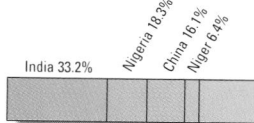

World total (1996): 29,563,000 tonnes

Sugars

Sugar cane: Confined to tropical regions, cane sugar accounts for the bulk of international trade in sugar. Most is produced as a food-stuff, but some countries, notably Brazil and South Africa, distill sugar cane to make motor fuels.

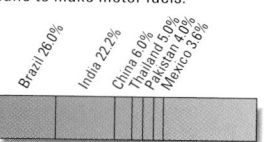

World total (1996): 1,192,555,000 tonnes

Cereals are grasses with starchy, edible seeds; every important civilization has depended on them as a source of food. The major cereal grains contain about 10% protein and 75% carbohydrate.
Grain contributes more than any other group of foods to the energy and protein content of human diet. Starchy tuber crops or root crops are second in importance after cereals as staple foods; easily cultivated, they provide high yields for little effort.

Rice: Thrives on the high humidity and temperatures of the Far East, where it is the traditional staple food of half the human race. Usually grown standing in water, rice responds well to continuous cultivation, with three or four crops annually.

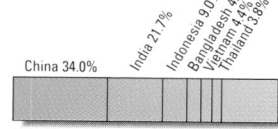

World total (1996): 562,259,000 tonnes

Potatoes: The most important of the edible tubers, potatoes grow in well-watered, temperate areas. Weight for weight less nutritious than grain, they are a human staple as well as an important animal feed.

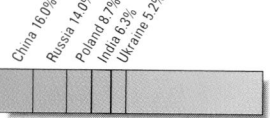

World total (1996): 294,834,000 tonnes

Soya: Beans from soya bushes are very high (30–40%) in protein. Most are processed into oil and proprietary protein foods. Consumption since 1950 has tripled, mainly due to the health-conscious developed world.

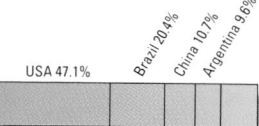

World total (1996): 130,302,000 tonnes

Cassava: A tropical shrub that needs high rainfall (over 1,000 mm annually) and a 10–30 month growing season to produce its large, edible tubers. Used as flour by humans, as cattle feed and in industrial starches.

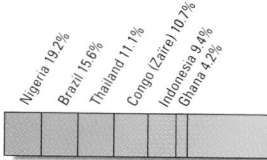

World total (1996): 162,942,000 tonnes

Sugar beet: Closely related to the beetroot, sugar beet's yield after processing is indistinguishable from cane sugar. It is replacing sugar-cane imports in Europe, to the detriment of the developing countries that rely on it as a major cash crop.

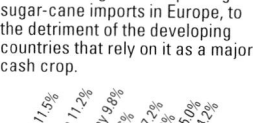

World total (1996): 255,500,000 tonnes

Food and Population

Comparison of food production and population by continent.

The left column indicates the % of world food production and the right shows population in proportion.

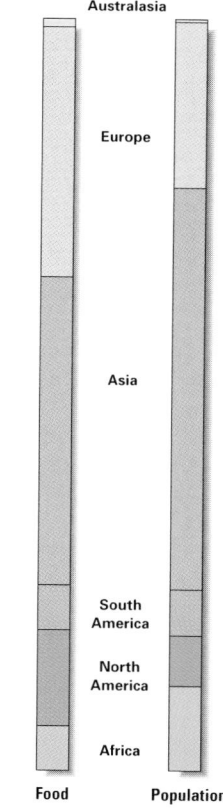

Australasia · Europe · Asia · South America · North America · Africa

Food — Population

Agricultural Population

Percentage of the total population dependent on agriculture for their livelihood (1997)

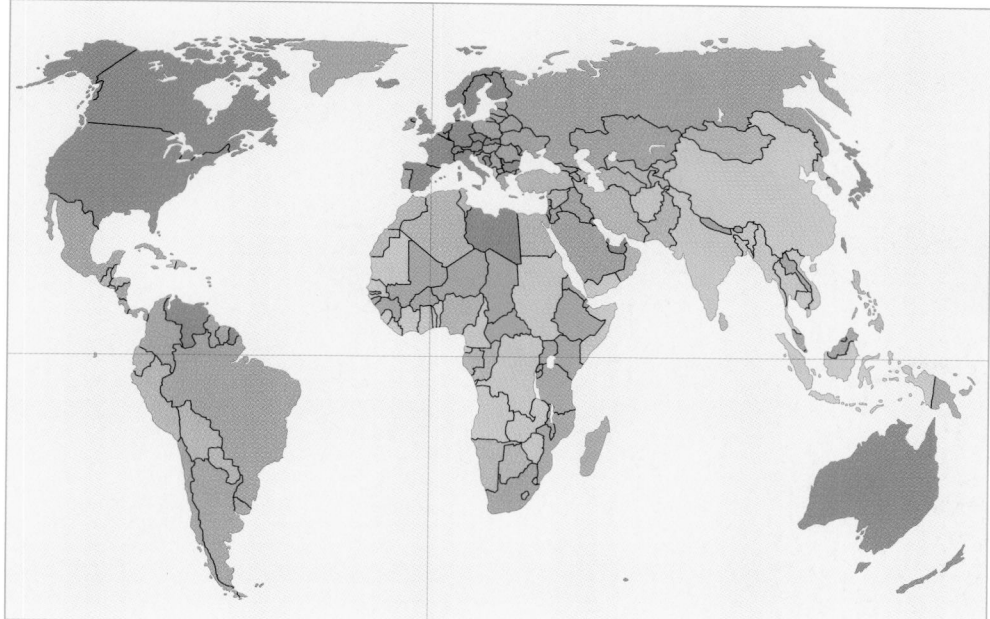

Over 75% dependent
50 – 75% dependent
25 – 50% dependent
10 – 25% dependent
Under 10% dependent

Top 5 countries (1997)		Bottom 5 countries (1997)	
Bhutan	94%	Singapore	0.2%
Nepal	93%	Kuwait	1.0%
Burkina Faso	92%	Brunei	1.0%
Rwanda	91%	Bahrain	1.3%
Burundi	91%	Qatar	1.7%

Animal Products

Traditionally, food animals subsisted on land unsuitable for cultivation, supporting agricultural production with their fertilizing dung. But free-ranging animals grow slowly and yield less meat than those more intensively reared; the demands of urban markets in the developed world have encouraged the growth of factory-like production methods. A large proportion of staple crops, especially cereals, are fed to animals, an inefficient way to produce protein but one likely to continue as long as people value meat and dairy products in their diet.

Cheese: Least perishable of all dairy products, cheese is milk fermented with selected bacterial strains to produce a foodstuff with a potentially immense range of flavours and textures. The vast majority of cheeses are made from cow's milk, although sheep and goat cheeses are highly prized.

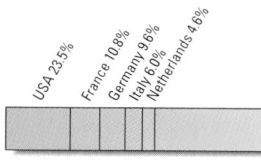

World total (1995): 14,754,000 tonnes

Beef and Veal: Most beef and veal is reared for home markets, and the top five producers are also the biggest consumers. The USA produces nearly a quarter of the world's beef and eats even more.

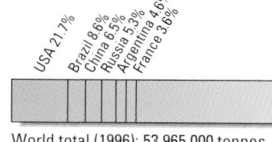

World total (1996): 53,965,000 tonnes

Milk: Many human groups, including most Asians, find raw milk indigestible after infancy, and it is often only the starting point for other dairy products such as butter, cheese and yoghurt. Most world production comes from cows, but sheep's milk and goats' milk are also important.

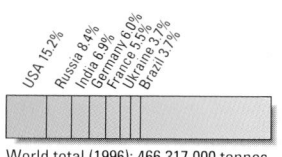

World total (1996): 466,317,000 tonnes

Butter: A traditional source of vitamin A as well as calories, butter has lost much popularity in the developed world for health reasons, although it remains a valuable food. Most butter from India, the world's largest producer, is clarified into ghee, which has religious as well as nutritional importance.

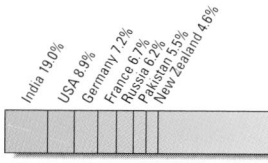

World total (1996): 6,565,000 tonnes

Pork: Although pork is forbidden to many millions, notably Muslims, on religious grounds, more is produced than any other meat in the world, mainly because it is the cheapest. It accounts for about 90% of China's meat output, although per capita meat consumption is relatively low.

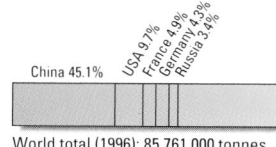

World total (1996): 85,761,000 tonnes

Crisis in Africa

Each year 40 million people, almost half of whom are children, die from starvation and related diseases. In 2000, 600 million people worldwide were estimated to be suffering from malnutrition. Africa suffers from more natural disasters than any other continent; pests such as locusts destroy crops, and tropical storms and flooding ruin harvests. Famines periodically affect parts of Africa causing widespread hardship, even though enough food is produced worldwide to feed everyone.

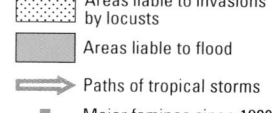

Areas liable to invasions by locusts
Areas liable to flood
Paths of tropical storms
Major famines since 1900 (with dates)

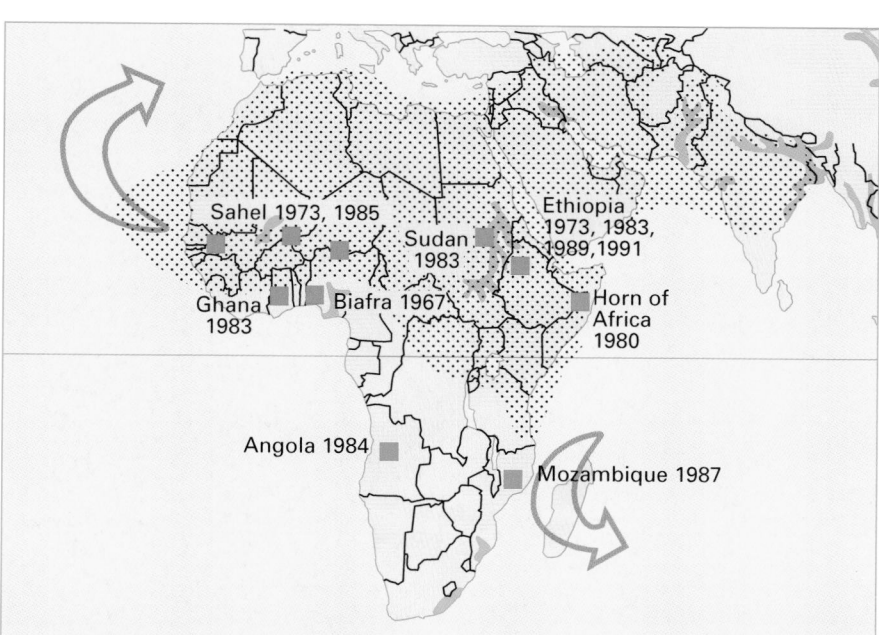

Sahel 1973, 1985 · Ethiopia 1973, 1983, 1989, 1991 · Sudan 1983 · Ghana 1983 · Biafra 1967 · Horn of Africa 1980 · Angola 1984 · Mozambique 1987

Energy

For more information:
22 Carbon dioxide
   Greenhouse power
   CO$_2$ producers
   Global warming
23 Water pollution
39 World shipping

Every year, the world's energy consumption is about the equivalent of what would come from burning 8,000 million tonnes of oil (8,000 MtOe) – a twenty-fold increase since 1850. Two-fifths of this total actually comes from burning oil and most of the rest comes from coal and natural gas.

The oil crises in the 1970s precipitated concern over dependence on finite fossil fuels as the primary source of energy, and growing environmental awareness has added impetus to the search for alternative energy resources.

Fossil fuel combustion damages the environment through the release of gases and particulate matter but two other major sources of energy, hydroelectricity and nuclear power, are also controversial. For example, hydro electricity production involves flooding large areas to create reservoirs, while nuclear power stations, which are costly to build, generate dangerous radioactive wastes, and can lead to disasters on an international scale.

Alternative energy resources may soon provide a much larger proportion of the world's energy consumption, especially in developing countries where millions of people currently have no access to electricity. Experts have predicted that solar and wind energy may have an important future in such countries as China and India, while other areas under development, such as tidal, wave and geothermal power, all have potential in appropriate areas. World Bank experts have calculated that solar power could, in theory, supply between five and ten times the present electricity supply of developing countries.

Conversions

For historical reasons, oil is still traded in barrels. The weight and volume equivalents shown below are all based on average density 'Arabian light' crude oil, and should be considered approximate.

The energy equivalents given for a tonne of oil are also somewhat imprecise: oil and coal of different qualities will have varying energy contents, a fact usually reflected in their price on world markets.

1 barrel:
0.136 tonnes
159 litres
35 Imperial gallons
42 US gallons

1 tonne:
7.33 barrels
1185 litres
256 Imperial gallons
261 US gallons

1 tonne oil:
1.5 tonnes hard coal
3.0 tonnes lignite
12,000 kWh

1 gallon (Imperial):
227,42 cubic inches
1.201 US gallons
4,546 litres

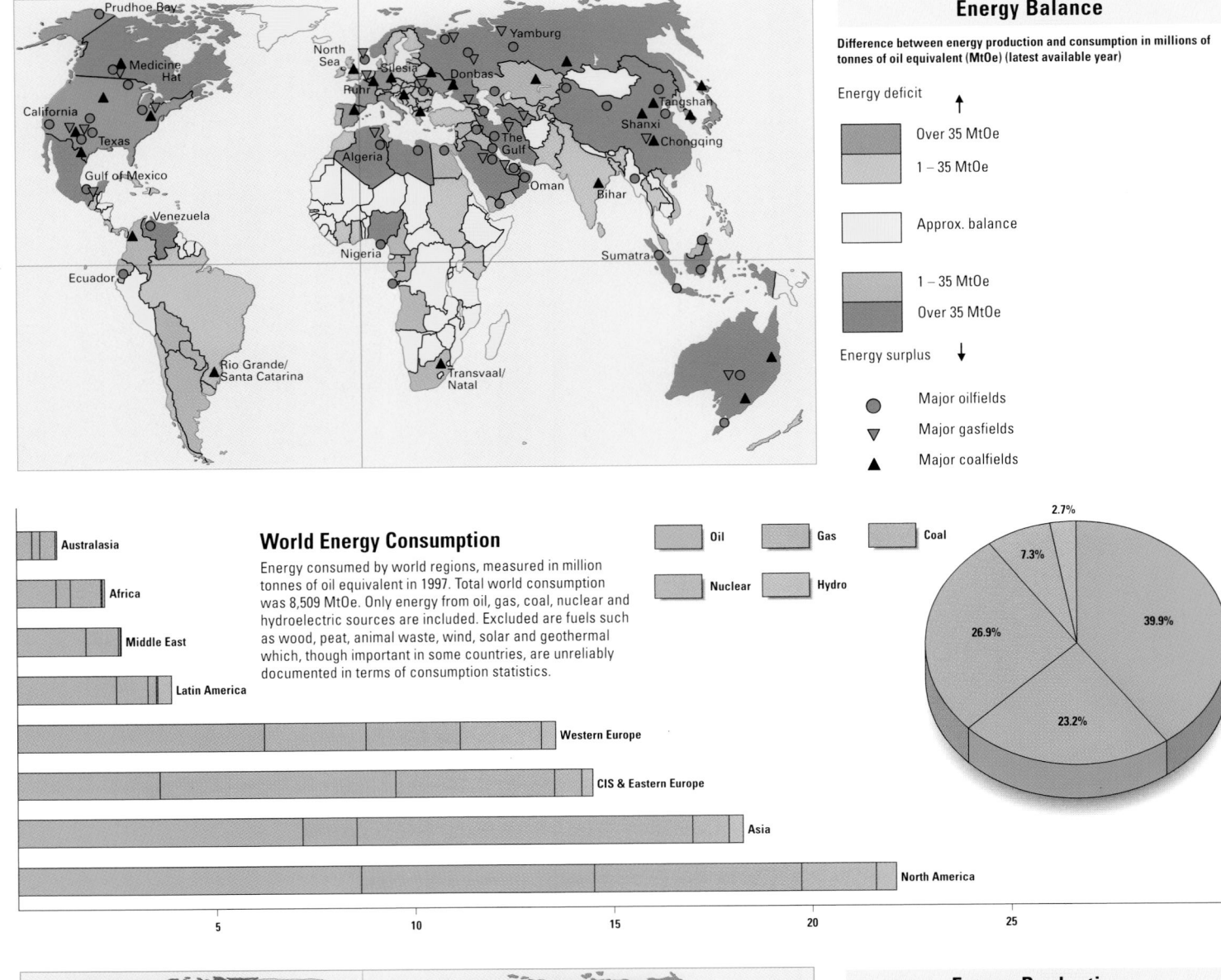

Energy Balance

Difference between energy production and consumption in millions of tonnes of oil equivalent (MtOe) (latest available year)

Energy deficit ↑

- Over 35 MtOe
- 1 – 35 MtOe
- Approx. balance
- 1 – 35 MtOe
- Over 35 MtOe

Energy surplus ↓

- ● Major oilfields
- ▽ Major gasfields
- ▲ Major coalfields

World Energy Consumption

Energy consumed by world regions, measured in million tonnes of oil equivalent in 1997. Total world consumption was 8,509 MtOe. Only energy from oil, gas, coal, nuclear and hydroelectric sources are included. Excluded are fuels such as wood, peat, animal waste, wind, solar and geothermal which, though important in some countries, are unreliably documented in terms of consumption statistics.

Oil   Gas   Coal   Nuclear   Hydro

Australasia
Africa
Middle East
Latin America
Western Europe
CIS & Eastern Europe
Asia
North America

Pie chart: 39.9%, 23.2%, 26.9%, 7.3%, 2.7%

Energy Production

Primary energy production expressed in kilograms of coal equivalent per person (1994)

In developing countries traditional fuels are still very important. These so-called biomass fuels include wood, charcoal and dried dung. The pie-chart highlights the importance of biomass in terms of energy consumption in Nigeria. Collecting fuelwood can be a time-consuming task, sometimes taking all day.

- Over 10,000 kg per person
- 1,000 – 10,000 kg per person
- 100 – 1,000 kg per person
- 10 – 100 kg per person
- Under 10 kg per person

Nigeria
Oil
Gas
Biomass

Oil Movements

Major world movements of oil in millions of tonnes (1997)

Middle East to Asia (not Japan)	294.4
Middle East to Japan	218.1
Middle East to Western Europe	187.9
South and Central America to USA	132.1
North Africa to Western Europe	97.9
CIS to Western Europe	90.8
Middle East to USA	86.9
Canada to USA	72.7
West Africa to USA	68.3
Mexico to USA	68.0
West Africa to Western Europe	40.1
Western Europe to USA	32.9
Middle East to Africa	32.0
CIS to Central Europe	31.8
Middle East to South and Central America	27.8
Middle East to Central Europe	19.3

Total world imports ....**1,978,900,000 million tonnes**

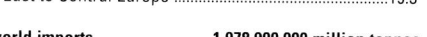

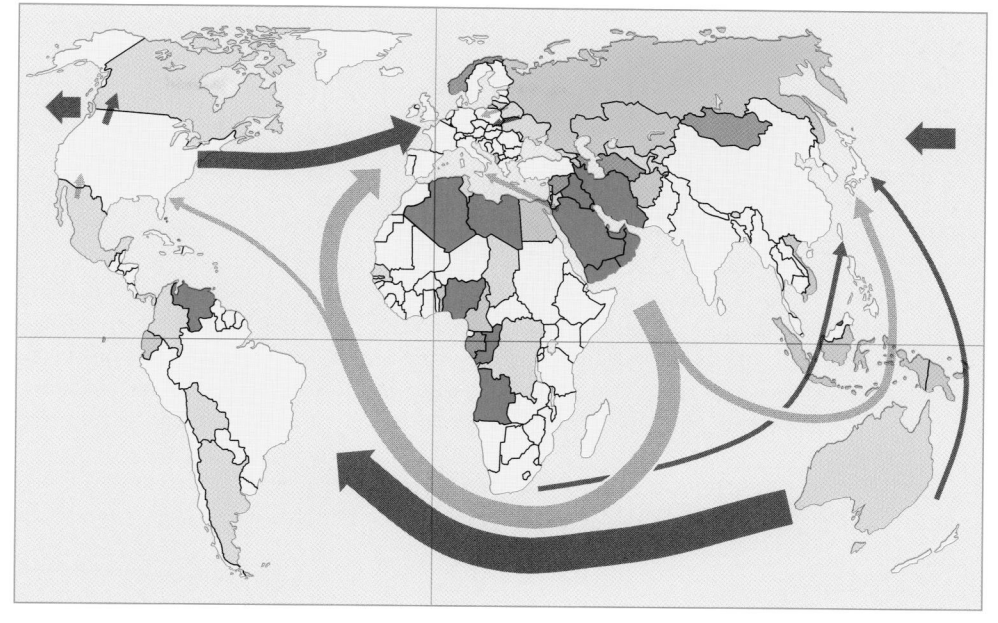

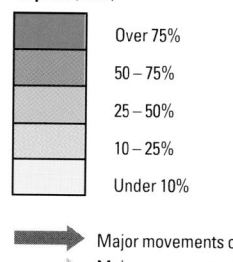

Fuel Exports

Fuels as a percentage of total value of exports (1996)

- Over 75%
- 50 – 75%
- 25 – 50%
- 10 – 25%
- Under 10%

→ Major movements of coal
→ Major movements of oil

In the 1970s, oil exports became a political issue when OPEC sought to increase the influence of developing countries in world affairs by raising oil prices and restricting production. But its power was short-lived, following a fall in demand for oil in the 1980s, due to an increase in energy efficiency and development of alternative resources.

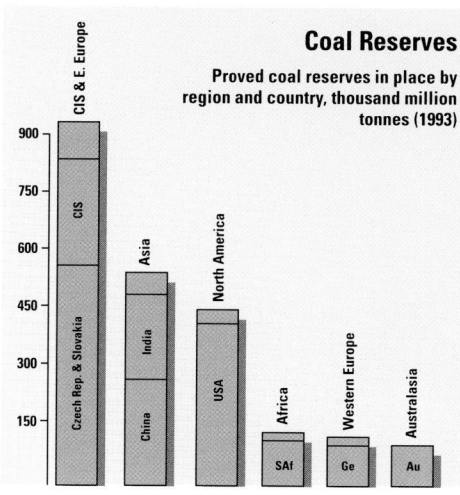

Coal Reserves

Proved coal reserves in place by region and country, thousand million tonnes (1993)

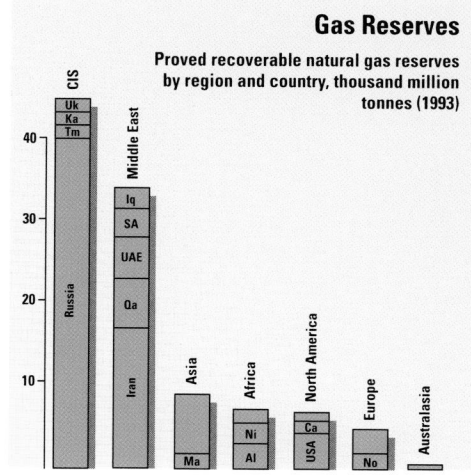

Gas Reserves

Proved recoverable natural gas reserves by region and country, thousand million tonnes (1993)

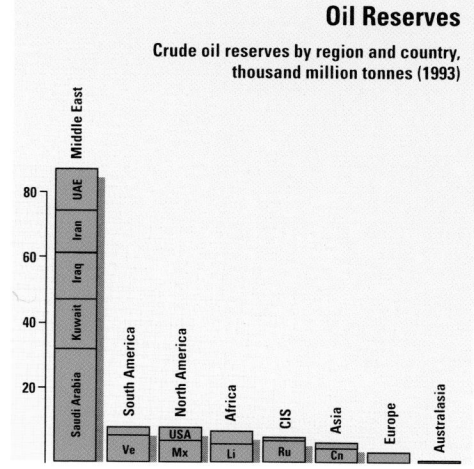

Oil Reserves

Crude oil reserves by region and country, thousand million tonnes (1993)

Al: Algeria
Au: Australia
Ca: Canada
Cn: China
Ge: Germany
Iq: Iraq
Ka: Kazakstan
Li: Libya
Ma: Malaysia
Mx: Mexico
Ni: Nigeria
No: Norway
Qa: Qatar
Ru: Russia
SA: Saudi Arabia
SAf: South Africa
Tm: Turkmenistan
Uk: Ukraine
Ve: Venezuela

Nuclear Power

Percentage of electricity generated by nuclear power stations, leading nations (1995)

1.	Lithuania	85%	11.	Spain	33%
2.	France	77%	12.	Finland	30%
3.	Belgium	56%	13.	Germany	29%
4.	Slovak Rep.	49%	14.	Japan	29%
5.	Sweden	48%	15.	UK	27%
6.	Bulgaria	41%	16.	Ukraine	27%
7.	Hungary	41%	17.	Czech Rep.	22%
8.	Switzerland	39%	18.	Canada	19%
9.	Slovenia	38%	19.	USA	18%
10.	South Korea	33%	20.	Russia	12%

Although the 1980s were a bad time for the nuclear power industry (major projects ran over budget and fears of long-term environmental damage were heavily reinforced by the 1986 disaster at Chernobyl), the industry picked up in the early 1990s. Whilst the number of reactors is still increasing, however, orders for new plants have shrunk. In 1997, the Swedish government began to decommission the country's 12 nuclear power plants; a bold environmental decision that could cost US $50 billion.

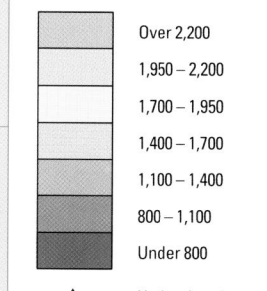

Renewable Energy

Average annual solar irradiance in kWh/m², with selected major hydroelectric and geothermal power stations

- Over 2,200
- 1,950 – 2,200
- 1,700 – 1,950
- 1,400 – 1,700
- 1,100 – 1,400
- 800 – 1,100
- Under 800

△ Hydroelectric plants
● Geothermal plants

Hydroelectricity

Percentage of electricity generated by hydroelectric power stations, leading nations (1995)

1.	Paraguay	99.9%	11.	Rwanda	97.6%
2.	Congo (D. Rep.)	99.7%	12.	Malawi	97.6%
3.	Bhutan	99.6%	13.	Cameroon	96.9%
4.	Zambia	99.5%	14.	Nepal	96.7%
5.	Norway	99.4%	15.	Laos	95.3%
6.	Ghana	99.3%	16.	Albania	95.2%
7.	Congo	99.3%	17.	Iceland	94.0%
8.	Uganda	99.1%	18.	Brazil	92.2%
9.	Burundi	98.3%	19.	Honduras	87.6%
10.	Uruguay	98.0%	20.	Tanzania	87.1%

The countries that are heavily reliant on hydroelectricity are usually small and non-industrial: a high proportion of hydroelectric power more often reflects a modest energy budget than vast hydroelectric resources. The USA, for instance, produces only 9% of power requirements from hydroelectricity; yet that 9% amounts to more than three times the hydropower generated by the whole of Africa.

Alternative Energy Resources

Solar: Each year the Sun bestows upon the Earth almost a million times as much energy as is locked up in all the planet's oil reserves, but only an insignificant fraction is trapped and used commercially. In a few installations around the world, mirrors focus the Sun's rays on to boilers, whose steam generates electricity by spinning turbines.

Wind: Caused by uneven heating of the Earth, winds are themselves a form of solar energy. Windmills have been used for centuries to turn wind power into mechanical work; recent models, often arranged in banks on wind-swept high ground, usually generate electricity. Figures for wind power worldwide are given in the table, right.

Tidal: The energy from tides is potentially enormous, although only a few installations have so far been built to exploit it. In theory at least, waves and currents could also provide almost unimaginable power, and the thermal differences in the ocean depths are another huge well of potential energy. But work on extracting it is still in the experimental stage.

Geothermal: The Earth's temperature rises by 1°C for every 30 metres descent, with much steeper temperature gradients in geologically active areas. El Salvador, for example, produces 39% of its electricity from geothermal power stations, whilst the USA, the world leader, produced 3,331 megawatts in 1993. Some of the oldest and most successful applications are in Iceland, where 86% of all households are heated by geothermal energy.

Biomass: The oldest of human fuels ranges from animal dung, still burned in cooking fires in much of North Africa and elsewhere, to sugar cane plantations feeding high-technology distilleries to produce ethanol for motor vehicle engines. In Brazil and South Africa, plant ethanol provides up to 25% of motor fuel. Throughout the developing world, most biomass energy comes from firewood: although accurate figures are impossible to obtain, it may yield as much as 10% of the world's total energy consumption.

Wind Power

World wind energy generating capacity, in megawatts

1980	10
1981	25
1982	90
1983	210
1984	600
1985	1,020
1986	1,270
1987	1,450
1988	1,580
1989	1,730
1990	1,930
1991	2,170
1992	2,510
1993	3,050
1994	3,710

Wind power is the fastest growing source of energy worldwide but still provides only 1% of the world's energy. Output grew by 33% in 1995.

Minerals

The use of metals played a vital part in the evolving technologies of early peoples. Copper first came into use around 10,000 years ago, bronze about 5,000 years ago, and iron 3,300 years ago. In the early stages of the Industrial Revolution, the location of coal, iron ore and water power usually determined the location of new industries. But due to continuing improvements in transport, including oil pipelines, industries can now be located almost anywhere.

Minerals are distributed unevenly and some industrial countries, lacking their own mineral resources, import most of the raw materials they need. Some imports come from mineral-rich countries, such as Australia but others come from developing countries, especially in Africa and South America. Most of the developing countries export unprocessed ores, losing out on the much higher revenues gained from exporting metals.

Most minerals come from land deposits, because undersea deposits, with the exception of oil reserves under the continental shelves, have been regarded as inaccessible. But shortages of terrestrial minerals may one day encourage exploitation of the ocean floor.

Mineral Exports

Minerals and metals as a percentage of total exports (latest available year)

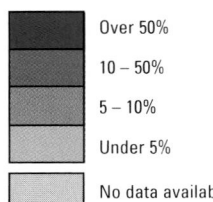

- Over 50%
- 10 – 50%
- 5 – 10%
- Under 5%
- No data available

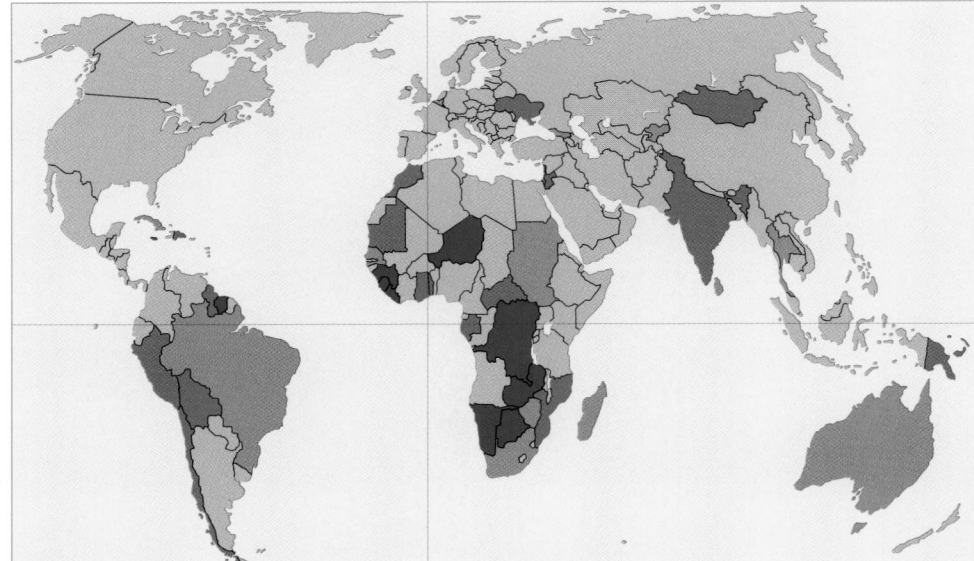

Uranium

In its pure state, uranium is an immensely heavy, white metal; but although spent uranium is employed as projectiles in anti-missile cannons, where its mass ensures a lethal punch, its main use is as a fuel in nuclear reactors, and in nuclear weaponry. Uranium is very scarce: the main source is the rare ore pitchblende, which itself contains only 0.2% uranium oxide. Only a minute fraction of that is the radioactive U^{235} isotope, though so-called breeder reactors can transmute the more common U^{238} into highly radioactive plutonium.

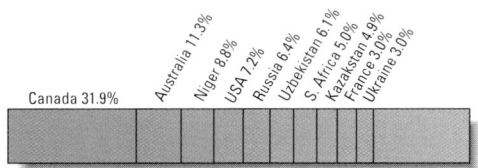

World total (1995): 32,976 tonnes

Metals

Figures for aluminium are for refined metal; all other figures refer to ore production.

The world's leading producers of aluminium ore (bauxite) in 1995 were as follows:

1. Australia 41.9%
2. Papua New Guinea 14.3%
3. Jamaica 10.8%
4. Brazil 10.1%
5. Russia 6.7%
6. China 5.7%
7. India 5.0%
8. Surinam 2.8%
9. Venezuela 2.6%
10. Greece 1.9%

The figures shown above are in stark contrast to the figures showing aluminium production on the right. Australia, for example, produces 41.9% of the world's bauxite but only 5.9% of the aluminium metal. Papua New Guinea and Jamaica account for 25% of the bauxite mined but have no smelters and export virtually all of it to countries like the USA and Canada.

Diamond

Most of the world's diamond is found in kimberlite, or 'blue ground', a basic peridotite rock; erosion may wash the diamond from its kimberlite matrix and deposit it with sand or gravel on river beds. Only a small proportion of the world's diamond, the most flawless, is cut into gemstones – 'diamonds'; most is used in industry, where the material's remarkable hardness and abrasion resistance finds a use in cutting tools, drills and dies, as well as in styluses. Australia, not among the top 12 producers at the beginning of the 1980s, had by 1986 become world leader and by 1993 was the source of 40.6% of world production. The other main producers were Congo (then Zaïre) (16.3%), Botswana (14.6%), Russia (11.4%) and South Africa (9.7%). Between them, these five nations accounted for over 82% of the world total of 100,850,000 carats.

Aluminium: Produced mainly from its oxide, bauxite, which yields 25% of its weight in aluminium. The cost of refining and production is often too high for producer-countries to bear, so bauxite is largely exported. Lightweight and corrosion resistant, aluminium alloys are widely used in aircraft, vehicles, cans and packaging.

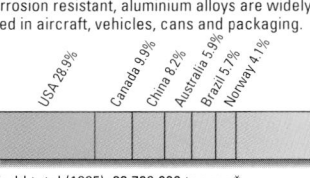

World total (1995): 22,706,000 tonnes *

Lead: A soft metal, obtained mainly from galena (lead sulphide), which occurs in veins associated with iron, zinc and silver sulphides. Its use in vehicle batteries accounts for the USA's prime consumer status; lead is also made into sheeting and piping. Its use as an additive to paints and petrol is decreasing.

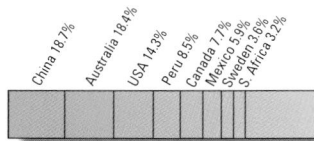

World total (1995): 2,751,000 tonnes *

Tin: Soft, pliable and non-toxic, used to coat 'tin' (tin-plated steel) cans, in the manufacture of foils and in alloys. The principal tin-bearing mineral is cassiterite (SnO_2), found in ore formed from molten rock. Producers and refiners were hit by a price collapse in 1991.

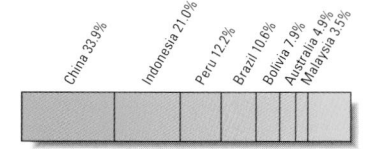

World total (1995): 182,518 tonnes *

Gold: Regarded for centuries as the most valuable metal in the world and used to make coins, gold is still recognized as the monetary standard. A soft metal, it is alloyed to make jewellery; the electronics industry values its corrosion resistance and conductivity.

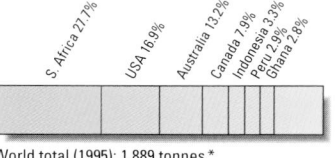

World total (1995): 1,889 tonnes *

Copper: Derived from low-yielding sulphide ores, copper is an important export for several developing countries. An excellent conductor of heat and electricity, it forms part of most electrical items, and is used in the manufacture of brass and bronze. Major importers include Japan and Germany.

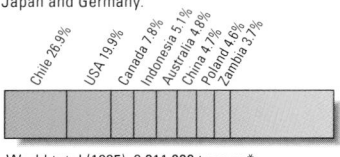

World total (1995): 9,311,000 tonnes *

Mercury: The only metal that is liquid at normal temperatures, most is derived from its sulphide, cinnabar, found only in small quantities in volcanic areas. Apart from its value in thermometers and other instruments, most mercury production is used in anti-fungal and anti-fouling preparations, and to make detonators.

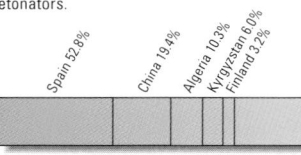

World total (1995): 2,837 tonnes *

Zinc: Often found in association with lead ores, zinc is highly resistant to corrosion, and about 40% of the refined metal is used to plate sheet steel, particularly vehicle bodies – a process known as galvanizing. Zinc is also used in dry batteries, paints and dyes.

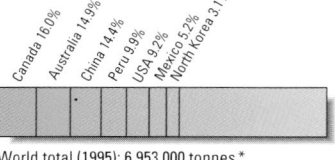

World total (1995): 6,953,000 tonnes *

Silver: Most silver comes from ores mined and processed for other metals (including lead and copper). Pure or alloyed with harder metals, it is used for jewellery and ornaments. Industrial use includes dentistry, electronics, photography and as a chemical catalyst.

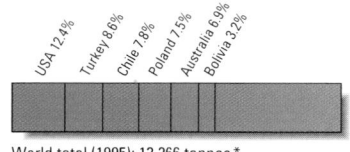

World total (1995): 13,266 tonnes *

Strategic Minerals

Ever since the art of high-temperature smelting was discovered, some time in the second millennium BC, iron has been by far the most important metal known to man. The earliest iron ploughs transformed primitive agriculture and led to the first human population explosion, while iron weapons – or the lack of them – ensured the rise or fall of entire cultures.

Widely distributed around the world, iron ores usually contain 25–60% iron; blast furnaces process the raw product into pig-iron, which is then alloyed with carbon and other minerals to produce steels of various qualities. From the time of the Industrial Revolution, steel has been almost literally the backbone of modern civilization, the prime structural material on which all else is built.

Iron smelting usually developed close to the sources of ore and, later, to the coalfields that fuelled the furnaces. Today, most ore comes from a few richly-endowed locations where large-scale mining is possible. Iron and steel plants are generally built at coastal sites so that giant ore carriers, which account for a sizeable proportion of the world's merchant fleet, can easily discharge their cargoes.

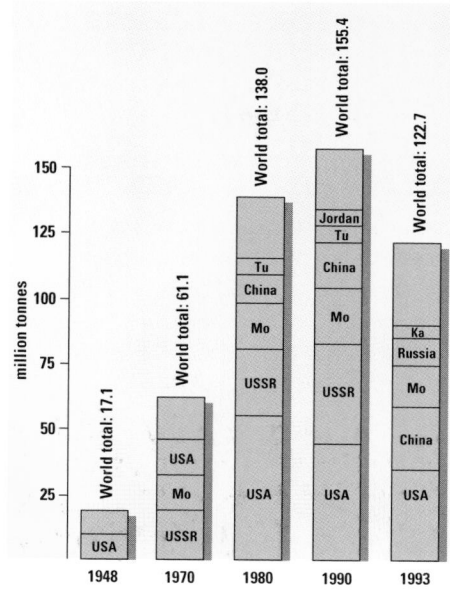

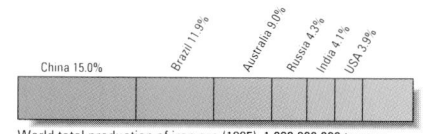

China 15.0% | Brazil 11.9% | Australia 9.0% | Russia 4.3% | India 4.1% | USA 3.9%

World total production of iron ore (1995): 1,020,000,000 tonnes

World production of phosphates in millions of tonnes (1993).
Phosphate production is vital to the economies of several small countries. Nauru, for example, is heavily dependent on phosphate exports – the island has one of the world's richest deposits. In 1994, 613,000 tonnes were mined, employing 1,000 people. In Togo, earnings from phosphate exports have superseded all agricultural exports.

Percentage of total world phosphate production (1994)

1.	USA	32.4%	7.	Israel	3.1%
2.	China	20.2%	8.	Brazil	2.6%
3.	Morocco	15.4%	9.	South Africa	2.0%
4.	Russia	6.2%	10.	Togo	1.7%
5.	Tunisia	4.4%	11.	Kazakstan	1.6%
6.	Jordan	3.3%	12.	Senegal	1.4%

World production of pig-iron and ferro-alloys (1995).
All countries with an annual output of more than 1 million tonnes are shown

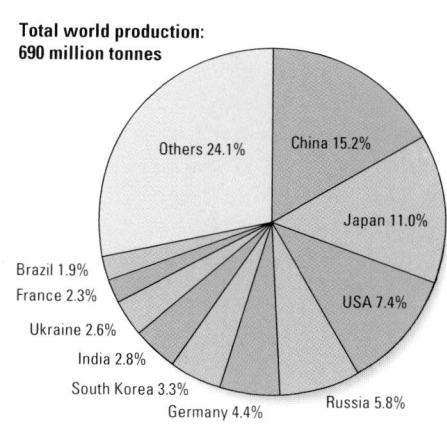

Total world production: 690 million tonnes

China 15.2% | Japan 11.0% | USA 7.4% | Russia 5.8% | Germany 4.4% | South Korea 3.3% | India 2.8% | Ukraine 2.6% | France 2.3% | Brazil 1.9% | Others 24.1%

Manganese: In its pure state, manganese is a hard, brittle metal. Alloyed with chrome, iron and nickel, it produces abrasion-resistant steels; manganese-aluminium alloys are light but tough. Found in batteries and inks, manganese is also used in glass production. Manganese ores are frequently found in the same location as sedimentary iron ores. Pyrolusite (MnO_2) and psilomelane are the main economically-exploitable sources.

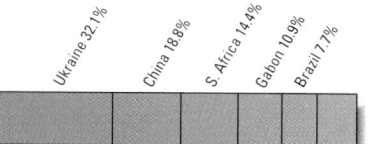

Ukraine 32.1% | China 18.8% | S. Africa 14.4% | Gabon 10.9% | Brazil 7.7%

World total (1994): 22,180,000 tonnes

Chromium: Most of the world's chromium production is alloyed with iron and other metals to produce steels with various different properties. Combined with iron, nickel, cobalt and tungsten, chromium produces an exceptionally hard steel, resistant to heat; chrome steels are used for many household items where utility must be matched with appearance – cutlery, for example. Chromium is also used in production of refractory bricks, and its salts for tanning and dyeing leather and cloth.

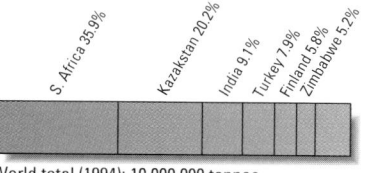

S. Africa 35.9% | Kazakstan 20.2% | India 9.1% | Turkey 7.9% | Finland 5.8% | Zimbabwe 5.2%

World total (1994): 10,000,000 tonnes

Nickel: Combined with chrome and iron, nickel produces stainless and high-strength steels; similar alloys go to make magnets and electrical heating elements. Nickel combined with copper is widely used to make coins; cupro-nickel alloy is very resistant to corrosion. Its ores yield only modest quantities of nickel – 0.5% to 3.0% – but also contain copper, iron and small amounts of precious metals. Japan, USA, UK, Germany and France are the principal importers.

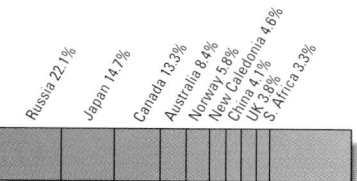

Russia 22.1% | Japan 14.7% | Canada 13.9% | Australia 8.4% | Norway 5.6% | New Caledonia 4.6% | China 4.1% | UK 3.6% | S. Africa 3.3%

World total (1995): 920,000 tonnes

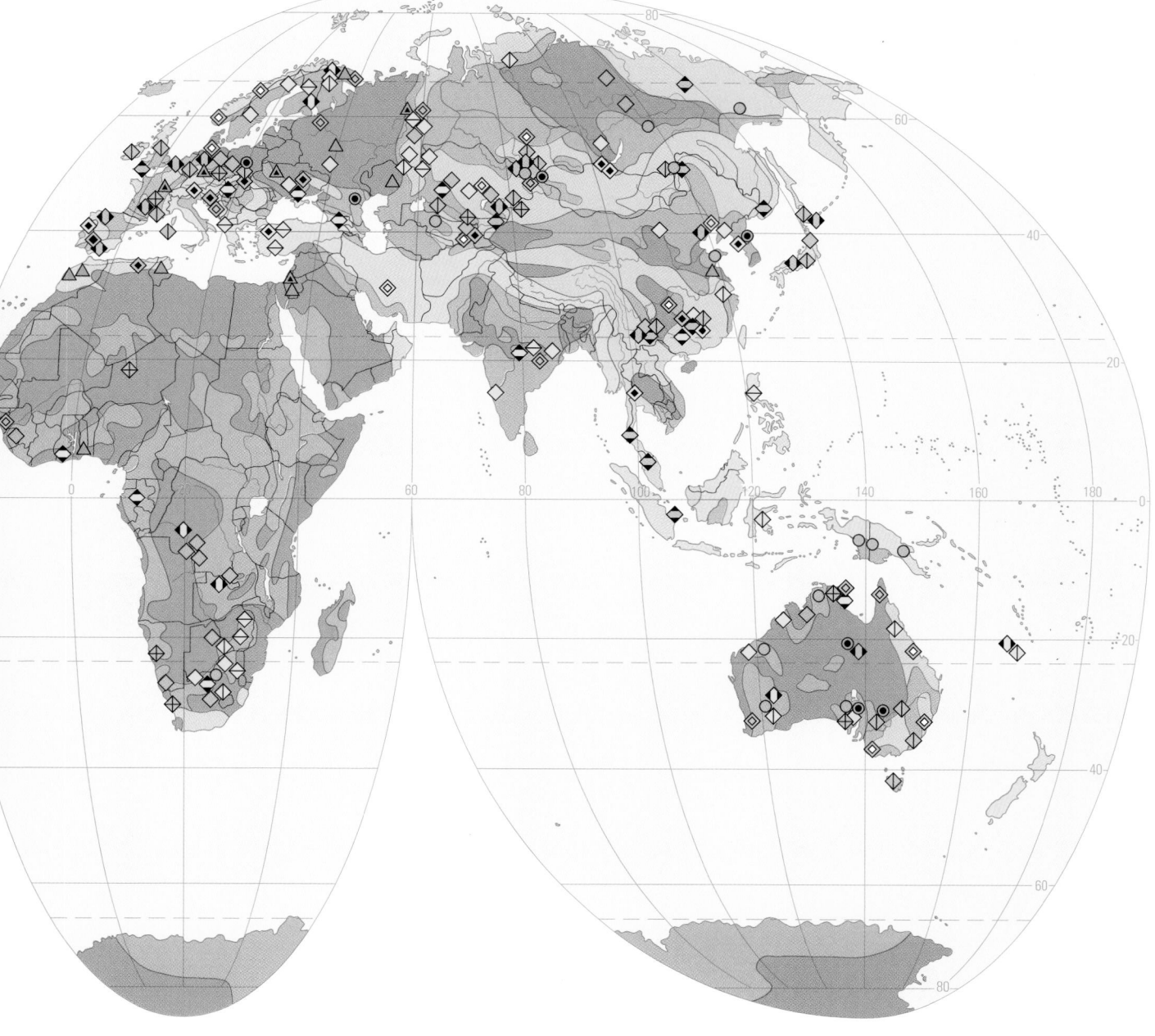

Distribution of Minerals

Structural Regions

- Pre-Cambrian shields
- Sedimentary cover on Pre-Cambrian shields
- Paleozoic (Caledonian and Hercynian) folding
- Sedimentary cover on Paleozoic folding
- Mesozoic folding
- Sedimentary cover on Mesozoic folding
- Cenozoic (Alpine) folding
- Sedimentary cover on Cenozoic folding
- Intensive Mesozoic and Cenozoic vulcanism

Distribution
Iron and ferro-alloys

- Chrome
- Cobalt
- Iron Ore
- Manganese
- Molybdenum
- Nickel Ore
- Tungsten

Non-ferrous metals

- Bauxite (Aluminium)
- Copper
- Lead
- Mercury
- Tin
- Zinc
- Uranium

Precious metals and stones

- Diamonds
- Gold
- Silver

Fertilizers

- Phosphates
- Potash

Manufacturing

The Industrial Revolution which began in Britain in the late 18th century, represented a major technological advance in the evolution of human society. It enabled a group of countries to become prosperous by replacing expensive human labour with increasingly sophisticated machinery. In economic terms, manufacturing is the transformation of raw materials, energy, labour and machines into finished goods, which have a higher value than the various elements used in production.

The economies of countries can be compared by reference to their per capita Gross National Products (or per capita GNPs), namely, the total value of goods and services produced in a country in a year, divided by the population.

The industrialized, or developed, countries accounted for 16% of the world's population in 1997 with an average per capita GNP of US $25,700. On the other hand, developing countries, with comparatively small industrial sectors and low-income economies, accounted for 35% of the world's population, with an average per capita GNP of just $350.

Kenya, with its low-income economy, had a per capita GNP in 1998 of $330. Agriculture employs 77% of the people, industry 8% and services 15%. The major industries are the processing of agricultural products and import substitution (the manufacture of such necessities as cement, footwear and textiles). Heavy industry plays a comparatively small part in the economy. By contrast, Germany, a major industrialized nation, had a per capita GNP in 1998 of $25,850. Agriculture employs only 1% of the population, with 32% in industry, and 67% in services. Germany's industrial sector differs greatly from Kenya's, with an emphasis on the manufacture of vehicles, machinery and chemicals.

Since the 1970s, some former developing countries in Asia have been transformed by rapid industrialization. These 'economic tigers', including China, Malaysia, South Korea, Singapore, Taiwan and Thailand, owe their success to low labour costs and substantial investment in education, together with advances in telecommunications, transport and computers, which have made technology more readily transferable around the world than ever before. They have also benefited from economic freedom and trade liberalization.

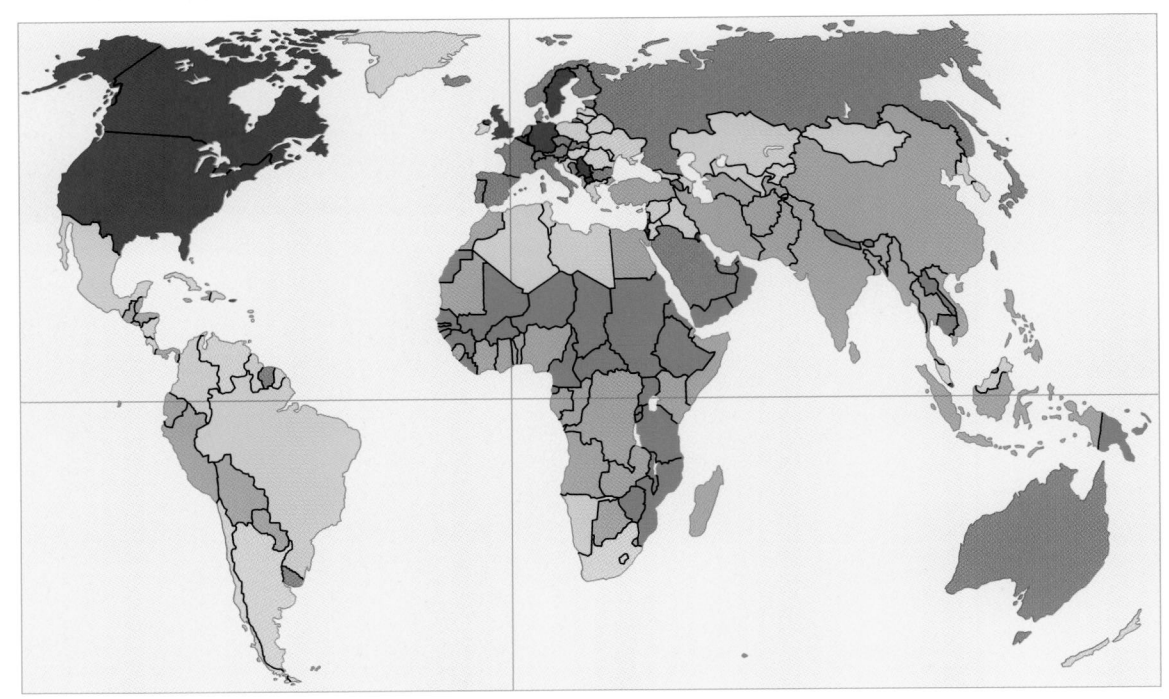

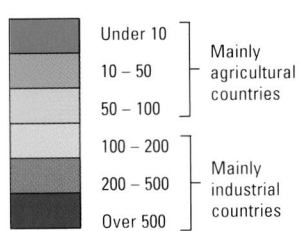

Employment

The number of workers employed in manufacturing for every 100 workers engaged in agriculture (latest available year)

Under 10	Mainly agricultural countries
10 – 50	
50 – 100	
100 – 200	Mainly industrial countries
200 – 500	
Over 500	

Selected countries (latest available year)

Singapore	8,860
UK	1,270
Belgium	820
Germany	800
Kuwait	767
Bahrain	660
USA	657
Israel	633

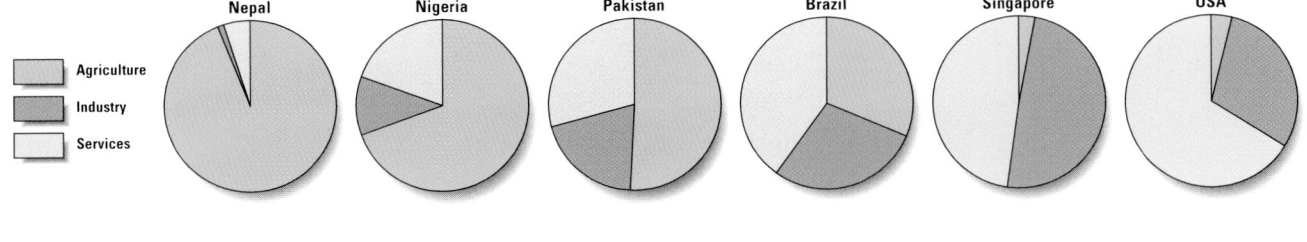

Nepal   Nigeria   Pakistan   Brazil   Singapore   USA

Agriculture
Industry
Services

Division of Employment

Distribution of workers between agriculture, industry and services, selected countries (latest available year)

The six countries selected illustrate the usual stages of economic development, from dependence on agriculture through industrial growth to the expansion of the service sector.

The Workforce

Percentages of men and women between 15 and 64 in employment, selected countries (latest available year)

The figures include employees and the self-employed, who in developing countries are often subsistence farmers. People in full-time education are excluded. Because of the population age structure in developing countries, the employed population has to support a far larger number of non-workers than its industrial equivalent. For example, more than 52% of Kenya's people are under 15, an age group that makes up less than a tenth of the UK population.

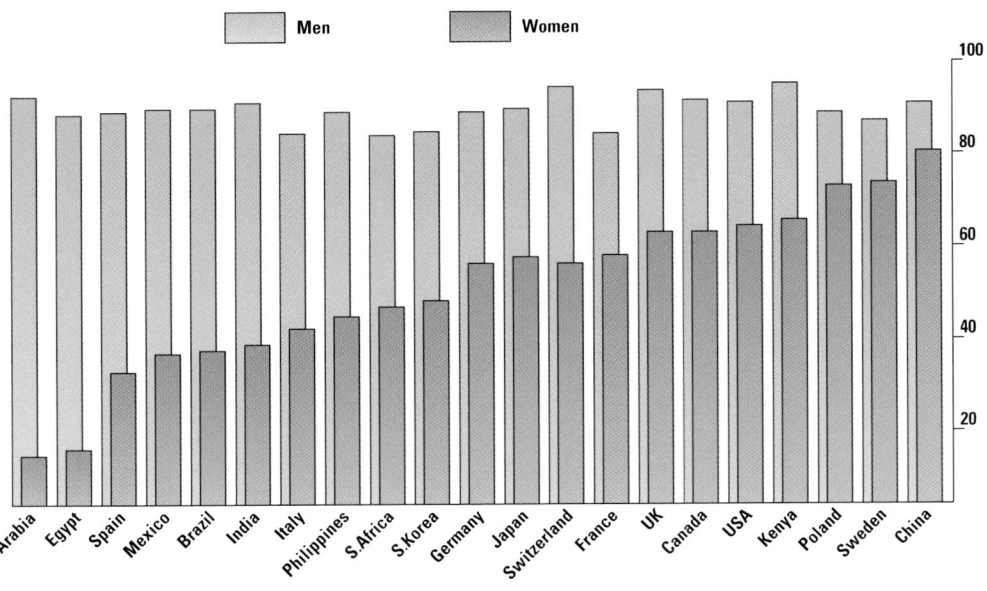

Men   Women

Saudi Arabia, Egypt, Spain, Mexico, Brazil, India, Italy, Philippines, S.Africa, S.Korea, Germany, Japan, Switzerland, France, UK, Canada, USA, Kenya, Poland, Sweden, China

Wealth Creation

The Gross National Product (GNP) of the world's largest economies, US $ million (1998)

1.	USA	7,922,651	21. Austria	217,163
2.	Japan	4,089,910	22. Turkey	200,505
3.	Germany	2,122,673	23. Saudi Arabia	186,000
4.	Italy	1,666,178	24. Denmark	176,374
5.	France	1,466,014	25. Hong Kong	158,286
6.	UK	1,263,777	26. Norway	152,082
7.	China	928,950	27. Poland	150,798
8.	Botswana	758,043	28. Indonesia	138,501
9.	Canada	612,332	29. Thailand	134,433
10.	Spain	553,690	30. Finland	124,293
11.	India	421,259	31. Greece	122,880
12.	Netherlands	388,682	32. South Africa	119,001
13.	Mexico	380,917	33. Iran	109,645
14.	Australia	380,625	34. Portugal	106,376
15.	South Korea	369,890	35. Colombia	106,090
16.	Russia	337,914	36. Israel	95,179
17.	Argentina	324,084	37. Singapore	95,095
18.	Switzerland	284,808	38. Venezuela	81,347
19.	Belgium	259,045	39. Malaysia	79,848
20.	Sweden	226,861	40. Egypt	79,208

Patterns of Production

Breakdown of industrial output by value, selected countries (latest available year)

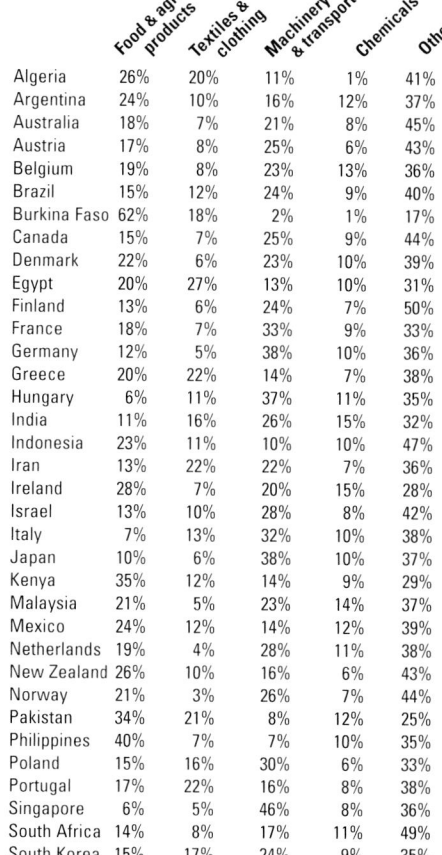

	Food & agric. products	Textiles & clothing	Machinery & transport	Chemicals	Other
Algeria	26%	20%	11%	1%	41%
Argentina	24%	10%	16%	12%	37%
Australia	18%	7%	21%	8%	45%
Austria	17%	8%	25%	6%	43%
Belgium	19%	8%	23%	13%	36%
Brazil	15%	12%	24%	9%	40%
Burkina Faso	62%	18%	2%	1%	17%
Canada	15%	7%	25%	9%	44%
Denmark	22%	6%	23%	10%	39%
Egypt	20%	27%	13%	10%	31%
Finland	13%	6%	24%	7%	50%
France	18%	7%	33%	9%	33%
Germany	12%	5%	38%	10%	36%
Greece	20%	22%	14%	7%	38%
Hungary	6%	11%	37%	11%	35%
India	11%	16%	26%	15%	32%
Indonesia	23%	11%	10%	10%	47%
Iran	13%	22%	22%	7%	36%
Ireland	28%	7%	20%	15%	28%
Israel	13%	10%	28%	8%	42%
Italy	7%	13%	32%	10%	38%
Japan	10%	6%	38%	10%	37%
Kenya	35%	12%	14%	9%	29%
Malaysia	21%	5%	23%	14%	37%
Mexico	24%	12%	14%	12%	39%
Netherlands	19%	4%	28%	11%	38%
New Zealand	26%	10%	16%	6%	43%
Norway	21%	3%	26%	7%	44%
Pakistan	34%	21%	8%	12%	25%
Philippines	40%	7%	7%	10%	35%
Poland	15%	16%	30%	6%	33%
Portugal	17%	22%	16%	8%	38%
Singapore	6%	5%	46%	8%	36%
South Africa	14%	8%	17%	11%	49%
South Korea	15%	17%	24%	9%	35%
Spain	17%	9%	22%	9%	43%
Sweden	10%	2%	35%	8%	44%
Thailand	30%	17%	14%	6%	33%
Turkey	20%	14%	15%	8%	43%
UK	14%	6%	32%	11%	36%
USA	12%	5%	35%	10%	38%
Venezuela	23%	8%	9%	11%	49%

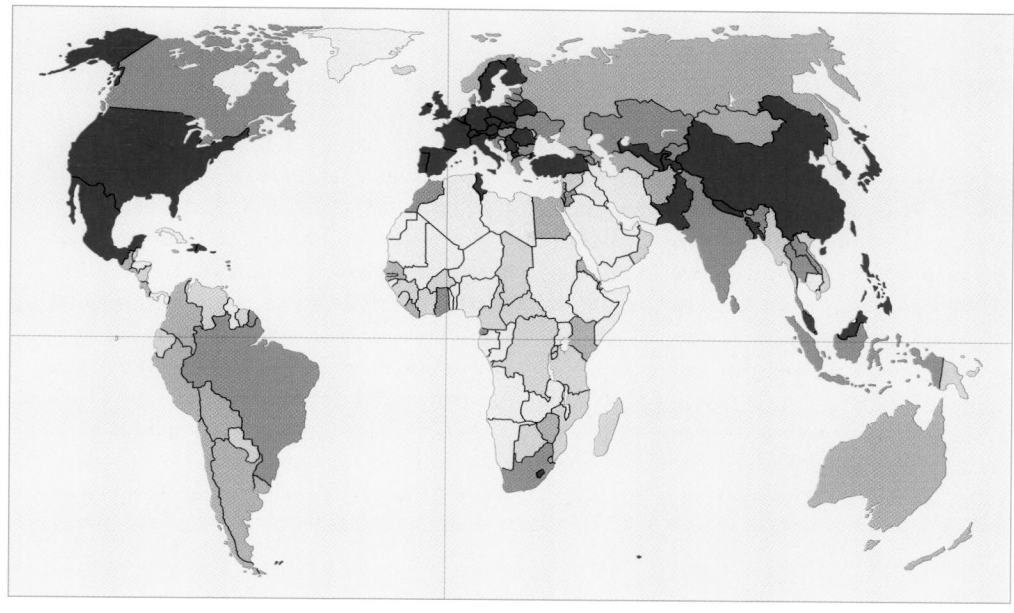

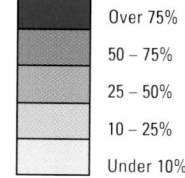

Industry and Trade

Manufactured goods (including machinery and transport) as a percentage of total exports (1996)

- Over 75%
- 50 – 75%
- 25 – 50%
- 10 – 25%
- Under 10%

The Far East and South-east Asia (Japan 98%, Macau 96%, Taiwan 95%, Hong Kong [now part of China] 94%, South Korea 94%) are most dominant, but many countries in Europe (e.g. Slovenia 93%) are also heavily dependent on manufactured goods.

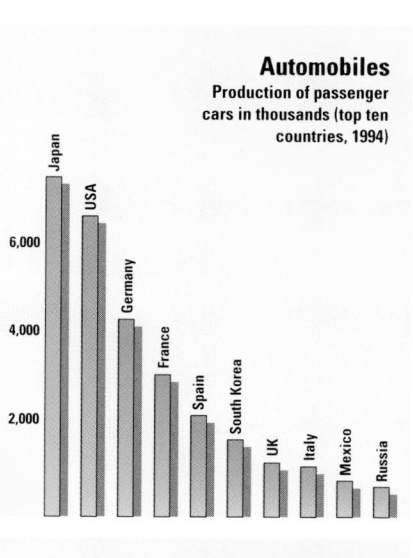

Automobiles
Production of passenger cars in thousands (top ten countries, 1994)

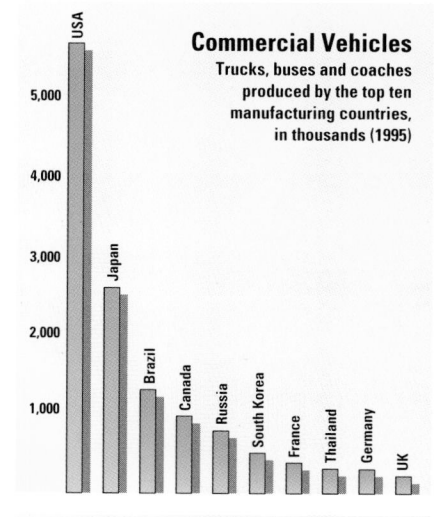

Commercial Vehicles
Trucks, buses and coaches produced by the top ten manufacturing countries, in thousands (1995)

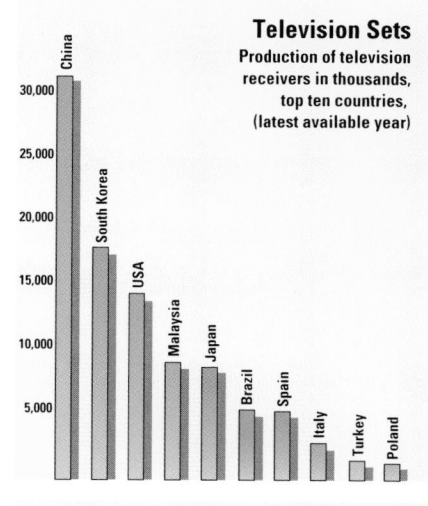

Television Sets
Production of television receivers in thousands, top ten countries, (latest available year)

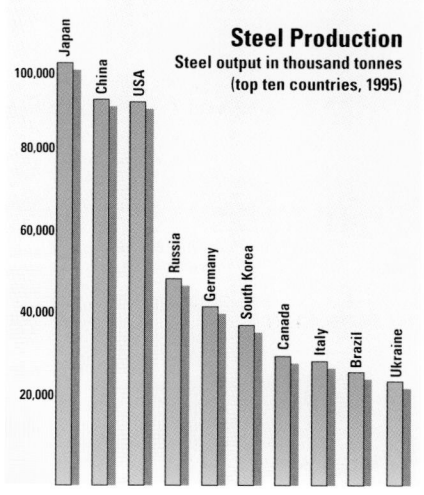

Steel Production
Steel output in thousand tonnes (top ten countries, 1995)

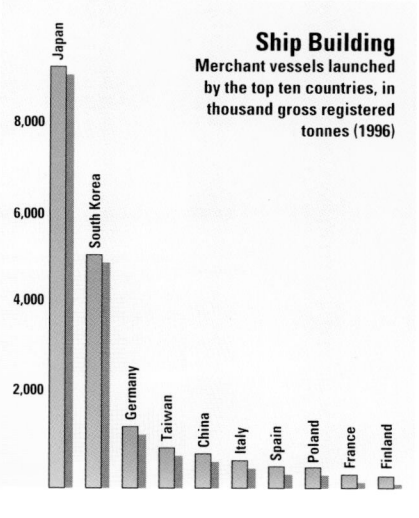

Ship Building
Merchant vessels launched by the top ten countries, in thousand gross registered tonnes (1996)

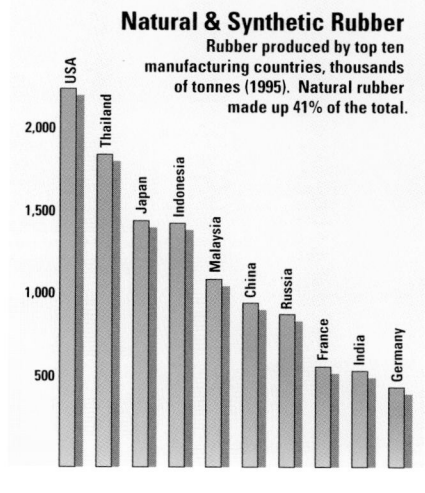

Natural & Synthetic Rubber
Rubber produced by top ten manufacturing countries, thousands of tonnes (1995). Natural rubber made up 41% of the total.

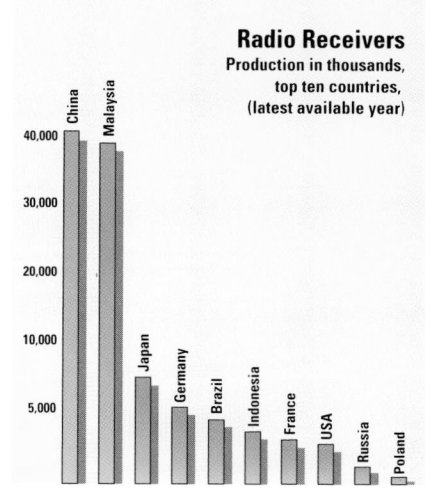

Radio Receivers
Production in thousands, top ten countries, (latest available year)

Industrial Output

Industrial output (mining, manufacturing, construction, energy and water production), US $ billion (1995)

		US $ bn				US $ bn
1.	Japan	1,941	21.	Sweden		73
2.	USA	1,808	22.	Saudi Arabia		67
3.	Germany	780	=	Thailand		67
4.	France	415	24.	Mexico		65
5.	UK	354	25.	Turkey		51
6.	Italy	337	26.	Denmark		50
7.	China	335	27.	Finland		46
8.	Brazil	255	=	Poland		46
9.	South Korea	196	29.	Norway		44
10.	Spain	187	30.	Malaysia		37
11.	Canada	174	=	Portugal		37
12.	Russia	131	32.	Ukraine		34
13.	Netherlands	107	33.	Greece		33
14.	Australia	98	34.	Singapore		30
15.	Switzerland	96	35.	Venezuela		29
16.	India	94	=	Israel		29
17.	Argentina	87	37.	Chile		24
18.	Belgium	83	=	Colombia		24
=	Indonesia	83	=	Hong Kong		24
20.	Austria	79	=	Philippines		24

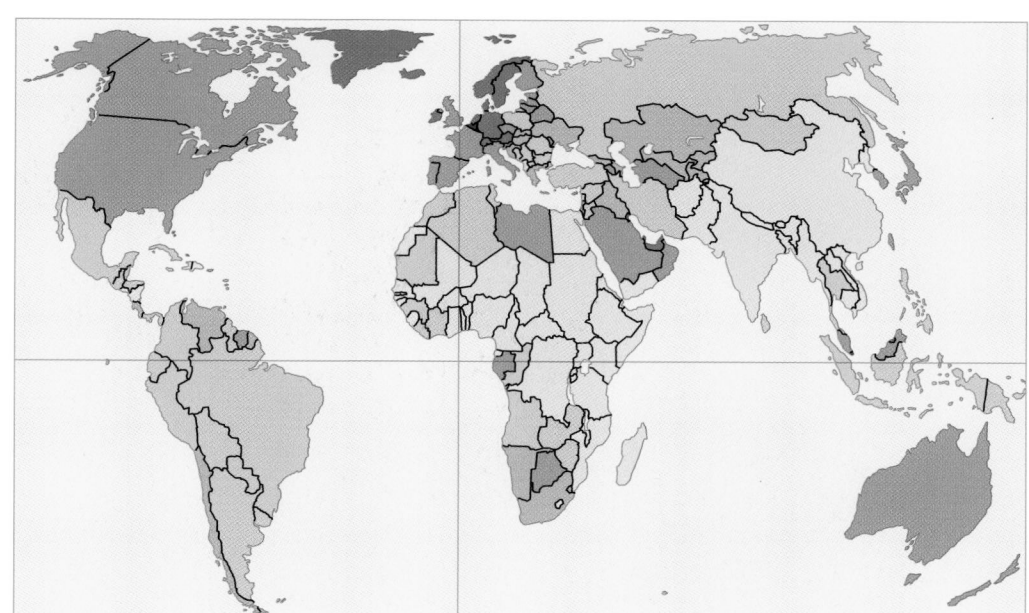

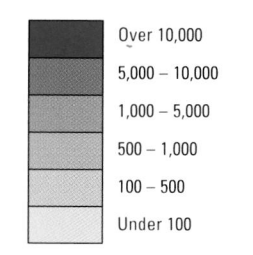

Exports Per Capita

Value of exports in US $, divided by total population (latest available year)

- Over 10,000
- 5,000 – 10,000
- 1,000 – 5,000
- 500 – 1,000
- 100 – 500
- Under 100

[UK 3,135] [USA 1,967]

Highest per capita exports (1993)

Singapore	25,787
Hong Kong	22,339
Benelux	12,295
Brunei	8,778
Netherlands	8,578
Switzerland	8,457

Trade

Trade played a vital role in the growth of early civilizations and it was later a spur to European exploration and colonization. The colonial powers grew rich by exporting cheap manufactures, such as clothing and footwear, while obtaining primary products from their colonies.

From the late 19th century to the early 1950s, as transport technology improved, primary products, especially oil in the later stages of this period, dominated world trade.

However, since that time, manufactures have become the chief commodities in world trade, which is dominated by the industrialized countries. Nearly half of all world trade flows between the developed market economies of the European Union, the United States and Japan, although the Asian 'tiger economies', notably Singapore, South Korea, Taiwan, Malaysia and Thailand, have increased their share in recent years. Recent predictions suggest that the next

'tigers' might include Argentina and Chile in South America, Indonesia, the Philippines and Vietnam in Asia, and the Czech Republic and Poland in Europe.

There is little trade between developing countries, although some mineral- and oil-rich nations obtain a high proportion of their GNP from export sales. Growth in world trade is regarded as a sign of economic health, as is a favourable balance of trade (or trade surplus) in any country.

World Trade

Percentage share of total world exports by value (1996)

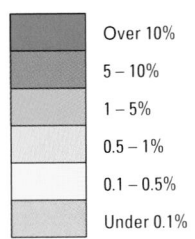

- Over 10%
- 5 – 10%
- 1 – 5%
- 0.5 – 1%
- 0.1 – 0.5%
- Under 0.1%

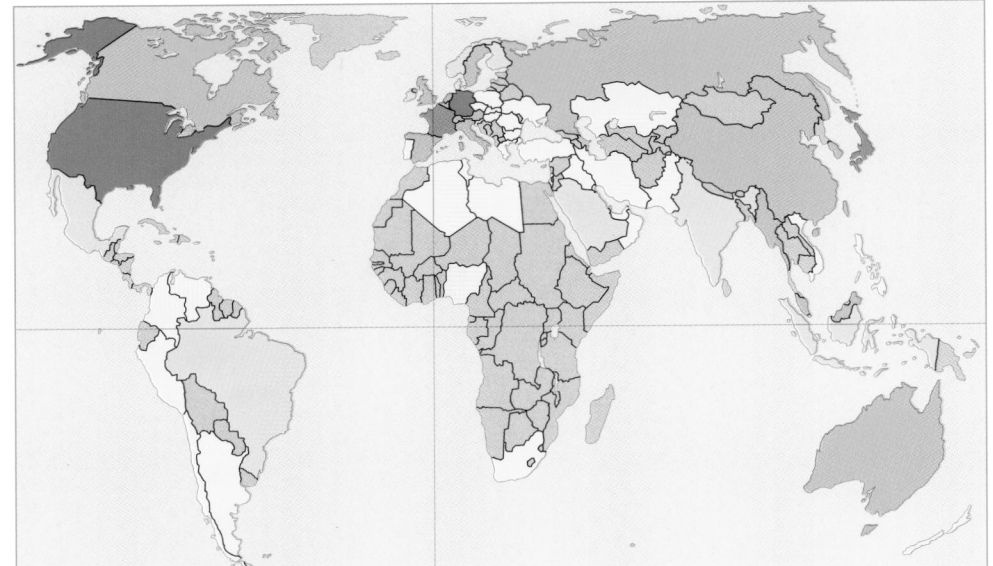

The Main Trading Nations

The imports and exports of the top ten trading nations as a percentage of world trade (1994). Each country's trade in manufactured goods is shown in dark blue. The graph shows that, in 1994, virtually all of Japan's imports and exports were manufactured goods.

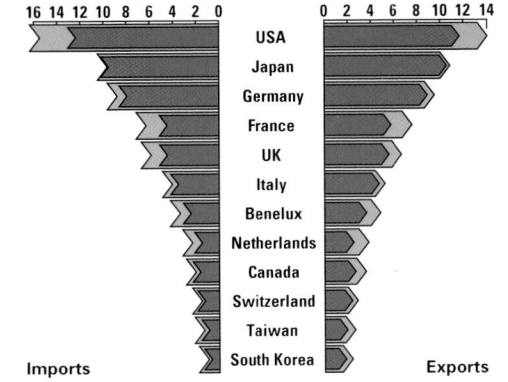

16 14 12 10 8 6 4 2 0   0 2 4 6 8 10 12 14

USA
Japan
Germany
France
UK
Italy
Benelux
Netherlands
Canada
Switzerland
Taiwan
South Korea

Imports   Exports

Dependence on Trade

Value of exports as a percentage of Gross Domestic Product (1997)

- Over 50% GDP from exports
- 40 – 50% GDP from exports
- 30 – 40% GDP from exports
- 20 – 30% GDP from exports
- 10 – 20% GDP from exports
- Under 10% GDP from exports

○ Most dependent on industrial exports (over 75% of total exports)
● Most dependent on fuel exports (over 75% of total exports)
◉ Most dependent on metal and mineral exports (over 75% of total exports)

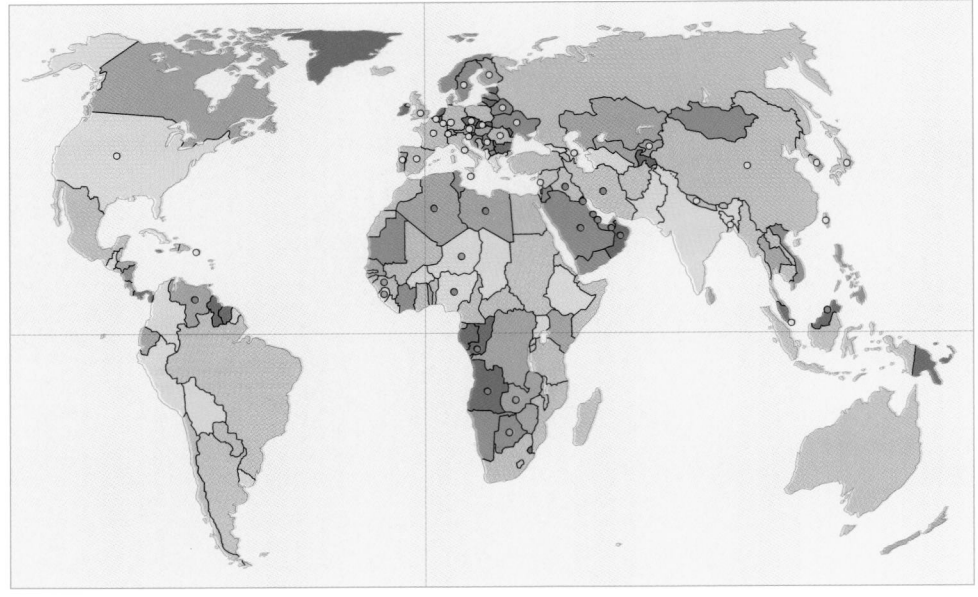

Major Exports

Leading manufactured items and their exporters, by percentage of world total in US $ (latest available year)

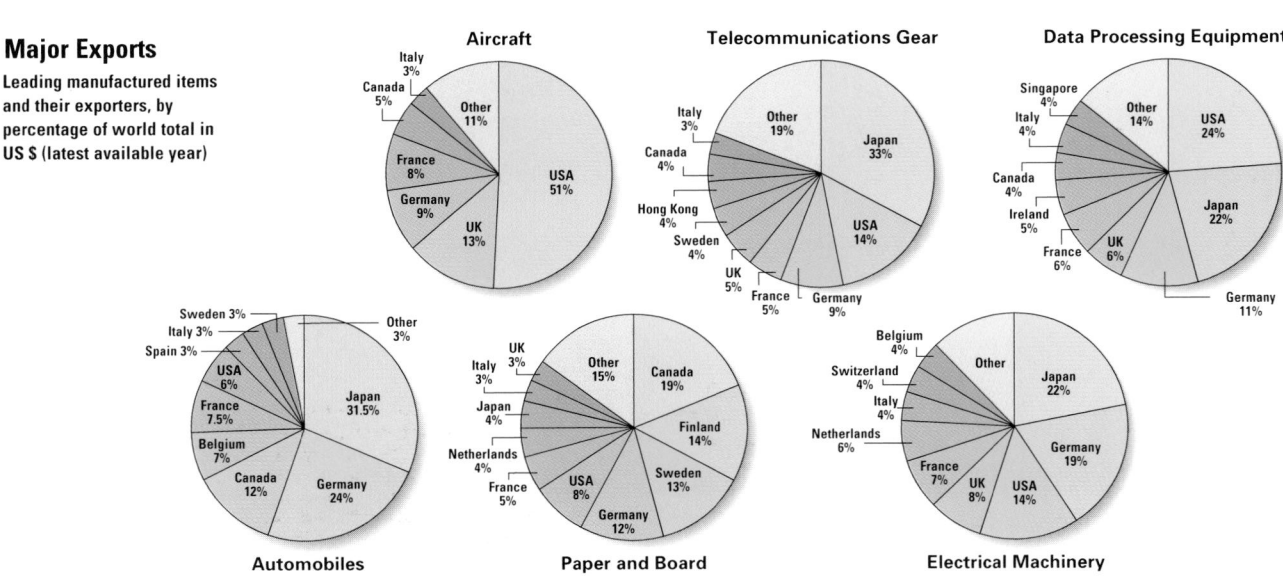

Aircraft
Italy 3%, Canada 5%, France 8%, Germany 9%, UK 13%, USA 51%, Other 11%

Telecommunications Gear
Italy 3%, Canada 4%, Hong Kong 4%, Sweden 4%, UK 5%, France 5%, Germany 9%, USA 14%, Japan 33%, Other 19%

Data Processing Equipment
Singapore 4%, Italy 4%, Canada 4%, Ireland 5%, France 6%, UK 6%, Germany 11%, Japan 22%, USA 24%, Other 14%

Automobiles
Sweden 3%, Italy 3%, Spain 3%, USA 6%, France 7.5%, Belgium 7%, Canada 12%, Germany 24%, Japan 31.5%, Other 3%

Paper and Board
UK 3%, Italy 3%, Japan 4%, Netherlands 4%, France 5%, USA 8%, Germany 12%, Sweden 13%, Finland 14%, Canada 19%, Other 15%

Electrical Machinery
Belgium 4%, Switzerland 4%, Italy 4%, Netherlands 6%, France 7%, UK 8%, USA 14%, Germany 19%, Japan 22%, Other

Traded Products

Top ten manufactures traded, by value in billions of US $ (latest available year)

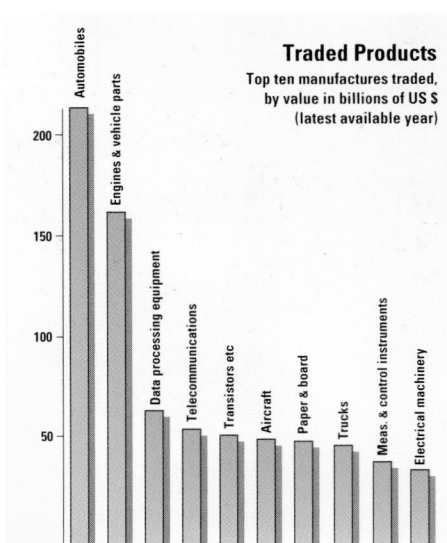

Automobiles
Engines & vehicle parts
Data processing equipment
Telecommunications
Transistors etc
Aircraft
Paper & board
Trucks
Meas. & control instruments
Electrical machinery

World Shipping

While ocean passenger traffic is nowadays relatively modest, sea transport still carries most of the world's trade. Oil and bulk carriers make up the majority of the world fleet, although the general cargo category is the fastest growing. Two innovations have revolutionized sea transport. The first is the development of the roll-on/roll-off (Ro-Ro) method where lorries or even trains loaded with freight are driven straight on to the ship, thus saving time. The second is containerization in which goods are packed into containers (the dimensions of which are fixed) at the factory, driven to the port and loaded on board by specialist machinery.

Almost 30% of world shipping sails under a 'flag of convenience', whereby owners take advantage of low taxes by registering their vessels in a foreign country the ships will never see, notably Panama and Liberia.

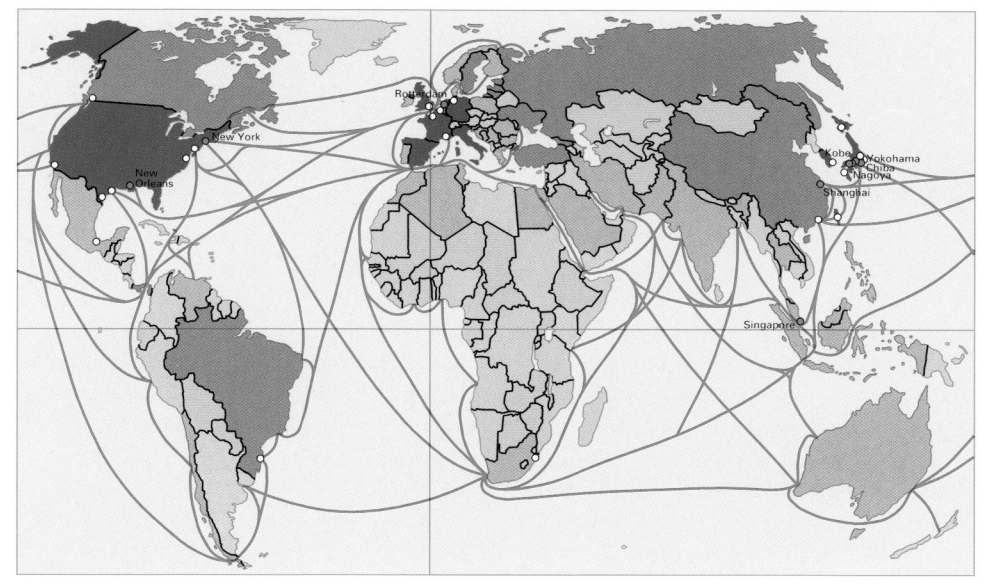

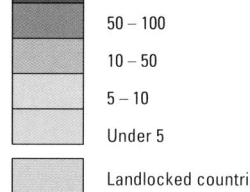

Freight

Freight unloaded in millions of tonnes (latest available year)

- Over 100
- 50 – 100
- 10 – 50
- 5 – 10
- Under 5
- Landlocked countries

Major seaports

- ● Over 100 million tonnes per year
- ○ 50 – 100 million tonnes per year
- ━━ major shipping routes

Merchant Fleets

Merchant fleets in thousand gross tonnage (1996). A large number of vessels are registered in Liberia and Panama but they are not part of the national fleet.

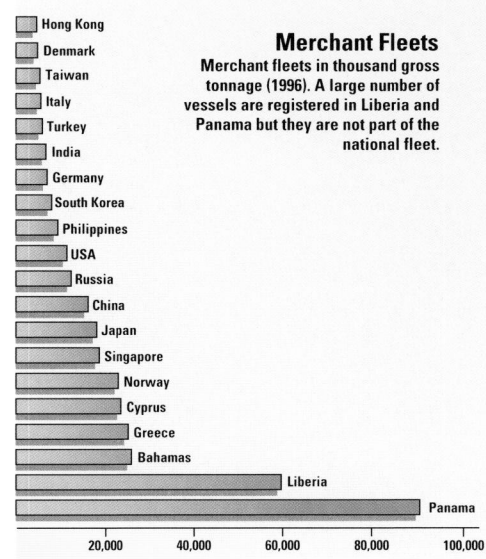

Hong Kong, Denmark, Taiwan, Italy, Turkey, India, Germany, South Korea, Philippines, USA, Russia, China, Japan, Singapore, Norway, Cyprus, Greece, Bahamas, Liberia, Panama

20,000 40,000 60,000 80,000 100,000

Types of Vessels

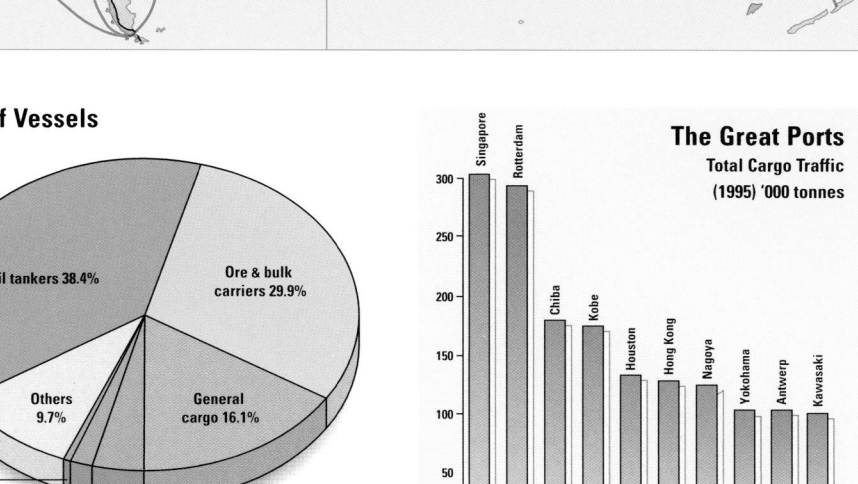

Oil tankers 38.4%
Ore & bulk carriers 29.9%
Others 9.7%
General cargo 16.1%
Ferries & passenger ships 0.5%
Liquid gas carriers 1.6%
Container ships 3.8%

The Great Ports

Total Cargo Traffic (1995) '000 tonnes

Singapore, Rotterdam, Chiba, Kobe, Houston, Hong Kong, Nagoya, Yokohama, Antwerp, Kawasaki

---

Trade in Primary Products

Primary products (excluding fuels, minerals and metals) as a percentage of total export value (latest available year)

- Over 75%
- 50 – 75%
- 25 – 50%
- 10 – 25%
- Under 10%

Primary products are raw materials or partly processed products which form the basis for manufacturing. They are the necessary requirements of industries and include agricultural products, minerals and timber, as well as semi-manufactured goods such as cotton, which has been spun but not woven, wood pulp or flour. Many developed countries have few natural resources and rely on imports for the majority of their primary products. The countries of South-east Asia export hardwoods to the rest of the world, whilst many South American countries are heavily dependent on coffee exports.

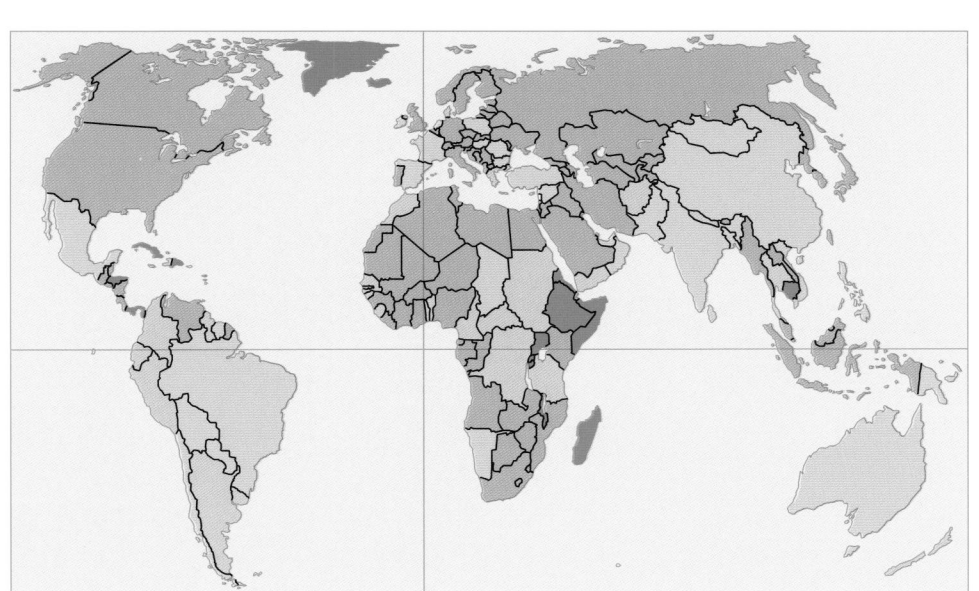

Air Freight

Trends in air freight in million tonne-km*, selected countries (1988–92)

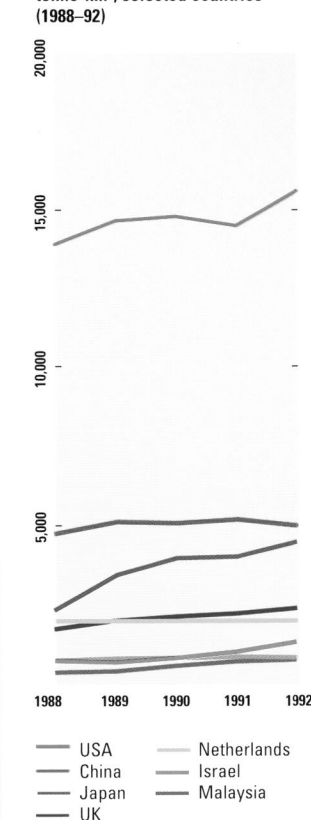

20,000
15,000
10,000
5,000

1988 1989 1990 1991 1992

- ━━ USA
- ━━ China
- ━━ Japan
- ━━ UK
- ━━ Netherlands
- ━━ Israel
- ━━ Malaysia

* Equivalent to million tonnes of air freight flown over 1 million kilometres per year.

Air transport is important to countries of considerable size; where ground terrain is difficult; when crossing short stretches of sea; and where goods are of high value, light in weight or perishable. Recent deregulation of airlines (in the USA since 1978 and the EU in 1993) has led to increased competition and lower fares.

Balance of Trade

Value of exports in proportion to the value of imports (1995)

- More than 40% ⬆ Exports exceed imports by:
- 10 – 40%
- 10% either side
- 10 – 40%
- More than 40% ⬇ Imports exceed exports by:

The total world trade balance should amount to zero, since exports must equal imports on a global scale. In practice, at least $100 billion in exports go unrecorded, leaving the world with an apparent deficit and many countries in a better position than public accounting reveals. However, a favourable trade balance is not necessarily a sign of prosperity: many poorer countries must maintain a high surplus in order to service debts, and do so by restricting imports below the levels needed to sustain successful economies.

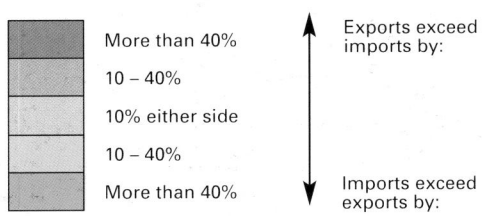

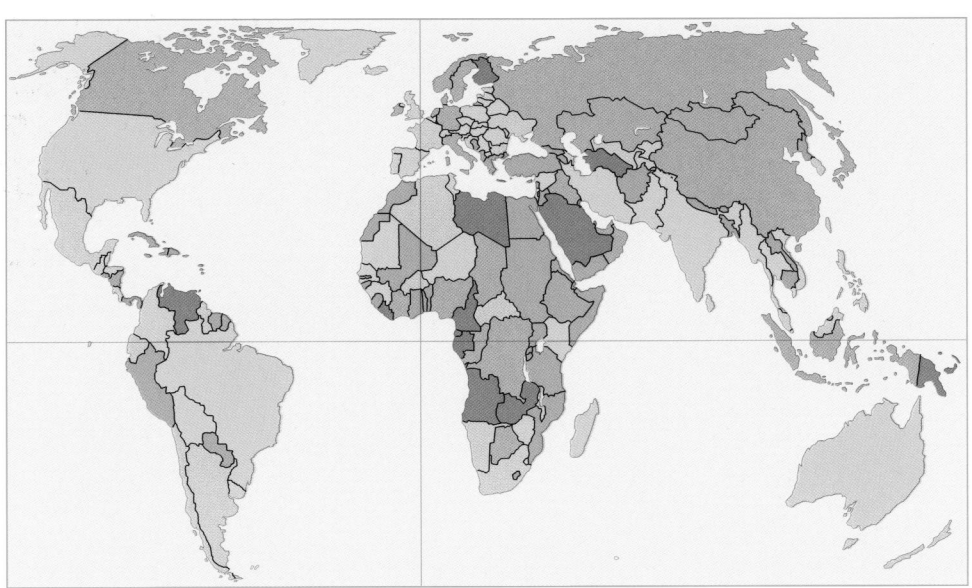

CARTOGRAPHY BY PHILIP'S. COPYRIGHT GEORGE PHILIP LTD

Health

Average life expectancies all over the world have never been higher. They range from an average of 77 years in high-income economies, to 67 years in middle-income economies and 63 in low-income economies. Even in poverty-stricken and strife-torn Burundi and Ethiopia, average life expectancies are around 50 years, as compared with less than 30 years for a citizen of Berlin in 1880.

In global terms, the radical improvements in health have much to do with improvements in agriculture and, hence, nutrition, as well as health education, an increase in sanitation and the quality of drinking water, together with advances in medicine. These radical changes have been responsible for falling death rates and rapid population growth, together with the expectation by most people that improvements in health will continue.

Health standards, life expectancies and causes of death vary greatly between the developed and developing world. The map below shows that in most of Africa, Asia and Latin America, the average daily calorie supply per person is so low as to cause malnutrition. (The daily requirement rated adequate by the World Health Organization is from 2,300 and 2,500 calories per person per day.) Malnutrition is a serious condition. For example, in pregnant women it causes high rates of child mortality.

Deficiency diseases occur when people do not have a balanced diet. Protein deficiency causes stunting and kwashiorkor, which can be fatal, especially among young children, while vitamin deficiencies cause such illnesses as beri beri, pellagra, scurvy and rickets. Iron deficiency causes anaemia, while a lack of iodine causes mental retardation. A UN report in the early 1990s reported that iodine deficiency affected 458 million women worldwide, as compared with 238 million men. Women's nutritional problems are especially acute in southern Asia. For example, the UN report stated that 88% of pregnant women in India were anaemic, as compared with 15% in developed countries.

Infectious diseases in association, directly or indirectly, with deficient diets, continue to affect people in developing countries, especially the 48 countries in the low human development category, where, in 1990–95, only 32% of the people had access to sanitation and 68% to safe water supplies.

A World Health report in 1996 stated that infectious diseases cause 17 million deaths per year. Most of the victims are young and otherwise fit people in developing countries. The major killers in 1995 were respiratory infections, including pneumonia (which caused 4.4 million deaths), cholera, typhoid, dysentery

(3.1 million together), tuberculosis (almost 3 million), malaria (2.1 million), hepatitis B (1.1 million), AIDS and measles (more than 1 million each). Many of these diseases are preventable and, according to the United Nations Children's Fund, an investment of US $25,000 million per year, about half the money spent annually on cigarettes in Europe alone, would save the lives of all the children who currently die from avoidable diseases.

Infectious diseases are much less important as causes of death in developed countries, where cancer and circulatory diseases, such as atherosclerosis and hypertension, which cause strokes and heart attacks, are the most common causes of fatality. Because these diseases tend to kill older people, they are relatively less important in developing countries where people have shorter lifespans.

Harmful habits are also generally practised more by the rich than the poor. For example, smoking is an important cause of death in developed countries, though, curiously, the Japanese, with an average life expectancy of 79 years in 1996, are among the highest tobacco consumers. Similarly, high alcohol consumption, although it has bad effects on health, does not seem to affect longevity. The leading consumers, the French, had a life expectancy of 78 in 1996.

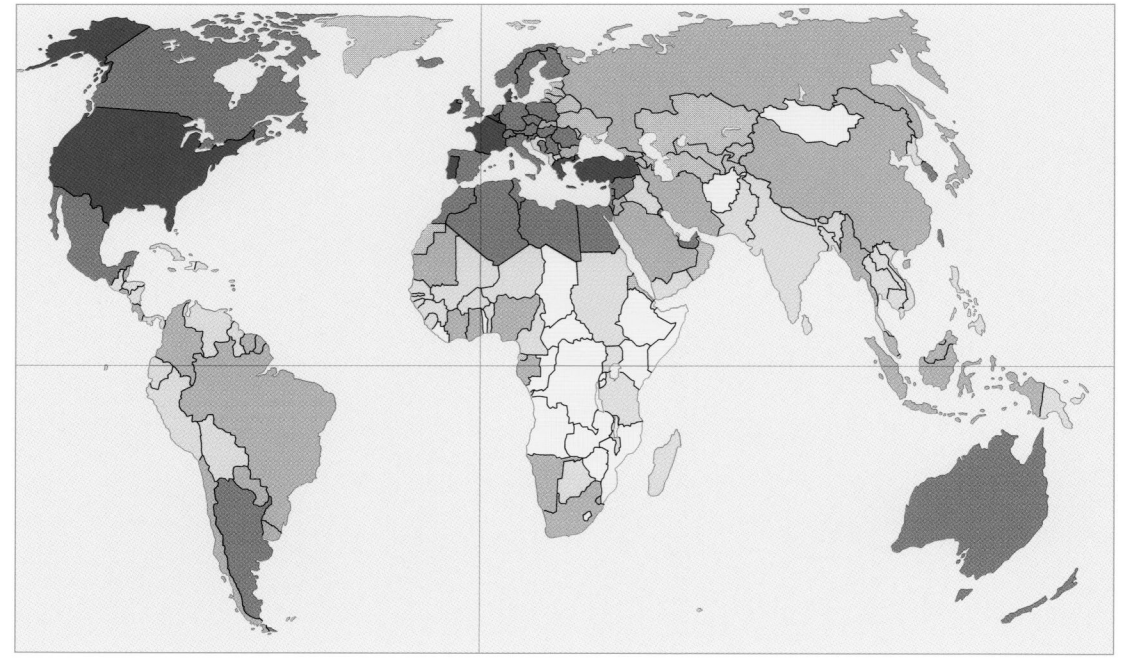

Food Consumption

Average daily food intake in calories per person (1995)

- Over 3,500 calories
- 3,000 – 3,500 calories
- 2,500 – 3,000 calories
- 2,000 – 2,500 calories
- Under 2,000 calories
- No available data

Top 5 countries

Cyprus . . . . 3,708 calories
Denmark . . . . 3,704 calories
Portugal . . . . 3,639 calories
Ireland . . . . 3,638 calories
USA . . . . 3,603 calories

Bottom 5 countries

Congo (D. Rep.) . . . . 1,879 calories
Djibouti . . . . 1,831 calories
Togo . . . . 1,754 calories
Burundi . . . . 1,749 calories
Mozambique . . . . 1,678 calories

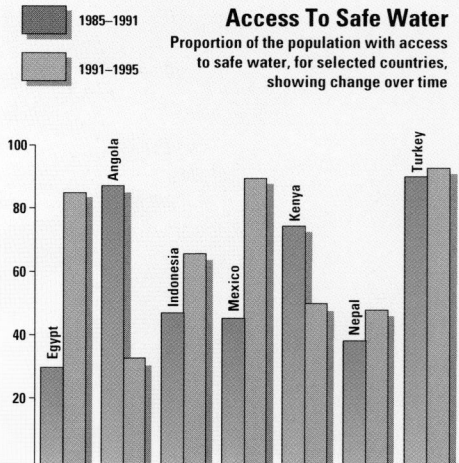

Access To Safe Water

1985–1991
1991–1995

Proportion of the population with access to safe water, for selected countries, showing change over time

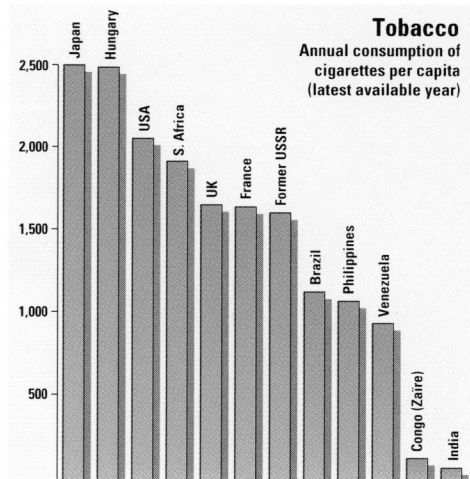

Tobacco

Annual consumption of cigarettes per capita (latest available year)

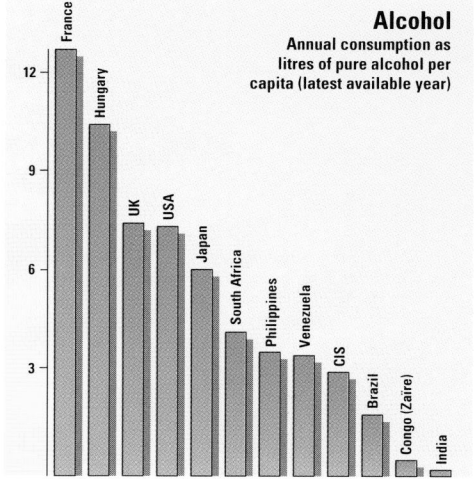

Alcohol

Annual consumption as litres of pure alcohol per capita (latest available year)

Life Expectancy

Years of life expectancy at birth, selected countries (1997)

The chart shows combined data for both sexes. On average, women live longer than men worldwide, even in developing countries with high maternal mortality rates. Overall, life expectancy is steadily rising, though the difference between rich and poor nations remains dramatic.

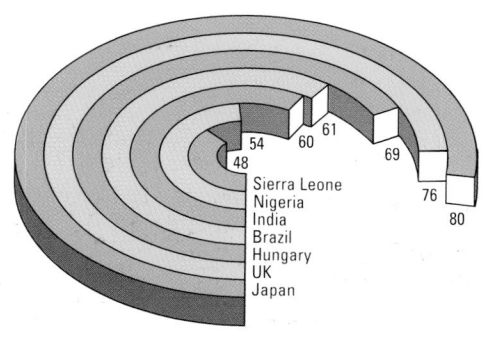

48 Sierra Leone
54 Nigeria
60 India
61 Brazil
69 Hungary
76 UK
80 Japan

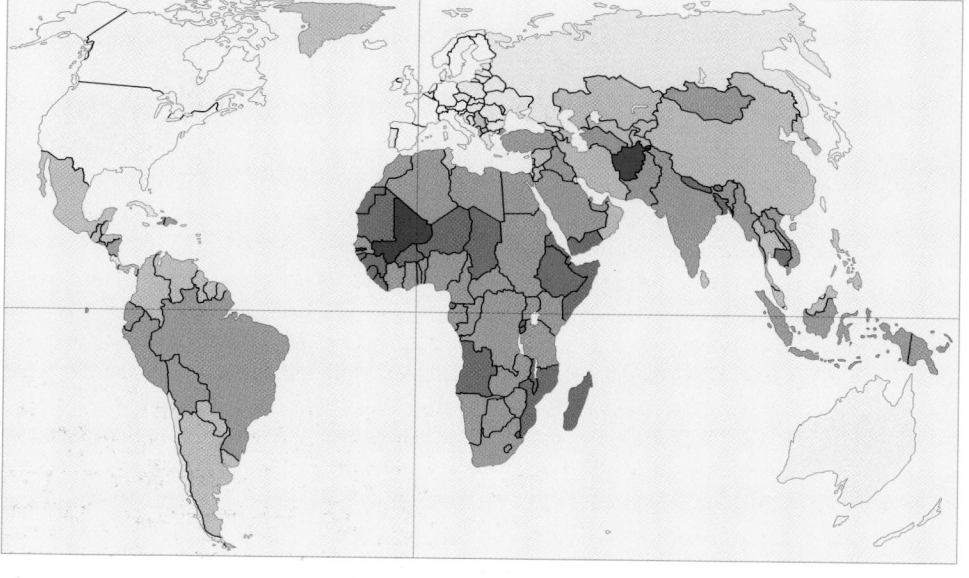

Child Mortality

Number of babies who will die under the age of one, per 1,000 births (average 1990–95)

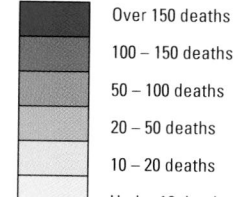

Over 150 deaths
100 – 150 deaths
50 – 100 deaths
20 – 50 deaths
10 – 20 deaths
Under 10 deaths

Highest child mortality

Afghanistan	162 deaths
Mali	159 deaths

Lowest child mortality

Iceland	5 deaths
Finland	5 deaths

[UK 8 deaths] [USA 8 deaths]

Expenditure on Health

Public expenditure on health as a percentage of GDP (1996)

Countries with the highest spending		Countries with the lowest spending	
USA	14.2	Sudan	0.3
Argentina	10.6	Cameroon	1.4
Germany	10.4	Ghana	1.4
Croatia	10.1	Nigeria	1.4
Switzerland	10.0	Indonesia	1.8
France	9.9	Sri Lanka	1.9
Canada	9.6	Eritrea	2.0
Czech Rep.	9.6	Bangladesh	2.4
Australia	8.9	Kenya	2.5

The allocation of limited funds for health care in developing countries is rarely evenly spread – the quality of treatment can vary enormously from place to place within the same country. Urban dwellers tend to have much better access to health provisions than those living in rural areas.

Medical Provision

Doctors per 100,000 population, selected countries (latest available year, 1996)

Although the ratio of people to doctors gives a good approximation of a country's health provision, it is not an absolute indicator. Raw numbers may mask inefficiency and other weaknesses: the high proportion of physicians in Hungary, for example, has not prevented infant mortality rates more than twice as high as in the United Kingdom.

The definition of a doctor also varies from nation to nation. As well as registered medical practitioners, it may include trained medical assistants – an especially important category in developing countries, where they provide many of the same services as fully qualified physicians, including simple operations.

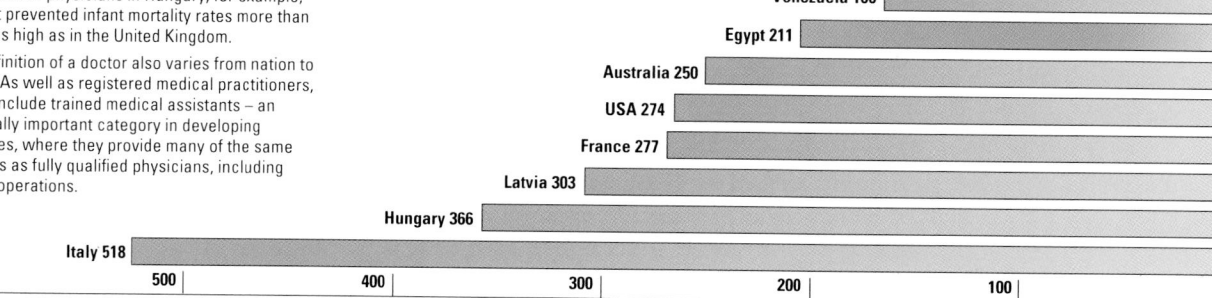

Ghana 4
Indonesia 15
Brazil 147
UK 156
Venezuela 160
Egypt 211
Australia 250
USA 274
France 277
Latvia 303
Hungary 366
Italy 518

500 400 300 200 100

The Aids Crisis

The Acquired Immune Deficiency Syndrome (AIDS) was first identified in 1981 when American doctors found otherwise healthy young men succumbing to rare infections. By 1984 the cause had been traced to the Human Immunodeficiency Virus (HIV) which can remain dormant for many years and perhaps indefinitely: only half of those known to carry the virus in 1981 had developed AIDS ten years later.

In Western countries in the mid-1990s, most AIDS deaths were among male homosexuals or needle-sharing drug-users. However, the disease is spreading fastest among heterosexual men and women, which is its usual vector in the developing world where most of its victims live.

The World Health Organization estimated that 1.3 million people died of AIDS in 1995 and that by the end of the same year 22 million people were HIV-positive. India has the largest number of HIV infections totalling more than 3 million, but two-thirds of all infections are in sub-Saharan Africa (where, unlike the rest of the world, more women are infected than men). It was estimated that two million African children would die of AIDS by the year 2000, and some 10 million would be orphaned.

Causes of Death

Accidents, poisoning & violence
Respiratory & digestive diseases
Nervous & circulatory diseases
Metabolic disorders
Cancers
Infectious & parasitic diseases

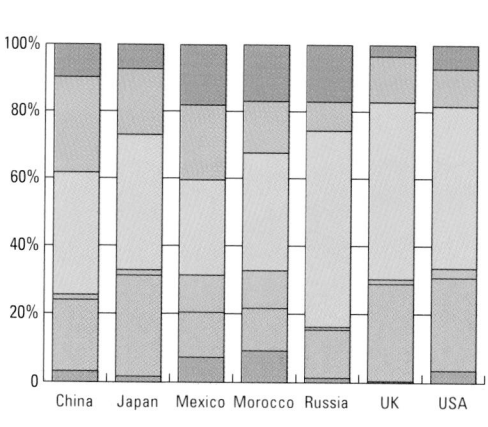

China   Japan   Mexico   Morocco   Russia   UK   USA

Circulatory Disease in Europe

Diseases of the circulatory system per 100,000 people (latest available year 1992–95)

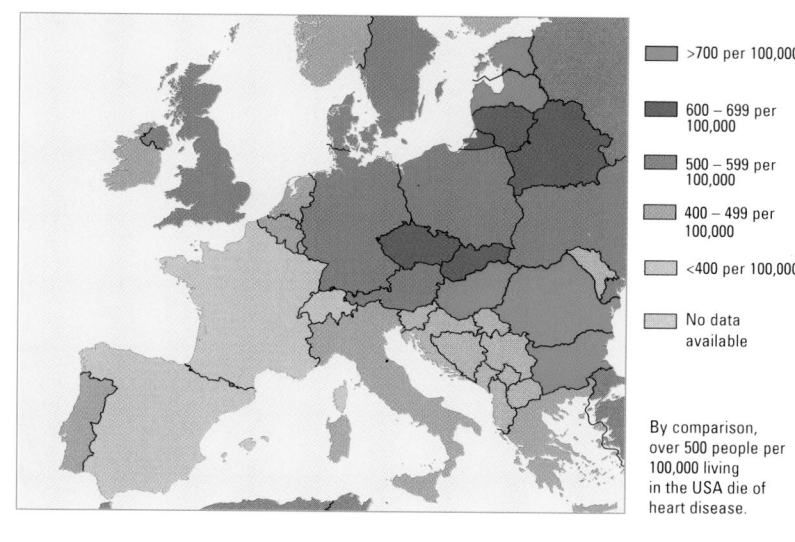

>700 per 100,000
600 – 699 per 100,000
500 – 599 per 100,000
400 – 499 per 100,000
<400 per 100,000
No data available

By comparison, over 500 people per 100,000 living in the USA die of heart disease.

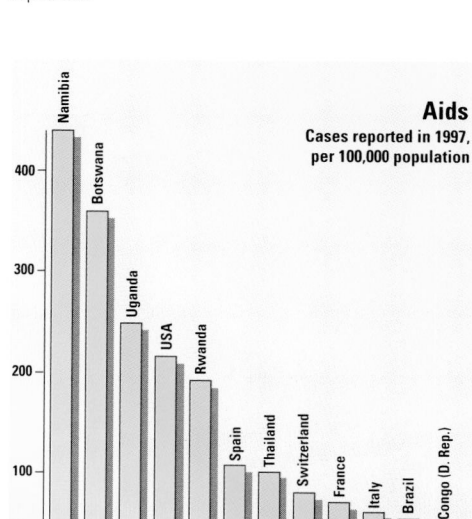

Aids
Cases reported in 1997, per 100,000 population

Namibia
Botswana
Uganda
USA
Rwanda
Spain
Thailand
Switzerland
France
Italy
Brazil
Congo (D. Rep.)

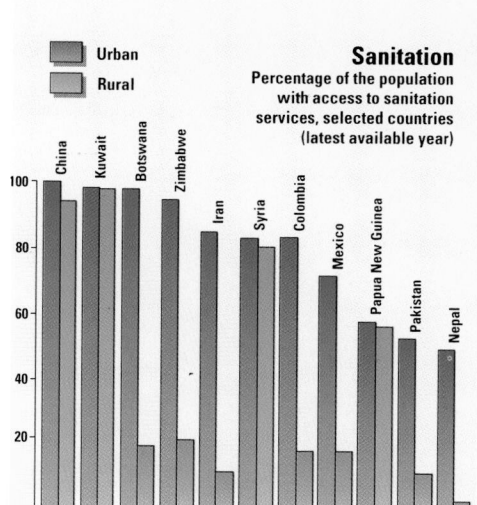

Sanitation

Urban
Rural

Percentage of the population with access to sanitation services, selected countries (latest available year)

China
Kuwait
Botswana
Zimbabwe
Iran
Syria
Colombia
Mexico
Papua New Guinea
Pakistan
Nepal

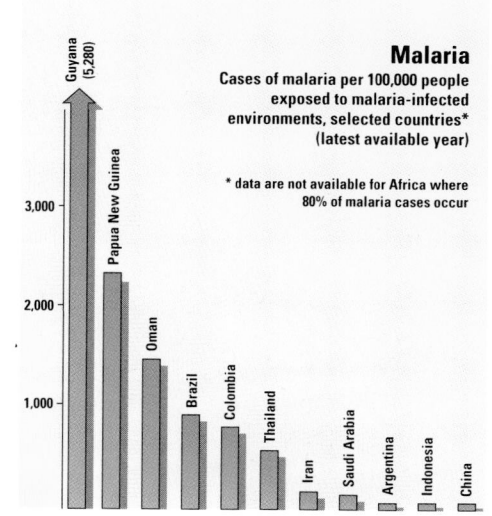

Malaria
Cases of malaria per 100,000 people exposed to malaria-infected environments, selected countries* (latest available year)

* data are not available for Africa where 80% of malaria cases occur

Guyana (5,280)
Papua New Guinea
Oman
Brazil
Colombia
Thailand
Iran
Saudi Arabia
Argentina
Indonesia
China

Infectious and parasitic diseases, such as malaria, which claimed 2.1 million lives in 1995, remain a scourge in the developing countries. Respiratory infections and injury also claim more lives in developing countries, which lack the drugs and the medical personnel to deal with them. Developing countries lack the basic services taken for granted in developed nations.

For example, in sub-Saharan Africa in 1990–95, only 31% of the population had access to sanitation and 45% to safe water, with the situation being worse in rural areas. By contrast, circulatory diseases and cancer are the main causes of death in the rich, industrialized countries.

For example, in the UK in the mid-1990s, circulatory diseases, which cause heart attacks and strokes, accounted for nearly half the deaths, with cancer accounting for nearly a quarter.

Wealth

Currencies

Currency units of the world's most powerful economies

1. USA: US dollar ($, US $)
   = 100 cents
2. Japan: Yen (Y, ¥)
   = 100 sen
3. Germany: Euro; Deutsche Mark
   (DM)= 100 Pfennig
4. France: Euro; French franc (Fr)
   = 100 centimes
5. Italy: Euro; Italian lira (L, £, Lit)
   = 100 centesimi
6. UK: Pound sterling (£)
   = 100 pence
7. Canada: Canadian dollar
   (C$, Can$) = 100 cents
8. China: Renminbi yuan
   (RMBY, $, Y) = 10 jiao = 100 fen
9. Brazil: Cruzeiro real (BRC)
   = 100 centavos
10. Spain: Euro; Peseta (Pta, Pa)
    = 100 céntimos
11. India: Indian rupee (Re, Rs)
    = 100 paisa
12. Australia: Australian dollar
    ($A) = 100 cents
13. Netherlands: Euro; Guilder,
    florin (Gld, f) = 100 centimes
14. Switzerland: Swiss franc
    (SFr, SwF) = 100 centimes
15. South Korea: Won (W)
    = 100 chon
16. Sweden: Swedish krona (SKr)
    = 100 ore
17. Mexico: Mexican peso
    (Mex$) = 100 centavos
18. Belgium: Euro; Belgian franc
    (BFr) = 100 centimes
19. Austria: Euro; Schilling (S, Sch)
    = 100 Groschen
20. Finland: Euro; Markka (FMk)
    = 100 penniä
21. Denmark: Danish krone (DKr)
    = 100 øre
22. Norway: Norwegian krone
    (NKr) = 100 øre
23. Saudi Arabia: Riyal (SAR, SRl$)
    = 100 halalah
24. Indonesia: Rupiah (Rp)
    = 100 sen
25. South Africa: Rand (R)
    = 100 cents

Perhaps the most glaring differences in the world today are those between the rich and the poor. The World Bank divides countries into three main groups based on average economic production expressed in terms of per capita GNP (Gross National Product). They are the low-income economies, including most African countries and much of Asia; the middle-income economies, including most of Latin America and the former USSR; and the high-income economies of Canada, the United States, Western Europe, Japan and Australia.

Per capita GNPs are a measure of the total goods and services produced by a country divided by the population, and converted into US dollars at official exchange rates. They are useful indicators of a country's prosperity, but, like all statistics, must be treated with care. For example, prices for goods and services in China are far cheaper than in the United States. China's per capita GNP in 1998 was $750 (as compared with $29,340 in the USA) but the PPP (Purchasing-Power Parity) estimate of China's per capita GNP was considerably higher at $3,570. Another problem with per capita GNPs is that they are averages, which often conceal wide internal variations.

The pattern of poverty varies from region to region. In Latin America, much progress has been made through industrialization, though startling inequalities still exist between rich and poor. In Asia, the 'tiger economies' have followed Japan's example in pursuing export-led industrial policies, while the success of China's Special Economic Zones, where foreign investment is encouraged, has led to a huge rise in China's per capita GNP, as shown on the map on page 45, bottom right.

Solutions to poverty in Africa are much harder to find because of its high population growth, civil wars, natural disasters and high inflation rates. Although Africa receives more aid than any other continent, aid is only a partial solution. Much aid has been wasted on overambitious projects, in the servicing of huge national debts, or lost by inexperienced or corrupt governments. One initiative in some African countries has been to improve the infrastructure and develop tourism, creating employment and providing much-needed foreign currency. But tourism alone cannot solve the problems of under-development.

The International Monetary Fund and the World Bank argue that real economic progress in Africa will be achieved only when African countries create market-friendly economies that encourage trade through export-led manufacturing, while at the same time strictly controlling public spending on welfare, the civil service and other areas.

Continental Shares

Shares of population and of wealth (GNP) by continent

These generalized continental figures show the startling difference between rich and poor but mask the successes or failures of individual countries. Japan, for example, with less than 4% of Asia's population, produces almost 70% of the continent's output. Within countries, the difference between rich and poor can also be startling. In Brazil, for example, the richest 20% of the population own 60% of the wealth.

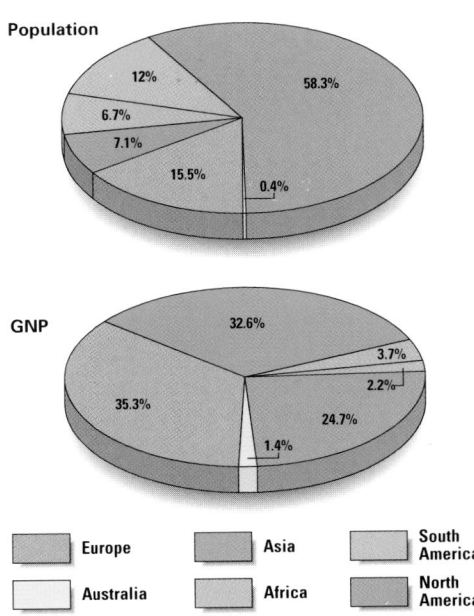

Population

GNP

| Europe | Asia | South America |
| Australia | Africa | North America |

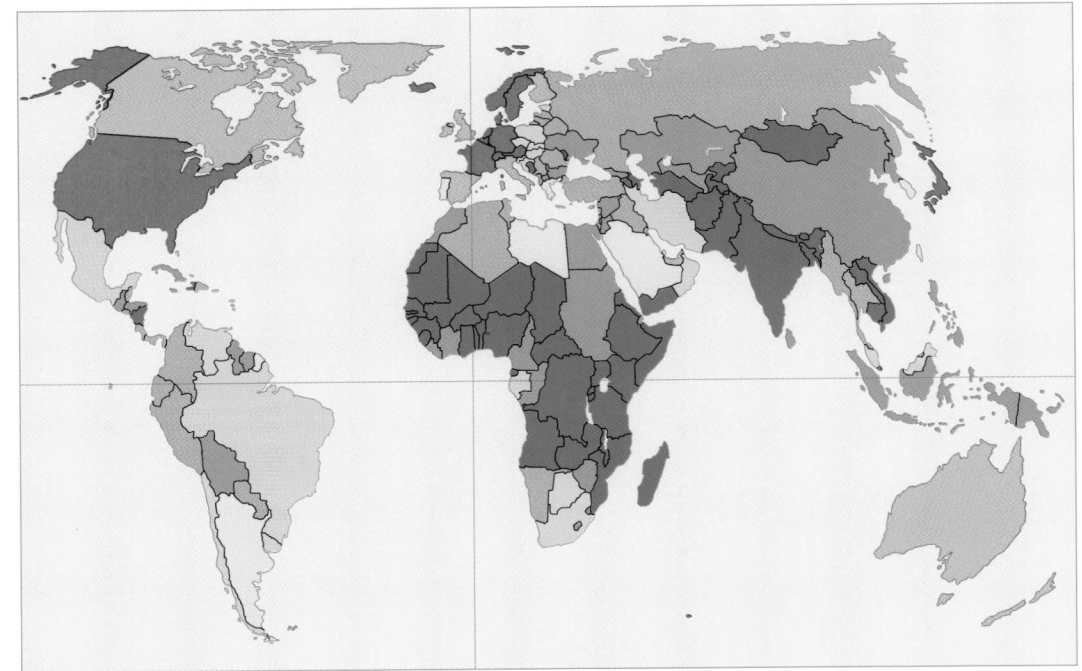

Levels of Income

Gross National Product per capita: the value of total production divided by the population (1997)

- Over 400% of world average
- 200 – 400%
- 100 – 200%
- 50 – 100%
- 25 – 50%
- 10 – 25%
- Under 10%

Top 5 countries

Luxembourg	$45,360
Switzerland	$44,220
Japan	$37,850
Norway	$36,090
Liechtenstein	$33,000

Bottom 5 countries

Mozambique	$90
Ethiopia	$110
Congo (Dem. Rep.)	$110
Burundi	$180
Sierra Leone	$200

The gap between the world's rich and poor is now so great that it is difficult to illustrate on a single graph. Within each income group (as defined by the World Bank), however, comparisons have some meaning; the Chinese, perhaps because of propaganda value, have more TV sets than Indians, whereas Nigerians prefer to spend their money on radios. However, the wealth gap in many developing countries is wide, with a small, rich class and a large, impoverished majority, while many high-income countries contain an underclass of unemployed and homeless people.

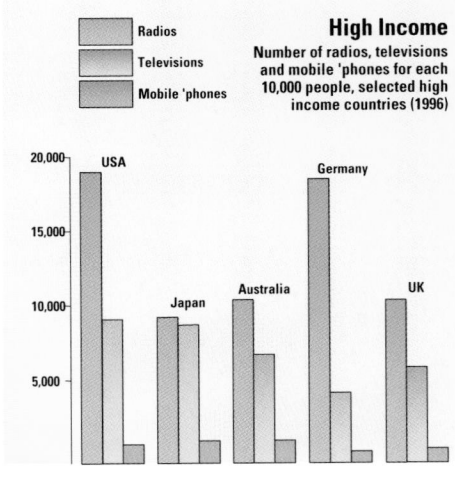

High Income
Radios
Televisions
Mobile 'phones
Number of radios, televisions and mobile 'phones for each 10,000 people, selected high income countries (1996)

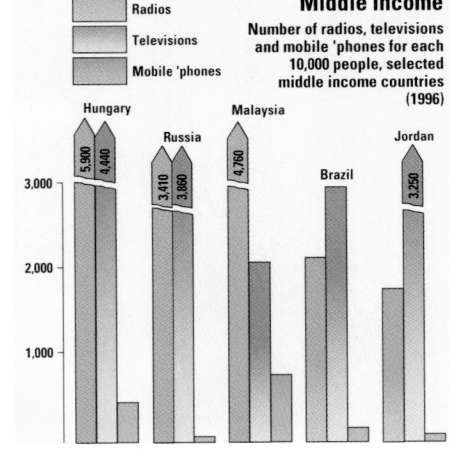

Middle Income
Radios
Televisions
Mobile 'phones
Number of radios, televisions and mobile 'phones for each 10,000 people, selected middle income countries (1996)

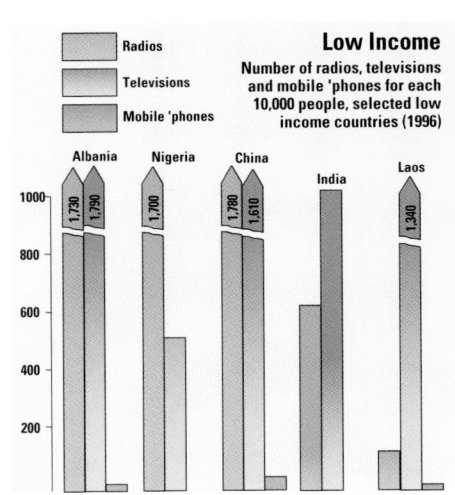

Low Income
Radios
Televisions
Mobile 'phones
Number of radios, televisions and mobile 'phones for each 10,000 people, selected low income countries (1996)

World Tourism

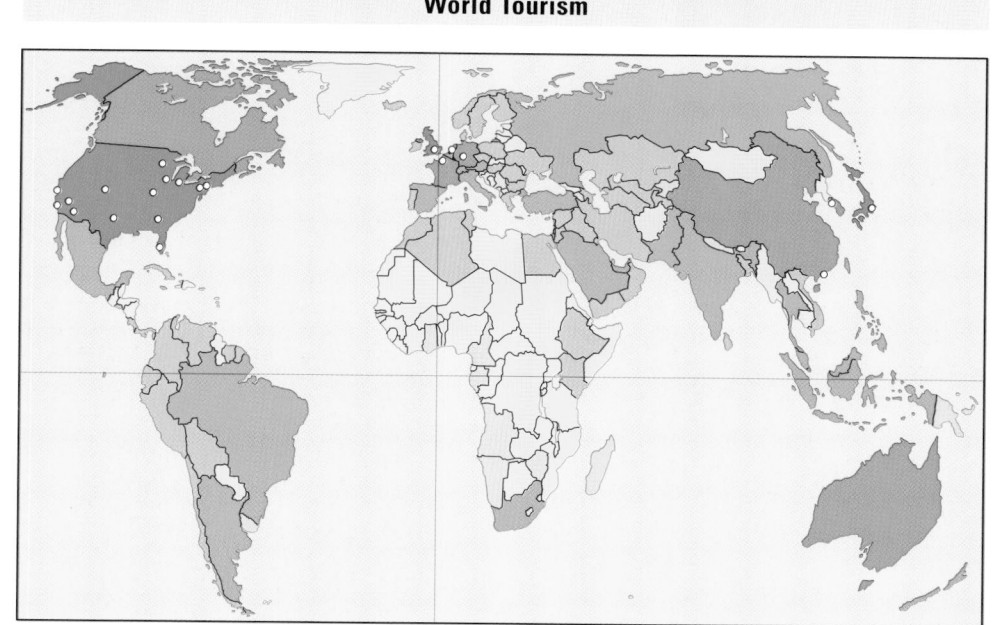

Passenger km flown (the number of passengers multiplied by the distance flown by each passenger from the airport of origin) (1997)

- Over 100,000 million
- 50,000 – 100,000 million
- 10,000 – 50,000 million
- 1,000 – 10,000 million
- 500 – 1,000 million
- Under 500 million
- ○ Major airports (handling over 25 million passengers in 2000)

Leisure and tourism is the world's second largest industry in terms of revenue generated. Small economies in attractive areas are often completely dominated by tourism: in some Caribbean islands, tourist spending provides over 90% of the total income and is the biggest foreign exchange earner. In cash terms the USA is the world leader: its 1999 earnings exceeded US $74 billion, though that sum amounted to approximately 0.9% of its total GDP. Of the 48 million visitors to the USA, 34% came from Canada and 25% from Mexico. Germany spends the most on overseas tourism; this amounts to over US $50,000 million. The next biggest spenders are the USA, Japan and the UK.

The world's busiest airport in terms of total number of passengers is Atlanta (78.1 million passengers in 1999); the busiest international airport is London's Heathrow Airport.

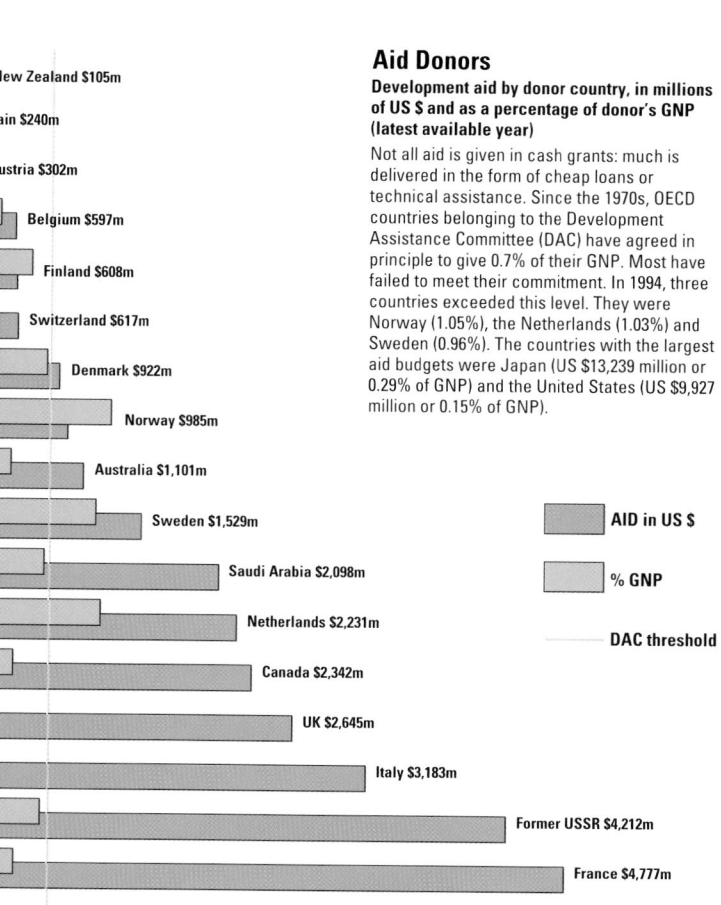

New Zealand $105m
Spain $240m
Austria $302m
Belgium $597m
Finland $608m
Switzerland $617m
Denmark $922m
Norway $985m
Australia $1,101m
Sweden $1,529m
Saudi Arabia $2,098m
Netherlands $2,231m
Canada $2,342m
UK $2,645m
Italy $3,183m
Former USSR $4,212m
France $4,777m
Germany $4,911m
USA $9,927m
Japan $13,239m

0.5%   1%   1.5%   2%   2.5%

Aid Donors

Development aid by donor country, in millions of US $ and as a percentage of donor's GNP (latest available year)

Not all aid is given in cash grants: much is delivered in the form of cheap loans or technical assistance. Since the 1970s, OECD countries belonging to the Development Assistance Committee (DAC) have agreed in principle to give 0.7% of their GNP. Most have failed to meet their commitment. In 1994, three countries exceeded this level. They were Norway (1.05%), the Netherlands (1.03%) and Sweden (0.96%). The countries with the largest aid budgets were Japan (US $13,239 million or 0.29% of GNP) and the United States (US $9,927 million or 0.15% of GNP).

- AID in US $
- % GNP
- DAC threshold

State Finance

Inflation rates, shown on the map, right, are an index of a country's financial stability and usually of its prosperity. Annual inflation rates above 20% are usually marked by slow or even negative growth of the GNP. Above 50%, it becomes hyperinflation and an economy is reeling. In the late 1980s and early 1990s, many high-income countries had to contend with annual inflation rates of 10% or more, while Japan, the growth leader, had an average inflation rate of 1.3% between 1985 and 1994.

The per capita GNP figures listed below are useful indicators of economic success or failure, but they do not account for living costs. Nor do they reveal the gaps between the rich and poor within countries.

Market-friendly policies, including low taxes and state spending, liberal trade policies and a welcome for foreign investors, are major factors in countries which have enjoyed rapid economic growth since 1980. For example, the setting up of Special Economic Zones in eastern China has led to a spectacular rise in the per capita GNP. Other successful countries include the 'tiger economies' of South Korea, Thailand and Singapore, although an Asian market crash in 1997 temporarily halted the dramatic economic expansion in these countries.

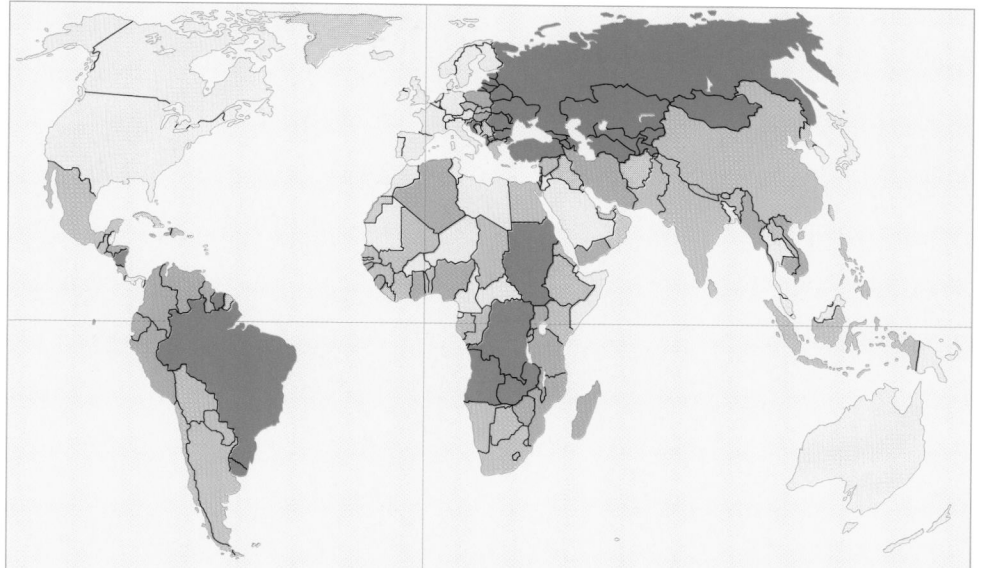

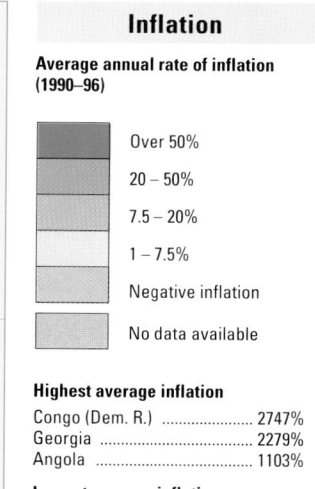

Inflation

Average annual rate of inflation (1990–96)

- Over 50%
- 20 – 50%
- 7.5 – 20%
- 1 – 7.5%
- Negative inflation
- No data available

Highest average inflation
Congo (Dem. R.) 2747%
Georgia 2279%
Angola 1103%

Lowest average inflation
Oman .... –3.0%
Bahrain .... –0.5%
Brunei .... –0.0%

The Wealth Gap

The world's richest and poorest countries, by Gross National Product per capita in US $ (1999 estimates)

1. Liechtenstein	50,000	1. Ethiopia	100
2. Luxembourg	44,640	2. Congo (D. Rep.)	110
3. Switzerland	38,350	3. Burundi	120
4. Bermuda	35,590	4. Sierra Leone	130
5. Norway	32,880	5. Guinea-Bissau	160
6. Japan	32,230	6. Niger	190
7. Denmark	32,030	7. Malawi	190
8. USA	30,600	8. Eritrea	200
9. Singapore	29,610	9. Chad	200
10. Iceland	29,280	10. Nepal	220
11. Austria	25,970	11. Angola	220
12. Germany	25,350	12. Mozambique	230
13. Sweden	25,040	13. Tanzania	240
14. Monaco	25,000	14. Burkina Faso	240
15. Belgium	24,510	15. Mali	240
16. Brunei	24,630	16. Rwanda	250
17. Netherlands	24,320	17. Madagascar	250
18. Finland	23,780	18. Cambodia	260
19. Hong Kong	23,520	19. São Tomé & Principe	270
20. France	23,480	20. Laos	280

GNP per capita is calculated by dividing a country's Gross National Product by its total population.

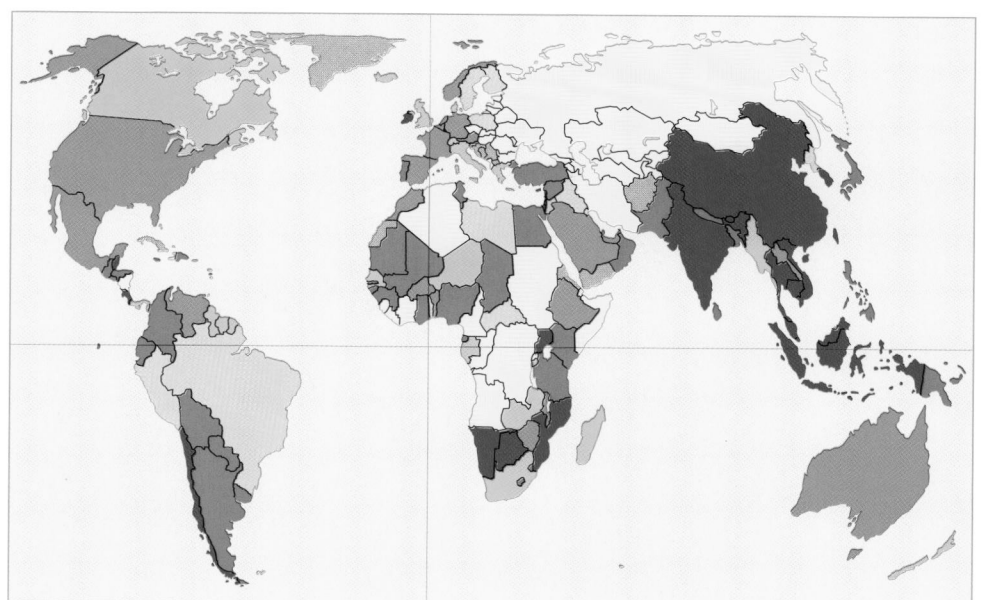

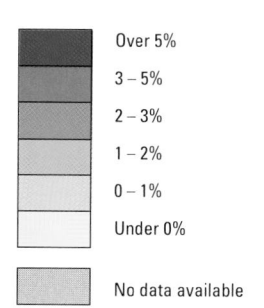

Growth in GNP

GNP per capita annual growth rate (1985–95)

- Over 5%
- 3 – 5%
- 2 – 3%
- 1 – 2%
- 0 – 1%
- Under 0%
- No data available

Countries with highest growth rates
Maldives 9.9%
Thailand 9.7%
China 9.3%
Botswana 9.0%
South Korea 8.5%

Standards of Living

Wealth is a basic factor in determining standards of living. Everywhere, the rich have more of everything, including higher average life expectancies, while the poor spend most of their income on basic human needs, such as food and clothing. Yet poverty and wealth are relative terms. Slum dwellers living on social security in an industrial society feel their poverty acutely, but they have far more resources than an average African living in a rural area.

In 1990 the United Nations Development Programme published its first Human Development Index (HDI), an attempt to construct a comparative scale by which a simplified form of well-being may be measured. The HDI, expressed as a value between 0 and 0.999, combines figures for life expectancy and literacy with a wealth scale, based on Purchasing-Power Parity. The world's countries are divided into three groups, those with a high HDI (0.800 and above); those with a medium HDI (0.500 to 0.799); and those with a low HDI (below 0.500).

National scores for 1993 ranged from 0.951 for Canada to a low of 0.204 in Niger. In fact, of the 48 countries with a low HDI, 37 were from Africa, 10 from Asia, plus Haiti from the Caribbean. Besides having low per capita GNPs, the average life expectancy in these countries was 56 years, while the adult literacy rate was 49%. By comparison, the average life expectancy at birth in countries in the high HDI group was 74 years, while the literacy rate was 97%.

Comparisons between countries with similar per capita GNPs reveal effects of government actions. For example, the World Bank classifies India and China as low income economies, but India's HDI at 0.436 is lower than that of China, at 0.609. This reflects not only China's economic progress in the 1980s and 1990s, but also differences in average life expectancies (61 years in India and 69 years in China), and adult literacy rates (51% in India and 80% in China).

Disparities in standards of living exist not only between countries but also between individuals, groups and regions within countries. For example, income distribution figures for 1995 show that, in the United States, the poorest 20% of households received less than 4% of the income.

Other contrasts exist in developing countries between rural communities, where incomes are low and basic services are often in short supply, and urban areas, where even those living in slums are generally better off than their rural neighbours. Other striking differences exist between men and women. For example, while adult literacy rates for men and women living in developed countries are more or less the same, large differences exist in many developing countries. In 1995, in countries in the lowest HDI category, only 37% of women were literate, as compared with 62% of men.

Female education is a factor in population control, especially as women's fertility rates appear to fall in direct proportion to the amount of secondary education they receive. This point was acknowledged in 1994 by the UN Population Fund, which defined four main objectives relating to women and population control. They were: the reduction of maternal, infant and child mortality; better education, especially for girls; universal access to reproductive health services; and gender equality.

Statistical analysis presents many problems of interpretation, especially when trying to define such intangible factors as a sense of well-being. For example, education helps create wealth; but are rich countries wealthy because their people are well-educated, or are they well-educated because they are rich?

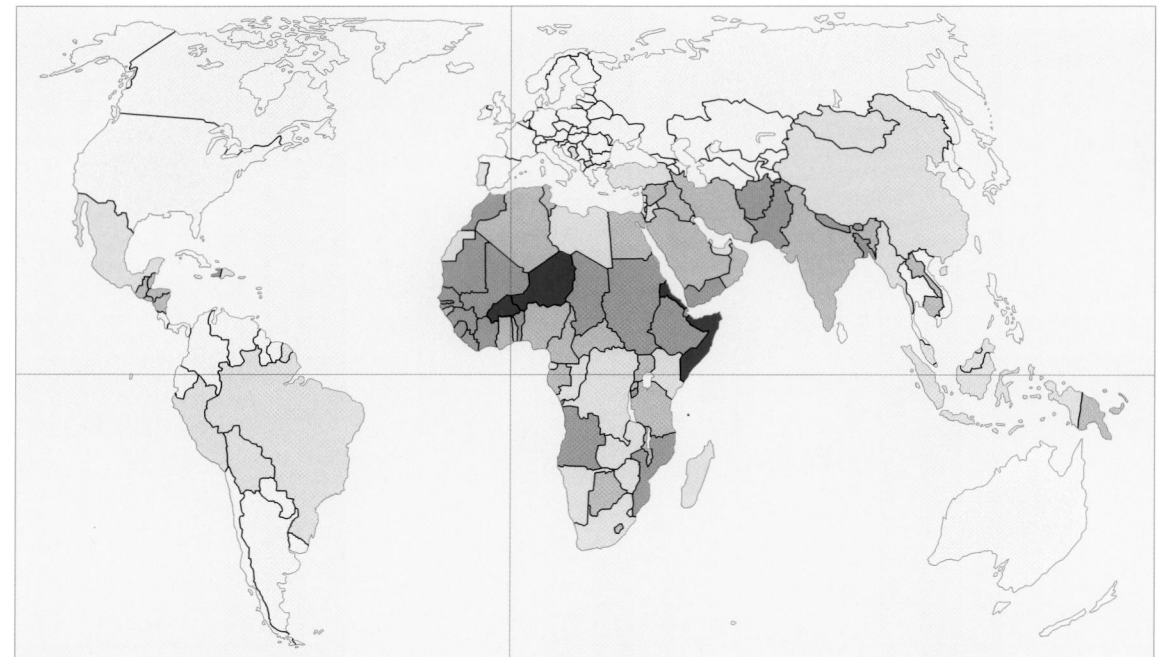

Illiteracy

% of the total population unable to read or write (1996)

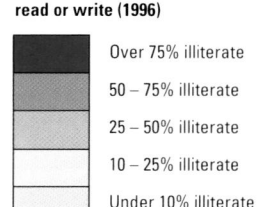

- Over 75% illiterate
- 50 – 75% illiterate
- 25 – 50% illiterate
- 10 – 25% illiterate
- Under 10% illiterate

Educational expenditure per person (latest available year)

Top 5 countries

Sweden	$997
Qatar	$989
Canada	$983
Norway	$971
Switzerland	$796

Bottom 5 countries

Chad	$2
Bangladesh	$3
Ethiopia	$3
Nepal	$4
Somalia	$4

Education

The developing countries made great efforts in the 1970s and 1980s to bring at least a basic education to their people. Primary school enrolments rose above 60% in all but the poorest nations. Figures often include teenagers or young adults, however, and there are still an estimated 300 million children worldwide who receive no schooling at all. A lack of resources has restricted the development of secondary and higher education. Most primary education is free in the poorer countries, but fees are often paid for secondary and higher education, thus heightening the differences between rich and poor.

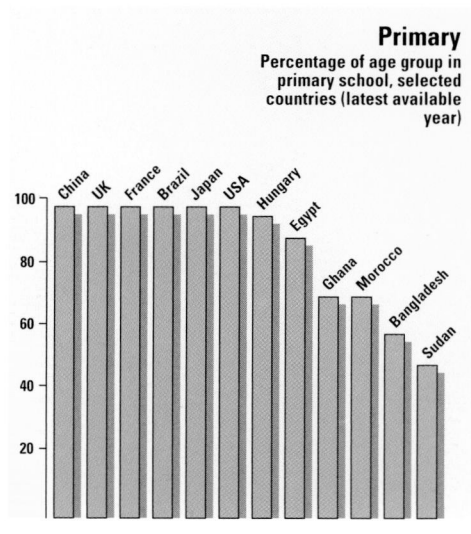

Primary
Percentage of age group in primary school, selected countries (latest available year)

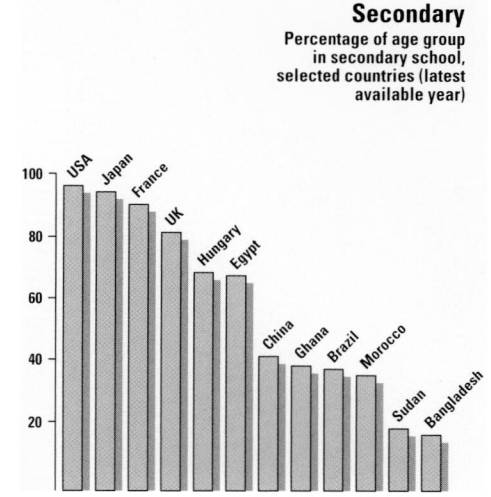

Secondary
Percentage of age group in secondary school, selected countries (latest available year)

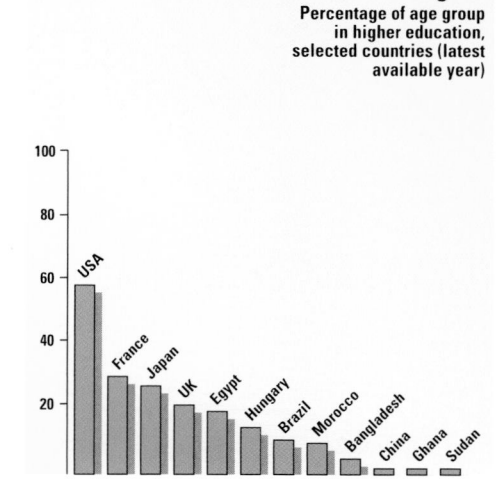

Higher
Percentage of age group in higher education, selected countries (latest available year)

Distribution of Spending

Percentage share of household spending (latest available year)

A high proportion of the average income of households in developing nations is spent on basic needs such as food and clothing. In most Western countries food and clothing account for less than 25% of expenditure.

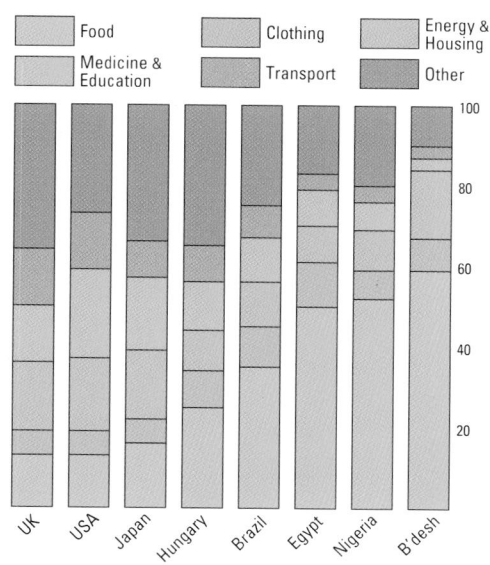

Legend:
- Food
- Clothing
- Energy & Housing
- Medicine & Education
- Transport
- Other

(UK, USA, Japan, Hungary, Brazil, Egypt, Nigeria, B'desh)

Distribution of Income

Percentage share of household income from poorest fifth to richest fifth, selected countries (latest available year)

The graph below shows that wealth is not distributed evenly throughout the population of the six countries. In every country worldwide the richest 20% of the population have a disproportionately high percentage of the income. This disparity between rich and poor is nowhere more pronounced than in Brazil, where the richest 20% of the population have over 60% of the income. The poorest 20%, on the other hand, have less than 5%.

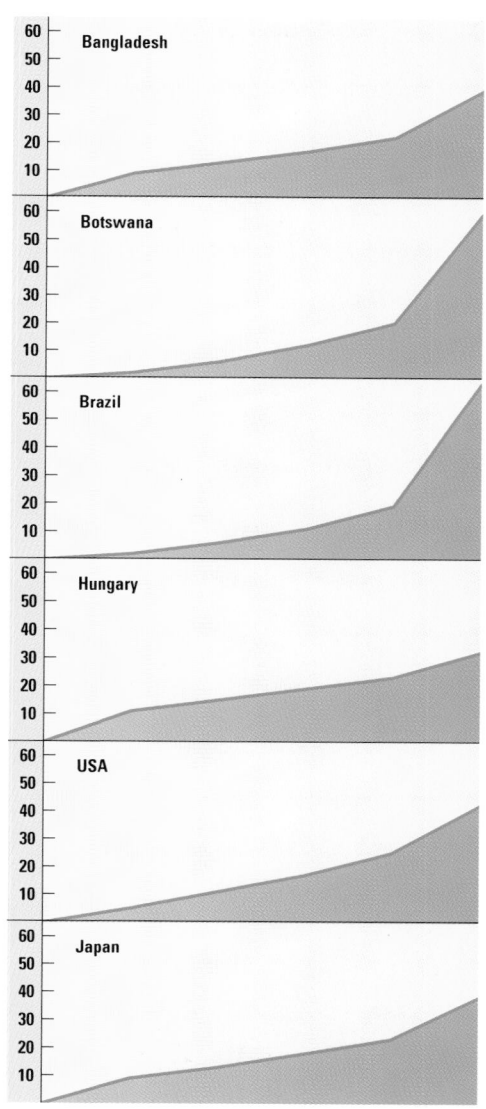

(Bangladesh, Botswana, Brazil, Hungary, USA, Japan)

Fertility and Education

Fertility rates compared with female education, selected countries (1992–95)

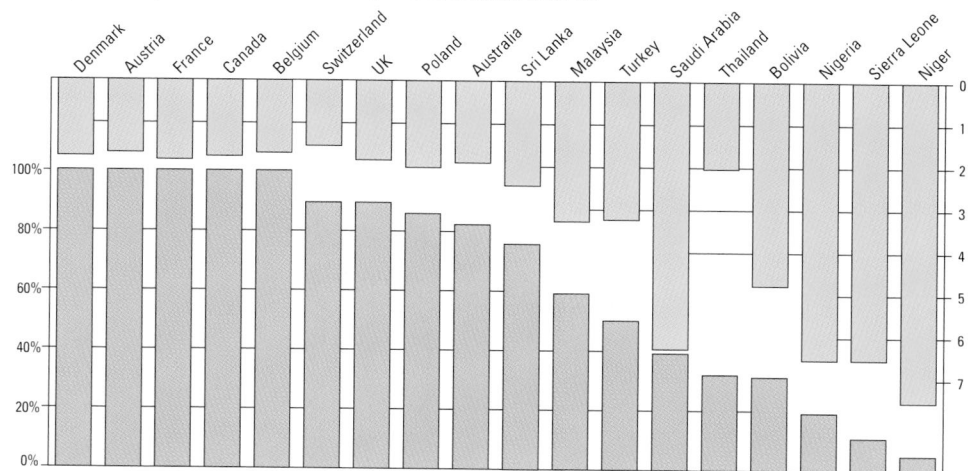

(Denmark, Austria, France, Canada, Belgium, Switzerland, UK, Poland, Australia, Sri Lanka, Malaysia, Turkey, Saudi Arabia, Thailand, Bolivia, Nigeria, Sierra Leone, Niger)

- Percentage of females aged 12–17 in secondary education
- Fertility rate: average number of children borne per woman

Access to secondary education is closely linked to low fertility rates in developed countries. By contrast, in many developing countries, women's lives are dominated by agriculture, or they lack access to secondary and higher education for cultural reasons, as in Muslim countries. Such disparities are reflected in women's parliamentary representation which is only one-seventh that of men, despite the emergence of such figures as Mrs Indira Gandhi, India's former prime minister. Female wages are also, on average, only two-thirds of those of men.

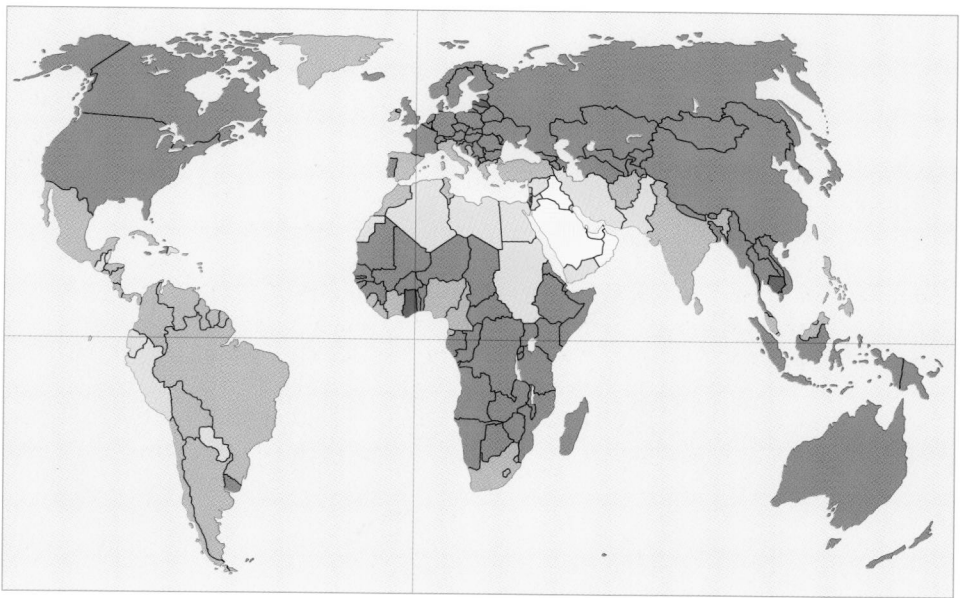

Women at Work

Women in paid employment as a percentage of the total workforce (1996)

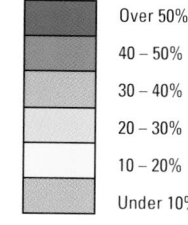

- Over 50%
- 40 – 50%
- 30 – 40%
- 20 – 30%
- 10 – 20%
- Under 10%

Most women in work

Cambodia	53%
Ghana	51%
Latvia	50%

Fewest women in work

Iraq	18%
Oman	15%
Saudi Arabia	14%

Car Ownership

Proportion of the world's vehicles, by region (1996)

(0, 10%, 20%, 30%, 40%)
- North America
- Western Europe
- Asia
- E Europe & CIS
- Others

TOTAL = 312 million vehicles

Motor cars per 100 people (1996)

Lebanon	73.1
Brunei	57.5
Italy	56.8
Luxembourg	56.1
USA	51.8

Standards of Living in the USA by Race, Age and Region

A comparison of measures of income and education, by selected characteristics (1995)

Median income per household (US $), by age and region

15–24 years	20,979
25–34 years	34,701
35–44 years	43,465
45–54 years	48,058
55–64 years	38,077
65 years and over	19,096
North-east	36,111
Mid-west	35,839
South	30,942
West	35,979

Per capita income (US $), by race and Hispanic origin of householder

ALL RACES	17,227
White	18,304
Black	10,982
Asian & Pacific Is.	16,567
Hispanic (any race)	9,300

The poorest 20% of households received just 3.6% of the income, whereas the richest 20% received 48.2%.

Percentage of persons aged 25 and over who have completed High School, by race or origin

ALL RACES	1975	62.5
	1995	81.7
White	1975	64.5
	1995	83.0
Black	1975	42.5
	1995	73.8
Hispanic	1975	37.9
	1995	53.4

Regional Inequality in Italy

Gross Domestic Product (GDP) per capita in Italy, by region (1993)

- Over US $20,000
- $16,000 – $19,999
- $12,000 – $15,999
- $8,000 – $11,999
- Under $8,000

Average GDP per capita for Italy was $18,878. The per capita GDP, by comparison, for the UK was $17,920; for the USA $25,650; and for the EU $25,900.

The number of inhabitants per doctor, another social indicator, varies from less than 500 in the north-west of Italy to over 800 in the far south, with a national average of 607.

The southern part of Italy, known as the *Mezzogiorno* (or 'Land of the midday sun'), has been described as the poorest part of the European Union. It is identifiable on the map, left, as all the regions with a GDP per capita of less than $12,000 (including the two islands of Sicily and Sardinia), plus Abruzzi whose capital is L'Aquila.

The *Mezzogiorno* region suffers from a lack of mineral and energy resources, industry, commerce, services and skilled labour. As a result, standards of living in the region are well below the rest of Italy and Europe. Employment is predominantly agricultural and small-scale.

The north of Italy accounts for 60% of the population but 80% of the GDP, whereas the *Mezzogiorno* accounts for 40% of the population and only 20% of the GDP. Manpower surpluses in the south led to emigration to other parts of Europe and the Americas. It has also led, especially in the last 50 years, to inter-regional migration from the islands and the southern mainland to the north. The main regions attracting migrants were the north-west – the prosperous Liguria–Piedmont–Lombardy triangle with its great industrial cities of Genoa, Milan and Turin – and the Venetia region in the north-east. As a result, the north has experienced much higher population growth rates than the rest of Italy.

In 1996 the Northern League, one of Italy's political parties, exploited the regional differences by declaring the north to be the independent 'Republic of Padania'. However, only a small minority of northerners supports secession.

– Mt Everest, China/Nepal –

Part of the Himalaya range, Mt Everest - the highest mountain in the world at 8,850 m (29,035 ft) - lies just north of centre in this image. The two arms of the Rongbuk glacier flow away from the triangular shaded north wall, with the Kangshung glacier due east. The international boundary between China and Nepal bisects the peak, which was first climbed on 28 May 1953.

WORLD MAPS

SETTLEMENTS

■ **PARIS**　　■ **Berne**　　◉ Livorno　　◉ Brugge　　◎ Algeciras　　○ *Frejus*　　○ *Oberammergau*　　○ *Thira*

Settlement symbols and type styles vary according to the scale of each map and indicate the importance of towns on the map rather than specific population figures

∴ Ruins or Archæological Sites　　　　　　⌣ Wells in Desert

ADMINISTRATION

—— International Boundaries

— — — International Boundaries (Undefined or Disputed)

·········· Internal Boundaries

National Parks

Country Names
NICARAGUA

Administrative Area Names
KENT
CALABRIA

International boundaries show the *de facto* situation where there are rival claims to territory

---

COMMUNICATIONS

—— Principal Roads

—— Other Roads

+--+ Road Tunnels

⋉ Passes

⊕ Airfields

—— Principal Railways

— ⌄ — Railways Under Construction

—— Other Railways

+--+ Railway Tunnels

·········· Principal Canals

PHYSICAL FEATURES

⌁ Perennial Streams

-⌁- Intermittent Streams

◯ Perennial Lakes

◯ Intermittent Lakes

Swamps and Marshes

Permanent Ice and Glaciers

▲ 8848 Elevations in metres

▼ 8500 Sea Depths in metres

1134 Height of Lake Surface Above Sea Level in metres

ELEVATION AND DEPTH TINTS

Height of Land above Sea Level

in metres　6000　4000　3000　2000　1500　1000　400　200　0

in feet　18 000　12 000　9000　6000　4500　3000　1200　600

Land Below Sea Level　　**Depth of Sea**

6000　12 000　15 000　18 000　24 000　in feet

0　200　2000　4000　5000　6000　8000　in metres

Some of the maps have different contours to highlight and clarify the principal relief features

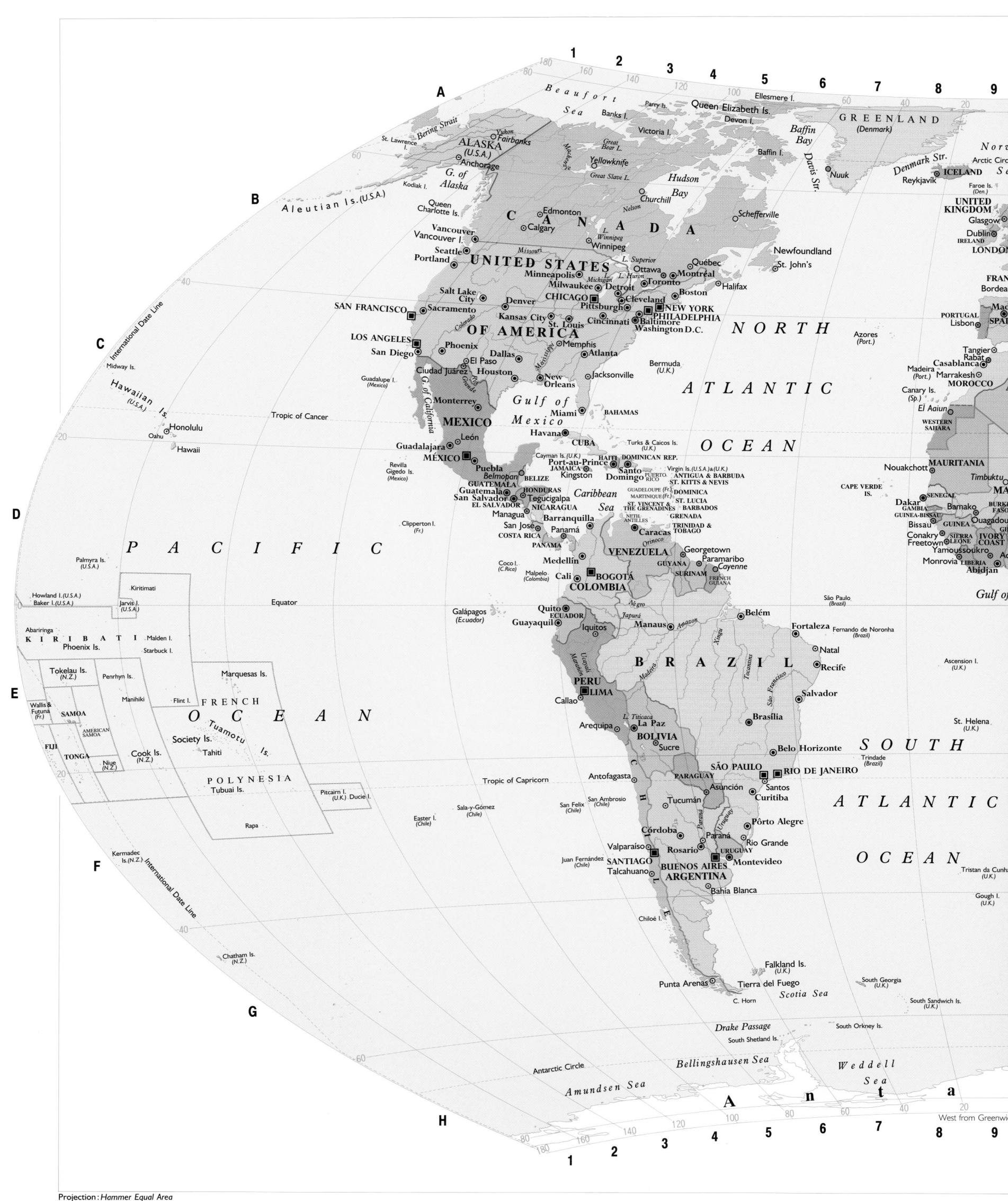

Projection: *Hammer Equal Area*

Hanoi ◉ Capital Cities

100 0 200 400 600 800 1000 1200 1400 km
100 0 200 400 600 800 1000 miles

| 18 | 17 | 16 | 15 |

JAPAN

PACIFIC OCEAN

Aleutian Islands
(U.S.A.)

Near Is.
(U.S.A.) ▽ 7822

Mys Lopatka

Kurilskiye Ostrova
(Russia)

La Perouse Str.

Hokkaidō

Dutch Harbor

Komandorskiye
Ostrova

Petropavlovsk-
Kamchatskiy

Unimak I.

B e r i n g S e a

D

Gora Klyuchevskaya
4750

Poluostrov Kamchatka

Sakhalin
(Russia)

Sakhalinskiy Zaliv

Bristol
Bay

Pribilof Is.
(U.S.A.)

International Date Line

60

Ostrov
Karaginskiy

Sea of
Okhotsk

Vanino

Kodiak I.

▽ 42

Mys Olyutorski

Amur

Nikolayevsk

G. of Alaska

Nunivak

St. Matthew
(U.S.A.)

Mys Navarin

Penzhinskaya G.
Gishiginskaya
Guba

Penzhino

Tauiskaya
Guba

Ulbanskiy
Zaliv

Khabarovsk

1

Seward
Prince
William Sd.

Cook Inlet

Alaska Pen.

St. Lawrence I.
(U.S.A.)

Anadyrskiy
Zaliv

Anadyr

Kolymskoye Nagorye

Okhotsk

Udskaya
Guba

14

Cordova

Anchorage

Mt. McKinley
6194

Norton Sd.

Bering Str.

Nome

Mys
Dezhneva

C

Chukotskoye
Nagorye

S

Prince Rupert

Mt. St. Elias
5489

Fairbanks

ALASKA
(U.S.A.)

C. Prince of Wales

Omolon

Nizhne
Kolymsk

Skagway
Mt. Logan
5959

Whitehorse

Yukon

Kotzebue Sd.

Pt. Hope

Proliv Longa

Kolyma

Srednekolymsk

Verkhoyansk

Stanovoy Khrebet

Rocky Mountains

Dawson

Kuskokwim

Yukon

Koyukuk

C. Lisburne

Chukchi
Sea

Ostrov
Vrangelya
(Russia)

Nizhne
Kolymsk

Indigirka

Yakutsk

120

Dawson Creek

Liard

Stewart

Peel

Noatak

Chaunskaya G.

Zashiversk

Aldan

Olekma

Fort
Simpson

Fort Yukon

Fort McPherson

Prudhoe Bay

Pt. Barrow

▽ 46

B

Yana

Kazachye

Zhigansk

120

Fort
Vermilion

Peace

Mackenzie

Herschel I.

Harrison Bay

Novosibirskiye
Ostrova

Lyakhovskiye
Ostrova

Lena

Bulun

Vilyuy

2

NORTH

Athabasca

Tulita

Good Hope

Mackenzie
Bay

Beaufort Sea

A R C T I C

Mendeleyev Ridge

O. Bennetta
(Russia)

O. Kotelnyy

Tiksi

Olenek

13

Yellowknife

Great Bear
Lake

Coppermine

C. Bathurst

3767

O C E A N

Laptev
Sea

Anabar

Athabasca
Lake

Great Slave
Lake

C. Kellett

3327

Ostrova Petra

Nordvik

Vilyuy

100

AMERICA

Kugluktuk

Coronation G.

Banks I.

C. Prince Alfred

Canada
Basin

Severnaya
Zemlya

Poluostrov
Taymyr

Kheta

100

Victoria
Island

M'Clure Str.

Prince
Patrick I.

3546

3849

Oktyabrskoy
Revolyutsii

Ozero Taymyr

Putorana

Gory

Melville I.

Alpha
Cordillera

4007

Lomonosov Ridge

4100

Nansen Cordillera

Pyasina

King
William I.

Prince
Albert
Pen.

Parry Is.

3700

NORTH
POLE

4484

3

Hudson
Bay

Boothia
Pen.

Prince of
Wales I.

Bathurst
I.

Borden I.

Ellef Ringnes I.

Makarov Basin

Fram Basin

Golchikha

Dudinka

Norilsk

Yenisey

Igarka

12

Somerset
I.

North
Magnetic
Pole
1995

Sverdrup Is.

2104

4418

3741

Nansen Basin

O. Uedineniya

O. Vise

Southampton I.

Gulf of
Boothia

Axel
Heiberg I.

Nansen Sd.

Eureka

Alert

Zemlya
Frantsa
Iosifa

O. Ushakova

Coats I.

Prince Regent Inlet

Devon I.

C. Columbia

O. Graham Bell

Mansel I.

Melville
Pen.

Lancaster Sd.

Lincoln
Sea

Z. Vilcheka

Foxe
Chan.

Barrow Str.

Jones Sound

Smith Sd.

Kane
Basin

Robeson Chan.

McKinley
Sea

Z. Aleksandry
(Russia)

O. Belyy

Kara
Sea

Poluostrov
Yamal

Urengoy

Novyy Port
Nadym

80

Foxe
Basin

Prince
Charles I.

Bylot
I.

Qaanaaq

Uummannaq

Peary
Land

Knud
Rasmussen
Land

Novaya
Zemlya

Baydaratskaya
Guba

Khabarovo

80

2399

K. York

Sermersuaq

K. Morris Jesup

Kong Frederik
VIII.s Land

Nordaustlandet

Zemlya

Vorkuta

Salekhard

Ob

Surgut

Nettilling L.

Baffin
Bay

Independence Fjord

Vestspitsbergen

Barents

Berezovo

4

Iqaluit

Frobisher B.

Upernavik

Kong Frederik
IX.s Land

2571

Longyearbyen

Svalbard
(Norway)

Edgeøya

Sea

O. Kolguyev

1894
Narodnaya

Uralskie

11

Resolution I.

C. Dyer

Qeqertarsuaq

Davis
Str.

Nordkapp

Greenland

Pechora

Gory

YEKATERINBURG

Labrador

C. Chidley

Ungava
Bay

Qeqertarsuaq

GREENLAND
(KALAALLIT NUNAAT)
(Denmark)

Sea

Bjørnøya

Mys
Kanin
Nos

PERM

Feuilles

Uummannaq

Kong
Christian Xs Land

Nordkapp

Varangerfjorden

Mezen

60

Nuuk

Mt.
Forel
3360

Kejser Franz Joseph Fd.

Vardø

UFA

Hamilton Inlet

Paamiut

Kong
Frederik VI.s Kyst

Kong
Christian IX.s Land

Kong Oscar Fjord

Hammerfest

Murmansk

Kolskiy
Poluostrov

Arkhangelsk

Beloye
More

SAMARA

60

Qaqortoq

Gunnbjørn
Fjeld 3700

Ittoqqortoormiit

Tromsø

Sev. Dvina

Volga

Alluitsup Paa

Kap Brewster

Jan Mayen
(Norway)

Kolskiy

Onega

Onezhskoye
Ozero

5

Kap Farvel
(Nunap Isua)

Tasiilaq

Denmark Str.

Iceland
Plateau

Norwegian

Arctic Circle

Trondheim

Ladozhskoye
Ozero

ST. PETERBURG

Saratov

10

Breiðafjörður

Horn

Fontur

Sea

FINLAND

Tornio

Chudskoye
Ozero

MOSKVA

Mid-Atlantic Ridge

Rockall
(U.K.)

Reykjavík
ICELAND

Orœfajökull
2119

3800

C

Helsinki

VOLGOGRAD

4755 ▽

Føroyar
(Den.)

Bergen

STOCKHOLM

Oslo

Gulf of Bothnia

G. of Finland

Tallinn

Riga

Wisła

EST.

LAT.

LITH.

Vilnius

BELARUS

KYYIV

ROSTOV

ATLANTIC OCEAN

Shetland Is.
(U.K.)

Orkney Is.
(U.K.)

North
Sea

KØBENHAVN

Skagerrak

Baltic Sea

Kaliningrad

WARSZAWA

UKRAINE

ODESA

Black Sea

UNITED
KINGDOM

Edinburgh

SCOTLAND

DENMARK

HAMBURG

BERLIN

POLAND

Belfast

Dublin
IRELAND

ENGLAND

WALES

D

NETH.
AMSTERDAM

GERMANY

Elbe

PRAHA

C. Clear

LONDON

| 6 | 7 | 8 | 9 |

**Maximum extent of
sea ice**

Summer extent of sea ice

**Ice caps and permanent
ice shelf**

Projection : Zenithal Equidistant

West from Greenwich East from Greenwich

COPYRIGHT GEORGE PHILIP LTD

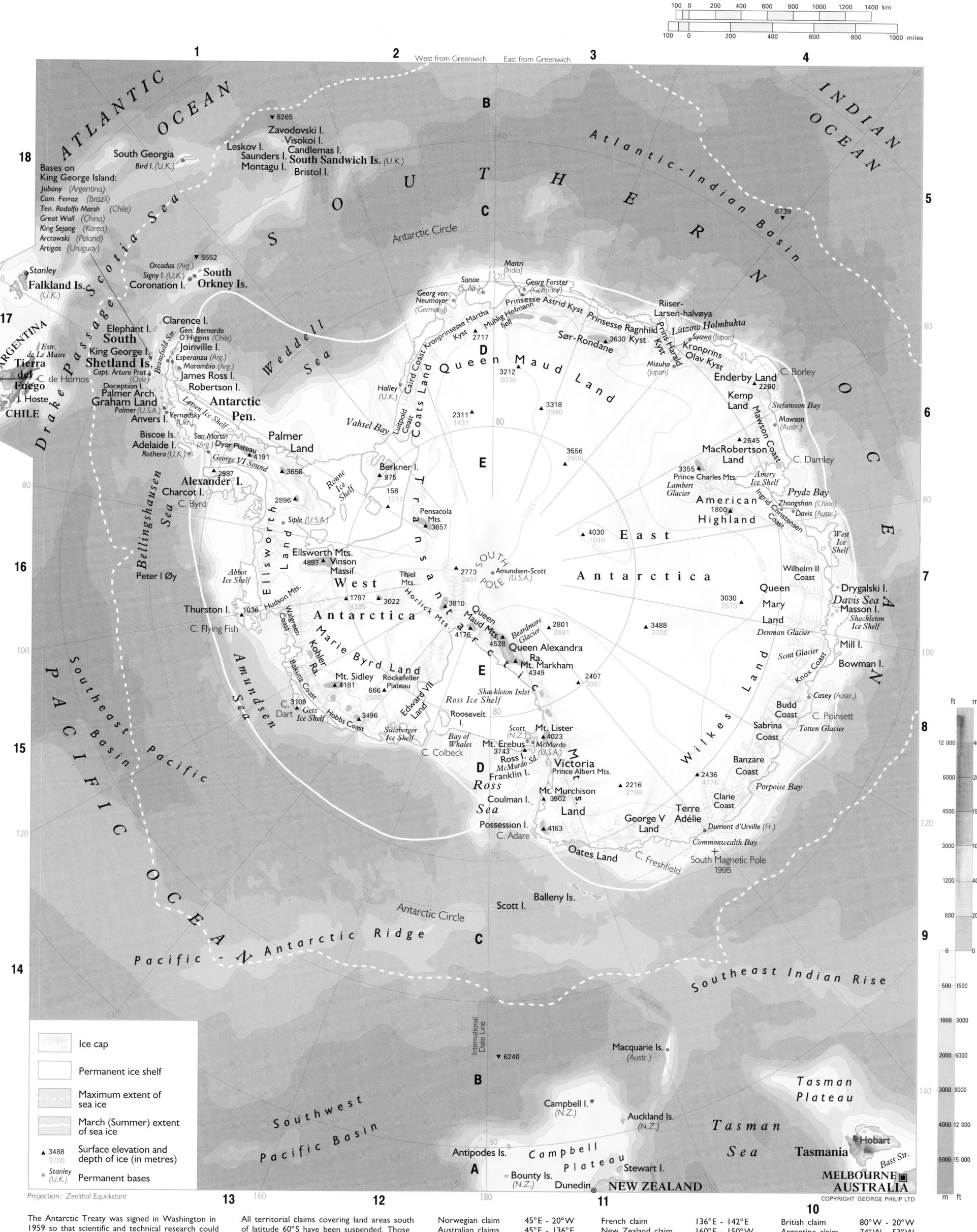

100 0 200 400 600 800 1000 1200 1400 km
100 0 200 400 600 800 1000 miles

West from Greenwich East from Greenwich

ATLANTIC OCEAN

18

Bases on
King George Island:
Jubany (Argentina)
Com. Ferraz (Brazil)
Ten. Rodolfo Marsh (Chile)
Great Wall (China)
King Sejong (Korea)
Arctowski (Poland)
Artigas (Uruguay)

South Georgia
Bird I. (U.K.)

▼8265
Zavodovski I.
Visokoi I.
Leskov I. Candlemas I.
Saunders I. **South Sandwich Is.** (U.K.)
Montagu I. Bristol I.

ATLANTIC–INDIAN BASIN

INDIAN OCEAN

6739

B

SOUTHERN

Antarctic Circle

C

17

Stanley
Falkland Is.
(U.K.)

ARGENTINA

Tierra
del
Fuego
I. Hoste

CHILE

Estr.
de Le Maire
C. de Hornos

Drake Passage

Scotia Sea

Orcadas (Arg.) ▼5552
Signy I. (U.K.) **South**
Coronation I. **Orkney Is.**

Clarence I.
Elephant I. Gen. Bernardo
South O'Higgins (Chile)
King George I. Joinville I.
Shetland Is. Esperanza (Arg.)
Capt. Arturo Prat (Chile) Marambio (Arg.)
Deception I. James Ross I.
Palmer Arch. Robertson I.
Graham Land
Palmer (U.S.A.) **Antarctic**
Anvers I. Vernadsky (Ukr.) **Pen.**
Biscoe Is. San Martin
Adelaide I. (Arg.) Dyer Plateau
Rothera (U.K.) George VI Sound ▲4191

Weddell Sea

Bellingshausen Sea

Alexander I.
Charcot I.
C. Byrd

Peter I Øy

Halley
(U.K.)

Vahsel Bay

Luitpold Coast

Berkner I. 975
Ronne
Ice 158
Shelf

▲3658
2896

Sanae
(S. Afr.) Maitri
(India)

Georg von
Neumayer
(Germany)

Georg Forster
(Germany)

Prinsesse Astrid Kyst
Kronprinsesse Martha
Kyst 2717

Prinsesse Ragnhild
Kyst

Mühlig Hofmann
fjell Sør-Rondane

Riiser-
Larsen-halvøya

Prins Harald
Kyst Lützow Holmbukta

3630 Kyst Syowa (Japan)
Kronprins
Olav Kyst
Mizuho
(Japan)

Queen Maud Land 3212
3039

Enderby Land
C. Borley

Kemp
Land 2260

Stefansson Bay

Mawson
(Austr.)

2311
1431

3318
2990

3556
2600

MacRobertson
Land 2645

C. Darnley

Prince Charles Mts. 3355
Lambert 3491
Glacier

Amery
Ice Shelf

Prydz Bay

Ingrid Christensen
Coast

Zhongshan (China)
Davis (Austr.)

B

C

D

16

West Siple (U.S.A.)

Ellsworth Mts.
4897 ▲Vinson
Massif

Thiel
Mts.

2773

Pensacola
Mts.
3657

4030
1040

East

Antarctica

South
Pole

Amundsen-Scott
(U.S.A.)

2407

American
Highland 1800

3030
2570

Queen
Mary

Wilhelm II
Coast

West
Ice Shelf

Drygalski I.
Davis Sea
Masson I.
Shackleton
Ice Shelf

Mill I.

Bowman I.

E

7

8

15

Thurston I. 1036
1797
C. Flying Fish

Abbot
Ice Shelf

Ellsworth Land

Hudson Mts.

3022

Horlick Mts.

3810
4176

Queen
Maud Mts.

4528

Beardmore
Glacier 2801

Mt. Markham
4349

Antarctica

3488
3700

Denman Glacier

Scott Glacier

Knox Coast

Totten Glacier

C. Poinsett

2407
3087

Land

Wilkes

Budd
Coast

Sabrina
Coast

Banzare
Coast

Antarctic

Marie Byrd Land Kohler Ra.

Amundsen Sea

Bakutis Coast

Mt. Sidley 4181

3109
Dart Getz
Ice Shelf

Rockefeller
Plateau 666
2080

3496

Hobbs Coast

Walgreen Coast

Edward VII
Land

Sulzberger
Ice Shelf

Ross Ice Shelf

Roosevelt
I.

Bay of
Whales

C. Colbeck

Scott
(N.Z.)

Mt. Lister
4023

Mt. Erebus
3743 McMurdo
Ross (U.S.A.)
McMurdo Sd.

Franklin I.

Queen Alexandra
Ra.

Shackleton Inlet

Victoria

Prince Albert Mts.

2216
2798

2436
4776

Porpoise Bay

Clarie
Coast

Terre
Adélie

E

C

D

14

Pacific-Antarctic Ridge

Southeast Pacific Basin

PACIFIC OCEAN

Ross
Sea

Coulman I.

Possession I.

C. Adare

Balleny Is.

Scott I.

Antarctic Circle

Mt. Murchison
3502 **Land**

4163

George V
Land

Commonwealth Bay
+ South Magnetic Pole
1995

Dumont d'Urville (Fr.)

C. Freshfield

Oates Land

Southeast Indian Rise

Southwest

Pacific Basin

International Date Line

▼6240

Macquarie Is.
(Austr.)

Tasman
Plateau

Campbell I.
(N.Z.)

Auckland Is.
(N.Z.)

Tasman

Sea

Tasmania

Hobart

Bass Str.

MELBOURNE
AUSTRALIA

B

A

Antipodes Is.

Bounty Is.
(N.Z.) Dunedin **NEW ZEALAND**

Campbell
Plateau

Stewart I.

COPYRIGHT GEORGE PHILIP LTD

ft m

12 000 400

6000 200

4500

3000

1200

600

0

500 1500

1000 3000

2000 6000

3000 9000

4000 12 000

5000 15 000

m ft

Legend:

	Ice cap
	Permanent ice shelf
	Maximum extent of sea ice
	March (Summer) extent of sea ice
▲3488 / 3700	Surface elevation and depth of ice (in metres)
• *Stanley* (U.K.)	Permanent bases

Projection : *Zenithal Equidistant*

The Antarctic Treaty was signed in Washington in 1959 so that scientific and technical research could continue unhampered by international politics.

All territorial claims covering land areas south of latitude 60°S have been suspended. Those claims were:

Norwegian claim 45°E – 20°W
Australian claims 45°E – 136°E
142°E – 160°E

French claim 136°E – 142°E
New Zealand claim 160°E – 150°W
Chilean claim 90°W – 53°W

British claim 80°W – 20°W
Argentine claim 74°W – 53°W

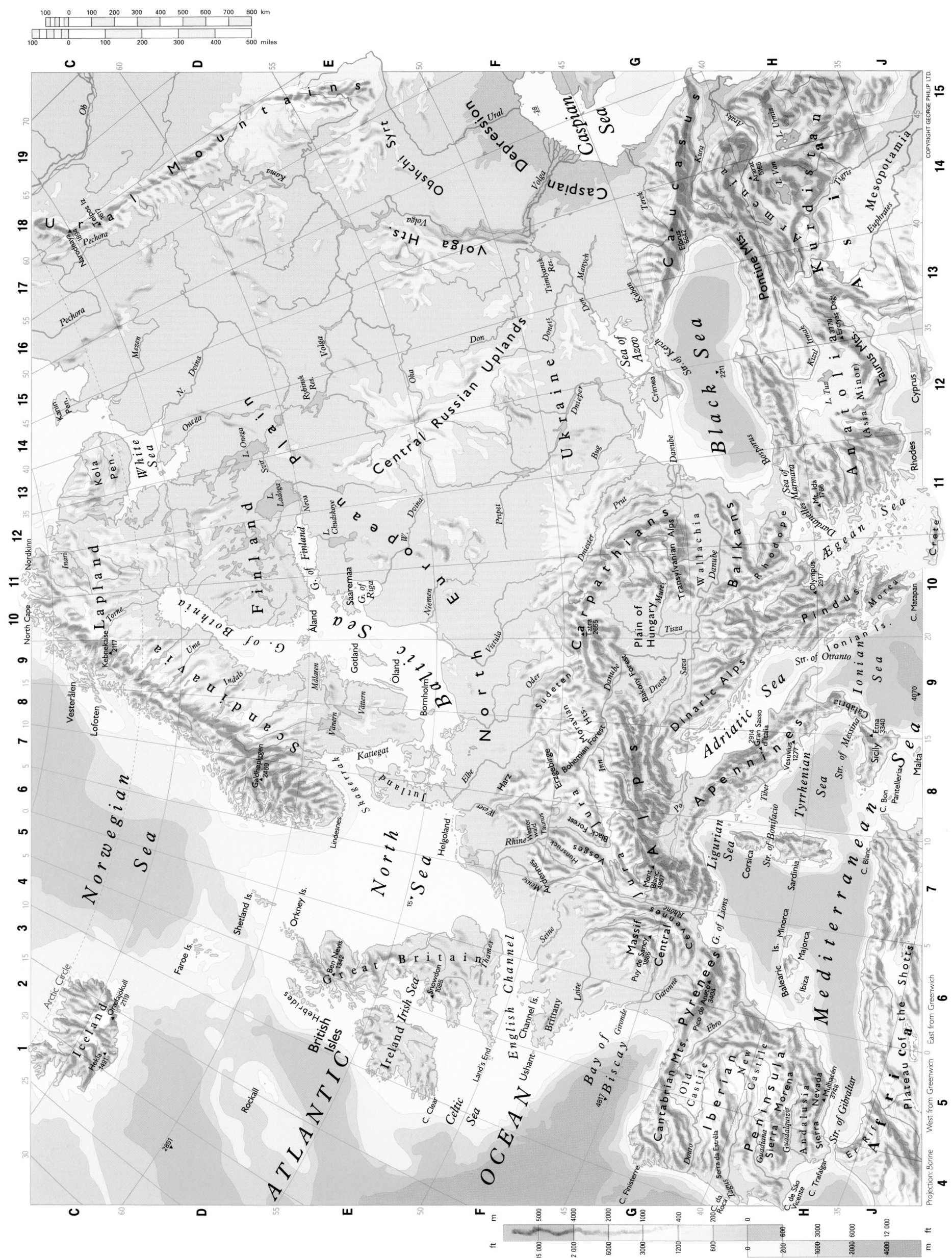

100 0 100 200 300 400 500 600 700 800 km
100 0 100 200 300 400 500 miles

Projection: Bonne

Ob

Ural Mountains

Obschi Syrt

Caspian Depression

Ural

Caspian Sea

Ural

Pechora

Kama

Volga Hts.

Volga

Caucasus

Pontine Mts.

Kura

Terek

Kuban

Pechora

Mezen

N. Dvina

Central Russian Uplands

Don

Donets

Sea of Azov

Kerch

Black Sea

Armenia

Kurdistan

Mesopotamia

Euphrates

Tigris

Elbruz 5642

Ararat 5165

L. Urmia

L. Van

Kanin Pen.

White Sea

Onega

L. Onega

Svir

Neva

L. Ladoga

L. Chudskoye

W. Dvina

Dnieper

Ukraine

Bug

Danube

Prut

Wallachia

Transylvanian Alps

Balkans

Rhodope

Bosporus

Sea of Marmara

Dardanelles

Anatolia (Asia Minor)

Taurus Mts.

Erciyes Dağı 3770

Kızıl Irmak

L. Tuz

Aegean Sea

Crete

Rhodes

Cyprus

Kola Pen.

Lapland

Inari

Nordkinn

North Cape

Vesterålen

Lofoten

Kebnekaise 2117

Torne

Finland

G. of Finland

Saaremaa

G. of Riga

Niemen

European Plain

North European Plain

Vistula

Carpathians

Tatra 2665

Plain of Hungary

Maros

Tisza

Drava

Dinaric Alps

Adriatic Sea

Pindus

Olympus 2917

Morea

C. Matapan

Ionian Is.

Ionian Sea

Str. of Otranto

Scandinavia

Galdhøpiggen 2469

Åland

Baltic Sea

Öland

Gotland

Bornholm

Jutland

Skagerrak

Kattegat

Jutland

Elbe

Oder

Sudeten Hts.

Moravian Hts.

Ergebirge

Bohemian Forest

Harz

Inn

Bakony Forest

Danube

Sava

Apennines

Gran Sasso d'Italia 2914

Vesuvius 1277

Tyrrhenian Sea

Str. of Messina

Etna 3340

Calabria

Sicily

Malta

Pantelleria

C. Bon

Norwegian Sea

Iceland

Hekla 1491

Öraefajökull 2119

Vesterålen

Faroe Is.

Rockall

Shetland Is.

Orkney Is.

Hebrides

Ben Nevis 1342

Great Britain

Snowdon 1085

Ireland

Irish Sea

North Sea

Weser

Ems

Helgoland

Rhine

Black Forest

Jura

Vosges

Taunus

Hunsrück

Ardennes

Meuse

Alps

Mont Blanc 4807

Po

Ligurian Sea

Corsica

Sardinia

Str. of Bonifacio

Mediterranean Sea

Cevennes

Rhône

Massif Central

Puy de Sancy 1886

Garonne

Loire

Seine

Thames

English Channel

Channel Is.

Brittany

Ushant

Bay of Biscay

Pyrenees

Pico de Aneto 3404

Ebro

Cantabrian Mts.

Old Castile

New Castile

Iberian Peninsula

Duero

Sierra de Estrela

Sierra Morena

Guadiana

Guadalquivir

Andalusia

Sierra Nevada

Mulhacén 3478

Str. of Gibraltar

Plateau of the Shotts

Atlas

Rif

Er Rif

C. de São Vicente

C. da Roca

C. Trafalgar

C. Finisterre

C. Clear

Land's End

Celtic Sea

English Channel

ATLANTIC OCEAN

British Isles

Arctic Circle

2851

4070

Balearic Is.

Minorca

Majorca

Ibiza

Gomera

Arctic Circle

West from Greenwich   East from Greenwich

m 5000 4000 2000 1000 400 200 0 200 400 1000 2000 4000 m

ft 15 000 12 000 6000 3000 1200 600 0 600 3000 6000 12 000 ft

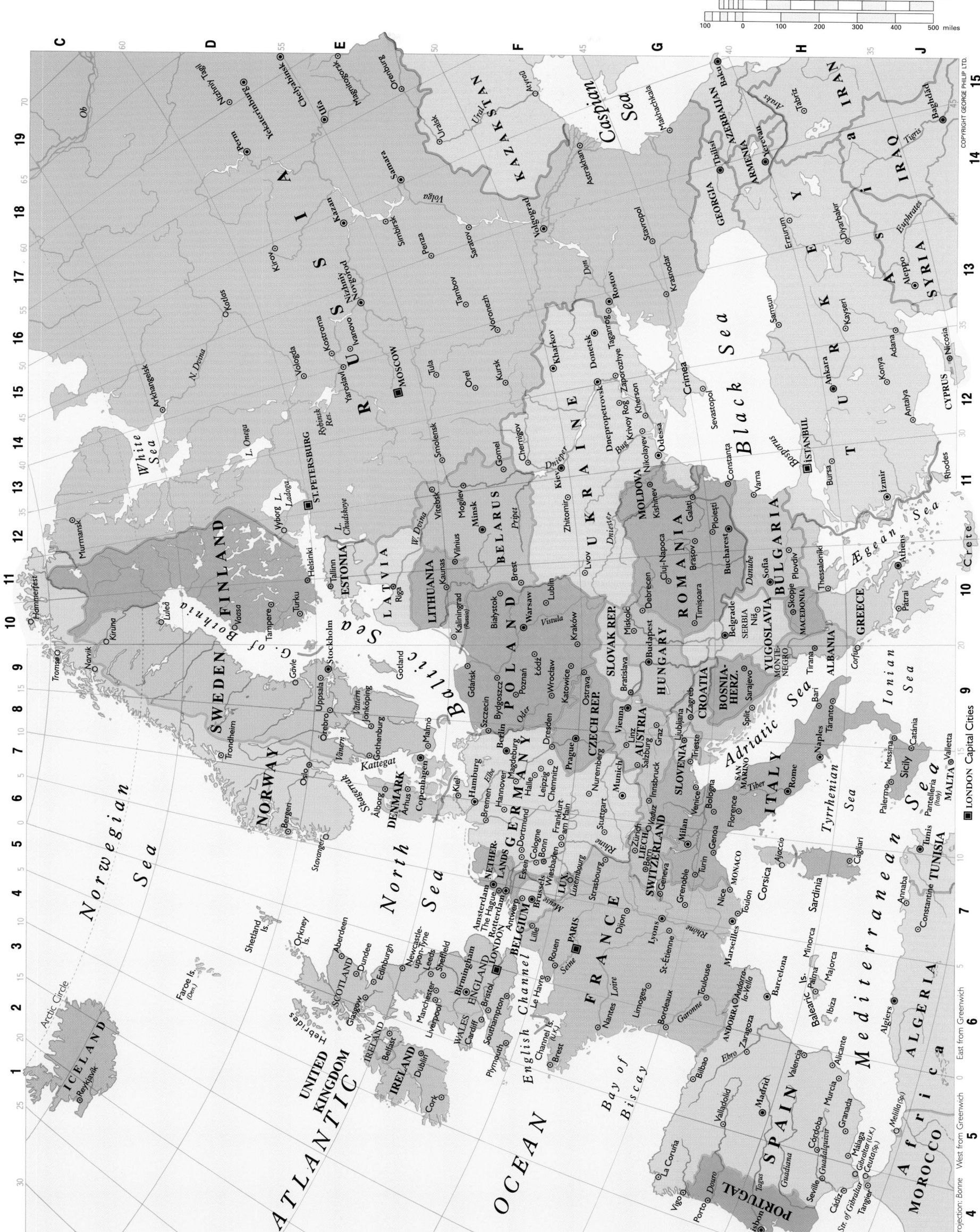

SCANDINAVIA 1:4 200 000

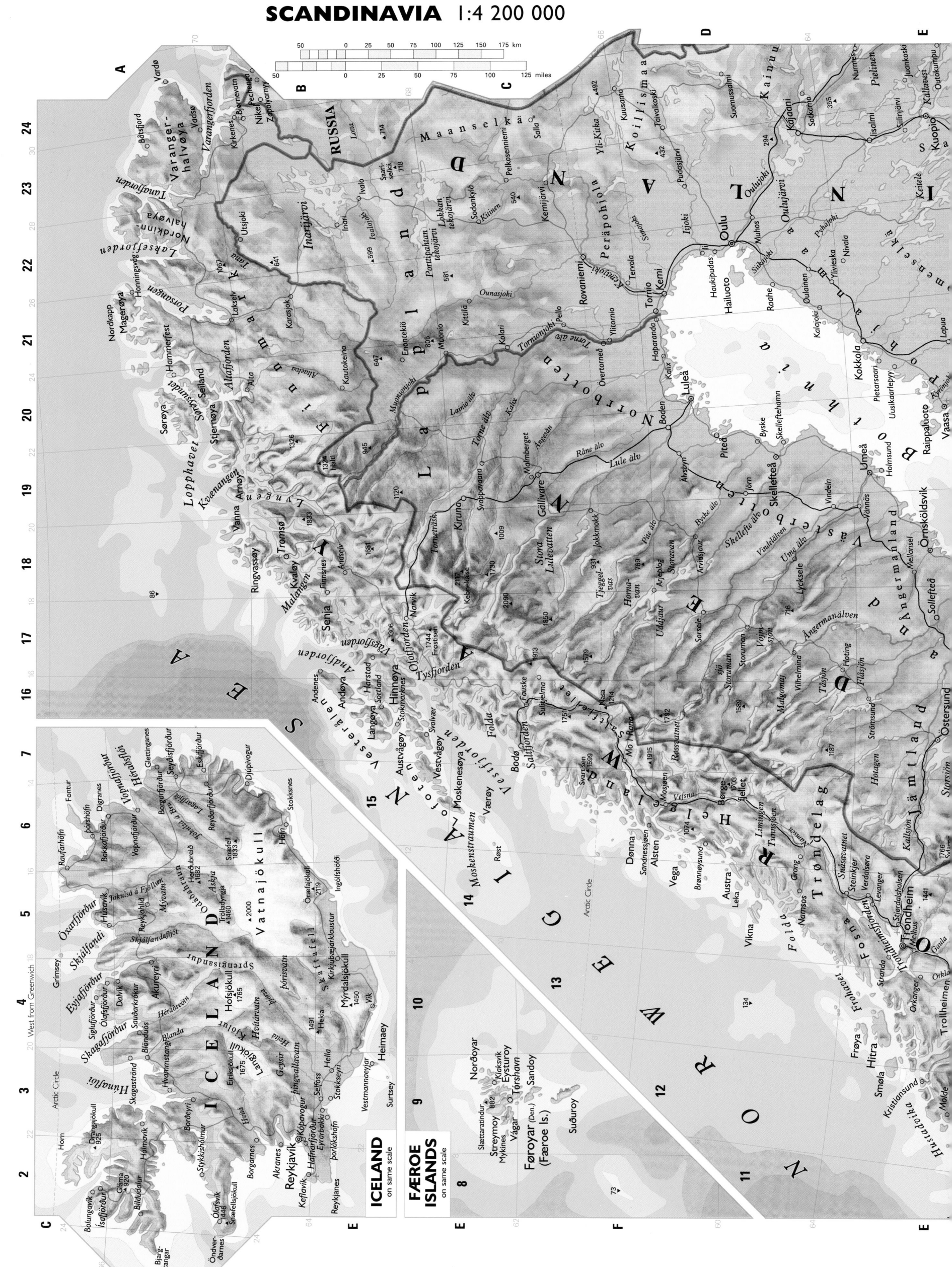

ICELAND
on same scale

FÆROE
ISLANDS
on same scale

FINLAND

ESTONIA

LATVIA

LITHUANIA

SWEDEN

NORWAY

DENMARK

GERMANY

POLAND

BELARUS

RUSSIA

BALTIC SEA

Gulf of Finland

Gulf of Riga

Gulf of Bothnia

Ålands hav

Skagerrak

Kattegat

Helsinki (Helsingfors) · Espoo · Vantaa · Tampere · Turku (Åbo) · Pori · Rauma · Lahti · Kotka · Hamina · Mikkeli · Savonlinna · Jyväskylä · Seinäjoki

Tallinn · Tartu · Pärnu · Narva · Hiiumaa (Dagö) · Saaremaa (Ösel) · Kuressaare

Riga · Jelgava · Daugavpils · Ventspils · Liepāja · Valmiera · Jēkabpils

Vilnius · Kaunas · Panevėžys · Šiauliai · Klaipėda · Kaliningrad (Russia) · Chernyakhovsk

STOCKHOLM · Uppsala · Västerås · Eskilstuna · Örebro · Norrköping · Linköping · Jönköping · Gävle · Sundsvall · Härnösand · Falun · Borlänge · Karlstad · Göteborg (Gothenburg) · Borås · Malmö · Helsingborg · Halmstad · Kalmar · Karlskrona · Visby

Gotland · Öland · Bornholm · Åland (Ahvenanmaa)

Oslo · Bergen · Stavanger · Kristiansand · Drammen · Hamar · Lillehammer · Hardangervidda · Jotunheimen · Dovrefjell · Rondane

KØBENHAVN (Copenhagen) · Odense · Ålborg · Århus · Esbjerg · Kolding · Sjælland · Fyn · Lolland · Falster · Bornholm

Kiel · Lübeck · Rostock · Flensburg · Schleswig · Holstein · Rügen · Usedom

Gdańsk · Gdynia · Sopot · Słupsk · Koszalin · Kołobrzeg · Elbląg · Malbork

Vänern · Vättern · Mälaren · Hjälmaren

Projection: Conical with two standard parallels

East from Greenwich

COPYRIGHT GEORGE PHILIP LTD.

10 0 10 20 30 40 50 60 70 80 90 km

10 0 10 20 30 40 50 60 miles

A B C D E

Gulf of Bothnia

NORRLANDS LÄN

VÄSTER-NORRLANDS LÄN

Husum
Örnsköldsvik
Kristiansund

JÄMTLANDS LÄN

Östersund
Storsjön

Storsjön

HÄRJEDALEN

HÄLSINGLAND

GÄVLEBORGS LÄN

GÄSTRIKLAND

Gävle
Sandviken

DALARNAS LÄN

Dalarna

Siljan

Falun
Borlänge

VÄSTMANLANDS LÄN

Västerås

UPPSALA LÄN

Uppland

Uppsala

STOCKHOLMS LÄN

STOCKHOLM

Södertälje

Mälaren

Mälaren

SÖDERMANLANDS LÄN

Eskilstuna

ÖREBRO LÄN

Örebro

NÄRKE

VÄRMLANDS LÄN

Karlstad

Vänern

SØR-TRØNDELAG

Trondheim

MØRE OG ROMSDAL

Dovrefjell

Rondane

Jotunheimen

OPPLAND

GUDBRANDSDALEN

Lillehammer

HEDMARK

ØSTERDALEN

Elverum

Hamar

AKERSHUS

OSLO

Drammen

BUSKERUD

TELEMARK

VESTFOLD

ØSTFOLD

Fredrikstad

Glomma

m ft
2000 6000
1500 4500
1000 3000
500 1500
200 600
0 0
50-150
100-300
200-600
500-1500

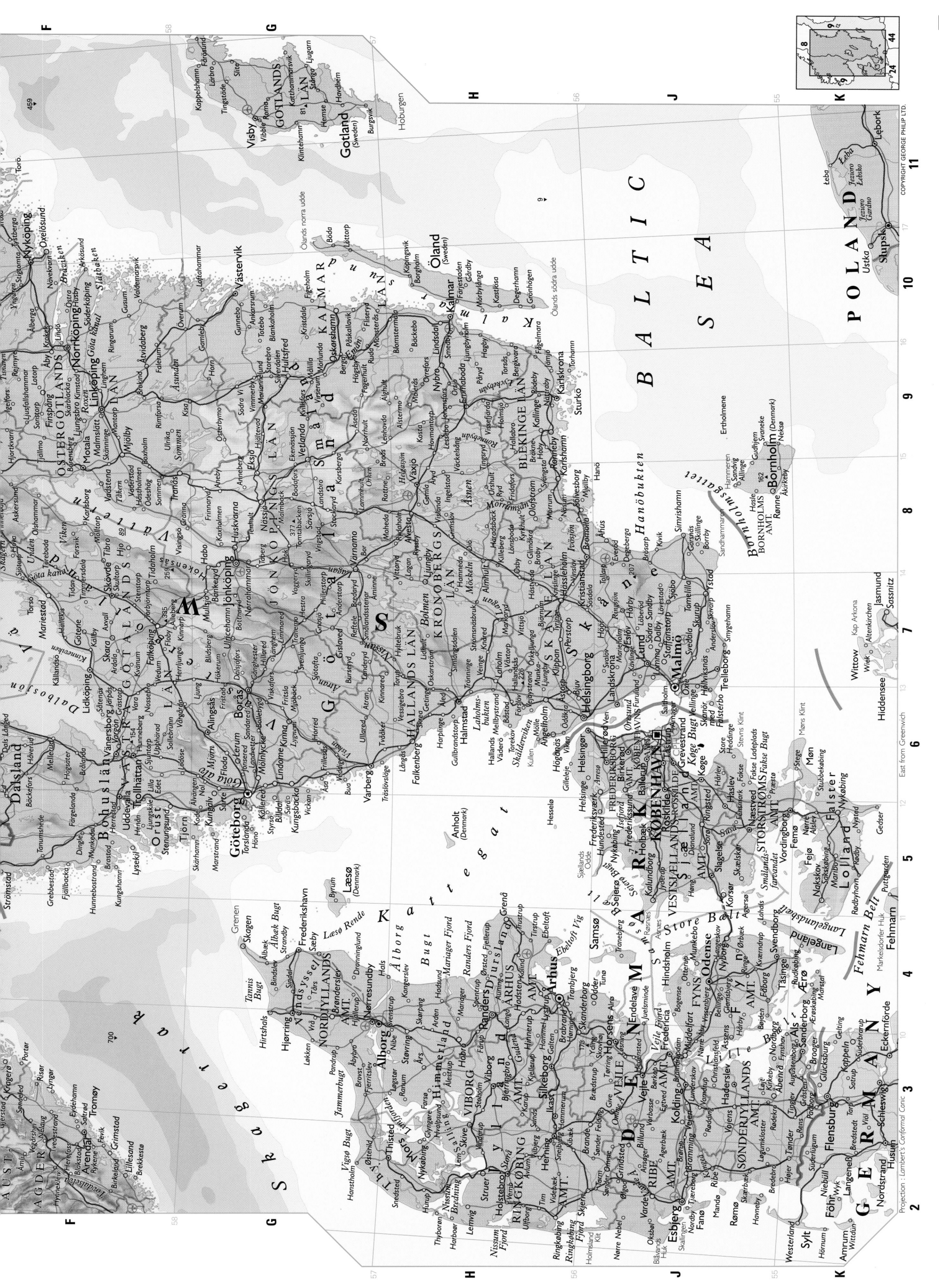

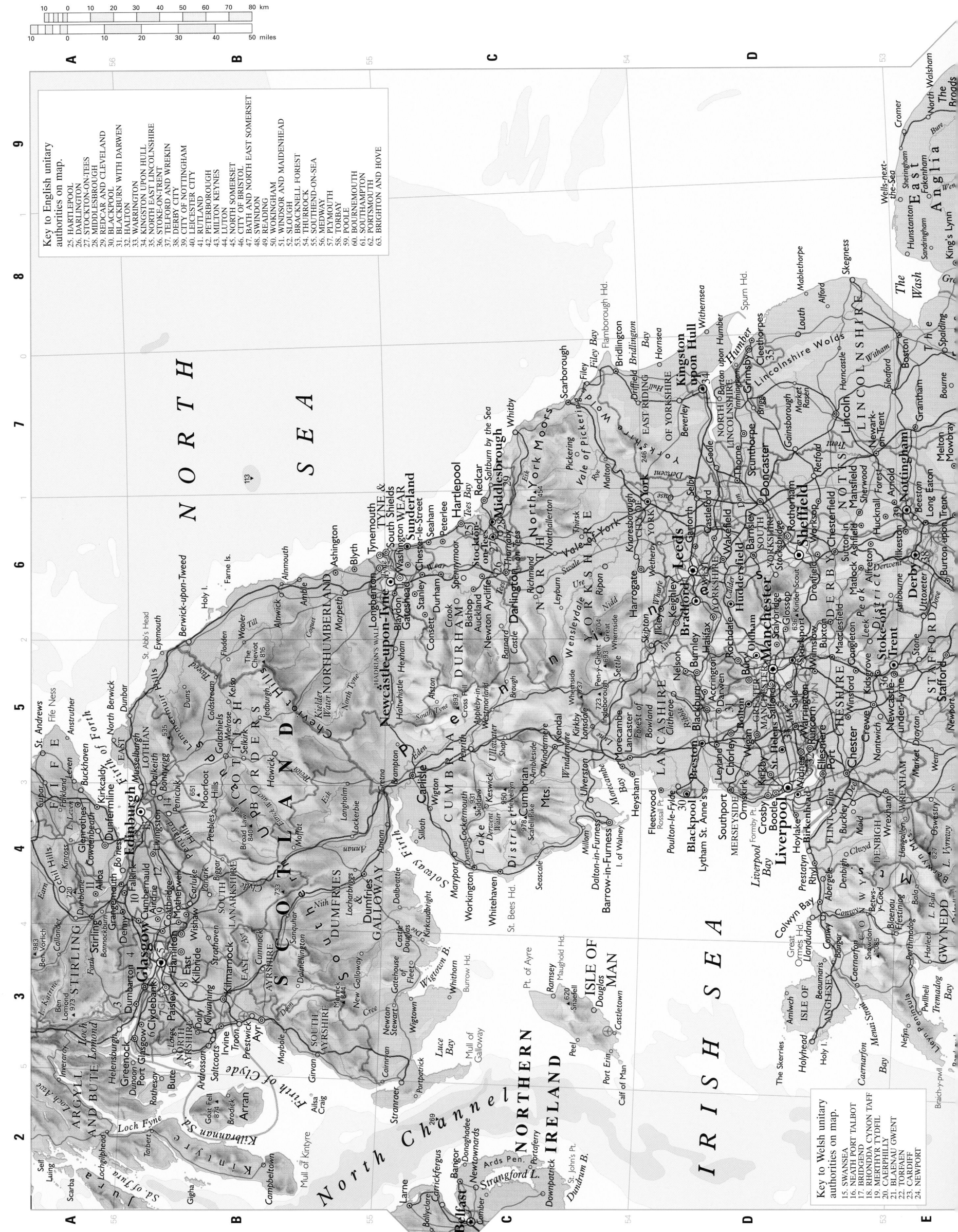

Key to English unitary authorities on map.
25. HARTLEPOOL
26. DARLINGTON
27. STOCKTON-ON-TEES
28. MIDDLESBROUGH
29. REDCAR AND CLEVELAND
30. BLACKPOOL
31. BLACKBURN WITH DARWEN
32. HALTON
33. WARRINGTON
34. KINGSTON UPON HULL
35. NORTH EAST LINCOLNSHIRE
36. NORTH LINCOLNSHIRE
37. TELFORD AND WREKIN
38. DERBY CITY
39. CITY OF NOTTINGHAM
40. LEICESTER CITY
41. RUTLAND
42. PETERBOROUGH
43. MILTON KEYNES
44. LUTON
45. NORTH SOMERSET
46. CITY OF BRISTOL
47. BATH AND NORTH EAST SOMERSET
48. SWINDON
49. READING
50. WOKINGHAM
51. WINDSOR AND MAIDENHEAD
52. SLOUGH
53. BRACKNELL FOREST
54. THURROCK
55. SOUTHEND-ON-SEA
56. MEDWAY
57. PLYMOUTH
58. TORBAY
59. POOLE
60. BOURNEMOUTH
61. SOUTHAMPTON
62. PORTSMOUTH
63. BRIGHTON AND HOVE

Key to Welsh unitary authorities on map.
15. SWANSEA
16. NEATH PORT TALBOT
17. BRIDGEND
18. RHONDDA CYNON TAFF
19. MERTHYR TYDFIL
20. CAERPHILLY
21. BLAENAU GWENT
22. TORFAEN
23. CARDIFF
24. NEWPORT

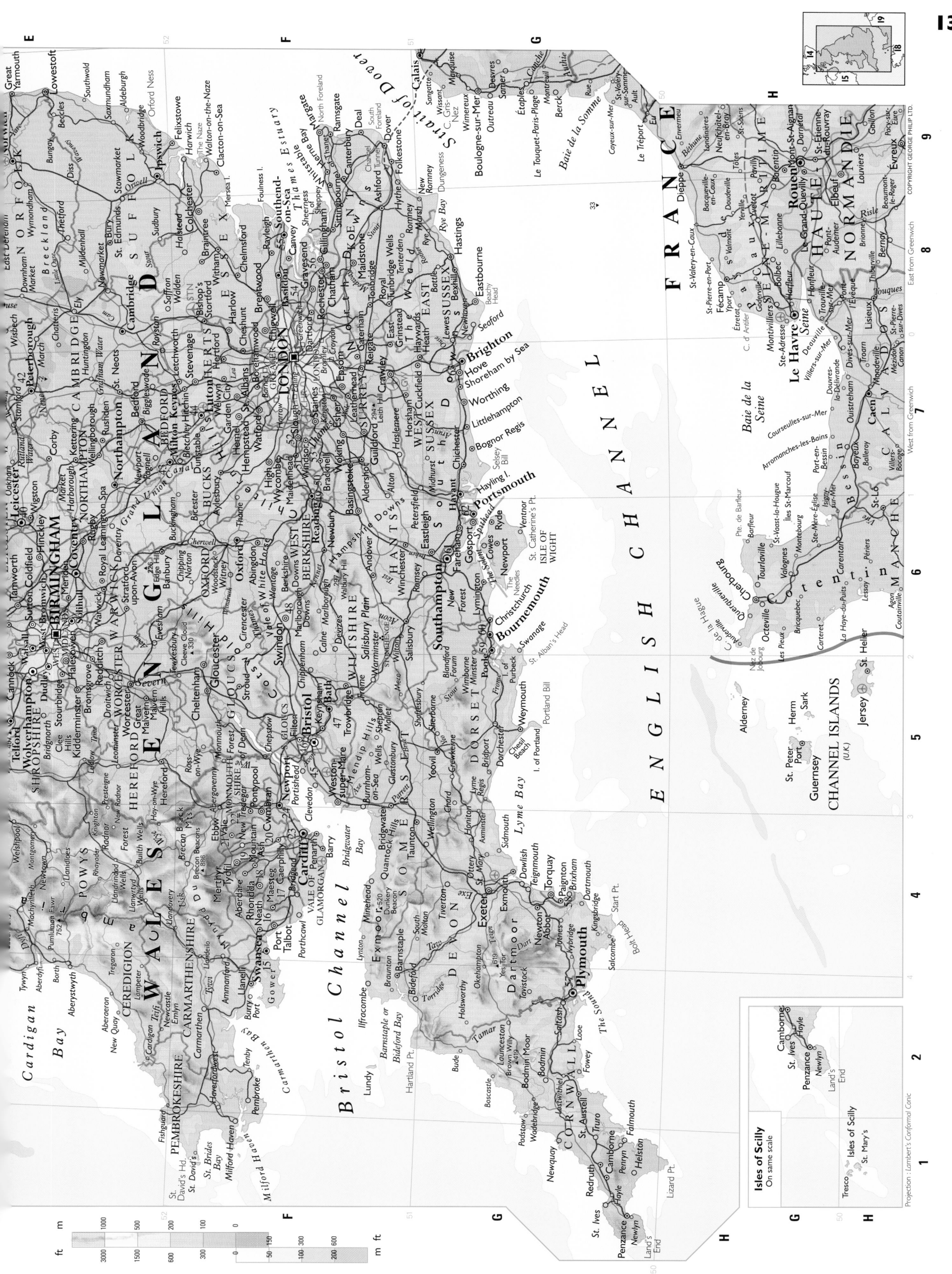

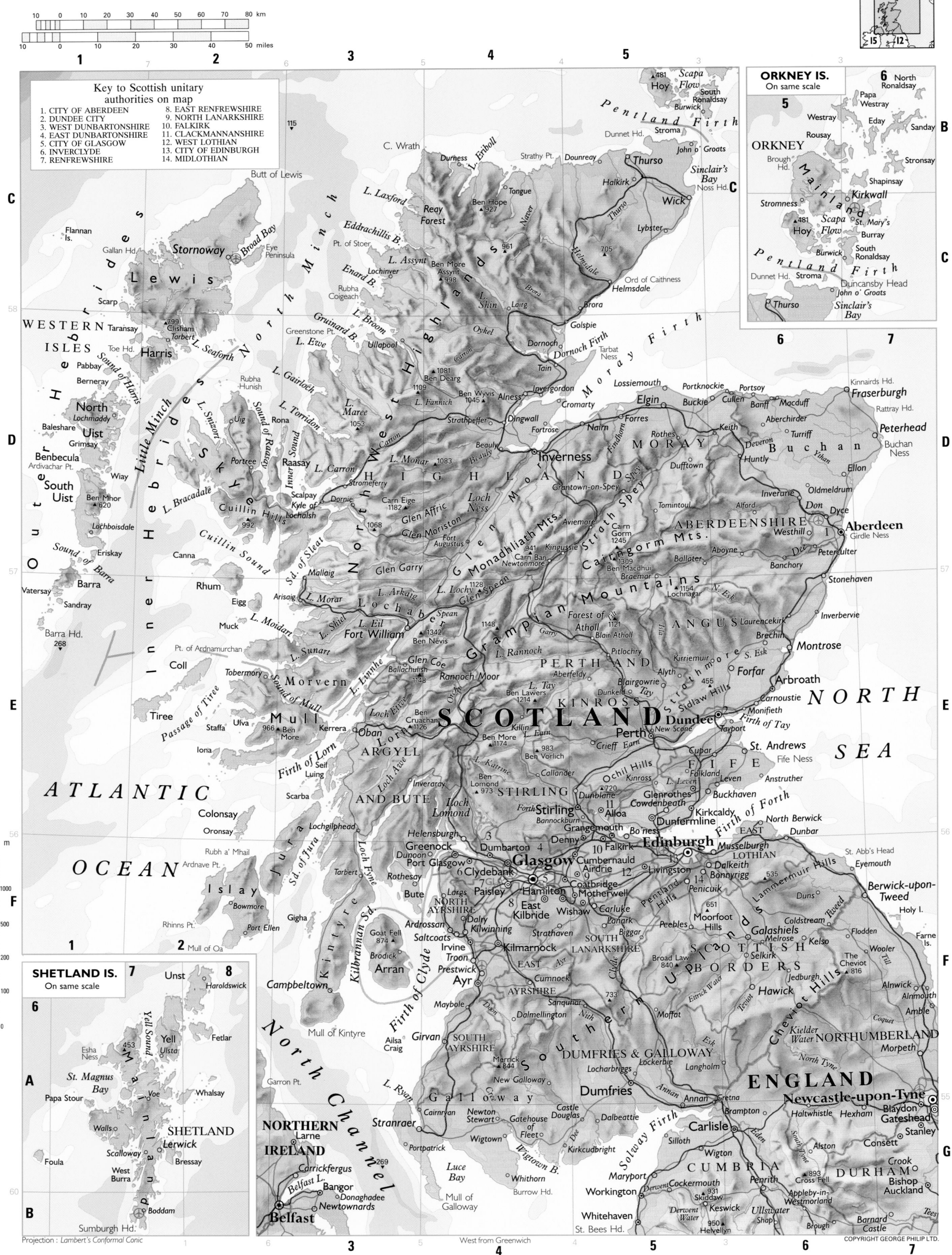

Key to Scottish unitary authorities on map

1. CITY OF ABERDEEN
2. DUNDEE CITY
3. WEST DUNBARTONSHIRE
4. EAST DUNBARTONSHIRE
5. CITY OF GLASGOW
6. INVERCLYDE
7. RENFREWSHIRE
8. EAST RENFREWSHIRE
9. NORTH LANARKSHIRE
10. FALKIRK
11. CLACKMANNANSHIRE
12. WEST LOTHIAN
13. CITY OF EDINBURGH
14. MIDLOTHIAN

ORKNEY IS. On same scale

SHETLAND IS. On same scale

Projection : Lambert's Conformal Conic

West from Greenwich

COPYRIGHT GEORGE PHILIP LTD.

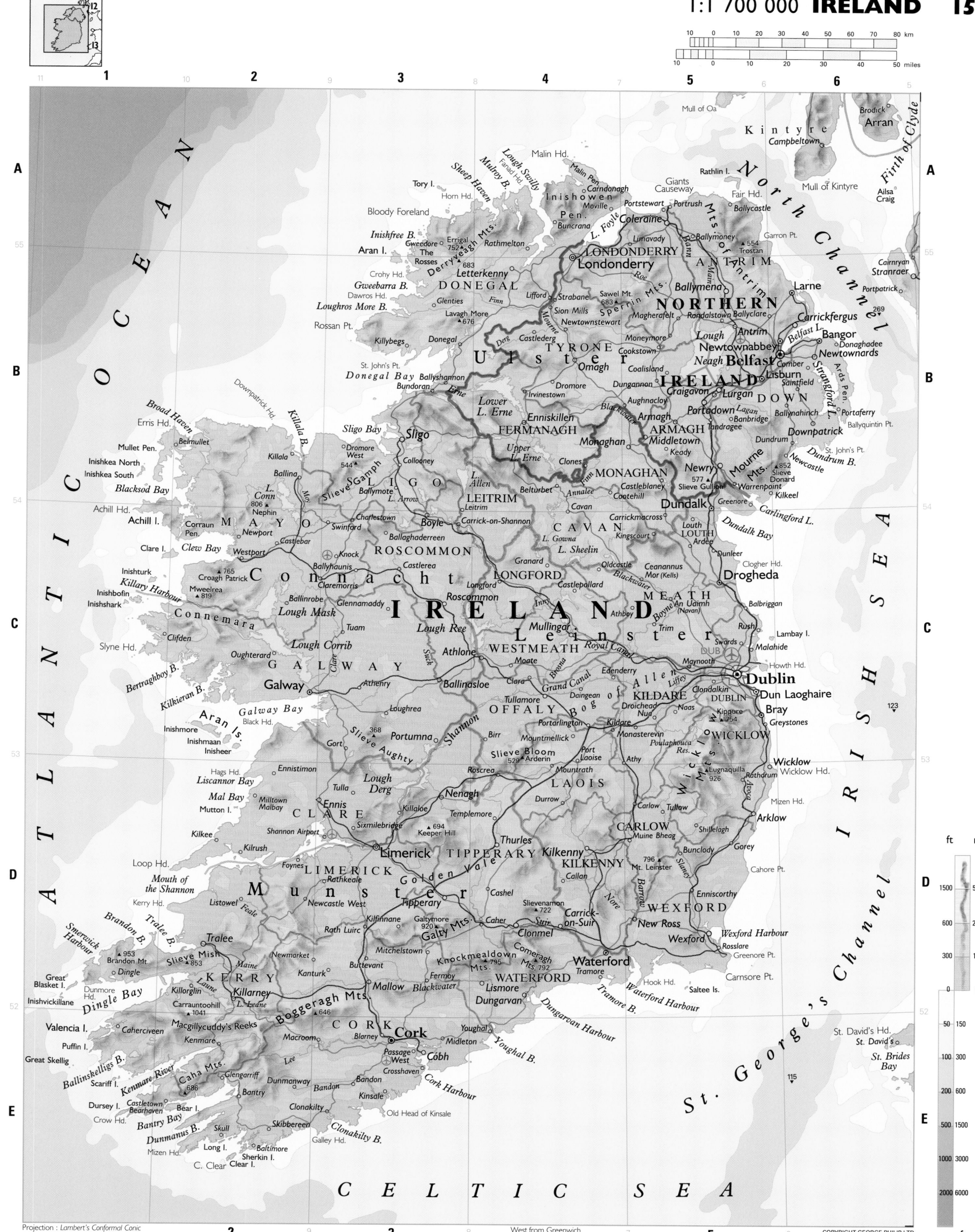

10 0 10 20 30 40 50 60 70 80 km
10 0 10 20 30 40 50 miles

A T L A N T I C   O C E A N

North Channel

Firth of Clyde

Kintyre

Brodick
Arran
Ailsa Craig

Mull of Oa
Mull of Kintyre
Campbeltown

Cairnryan
Stranraer
Portpatrick

Malin Hd.
Lough Swilly
Fanad Hd.
Mulroy B.
Malin Pen.
Carndonagh
Giants Causeway
Rathlin I.
Garron Pt.
Fair Hd.
Ballycastle

Tory I.
Sheep Haven
Horn Hd.
Inishowen Pen.
Moville
Buncrana
Portstewart
Portrush
L. Foyle
Coleraine
Ballymoney
554 Trostan
Larne

Bloody Foreland
Inishfree B.
Aran I.
Gweedore
Errigal 752
Derryveagh Mts.
The Rosses
683
Rathmelton
Letterkenny
LONDONDERRY
Londonderry
Limavady
Ballymena
ANTRIM
Portpatrick

Crohy Hd.
Gweebarra B.
Dawros Hd.
Glenties
DONEGAL
Lifford
Strabane
Sawel Mt. 683
Sperrin Mts.
Roe
Magherafelt
Randalstown Ballyclare
Garron Pt.
Carrickfergus
Belfast L. 269
Bangor
Newtownabbey
Newtownards
Comber
Belfast

Loughros More B.
Rossan Pt.
Lavagh More 676
Killybegs
Donegal
Ulster
Castlederg
Newtownstewart
TYRONE
Omagh
Cookstown
Moneymore
Coalisland
Dungannon
Lough Neagh
Antrim
IRELAND
Lisburn
Saintfield
Donaghadee
Ards Pen.

St. John's Pt.
Donegal Bay
Ballyshannon
Bundoran
Ballintra
Erne
Lower L. Erne
Enniskillen
FERMANAGH
Upper L. Erne
Clones
Monaghan
Irvinestown
Dromore
Blackwater
Aughnacloy
Middletown
Keady
Armagh
ARMAGH
Portadown
Lagan
Lurgan
Craigavon
Banbridge
Tandragee
DOWN
Ballynahinch
Downpatrick
St. John's Pt.
Dundrum B.

NORTHERN

Broad Haven
Erris Hd.
Downpatrick Hd.
Killala B.
Sligo Bay
Sligo
Colloney
L. Allen
Belturbet
Annalee
MONAGHAN
577 Slieve Gullion
Castleblaney
Cootehill
Cavan
Carrickmacross
Kingscourt
Newry
Mourne Mts.
852 Slieve Donard
Warrenpoint
Kilkeel
Greenore
Carlingford L.
Dundrum

Mullet Pen.
Belmullet
Inishkea North
Inishkea South
Blacksod Bay
Killala
Ballina
Dromore West
544
S Gamph
Slieve
Ballymote
L. Arrow
SLIGO
LEITRIM
Leitrim
L. Gowna
Granard
L. Sheelin
CAVAN
Oldcastle
Ceanannus Mor (Kells)
Blackwater
Ardee
LOUTH
Louth
Dunleer
Clogher Hd.
Dundalk
Dundalk Bay
Drogheda

Achill Hd.
Achill I.
Clare I.
Corraun Pen.
Newport
Castlebar
MAYO
L. Conn 806
Nephin
Mox
Swinford
Charlestown
Ballaghaderreen
ROSCOMMON
Castlerea
Boyle
Carrick-on-Shannon
Carrickmacross

Inishturk
Inishbofin
Inishshark
Killary Harbour
Mweelrea 819
765 Croagh Patrick
Westport
Knock
Claremorris
Ballinrobe
Ballyhaunis
Castlerea
Roscommon
LONGFORD
Longford
Castlepollard
MEATH
An Uaimh (Navan)
Balbriggan
Rush
Lambay I.

Connacht
Lough Mask
Glennamaddy
Roscommon
Inny
Athboy
Boyne
Trim
Swords
Malahide
Howth Hd.

Slyne Hd.
Clifden
Connemara
Oughterard
Lough Corrib
Tuam
Lough Ree
WESTMEATH
Mullingar
Moate
Royal Canal
Maynooth
Clondalkin
Dublin
DUBLIN
Dun Laoghaire

Bertraghboy B.
Kilkieran B.
GALWAY
Galway
Athenry
Loughrea
Ballinasloe
Clara
Athlone
IRELAND
Leinster
Edenderry
Allen
KILDARE
Naas
DUB
Bray

Aran Is.
Inishmore
Inishmaan
Inisheer
Galway Bay
Black Hd.
Gort
368
Slieve Aughty
Portumna
Shannon
Birr
OFFALY
Tullamore
Daingean
Bog of Allen
Kildare
Droichead Nua
Monasterevin
Grand Canal
Portarlington
Mountmellick
Port Laoise
Poulaphouca Res.
Kippure 754
WICKLOW
Greystones

Hags Hd.
Liscannor Bay
Ennistimon
Mal Bay
Mutton I.
Tulla
Lough Derg
Slieve Bloom 529 Arderin
Roscrea
Mountrath
LAOIS
Durrow
Athy
Carlow
Lugnaquilla 926
Rathdrum
Wicklow
Wicklow Hd.
Mizen Hd.

Loop Hd.
Kilkee
Kilrush
CLARE
Ennis
Sixmilebridge
Milltown Malbay
Shannon Airport
694
Keeper Hill
Nenagh
Killaloe
Templemore
Thurles
Kilkenny
KILKENNY
Muine Bheag
Tullow
Bunclody
Shillelagh
Gorey
Arklow

Mouth of the Shannon
Kerry Hd.
Foynes
Rathkeale
LIMERICK
Limerick
TIPPERARY
Golden Vale
Tipperary
Cashel
Callan
796 Mt. Leinster
Cahore Pt.
Enniscorthy

Brandon B.
Tralee B.
Smerwick Harbour
Brandon Pt.
953
Brandon Mt. 853
Slieve Mish
Tralee
Listowel
Feale
Newcastle West
Munster
Rath Luirc
Sheppy
Thurles
Slievenamon 722
Carrick-on-Suir
Clonmel
WEXFORD
New Ross
Wexford Harbour
Rosslare

Great Blasket I.
Dunmore Hd.
Inishvickillane
Dingle
Dingle Bay
KERRY
Killorglin
Killarney
Newmarket
Kanturk
Mitchelstown
Fermoy
Buttevant
Mallow
Galtymore 920
Galty Mts.
Caher
Knockmealdown Mts. 795 792
Lismore
Dungarvan
WATERFORD
Waterford
Tramore
Tramore B.
Hook Hd.
Saltee Is.
Carnsore Pt.

Valencia I.
Puffin I.
Great Skellig
Cahirciveen
Macgillycuddy's Reeks
Carrauntoohill 1041
L. Leane
Kenmare
Macroom
Boggeragh Mts. 646
Blarney
CORK
Cork
Lee
Blackwater
Youghal
Midleton
Youghal B.
Dungarvan Harbour
Waterford Harbour
Greenore Pt.

Ballinskelligs B.
Scariff I.
Dursey I.
Crow Hd.
Castletown Bearhaven
Bear I.
Bantry Bay
Kenmare River
Caha Mts. 686
Glengarriff
Bantry
Dunmanway
Bandon
Bandon
Clonakilty
Kinsale
Passage West
Cobh
Cork Harbour
Old Head of Kinsale

St. David's Hd.
St. David's
St. Brides Bay

Mizen Hd.
Dunmanus B.
Long I.
Skull
Baltimore
Sherkin I.
Skibbereen
Clonakilty B.
Galley Hd.
C. Clear
Clear I.

C E L T I C   S E A

I R I S H   S E A

St. George's Channel

123

115

ft   m
1500   500
600   300
300
0   0
50   150
100   200
200   500
500   1000
1000   3000
2000   6000
m   ft

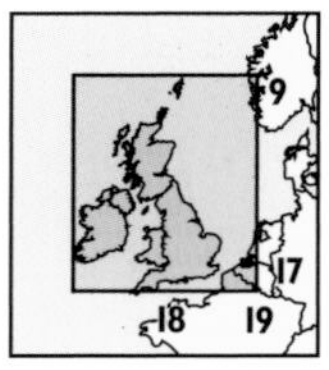

50 25 0 25 50 75 100 125 150 175 km
50   0   25   50   75   100   125 miles

1   2   3   4   5   6   7   8   9

A — Shetland Is. — Yell — Unst — Fetlar — Foula — Mainland — Lerwick — Fair Isle — Askøy — Bergen — Osøyro — NORWAY — Haugesund — Kopervik — Åkrahamn — Stord — Bømlo — Stavanger — Boknafjo — Sandnes — Bryne — Nærbø

B — Orkney Is. — Westray — Sanday — Stronsay — Mainland — Kirkwall — Hoy — South Ronaldsay — Pentland Firth

ATLANTIC OCEAN — 316 — 1224

C — Outer Hebrides — Lewis — Stornoway — Harris — St. Kilda — North Uist — Benbecula — South Uist — North Minch — C. Wrath — Thurso — Wick — North West Highlands — Ullapool — Lairg — Helmsdale — Golspie — Tain — Invergordon — Dingwall — Moray Firth — Buckie — Banff — Fraserburgh — Peterhead — Nairn — Elgin — Huntly — Inverurie — Inverness — Aviemore — Aberdeen — L. Ness — 1182 — Spey — Grampian Mts. — Don — SCOTLAND — Dee — 1311 — Ballater — Stonehaven — Ben Nevis 1342 — Fort William — Rhum — Eigg — Coll — Tobermory — Forfar — Arbroath — Skye — Portree — Mallaig — 789 — Inner Hebrides — Oban — 1214 — Perth — Dundee — St. Andrews

NORTH SEA — 238

D — Mull — Colonsay — L. Lomond — 973 — Stirling — Dunfermline — Kirkcaldy — Jura — Greenock — Glasgow — Edinburgh — Islay — Paisley — East Kilbride — Hamilton — Berwick-upon-Tweed — Arran — Kilmarnock — Galashiels — Campbeltown — Ayr — Southern Uplands — 840 Jedburgh — 816 — Alnwick — Hawick — Cheviot Hills — Newcastle-upon-Tyne — South Shields — Sunderland — Dumfries — Hexham — Gateshead — Durham — Hartlepool — Redcar — Buncrana — Letterkenny — Coleraine — Annan — Carlisle — 893 — Darlington — Middlesbrough — Aran I. — Lifford — Londonderry — Ballymena — Larne — Kirkcudbright — Workington — Stockton-on-Tees — Donegal — Omagh — Antrim — Bangor — Whitehaven — Cumbrian Mts. — 978 — Scarborough

E — Bundoran — Lower L. Erne — Enniskillen — Clones — Armagh — Newry — Belfast — Lisburn — Lurgan — Mull of Galloway — Barrow-in-Furness — Lancaster — Bridlington — Ballina — L. Conn — Sligo — Leitrim — Cavan — Castleblaney — Dundalk — Douglas — I. of Man — Harrogate — York — Beverley — Achill I. — Castlebar — Roscommon — Longford — Monaghan — Drogheda — UNITED — Kingston upon Hull — Westport — L. Mask — Lough Ree — Mullingar — Boyne — KINGDOM — Blackpool — Keighley — Leeds — Louth — Connemara — Lough Corrib — Athlone — Ballinasloe — Tullamore — Liffey — Dublin — IRISH — Preston — Burnley — Bradford — Huddersfield — Barnsley — Doncaster — Grimsby — Galway B. — Galway — Aran Is. — Birr — Port Laoise — Dun Laoghaire — Holyhead — SEA — Blackburn — Halifax — Bolton — Manchester — Oldham — Rotherham — Humber — Ennis — Lough Derg — Nenagh — Carlow — Kilkenny — Athy — Arklow — Anglesey — Liverpool — Warrington — Stockport — Sheffield — Lincoln — Skegness — The Wash — Kilrush — Limerick — Thurles — Tipperary — Carrick-on-Suir — Wexford — Bangor — Colwyn Bay — Chester — Crewe — Chesterfield — Mansfield — Boston — Cromer

F — 953 — Dingle — Listowel — Mallow — Clonmel — Rosslare — 1085 — Snowdon — Wrexham — Derby — Nottingham — Grantham — King's Lynn — Norwich — Great Yarmouth — Lowestoft — Carrauntoohill 1041 — Tralee — Killarney — Waterford — Pwllheli — Cambrian Mts. — Stoke on Trent — Stafford — Telford — ENGLAND — Leicester — Corby — Peterborough — Thetford — Macgillycuddy's Reeks — Valencia I. — Kilgarvan — Dungarvan — Youghal — Cardigan Bay — Aberystwyth — Welshpool — Shrewsbury — Wolverhampton — Nuneaton — Ely — Bury St. Edmunds — Ipswich — Bantry — Cork — Cóbh — Kinsale — WALES — BIRMINGHAM — Coventry — Rugby — Northampton — Cambridge — Felixstowe — C. Clear — 99 — Fishguard — Carmarthen — Brecon — 886 — Redditch — Worcester — Royal Leamington Spa — Milton Keynes — Stevenage — Harwich — Colchester — Chelmsford — Haverfordwest — Milford Haven — Pembroke — Merthyr Tydfil — Neath — Hereford — Gloucester — Cheltenham — Oxford — Luton — Harlow — St. George's Channel — Llanelli — Rhondda — Cwmbran — Newport — Cotswold Hills — High Wycombe — Hemel Hempstead — Watford — Slough — Basildon — Southend-on-Sea — Margate — Swansea — Cardiff — Bristol — Bath — Swindon — Newbury — Reading — LONDON — Chatham — Canterbury — Dover — Port Talbot — Barry — Weston-super-Mare — Thames — Reigate — Maidstone — 36

Bristol Channel — Exmoor — Taunton — Salisbury — Basingstoke — Guildford — Winchester — Crawley — Ashford — Folkestone — Str. of Dover — Calais — BELGIUM

G — CELTIC SEA — Barnstaple — Bude — 618 — Dartmoor — Exmouth — Yeovil — Southampton — Fareham — Havant — Brighton — Eastbourne — Hastings — Boulogne — Newquay — Truro — St. Austell — Plymouth — Torbay — Bournemouth — Poole — Weymouth — Newport — Isle of Wight — Portsmouth — Worthing — Land's End — Penzance — Falmouth — Isles of Scilly — English Channel

FRANCE — Alderney — C. de la Hague — Pte. de Barfleur — Fécamp — Dieppe — Amiens — Guernsey — St. Peter Port — Sark — Cherbourg — Valognes — Le Havre — Rouen — Channel Is. (U.K.) — St. Helier — Jersey — Trouville-sur-Mer — Bayeux — Caen — Lisieux

West from Greenwich

Projection: Conical with two standard parallels
East from Greenwich
COPYRIGHT GEORGE PHILIP LTD.

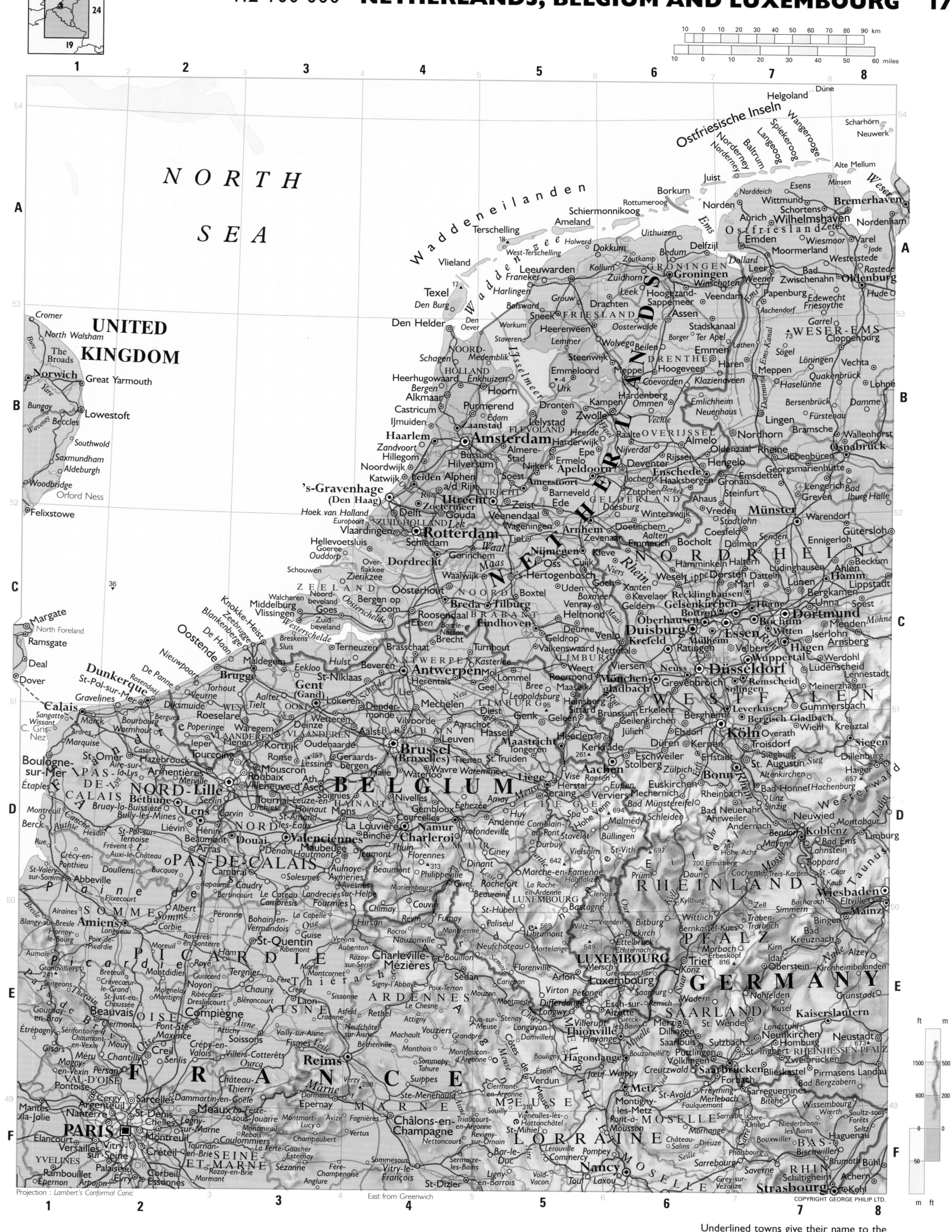

Underlined towns give their name to the
administrative area in which they stand.

DÉPARTEMENTS IN THE PARIS AREA
1. Ville de Paris   3. Val-de-Marne
2. Seine-St-Denis   4. Hauts-de-Seine

Underlined towns give their name to the
administrative area in which they stand.

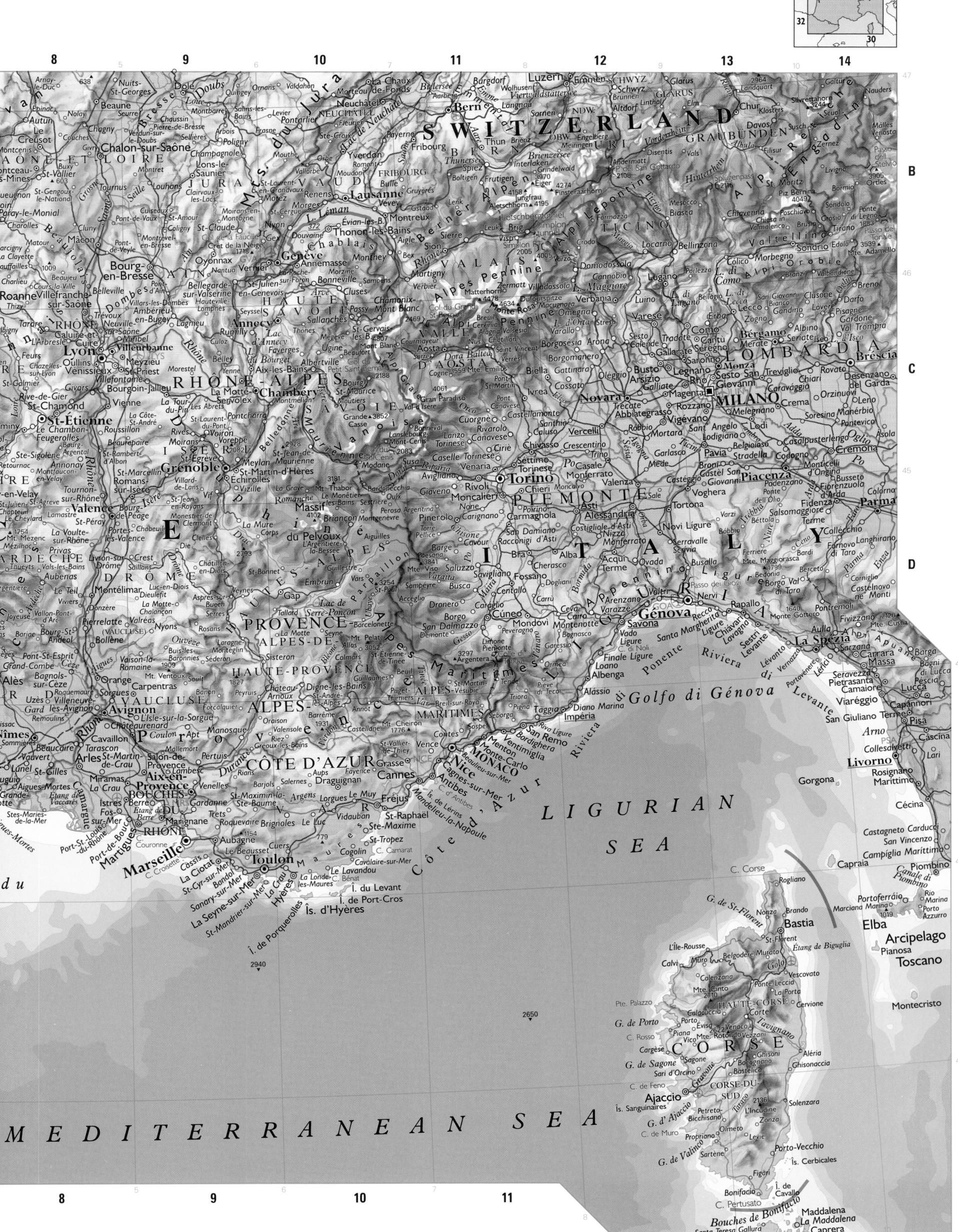

LIGURIAN
SEA

MEDITERRANEAN SEA

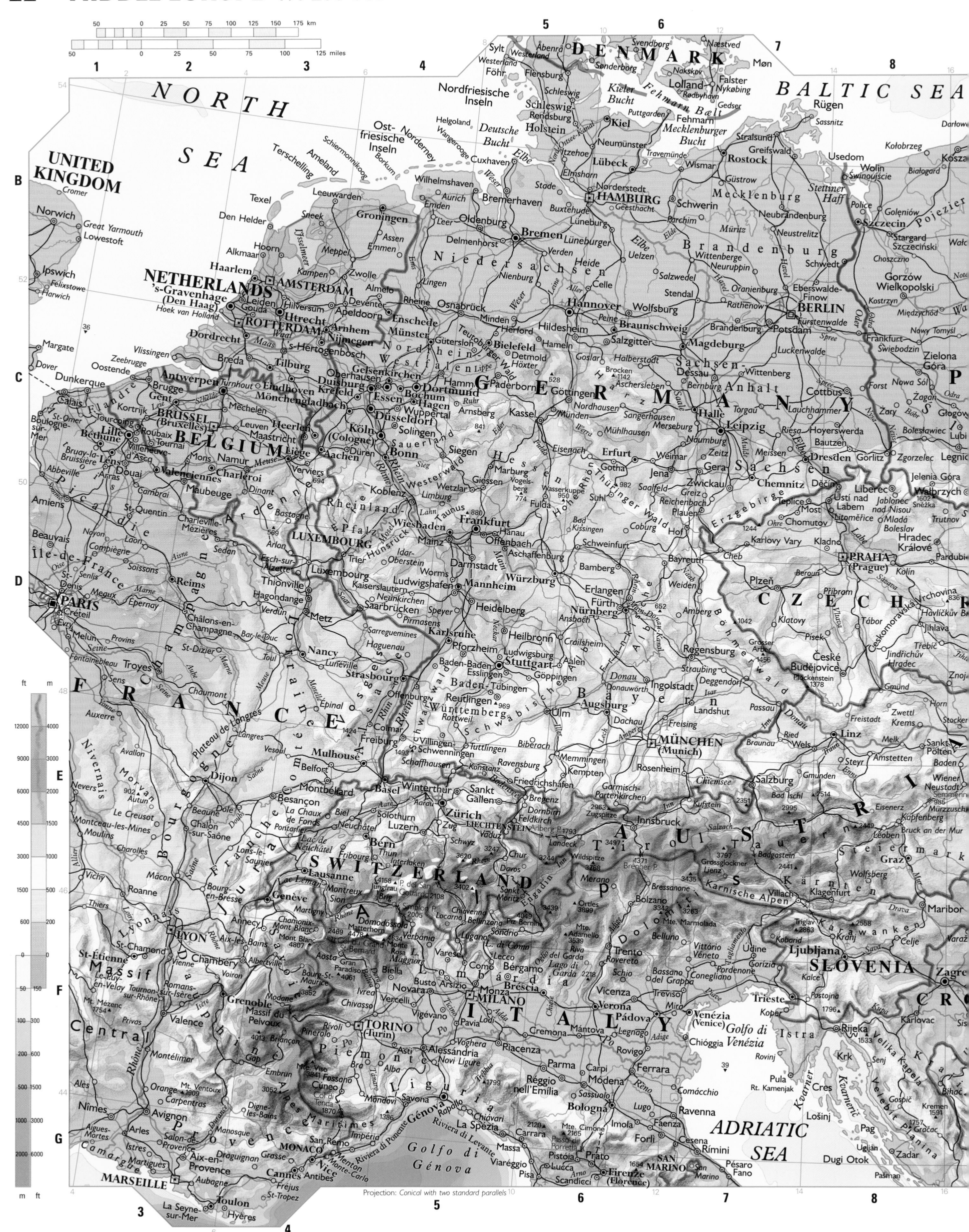

Projection: Conical with two standard parallels

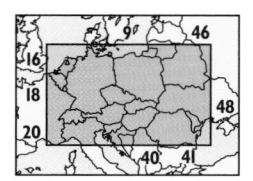

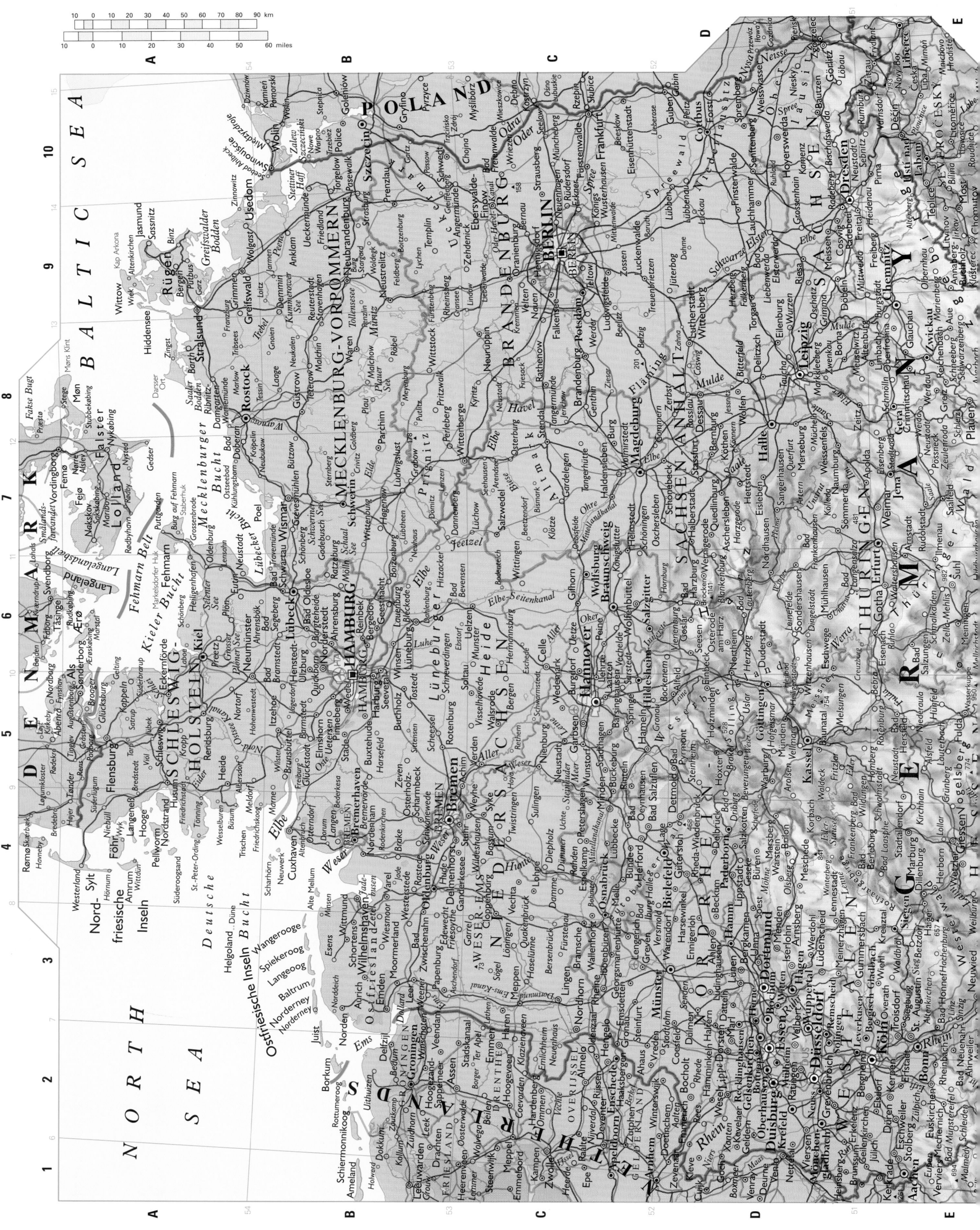

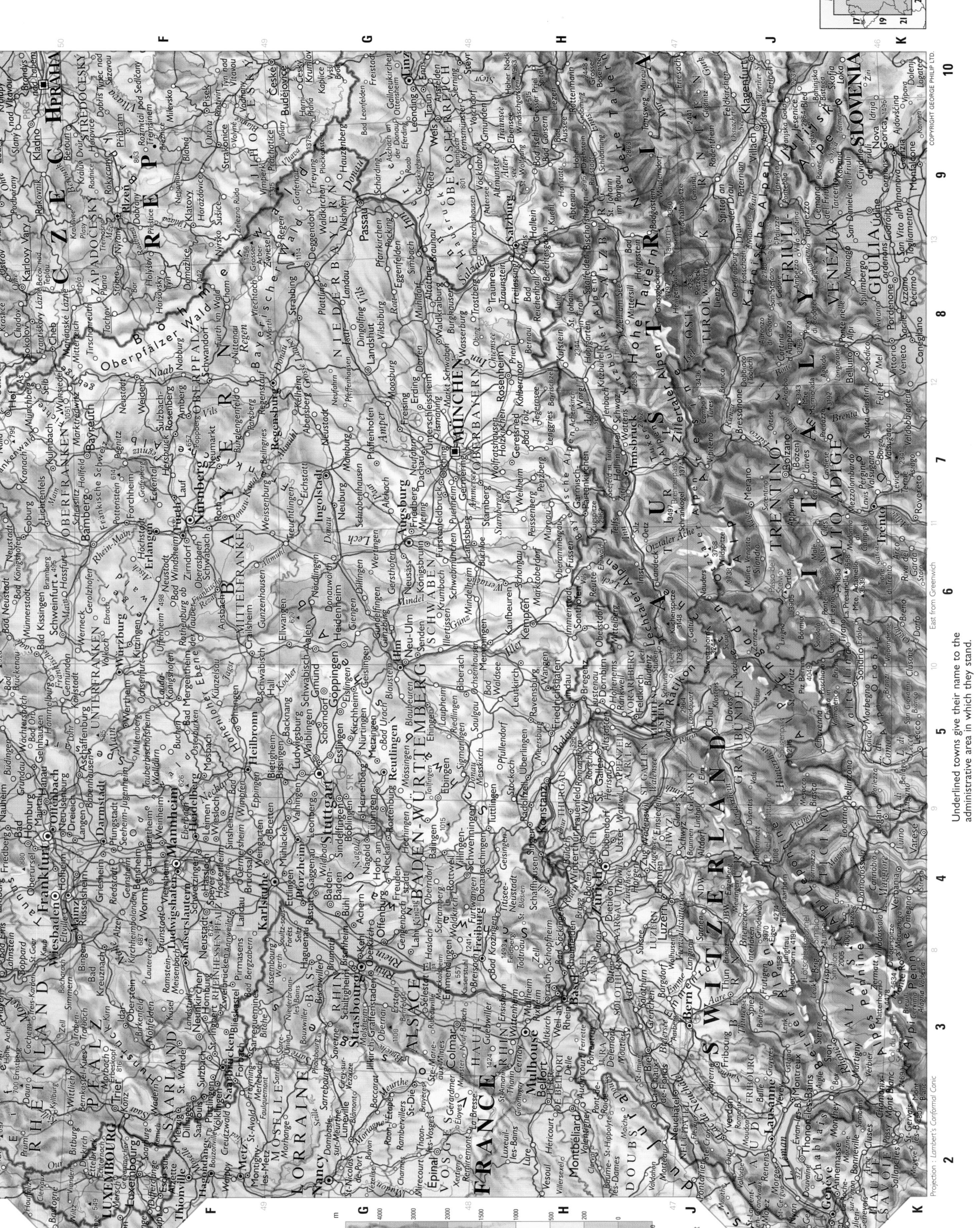

Underlined towns give their name to the
administrative area in which they stand.

Projection : Lambert's Conformal Conic

East from Greenwich

COPYRIGHT GEORGE PHILIP LTD.

Underlined towns give their name to the
administrative area in which they stand.

COPYRIGHT GEORGE PHILIP LTD.

East from Greenwich

Underlined towns give their name to the
administrative area in which they stand.

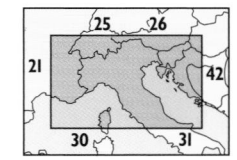

Administrative divisions in Croatia:

Brodsko-Posavska   4. Medimurska   8. Virovitičko-Podravska
Koprivničko-Križevačka   6. Požeško-Slavonska   10. Zagrebačka
Krapinsko-Zagorska   7. Varaždinska

Inter-entity boundaries as agreed
at the 1995 Dayton Peace Agreement.

COPYRIGHT GEORGE PHILIP LTD.

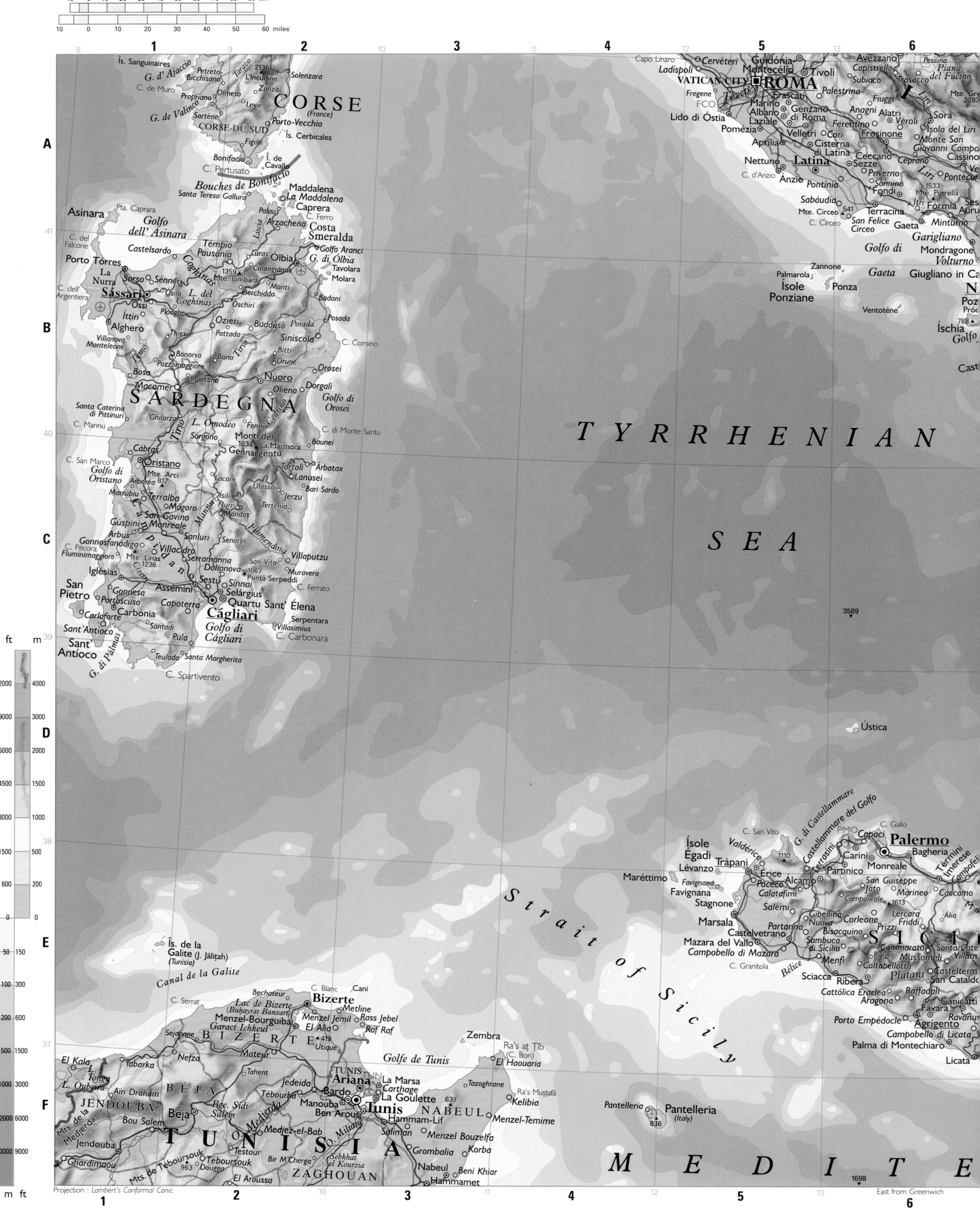

CORSE
(France)

Ís. Sanguinaires
G. d'Ajaccio
Petreto-
Bicchisano
L'Incudine
Zonza
Solenzara
Propriano
Olmeto
Levie
Sartène
Porto-Vecchio
Bonifácio
Figari
C. de Muro
G. de Valinco
CORSE-DU-SUD
Î. de Cavallo
C. Pertusato
Bouches de Bonifacio
Maddalena
La Maddalena
Santa Teresa Gallura
Caprera
Asinara
Palau
Arzachena
C. Ferro
Golfo
dell' Asinara
Costa
Smeralda
C. del
Falcone
Castelsardo
Têmpio
Pausânia
Golfo Aranci
G. di Olbia
Porto Tôrres
Luras
Olbia
Tavolara
La
Nurra
Sorso
Sénnori
Calangiánus
Monti
Molara
C. dell'
Argentiera
Sássari
Ósilo
Mte. Limbara
Berchidda
Budoni
Ittiri
Óssi
Ploaghe
Ozieri
Posada
Alghero
Thiesi
Pattada
Buddusò
Siniscola
C. Comino
Villanova
Monteleóne
Bonorva
Bano Tirso
Bitti
Orune
Bosa
Pozzomaggiore
Búlzi
Macomer
Núoro
Oliena
Orosei
Bolotana
Dorgali
SARDEGNA
Santa Caterina
di Pittinuri
Ghilarza
L. Omodeo
Fonni
Golfo di
Orosei
Sórgono
C. Mannu
Cúglieri
Monti del
Gennargentu
C. di Monte Santu
Mte. Arci
1834
La Mármora
Baunei
Oristano
812
Arbórea
Lácóni
Tortolì
Árbatax
Marrúbiu
Lanusei
Golfo di
Oristano
Terralba
Mógoro
Ulassai
Jerzu
Isili
Mándas
Bari Sardo
Nurri
Tertenia
Gúspini
San Gavino
Monreale
Sanluri
Senorbì
Arbus
Villacidro
Serramanna
Gonnosfanádiga
Mte. Linas
1236
Dolianova
Villaputzu
C. Pécora
Fluminimaggiore
Sestu
Sínnai
Muravera
Iglésias
Selárgius
San Vito
Assémini
Quartu Sant' Élena
Punta Serpeddi
1067
San
Pietro
Gonnesa
Capoterra
Serpentara
Portoscuso
Cágliari
C. Ferrato
Sant'Antíoco
Carbónia
Villasimius
Carloforte
Santadi
Golfo di
Cágliari
Sant'
Antíoco
Teulada
Pula
C. Carbonara
Santa Margherita
G. di Palmas
C. Spartivento

T Y R R H E N I A N

S E A

3589

Capo Linaro
Cervéteri
Ladíspoli
GUIDÓNIA
Montecélio
Tivoli
Avezzano
Capistrello
Piana
del Fúcino
VATICAN CITY
FCO
Fregene
ROMA
Palestrina
Subiaco
Trasacco
Mte. Gr
2283
Frascati
Marino
Anagni
Albano
Genzano
di Roma
Fiuggi
Alatri
Sora
Laziale
Velletri
Cori
Ferentino
Isola del Liri
Pomézia
Lido di Óstia
Cisterna
di Latina
Frosinone
Monte San
Giovanni Campa
C. d'Anzio
Ánzio
Ceccano
Ceprano
Cassino
Nettuno
Pontínia
Aprília
Sabáudia
Priverno
Sezze
1533
Fondi
Sómino
Itri
Formia
Mte. Petrella
Terracina
San Felice
Circeo
Mte. Circeo
541
Gaeta
Minturno
Auru
C. Circeo
Garigliano
Golfo di
Mondragone
Giugliano in Ca
Zannone
Gaeta
Volturno
Palmarola
Ísole
Ponziane
Ponza
N
Poz
Próc
Ventoténe
788
Íschia
Golfo
Cast

Ústica

ISOLE
ÉGADI
C. San Vito
G. di Castellammare del Golfo
C. Gallo
PMO
Capaci
Palermo
Valdérice
Castellammare
del Golfo
Bagheria
Lévanzo
1110
Terrasini
Carini
Monreale
Termini
Imerese
Maréttimo
Trápani
Érice
Alcamo
Partinico
San Guiseppe
Jato
Camporéale
Mineo
Cáccamo
Favignana
Paceco
Marineo
Favara
Stagnone
Calatafimi
Gibellina
1613
Lercara
Friddi
Ália
Marsala
Salemi
Nuova
Corleone
Bisacquino
SICI
Mazara del Vallo
Castelvetrano
Partanna
Prizzi
Cammarata
Santa Cate
Villam
Campobello di Mazara
Sambuca
di Sícilia
Búrgio
Mussomeli
Menfi
Castelterm
San Cataldo
C. Granitola
Bélice
Ribera
Caltabellotta
Plátani
Sciacca
Cattólica Eraclea
Raffadali
Canicatt
Aragona
Favara
Ravanu
Porto Empédocle
Agrigento
Campobello di Licata
Palma di Montechiaro
Licata

Strait of Sicily

S t r a i t   o f   S i c i l y

Ís. de la
Galite (J. Jálitah)
(Tunisia)
Canal de la Galite
C. Serrat
Cani
C. Blanc
Bechateur
Metline
Rass Jebel
Bizerte
Menzel Jemil
Raf Raf
Menzel-Bourguiba
(Buhayrat Banzart)
El Alia
Lac de Bizerte
Zembra
Sejnane
Garet Ichkeul
Útique
419
Ra's aṭ Ṭīb
(C. Bon)
Nefza
Mateur
BIZERTE
Tahent
El Haouaria
El Kala
Tabarka
Nefza
Golfe de Tunis
L. Ichkeul
Tazoghrane
637
Aïn Draham
BÉJA
Jedeida
Téboursouk
TUNIS
La Marsa
Ra's Muṣṭafá
Kelibia
Roma
Ariana
Carthage
L. Ouberia
Bardo
La Goulette
Tébourba
Manouba
NABEUL
Menzel-Temime
JENDOUBA
Béja
Bée. Sidi
Salem
Medjerda
Tunis
Ben Arous
Hammam-Lif
Soliman
Menzel Bouzelfa
Jendouba
Bou Salem
Mts. de la
Medjerda
Medjez-el-Bab
Testour
Grombalia
Korba
Ghardimaou
Bir M'Cherga
Soliman
Nabeul
Beni Khiar
Mts. de Téboursouk
963
El Kourzia
Hammamet
T U N I S I A
El Aroussa
Dougga
ZAGHOUAN

Pantelleria
Pantelleria
(Italy)
836
1698

M E D I T E

M E D I T E R

East from Greenwich

Projection: Lambert's Conformal Conic

ADRIATIC SEA

IONIAN SEA

STRAIT OF OTRANTO

GREECE

ALBANIA

Tiranë
Durrës
Vlorë

MOLISE
APULIA
BASILICATA
CALÁBRIA

Fóggia
Bari
Táranto
Lecce
Brindisi
Matera
Potenza
Salerno
Cosenza
Catanzaro
Reggio di Calábria
Messina
Catánia
Siracusa

Golfo di Manfredónia
Golfo di Táranto
Golfo di Squillace
Golfo di Sant' Eufémia
Golfo di Gióia

KÉRKIRA
Kérkira (Corfu)

ISOLE EÓLIE

Underlined towns give their name to the
administrative area in which they stand.

COPYRIGHT GEORGE PHILIP LTD.

Projection : Lambert's Conformal Conic

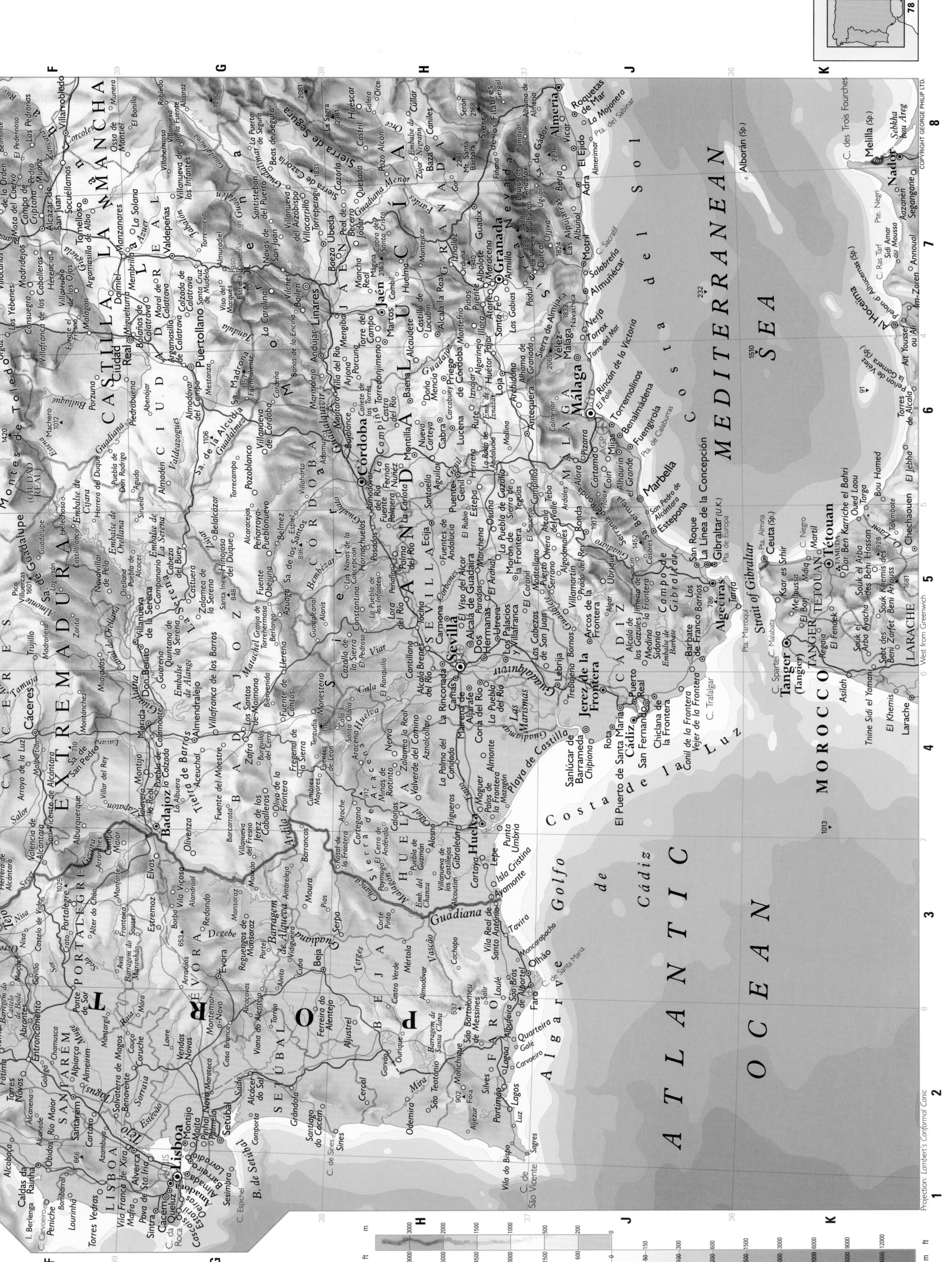

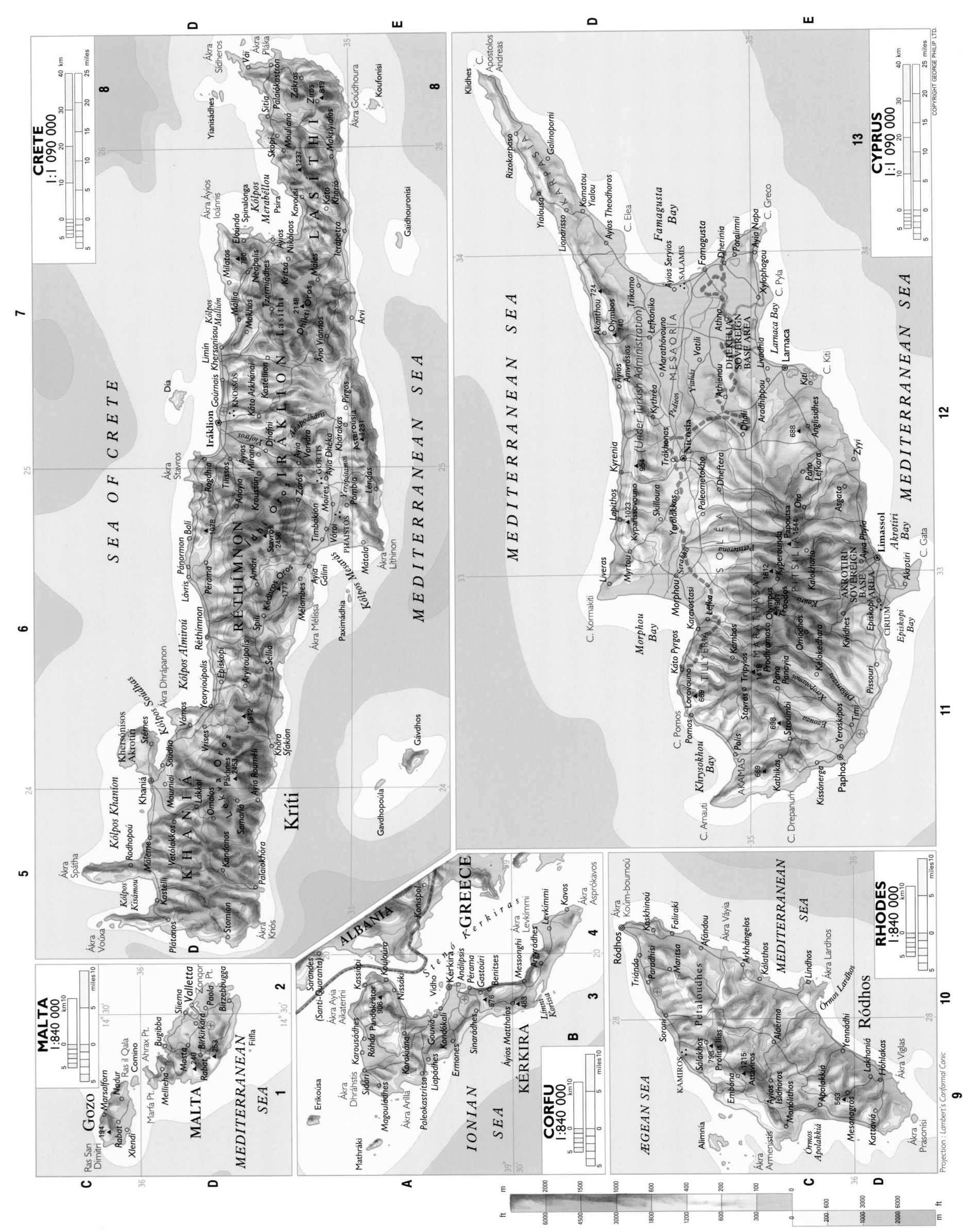

CRETE
1:1 090 000

MALTA
1:840 000

CORFU
1:840 000

RHODES
1:840 000

CYPRUS
1:1 090 000

Projection: Lambert's Conformal Conic

COPYRIGHT GEORGE PHILIP LTD.

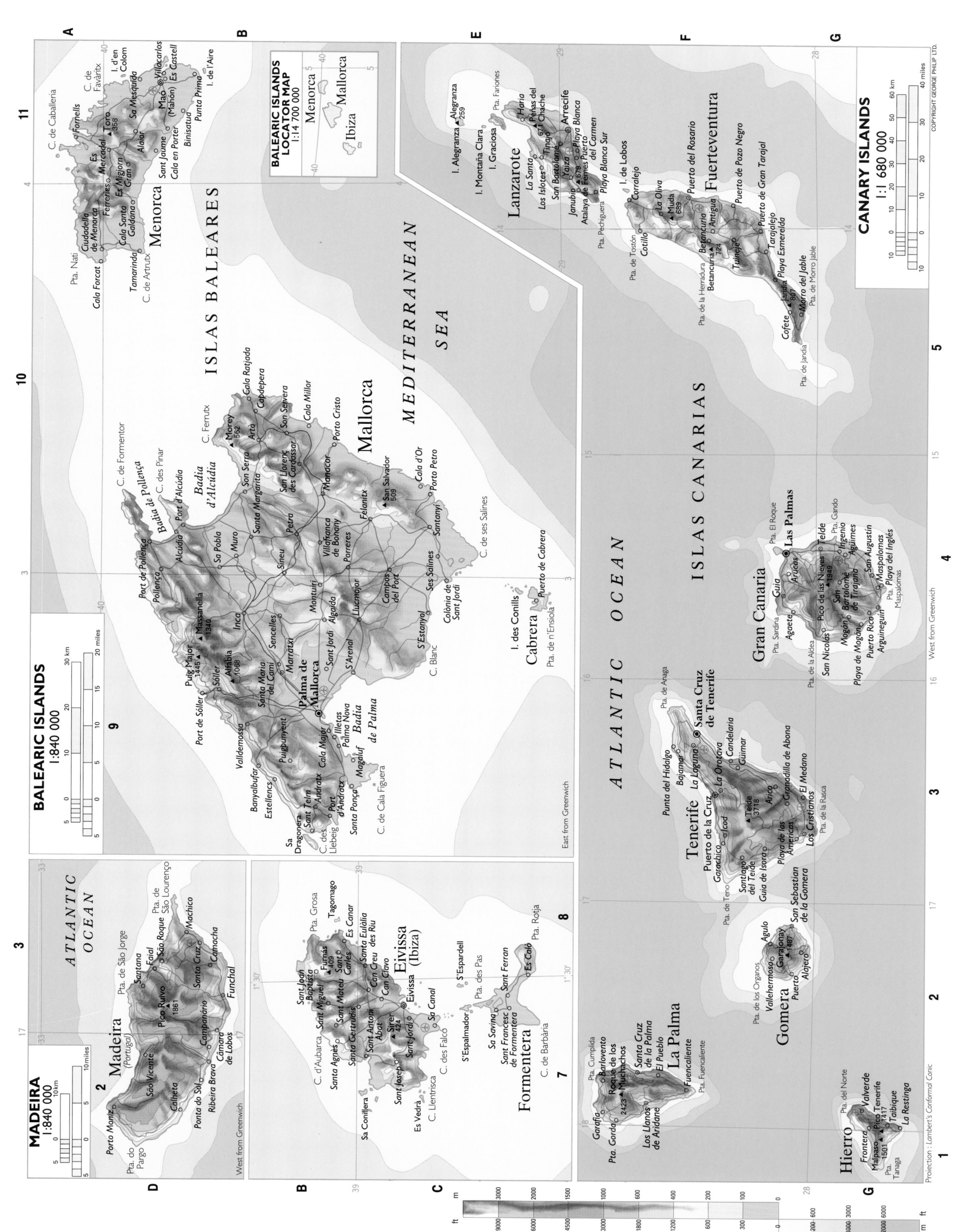

MADEIRA
1:840 000

BALEARIC ISLANDS
1:840 000

BALEARIC ISLANDS LOCATOR MAP
1:14 700 000

Menorca
Mallorca
Ibiza

CANARY ISLANDS
1:1 680 000

COPYRIGHT GEORGE PHILIP LTD.

Projection: Lambert's Conformal Conic

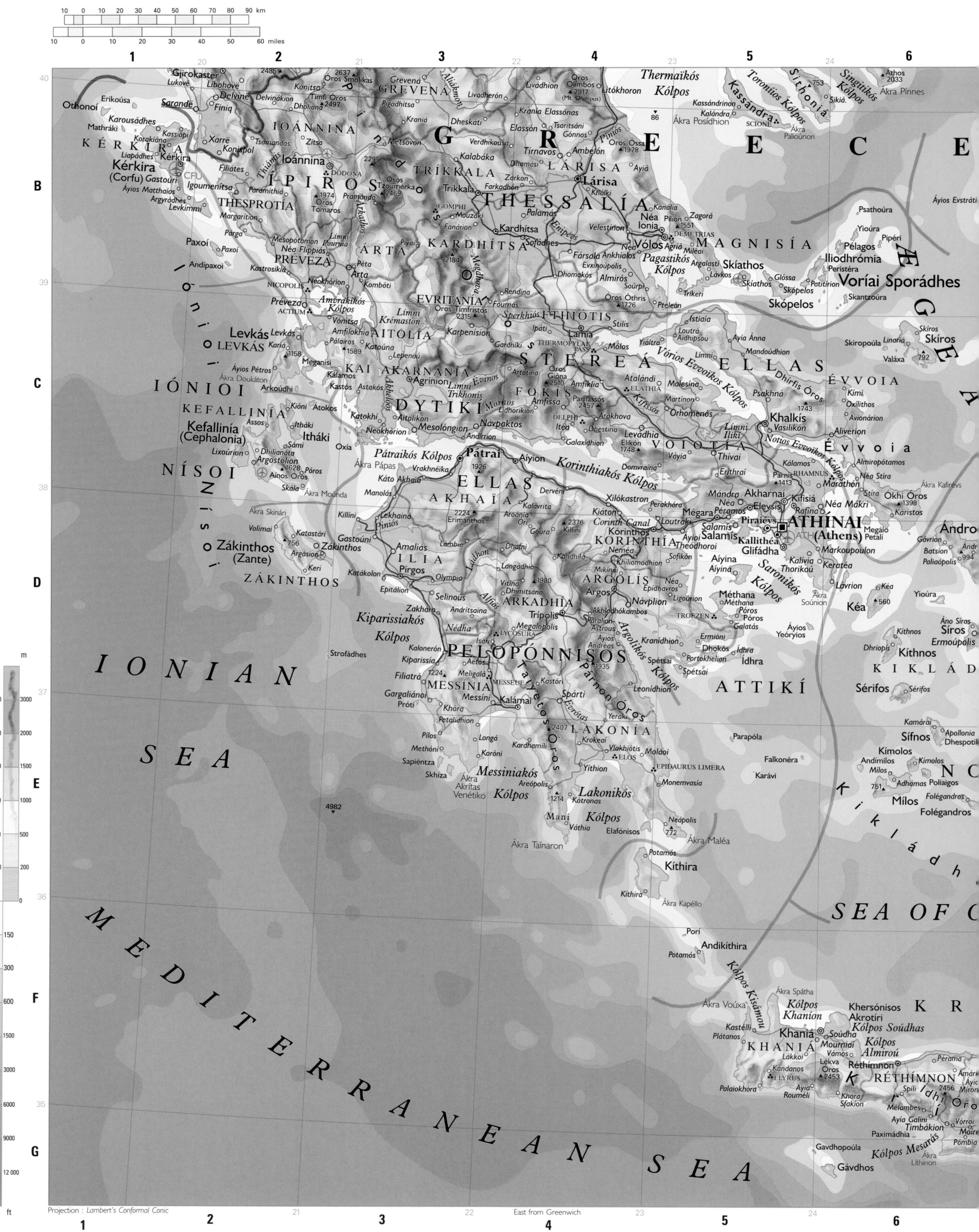

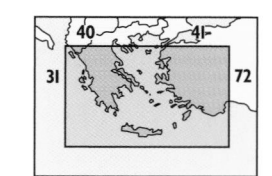

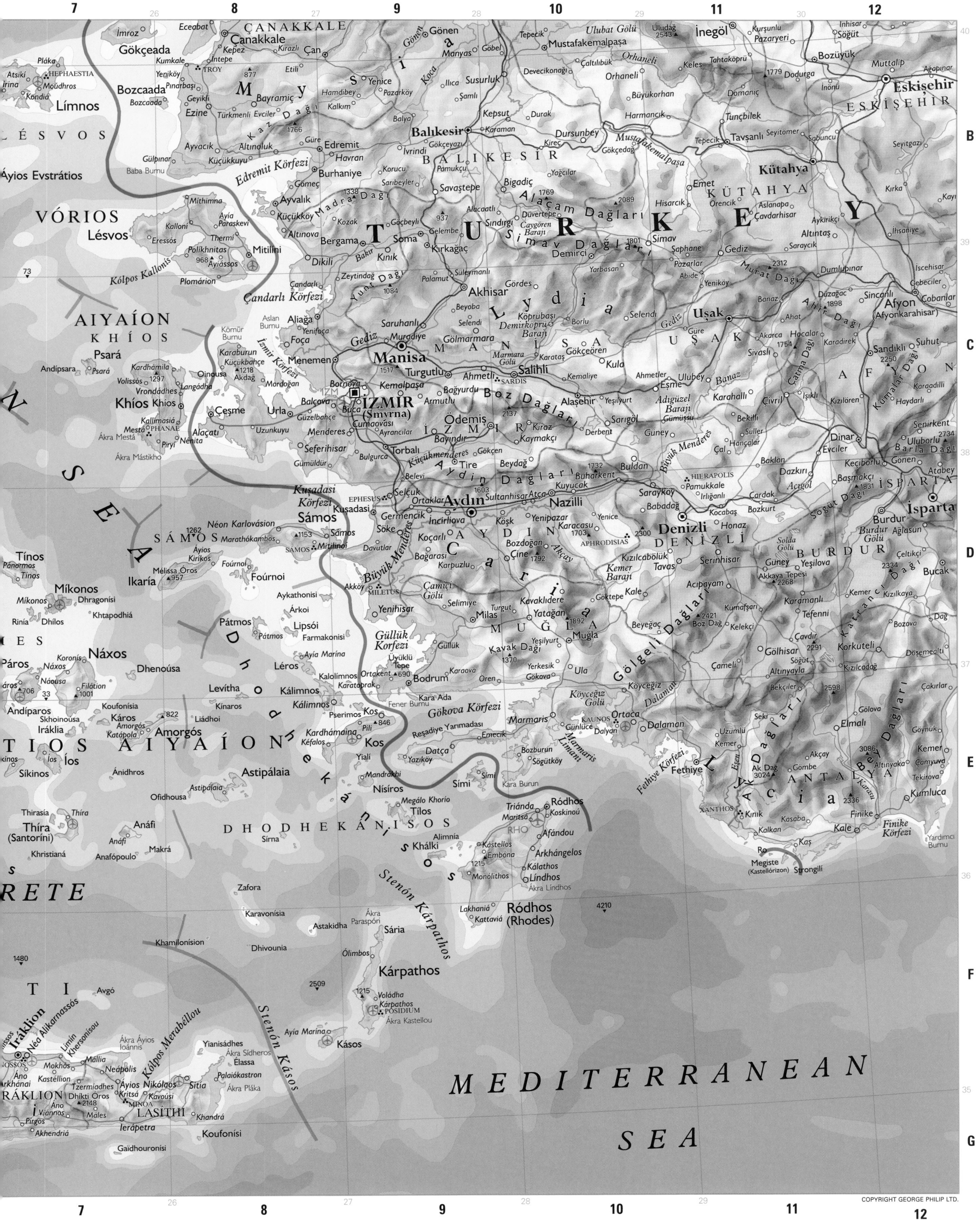

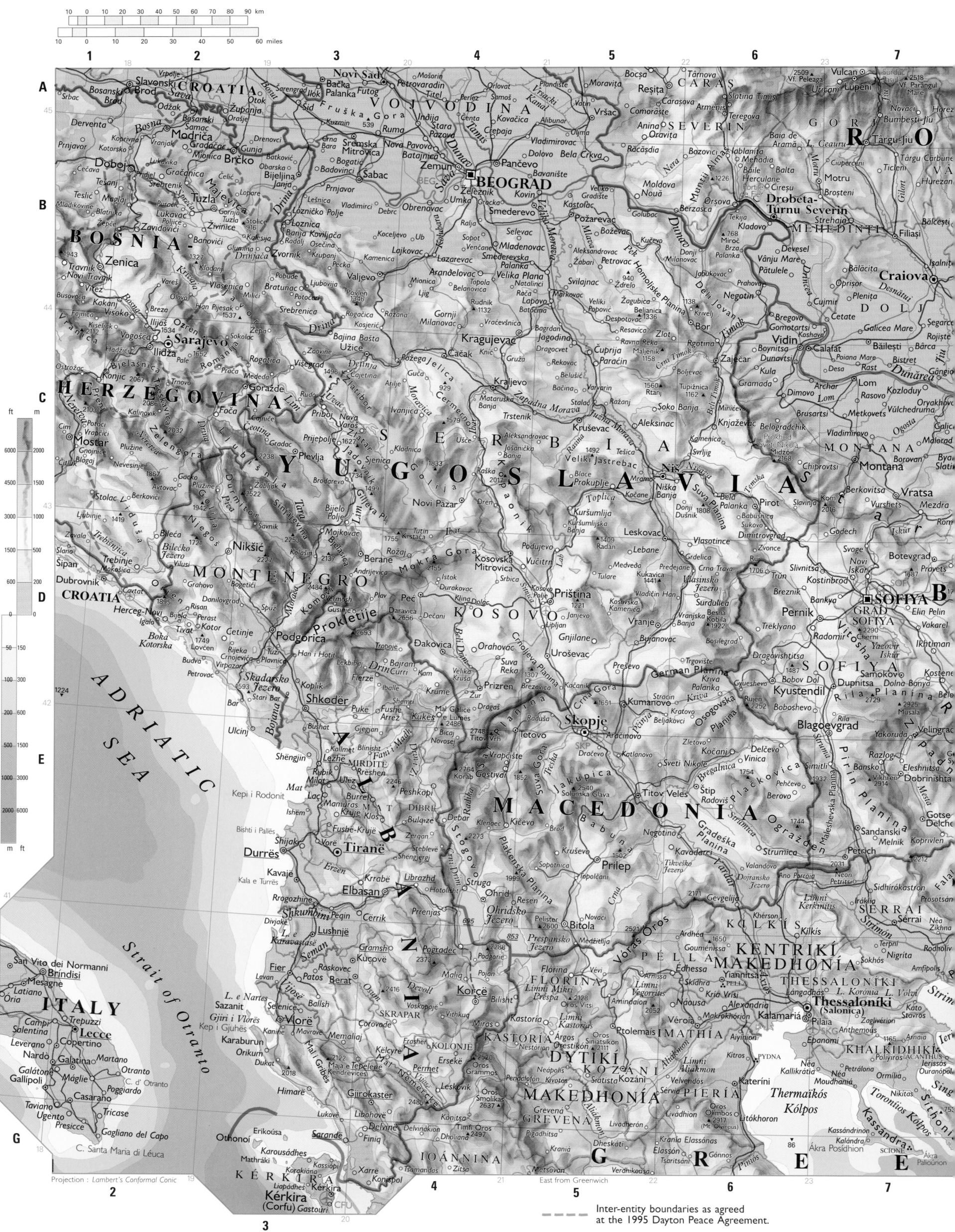

East from Greenwich

_ _ _ _ _ Inter-entity boundaries as agreed
at the 1995 Dayton Peace Agreement.

Underlined towns give their name to the
administrative area in which they stand.

Projection : Lambert's Conformal Conic

East from Greenwich

Administrative divisions in Croatia:
1. Brodsko-Posavska   5. Osiječko-Baranjska   9. Vukovarsko-Srijemska
2. Koprivničko-Križevačka   6. Požeško-Slavonska
4. Medimurska   8. Virovitičko-Podravska

– – – – Inter-entity boundaries as agreed
at the 1995 Dayton Peace Agreement.

Underlined towns give their name to the administrative area in which they stand.

COPYRIGHT GEORGE PHILIP LTD.

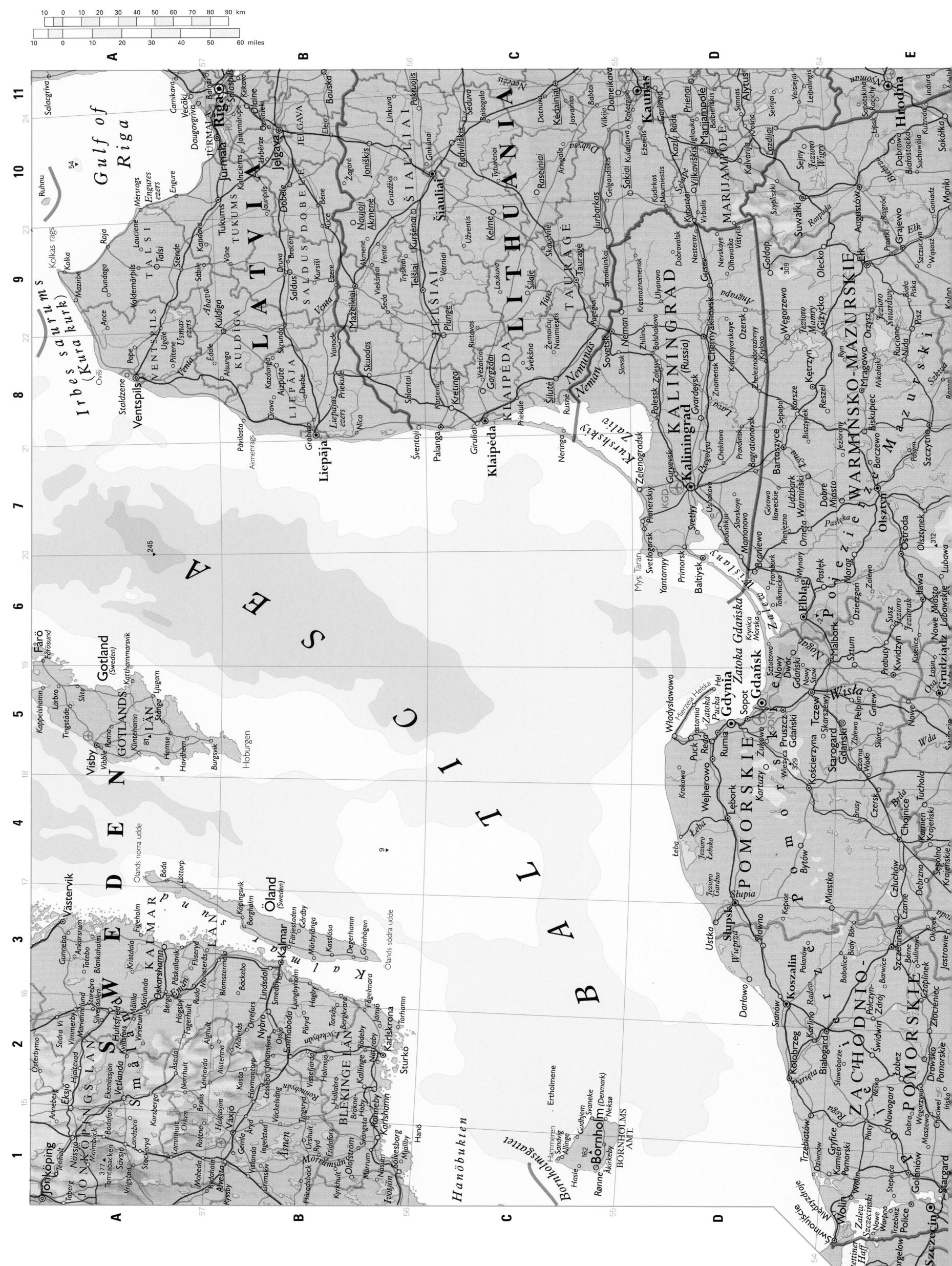

Underlined towns give their name to the administrative area in which they stand.

COPYRIGHT GEORGE PHILIP LTD.

East from Greenwich

Projection : Lambert's Conformal Conic

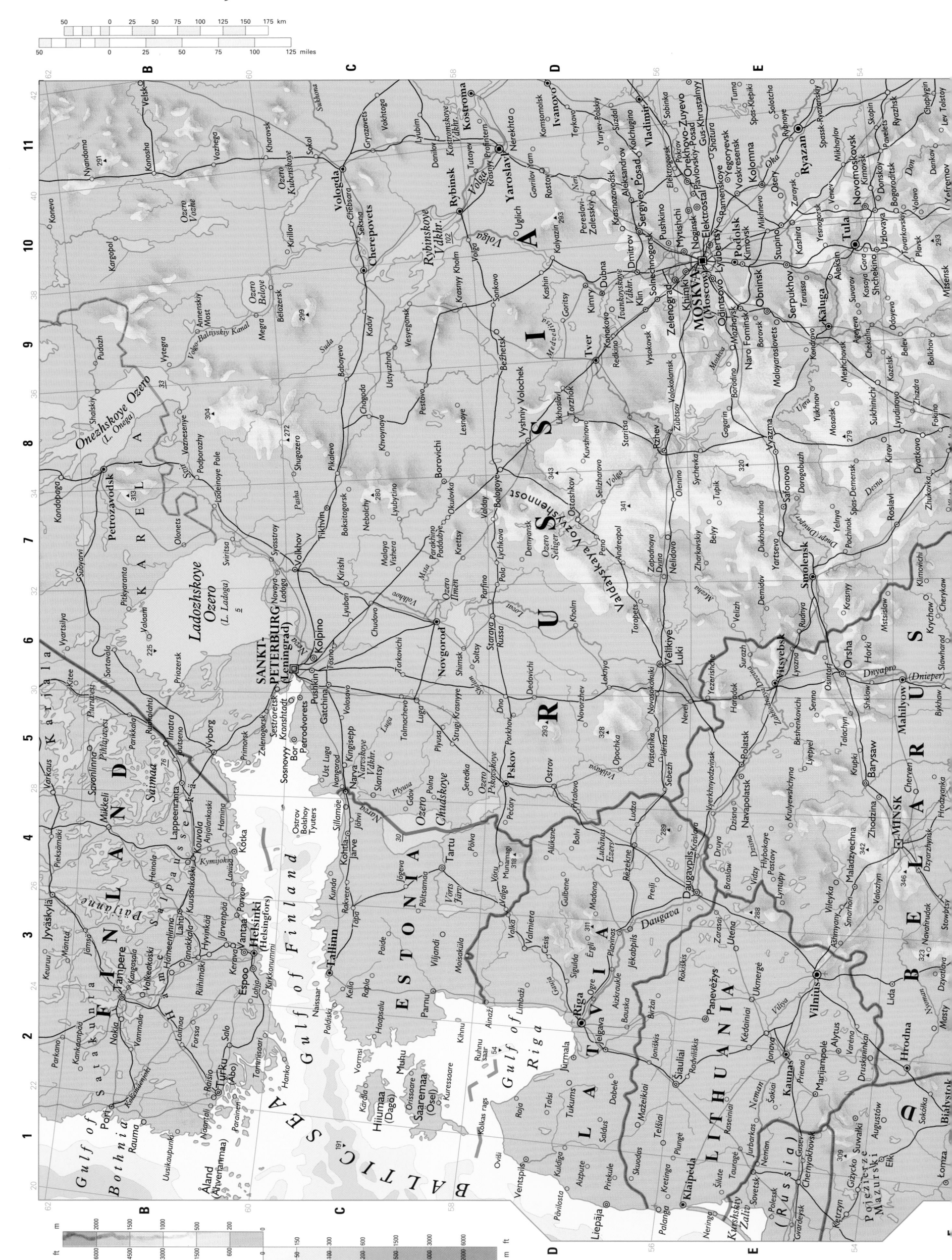

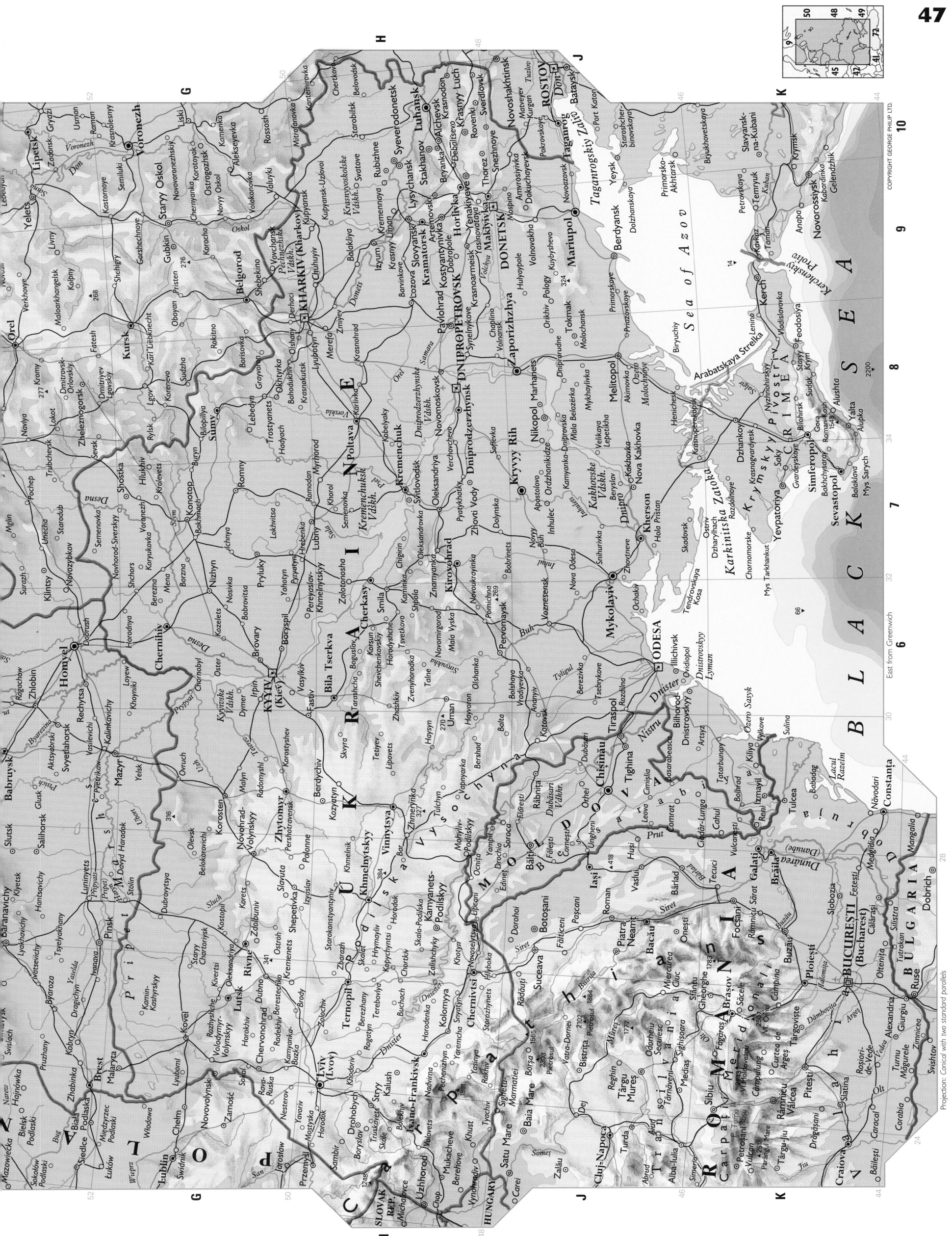

Projection: Conical with two standard parallels

East from Greenwich

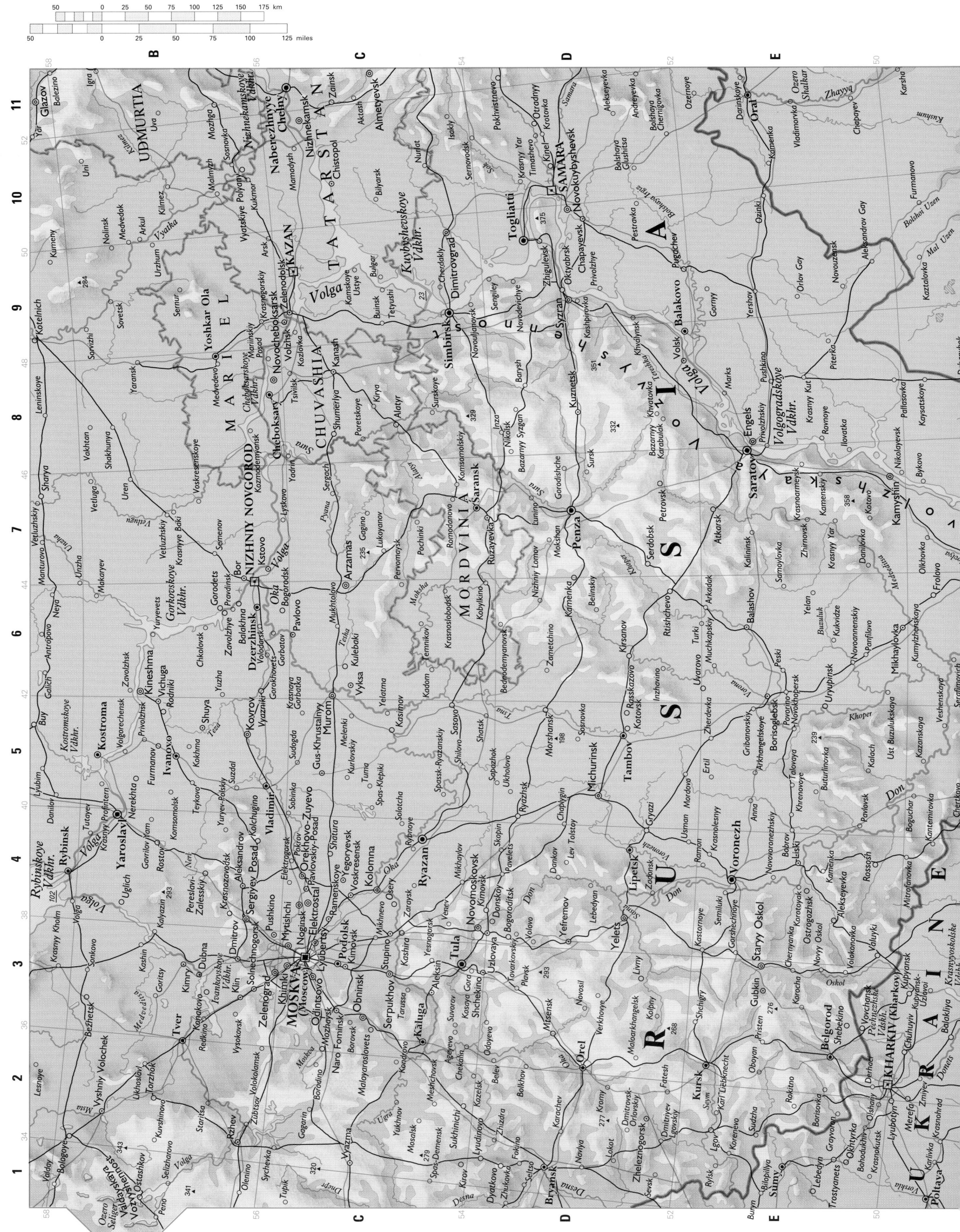

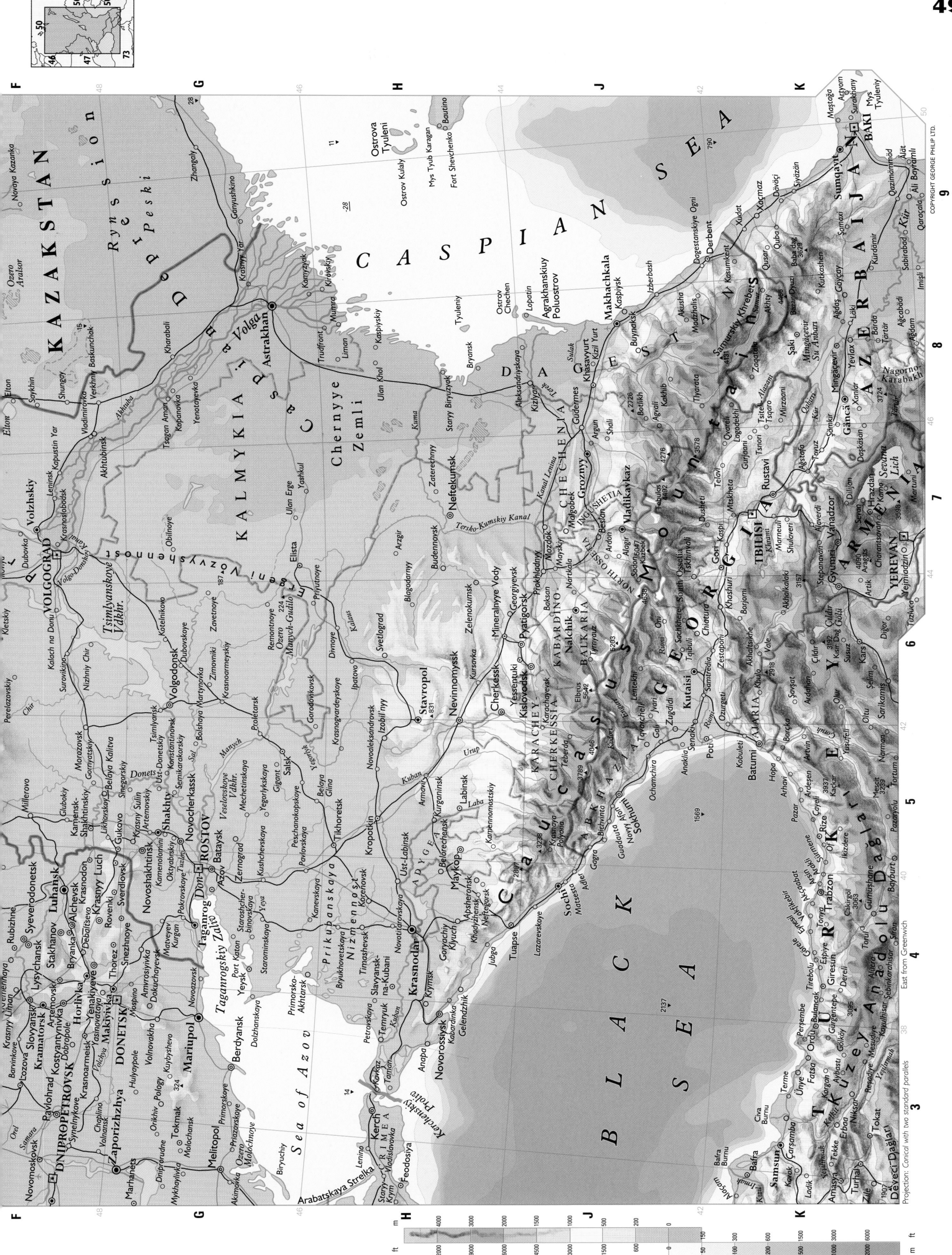

C A S P I A N   S E A

B L A C K   S E A

KAZAKSTAN

AZERBAIJAN

GEORGIA

ARMENIA

DAGESTAN

CHECHENIA

KALMYKIA

Chernyye Zemli

Caucasus Mountains

Sea of Azov

VOLGOGRAD

DNIPROPETROVSK

DONETSK

ROSTOV

Astrakhan

Makhachkala

Grozny

TBILISI

YEREVAN

BAKI

Sumqayit

Projection: Conical with two standard parallels

East from Greenwich

RUSSIA	
1	Adygea
2	Karachey-Cherkessia
3	Kabardino-Balkaria
4	North Ossetia
5	Ingushetia
6	Chechenia
7	Dagestan
8	Mordvinia
9	Chuvashia
10	Mari El
11	Tatarstan
12	Udmurtia
13	Khakassia
AZERBAIJAN	
14	Naxçıvan
GEORGIA	UKRAINE
15 Ajaria	17 Crimea
16 Abkhazia	

Projection: Conical Orthomorphic with two standard parallels

East from Greenwich

500 0 250 500 750 1000 1250 1500 1750 km
500 0 250 500 750 1000 1250 miles

Projection: Bonne

East of Greenwich

PACIFIC OCEAN

ARCTIC OCEAN

ATLANTIC OCEAN

INDIAN OCEAN

Siberia

Europe

Africa

Arabia

China

Himalaya

Plateau of Tibet

Mt. Everest 8850

Caspian Sea

Bay of Bengal

Arabian Sea

South China Sea

East Indies

Australia

New Guinea

m   ft
4000 12 000
3000 9000
2000 6000
1000 3000
500 1500
200 600
0
200 - 600
1000 3000
2000 6000
4000 12 000
6000 18 000
8000 24 000
ft   m

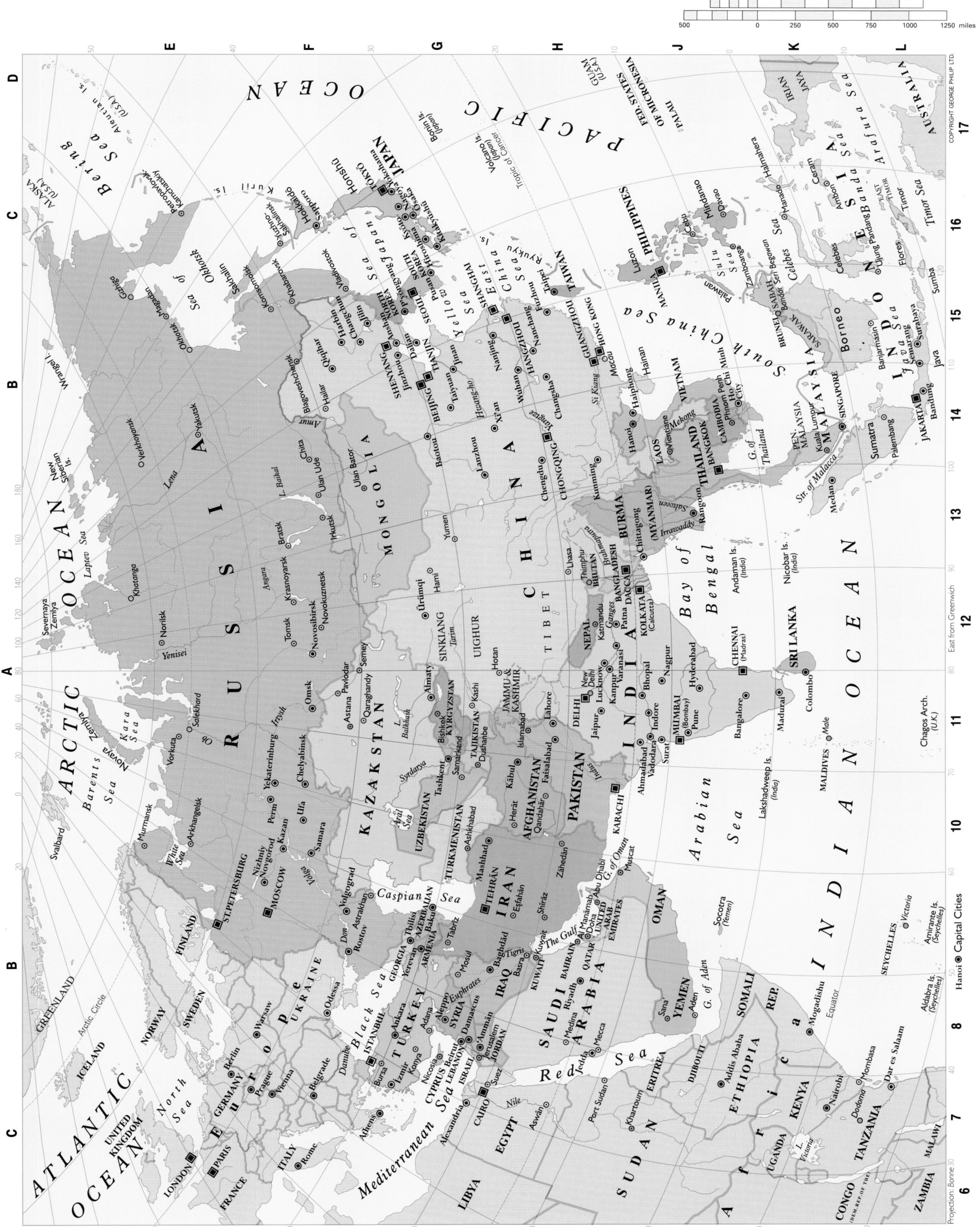

JAPAN 1:4 200 000

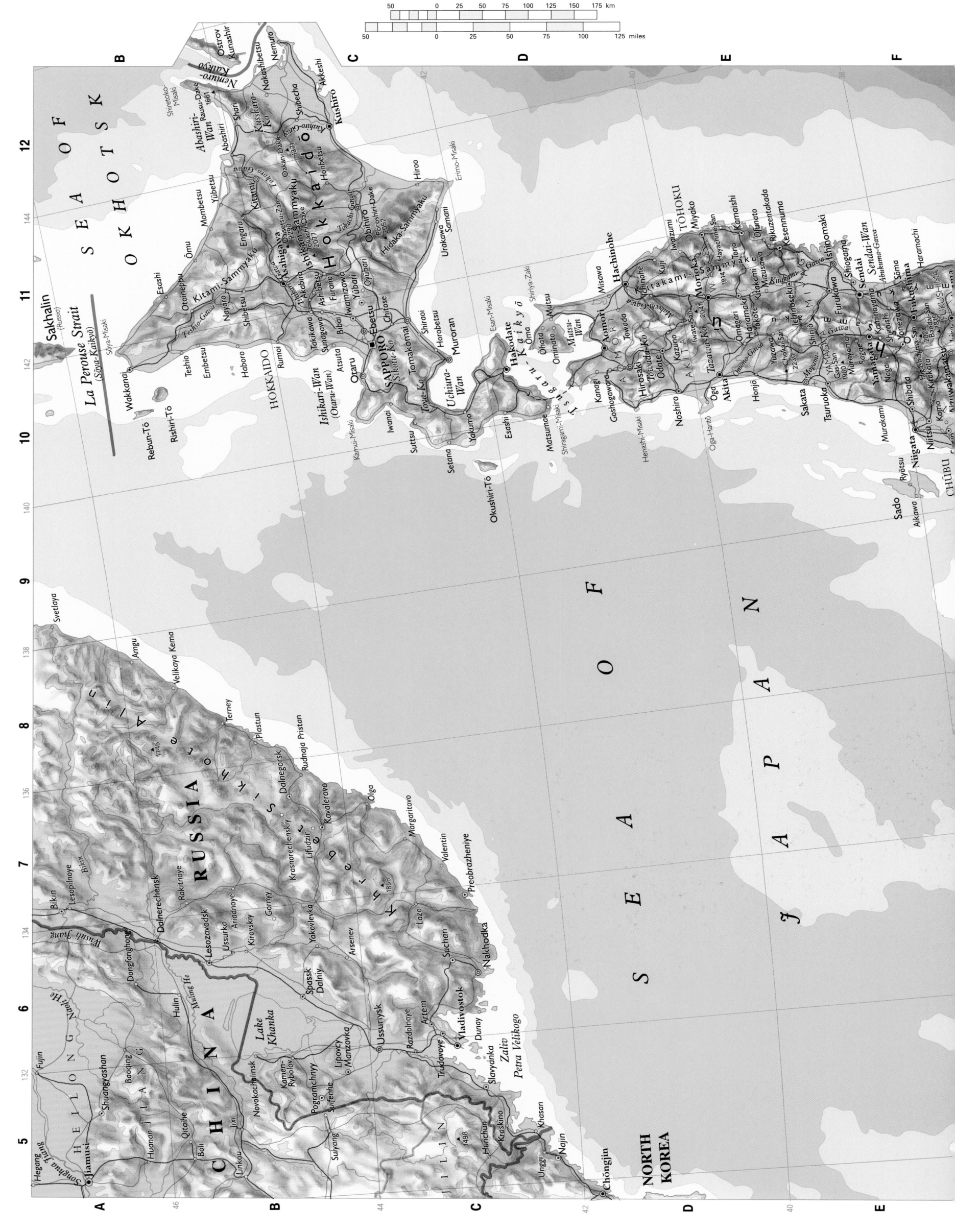

SEA OF OKHOTSK

Sakhalin (Russia)

La Perouse Strait
(Sōya-Kaikyō)

Ostrov Kunashir

Nemuro-Kaikyō

Shiretoko-Misaki

Abashiri-Wan
Abashiri
Shari
Rausu-Dake 1661
Nakashibetsu
Nemuro
Akkeshi
Shibecha
Kushiro-Kō
Kushiro
Kitami
Mombetsu
Engaru
Ōmu
Esashi
Kitami-Sammyaku
Otoineppu
Noyoro
Teshio-gawa
Shibetsu
Takikawa
Sunagawa
Bibai
Iwamizawa
Yūbari
Furano
Ashibetsu
Asahigawa
Asahi-Dake 2290
Ishikari-Sammyaku
Daisetsu-zan
Tokoro-Gawa
Akan-Dake
Tokachi-Dake 2077
Obihiro
Poroshiri-Dake 2052
Hidaka-Sammyaku
Urakawa
Samani
Hiroo
Erimo-Misaki

HOKKAIDO

Wakkanai
Rebun-Tō
Rishiri-Tō
Teshio
Embetsu
Haboro
Rumoi
Ishikari-Wan
(Otaru-Wan)
Otaru
Ishikari
SAPPORO
Chitose
Ebetsu
Sikotu-Ko
Tomakomai
Toya-Ko
Uchiura-Wan
Shiraoi
Horobetsu
Muroran

Kamui-Misaki
Iwanai
Setana
Suttsu
Yakumo
Esashi
Okushiri-Tō

Matsumae
Shirakami-Misaki
Shiriya-Zaki
Esan-Misaki
Hakodate
Tsugaru-Kaikyō
Ōma
Ōhata
Ōminato
Mutsu
Mutsu-Wan

Tsugaru-Hantō

Kanagi
Goshogawara
Henashi-Misaki
Oga-Hantō
Oga
Noshiro

AKITA
Akita
Honjō

TOHOKU
Miyako
Iwaizumi
Hayachine-San 1914
Tōno
Kamaishi
Ōfunato
Rikuzentakada
Kesennuma

MORI
AOMORI
Aomori
Misawa
Hachinohe
Towada
Towada-Ko
Kuji
Kitakami
Ninohe
Ōdate
Kazuno
Iwate-San 2041
Kitakami-Sammyaku
Morioka
Hanamaki
Mizusawa
Ichinoseki

YAMAGATA
Gassan 1980
Nagai
Yonezawa
Furukawa
Shiogama
Sendai
Sendai-Wan
Abukuma-Gawa
Shiroishi
Haramachi

Sakata
Tsuruoka
Murakami

Niitsu
Niigata
Ryōtsu
Sado
Aikawa

CHŪBU

FUKUSHIMA
Fukushima
Nihommatsu
Kōriyama

SEA OF JAPAN

RUSSIA

Svetlaya
Amgu
Velikaya Kema
Kema
Terney
Plastun
Rudnaja Pristan
Dalnegorsk
Kavalerovo
Olga
Margaritovo
Valentin
Preobrazheniye

Sikhote Alin
1745
1856

Dalnerechensk
Krasnorechenskiy
Lifudzin
Yakovlevka
Arsenev
Lazo
Suchan
Nakhodka

Bikin
Lesopilnoye
Bikin
Rakitnoye
Gornyy
Kirovskiy
Spassk Dalniy

HEILONGJIANG

CHINA

Hegang
Songhua Jiang
Jiamusi
Fujin
Shuangyashan
Huanan
Boli
Qitaihe
Jixi
Linkou
Mudan He
Mudanjiang
Hulin
Lake Khanka
Novokachalinsk
Kamen-Rybolov
Poganichnyy
Sujfun
Ussuriysk
Razdolnoye
Artem
Trudovoye
Vladivostok
Dunay
Zaliv
Petra Velikogo
Slavyanka
Kraskino
Khasan

JILIN

Baoqing
Dongfanghong
Wusuli Jiang
Naoli He
Hunchun
Unggi
Najin

NORTH KOREA

Chongjin
449
Suifang
Lipovcy
Manzovka

SEA OF JAPAN

Dunhua

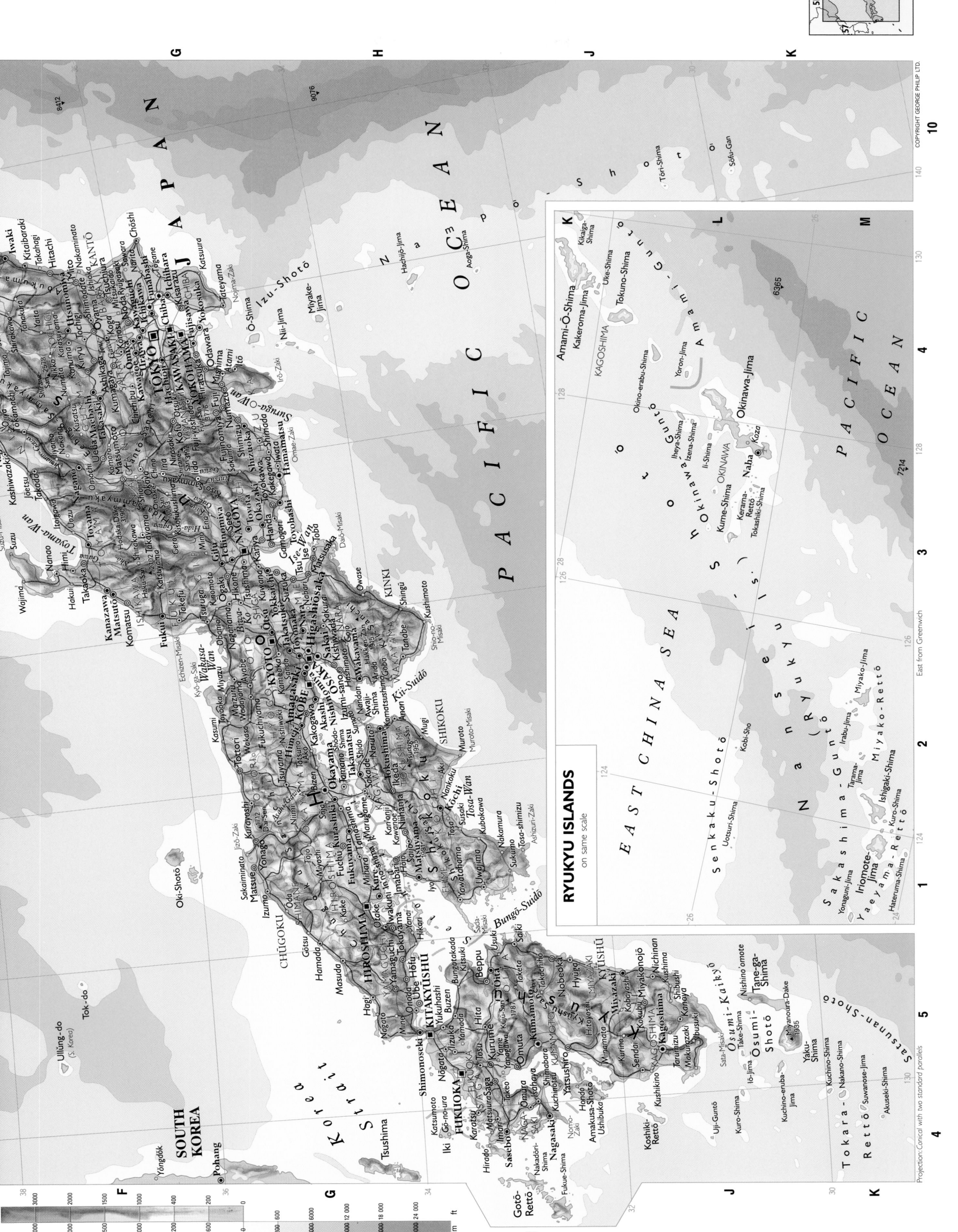

RYUKYU ISLANDS
on same scale

SOUTH
KOREA

JAPAN

PACIFIC OCEAN

EAST CHINA SEA

PACIFIC OCEAN

Projection: Conical with two standard parallels

Projection: Conical with two standard parallels

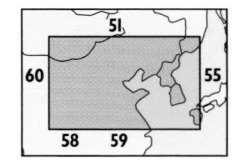

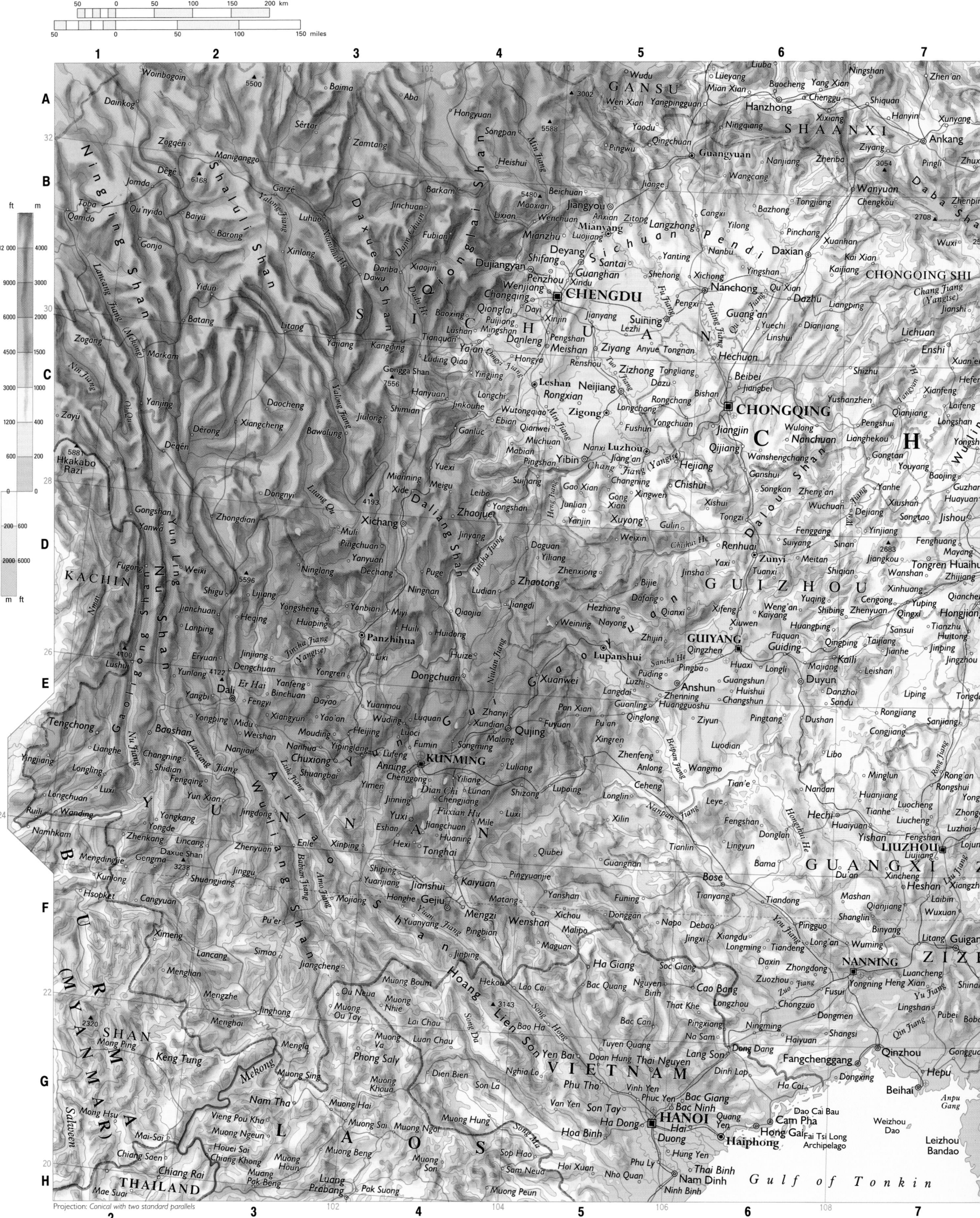

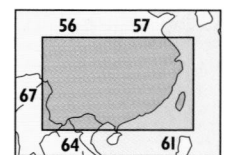

COPYRIGHT GEORGE PHILIP LTD.

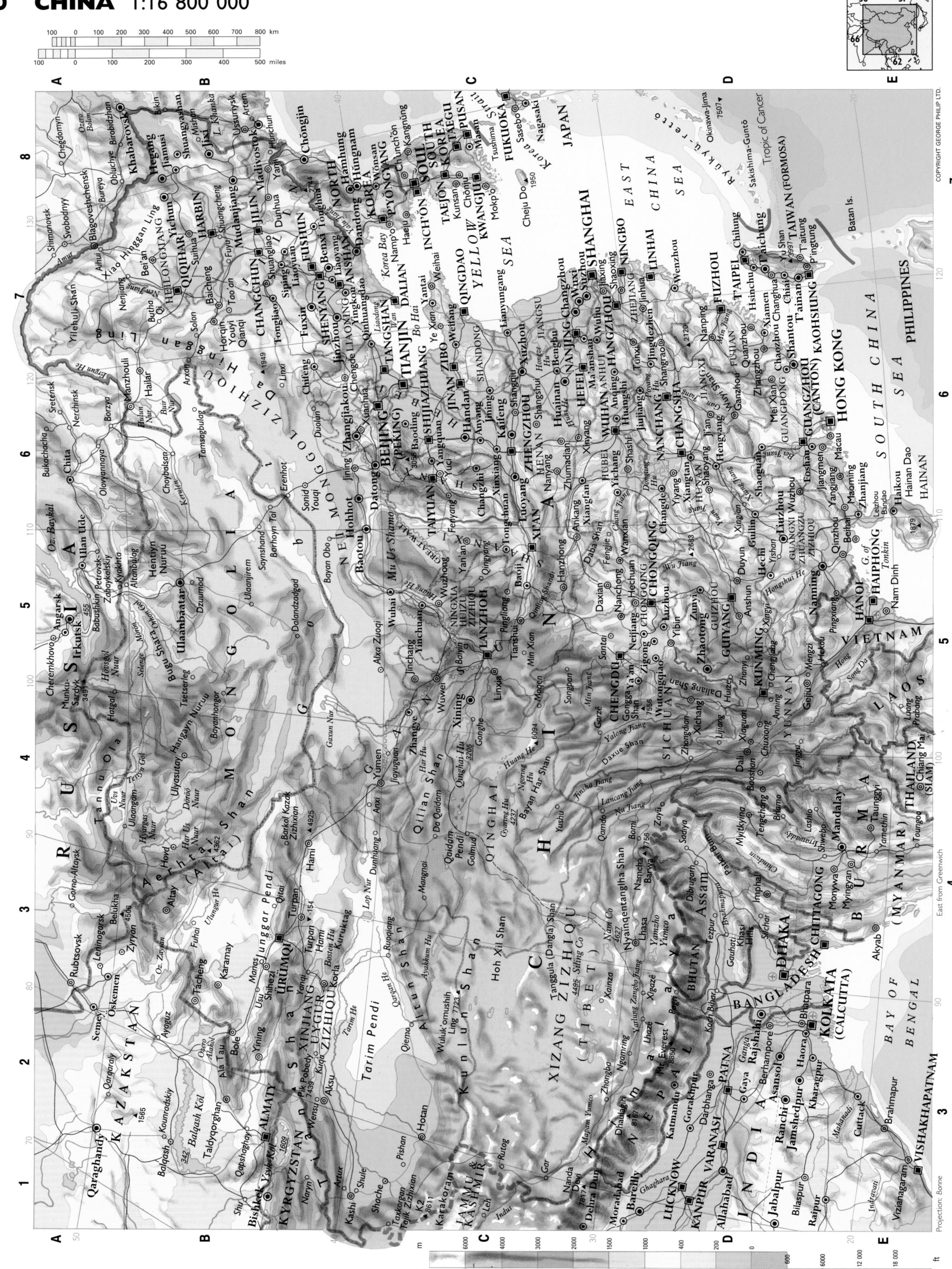

Projection: Borne

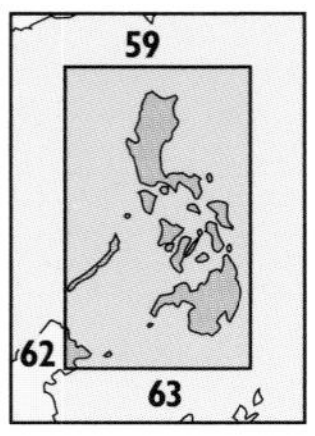

59
62 63

50 0 100 150 200 250 300 km
50 0 50 100 150 200 miles

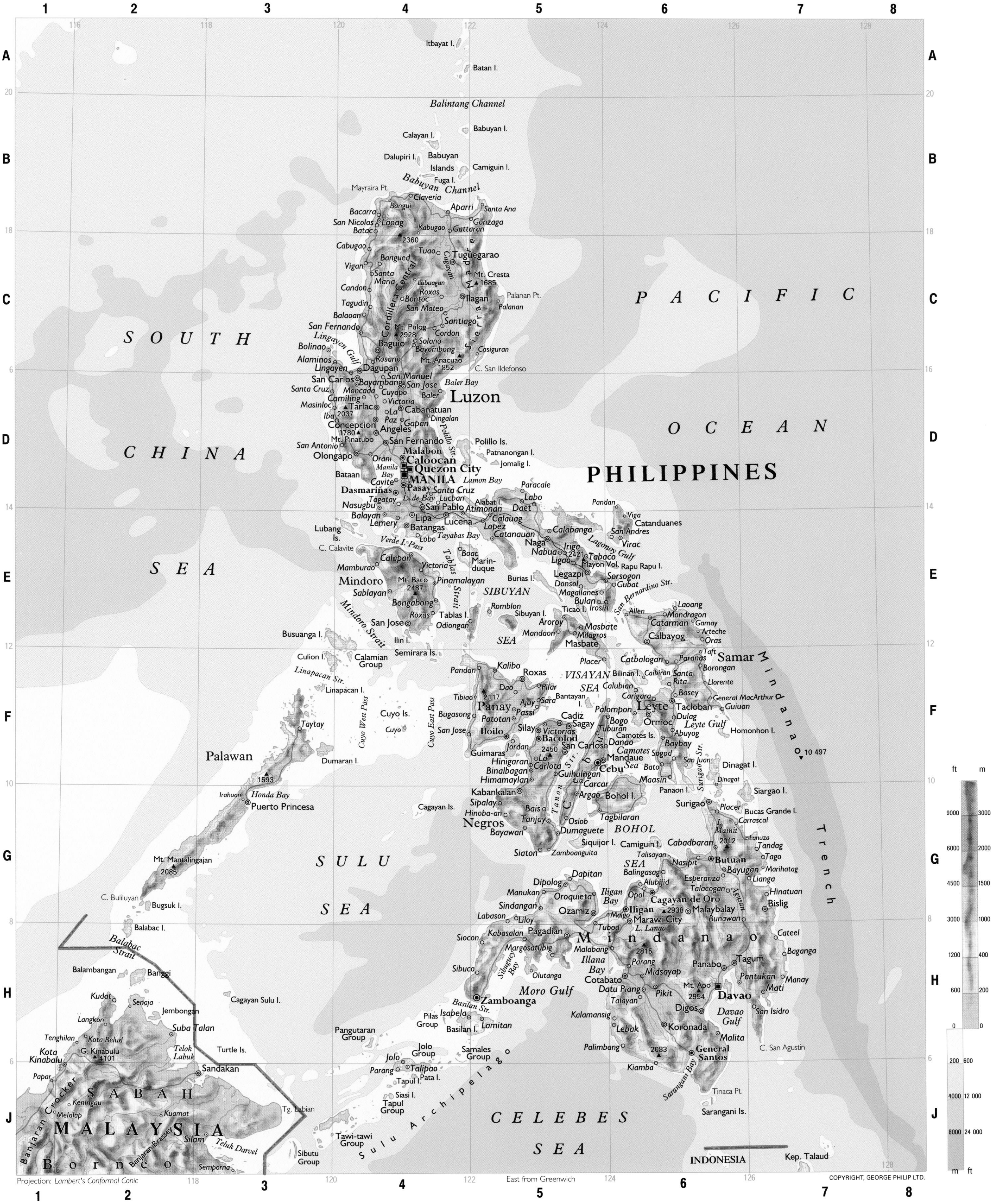

| 1 | 2 | 3 | 4 | 5 | 6 | 7 | 8 |

116 118 120 122 124 126 128

A
Itbayat I.
Batan I.
20

Balintang Channel

B
Calayan I. Babuyan I.
Dalupiri I. Babuyan Islands Camiguin I.
Fuga I.
Mayraira Pt. *Babuyan Channel*
Claveria Aparri Santa Ana
Bacarra Laoag Gonzaga
San Nicolas Batac Kabugao Gattaran
18 ▲2360 Tuao
Cabugao Bangued Tuguegarao
Vigan Tuao Cuyuan
Santa Mt. Cresta
Maria Lubuagan ▲1685
Candon Roxas
Tagudin Bontoc Ilagan Palanan Pt.
Balaoan San Mateo Palanan
C
San Fernando Santiago
Lingayen Gulf Mt. Pulog Cordon
Bolinao ▲2928
Baguio Bayombong Casiguran
Alaminos Rosario Mt. Anacuao
Lingayen Dagupan ▲1852 C. San Ildefonso
16

P A C I F I C

San Manuel Baler Bay
San Carlos San Jose
Bayambang San Jose Baler
Santa Cruz Moncada Cuyapo
Camiling Victoria **Luzon**
Masinloc ▲Tarlac La Cabanatuan
▲2037 Paz Gapan Dingalan
Concepcion Angeles
▲1780 San Fernando
Mt. Pinatubo Polillo Is.
San Antonio Patnanongan I.
Olongapo Orani Malabon Jomalig I.
Bataan **Caloocan**
Manila **Quezon City**
Bay **MANILA** Lamon Bay
Dasmariñas **Pasay** Santa Cruz Paracale
Cavite Labo
Tagaytay Is. de Bay Lucban Alabat I. Daet Pandan
Nasugbu San Pablo Atimonan
Balayan Lipa Lucena Viga Catanduanes
Lemery Lopez Calabanga San Andres
Batangas Catanauan Naga Virac
Lubang Tayabas Bay Iriga
Is. Calauag Nabua Tabaco Rapu Rapu I.
C. Calavite Boac Ligao Mayon Vol.
Verde I. Pass Marin- Legazpi Sorsogon
Calapan duque Donsol San Bernardino Str.
Mindoro Victoria Magallanes Gubat
Mt. Baco Pinamalayan Bulan Laoang
Sablayan ▲2487 Burias I. Irosin Catarman Gamay
Bongabong *SIBUYAN* Ticao I. Allen Arteche
San Jose Romblon Masbate Calbayog Oras
Roxas Tablas I. Mandaon Mondragon
Busuanga I. Ilin I. Odiongan Milagros Taft
Culion I. Semirara Is. *SEA* Masbate Catbalogan **Samar**
Calamian Pandan Placer Paranas Borongan
Group Kalibo *VISAYAN* Basey
Linapacan Str. Dao Roxas *SEA* Bilinan I. Caibiran Santa Llorente
Linapacan I. Tibiao ▲2117 Pilar Calubian Rita General MacArthur
Cuyo West Pass Ajuy Sara Bantayan Carigara Guiuan
Taytay **Panay** Passi Palompon **Leyte** Homonhon I.
Cuyo Is. Bugasong Cadiz Bogo Ormoc Abuyog
Cuyo Patotan Sagay Tuburan Dulag
Cuyo East Pass Silay Camotes Is. Leyte Gulf
Palawan San Jose Iloilo Victorias Camotes Baybay
Dumaran I. Guimaras Jordan Bacolod San Carlos Sea Bato San Juan Dinagat I.
Binalbagan ▲2450 Sogod Siargao I.
Himamaylan Mandaue Surigao Str.
Mt. Mantalingajan Kabankalan **Cebu** Panaon I. Dinagat
▲2085 Sipalay Guihulngan Maasin Surigao Placer
C. Buliluyan Cagayan I. Bais Carcar Bucas Grande I.
Bugsuk I. Hinoba-an Argao Bohol I. Carrascal
Tanjay Oslob Tagbilaran Mainit
Balabac I. **Negros** Dumaguete *BOHOL* L. Cabadbaran
Bayawan Siquijor I. ▲2012 Tandag
Balabac Siaton Zamboanguita Camiguin I. **Butuan** Tago
Strait Talisayan Nasipit Bayugan Marihatag
Balambangan Dipolog *SEA* Bislig Lianga
Banggi Dapitan Balingasag Esperanza Hinatuan
Cagayan Sulu I. Manukan Alubijid Opol Talacogon
Kudat Sindangan Oroquieta Iligan **Cagayan de Oro** Asuson Cateel
Langkon Iligan Bay Ozamiz Bay **Iligan** ▲2938 Malaybalay Baganga
SABAH Labason Liloy Tubod Marawi City Bunawan
Tenghilan Jembongan Siocon Kabasalan Pagadian L. Lanao Panabo
Kota Belus Suba Talan Margosatubig ▲2815 Parang Tagum
Kota G. Kinabalu Turtle Is. Sibuco Illana Midsayap Pantukan Manay
Kinabalu ▲4101 Olutanga Bay **Mindanao** Mati
Papar Sandakan Pilas Basilan Cotabato Mt. Apo **Davao**
MALAYSIA Group Strait Datu Piang Pikit ▲2954 Davao
Melalap Isabela Talayan Digos Gulf San Isidro
Borneo Pangutaran Basilan I. Kalamansig Koronadal
Group Lamitan Lebak Palimbang
Jolo Palimbang ▲2083 **General**
Parang Jolo Samales Kiamba **Santos**
Group Group Sarangani Bay Tinaca Pt.
Siasi Talipao C. San Agustin
Tapul Pata I. *CELEBES* Sarangani Is.
Group **INDONESIA**
Tawi-tawi Siasi *SEA* Kep. Talaud
Group Tapul Sulu Archipelago
Sibutu
Semporna Group

SOUTH
CHINA
SEA

Irahuon Honda Bay
Puerto Princesa

SULU
SEA

MORO GULF

CELEBES
SEA

PHILIPPINES

Mindanao Trench
10 497

ft m
9000 3000
6000 2000
4500 1500
3000 1000
1200 400
600 200
0 0
200 600
4000 12 000
8000 24 000
m ft

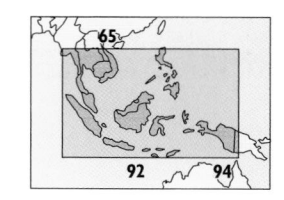

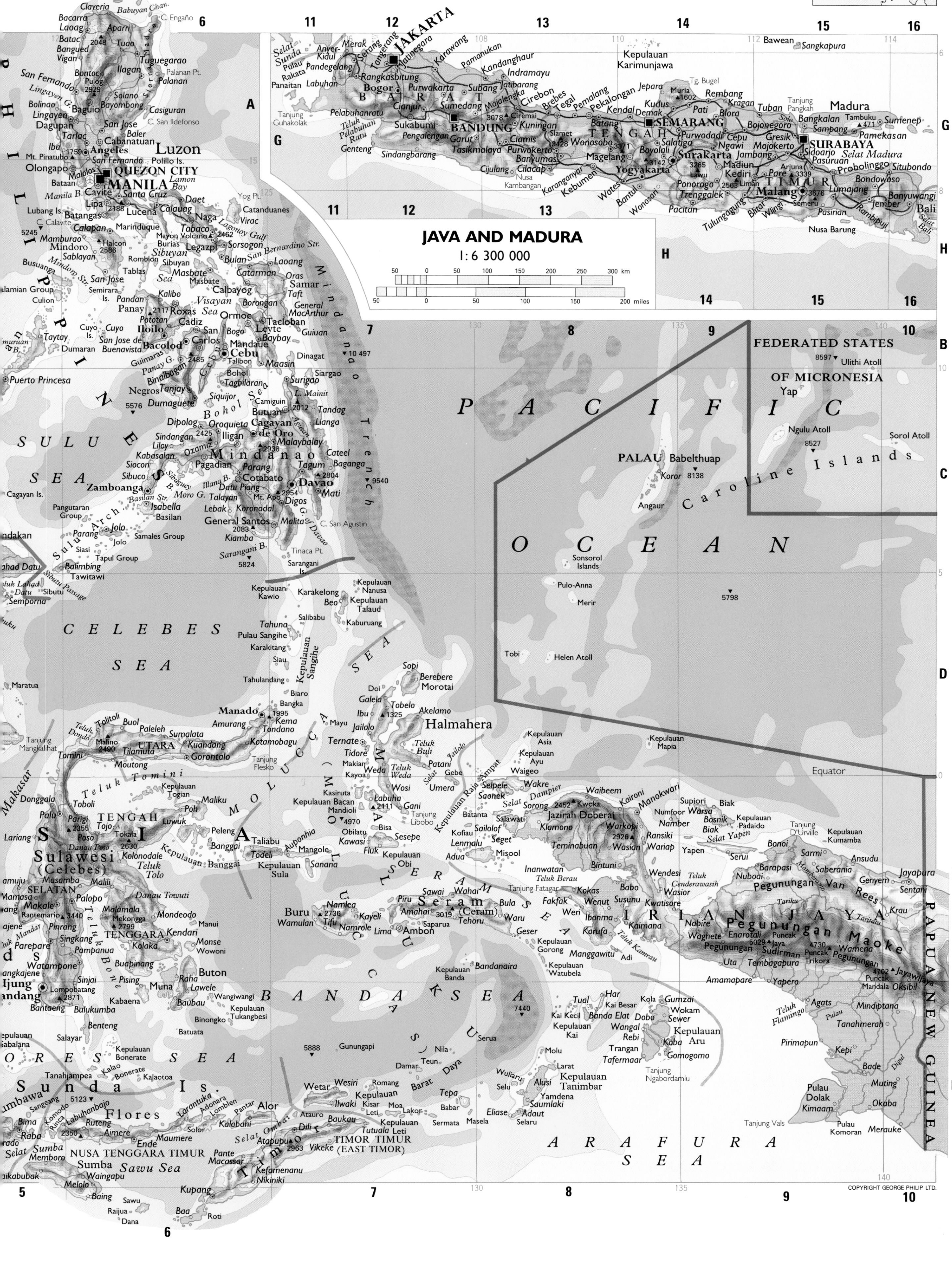

JAVA AND MADURA
1: 6 300 000

50 0 50 100 150 200 250 300 km
50 0 50 100 150 200 miles

PACIFIC

OCEAN

FEDERATED STATES
OF MICRONESIA

PALAU   Babelthuap

Caroline Islands

Yap

Ulithi Atoll

Ngulu Atoll

Sorol Atoll

CELEBES SEA

SULU SEA

BANDA SEA

MOLUCCA SEA

CERAM SEA

ARAFURA SEA

FLORES SEA

SAWU SEA

Luzon

QUEZON CITY
MANILA

Mindanao

Davao

Zamboanga

Cebu

Iloilo

Bacolod

General Santos

Manado

**Sulawesi
(Celebes)**

TENGAH

SELATAN

TENGGARA

UTARA

**Ujung
Pandang**

Halmahera

Ternate
Tidore

**Seram
(Ceram)**

Buru

Ambon

IRIAN JAYA

Pegunungan Maoke

Jayapura

PAPUA NEW GUINEA

Flores

Sumba

NUSA TENGGARA TIMUR

TIMOR TIMUR
(EAST TIMOR)

Kupang

Equator

COPYRIGHT GEORGE PHILIP LTD.

JAKARTA

BANDUNG

SEMARANG

SURABAYA

BARAT

TENGAH

TIMUR

Yogyakarta

Surakarta

Madura

Bali

Bogor

Sukabumi

Cirebon

Tegal

Pekalongan

Cilacap

Malang

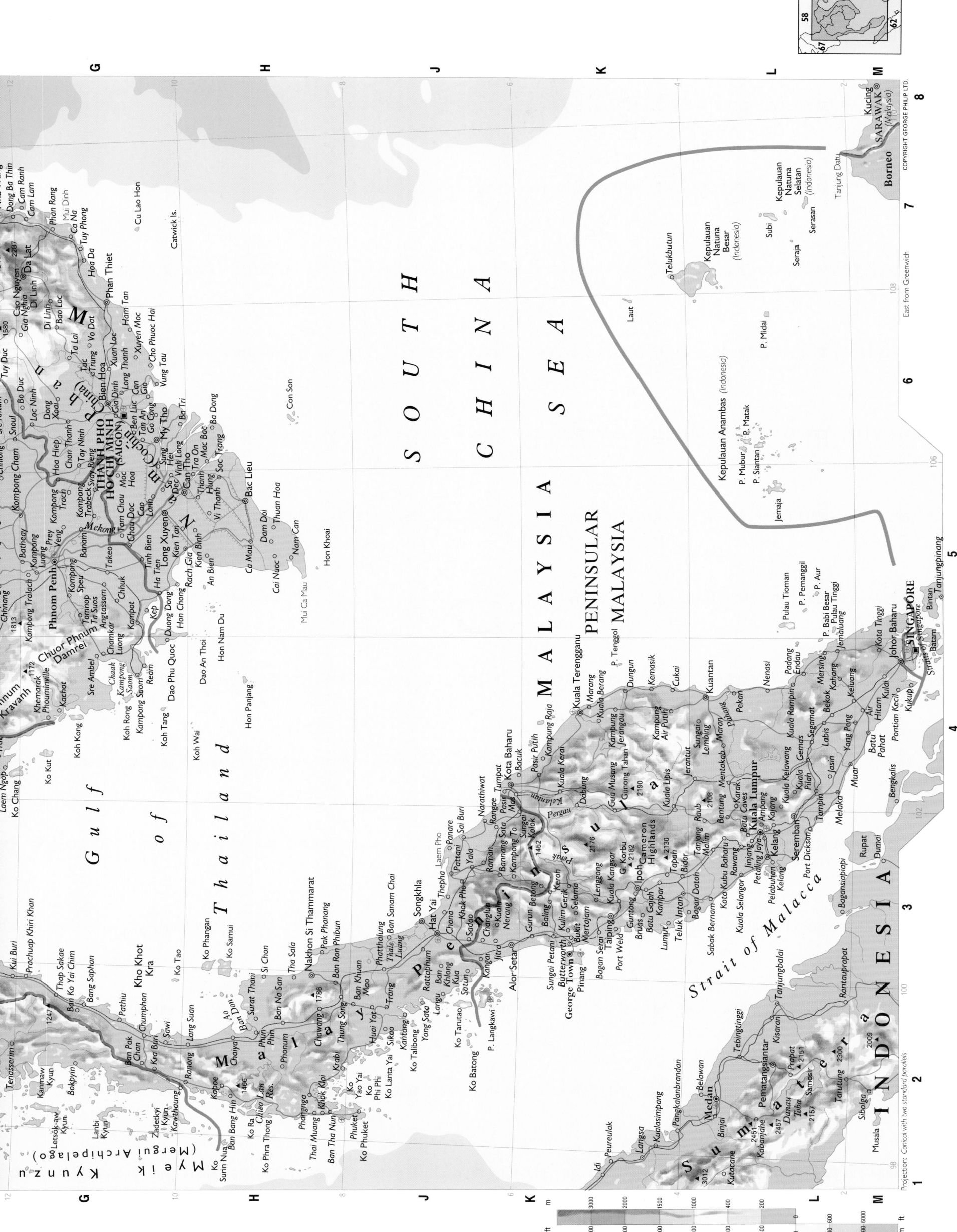

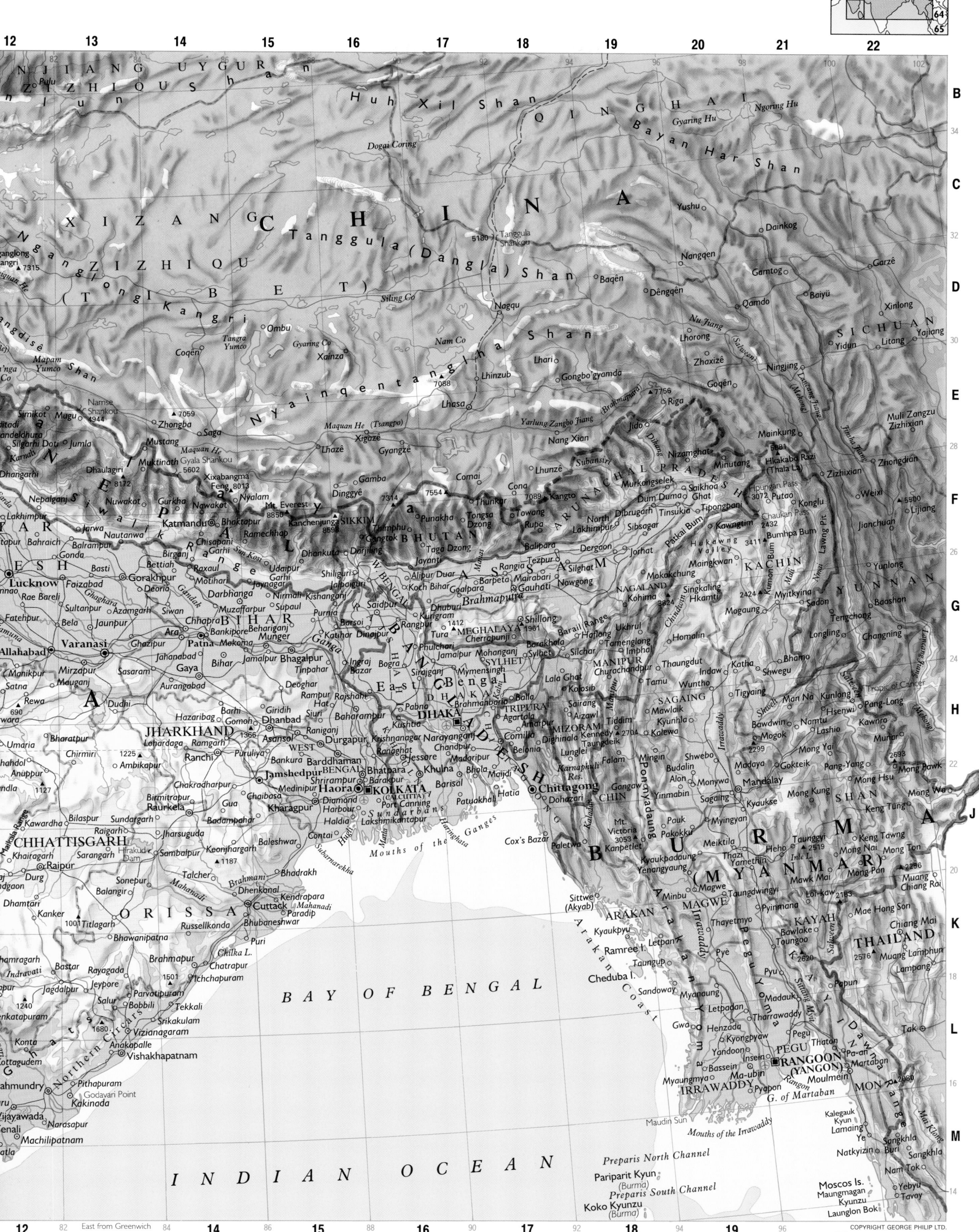

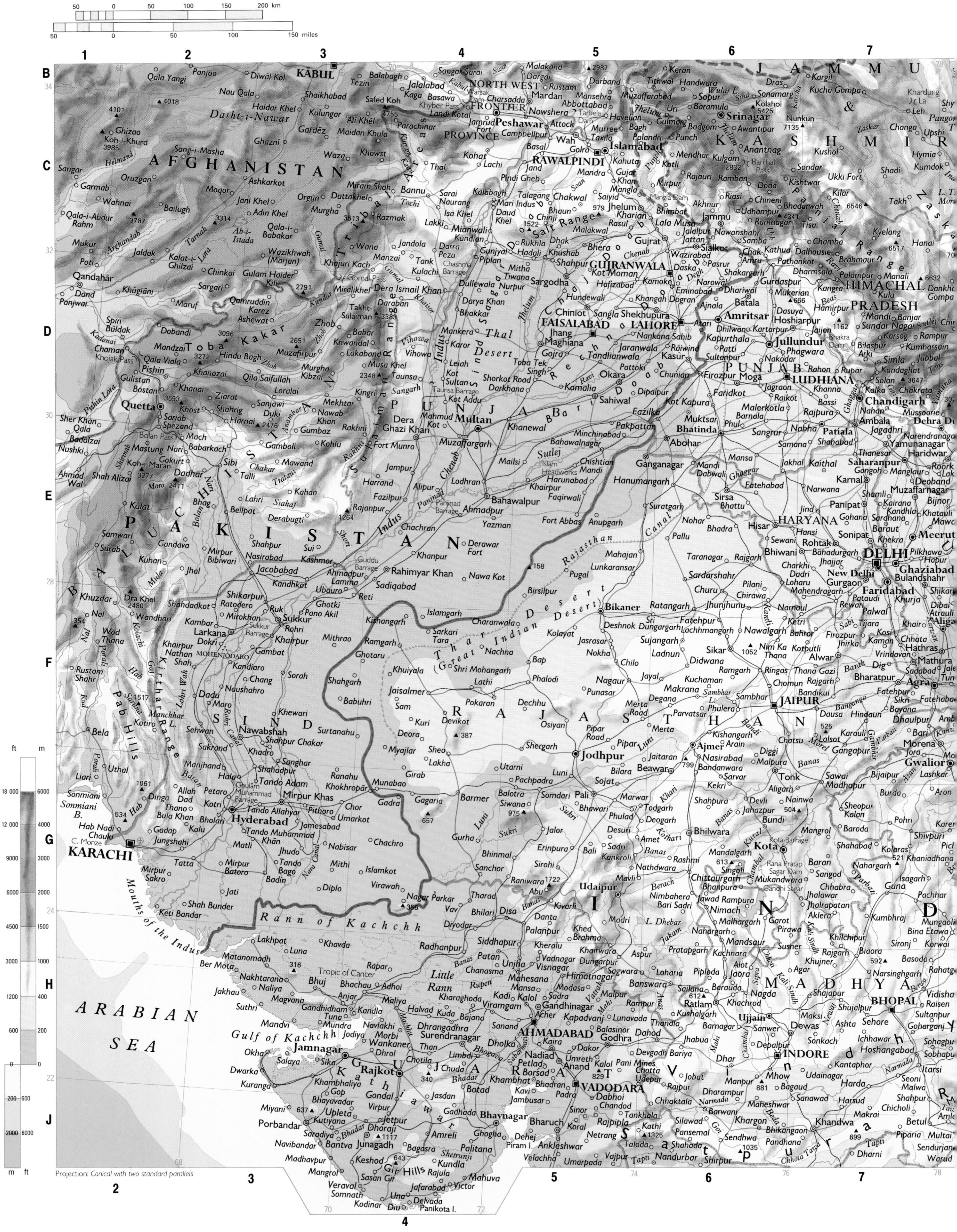

50 0 50 100 150 200 km
50 0 50 100 150 miles

AFGHANISTAN
PAKISTAN
BALUCHISTAN
SIND
PUNJAB
NORTH WEST FRONTIER PROVINCE
JAMMU & KASHMIR
HIMACHAL PRADESH
PUNJAB
HARYANA
RAJASTHAN
GUJARAT
MADHYA PRADESH

KABUL
Islamabad
RAWALPINDI
Peshawar
Srinagar
LAHORE
FAISALABAD
GUJRANWALA
Amritsar
Jullundur
LUDHIANA
Chandigarh
Patiala
Quetta
Multan
Bhatinda
DELHI
New Delhi
Ghaziabad
Faridabad
Meerut
JAIPUR
Agra
Gwalior
Ajmer
Jodhpur
Bikaner
Udaipur
Kota
KARACHI
Hyderabad
Mirpur Khas
Sukkur
Larkana
Jamnagar
Rajkot
AHMADABAD
Gandhinagar
VADODARA
Bhavnagar
Junagadh
Porbandar
INDORE
BHOPAL
Ujjain

ARABIAN SEA
Gulf of Kachchh
Rann of Kachchh
Little Rann
Mouths of the Indus
Thar Desert (Great Indian Desert)
Dasht-i-Nawar
Thal Desert
Gir Hills
Kathiawar

Indus
Chenab
Sutlej
Jhelum
Ravi
Luni
Narmada
Tapti
Chambal

Tropic of Cancer

ft m
18 000 6000
12 000 4000
9000 3000
6000 2000
4500 1500
3000 1000
1200 400
600 200
0 0
200 600
2000 6000
m ft

Projection: Conical with two standard parallels

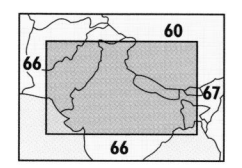

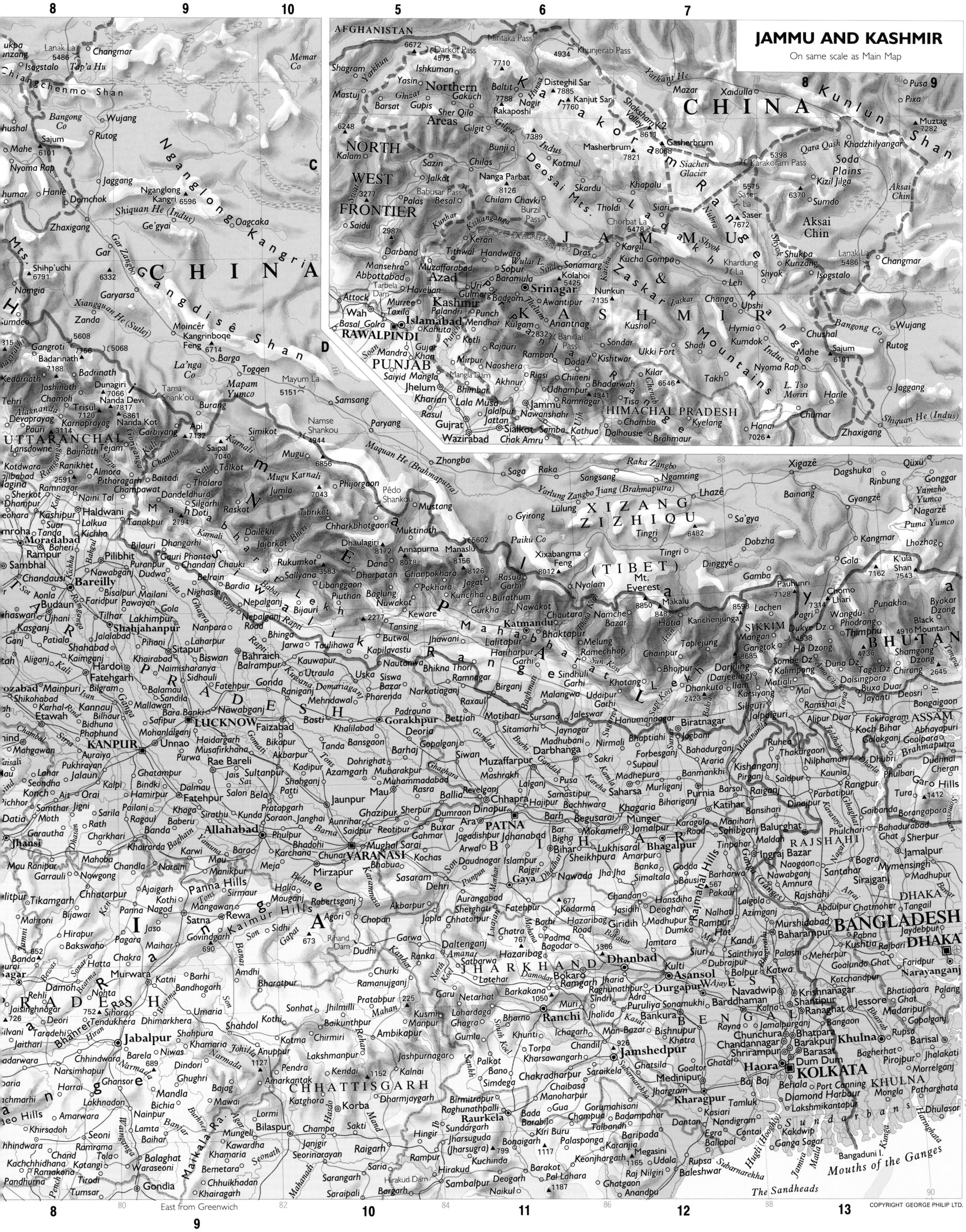

JAMMU AND KASHMIR
On same scale as Main Map

East from Greenwich

COPYRIGHT GEORGE PHILIP LTD.

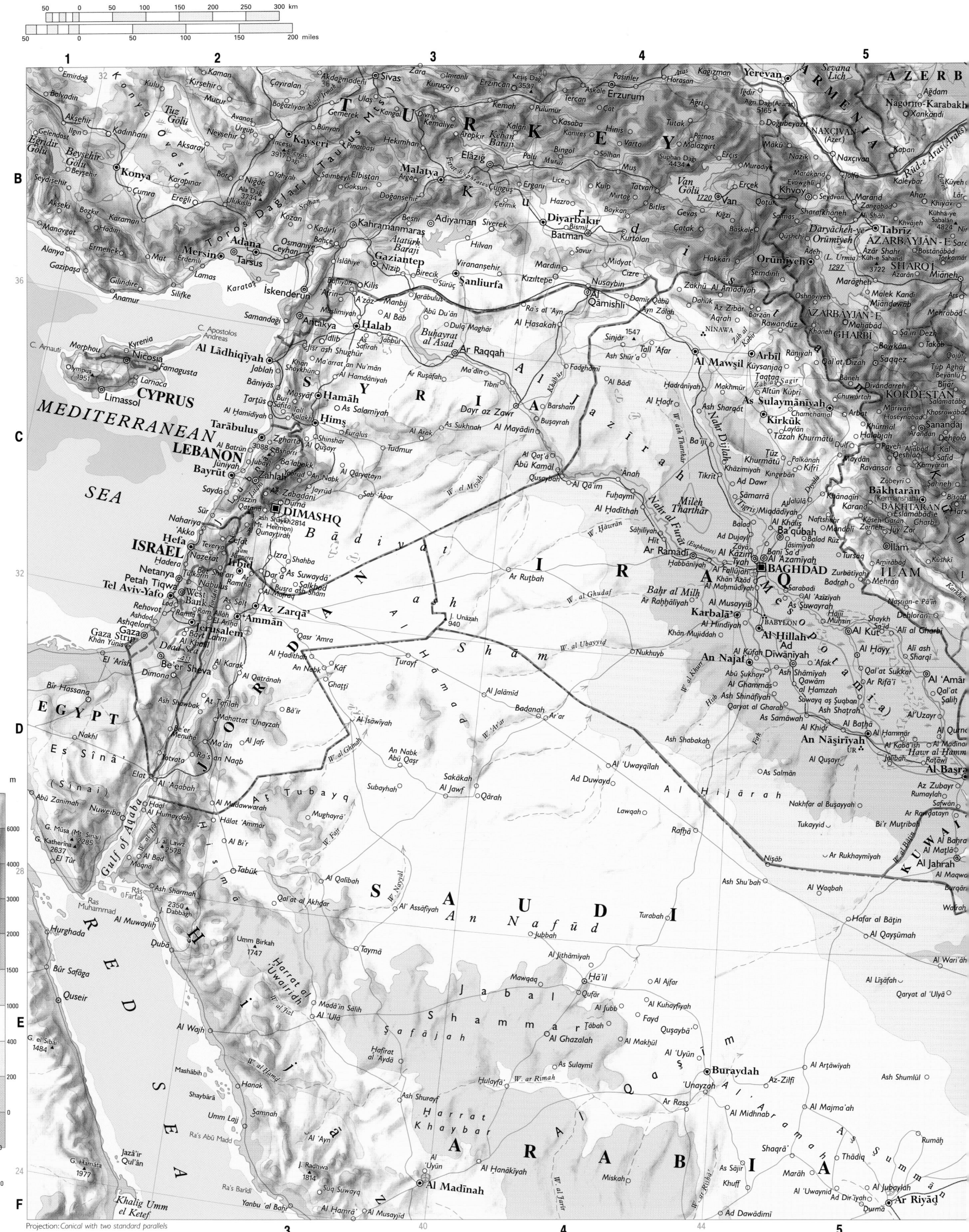

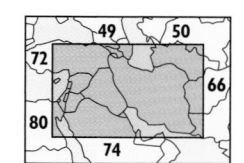

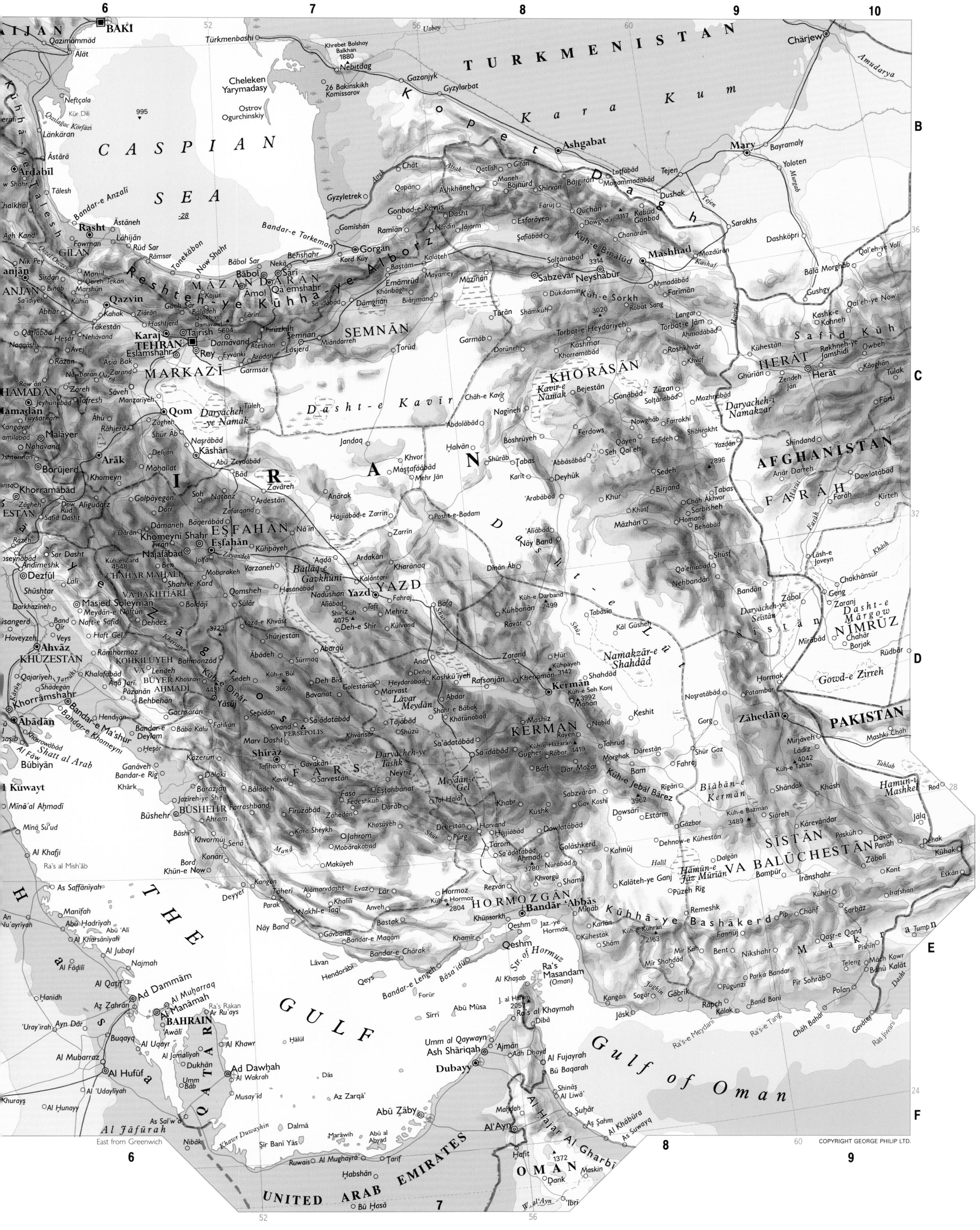

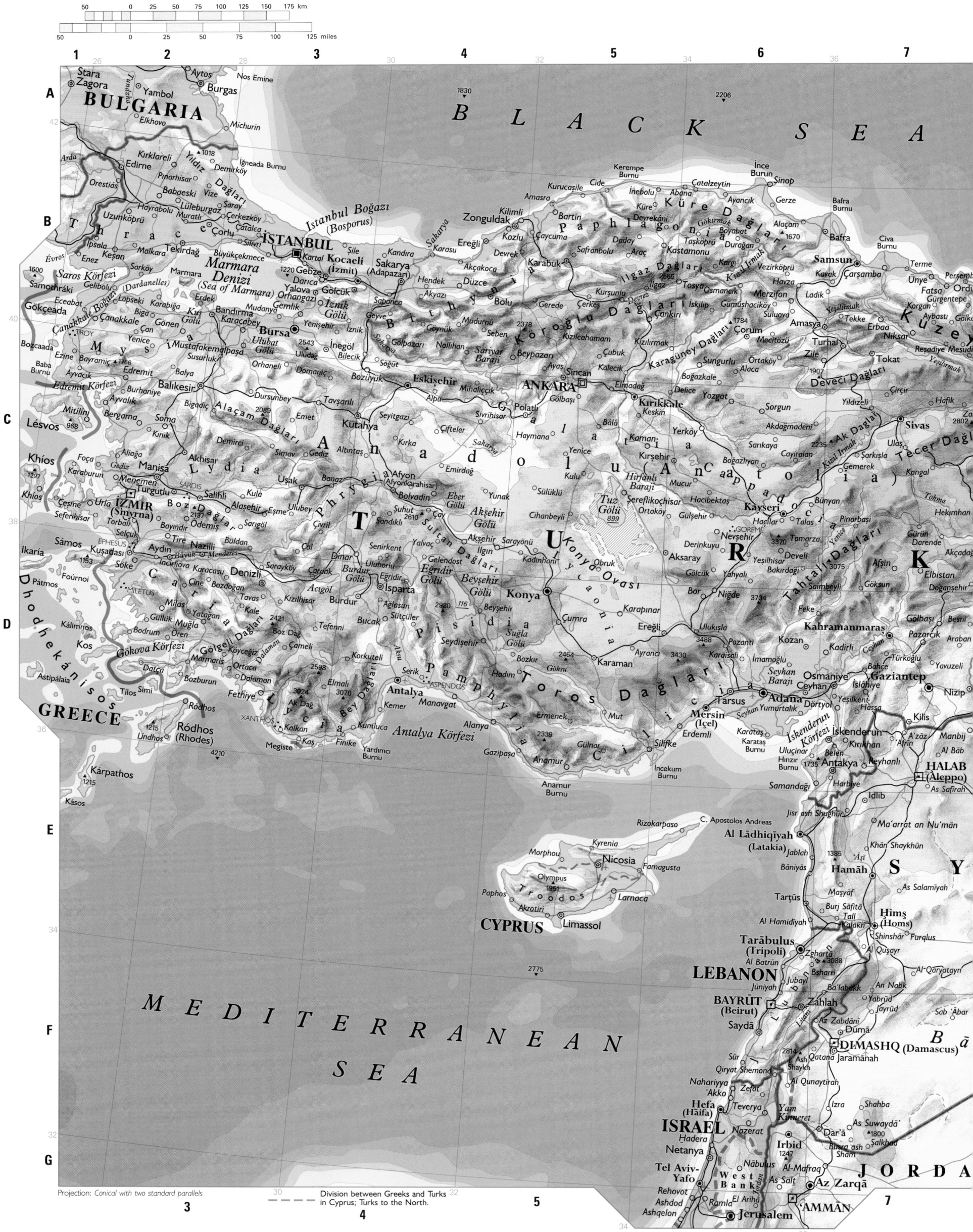

Division between Greeks and Turks
in Cyprus; Turks to the North.

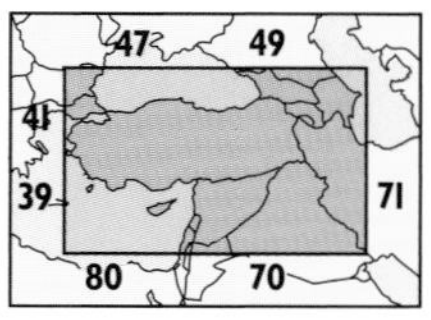

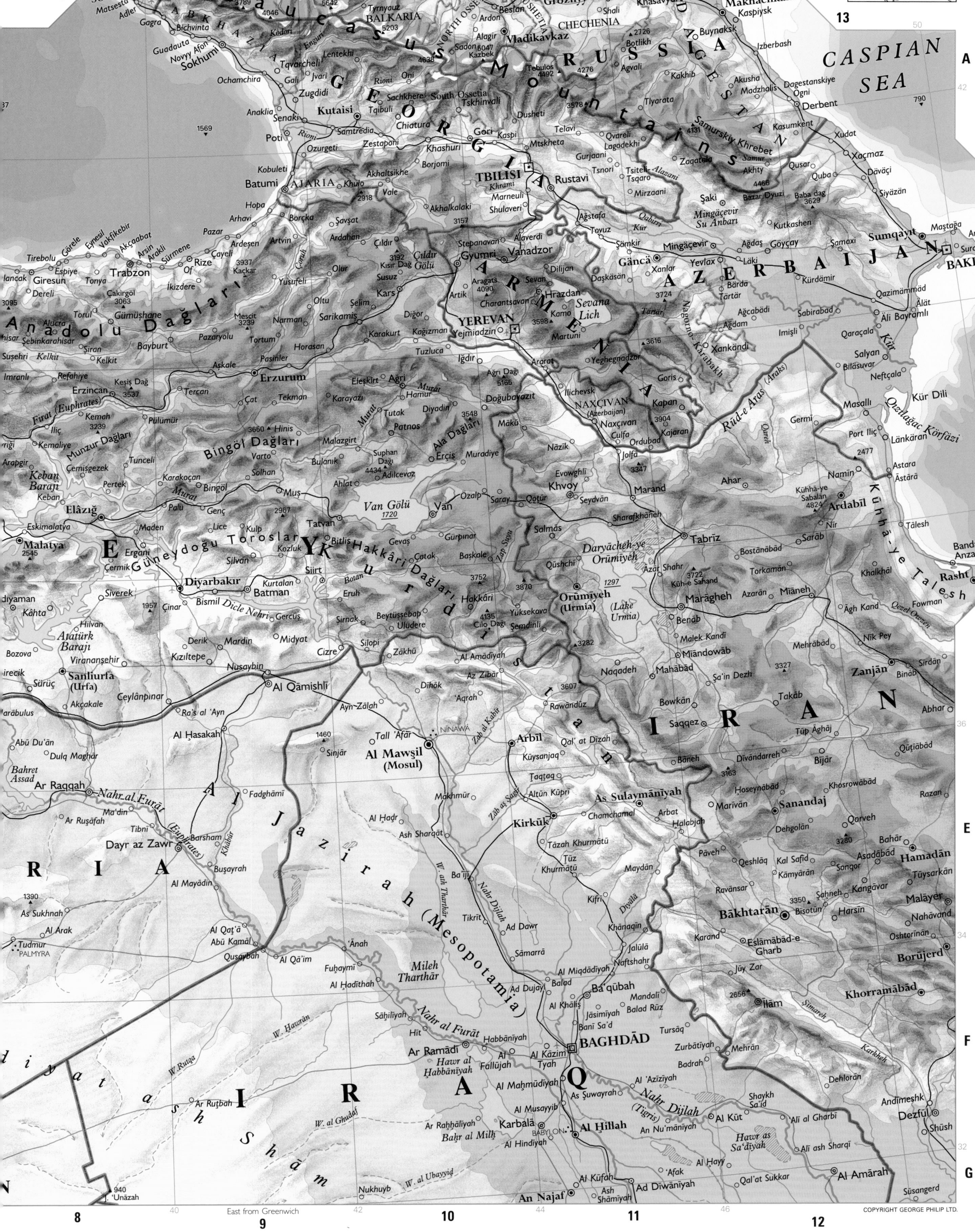

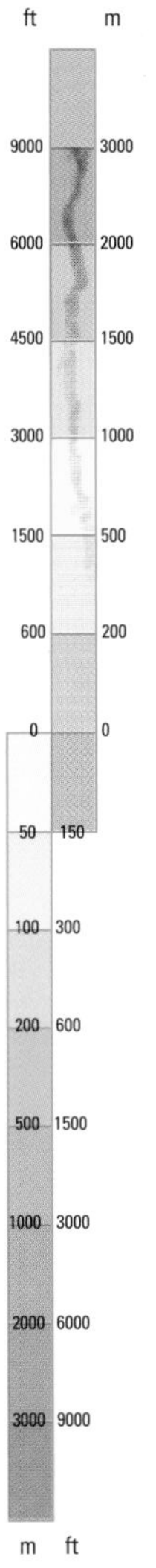

47 49
41 71
39
80 70

CASPIAN SEA

8
Sochi
Matsesta
Adler
Gagra
Bíchvinta
Novvy Afon
Guadauta
Sokhumi
Ochamchira
Anaklia
Senaki
Poti
Kobuleti
Batumi
ADJARIA
Hopa
Borçka
Arhavi
Pazar
Çayeli
Rize
Of
İkizdere
Trabzon
Çakirgöl 3063
Tonya
Sürmene
Arsin
Araklı
Vakfıkebir
Görele
Eynesil
Tirebolu
Espiye
Giresun
Bulancak
Dereli
Keşap

CAUCASUS Mountains
3789 Teberda Elbrus 5642
4046 KABARDINO-BALKARIA
Tyrnyauz
5203
NORTH OSSETIA
4638 Lentekhi
Tqvarcheli
Jvari
Zugdidi
Gali
Kutaisi
Samtredia
Sachkhere
Chiatura
South Ossetia
Tskhinvali
Gori
1569
Ozurgeti
Zestaponi
Rioni
Khashuri
Borjomi
Akhaltsikhe
Khulo
Vale
2918
Ardahan
Çıldır
3157
Akhalkalaki

GEORGIA
TBILISI
Khrami
Marneuli
Shulaveri
Rustavi

Tebulos 4492
Botlish
Agvali
4276
4131
Samurskiy Khrebet
Samut
Zaqatala
Şaki
Baba dag 3629
Bazar Dyuzi 4466
Qusar
Xudat
Xaçmaz
Siyäzän
Maştağa
Surakhany
BAKI
Sumqayıt

RUSSIA
Beslan
NGUSHETIA
Argun
Groznyy
Shali
CHECHENIA
2726
Kizil Yurt
Khasavyurt
Buynaksk
Makhachkala
Kaspiysk
Izberbash
Akusha
Madzhalis
Dagestanskiye Ogni
Derbent
790
DAGESTAN

Vladikavkaz
Sadon 5047
Kazbek
Dusheti
Telavi
Mtskheta
Kaspi
Gurjaani
Lagodekhi
Qvareli
Tsnori
Tsiteli-Alasani
Mirzaani

Ağstafa
Tovuz
Şämkir
Mingäçevir Su Anbarı
Kutkashen
Şamaxı
Mingäçevir
Ağdaş
Göyçay
Läki

AZERBAIJAN

Ağsu
Şamaxı
Artyom

Stepanavan
Vanadzor
Dilijan
Gyumri
Aragats 4090
Artik
Charantsavan
Sevan
Sevana Lich
Hrazdan
3724
3598
Nagorno-Karabakh
Gäncä
Xanlar
Yevlax
Bärdä
Tärtär
Ağcäbädi
Qazımämmäd
Kürdämir
Sabirabad
Äli Bayramlı
Imişli
Qaraçala
Salyan
Biläsuvar
Neftçala
Qızılağac Körfäzi

ARMENIA
YEREVAN
Yejmiadzin
Kağızman
Kamo
Martuni
Ararat
Yeghegnadzor
3616
Goris
Kapan
Kajaran
Rüd-e Aras (Araks)
Qarälı
Germi
Port İliç
Länkäran
Astara

NAXÇIVAN (Azerbaijan)
Naxçıvan
Culfa
Ordubad
Jolfa
3904
3347
2477
Namīn

Kars
Selim
Sarıkamış
Digor
Tuzluca
İğdır
Ağrı Dağı 5165
Doğubayazıt
Mākū
Khvoy
Nāzik
Marand
Ahar
Kühhā-ye Sabalān 4824
Ardabīl
Nir
Tälesh
Astārā
Bandar-e Anzalī
Rasht
Kühhā-ye Talesh

Erzurum
Aşkale
Tekman
Karayazı
Hınıs
3537
Tercan
Çat
Eleşkirt
Ağrı
Murat
Tutak
Patnos
3548
Diyadin
Suphan Dağı 4434
Adilcevaz
Ahlat
Erciş
Muradiye
Özalp
Saray
Qotūr
Seydvān
Sharafkhāneh
Salmās
Tabrīz
Bostānābād
Sarāb
Torkamān
Mīāneh
Āzarān
Marāgheh
Kūh-e Sahand 3710
Azar Shahr
Qūshchī
1297
Orūmīyeh (Urmia)
Daryācheh-ye Orūmīyeh (Lake Urmia)

Bingöl Dağları
Varto
Malazgirt
Bulanık
Muş
Solhan
Genç
Bingöl
Van Gölü 1720
Tatvan
Bitlis
Gevaş
Van
Gürpınar
Zap Suyu
Çatak
Başkale
Şemdinli
Hakkâri
Cilo Dağı 4135
Yüksekova
Uludere
3282
3607
Rawāndūz
Naqadeh
Şa'in Dezh
Mahābād
Bowkān
Saqqez
Bāneh
3327
Zanjān
Sīrdān
Bināb
Takāb
Tūp Āghāj
Abhar

Elâzığ
Eskimalatya
Malatya 2545
Ergani
Çermik
Maden
Lice
Kulp
Güneydoğu Toroslar
Silvan
Diyarbakır
Kurtalan
Batman
Siirt
Eruh
Hakkâri Dağları
Beytüşşebap
Şırnak
Silopi
Cizre
Zākhū
Al Amādīyah
Az Zībār
'Aqrah
Dīhōk
Arbīl
Qal'at Dīzah
Küysanjaq
3752
3870

Siverek
Viranşehir
Derik
Mardin
Kızıltepe
Midyat
Nusaybin
Al Qāmishlī
Ra's al 'Ayn
Ayn-Zālah
Tall 'Afar
NĪNAWĀ
Al Mawşil (Mosul)
Makhmūr
Al Ḥaḑr
Ash Sharqāt
Zāb as Saġīr
Altūn Kūprī
Ţaqţaq
As Sulaymānīyah
Chamchamal
Arbat
Halabjah
Pāveh
3163
Mariwān
Sanandaj
Qorveh
Dehgolān
3280
Bahār
Asadābād
Hamadān
Tūysarkān
Malāyer
Nahāvand
Oshtorīnān
Borūjerd

Şanlıurfa (Urfa)
Akçakale
Ceylanpınar
1460
Sinjār
Al Ḥasakah
Dulq Maghār
Bahret Assad
Ar Raqqah
Nahr al Furāt (Euphrates)
Ma'din
Ar Ruşāfah
Tibnī
Barsham
Khābūr
Būşayrah
Dayr az Zawr
Al Mayādin
1390
As Sukhnah
Al 'Arak
Tudmur (PALMYRA)
Al Qaţ'ā
Abū Kamāl
Qusaybah
Al Qā'im
Fuḩaymī
Al Hadīthah
'Ānah

Al Jazīra (Mesopotamia)
Fadghamī
Makhmūr
Ash Sharqāt
Tikrīt
Ad Dawr
Sāmarrā
Nahr Dijlah
Kirkūk
Tāzah Khurmātū
Tūz Khurmātū
Kifrī
Diyālā
Khānaqīn
Jalūlā
Naftshahr
Eslāmābād-e Gharb
Karand
Bīsotūn
3350
Şahneh
Kangāvar
Harsin
Bākhtarān
Kermānshāh
Māhīdasht
Ravānsar
Qeshlāq
Kāmyārān
Songor
Dīvāndarreh
Bijār
Khosrowābād
Razan
Qūţīābād

Mileh Tharthār
W. ath Tharthār
Ba'ījī
Balad
Ad Dujayl
Al Miqdādīyah
Mandalī
Balad Rūz
2856
Īlām
Sīmareh
Khorramābād
Dehlorān
Andīmeshk
Dezfūl
Shūsh

IRAN

SYRIA
RIA
Abū Du'ān
arābulus
Dulq Maghār
Ar Ruţbah
iyat
940 'Unāzah

IRAQ
Nahr al Furāt
Sāḩilīyah
Hīt
Habbānīyah
Al Kāzim
Tyah
BAGHDAD
Ar Ramādī
Al Fallūjah
Hawr al Ḥabbānīyah
Al Maḩmūdīyah
Al Musayyib
Karbalā
BABYLON
Al Hillah
An Najaf
Al Kūfah
Ash Shāmīyah
Ad Dīwānīyah
Al 'Azīzīyah
As Suwayrah
Nahr Dijlah (Tigris)
Al Kūt
Qal'at Sukkar
Al Ḩayy
Al Amārah
Zurbāţīyah
Mehrān
Badrah
Shaykh Sa'd
Alī al Gharbī
Alī ash Sharqī
Hawr as Sa'dīyah
Karkheh
Sūsangerd
Jāsimīyah
Banī Sa'd
Tursāq
Ba'qūbah
Al Khāliş

Anadolu Dağları
3095
Fırat (Euphrates)
Kemah 3239
İliç
Kemaliye
Arapgir
Keban Barajı
Keban
Çemişgezek
Karakoçan
Pertek
Tunceli
Palu
Murat
Kâhta
Bozova
Atatürk Barajı
Hilvan
1957
Çınar
Bismil
Dicle Nehri
Gercüş
Adıyaman
diyaman
irecik
Süruç

Münzur Dağları
Refahiye
Erzincan
Pülümür
Şebinkarahisar
Suşehri
Kelkit
Şiran
Bayburt
Gümüşhane
İmranlı
Refahiye
Torul
Köse
Mescit 3239
Narman
Oltu
Olur
Şavşat
Artvin
Ardanuç
Yusufeli
3937
Kaçkar
3192 Kısır Dağ
Çıldır Gölü
Susuz
Gyumri
Kağızman
Karakurt
Horasan
Pasinler
Karabulak

Şiran
Kelkit
Şebinkarahisar

COPYRIGHT GEORGE PHILIP LTD.

8 9 10 11 12
East from Greenwich

ft m
9000 3000
6000 2000
4500 1500
3000
1500 500
600 200
0 0
50 150
100 300
200 600
500 1500
1000 3000
2000 6000
3000 9000
m ft

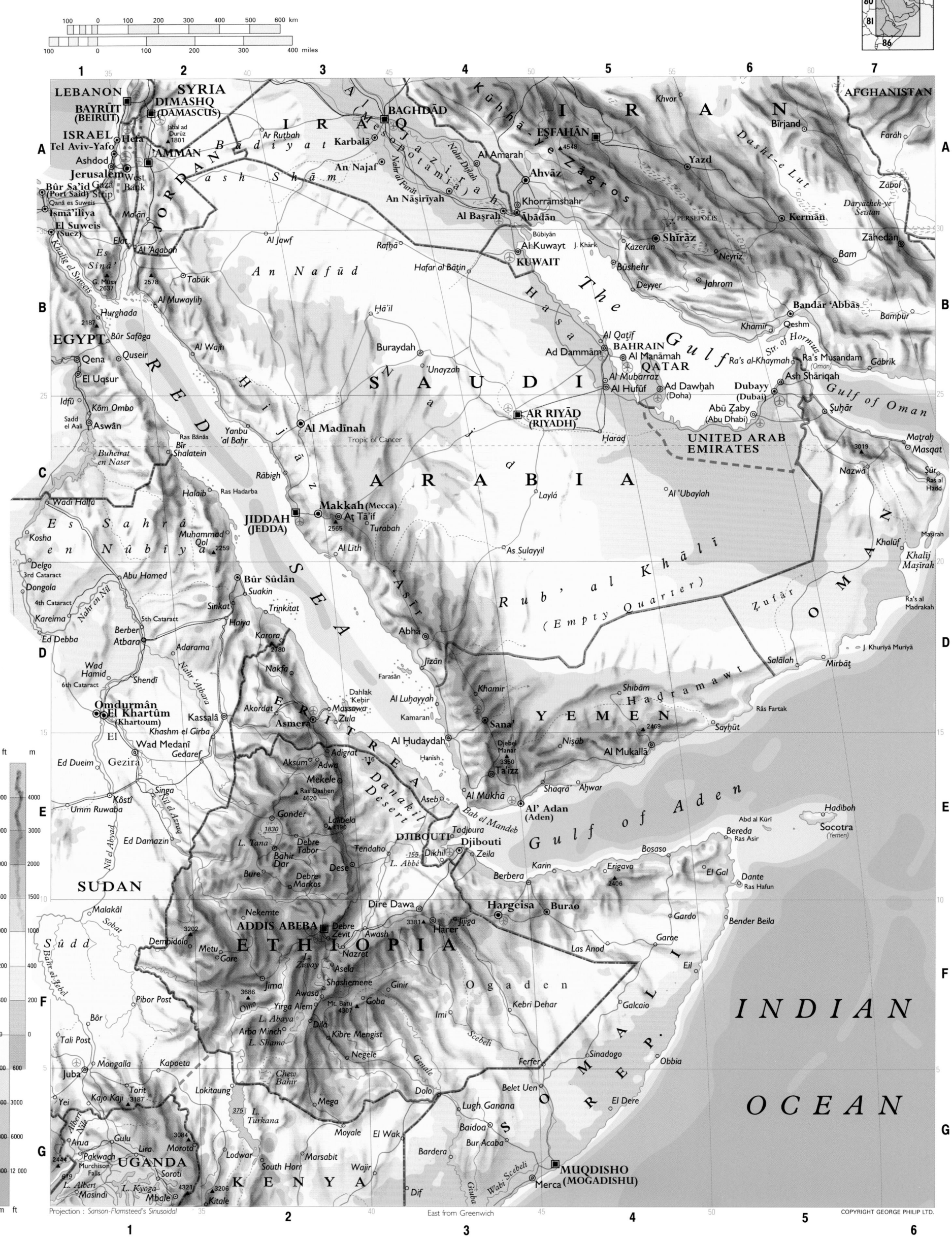

100 0 100 200 300 400 500 600 km
100 0 100 200 300 400 miles

1 2 3 4 5 6 7

LEBANON   SYRIA
BAYRŪT   DIMASHQ
(BEIRUT)   (DAMASCUS)   AFGHANISTAN
ISRAEL   Khvor
Tel Aviv-Yafo   Hefa   Birjand
Ashdod   AMMĀN   Ar Ruṭbah   Farāh
Jerusalem   West   Yazd
Bûr Sa'îd Gaza Bank   Karbalā'   Zābol
(Port Said) Strip   An Najaf   Daryācheh-ye
Ismâ'iliya   Ma'ān   Seistan
El Suweis   Elat   An Nāṣirīyah   Kermān
(Suez)   Al 'Aqabah   Al Baṣrah   Ābādān   Zāhedān

A   Al Jawf   Rafḥā'   Al Kuwayt   Shīrāz   Bam   **A**
EGYPT   Hurghada   Ḥā'il   Hafar al Bāṭin KUWAIT   Būshehr Jahrom
        Al Muwayliḥ   Deyyer
Qena   Bûr Safâga   Bandar 'Abbās
El Uqsur   Buraydah   Al Qaṭīf BAHRAIN Qeshm   Bampūr
        Al Wajh   'Unayzah   Ad Dammām Al Manāmah Ra's Musandam
Idfû   QATAR   Ash Shāriqah
Kôm Ombo Al Bânâs   Al Mubarraz Ad Dawḥah Dubayy   Gulf of Oman
Aswân   Ras Bânâs   Yanbu   AR RIYĀD Al Hufūf (Doha) (Dubai) Ṣuḥār
        Bîr Shalatein 'al Baḥr   (RIYADH) Abū Ẓaby Nazwā   Maṭraḥ
C   Al Madīnah   Ḥaraḍ   (Abu Dhabi)   Masqat   **C**
Buheirat Wadi Halfa   Tropic of Cancer   UNITED ARAB   3019
en Naser   EMIRATES   Ṣūr
        Halaib   Ras Hadarba   Laylá   Al 'Ubaylah   Ras al Hadd
        Muhammad Rābigh   Khalūf
        Qol   2259   Al Līth   As Sulayyil   Khalīj
JIDDAH   Maṣīrah
(JEDDA) MAKKAH (Mecca)   J. Khuriyā Muriyā
         Aṭ Ṭā'if Turabah
D   Bûr Sûdân   2565   Salālah Mirbāṭ   **D**
SUDAN   Suakin   Shibām   Ras al
        Sinkat   Trinkitat   Abhā   Khamir   Hadramawt   Madrakah
Berber Haiya Karora 2780 Jīzān   YEMEN   Rās Fartak
Atbara   Farasān   Al Luḥayyah Sanā'
        Adarama   Nakfa   Dahlak Kebir   Nişāb Al Mukallā
E   Omdurmân ERITREA Massawa Al Hudaydah 2469   **E**
El Khartûm Kassalā Asmera Kamaran Djebel Ta'izz Sayḥūt
(Khartoum)   Manār 3350
SUDAN   Asmera   Adigrat Al Mukhā Shaqrā Aḥwar Gulf of Aden
        Aksum Adwa   Al' Adan Socotra
        Mekele Aseb Bab el Mandeb (Aden) (Yemen)
ETHIOPIA Ras Dashen DJIBOUTI Hadiboh
        4620   Djibouti Bereda Ras Asir
ADDIS ABEBA Dikhil Zeila Bosaso
F   Berbera   Dante   INDIAN   **F**
        Hargeisa Burao
        Dire Dawa   El Gal   Ras Hafun
        Harer Jijiga   Bender Beila
        Nazret 3381   Gardo
ETHIOPIA   Ogaden   Garoe   OCEAN
        Goba Kebri Dehar   Las Anod
        Ginir
G   **G**
UGANDA KENYA   Moyale   Baidoa   MUQDISHO
                El Wak   Bur Acaba (MOGADISHU)
                           Merca

Projection : Sanson-Flamsteed's Sinusoidal   East from Greenwich   COPYRIGHT GEORGE PHILIP LTD.

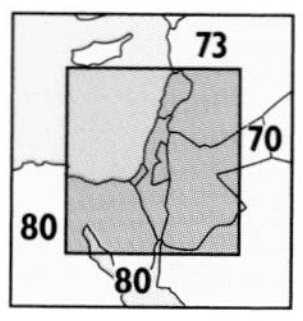

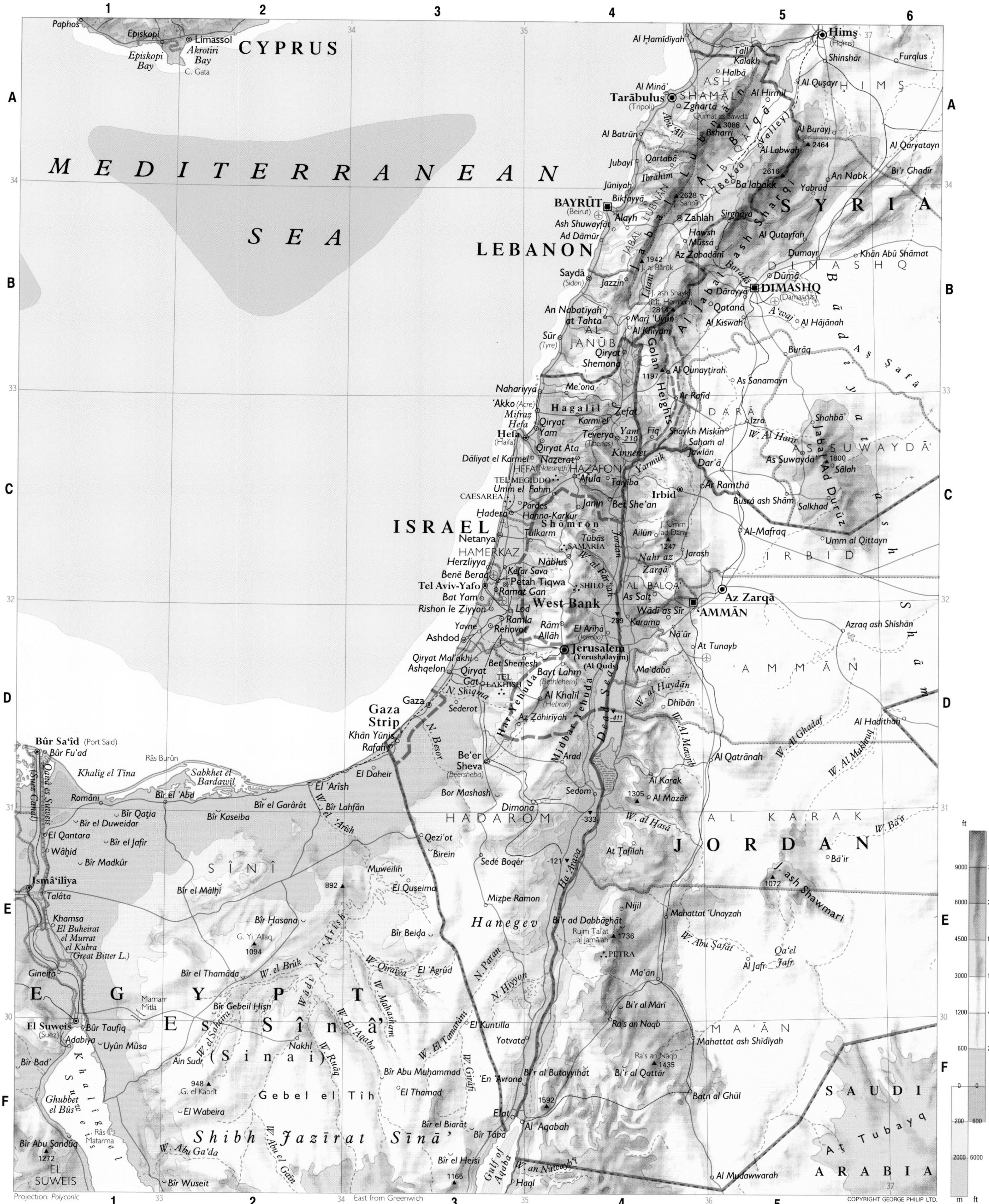

CYPRUS
Paphos
Episkopi
Limassol
Akrotiri Bay
Episkopi Bay
C. Gata
MEDITERRANEAN
SEA
LEBANON
ISRAEL
SYRIA
JORDAN
EGYPT
SAUDI ARABIA
Hims
(Homs)
Furqlus
Shinshār
Al Quşayr
Al Ḥamīdīyah
Tall Kalakh
Halbā
Al Minā'
Tarābulus
(Tripoli)
Zghartā
Qurnat as Sawdā'
3088
Bsharri
Al Hirmil
Al Batrūn
Al Labwah
Al Burayj
2464
Al Qaryatayn
Jubayl
Qartabā
Ibrāhīm
Jūniyah
2628
Sannin
2616
Ba'labakk
An Nabk
Bi'r Ghadir
Yabrūd
BAYRŪT
(Beirut)
Bikfayyā
'Alayh
Zahlah
Sirghāyā
Ash Shuwayfāt
Ad Dāmūr
Hawsh Mūssá
Az Zabadānī
Al Qutayfah
Dumayr
Khān Abū Shāmat
1942
J. al Bārūk
Saydā
(Sidon)
Jazzīn
DIMASHQ
(Damascus)
Dūmā
Dārayyā
J. ash Shaykh
(Mt. Hermon)
2814
Qatanā
An Nabaţīyah at Tahta
Marj 'Uyūn
Al Kiswah
Al Hājānah
Al Khiyām
Şūr
(Tyre)
AL JANŪB
Qiryat Shemona
Burāq
Golan Heights
Al Qunayţirah
1197
Aş Şanamayn
Nahariyya
Me'ona
Ar Rafid
'Akko (Acre)
Hagalil
Karmi'el
Zefat
DAR'Ā
Mifraz Hefa
Qiryat Yam
Hefa
(Haifa)
Yam
-210
Fiq
Shaykh Miskin
Izra
Shahbā'
Qiryat Ata
Kinneret
Saham al Jawlān
Dāliyat el Karmel
Nazerat
(Nazareth)
HEFA
HAZAFON
Dar'ā
As Suwaydā'
1800
Şalah
AS SUWAYDĀ'
TEL MEGIDDO
Umm el Fahm
'Afula
Taiyiba
Yarmūk
Ar Ramthā
CAESAREA
Pardes Hanna-Karkur
Jenin
Bet She'an
Irbid
Buşrá ash Shām
Salkhad
Hadera
Shomron
Umm ad Darai
1247
Al-Mafraq
Netanya
Tulkarm
Tūbās
SAMARIA
Ailūn
Umm al Qittayn
HAMERKAZ
Jarash
IRBID
Herzliyya
Nāblus
Nahr az Zarqā'
Benē Beraq
Kefar Sava
Petah Tiqwa
SHILO
AL BALQĀ'
Tel Aviv-Yafo
Ramat Gan
Az Zarqā
Bat Yam
West Bank
As Salţ
Rishon le Ziyyon
Lod
Wādī as Sīr
'AMMĀN
Yavne
Ramla
Rehovot
-289
Karama
Azraq ash Shīshān
Rām Allāh
El Arīḥā
(Jericho)
Nā'ūr
Ashdod
Jerusalem
(Yerushalayim)
(Al Quds)
At Tunayb
Qiryat Mal'akhi
Bet Shemesh
Ashqelon
Bayt Lahm
(Bethlehem)
Ma'dabā
'AMMĀN
Qiryat Gat
TEL LAKHISH
Al Khalīl
(Hebron)
W. al Haydān
Gaza
N. Shiqma
Gaza Strip
Sederot
Dhībān
Az Zāhirīyah
-411
Al Hadithah
Khān Yūnis
Rafah
W. Al Mawjib
W. Al Ghadaf
Har Yehuda
Midbar Yehuda
Dead Sea
Jordan
N. Besor
Be'er Sheva
(Beersheba)
Arad
Al Qatrānah
W. Al Makhruq
Bûr Sa'îd (Port Said)
Bûr Fu'ad
Râs Burûn
Sabkhet el Bardawîl
Khalîg el Tîna
El 'Arîsh
El Daheir
Al Karak
Qanâ es Suweis (Suez Canal)
Români
Bîr el 'Abd
Bîr el Garârât
Bîr Lahfân
Bor Mashash
Sedom
1305
Al Mazār
Bîr Qaţia
Bîr Kaseiba
Dimona
Bîr el Duweidar
W. el 'Arîsh
HADAROM
-333
AL KARAK
W. Ba'ir
El Qantara
Bîr el Jafir
Qezi'ot
W. al Hasā
Wâhid
Birein
At Ţafilah
Bîr Madkûr
SÎNÎ
Sedé Boqér
Bā'ir
Muweilih
-121
Ha 'Arava
Ismâ'ilîya
892
El Quseima
J. ash Shawmari
1072
Bîr el Mâlhi
Talâta
Mizpe Ramon
Nijil
Khamsa
Bîr Hasana
Bi'r ad Dabbāghāt
Mahattat 'Unayzah
El Buheirat el Murrat el Kubra
(Great Bitter L.)
Hanegev
G. Yi 'Allaq
1094
Bîr Beiḍa
Rujm Tal'at al Jamā'ah
1736
PETRA
W. Abu Şafāt
Qa'el Jafr
Al Jafr
Gineifa
Bîr el Thamâda
W. el Brûk
W. Qiraiya
El 'Agrûd
N. Paran
Ma'ān
Mamarr Mitlâ
N. Hiyyon
Wâdi el 'Arîsh
W. Mahashsham
Bîr Gebeil Hişn
Bi'r al Mārī
El Suweis
(Suez)
Bûr Taufiq
W. El 'Aqaba
El Kuntilla
Ra's an Naqb
MA'ĀN
Adabiya
Uyûn Mûsa
W. el Sahéira
Es Sînâ'
(Sinai)
Nakhl
W. Ruâg
W. El Tamarâni
Yotvata
Mahattat ash Shidīyah
Bîr Bad'
Ain Sudr
W. Girafi
Ra's an Naqb
1435
Khalîg el Suweis
Bîr Abu Muḥammad
'En 'Avrona
Bi'r al Butayyihāt
Bi'r al Qattār
948
G. el Kabrît
El Thamad
Gebel el Tîh
Ghubbet el Bûs
1592
Baţn al Ghūl
El Wabeira
Elat
Bîr el Biarât
Al 'Aqabah
Bîr Tâba
Râs Matarma
Shibh Jazīrat Sīnā'
Aţ Ţubayq
Bîr Abu Sandûq
W. Abu Ga'da
W. Abu el Gaîn
1272
Bîr el Heisi
W. an Nuwaybi
Gulf of Aqaba
EL SUWEIS
Bîr Wuseit
1165
Haql
Al Mudawwarah
Projection: Polyconic
East from Greenwich

1974 Cease Fire Lines

COPYRIGHT GEORGE PHILIP LTD.

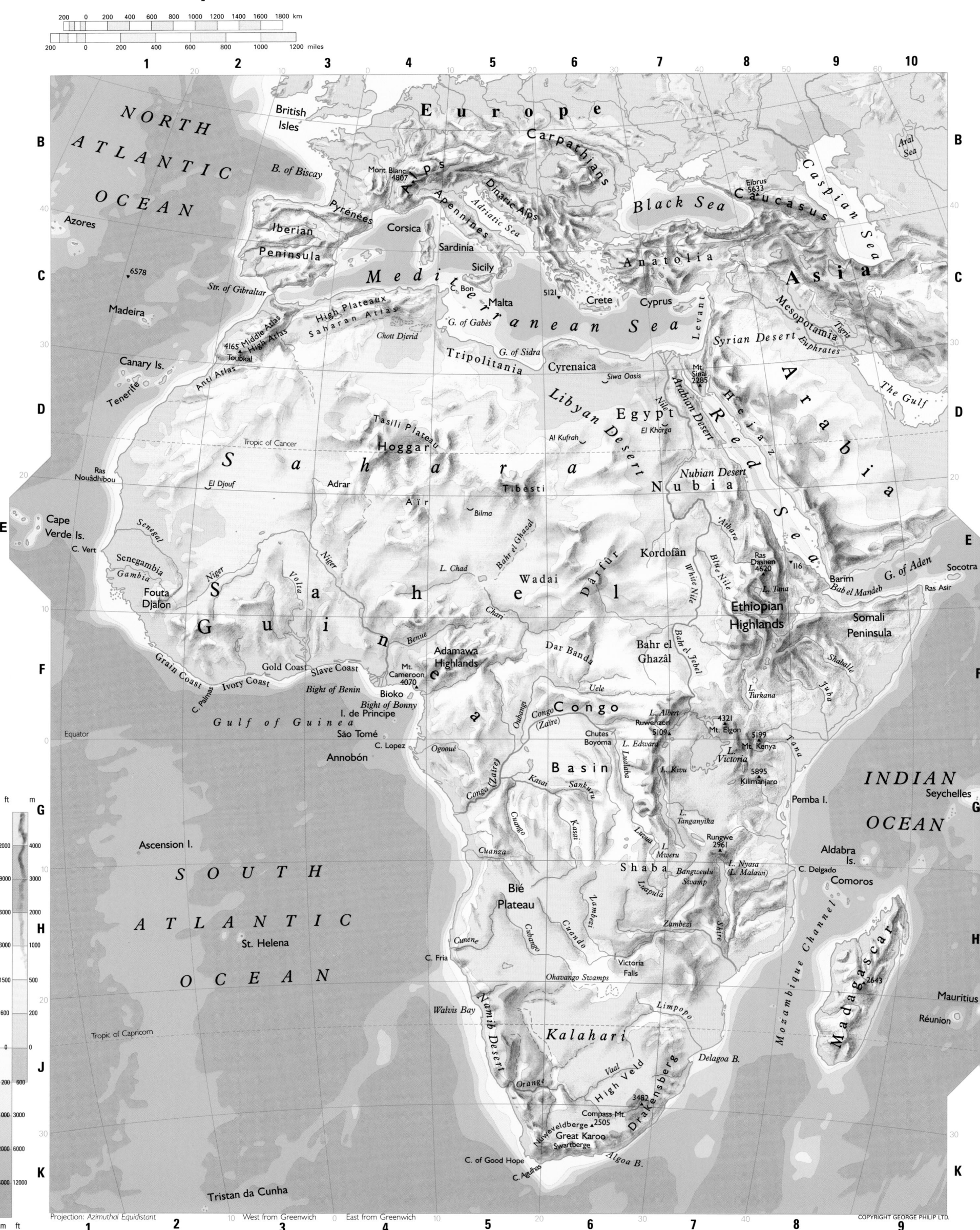

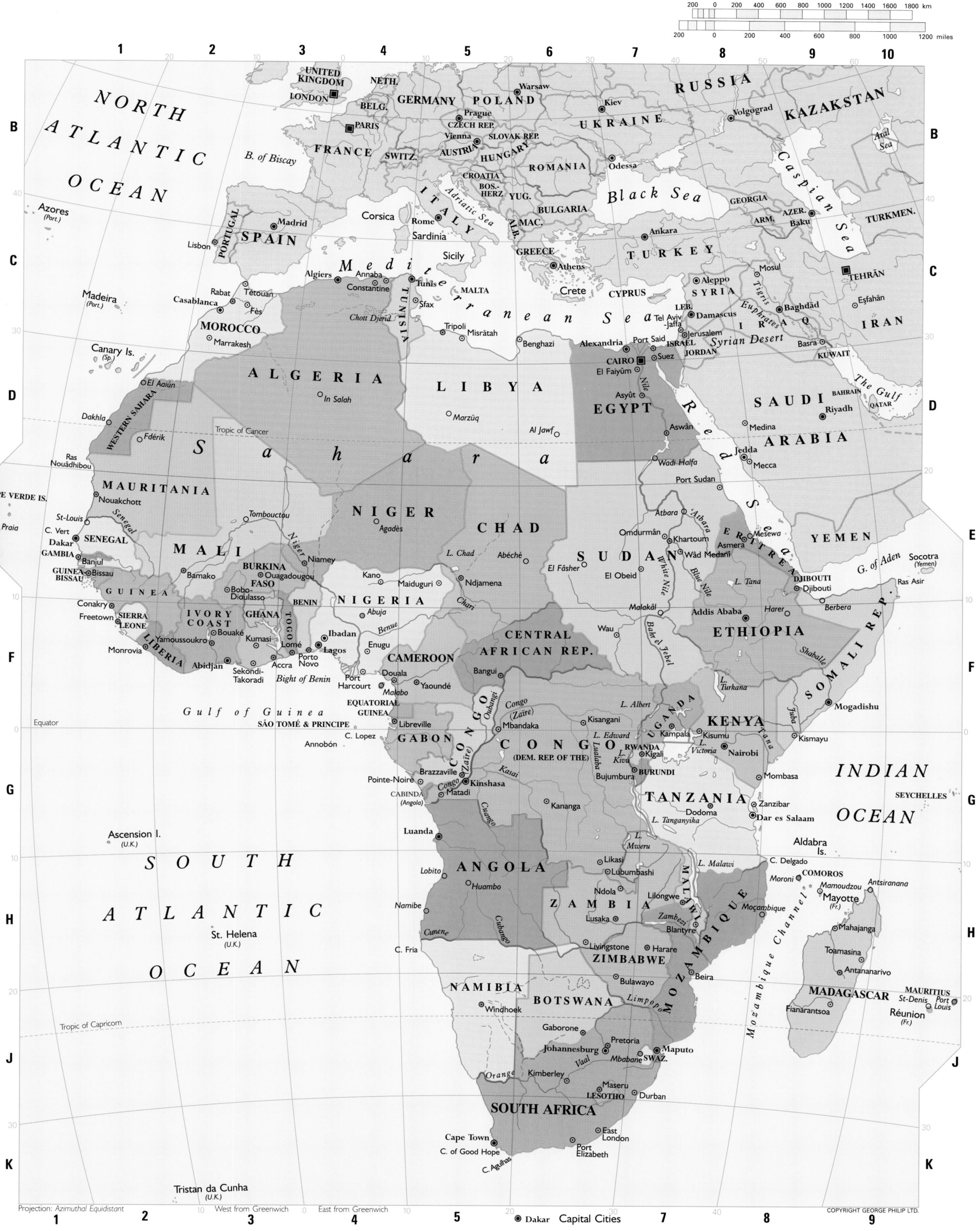

200 0 200 400 600 800 1000 1200 1400 1600 1800 km

200 0 200 400 600 800 1000 1200 miles

B

NORTH
ATLANTIC
OCEAN

UNITED
KINGDOM
LONDON
NETH.
BELG.
GERMANY POLAND
Warsaw
RUSSIA
KAZAKSTAN

PARIS
FRANCE
SWITZ.
Prague
CZECH REP.
Vienna
AUSTRIA
SLOVAK REP.
HUNGARY
ROMANIA
Kiev
UKRAINE
Odessa
Volgograd
Aral
Sea
Caspian Sea

B. of Biscay

CROATIA
BOS.-
HERZ.
YUG.
BULGARIA
Black Sea
GEORGIA
ARM.
AZER.
Baku
TURKMEN.

PORTUGAL
SPAIN
Madrid
Corsica
Rome
ITALY
Adriatic Sea
ALB.
MAC.
GREECE
Athens
TURKEY
Ankara
Esfahān
TEHRĀN

Lisbon
Sardinia
Sicily
Crete
CYPRUS
Aleppo
SYRIA
Mosul
Baghdād

Madeira
(Port.)
Algiers
Annaba
Constantine
TUNISIA
Tunis
MALTA
LEB.
Tel Aviv
-Jaffa
Damascus
I R A Q
Basra
IRAN

Casablanca
Rabat
Tétouan
Fès
MOROCCO
Sfax
Tripoli
Misrātah
Benghazi
Alexandria
Port Said
ISRAEL
Jerusalem
JORDAN
Syrian Desert
KUWAIT

Canary Is.
(Sp.)
Marrakesh
Chott Djerid
CAIRO
Suez
El Faiyûm
SAUDI
BAHRAIN
QATAR
The Gulf

El Aaiún
WESTERN SAHARA
ALGERIA
LIBYA
EGYPT
Asyût
Aswân
Medina
ARABIA
Riyadh

Dakhla
Fdérik
In Salah
Tropic of Cancer
Marzūq
Al Jawf
Jedda
Mecca
Wadi Halfa

Ras
Nouâdhibou
S a h a r a
Red
Sea
Port Sudan
YEMEN
Socotra
(Yemen)

PE VERDE IS.
MAURITANIA
Nouakchott
NIGER
CHAD
Atbara
Omdurmân
Khartoum
ERITREA
Mesewa
Asmera
G. of Aden
Ras Asir

St-Louis
Senegal
Tombouctou
Agadès
SUDAN
Wâd Medani
DJIBOUTI
Djibouti
Berbera

C. Vert
Dakar
SENEGAL
MALI
Niamey
L. Chad
Abéché
Ndjamena
El Fâsher
El Obeid
White Nile
Blue Nile
L. Tana
Harer

Praia
GAMBIA
Banjul
GUINEA-
BISSAU
Bissau
Bámako
BURKINA
FASO
Ouagadougou
Kano
Maiduguri
Chari
Malakâl
Addis Ababa
ETHIOPIA

Conakry
GUINEA
Bobo
Dioulasso
BENIN
NIGERIA
Abuja
Wau
Bahr el Jebel
L.
Turkana

Freetown
SIERRA
LEONE
IVORY
COAST
GHANA
TOGO
Ibadan
Enugu
Benue
CENTRAL
AFRICAN REP.
L. Albert
UGANDA
KENYA
Mogadishu

Monrovia
Yamoussoukro
Bouaké
Kumasi
Lomé
Porto
Novo
Lagos
CAMEROON
Bangui
Oubangi
L. Edward
RWANDA
Kigali
Kampala
L.
Victoria
Kisumu
Nairobi
Kismayu

LIBERIA
Abidjan
Sekondi-
Takoradi
Accra
Port
Harcourt
Douala
Yaoundé
Congo
(Zaïre)
Mbandaka
Kisangani
L. Kivu
BURUNDI
Bujumbura
Juba

Bight of Benin
EQUATORIAL
GUINEA
Malabo
CONGO
(DEM. REP. OF THE)
Mombasa
INDIAN

Gulf of Guinea
SÃO TOMÉ & PRINCIPE
Libreville
GABON
C. Lopez
CONGO
Brazzaville
Kinshasa
Matadi
Kasai
Kananga
TANZANIA
Zanzibar
Dodoma
Dar es Salaam
OCEAN
SEYCHELLES

Equator
Annobón
Pointe-Noire
CABINDA
(Angola)
L. Tanganyika

Ascension I.
(U.K.)
Luanda
Chiumbe
Cuango
L.
Mweru
L. Malawi
C. Delgado
Mayotte
(Fr.)
COMOROS
Moroni
Mamoudzou
Antsiranana

SOUTH
ATLANTIC
OCEAN
Lobito
ANGOLA
Huambo
Likasi
Lubumbashi
Ndola
MALAWI
Lilongwe
MOZAMBIQUE
Moçambique
Mahajanga

St. Helena
(U.K.)
Namibe
ZAMBIA
Lusaka
Zambezi
Blantyre
Toamasina

C. Fria
Cunene
Cubango
Livingstone
Harare
Beira
Antananarivo
MAURITIUS
MADAGASCAR

Cuando
Limpopo
Bulawayo
ZIMBABWE
Fianarantsoa
St-Denis
Réunion
(Fr.)
Port
Louis

Tropic of Capricorn
NAMIBIA
BOTSWANA
Windhoek
Gaborone
Pretoria
Maputo
Mbabane
SWAZ.
Mozambique Channel
Aldabra
Is.

Johannesburg
Vaal
Kimberley
Maseru
LESOTHO
Durban

Orange
SOUTH AFRICA
East
London
Port
Elizabeth

Cape Town
C. of Good Hope
C. Agulhas

Tristan da Cunha
(U.K.)

Projection: Azimuthal Equidistant

West from Greenwich   East from Greenwich

Dakar Capital Cities

COPYRIGHT GEORGE PHILIP LTD.

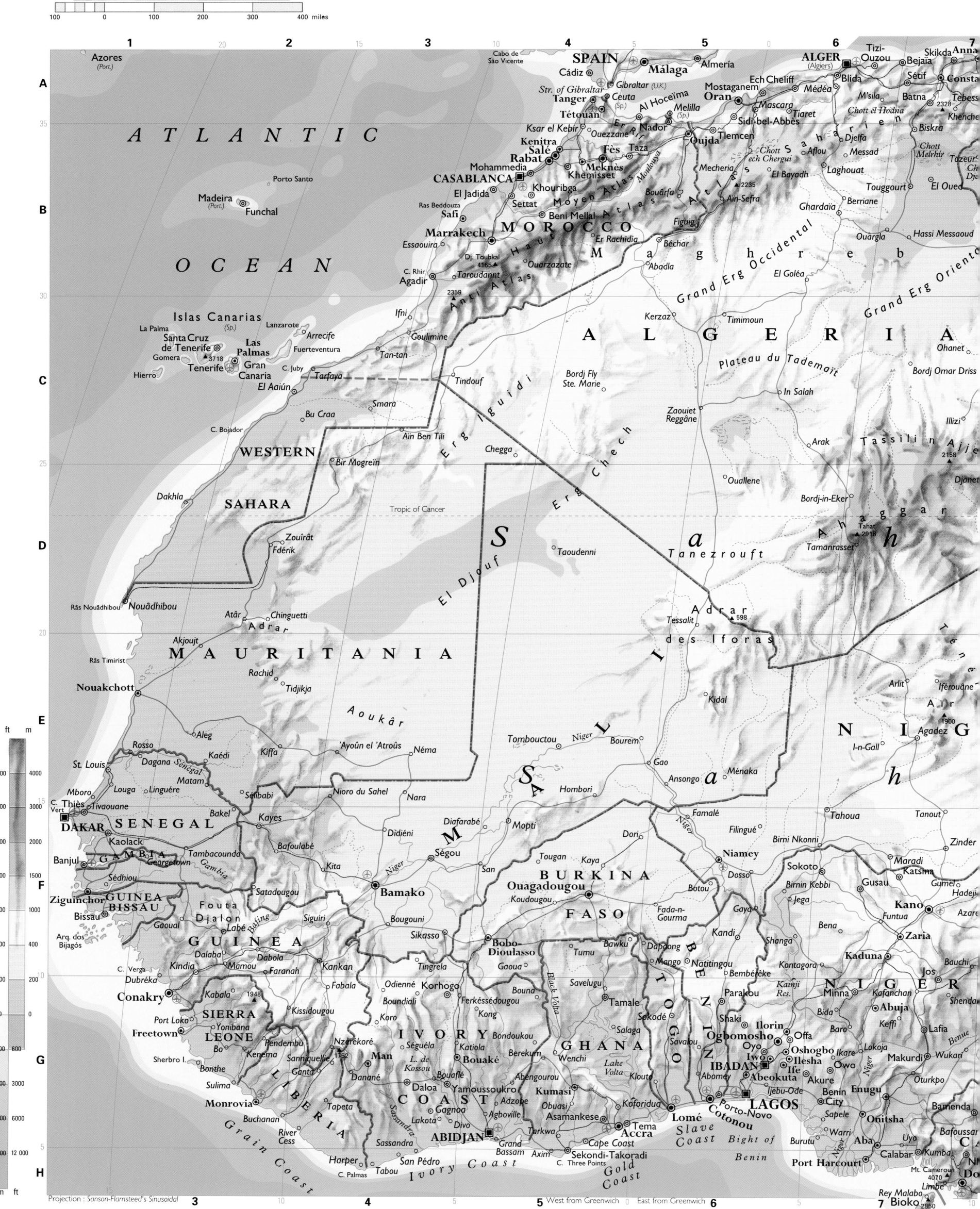

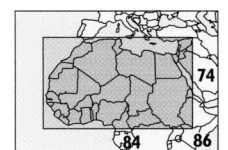

MEDITERRANEAN SEA

TURKEY Antalya **ADANA**
Antakya **HALAB**
Al Lādhiqiyah
GREECE Ródhos CYPRUS Nicosia **SYRIA**
Kríti Tarābulus Hims Nahr al Furāt
Iráklion LEBANON
BAYRŪT **DIMASHQ** **IRAQ**
(Beirut) (Damascus) Ar Ruţbah
ISRAEL Hefa Jabal ad Durūz Bādiyat
Tel Aviv-Yafo **AMMÂN** ash Shām
Ashdod West Bank
Bizerte Ariana **CARTHAGE**
Béja **TUNIS** Nabeul Sicilia **MALTA**
Kairouan Sousse Valletta Zāwiyat al Baydā Darnah Al Jaghbūb El Mahalla el Kubra Dumyât **JERUSALEM**
Mahdia Banghāzī Al Marj Tubruq Damanhûr Bûr Sa'îd
Sfax Al Khums Misrātah Suluq Bardīyah Salūm **EL ISKANDARÎYA** **El Mansûra** Jordan
Golfe de Gabès **Tarābulus** (Tripoli) Surt Marsâ Matrûh El Alamein (Alexandria) Tanta Ismâ'ilîya Ma'ān Al Jawf
Île de Djerba Az Zāwiyah Gharyān 968 Khalīj Surt Ajdābiyā Zagazig Isma'ilîya
Zarzis Mizdah Tripolitania Cyrenaica **EL GÎZA** **EL QAHIRA** El Suweis Elat Al 'Aqabah **SAUDI**
Médenine Daraj Hūn Awjilah Sîwa Munkhafed el Qattâra Helwan El Suweis Es Sînā' Tabūk **ARABIA**
Ghudāmis Brach El Faiyûm Beni Suef G. Mûsa 2578
Idehan **LIBYA** Zillah Sahrâ' Maghâgha 2637 Al Muwayliħ
Awbārī Sabhah 1200 El Minyâ Es Sahrâ Hurghada
Awbārī Marzūq Libîya Mallawi Esh Sharqîya Bûr Safâga Al Wajh
Fezzan Wāw al Kabīr Qasr Farâfra Manfalût **Asyût** 2187 Quseir
Ghat Al Qaţrūn Qena Quseir Al Wajh
Sahrâ' Al Kufrah Mût El Wâhât el-Dakhla Tahta Sohâg Girga THEBES KARNAK Al Wajh
Rebiana Al Jawf El Wâhât el-Khârga Idfû El Uqsur
Toummo El Wâhât el-Khârga Kom Ombo RED
1082 Sadd el Aali Aswân
Madama Aozou J. Uweinat 1893 Buheirat Ras Bānās HIJAZ
Chirfa Bardai Pic Toussidé 3265 Tarso Emissi 3150 Ma'tan as Sārra en Naser Bîr Shalatein Yanbu al Baħr
Tibesti Zouar ABU SIMBEL Râbigh
Emi Koussi 3415 Strip El Wâhât el Selîma Wadi Halfa Halaib Ras Hadarba SEA
Fachi Bilma Borkou Ounianga Sérir Bir 'Atrun Es Sahrâ Muhammad
Grand Erg du Bilma Faya-Largeau Dépression du Mourdi Delgo en Nûbîya Qol 2259
Erg du Djourab Fada Ennedi 1310 3rd Cataract Kosha Bûr
ER Zagaoua Dongola Abu Hamed Sûdân
Zigey Bahr el Ghazal Biltine Oum Chalouba SUDAN 4th Cataract Kareima Suakin
Nguigmi Mao Lac Tchad Moussoro Ati Malha Kutum Umm Keddada Nahr en Nil Berber 5th Cataract Sinkat Trinkitat
Bosso Gashua Massakory Abéché 1954 El Fâsher Atbara Adarama Haiya Karora 2780
Nguru Geidam Ndjamena Bokoro Mongo Goz Beïda Al Junaynah Zalingei Jebel Mara 3088 Nyâlâ El Wuz Sodiri En Nahud Umm Ruwaba Wad Hamid Shendî 6th Cataract ERITREA Nakfa
Maiduguri Kousseri CHAD Massenya Abou-Deïa Am Timan Darfur Nyâlâ El Fâsher El Obeid Kâdugli Omdurmân **El Khartûm** Kassalâ Akordat
Potiskum Bama Maroua Guider Chari Bongor Birao Songa Kordofân Abū Zabad 1325 Ed Dueim El Gezira Wâd Medanî Khashm el Girba Gedaref
Bajoga Biu Mubi Garoua Laï Sarh Ndélé 1226 Sa'id Bundas Bahr el Arab Abū Zabad Er Rahad Nil el Abyad Ed Damazin 1830
Numan Yola Pala Moundou Doba Koumra Birao Bahr el Ghazâl Raga Wâw Gogriâl Sûdd 3202 ETHIOPIA
Baïbokoum Ngaoundéré Kaga Bandoro Yalinga Ghazâl Tonj Rumbêk Bôr L. Tana
Gashaka Banyo Bossangoa Ippy Bakouma Obo Rumbêk Pibor Post 3886 L. Abaya
Massif de Adamaoua Bétaré Oya **CENTRAL AFRICAN REPUBLIC** Bambari Amâdi Tali Post Juba Bahir Dar Debre Markos
Foumban Yoko Bouar Bozoum Sibut Kaga Bandoro Bangassou El Istiwâ'iya Mongalla Nekemte Metu Gore Jima
CAMEROON Batouri Carnot Bossembélé Bambari Bomu Yâmbiô Yei Dungu Faradje Kapoeta Dembidolo Arba Minch L. Shamo
Yaoundé Abong-Mbang Berbérati Mbaïki **Bangui** Zongo Bosobolo Mobaye Mobayi Bondo Uele Kajo Kaji Torit 3181 Lokitaung L. Turkana Chew Bahr
375

COPYRIGHT GEORGE PHILIP LTD.

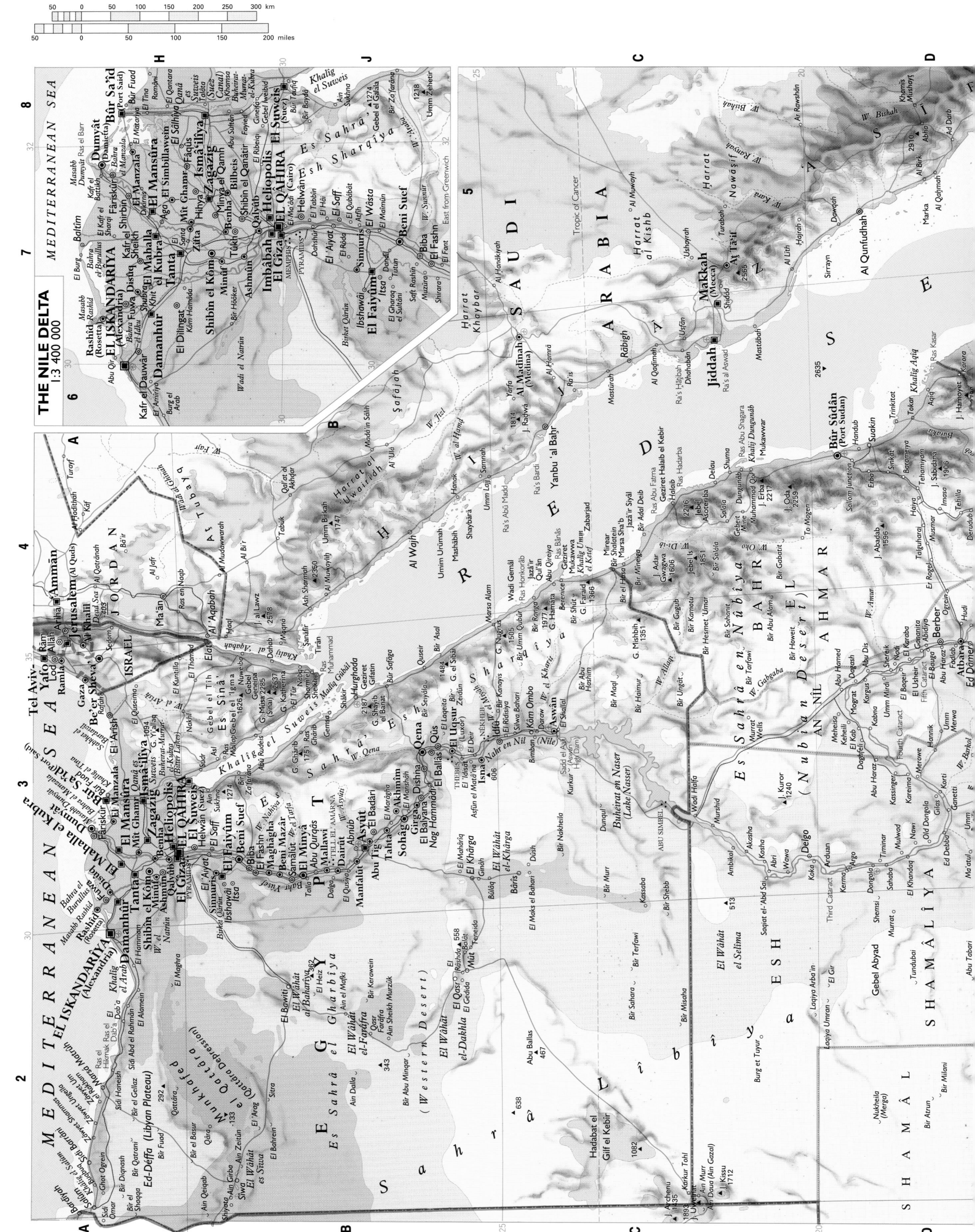

THE NILE DELTA
1:3 400 000

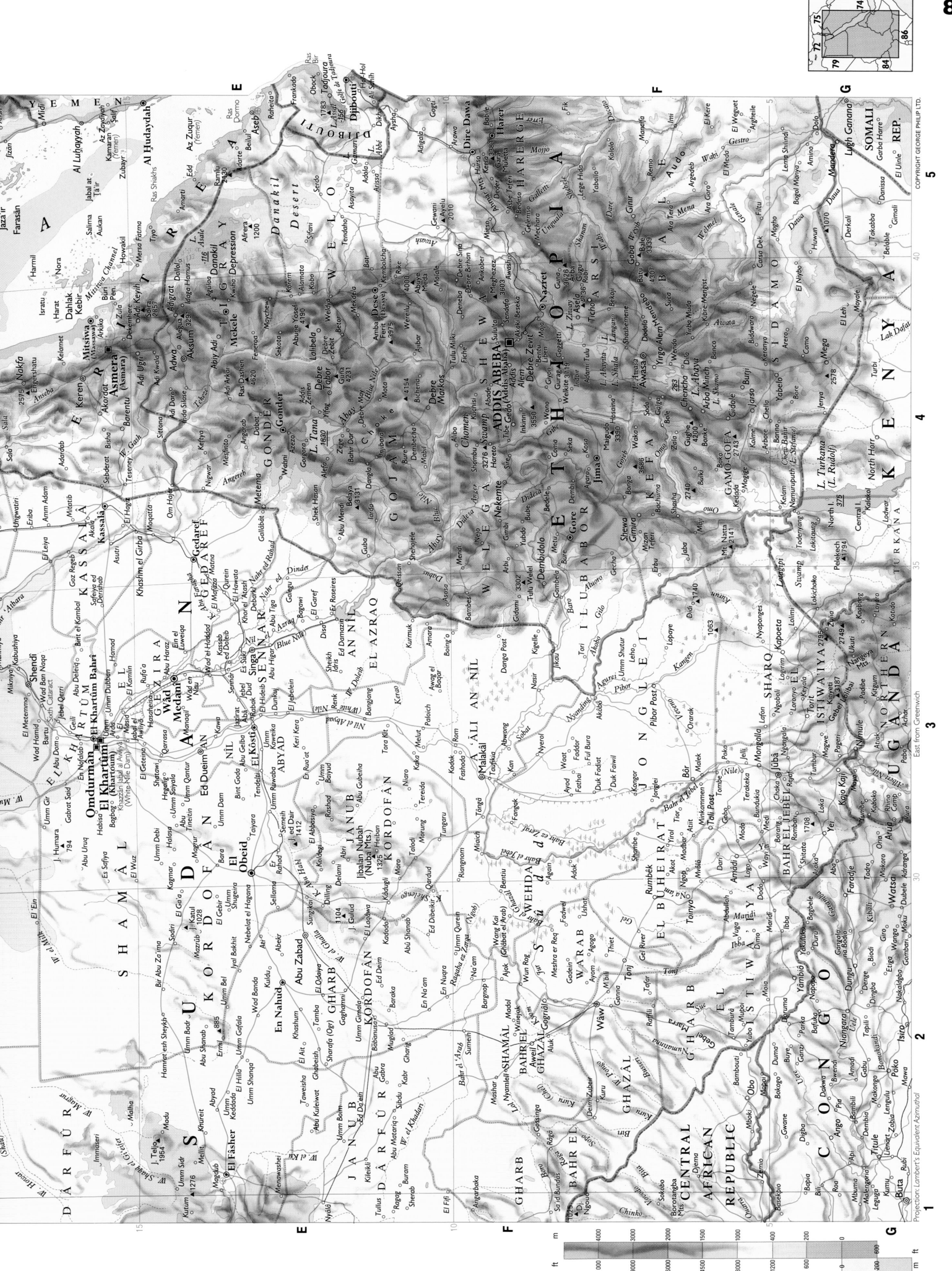

Projection: Lambert's Equivalent Azimuthal

East from Greenwich

50   0   50   100   150   200   250   300 km

50   0   50   100   150   200 miles

1   **2**   **3**

ft   m

12 000   4000

9000   3000

6000   2000

4500   1500

3000   1000

1200   400

600   200

0   0

200   600

2000   6000

4000   12 000

6000   18 000

m   ft

Et Tidra

Râs Timirist

Nouâmghâr

Bennichâb

Akjoujt

M A U R I T A N I A

El Mreyye

Azao

Araouane

Bou Djébéha

In-Aleï

Dayet en Nâharat

Tombouctou (Timbuktu)

L. Faguibine

Ras el Mâ

Goundam

Koriumbé

Diré

Kabara

Niafounké

Saréyamou

Bamba

L. Débo

L. Korarou

A

L. Korarou

791

Douentza

M

Mopti

Bandiagara

Dougani

Bankas

Koro

Ouahigouya

B U

B

Nouakchott

Tidjikja

Gânet

Tîchît

Akreijit

Arâtâne

Tagânt

Aoukâr

Moudjeria

Boûmdeïd

Togba

Tâmchekket

Oualâta

Néma

Timbedgha

Bassikounou

Nampala

Akka

Kona

Mederdra

Boutilimit

Magta Lahjar

Aleg

Mâl

Kiffa

'Ayoûn el 'Akroûs

L. Faguibine

Rachid

420

Tidjikja

Gânet

Kobenni

Boulouli

Guirel

Nioro du Sahel

Ballé

Karounga

Nara

Douna

Macina

Diabaly

Tenenkou

Manimpé

Niono

Diafarabé

Ké-Macina

Sofara

Djenné

Say

ATLANTIC

OCEAN

G U L F

Projection : Lambert's Equivalent Azimuthal

1   **2**   **3**   **4**

West from Greenw

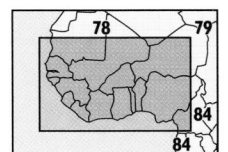

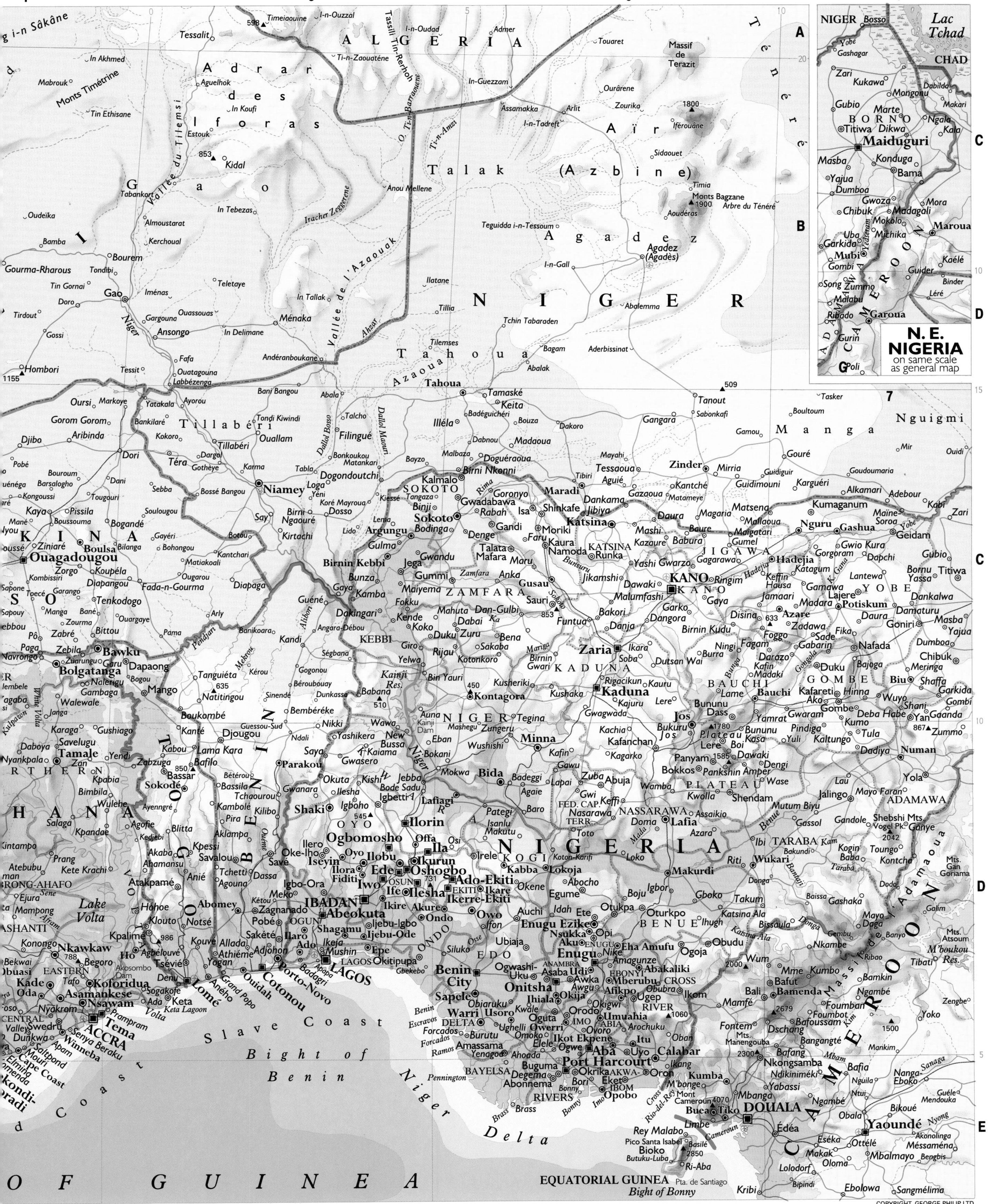

N. E. NIGERIA on same scale as general map

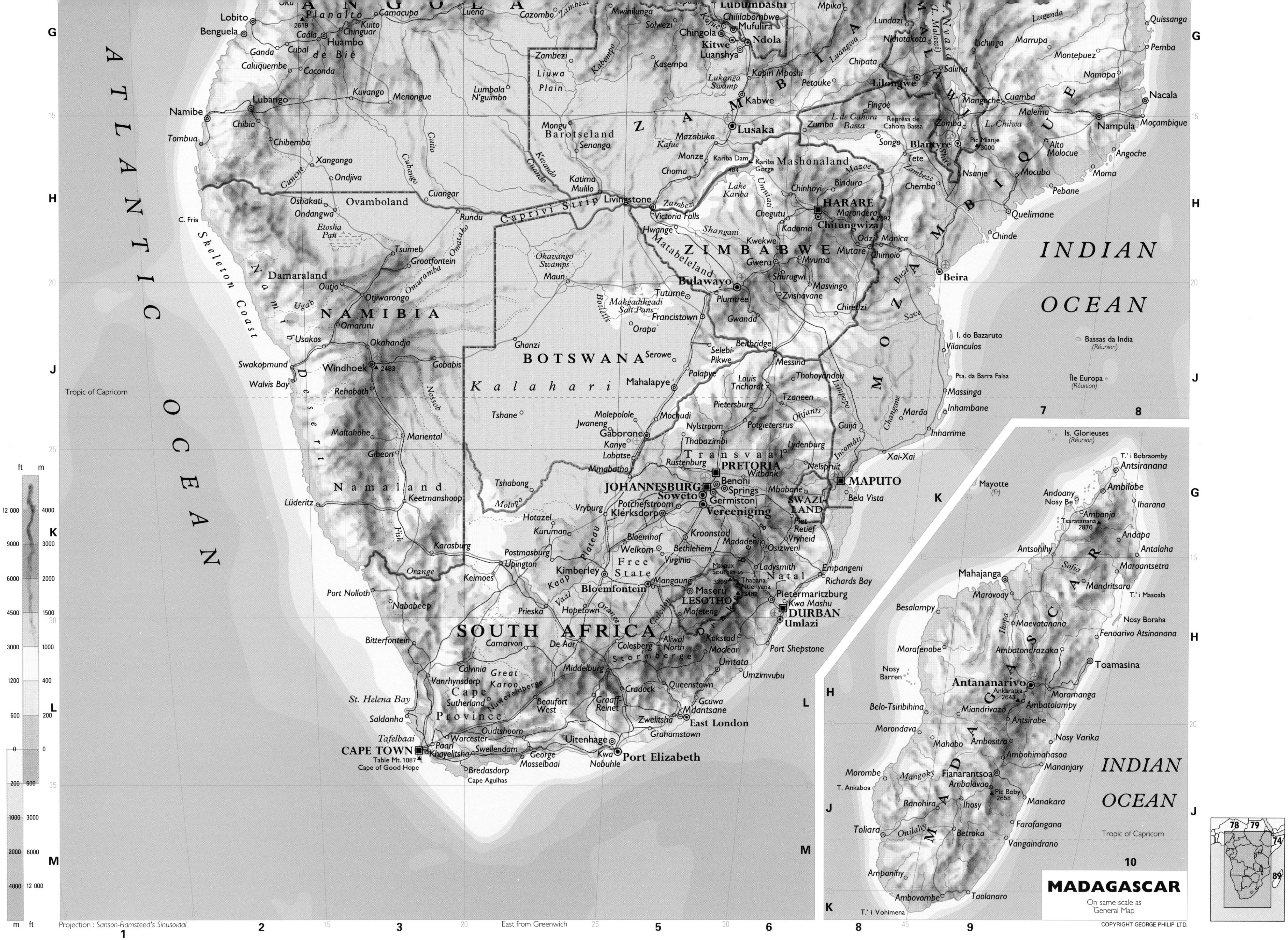

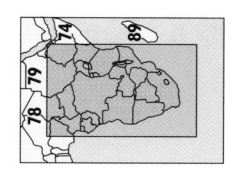

MADAGASCAR
On same scale as
General Map

Projection : Sanson-Flamsteed's Sinusoidal

East from Greenwich

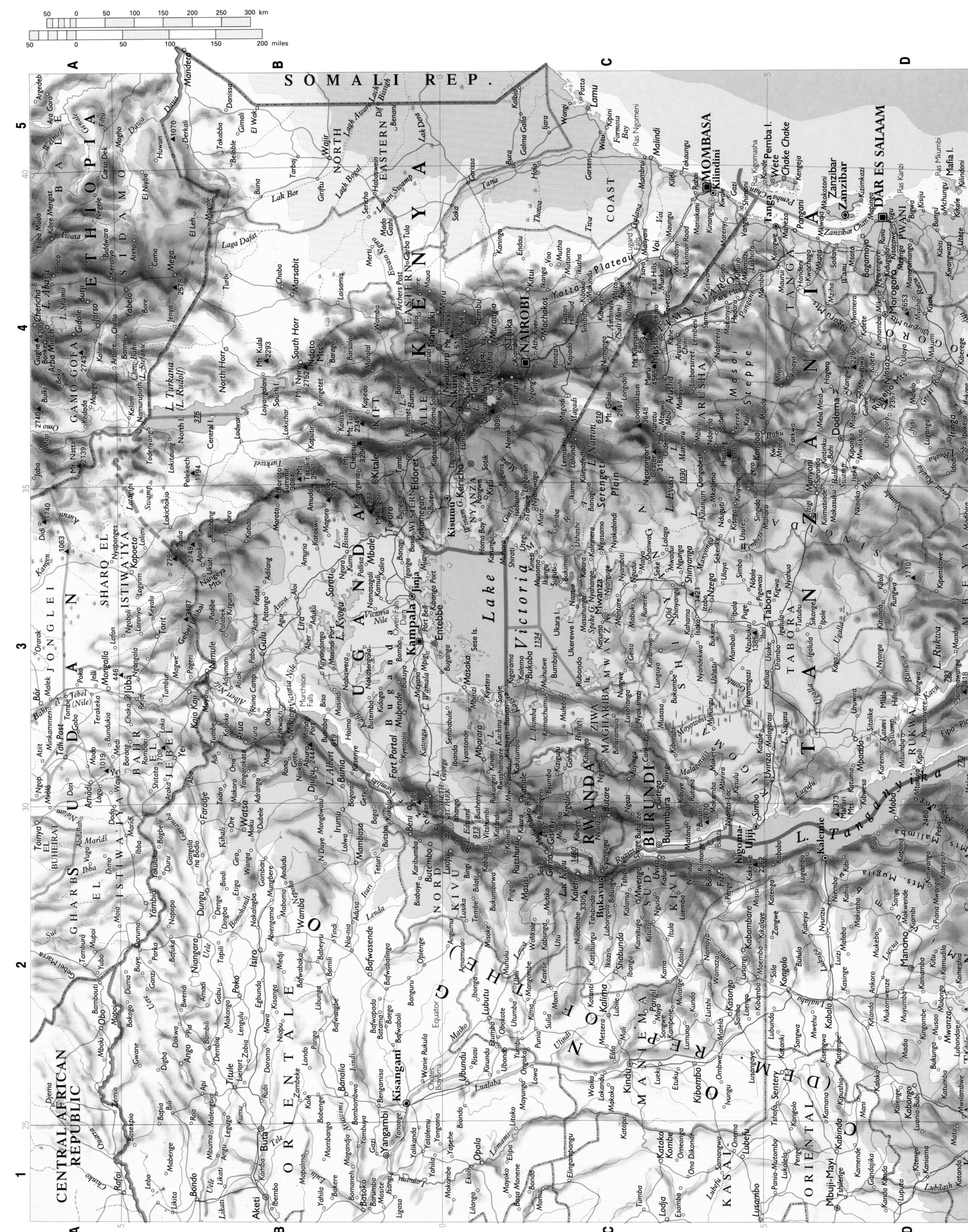

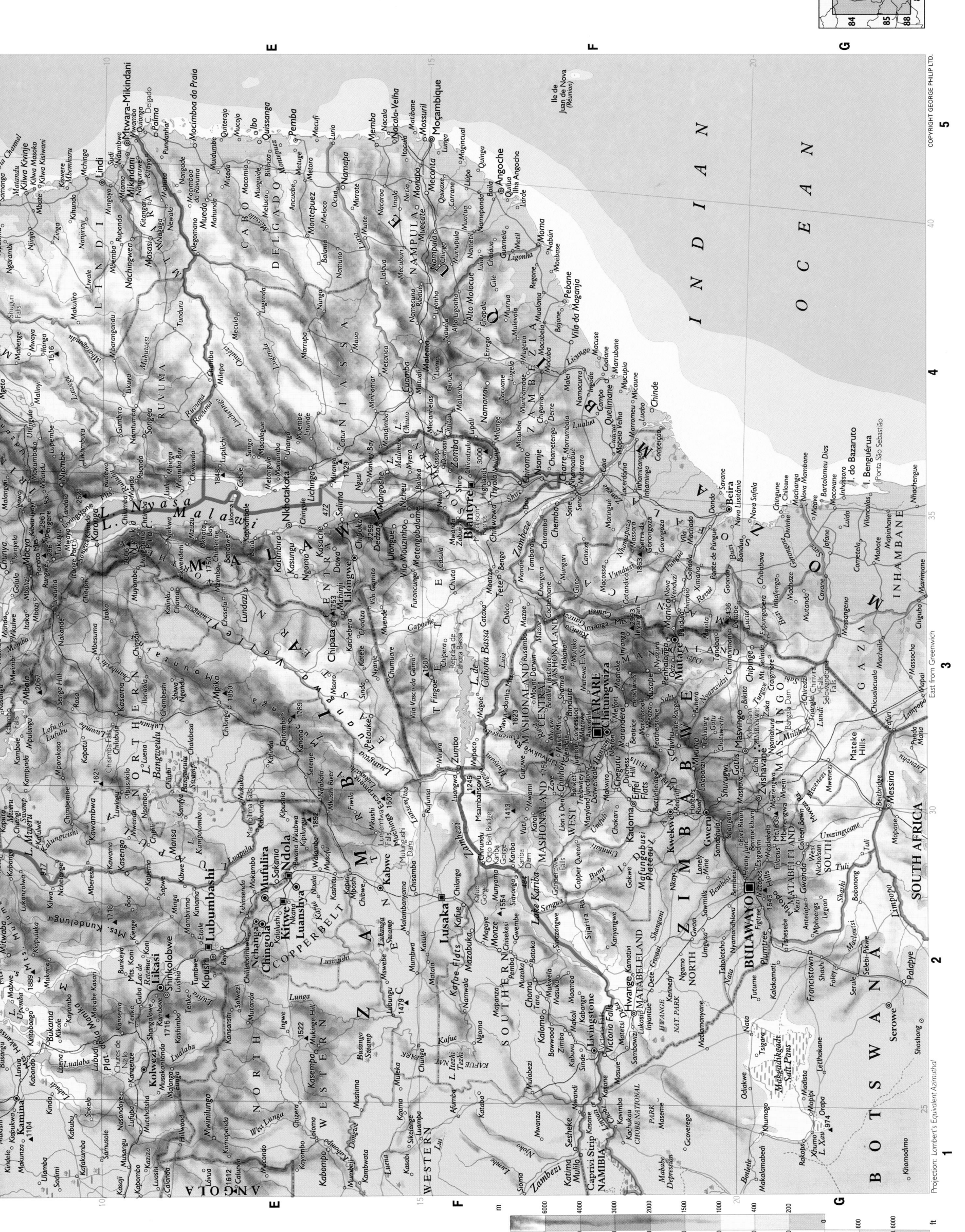

Projection: Lambert's Equivalent Azimuthal

East from Greenwich

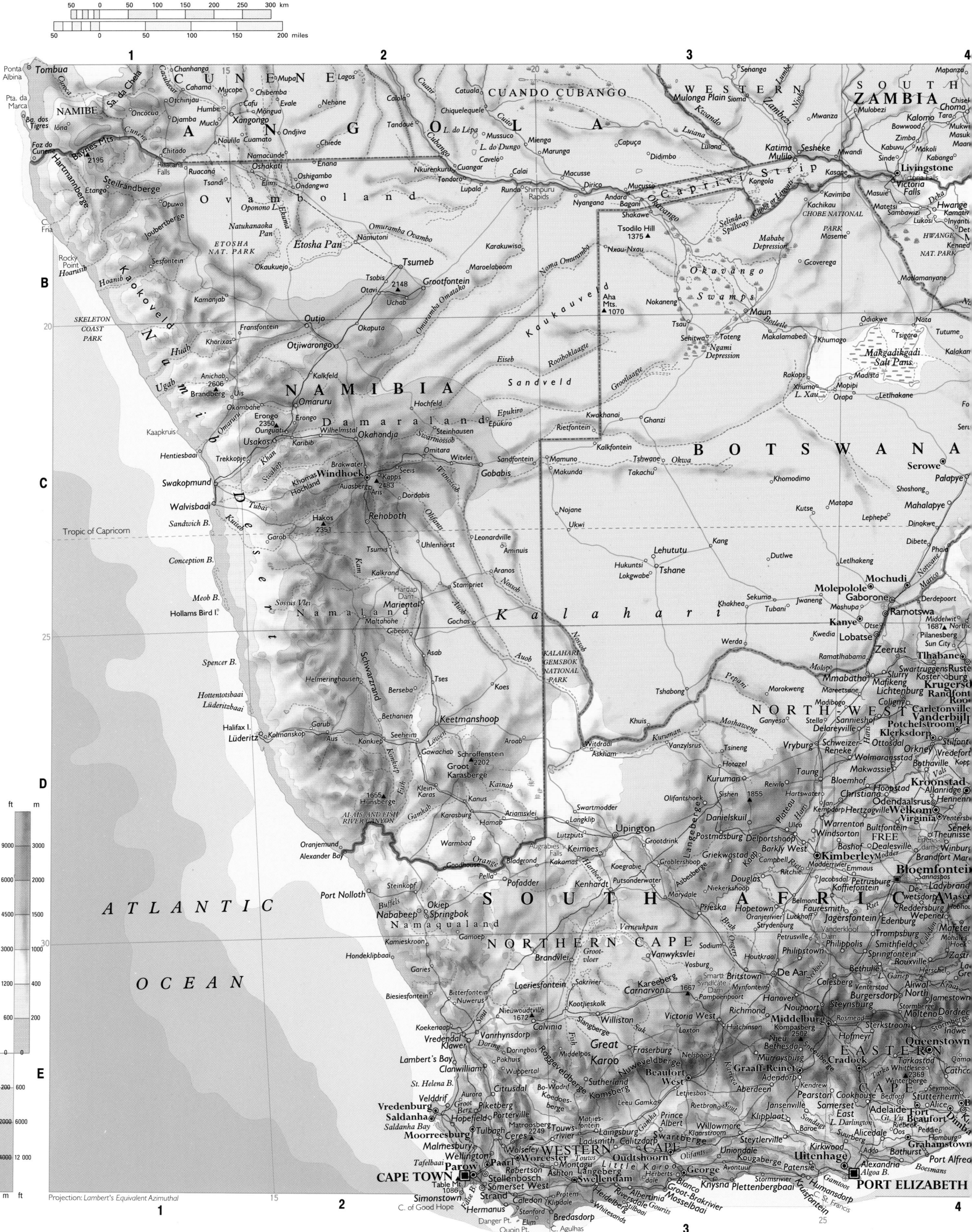

ft   m

9000 3000

6000 2000

4500 1500

3000 1000

1200   400

600   200

0   0

200   600
2000 6000
4000 12 000

m   ft

Projection: Lambert's Equivalent Azimuthal

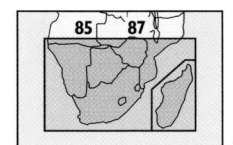

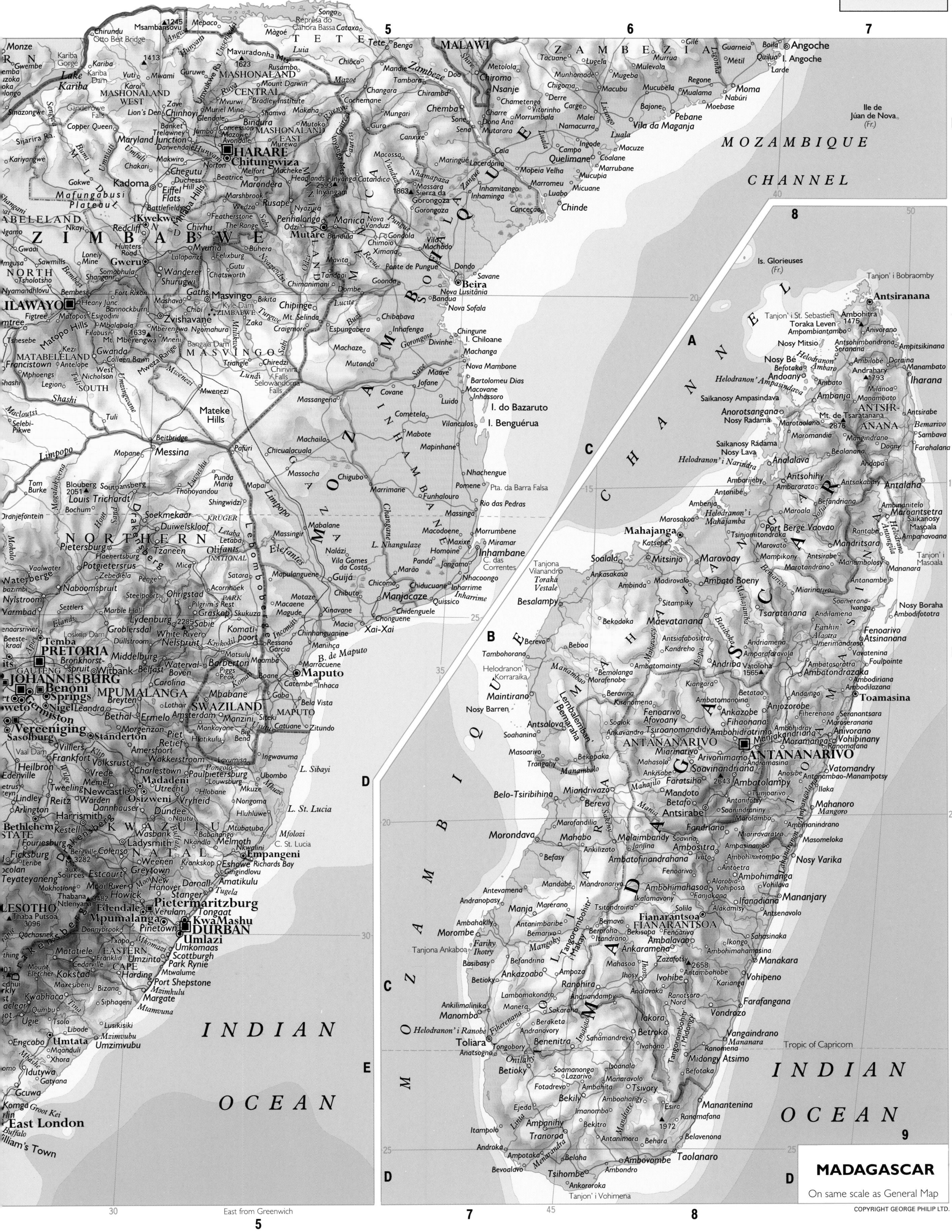

MADAGASCAR

On same scale as General Map

COPYRIGHT GEORGE PHILIP LTD.

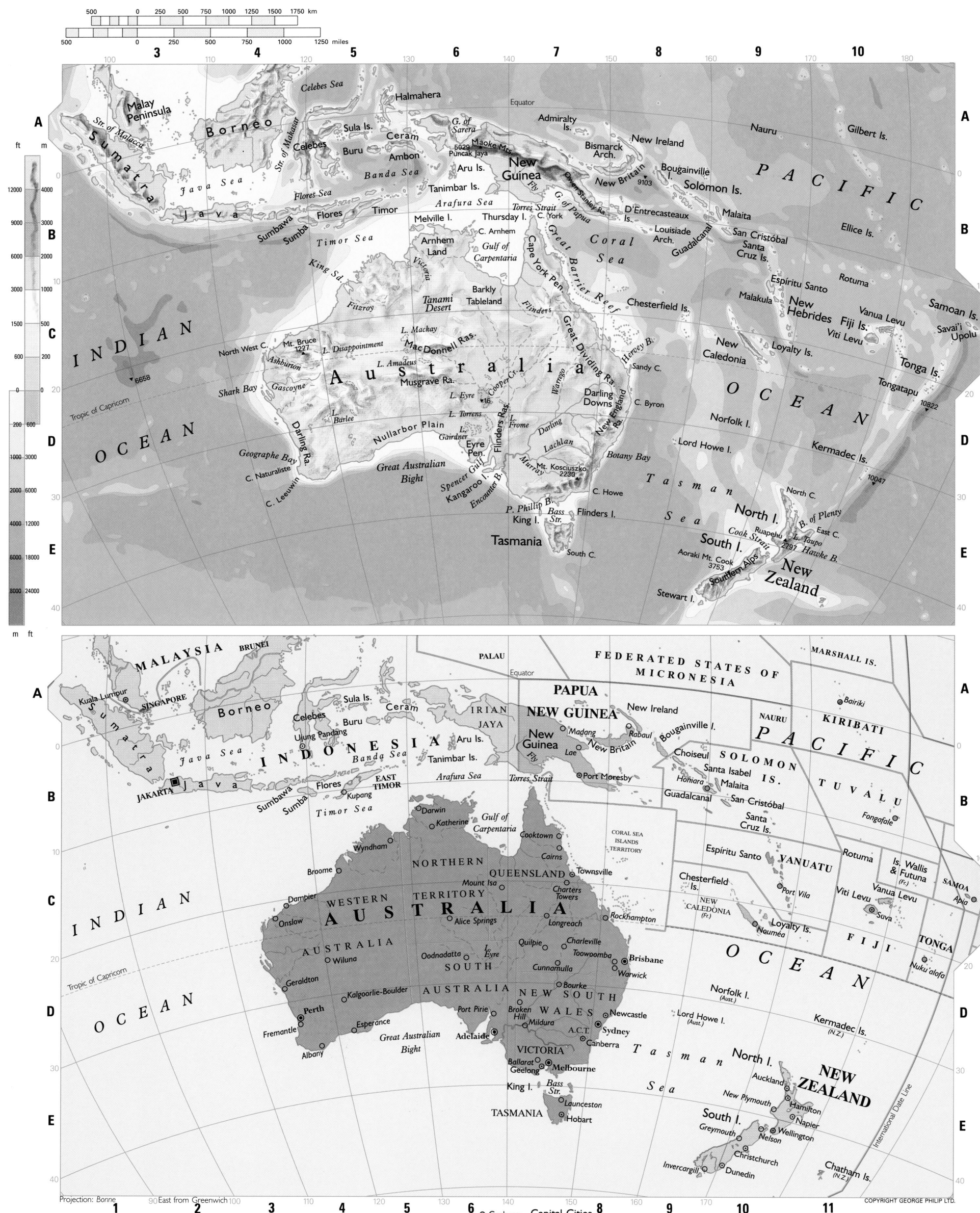

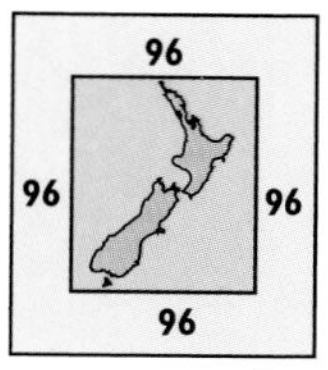
96
96
96
96

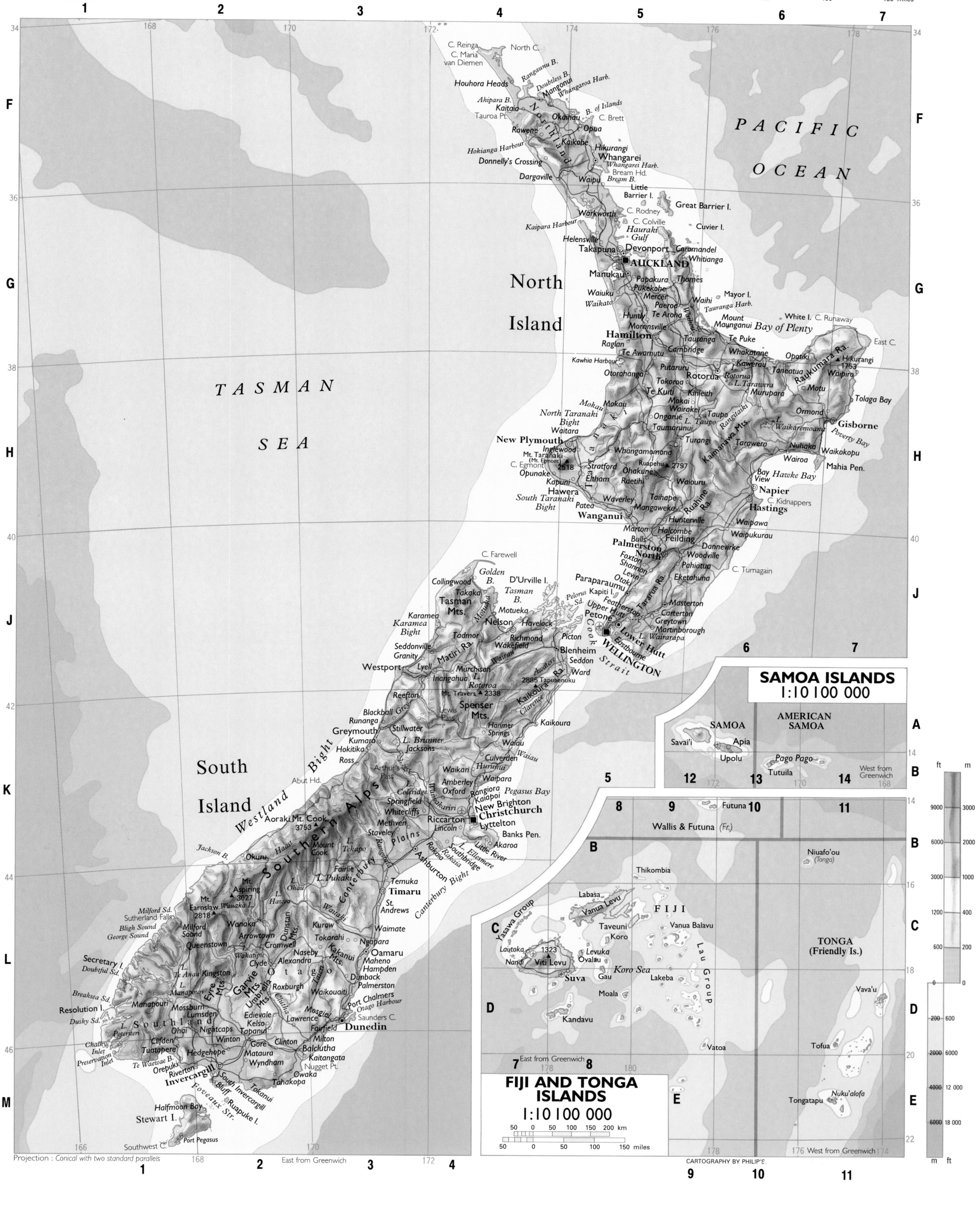
50 0 50 100 150 200 km
50 0 50 100 150 miles
PACIFIC OCEAN
TASMAN SEA
North Island
South Island
C. Reinga
C. Maria van Diemen
North C.
Rangaunu B.
Houhora Heads
Doubtless B.
Mangonui
Whangaroa Harb.
Ahipara B.
Kaitaia
Tauroa Pt.
B. of Islands
Okaihau
C. Brett
Northland
Rawene
Opua
Kaikohe
Hokianga Harbour
Hikurangi
Whangarei
Whangarei Harb.
Donnelly's Crossing
Bream Hd.
Bream B.
Dargaville
Waipu
Little Barrier I.
Great Barrier I.
Warkworth
C. Rodney
C. Colville
Kaipara Harbour
Hauraki Gulf
Cuvier I.
Helensville
Takapuna
Devonport
Coromandel
AUCKLAND
Whitianga
Manukau
Papakura
Thames
Pukekohe
Waiuku
Mercer
Waikato
Mayor I.
Paeroa
Waihi
Tauranga Harb.
Huntly
Te Aroha
White I.
C. Runaway
Morrinsville
Mount Maunganui
Bay of Plenty
Hamilton
Tauranga
Te Puke
East C.
Raglan
Cambridge
Whakatane
Opotiki
Te Awamutu
Kawerau
Raukumara Ra.
Kawhia Harbour
Putaruru
Rotorua
Hikurangi 1753
Otorohanga
L. Rotorua
Te Kaha
Waipiro
Tokoroa
L. Tarawera
Te Kuiti
Kinleith
Murupara
Motu
Mokau
Mokai
Tolaga Bay
Wairakei
North Taranaki Bight
Ongarue
Taupo
Ormond
Waitara
Taumarunui
L. Taupo
Gisborne
New Plymouth
L. Waikaremoana
Inglewood
Whangamomona
Turangi
Tarawera
Poverty Bay
Mt. Taranaki (Mt. Egmont) 2518
Nuhaka
Waikokopu
C. Egmont
Stratford
Ruapehu 2797
Wairoa
Mahia Pen.
Opunake
Ohakune
Eltham
Raetihi
Waiouru
Bay View
Hawke Bay
Kapuni
Napier
Hawera
Taihape
C. Kidnappers
South Taranaki Bight
Patea
Waverley
Mangaweka
Hastings
Wanganui
Hunterville
Waipawa
Marton
Halcombe
Waipukurau
Bulls
Feilding
Palmerston North
Dannevirke
C. Farewell
Foxton
Woodville
Shannon
Pahiatua
Golden B.
D'Urville I.
Levin
C. Turnagain
Collingwood
Takaka
Tasman B.
Otaki
Eketahuna
Paraparaumu
Kapiti I.
Tasman Mts.
Motueka
Pelorus Sd.
Masterton
Karamea
Nelson
Havelock
Upper Hutt
Featherston
Carterton
Karamea Bight
Petone
Greytown
Lower Hutt
Martinborough
Tadmor
Richmond
Picton
Eastbourne
WELLINGTON
L. Wairarapa
Seddonville
Wakefield
Blenheim
Cook Strait
Granity
Seddon
Westport
Lyell
Matiri Ra.
Ward
Murchison
Inangahua
L. Rotoroa
2885 Tapuaenuku
Mt. Travers 2338
Reefton
Spenser Mts.
Kaikoura Ra.
Clarence
Blackball
Lewis Pass
Runanga
Hanmer Springs
Kaikoura
Greymouth
Stillwater
Kumara
L. Brunner
Waiau
Hokitika
Jacksons
Ross
Culverden
Arthur's Pass
Hurunui
Waikari
Westland Bight
Abut Hd.
Waipara
Amberley
Oxford
Rangiora
Kaiapoi
Pegasus Bay
L. Coleridge
Springfield
New Brighton
Whitecliffs
Christchurch
Riccarton
Aoraki Mt. Cook 3753
Methven
Lyttelton
Lincoln
Banks Pen.
Staveley
Plains
Southern Alps
Mount Cook
L. Tekapo
Rakaia
L. Ellesmere
Akaroa
Little River
Jackson B.
Okuru
Haast
Southbridge
Ashburton
Canterbury Bight
Mt. Aspiring 3027
L. Pukaki
Temuka
L. Ohau
Timaru
Mt. Earnslaw 2818
Wanaka L.
L. Hawea
Canterbury
St. Andrews
Milford Sd.
Sutherland Falls
Bligh Sound
Milford Sound
Wanaka
Dunstan Mts.
Waimate
George Sound
Arrowtown
Kurow
Queenstown
Cromwell
Tokarahi
Ngapara
L. Wakatipu
Naseby
Oamaru
Secretary I.
Doubtful Sd.
Clyde
Alexandra
Kakanui Mts.
Maheno
Te Anau
Kingston
Otago
Hampden
L. Manapouri
Eyre Mts.
Garvie Mts.
Umbrella Mts.
Dunback
Palmerston
Breaksea Sd.
Roxburgh
Waikouaiti
Manapouri
Resolution I.
Mossburn
Lumsden
Port Chalmers
Otago Harbour
Dusky Sd.
Southland
Edievale
Kelso
Lawrence
Mosgiel
Saunders C.
Nightcaps
Tapanui
Dunedin
L. Poteriteri
Ohai
Winton
Fairfield
Clifden
Milton
Tuatapere
Gore
Clinton
Chalky Inlet
Hedgehope
Balclutha
Preservation Inlet
Te Waewae B.
Mataura
Kaitangata
Orepuki
Wyndham
Nugget Pt.
Riverton
Owaka
Invercargill
Tahakopa
South Invercargill
Foveaux Str.
Tokanui
Bluff
Ruapuke I.
Halfmoon Bay
Stewart I.
Port Pegasus
Southwest C.
Projection : Conical with two standard parallels
East from Greenwich
SAMOA ISLANDS
1:10 100 000
SAMOA
AMERICAN SAMOA
Savai'i
Apia
Upolu
Pago Pago
Tutuila
West from Greenwich
Futuna
Wallis & Futuna (Fr.)
Niuafo'ou (Tonga)
Thikombia
Labasa
Vanua Levu
FIJI
Yasawa Group
Taveuni
Vanua Balavu
Koro
Lau Group
TONGA (Friendly Is.)
Lautoka
1323
Viti Levu
Levuka
Ovalau
Nandi
Koro Sea
Suva
Gau
Lakeba
Moala
Vava'u
Kandavu
Vatoa
Tofua
East from Greenwich
FIJI AND TONGA ISLANDS
1:10 100 000
50 0 50 100 150 200 km
50 0 50 100 150 miles
Nuku'alofa
Tongatapu
176 West from Greenwich
CARTOGRAPHY BY PHILIP'S
ft m
9000 3000
6000 2000
3000 1000
1200 400
600 200
0 0
200 600
2000 6000
4000 12 000
6000 18 000
m ft

50 0 50 100 150 200 250 300 km
50 0 50 100 150 200 miles

INDONESIA

Bali
Lombok
Sumbawa
Sumba
Waingapu
Waikabubak
Melolo
Baing
Dana
Raijua
Sawu
Roti
Semau
Kupang
Timor

TIMOR SEA

Sennapatam Reef
Scott Reef
Hibernia Reef
Ashmore Reef
Cartier I.
Browse I.
Lynher Reef
Mermaid Reef
Clerke Reef
Rowley Shoals
Imperieuse Reef

INDIAN OCEAN

C. Croker
C. Don
McCluer Gulf
Grant I.
Croker I.
Cobourg Pen.
Murganella
P. Essington
C. Gambier I.
Endyalgout I.
Van Diemen Gulf
C. Hotham
Nguiu
Melville I.
Bathurst I.
Milikapiti
Pularumpi
Snake Bay
C. Fourcroy
Pt. Fawcett
C. Gambier
Gordan B.
Peron Is.
Anson B.
Port Darwin
Darwin
Mandorah
Noonamah
Batchelor
Adelaide River
Hayes Creek
Pine Creek
Oenpelli
Jabiru
480
Cooinda
KAKADU NAT. PARK
Rum Jungle
Katherine Gorge
Katherine
Tindal
Maranboy
Beswick
Birdum Creek
Larrimah
Daly River
Daly
Wadeye
C. Scott
Mt. Greenwood 152
C. Hay
Quoin I.
Wingate Mts.
Fitzmaurice
Port Keats
Queen Chan.
Cambridge Gulf
Joseph Bonaparte Gulf
Victoria River
Wyndham
Kununurra
Victoria
Newcastle Ra.
Stokes Ra.
Timber Creek
West Baines
Kalkaringi
Hooker Creek
Top Springs
Victoria
Daguragu
Nicholson

NORTHERN TERRITORY

Tanami Desert
Tanami
Lander
Horden Hills
Lewis Ra.
Mt. Singleton 808
Yuendumu
Reynolds Ra.
Stuart Bluff Ra.
Mt. Liebig 1524
Papunya
Mt. Zeil 1510
MacDonnell Ranges
Hermannsburg
James Ranges
George Gill Ra.
Haast Bluff
L. Neale
Kintore
Mt. Leisler 901
L. Macdonald
Banython Ra.
L. Bennett
L. White
L. Wills
Stansmore Ra.
Lake Mackay
L. Hazlett
Angas Hills
Gregory Lake
Billiluna
Balgo
Halls Creek
McClintock Ra.
Denison Plains
Flora Valley
Nicholson
Gordon Downs
Sturt Creek
Christmas Cr.
Gregory Ra.
Stretch Ra.
Percival Lakes
L. Tobin
L. Auld
L. Dora
Isabella Ra.
Telfer Mineorn
Gibson Desert
Tropic of Capricorn
L. Disappointment
L. Blanche
L. George
Broadhurst Ra.
McKay Ra.
Paterson Ra.
Throssell Ra.
Poisonbush Ra.
Gregory Ra.
Robertson Ra.
Rudall
Nullagine
Jigalong
Balfour Downs
L. Waukarlycarly
Mundiwindi

Kimberley
Carr Boyd Ra.
L. Argyle
Turkey Creek
Albert Edward Ra.
Halls Creek
Durack Ra.
Black Ra.
Chamberlain Ra.
Cockburn Ra.
Mueller Ra.
Mt. Wells 970
Gibb River
King Edward R.
Mt. Hann 776
Hann Ra.
Mt. Ord 937
Iddell
Hann
Durack River
Fitzroy Crossing
Margaret
St. George Ra.
King Leopold Ranges
Princess May Ras.
Harding Ra.
Synnot Ra.
Oombulgurri
Mt. Barnett
Kalumburu

Bonaparte Archipelago
Joseph Bonaparte Gulf
Napier Broome B.
Sir Graham Moore Is.
Eclipse Is.
Institut B.
Long Reef
Admiralty Gulf
Montague Sd.
C. Voltaire
C. Bougainville
Bigge I.
York Sd.
Coronation Is.
Brunswick B.
Camden Sd.
Prince Frederick Hr.
Augustus I.
St. George Basin
Prince Regent R.
Kuri Bay
Walcott Inlet
Collier B.
Raft Pt.
Wood Eagle Is.
King
King Sound
Kimbolton
Yampi Sd.
C. Leveque
Pender B.
Lombadina
Buccaneer Archipelago
Beagle Bay
Carnot B.
C. Boileau
Broome
Roebuck B.
C. Latouche Treville
Lagrange B.
Lagrange
Eighty Mile Beach
Sandfire Roadhouse
Mowanjum
Derby
Camballin
Looma
Fitzroy
Greeull.
Liveringa
Lesser I.
C. Rulhieres
Anjo Pen.
Cape Londonderry
Dampier Pen.
Adele I.
Lacepede Is.

Poissonnier Pt.
Port Hedland
Goldsworthy
Shay Gap
De Grey
Marble Bar
Shaw
Pippingarra
Whim Creek
Yule
Roebourne
Point Samson
Wickham
Dampier
Karratha
Nickol B.
C. Preston
Enderby I.
Legendre I.
C. Thouin
Delambre I.
Dampier Archipelago
Monte Bello Is.
Barrow I.
Pasco I.
Onslow
Ashburton
North West C.
Exmouth
Exmouth Gulf
Learmonth
C. Cuvier
Yannarie
Pannawonica
Fortescue
Nanutarra Roadhouse
Barradale Roadhouse
Paraburdoo
Tom Price
Hamersley Range
Mt. Bruce 1235
Mt. Meharry 1251
Wittenoom
Mt. Newman
Chichester Ra.
Ophthalmia Ra. 1053
Newman
Nullagine
Roy

Great Sandy Desert

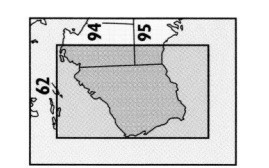

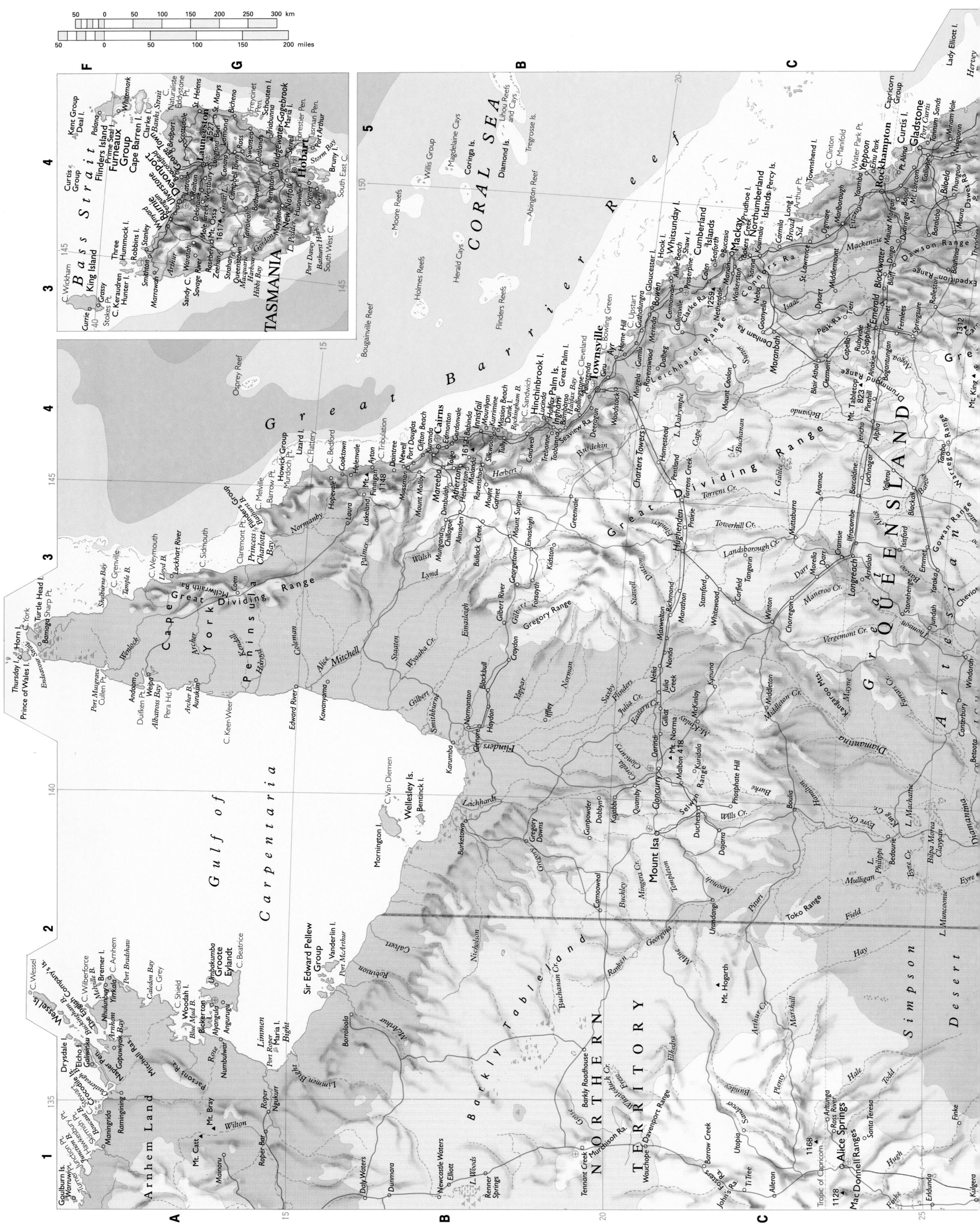

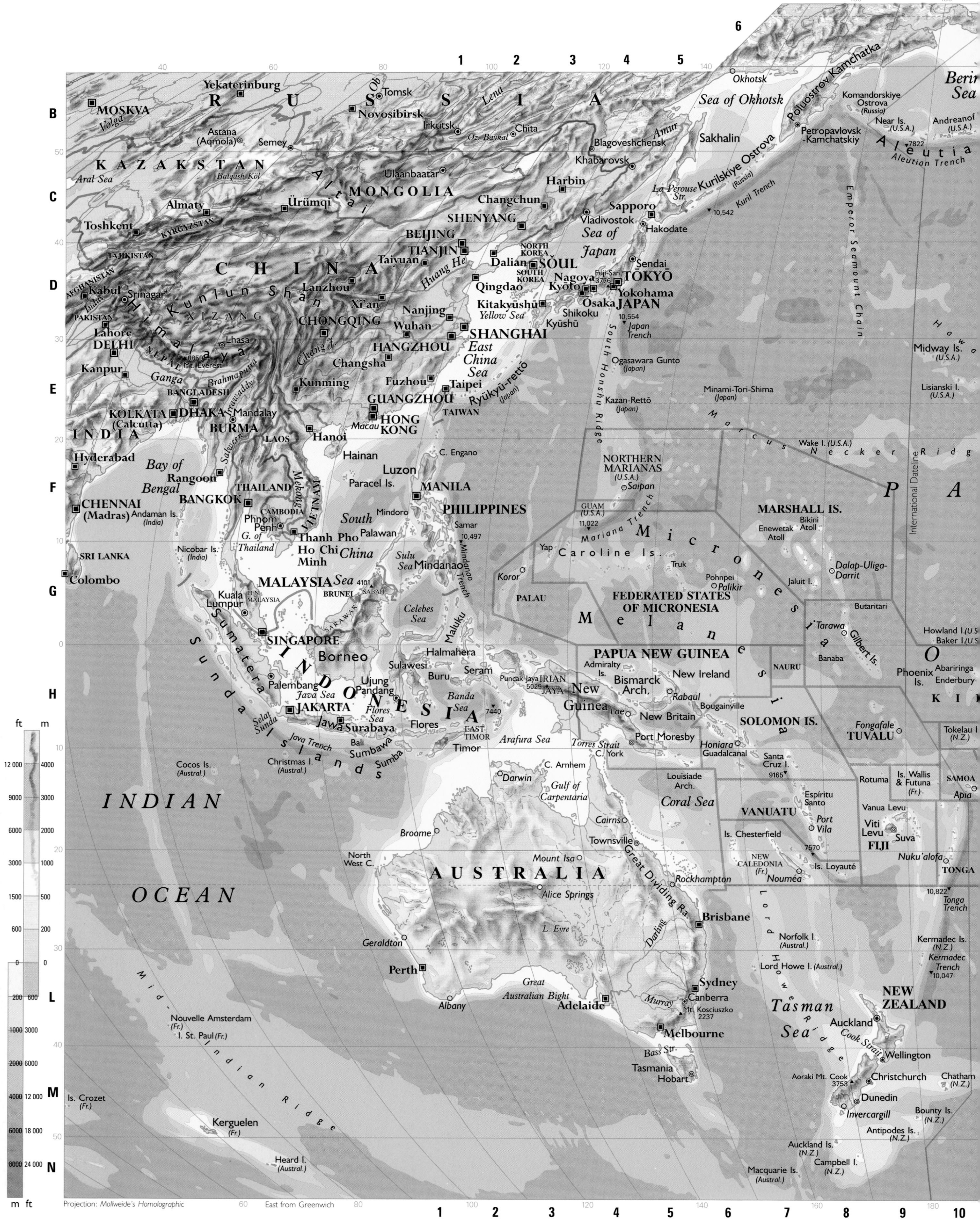

7 8 9 10
6
1 2 3 4 5

Bering Sea

MOSKVA Yekaterinburg
Volga Tomsk
R U S S I A
Novosibirsk *Lena* Sea of Okhotsk
Irkutsk Chita Okhotsk Komandorskiye Ostrova (Russia)
Oz. Baykal Blagoveshchensk *Amur* Petropavlovsk-Kamchatskiy Near Is. (U.S.A.) Andreanof (U.S.A.)
Astana (Aqmola) Semey Khabarovsk Sakhalin 7822
K A Z A K S T A N Ulaanbaatar La Perouse Kurilskiye Ostrova (Russia) *Aleutian Trench*
Aral Sea *Balqash Kol* M O N G O L I A Str. Kuril Trench *Aleutia*
Almaty Changchun Sapporo 10,542
Toshkent Ürümqi *Altai* SHENYANG Vladivostok Hakodate *Emperor Seamount Chain*
KYRGYZSTAN Harbin
TAJIKISTAN BEIJING *Sea of Japan*
Kunlun Shan Taiyuan NORTH KOREA Sendai
AFGHANISTAN Kabul Srinagar C H I N A Dalian SÖUL Fuji-San Midway Is. (U.S.A.)
Indus Lanzhou Huang He SOUTH KOREA Nagoya Kyoto TOKYO
PAKISTAN *Himalaya* XIZANG Xi'an Qingdao Osaka Yokohama
Lahore Nanjing *Yellow Sea* Shikoku JAPAN 10,554
DELHI NEPAL Lhasa Wuhan Kyūshū *Japan Trench*
Mt. Everest 8850 CHONGQING SHANGHAI Lisianski I. (U.S.A.)
Kanpur *Ganga* *Brahmaputra* *Chang J.* HANGZHOU *East China Sea* Ogasawara Gunto (Japan)
Changsha *South Honshu Ridge* Minami-Tori-Shima (Japan)
Irrawaddy Kunming Fuzhou Kazan-Rettō (Japan)
KOLKATA DHAKA Mandalay GUANGZHOU Taipei *Marcus* Wake I. (U.S.A.) *Necker Ridge*
(Calcutta) HONG TAIWAN *Ryūkyū-rettō* NORTHERN MARIANAS
I N D I A BURMA KONG Macau (Japan) (U.S.A.) P A
Salween LAOS Hanoi Saipan MARSHALL IS.
Hyderabad Hainan Luzon GUAM (U.S.A.) Bikini
Bay of Bengal Rangoon THAILAND Paracel Is. MANILA 11,022 Enewetak Atoll Atoll
CHENNAI BANGKOK Mindoro PHILIPPINES Yap *Mariana Trench* *Micronesia*
(Madras) Andaman Is. CAMBODIA Samar *Caroline Is.*
(India) Phnom Palawan 10,497 Truk Pohnpei Dalap-Uliga-Darrit
SRI LANKA Penh *South China Sea* Koror Palikir Jaluit I.
Nicobar Is. Thanh Pho *Sulu Sea* Mindanao PALAU FEDERATED STATES *Melan* Tarawa Butaritari
(India) *G. of Thailand* Ho Chi Minh 4101 *Mindanao Trench* OF MICRONESIA Gilbert Is. Banaba Howland I. (U.S.
Colombo MALAYSIA Sea NAURU Baker I. (U.S.
Kuala PEN. BRUNEI SABAH *Celebes Sea* PAPUA NEW GUINEA *esia* Phoenix Abariringa O
Lumpur MALAYSIA Halmahera Admiralty Is. New Ireland Is. Enderbury
SINGAPORE SARAWAK Sulawesi Buru Seram Puncak Jaya IRIAN New Bismarck Rabaul *Melanesia* K I
Sunda Borneo 5029 JAYA Guinea Arch. NAURU
Sumatera Palembang Ujung *Banda Sea* New Britain Fongafale
INDONESIA Pandang 7440 East Lae Bougainville SOLOMON IS. TUVALU Tokelau
Java Sea *Flores* Flores Timor *Arafura Sea* Port Moresby Honiara (N.Z.)
JAKARTA Surabaya *Sumbawa* TIMOR *Torres Strait* Guadalcanal Santa Rotuma Is. Wallis SAMOA
Jawa Bali *Sumba* C. York Cruz I. & Futuna Apia
Selat Sunda *Java Trench* *Sunda Islands* C. Arnhem 9165 (Fr.)
Christmas I. Darwin *Gulf of* VANUATU Espiritu Vanua Levu
(Austral.) *Carpentaria* Santo Viti Suva
Cocos Is. *Coral Sea* Port Levu FIJI
(Austral.) North Cairns Is. Chesterfield Vila *Nuku'alofa*
I N D I A N West C. Townsville NEW 7570 TONGA
Broome Mount Isa *Great Dividing Ra.* CALEDONIA Norfolk I. 10,822
A U S T R A L I A Rockhampton (Fr.) Nouméa (Austral.) *Tonga Trench*
Alice Springs Brisbane Is. Loyauté Kermadec Is.
O C E A N *Darling* (N.Z.)
Geraldton *L. Eyre* Lord Howe I. (Austral.) *Kermadec Trench* 10,047
Perth *Great Australian Bight* *Murray* Sydney
Albany Adelaide Canberra Mt. Kosciuszko 2237 NEW ZEALAND
Nouvelle Amsterdam Melbourne *Tasman Sea*
(Fr.) *Bass Str.* Auckland *Cook Strait*
I. St. Paul (Fr.) Tasmania Wellington
Hobart Aoraki Mt. Cook 3753 Christchurch Chatham (N.Z.)
Is. Crozet Dunedin Bounty Is. (N.Z.)
(Fr.) Invercargill Antipodes Is. (N.Z.)
Kerguelen Macquarie I. Auckland Is.
(Fr.) (Austral.) (N.Z.) Campbell I. (N.Z.)
Heard I.
(Austral.)

Mid-Indian Ridge

ft m
12 000 4000
9000 3000
6000 2000
3000 1000
1500 500
600 200
0 0
200 600
1000 3000
2000 6000
4000 12 000
6000 18 000
8000 24 000
m ft

Projection: Mollweide's Homolographic East from Greenwich
60 80 100 120 140 160 180
1 2 3 4 5 6 7 8 9 10

B
C
D
E
F
G
H
L
M
N

Arctic Circle

ALASKA
(U.S.A.)
Anchorage

16 120 17 100 18 19 80 20

60 40 20

B

Bristol Bay

5959

Gulf of Alaska

. (U.S.A.)

Juneau

Prince of Wales I.
(U.S.A.) Prince Rupert
Queen Charlotte Is.
(Canada)

Edmonton

C A N A D A

L. Winnipeg

St. Lawrence

Newfoundland

N O R T H

Vancouver
Vancouver I.
Victoria
Seattle
Portland

Calgary
Regina
Winnipeg

L. Superior

Québec
Montréal
Ottawa
Toronto

St. John's

50

C

Snake

Boise

Missouri

Minneapolis

L. Michigan
L. Huron
L. Ontario

Detroit
CHICAGO
Pittsburgh
L. Erie
Buffalo
Boston

Salt Lake
City
Denver
Kansas City

St. Louis
Cincinnati

NEW YORK CITY
PHILADELPHIA
Baltimore
Washington D.C.

A T L A N T I C

40

C. Mendocino

Sacramento
SAN FRANCISCO

4418

Colorado

UNITED STATES

Memphis

Appalachian Mts.

Atlanta

C. Hatteras

D

6741

LOS ANGELES
San Diego

Phoenix

Oklahoma City

Dallas

Houston
San Antonio

Mississippi

New
Orleans

Jacksonville

Bermuda
(U.K.)

Sargasso Sea

O C E A N

30

Guadalupe
(Mex.)

Ciudad
Juárez

Gulf of Mexico

Miami

BAHAMAS

West Indies

E

Tropic of Cancer

Monterrey

Florida Str.

C U B A

C. San Lucas

Gulf of California

La Habana

Canal de Yucatán

HAITI
DOMINICAN REP.

9200

Leeward
Is.

20

Honolulu
Oahu
4205
HAWAIIAN IS.
(U.S.A.)
Hawaii

Is. Revilla Gigedo
(Mex.)

Guadalajara

MEXICO
5700
Puebla

Mérida

7680

JAMAICA
Kingston

PUERTO
RICO
(U.S.A.)

BARBADOS

F

C I F I C

Acapulco

GUATEMALA

BELIZE

HONDURAS

Caribbean Sea

Windward Is.

10

I. Clipperton
(Fr.)

Guatemala
San Salvador
EL SALVADOR
Managua

NICARAGUA

Barranquilla
San José

Maracaibo

Caracas

North West Christmas Ridge

COSTA
RICA

Colón
Panamá
PANAMA

Orinoco

VENEZUELA

G

Palmyra Is.
(U.S.A.)

I. del Coco
(Costa Rica)

Medellín

Bogotá
Cali

COLOMBIA

Teraina
Tabuaeran
Kiritimati

I. de Malpelo
(Colombia)

Jarvis I.
(U.S.A.)

Equator

Galápagos
(Ecuador)

Quito
ECUADOR

0

E A N

Amazonas

H

B A T I

Malden I.
Starbuck I.

Guayaquil
C. Pariñas

Iquitos

BRAZIL

Pukapuka
Manihiki

Caroline I.

Trujillo

Tongareva

Vostok I.

Suwarrow Is.
Flint I.

6369

PERU

10

Is. de la
Société

Is. Marquises

Cook Is.
(N.Z.)

Papeete
Tahiti

FRENCH POLYNESIA

Is. Tuamotu

East Pacific Ridge

LIMA
Cuzco

L. Titicaca
6550

Nevada Ancohuma

J

Arequipa
6866

Australseamount Chain

Rarotonga

Is. Tubuai

Mururoa

Tuamotu Ridge

Tropic of Capricorn

Peru-
Arica

8050
Trench

La Paz
BOLIVIA

Iquique
Chile

20

Ducie I.

Sala-y-Gómez
(Chile)

San Felix
(Chile)

San Ambrosio
(Chile)

Antofagasta

PARAGUAY

Asunción

K

Pitcairn I.
(U.K.)

Rapa

I. de Pascua
(Chile)

Chile Rise

Arch. de
Juan Fernández
(Chile)

Valparaíso

Córdoba
Aconcagua
6960
Rosario

San Miguel
de Tucumán

Pôrto
Alegre

30

URUGUAY
Montevideo

L

Pacific Antarctic Ridge

SANTIAGO
Concepción

ARGENTINA

BUENOS
AIRES

Río de la Plata

40

SOUTH

M

ATLANTIC

6212 OCEAN

Falkland Is.
(U.K.)

Punta Arenas
Est. de Magallanes
Tierra del Fuego

South Georgia
(U.K.)

50

N

C. de Hornos

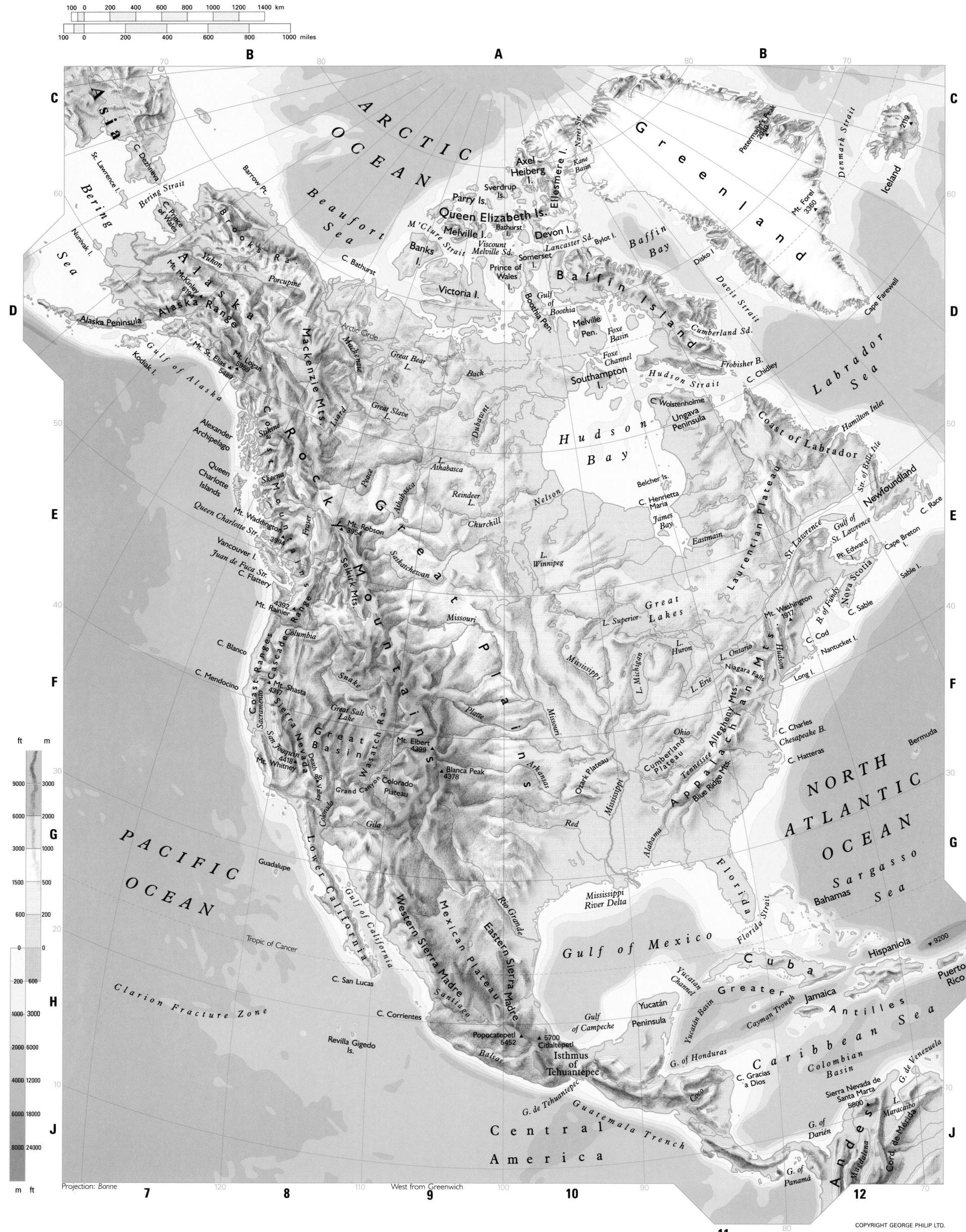

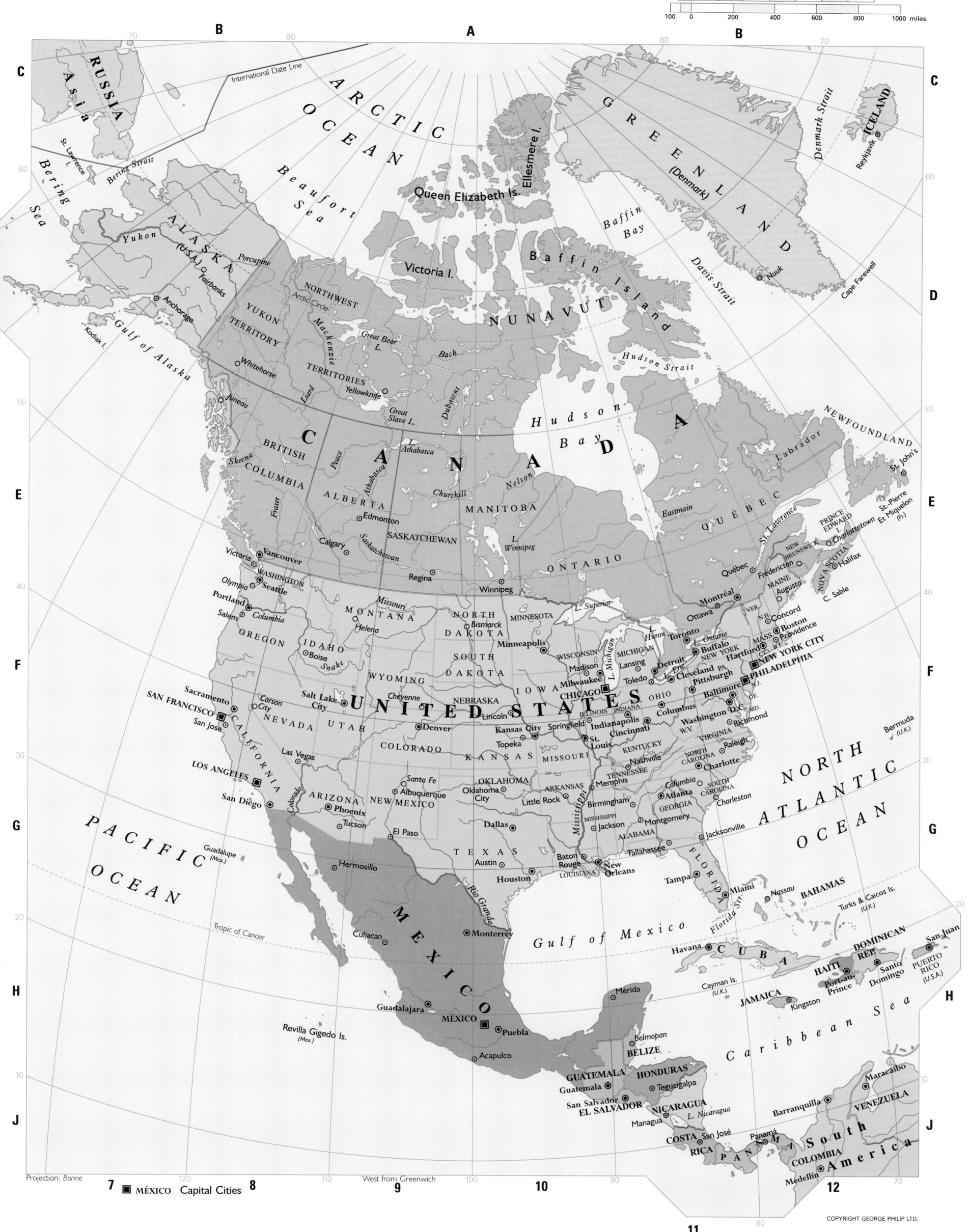

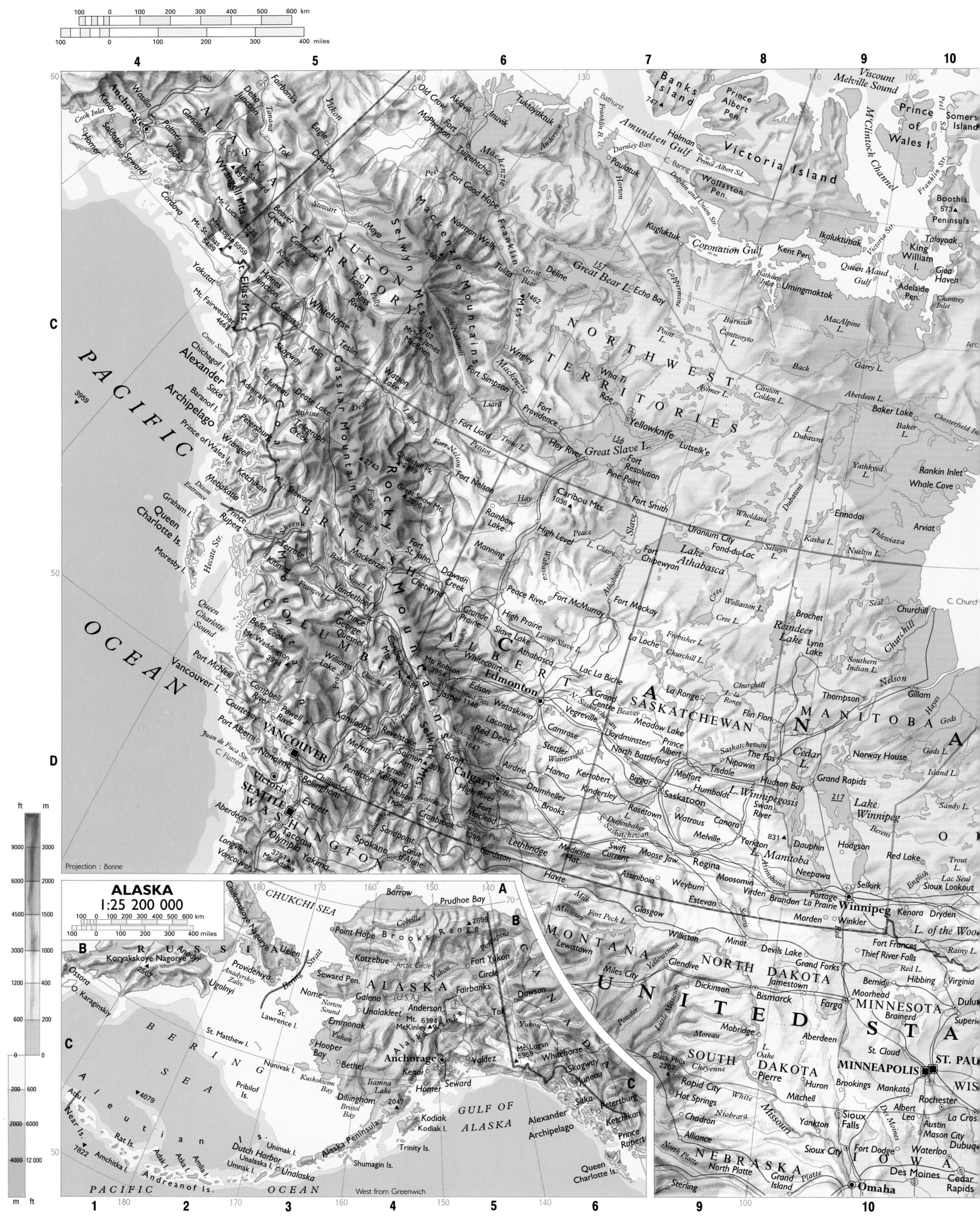

Projection : Bonne

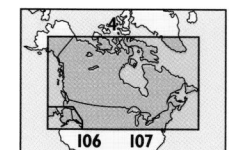

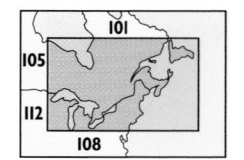

COPYRIGHT GEORGE PHILIP LTD.

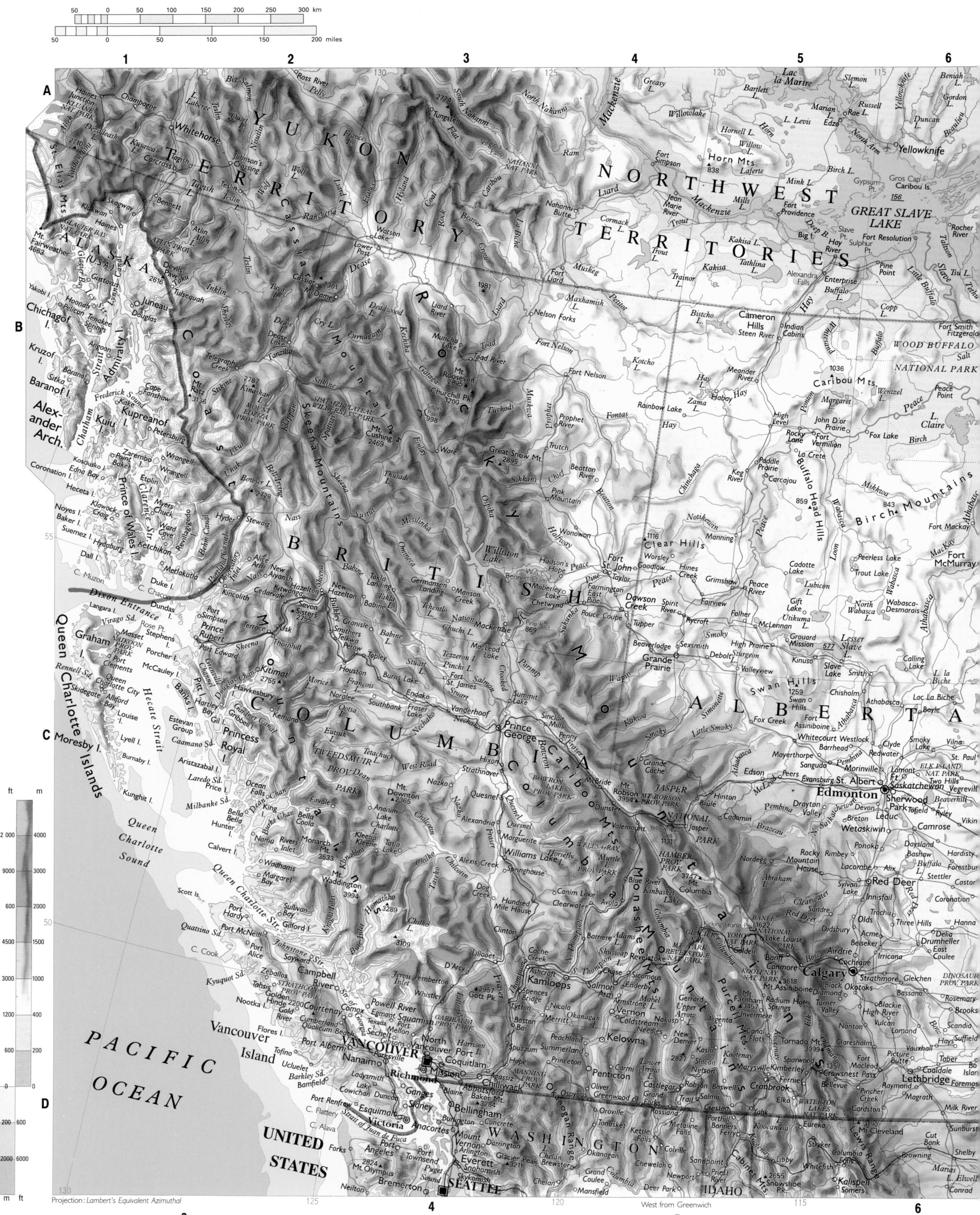

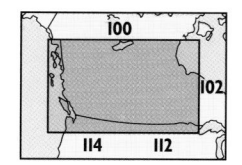

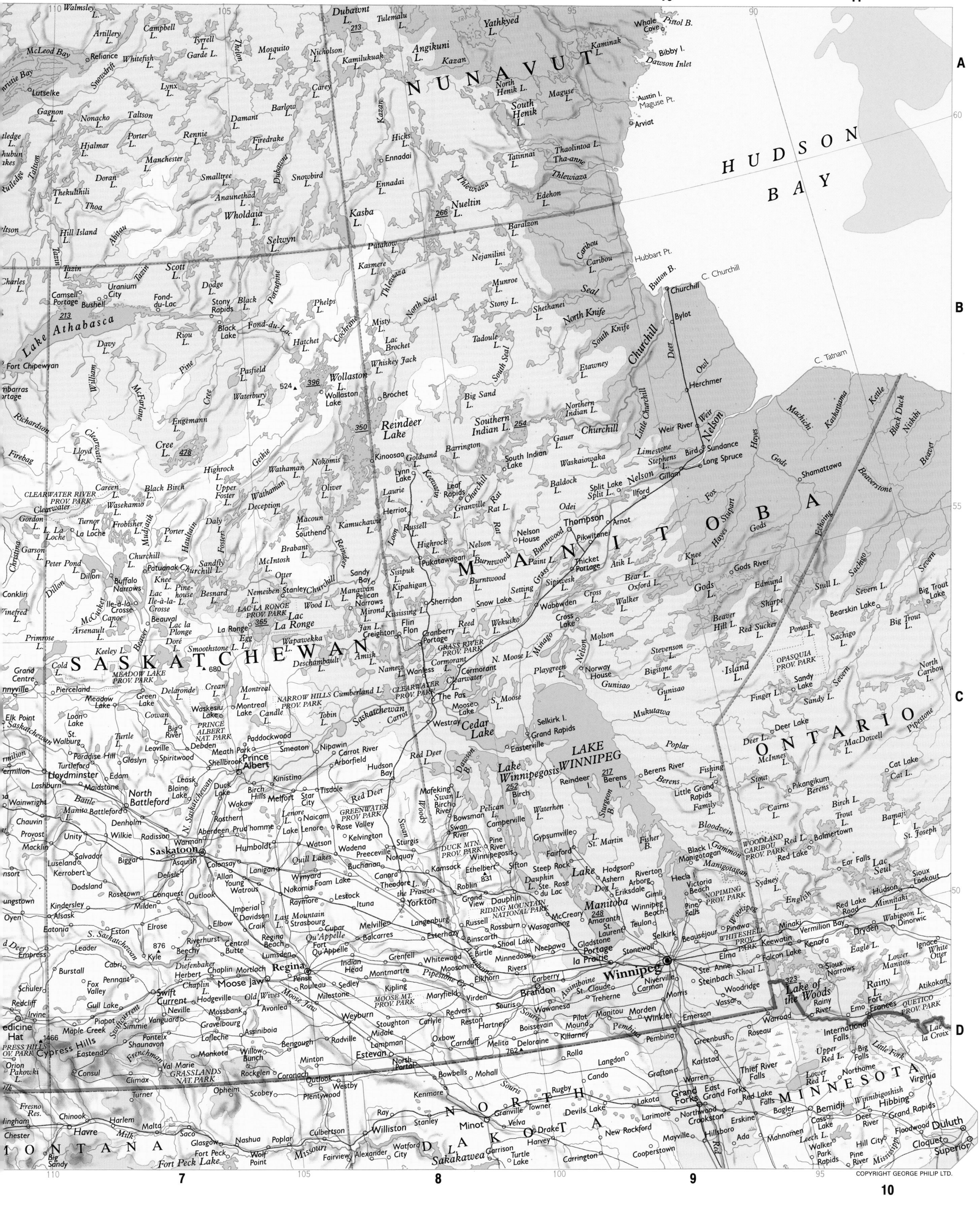

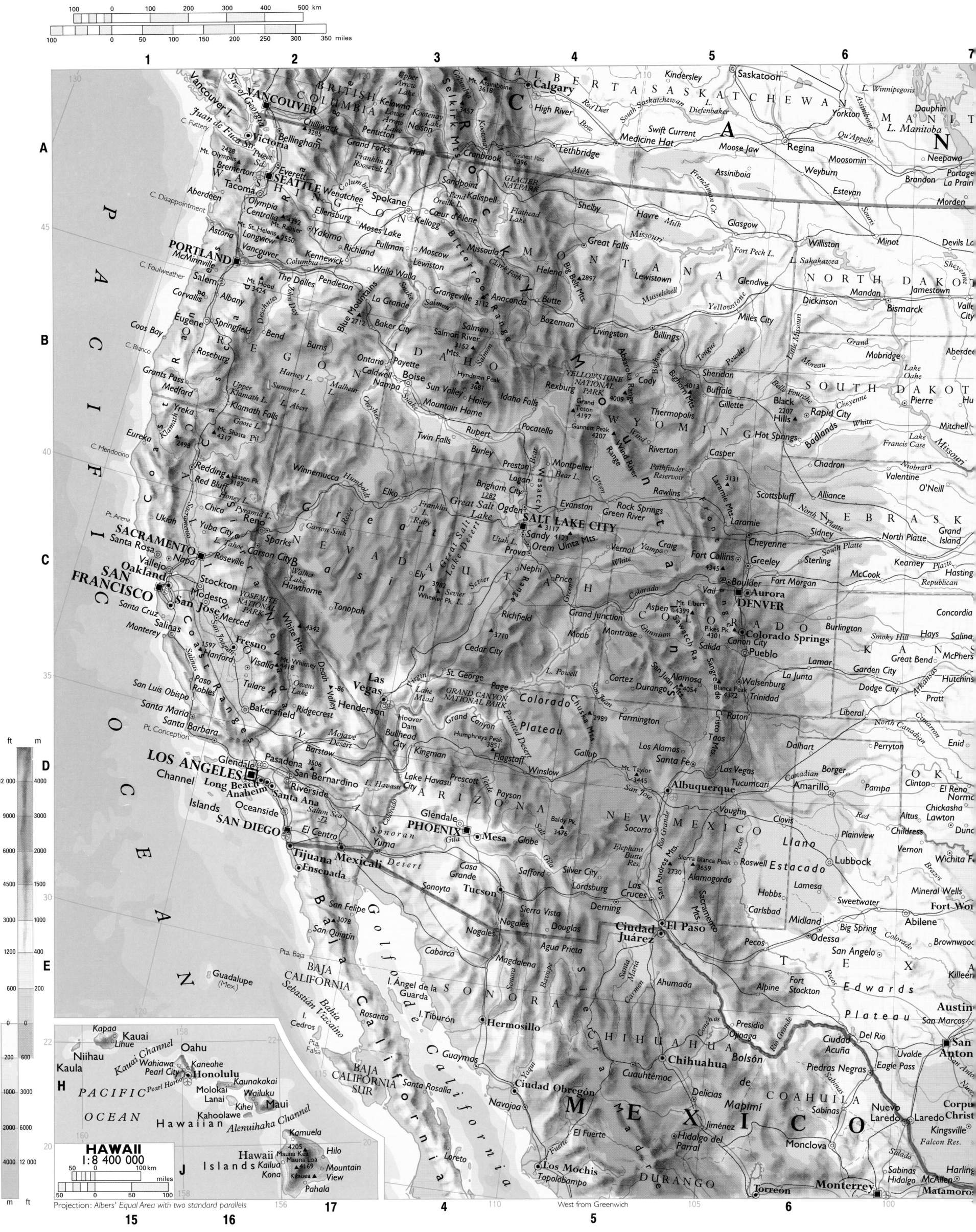

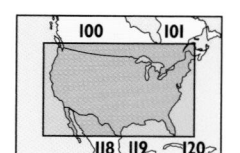

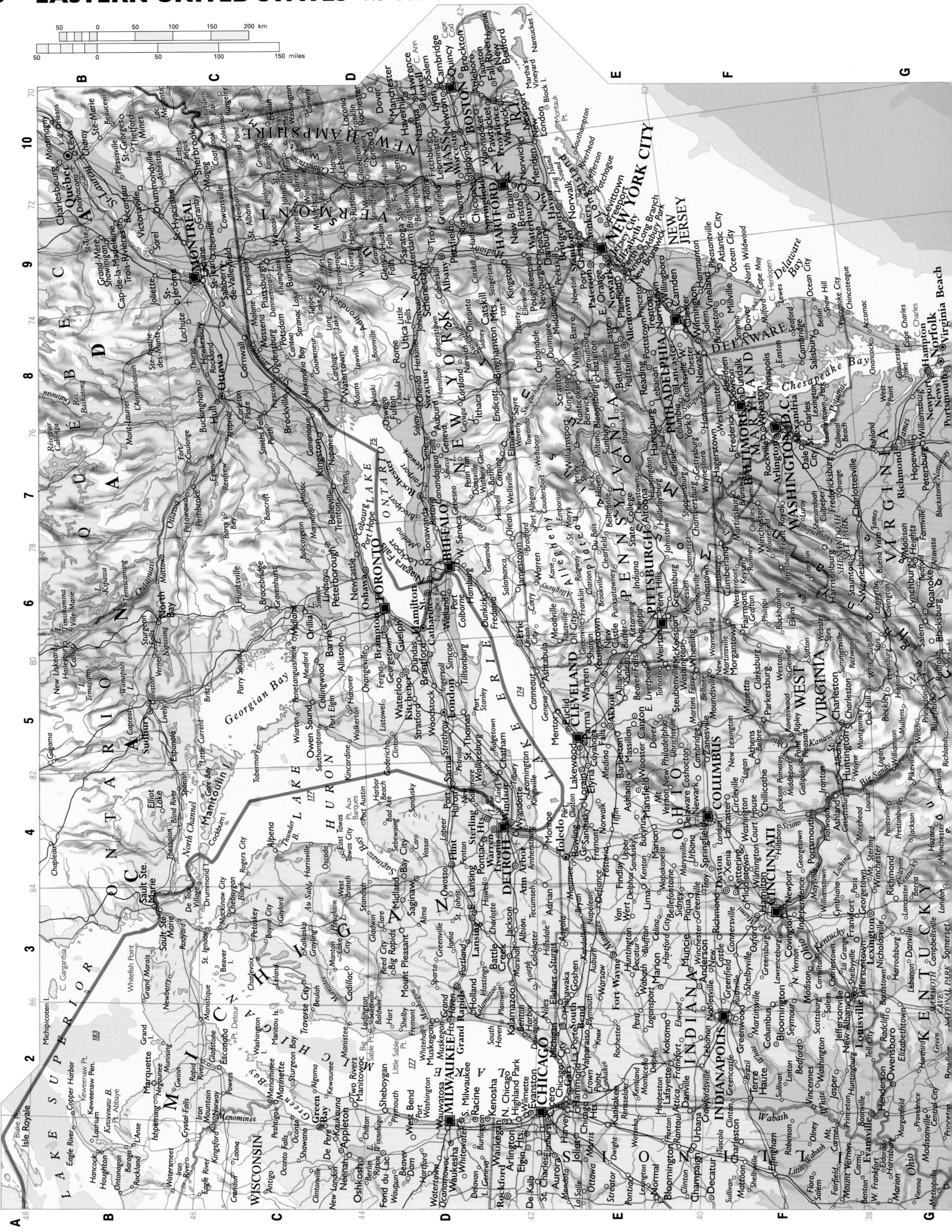

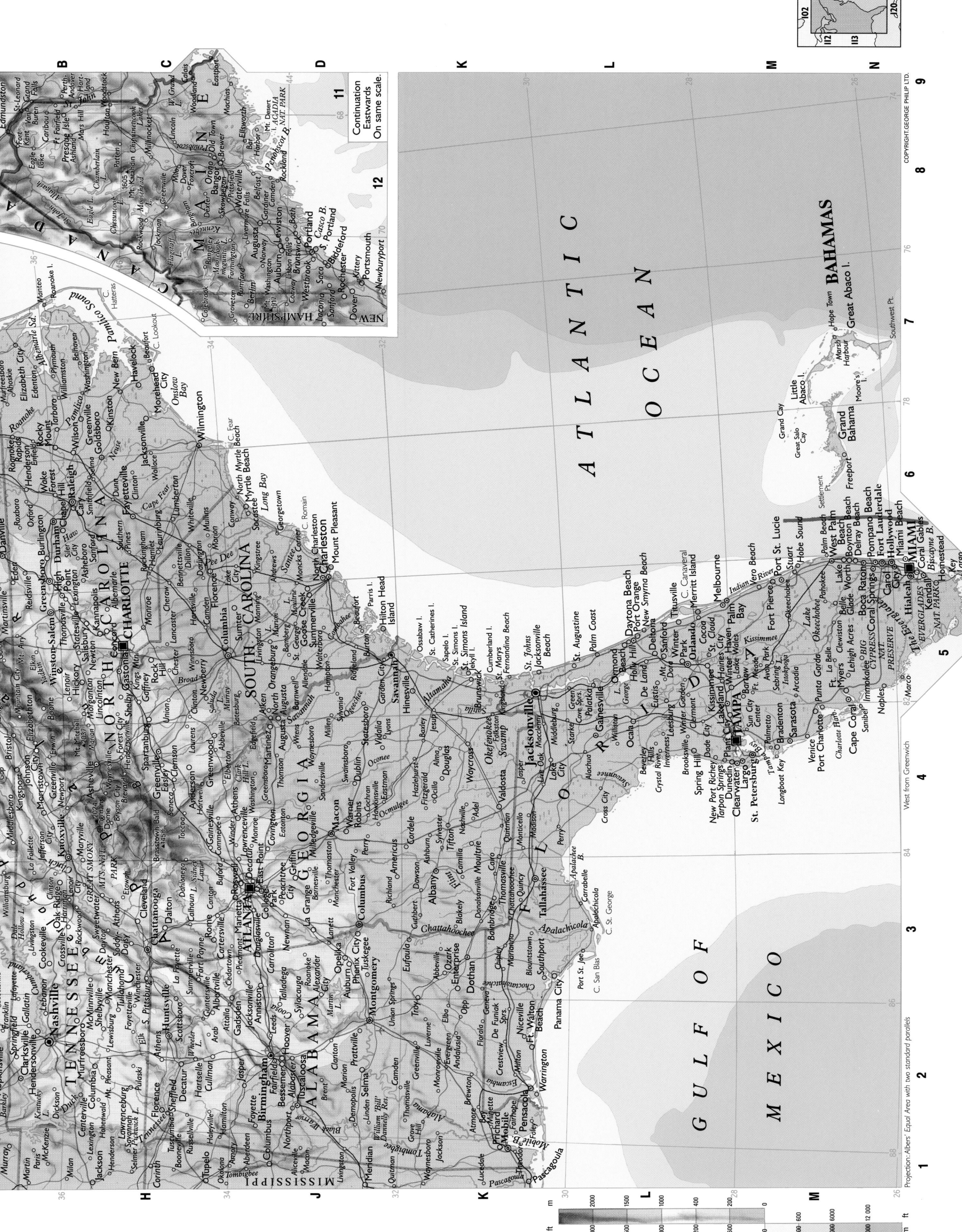

Continuation
Eastwards
On same scale.

ATLANTIC

OCEAN

BAHAMAS

GULF OF

MEXICO

Projection: Albers' Equal Area with two standard parallels

West from Greenwich

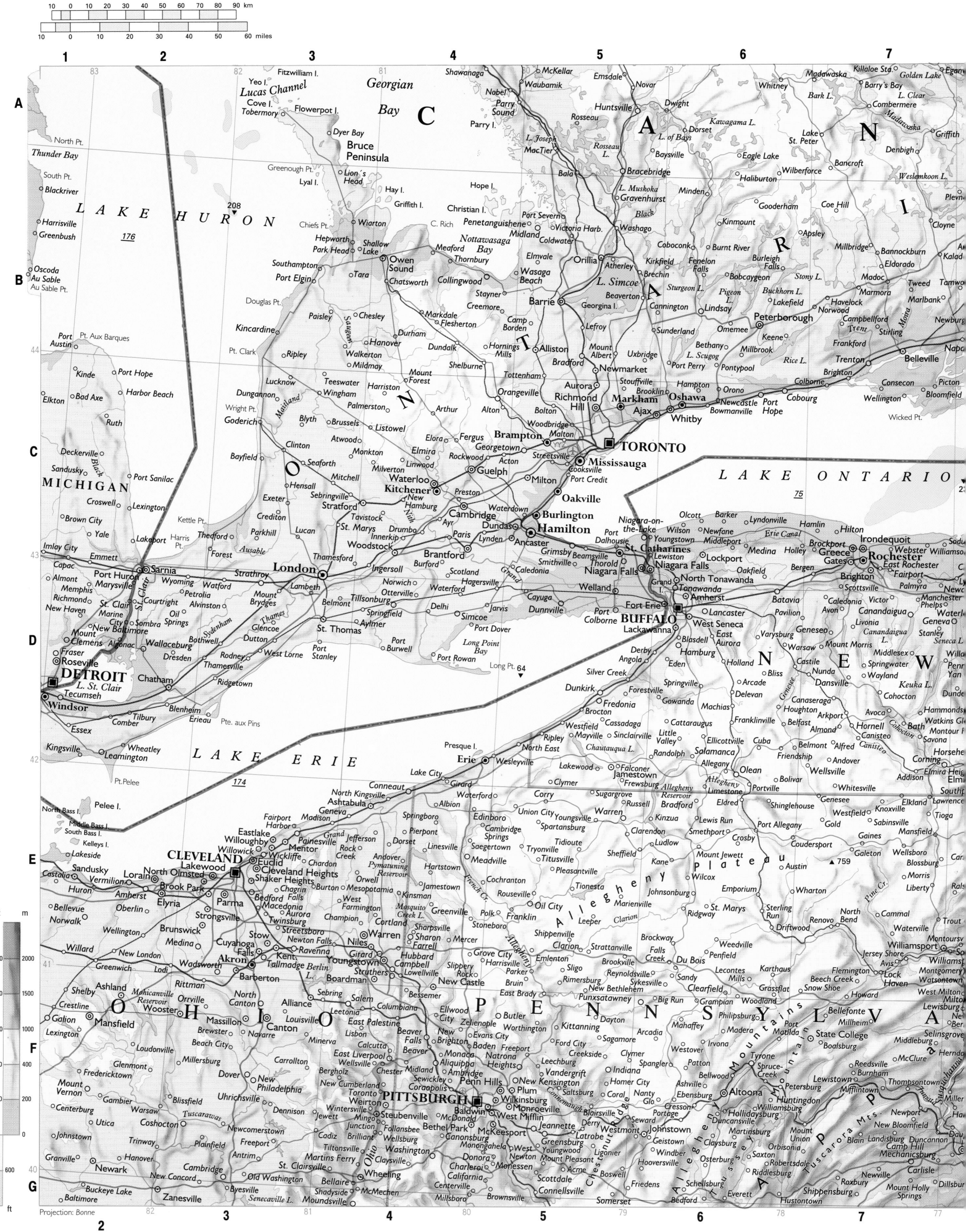

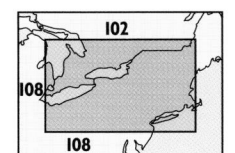

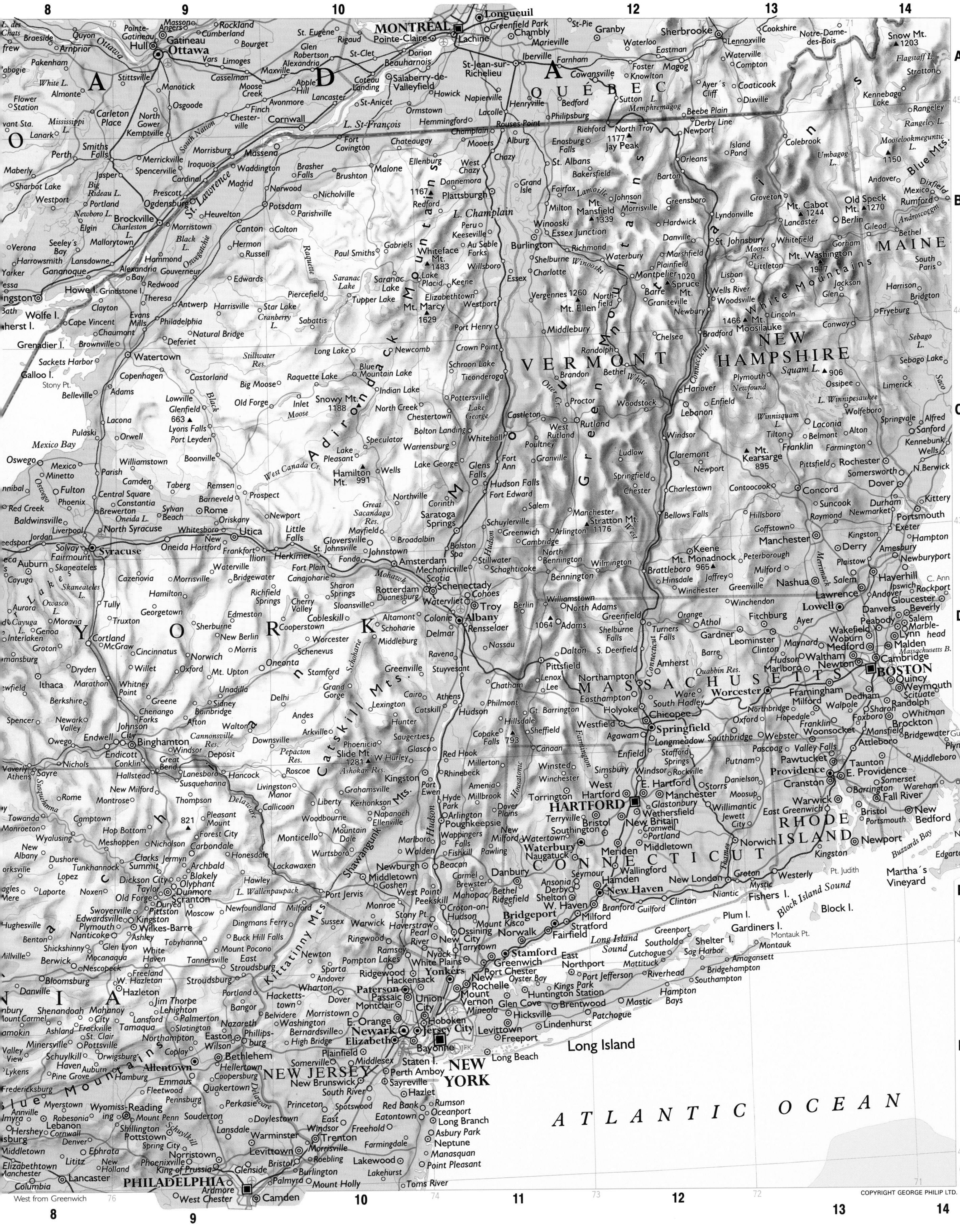

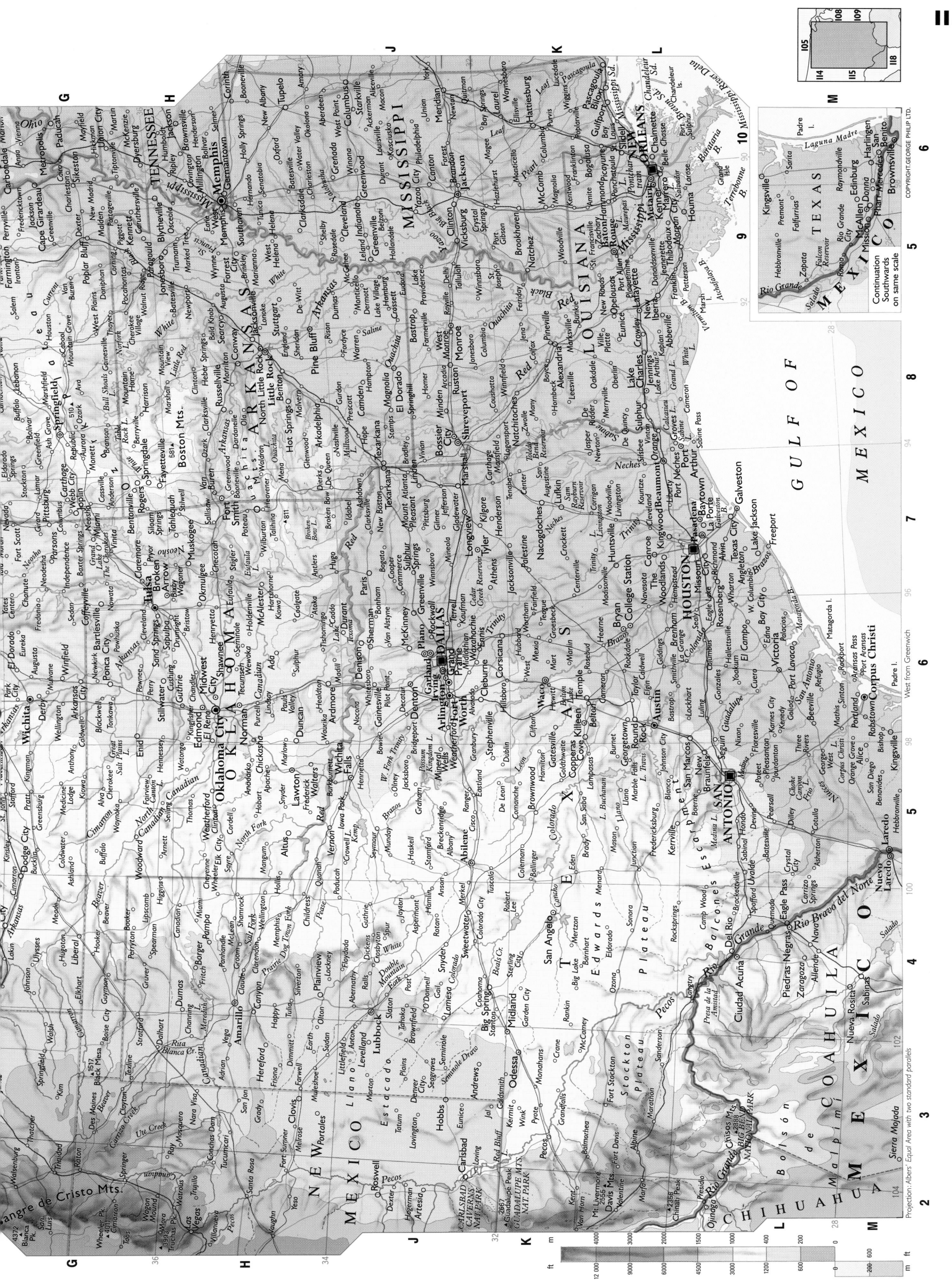

WESTERN UNITED STATES 1:5 000 000

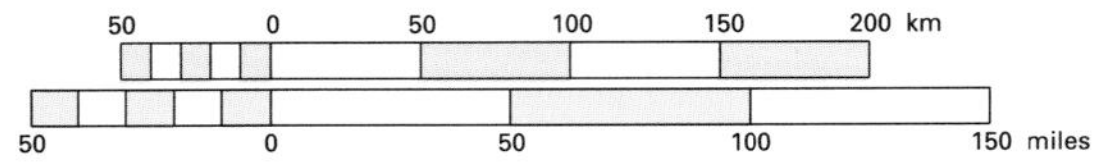

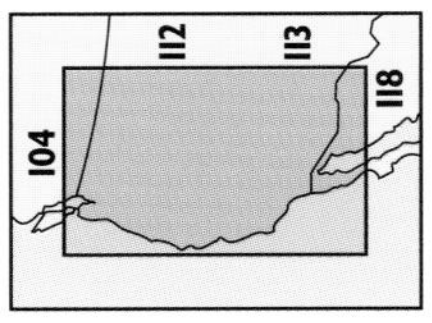

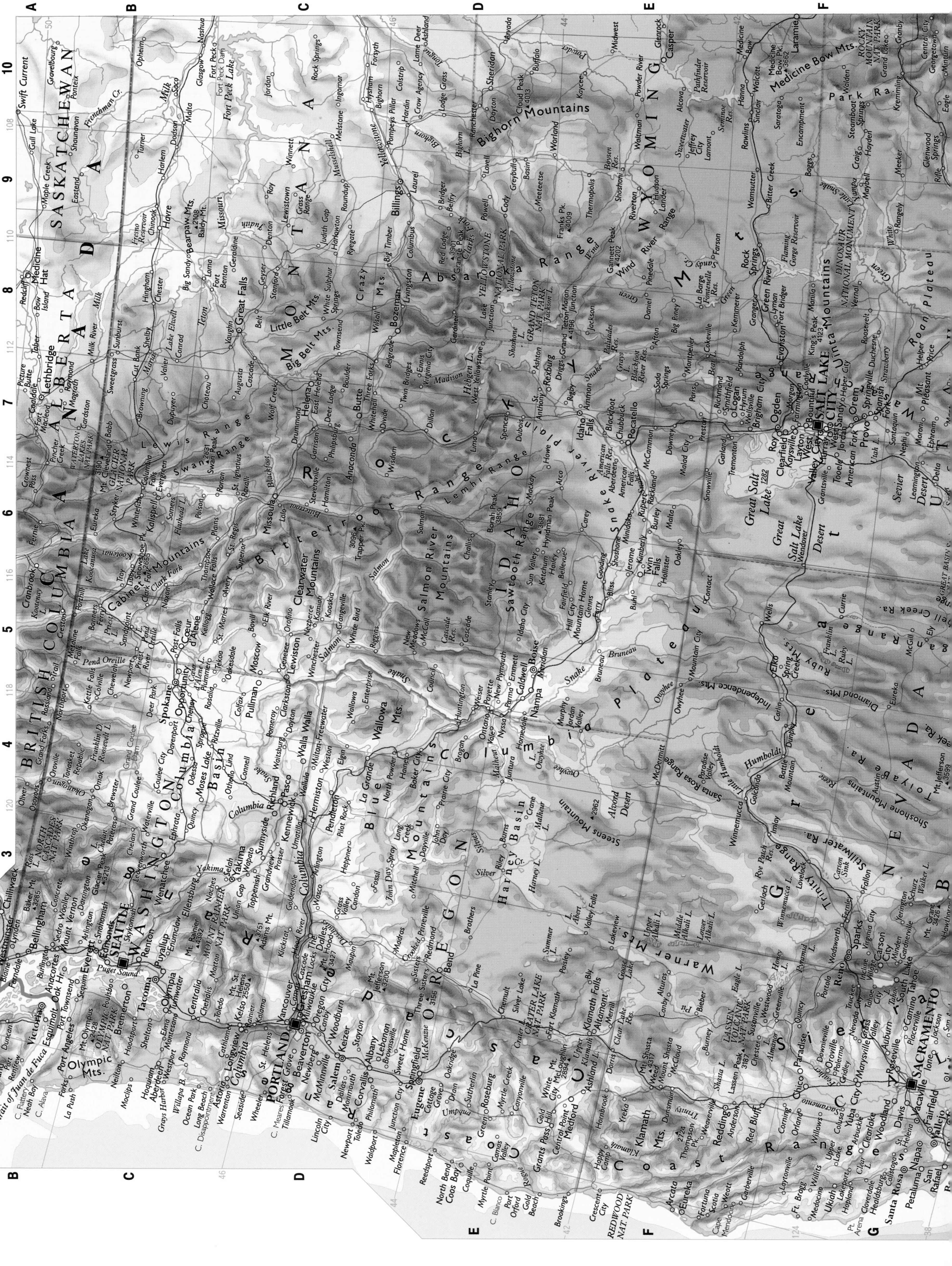

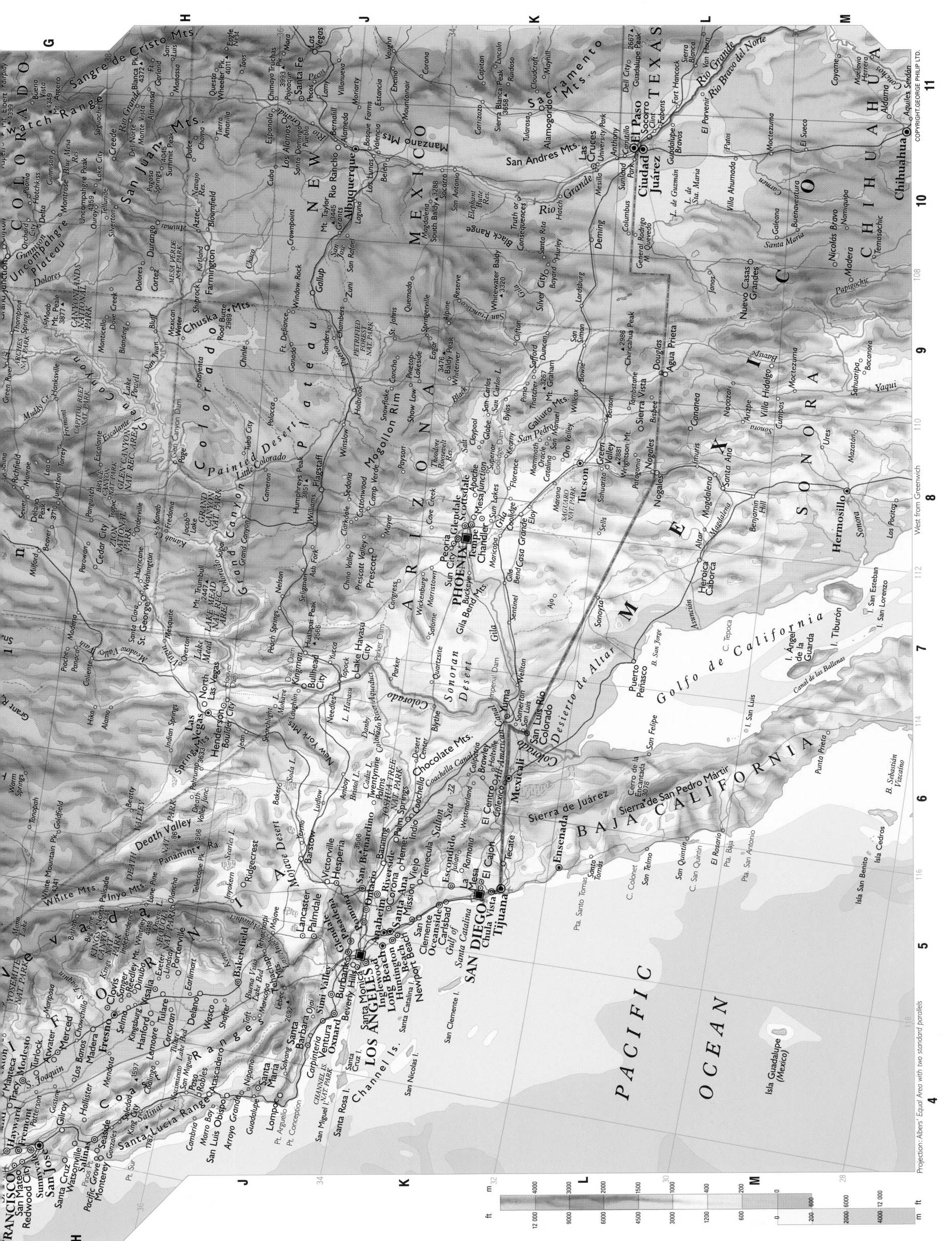

Projection: Albers' Equal Area with two standard parallels

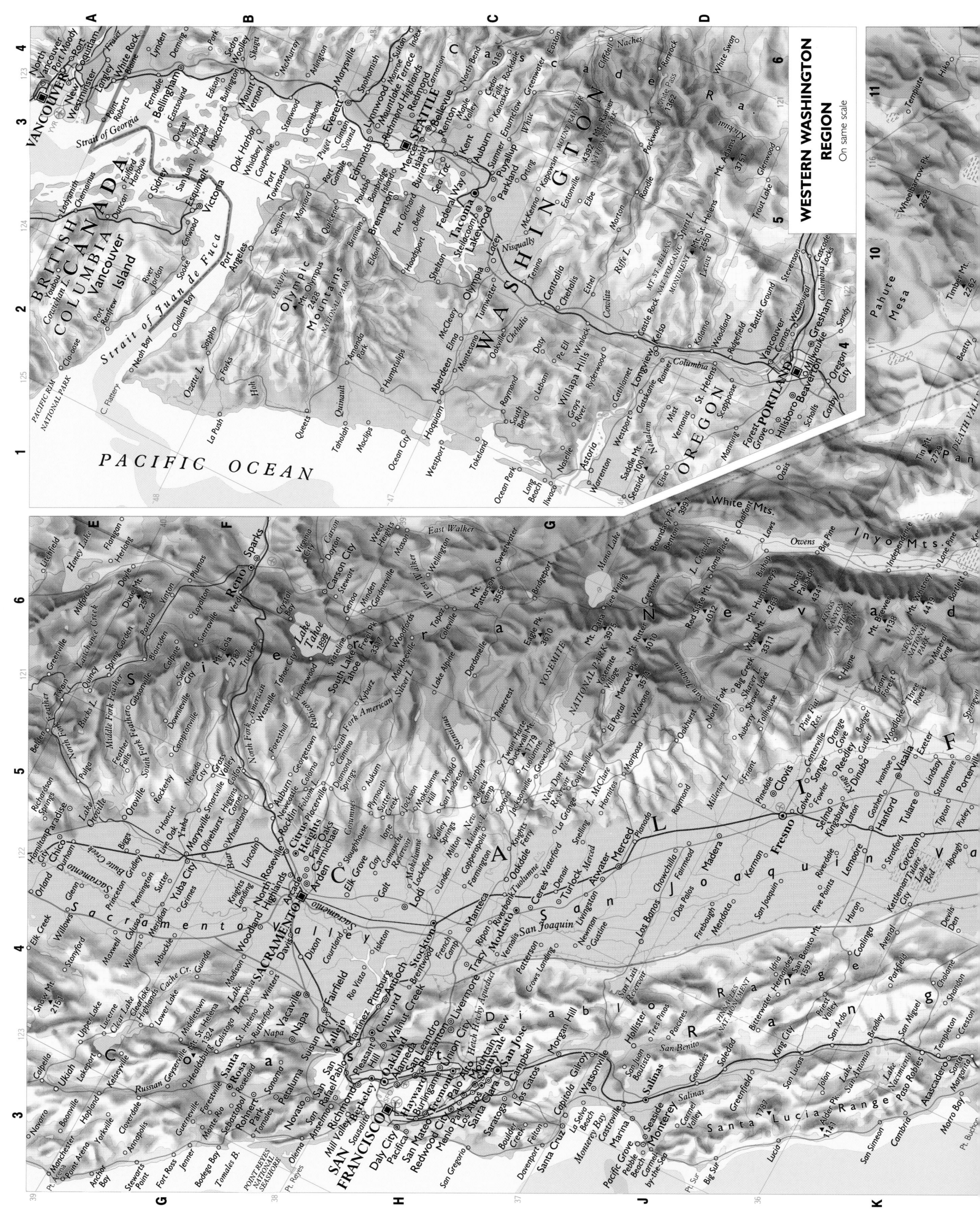

WESTERN WASHINGTON REGION
On same scale

50 0 50 100 150 200 250 300 km
50 0 50 100 150 200 miles

REFERENCE TO NUMBERS

1 Distrito Federal
2 Aguascalientes
3 Guanajuato
4 Hidalgo
5 México
6 Morelos
7 Querétaro
8 Tlaxcala

Projection: Bi-polar oblique Conical Orthomorphic

West from Greenwich

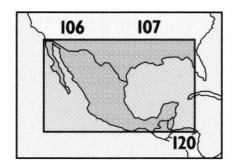

A B C D E

1 2 3 4

GULF OF MEXICO

I. Desterrada
I. Pérez (Mexico)

U.S.A. Fort Myers · Naples · C. Romano · Hialeah · **MIAMI** · Dry Tortugas (U.S.A.) · Key West · Florida Keys
West Palm Beach · Boca Raton · Fort Lauderdale · West End · Freeport · Grand Bahama · Hope Town · Little Abaco I.
Great Abaco I. · Northwest Providence Channel · Bimini Is. · Berry Is. · Nassau · New Providence · Adelaide · Andros Town · Nicolls Town · Eleuthera · Governor · New · Andros Island · Exuma (Rock Sound) · Great Exuma I. · Great Guana Cay

BAH · Great Exuma I. · Jumentos Cays · Dunmore Town

Straits of Florida · Santaren Channel

LA HABANA (Havana) · **MARIANAO** · Guanabacoa · Bahía Honda · Guanajay · La Esperanza · Los Palacios · San Antonio de los Baños · **Pinar del Río** · Guane · San Luis · La Fé · Corrientes · C. San Antonio
Matanzas · Cárdenas · Jovellanos · Colón · Sagua la Grande · Caibarién · Morón · Cayo Romano
Güines · Batabanó · Jagüey Grande · **Santa Clara** · Placetas · Ciego de Avila · Nueva Gerona · I. de la Juventud · Cienfuegos · Trinidad · Sancti Spíritus · Júcaro · Tunas de Zaza · Florida · **Camagüey** · Nuevitas
Arch. de los Canarreos · Santa Cruz del Sur · Arch. de Jardines de la Reina · Golfo de Guacanayabo · Bayamo · Manzanillo · Gibara · **HOLGUÍN** · Puerto Manotí · Puerto Padr
Victoria de las Tunas · Sierra Maestra · 2000 · **SANTIAGO DE CUBA** · C. Cruz

CUBA · **Greater**

Cay Sal Bank · Canal Nicholás · Canal Viejo de Bahama

Cayman Islands (U.K.) · Cayman Brac · Little Cayman · Georgetown · Grand Cayman · 7680

Montego Bay · Lucea · Negril · South Negril Pt. · Savanna-la-Mar · **JAMAICA** · Cambridge · Black River · Mandeville · May Pen · Spanish Town · **KINGSTON** · St. Ann's Bay · Port Maria · Annotto Bay · Port Antonio · Port Moran · Falmouth · Mora Cay (Jamaica) · Pedro Cays (Jamaica)

GULF OF MEXICO

Progreso · Dzilam de Bravo · Río Lagartos · El Cuyo · C. Catoche · Cancún · Punta Yalkubul · Temax · Tizimín · Puerto Juárez · Dzibilchaltún · Motul · Izamal · Espita · **Mérida** · Valladolid · Maxcanú · Ticul · Chichén Itzá · Puerto Morelos · Calkini · Tenabo · Sotuta · Peto · Cozumel · Isla Cozumel · Hopelchén · Mayapán · Uxmal · Bolonchenticul · Vigía Chico
Campeche · San José Carpizo · Felipe Carrillo Puerto · B. de la Ascensión · Champotón · Hecelchakán · Chenkán · B. del Espíritu Santo
Ciudad del Carmen · L. de Términos · Palizada · Matamoros · Bacalar · Banco Chinchorro · Balancán · Concepción · Chetumal · Corozal · B. de Chetumal · Hondo · Orange Walk · Ambergris Cay

MEXICO · **CAMPECHE** · **QUINTANA ROO**

Palenque · Tenosique · Uaxactún · Belmopan · Turneffe Is. · **Belize City** · Ocosingo · San Ignacio · Benque Viejo · **BELIZE** · Middlesex · La Independencia · L. Petén Itzá · La Libertad · Flores · Dangriga · Comitán · Lacantún · Sebol · Maya Mts. · Golfo de Honduras · Monkey River · Is. de la Bahía
San Luis · San Antonio · Roatán · Swan Islands (U.S.A. & Honduras)

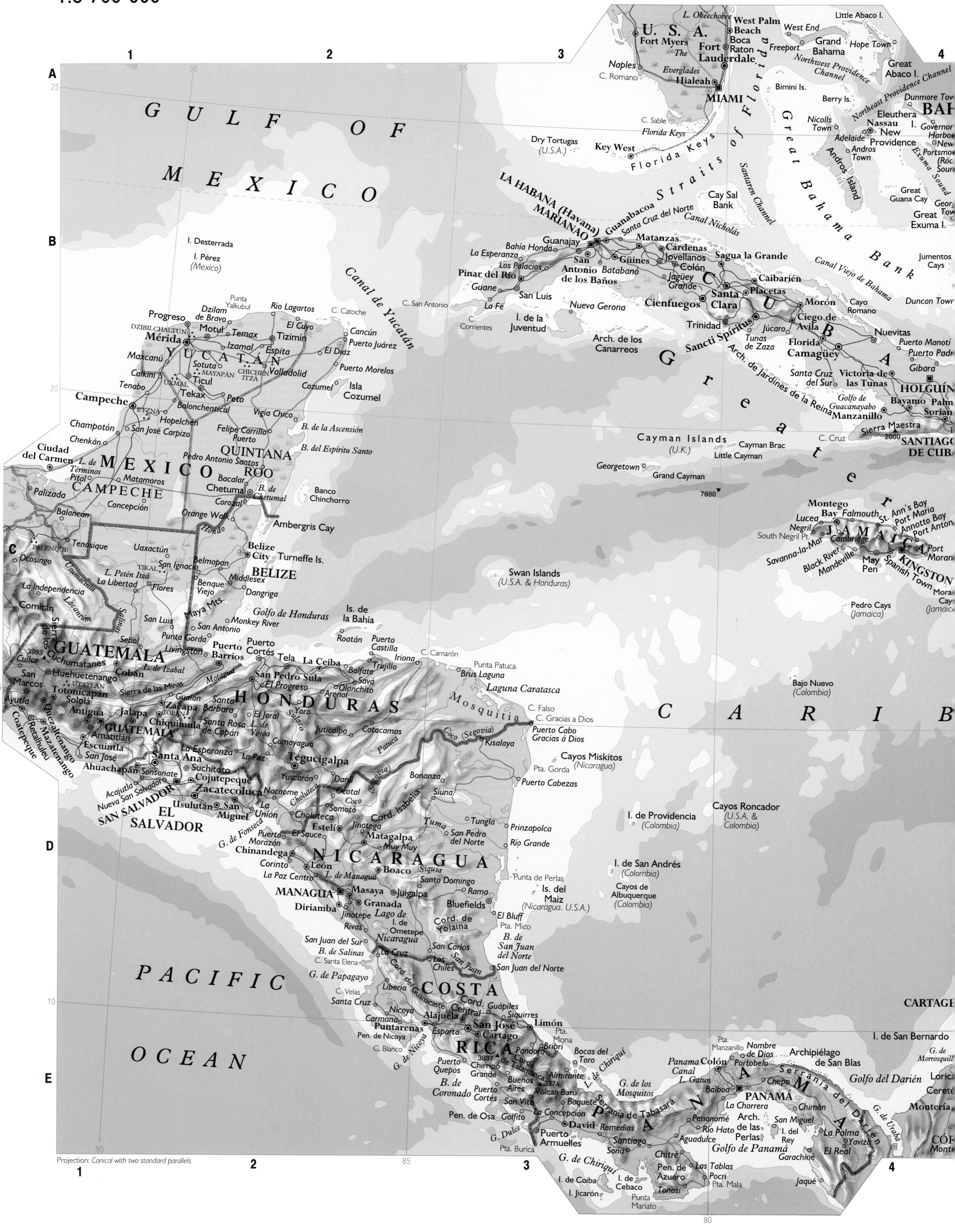

GUATEMALA · Cuilco · 3993 · Cuchumatanes · Coban · L. de Izabal · Livingston · Punta Gorda · Puerto Barrios · Puerto Cortés · Tela · La Ceiba · Balfate · Trujillo · Iriona · C. Camarón · Punta Patuca
San Marcos · Huehuetenango · Totonicapán · Sierra de las Minas · Gualán · Motagua · **San Pedro Sula** · El Progreso · Olanchito · Arenal · Brus Laguna
Ayutla · Quezaltenango · Sololá · Antigua · Zacapa · Santa Bárbara · Yoro · Sulaco · **HONDURAS** · Catacamas · Laguna Caratasca
Coatepeque · Mazatenango · Jalapa · Chiquimula · Santa Rosa de Copán · L. de Yojoa · Juticalpa · Mosquitia · C. Falso
Retalhuleu · Amatitlán · Copán · La Esperanza · Comayagua · Panca · Puerto Cabo Gracias á Dios
Escuintla · **GUATEMALA** · La Paz · **Tegucigalpa** · Coco (Segovia) · Kisalaya · C. Gracias a Dios
San José · Ahuachapán · Suchitoto · Yuscarán · Danlí · Ocotal · Somoto · Bonanza · Cayos Miskitos (Nicaragua)
Acajutla · Sonsonate · **Santa Ana** · Cojutepeque · Nacaome · Choluteca · Coco · Siuna · Pta. Gorda
Nueva San Salvador · **SAN SALVADOR** · Zacatecoluca · La Unión · Somoto · Cord. Isabelia · Puerto Cabezas
EL SALVADOR · Usulután · San Miguel · G. de Fonseca · Estelí · Jinotega · Tuma · Tungla
Puerto Morazán · El Sauce · Matagalpa · Muy Muy · San Pedro del Norte · Prinzapolca
Chinandega · **NICARAGUA** · Boaco · Siquia · Santo Domingo · Río Grande · Punta de Perlas
Corinto · León · L. de Managua · Juigalpa · Rama · Is. del Maiz (Nicaragua, U.S.A.)
La Paz Centro · **MANAGUA** · Masaya · Granada · Bluefields · Cayos de Albuquerque (Colombia)
Diriamba · Jinotepe · Lago de Nicaragua · El Bluff · Pta. Mico
Rivas · I. de Ometepe · Cord. de Yolaina
San Juan del Sur · B. de Salinas · La Cruz · San Carlos · B. de San Juan del Norte · San Juan del Norte
C. Santa Elena · San Juan · Los Chiles · Cord. de Guanacaste · Cord. Central
G. de Papagayo · Liberia · **COSTA RICA** · Guápiles · Siquirres · Limón
G. de Nicoya · Nicoya · Alajuela · Pta. Mona · I. de San Andrés (Colombia)
Santa Cruz · **San José** · Cartago · Bribri · Bocas del Toro · Cayos Roncador (U.S.A. & Colombia)
Puntarenas · Carmona · Pen. de Nicoya · C. Blanco · Pandora · 3837 · Almirante · Panama Canal · Colón · Portobelo · Nombre de Dios · Archipiélago de San Blas
Esparza · Puerto Quepos · Chirripó Grande · Cord. de Talamanca · Buenos Aires · 3374 · Volcán Barú · La Chorrera · **PANAMÁ** · Serranía del Darién · Golfo del Darién
B. de Coronado · Puerto Cortés · San Vito · Boquete · **PANAMA** · Chepo · Chimán · El Real
Pen. de Osa · Golfito · La Concepción · Penonomé · Río Hato · San Miguel · I. del Rey · La Palma · Yaviza
Puerto Armuelles · David · Remedios · Aguadulce · Arch. de las Perlas · Jaqué
Pta. Burica · Santiago · Soná · Chitré · Golfo de Panamá · Garachiné
G. de Chiriquí · Pen. de Azuero · Las Tablas · Pocrí
I. de Coiba · I. de Cebaco · Tonosí · Punta Mariato · Pta. Mala

PACIFIC OCEAN

CARIB (Caribbean)

Swan Islands (U.S.A. & Honduras)

Bajo Nuevo (Colombia)

I. de Providencia (Colombia)

Cayos Roncador (U.S.A. & Colombia)

CARTAG

I. de San Bernardo · G. de Morrosquill · Lorica · Cereté · Montería · **CÓR** Mont

ATLANTIC

OCEAN

Tropic of Cancer

MAS

Arthur's Town
The Bight
Cat I.
San Salvador I.
Conception I.
Rum Cay
Long I.
Clarence Town
Samana Cay
Crooked I. Passage
Crooked I.
Plana Cays
Albert Town
Snug Corner
Mayaguana I.
Acklins I.
Cay Verde
Mira por vos Cay
ay Santa
omingo
Hogsty Reef
Little Inagua I.
Caicos Passage
Caicos Is.
Turks & Caicos (U.K.)
nes
Lake Rosa
Great Inagua I.
Turks Island Passage
Turks Is.
tilla
Moa
Matthew Town
ayari
Baracoa
Pta. de Maisí
Î. de la Tortue
Monte Cristi
LA ISABELA
uantánamo
Paso de los Vientos
(Windward Passage)
Cap-Haïtien
Santiago de los Cabelleros
San Francisco de Macorís
Puerto Rico Trench
Jean Rabel
Port-de-Paix
Puerto Plata
Milwaukee Deep 9200
Cap-à-Foux
Fort Liberté
Cord. La Vega
Nagua
Samana
G. de la Gonâve
Gonaïves
Hinche
Central
Sánchez
Sabana de la Mar
Bayamón
SAN JUAN
Virgin Gorda
Anegada
St-Marc
3175
Hato Mayor
C. Engaño
Carolina
Tortola
Virgin Is. (U.K.)
Sombrero (U.K.)
HAITI
DOMINICAN
Arecibo
St. Thomas
Road Town
Anguilla (U.K.)
Î. de la Gonâve
PORT-
AU-PRINCE
REP.
San Pedro de Macorís
Higüey
Aguadilla
1338
Fajardo
Charlotte Amalie
Virgin Is. (U.S.A.)
St.-Martin (Fr.)
Jérémie
San Juan
L. Enriquillo
Ponce
Caguas
St.-Barthélemy (Fr.)
Hnassa I. (U.S.A.)
Dame Marie
2280
SANTO DOMINGO
Mayagüez
Guayama
Christiansted
St. Maarten (Neth.)
Saba (Neth.)
Barbuda
Massif de la Hotte
Les Cayes
Aquin
Petit Goâve
Jacmel
Barahona
B. de Yuma
Isla Mona (U.S.A.)
PUERTO
Frederiksted
St. Croix
St. Eustatius (Neth.)
ANTIGUA & BARBUDA
C. Carcasse
Î. à Vache
Compostela
San Cristóbal
I. Saona
RICO
Basseterre
ST. KITTS & NEVIS
St. John's
Pointe-à- Gravois
Pedernales
(U.S.A.)
Nevis
Antigua
Hispaniola
I. Beata
C. Beata
Redonda
Montserrat (U.K.)
Guadeloupe Passage
A n t i l l e s
Ste.-Rose (Fr.)
Le Moule
La Désirade
GUADELOUPE
Pointe-à-Pitre
Basse-Terre
Marie-Galante (Fr.)
Grand-Bourg
I. de Aves
(Venezuela)
I. des Saintes (Fr.)
Dominica Passage
Portsmouth
DOMINICA
Roseau
Martinique Passage
Mt. Pelée 1397
Ste.-Marie
B **E** **A** **N** **S** **E** **A**
Fort-de-France
Le François
Rivière-Pilote
MARTINIQUE
St. Lucia Channel (Fr.)
Castries
ST. LUCIA
Soufrière
St. Vincent Passage
La Soufrière 1234
ST. VINCENT
Speightstown
Kingstown
Bridgetown
Grenadines & THE **BARBADOS**
L e s s e r
Hillsborough
GRENADINES
Aruba (Neth.)
Curaçao
A n t i l l e s
St. George's
GRENADA
Bonaire
Pta. Gallinas
C. San Román
Pen. de Paraguaná
NETH. ANTILLES
Willemstad
Is. Las Aves (Ven.)
I. Orchila (Ven.)
I. Blanquilla (Ven.)
Tobago
Pta. Espada
Punta Cardón
Is. Los Roques (Ven.)
Is. Los Hermanos (Ven.)
Is. Los Testigos (Ven.)
Scarborough
Pen. de la Guajira
Puerto Fijo
Puerto Cumarebo
Dragon's Mouth
Port of Spain
Galera Point
SANTA MARTA
Ríohacha
Uribia
GUAJIRA
Golfo de Venezuela
Cora La Vela de Coro
I. de Margarita
La Asunción
NUEVA ESPARTA
Porlamar
Trinidad
Arima
ARRAN-
QUILLA
Baranoa
Cienaga
Sierra Nevada de Santa Marta 5800
San Rafael
FALCÓN
Tucacas
Puerto Cabello
Maiquetía
La Guaira
CARACAS
La Tortuga (Ven.)
Cumaná
Carúpano
Caribe
Río Claro
Güiria
G. de Paria
TRINIDAD
Soledad
LÁNTICO
Sabanalarga
Altagracia
Mene de Mauroa
Maracay
DISTRITO FEDERAL
SUCRE
San Fernando
& TOBAGO
Fundación
Calamar
Valledupar
La Concepción
MARACAIBO
Santa Rita
Barquita
San Felipe
YARACUY
Valencia
Villa de Cura
Higuerote
Puerto La Cruz
Caripito
Serpent's Mouth
MAGDALENA
Plato
Agustín Codazzi
Ciudad Ojeda
CABIMAS
Carora
CARABOBO
San Juan de los Morros
Barcelona
Caicara
SUCRE
Maturín
Sincé
Zambrano
CÉSAR
Machiques
Mene Grande
Santa Cruz
Yaritagua de los Morros
San Carlos
Aragua de Barcelona
Anaco
MONAGAS
DELTA
enceo
Corozal
ZULIA
Lago de Maracaibo
TRUJILLO
Acarigua
COJEDES
El Sombrero
Cantaura
El Tigre
AMACURO
San Marcos Planeta Rica
Magangué
El Banco
Entcontrados
Trujillo
PORTUGUESA
El Baúl
Calabozo
GUÁRICO
Valle de la Pascua
Pariaguán
Los Barrancos
Tucupita
Ayapel
BOLÍVAR
Mompós
NORTE DE OCAÑA
Valera
San Carlos del Zulia
Betijoque
Guanare
Portuguesa
Santa Maria de Ipire
El Pao
Sierra Imataca
Caucasia
SANTANDER
Simití
Ciudad Bolivia
MÉRIDA
Barinas
San Fernando de Apure
Soledad
Ciudad Guayana
Cúcuta
TÁCHIRA
Santa Bárbara
Libertad
BARINAS
Puerto de Nutrias
Achaguas
V E N E Z U E L A
Apure
Orinoco
Caicara
Ciudad Bolívar
Upata
Embalse de Guri
Guasipati
El Callao
Tumeremo

50 0 50 100 150 200 250 300 km
50 0 50 100 150 200 miles

100 0   200   400   600   800 1000 1200 1400 km

100   0   200   400   600   800   1000 miles

COPYRIGHT GEORGE PHILIP LTD.

100 0   200   400   600   800   1000   1200   1400 km

100 0   200   400   600   800   1000 miles

1 90 **2** 80 **3** 70 **4** 60 **5** 50 **6** 40 **7**

A   Tropic of Cancer   A

Havana ⊙ ‿C U B A   BAHAMAS   Turks & Caicos Is.   *N O R T H*

(U.K.)

20   **20**

JAMAICA   Kingston Port-au-   Virgin Is.   *A T L A N T I C*
                    Prince   San Juan *(U.K.)*
HAITI   DOMINICAN
          REP.   ANTIGUA &
MEXICO   PUERTO ST. KITTS BARBUDA
                     RICO   & NEVIS
BELIZE   *(U.S.A.)* Basse-Terre ⊙ GUADELOUPE   *O C E A N*
GUATEMALA HONDURAS   *(Fr.)*
                          DOMINICA   MARTINIQUE
B Guatemala ⊙ Tegucigalpa *Caribbean Sea* Fort-de-France *(Fr.)*   B
   San Salvador ⊙   Castries ⊙ ST. LUCIA
EL SALVADOR NICARAGUA   ST. VINCENT   BARBADOS
         Managua   Kingstown ⊙ ⊙ Bridgetown
                                   GRENADA ⊙ St. George's
COSTA ⊙ San José   Aruba   Port of
RICA   Panamá   ‿   Curaçao   Spain ⊙ TRINIDAD &
         ⊙ P A N A M A   C. de   TOBAGO
             Barranquilla ⊙ la Aguja
10   G. of   Maracaibo ⊙ Caracas   **10**
           Darién Cartagena ⊙   ⊙ ⊙ Valencia
           Gulf of   Barquisimeto
           Panamá   Cúcuta ⊙ San Cristóbal   Orinoco
C   Bucaramanga ⊙   V E N E Z U E L A   Ciudad Guayana ⊙   C
Medellín ⊙   Georgetown ⊙
         Cali ⊙ Bógota ⊙   GUYANA   Paramaribo ⊙
                                        SURINAM Cayenne ⊙
C O L O M B I A   RORAIMA   FRENCH C. Orange
                                         GUIANA
                      ⊙ Quito   AMAPÁ
Galapagos Is. E C U A D O R   *Equator*
0 *(Ecuador)* Guayaquil ⊙   Japurá   Manaus ⊙ Marajó ⊙ Belém **0**
         G. of Guayaquil Napo Putumayo   Amazon I.
                  Iquitos ⊙ A M A Z O N A S Santarém ⊙ ⊙ São Luís
              Marañón   Fortaleza ⊙
D Chiclayo ⊙   Juruá Purus Madeira P A R Á MARANHÃO   C. de D
   Trujillo ⊙   ACRE   Teresina ⊙ São Roque
   Chimbote ⊙   Pôrto Velho ⊙ RONDÔNIA   PIAUÍ   RIO G. Natal
                                              CEARÁ DO NORTE
P E R U Callao □ LIMA   Madre de Dios B R A Z I L Campina Grande ⊙
10   Cuzco ⊙   RONDÔNIA   TOCANTINS PERNAMBUCO Recife ⊙ **10**
         L. Titicaca Mamoré MATO GROSSO   ALAGOAS Maceió ⊙
                                         GOIÁS SERGIPE
B O L I V I A La Paz ⊙ Santa Cruz Cuiabá ⊙ DIS. FED ⊙ Brasília Aracaju ⊙
   Arequipa ⊙ ⊙ Cochabamba   Goiânia ⊙ B A H Í A Salvador ⊙
E   Sucre ⊙   MINAS GERAIS   E
                      MATO GROSSO   Belo   ESPÍRITO
Iquique ⊙   DO SUL   Ribeirão Horizonte ⊙ SANTO
                                     Prêto ⊙ Juiz Vitória ⊙
                      Paraná   SÃO PAULO de Fora Campos ⊙
20 Antofagasta ⊙   PARAGUAY   Campinas ⊙ R. DE J. **20**
                            Pilcomayo P A R A N Á SÃO Niterói
Tropic of Capricorn   Asunción ⊙   PAULO □ RIO DE
San Félix   Salta ⊙   JANEIRO
(Chile) San Ambrosio San Miguel   SANTA CATARINA Curitiba ⊙
F *(Chile)*   de Tucumán Saladó Resistencia ⊙ RIO GRANDE F
                    ⊙ Corrientes DO SUL
                  Córdoba ⊙   Pôrto Alegre ⊙
Arch. de Juan Fernández San Juan ⊙   Santa Fe ⊙ Paraná Pelotas ⊙
(Chile)   Viña del Mar ⊙ Mendoza ⊙ Rosario ⊙ URUGUAY
30 Valparaíso □   A R G E N T I N A Montevideo ⊙ **30**
         SANTIAGO □   BUENOS AIRES □
         Talca ⊙   La Plata Rio de la Plata
G Concepción ⊙   C H I L E   Bahía   *S O U T H* G
         Valdivia ⊙   Colorado Blanca ⊙ Mar del Plata
                   Negro ⊙ Viedma   *A T L A N T I C*
Puerto Montt ⊙   Chubut
                              O C E A N
H   H
              West Falkland FALKLAND IS.
Punta Arenas ⊙ Magellan's Str. *(U.K.)* ⊙ Stanley
           Tierra del Fuego   East Falkland
                    C. Horn   South Georgia
Projection: Lambert's Azimuthal Equal Area   *(U.K.)*

P A C I F I C   **O C E A N**

□ LIMA Capital Cities

West from Greenwich

COPYRIGHT GEORGE PHILIP LTD.

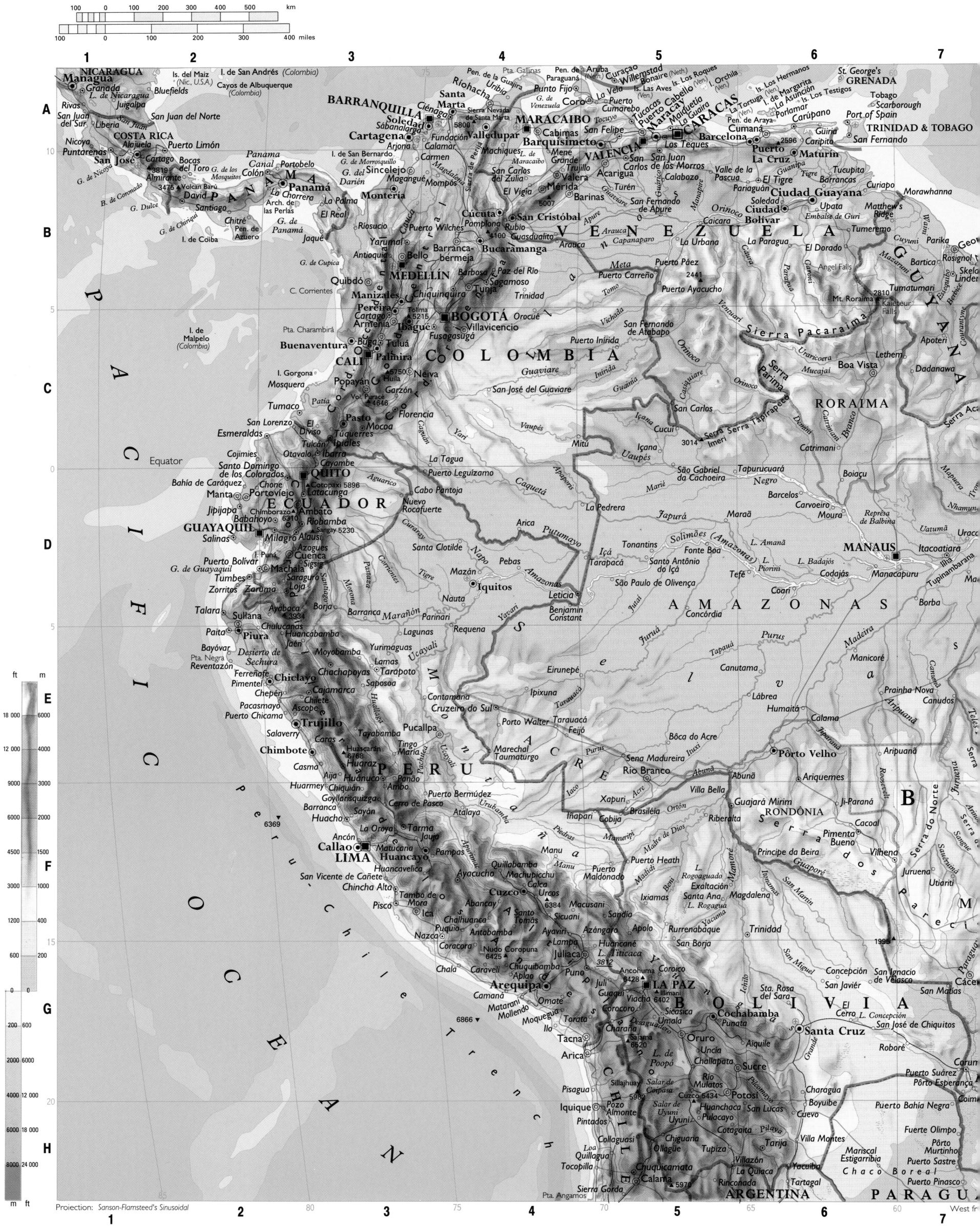

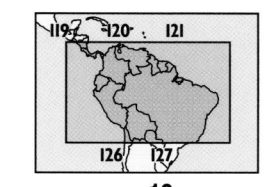

8   9   10   11   12   13

A

A T L A N T I C

10

B

O C E A N

5

0

São Paulo
(Braz.)

C

Equator

AMAPÁ

Serra do
Navio

Meriruma

Macapá
I. Caviana
I. Mexiana
C. Maguarinho

Mazagão
Afuá Chaves
Curuçá Salinópolis
Vigia Bragança

Fernando de Noronha
(Braz.)

D

Rocas

I. de Maracá

I. Caviana

I. de Soure
Marajó BELÉM
Breves Castanhal
Curralinho Abaetetuba
Cametá

Viseu
Turiaçu

Alcântara São Luís
B. de São Marcos
Barreirinhas
Tutóia

Luís Correia
Camocim

Rosário
Itapecuru-
Mirim
Parnaíba
Granja Itapipoca

Caucaia

FORTALEZA

5

Amapá

SURINAM

FRENCH
GUIANA

C. Orange

St-Georges
Oiapoque

Camopi

Serra Tumucumaque

Kwakoegron Albina Sinnamary
Totness Paramaribo Nieuw Amsterdam Kourou
Moengo St-Laurent Iracoubo Cayenne
Kaw Approuague

Amsterdam
New Nickerie
Nieuw Amsterdam
Prof. Van
Blommesteinmeer
1230

PARÁ

Óbidos Monte Prainha
Alegre
Alenquer
Juruti
Santarém Altamira
Belterra
Brasília Legal
Itaituba Irri

Almeirim
I. Grande
de Gurupá Pôrto de Móz
Baião
Capim

Turiaçu
Viana Pinheiro
Santa Inês
Bacabal
Grajaú
Codó
Coroatá
Caxias

Piracuruca
Brejo
Campo Oiticica
Maior

Piripiri
Cedro
Ipu Quixadá
Sobral Cascavel
Maranguape Aracati
Baturité
Russas
Areia Branca
Macau
Ceará Mirim

Mossoró

Sobradinho

Parintins
Santarém
Aveiro

Represa de
Tucuruí
Tucuruí

Açailândia
Pedreiras

Crateús
Senador Pompeu

RIO GRANDE
DO NORTE Natal

C. de São Roque

G

Marabá Imperatriz
São João do
Araguaia
Carajás
Tocantinópolis

MARANHÃO
Barra
do Corda
Colinas
Floriano
Nova Iorque
Loreto
Riachão
Carolina

Teresina

Amarante Valença
do Piauí
Oeiras
Picos
Juazeiro

Senhor do Norte
Crato
Cajàzeiras
Sousa Patos
Caicó
Currais
Novos

Canguaretama
Mamanguape
Cabedelo

João Pessoa
Olinda
RECIFE
Jaboatão

Serra dos Carajás
Conceição do
Araguaia
Araguaína

PIAUÍ
São João
do Piauí
Caracol
Nova Casa
Nova
Novo Remanso
Represa de
Sobradinho

Chapada do
Araripe
Ouricuri
Paulistana
Salgueiro
Pesqueira
Garanhuns
Caruaru
Palmares
Palmeira
dos Indios

Vitória de Santo Antão
PERNAMBUCO
Capela
Arapiraca

Maceió

10

Araguacema

Serra do Cachimbo

Palmas
Pôrto Nacional

TOCANTINS
Santa Isabel
do Morro
Gurupi
Peixe
Paranã

Pedro Afonso

Sono

Barra
Xique-Xique
Mundo
Novo
Jacobina
Queimadas

São Francisco
Paulo Afonso
ALAGOAS
Penedo
Propriá
SERGIPE

Aracaju
São Cristóvão
Estância
Serrinha

6059

F

MATO GROSSO

Santa
Filomena
Parnaguá

Taguatinga
Paranã

Barreiras
Santa Maria
da Vitória
São Domingos

Ibotirama

B A H I A
Itaberaba

Feira de
Santana
Alagoinhas
Santo Amaro

15

Planalto do

Barra do Garças

Aruanã
Niquelândia

1678

Campos Belos
Posse
Carinhana

Bom Jesus
da Lapa
Castro
Alves

Itaberaba
Cachoeira
Jequié
Valença
Nazaré
B. de Todos os Santos

SALVADOR

Cuiabá **Mato Grosso**
Santo Antonio

**MATO GROSSO
DO SUL**

GOIÁS
Goiás Taguatinga
Anápolis **BRASÍLIA**
Luziânia
Goiânia
Vianópolis
Alto Araguaia
Morrinhos
Rio Verde
Jataí
Quirinópolis

DIST.
FED.
Formosa
São Francisco

Januária
Montes
Claros
Janaúba
Salinas
Araçuaí

Carinhanha
Condeúba
Vitória da
Conquista

Brumado
Ubaíba
Itabuna
Ilhéus
Canavieiras
Belmonte

Pedra Azul
Jequitinhonha
Itamaraju
Prado
Caravelas

Pôrto Seguro

G

Campo
Grande
Miranda
Aquidauana

Coxim

Rondonópolis

Paracatu
Ipameri
Catalão
Patos de
Minas
Araguari
Ituiutaba Araxá
Uberaba

MINAS GERAIS
Pirapora
Corinto
Diamantina

Teófilo Otoni
Nova
Venécia
Colatina
Linhares

Governador
Valadares
Ipatinga
Itabira

Nanuque
Mucuri
Conceição da Barra
São Mateus

Trindade
(Braz.)

20

**Campo
Grande**
Três Lagoas
Rio Prêto

Uberlândia
Paranaíba
Santa Fé do Sul
Água Clara
São José do
Rio Prêto

BELO HORIZONTE
Divinópolis
Sabará
Nova
Lima
Ouro
Prêto
Caratinga
Ponte Nova

Vitória
Cariacica
Vila Velha
Cachoeiro de Itapemirim

H

Dourados
Ponta Porã

Pedro Juan
Caballero

Presidente Epitácio
Presidente
Prudente
Marília
Assis

Penápolis
Araçatuba
Andradina
Catanduva
Lins
Bauru Jaú **SÃO
PAULO**
Araraquara
São Carlos
Piracicaba
Limeira
Campinas
Botucatu
Moji-Mirim

Franca
Ribeirão Prêto
Guaxupé
Poços de
Caldas
São João
del Rei
Barbacena
Juiz de Fora

Conselheiro
Lafaiete
São
Lourenço
Volta
Redonda
RIO DE JANEIRO
Niterói

Itaperuna
Três Rios
Nova Friburgo
Petrópolis
Cabo Frio

Campos

COPYRIGHT GEORGE PHILIP LTD.

8   9   10   11   12   13

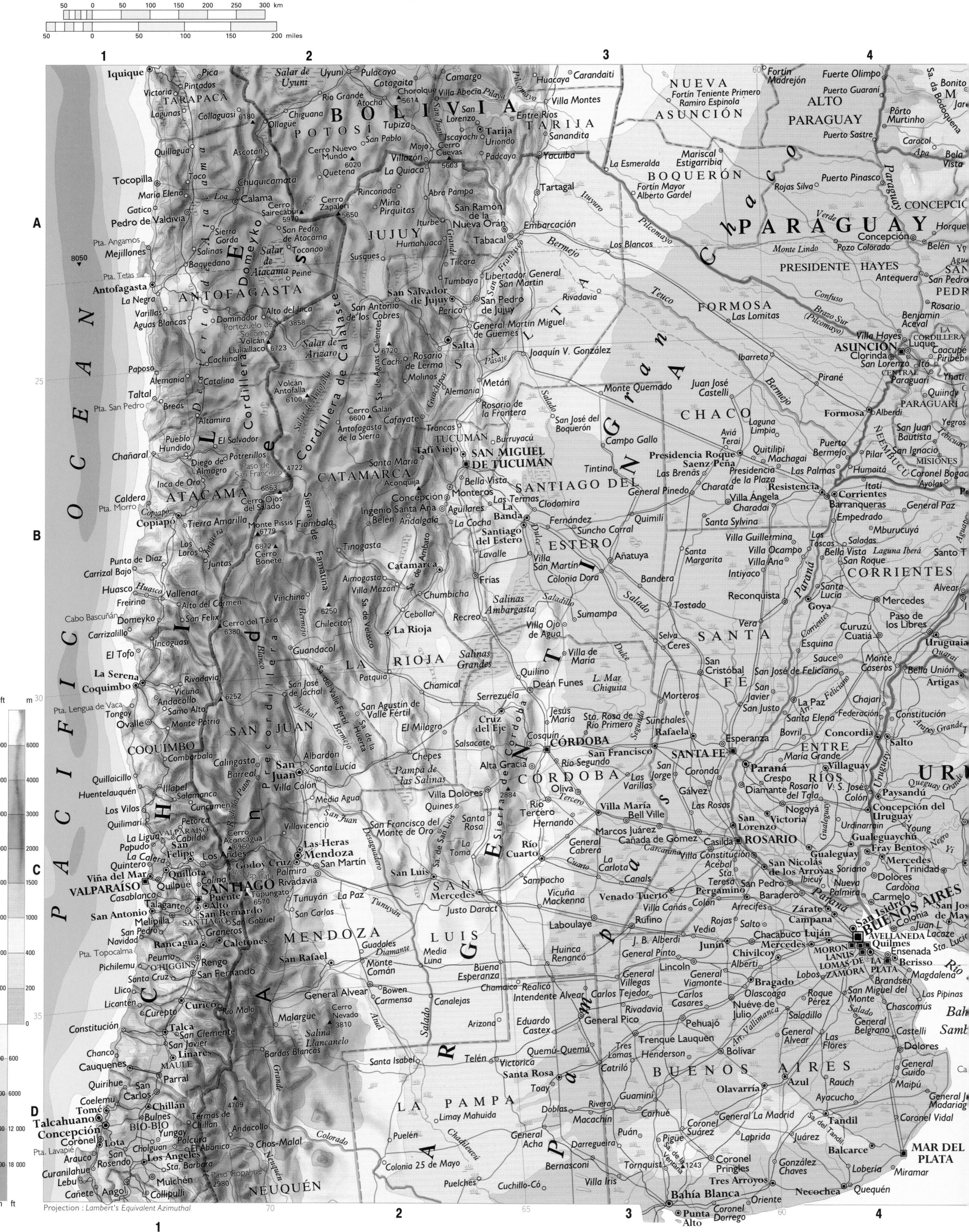

A

B

C

D

5 6 7

ATLANTIC

OCEAN

BRAZIL

MATO GROSSO DO SUL

SÃO PAULO

PARANÁ

SANTA CATARINA

RIO GRANDE DO SUL

MISIONES

URUGUAY

BELO HORIZONTE

RIO DE JANEIRO

SÃO PAULO

CURITIBA

PÔRTO ALEGRE

MONTEVIDEO

Tropic of Capricorn

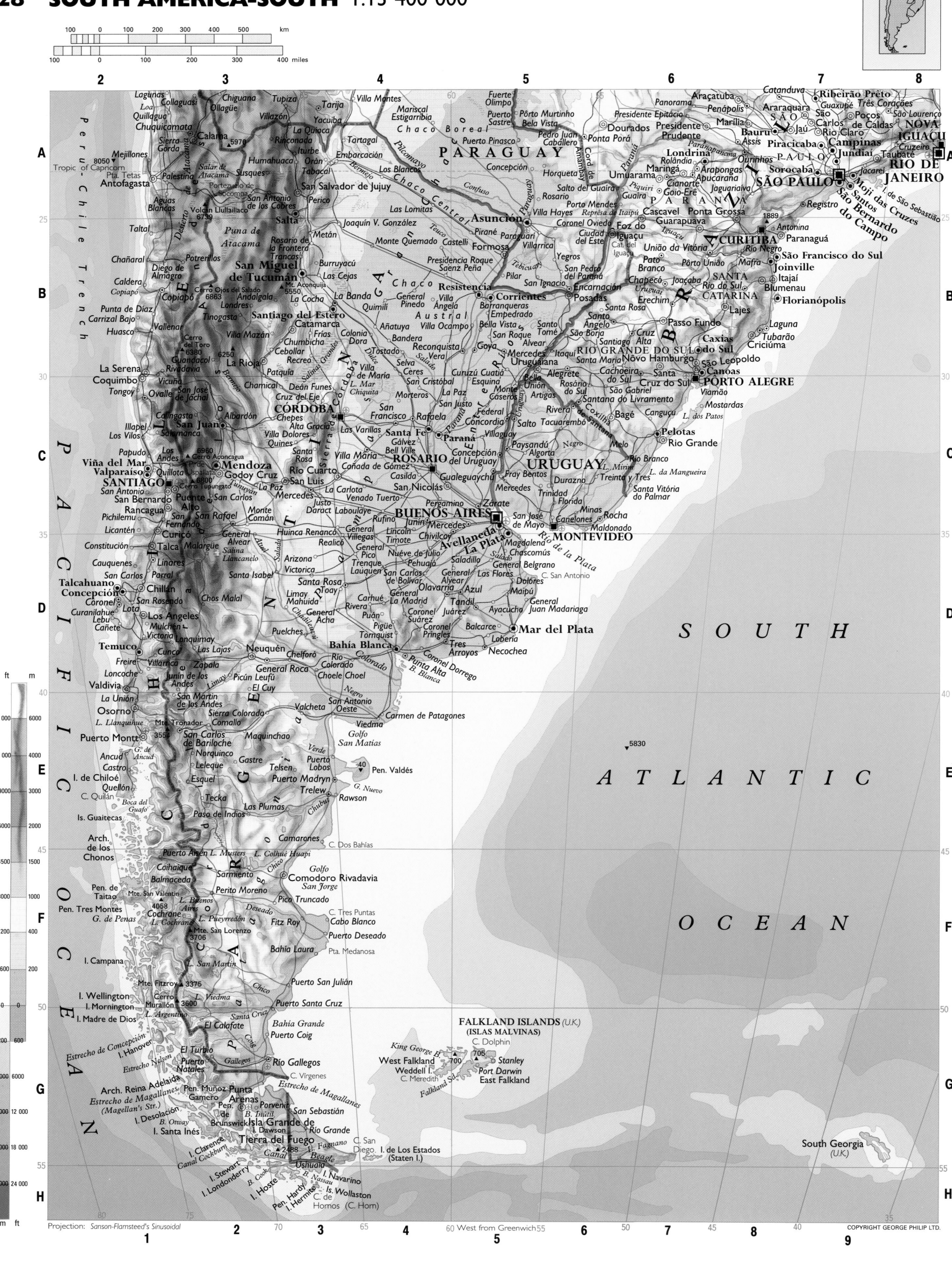

Projection: Sanson-Flamsteed's Sinusoidal

INDEX

How to use the index

The index contains the names of all the principal places and features shown on the World Maps. Each name is followed by an additional entry in italics giving the country or region within which it is located. The alphabetical order of names composed of two or more words is governed primarily by the first word and then by the second. This is an example of the rule:

Mīr Kūh, *Iran*	. . . .	**71 E8**	26 22N 58 55 E
Mīr Shahdād, *Iran*	. . . .	**71 E8**	26 15N 58 29 E
Mira, *Italy*	. . . .	**29 B5**	45 26N 12 8 E
Mira por vos Cay, *Bahamas*	. .	**121 B5**	22 9N 74 30W
Miraj, *India*	. . . .	**66 L9**	16 50N 74 45 E

Physical features composed of a proper name (Erie) and a description (Lake) are positioned alphabetically by the proper name. The description is positioned after the proper name and is usually abbreviated:

Erie, L., *N. Amer.* **110 D4**   42 15N 81 0W

Where a description forms part of a settlement or administrative name however, it is always written in full and put in its true alphabetic position:

Mount Morris, *U.S.A.* **110 D7**   42 44N 77 52W

Names beginning with M' and Mc are indexed as if they were spelled Mac. Names beginning St. are alphabetised under Saint, but Sankt, Sint, Sant', Santa and San are all spelt in full and are alphabetised accordingly. If the same place name occurs two or more times in the index and all are in the same country, each is followed by the name of the administrative subdivision in which it is located.

The number in bold type which follows each name in the index refers to the number of the map page where that feature or place will be found. This is usually the largest scale at which the place or feature appears.

The letter and figure which are in bold type immediately after the page number give the grid square on the map page, within which the feature is situated. The letter represents the latitude and the figure the longitude.

In some cases the feature itself may fall within the specified square, while the name is outside. This is usually the case only with features which are larger than a grid square.

The geographical co-ordinates which follow the letter-figure references give the latitude and longitude of each place. The first co-ordinate indicates latitude – the distance north of the Equator. The second co-ordinate indicates longitude – the distance east or west of the Greenwich Meridian. Both latitude and longitude are measured in degrees and minutes (there are 60 minutes in a degree).

The latitude is followed by N(orth) or S(outh) and the longitude by E(ast) or W(est).

Rivers are indexed to their mouths or confluences, and carry the symbol → after their names. A solid square ■ follows the name of a country, while an open square □ refers to a first order administrative area.

How to pronounce place names

English-speaking people usually have no difficulty in reading and pronouncing correctly English place names. However, foreign place name pronunciations may present many problems. Such problems can be minimised by following some simple rules. However, these rules cannot be applied to all situations, and there will be many exceptions.

1. In general, stress each syllable equally, unless your experience suggests otherwise.
2. Pronounce the letter 'a' as a broad 'a' as in 'arm'.
3. Pronounce the letter 'e' as a short 'e' as in 'elm'.
4. Pronounce the letter 'i' as a cross between a short 'i' and long 'e', as the two 'i's in 'California'.
5. Pronounce the letter 'o' as an intermediate 'o' as in 'soft'.
6. Pronounce the letter 'u' as an intermediate 'u' as in 'sure'.
7. Pronounce consonants hard, except in the Romance-language areas where 'g's are likely to be pronounced softly like 'j' in 'jam'; 'j' itself may be pronounced as 'y'; and 'x's may be pronounced as 'h'.
8. For names in mainland China, pronounce 'q' like the 'ch' in 'chin', 'x' like the 'sh' in 'she', 'zh' like the 'j' in 'jam', and 'z' as if it were spelled 'dz'. In general pronounce 'a' as in 'father', 'e' as in 'but', 'i' as in 'keep', 'o' as in 'or', and 'u' as in 'rule'.

Moreover, English has no diacritical marks (accent and pronunciation signs), although some languages do. The following is a brief and general guide to the pronunciation of those most frequently used in the principal Western European languages.

		Pronunciation as in
French	é	day and shows that the e is to be pronounced; e.g. Orléans.
	è	mare
	î	used over any vowel and does not affect pronunciation; shows contraction of the name, usually omission of 's' following a vowel.
	ç	's' before 'a', 'o' and 'u'.
	ë, ï, ü	over 'e', 'i' and 'u' when they are used with another vowel and shows that each is to be pronounced.
German	ä	fate
	ö	fur
	ü	no English equivalent; like French 'tu'
Italian	à, é	over vowels and indicates stress.
Portuguese	ã, õ	vowels pronounced nasally.
	ç	boss
	á	shows stress
	ô	shows that a vowel has an 'i' or 'u' sound combined with it.
Spanish	ñ	canyon
	ü	pronounced as w and separately from adjoining vowels.
	á	usually indicates that this is a stressed vowel.

Abbreviations

A.C.T. – Australian Capital Territory	E. Salv. – El Salvador	Mass. – Massachusetts	Or. – Orientale	Sd. – Sound
A.R. – Autonomous Region	Eq. Guin. – Equatorial Guinea	Md. – Maryland	Oreg. – Oregon	Sev. – Severnaya
Afghan. – Afghanistan	Est. – Estrecho	Me. – Maine	Os. – Ostrov	Sib. – Siberia
Ala. – Alabama	Falk. Is. – Falkland Is.	Medit. S. – Mediterranean Sea	Oz. – Ozero	Sprs. – Springs
Alta. – Alberta	Fd. – Fjord	Mich. – Michigan	P. – Pass, Passo, Pasul, Pulau	St. – Saint
Amer. – America(n)	Fla. – Florida	Minn. – Minnesota	P.E.I. – Prince Edward Island	Sta. – Santa
Arch. – Archipelago	Fr. – French	Miss. – Mississippi	Pa. – Pennsylvania	Ste. – Sainte
Ariz. – Arizona	G. – Golfe, Golfo, Gulf, Guba, Gebel	Mo. – Missouri	Pac. Oc. – Pacific Ocean	Sto. – Santo
Ark. – Arkansas	Ga. – Georgia	Mont. – Montana	Papua N.G. – Papua New Guinea	Str. – Strait, Stretto
Atl. Oc. – Atlantic Ocean	Gt. – Great, Greater	Mozam. – Mozambique	Pass. – Passage	Switz. – Switzerland
B. – Baie, Bahía, Bay, Bucht, Bugt	Guinea-Biss. – Guinea-Bissau	Mt.(s) – Mont, Montaña, Mountain	Pen. – Peninsula, Péninsule	Tas. – Tasmania
B.C. – British Columbia	H.K. – Hong Kong	Mte. – Monte	Phil. – Philippines	Tenn. – Tennessee
Bangla. – Bangladesh	H.P. – Himachal Pradesh	Mti. – Monti	Pk. – Peak	Terr. – Territory, Territoire
Barr. – Barrage	Hants. – Hampshire	N. – Nord, Norte, North, Northern,	Plat. – Plateau	Tex. – Texas
Bos.-H. – Bosnia-Herzegovina	Harb. – Harbor, Harbour	Nouveau	Prov. – Province, Provincial	Tg. – Tanjung
C. – Cabo, Cap, Cape, Coast	Hd. – Head	N.B. – New Brunswick	Pt. – Point	Trin. & Tob. – Trinidad & Tobago
C.A.R. – Central African Republic	Hts. – Heights	N.C. – North Carolina	Pta. – Ponta, Punta	U.A.E. – United Arab Emirates
C. Prov. – Cape Province	I.(s). – Île, Ilha, Insel, Isla, Island, Isle	N. Cal. – New Caledonia	Pte. – Pointe	U.K. – United Kingdom
Calif. – California	Ill. – Illinois	N. Dak. – North Dakota	Qué. – Québec	U.S.A. – United States of America
Cat. – Catarata	Ind. – Indiana	N.H. – New Hampshire	Queens. – Queensland	Ut. P. – Uttar Pradesh
Cent. – Central	Ind. Oc. – Indian Ocean	N.I. – North Island	R. – Rio, River	Va. – Virginia
Chan. – Channel	Ivory C. – Ivory Coast	N.J. – New Jersey	R.I. – Rhode Island	Vdkhr. – Vodokhranilishche
Colo. – Colorado	J. – Jabal, Jebel	N. Mex. – New Mexico	Ra. – Range	Vdskh. – Vodoskhovyshche
Conn. – Connecticut	Jaz. – Jazīrah	N.S. – Nova Scotia	Raj. – Rajasthan	Vf. – Virful
Cord. – Cordillera	Junc. – Junction	N.S.W. – New South Wales	Récr. – Récréatif	Vic. – Victoria
Cr. – Creek	K. – Kap, Kapp	N.W.T. – North West Territory	Reg. – Region	Vol. – Volcano
Czech. – Czech Republic	Kans. – Kansas	N.Y. – New York	Rep. – Republic	Vt. – Vermont
D.C. – District of Columbia	Kep. – Kepulauan	N.Z. – New Zealand	Res. – Reserve, Reservoir	W. – Wadi, West
Del. – Delaware	Ky. – Kentucky	Nat. – National	Rhld-Pfz. – Rheinland-Pfalz	W. Va. – West Virginia
Dem. – Democratic	L. – Lac, Lacul, Lago, Lagoa, Lake, Limni,	Nebr. – Nebraska	S. – South, Southern, Sur	Wall. & F. Is. – Wallis and Futuna Is.
Dep. – Dependency	Loch, Lough	Neths. – Netherlands	Si. Arabia – Saudi Arabia	Wash. – Washington
Des. – Desert	La. – Louisiana	Nev. – Nevada	S.C. – South Carolina	Wis. – Wisconsin
Dét. – Détroit	Ld. – Land	Nfld. – Newfoundland	S. Dak. – South Dakota	Wlkp. – Wielkopolski
Dist. – District	Liech. – Liechtenstein	Nic. – Nicaragua	S.I. – South Island	Wyo. – Wyoming
Dj. – Djebel	Lux. – Luxembourg	O. – Oued, Ouadi	S. Leone – Sierra Leone	Yorks. – Yorkshire
Domin. – Dominica	Mad. P. – Madhya Pradesh	Occ. – Occidentale	Sa. – Serra, Sierra	Yug. – Yugoslavia
Dom. Rep. – Dominican Republic	Madag. – Madagascar	Okla. – Oklahoma	Sask. – Saskatchewan	
E. – East	Man. – Manitoba	Ont. – Ontario	Scot. – Scotland	

A Baña

A

A Baña, *Spain* **34 C2** 42 58N 8 46W
A Cañiza, *Spain* **34 C2** 42 13N 8 16W
A Coruña, *Spain* **34 B2** 43 20N 8 25W
A Estrada, *Spain* **34 C2** 42 43N 8 27W
A Fonsagrada, *Spain* **34 B3** 43 8N 7 4W
A Guarda, *Spain* **34 D2** 41 56N 8 52W
A Gudiña, *Spain* **34 C3** 42 4N 7 8W
A Rúa, *Spain* **34 C3** 42 24N 7 6W
Aachen, *Germany* **24 E2** 50 45N 6 6 E
Aalborg = Ålborg, *Denmark* **11 G3** 57 2N 9 54 E
Aalen, *Germany* **25 G6** 48 51N 10 6 E
A'āli an Nīl □, *Sudan* **81 F3** 9 30N 33 0 E
Aalst, *Belgium* **17 D4** 50 56N 4 2 E
Aalten, *Neths.* **17 C6** 51 56N 6 35 E
Aalter, *Belgium* **17 C3** 51 5N 3 28 E
Äänekoski, *Finland* **9 E21** 62 36N 25 44 E
Aarau, *Switz.* **25 H4** 47 23N 8 4 E
Aarberg, *Switz.* **25 H3** 47 2N 7 16 E
Aare →, *Switz.* **25 H4** 47 33N 8 14 E
Aargau □, *Switz.* **25 H4** 47 26N 8 10 E
Aarhus = Århus, *Denmark* **11 H4** 56 8N 10 11 E
Aarschot, *Belgium* **17 D4** 50 59N 4 49 E
Aba, *China* **58 A3** 32 59N 101 42 E
Aba, *Dem. Rep. of the Congo* **86 B3** 3 58N 30 17 E
Aba, *Nigeria* **83 D6** 5 10N 7 19 E
Âbâ, Jazîrat, *Sudan* **81 E3** 13 30N 32 31 E
Abadab, J., *Sudan* **80 D4** 18 54N 35 56 E
Ābādān, *Iran* **71 D6** 30 22N 48 20 E
Abade, *Ethiopia* **81 F4** 9 22N 38 3 E
Ābādeh, *Iran* **71 D7** 31 8N 52 40 E
Abadin, *Spain* **34 B3** 43 21N 7 29W
Abadla, *Algeria* **78 B5** 31 2N 2 45W
Abaetetuba, *Brazil* **125 D9** 1 40 S 48 50W
Abagnar Qi, *China* **56 C9** 43 52N 116 2 E
Abai, *Paraguay* **127 B4** 25 58 S 55 54W
Abak, *Nigeria* **83 E6** 4 58N 7 50 E
Abakaliki, *Nigeria* **83 D6** 6 22N 8 2 E
Abakan, *Russia* **51 D10** 53 40N 91 10 E
Abala, *Niger* **83 C5** 14 56N 3 22 E
Abalak, *Niger* **83 B6** 15 22N 6 21 E
Abalemma, *Niger* **83 B6** 16 12N 7 50 E
Abana, *Turkey* **72 B6** 41 59N 34 1 E
Abancay, *Peru* **124 F4** 13 35 S 72 55W
Abano Terme, *Italy* **29 C8** 45 22N 11 46 E
Abarán, *Spain* **33 G3** 38 12N 1 23W
Abariringa, *Kiribati* **96 H10** 2 50 S 171 40W
Abarqū, *Iran* **71 D7** 31 10N 53 20 E
Abashiri, *Japan* **54 B12** 44 0N 144 15 E
Abashiri-Wan, *Japan* **54 C12** 44 0N 144 30 E
Abaújszántó, *Hungary* **42 B6** 48 16N 21 12 E
Abava →, *Latvia* **44 A8** 57 6N 21 54 E
Ābay = Nîl el Azraq →, *Sudan* **81 D3** 15 38N 32 31 E
Abay, *Kazakhstan* **50 E8** 49 38N 72 53 E
Abaya, L., *Ethiopia* **81 F4** 6 30N 37 50 E
Abaza, *Russia* **50 D9** 52 39N 90 6 E
Abbadia San Salvatore, *Italy* **29 F8** 42 53N 11 41 E
'Abbāsābād, *Iran* **71 C8** 33 34N 58 23 E
Abbay = Nîl el Azraq →, *Sudan* **81 D3** 15 38N 32 31 E
Abbaye, Pt., *U.S.A.* **108 B1** 46 58N 88 8W
Abbé, L., *Ethiopia* **81 E5** 11 8N 41 47 E
Abbeville, *France* **19 B8** 50 6N 1 49 E
Abbeville, *Ala., U.S.A.* **109 K3** 31 34N 85 15W
Abbeville, *La., U.S.A.* **113 L8** 29 58N 92 8W
Abbeville, *S.C., U.S.A.* **109 H4** 34 11N 82 23W
Abbiategrasso, *Italy* **28 C5** 45 24N 8 54 E
Abbot Ice Shelf, *Antarctica* **5 D16** 73 0 S 92 0W
Abbottabad, *Pakistan* **68 B5** 34 10N 73 15 E
Abd al Kūrī, *Ind. Oc.* **74 E5** 12 5N 52 20 E
Ābdar, *Iran* **71 D7** 30 16N 55 19 E
'Abdolābād, *Iran* **71 C8** 34 12N 56 30 E
Abdulpur, *Bangla.* **69 G13** 24 15N 88 59 E
Abéché, *Chad* **79 F10** 13 50N 20 35 E
Abejar, *Spain* **32 D2** 41 48N 2 47W
Abekr, *Sudan* **81 E2** 12 45N 28 50 E
Abengourou, *Ivory C.* **82 D4** 6 42N 3 27W
Abenójar, *Spain* **35 G6** 38 53N 4 21W
Åbenrå, *Denmark* **11 J3** 55 3N 9 25 E
Abensberg, *Germany* **25 G7** 48 48N 11 51 E
Abeokuta, *Nigeria* **83 D5** 7 3N 3 19 E
Aber, *Uganda* **86 B3** 2 12N 32 25 E
Aberaeron, *U.K.* **13 E3** 52 15N 4 15W
Aberayron = Aberaeron, *U.K.* **13 E3** 52 15N 4 15W
Aberchirder, *U.K.* **14 D6** 57 34N 2 37W
Abercorn = Mbala, *Zambia* **87 D3** 8 46 S 31 24 E
Abercorn, *Australia* **95 D5** 25 12 S 151 5 E
Aberdare, *U.K.* **13 F4** 51 43N 3 27W
Aberdare Ra., *Kenya* **86 C4** 0 15 S 36 50 E
Aberdeen, *Australia* **95 E5** 32 9 S 150 56 E
Aberdeen, *Canada* **105 C7** 52 20N 106 8W
Aberdeen, *S. Africa* **88 E3** 32 28 S 24 2 E
Aberdeen, *U.K.* **14 D6** 57 9N 2 5W
Aberdeen, *Ala., U.S.A.* **109 J1** 33 49N 88 33W
Aberdeen, *Idaho, U.S.A.* **114 E7** 42 57N 112 50W
Aberdeen, *Md., U.S.A.* **108 F7** 39 31N 76 10W
Aberdeen, *S. Dak., U.S.A.* **112 C5** 45 28N 98 29W
Aberdeen, *Wash., U.S.A.* **116 D3** 46 59N 123 50W
Aberdeen, City of □, *U.K.* **14 D6** 57 10N 2 10W
Aberdeenshire □, *U.K.* **14 D6** 57 17N 2 36W
Aberdovey = Aberdyfi, *U.K.* **13 E3** 52 33N 4 3W
Aberdyfi, *U.K.* **13 E3** 52 33N 4 3W
Aberfeldy, *U.K.* **14 E5** 56 37N 3 51W
Abergavenny, *U.K.* **13 F4** 51 49N 3 1W
Abergele, *U.K.* **12 D4** 53 17N 3 35W
Abernathy, *U.S.A.* **113 J4** 33 50N 101 51W
Abert, L., *U.S.A.* **114 E3** 42 38N 120 14W
Aberystwyth, *U.K.* **13 E3** 52 25N 4 5W
Abhā, *Si. Arabia* **74 D3** 18 0N 42 34 E
Abhar, *Iran* **71 B6** 36 9N 49 13 E
Abhayapuri, *India* **69 F14** 26 24N 90 38 E
Abia □, *Nigeria* **83 D6** 5 30N 7 35 E
Abide, *Turkey* **39 C11** 38 55N 29 20 E
Abidiya, *Sudan* **80 D3** 18 18N 34 3 E
Abidjan, *Ivory C.* **82 D4** 5 26N 3 58W
Abilene, *Kans., U.S.A.* **112 F6** 38 55N 97 13W
Abilene, *Tex., U.S.A.* **113 J5** 32 28N 99 43W
Abingdon, *U.K.* **13 F6** 51 40N 1 17W
Abingdon, *U.S.A.* **109 G5** 36 43N 81 59W
Abington Reef, *Australia* **94 B4** 18 0 S 149 35 E
Abitau →, *Canada* **105 B7** 59 53N 109 3W
Abitibi →, *Canada* **102 B3** 51 3N 80 55W
Abitibi, L., *Canada* **102 C4** 48 40N 79 40W
Abiy Adi, *Ethiopia* **81 E4** 13 39N 39 3 E
Abkhaz Republic = Abkhazia □, *Georgia* **49 J5** 43 12N 41 5 E
Abkhazia □, *Georgia* **49 J5** 43 12N 41 5 E
Abminga, *Australia* **95 D1** 26 8 S 134 51 E
Abnûb, *Egypt* **80 B3** 27 18N 31 4 E
Åbo = Turku, *Finland* **9 F20** 60 30N 22 19 E
Abocho, *Nigeria* **83 D6** 7 35N 6 56 E
Abohar, *India* **68 D6** 30 10N 74 10 E
Aboisso, *Ivory C.* **82 D4** 5 30N 3 5W
Abomey, *Benin* **83 D5** 7 10N 2 5 E
Abong-Mbang, *Cameroon* **84 D2** 4 0N 13 8 E
Abonnema, *Nigeria* **83 E6** 4 41N 6 49 E
Abony, *Hungary* **42 C5** 47 12N 20 3 E
Aboso, *Ghana* **82 D4** 5 23N 1 57W
Abou-Deïa, *Chad* **79 F9** 11 20N 19 20 E
Aboyne, *U.K.* **14 D6** 57 4N 2 47W
Abra Pampa, *Argentina* **126 A2** 22 43 S 65 42W
Abraham L., *Canada* **104 C5** 52 15N 116 35W
Abrantes, *Portugal* **35 F2** 39 24N 8 7W
Abreojos, Pta., *Mexico* **118 B2** 26 50N 113 40W
Abri, *Esh Shamâliya, Sudan* **80 C3** 20 50N 30 27 E
Abri, *Janub Kordofân, Sudan* **81 E3** 11 40N 30 21 E
Abrud, *Romania* **42 D8** 46 19N 23 5 E
Abruzzo □, *Italy* **29 F10** 42 15N 14 0 E
Absaroka Range, *U.S.A.* **114 D9** 44 45N 109 50W
Abtenau, *Austria* **26 D6** 47 33N 13 21 E
Abu, *India* **68 G5** 24 41N 72 50 E
Abū al Abyad, *U.A.E.* **71 E7** 24 11N 53 50 E
Abū al Khaşīb, *Iraq* **71 D6** 30 25N 48 0 E
Abū 'Alī, *Si. Arabia* **71 E6** 27 20N 49 27 E
Abū 'Alī →, *Lebanon* **75 A4** 34 25N 35 50 E
Abu Ballas, *Egypt* **80 C2** 24 26N 27 36 E
Abu Deleiq, *Sudan* **81 D3** 15 57N 33 48 E
Abu Dhabi = Abū Z̧āby, *U.A.E.* **71 E7** 24 28N 54 22 E
Abu Dis, *Sudan* **80 D3** 19 12N 33 38 E
Abu Dom, *Sudan* **81 D3** 16 18N 32 25 E
Abū Du'ān, *Syria* **70 B3** 36 25N 38 15 E
Abu el Gairi, W. →, *Egypt* **75 F2** 29 35N 33 30 E
Abu Fatma, Ras, *Sudan* **80 C4** 22 25N 36 25 E
Abu Gabra, *Sudan* **81 E2** 11 2N 26 50 E
Abu Ga'da, W. →, *Egypt* **75 F1** 29 15N 32 53 E
Abu Gelba, *Sudan* **81 E3** 13 11N 31 52 E
Abu Gubeiha, *Sudan* **81 E3** 11 30N 31 15 E
Abu Habl, Khawr →, *Sudan* **81 E3** 12 37N 31 0 E
Abū Ḩadrīyah, *Si. Arabia* **71 E6** 27 20N 48 58 E
Abu Hamed, *Sudan* **80 D3** 19 32N 33 13 E
Abu Haraz, *An Nîl el Azraq, Sudan* **80 D3** 18 1N 33 58 E
Abu Haraz, *El Gezira, Sudan* **81 E3** 14 35N 33 30 E
Abu Haraz, *Esh Shamâliya, Sudan* **80 D3** 19 8N 32 18 E
Abu Higar, *Sudan* **81 E3** 12 50N 33 59 E
Abū Kamāl, *Syria* **70 C4** 34 30N 41 0 E
Abu Kuleiwat, *Sudan* **81 E2** 12 20N 26 0 E
Abū Madd, Ra's, *Si. Arabia* **70 E3** 24 50N 37 7 E
Abu Matariq, *Sudan* **81 E2** 10 59N 26 9 E
Abu Mendi, *Ethiopia* **81 E4** 11 48N 35 42 E
Abū Mūsā, *U.A.E.* **71 E7** 25 52N 55 3 E
Abū Qaşr, *Si. Arabia* **70 D3** 30 21N 38 34 E
Abu Qir, *Egypt* **80 H7** 31 18N 30 0 E
Abu Qireiya, *Egypt* **80 C4** 24 5N 35 28 E
Abu Qurqâs, *Egypt* **80 B3** 28 1N 30 44 E
Abu Şafāt, W. →, *Jordan* **75 E5** 30 24N 36 7 E
Abu Shagara, Ras, *Sudan* **80 C4** 21 4N 37 19 E
Abu Shanab, *Sudan* **81 E2** 13 58N 27 49 E
Abu Simbel, *Egypt* **80 C3** 22 18N 31 40 E
Abū Şukhayr, *Iraq* **70 D5** 31 54N 44 30 E
Abu Sultân, *Egypt* **80 H8** 30 24N 32 21 E
Abu Tabari, *Sudan* **80 D2** 17 32N 28 32 E
Abu Tig, *Egypt* **80 B3** 27 4N 31 15 E
Abu Tiga, *Sudan* **81 E3** 12 47N 34 12 E
Abu Tineitin, *Sudan* **81 E3** 14 24N 31 1 E
Abu Uruq, *Sudan* **81 D3** 15 52N 30 25 E
Abu Zabad, *Sudan* **81 E2** 12 25N 29 10 E
Abū Z̧āby, *U.A.E.* **71 E7** 24 28N 54 22 E
Abū Zeydābād, *Iran* **71 C6** 33 54N 51 45 E
Abuja, *Nigeria* **83 D6** 9 16N 7 2 E
Abukuma-Gawa →, *Japan* **54 E10** 38 6N 140 52 E
Abukuma-Sammyaku, *Japan* **54 F10** 37 30N 140 45 E
Abunã, *Brazil* **124 E5** 9 40 S 65 20W
Abunã →, *Brazil* **124 E5** 9 41 S 65 20W
Abune Yosef, *Ethiopia* **81 E4** 12 5N 39 12 E
Aburo, *Dem. Rep. of the Congo* **86 B3** 2 4N 30 53 E
Abut Hd., *N.Z.* **91 K3** 43 7 S 170 15 E
Abuye Meda, *Ethiopia* **81 E4** 10 30N 39 49 E
Abwong, *Sudan* **81 F3** 9 2N 32 14 E
Åby, *Sweden* **11 F10** 58 40N 16 10 E
Aby, Lagune, *Ivory C.* **82 D4** 5 15N 3 14W
Abyad, *Sudan* **81 E2** 13 47N 26 24 E
Åbybro, *Denmark* **11 G3** 57 10N 9 44 E
Acadia National Park, *U.S.A.* **109 C11** 44 20N 68 13W
Açailândia, *Brazil* **125 D9** 4 57 S 47 0W
Acajutla, *El Salv.* **120 D2** 13 36N 89 50W
Acámbaro, *Mexico* **118 D4** 20 0N 100 40W
Acanthus, *Greece* **40 F7** 40 27N 23 47 E
Acaponeta, *Mexico* **118 C3** 22 30N 105 20W
Acapulco, *Mexico* **119 D5** 16 51N 99 56W
Acarai, Serra, *Brazil* **124 C7** 1 50N 57 50W
Acarigua, *Venezuela* **124 B5** 9 33N 69 12W
Acatlán, *Mexico* **119 D5** 18 10N 98 3W
Acayucan, *Mexico* **119 D6** 17 59N 94 58W
Accéglio, *Italy* **28 D4** 44 28N 7 0 E
Accomac, *U.S.A.* **108 G8** 37 43N 75 40W
Accous, *France* **20 E3** 43 0N 0 36W
Accra, *Ghana* **83 D4** 5 35N 0 6W
Accrington, *U.K.* **12 D5** 53 45N 2 22W
Acebal, *Argentina* **126 C3** 33 20 S 60 50W
Aceh □, *Indonesia* **62 D1** 4 15N 97 30 E
Acerra, *Italy* **31 B7** 40 57N 14 22 E
Aceuchal, *Spain* **35 G4** 38 39N 6 30W
Achalpur, *India* **66 J10** 21 22N 77 32 E
Acheng, *China* **57 B14** 45 30N 126 58 E
Achenkirch, *Austria* **26 D4** 47 32N 11 45 E
Achensee, *Austria* **26 D4** 47 26N 11 45 E
Acher, *India* **68 H5** 23 10N 72 32 E
Achern, *Germany* **25 G4** 48 37N 8 4 E
Achill Hd., *Ireland* **15 C1** 53 58N 10 15W
Achill I., *Ireland* **15 C1** 53 58N 10 1W
Achim, *Germany* **24 B5** 53 1N 9 3 E
Achinsk, *Russia* **51 D10** 56 20N 90 20 E
Acıgöl, *Turkey* **39 D11** 37 50N 29 50 E
Acıpayam, *Turkey* **39 D11** 37 26N 29 22 E
Acireale, *Italy* **31 E8** 37 37N 15 10 E
Ackerman, *U.S.A.* **113 J10** 33 19N 89 11W
Acklins I., *Bahamas* **121 B5** 22 30N 74 0W
Acme, *Canada* **104 C6** 51 33N 113 30W
Acme, *U.S.A.* **110 F5** 40 8N 79 26W
Aconcagua, Cerro, *Argentina* **126 C2** 32 39 S 70 0W
Aconquija, Mt., *Argentina* **126 B2** 27 0 S 66 0W
Açores, Is. dos = Azores, *Atl. Oc.* **78 A1** 38 44N 29 0W
Acornhoek, *S. Africa* **89 C5** 24 37 S 31 2 E
Acquapendente, *Italy* **29 F8** 42 44N 11 52 E
Acquasanta Terme, *Italy* **29 F10** 42 46N 13 24 E
Acquasparta, *Italy* **29 F9** 42 41N 12 33 E
Acquaviva delle Fonti, *Italy* **31 B9** 40 54N 16 50 E
Ácqui Terme, *Italy* **28 D5** 44 41N 8 28 E
Acraman, L., *Australia* **95 E2** 32 2 S 135 23 E
Acre = 'Akko, *Israel* **75 C4** 32 55N 35 4 E
Acre □, *Brazil* **124 E4** 9 1 S 71 0W
Acre →, *Brazil* **124 E5** 8 45 S 67 22W
Acri, *Italy* **31 C9** 39 29N 16 23 E
Acs, *Hungary* **42 C3** 47 42N 18 2 E
Actium, *Greece* **38 C2** 38 57N 20 45 E
Acton, *Canada* **110 C4** 43 38N 80 3W
Acuña, *Mexico* **118 B4** 29 18N 100 55W
Ad Dammām, *Si. Arabia* **71 E6** 26 20N 50 5 E
Ad Dāmūr, *Lebanon* **75 B4** 33 44N 35 27 E
Ad Dawādimī, *Si. Arabia* **70 E5** 24 35N 44 15 E
Ad Dawḩah, *Qatar* **71 E6** 25 15N 51 35 E
Ad Dawr, *Iraq* **70 C4** 34 27N 43 47 E
Ad Dir'īyah, *Si. Arabia* **70 E5** 24 44N 46 35 E
Ad Dīwānīyah, *Iraq* **70 D5** 32 0N 45 0 E
Ad Dujayl, *Iraq* **70 C5** 33 51N 44 14 E
Ad Duwayd, *Si. Arabia* **70 D4** 30 15N 42 17 E
Ada, *Ghana* **83 D5** 5 44N 0 40 E
Ada, *Serbia, Yug.* **42 E5** 45 49N 20 9 E
Ada, *Minn., U.S.A.* **112 B6** 47 18N 96 31W
Ada, *Okla., U.S.A.* **113 H6** 34 46N 96 41W
Adabiya, *Egypt* **75 F1** 29 53N 32 28 E
Adair, C., *Canada* **101 A12** 71 31N 71 24W
Adaja →, *Spain* **34 D6** 41 32N 4 52W
Adak I., *U.S.A.* **100 C2** 51 45N 176 45W
Adamaoua, Massif de l', *Cameroon* **83 D7** 7 20N 12 20 E
Adamawa □, *Nigeria* **83 D7** 9 20N 12 30 E
Adamawa Highlands = Adamaoua, Massif de l', *Cameroon* **83 D7** 7 20N 12 20 E
Adamello, Mte., *Italy* **28 B7** 46 9N 10 30 E
Adami Tulu, *Ethiopia* **81 F4** 7 53N 38 41 E
Adaminaby, *Australia* **95 F4** 36 0 S 148 45 E
Adams, *Mass., U.S.A.* **111 D11** 42 38N 73 7W
Adams, *N.Y., U.S.A.* **111 C8** 43 49N 76 1W
Adams, *Wis., U.S.A.* **112 D10** 43 57N 89 49W
Adam's Bridge, *Sri Lanka* **66 Q11** 9 15N 79 40 E
Adams L., *Canada* **104 C5** 51 10N 119 40W
Adams Mt., *U.S.A.* **116 D5** 46 12N 121 30W
Adam's Peak, *Sri Lanka* **66 R12** 6 48N 80 30 E
Adamuz, *Spain* **35 G6** 38 2N 4 32W
Adana, *Turkey* **70 B2** 37 0N 35 16 E
Adanero, *Spain* **34 E6** 40 56N 4 36W
Adapazarı = Sakarya, *Turkey* **72 B4** 40 48N 30 25 E
Adar Gwagwa, J., *Sudan* **80 C4** 22 15N 35 20 E
Adarama, *Sudan* **81 D3** 17 10N 34 52 E
Adare, C., *Antarctica* **5 D11** 71 0 S 171 0 E
Adarte, *Eritrea* **81 E5** 13 18N 42 8 E
Adaut, *Indonesia* **63 F8** 8 8 S 131 7 E
Adavale, *Australia* **95 D3** 25 52 S 144 32 E
Adda →, *Italy* **28 C6** 45 8N 9 53 E
Addis Ababa = Addis Abeba, *Ethiopia* **81 F4** 9 2N 38 42 E
Addis Abeba, *Ethiopia* **81 F4** 9 2N 38 42 E
Addis Alem, *Ethiopia* **81 F4** 9 0N 38 17 E
Addis Zemen, *Ethiopia* **81 E4** 12 7N 37 47 E
Addison, *U.S.A.* **110 D7** 42 1N 77 14W
Addo, *S. Africa* **88 E4** 33 32 S 25 45 E
Adebour, *Niger* **83 C7** 13 17N 11 50 E
Ādeh, *Iran* **70 B5** 37 42N 45 11 E
Adel, *U.S.A.* **109 K4** 31 8N 83 25W
Adelaide, *Australia* **95 E2** 34 52 S 138 30 E
Adelaide, *Bahamas* **120 A4** 25 4N 77 31W
Adelaide, *S. Africa* **88 E4** 32 42 S 26 20 E
Adelaide I., *Antarctica* **5 C17** 67 15 S 68 30W
Adelaide Pen., *Canada* **100 B10** 68 15N 97 30W
Adelaide River, *Australia* **92 B5** 13 15 S 131 7 E
Adelanto, *U.S.A.* **117 L9** 34 35N 117 22W
Adele I., *Australia* **92 C3** 15 32 S 123 9 E
Adélie, Terre, *Antarctica* **5 C10** 68 0 S 140 0 E
Adélie Land = Adélie, Terre, *Antarctica* **5 C10** 68 0 S 140 0 E
Ademuz, *Spain* **32 E3** 40 5N 1 13W
Aden = Al 'Adan, *Yemen* **74 E4** 12 45N 45 0 E
Aden, G. of, *Asia* **74 E4** 12 30N 47 30 E
Adendorp, *S. Africa* **88 E3** 32 15 S 24 30 E
Aderbissinat, *Niger* **83 B6** 15 34N 7 54 E
Adh Dhayd, *U.A.E.* **71 E7** 25 17N 55 53 E
Adhoi, *India* **68 H4** 23 26N 70 32 E
Adi, *Indonesia* **63 E8** 4 15 S 133 30 E
Adi Arkai, *Ethiopia* **81 E4** 13 35N 37 57 E
Adi Daro, *Ethiopia* **81 E4** 14 20N 38 14 E
Adi Keyih, *Eritrea* **81 E4** 14 51N 39 22 E
Adi Kwala, *Eritrea* **81 E4** 14 38N 38 48 E
Adi Ugri, *Eritrea* **81 E4** 14 58N 38 48 E
Adieu, C., *Australia* **93 F5** 32 0 S 132 10 E
Adieu Pt., *Australia* **92 C3** 15 14 S 124 35 E
Adigala, *Ethiopia* **81 E5** 10 24N 42 15 E
Adige →, *Italy* **29 C9** 45 9N 12 20 E
Adigrat, *Ethiopia* **81 E4** 14 20N 39 26 E
Adıgüzel Barajı, *Turkey* **39 C11** 38 13N 29 14 E
Adilabad, *India* **66 K11** 19 33N 78 20 E
Adilcevaz, *Turkey* **73 C10** 38 47N 42 43 E
Adirondack Mts., *U.S.A.* **111 C10** 44 0N 74 0W
Adıyaman, *Turkey* **73 D8** 37 45N 38 16 E
Adjohon, *Benin* **83 D5** 6 41N 2 32 E
Adjud, *Romania* **43 D12** 46 7N 27 10 E
Adjumani, *Uganda* **86 B3** 3 20N 31 50 E
Adlavik Is., *Canada* **103 A8** 55 0N 58 40W
Adler, *Russia* **49 J4** 43 28N 39 52 E
Admer, *Algeria* **83 A6** 20 21N 5 27 E
Admiralty G., *Australia* **92 B4** 14 20 S 125 55 E
Admiralty I., *U.S.A.* **104 B2** 57 30N 134 30W
Admiralty Is., *Papua N. G.* **96 H6** 2 0 S 147 0 E
Ado, *Nigeria* **83 D5** 6 36N 2 56 E
Ado-Ekiti, *Nigeria* **83 D6** 7 38N 5 12 E
Adok, *Sudan* **81 F3** 8 10N 30 20 E
Adola, *Ethiopia* **81 E5** 11 14N 41 44 E
Adonara, *Indonesia* **63 F6** 8 15 S 123 5 E
Adoni, *India* **66 M10** 15 33N 77 18 E
Adony, *Hungary* **42 C3** 47 6N 18 52 E
Adour →, *France* **20 E2** 43 32N 1 32W
Adra, *India* **69 H12** 23 30N 86 42 E
Adra, *Spain* **35 J7** 36 43N 3 3W
Adrano, *Italy* **31 E7** 37 40N 14 50 E
Adrar, *Mauritania* **78 D3** 20 30N 7 30 E
Adrar des Iforas, *Algeria* **78 C5** 27 51N 0 11 E
Ádria, *Italy* **29 C9** 45 3N 12 3 E
Adrian, *Mich., U.S.A.* **108 E3** 41 54N 84 2W
Adrian, *Tex., U.S.A.* **113 H3** 35 16N 102 40W
Adriatic Sea, *Medit. S.* **6 G9** 43 0N 16 0 E
Adua, *Indonesia* **63 E7** 1 45 S 129 50 E
Adwa, *Ethiopia* **81 E4** 14 15N 38 52 E
Adygea □, *Russia* **49 H5** 45 0N 40 0 E
Adzhar Republic = Ajaria □, *Georgia* **49 K6** 41 30N 42 0 E
Adzopé, *Ivory C.* **82 D4** 6 7N 3 49W
Ægean Sea, *Medit. S.* **39 C7** 38 30N 25 0 E
Aerhtai Shan, *Mongolia* **60 B4** 46 40N 92 45 E
Ærø, *Denmark* **11 K4** 54 52N 10 25 E
Ærøskøbing, *Denmark* **11 K4** 54 53N 10 24 E
Aëtós, *Greece* **38 D3** 37 15N 21 50 E
'Afak, *Iraq* **70 C5** 32 4N 45 15 E
Afándou, *Greece* **36 C10** 36 18N 28 12 E
Afghanistan ■, *Asia* **66 C4** 33 0N 65 0 E
Afikpo, *Nigeria* **83 D6** 5 53N 7 54 E
Aflou, *Algeria* **78 B6** 34 7N 2 3 E
Afragóla, *Italy* **31 B7** 40 55N 14 18 E
Afram →, *Ghana* **83 D4** 7 0N 0 52W
Afrera, *Ethiopia* **81 E5** 13 16N 41 5 E
Africa **76 E6** 10 0N 20 0 E
'Afrīn, *Syria* **70 B3** 36 32N 36 50 E
Afşin, *Turkey* **72 C7** 38 14N 36 55 E
Afton, *N.Y., U.S.A.* **111 D9** 42 14N 75 32W
Afton, *Wyo., U.S.A.* **114 E8** 42 44N 110 56W
Afuá, *Brazil* **125 D8** 0 15 S 50 20W
'Afula, *Israel* **75 C4** 32 37N 35 17 E
Afyon, *Turkey* **39 C12** 38 45N 30 33 E
Afyon □, *Turkey* **39 C12** 38 25N 30 30 E
Afyonkarahisar = Afyon, *Turkey* **39 C12** 38 45N 30 33 E
Aga, *Egypt* **80 H7** 30 55N 31 10 E
Agadès = Agadez, *Niger* **83 B6** 16 58N 7 59 E
Agadez, *Niger* **83 B6** 16 58N 7 59 E
Agadir, *Morocco* **78 B4** 30 28N 9 55W
Agaete, *Canary Is.* **37 F4** 28 6N 15 43W
Agaie, *Nigeria* **83 D6** 9 1N 6 18 E
Again, *Sudan* **81 F2** 8 28N 29 55 E
Ağapınar, *Turkey* **39 B12** 39 48N 30 47 E
Agar, *India* **68 H7** 23 40N 76 2 E
Agaro, *Ethiopia* **81 F4** 7 50N 36 38 E
Agartala, *India* **67 H17** 23 50N 91 23 E
Agăş, *Romania* **43 D11** 46 28N 26 15 E
Agassiz, *Canada* **104 D4** 49 14N 121 46W
Agats, *Indonesia* **63 F9** 5 33 S 138 0 E
Agawam, *U.S.A.* **111 D12** 42 5N 72 37W
Agbélouvé, *Togo* **83 D5** 6 35N 1 14 E
Agboville, *Ivory C.* **82 D4** 5 55N 4 15W
Ağcabädi, *Azerbaijan* **49 K8** 40 5N 47 27 E
Ağdam, *Azerbaijan* **49 L8** 40 0N 46 58 E
Ağdaş, *Azerbaijan* **49 K8** 40 44N 47 22 E
Agde, *France* **20 E7** 43 19N 3 28 E
Agde, C. d', *France* **20 E7** 43 16N 3 28 E
Agdzhabedi = Ağcabädi, *Azerbaijan* **49 K8** 40 5N 47 27 E
Agen, *France* **20 D4** 44 12N 0 38 E
Agerbæk, *Denmark* **11 J2** 55 36N 8 48 E
Agersø, *Denmark* **11 J5** 55 13N 11 12 E
Ageyevo, *Russia* **46 E9** 54 10N 36 27 E
Āgh Kand, *Iran* **71 B6** 37 15N 48 4 E
Aghireşu, *Romania* **43 D8** 46 53N 23 15 E
Aginskoye, *Russia* **51 D12** 51 6N 114 32 E
Ağlasun, *Turkey* **39 D12** 37 39N 30 31 E
Agly →, *France* **20 F7** 42 46N 3 3 E
Agnew, *Australia* **93 E3** 28 1 S 120 31 E
Agnibilékrou, *Ivory C.* **82 D4** 7 10N 3 11W
Agnita, *Romania* **43 E9** 45 59N 24 40 E
Agnone, *Italy* **29 G11** 41 48N 14 22 E
Agofie, *Ghana* **83 D5** 8 27N 0 15 E
Agogna →, *Italy* **28 C5** 45 4N 8 54 E
Agogo, *Sudan* **81 F2** 7 50N 28 45 E
Agön, *Sweden* **10 C11** 61 34N 17 23 E
Agon Coutainville, *France* **18 C5** 49 2N 1 34W
Ágordo, *Italy* **29 B9** 46 18N 12 2 E
Agori, *India* **69 G10** 24 33N 82 57 E
Agouna, *Benin* **83 D5** 7 39N 1 47 E
Agout →, *France* **20 E5** 43 47N 1 41 E
Agra, *India* **68 F7** 27 17N 77 58 E
Agrakhanskiuy Poluostrov, *Russia* **49 J8** 43 42N 47 36 E
Agramunt, *Spain* **32 D6** 41 48N 1 6 E
Agreda, *Spain* **32 D3** 41 51N 1 55W
Ağri, *Turkey* **73 C10** 39 44N 43 3 E
Agri →, *Italy* **31 B9** 40 13N 16 44 E
Ağrı Dağı, *Turkey* **70 B5** 39 50N 44 15 E
Ağri Karakose = Ağri, *Turkey* **73 C10** 39 44N 43 3 E
Agriá, *Greece* **38 B5** 39 20N 23 1 E
Agrigento, *Italy* **30 E6** 37 19N 13 34 E
Agrínion, *Greece* **38 C3** 38 37N 21 27 E
Agrópoli, *Italy* **31 B7** 40 21N 14 59 E
Ağstafa, *Azerbaijan* **49 K7** 41 7N 45 27 E
Agua Caliente, *Baja Calif., Mexico* **117 N10** 32 29N 116 59W
Agua Caliente, *Sinaloa, Mexico* **118 B3** 26 30N 108 20W
Agua Caliente Springs, *U.S.A.* **117 N10** 32 56N 116 19W
Água Clara, *Brazil* **125 H8** 20 25 S 52 45W
Agua Hechicero, *Mexico* **117 N10** 32 26N 116 14W
Agua Prieta, *Mexico* **118 A3** 31 20N 109 32W
Aguadilla, *Puerto Rico* **121 C6** 18 26N 67 10W
Aguadulce, *Panama* **120 E3** 8 15N 80 32W
Aguanga, *U.S.A.* **117 M10** 33 27N 116 51W
Aguanish, *Canada* **103 B7** 50 14N 62 2W
Aguanus →, *Canada* **103 B7** 50 13N 62 5W
Aguapey →, *Argentina* **126 B4** 29 7 S 56 36W
Aguaray Guazú →, *Paraguay* **126 A4** 24 47 S 57 19W
Aguarico →, *Ecuador* **124 D3** 0 59 S 75 11W
Aguas →, *Spain* **32 D4** 41 20N 0 30W
Aguas Blancas, *Chile* **126 A2** 24 15 S 69 55W
Aguas Calientes, Sierra de, *Argentina* **126 B2** 25 26 S 66 40W
Aguascalientes, *Mexico* **118 C4** 21 53N 102 12W
Aguascalientes □, *Mexico* **118 C4** 22 0N 102 20W
Agudo, *Spain* **35 G6** 38 59N 4 52W
Águeda, *Portugal* **34 E2** 40 34N 8 27W
Agueda →, *Spain* **34 D4** 41 2N 6 56W
Aguelhok, *Mali* **83 B5** 19 29N 0 52 E
Aguié, *Niger* **83 C6** 13 31N 7 46 E
Aguilafuente, *Spain* **34 D6** 41 13N 4 7W
Aguilar, *Spain* **35 H6** 37 31N 4 40W
Aguilar de Campóo, *Spain* **34 C6** 42 47N 4 15W
Aguilares, *Argentina* **126 B2** 27 26 S 65 35W
Aguilas, *Spain* **33 H3** 37 23N 1 35W
Agüimes, *Canary Is.* **37 G4** 27 58N 15 27W
Aguja, C. de la, *Colombia* **122 B3** 11 18N 74 12W
Agulaa, *Ethiopia* **81 E4** 13 40N 39 40 E
Agulhas, C., *S. Africa* **88 E3** 34 52 S 20 0 E
Agulo, *Canary Is.* **37 F2** 28 11N 17 12W
Agung, *Indonesia* **62 F5** 8 20 S 115 28 E
Agur, *Uganda* **86 B3** 2 28N 32 55 E
Agusan →, *Phil.* **61 G6** 9 0N 125 30 E
Ağva, *Turkey* **41 E13** 41 8N 29 51 E
Agvali, *Russia* **49 J8** 42 36N 46 8 E
Aha Mts., *Botswana* **88 B3** 19 45 S 21 0 E
Ahaggar, *Algeria* **78 D7** 23 0N 6 30 E
Ahamansu, *Ghana* **83 D5** 7 38N 0 35 E
Ahar, *Iran* **70 B5** 38 35N 47 0 E
Ahat, *Turkey* **39 C11** 38 39N 29 47 E
Ahaus, *Germany* **24 C2** 52 4N 7 0 E
Ahipara B., *N.Z.* **91 F4** 35 5 S 173 5 E
Ahir Dağı, *Turkey* **39 C12** 38 45N 30 10 E
Ahiri, *India* **66 K12** 19 30N 80 0 E
Ahlat, *Turkey* **73 C10** 38 45N 42 29 E
Ahlen, *Germany* **24 D3** 51 45N 7 53 E
Ahmad Wal, *Pakistan* **68 E1** 29 18N 65 58 E
Ahmadabad, *India* **68 H5** 23 0N 72 40 E
Aḩmadābād, *Khorāsān, Iran* **71 C9** 35 3N 60 50 E
Aḩmadābād, *Khorāsān, Iran* **71 C8** 35 49N 59 42 E
Aḩmadī, *Iran* **71 E8** 27 56N 56 42 E
Ahmadnagar, *India* **66 K9** 19 7N 74 46 E
Ahmadpur, *Pakistan* **68 E4** 29 12N 71 10 E
Ahmadpur Lamma, *Pakistan* **68 E4** 28 19N 70 3 E
Ahmar, *Ethiopia* **81 F5** 9 20N 41 15 E
Ahmedabad = Ahmadabad, *India* **68 H5** 23 0N 72 40 E
Ahmednagar = Ahmadnagar, *India* **66 K9** 19 7N 74 46 E
Ahmetbey, *Turkey* **41 E11** 41 26N 27 34 E
Ahmetler, *Turkey* **39 C11** 38 28N 29 5 E
Ahmetli, *Turkey* **39 C9** 38 32N 27 57 E
Ahoada, *Nigeria* **83 D6** 5 8N 6 36 E
Ahome, *Mexico* **118 B3** 25 55N 109 11W
Ahoskie, *U.S.A.* **109 G7** 36 17N 76 59W
Ahr →, *Germany* **24 E3** 50 32N 7 16 E
Ahram, *Iran* **71 D6** 28 52N 51 16 E
Ahrax Pt., *Malta* **36 D1** 35 59N 14 22 E
Ahrensbök, *Germany* **24 A6** 54 2N 10 35 E
Ahrensburg, *Germany* **24 B6** 53 40N 10 13 E
Āhū, *Iran* **71 C6** 34 33N 50 2 E
Ahuachapán, *El Salv.* **120 D2** 13 54N 89 52W
Ahun, *France* **19 F9** 46 4N 2 5 E
Åhus, *Sweden* **11 J8** 55 56N 14 18 E
Ahvāz, *Iran* **71 D6** 31 20N 48 40 E
Ahvenanmaa = Åland, *Finland* **9 F19** 60 15N 20 0 E
Aḩwar, *Yemen* **74 E4** 13 30N 46 40 E
Ahzar →, *Mali* **83 B5** 15 30N 3 20 E
Ai →, *India* **69 F14** 26 26N 90 44 E
Ai-Ais, *Namibia* **88 D2** 27 54 S 17 59 E
Aichach, *Germany* **25 G7** 48 27N 11 8 E
Aichi □, *Japan* **55 G8** 35 0N 137 15 E
Aigle, *Switz.* **25 J2** 46 18N 6 58 E
Aignay-le-Duc, *France* **19 E11** 47 40N 4 43 E
Aigoual, Mt., *France* **20 D7** 44 8N 3 35 E
Aigre, *France* **20 C4** 45 54N 0 1 E
Aigua, *Uruguay* **127 C5** 34 13 S 54 46W
Aigueperse, *France* **19 F10** 46 3N 3 13 E
Aigues →, *France* **21 D8** 44 7N 4 43 E
Aigues-Mortes, *France* **21 E8** 43 35N 4 12 E
Aigues-Mortes, G. d', *France* **21 E8** 43 31N 4 3 E
Aiguilles, *France* **21 D10** 44 47N 6 51 E
Aiguillon, *France* **20 D4** 44 18N 0 21 E
Aigurande, *France* **19 F8** 46 27N 1 49 E
Aihui, *China* **60 A7** 50 10N 127 30 E
Aija, *Peru* **124 E3** 9 50 S 77 45W
Aikawa, *Japan* **54 E9** 38 2N 138 15 E
Aiken, *U.S.A.* **109 J5** 33 34N 81 43W
Ailao Shan, *China* **58 F3** 24 0N 101 20 E
Aileron, *Australia* **94 C1** 22 39 S 133 20 E
Aillant-sur-Tholon, *France* **19 E10** 47 52N 3 20 E
Aillik, *Canada* **103 A8** 55 11N 59 18W
Ailsa Craig, *U.K.* **14 F3** 55 15N 5 6W
'Ailūn, *Jordan* **75 C4** 32 18N 35 47 E
Aim, *Russia* **51 D14** 59 0N 133 55 E
Aimere, *Indonesia* **63 F6** 8 45 S 121 3 E
Aimogasta, *Argentina* **126 B2** 28 33 S 66 50W
Ain □, *France* **19 F12** 46 5N 5 20 E
Ain →, *France* **21 C9** 45 45N 5 11 E
Aïn Ben Tili, *Mauritania* **78 C4** 25 59N 9 27W
Ain Dalla, *Egypt* **80 B2** 27 20N 27 23 E
Ain el Mafki, *Egypt* **80 B2** 27 30N 28 15 E
Ain Girba, *Egypt* **80 B2** 29 20N 25 14 E
Ain Murr, *Sudan* **80 C2** 21 50N 25 9 E
Ain Qeiqab, *Egypt* **80 B1** 29 42N 24 55 E
Aïn Sefra, *Algeria* **78 B5** 32 47N 0 37W
Ain Sheikh Murzûk, *Egypt* **80 B2** 26 47N 27 45 E
Ain Sudr, *Egypt* **75 F2** 29 50N 33 6 E
Ain Sukhna, *Egypt* **80 J8** 29 32N 32 20 E
Ain Zeitûn, *Egypt* **80 B2** 29 10N 25 48 E

Alexandria

Ainaži, *Latvia* **9 H21** 57 50N 24 24 E
Aínos Óros, *Greece* **38 C2** 38 10N 20 35 E
Ainsworth, *U.S.A.* **112 D5** 42 33N 99 52W
Aiquile, *Bolivia* **124 G5** 18 10 S 65 10W
Aïr, *Niger* **83 B6** 18 30N 8 0 E
Air Force I., *Canada* **101 B12** 67 58N 74 5W
Air Hitam, *Malaysia* **65 M4** 1 55N 103 11 E
Airaines, *France* **19 C8** 49 58N 1 55 E
Airdrie, *Canada* **104 C6** 51 18N 114 2W
Airdrie, *U.K.* **14 F5** 55 52N 3 57W
Aire →, *France* **19 C11** 49 18N 4 49 E
Aire →, *U.K.* **12 D7** 53 43N 0 55W
Aire, I. de l', *Spain* **37 B11** 39 48N 4 16 E
Aire-sur-la-Lys, *France* **19 B9** 50 37N 2 22 E
Aire-sur-l'Adour, *France* **20 E3** 43 42N 0 15W
Airlie Beach, *Australia* **94 C4** 20 16 S 148 43 E
Airvault, *France* **18 F6** 46 50N 0 8W
Aisch →, *Germany* **25 F6** 49 49N 10 58 E
Aisne □, *France* **19 C10** 49 42N 3 40 E
Aisne →, *France* **19 C9** 49 26N 2 50 E
Ait, *India* **69 G8** 25 54N 79 14 E
Aitana, Sierra de, *Spain* **33 G4** 38 35N 0 24W
Aitkin, *U.S.A.* **112 B8** 46 32N 93 42W
Aitolía Kai Akarnanía □, *Greece* **38 C3** 38 45N 21 18 E
Aitolikón, *Greece* **38 C3** 38 26N 21 21 E
Aiud, *Romania* **43 D8** 46 19N 23 44 E
Aix-en-Provence, *France* **21 E9** 43 32N 5 27 E
Aix-la-Chapelle = Aachen, *Germany* **24 E2** 50 45N 6 6 E
Aix-les-Bains, *France* **21 C9** 45 41N 5 53 E
Aixe-sur-Vienne, *France* **20 C5** 45 47N 1 9 E
Áíyina, *Greece* **38 D5** 37 45N 23 26 E
Aiyínion, *Greece* **40 F6** 40 28N 22 28 E
Aíyion, *Greece* **38 C4** 38 15N 22 5 E
Aizawl, *India* **67 H18** 23 40N 92 44 E
Aizenay, *France* **18 F5** 46 44N 1 38W
Aizkraukle, *Latvia* **9 H21** 56 36N 25 11 E
Aizpute, *Latvia* **9 H19** 56 43N 21 40 E
Aizuwakamatsu, *Japan* **54 F9** 37 30N 139 56 E
Ajaccio, *France* **21 G12** 41 55N 8 40 E
Ajaccio, G. d', *France* **21 G12** 41 52N 8 40 E
Ajaigarh, *India* **69 G9** 24 52N 80 16 E
Ajalpan, *Mexico* **119 D5** 18 22N 97 15W
Ajanta Ra., *India* **66 J9** 20 28N 75 50 E
Ajari Rep. = Ajaria □, *Georgia* **49 K6** 41 30N 42 0 E
Ajaria □, *Georgia* **49 K6** 41 30N 42 0 E
Ajax, *Canada* **110 C5** 43 50N 79 1W
Ajdâbiyâ, *Libya* **79 B10** 30 54N 20 4 E
Ajdovščina, *Slovenia* **29 C10** 45 54N 13 54 E
Ajibar, *Ethiopia* **81 E4** 10 35N 38 36 E
Ajka, *Hungary* **42 C2** 47 4N 17 31 E
'Ajmān, *U.A.E.* **71 E7** 25 25N 55 30 E
Ajmer, *India* **68 F6** 26 28N 74 37 E
Ajnala, *India* **68 D6** 31 50N 74 48 E
Ajo, *U.S.A.* **115 K7** 32 22N 112 52W
Ajo, C. de, *Spain* **34 B7** 43 31N 3 35W
Ajok, *Sudan* **81 F2** 9 15N 28 28 E
Ajuy, *Phil.* **61 F5** 11 10N 123 1 E
Ak Dağ, *Turkey* **39 E11** 36 30N 29 32 E
Ak Dağları, *Muğla, Turkey* **39 E11** 36 30N 29 30 E
Ak Dağları, *Sivas, Turkey* **72 C7** 39 32N 36 12 E
Akaba, *Togo* **83 D5** 8 10N 1 2 E
Akabira, *Japan* **54 C11** 43 33N 142 5 E
Akaki Beseka, *Ethiopia* **81 F4** 8 55N 38 45 E
Akala, *Sudan* **81 D4** 15 39N 36 13 E
Akamas □, *Cyprus* **36 D11** 35 3N 32 18 E
Akanthou, *Cyprus* **36 D12** 35 22N 33 45 E
Akarca, *Turkey* **39 C11** 38 35N 29 35 E
Akaroa, *N.Z.* **91 K4** 43 49 S 172 59 E
Akasha, *Sudan* **80 C3** 21 10N 30 32 E
Akashi, *Japan* **55 G7** 34 45N 134 58 E
Akbarpur, *Bihar, India* **69 G10** 24 39N 83 58 E
Akbarpur, *Ut. P., India* **69 F10** 26 25N 82 32 E
Akçaabat, *Turkey* **73 B8** 41 1N 39 34 E
Akçadağ, *Turkey* **72 C7** 38 27N 37 43 E
Akçakale, *Turkey* **73 D8** 36 41N 38 56 E
Akçakoca, *Turkey* **72 B4** 41 5N 31 8 E
Akçaova, *Turkey* **41 E13** 41 3N 29 57 E
Akçay, *Turkey* **39 E11** 36 36N 29 45 E
Akçay →, *Turkey* **39 D10** 37 50N 28 15 E
Akdağ, *Turkey* **39 C8** 38 33N 26 30 E
Akdağmadeni, *Turkey* **72 C6** 39 39N 35 53 E
Akelamo, *Indonesia* **63 D7** 1 35N 129 40 E
Åkers styckebruk, *Sweden* **10 E11** 59 15N 17 5 E
Åkersberga, *Sweden* **10 E12** 59 29N 18 18 E
Aketi, *Dem. Rep. of the Congo* **84 D4** 2 38N 23 47 E
Akhaïa □, *Greece* **38 C3** 38 5N 21 45 E
Akhalkalaki, *Georgia* **49 K6** 41 27N 43 25 E
Akhaltsikhe, *Georgia* **49 K6** 41 40N 43 0 E
Akharnaí, *Greece* **38 C5** 38 5N 23 44 E
Akhelóös →, *Greece* **38 C3** 38 19N 21 7 E
Akhendriá, *Greece* **39 G7** 34 59N 25 13 E
Akhisar, *Turkey* **39 C9** 38 56N 27 48 E
Akhladhókambos, *Greece* **38 D4** 37 31N 22 35 E
Akhmîm, *Egypt* **80 B3** 26 31N 31 47 E
Akhnur, *India* **69 C6** 32 52N 74 45 E
Akhtopol, *Bulgaria* **41 D11** 42 6N 27 56 E
Akhtuba →, *Russia* **49 G8** 47 41N 46 55 E
Akhtubinsk, *Russia* **49 F8** 48 13N 46 7 E
Akhty, *Russia* **49 K8** 41 30N 47 45 E
Akhtyrka = Okhtyrka, *Ukraine* **47 G8** 50 25N 35 0 E
Aki, *Japan* **55 H6** 33 30N 133 54 E
Akimiski I., *Canada* **102 B3** 52 50N 81 30W
Akimovka, *Ukraine* **47 J8** 46 44N 35 0 E
Åkirkeby, *Denmark* **11 J8** 55 4N 14 55 E
Akita, *Japan* **54 E10** 39 45N 140 7 E
Akita □, *Japan* **54 E10** 39 40N 140 30 E
Akjoujt, *Mauritania* **82 B2** 19 45N 14 15W
Akka, *Mali* **82 B4** 15 24N 4 11W
Akkaya Tepesi, *Turkey* **39 D11** 37 25N 29 38 E
Akkeshi, *Japan* **54 C12** 43 2N 144 51 E
'Akko, *Israel* **75 C4** 32 55N 35 4 E
Akköy, *Turkey* **39 D9** 37 29N 27 15 E
Aklampa, *Benin* **83 D5** 8 15N 2 10 E
Aklavik, *Canada* **100 B6** 68 12N 135 0W
Aklera, *India* **68 G7** 24 26N 76 32 E
Akmenė, *Lithuania* **44 B9** 56 15N 22 45 E
Akmenrags, *Latvia* **44 B8** 56 50N 21 4 E
Akmolinsk = Astana, *Kazakhstan* **50 D8** 51 10N 71 30 E
Akmonte = Almonte, *Spain* **35 H4** 37 13N 6 38W
Akō, *Japan* **55 G7** 34 45N 134 24 E
Ako, *Nigeria* **83 C7** 10 19N 10 48 E
Akôbô, *Sudan* **81 F3** 7 47N 33 1 E
Akobo →, *Ethiopia* **81 F3** 7 48N 33 3 E
Akola, *India* **66 J10** 20 42N 77 2 E
Akonolinga, *Cameroon* **83 E7** 3 50N 12 18 E
Akor, *Mali* **82 C3** 14 59N 6 58W
Akordat, *Eritrea* **81 D4** 15 30N 37 40 E
Akosombo Dam, *Ghana* **83 D5** 6 20N 0 5 E
Akot, *Sudan* **81 F3** 6 31N 30 9 E
Akoupé, *Ivory C.* **82 D4** 6 23N 3 54W
Akpatok I., *Canada* **101 B13** 60 25N 68 8W
Åkrahamn, *Norway* **9 G11** 59 15N 5 10 E
Akranes, *Iceland* **8 D2** 64 19N 22 5W
Akreïjit, *Mauritania* **82 B3** 18 19N 9 11W
Akrítas Venétiko, Ákra, *Greece* **38 E3** 36 43N 21 54 E
Akron, *Colo., U.S.A.* **112 E3** 40 10N 103 13W
Akron, *Ohio, U.S.A.* **110 E3** 41 5N 81 31W
Akrotiri, *Cyprus* **36 E11** 34 36N 32 57 E
Akrotíri, Ákra, *Greece* **41 F9** 40 26N 25 27 E
Akrotiri Bay, *Cyprus* **36 E12** 34 35N 33 10 E
Aksai Chin, *India* **69 B8** 35 15N 79 55 E
Aksaray, *Turkey* **70 B2** 38 25N 34 2 E
Aksay, *Kazakhstan* **50 D6** 51 11N 53 0 E
Akşehir, *Turkey* **70 B1** 38 18N 31 30 E
Akşehir Gölü, *Turkey* **72 C4** 38 30N 31 25 E
Akstafa = Ağstafa, *Azerbaijan* **49 K7** 41 7N 45 27 E
Aksu, *China* **60 B3** 41 5N 80 10 E
Aksu →, *Turkey* **72 D4** 36 52N 30 57 E
Aksum, *Ethiopia* **81 E4** 14 5N 38 40 E
Aktash, *Russia* **48 C11** 55 2N 52 0 E
Aktogay, *Kazakhstan* **50 E8** 46 57N 79 40 E
Aktsyabrski, *Belarus* **47 F5** 52 38N 28 53 E
Aktyubinsk = Aqtöbe, *Kazakhstan* **50 D6** 50 17N 57 10 E
Aku, *Nigeria* **83 D6** 6 40N 7 18 E
Akure, *Nigeria* **83 D6** 7 15N 5 5 E
Akureyri, *Iceland* **8 D4** 65 40N 18 6W
Akuseki-Shima, *Japan* **55 K4** 29 27N 129 37 E
Akusha, *Russia* **49 J8** 42 18N 47 30 E
Akwa-Ibom □, *Nigeria* **83 E6** 4 30N 7 30 E
Akyab = Sittwe, *Burma* **67 J18** 20 18N 92 45 E
Akyazı, *Turkey* **72 B4** 40 40N 30 38 E
Al 'Adan, *Yemen* **74 E4** 12 45N 45 0 E
Al Aḩsā = Hasa □, *Si. Arabia* **71 E6** 25 50N 49 0 E
Al Ajfar, *Si. Arabia* **70 E4** 27 26N 43 0 E
Al Amādīyah, *Iraq* **70 B4** 37 5N 43 30 E
Al 'Amārah, *Iraq* **70 D5** 31 55N 47 15 E
Al 'Aqabah, *Jordan* **75 F4** 29 31N 35 0 E
Al Arak, *Syria* **70 C3** 34 38N 38 35 E
Al 'Aramah, *Si. Arabia* **70 E5** 25 30N 46 0 E
Al Arṭāwīyah, *Si. Arabia* **70 E5** 26 31N 45 20 E
Al 'Āşimah = 'Ammān □, *Jordan* **75 D5** 31 40N 36 30 E
Al 'Assāfīyah, *Si. Arabia* **70 D3** 28 17N 38 59 E
Al 'Ayn, *Oman* **71 E7** 24 15N 55 45 E
Al 'Ayn, *Si. Arabia* **70 E3** 25 4N 38 6 E
Al 'Aẓamīyah, *Iraq* **70 C5** 33 22N 44 22 E
Al 'Azīzīyah, *Iraq* **70 C5** 32 54N 45 4 E
Al Bāb, *Syria* **70 B3** 36 23N 37 29 E
Al Bad', *Si. Arabia* **70 D2** 28 28N 35 1 E
Al Bādī, *Iraq* **70 C4** 35 56N 41 32 E
Al Baḩrah, *Kuwait* **70 D5** 29 40N 47 52 E
Al Baḩral Mayyit = Dead Sea, *Asia* **75 D4** 31 30N 35 30 E
Al Balqā' □, *Jordan* **75 C4** 32 5N 35 45 E
Al Bārūk, J., *Lebanon* **75 B4** 33 39N 35 40 E
Al Başrah, *Iraq* **70 D5** 30 30N 47 50 E
Al Baṭḩā, *Iraq* **70 D5** 31 6N 45 53 E
Al Batrūn, *Lebanon* **75 A4** 34 15N 35 40 E
Al Bayḑā, *Libya* **79 B10** 32 50N 21 44 E
Al Biqā, *Lebanon* **75 A5** 34 10N 36 10 E
Al Bi'r, *Si. Arabia* **70 D3** 28 51N 36 16 E
Al Burayj, *Syria* **75 A5** 34 15N 36 46 E
Al Faḑilī, *Si. Arabia* **71 E6** 26 58N 49 10 E
Al Fallūjah, *Iraq* **70 C4** 33 20N 43 55 E
Al Fāw, *Iraq* **71 D6** 30 0N 48 30 E
Al Fujayrah, *U.A.E.* **71 E8** 25 7N 56 18 E
Al Ghadaf, W. →, *Jordan* **75 D5** 31 26N 36 43 E
Al Ghammās, *Iraq* **70 D5** 31 45N 44 37 E
Al Ghazālah, *Si. Arabia* **70 E4** 26 48N 41 19 E
Al Ḩadīthah, *Iraq* **70 C4** 34 0N 41 13 E
Al Ḩadīthah, *Si. Arabia* **75 D6** 31 28N 37 8 E
Al Ḩaḑr, *Iraq* **70 C4** 35 35N 42 44 E
Al Ḩājānah, *Syria* **75 B5** 33 20N 36 33 E
Al Hajar al Gharbi, *Oman* **71 E8** 24 10N 56 15 E
Al Hāmad, *Si. Arabia* **70 D3** 31 30N 39 30 E
Al Hamdānīyah, *Syria* **70 C3** 35 25N 36 50 E
Al Ḩamīdīyah, *Syria* **75 A4** 34 42N 35 57 E
Al Ḩammār, *Iraq* **70 D5** 30 57N 46 51 E
Al Ḩamrā', *Si. Arabia* **70 E3** 24 2N 38 55 E
Al Ḩanākīyah, *Si. Arabia* **70 E4** 24 51N 40 31 E
Al Harīr, W. →, *Syria* **75 C4** 32 44N 35 59 E
Al Ḩasā, W. →, *Jordan* **75 D4** 31 4N 35 29 E
Al Ḩasakah, *Syria* **70 B4** 36 35N 40 45 E
Al Haydān, W. →, *Jordan* **75 D4** 31 29N 35 34 E
Al Ḩayy, *Iraq* **70 C5** 32 5N 46 5 E
Al Ḩijarah, *Asia* **70 D4** 30 0N 44 0 E
Al Ḩillah, *Iraq* **70 C5** 32 30N 44 25 E
Al Ḩillah, *Si. Arabia* **74 B4** 23 35N 46 50 E
Al Hindīyah, *Iraq* **70 C5** 32 30N 44 10 E
Al Hirmil, *Lebanon* **75 A5** 34 26N 36 24 E
Al Hoceïma, *Morocco* **78 A5** 35 8N 3 58W
Al Ḩudaydah, *Yemen* **74 E3** 14 50N 43 0 E
Al Hufūf, *Si. Arabia* **71 E6** 25 25N 49 45 E
Al Ḩumaydah, *Si. Arabia* **70 D2** 29 14N 34 56 E
Al Ḩunayy, *Si. Arabia* **71 E6** 25 58N 48 45 E
Al Īsāwīyah, *Si. Arabia* **70 D3** 30 43N 37 59 E
Al Jafr, *Jordan* **75 E5** 30 18N 36 14 E
Al Jāfūrah, *Si. Arabia* **71 E7** 25 0N 50 15 E
Al Jaghbūb, *Libya* **79 C10** 29 42N 24 38 E
Al Jahrah, *Kuwait* **70 D5** 29 25N 47 40 E
Al Jalāmīd, *Si. Arabia* **70 D3** 31 20N 40 6 E
Al Jamalīyah, *Qatar* **71 E6** 25 37N 51 5 E
Al Janūb □, *Lebanon* **75 B4** 33 20N 35 20 E
Al Jawf, *Libya* **79 D10** 24 10N 23 24 E
Al Jawf, *Si. Arabia* **70 D3** 29 55N 39 40 E
Al Jazirah, *Iraq* **70 C5** 33 30N 44 0 E
Al Jithāmīyah, *Si. Arabia* **70 E4** 27 41N 41 43 E
Al Jubayl, *Si. Arabia* **71 E6** 27 0N 49 50 E
Al Jubaylah, *Si. Arabia* **70 E5** 24 55N 46 25 E
Al Jubb, *Si. Arabia* **70 E4** 27 11N 42 17 E
Al Junaynah, *Sudan* **79 F10** 13 27N 22 45 E
Al Kabā'ish, *Iraq* **70 D5** 30 58N 47 0 E
Al Karak, *Jordan* **75 D4** 31 11N 35 42 E
Al Karak □, *Jordan* **75 E5** 31 0N 36 0 E
Al Kāẓim Tyah, *Iraq* **70 C5** 33 22N 44 12 E
Al Khābūra, *Oman* **71 F8** 23 57N 57 5 E
Al Khafji, *Si. Arabia* **71 E6** 28 24N 48 29 E
Al Khalīl, *West Bank* **75 D4** 31 32N 35 6 E
Al Khāliş, *Iraq* **70 C5** 33 49N 44 32 E
Al Kharsānīyah, *Si. Arabia* **71 E6** 27 13N 49 18 E
Al Khaşab, *Oman* **71 E8** 26 14N 56 15 E
Al Khawr, *Qatar* **71 E6** 25 41N 51 30 E
Al Khiḑr, *Iraq* **70 D5** 31 12N 45 33 E
Al Khiyām, *Lebanon* **75 B4** 33 20N 35 36 E
Al Kiswah, *Syria* **75 B5** 33 23N 36 14 E
Al Kūfah, *Iraq* **70 C5** 32 2N 44 24 E
Al Kufrah, *Libya* **79 D10** 24 17N 23 15 E
Al Kuhayfīyah, *Si. Arabia* **70 E4** 27 12N 43 3 E
Al Kūt, *Iraq* **70 C5** 32 30N 46 0 E
Al Kuwayt, *Kuwait* **70 D5** 29 30N 48 0 E
Al Labwah, *Lebanon* **75 A5** 34 11N 36 20 E
Al Lādhiqīyah, *Syria* **70 C2** 35 30N 35 45 E
Al Līth, *Si. Arabia* **74 C3** 20 9N 40 15 E
Al Liwā', *Oman* **71 E8** 24 31N 56 36 E
Al Luḩayyah, *Yemen* **74 D3** 15 45N 42 40 E
Al Madīnah, *Iraq* **70 D5** 30 57N 47 16 E
Al Madīnah, *Si. Arabia* **70 E3** 24 35N 39 52 E
Al Mafraq, *Jordan* **75 C5** 32 17N 36 14 E
Al Maḩmūdīyah, *Iraq* **70 C5** 33 3N 44 21 E
Al Majma'ah, *Si. Arabia* **70 E5** 25 57N 45 22 E
Al Makhruq, W. →, *Jordan* **75 D6** 31 28N 37 0 E
Al Makḩūl, *Si. Arabia* **70 E4** 26 37N 42 39 E
Al Manāmah, *Bahrain* **71 E6** 26 10N 50 30 E
Al Maqwa', *Kuwait* **70 D5** 29 10N 47 59 E
Al Marj, *Libya* **79 B10** 32 25N 20 30 E
Al Maṭlā, *Kuwait* **70 D5** 29 24N 47 40 E
Al Mawjib, W. →, *Jordan* **75 D4** 31 28N 35 36 E
Al Mawşil, *Iraq* **70 B4** 36 15N 43 5 E
Al Mayādin, *Syria* **70 C4** 35 1N 40 27 E
Al Mazār, *Jordan* **75 D4** 31 4N 35 41 E
Al Midhnab, *Si. Arabia* **70 E5** 25 50N 44 18 E
Al Minā', *Lebanon* **75 A4** 34 24N 35 49 E
Al Miqdādīyah, *Iraq* **70 C5** 34 0N 45 0 E
Al Mubarraz, *Si. Arabia* **71 E6** 25 30N 49 40 E
Al Mudawwarah, *Jordan* **75 F5** 29 19N 36 0 E
Al Mughayrā', *U.A.E.* **71 E7** 24 5N 53 32 E
Al Muḩarraq, *Bahrain* **71 E6** 26 15N 50 40 E
Al Mukallā, *Yemen* **74 E4** 14 33N 49 2 E
Al Mukhā, *Yemen* **74 E3** 13 18N 43 15 E
Al Musayjīd, *Si. Arabia* **70 E3** 24 5N 39 5 E
Al Musayyib, *Iraq* **70 C5** 32 49N 44 20 E
Al Muwayh, *Si. Arabia* **80 C5** 22 41N 41 37 E
Al Muwayliḩ, *Si. Arabia* **70 E2** 27 40N 35 30 E
Al Owuho = Otukpa, *Nigeria* **83 D6** 7 9N 7 41 E
Al Qā'im, *Iraq* **70 C4** 34 21N 41 7 E
Al Qalībah, *Si. Arabia* **70 D3** 28 24N 37 42 E
Al Qāmishlī, *Syria* **70 B4** 37 2N 41 14 E
Al Qaryatayn, *Syria* **75 A6** 34 12N 37 13 E
Al Qaşīm, *Si. Arabia* **70 E4** 26 0N 43 0 E
Al Qaṭ'ā, *Syria* **70 C4** 34 40N 40 48 E
Al Qaṭīf, *Si. Arabia* **71 E6** 26 35N 50 0 E
Al Qatrānah, *Jordan* **75 D5** 31 12N 36 6 E
Al Qaṭrūn, *Libya* **79 D9** 24 56N 15 3 E
Al Qayşūmah, *Si. Arabia* **70 D5** 28 20N 46 7 E
Al Quds = Jerusalem, *Israel* **75 D4** 31 47N 35 10 E
Al Qunayṭirah, *Syria* **75 C4** 32 55N 35 45 E
Al Qunfudhah, *Si. Arabia* **80 D5** 19 3N 41 4 E
Al Qurnah, *Iraq* **70 D5** 31 1N 47 25 E
Al Quşayr, *Iraq* **70 D5** 30 39N 45 50 E
Al Quşayr, *Syria* **75 A5** 34 31N 36 34 E
Al Qutayfah, *Syria* **75 B5** 33 44N 36 36 E
Al 'Ubaylah, *Si. Arabia* **74 C5** 21 59N 50 57 E
Al 'Uḑaylīyah, *Si. Arabia* **71 E6** 25 8N 49 18 E
Al 'Ulā, *Si. Arabia* **70 E3** 26 35N 38 0 E
Al 'Uqayr, *Si. Arabia* **71 E6** 25 40N 50 15 E
Al 'Uwaynid, *Si. Arabia* **70 E5** 24 50N 46 0 E
Al 'Uwayqīlah, *Si. Arabia* **70 D4** 30 30N 42 10 E
Al 'Uyūn, *Ḩijāz, Si. Arabia* **70 E3** 24 33N 39 35 E
Al 'Uyūn, *Najd, Si. Arabia* **70 E4** 26 30N 43 50 E
Al 'Uzayr, *Iraq* **70 D5** 31 19N 47 25 E
Al Wajh, *Si. Arabia* **70 E3** 26 10N 36 30 E
Al Wakrah, *Qatar* **71 E6** 25 10N 51 40 E
Al Waqbah, *Si. Arabia* **70 D5** 28 48N 45 33 E
Al Wari'āh, *Si. Arabia* **70 E5** 27 51N 47 25 E
Ala, *Italy* **28 C8** 45 45N 11 0 E
Ala Dağ, *Turkey* **72 D6** 37 44N 35 9 E
Ala Dağları, *Turkey* **73 C10** 39 15N 43 33 E
Alabama □, *U.S.A.* **109 J2** 33 0N 87 0W
Alabama →, *U.S.A.* **109 K2** 31 8N 87 57W
Alabaster, *U.S.A.* **109 J2** 33 15N 86 49W
Alaca, *Turkey* **72 B6** 40 10N 34 51 E
Alacaatlı, *Turkey* **39 B10** 39 15N 28 3 E
Alaçam, *Turkey* **72 B6** 41 36N 35 36 E
Alaçam Dağları, *Turkey* **39 B10** 39 18N 28 49 E
Alaçatı, *Turkey* **39 C8** 38 16N 26 22 E
Alachua, *U.S.A.* **109 L4** 29 47N 82 30W
Alaejos, *Spain* **34 D5** 41 18N 5 13W
Alaérma, *Greece* **36 C9** 36 9N 27 57 E
Alagir, *Russia* **49 J7** 43 3N 44 14 E
Alagna Valsésia, *Italy* **28 C4** 45 51N 7 56 E
Alagoa Grande, *Brazil* **125 E11** 7 3 S 35 35W
Alagoas □, *Brazil* **125 E11** 9 0 S 36 0W
Alagoinhas, *Brazil* **125 F11** 12 7 S 38 20W
Alagón, *Spain* **32 D3** 41 46N 1 12W
Alagón →, *Spain* **34 F4** 39 44N 6 53W
Alaior, *Spain* **37 B11** 39 57N 4 8 E
Alajero, *Canary Is.* **37 F2** 28 3N 17 13W
Alajuela, *Costa Rica* **120 D3** 10 2N 84 8W
Alakamisy, *Madag.* **89 C8** 21 19 S 47 14 E
Alaknanda →, *India* **69 D8** 30 8N 78 36 E
Alakol, Ozero, *Kazakhstan* **60 B3** 46 0N 81 5 E
Alamarvdasht, *Iran* **71 E7** 27 37N 52 59 E
Alamata, *Ethiopia* **81 E4** 12 25N 39 33 E
Alameda, *Calif., U.S.A.* **116 H4** 37 46N 122 15W
Alameda, *N. Mex., U.S.A.* **115 J10** 35 11N 106 37W
Alaminos, *Phil.* **61 C3** 16 10N 119 59 E
Alamo, *U.S.A.* **117 J11** 37 22N 115 10W
Alamo Crossing, *U.S.A.* **117 L13** 34 16N 113 33W
Alamogordo, *U.S.A.* **115 K11** 32 54N 105 57W
Alamos, *Mexico* **118 B3** 27 0N 109 0W
Alamosa, *U.S.A.* **115 H11** 37 28N 105 52W
Åland, *Finland* **9 F19** 60 15N 20 0 E
Alandroal, *Portugal* **35 G3** 38 41N 7 24W
Ålands hav, *Sweden* **9 F18** 60 0N 19 30 E
Alange, Presa de, *Spain* **35 G4** 38 45N 6 18W
Alania = North Ossetia □, *Russia* **49 J7** 43 30N 44 30 E
Alanís, *Spain* **35 G5** 38 3N 5 43W
Alanya, *Turkey* **70 B1** 36 38N 32 0 E
Alaotra, Farihin', *Madag.* **89 B8** 17 30 S 48 30 E
Alapayevsk, *Russia* **50 D7** 57 52N 61 42 E
Alappuzha = Alleppey, *India* **66 Q10** 9 30N 76 28 E
Alar del Rey, *Spain* **34 C6** 42 38N 4 20W
Alaraz, *Spain* **34 E5** 40 45N 5 17W
Alarcón, Embalse de, *Spain* **32 F2** 39 36N 2 10W
Alarobia-Vohiposa, *Madag.* **89 C8** 20 59 S 47 9 E
Alaşehir, *Turkey* **39 C10** 38 23N 28 30 E
Alaska □, *U.S.A.* **100 B5** 64 0N 154 0W
Alaska, G. of, *Pac. Oc.* **100 C5** 58 0N 145 0W
Alaska Peninsula, *U.S.A.* **100 C4** 56 0N 159 0W
Alaska Range, *U.S.A.* **100 B4** 62 50N 151 0W
Alássio, *Italy* **28 E5** 44 0N 8 10 E
Älät, *Azerbaijan* **49 L9** 39 58N 49 25 E
Alatri, *Italy* **29 G10** 41 43N 13 21 E
Alatyr, *Russia* **48 C8** 54 55N 46 35 E
Alatyr →, *Russia* **48 C8** 54 52N 46 36 E
Alausi, *Ecuador* **124 D3** 2 0 S 78 50W
Álava □, *Spain* **32 C2** 42 48N 2 28W
Alava, C., *U.S.A.* **114 B1** 48 10N 124 44W
Alaverdi, *Armenia* **49 K7** 41 15N 44 37 E
Alavus, *Finland* **9 E20** 62 35N 23 36 E
Alawoona, *Australia* **95 E3** 34 45 S 140 30 E
'Alayh, *Lebanon* **75 B4** 33 46N 35 33 E
Alazani →, *Azerbaijan* **49 K8** 41 5N 46 40 E
Alba, *Italy* **28 D5** 44 42N 8 2 E
Alba □, *Romania* **43 D8** 46 10N 23 30 E
Alba Adriática, *Italy* **29 F10** 42 50N 13 56 E
Alba de Tormes, *Spain* **34 E5** 40 50N 5 30W
Alba-Iulia, *Romania* **43 D8** 46 8N 23 39 E
Albac, *Romania* **42 D7** 46 28N 22 58 E
Albacete, *Spain* **33 F3** 39 0N 1 50W
Albacete □, *Spain* **33 G3** 38 50N 2 0W
Albacutya, L., *Australia* **95 F3** 35 45 S 141 58 E
Ålbæk, *Denmark* **11 G4** 57 36N 10 25 E
Ålbæk Bugt, *Denmark* **11 G4** 57 35N 10 40 E
Albaida, *Spain* **33 G4** 38 51N 0 31W
Albalate de las Nogueras, *Spain* **32 E2** 40 22N 2 18W
Albalate del Arzobispo, *Spain* **32 D4** 41 6N 0 31W
Alban, *France* **20 E6** 43 53N 2 28 E
Albanel, L., *Canada* **102 B5** 50 55N 73 12W
Albania ■, *Europe* **40 E4** 41 0N 20 0 E
Albano Laziale, *Italy* **29 G9** 41 44N 12 39 E
Albany, *Australia* **93 G2** 35 1 S 117 58 E
Albany, *Ga., U.S.A.* **109 K3** 31 35N 84 10W
Albany, *N.Y., U.S.A.* **111 D11** 42 39N 73 45W
Albany, *Oreg., U.S.A.* **114 D2** 44 38N 123 6W
Albany, *Tex., U.S.A.* **113 J5** 32 44N 99 18W
Albany →, *Canada* **102 B3** 52 17N 81 31W
Albardón, *Argentina* **126 C2** 31 20 S 68 30W
Albarracín, *Spain* **32 E3** 40 25N 1 26W
Albarracín, Sierra de, *Spain* **32 E3** 40 30N 1 30W
Albatera, *Spain* **33 G4** 38 11N 0 52W
Albatross B., *Australia* **94 A3** 12 45 S 141 30 E
Albegna →, *Italy* **29 F8** 42 30N 11 11 E
Albemarle, *U.S.A.* **109 H5** 35 21N 80 11W
Albemarle Sd., *U.S.A.* **109 H7** 36 5N 76 0W
Albenga, *Italy* **28 D5** 44 3N 8 13 E
Alberche →, *Spain* **34 F6** 39 58N 4 46W
Alberdi, *Paraguay* **126 B4** 26 14 S 58 20W
Alberes, Mts., *France* **20 F6** 42 28N 2 56 E
Ålberga, *Sweden* **11 F10** 58 44N 16 35 E
Albersdorf, *Germany* **24 A5** 54 8N 9 17 E
Albert, *France* **19 C9** 50 0N 2 38 E
Albert, L., *Africa* **86 B3** 1 30N 31 0 E
Albert, L., *Australia* **95 F2** 35 30 S 139 10 E
Albert Edward Ra., *Australia* **92 C4** 18 17 S 127 57 E
Albert Lea, *U.S.A.* **112 D8** 43 39N 93 22W
Albert Nile →, *Uganda* **86 B3** 3 36N 32 2 E
Albert Town, *Bahamas* **121 B5** 22 37N 74 33W
Alberta □, *Canada* **104 C6** 54 40N 115 0W
Alberti, *Argentina* **126 D3** 35 1 S 60 16W
Albertinia, *S. Africa* **88 E3** 34 11 S 21 34 E
Albertirsa, *Hungary* **42 C4** 47 14N 19 37 E
Alberton, *Canada* **103 C7** 46 50N 64 0W
Albertville = Kalemie, *Dem. Rep. of the Congo* **86 D2** 5 55 S 29 9 E
Albertville, *France* **21 C10** 45 40N 6 22 E
Albertville, *U.S.A.* **109 H2** 34 16N 86 13W
Albi, *France* **20 E6** 43 56N 2 9 E
Albia, *U.S.A.* **112 E8** 41 2N 92 48W
Albina, *Suriname* **125 B8** 5 37N 54 15W
Albina, Ponta, *Angola* **88 B1** 15 52 S 11 44 E
Albino, *Italy* **28 C6** 45 46N 9 47 E
Albion, *Mich., U.S.A.* **108 D3** 42 15N 84 45W
Albion, *Nebr., U.S.A.* **112 E6** 41 42N 98 0W
Albion, *Pa., U.S.A.* **110 E4** 41 53N 80 22W
Albocácer, *Spain* **32 E5** 40 21N 0 1 E
Albolote, *Spain* **35 H7** 37 14N 3 39W
Alborán, *Medit. S.* **35 K7** 35 57N 3 0W
Alborea, *Spain* **33 F3** 39 17N 1 24W
Ålborg, *Denmark* **11 G3** 57 2N 9 54 E
Ålborg Bugt, *Denmark* **11 H4** 56 50N 10 35 E
Alborz, Reshteh-ye Kūhhā-ye, *Iran* **71 C7** 36 0N 52 0 E
Albox, *Spain* **33 H2** 37 23N 2 8W
Albufeira, *Portugal* **35 H2** 37 5N 8 15W
Albula →, *Switz.* **25 J5** 46 38N 9 28 E
Albuñol, *Spain* **35 J7** 36 48N 3 11W
Albuquerque, *U.S.A.* **115 J10** 35 5N 106 39W
Albuquerque, Cayos de, *Caribbean* **120 D3** 12 10N 81 50W
Alburg, *U.S.A.* **111 B11** 44 59N 73 18W
Alburno, Mte., *Italy* **31 B8** 40 33N 15 17 E
Alburquerque, *Spain* **35 F4** 39 15N 6 59W
Albury = Albury-Wodonga, *Australia* **95 F4** 36 3 S 146 56 E
Albury-Wodonga, *Australia* **95 F4** 36 3 S 146 56 E
Alcácer do Sal, *Portugal* **35 G2** 38 22N 8 33W
Alcáçovas, *Portugal* **35 G2** 38 23N 8 9W
Alcalá de Chivert, *Spain* **32 E5** 40 19N 0 13 E
Alcalá de Guadaira, *Spain* **35 H5** 37 20N 5 50W
Alcalá de Henares, *Spain* **34 E7** 40 28N 3 22W
Alcalá de los Gazules, *Spain* **35 J5** 36 29N 5 43W
Alcalá del Júcar, *Spain* **33 F3** 39 12N 1 26W
Alcalá del Río, *Spain* **35 H5** 37 31N 5 59W
Alcalá del Valle, *Spain* **35 J5** 36 54N 5 10W
Alcalá la Real, *Spain* **35 H7** 37 27N 3 57W
Álcamo, *Italy* **30 E5** 37 59N 12 55 E
Alcanadre, *Spain* **32 C2** 42 24N 2 7W
Alcanadre →, *Spain* **32 D4** 41 43N 0 12W
Alcanar, *Spain* **32 E5** 40 33N 0 28 E
Alcanede, *Portugal* **35 F2** 39 25N 8 49W
Alcanena, *Portugal* **35 F2** 39 27N 8 40W
Alcañices, *Spain* **34 D4** 41 41N 6 21W
Alcañiz, *Spain* **32 D4** 41 2N 0 8W
Alcântara, *Brazil* **125 D10** 2 20 S 44 30W
Alcántara, *Spain* **34 F4** 39 41N 6 57W
Alcántara, Embalse de, *Spain* **34 F4** 39 44N 6 50W
Alcantarilla, *Spain* **33 H3** 37 59N 1 12W
Alcaracejos, *Spain* **35 G6** 38 24N 4 58W
Alcaraz, *Spain* **33 G2** 38 40N 2 29W
Alcaraz, Sierra de, *Spain* **33 G2** 38 40N 2 20W
Alcaudete, *Spain* **35 H6** 37 35N 4 5W
Alcázar de San Juan, *Spain* **35 F7** 39 24N 3 12W
Alchevsk, *Ukraine* **47 H10** 48 30N 38 45 E
Alcira = Alzira, *Spain* **33 F4** 39 9N 0 30W
Alcobaça, *Portugal* **35 F2** 39 32N 8 58W
Alcobendas, *Spain* **34 E7** 40 32N 3 38W
Alcolea del Pinar, *Spain* **32 D2** 41 2N 2 28W
Alcora, *Spain* **32 E4** 40 5N 0 14W
Alcorcón, *Spain* **34 E7** 40 20N 3 50W
Alcoutim, *Portugal* **35 H3** 37 25N 7 28W
Alcova, *U.S.A.* **114 E10** 42 34N 106 43W
Alcoy, *Spain* **33 G4** 38 43N 0 30W
Alcubierre, Sierra de, *Spain* **32 D4** 41 45N 0 22W
Alcublas, *Spain* **32 F4** 39 48N 0 43W
Alcúdia, *Spain* **37 B10** 39 51N 3 7 E
Alcúdia, B. d', *Spain* **37 B10** 39 47N 3 15 E
Alcudia, Sierra de la, *Spain* **35 G6** 38 34N 4 30W
Aldabra Is., *Seychelles* **77 G8** 9 22 S 46 28 E
Aldama, *Mexico* **119 C5** 23 0N 98 4W
Aldan, *Russia* **51 D13** 58 40N 125 30 E
Aldan →, *Russia* **51 C13** 63 28N 129 35 E
Aldea, Pta. de la, *Canary Is.* **37 G4** 28 0N 15 50W
Aldeburgh, *U.K.* **13 E9** 52 10N 1 37 E
Alder Pk., *U.S.A.* **116 K5** 35 53N 121 22W
Alderney, *U.K.* **13 H5** 49 42N 2 11W
Aldershot, *U.K.* **13 F7** 51 15N 0 44W
Åled, *Sweden* **11 H6** 56 44N 12 57 E
Aledo, *U.S.A.* **112 E9** 41 12N 90 45W
Alefa, *Ethiopia* **81 E4** 11 55N 36 55 E
Aleg, *Mauritania* **82 B2** 17 3N 13 55W
Alegranza, *Canary Is.* **37 E6** 29 23N 13 32W
Alegranza, I., *Canary Is.* **37 E6** 29 23N 13 32W
Alegre, *Brazil* **127 A7** 20 50 S 41 30W
Alegrete, *Brazil* **127 B4** 29 40 S 56 0W
Aleisk, *Russia* **50 D9** 52 40N 83 0 E
Aleksandriya = Oleksandriya, *Kirovohrad, Ukraine* **47 H7** 48 42N 33 3 E
Aleksandriya = Oleksandriya, *Rivne, Ukraine* **47 G4** 50 37N 26 19 E
Aleksandriyskaya, *Russia* **49 J8** 43 58N 47 14 E
Aleksandrov, *Russia* **46 D10** 56 23N 38 44 E
Aleksandrov Gay, *Russia* **48 E9** 50 9N 48 34 E
Aleksandrovac, *Serbia, Yug.* **40 C5** 43 28N 21 3 E
Aleksandrovac, *Serbia, Yug.* **40 B5** 44 28N 21 13 E
Aleksandrovka = Oleksandrovka, *Ukraine* **47 H7** 48 55N 32 20 E
Aleksandrovo, *Bulgaria* **41 C8** 43 14N 24 51 E
Aleksandrovsk-Sakhalinskiy, *Russia* **51 D15** 50 50N 142 20 E
Aleksandrów Kujawski, *Poland* **45 F5** 52 53N 18 43 E
Aleksandrów Łódźki, *Poland* **45 G6** 51 49N 19 17 E
Alekseyevka, *Samara, Russia* **48 D10** 52 35N 51 17 E
Alekseyevka, *Voronezh, Russia* **47 G10** 50 43N 38 40 E
Aleksin, *Russia* **46 E9** 54 31N 37 9 E
Aleksinac, *Serbia, Yug.* **40 C5** 43 31N 21 42 E
Além Paraíba, *Brazil* **127 A7** 21 52 S 42 41W
Alemania, *Argentina* **126 B2** 25 40 S 65 30W
Alemania, *Chile* **126 B2** 25 10 S 69 55W
Alençon, *France* **18 D7** 48 27N 0 4 E
Alenquer, *Brazil* **125 D8** 1 56 S 54 46W
Alenuihaha Channel, *U.S.A.* **106 H17** 20 30N 156 0W
Alépé, *Ivory C.* **82 D4** 5 29N 3 40W
Aleppo = Ḩalab, *Syria* **70 B3** 36 10N 37 15 E
Aléria, *France* **21 F13** 42 5N 9 26 E
Alès, *France* **21 D8** 44 9N 4 5 E
Aleşd, *Romania* **42 C7** 47 3N 22 22 E
Alessándria, *Italy* **28 D5** 44 54N 8 37 E
Ålestrup, *Denmark* **11 H3** 56 42N 9 29 E
Ålesund, *Norway* **9 E12** 62 28N 6 12 E
Alet-les-Bains, *France* **20 F6** 42 59N 2 14 E
Aletschhorn, *Switz.* **25 J4** 46 28N 8 0 E
Aleutian Is., *Pac. Oc.* **100 C2** 52 0N 175 0W
Aleutian Trench, *Pac. Oc.* **96 C10** 48 0N 180 0 E
Alexander, *U.S.A.* **112 B3** 47 51N 103 39W
Alexander, Mt., *Australia* **93 E3** 28 58 S 120 16 E
Alexander Arch., *U.S.A.* **100 C6** 56 0N 136 0W
Alexander Bay, *S. Africa* **88 D2** 28 40 S 16 30 E
Alexander City, *U.S.A.* **109 J3** 32 56N 85 58W
Alexander I., *Antarctica* **5 C17** 69 0 S 70 0W
Alexandra, *Australia* **95 F4** 37 8 S 145 40 E
Alexandra, *N.Z.* **91 L2** 45 14 S 169 25 E
Alexandra Falls, *Canada* **104 A5** 60 29N 116 18W
Alexandria = El Iskandarîya, *Egypt* **80 H7** 31 13N 29 58 E

Alexandria

Aransas Pass

An Uaimh, Ireland 15 C5 53 39N 6 41W
Anabar ➛, Russia 51 B12 73 8N 113 36 E
'Anabtā, West Bank 75 C4 32 19N 35 7 E
Anaconda, U.S.A. 114 C7 46 8N 112 57W
Anacortes, U.S.A. 116 B4 48 30N 122 37W
Anacuao, Mt., Phil. 61 C4 16 16N 121 53 E
Anadarko, U.S.A. 113 H5 35 4N 98 15W
Anadia, Portugal 34 E2 40 26N 8 27W
Anadolu, Turkey 72 C5 39 0N 30 0 E
Anadyr, Russia 51 C18 64 35N 177 20 E
Anadyr ➛, Russia 51 C18 64 55N 176 5 E
Anadyrskiy Zaliv, Russia 51 C19 64 0N 180 0 E
Anáfi, Greece 39 E7 36 22N 25 48 E
Anafópoulo, Greece 39 E7 36 17N 25 50 E
Anaga, Pta. de, Canary Is. 37 F3 28 34N 16 9W
Anagni, Italy 29 G10 41 44N 13 9 E
'Ānah, Iraq 70 C4 34 25N 42 0 E
Anaheim, U.S.A. 117 M9 33 50N 117 55W
Anahim Lake, Canada 104 C3 52 28N 125 18W
Anáhuac, Mexico 118 B4 27 14N 100 9W
Anakapalle, India 67 L13 17 42N 83 6 E
Anakie, Australia 94 C4 23 32 S 147 45 E
Anaklia, Georgia 49 J5 42 22N 41 35 E
Analalava, Madag. 89 A8 14 35 S 48 0 E
Analavoka, Madag. 89 C8 22 23 S 46 30 E
Análipsis, Greece 36 A3 39 36N 19 55 E
Anambar ➛, Pakistan 68 D3 30 15N 68 50 E
Anambas, Kepulauan, Indonesia 65 L6 3 20N 106 30 E
Anambas Is. = Anambas, Kepulauan, Indonesia 65 L6 3 20N 106 30 E
Anambra □, Nigeria 83 D6 6 20N 7 0 E
Anamosa, U.S.A. 112 D9 42 7N 91 17W
Anamur, Turkey 70 B2 36 8N 32 58 E
Anamur Burnu, Turkey 72 D5 36 2N 32 47 E
Anan, Japan 55 H7 33 54N 134 40 E
Anand, India 68 H5 22 32N 72 59 E
Anánes, Greece 38 E6 36 33N 24 9 E
Anantnag, India 69 C6 33 45N 75 10 E
Ananyiv, Ukraine 47 J5 47 44N 29 58 E
Anapa, Russia 47 K9 44 55N 37 25 E
Anapodháris ➛, Greece 36 E7 34 59N 25 20 E
Anápolis, Brazil 125 G9 16 15 S 48 50W
Anapu ➛, Brazil 125 D8 1 53 S 50 53W
Anār, Iran 71 D7 30 55N 55 13 E
Anārak, Iran 71 C7 33 25N 53 40 E
Anarisfjällen, Sweden 10 A7 63 6N 13 10 E
Anas ➛, India 68 H5 23 26N 74 0 E
Anatolia = Anadolu, Turkey 72 C5 39 0N 30 0 E
Anatsogno, Madag. 89 C7 23 33 S 43 46 E
Añatuya, Argentina 126 B3 28 20 S 62 50W
Anaunethad L., Canada 105 A8 60 55N 104 25W
Anbyŏn, N. Korea 57 E14 39 1N 127 35 E
Ancares, Sierra de, Spain 34 C4 42 51N 6 52W
Ancaster, Canada 110 C5 43 13N 79 59W
Ancenis, France 18 E5 47 21N 1 10W
Anchor Bay, U.S.A. 116 G3 38 48N 123 34W
Anchorage, U.S.A. 100 B5 61 13N 149 54W
Anci, China 56 E9 39 20N 116 40 E
Ancohuma, Nevada, Bolivia 122 E4 16 0 S 68 50W
Ancón, Peru 124 F3 11 50 S 77 10W
Ancona, Italy 29 E10 43 38N 13 30 E
Ancud, Chile 128 E2 42 0 S 73 50W
Ancud, G. de, Chile 128 E2 42 0 S 73 0W
Ancy-le-Franc, France 19 E11 47 46N 4 10 E
Andacollo, Argentina 126 D1 37 10 S 70 42W
Andacollo, Chile 126 C1 30 14 S 71 6W
Andaingo, Madag. 89 B8 18 12 S 48 17 E
Andalgalá, Argentina 126 B2 27 40 S 66 30W
Åndalsnes, Norway 9 E12 62 35N 7 43 E
Andalucía □, Spain 35 H6 37 35N 5 0W
Andalusia = Andalucía □, Spain 35 H6 37 35N 5 0W
Andalusia, U.S.A. 109 K2 31 18N 86 29W
Andaman Is., Ind. Oc. 52 H13 12 30N 92 30 E
Andaman Sea, Ind. Oc. 62 B1 13 0N 96 0 E
Andamooka Opal Fields, Australia 95 E2 30 27 S 137 9 E
Andapa, Madag. 89 A8 14 39 S 49 39 E
Andara, Namibia 88 B3 18 2 S 21 9 E
Andelot-Blancheville, France 19 D12 48 15N 5 18 E
Andenes, Norway 8 B17 69 19N 16 18 E
Andenne, Belgium 17 D5 50 28N 5 5 E
Andéranboukane, Mali 83 B5 15 26N 3 2 E
Andermatt, Switz. 25 J4 46 38N 8 35 E
Andernach, Germany 24 E3 50 26N 7 24 E
Andernos-les-Bains, France 20 D2 44 44N 1 6W
Anderslöv, Sweden 11 J7 55 26N 13 19 E
Anderson, Alaska, U.S.A. 100 B5 64 25N 149 15W
Anderson, Calif., U.S.A. 114 F2 40 27N 122 18W
Anderson, Ind., U.S.A. 108 E3 40 10N 85 41W
Anderson, Mo., U.S.A. 113 G7 36 39N 94 27W
Anderson, S.C., U.S.A. 109 H4 34 31N 82 39W
Anderson ➛, Canada 100 B7 69 42N 129 0W
Anderstorp, Sweden 11 G7 57 19N 13 39 E
Andes, U.S.A. 111 D10 42 12N 74 47W
Andes, Cord. de los, S. Amer. 122 F4 20 0 S 68 0W
Andfjorden, Norway 8 B17 69 10N 16 20 E
Andhra Pradesh □, India 66 L11 18 0N 79 0 E
Andijon, Uzbekistan 50 E8 41 10N 72 15 E
Andikíthira, Greece 38 F5 35 52N 23 15 E
Andilamena, Madag. 89 B8 17 1 S 48 35 E
Andīmeshk, Iran 71 C6 32 27N 48 21 E
Andímilos, Greece 38 E6 36 47N 24 12 E
Andíparos, Greece 39 D7 37 0N 25 3 E
Andípaxoi, Greece 38 B2 39 9N 20 13 E
Andípsara, Greece 39 C7 38 30N 25 29 E
Andírrion, Greece 38 C3 38 20N 21 46 E
Andizhan = Andijon, Uzbekistan 50 E8 41 10N 72 15 E
Andoain, Spain 32 B2 43 13N 2 1W
Andoany, Madag. 89 A8 13 25 S 48 16 E
Andong, S. Korea 57 F15 36 40N 128 43 E
Andongwei, China 57 G10 35 6N 119 20 E
Andoom, Australia 94 A3 12 25 S 141 53 E
Andorra, Spain 32 E4 40 59N 0 28W
Andorra ■, Europe 20 F5 42 30N 1 30 E
Andorra La Vella, Andorra 20 F5 42 31N 1 32 E
Andover, U.K. 13 F6 51 12N 1 29W
Andover, Maine, U.S.A. 111 B14 44 38N 70 45W
Andover, Mass., U.S.A. 111 D13 42 40N 71 8W
Andover, N.J., U.S.A. 111 F10 40 59N 74 45W
Andover, N.Y., U.S.A. 110 D7 42 10N 77 48W
Andover, Ohio, U.S.A. 110 E4 41 36N 80 34W
Andøya, Norway 8 B16 69 10N 15 50 E
Andradina, Brazil 125 H8 20 54 S 51 23W
Andrahary, Mt., Madag. 89 A8 13 37 S 49 17 E
Andramasina, Madag. 89 B8 19 11 S 47 35 E
Andranopasy, Madag. 89 C7 21 17 S 43 44 E
Andranovory, Madag. 89 C7 23 8 S 44 10 E
Andratx, Spain 37 B9 39 39N 2 25 E
Andreanof Is., U.S.A. 100 C2 51 30N 176 0W
Andreapol, Russia 46 D7 56 40N 32 17 E
Andrews, S.C., U.S.A. 109 J6 33 27N 79 34W
Andrews, Tex., U.S.A. 113 J3 32 19N 102 33W
Andreyevka, Russia 48 D10 52 19N 51 55 E
Ándria, Italy 31 A9 41 13N 16 17 E
Andriamena, Madag. 89 B8 17 26 S 47 30 E
Andriandampy, Madag. 89 C8 22 45 S 45 41 E
Andriba, Madag. 89 B8 17 30 S 46 58 E
Andrijevica, Montenegro, Yug. 40 D3 42 45N 19 48 E
Andrítsaina, Greece 38 D3 37 29N 21 52 E
Androka, Madag. 89 C7 24 58 S 44 2 E
Andropov = Rybinsk, Russia 46 C10 58 5N 38 50 E
Ándros, Greece 38 D6 37 50N 24 57 E
Andros I., Bahamas 120 B4 24 30N 78 0W
Andros Town, Bahamas 120 B4 24 43N 77 47W
Androscoggin ➛, U.S.A. 111 C14 43 58N 70 0W
Andrychów, Poland 45 J6 49 51N 19 18 E
Andselv, Norway 8 B18 69 4N 18 34 E
Andújar, Spain 35 G6 38 3N 4 5W
Andulo, Angola 84 G3 11 25 S 16 45 E
Aneby, Sweden 11 G8 57 48N 14 49 E
Anegada I., U.S. Virgin Is. 121 C7 18 45N 64 20W
Anegada Passage, W. Indies 121 C7 18 15N 63 45W
Anécho, Togo 83 D5 6 12N 1 34 E
Anenni-Noi, Moldova 43 D14 46 53N 29 15 E
Aneto, Pico de, Spain 32 C5 42 37N 0 40 E
Anfu, China 59 D10 27 21N 114 40 E
Ang Thong, Thailand 64 E3 14 35N 100 31 E
Angamos, Punta, Chile 126 A1 23 1 S 70 32W
Angara ➛, Russia 51 D10 58 5N 94 20 E
Angara-Débou, Benin 83 C5 11 19N 3 3 E
Angarab, Ethiopia 81 E4 13 11N 37 7 E
Angarbaka, Sudan 81 F1 9 44N 24 44 E
Angarsk, Russia 51 D11 52 30N 104 0 E
Angas Hills, Australia 92 D4 23 0 S 127 50 E
Angaston, Australia 95 E2 34 30 S 139 8 E
Angaur I., Pac. Oc. 63 C8 6 54N 134 9 E
Ånge, Sweden 10 B9 62 31N 15 35 E
Ángel, Salto = Angel Falls, Venezuela 124 B6 5 57N 62 30W
Ángel de la Guarda, I., Mexico 118 B2 29 30N 113 30W
Angel Falls, Venezuela 124 B6 5 57N 62 30W
Angeles, Phil. 61 D4 15 9N 120 33 E
Ängelholm, Sweden 11 H6 56 15N 12 58 E
Angels Camp, U.S.A. 116 G6 38 4N 120 32W
Ängelsberg, Sweden 10 E10 59 58N 16 0 E
Anger ➛, Ethiopia 81 F4 9 37N 36 6 E
Angereb ➛, Ethiopia 81 E4 13 45N 36 40 E
Ångermanälven ➛, Sweden 10 B11 62 40N 18 0 E
Ångermanland, Sweden 8 E18 63 36N 17 45 E
Angermünde, Germany 24 B9 53 0N 14 0 E
Angers, Canada 111 A9 45 31N 75 29W
Angers, France 18 E6 47 30N 0 35W
Angerville, France 19 D9 48 19N 2 0 E
Ängesån ➛, Sweden 8 C20 66 16N 22 47 E
Angikuni L., Canada 105 A9 62 0N 100 0W
Angkor, Cambodia 64 F4 13 22N 103 50 E
Anglès, Spain 32 D7 41 57N 2 38 E
Anglesey, Isle of □, U.K. 12 D3 53 16N 4 18W
Anglet, France 20 E2 43 29N 1 31W
Angleton, U.S.A. 113 L7 29 10N 95 26W
Anglin ➛, France 20 B4 46 42N 0 52 E
Anglisidhes, Cyprus 36 E12 34 51N 33 27 E
Anglure, France 19 D10 48 35N 3 50 E
Angmagssalik = Tasiilaq, Greenland 4 C6 65 40N 37 20W
Ango, Dem. Rep. of the Congo 86 B2 4 10N 26 5 E
Angoche, Mozam. 87 F4 16 8 S 39 55 E
Angoche, I., Mozam. 87 F4 16 20 S 39 50 E
Angol, Chile 126 D1 37 56 S 72 45W
Angola, Ind., U.S.A. 108 E3 41 38N 85 0W
Angola, N.Y., U.S.A. 110 D5 42 38N 79 2W
Angola ■, Africa 85 G3 12 0 S 18 0 E
Angoulême, France 20 C4 45 39N 0 10 E
Angoumois, France 20 C4 45 50N 0 25 E
Angra dos Reis, Brazil 127 A7 23 0 S 44 10W
Angren, Uzbekistan 50 E8 41 1N 70 12 E
Angtassom, Cambodia 65 G5 11 1N 104 41 E
Angu, Dem. Rep. of the Congo 86 B1 3 23N 24 30 E
Anguang, China 57 B12 45 15N 123 45 E
Anguilla ■, W. Indies 121 C7 18 14N 63 5W
Anguo, China 56 E8 38 28N 115 15 E
Angurugu, Australia 94 A2 14 0 S 136 25 E
Angus □, U.K. 14 E6 56 46N 2 56W
Angwa ➛, Zimbabwe 89 B5 16 0 S 30 23 E
Anhanduí ➛, Brazil 127 A5 21 46 S 52 9W
Anholt, Denmark 11 H5 56 42N 11 33 E
Anhua, China 59 C8 28 23N 111 12 E
Anhui □, China 59 B11 32 0N 117 0 E
Anhwei = Anhui □, China 59 B11 32 0N 117 0 E
Anichab, Namibia 88 C1 21 0 S 14 46 E
Anidhros, Greece 39 E7 36 38N 25 43 E
Anié, Togo 83 D5 7 42N 1 8 E
Animas ➛, U.S.A. 115 H9 36 43N 108 13W
Anina, Romania 42 E6 45 6N 21 51 E
Aninoasa, Romania 43 F9 44 47N 24 10 E
Anivorano, Madag. 89 B8 18 44 S 48 58 E
Anjalankoski, Finland 9 F22 60 45N 26 51 E
Anjar, India 68 H4 23 6N 70 10 E
Anji, China 59 B12 30 46N 119 40 E
Anjou, France 18 E6 47 20N 0 15W
Anjozorobe, Madag. 89 B8 18 22 S 47 52 E
Anju, N. Korea 57 E13 39 36N 125 40 E
Anka, Nigeria 83 C6 12 13N 5 58 E
Ankaboa, Tanjona, Madag. 89 C7 21 58 S 43 20 E
Ankang, China 56 H5 32 40N 109 1 E
Ankara, Turkey 72 C5 39 57N 32 54 E
Ankaramena, Madag. 89 C8 21 57 S 46 39 E
Ankaratra, Madag. 85 H9 19 25 S 47 12 E
Ankarsrum, Sweden 11 G10 57 41N 16 20 E
Ankasakasa, Madag. 89 B7 16 21 S 44 52 E
Ankavandra, Madag. 89 B8 18 46 S 45 18 E
Ankazoabo, Madag. 89 C7 22 18 S 44 31 E
Ankazobe, Madag. 89 B8 18 20 S 47 10 E
Ankeny, U.S.A. 112 E8 41 44N 93 36W
Ankilimalinika, Madag. 89 C7 22 58 S 43 45 E
Ankilizato, Madag. 89 C8 20 25 S 45 1 E
Ankisabe, Madag. 89 B8 19 17 S 46 29 E
Anklam, Germany 24 B9 53 51N 13 41 E
Ankober, Ethiopia 81 F4 9 35N 39 40 E
Ankoro, Dem. Rep. of the Congo 86 D2 6 45 S 26 55 E
Ankororoka, Madag. 89 D8 25 30 S 45 11 E
Anlong, China 58 E5 25 2N 105 27 E
Anlu, China 59 B9 31 15N 113 45 E
Anmyŏn-do, S. Korea 57 F14 36 25N 126 25 E
Ånn, Sweden 10 A6 63 19N 12 34 E
Ann, C., U.S.A. 111 D14 42 38N 70 35W
Ann Arbor, U.S.A. 108 D4 42 17N 83 45W
Anna, Russia 48 E5 51 28N 40 23 E
Anna, U.S.A. 113 G10 37 28N 89 15W
Annaba, Algeria 78 A7 36 50N 7 46 E
Annaberg-Buchholz, Germany 24 E9 50 34N 13 0 E
Annalee ➛, Ireland 15 B4 54 2N 7 24W
Annam, Vietnam 64 E7 16 0N 108 0 E
Annamitique, Chaîne, Asia 64 D6 17 0N 106 0 E
Annan, U.K. 14 G5 54 59N 3 16W
Annan ➛, U.K. 14 G5 54 58N 3 16W
Annapolis, U.S.A. 108 F7 38 59N 76 30W
Annapolis Royal, Canada 103 D6 44 44N 65 32W
Annapurna, Nepal 69 E10 28 34N 83 50 E
Annean, L., Australia 93 E2 26 54 S 118 14 E
Anneberg, Sweden 11 G8 57 44N 14 49 E
Annecy, France 21 C10 45 55N 6 8 E
Annecy, Lac d', France 21 C10 45 52N 6 10 E
Annemasse, France 19 F13 46 12N 6 16 E
Annenskiy Most, Russia 46 B9 60 45N 37 10 E
Anning, China 58 E4 24 55N 102 26 E
Anniston, U.S.A. 109 J3 33 39N 85 50W
Annobón, Atl. Oc. 77 G4 1 25 S 5 36 E
Annonay, France 21 C8 45 15N 4 40 E
Annot, France 21 E10 43 58N 6 38 E
Annotto Bay, Jamaica 120 C4 18 17N 76 45W
Ånnsjön, Sweden 10 A6 63 16N 12 34 E
Annville, U.S.A. 111 F8 40 20N 76 31W
Annweiler, Germany 25 F3 49 12N 7 57 E
Áno Arkhánai, Greece 39 F7 35 16N 25 11 E
Áno Porróia, Greece 40 E7 41 17N 23 2 E
Áno Síros, Greece 38 D6 37 29N 24 56 E
Áno Viánnos, Greece 36 D7 35 2N 25 21 E
Anorotsangana, Madag. 89 A8 13 56 S 47 55 E
Anosibe, Madag. 89 B8 19 26 S 48 13 E
Anou Mellene, Mali 83 B5 17 29N 0 33 E
Anoumaba, Ivory C. 82 D4 6 23N 4 38W
Anóyia, Greece 36 D6 35 16N 24 52 E
Anping, Hebei, China 56 E8 38 15N 115 30 E
Anping, Liaoning, China 57 D12 41 5N 123 30 E
Anpu Gang, China 58 G7 21 25N 109 50 E
Anqing, China 59 B11 30 30N 117 3 E
Anqiu, China 57 F10 36 25N 119 10 E
Anren, China 59 D9 26 43N 113 18 E
Ansager, Denmark 11 J2 55 43N 8 45 E
Ansai, China 56 F5 36 50N 109 20 E
Ansbach, Germany 25 F6 49 28N 10 34 E
Anseba ➛, Eritrea 81 D4 16 0N 38 30 E
Ansfelden, Austria 26 C7 48 12N 14 17 E
Anshan, China 57 D12 41 5N 122 58 E
Anshun, China 58 D5 26 18N 105 57 E
Ansião, Portugal 34 F2 39 56N 8 27W
Ansley, U.S.A. 112 E5 41 18N 99 23W
Ansó, Spain 32 C4 42 51N 0 48W
Ansoain, Spain 32 C3 42 50N 1 38W
Anson, U.S.A. 113 J5 32 45N 99 54W
Anson B., Australia 92 B5 13 20 S 130 6 E
Ansongo, Mali 83 B5 15 25N 0 35 E
Ansonia, U.S.A. 111 E11 41 21N 73 5W
Anstruther, U.K. 14 E6 56 14N 2 41W
Ansudu, Indonesia 63 E9 2 11 S 139 22 E
Antabamba, Peru 124 F4 14 40 S 73 0W
Antakya, Turkey 70 B3 36 14N 36 10 E
Antalaha, Madag. 89 A9 14 57 S 50 20 E
Antalya, Turkey 72 D4 36 52N 30 45 E
Antalya □, Turkey 39 E12 36 30N 30 0 E
Antalya Körfezi, Turkey 72 D4 36 15N 31 30 E
Antambohobe, Madag. 89 C8 22 20 S 46 47 E
Antanambao-Manampotsy, Madag. 89 B8 19 29 S 48 34 E
Antanambe, Madag. 89 B8 16 26 S 49 52 E
Antananarivo, Madag. 89 B8 18 55 S 47 31 E
Antananarivo □, Madag. 89 B8 19 0 S 47 0 E
Antanifotsy, Madag. 89 B8 19 39 S 47 19 E
Antanimbaribe, Madag. 89 C7 21 30 S 44 48 E
Antanimora, Madag. 89 C8 24 49 S 45 40 E
Antarctic Pen., Antarctica 5 C18 67 0 S 60 0W
Antarctica 5 E3 90 0 S 0 0W
Antelope, Zimbabwe 87 G2 21 2 S 28 31 E
Antequera, Paraguay 126 A4 24 8 S 57 7W
Antequera, Spain 35 H6 37 5N 4 33W
Antero, Mt., U.S.A. 115 G10 38 41N 106 15W
Antevamena, Madag. 89 C7 21 2 S 44 8 E
Anthemoús, Greece 40 F7 40 31N 23 15 E
Anthony, Kans., U.S.A. 113 G5 37 9N 98 2W
Anthony, N. Mex., U.S.A. 115 K10 32 0N 106 36W
Anti Atlas, Morocco 78 C4 30 0N 8 30W
Anti-Lebanon = Ash Sharqi, Al Jabal, Lebanon 75 B5 33 40N 36 10 E
Antibes, France 21 E11 43 34N 7 6 E
Antibes, C. d', France 21 E11 43 31N 7 7 E
Anticosti, Î. d', Canada 103 C7 49 30N 63 0W
Antifer, C. d', France 18 C7 49 41N 0 10 E
Antigo, U.S.A. 112 C10 45 9N 89 9W
Antigonish, Canada 103 C7 45 38N 61 58W
Antigua, Canary Is. 37 F5 28 24N 14 1W
Antigua, W. Indies 121 C7 17 0N 61 50W
Antigua & Barbuda ■, W. Indies 121 C7 17 20N 61 48W
Antigua Guatemala, Guatemala 120 D1 14 34N 90 41W
Antilla, Cuba 120 B4 20 40N 75 50W
Antilles = West Indies, Cent. Amer. 121 D7 15 0N 65 0W
Antioch, U.S.A. 116 G5 38 1N 121 48W
Antioche, Pertuis d', France 20 B2 46 6N 1 20W
Antioquia, Colombia 124 B3 6 40N 75 55W
Antipodes Is., Pac. Oc. 96 M9 49 45 S 178 40 E
Antlers, U.S.A. 113 H7 34 14N 95 37W
Antoetra, Madag. 89 C8 20 46 S 47 20 E
Antofagasta, Chile 126 A1 23 50 S 70 30W
Antofagasta □, Chile 126 A2 24 0 S 69 0W
Antofagasta de la Sierra, Argentina 126 B2 26 5 S 67 20W
Antofalla, Argentina 126 B2 25 30 S 68 5W
Antofalla, Salar de, Argentina 126 B2 25 40 S 67 45W
Anton, U.S.A. 113 J3 33 49N 102 10W
Antongila, Helodrano, Madag. 89 B8 15 30 S 49 50 E
Antonibé, Madag. 89 B8 15 7 S 47 24 E
Antonibé, Presqu'île d', Madag. 89 A8 14 55 S 47 20 E
Antonina, Brazil 127 B6 25 26 S 48 42W
Antrain, France 18 D5 48 28N 1 30W
Antrim, U.K. 15 B5 54 43N 6 14W
Antrim, U.S.A. 110 F3 40 7N 81 21W
Antrim □, U.K. 15 B5 54 56N 6 25W
Antrim, Mts. of, U.K. 15 A5 55 3N 6 14W
Antrim Plateau, Australia 92 C4 18 8 S 128 20 E
Antrodoco, Italy 29 F10 42 25N 13 5 E
Antropovo, Russia 48 A6 58 24N 43 6 E
Antsakabary, Madag. 89 B8 15 3 S 48 56 E
Antsalova, Madag. 89 B7 18 40 S 44 37 E
Antsenavolo, Madag. 89 C8 21 24 S 48 3 E
Antsiafabositra, Madag. 89 B8 17 18 S 46 57 E
Antsirabe, Antananarivo, Madag. 89 B8 19 55 S 47 2 E
Antsirabe, Antsiranana, Madag. 89 A8 14 0 S 49 59 E
Antsirabe, Mahajanga, Madag. 89 B8 15 57 S 48 58 E
Antsiranana, Madag. 89 A8 12 25 S 49 20 E
Antsiranana □, Madag. 89 A8 12 16 S 49 17 E
Antsohihy, Madag. 89 A8 14 50 S 47 59 E
Antsohimbondrona Seranana, Madag. 89 A8 13 7 S 48 48 E
Antu, China 57 C15 42 30N 128 20 E
Antwerp = Antwerpen, Belgium 17 C4 51 13N 4 25 E
Antwerp, U.S.A. 111 B9 44 12N 75 37W
Antwerpen, Belgium 17 C4 51 13N 4 25 E
Antwerpen □, Belgium 17 C4 51 15N 4 40 E
Anupgarh, India 68 E5 29 10N 73 10 E
Anuppur, India 69 H9 23 6N 81 41 E
Anuradhapura, Sri Lanka 66 Q12 8 22N 80 28 E
Anveh, Iran 71 E7 27 23N 54 11 E
Anvers = Antwerpen, Belgium 17 C4 51 13N 4 25 E
Anvers I., Antarctica 5 C17 64 30 S 63 40W
Anwen, China 59 C13 29 4N 120 26 E
Anxi, Fujian, China 59 E12 25 2N 118 12 E
Anxi, Gansu, China 60 B4 40 30N 95 43 E
Anxian, China 58 B5 31 40N 104 25 E
Anxiang, China 59 C9 29 27N 112 11 E
Anxious B., Australia 95 E1 33 24 S 134 45 E
Anyama, Ivory C. 82 D4 5 30N 4 3W
Anyang, China 56 F8 36 5N 114 21 E
Anyer-Kidul, Indonesia 63 G11 6 4 S 105 53 E
Anyi, Jiangxi, China 59 C10 28 49N 115 25 E
Anyi, Shanxi, China 56 G6 35 2N 111 2 E
Anyuan, China 59 E10 25 9N 115 21 E
Anyue, China 58 B5 30 9N 105 50 E
Anza, U.S.A. 117 M10 33 35N 116 39W
Anze, China 56 F7 36 10N 112 12 E
Anzhero-Sudzhensk, Russia 50 D9 56 10N 86 0 E
Ánzio, Italy 30 A5 41 27N 12 37 E
Aoga-Shima, Japan 55 H9 32 28N 139 46 E
Aoiz, Spain 32 C3 42 46N 1 22W
Aomen = Macau □, China 59 F9 22 16N 113 35 E
Aomori, Japan 54 D10 40 45N 140 45 E
Aomori □, Japan 54 D10 40 45N 140 40 E
Aonla, India 69 E8 28 16N 79 11 E
Aoraki Mount Cook, N.Z. 91 K3 43 36 S 170 9 E
Aosta, Italy 28 C4 45 45N 7 20 E
Aoudéras, Niger 83 B6 17 45N 8 20 E
Aoukâr, Mauritania 82 B3 17 40N 10 0W
Apa ➛, S. Amer. 126 A4 22 6 S 58 2W
Apache, U.S.A. 113 H5 34 54N 98 22W
Apache Junction, U.S.A. 115 K8 33 25N 111 33W
Apalachee B., U.S.A. 109 L4 30 0N 84 0W
Apalachicola, U.S.A. 109 L3 29 43N 84 59W
Apalachicola ➛, U.S.A. 109 L3 29 43N 84 58W
Apam, Ghana 83 D4 5 19N 0 42W
Apapa, Nigeria 83 D5 6 25N 3 25 E
Apaporis ➛, Colombia 124 D5 1 23 S 69 25W
Aparri, Phil. 61 B4 18 22N 121 38 E
Apateu, Romania 42 D6 46 36N 21 47 E
Apatin, Serbia, Yug. 42 E4 45 40N 19 0 E
Apatity, Russia 50 C4 67 34N 33 22 E
Apatzingán, Mexico 118 D4 19 0N 102 20W
Apeldoorn, Neths. 17 B5 52 13N 5 57 E
Apen, Germany 24 B3 53 13N 7 48 E
Apennines = Appennini, Italy 28 E7 44 0N 10 0 E
Aphrodisias, Turkey 39 D10 37 42N 28 46 E
Apia, Samoa 91 A13 13 50 S 171 50W
Apiacás, Serra dos, Brazil 124 E7 9 50 S 57 0W
Apies ➛, S. Africa 89 D4 25 15 S 28 8 E
Apizaco, Mexico 119 D5 19 26N 98 9W
Aplao, Peru 124 G4 16 0 S 72 40W
Apo, Mt., Phil. 63 C7 6 53N 125 14 E
Apolakkiá, Greece 36 C9 36 5N 27 48 E
Apolakkiá, Órmos, Greece 36 C9 36 5N 27 45 E
Apolda, Germany 24 D7 51 2N 11 32 E
Apollonia, Greece 38 E6 36 58N 24 43 E
Apolo, Bolivia 124 F5 14 30 S 68 30W
Aporé ➛, Brazil 125 G8 19 27 S 50 57W
Apostle Is., U.S.A. 112 B9 47 0N 90 40W
Apóstoles, Argentina 127 B4 28 0 S 56 0W
Apostolos Andreas, C., Cyprus 36 D13 35 42N 34 35 E
Apostolovo, Ukraine 47 J7 47 39N 33 39 E
Apoteri, Guyana 124 C7 4 2N 58 32W
Appalachian Mts., U.S.A. 108 G6 38 0N 80 0W
Äppelbo, Sweden 10 D8 60 29N 14 1 E
Appennini, Italy 28 E7 44 0N 10 0 E
Appennino Ligure, Italy 28 D6 44 30N 9 0 E
Appenzell-Ausser Rhoden □, Switz. 25 H5 47 23N 9 23 E
Appenzell-Inner Rhoden □, Switz. 25 H5 47 20N 9 25 E
Appiano, Italy 29 B8 46 28N 11 15 E
Apple Hill, Canada 111 A10 45 13N 74 46W
Apple Valley, U.S.A. 117 L9 34 32N 117 14W
Appleby-in-Westmorland, U.K. 12 C5 54 35N 2 29W
Appleton, U.S.A. 108 C1 44 16N 88 25W
Approuague ➛, Fr. Guiana 125 C8 4 30N 51 57W
Apricena, Italy 29 G12 41 47N 15 27 E
Aprília, Italy 30 A5 41 36N 12 39 E
Apsheronsk, Russia 49 H4 44 28N 39 42 E
Apsley, Canada 110 B6 44 45N 78 6W
Apt, France 21 E9 43 53N 5 24 E
Apuane, Alpi, Italy 28 D7 44 7N 10 14 E
Apucarana, Brazil 127 A5 23 55 S 51 33W
Apulia = Púglia □, Italy 31 A9 41 15N 16 15 E
Apure ➛, Venezuela 124 B5 7 37N 66 25W
Apurimac ➛, Peru 124 F4 12 17 S 73 56W
Apuseni, Munţii, Romania 42 D7 46 30N 22 45 E
Āqā Jarī, Iran 71 D6 30 42N 49 50 E
Aqaba = Al 'Aqabah, Jordan 75 F4 29 31N 35 0 E
Aqaba, G. of, Red Sea 70 D2 28 15N 33 20 E
'Aqaba, Khalīj al = Aqaba, G. of, Red Sea 70 D2 28 15N 33 20 E
'Aqdā, Iran 71 C7 32 26N 53 37 E
Aqīq, Sudan 80 D4 18 14N 38 12 E
Aqīq, Khalīg, Sudan 80 D4 18 20N 38 10 E
Aqmola = Astana, Kazakhstan 50 D8 51 10N 71 30 E
'Aqrah, Iraq 70 B4 36 46N 43 45 E
Aqtaū, Kazakhstan 50 E6 43 39N 51 12 E
Aqtöbe, Kazakhstan 50 D6 50 17N 57 10 E
Aquidauana, Brazil 125 H7 20 30 S 55 50W
Aquiles Serdán, Mexico 118 B3 28 37N 105 54W
Aquin, Haiti 121 C5 18 16N 73 24W
Aquitaine □, France 20 D3 44 25N 0 30W
Aqviligjuaq = Pelly Bay, Canada 101 B11 68 38N 89 50W
Ar Rachidiya = Er Rachidia, Morocco 78 B5 31 58N 4 20W
Ar Rafīd, Syria 75 C4 32 57N 35 52 E
Ar Raḥḥālīyah, Iraq 70 C4 32 44N 43 23 E
Ar Ramādī, Iraq 70 C4 33 25N 43 20 E
Ar Ramthā, Jordan 75 C5 32 34N 36 0 E
Ar Raqqah, Syria 70 C3 35 59N 39 8 E
Ar Rass, Si. Arabia 70 E4 25 50N 43 40 E
Ar Rawshān, Si. Arabia 80 C5 20 2N 42 36 E
Ar Rifā'ī, Iraq 70 D5 31 50N 46 10 E
Ar Riyāḍ, Si. Arabia 70 E5 24 41N 46 42 E
Ar Ru'ays, Qatar 71 E6 26 8N 51 12 E
Ar Rukhaymīyah, Iraq 70 D5 29 22N 45 38 E
Ar Ruṣāfah, Syria 70 C3 35 45N 38 49 E
Ar Ruṭbah, Iraq 70 C4 33 0N 40 15 E
Ara, India 69 G11 25 35N 84 32 E
Ara Goro, Ethiopia 81 F5 5 48N 41 18 E
Ara Tera, Ethiopia 81 F5 6 38N 40 57 E
Arab, U.S.A. 109 H2 34 19N 86 30W
'Arab, Bahr el ➛, Sudan 81 F2 9 0N 29 30 E
Arab, Khalîg el, Egypt 80 A2 30 55N 29 0 E
Arab, Shatt al ➛, Asia 71 D6 30 0N 48 31 E
'Araba, W. ➛, Egypt 80 J8 28 19N 33 31 E
'Arabābād, Iran 71 C8 33 2N 57 41 E
Araban, Turkey 72 D7 37 28N 37 44 E
Arabatskaya Strelka, Ukraine 47 K8 45 40N 35 0 E
Arabba, Italy 29 B8 46 30N 11 52 E
Arabia, Asia 52 G8 25 0N 45 0 E
Arabian Desert = Es Sahrâ' Esh Sharqîya, Egypt 80 B3 27 30N 32 30 E
Arabian Gulf = Gulf, The, Asia 71 E6 27 0N 50 0 E
Arabian Sea, Ind. Oc. 52 H10 16 0N 65 0 E
Araç, Turkey 72 B5 41 15N 33 21 E
Aracaju, Brazil 125 F11 10 55 S 37 4W
Aracati, Brazil 125 D11 4 30 S 37 44W
Araçatuba, Brazil 127 A5 21 10 S 50 30W
Aracena, Spain 35 H4 37 53N 6 38W
Aracena, Sierra de, Spain 35 H4 37 50N 6 50W
Aračinovo, Macedonia 40 D5 42 1N 21 34 E
Araçuaí, Brazil 125 G10 16 52 S 42 4W
'Arad, Israel 75 D4 31 15N 35 12 E
Arad, Romania 42 D6 46 10N 21 20 E
Arad □, Romania 42 D6 46 20N 22 0 E
Arādān, Iran 71 C7 35 21N 52 30 E
Aradhippou, Cyprus 36 E12 34 57N 33 36 E
Arafura Sea, E. Indies 52 K17 9 0 S 135 0 E
Aragats, Armenia 49 K7 40 30N 44 15 E
Aragón □, Spain 32 D4 41 25N 0 40W
Aragón ➛, Spain 32 C3 42 13N 1 44W
Aragona, Italy 30 E6 37 24N 13 37 E
Araguacema, Brazil 125 E9 8 50 S 49 20W
Araguaia ➛, Brazil 122 D6 5 21 S 48 41W
Araguaína, Brazil 125 E9 7 12 S 48 12W
Araguari, Brazil 125 G9 18 38 S 48 11W
Araguari ➛, Brazil 125 C9 1 15N 49 55W
Arain, India 68 F6 26 27N 75 2 E
Arak, Algeria 78 C6 25 20N 3 45 E
Arāk, Iran 71 C6 34 0N 49 40 E
Araka, Sudan 81 G3 4 20N 30 23 E
Arakan Coast, Burma 67 K19 19 0N 94 0 E
Arakan Yoma, Burma 67 K19 20 0N 94 40 E
Arákhova, Greece 38 C4 38 28N 22 35 E
Arakli, Turkey 73 B8 41 6N 40 2 E
Araks = Aras, Rūd-e ➛, Asia 49 K9 40 5N 48 29 E
Aral, Kazakhstan 50 E7 46 41N 61 45 E
Aral Sea, Asia 50 E7 44 30N 60 0 E
Aral Tengizi = Aral Sea, Asia 50 E7 44 30N 60 0 E
Aralsk = Aral, Kazakhstan 50 E7 46 41N 61 45 E
Aralskoye More = Aral Sea, Asia 50 E7 44 30N 60 0 E
Aralsor, Ozero, Kazakhstan 49 F9 49 5N 48 12 E
Aramac, Australia 94 C4 22 58 S 145 14 E
Aran I., Ireland 15 A3 55 0N 8 30W
Aran Is., Ireland 15 C2 53 6N 9 38W
Aranda de Duero, Spain 34 D7 41 39N 3 42W
Arandān, Iran 70 C5 35 23N 46 55 E
Aranđelovac, Serbia, Yug. 40 B4 44 18N 20 34 E
Aranjuez, Spain 34 E7 40 1N 3 40W
Aranos, Namibia 88 C2 24 9 S 19 7 E
Aransas Pass, U.S.A. 113 M6 27 55N 97 9W

Aranyaprathet

Aranyaprathet, *Thailand* **64 F4** 13 41N 102 30 E
Araouane, *Mali* **82 B4** 18 55N 3 30W
Arapahoe, *U.S.A.* **112 E5** 40 18N 99 54W
Arapey Grande →, *Uruguay* **126 C4** 30 55 S 57 49W
Arapgir, *Turkey* **70 B3** 39 5N 38 30 E
Arapiraca, *Brazil* **125 E11** 9 45 S 36 39W
Arapongas, *Brazil* **127 A5** 23 29 S 51 28W
Ar'ar, *Si. Arabia* **70 D4** 30 59N 41 2 E
Araranguá, *Brazil* **127 B6** 29 0 S 49 30W
Araraquara, *Brazil* **125 H9** 21 50 S 48 0W
Ararás, Serra das, *Brazil* **127 B5** 25 0 S 53 10W
Ararat, *Armenia* **73 C11** 39 48N 44 50 E
Ararat, *Australia* **95 F3** 37 16 S 143 0 E
Ararat, Mt. = Ağrı Dağı, *Turkey* **70 B5** 39 50N 44 15 E
Araria, *India* **69 F12** 26 9N 87 33 E
Araripe, Chapada do, *Brazil* **125 E11** 7 20 S 40 0W
Araruama, L. de, *Brazil* **127 A7** 22 53 S 42 12W
Aras, Rūd-e →, *Asia* **49 K9** 40 5N 48 29 E
Aratāne, *Mauritania* **82 B3** 18 24N 8 32W
Arauca, *Colombia* **124 B4** 7 0N 70 40W
Arauca →, *Venezuela* **124 B5** 7 24N 66 35W
Arauco, *Chile* **126 D1** 37 16 S 73 25W
Arawa, *Ethiopia* **81 F5** 9 57N 41 58 E
Araxá, *Brazil* **125 G9** 19 35 S 46 55W
Araya, Pen. de, *Venezuela* **124 A6** 10 40N 64 0W
Arba Gugu, *Ethiopia* **81 F5** 8 40N 40 15 E
Arba Minch, *Ethiopia* **81 F4** 6 0N 37 30 E
Arbat, *Iraq* **70 C5** 35 25N 45 35 E
Árbatax, *Italy* **30 C2** 39 56N 9 42 E
Arbi, *Ethiopia* **81 F4** 9 4N 35 7 E
Arbīl, *Iraq* **70 B5** 36 15N 44 5 E
Arboga, *Sweden* **10 E9** 59 24N 15 52 E
Arbois, *France* **19 F12** 46 55N 5 46 E
Arbore, *Ethiopia* **81 F4** 5 3N 36 50 E
Arborèa, *Italy* **30 C1** 39 46N 8 35 E
Arborfield, *Canada* **105 C8** 53 6N 103 39W
Arborg, *Canada* **105 C9** 50 54N 97 13W
Arbre du Ténéré, *Niger* **83 B7** 17 50N 10 4 E
Arbroath, *U.K.* **14 E6** 56 34N 2 35W
Arbuckle, *U.S.A.* **116 F4** 39 1N 122 3W
Arbus, *Italy* **30 C1** 39 30N 8 33 E
Arc →, *France* **21 C10** 45 34N 6 12 E
Arc-lès-Gray, *France* **19 E12** 47 28N 5 34 E
Arcachon, *France* **20 D2** 44 40N 1 10W
Arcachon, Bassin d', *France* **20 D2** 44 42N 1 10W
Arcade, *Calif., U.S.A.* **117 L8** 34 2N 118 15W
Arcade, *N.Y., U.S.A.* **110 D6** 42 32N 78 25W
Arcadia, *Fla., U.S.A.* **109 M5** 27 13N 81 52W
Arcadia, *La., U.S.A.* **113 J8** 32 33N 92 55W
Arcadia, *Pa., U.S.A.* **110 F6** 40 47N 78 51W
Arcata, *U.S.A.* **114 F1** 40 52N 124 5W
Arcévia, *Italy* **29 E9** 43 30N 12 56 E
Archangel = Arkhangelsk, *Russia* **50 C5** 64 38N 40 36 E
Archar, *Bulgaria* **40 C6** 43 50N 22 54 E
Archbald, *U.S.A.* **111 E9** 41 30N 75 32W
Archena, *Spain* **33 G3** 38 9N 1 16W
Archer →, *Australia* **94 A3** 13 28 S 141 41 E
Archer B., *Australia* **94 A3** 13 20 S 141 30 E
Archers Post, *Kenya* **86 B4** 0 35N 37 35 E
Arches National Park, *U.S.A.* **115 G9** 38 45N 109 25W
Archidona, *Spain* **35 H6** 37 6N 4 22W
Arci, Mte., *Italy* **30 C1** 39 47N 8 45 E
Arcidosso, *Italy* **29 F8** 42 52N 11 33 E
Arcis-sur-Aube, *France* **19 D11** 48 32N 4 10 E
Arckaringa Cr. →, *Australia* **95 D2** 28 10 S 135 22 E
Arco, *Italy* **28 C7** 45 55N 10 53 E
Arco, *U.S.A.* **114 E7** 43 38N 113 18W
Arcos = Arcos de Jalón, *Spain* **32 D2** 41 12N 2 16W
Arcos de Jalón, *Spain* **32 D2** 41 12N 2 16W
Arcos de la Frontera, *Spain* **35 J5** 36 45N 5 49W
Arcos de Valdevez, *Portugal* **34 D2** 41 55N 8 22W
Arcot, *India* **66 N11** 12 53N 79 20 E
Arcozelo, *Portugal* **34 E3** 40 32N 7 47W
Arctic Bay, *Canada* **101 A11** 73 1N 85 7W
Arctic Ocean, *Arctic* **4 B18** 78 0N 160 0W
Arctic Red River = Tsiigehtchic, *Canada* **100 B6** 67 15N 134 0W
Arda →, *Bulgaria* **41 E10** 41 40N 26 30 E
Arda →, *Italy* **28 C7** 45 2N 10 2 E
Ardabīl, *Iran* **71 B6** 38 15N 48 18 E
Ardahan, *Turkey* **73 B10** 41 7N 42 41 E
Ardakān = Sepīdān, *Iran* **71 D7** 30 20N 52 5 E
Ardakān, *Iran* **71 C7** 32 19N 53 59 E
Ardala, *Sweden* **11 F7** 58 22N 13 19 E
Ardales, *Spain* **35 J6** 36 53N 4 51W
Ardèche □, *France* **21 D8** 44 42N 4 16 E
Ardèche →, *France* **21 D8** 44 16N 4 39 E
Ardee, *Ireland* **15 C5** 53 52N 6 33W
Arden, *Canada* **110 B8** 44 43N 76 56W
Arden, *Denmark* **11 H3** 56 46N 9 52 E
Arden, *Calif., U.S.A.* **116 G5** 38 36N 121 33W
Arden, *Nev., U.S.A.* **117 J11** 36 1N 115 14W
Ardenne, *Belgium* **6 F7** 49 50N 5 5 E
Ardennes = Ardenne, *Belgium* **6 F7** 49 50N 5 5 E
Ardennes □, *France* **19 C11** 49 35N 4 40 E
Ardentes, *France* **19 F8** 46 45N 1 50 E
Arderin, *Ireland* **15 C4** 53 2N 7 39W
Ardeşen, *Turkey* **73 B9** 41 12N 41 2 E
Ardestān, *Iran* **71 C7** 33 20N 52 25 E
Árdhas →, *Greece* **41 E10** 41 40N 26 30 E
Ardhéa, *Greece* **40 F6** 40 58N 22 3 E
Ardila →, *Portugal* **35 G3** 38 12N 7 28W
Ardino, *Bulgaria* **41 E9** 41 34N 25 9 E
Ardivachar Pt., *U.K.* **14 D1** 57 23N 7 26W
Ardlethan, *Australia* **95 E4** 34 22 S 146 53 E
Ardmore, *Okla., U.S.A.* **113 H6** 34 10N 97 8W
Ardmore, *Pa., U.S.A.* **111 G9** 39 58N 75 18W
Ardnamurchan, Pt. of, *U.K.* **14 E2** 56 43N 6 14W
Ardnave Pt., *U.K.* **14 F2** 55 53N 6 20W
Ardon, *Russia* **49 J7** 43 10N 44 18 E
Ardore, *Italy* **31 D9** 38 11N 16 10 E
Ardres, *France* **19 B8** 50 50N 1 59 E
Ardrossan, *Australia* **95 E2** 34 26 S 137 53 E
Ardrossan, *U.K.* **14 F4** 55 39N 4 49W
Ards Pen., *U.K.* **15 B6** 54 33N 5 34W
Arduan, *Sudan* **80 D3** 19 54N 30 20 E
Ardud, *Romania* **42 C7** 47 37N 22 52 E
Åre, *Sweden* **10 A7** 63 22N 13 15 E
Arecibo, *Puerto Rico* **121 C6** 18 29N 66 43W
Areia Branca, *Brazil* **125 E11** 5 0 S 37 0W
Arena, Pt., *U.S.A.* **116 G3** 38 57N 123 44W
Arenal, *Honduras* **120 C2** 15 21N 86 50W
Arenas = Las Arenas, *Spain* **34 B6** 43 17N 4 50W
Arenas de San Pedro, *Spain* **34 E5** 40 12N 5 5W
Arendal, *Norway* **9 G13** 58 28N 8 46 E
Arendsee, *Germany* **24 C7** 52 52N 11 27 E
Arenys de Mar, *Spain* **32 D7** 41 35N 2 33 E
Arenzano, *Italy* **28 D5** 44 24N 8 41 E
Areópolis, *Greece* **38 E4** 36 40N 22 22 E
Arequipa, *Peru* **124 G4** 16 20 S 71 30W
Arero, *Ethiopia* **81 G4** 4 41N 38 50 E
Arès, *France* **20 D2** 44 47N 1 8W
Arévalo, *Spain* **34 D6** 41 3N 4 43W
Arezzo, *Italy* **29 E8** 43 25N 11 53 E
Arga, *Turkey* **70 B3** 38 21N 37 59 E
Arga →, *Spain* **32 C3** 42 18N 1 47W
Argalastí, *Greece* **38 B5** 39 13N 23 13 E
Argamasilla de Alba, *Spain* **35 F7** 39 8N 3 5W
Argamasilla de Calatrava, *Spain* **35 G6** 38 44N 4 4W
Arganda, *Spain* **34 E7** 40 19N 3 26W
Arganil, *Portugal* **34 E2** 40 13N 8 3W
Argedeb, *Ethiopia* **81 F5** 6 11N 41 13 E
Argelès-Gazost, *France* **20 E3** 43 0N 0 6W
Argelès-sur-Mer, *France* **20 F7** 42 34N 3 1 E
Argens →, *France* **21 E10** 43 24N 6 44 E
Argent-sur-Sauldre, *France* **19 E9** 47 33N 2 25 E
Argenta, *Canada* **104 C5** 50 11N 116 56W
Argenta, *Italy* **29 D8** 44 37N 11 50 E
Argentan, *France* **18 D6** 48 45N 0 1W
Argentário, Mte., *Italy* **29 F8** 42 24N 11 9 E
Argentat, *France* **20 C5** 45 6N 1 56 E
Argentera, *Italy* **28 D4** 44 12N 7 5 E
Argenteuil, *France* **19 D9** 48 57N 2 14 E
Argentia, *Canada* **103 C9** 47 18N 53 58W
Argentiera, C. dell', *Italy* **30 B1** 40 44N 8 8 E
Argentina ■, *S. Amer.* **128 D3** 35 0 S 66 0W
Argentina Is., *Antarctica* **5 C17** 66 0 S 64 0W
Argentino, L., *Argentina* **128 G2** 50 10 S 73 0W
Argenton-Château, *France* **18 F6** 46 59N 0 27W
Argenton-sur-Creuse, *France* **19 F8** 46 36N 1 30 E
Argeş □, *Romania* **43 F9** 45 0N 24 45 E
Argeş →, *Romania* **43 F11** 44 5N 26 38 E
Arghandab →, *Afghan.* **68 D1** 31 30N 64 15 E
Argheile, *Ethiopia* **81 F5** 5 19N 42 4 E
Argo, *Sudan* **80 D3** 19 28N 30 30 E
Argolikós Kólpos, *Greece* **38 D4** 37 20N 22 52 E
Argolís □, *Greece* **38 D4** 37 38N 22 50 E
Argonne, *France* **19 C12** 49 10N 5 0 E
Árgos, *Greece* **38 D4** 37 40N 22 43 E
Árgos Orestikón, *Greece* **40 F5** 40 27N 21 18 E
Argostólion, *Greece* **38 C2** 38 12N 20 33 E
Arguedas, *Spain* **32 C3** 42 11N 1 36W
Arguello, Pt., *U.S.A.* **117 L6** 34 35N 120 39W
Arguineguín, *Canary Is.* **37 G4** 27 46N 15 41W
Argun, *Russia* **49 J7** 43 18N 45 52 E
Argun →, *Russia* **51 D13** 53 20N 121 28 E
Argungu, *Nigeria* **83 C5** 12 40N 4 31 E
Argus Pk., *U.S.A.* **117 K9** 35 52N 117 26W
Argyle, L., *Australia* **92 C4** 16 20 S 128 40 E
Argyll & Bute □, *U.K.* **14 E3** 56 13N 5 28W
Arhavi, *Turkey* **73 B9** 41 21N 41 18 E
Århus, *Denmark* **11 H4** 56 8N 10 11 E
Århus Amtskommune □, *Denmark* **11 H4** 56 15N 10 15 E
Ariadnoye, *Russia* **54 B7** 45 8N 134 25 E
Ariamsvlei, *Namibia* **88 D2** 28 9 S 19 51 E
Ariano Irpino, *Italy* **31 A8** 41 9N 15 5 E
Aribinda, *Burkina Faso* **83 C4** 14 17N 0 52W
Arica, *Chile* **124 G4** 18 32 S 70 20W
Arica, *Colombia* **124 D4** 2 0 S 71 50W
Arico, *Canary Is.* **37 F3** 28 9N 16 29W
Arid, C., *Australia* **93 F3** 34 1 S 123 10 E
Arida, *Japan* **55 G7** 34 5N 135 8 E
Ariège □, *France* **20 F5** 42 56N 1 30 E
Ariège →, *France* **20 E5** 43 30N 1 25 E
Arieş →, *Romania* **43 D8** 46 24N 23 20 E
Arihā, *Israel* **80 A4** 31 51N 35 27 E
Arilje, *Serbia, Yug.* **40 C4** 43 44N 20 7 E
Arílla, Ákra, *Greece* **36 A3** 39 43N 19 39 E
Arima, *Trin. & Tob.* **121 D7** 10 38N 61 17W
Arinos →, *Brazil* **122 E5** 10 25 S 58 20W
Ario de Rosales, *Mexico* **118 D4** 19 12N 102 0W
Ariogala, *Lithuania* **44 C10** 55 16N 23 28 E
Aripuanã, *Brazil* **124 E6** 9 25 S 60 30W
Aripuanã →, *Brazil* **122 D4** 5 7 S 60 25W
Ariquemes, *Brazil* **124 E6** 9 55 S 63 6W
Arisaig, *U.K.* **14 E3** 56 55N 5 51W
Arîsh, W. el →, *Egypt* **80 A3** 31 9N 33 49 E
Arissa, *Ethiopia* **81 E5** 11 10N 41 35 E
Aristazabal I., *Canada* **104 C3** 52 40N 129 10W
Arivonimamo, *Madag.* **89 B8** 19 1 S 47 11 E
Ariza, *Spain* **32 D2** 41 19N 2 3W
Arizaro, Salar de, *Argentina* **126 A2** 24 40 S 67 50W
Arizona, *Argentina* **126 D2** 35 45 S 65 25W
Arizona □, *U.S.A.* **115 J8** 34 0N 112 0W
Arizpe, *Mexico* **118 A2** 30 20N 110 11W
Årjäng, *Sweden* **10 E6** 59 24N 12 8 E
Arjeplog, *Sweden* **8 D18** 66 3N 18 2 E
Arjona, *Colombia* **124 A3** 10 14N 75 22W
Arjona, *Spain* **35 H6** 37 56N 4 4W
Arjuna, *Indonesia* **63 G15** 7 49 S 112 34 E
Arka, *Russia* **51 C15** 60 15N 142 0 E
Arkadak, *Russia* **48 E6** 51 58N 43 30 E
Arkadelphia, *U.S.A.* **113 H8** 34 7N 93 4W
Arkadhía □, *Greece* **38 D4** 37 30N 22 20 E
Arkaig, L., *U.K.* **14 E3** 56 59N 5 10W
Arkalyk = Arqalyk, *Kazakhstan* **50 D7** 50 13N 66 50 E
Arkansas □, *U.S.A.* **113 H8** 35 0N 92 30W
Arkansas →, *U.S.A.* **113 J9** 33 47N 91 4W
Arkansas City, *U.S.A.* **113 G6** 37 4N 97 2W
Arkaroola, *Australia* **95 E2** 30 20 S 139 22 E
Árkathos →, *Greece* **38 B3** 39 20N 21 4 E
Arkhángelos, *Greece* **36 C10** 36 13N 28 7 E
Arkhangelsk, *Russia* **50 C5** 64 38N 40 36 E
Arkhangelskoye, *Russia* **48 E5** 51 32N 40 58 E
Arki, *India* **68 D7** 31 9N 76 58 E
Arkiko, *Eritrea* **81 D4** 15 33N 39 30 E
Arklow, *Ireland* **15 D5** 52 48N 6 10W
Árkoi, *Greece* **39 D8** 37 24N 26 44 E
Arkona, Kap, *Germany* **24 A9** 54 42N 13 26 E
Arkösund, *Sweden* **11 F10** 58 29N 16 56 E
Arkoúdhi, *Greece* **38 C2** 38 33N 20 43 E
Arkport, *U.S.A.* **110 D7** 42 24N 77 42W
Arkticheskiy, Mys, *Russia* **51 A10** 81 10N 95 0 E
Arkul, *Russia* **48 B10** 57 17N 50 3 E
Arkville, *U.S.A.* **111 D10** 42 9N 74 37W
Årla, *Sweden* **10 E10** 59 17N 16 40 E
Arlanza →, *Spain* **34 C6** 42 6N 4 9W
Arlanzón →, *Spain* **34 C6** 42 3N 4 17W
Arlbergpass, *Austria* **26 D3** 47 9N 10 12 E
Arles, *France* **21 E8** 43 41N 4 40 E
Arlington, *S. Africa* **89 D4** 28 1 S 27 53 E
Arlington, *N.Y., U.S.A.* **111 E11** 41 42N 73 54W
Arlington, *Oreg., U.S.A.* **114 D3** 45 43N 120 12W
Arlington, *S. Dak., U.S.A.* **112 C6** 44 22N 97 8W
Arlington, *Tex., U.S.A.* **113 J6** 32 44N 97 7W
Arlington, *Va., U.S.A.* **108 F7** 38 53N 77 7W
Arlington, *Vt., U.S.A.* **111 C11** 43 5N 73 9W
Arlington, *Wash., U.S.A.* **116 B4** 48 12N 122 8W
Arlington Heights, *U.S.A.* **108 D2** 42 5N 87 59W
Arlit, *Niger* **78 E7** 19 0N 7 38 E
Arlon, *Belgium* **17 E5** 49 42N 5 49 E
Arltunga, *Australia* **94 C1** 23 26 S 134 41 E
Arly, *Burkina Faso* **83 C5** 11 35N 1 28 E
Armagh, *U.K.* **15 B5** 54 21N 6 39W
Armagh □, *U.K.* **15 B5** 54 18N 6 37W
Armagnac, *France* **20 E4** 43 50N 0 10 E
Armançon →, *France* **19 E10** 47 59N 3 30 E
Armavir, *Russia* **49 H5** 45 2N 41 7 E
Armenia, *Colombia* **124 C3** 4 35N 75 45W
Armenia ■, *Asia* **49 K7** 40 20N 45 0 E
Armeniş, *Romania* **42 E7** 45 13N 22 17 E
Armenistís, Ákra, *Greece* **36 C9** 36 8N 27 42 E
Armentières, *France* **19 B9** 50 40N 2 50 E
Armidale, *Australia* **95 E5** 30 30 S 151 40 E
Armilla, *Spain* **35 H7** 37 9N 3 37W
Armour, *U.S.A.* **112 D5** 43 19N 98 21W
Armstrong, *B.C., Canada* **104 C5** 50 25N 119 10W
Armstrong, *Ont., Canada* **102 B2** 50 18N 89 4W
Armutlu, *Bursa, Turkey* **41 F12** 40 31N 28 50 E
Armutlu, *İzmir, Turkey* **39 C9** 38 24N 27 34 E
Arnaía, *Greece* **40 F7** 40 30N 23 38 E
Arnarfjörður, *Iceland* **8 D2** 65 48N 23 40W
Arnaud →, *Canada* **101 B12** 60 0N 70 0W
Arnauti, C., *Cyprus* **36 D11** 35 6N 32 17 E
Arnay-le-Duc, *France* **19 E11** 47 10N 4 27 E
Arnedillo, *Spain* **32 C2** 42 13N 2 14W
Arnedo, *Spain* **32 C2** 42 12N 2 5W
Arnett, *U.S.A.* **113 G5** 36 8N 99 46W
Arnhem, *Neths.* **17 C5** 51 58N 5 55 E
Arnhem, C., *Australia* **94 A2** 12 20 S 137 30 E
Arnhem B., *Australia* **94 A2** 12 20 S 136 10 E
Arnhem Land, *Australia* **94 A1** 13 10 S 134 30 E
Árnissa, *Greece* **40 F5** 40 47N 21 49 E
Arno →, *Italy* **28 E7** 43 41N 10 17 E
Arno Bay, *Australia* **95 E2** 33 54 S 136 34 E
Arnold, *U.K.* **12 D6** 53 1N 1 7W
Arnold, *U.S.A.* **116 G6** 38 15N 120 20W
Arnoldstein, *Austria* **26 E6** 46 33N 13 43 E
Arnon →, *France* **19 E9** 47 13N 2 1 E
Arnot, *Canada* **105 B9** 55 56N 96 41W
Arnøy, *Norway* **8 A19** 70 9N 20 40 E
Arnprior, *Canada* **102 C4** 45 26N 76 21W
Arnsberg, *Germany* **24 D4** 51 24N 8 5 E
Arnstadt, *Germany* **24 E6** 50 50N 10 56 E
Aroab, *Namibia* **88 D2** 26 41 S 19 39 E
Aroánia Óri, *Greece* **38 D4** 37 56N 22 12 E
Aroche, *Spain* **35 H4** 37 56N 6 57W
Arochuku, *Nigeria* **83 D6** 5 21N 7 54 E
Arolsen, *Germany* **24 D5** 51 23N 9 2 E
Aron, *India* **68 G6** 25 57N 77 56 E
Aron →, *France* **19 F10** 46 50N 3 28 E
Arona, *Italy* **28 C5** 45 46N 8 34 E
Aroroy, *Phil.* **61 E5** 12 31N 123 24 E
Arosa, Ría de, *Spain* **34 C2** 42 28N 8 57W
Arpajon, *France* **19 D9** 48 36N 2 15 E
Arpajon-sur-Cère, *France* **20 D6** 44 53N 2 28 E
Arpaşu de Jos, *Romania* **43 E9** 45 47N 24 37 E
Arqalyk, *Kazakhstan* **50 D7** 50 13N 66 50 E
Arrah = Ara, *India* **69 G11** 25 35N 84 32 E
Arrah, *Ivory C.* **82 D4** 6 40N 3 58W
Arraiolos, *Portugal* **35 G3** 38 44N 7 59W
Arran, *U.K.* **14 F3** 55 34N 5 12W
Arras, *France* **19 B9** 50 17N 2 46 E
Arrasate, *Spain* **32 B2** 43 4N 2 30W
Arrats →, *France* **20 D4** 44 6N 0 52 E
Arreau, *France* **20 F4** 42 54N 0 22 E
Arrecife, *Canary Is.* **37 F6** 28 57N 13 37W
Arrecifes, *Argentina* **126 C3** 34 6 S 60 9W
Arrée, Mts. d', *France* **18 D3** 48 26N 3 55W
Arresø, *Denmark* **11 J6** 55 58N 12 6 E
Arriaga, *Chiapas, Mexico* **119 D6** 16 15N 93 52W
Arriaga, *San Luis Potosí, Mexico* **118 C4** 21 55N 101 23W
Arrilalah, *Australia* **94 C3** 23 43 S 143 54 E
Arrino, *Australia* **93 E2** 29 30 S 115 40 E
Arriondas, *Spain* **34 B5** 43 23N 5 11W
Arromanches-les-Bains, *France* **18 C6** 49 20N 0 38W
Arronches, *Portugal* **35 F3** 39 8N 7 16W
Arros →, *France* **20 E3** 43 40N 0 2W
Arrow, L., *Ireland* **15 B3** 54 3N 8 19W
Arrowhead, L., *U.S.A.* **117 L9** 34 16N 117 10W
Arrowtown, *N.Z.* **91 L2** 44 57 S 168 50 E
Arroyo de la Luz, *Spain* **35 F4** 39 30N 6 38W
Arroyo Grande, *U.S.A.* **117 K6** 35 7N 120 35W
Års, *Denmark* **11 H3** 56 48N 9 30 E
Ars, *Iran* **70 B5** 37 9N 47 46 E
Ars-sur-Moselle, *France* **19 C13** 49 5N 6 4 E
Arsenault L., *Canada* **105 B7** 55 6N 108 32W
Arsenev, *Russia* **54 B6** 44 10N 133 15 E
Arsi □, *Ethiopia* **81 F4** 7 45N 39 0 E
Arsiero, *Italy* **29 C8** 45 48N 11 21 E
Arsin, *Turkey* **73 B8** 41 8N 39 55 E
Arsk, *Russia* **48 B9** 56 10N 49 50 E
Årsunda, *Sweden* **10 D10** 60 31N 16 45 E
Árta, *Greece* **38 B3** 39 8N 21 2 E
Artà, *Spain* **37 B10** 39 41N 3 21 E
Árta □, *Greece* **38 B3** 39 15N 21 5 E
Arteaga, *Mexico* **118 D4** 18 50N 102 20W
Arteche, *Phil.* **61 E6** 12 17N 125 22 E
Arteijo = Arteixo, *Spain* **34 B2** 43 19N 8 29W
Arteixo, *Spain* **34 B2** 43 19N 8 29W
Artem = Artyom, *Azerbaijan* **49 K10** 40 28N 50 20 E
Artem, *Russia* **54 C6** 43 22N 132 13 E
Artemovsk, *Russia* **51 D10** 54 45N 93 35 E
Artemovsk, *Ukraine* **47 H9** 48 35N 38 0 E
Artemovskiy, *Russia* **49 G5** 47 45N 40 16 E
Artenay, *France* **19 D8** 48 5N 1 50 E
Artern, *Germany* **24 D7** 51 22N 11 18 E
Artesa de Segre, *Spain* **32 D6** 41 54N 1 3 E
Artesia = Mosomane, *Botswana* **88 C4** 24 2 S 26 19 E
Artesia, *U.S.A.* **113 J2** 32 51N 104 24W
Arthington, *Liberia* **82 D2** 6 35N 10 45W
Arthur, *Canada* **110 C4** 43 50N 80 32W
Arthur →, *Australia* **94 G3** 41 2 S 144 40 E
Arthur Cr. →, *Australia* **94 C2** 22 30 S 136 25 E
Arthur Pt., *Australia* **94 C5** 22 7 S 150 3 E
Arthur River, *Australia* **93 F2** 33 20 S 117 2 E
Arthur's Pass, *N.Z.* **91 K3** 42 54 S 171 35 E
Arthur's Town, *Bahamas* **121 B4** 24 38N 75 42W
Artigas, *Uruguay* **126 C4** 30 20 S 56 30W
Artik, *Armenia* **49 K6** 40 38N 43 58 E
Artillery L., *Canada* **105 A7** 63 9N 107 52W
Artois, *France* **19 B9** 50 20N 2 30 E
Artotína, *Greece* **38 C4** 38 42N 22 2 E
Artrutx, C. de, *Spain* **37 B10** 39 55N 3 49 E
Artsyz, *Ukraine* **47 J5** 46 4N 29 26 E
Artvin, *Turkey* **73 B9** 41 14N 41 44 E
Artyom, *Azerbaijan* **49 K10** 40 28N 50 20 E
Aru, Kepulauan, *Indonesia* **63 F8** 6 0 S 134 30 E
Aru Is. = Aru, Kepulauan, *Indonesia* **63 F8** 6 0 S 134 30 E
Arua, *Uganda* **86 B3** 3 1N 30 58 E
Aruanã, *Brazil* **125 F8** 14 54 S 51 10W
Aruba ■, *W. Indies* **121 D6** 12 30N 70 0W
Arucas, *Canary Is.* **37 F4** 28 7N 15 32W
Arudy, *France* **20 E3** 43 7N 0 28W
Arun →, *Nepal* **69 F12** 26 55N 87 10 E
Arun →, *U.K.* **13 G7** 50 49N 0 33W
Arunachal Pradesh □, *India* **67 F19** 28 0N 95 0 E
Arusha, *Tanzania* **86 C4** 3 20 S 36 40 E
Arusha □, *Tanzania* **86 C4** 4 0 S 36 30 E
Arusha Chini, *Tanzania* **86 C4** 3 32 S 37 20 E
Aruwimi →, *Dem. Rep. of the Congo* **86 B1** 1 13N 23 36 E
Arvada, *Colo., U.S.A.* **112 F2** 39 48N 105 5W
Arvada, *Wyo., U.S.A.* **114 D10** 44 39N 106 8W
Arve →, *France* **19 F13** 46 11N 6 8 E
Árvi, *Greece* **36 E7** 34 59N 25 28 E
Arviat, *Canada* **105 A10** 61 6N 93 59W
Arvidsjaur, *Sweden* **8 D18** 65 35N 19 10 E
Arvika, *Sweden* **10 E6** 59 40N 12 36 E
Arvin, *U.S.A.* **117 K8** 35 12N 118 50W
Arwal, *India* **69 G11** 25 15N 84 41 E
Arxan, *China* **60 B6** 47 11N 119 57 E
Äryd, *Sweden* **11 H8** 56 49N 14 59 E
Aryirádhes, *Greece* **36 B3** 39 27N 19 58 E
Aryiroúpolis, *Greece* **36 D6** 35 17N 24 20 E
Arys, *Kazakhstan* **50 E7** 42 26N 68 48 E
Arzachena, *Italy* **30 A2** 41 5N 9 23 E
Arzamas, *Russia* **48 C6** 55 27N 43 55 E
Arzgir, *Russia* **49 H7** 45 18N 44 23 E
Arzignano, *Italy* **29 C8** 45 31N 11 20 E
Arzúa, *Spain* **34 C2** 42 56N 8 9W
Aš, *Czech Rep.* **26 A5** 50 13N 12 12 E
Ås, *Sweden* **10 A8** 63 15N 14 34 E
As Pontes de García Rodríguez, *Spain* **34 B3** 43 27N 7 50W
Aş Şafā, *Syria* **75 B6** 33 10N 37 0 E
As Saffānīyah, *Si. Arabia* **71 E6** 27 55N 48 50 E
As Safīrah, *Syria* **70 B3** 36 5N 37 21 E
Aş Şahm, *Oman* **71 E8** 24 10N 56 53 E
As Sājir, *Si. Arabia* **70 E5** 25 11N 44 36 E
As Salamīyah, *Syria* **70 C3** 35 1N 37 2 E
As Salmān, *Iraq* **70 D5** 30 30N 44 32 E
As Salt, *Jordan* **75 C4** 32 2N 35 43 E
As Sal'w'a, *Qatar* **71 E6** 24 23N 50 50 E
As Samāwah, *Iraq* **70 D5** 31 15N 45 15 E
As Sanamayn, *Syria* **75 B5** 33 3N 36 10 E
As Sohar = Şuḩār, *Oman* **71 E8** 24 20N 56 40 E
As Sukhnah, *Syria* **70 C3** 34 52N 38 52 E
As Sulaymānīyah, *Iraq* **70 C5** 35 35N 45 29 E
As Sulaymī, *Si. Arabia* **70 E4** 26 17N 41 21 E
As Sulayyil, *Si. Arabia* **74 C4** 20 27N 45 34 E
As Summān, *Si. Arabia* **70 E5** 25 0N 47 0 E
As Suwaydā', *Syria* **75 C5** 32 40N 36 30 E
As Suwaydā' □, *Syria* **75 C5** 32 45N 36 45 E
As Suwayq, *Oman* **71 F8** 23 51N 57 26 E
Aş Şuwayrah, *Iraq* **70 C5** 32 55N 45 0 E
Åsa, *Sweden* **11 G6** 57 21N 12 8 E
Asab, *Namibia* **88 D2** 25 30 S 18 0 E
Asaba, *Nigeria* **83 D6** 6 12N 6 38 E
Asad, Buḩayrat al, *Syria* **70 C3** 36 0N 38 15 E
Asadābād, *Iran* **73 E13** 34 47N 48 7 E
Asafo, *Ghana* **82 D4** 6 20N 2 40W
Asahi-Gawa →, *Japan* **55 G6** 34 36N 133 58 E
Asahigawa, *Japan* **54 C11** 43 46N 142 22 E
Asale, L., *Ethiopia* **81 E5** 14 0N 40 20 E
Asamankese, *Ghana* **83 D4** 5 50N 0 40W
Asan →, *India* **69 F8** 26 37N 78 24 E
Asansol, *India* **69 H12** 23 40N 87 1 E
Åsarna, *Sweden* **10 B8** 62 39N 14 22 E
Asayita, *Ethiopia* **81 E5** 11 35N 41 23 E
Asbe Teferi, *Ethiopia* **81 F5** 9 4N 40 49 E
Asbesberge, *S. Africa* **88 D3** 29 0 S 23 0 E
Asbestos, *Canada* **103 C5** 45 47N 71 58W
Asbury Park, *U.S.A.* **111 F10** 40 13N 74 1W
Ascea, *Italy* **31 B8** 40 8N 15 11 E
Ascensión, *Mexico* **118 A3** 31 6N 107 59W
Ascensión, B. de la, *Mexico* **119 D7** 19 50N 87 20W
Ascension I., *Atl. Oc.* **77 G2** 8 0 S 14 15W
Aschach an der Donau, *Austria* **26 C7** 48 22N 14 2 E
Aschaffenburg, *Germany* **25 F5** 49 58N 9 6 E
Aschendorf, *Germany* **24 B3** 53 3N 7 19 E
Aschersleben, *Germany* **24 D7** 51 45N 11 29 E
Asciano, *Italy* **29 E8** 43 14N 11 33 E
Ascoli Piceno, *Italy* **29 F10** 42 51N 13 34 E
Ascoli Satriano, *Italy* **31 A8** 41 11N 15 32 E
Ascope, *Peru* **124 E3** 7 46 S 79 8W
Ascotán, *Chile* **126 A2** 21 45 S 68 17W
Aseb, *Eritrea* **81 E5** 13 0N 42 40 E
Åseda, *Sweden* **11 G9** 57 10N 15 20 E
Asela, *Ethiopia* **81 F4** 8 0N 39 0 E
Åsen, *Sweden* **10 C7** 61 17N 13 50 E
Asenovgrad, *Bulgaria* **41 D8** 42 1N 24 51 E
Aserradero, *Mexico* **118 C3** 23 40N 105 43W
Asfeld, *France* **19 C11** 49 27N 4 5 E
Asfûn el Matâ'na, *Egypt* **80 B3** 25 26N 32 30 E
Asgata, *Cyprus* **36 E12** 34 46N 33 15 E
Ash Fork, *U.S.A.* **115 J7** 35 13N 112 29W
Ash Grove, *U.S.A.* **113 G8** 37 19N 93 35W
Ash Shabakah, *Iraq* **70 D4** 30 49N 43 39 E
Ash Shamāl □, *Lebanon* **75 A5** 34 25N 36 0 E
Ash Shāmīyah, *Iraq* **70 D5** 31 55N 44 35 E
Ash Shāriqah, *U.A.E.* **71 E7** 25 23N 55 26 E
Ash Sharmah, *Si. Arabia* **70 D2** 28 1N 35 16 E
Ash Sharqāt, *Iraq* **70 C4** 35 27N 43 16 E
Ash Sharqi, Al Jabal, *Lebanon* **75 B5** 33 40N 36 10 E
Ash Shaṭrah, *Iraq* **70 D5** 31 30N 46 10 E
Ash Shawbak, *Jordan* **70 D2** 30 32N 35 34 E
Ash Shawmari, J., *Jordan* **75 E5** 30 35N 36 35 E
Ash Shināfīyah, *Iraq* **70 D5** 31 35N 44 39 E
Ash Shu'bah, *Si. Arabia* **70 D5** 28 54N 44 44 E
Ash Shumlūl, *Si. Arabia* **70 E5** 26 31N 47 20 E
Ash Shūr'a, *Iraq* **70 C4** 35 58N 43 13 E
Ash Shurayf, *Si. Arabia* **70 E3** 25 43N 39 14 E
Ash Shuwayfāt, *Lebanon* **75 B4** 33 45N 35 30 E
Ashanti □, *Ghana* **83 D4** 7 30N 1 30W
Ashau, *Vietnam* **64 D6** 16 6N 107 22 E
Ashbourne, *U.K.* **12 D6** 53 2N 1 43W
Ashburn, *U.S.A.* **109 K4** 31 43N 83 39W
Ashburton, *N.Z.* **91 K3** 43 53 S 171 48 E
Ashburton →, *Australia* **92 D1** 21 40 S 114 56 E
Ashcroft, *Canada* **104 C4** 50 40N 121 20W
Ashdod, *Israel* **75 D3** 31 49N 34 35 E
Ashdown, *U.S.A.* **113 J7** 33 40N 94 8W
Asheboro, *U.S.A.* **109 H6** 35 43N 79 49W
Ashern, *Canada* **105 C9** 51 11N 98 21W
Asherton, *U.S.A.* **113 L5** 28 27N 99 46W
Asheville, *U.S.A.* **109 H4** 35 36N 82 33W
Ashewat, *Pakistan* **68 D3** 31 22N 68 32 E
Asheweig →, *Canada* **102 B2** 54 17N 87 12W
Ashford, *Australia* **95 D5** 29 15 S 151 3 E
Ashford, *U.K.* **13 F8** 51 8N 0 53 E
Ashgabat, *Turkmenistan* **50 F6** 38 0N 57 50 E
Ashibetsu, *Japan* **54 C11** 43 31N 142 11 E
Ashikaga, *Japan* **55 F9** 36 28N 139 29 E
Ashington, *U.K.* **12 B6** 55 11N 1 33W
Ashizuri-Zaki, *Japan* **55 H6** 32 44N 133 0 E
Ashkarkot, *Afghan.* **68 C2** 33 3N 67 58 E
Ashkhabad = Ashgabat, *Turkmenistan* **50 F6** 38 0N 57 50 E
Āshkhāneh, *Iran* **71 B8** 37 26N 56 55 E
Ashland, *Kans., U.S.A.* **113 G5** 37 11N 99 46W
Ashland, *Ky., U.S.A.* **108 F4** 38 28N 82 38W
Ashland, *Mont., U.S.A.* **114 D10** 45 36N 106 16W
Ashland, *Ohio, U.S.A.* **110 F2** 40 52N 82 19W
Ashland, *Oreg., U.S.A.* **114 E2** 42 12N 122 43W
Ashland, *Pa., U.S.A.* **111 F8** 40 45N 76 22W
Ashland, *Va., U.S.A.* **108 G7** 37 46N 77 29W
Ashland, *Wis., U.S.A.* **112 B9** 46 35N 90 53W
Ashley, *N. Dak., U.S.A.* **112 B5** 46 2N 99 22W
Ashley, *Pa., U.S.A.* **111 E9** 41 12N 75 55W
Ashmore Reef, *Australia* **92 B3** 12 14 S 123 5 E
Ashmûn, *Egypt* **80 H7** 30 18N 30 55 E
Ashmyany, *Belarus* **9 J21** 54 26N 25 52 E
Ashokan Reservoir, *U.S.A.* **111 E10** 41 56N 74 13W
Ashqelon, *Israel* **75 D3** 31 42N 34 35 E
Ashta, *India* **68 H7** 23 1N 76 43 E
Ashtabula, *U.S.A.* **110 E4** 41 52N 80 47W
Ashton, *S. Africa* **88 E3** 33 50 S 20 5 E
Ashton, *U.S.A.* **114 D8** 44 4N 111 27W
Ashuanipi, L., *Canada* **103 B6** 52 45N 66 15W
Ashville, *U.S.A.* **110 F6** 40 34N 78 33W
'Āṣī →, *Asia* **72 D6** 36 1N 35 59 E
Asia **52 E11** 45 0N 75 0 E
Asia, Kepulauan, *Indonesia* **63 D8** 1 0N 131 13 E
Āsīā Bak, *Iran* **71 C6** 35 19N 50 30 E
Asiago, *Italy* **29 C8** 45 52N 11 30 E
Asifabad, *India* **66 K11** 19 20N 79 24 E
Asinara, *Italy* **30 A1** 41 4N 8 16 E
Asinara, G. dell', *Italy* **30 A1** 41 0N 8 30 E
Asino, *Russia* **50 D9** 57 0N 86 0 E
Asipovichy, *Belarus* **46 F5** 53 19N 28 33 E
'Asīr □, *Si. Arabia* **74 D3** 18 40N 42 30 E
Asir, Ras, *Somali Rep.* **74 E5** 11 55N 51 10 E
Aşkale, *Turkey* **73 C9** 39 55N 40 41 E
Askersund, *Sweden* **11 F8** 58 53N 14 55 E
Askham, *S. Africa* **88 D3** 26 59 S 20 47 E
Askim, *Norway* **9 G14** 59 35N 11 10 E
Askja, *Iceland* **8 D5** 65 3N 16 48W
Askøy, *Norway* **9 F11** 60 29N 5 10 E
Asl, *Egypt* **80 B3** 29 33N 32 44 E
Aslan Burnu, *Turkey* **39 C8** 38 44N 26 45 E
Aslanapa, *Turkey* **39 B11** 39 13N 29 52 E
Asmara = Asmera, *Eritrea* **81 D4** 15 19N 38 55 E
Asmera, *Eritrea* **81 D4** 15 19N 38 55 E
Asnæs, *Denmark* **11 J4** 55 40N 11 0 E
Åsnen, *Sweden* **11 H8** 56 37N 14 45 E
Ásola, *Italy* **28 C7** 45 13N 10 24 E
Asosa, *Ethiopia* **81 E3** 10 3N 34 32 E
Asoteriba, Jebel, *Sudan* **80 C4** 21 51N 36 30 E
Aspe, *Spain* **33 G4** 38 20N 0 40W
Aspen, *U.S.A.* **115 G10** 39 11N 106 49W
Aspendos, *Turkey* **72 D4** 36 54N 31 7 E
Aspermont, *U.S.A.* **113 J4** 33 8N 100 14W
Aspet, *France* **20 E4** 43 1N 0 48 E
Aspiring, Mt., *N.Z.* **91 L2** 44 23 S 168 46 E
Aspres-sur-Buëch, *France* **21 D9** 44 32N 5 44 E
Asprókavos, Ákra, *Greece* **36 B4** 39 21N 20 6 E
Aspromonte, *Italy* **31 D9** 38 10N 16 0 E
Aspur, *India* **68 H6** 23 58N 74 7 E
Asquith, *Canada* **105 C7** 52 8N 107 13W
Assâba, Massif de l', *Mauritania* **82 B2** 16 10N 11 45W
Assaikio, *Nigeria* **83 D6** 8 34N 8 55 E

Bacuag

Assal, L., Djibouti 81 E5 11 40N 42 26 E
Assam □, India 67 G18 26 0N 93 0 E
Assamakka, Niger 83 B6 19 21N 5 38 E
Asse, Belgium 17 D4 50 24N 4 10 E
Assémini, Italy 30 C1 39 17N 9 0 E
Assen, Neths. 17 A6 53 0N 6 35 E
Assens, Denmark 11 J3 55 16N 9 55 E
Assini, Ivory C. 82 D4 5 9N 3 17W
Assiniboia, Canada 105 D7 49 40N 105 59W
Assiniboine →, Canada 105 D9 49 53N 97 8W
Assiniboine, Mt., Canada 104 C5 50 52N 115 39W
Assis, Brazil 127 A5 22 40 S 50 20W
Assisi, Italy 29 E9 43 4N 12 37 E
Ássos, Greece 38 C2 38 22N 20 33 E
Assynt, L., U.K. 14 C3 58 10N 5 3W
Astaffort, France 20 D4 44 4N 0 40 E
Astakidha, Greece 39 F8 35 53N 26 50 E
Astakós, Greece 38 C3 38 32N 21 5 E
Astana, Kazakhstan 50 D8 51 10N 71 30 E
Āstāneh, Iran 71 B6 37 17N 49 59 E
Astara, Azerbaijan 71 B6 38 30N 48 50 E
Āstārā, Iran 73 C13 38 20N 48 52 E
Asteroúsia, Greece 36 E7 34 59N 25 3 E
Asti, Italy 28 D5 44 54N 8 12 E
Astipálaia, Greece 39 E8 36 32N 26 22 E
Astorga, Spain 34 C4 42 29N 6 8W
Astoria, U.S.A. 116 D3 46 11N 123 50W
Åstorp, Sweden 11 H6 56 6N 12 55 E
Astrakhan, Russia 49 G9 46 25N 48 5 E
Astudillo, Spain 34 C6 42 12N 4 22W
Asturias □, Spain 34 B5 43 15N 6 0W
Asunción, Paraguay 126 B4 25 10 S 57 30W
Asunción Nochixtlán, Mexico 119 D5 17 28N 97 14W
Åsunden, Sweden 11 F9 58 0N 15 51 E
Asutri, Sudan 81 D4 15 25N 35 45 E
Aswa →, Uganda 86 B3 3 43N 31 55 E
Aswad, Ra's al, Si. Arabia 80 C4 21 20N 39 0 E
Aswân, Egypt 80 C3 24 4N 32 57 E
Aswân High Dam = Sadd el Aali, Egypt 80 C3 23 54N 32 54 E
Asyût, Egypt 80 B3 27 11N 31 4 E
Asyûti, Wadi →, Egypt 80 B3 27 11N 31 16 E
Aszód, Hungary 42 C4 47 39N 19 28 E
At Ţafilah, Jordan 75 E4 30 45N 35 30 E
Aţ Ţā'if, Si. Arabia 74 C3 21 5N 40 27 E
Aţ Ţirāq, Si. Arabia 70 E5 27 19N 44 33 E
Aţ Tubayq, Si. Arabia 70 D3 29 30N 37 0 E
Atabey, Turkey 39 D12 37 57N 30 39 E
Atacama □, Chile 126 B2 27 30 S 70 0W
Atacama, Desierto de, Chile 126 A2 24 0 S 69 20W
Atacama, Salar de, Chile 126 A2 23 30 S 68 20W
Atakpamé, Togo 83 D5 7 31N 1 13 E
Atalándi, Greece 38 C4 38 39N 22 58 E
Atalaya, Peru 124 F4 10 45 S 73 50W
Atalaya de Femes, Canary Is. 37 F6 28 56N 13 47W
Atami, Japan 55 G9 35 5N 139 4 E
Atapupu, Indonesia 63 F6 9 0 S 124 51 E
Atâr, Mauritania 78 D3 20 30N 13 5W
Atarfe, Spain 35 H7 37 13N 3 40W
Atari, Pakistan 68 D6 30 56N 74 2 E
Atascadero, U.S.A. 116 K6 35 29N 120 40W
Atasu, Kazakhstan 50 E8 48 30N 71 0 E
Atatürk Barajı, Turkey 73 D8 37 28N 38 30 E
Atauro, Indonesia 63 F7 8 10 S 125 30 E
'Atbara, Sudan 80 D3 17 42N 33 59 E
'Atbara, Nahr →, Sudan 80 D3 17 40N 33 56 E
Atbasar, Kazakhstan 50 D7 51 48N 68 20 E
Atça, Turkey 39 D10 37 53N 28 13 E
Atchafalaya B., U.S.A. 113 L9 29 25N 91 25W
Atchison, U.S.A. 112 F7 39 34N 95 7W
Atebubu, Ghana 83 D4 7 47N 1 0W
Ateca, Spain 32 D3 41 20N 1 49W
Aterno →, Italy 29 F10 42 11N 13 51 E
Āteshān, Iran 71 C7 35 35N 52 37 E
Atesine, Alpi, Italy 29 B8 46 55N 11 30 E
Atessa, Italy 29 F11 42 4N 14 27 E
Atfîh, Egypt 80 J7 29 25N 31 15 E
Ath, Belgium 17 D3 50 38N 3 47 E
Athabasca, Canada 104 C6 54 45N 113 20W
Athabasca →, Canada 105 B6 58 40N 110 50W
Athabasca, L., Canada 105 B7 59 15N 109 15W
Athboy, Ireland 15 C5 53 37N 6 56W
Athenry, Ireland 15 C3 53 18N 8 44W
Athens = Athínai, Greece 38 D5 37 58N 23 46 E
Athens, Ala., U.S.A. 109 H2 34 48N 86 58W
Athens, Ga., U.S.A. 109 J4 33 57N 83 23W
Athens, N.Y., U.S.A. 111 D11 42 16N 73 49W
Athens, Ohio, U.S.A. 108 F4 39 20N 82 6W
Athens, Pa., U.S.A. 111 E8 41 57N 76 31W
Athens, Tenn., U.S.A. 109 H3 35 27N 84 36W
Athens, Tex., U.S.A. 113 J7 32 12N 95 51W
Atherley, Canada 110 B5 44 37N 79 20W
Atherton, Australia 94 B4 17 17 S 145 30 E
Athiéme, Benin 83 D5 6 37N 1 40 E
Athienou, Cyprus 36 D12 35 3N 33 32 E
Athínai, Greece 38 D5 37 58N 23 46 E
Athlone, Ireland 15 C4 53 25N 7 56W
Athna, Cyprus 36 D12 35 3N 33 47 E
Athol, U.S.A. 111 D12 42 36N 72 14W
Atholl, Forest of, U.K. 14 E5 56 51N 3 50W
Atholville, Canada 103 C6 47 59N 66 43W
Áthos, Greece 41 F8 40 9N 24 22 E
Athy, Ireland 15 C5 53 0N 7 0W
Ati, Chad 79 F9 13 13N 18 20 E
Ati, Sudan 81 E2 13 5N 29 2 E
Atiak, Uganda 86 B3 3 12N 32 2 E
Atienza, Spain 32 D2 41 12N 2 52W
Atiit, Sudan 81 F3 6 10N 30 35 E
Atik L., Canada 105 B9 55 15N 96 0W
Atikameg →, Canada 102 B3 52 30N 82 46W
Atikokan, Canada 102 C1 48 45N 91 37W
Atikonak L., Canada 103 B7 52 40N 64 32W
Atimonan, Phil. 61 E4 14 0N 121 55 E
Atka, Russia 51 C16 60 50N 151 48 E
Atka I., U.S.A. 100 C2 52 7N 174 30W
Atkarsk, Russia 48 E7 51 55N 45 2 E
Atkinson, U.S.A. 112 D5 42 32N 98 59W
Atlanta, Ga., U.S.A. 109 J3 33 45N 84 23W
Atlanta, Tex., U.S.A. 113 J7 33 7N 94 10W
Atlantic, U.S.A. 112 E7 41 24N 95 1W
Atlantic City, U.S.A. 108 F8 39 21N 74 27W
Atlantic Ocean 2 E9 0 0 20 0W
Atlas Mts. = Haut Atlas, Morocco 78 B4 32 30N 5 0W
Atlin, Canada 104 B2 59 31N 133 41W
Atlin, L., Canada 104 B2 59 26N 133 45W
Atlin Prov. Park, Canada 104 B2 59 10N 134 30W
Atmore, U.S.A. 109 K2 31 2N 87 29W
Atoka, U.S.A. 113 H6 34 23N 96 8W
Átokos, Greece 38 C2 38 28N 20 49 E
Atolia, U.S.A. 117 K9 35 19N 117 37W
Atrai →, Bangla. 69 G13 24 7N 89 22 E
Atrak = Atrek →, Turkmenistan 71 B8 37 35N 53 58 E
Ätran, Sweden 11 G6 57 7N 12 57 E
Ätran →, Sweden 11 H6 56 53N 12 30 E
Atrauli, India 68 E8 28 2N 78 20 E
Atrek →, Turkmenistan 71 B8 37 35N 53 58 E
Atri, Italy 29 F10 42 35N 13 58 E
Atsikí, Greece 39 B7 39 56N 25 13 E
Atsoum, Mts., Cameroon 83 D7 6 41N 12 57 E
Atsuta, Japan 54 C10 43 24N 141 26 E
Attalla, U.S.A. 109 H2 34 1N 86 6W
Attapu, Laos 64 E6 14 48N 106 50 E
Attáviros, Greece 36 C9 36 12N 27 50 E
Attawapiskat, Canada 102 B3 52 56N 82 24W
Attawapiskat →, Canada 102 B3 52 57N 82 18W
Attawapiskat L., Canada 102 B2 52 18N 87 54W
Attersee, Austria 26 D6 47 55N 13 32 E
Attica, Ind., U.S.A. 108 E2 40 18N 87 15W
Attica, Ohio, U.S.A. 110 E2 41 4N 82 53W
Attichy, France 19 C10 49 25N 3 3 E
Attigny, France 19 C11 49 28N 4 35 E
Attika = Attikí □, Greece 38 D5 37 10N 23 40 E
Attikamagen L., Canada 103 B6 55 0N 66 30W
Attikí □, Greece 38 D5 37 10N 23 40 E
Attleboro, U.S.A. 111 E13 41 57N 71 17W
Attock, Pakistan 68 C5 33 52N 72 20 E
Attopeu = Attapu, Laos 64 E6 14 48N 106 50 E
Attu I., U.S.A. 100 C1 52 55N 172 55 E
Attur, India 66 P11 11 35N 78 30 E
Atuel →, Argentina 126 D2 36 17 S 66 50W
Åtvidaberg, Sweden 11 F10 58 12N 16 0 E
Atwater, U.S.A. 116 H6 37 21N 120 37W
Atwood, Canada 110 C3 43 40N 81 1W
Atwood, U.S.A. 112 F4 39 48N 101 3W
Atyraū, Kazakhstan 50 E6 47 5N 52 0 E
Au Sable, U.S.A. 110 B1 44 25N 83 20W
Au Sable →, U.S.A. 108 C4 44 25N 83 20W
Au Sable Forks, U.S.A. 111 B11 44 27N 73 41W
Au Sable Pt., U.S.A. 110 B1 44 20N 83 20W
Aubagne, France 21 E9 43 17N 5 37 E
Aubarca, C. d', Spain 37 B7 39 4N 1 22 E
Aube □, France 19 D11 48 15N 4 10 E
Aube →, France 19 D10 48 34N 3 43 E
Aubenas, France 21 D8 44 37N 4 24 E
Aubenton, France 19 C11 49 50N 4 12 E
Auberry, U.S.A. 116 H7 37 7N 119 29W
Aubigny-sur-Nère, France 19 E9 47 30N 2 24 E
Aubin, France 20 D6 44 33N 2 15 E
Aubrac, Mts. d', France 20 D7 44 40N 3 2 E
Auburn, Ala., U.S.A. 109 J3 32 36N 85 29W
Auburn, Calif., U.S.A. 116 G5 38 54N 121 4W
Auburn, Ind., U.S.A. 108 E3 41 22N 85 4W
Auburn, Maine, U.S.A. 109 C10 44 6N 70 14W
Auburn, N.Y., U.S.A. 111 D8 42 56N 76 34W
Auburn, Nebr., U.S.A. 112 E7 40 23N 95 51W
Auburn, Pa., U.S.A. 111 F8 40 36N 76 6W
Auburn, Wash., U.S.A. 116 C4 47 18N 122 14W
Auburn Ra., Australia 95 D5 25 15 S 150 30 E
Auburndale, U.S.A. 109 L5 28 4N 81 48W
Aubusson, France 20 C6 45 57N 2 11 E
Auce, Latvia 44 B9 56 28N 22 53 E
Auch, France 20 E4 43 39N 0 36 E
Auchi, Nigeria 83 D6 7 6N 6 13 E
Auckland, N.Z. 91 G5 36 52 S 174 46 E
Auckland Is., Pac. Oc. 96 N8 50 40 S 166 5 E
Aude □, France 20 E6 43 8N 2 28 E
Aude →, France 20 E7 43 13N 3 14 E
Auden, Canada 102 B2 50 14N 87 53W
Auderville, France 18 C5 49 43N 1 57W
Audierne, France 18 D2 48 1N 4 34W
Audincourt, France 19 E13 47 30N 6 50 E
Audo, Ethiopia 81 F5 6 20N 41 50 E
Audubon, U.S.A. 112 E7 41 43N 94 56W
Aue, Germany 24 E8 50 35N 12 41 E
Auerbach, Germany 24 E8 50 30N 12 24 E
Augathella, Australia 95 D4 25 48 S 146 35 E
Aughnacloy, U.K. 15 B5 54 25N 6 59W
Augrabies Falls, S. Africa 88 D3 28 35 S 20 20 E
Augsburg, Germany 25 G6 48 25N 10 52 E
Augusta, Australia 93 F2 34 19 S 115 9 E
Augusta, Italy 31 E8 37 13N 15 13 E
Augusta, Ark., U.S.A. 113 H9 35 17N 91 22W
Augusta, Ga., U.S.A. 109 J5 33 28N 81 58W
Augusta, Kans., U.S.A. 113 G6 37 41N 96 59W
Augusta, Maine, U.S.A. 101 D13 44 19N 69 47W
Augusta, Mont., U.S.A. 114 C7 47 30N 112 24W
Augustenborg, Denmark 11 K3 54 57N 9 53 E
Augustów, Poland 44 E9 53 51N 23 0 E
Augustus, Mt., Australia 93 D2 24 20 S 116 50 E
Augustus I., Australia 92 C3 15 20 S 124 30 E
Aukan, Eritrea 81 D5 15 29N 40 50 E
Aukum, U.S.A. 116 G6 38 34N 120 43W
Auld, L., Australia 92 D3 22 25 S 123 50 E
Aulla, Italy 28 D6 44 12N 9 58 E
Aulnay, France 20 B3 46 2N 0 22W
Aulne →, France 18 D2 48 17N 4 16W
Aulnoye-Aymeries, France 19 B10 50 12N 3 50 E
Ault, France 18 B8 50 8N 1 26 E
Ault, U.S.A. 112 E2 40 35N 104 44W
Aulus-les-Bains, France 20 F5 42 49N 1 19 E
Aumale, France 19 C8 49 46N 1 46 E
Aumont-Aubrac, France 20 D7 44 43N 3 17 E
Auna, Nigeria 83 C5 10 9N 4 42 E
Auning, Denmark 11 H4 56 26N 10 22 E
Aunis, France 20 B3 46 5N 0 50W
Auponhia, Indonesia 63 E7 1 58 S 125 27 E
Aups, France 21 E10 43 37N 6 15 E
Aur, Pulau, Malaysia 65 L5 2 35N 104 10 E
Auraiya, India 69 F8 26 28N 79 33 E
Aurangabad, Bihar, India 69 G11 24 45N 84 18 E
Aurangabad, Maharashtra, India 66 K9 19 50N 75 23 E
Auray, France 18 E4 47 40N 2 59W
Aurich, Germany 24 B3 53 28N 7 28 E
Aurillac, France 20 D6 44 55N 2 26 E
Auronzo di Cadore, Italy 29 B9 46 33N 12 26 E
Aurora, Canada 110 C5 44 0N 79 28W
Aurora, S. Africa 88 E2 32 40 S 18 29 E
Aurora, Colo., U.S.A. 112 F2 39 44N 104 52W
Aurora, Ill., U.S.A. 108 E1 41 45N 88 19W
Aurora, Mo., U.S.A. 113 G8 36 58N 93 43W
Aurora, N.Y., U.S.A. 111 D8 42 45N 76 42W
Aurora, Nebr., U.S.A. 112 E6 40 52N 98 0W
Aurora, Ohio, U.S.A. 110 E3 41 21N 81 20W
Aurukun, Australia 94 A3 13 20 S 141 45 E
Aus, Namibia 88 D2 26 35 S 16 12 E
Ausable →, Canada 110 C3 43 19N 81 46W
Auschwitz = Oświęcim, Poland 45 H6 50 2N 19 11 E
Austerlitz = Slavkov u Brna, Czech Rep. 27 B9 49 10N 16 52 E
Austin, Minn., U.S.A. 112 D8 43 40N 92 58W
Austin, Nev., U.S.A. 114 G5 39 30N 117 4W
Austin, Pa., U.S.A. 110 E6 41 38N 78 6W
Austin, Tex., U.S.A. 113 K6 30 17N 97 45W
Austin, L., Australia 93 E2 27 40 S 118 0 E
Austin I., Canada 105 A10 61 10N 94 0W
Austra, Norway 8 D14 65 8N 11 55 E
Austral Is. = Tubuai Is., Pac. Oc. 97 K13 25 0 S 150 0W
Austral Seamount Chain, Pac. Oc. 97 K13 24 0 S 150 0W
Australia ■, Oceania 96 K5 23 0 S 135 0 E
Australian Capital Territory □, Australia 95 F4 35 30 S 149 0 E
Australind, Australia 93 F2 33 17 S 115 42 E
Austria ■, Europe 26 E7 47 0N 14 0 E
Austvågøy, Norway 8 B16 68 20N 14 40 E
Auterive, France 20 E5 43 21N 1 29 E
Authie →, France 19 B8 50 22N 1 38 E
Authon-du-Perche, France 18 D7 48 12N 0 54 E
Autlán, Mexico 118 D4 19 40N 104 30W
Autun, France 19 F11 46 58N 4 17 E
Auvergne, France 20 C7 45 20N 3 15 E
Auvergne, Mts. d', France 20 C6 45 20N 2 55 E
Auvézère →, France 20 C4 45 12N 0 50 E
Auxerre, France 19 E10 47 48N 3 32 E
Auxi-le-Château, France 19 B9 50 15N 2 8 E
Auxonne, France 19 E12 47 10N 5 20 E
Auzances, France 19 F9 46 2N 2 30 E
Ava, U.S.A. 113 G8 36 57N 92 40W
Avallon, France 19 E10 47 30N 3 53 E
Avalon, U.S.A. 117 M8 33 21N 118 20W
Avalon Pen., Canada 103 C9 47 30N 53 20W
Avanos, Turkey 70 B2 38 43N 34 51 E
Avaré, Brazil 127 A6 23 4 S 48 58W
Ávas, Greece 41 F9 40 57N 25 56 E
Avawatz Mts., U.S.A. 117 K10 35 40N 116 30W
Avdan Daği, Turkey 41 F13 40 23N 29 46 E
Aveiro, Brazil 125 D7 3 10 S 55 5W
Aveiro, Portugal 34 E2 40 37N 8 38W
Aveiro □, Portugal 34 E2 40 40N 8 35W
Āvej, Iran 71 C6 35 40N 49 15 E
Avellaneda, Argentina 126 C4 34 50 S 58 10W
Avellino, Italy 31 B7 40 54N 14 47 E
Avenal, U.S.A. 116 K6 36 0N 120 8W
Aversa, Italy 31 B7 40 58N 14 12 E
Avery, U.S.A. 114 C6 47 15N 115 49W
Aves, Is. las, Venezuela 121 D6 12 0N 67 30W
Avesnes-sur-Helpe, France 19 B10 50 8N 3 55 E
Avesta, Sweden 10 D10 60 9N 16 10 E
Aveyron □, France 20 D6 44 22N 2 45 E
Aveyron →, France 20 D5 44 5N 1 16 E
Avezzano, Italy 29 F10 42 2N 13 25 E
Avgó, Greece 39 F7 35 33N 25 37 E
Aviá Terai, Argentina 126 B3 26 45 S 60 50W
Aviano, Italy 29 B9 46 4N 12 36 E
Aviemore, U.K. 14 D5 57 12N 3 50W
Avigliana, Italy 28 C4 45 5N 7 23 E
Avigliano, Italy 31 B8 40 44N 15 43 E
Avignon, France 21 E8 43 57N 4 50 E
Ávila, Spain 34 E6 40 39N 4 43W
Ávila □, Spain 34 E6 40 30N 5 0W
Ávila, Sierra de, Spain 34 E5 40 40N 5 15W
Avila Beach, U.S.A. 117 K6 35 11N 120 44W
Avilés, Spain 34 B5 43 35N 5 57W
Avintes, Portugal 34 D2 41 7N 8 33W
Avionárion, Greece 38 C6 38 31N 24 8 E
Avis, Portugal 35 F3 39 4N 7 53W
Avis, U.S.A. 110 E7 41 11N 77 19W
Avísio →, Italy 28 B8 46 7N 11 5 E
Aviz = Avis, Portugal 35 F3 39 4N 7 53W
Avize, France 19 D11 48 59N 4 1 E
Avlum, Denmark 11 H2 56 16N 8 47 E
Avoca, U.S.A. 110 D7 42 25N 77 25W
Avoca →, Australia 95 F3 35 40 S 143 43 E
Avoca →, Ireland 15 D5 52 48N 6 10W
Avola, Canada 104 C5 51 45N 119 19W
Avola, Italy 31 F8 36 56N 15 7 E
Avon, U.S.A. 110 D7 42 55N 77 45W
Avon →, Australia 93 F2 31 40 S 116 7 E
Avon →, Bristol, U.K. 13 F5 51 29N 2 41W
Avon →, Dorset, U.K. 13 G6 50 44N 1 46W
Avon →, Warks., U.K. 13 E5 52 0N 2 8W
Avon Park, U.S.A. 109 M5 27 36N 81 31W
Avondale, Zimbabwe 87 F3 17 43 S 30 58 E
Avonlea, Canada 105 D8 50 0N 105 0W
Avonmore, Canada 111 A10 45 10N 74 58W
Avramov, Bulgaria 41 D10 42 45N 26 38 E
Avranches, France 18 D5 48 40N 1 20W
Avre →, France 18 D8 48 47N 1 22 E
Avrig, Romania 43 E9 45 43N 24 21 E
Avrillé, France 18 E6 47 30N 0 35W
Avtovac, Bos.-H. 40 C2 43 9N 18 35 E
Awag el Baqar, Sudan 81 E3 10 10N 33 10 E
A'waj →, Syria 75 B5 33 23N 36 20 E
Awaji-Shima, Japan 55 G7 34 30N 134 50 E
'Awālī, Bahrain 71 E6 26 0N 50 30 E
Awantipur, India 69 C6 33 55N 75 3 E
Awasa, Ethiopia 81 F4 7 2N 38 28 E
Awasa, L., Ethiopia 81 F4 7 0N 38 30 E
Awash, Ethiopia 81 F5 9 1N 40 10 E
Awash →, Ethiopia 81 E5 11 45N 41 5 E
Awaso, Ghana 82 D4 6 15N 2 22W
Awatere →, N.Z. 91 J5 41 37 S 174 10 E
Awbārī, Libya 79 C8 26 46N 12 57 E
Awe, L., U.K. 14 E3 56 17N 5 16W
Aweil, Sudan 81 F2 8 42N 27 20 E
Awgu, Nigeria 83 D6 6 4N 7 24 E
Awjilah, Libya 79 C10 29 8N 21 7 E
Awka, Nigeria 83 D6 6 12N 7 5 E
Ax-les-Thermes, France 20 F5 42 44N 1 50 E
Axat, France 20 F6 42 48N 2 13 E
Axe →, U.K. 13 F5 50 42N 3 4W
Axel Heiberg I., Canada 4 B3 80 0N 90 0W
Axim, Ghana 82 E4 4 51N 2 15W
Axintele, Romania 43 F11 44 37N 26 47 E
Axiós →, Greece 40 F6 40 57N 22 35 E
Axminster, U.K. 13 G4 50 46N 3 0W
Axvall, Sweden 11 F7 58 23N 13 34 E
Ay, France 19 C11 49 3N 4 1 E
Ayabaca, Peru 124 D3 4 40 S 79 53W
Ayabe, Japan 55 G7 35 20N 135 20 E
Ayacucho, Argentina 126 D4 37 5 S 58 20W
Ayacucho, Peru 124 F4 13 0 S 74 0W
Ayaguz, Kazakhstan 50 E9 48 10N 80 10 E
Ayamé, Ivory C. 82 D4 5 35N 3 9W
Ayamonte, Spain 35 H3 37 12N 7 24W
Ayan, Russia 51 D14 56 30N 138 16 E
Ayancık, Turkey 72 B6 41 57N 34 35 E
Ayas, Turkey 72 B5 40 2N 32 21 E
Ayaviri, Peru 124 F4 14 50 S 70 35W
Aybastı, Turkey 72 B7 40 41N 37 23 E
Aydın, Turkey 72 D2 37 51N 27 51 E
Aydin □, Turkey 39 D9 37 50N 28 0 E
Aydin Dağları, Turkey 39 D10 38 0N 28 0 E
Ayelu, Ethiopia 81 E5 10 5N 40 42 E
Ayenngré, Togo 83 D5 8 40N 1 1 E
Ayer, U.S.A. 111 D13 42 34N 71 35W
Ayerbe, Spain 32 C4 42 17N 0 41W
Ayer's Cliff, Canada 111 A12 45 10N 72 3W
Ayers Rock, Australia 93 E5 25 23 S 131 5 E
Ayiá, Greece 38 B4 39 43N 22 45 E
Ayia Aikateríni, Ákra, Greece 36 A3 39 50N 19 50 E
Ayía Ánna, Greece 38 C5 38 52N 23 24 E
Ayia Dhéka, Greece 36 D6 35 3N 24 58 E
Ayia Gálini, Greece 36 D6 35 6N 24 41 E
Ayía Marína, Kásos, Greece 39 F8 35 27N 26 53 E
Ayía Marína, Léros, Greece 39 D8 37 11N 26 48 E
Áyia Napa, Cyprus 36 E13 34 59N 34 0 E
Ayía Paraskeví, Greece 39 B8 39 14N 26 21 E
Áyia Phyla, Cyprus 36 E12 34 43N 33 1 E
Ayía Rouméli, Greece 38 F5 35 14N 23 58 E
Ayia Varvára, Greece 36 D7 35 8N 25 1 E
Ayiássos, Greece 39 B8 39 5N 26 23 E
Áyioi Theódhoroi, Greece 38 D5 37 55N 23 9 E
Áyion Óros □, Greece 41 F8 40 25N 24 6 E
Áyios Amvrósios, Cyprus 36 D12 35 20N 33 35 E
Áyios Andréas, Greece 38 D4 37 21N 22 45 E
Áyios Evstrátios, Greece 38 B6 39 34N 24 58 E
Áyios Ioánnis, Ákra, Greece 36 D7 35 20N 25 40 E
Áyios Isidhoros, Greece 36 C9 36 9N 27 51 E
Áyios Kiríkos, Greece 39 D8 37 34N 26 17 E
Áyios Matthaíos, Greece 36 B3 39 30N 19 47 E
Áyios Míronos, Greece 39 F7 35 15N 25 1 E
Áyios Nikólaos, Greece 36 D7 35 11N 25 41 E
Áyios Pétros, Greece 38 C2 38 38N 20 33 E
Áyios Seryios, Cyprus 36 D12 35 12N 33 53 E
Áyios Theodhoros, Cyprus 36 D13 35 22N 34 1 E
Áyios Yeóryios, Greece 38 D5 37 28N 23 57 E
Aykathonisi, Greece 39 D8 37 28N 27 0 E
Aykirikçi, Turkey 39 B12 39 8N 30 9 E
Aylesbury, U.K. 13 F7 51 49N 0 49W
Aylmer, Canada 110 D4 42 46N 80 59W
Aylmer, L., Canada 100 B8 64 0N 110 8W
'Ayn, Wādī al, Oman 71 F7 22 15N 55 28 E
Ayn Dār, Si. Arabia 71 E7 25 55N 49 10 E
Ayn Zālah, Iraq 70 B4 36 45N 42 35 E
Ayna, Spain 33 G2 38 34N 2 3W
Ayod, Sudan 81 F3 8 7N 31 26 E
Ayolas, Paraguay 126 B4 27 10 S 56 59W
Ayom, Sudan 81 F2 7 49N 28 23 E
Ayon, Ostrov, Russia 51 C17 69 50N 169 0 E
Ayora, Spain 33 F3 39 3N 1 3W
Ayorou, Niger 83 C5 14 53N 1 0 E
'Ayoûn el 'Atroûs, Mauritania 82 B3 16 38N 9 37W
Ayr, Australia 94 B4 19 35 S 147 25 E
Ayr, Canada 110 C4 43 17N 80 27W
Ayr, U.K. 14 F4 55 28N 4 38W
Ayr →, U.K. 14 F4 55 28N 4 38W
Ayrancı, Turkey 72 D5 37 21N 33 41 E
Ayrancılar, Turkey 39 C9 38 15N 27 18 E
Ayre, Pt. of, U.K. 12 C3 54 25N 4 21W
Aysha, Ethiopia 81 E5 10 50N 42 23 E
Ayton, Australia 94 B4 15 56 S 145 22 E
Aytos, Bulgaria 41 D11 42 42N 27 16 E
Aytoska Planina, Bulgaria 41 D11 42 45N 27 30 E
Ayu, Kepulauan, Indonesia 63 D8 0 35N 131 5 E
Ayutla, Guatemala 120 D1 14 40N 92 10W
Ayutla, Mexico 119 D5 16 58N 99 17W
Ayvacık, Turkey 72 C2 39 36N 26 24 E
Ayvalık, Turkey 39 B8 39 20N 26 46 E
Az Zabadānī, Syria 75 B5 33 43N 36 5 E
Az Zāhirīyah, West Bank 75 D3 31 25N 34 58 E
Az Zahrān, Si. Arabia 71 E6 26 10N 50 7 E
Az Zarqā, Jordan 75 C5 32 5N 36 4 E
Az Zarqā', U.A.E. 71 E7 24 53N 53 4 E
Az Zībār, Iraq 70 B5 36 52N 44 4 E
Az Zilfī, Si. Arabia 70 E5 26 12N 44 52 E
Az Zubayr, Iraq 70 D5 30 26N 47 40 E
Az Zuqur, Yemen 81 E5 14 0N 42 45 E
Azambuja, Portugal 35 F2 39 4N 8 51W
Azamgarh, India 69 F10 26 5N 83 13 E
Azangaro, Peru 124 F4 14 55 S 70 13W
Azaouak, Niger 83 B5 15 50N 4 0 E
Azaouad, Mali 82 B4 19 0N 3 0W
Azaouak, Vallée de l', Mali 83 B5 15 50N 3 20 E
Āzār Shahr, Iran 70 B5 37 45N 45 59 E
Azara, Nigeria 83 D6 8 22N 9 12 E
Azarān, Iran 70 B5 37 25N 47 16 E
Azärbayjan = Azerbaijan ■, Asia 49 K9 40 20N 48 0 E
Āzarbāyjān-e Gharbī □, Iran 70 B5 37 0N 44 30 E
Āzarbāyjān-e Sharqī □, Iran 70 B5 37 20N 47 0 E
Azare, Nigeria 83 C7 11 55N 10 10 E
Azay-le-Rideau, France 18 E7 47 16N 0 30 E
A'zāz, Syria 70 B3 36 36N 37 4 E
Azbine = Aïr, Niger 83 B6 18 30N 8 0 E
Azerbaijan ■, Asia 49 K9 40 20N 48 0 E
Azerbaijchan = Azerbaijan ■, Asia 49 K9 40 20N 48 0 E
Azezo, Ethiopia 81 E4 12 28N 37 15 E
Azimganj, India 69 G13 24 14N 88 16 E
Aznalcóllar, Spain 35 H4 37 32N 6 17W
Azogues, Ecuador 124 D3 2 35 S 78 0W
Azores, Atl. Oc. 78 A1 38 44N 29 0W
Azov, Russia 49 G4 47 3N 39 25 E
Azov, Sea of, Europe 47 J9 46 0N 36 30 E
Azovskoye More = Azov, Sea of, Europe 47 J9 46 0N 36 30 E
Azpeitia, Spain 32 B2 43 12N 2 19W
Azraq ash Shīshān, Jordan 75 D5 31 50N 36 49 E
Aztec, U.S.A. 115 H10 36 49N 107 59W
Azúa de Compostela, Dom. Rep. 121 C5 18 25N 70 44W
Azuaga, Spain 35 G5 38 16N 5 39W
Azuara, Spain 32 D4 41 15N 0 53W
Azuer →, Spain 35 F7 39 8N 3 36W
Azuero, Pen. de, Panama 120 E3 7 30N 80 30W
Azuga, Romania 43 E10 45 27N 25 33 E
Azul, Argentina 126 D4 36 42 S 59 43W
Azusa, U.S.A. 117 L9 34 8N 117 52W
Azzano Décimo, Italy 29 C9 45 52N 12 56 E

B

Ba Don, Vietnam 64 D6 17 45N 106 26 E
Ba Dong, Vietnam 65 H6 9 40N 106 33 E
Ba Ngoi = Cam Lam, Vietnam 65 G7 11 54N 109 10 E
Ba Tri, Vietnam 65 G6 10 2N 106 36 E
Ba Xian = Bazhou, China 56 E9 39 8N 116 22 E
Baa, Indonesia 63 F6 10 50 S 123 0 E
Baamonde, Spain 34 B3 43 7N 7 44W
Baarle-Nassau, Belgium 17 C4 51 27N 4 56 E
Bab el Mandeb, Red Sea 74 E3 12 35N 43 25 E
Baba, Bulgaria 40 D7 42 44N 23 59 E
Bābā, Koh-i-, Afghan. 66 B5 34 30N 67 0 E
Baba Burnu, Turkey 39 B8 39 29N 26 2 E
Baba dag, Azerbaijan 49 K9 41 0N 48 19 E
Bābā Kalū, Iran 71 D6 30 7N 50 49 E
Babadag, Romania 43 F13 44 53N 28 44 E
Babadağ, Turkey 39 D10 37 49N 28 52 E
Babadayhan, Turkmenistan 50 F7 37 42N 60 23 E
Babaeski, Turkey 41 E11 41 26N 27 6 E
Babahoyo, Ecuador 124 D3 1 40 S 79 30W
Babai = Sarju →, India 69 F9 27 21N 81 23 E
Babana, Nigeria 83 C5 10 31N 3 46 E
Babanusa, Sudan 81 E2 11 20N 27 48 E
Babar, Indonesia 63 F7 8 0 S 129 30 E
Babar, Pakistan 68 D3 31 7N 69 32 E
Babarkach, Pakistan 68 E3 29 45N 68 0 E
Babayevo, Russia 46 C8 59 24N 35 55 E
Babb, U.S.A. 114 B7 48 51N 113 27W
Babelthuap, Pac. Oc. 63 C8 7 30N 134 30 E
Babenhausen, Germany 25 F4 49 57N 8 57 E
Băbeni, Romania 43 F9 44 59N 24 11 E
Baberu, India 69 G9 25 33N 80 43 E
Babi Besar, Pulau, Malaysia 65 L4 2 25N 103 59 E
Babia Gora, Europe 45 J6 49 38N 19 38 E
Babian Jiang →, China 58 F3 22 55N 101 47 E
Babile, Ethiopia 81 F5 9 16N 42 11 E
Babimost, Poland 45 F2 52 10N 15 49 E
Babinda, Australia 94 B4 17 20 S 145 56 E
Babine, Canada 104 B3 55 22N 126 37W
Babine →, Canada 104 B3 55 45N 127 44W
Babine L., Canada 104 C3 54 48N 126 0W
Babo, Indonesia 63 E8 2 30 S 133 30 E
Babócsa, Hungary 42 D2 46 2N 17 21 E
Bābol, Iran 71 B7 36 40N 52 50 E
Bābol Sar, Iran 71 B7 36 45N 52 45 E
Baborów, Poland 45 H5 50 7N 18 1 E
Babruysk, Belarus 47 F5 53 10N 29 15 E
Babuhri, India 68 F3 26 49N 69 43 E
Babuna, Macedonia 40 E5 41 30N 21 40 E
Babura, Nigeria 83 C6 12 51N 8 59 E
Babusar Pass, Pakistan 69 B5 35 12N 73 59 E
Babushkin, Russia 60 A5 52 0N 155 50 E
Babušnica, Serbia, Yug. 40 C6 43 7N 22 27 E
Babuyan Chan., Phil. 61 B4 18 40N 121 30 E
Babylon, Iraq 70 C5 32 34N 44 22 E
Bač, Serbia, Yug. 42 E4 45 29N 19 17 E
Bâc →, Moldova 43 D14 46 55N 29 26 E
Bac Can, Vietnam 58 F5 22 8N 105 49 E
Bac Giang, Vietnam 58 G6 21 16N 106 11 E
Bac Lieu, Vietnam 65 H5 9 17N 105 43 E
Bac Ninh, Vietnam 58 G6 21 13N 106 4 E
Bac Phan, Vietnam 64 B5 22 0N 105 0 E
Bac Quang, Vietnam 58 F5 22 30N 104 48 E
Bacabal, Brazil 125 D10 4 15 S 44 45W
Bacalar, Mexico 119 D7 18 50N 87 27W
Bacan, Kepulauan, Indonesia 63 E7 0 35 S 127 30 E
Bacarra, Phil. 61 B4 18 15N 120 37 E
Bacău, Romania 43 D11 46 35N 26 55 E
Bacău □, Romania 43 D11 46 30N 26 45 E
Baccarat, France 19 D13 48 28N 6 42 E
Bacerac, Mexico 118 A3 30 18N 108 50W
Băceşti, Romania 43 D12 46 50N 27 11 E
Bach Long Vi, Dao, Vietnam 64 B6 20 10N 107 40 E
Bacharach, Germany 25 E3 50 3N 7 44 E
Bachelina, Russia 50 D7 57 45N 67 20 E
Bachhwara, India 69 G11 25 35N 85 54 E
Bachuma, Ethiopia 81 F4 6 48N 35 53 E
Bačina, Serbia, Yug. 40 C5 43 42N 21 23 E
Back →, Canada 100 B9 65 10N 104 0W
Bačka Palanka, Serbia, Yug. 42 E4 45 17N 19 27 E
Bačka Topola, Serbia, Yug. 42 E4 45 49N 19 39 E
Bäckebo, Sweden 11 H10 56 53N 16 4 E
Bäckefors, Sweden 11 F6 58 48N 12 9 E
Bäckhammar, Sweden 10 E8 59 10N 14 11 E
Bački Petrovac, Serbia, Yug. 42 E4 45 29N 19 32 E
Backnang, Germany 25 G5 48 56N 9 26 E
Baco, Mt., Phil. 61 E4 12 49N 121 10 E
Bacolod, Phil. 61 F5 10 40N 122 57 E
Bacqueville-en-Caux, France 18 C8 49 47N 1 0 E
Bács-Kiskun □, Hungary 42 D4 46 43N 19 30 E
Bácsalmás, Hungary 42 D4 46 8N 19 17 E
Bacuag = Placer, Phil. 61 G6 9 36N 125 38 E

Bacuk

Bacuk, *Malaysia* ..... **65 J4** 6 4N 102 25 E
Bād, *Iran* .... **71 C7** 33 41N 52 1 E
Bad →, *U.S.A.* **112 C4** 44 21N 100 22W
Bad Aussee, *Austria* .. **26 D6** 47 43N 13 45 E
Bad Axe, *U.S.A.* **110 C2** 43 48N 83 0W
Bad Bergzabern, *Germany* .... **25 F3** 49 6N 7 59 E
Bad Berleburg, *Germany* .... **24 D4** 51 2N 8 26 E
Bad Bevensen, *Germany* .... **24 B6** 53 5N 10 35 E
Bad Bramstedt, *Germany* .... **24 B5** 53 55N 9 53 E
Bad Brückenau, *Germany* .... **25 E5** 50 18N 9 47 E
Bad Doberan, *Germany* **24 A7** 54 6N 11 53 E
Bad Driburg, *Germany* **24 D5** 51 43N 9 1 E
Bad Ems, *Germany* ... **25 E3** 50 20N 7 43 E
Bad Frankenhausen, *Germany* .... **24 D7** 51 21N 11 5 E
Bad Freienwalde, *Germany* .... **24 C10** 52 46N 14 1 E
Bad Goisern, *Austria* . **26 D6** 47 38N 13 38 E
Bad Harzburg, *Germany* .... **24 D6** 51 52N 10 34 E
Bad Hersfeld, *Germany* **24 E5** 50 52N 9 42 E
Bad Hofgastein, *Austria* **26 D6** 47 17N 13 6 E
Bad Homburg, *Germany* .... **25 E4** 50 13N 8 38 E
Bad Honnef, *Germany* **24 E3** 50 38N 7 13 E
Bad Iburg, *Germany* .. **24 C4** 52 10N 8 3 E
Bad Ischl, *Austria* .... **26 D6** 47 44N 13 38 E
Bad Kissingen, *Germany* .... **25 E6** 50 11N 10 4 E
Bad Königshofen, *Germany* .... **25 E6** 50 17N 10 28 E
Bad Kreuznach, *Germany* .... **25 F3** 49 50N 7 51 E
Bad Krozingen, *Germany* .... **25 H3** 47 54N 7 42 E
Bad Laasphe, *Germany* **24 E4** 50 56N 8 25 E
Bad Lands, *U.S.A.* ... **112 D3** 43 40N 102 10W
Bad Langensalza, *Germany* .... **24 D6** 51 5N 10 38 E
Bad Lauterberg, *Germany* .... **24 D6** 51 38N 10 28 E
Bad Leonfelden, *Austria* .... **26 C7** 48 31N 14 18 E
Bad Liebenwerda, *Germany* .... **24 D9** 51 31N 13 24 E
Bad Mergentheim, *Germany* .... **25 F5** 49 28N 9 42 E
Bad Münstereifel, *Germany* .... **24 E2** 50 33N 6 46 E
Bad Nauheim, *Germany* .... **25 E4** 50 21N 8 43 E
Bad Neuenahr-Ahrweiler, *Germany* **24 E3** 50 32N 7 5 E
Bad Neustadt, *Germany* **25 E6** 50 18N 10 13 E
Bad Oeynhausen, *Germany* .... **24 C4** 52 12N 8 46 E
Bad Oldesloe, *Germany* **24 B6** 53 48N 10 22 E
Bad Orb, *Germany* ... **25 E5** 50 12N 9 22 E
Bad Pyrmont, *Germany* **24 D5** 51 59N 9 16 E
Bad Reichenhall, *Germany* .... **25 H8** 47 43N 12 54 E
Bad Säckingen, *Germany* .... **25 H3** 47 33N 7 56 E
Bad Salzuflen, *Germany* .... **24 C4** 52 5N 8 45 E
Bad Salzungen, *Germany* .... **24 E6** 50 48N 10 14 E
Bad Schwartau, *Germany* .... **24 B6** 53 55N 10 41 E
Bad Segeberg, *Germany* .... **24 B6** 53 56N 10 17 E
Bad St. Leonhard, *Austria* .... **26 E7** 46 58N 14 47 E
Bad Tölz, *Germany* ... **25 H7** 47 45N 11 34 E
Bad Urach, *Germany* . **25 G5** 48 29N 9 23 E
Bad Vöslau, *Austria* .. **27 D9** 47 58N 16 12 E
Bad Waldsee, *Germany* **25 H5** 47 55N 9 45 E
Bad Wildungen, *Germany* .... **24 D5** 51 6N 9 7 E
Bad Wimpfen, *Germany* .... **25 F5** 49 13N 9 11 E
Bad Windsheim, *Germany* .... **25 F6** 49 36N 10 25 E
Bad Zwischenahn, *Germany* .... **24 B4** 53 12N 8 1 E
Bada Barabil, *India* ... **69 H11** 22 7N 85 24 E
Badagara, *India* ...... **66 P9** 11 35N 75 40 E
Badagri, *Nigeria* ..... **83 D5** 6 25N 2 55 E
Badajós, L., *Brazil* ... **124 D6** 3 15 S 62 50W
Badajoz, *Spain* **35 G4** 38 50N 6 59W
Badajoz □, *Spain* **35 G4** 38 40N 6 30W
Badakhshān □, *Afghan.* **66 A7** 36 30N 71 0 E
Badalona, *Spain* ..... **32 D7** 41 26N 2 15 E
Badalzai, *Afghan.* .... **68 E1** 29 50N 65 35 E
Badampahar, *India* ... **67 H15** 22 10N 86 10 E
Badanah, *Si. Arabia* .. **70 D4** 30 58N 41 30 E
Badarinath, *India* .... **69 D8** 30 45N 79 30 E
Badas, Kepulauan, *Indonesia* .... **62 D3** 0 45N 107 5 E
Baddo →, *Pakistan* .. **66 F4** 28 0N 64 20 E
Bade, *Indonesia* ..... **63 F9** 7 10 S 139 35 E
Badeggi, *Nigeria* ..... **83 D6** 9 1N 6 8 E
Badéguichéri, *Niger* .. **83 C6** 14 30N 5 22 E
Baden, *Austria* ...... **27 C9** 48 1N 16 13 E
Baden, *Switz.* .... **25 H4** 47 28N 8 18 E
Baden, *U.S.A.* **110 F4** 40 38N 80 14W
Baden-Baden, *Germany* **25 G4** 48 44N 8 13 E
Baden-Württemberg □, *Germany* .... **25 G4** 48 20N 8 40 E
Badgastein, *Austria* ... **26 D6** 47 7N 13 9 E
Badger, *Canada* **103 C8** 49 0N 56 4W
Badger, *U.S.A.* **116 J7** 36 38N 119 1W
Bādghīs □, *Afghan.* .. **66 B3** 35 0N 63 0 E
Badgom, *India* .... **69 B6** 34 1N 74 45 E
Badia Polésine, *Italy* .. **29 C8** 45 5N 11 29 E
Badin, *Pakistan* ...... **68 G3** 24 38N 68 54 E
Badlands National Park, *U.S.A.* **112 D3** 43 38N 102 56W
Badogo, *Mali* **82 C3** 11 2N 8 13W
Badoumbé, *Mali* **82 C2** 13 42N 10 15W
Badrah, *Iraq* .... **70 C5** 33 6N 45 58 E
Badrinath, *India* ..... **69 D8** 30 44N 79 29 E
Badulla, *Sri Lanka* ... **66 R12** 7 1N 81 7 E
Baena, *Spain* **35 H6** 37 37N 4 20W
Baeza, *Spain* **35 H7** 37 57N 3 25W
Bafang, *Cameroon* ... **83 D7** 5 9N 10 11 E
Bafatá, *Guinea-Biss.* .. **82 C2** 12 8N 14 40W
Baffin B., *Canada* **101 A13** 72 0N 64 0W
Baffin I., *Canada* **101 B12** 68 0N 75 0W
Bafia, *Cameroon* ..... **83 E7** 4 40N 11 10 E
Bafilo, *Togo* .... **83 D5** 9 22N 1 22 E
Bafing →, *Mali* **82 C2** 13 49N 10 50W
Bafliyūn, *Syria* ...... **70 B3** 36 37N 36 59 E
Bafoulabé, *Mali* **82 C2** 13 50N 10 55W
Bafoussam, *Cameroon* **83 D7** 5 28N 10 25 E
Bāfq, *Iran* .... **71 D7** 31 40N 55 25 E
Bafra, *Turkey* .... **72 B6** 41 34N 35 54 E
Bafra Burnu, *Turkey* . **72 B7** 41 45N 36 2 E
Bāft, *Iran* .... **71 D8** 29 15N 56 38 E
Bafut, *Cameroon* ..... **83 D7** 6 6N 10 2 E
Bafwasende, *Dem. Rep. of the Congo* ..... **86 B2** 1 3N 27 5 E
Bagam, *Niger* .... **83 B6** 15 43N 6 35 E
Bagamoyo, *Tanzania* . **86 D4** 6 28 S 38 55 E
Bagan Datoh, *Malaysia* **65 L3** 3 59N 100 47 E
Bagan Serai, *Malaysia* **65 K3** 5 1N 100 32 E
Baganga, *Phil.* ...... **61 H7** 7 34N 126 33 E
Bagani, *Namibia* ..... **88 B3** 18 7 S 21 41 E
Bagansiapiapi, *Indonesia* .... **62 D2** 2 12N 100 50 E
Bagasra, *India* ...... **68 J4** 21 30N 71 0 E
Bagaud, *India* ...... **68 H6** 22 19N 75 53 E
Bagawi, *Sudan* ...... **81 E3** 12 20N 34 18 E
Bagbag, *Sudan* ...... **81 D3** 15 23N 31 30 E
Bagdad, *U.S.A.* **117 L11** 34 35N 115 53W
Bagdarin, *Russia* .... **51 D12** 54 26N 113 36 E
Bagé, *Brazil* .... **127 C5** 31 20 S 54 15W
Bagenalstown = Muine Bheag, *Ireland* **15 D5** 52 42N 6 58W
Baggs, *U.S.A.* **114 F10** 41 2N 107 39W
Bagh, *Pakistan* ...... **69 C5** 33 59N 73 45 E
Baghain →, *India* .... **69 G9** 25 32N 81 1 E
Baghdād, *Iraq* .... **70 C5** 33 20N 44 30 E
Bagheria, *Italy* ...... **30 D6** 38 5N 13 30 E
Baghlān, *Afghan.* .... **66 A6** 36 12N 69 0 E
Baghlān □, *Afghan.* .. **66 B6** 36 0N 68 30 E
Bagley, *U.S.A.* **112 B7** 47 32N 95 24W
Bagnara Cálabra, *Italy* **31 D8** 38 17N 15 48 E
Bagnasco, *Italy* ...... **28 D5** 44 18N 8 2 E
Bagnères-de-Bigorre, *France* .... **20 E4** 43 5N 0 9 E
Bagnères-de-Luchon, *France* .... **20 F4** 42 47N 0 38 E
Bagni di Lucca, *Italy* .. **28 D7** 44 1N 10 35 E
Bagno di Romagna, *Italy* .... **29 E8** 43 50N 11 57 E
Bagnoles-de-l'Orne, *France* **18 D6** 48 32N 0 25W
Bagnols-sur-Cèze, *France* .... **21 D8** 44 10N 4 36 E
Bagnorégio, *Italy* .... **29 F9** 42 37N 12 5 E
Bago = Pegu, *Burma* . **67 L20** 17 20N 96 29 E
Bagodar, *India* ...... **69 G11** 24 5N 85 52 E
Bagrationovsk, *Russia* **9 J19** 54 23N 20 39 E
Bagrdan, *Serbia, Yug.* . **40 B5** 44 5N 21 11 E
Baguio, *Phil.* .... **61 C4** 16 26N 120 34 E
Bağyurdu, *Turkey* .... **39 C9** 38 25N 27 41 E
Bagzane, Monts, *Niger* **83 B6** 17 43N 8 45 E
Bah, *India* .... **69 F8** 26 53N 78 36 E
Bahabón de Esgueva, *Spain* **34 D7** 41 52N 3 43W
Bahadurganj, *India* ... **69 F12** 26 16N 87 49 E
Bahadurgarh, *India* ... **68 E7** 28 40N 76 57 E
Bahama, Canal Viejo de, *W. Indies* **120 B4** 22 10N 77 30W
Bahamas ■, *N. Amer.* . **121 B5** 24 0N 75 0W
Bahār, *Iran* .... **73 E13** 34 54N 48 26 E
Baharampur, *India* ... **69 G13** 24 2N 88 27 E
Baharîya, El Wâhât al, *Egypt* .... **80 B2** 28 0N 28 50 E
Bahawalnagar, *Pakistan* **68 E5** 30 0N 73 15 E
Bahawalpur, *Pakistan* . **68 E4** 29 24N 71 40 E
Bahçe, *Turkey* ...... **72 D7** 37 13N 36 34 E
Bahçecik, *Turkey* ..... **41 F13** 40 41N 29 44 E
Baheri, *India* .... **69 E8** 28 45N 79 34 E
Bahgul →, *India* ..... **69 F8** 27 45N 79 36 E
Bahi, *Tanzania* ...... **86 D4** 5 58 S 35 21 E
Bahi Swamp, *Tanzania* **86 D4** 6 10 S 35 0 E
Bahía = Salvador, *Brazil* .... **125 F11** 13 0 S 38 30W
Bahía □, *Brazil* ..... **125 F10** 12 0 S 42 0W
Bahía, Is. de la, *Honduras* **120 C2** 16 45N 86 15W
Bahía Blanca, *Argentina* .... **126 D3** 38 35 S 62 13W
Bahía de Caráquez, *Ecuador* .... **124 D2** 0 40 S 80 27W
Bahía Honda, *Cuba* ... **120 B3** 22 54N 83 10W
Bahía Laura, *Argentina* **128 F3** 48 10 S 66 30W
Bahía Negra, *Paraguay* **124 H7** 20 5 S 58 5W
Bahir Dar, *Ethiopia* ... **81 E4** 11 37N 37 10 E
Bahmanzād, *Iran* ..... **71 D6** 31 15N 51 47 E
Bahr el Ahmar □, *Sudan* .... **80 D4** 20 0N 35 0 E
Bahr el Ghazâl □, *Sudan* .... **81 F2** 7 0N 28 0 E
Bahr el Jabal □, *Sudan* **81 G3** 4 0N 31 0 E
Bahr Yûsef →, *Egypt* . **80 B3** 28 25N 30 35 E
Bahraich, *India* ...... **69 F9** 27 38N 81 37 E
Bahrain ■, *Asia* ...... **71 E6** 26 0N 50 35 E
Bahror, *India* .... **68 F7** 27 51N 76 20 E
Bāhū Kalāt, *Iran* .... **71 E9** 25 43N 61 25 E
Bai, *Mali* **82 C4** 13 35N 3 28W
Bai Bung, Mui = Ca Mau, Mui, *Vietnam* . **65 H5** 8 38N 104 44 E
Bai Duc, *Vietnam* .... **64 C5** 18 3N 105 49 E
Bai Thuong, *Vietnam* . **64 C5** 19 54N 105 23 E
Baia de Aramă, *Romania* .... **42 E7** 45 0N 22 50 E
Baia Mare, *Romania* .. **43 C8** 47 40N 23 35 E
Baia-Sprie, *Romania* .. **43 C8** 47 41N 23 43 E
Baião, *Brazil* .... **125 D9** 2 40 S 49 40W
Baïbokoum, *Chad* .... **79 G9** 7 46N 15 43 E
Baicheng, *China* ..... **57 B12** 45 38N 122 42 E
Băicoi, *Romania* ..... **43 E10** 45 3N 25 52 E
Baidoa, *Somali Rep.* .. **74 G3** 3 8N 43 30 E
Baie Comeau, *Canada* **103 C6** 49 12N 68 10W
Baie-St-Paul, *Canada* . **103 C5** 47 28N 70 32W
Baie Trinité, *Canada* . **103 C6** 49 25N 67 20W
Baie Verte, *Canada* .. **103 C8** 49 55N 56 12W
Baignes-Ste-Radegonde, *France* . **20 C3** 45 23N 0 25W
Baigneux-les-Juifs, *France* .... **19 E11** 47 31N 4 39 E
Baihar, *India* .... **69 H9** 22 6N 80 33 E
Baihe, *China* .... **56 H6** 32 50N 110 5 E
Ba'ījī, *Iraq* .... **70 C4** 35 0N 43 30 E
Baijnath, *India* ..... **69 E8** 29 55N 79 37 E
Baikal, L. = Baykal, Oz., *Russia* .... **51 D11** 53 0N 108 0 E
Baikunthpur, *India* ... **69 H10** 23 15N 82 33 E
Baile Atha Cliath = Dublin, *Ireland* **15 C5** 53 21N 6 15W
Băile Govora, *Romania* **43 E9** 45 5N 24 11 E
Băile Herculane, *Romania* .... **42 F7** 44 53N 22 26 E
Băile Olănești, *Romania* .... **43 E9** 45 12N 24 14 E
Băile Tușnad, *Romania* **43 D10** 46 9N 25 51 E
Bailén, *Spain* **35 G7** 38 8N 3 48W
Băilești, *Romania* .... **43 F8** 44 1N 23 20 E
Baima, *China* .... **58 A3** 33 0N 100 26 E
Bain-de-Bretagne, *France* **18 E5** 47 50N 1 40W
Bainbridge, *Ga., U.S.A.* **109 K3** 30 55N 84 35W
Bainbridge, *N.Y., U.S.A.* **111 D9** 42 18N 75 29W
Baing, *Indonesia* .... **63 F6** 10 14 S 120 34 E
Bainiu, *China* ...... **56 H7** 32 50N 112 15 E
Baiona, *Spain* **34 C2** 42 6N 8 52W
Bā'ir, *Jordan* ...... **75 E5** 30 45N 36 55 E
Bairin Youqi, *China* .. **57 C10** 43 30N 118 35 E
Bairin Zuoqi, *China* .. **57 C10** 43 58N 119 15 E
Bairnsdale, *Australia* . **95 F4** 37 48 S 147 36 E
Bais, *Phil.* .... **61 G5** 9 35N 123 7 E
Baisha, *China* ...... **56 G7** 34 20N 112 32 E
Baissa, *Nigeria* ..... **83 D7** 7 14N 10 38 E
Baitadi, *Nepal* ...... **69 E9** 29 35N 80 25 E
Baiyin, *China* ...... **56 F3** 36 45N 104 14 E
Baiyü, *China* .... **58 B2** 31 16N 98 50 E
Baiyu Shan, *China* ... **56 F4** 37 15N 107 30 E
Baiyuda, *Sudan* ..... **80 D3** 17 35N 32 7 E
Baj Baj, *India* ...... **69 H13** 22 30N 88 5 E
Baja, *Hungary* ...... **42 D3** 46 12N 18 59 E
Baja, Pta., *Mexico* ... **118 B1** 29 50N 116 0W
Baja California, *Mexico* **118 A1** 31 10N 115 12W
Baja California □, *Mexico* **118 B2** 30 0N 115 0W
Baja California Sur □, *Mexico* **118 B2** 25 50N 111 50W
Bajag, *India* .... **69 H9** 22 40N 81 21 E
Bajamar, *Canary Is.* .. **37 F3** 28 33N 16 20W
Bajana, *India* ...... **68 H4** 23 7N 71 49 E
Bājgīrān, *Iran* ...... **71 B8** 37 36N 58 24 E
Bajimba, Mt., *Australia* **95 D5** 29 17 S 152 6 E
Bajina Bašta, *Serbia, Yug.* .... **40 C3** 43 58N 19 35 E
Bajmok, *Serbia, Yug.* . **42 E4** 45 57N 19 24 E
Bajo Nuevo, *Caribbean* **120 C4** 15 40N 78 50W
Bajoga, *Nigeria* ..... **83 C7** 10 57N 11 20 E
Bajool, *Australia* .... **94 C5** 23 40 S 150 35 E
Bak, *Hungary* ...... **42 D1** 46 43N 16 51 E
Bakar, *Croatia* ..... **29 C11** 45 18N 14 32 E
Bakel, *Senegal* **82 C2** 14 56N 12 20W
Baker, *Calif., U.S.A.* . **117 K10** 35 16N 116 4W
Baker, *Mont., U.S.A.* . **112 B2** 46 22N 104 17W
Baker, L., *Canada* ... **100 B10** 64 0N 96 0W
Baker City, *U.S.A.* ... **114 D5** 44 47N 117 50W
Baker I., *Pac. Oc.* **96 G10** 0 10N 176 35W
Baker I., *U.S.A.* **104 B2** 55 20N 133 40W
Baker L., *Australia* ... **93 E4** 26 54 S 126 5 E
Baker Lake, *Canada* .. **100 B10** 64 20N 96 3W
Baker Mt., *U.S.A.* ... **114 B3** 48 50N 121 49W
Bakers Creek, *Australia* **94 C4** 21 13 S 149 7 E
Baker's Dozen Is., *Canada* **102 A4** 56 45N 78 45W
Bakersfield, *Calif., U.S.A.* **117 K8** 35 23N 119 1W
Bakersfield, *Vt., U.S.A.* **111 B12** 44 45N 72 48W
Bakhchysaray, *Ukraine* **47 K7** 44 40N 33 45 E
Bakhmach, *Ukraine* ... **47 G7** 51 10N 32 45 E
Bākhtarān, *Iran* ..... **70 C5** 34 23N 47 0 E
Bākhtarān □, *Iran* .... **70 C5** 34 0N 46 30 E
Bakı, *Azerbaijan* ..... **49 K9** 40 29N 49 56 E
Bakır →, *Turkey* ..... **39 C9** 38 55N 27 0 E
Bakırdaği, *Turkey* .... **72 C6** 38 13N 35 46 E
Bakkafjörður, *Iceland* **8 C6** 66 2N 14 48W
Baklan, *Turkey* ..... **39 C11** 38 0N 29 36 E
Bako, *Ethiopia* ..... **81 F4** 5 51N 36 23 E
Bako, *Ivory C.* **82 D3** 9 8N 7 40W
Bakony, *Hungary* .... **42 C2** 47 10N 17 30 E
Bakony Forest = Bakony, *Hungary* .... **42 C2** 47 10N 17 30 E
Bakori, *Nigeria* ..... **83 C6** 11 34N 7 25 E
Bakouma, *C.A.R.* .... **84 C4** 5 40N 22 56 E
Baksan, *Russia* ..... **49 J6** 43 42N 43 32 E
Bakswaho, *India* .... **69 G8** 24 15N 79 18 E
Baku = Bakı, *Azerbaijan* .... **49 K9** 40 29N 49 56 E
Bakundi, *Nigeria* .... **83 D7** 8 2N 10 45 E
Bakutis Coast, *Antarctica* .... **5 D15** 74 0 S 120 0W
Baky = Bakı, *Azerbaijan* .... **49 K9** 40 29N 49 56 E
Bala, *Canada* **110 A5** 45 1N 79 37W
Bala, *Senegal* **82 C2** 14 1N 13 8W
Bâlâ, *Turkey* ...... **72 C5** 39 32N 33 6 E
Bala, *U.K.* **12 E4** 52 54N 3 36W
Bala, L., *U.K.* **12 E4** 52 53N 3 37W
Balabac I., *Phil.* .... **62 C5** 8 0N 117 0 E
Balabac Str., *E. Indies* **62 C5** 7 53N 117 5 E
Balabagh, *Afghan.* ... **68 B4** 34 25N 70 12 E
Ba'labakk, *Lebanon* .. **75 B5** 34 0N 36 10 E
Balabalangan, Kepulauan, *Indonesia* **62 E5** 2 20 S 117 30 E
Bălăcița, *Romania* ... **43 F8** 44 23N 23 8 E
Balad, *Iraq* .... **70 C5** 34 1N 44 9 E
Balad Rūz, *Iraq* ..... **70 C5** 33 42N 45 5 E
Bālādeh, *Fārs, Iran* .. **71 D6** 29 17N 51 56 E
Bālādeh, *Māzandaran, Iran* .... **71 B6** 36 12N 51 48 E
Balaghat, *India* ..... **66 J12** 21 49N 80 12 E
Balaghat Ra., *India* .. **66 K10** 18 50N 76 30 E
Balaguer, *Spain* .... **32 D5** 41 50N 0 50 E
Balakhna, *Russia* ... **48 B6** 56 25N 43 32 E
Balaklava, *Ukraine* .. **47 K7** 44 30N 33 30 E
Balakliya, *Ukraine* .. **47 H9** 49 28N 36 55 E
Balakovo, *Russia* ... **48 D8** 52 4N 47 55 E
Balamau, *India* .... **69 F9** 27 10N 80 21 E
Bălan, *Romania* .... **43 D10** 46 39N 25 48 E
Balancán, *Mexico* ... **119 D6** 17 48N 91 32W
Balashov, *Russia* ... **48 E6** 51 30N 43 10 E
Balasinor, *India* .... **68 H5** 22 57N 73 23 E
Balasore = Baleshwar, *India* .... **67 J15** 21 35N 87 3 E
Balassagyarmat, *Hungary* .... **42 B4** 48 4N 19 15 E
Balât, *Egypt* .... **80 B2** 25 36N 29 19 E
Balaton, *Hungary* ... **42 D2** 46 50N 17 40 E
Balatonboglár, *Hungary* .... **42 D2** 46 46N 17 40 E
Balatonfüred, *Hungary* **42 D2** 46 58N 17 54 E
Balatonszentgyörgy, *Hungary* .... **42 D2** 46 41N 17 19 E
Balayan, *Phil.* ..... **61 E4** 13 57N 120 44 E
Balazote, *Spain* **33 G2** 38 54N 2 9W
Balbieriškis, *Lithuania* **44 D10** 54 32N 23 53 E
Balbigny, *France* ..... **21 C8** 45 49N 4 11 E
Balbina, Represa de, *Brazil* .... **124 D7** 2 0 S 59 30W
Balboa, *Panama* **120 E4** 8 57N 79 34W
Balbriggan, *Ireland* ... **15 C5** 53 37N 6 11W
Balcarce, *Argentina* ... **126 D4** 38 0 S 58 10W
Balcarres, *Canada* **105 C8** 50 50N 103 35W
Bălcești, *Romania* .... **43 F8** 44 37N 23 57 E
Balchik, *Bulgaria* .... **41 C12** 43 28N 28 11 E
Balclutha, *N.Z.* ..... **91 M2** 46 15 S 169 45 E
Balcones Escarpment, *U.S.A.* **113 L5** 29 30N 99 15W
Balçova, *Turkey* ..... **39 C9** 38 22N 27 4 E
Bald Hd., *Australia* ... **93 G2** 35 6 S 118 1 E
Bald I., *Australia* .... **93 F2** 34 57 S 118 27 E
Bald Knob, *U.S.A.* ... **113 H9** 35 19N 91 34W
Baldock L., *Canada* .. **105 B9** 56 33N 97 57W
Baldwin, *Mich., U.S.A.* **108 D3** 43 54N 85 51W
Baldwin, *Pa., U.S.A.* .. **110 F5** 40 23N 79 59W
Baldwinsville, *U.S.A.* . **111 C8** 43 10N 76 20W
Baldy Mt., *U.S.A.* ... **114 B9** 48 9N 109 39W
Baldy Peak, *U.S.A.* ... **115 K9** 33 54N 109 34W
Bale, *Croatia* .... **29 C10** 45 4N 13 46 E
Bale, *Ethiopia* ...... **81 F5** 6 57N 40 8 E
Bale □, *Ethiopia* .... **81 F5** 6 20N 41 30 E
Baleares, Is., *Spain* ... **37 B10** 39 30N 3 0 E
Balearic Is. = Baleares, Is., *Spain* .... **37 B10** 39 30N 3 0 E
Baleine = Whale →, *Canada* **103 A6** 58 15N 67 40W
Băleni, *Romania* ..... **43 E12** 45 48N 27 51 E
Baler, *Phil.* .... **61 D4** 15 46N 121 34 E
Baler Bay, *Phil.* ..... **61 D4** 15 50N 121 35 E
Baleshare, *U.K.* **14 D1** 57 31N 7 22W
Baleshwar, *India* ..... **67 J15** 21 35N 87 3 E
Balezino, *Russia* .... **48 B11** 58 2N 53 6 E
Balfate, *Honduras* ... **120 C2** 15 48N 86 25W
Bali, *Cameroon* ..... **83 D7** 5 54N 10 0 E
Balí, *Greece* .... **36 D6** 35 25N 24 47 E
Bali, *India* .... **68 G5** 25 11N 73 17 E
Bali, *Indonesia* ..... **62 F4** 8 20 S 115 0 E
Bali □, *Indonesia* ... **62 F5** 8 20 S 115 0 E
Bali, Selat, *Indonesia* **63 H16** 8 18 S 114 25 E
Balia, *S. Leone* **82 D2** 9 22N 11 1W
Baliapal, *India* ..... **69 J12** 21 40N 87 17 E
Baligród, *Poland* .... **45 J9** 49 20N 22 17 E
Balikeşir, *Turkey* .... **39 B9** 39 39N 27 53 E
Balikeşir □, *Turkey* .. **39 B9** 39 45N 28 0 E
Balıklıçeşme, *Turkey* . **41 F11** 40 18N 27 5 E
Balikpapan, *Indonesia* **62 E5** 1 10 S 116 55 E
Balimbing, *Phil.* ..... **63 C5** 5 5N 119 58 E
Baling, *Malaysia* .... **65 K3** 5 41N 100 55 E
Balingen, *Germany* ... **25 G4** 48 16N 8 51 E
Balinț, *Romania* .... **42 E6** 45 48N 21 54 E
Balintang Channel, *Phil.* .... **61 B4** 19 49N 121 40 E
Balipara, *India* ..... **67 F18** 26 50N 92 45 E
Balkan Mts. = Stara Planina, *Bulgaria* ... **40 C7** 43 15N 23 0 E
Balkhash = Balqash, *Kazakhstan* .... **50 E8** 46 50N 74 50 E
Balkhash, Ozero = Balqash Köl, *Kazakhstan* .... **50 E8** 46 0N 74 50 E
Balla, *Bangla.* ...... **67 G17** 24 10N 91 35 E
Ballachulish, *U.K.* ... **14 E3** 56 41N 5 8W
Balladonia, *Australia* . **93 F3** 32 27 S 123 51 E
Ballaghaderreen, *Ireland* **15 C3** 53 55N 8 34W
Ballarat, *Australia* ... **95 F3** 37 33 S 143 50 E
Ballard, L., *Australia* . **93 E3** 29 20 S 120 40 E
Ballater, *U.K.* **14 D5** 57 3N 3 3W
Ballé, *Mali* **82 B3** 15 18N 8 33W
Ballenas, Canal de, *Mexico* **118 B2** 29 10N 113 45W
Balleny Is., *Antarctica* **5 C11** 66 30 S 163 0 E
Balleroy, *France* **18 C6** 49 11N 0 50W
Ballerup, *Denmark* ... **11 J6** 55 44N 12 21 E
Ballı, *Turkey* .... **41 F11** 40 50N 27 3 E
Ballia, *India* .... **69 G11** 25 46N 84 12 E
Ballina, *Australia* .... **95 D5** 28 50 S 153 31 E
Ballina, *Ireland* **15 B2** 54 7N 9 9W
Ballinasloe, *Ireland* .. **15 C3** 53 20N 8 13W
Ballinger, *U.S.A.* **113 K5** 31 45N 99 57W
Ballinrobe, *Ireland* ... **15 C2** 53 38N 9 13W
Ballinskelligs B., *Ireland* **15 E1** 51 48N 10 13W
Ballon, *France* ...... **18 D7** 48 10N 0 14 E
Ballsh, *Albania* ..... **40 F3** 40 36N 19 44 E
Ballston Spa, *U.S.A.* . **111 D11** 43 0N 73 51W
Ballycastle, *U.K.* **15 A5** 55 12N 6 15W
Ballyclare, *U.K.* **15 B5** 54 46N 6 0W
Ballyhaunis, *Ireland* .. **15 C3** 53 46N 8 46W
Ballymena, *U.K.* **15 B5** 54 52N 6 17W
Ballymoney, *U.K.* ... **15 A5** 55 5N 6 31W
Ballymote, *Ireland* ... **15 B3** 54 5N 8 31W
Ballynahinch, *U.K.* .. **15 B6** 54 24N 5 54W
Ballyquintin Pt., *U.K.* . **15 B6** 54 20N 5 30W
Ballyshannon, *Ireland* . **15 B3** 54 30N 8 11W
Balmaceda, *Chile* .... **128 F2** 46 0 S 71 50W
Balmaseda, *Spain* ... **32 B1** 43 11N 3 12W
Balmazújváros, *Hungary* .... **42 C6** 47 37N 21 21 E
Balmertown, *Canada* . **105 C10** 51 4N 93 41W
Balmoral, *Australia* .. **95 F3** 37 15 S 141 48 E
Balmorhea, *U.S.A.* ... **113 K3** 30 59N 103 45W
Balonne →, *Australia* . **95 D4** 28 47 S 147 56 E
Balotra, *India* ...... **68 G5** 25 50N 72 14 E
Balqash, *Kazakhstan* .. **50 E8** 46 50N 74 50 E
Balqash Köl, *Kazakhstan* .... **50 E8** 46 0N 74 50 E
Balrampur, *India* .... **69 F10** 27 30N 82 20 E
Balranald, *Australia* .. **95 E3** 34 38 S 143 33 E
Balș, *Romania* ...... **43 F9** 44 22N 24 5 E
Balsas, *Mexico* **119 D5** 18 0N 99 40W
Balsas →, *Brazil* .... **125 E9** 7 15 S 44 35W
Balsas →, *Mexico* ... **118 D4** 17 55N 102 10W
Bålsta, *Sweden* ..... **10 E11** 59 35N 17 30 E
Balston Spa, *U.S.A.* . **111 D11** 43 0N 73 52W
Balta, *Romania* ..... **42 F7** 44 54N 22 38 E
Balta, *Ukraine* ..... **47 H5** 48 2N 29 45 E
Baltanás, *Spain* **34 D6** 41 56N 4 15W
Bălți, *Moldova* ..... **43 C12** 47 48N 27 58 E
Baltic Sea, *Europe* ... **9 H18** 57 0N 19 0 E
Baltîm, *Egypt* ...... **80 H7** 31 35N 31 10 E
Baltimore, *Ireland* ... **15 E2** 51 29N 9 22W
Baltimore, *Md., U.S.A.* **108 F7** 39 17N 76 37W
Baltimore, *Ohio, U.S.A.* **110 G2** 39 51N 82 36W
Baltit, *Pakistan* ..... **69 A6** 36 15N 74 40 E
Baltiysk, *Russia* ..... **9 J18** 54 41N 19 58 E
Baltrum, *Germany* ... **24 B3** 53 43N 7 24 E
Baluchistan □, *Pakistan* **66 F4** 27 30N 65 0 E
Balurghat, *India* ..... **69 G13** 25 15N 88 44 E
Balvi, *Latvia* .... **9 H22** 57 8N 27 15 E
Balya, *Turkey* ...... **39 B9** 39 44N 27 35 E
Bam, *Iran* .... **71 D8** 29 7N 58 14 E
Bama, *China* .... **58 E6** 24 8N 107 12 E
Bama, *Nigeria* ..... **83 C7** 11 33N 13 41 E
Bamaga, *Australia* ... **94 A3** 10 50 S 142 25 E
Bamaji L., *Canada* ... **102 B1** 51 9N 91 25W
Bamako, *Mali* **82 C3** 12 34N 7 55W
Bamba, *Mali* **83 B4** 17 5N 1 24W
Bambara Maoundé, *Mali* **82 B4** 13 26N 4 3W
Bambari, *C.A.R.* .... **84 C4** 5 40N 20 35 E
Bambaroo, *Australia* .. **94 B4** 18 50 S 146 10 E
Bambaya, *Guinea* **82 D2** 10 55N 13 38W
Bamberg, *Germany* ... **25 F6** 49 54N 10 54 E
Bamberg, *U.S.A.* **109 J5** 33 18N 81 2W
Bambesi, *Ethiopia* ... **81 F3** 9 45N 34 40 E
Bambey, *Senegal* **82 C1** 14 42N 16 28W
Bambili, *Dem. Rep. of the Congo* .... **86 B2** 3 40N 26 0 E
Bamboi, *Ghana* **82 D4** 8 13N 2 1W
Bamenda, *Cameroon* . **83 D7** 5 57N 10 11 E
Bamfield, *Canada* ... **104 D3** 48 45N 125 10W
Bāmīān □, *Afghan.* ... **66 B5** 35 0N 67 0 E
Bamiancheng, *China* .. **57 C13** 43 15N 124 2 E
Bamkin, *Cameroon* ... **83 D7** 6 3N 11 27 E
Bampūr, *Iran* ...... **71 E9** 27 15N 60 21 E
Ban, *Burkina Faso* ... **82 C4** 14 5N 2 27W
Ban Ban, *Laos* ..... **64 C4** 19 31N 103 30 E
Ban Bang Hin, *Thailand* .... **65 H2** 9 32N 98 35 E
Ban Chiang Klang, *Thailand* .... **64 C3** 19 25N 100 55 E
Ban Chik, *Laos* .... **64 D4** 17 15N 102 22 E
Ban Choho, *Thailand* . **64 E4** 15 2N 102 9 E
Ban Dan Lan Hoi, *Thailand* .... **64 D2** 17 0N 99 35 E
Ban Don = Surat Thani, *Thailand* .... **65 H2** 9 6N 99 20 E
Ban Don, *Vietnam* ... **64 F6** 12 53N 107 48 E
Ban Don, Ao →, *Thailand* .... **65 H2** 9 20N 99 25 E
Ban Dong, *Thailand* .. **64 C3** 19 30N 100 59 E
Ban Hong, *Thailand* .. **64 C2** 18 18N 98 50 E
Ban Kaeng, *Thailand* . **64 D3** 17 29N 100 7 E
Ban Kantang, *Thailand* **65 J2** 7 25N 99 31 E
Ban Keun, *Laos* .... **64 C4** 18 22N 102 35 E
Ban Khai, *Thailand* .. **64 F3** 12 46N 101 18 E
Ban Kheun, *Laos* ... **64 B3** 20 13N 101 7 E
Ban Khlong Kua, *Thailand* .... **65 J3** 6 57N 100 8 E
Ban Khuan Mao, *Thailand* .... **65 J2** 7 50N 99 37 E
Ban Ko Yai Chim, *Thailand* .... **65 G2** 11 17N 99 26 E
Ban Kok, *Thailand* .. **64 D4** 16 40N 103 40 E
Ban Laem, *Thailand* . **64 F2** 13 13N 99 59 E
Ban Lao Ngam, *Laos* . **64 E6** 15 28N 106 10 E
Ban Le Kathe, *Thailand* **64 E2** 15 49N 98 53 E
Ban Mae Chedi, *Thailand* .... **64 C2** 19 11N 99 31 E
Ban Mae Laeng, *Thailand* .... **64 B2** 20 1N 99 17 E
Ban Mae Sariang, *Thailand* .... **64 C1** 18 10N 97 56 E
Ban Mê Thuôt = Buon Ma Thuot, *Vietnam* . **64 F7** 12 40N 108 3 E
Ban Mi, *Thailand* ... **64 E3** 15 3N 100 32 E
Ban Muong Mo, *Laos* . **64 C4** 19 4N 103 58 E
Ban Na Mo, *Laos* ... **64 D5** 17 7N 105 40 E
Ban Na San, *Thailand* **65 H2** 8 53N 99 52 E
Ban Na Tong, *Laos* .. **64 B3** 20 56N 101 47 E
Ban Nam Bac, *Laos* .. **64 B4** 20 38N 102 20 E
Ban Nam Ma, *Laos* .. **64 A3** 22 2N 101 37 E
Ban Ngang, *Laos* ... **64 E6** 15 59N 106 11 E
Ban Nong Bok, *Laos* . **64 D5** 17 5N 104 48 E
Ban Nong Boua, *Laos* **64 E6** 15 40N 106 33 E
Ban Nong Pling, *Thailand* .... **64 E3** 15 40N 100 10 E
Ban Pak Chan, *Thailand* .... **65 G2** 10 32N 98 51 E
Ban Phai, *Thailand* .. **64 D4** 16 4N 102 44 E
Ban Pong, *Thailand* .. **64 F2** 13 50N 99 55 E
Ban Ron Phibun, *Thailand* .... **65 H2** 8 9N 99 51 E
Ban Sanam Chai, *Thailand* .... **65 J3** 7 33N 100 25 E
Ban Sangkha, *Thailand* **64 E4** 14 37N 103 52 E
Ban Tak, *Thailand* .. **64 D2** 17 2N 99 4 E
Ban Tako, *Thailand* .. **64 E4** 14 5N 102 40 E
Ban Tha Dua, *Thailand* **64 D2** 17 59N 98 39 E
Ban Tha Li, *Thailand* . **64 D3** 17 37N 101 25 E
Ban Tha Nun, *Thailand* **65 H2** 8 12N 98 18 E
Ban Thahine, *Laos* .. **64 E5** 14 12N 105 33 E
Ban Xien Kok, *Laos* .. **64 B3** 20 54N 100 39 E
Ban Yen Nhan, *Vietnam* .... **64 B6** 20 57N 106 2 E
Banaba, *Kiribati* .... **96 H8** 0 45 S 169 50 E
Banalia, *Dem. Rep. of the Congo* .... **86 B2** 1 32N 25 5 E
Banam, *Cambodia* ... **65 G5** 11 20N 105 17 E
Banamba, *Mali* **82 C3** 13 29N 7 22W
Banana Is., *S. Leone* . **82 D2** 8 7N 13 15W
Bananal, I. do, *Brazil* **125 F8** 11 30 S 50 30W
Banaras = Varanasi, *India* .... **69 G10** 25 22N 83 0 E
Banas →, *Gujarat, India* .... **68 H4** 23 45N 71 25 E
Banas →, *Mad. P., India* .... **69 G9** 24 15N 81 30 E
Bânâs, Ras, *Egypt* ... **80 C4** 23 57N 35 59 E
Banaz, *Turkey* ..... **39 C11** 38 46N 29 46 E
Banaz →, *Turkey* ... **39 C11** 38 18N 29 14 E
Banbridge, *U.K.* **15 B5** 54 22N 6 16W
Banbury, *U.K.* **13 E6** 52 4N 1 20W
Banchory, *U.K.* **14 D6** 57 3N 2 29W
Banco, *Ethiopia* .... **81 F4** 6 12N 38 13 E
Bancroft, *Canada* ... **102 C4** 45 3N 77 51W
Band, *Romania* .... **43 D9** 46 30N 24 25 E
Band Bonī, *Iran* .... **71 E8** 25 30N 59 33 E
Band Qīr, *Iran* ..... **71 D6** 31 39N 48 53 E
Banda, *Mad. P., India* . **69 G8** 24 3N 78 57 E
Banda, *Ut. P., India* .. **69 G9** 25 30N 80 26 E
Banda, Kepulauan, *Indonesia* .... **63 E7** 4 37 S 129 50 E
Banda Aceh, *Indonesia* **62 C1** 5 35N 95 20 E
Banda Banda, Mt., *Australia* .... **95 E5** 31 10 S 152 28 E
Banda Elat, *Indonesia* **63 F8** 5 40 S 133 5 E
Banda Is. = Banda, Kepulauan, *Indonesia* **63 E7** 4 37 S 129 50 E
Banda Sea, *Indonesia* . **63 F7** 6 0 S 130 0 E
Bandai-San, *Japan* .. **54 F10** 37 36N 140 4 E
Bandama →, *Ivory C.* **82 D3** 6 32N 4 30W

Bátonyterenye

Bandama Blanc →, *Ivory C.* **82 D3** 6 55N 5 30W
Bandama Rouge →, *Ivory C.* **82 D4** 6 55N 5 30W
Bandān, *Iran* **71 D9** 31 23N 60 44 E
Bandanaira, *Indonesia* **63 E7** 4 32 S 129 54 E
Bandanwara, *India* **68 F6** 26 9N 74 38 E
Bandar = Machilipatnam, *India* **67 L12** 16 12N 81 8 E
Bandār 'Abbās, *Iran* **71 E8** 27 15N 56 15 E
Bandar-e Anzalī, *Iran* **71 B6** 37 30N 49 30 E
Bandar-e Bushehr = Būshehr, *Iran* **71 D6** 28 55N 50 55 E
Bandar-e Chārak, *Iran* **71 E7** 26 45N 54 20 E
Bandar-e Deylam, *Iran* **71 D6** 30 5N 50 10 E
Bandar-e Khomeynı, *Iran* **71 D6** 30 30N 49 5 E
Bandar-e Lengeh, *Iran* **71 E7** 26 35N 54 58 E
Bandar-e Maqām, *Iran* **71 E7** 26 56N 53 29 E
Bandar-e Ma'shur, *Iran* **71 D6** 30 35N 49 10 E
Bandar-e Rīg, *Iran* **71 D6** 29 29N 50 38 E
Bandar-e Torkeman, *Iran* **71 B7** 37 0N 54 10 E
Bandar Maharani = Muar, *Malaysia* **65 L4** 2 3N 102 34 E
Bandar Penggaram = Batu Pahat, *Malaysia* **65 M4** 1 50N 102 56 E
Bandar Seri Begawan, *Brunei* **62 C4** 4 52N 115 0 E
Bandar Sri Aman, *Malaysia* **62 D4** 1 15N 111 32 E
Bandawe, *Malawi* **87 E3** 11 58 S 34 5 E
Bande, *Spain* **34 C3** 42 3N 7 58W
Bandeira, Pico da, *Brazil* **127 A7** 20 26 S 41 47W
Bandera, *Argentina* **126 B3** 28 55 S 62 20W
Banderas, B. de, *Mexico* **118 C3** 20 40N 105 30W
Bandhogarh, *India* **69 H9** 23 40N 81 2 E
Bandi →, *India* **68 F6** 26 12N 75 47 E
Bandiagara, *Mali* **82 C4** 14 12N 3 29W
Bandikui, *India* **68 F7** 27 3N 76 34 E
Bandırma, *Turkey* **41 F11** 40 20N 28 0 E
Bandol, *France* **21 E9** 43 8N 5 46 E
Bandon, *Ireland* **15 E3** 51 44N 8 44W
Bandon →, *Ireland* **15 E3** 51 43N 8 37W
Bandula, *Mozam.* **87 F3** 19 0 S 33 7 E
Bandundu, *Dem. Rep. of the Congo* **84 E3** 3 15 S 17 22 E
Bandung, *Indonesia* **62 F3** 6 54 S 107 36 E
Bané, *Burkina Faso* **83 C4** 11 42N 0 15W
Băneasa, *Romania* **43 E12** 45 56N 27 55 E
Bāneh, *Iran* **70 C5** 35 59N 45 53 E
Bañeres, *Spain* **33 G4** 38 44N 0 38W
Banes, *Cuba* **121 B4** 21 0N 75 42W
Banff, *Canada* **104 C5** 51 10N 115 34W
Banff, *U.K.* **14 D6** 57 40N 2 33W
Banff Nat. Park, *Canada* **104 C5** 51 30N 116 15W
Banfora, *Burkina Faso* **82 C4** 10 40N 4 40W
Bang Fai →, *Laos* **64 D5** 16 57N 104 45 E
Bang Hieng →, *Laos* **64 D5** 16 10N 105 10 E
Bang Krathum, *Thailand* **64 D3** 16 34N 100 18 E
Bang Lamung, *Thailand* **64 F3** 13 3N 100 56 E
Bang Mun Nak, *Thailand* **64 D3** 16 2N 100 23 E
Bang Pa In, *Thailand* **64 E3** 14 14N 100 35 E
Bang Rakam, *Thailand* **64 D3** 16 45N 100 7 E
Bang Saphan, *Thailand* **65 G2** 11 14N 99 28 E
Bangaduni I., *India* **69 J13** 21 34N 88 52 E
Bangala Dam, *Zimbabwe* **87 G3** 21 7 S 31 25 E
Bangalore, *India* **66 N10** 12 59N 77 40 E
Banganga →, *India* **68 F6** 27 6N 77 25 E
Bangangté, *Cameroon* **83 D7** 5 8N 10 32 E
Bangaon, *India* **69 H13** 23 0N 88 47 E
Bangassou, *C.A.R.* **84 D4** 4 55N 23 7 E
Banggai, *Indonesia* **63 E6** 1 34 S 123 30 E
Banggai, Kepulauan, *Indonesia* **63 E6** 1 40 S 123 30 E
Banggai Arch. = Banggai, Kepulauan, *Indonesia* **63 E6** 1 40 S 123 30 E
Banggi, *Malaysia* **62 C5** 7 17N 117 12 E
Banghāzī, *Libya* **79 B10** 32 11N 20 3 E
Bangjang, *Sudan* **81 E3** 11 23N 32 41 E
Bangka, *Sulawesi, Indonesia* **63 D7** 1 50N 125 5 E
Bangka, *Sumatera, Indonesia* **62 E3** 2 0 S 105 50 E
Bangka, Selat, *Indonesia* **62 E3** 2 30 S 105 30 E
Bangkalan, *Indonesia* **63 G15** 7 2 S 112 46 E
Bangkinang, *Indonesia* **62 D2** 0 18N 101 5 E
Bangko, *Indonesia* **62 E2** 2 5 S 102 9 E
Bangkok, *Thailand* **64 F3** 13 45N 100 35 E
Bangladesh ■, *Asia* **67 H17** 24 0N 90 0 E
Bangolo, *Ivory C.* **82 D3** 7 1N 7 29W
Bangong Co, *India* **69 B8** 35 50N 79 20 E
Bangor, *Down, U.K.* **15 B6** 54 40N 5 40W
Bangor, *Gwynedd, U.K.* **12 D3** 53 14N 4 8W
Bangor, *Maine, U.S.A.* **101 D13** 44 48N 68 46W
Bangor, *Pa., U.S.A.* **111 F9** 40 52N 75 13W
Bangued, *Phil.* **61 C4** 17 40N 120 37 E
Bangui, *C.A.R.* **84 D3** 4 23N 18 35 E
Bangui, *Phil.* **61 B4** 18 32N 120 46 E
Banguru, *Dem. Rep. of the Congo* **86 B2** 0 30N 27 10 E
Bangweulu, L., *Zambia* **87 E3** 11 0 S 30 0 E
Bangweulu Swamp, *Zambia* **87 E3** 11 20 S 30 15 E
Bani, *Dom. Rep.* **121 C5** 18 16N 70 22W
Bani →, *Mali* **82 C4** 14 30N 4 12W
Bani Bangou, *Niger* **83 B5** 15 3N 2 42 E
Banī Sa'd, *Iraq* **70 C5** 33 34N 44 32 E
Bania, *Ivory C.* **82 D4** 9 4N 3 6W
Banihal Pass, *India* **69 C6** 33 30N 75 12 E
Banikoara, *Benin* **83 C5** 11 18N 2 26 E
Bāniyās, *Syria* **70 C3** 35 10N 36 0 E
Banja Luka, *Bos.-H.* **42 F2** 44 49N 17 11 E
Banjar, *India* **68 D7** 31 38N 77 21 E
Banjar →, *India* **69 H9** 22 36N 80 22 E
Banjarmasin, *Indonesia* **62 E4** 3 20 S 114 35 E
Banjul, *Gambia* **82 C1** 13 28N 16 40W
Banka, *India* **69 G12** 24 53N 86 55 E
Bankas, *Mali* **82 C4** 14 4N 3 31W
Bankeryd, *Sweden* **11 G8** 57 53N 14 6 E
Banket, *Zimbabwe* **87 F3** 17 27 S 30 19 E
Bankilaré, *Niger* **83 C5** 14 35N 0 44 E
Bankipore, *India* **67 G14** 25 35N 85 10 E
Banks I., *B.C., Canada* **104 C3** 53 20N 130 0W
Banks I., *N.W.T., Canada* **100 A7** 73 15N 121 30W
Banks Pen., *N.Z.* **91 K4** 43 45 S 173 15 E
Banks Str., *Australia* **94 G4** 40 40 S 148 10 E
Bankura, *India* **69 H12** 23 11N 87 18 E
Bankya, *Bulgaria* **40 D7** 42 43N 23 8 E
Banmankhi, *India* **69 G12** 25 53N 87 11 E
Bann →, *Arm., U.K.* **15 B5** 54 30N 6 31W
Bann →, *L'derry., U.K.* **15 A5** 55 8N 6 41W
Bannalec, *France* **18 E3** 47 57N 3 42W
Bannang Sata, *Thailand* **65 J3** 6 16N 101 16 E
Banning, *U.S.A.* **117 M10** 33 56N 116 53W
Banningville = Bandundu, *Dem. Rep. of the Congo* **84 E3** 3 15 S 17 22 E
Banno, *Ethiopia* **81 G4** 4 51N 37 24 E
Bannockburn, *Canada* **110 B7** 44 39N 77 33W
Bannockburn, *U.K.* **14 E5** 56 5N 3 55W
Bannockburn, *Zimbabwe* **87 G2** 20 17 S 29 48 E
Bannu, *Pakistan* **66 C7** 33 0N 70 18 E
Bano, *India* **69 H11** 22 40N 84 55 E
Bañolas = Banyoles, *Spain* **32 C7** 42 16N 2 44 E
Banon, *France* **21 D9** 44 2N 5 38 E
Baños de la Encina, *Spain* **35 G7** 38 10N 3 46W
Baños de Molgas, *Spain* **34 C3** 42 15N 7 40W
Bánovce nad Bebravou, *Slovak Rep.* **27 C11** 48 44N 18 16 E
Banovići, *Bos.-H.* **42 F3** 44 25N 18 32 E
Bansgaon, *India* **69 F10** 26 33N 83 21 E
Banská Bystrica, *Slovak Rep.* **27 C12** 48 46N 19 14 E
Banská Štiavnica, *Slovak Rep.* **27 C11** 48 25N 18 55 E
Bansko, *Bulgaria* **40 E7** 41 52N 23 28 E
Banskobystrický □, *Slovak Rep.* **27 C12** 48 20N 19 0 E
Banswara, *India* **68 H6** 23 32N 74 24 E
Bantaeng, *Indonesia* **63 F5** 5 32 S 119 56 E
Bantaji, *Nigeria* **83 D7** 8 6N 10 5 E
Bantayan, *Phil.* **61 F5** 11 10N 123 43 E
Bantry, *Ireland* **15 E2** 51 41N 9 27W
Bantry B., *Ireland* **15 E2** 51 37N 9 44W
Bantul, *Indonesia* **63 G14** 7 55 S 110 19 E
Bantva, *India* **68 J4** 21 29N 70 12 E
Banya, *Bulgaria* **41 D8** 42 33N 24 50 E
Banyak, Kepulauan, *Indonesia* **62 D1** 2 10N 97 10 E
Banyalbufar, *Spain* **37 B9** 39 42N 2 31 E
Banyo, *Cameroon* **83 D7** 6 52N 11 45 E
Banyoles, *Spain* **32 C7** 42 16N 2 44 E
Banyuls-sur-Mer, *France* **20 F7** 42 28N 3 8 E
Banyumas, *Indonesia* **63 G13** 7 32 S 109 18 E
Banyuwangi, *Indonesia* **63 H16** 8 13 S 114 21 E
Banzare Coast, *Antarctica* **5 C9** 68 0 S 125 0 E
Banzyville = Mobayi, *Dem. Rep. of the Congo* **84 D4** 4 15N 21 8 E
Bao Ha, *Vietnam* **58 F5** 22 11N 104 21 E
Bao Lac, *Vietnam* **64 A5** 22 57N 105 40 E
Bao Loc, *Vietnam* **65 G6** 11 32N 107 48 E
Bao'an = Shenzhen, *China* **59 F10** 22 27N 114 10 E
Baocheng, *China* **56 H4** 33 12N 106 56 E
Baode, *China* **56 E6** 39 1N 111 5 E
Baodi, *China* **57 E9** 39 38N 117 20 E
Baoding, *China* **56 E8** 38 50N 115 28 E
Baoji, *China* **56 G4** 34 20N 107 5 E
Baojing, *China* **58 C7** 28 45N 109 41 E
Baokang, *China* **59 B8** 31 54N 111 12 E
Baoshan, *Shanghai, China* **59 B13** 31 27N 121 26 E
Baoshan, *Yunnan, China* **58 E2** 25 10N 99 5 E
Baotou, *China* **56 D6** 40 32N 110 2 E
Baoxing, *China* **58 B4** 30 24N 102 50 E
Baoying, *China* **57 H10** 33 17N 119 20 E
Bap, *India* **68 F5** 27 23N 72 18 E
Bapatla, *India* **67 M12** 15 55N 80 30 E
Bapaume, *France* **19 B9** 50 7N 2 50 E
Bāqerābād, *Iran* **71 C6** 33 2N 51 58 E
Ba'qūbah, *Iraq* **70 C5** 33 45N 44 50 E
Baquedano, *Chile* **126 A2** 23 20 S 69 52W
Bar, *Montenegro, Yug.* **40 D3** 42 8N 19 6 E
Bar, *Ukraine* **47 H4** 49 4N 27 40 E
Bar Bigha, *India* **69 G11** 25 21N 85 47 E
Bar Harbor, *U.S.A.* **109 C11** 44 23N 68 13W
Bar-le-Duc, *France* **19 D12** 48 47N 5 10 E
Bar-sur-Aube, *France* **19 D11** 48 14N 4 40 E
Bar-sur-Seine, *France* **19 D11** 48 7N 4 20 E
Bara, *India* **69 G9** 25 16N 81 43 E
Bâra, *Romania* **43 C12** 47 2N 27 3 E
Bara Banki, *India* **69 F9** 26 55N 81 12 E
Barabai, *Indonesia* **62 E5** 2 32 S 115 34 E
Baraboo, *U.S.A.* **112 D10** 43 28N 89 45W
Baracoa, *Cuba* **121 B5** 20 20N 74 30W
Baradā →, *Syria* **75 B5** 33 33N 36 34 E
Baradero, *Argentina* **126 C4** 33 52 S 59 29W
Baraga, *U.S.A.* **112 B10** 46 47N 88 30W
Bărăganul, *Romania* **43 F12** 44 49N 27 31 E
Barah →, *India* **68 F6** 27 42N 77 5 E
Barahona, *Dom. Rep.* **121 C5** 18 13N 71 7W
Barahona, *Spain* **32 D2** 41 17N 2 39W
Barail Range, *India* **67 G18** 25 15N 93 20 E
Baraka, *Sudan* **81 E2** 10 59N 27 59 E
Baraka →, *Sudan* **80 D4** 18 13N 37 35 E
Barakaldo, *Spain* **32 B2** 43 18N 2 59W
Barakar →, *India* **69 G12** 24 7N 86 14 E
Barakhola, *India* **67 G18** 25 0N 92 45 E
Barakot, *India* **69 J11** 21 33N 84 59 E
Barakpur, *India* **69 H13** 22 44N 88 30 E
Baralaba, *Australia* **94 C4** 24 13 S 149 50 E
Baralla, *Spain* **34 C3** 42 53N 7 15W
Baralzon L., *Canada* **105 B9** 60 0N 98 3W
Barameiya, *Sudan* **80 D4** 18 32N 36 38 E
Baramula, *India* **69 B6** 34 15N 74 20 E
Baran, *India* **68 G7** 25 9N 76 40 E
Baran →, *Pakistan* **68 G3** 25 13N 68 17 E
Barañain, *Spain* **32 C3** 42 48N 1 40W
Baranavichy, *Belarus* **47 F4** 53 10N 26 0 E
Barani, *Burkina Faso* **82 C4** 13 9N 3 51W
Baranof, *U.S.A.* **104 B2** 57 5N 134 50W
Baranof I., *U.S.A.* **100 C6** 57 0N 135 0W
Baranów Sandomierski, *Poland* **45 H8** 50 29N 21 30 E
Baranya □, *Hungary* **42 E3** 46 0N 18 15 E
Baraolt, *Romania* **43 D10** 46 5N 25 34 E
Barapasi, *Indonesia* **63 E9** 2 15 S 137 5 E
Barasat, *India* **69 H13** 22 46N 88 31 E
Barat Daya, Kepulauan, *Indonesia* **63 F7** 7 30 S 128 0 E
Barataria B., *U.S.A.* **113 L10** 29 20N 89 55W
Barauda, *India* **68 H6** 23 33N 75 15 E
Baraut, *India* **68 E7** 29 13N 77 7 E
Barbacena, *Brazil* **127 A7** 21 15 S 43 56W
Barbados ■, *W. Indies* **121 D8** 13 10N 59 30W
Barban, *Croatia* **29 C11** 45 5N 14 2 E
Barbària, C. de, *Spain* **37 C7** 38 39N 1 24 E
Barbaros, *Turkey* **41 F11** 40 54N 27 27 E
Barbastro, *Spain* **32 C5** 42 2N 0 5 E
Barbate = Barbate de Franco, *Spain* **35 J5** 36 13N 5 56W
Barbate de Franco, *Spain* **35 J5** 36 13N 5 56W
Barberino di Mugello, *Italy* **29 E8** 44 0N 11 15 E
Barberton, *S. Africa* **89 D5** 25 42 S 31 2 E
Barberton, *U.S.A.* **110 E3** 41 0N 81 39W
Barbezieux-St-Hilaire, *France* **20 C3** 45 28N 0 9W
Barbosa, *Colombia* **124 B4** 5 57N 73 37W
Barbourville, *U.S.A.* **109 G4** 36 52N 83 53W
Barbuda, *W. Indies* **121 C7** 17 30N 61 40W
Bârca, *Romania* **43 G8** 43 59N 23 36 E
Barcaldine, *Australia* **94 C4** 23 43 S 145 6 E
Barcarrota, *Spain* **35 G4** 38 31N 6 51W
Barcellona Pozzo di Gotto, *Italy* **31 D8** 38 9N 15 13 E
Barcelona, *Spain* **32 D7** 41 21N 2 10 E
Barcelona, *Venezuela* **124 A6** 10 10N 64 40W
Barcelona □, *Spain* **32 D7** 41 30N 2 0 E
Barcelonette, *France* **21 D10** 44 23N 6 40 E
Barcelos, *Brazil* **124 D6** 1 0 S 63 0W
Barcin, *Poland* **45 F4** 52 52N 17 55 E
Barclayville, *Liberia* **82 E3** 4 48N 8 10W
Barcoo →, *Australia* **94 D3** 25 30 S 142 50 E
Barcs, *Hungary* **42 E2** 45 58N 17 28 E
Barczewo, *Poland* **44 E7** 53 50N 20 42 E
Bärdä, *Azerbaijan* **49 K8** 40 25N 47 10 E
Bardaï, *Chad* **79 D9** 21 25N 17 0 E
Bardas Blancas, *Argentina* **126 D2** 35 49 S 69 45W
Barddhaman, *India* **69 H12** 23 14N 87 39 E
Bardejov, *Slovak Rep.* **27 B14** 49 18N 21 15 E
Bardera, *Somali Rep.* **74 G3** 2 20N 42 27 E
Bardi, *Italy* **28 D6** 44 38N 9 44 E
Bardīyah, *Libya* **79 B10** 31 45N 25 5 E
Bardolino, *Italy* **28 C7** 45 33N 10 43 E
Bardonécchia, *Italy* **28 C3** 45 5N 6 42 E
Bardsey I., *U.K.* **12 E3** 52 45N 4 47W
Bardstown, *U.S.A.* **108 G3** 37 49N 85 28W
Bareilly, *India* **69 E8** 28 22N 79 27 E
Barela, *India* **69 H9** 23 6N 80 3 E
Barentin, *France* **18 C7** 49 33N 0 58 E
Barenton, *France* **18 D6** 48 38N 0 50W
Barents Sea, *Arctic* **4 B9** 73 0N 39 0 E
Barentu, *Eritrea* **81 D4** 15 2N 37 35 E
Barfleur, *France* **18 C5** 49 40N 1 17W
Barfleur, Pte. de, *France* **18 C5** 49 42N 1 16W
Barga, *Italy* **28 D7** 44 4N 10 29 E
Bargara, *Australia* **94 C5** 24 50 S 152 25 E
Bargas, *Spain* **34 F6** 39 56N 4 3W
Bârgăului Bistriţa, *Romania* **43 C9** 47 13N 24 46 E
Barge, *Italy* **28 D4** 44 43N 7 20 E
Bargnop, *Sudan* **81 F2** 9 32N 28 25 E
Bargteheide, *Germany* **24 B6** 53 44N 10 14 E
Barguzin, *Russia* **51 D11** 53 37N 109 37 E
Barh, *India* **69 G11** 25 29N 85 46 E
Barhaj, *India* **69 F10** 26 18N 83 44 E
Barharwa, *India* **69 G12** 24 52N 87 47 E
Barhi, *India* **69 G11** 24 15N 85 25 E
Bari, *India* **68 F7** 26 39N 77 39 E
Bari, *Italy* **31 A9** 41 8N 16 51 E
Bari Doab, *Pakistan* **68 D5** 30 20N 73 0 E
Bari Sadri, *India* **68 G6** 24 28N 74 30 E
Bari Sardo, *Italy* **30 C2** 39 50N 9 38 E
Barīdī, Ra's, *Si. Arabia* **70 E3** 24 17N 37 31 E
Barīm, *Yemen* **76 E8** 12 39N 43 25 E
Barinas, *Venezuela* **124 B4** 8 36N 70 15W
Baring, C., *Canada* **100 B8** 70 0N 117 30W
Baringo, *Kenya* **86 B4** 0 47N 36 16 E
Baringo, L., *Kenya* **86 B4** 0 47N 36 16 E
Bârîs, *Egypt* **80 C3** 24 42N 30 31 E
Barisal, *Bangla.* **67 H17** 22 45N 90 20 E
Barisal □, *Bangla.* **67 H17** 22 40N 90 20 E
Barisan, Bukit, *Indonesia* **62 E2** 3 30 S 102 15 E
Barito →, *Indonesia* **62 E4** 4 0 S 114 50 E
Barjac, *France* **21 D8** 44 20N 4 22 E
Barjols, *France* **21 E10** 43 34N 6 2 E
Bark L., *Canada* **110 A7** 45 27N 77 51W
Barka = Baraka →, *Sudan* **80 D4** 18 13N 37 35 E
Barkakana, *India* **69 H11** 23 37N 85 29 E
Barkam, *China* **58 B4** 31 51N 102 28 E
Barker, *U.S.A.* **110 C6** 43 20N 78 33W
Barkley, L., *U.S.A.* **109 G2** 37 1N 88 14W
Barkley Sound, *Canada* **104 D3** 48 50N 125 10W
Barkly East, *S. Africa* **88 E4** 30 58 S 27 33 E
Barkly Roadhouse, *Australia* **94 B2** 19 52 S 135 50 E
Barkly Tableland, *Australia* **94 B2** 17 50 S 136 40 E
Barkly West, *S. Africa* **88 D3** 28 5 S 24 31 E
Barkol, Wadi →, *Sudan* **80 D3** 17 40N 32 0 E
Barla Dağı, *Turkey* **39 C12** 38 5N 30 40 E
Bârlad, *Romania* **43 D12** 46 15N 27 38 E
Bârlad →, *Romania* **43 E12** 45 38N 27 32 E
Barlee, L., *Australia* **93 E2** 29 15 S 119 30 E
Barlee, Mt., *Australia* **93 D4** 24 38 S 128 13 E
Barletta, *Italy* **31 A9** 41 19N 16 17 E
Barlinek, *Poland* **45 F2** 53 0N 15 15 E
Barlovento, *Canary Is.* **37 F2** 28 48N 17 48W
Barlow L., *Canada* **105 A8** 62 0N 103 0W
Barmedman, *Australia* **95 E4** 34 9 S 147 21 E
Barmer, *India* **68 G4** 25 45N 71 20 E
Barmera, *Australia* **95 E3** 34 15 S 140 28 E
Barmouth, *U.K.* **12 E3** 52 44N 4 4W
Barmstedt, *Germany* **24 B5** 53 47N 9 46 E
Barna →, *India* **69 G10** 25 21N 83 3 E
Barnagar, *India* **68 H6** 23 7N 75 19 E
Barnala, *India* **68 D6** 30 23N 75 33 E
Barnard Castle, *U.K.* **12 C6** 54 33N 1 55W
Barnaul, *Russia* **50 D9** 53 20N 83 40 E
Barnesville, *U.S.A.* **109 J3** 33 3N 84 9W
Barnet □, *U.K.* **13 F7** 51 38N 0 9W
Barneveld, *Neths.* **17 B5** 52 7N 5 36 E
Barneveld, *U.S.A.* **111 C9** 43 16N 75 14W
Barneville-Cartevert, *France* **18 C5** 49 23N 1 46W
Barnhart, *U.S.A.* **113 K4** 31 8N 101 10W
Barnsley, *U.K.* **12 D6** 53 34N 1 27W
Barnstaple, *U.K.* **13 F3** 51 5N 4 4W
Barnstaple Bay = Bideford Bay, *U.K.* **13 F3** 51 5N 4 20W
Barnsville, *U.S.A.* **112 B6** 46 43N 96 28W
Barnwell, *U.S.A.* **109 J5** 33 15N 81 23W
Baro, *Nigeria* **83 D6** 8 35N 6 18 E
Baro →, *Ethiopia* **81 F3** 8 26N 33 13 E
Baroda = Vadodara, *India* **68 H5** 22 20N 73 10 E
Baroda, *India* **68 G7** 25 29N 76 35 E
Baroe, *S. Africa* **88 E3** 33 13 S 24 33 E
Baron Ra., *Australia* **92 D4** 23 30 S 127 45 E
Barong, *China* **58 B2** 31 3N 99 20 E
Barotseland, *Zambia* **85 H4** 15 0 S 24 0 E
Barouéli, *Mali* **82 C3** 13 4N 6 50W
Barpeta, *India* **67 F17** 26 20N 91 10 E
Barques, Pt. Aux, *U.S.A.* **110 B2** 44 4N 82 58W
Barquísimeto, *Venezuela* **124 A5** 10 4N 69 19W
Barr, Ras el, *Egypt* **80 H7** 31 32N 31 50 E
Barr Smith Range, *Australia* **93 E3** 27 4 S 120 20 E
Barra, *Brazil* **125 F10** 11 5 S 43 10W
Barra, *U.K.* **14 E1** 57 0N 7 29W
Barra, Sd. of, *U.K.* **14 D1** 57 4N 7 25W
Barra de Navidad, *Mexico* **118 D4** 19 12N 104 41W
Barra do Corda, *Brazil* **125 E9** 5 30 S 45 10W
Barra do Piraí, *Brazil* **127 A7** 22 30 S 43 50W
Barra Falsa, Pta. da, *Mozam.* **89 C6** 22 58 S 35 37 E
Barra Hd., *U.K.* **14 E1** 56 47N 7 40W
Barra Mansa, *Brazil* **127 A7** 22 35 S 44 12W
Barraba, *Australia* **95 E5** 30 21 S 150 35 E
Barrackpur = Barakpur, *India* **69 H13** 22 44N 88 30 E
Barradale Roadhouse, *Australia* **92 D1** 22 42 S 114 58 E
Barrafranca, *Italy* **31 E7** 37 22N 14 12 E
Barraigh = Barra, *U.K.* **14 E1** 57 0N 7 29W
Barranca, *Lima, Peru* **124 F3** 10 45 S 77 50W
Barranca, *Loreto, Peru* **124 D3** 4 50 S 76 50W
Barrancabermeja, *Colombia* **124 B4** 7 0N 73 50W
Barrancas, *Venezuela* **124 B6** 8 55N 62 5W
Barrancos, *Portugal* **35 G4** 38 10N 6 58W
Barranqueras, *Argentina* **126 B4** 27 30 S 59 0W
Barranquilla, *Colombia* **124 A4** 11 0N 74 50W
Barraute, *Canada* **102 C4** 48 26N 77 38W
Barre, *Mass., U.S.A.* **111 D12** 42 25N 72 6W
Barre, *Vt., U.S.A.* **111 B12** 44 12N 72 30W
Barreal, *Argentina* **126 C2** 31 33 S 69 28W
Barreiras, *Brazil* **125 F10** 12 8 S 45 0W
Barreirinhas, *Brazil* **125 D10** 2 30 S 42 50W
Barreiro, *Portugal* **35 G1** 38 40N 9 6W
Barrême, *France* **21 E10** 43 57N 6 23 E
Barren, Nosy, *Madag.* **89 B7** 18 25 S 43 40 E
Barretos, *Brazil* **125 H9** 20 30 S 48 35W
Barrhead, *Canada* **104 C6** 54 10N 114 24W
Barrie, *Canada* **102 D4** 44 24N 79 40W
Barrier Ra., *Australia* **95 E3** 31 0 S 141 30 E
Barrière, *Canada* **104 C4** 51 12N 120 7W
Barrington, *U.S.A.* **111 E13** 41 44N 71 18W
Barrington L., *Canada* **105 B8** 56 55N 100 15W
Barrington Tops, *Australia* **95 E5** 32 6 S 151 28 E
Barringun, *Australia* **95 D4** 29 1 S 145 41 E
Barro do Garças, *Brazil* **125 G8** 15 54 S 52 16W
Barron, *U.S.A.* **112 C9** 45 24N 91 51W
Barrow, *U.S.A.* **100 A4** 71 18N 156 47W
Barrow →, *Ireland* **15 D5** 52 25N 6 58W
Barrow, Pt., *U.S.A.* **98 B4** 71 10N 156 20W
Barrow Creek, *Australia* **94 C1** 21 30 S 133 55 E
Barrow I., *Australia* **92 D2** 20 45 S 115 20 E
Barrow-in-Furness, *U.K.* **12 C4** 54 7N 3 14W
Barrow Pt., *Australia* **94 A3** 14 20 S 144 40 E
Barrow Ra., *Australia* **93 E4** 26 0 S 127 40 E
Barrow Str., *Canada* **4 B3** 74 20N 95 0W
Barruecopardo, *Spain* **34 D4** 41 4N 6 40W
Barruelo de Santullán, *Spain* **34 C6** 42 54N 4 17W
Barry, *U.K.* **13 F4** 51 24N 3 16W
Barry's Bay, *Canada* **102 C4** 45 29N 77 41W
Barsalogho, *Burkina Faso* **83 C4** 13 25N 1 3W
Barsat, *Pakistan* **69 A5** 36 10N 72 45 E
Barsham, *Syria* **70 C4** 35 21N 40 33 E
Barsi, *India* **66 K9** 18 10N 75 50 E
Barsinghausen, *Germany* **24 C5** 52 18N 9 28 E
Barsoi, *India* **67 G15** 25 48N 87 57 E
Barstow, *U.S.A.* **117 L9** 34 54N 117 1W
Barth, *Germany* **24 A8** 54 22N 12 42 E
Barthélemy, Col, *Vietnam* **64 C5** 19 26N 104 6 E
Bartica, *Guyana* **124 B7** 6 25N 58 40W
Bartin, *Turkey* **72 B5** 41 38N 32 21 E
Bartlesville, *U.S.A.* **113 G7** 36 45N 95 59W
Bartlett, *U.S.A.* **116 J8** 36 29N 118 2W
Bartlett, L., *Canada* **104 A5** 63 5N 118 20W
Bartolomeu Dias, *Mozam.* **87 G4** 21 10 S 35 8 E
Barton, *U.S.A.* **111 B12** 44 45N 72 11W
Barton upon Humber, *U.K.* **12 D7** 53 41N 0 25W
Bartoszyce, *Poland* **44 D7** 54 15N 20 55 E
Bartow, *U.S.A.* **109 M5** 27 54N 81 50W
Barú, Volcan, *Panama* **120 E3** 8 55N 82 35W
Barumba, *Dem. Rep. of the Congo* **86 B1** 1 3N 23 37 E
Baruth, *Germany* **24 C9** 52 4N 13 30 E
Baruunsuu, *Mongolia* **56 C3** 43 43N 105 35 E
Barvinkove, *Ukraine* **47 H9** 48 57N 37 0 E
Barwani, *India* **68 H6** 22 2N 74 57 E
Barwice, *Poland* **44 E3** 53 44N 16 21 E
Barycz →, *Poland* **45 G3** 51 42N 16 15 E
Barysaw, *Belarus* **46 E5** 54 17N 28 28 E
Barysh, *Russia* **48 D8** 53 39N 47 8 E
Barzān, *Iraq* **70 B5** 36 55N 44 3 E
Bârzava, *Romania* **42 D6** 46 7N 21 59 E
Bas-Rhin □, *France* **19 D14** 48 40N 7 30 E
Bašaid, *Serbia, Yug.* **42 E5** 45 38N 20 25 E
Bāsa'idū, *Iran* **71 E7** 26 35N 55 20 E
Basal, *Pakistan* **68 C5** 33 33N 72 13 E
Basankusa, *Dem. Rep. of the Congo* **84 D3** 1 5N 19 50 E
Basarabeasca, *Moldova* **43 D13** 46 21N 28 58 E
Basarabi, *Romania* **43 F13** 44 10N 28 26 E
Basauri, *Spain* **32 B2** 43 13N 2 53W
Basawa, *Afghan.* **68 B4** 34 15N 70 50 E
Bascuñán, C., *Chile* **126 B1** 28 52 S 71 35W
Basel, *Switz.* **25 H3** 47 35N 7 35 E
Basel-Landschaft □, *Switz.* **25 H3** 47 26N 7 45 E
Basento →, *Italy* **31 B9** 40 20N 16 49 E
Bashākerd, Kūhhā-ye, *Iran* **71 E8** 26 42N 58 35 E
Bashaw, *Canada* **104 C6** 52 35N 112 58W
Bāshī, *Iran* **71 D6** 28 41N 51 4 E
Bashkir Republic = Bashkortostan □, *Russia* **50 D6** 54 0N 57 0 E
Bashkortostan □, *Russia* **50 D6** 54 0N 57 0 E
Basibasy, *Madag.* **89 C7** 22 10 S 43 40 E
Basilan I., *Phil.* **61 H5** 6 35N 122 0 E
Basilan Str., *Phil.* **61 H5** 6 50N 122 0 E
Basildon, *U.K.* **13 F8** 51 34N 0 28 E
Basile, *Eq. Guin.* **83 E6** 3 42N 8 48 E
Basilicata □, *Italy* **31 B9** 40 30N 16 30 E
Basim = Washim, *India* **66 J10** 20 3N 77 0 E
Basin, *U.S.A.* **114 D9** 44 23N 108 2W
Basingstoke, *U.K.* **13 F6** 51 15N 1 5W
Baška, *Croatia* **29 D11** 44 58N 14 45 E
Başkale, *Turkey* **73 C10** 38 2N 43 59 E
Baskatong, Rés., *Canada* **102 C4** 46 46N 75 50W
Basle = Basel, *Switz.* **25 H3** 47 35N 7 35 E
Başmakçı, *Turkey* **39 D12** 37 54N 30 1 E
Basoda, *India* **68 H7** 23 52N 77 54 E
Basoka, *Dem. Rep. of the Congo* **86 B1** 1 16N 23 40 E
Basque, Pays, *France* **20 E2** 43 15N 1 20W
Basque Provinces = País Vasco □, *Spain* **32 C2** 42 50N 2 45W
Basra = Al Başrah, *Iraq* **70 D5** 30 30N 47 50 E
Bass Str., *Australia* **94 F4** 39 15 S 146 30 E
Bassano, *Canada* **104 C6** 50 48N 112 20W
Bassano del Grappa, *Italy* **29 C8** 45 46N 11 44 E
Bassar, *Togo* **83 D5** 9 19N 0 57 E
Bassas da India, *Ind. Oc.* **85 J7** 22 0 S 39 0 E
Basse-Normandie □, *France* **18 D6** 48 45N 0 30W
Basse Santa-Su, *Gambia* **82 C2** 13 13N 14 15W
Basse-Terre, *Guadeloupe* **121 C7** 16 0N 61 44W
Bassein, *Burma* **67 L19** 16 45N 94 30 E
Basseterre, *St. Kitts & Nevis* **121 C7** 17 17N 62 43W
Bassett, *U.S.A.* **112 D5** 42 35N 99 32W
Bassi, *India* **68 D7** 30 44N 76 21 E
Bassigny, *France* **19 E12** 48 0N 5 30 E
Bassikounou, *Mauritania* **82 B3** 15 55N 6 1W
Bassila, *Benin* **83 D5** 9 1N 1 46 E
Bassum, *Germany* **24 C4** 52 50N 8 40 E
Båstad, *Sweden* **11 H6** 56 25N 12 51 E
Bastak, *Iran* **71 E7** 27 15N 54 25 E
Baştām, *Iran* **71 B7** 36 29N 55 4 E
Bastar, *India* **67 K12** 19 15N 81 40 E
Bastelica, *France* **21 F13** 42 1N 9 3 E
Basti, *India* **69 F10** 26 52N 82 55 E
Bastia, *France* **21 F13** 42 40N 9 30 E
Bastogne, *Belgium* **17 D5** 50 1N 5 43 E
Bastrop, *La., U.S.A.* **113 J9** 32 47N 91 55W
Bastrop, *Tex., U.S.A.* **113 K6** 30 7N 97 19W
Bat Yam, *Israel* **75 C3** 32 2N 34 44 E
Bata, *Eq. Guin.* **84 D1** 1 57N 9 50 E
Bata, *Romania* **42 D7** 46 1N 22 4 E
Bataan □, *Phil.* **61 D4** 14 40N 120 25 E
Batabanó, *Cuba* **120 B3** 22 40N 82 20W
Batabanó, G. de, *Cuba* **120 B3** 22 30N 82 30W
Batac, *Phil.* **61 B4** 18 3N 120 34 E
Batagai, *Russia* **51 C14** 67 38N 134 38 E
Batajnica, *Serbia, Yug.* **40 B4** 44 54N 20 17 E
Batak, *Bulgaria* **41 E8** 41 57N 24 12 E
Batala, *India* **68 D6** 31 48N 75 12 E
Batalha, *Portugal* **34 F2** 39 40N 8 50W
Batama, *Dem. Rep. of the Congo* **86 B2** 0 58N 26 33 E
Batamay, *Russia* **51 C13** 63 30N 129 15 E
Batang, *China* **58 B2** 30 1N 99 0 E
Batang, *Indonesia* **63 G13** 6 55 S 109 45 E
Batangas, *Phil.* **61 E4** 13 35N 121 10 E
Batanta, *Indonesia* **63 E8** 0 55 S 130 40 E
Batatais, *Brazil* **127 A6** 20 54 S 47 37W
Batavia, *U.S.A.* **110 D6** 43 0N 78 11W
Bataysk, *Russia* **47 J10** 47 3N 39 45 E
Batchelor, *Australia* **92 B5** 13 4 S 131 1 E
Batdambang, *Cambodia* **64 F4** 13 7N 103 12 E
Batemans B., *Australia* **95 F5** 35 40 S 150 12 E
Batemans Bay, *Australia* **95 F5** 35 44 S 150 11 E
Bates Ra., *Australia* **93 E3** 27 27 S 121 5 E
Batesburg-Leesville, *U.S.A.* **109 J5** 33 54N 81 33W
Batesville, *Ark., U.S.A.* **113 H9** 35 46N 91 39W
Batesville, *Miss., U.S.A.* **113 H10** 34 19N 89 57W
Batesville, *Tex., U.S.A.* **113 L5** 28 58N 99 37W
Bath, *Canada* **111 B8** 44 11N 76 47W
Bath, *U.K.* **13 F5** 51 23N 2 22W
Bath, *Maine, U.S.A.* **109 D11** 43 55N 69 49W
Bath, *N.Y., U.S.A.* **110 D7** 42 20N 77 19W
Bath & North East Somerset □, *U.K.* **13 F5** 51 21N 2 27W
Batheay, *Cambodia* **65 G5** 11 59N 104 57 E
Bathurst = Banjul, *Gambia* **82 C1** 13 28N 16 40W
Bathurst, *Australia* **95 E4** 33 25 S 149 31 E
Bathurst, *Canada* **103 C6** 47 37N 65 43W
Bathurst, *S. Africa* **88 E4** 33 30 S 26 50 E
Bathurst, C., *Canada* **100 A7** 70 34N 128 0W
Bathurst B., *Australia* **94 A3** 14 16 S 144 25 E
Bathurst Harb., *Australia* **94 G4** 43 15 S 146 10 E
Bathurst I., *Australia* **92 B5** 11 30 S 130 10 E
Bathurst I., *Canada* **4 B2** 76 0N 100 30W
Bathurst Inlet, *Canada* **100 B9** 66 50N 108 1W
Bati, *Ethiopia* **81 E5** 11 10N 40 0 E
Batie, *Burkina Faso* **82 D4** 9 53N 2 53W
Batlow, *Australia* **95 F4** 35 31 S 148 9 E
Batman, *Turkey* **70 B4** 37 55N 41 5 E
Baṭn al Ghūl, *Jordan* **75 F4** 29 36N 35 56 E
Batna, *Algeria* **78 A7** 35 34N 6 15 E
Batobato = San Isidro, *Phil.* **61 H7** 6 50N 126 5 E
Batočina, *Serbia, Yug.* **40 B5** 44 7N 21 5 E
Batoka, *Zambia* **87 F2** 16 45 S 27 15 E
Baton Rouge, *U.S.A.* **113 K9** 30 27N 91 11W
Batong, Ko, *Thailand* **65 J2** 6 32N 99 12 E
Bátonyterenye, *Hungary* **42 C4** 47 59N 19 50 E

Binzert

Binzert = Bizerte, Tunisia 79 A7 37 15N 9 50 E
Binzhou, China 57 F10 37 20N 118 2 E
Bío Bío □, Chile 126 D1 37 35 S 72 0W
Biograd na Moru, Croatia 29 E12 43 56N 15 29 E
Bioko, Eq. Guin. 83 E6 3 30N 8 40 E
Biokovo, Croatia 29 E14 43 23N 17 0 E
Bipindi, Cameroon 83 E7 3 6N 10 30 E
Bir, India 66 K9 19 4N 75 46 E
Bir, Ras, Djibouti 81 E5 12 0N 43 20 E
Bîr Abu Hashim, Egypt 80 C3 23 42N 34 6 E
Bîr Abu Minqar, Egypt 80 B2 26 33N 27 33 E
Bîr Abu Muḥammad, Egypt 75 F3 29 44N 34 14 E
Bi'r ad Dabbāghāt, Jordan 75 E4 30 26N 35 32 E
Bîr Adal Deib, Sudan 80 C4 22 35N 36 10 E
Bi'r al Butayyihāt, Jordan 75 F4 29 47N 35 20 E
Bi'r al Mārī, Jordan 75 E4 30 4N 35 33 E
Bi'r al Qattār, Jordan 75 F4 29 47N 35 32 E
Bîr 'Asal, Egypt 80 B3 25 55N 34 20 E
Bîr Atrun, Sudan 80 D2 18 15N 26 40 E
Bîr Beiḍa, Egypt 75 E3 30 25N 34 29 E
Bîr Diqnash, Egypt 80 A2 31 3N 25 23 E
Bîr el 'Abd, Egypt 75 D2 31 2N 33 0 E
Bîr el Basur, Egypt 80 B2 29 51N 25 49 E
Bîr el Biarât, Egypt 75 F3 29 30N 34 43 E
Bîr el Duweidar, Egypt 75 E1 30 56N 32 32 E
Bîr el Garârât, Egypt 75 D2 31 3N 33 34 E
Bîr el Gellaz, Egypt 80 A2 30 50N 26 40 E
Bîr el Heisi, Egypt 75 F3 29 22N 34 36 E
Bîr el Jafir, Egypt 75 E1 30 50N 32 41 E
Bîr el Mâlḥi, Egypt 75 E2 30 38N 33 19 E
Bîr el Shaqqa, Egypt 80 A2 30 54N 25 1 E
Bîr el Thamâda, Egypt 75 E2 30 12N 33 27 E
Bîr Fuad, Egypt 80 A2 30 35N 26 28 E
Bîr Gebeil Ḥiṣn, Egypt 75 E2 30 2N 33 18 E
Bi'r Ghadīr, Syria 75 A6 34 6N 37 3 E
Bîr Haimur, Egypt 80 C3 22 45N 33 40 E
Bîr Ḥasana, Egypt 75 E2 30 29N 33 46 E
Bîr Hööker, Egypt 80 H7 30 22N 30 21 E
Bîr Kanayis, Egypt 80 C3 24 59N 33 15 E
Bîr Kaseiba, Egypt 75 E2 31 0N 33 17 E
Bîr Kerawein, Egypt 80 B2 27 10N 28 25 E
Bîr Lahfân, Egypt 75 E2 31 0N 33 51 E
Bîr Madkûr, Egypt 75 E1 30 44N 32 33 E
Bîr Maql, Egypt 80 C3 23 7N 33 40 E
Bîr Mîneiga, Sudan 80 C4 22 47N 35 12 E
Bîr Misaha, Egypt 80 C2 22 13N 27 59 E
Bîr Mogreïn, Mauritania 78 C3 25 10N 11 25W
Bîr Murr, Egypt 80 C3 23 28N 30 10 E
Bi'r Muṭribah, Kuwait 70 D5 29 54N 47 17 E
Bîr Nakheila, Egypt 80 C3 24 1N 30 50 E
Bîr Qaṭia, Egypt 75 E1 30 58N 32 45 E
Bîr Qatrani, Egypt 80 A2 30 55N 26 10 E
Bîr Ranga, Egypt 80 C4 24 25N 35 15 E
Bîr Sahara, Egypt 80 C2 22 54N 28 40 E
Bîr Seiyâla, Egypt 80 B3 26 10N 33 50 E
Bîr Shalatein, Egypt 80 C4 23 5N 35 25 E
Bîr Shebb, Egypt 80 C2 22 25N 29 40 E
Bîr Shût, Egypt 80 C4 23 50N 35 15 E
Bîr Terfawi, Egypt 80 C2 22 57N 28 55 E
Bîr Umm Qubûr, Egypt 80 C3 24 35N 34 2 E
Bîr Ungât, Egypt 80 C3 22 8N 33 48 E
Bîr Za'farâna, Egypt 80 J8 29 10N 32 40 E
Bîr Zeidûn, Egypt 80 B3 25 45N 33 40 E
Biramféro, Guinea 82 C3 11 40N 9 10W
Biratnagar, Nepal 69 F12 26 27N 87 17 E
Birawa, Dem. Rep. of the Congo 86 C2 2 20 S 28 48 E
Birch →, Canada 104 B6 58 28N 112 17W
Birch Hills, Canada 105 C7 52 59N 105 25W
Birch I., Canada 105 C9 52 26N 99 54W
Birch L., N.W.T., Canada 104 A5 62 4N 116 33W
Birch L., Ont., Canada 102 B1 51 23N 92 18W
Birch Mts., Canada 104 B6 57 30N 113 10W
Birch River, Canada 105 C8 52 24N 101 6W
Birchip, Australia 95 F3 35 56 S 142 55 E
Birchiş, Romania 42 E7 45 58N 22 9 E
Bird, Canada 105 B10 56 30N 94 13W
Bird I. = Las Aves, Is., W. Indies 121 C7 15 45N 63 55W
Birdsville, Australia 94 D2 25 51 S 139 20 E
Birdum Cr. →, Australia 92 C5 15 14 S 133 0 E
Birecik, Turkey 70 B3 37 2N 38 0 E
Birein, Israel 75 E3 30 50N 34 28 E
Bireuen, Indonesia 62 C1 5 14N 96 39 E
Biri →, Sudan 81 F2 7 56N 26 33 E
Birifo, Gambia 82 C2 13 30N 14 0W
Birigui, Brazil 127 A5 21 18 S 50 16W
Birjand, Iran 71 C8 32 53N 59 13 E
Birkenfeld, Germany 25 F3 49 38N 7 9 E
Birkenhead, U.K. 12 D4 53 23N 3 2W
Birkerød, Denmark 11 J6 55 50N 12 25 E
Birket Qârûn, Egypt 80 J7 29 30N 30 40 E
Birkfeld, Austria 26 D8 47 21N 15 45 E
Bîrlad = Bârlad, Romania 43 D12 46 15N 27 38 E
Birmingham, U.K. 13 E6 52 29N 1 52W
Birmingham, U.S.A. 109 J2 33 31N 86 48W
Birmitrapur, India 67 H14 22 24N 84 46 E
Birni Ngaouré, Niger 83 C5 13 5N 2 51 E
Birni Nkonni, Niger 83 C6 13 55N 5 15 E
Birnin Gwari, Nigeria 83 C6 11 0N 6 45 E
Birnin Kebbi, Nigeria 83 C5 12 32N 4 12 E
Birnin Kudu, Nigeria 83 C6 11 30N 9 29 E
Birobidzhan, Russia 51 E14 48 50N 132 50 E
Birr, Ireland 15 C4 53 6N 7 54W
Birrie →, Australia 95 D4 29 43 S 146 37 E
Birsilpur, India 68 E5 28 11N 72 15 E
Birsk, Russia 50 D6 55 25N 55 30 E
Birštonas, Lithuania 44 D11 54 37N 24 2 E
Birtle, Canada 105 C8 50 30N 101 5W
Birur, India 66 N9 13 30N 75 55 E
Biryuchiy, Ukraine 47 J8 46 10N 35 0 E
Biržai, Lithuania 9 H21 56 11N 24 45 E
Birzebbugga, Malta 36 D2 35 49N 14 32 E
Bisa, Indonesia 63 E7 1 15 S 127 28 E
Bisáccia, Italy 31 A8 41 1N 15 22 E
Bisacquino, Italy 30 E6 37 42N 13 15 E
Bisalpur, India 69 E8 28 14N 79 48 E
Bisbee, U.S.A. 115 L9 31 27N 109 55W
Biscarrosse, France 20 D2 44 22N 1 20W
Biscarrosse et de Parentis, Étang de, France 20 D2 44 21N 1 10W
Biscay, B. of, Atl. Oc. 6 F5 45 0N 2 0W
Biscayne B., U.S.A. 109 N5 25 40N 80 12W
Biscéglie, Italy 31 A9 41 14N 16 30 E
Bischheim, France 19 D14 48 37N 7 46 E
Bischofshofen, Austria 26 D6 47 26N 13 14 E
Bischofswerda, Germany 24 D10 51 7N 14 10 E
Bischwiller, France 19 D14 48 46N 7 50 E
Biscoe Bay, Antarctica 5 D13 77 0 S 152 0W
Biscoe Is., Antarctica 5 C17 66 0 S 67 0W
Biscostasing, Canada 102 C3 47 18N 82 9W
Biševo, Croatia 29 F13 42 57N 16 3 E
Bisha, Eritrea 81 D4 15 30N 37 31 E
Bishah, W. →, Si. Arabia 80 C5 21 24N 43 26 E
Bishan, China 58 C6 29 33N 106 12 E
Bishkek, Kyrgyzstan 50 E8 42 54N 74 46 E
Bishnupur, India 69 H12 23 8N 87 20 E
Bisho, S. Africa 89 E4 32 50 S 27 23 E
Bishop, Calif., U.S.A. 116 H8 37 22N 118 24W
Bishop, Tex., U.S.A. 113 M6 27 35N 97 48W
Bishop Auckland, U.K. 12 C6 54 39N 1 40W
Bishop's Falls, Canada 103 C8 49 2N 55 30W
Bishop's Stortford, U.K. 13 F8 51 52N 0 10 E
Bisignano, Italy 31 C9 39 31N 16 17 E
Bisina, L., Uganda 86 B3 1 38N 33 56 E
Biskra, Algeria 78 B7 34 50N 5 44 E
Biskupiec, Poland 44 E7 53 53N 20 58 E
Bismarck, U.S.A. 112 B4 46 48N 100 47W
Bismarck Arch., Papua N. G. 96 H7 2 30 S 150 0 E
Bismark, Germany 24 C7 52 40N 11 33 E
Bismil, Turkey 73 D9 37 51N 40 40 E
Biso, Uganda 86 B3 1 44N 31 26 E
Bison, U.S.A. 112 C3 45 31N 102 28W
Bīsotūn, Iran 70 C5 34 23N 47 26 E
Bispgården, Sweden 10 A10 63 2N 16 40 E
Bissagos = Bijagós, Arquipélago dos, Guinea-Biss. 82 C1 11 15N 16 10W
Bissau, Guinea-Biss. 82 C1 11 45N 15 45W
Bissaula, Nigeria 83 D7 7 0N 10 27 E
Bissikrima, Guinea 82 C2 10 50N 10 58W
Bissorã, Guinea-Biss. 82 C1 12 16N 15 35W
Bistcho L., Canada 104 B5 59 45N 118 50W
Bistreţ, Romania 43 G8 43 54N 23 23 E
Bistrica = Ilirska-Bistrica, Slovenia 29 C11 45 34N 14 14 E
Bistriţa, Romania 43 C9 47 9N 24 35 E
Bistriţa →, Romania 43 D11 46 30N 26 57 E
Bistriţa Năsăud □, Romania 43 C9 47 15N 24 30 E
Bistriţei, Munţii, Romania 43 C10 47 15N 25 40 E
Biswan, India 69 F9 27 29N 81 2 E
Bisztynek, Poland 44 D7 54 8N 20 53 E
Bitburg, Germany 25 F2 49 58N 6 31 E
Bitche, France 19 C14 49 2N 7 25 E
Bithynia, Turkey 72 B4 40 40N 31 0 E
Bitlis, Turkey 70 B4 38 20N 42 3 E
Bitola, Macedonia 40 E5 41 1N 21 20 E
Bitolj = Bitola, Macedonia 40 E5 41 1N 21 20 E
Bitonto, Italy 31 A9 41 6N 16 41 E
Bitter Creek, U.S.A. 114 F9 41 33N 108 33W
Bitter L. = Buheirat-Murrat-el-Kubra, Egypt 80 H8 30 18N 32 26 E
Bitterfeld, Germany 24 D8 51 37N 12 20 E
Bitterfontein, S. Africa 88 E2 31 1 S 18 32 E
Bitterroot →, U.S.A. 114 C6 46 52N 114 7W
Bitterroot Range, U.S.A. 114 D6 46 0N 114 20W
Bitterwater, U.S.A. 116 J6 36 23N 121 0W
Bitti, Italy 30 B2 40 29N 9 23 E
Bittou, Burkina Faso 83 C4 11 17N 0 18W
Biu, Nigeria 83 C7 10 40N 12 3 E
Bivolari, Romania 43 C12 47 31N 27 27 E
Bivolu, Vf., Romania 43 C10 47 16N 25 58 E
Biwa-Ko, Japan 55 G8 35 15N 136 10 E
Biwabik, U.S.A. 112 B8 47 32N 92 21W
Bixad, Romania 43 C8 47 56N 23 28 E
Bixby, U.S.A. 113 H7 35 57N 95 53W
Biyang, China 56 H7 32 38N 113 21 E
Biysk, Russia 50 D9 52 40N 85 0 E
Bizana, S. Africa 89 E4 30 50 S 29 52 E
Bizen, Japan 55 G7 34 43N 134 8 E
Bizerte, Tunisia 79 A7 37 15N 9 50 E
Bjargtangar, Iceland 8 D1 65 30N 24 30W
Bjärnum, Sweden 11 H7 56 17N 13 43 E
Bjästa, Sweden 10 A12 63 12N 18 29 E
Bjelasica, Montenegro, Yug. 40 D3 42 50N 19 40 E
Bjelašnica, Bos.-H. 42 G3 43 43N 18 9 E
Bjelovar, Croatia 29 C13 45 56N 16 49 E
Bjerringbro, Denmark 11 H3 56 23N 9 39 E
Björbo, Sweden 10 D8 60 27N 14 44 E
Björklinge, Sweden 10 D11 60 2N 17 33 E
Björneborg, Sweden 10 E8 59 14N 14 16 E
Bjørnevatn, Norway 8 B23 69 40N 30 0 E
Bjørnøya, Arctic 4 B8 74 30N 19 0 E
Bjursås, Sweden 10 D9 60 44N 15 25 E
Bjuv, Sweden 11 H6 56 5N 12 55 E
Bla, Mali 82 C3 12 56N 5 47W
Blace, Serbia, Yug. 40 C5 43 18N 21 17 E
Blachownia, Poland 45 H5 50 49N 18 56 E
Black = Da →, Vietnam 58 G5 21 15N 105 20 E
Black →, Canada 110 B5 44 42N 79 19W
Black →, Ariz., U.S.A. 115 K8 33 44N 110 13W
Black →, Ark., U.S.A. 113 H9 35 38N 91 20W
Black →, Mich., U.S.A. 110 D2 42 59N 82 27W
Black →, N.Y., U.S.A. 111 C8 43 59N 76 4W
Black →, Wis., U.S.A. 112 D9 43 57N 91 22W
Black Bay Pen., Canada 102 C2 48 38N 88 21W
Black Birch L., Canada 105 B7 56 53N 107 45W
Black Diamond, Canada 104 C6 50 45N 114 14W
Black Duck →, Canada 102 A2 56 51N 89 2W
Black Forest = Schwarzwald, Germany 25 G4 48 30N 8 20 E
Black Forest, U.S.A. 112 F2 39 0N 104 43W
Black Hd., Ireland 15 C2 53 9N 9 16W
Black Hills, U.S.A. 112 D3 44 0N 103 45W
Black I., Canada 105 C9 51 12N 96 30W
Black L., Canada 105 B7 59 12N 105 15W
Black L., Mich., U.S.A. 108 C3 45 28N 84 16W
Black L., N.Y., U.S.A. 111 B9 44 31N 75 36W
Black Lake, Canada 105 B7 59 11N 105 20W
Black Mesa, U.S.A. 113 G3 36 58N 102 58W
Black Mt. = Mynydd Du, U.K. 13 F4 51 52N 3 50W
Black Mts., U.K. 13 F4 51 55N 3 7W
Black Range, U.S.A. 115 K10 33 15N 107 50W
Black River, Jamaica 120 C4 18 0N 77 50W
Black River Falls, U.S.A. 112 C9 44 18N 90 51W
Black Sea, Eurasia 6 G12 43 30N 35 0 E
Black Tickle, Canada 103 B8 53 28N 55 45W
Black Volta →, Africa 82 D4 8 41N 1 33W
Black Warrior →, U.S.A. 109 J2 32 32N 87 51W
Blackall, Australia 94 C4 24 25 S 145 45 E
Blackball, N.Z. 91 K3 42 22 S 171 26 E
Blackbull, Australia 94 B3 17 55 S 141 45 E
Blackburn, U.K. 12 D5 53 45N 2 29W
Blackburn with Darwen □, U.K. 12 D5 53 45N 2 29W
Blackfoot, U.S.A. 114 E7 43 11N 112 21W
Blackfoot →, U.S.A. 114 C7 46 52N 113 53W
Blackfoot River Reservoir, U.S.A. 114 E8 43 0N 111 43W
Blackpool, U.K. 12 D4 53 49N 3 3W
Blackpool □, U.K. 12 D4 53 49N 3 3W
Blackriver, U.S.A. 110 B1 44 46N 83 17W
Blacks Harbour, Canada 103 C6 45 3N 66 49W
Blacksburg, U.S.A. 108 G5 37 14N 80 25W
Blacksod B., Ireland 15 B1 54 6N 10 0W
Blackstone, U.S.A. 108 G7 37 4N 78 0W
Blackstone Ra., Australia 93 E4 26 0 S 128 30 E
Blackwater, Australia 94 C4 23 35 S 148 53 E
Blackwater →, Meath, Ireland 15 C4 53 39N 6 41W
Blackwater →, Waterford, Ireland 15 D4 52 4N 7 52W
Blackwater →, U.K. 15 B5 54 31N 6 35W
Blackwell, U.S.A. 113 G6 36 48N 97 17W
Blackwells Corner, U.S.A. 117 K7 35 37N 119 47W
Blaenau Ffestiniog, U.K. 12 E4 53 0N 3 56W
Blaenau Gwent □, U.K. 13 F4 51 48N 3 12W
Blagaj, Bos.-H. 40 C1 43 16N 17 55 E
Blagnac, France 20 E5 43 37N 1 23 E
Blagodarnoye = Blagodarnyy, Russia 49 H6 45 7N 43 37 E
Blagodarnyy, Russia 49 H6 45 7N 43 37 E
Blagoevgrad, Bulgaria 40 D7 42 2N 23 5 E
Blagoveshchensk, Russia 51 D13 50 20N 127 30 E
Blain, France 18 E5 47 29N 1 45W
Blain, U.S.A. 110 F7 40 20N 77 31W
Blaine, Minn., U.S.A. 112 C8 45 10N 93 13W
Blaine, Wash., U.S.A. 116 B4 48 59N 122 45W
Blaine Lake, Canada 105 C7 52 51N 106 52W
Blair, U.S.A. 112 E6 41 33N 96 8W
Blair Athol, Australia 94 C4 22 42 S 147 31 E
Blair Atholl, U.K. 14 E5 56 46N 3 50W
Blairgowrie, U.K. 14 E5 56 35N 3 21W
Blairsden, U.S.A. 116 F6 39 47N 120 37W
Blairsville, U.S.A. 110 F5 40 26N 79 16W
Blaj, Romania 43 D8 46 10N 23 57 E
Blake Pt., U.S.A. 112 A10 48 11N 88 25W
Blakely, Ga., U.S.A. 109 K3 31 23N 84 56W
Blakely, Pa., U.S.A. 111 E9 41 28N 75 37W
Blâmont, France 19 D13 48 35N 6 50 E
Blanc, C., Spain 37 B9 39 21N 2 51 E
Blanc, Mont, Alps 21 C10 45 48N 6 50 E
Blanc-Sablon, Canada 103 B8 51 24N 57 12W
Blanca, B., Argentina 122 G4 39 10 S 61 30W
Blanca Peak, U.S.A. 115 H11 37 35N 105 29W
Blanche, C., Australia 95 E1 33 1 S 134 9 E
Blanche, L., S. Austral., Australia 95 D2 29 15 S 139 40 E
Blanche, L., W. Austral., Australia 92 D3 22 25 S 123 17 E
Blanco, S. Africa 88 E3 33 55 S 22 23 E
Blanco, U.S.A. 113 K5 30 6N 98 25W
Blanco →, Argentina 126 C2 30 20 S 68 42W
Blanco, C., Costa Rica 120 E2 9 34N 85 8W
Blanco, C., U.S.A. 114 E1 42 51N 124 34W
Blanda →, Iceland 8 D3 65 37N 20 9W
Blandford Forum, U.K. 13 G5 50 51N 2 9W
Blanding, U.S.A. 115 H9 37 37N 109 29W
Blanes, Spain 32 D7 41 40N 2 48 E
Blangy-sur-Bresle, France 19 C8 49 55N 1 37 E
Blanice →, Czech Rep. 26 B7 49 10N 14 5 E
Blankaholm, Sweden 11 G10 57 36N 16 31 E
Blankenberge, Belgium 17 C3 51 20N 3 9 E
Blankenburg, Germany 24 D6 51 47N 10 57 E
Blanquefort, France 20 D3 44 55N 0 38W
Blanquilla, I., Venezuela 121 D7 11 51N 64 37W
Blanquillo, Uruguay 127 C4 32 53 S 55 37W
Blansko, Czech Rep. 27 B9 49 22N 16 40 E
Blantyre, Malawi 87 F4 15 45 S 35 0 E
Blarney, Ireland 15 E3 51 56N 8 33W
Blasdell, U.S.A. 110 D6 42 48N 78 50W
Błaszki, Poland 45 G5 51 38N 18 30 E
Blatná, Czech Rep. 26 B6 49 25N 13 52 E
Blato, Croatia 29 F13 42 56N 16 48 E
Blaubeuren, Germany 25 G5 48 24N 9 46 E
Blaustein, Germany 25 G5 48 25N 9 53 E
Blåvands Huk, Denmark 11 J2 55 33N 8 4 E
Blaydon, U.K. 12 C6 54 58N 1 42W
Blaye, France 20 C3 45 8N 0 40W
Blaye-les-Mines, France 20 D6 44 1N 2 8 E
Blayney, Australia 95 E4 33 32 S 149 14 E
Blaze, Pt., Australia 92 B5 12 56 S 130 11 E
Błażowa, Poland 45 J9 49 53N 22 7 E
Bleckede, Germany 24 B6 53 17N 10 43 E
Bled, Slovenia 29 B11 46 27N 14 7 E
Bleiburg, Austria 26 E7 46 35N 14 49 E
Blejeşti, Romania 43 F10 44 19N 25 27 E
Blekinge, Sweden 9 H16 56 25N 15 20 E
Blekinge län □, Sweden 11 H9 56 20N 15 20 E
Blenheim, Canada 110 D3 42 20N 82 0W
Blenheim, N.Z. 91 J4 41 38 S 173 57 E
Bléone →, France 21 D10 44 5N 6 0 E
Blérancourt, France 19 C10 49 31N 3 9 E
Bletchley, U.K. 13 F7 51 59N 0 44W
Blida, Algeria 78 A6 36 30N 2 49 E
Blidö, Sweden 10 E12 59 37N 18 53 E
Blidsberg, Sweden 11 G7 57 56N 13 30 E
Blieskastel, Germany 25 F3 49 14N 7 12 E
Bligh Sound, N.Z. 91 L1 44 47 S 167 32 E
Blind River, Canada 102 C3 46 10N 82 58W
Blinisht, Albania 40 E3 41 52N 19 59 E
Bliss, Idaho, U.S.A. 114 E6 42 56N 114 57W
Bliss, N.Y., U.S.A. 110 D6 42 34N 78 15W
Blissfield, U.S.A. 110 F3 40 24N 81 58W
Blitar, Indonesia 63 H15 8 5 S 112 11 E
Blitta, Togo 83 D5 8 23N 1 6 E
Block I., U.S.A. 111 E13 41 11N 71 35W
Block Island Sd., U.S.A. 111 E13 41 15N 71 40W
Blodgett Iceberg Tongue, Antarctica 5 C9 66 8 S 130 35 E
Bloemfontein, S. Africa 88 D4 29 6 S 26 7 E
Bloemhof, S. Africa 88 D4 27 38 S 25 32 E
Blois, France 18 E8 47 35N 1 20 E
Blomskog, Sweden 10 E6 59 16N 12 2 E
Blomstermåla, Sweden 11 H10 56 59N 16 21 E
Blönduós, Iceland 8 D3 65 40N 20 12W
Błonie, Poland 45 F7 52 12N 20 37 E
Bloodvein →, Canada 105 C9 51 47N 96 43W
Bloody Foreland, Ireland 15 A3 55 10N 8 17W
Bloomer, U.S.A. 112 C9 45 6N 91 29W
Bloomfield, Canada 110 C7 43 59N 77 14W
Bloomfield, Iowa, U.S.A. 112 E8 40 45N 92 25W
Bloomfield, N. Mex., U.S.A. 115 H10 36 43N 107 59W
Bloomfield, Nebr., U.S.A. 112 D6 42 36N 97 39W
Bloomington, Ill., U.S.A. 112 E10 40 28N 89 0W
Bloomington, Ind., U.S.A. 108 F2 39 10N 86 32W
Bloomington, Minn., U.S.A. 112 C8 44 50N 93 17W
Bloomsburg, U.S.A. 111 F8 41 0N 76 27W
Blora, Indonesia 63 G14 6 57 S 111 25 E
Blossburg, U.S.A. 110 E7 41 41N 77 4W
Blouberg, S. Africa 89 C4 23 8 S 28 59 E
Blountstown, U.S.A. 109 K3 30 27N 85 3W
Bludenz, Austria 26 D2 47 10N 9 50 E
Blue Earth, U.S.A. 112 D8 43 38N 94 6W
Blue Mesa Reservoir, U.S.A. 115 G10 38 28N 107 20W
Blue Mountain Lake, U.S.A. 111 C10 43 52N 74 30W
Blue Mts., Maine, U.S.A. 111 B14 44 50N 70 35W
Blue Mts., Oreg., U.S.A. 114 D4 45 15N 119 0W
Blue Mts., Pa., U.S.A. 111 F8 40 30N 76 30W
Blue Mud B., Australia 94 A2 13 30 S 136 0 E
Blue Nile = Nîl el Azraq →, Sudan 81 D3 15 38N 32 31 E
Blue Rapids, U.S.A. 112 F6 39 41N 96 39W
Blue Ridge Mts., U.S.A. 109 G5 36 30N 80 15W
Blue River, Canada 104 C5 52 6N 119 18W
Bluefield, U.S.A. 108 G5 37 15N 81 17W
Bluefields, Nic. 120 D3 12 20N 83 50W
Bluff, Australia 94 C4 23 35 S 149 4 E
Bluff, N.Z. 91 M2 46 37 S 168 20 E
Bluff, U.S.A. 115 H9 37 17N 109 33W
Bluff Knoll, Australia 93 F2 34 24 S 118 15 E
Bluff Pt., Australia 93 E1 27 50 S 114 5 E
Bluffton, U.S.A. 108 E3 40 44N 85 11W
Blumenau, Brazil 127 B6 27 0 S 49 0W
Blunt, U.S.A. 112 C5 44 31N 99 59W
Bly, U.S.A. 114 E3 42 24N 121 3W
Blyth, Canada 110 C3 43 44N 81 26W
Blyth, U.K. 12 B6 55 8N 1 31W
Blythe, U.S.A. 117 M12 33 37N 114 36W
Blytheville, U.S.A. 113 H10 35 56N 89 55W
Bo, S. Leone 82 D2 7 55N 11 50W
Bo Duc, Vietnam 65 G6 11 58N 106 50 E
Bo Hai, China 57 E10 39 0N 119 0 E
Bo Xian = Bozhou, China 56 H8 33 55N 115 41 E
Boa Vista, Brazil 124 C6 2 48N 60 30W
Boac, Phil. 61 E4 13 27N 121 50 E
Boaco, Nic. 120 D2 12 29N 85 35W
Bo'ai, China 56 G7 35 10N 113 3 E
Boal, Spain 34 B4 43 25N 6 49W
Boalsburg, U.S.A. 110 F7 40 46N 77 47W
Boane, Mozam. 89 D5 26 6 S 32 19 E
Boardman, U.S.A. 110 E4 41 2N 80 40W
Bobadah, Australia 95 E4 32 19 S 146 41 E
Bobai, China 58 F7 22 17N 109 59 E
Bobbili, India 67 K13 18 35N 83 30 E
Bóbbio, Italy 28 D6 44 46N 9 23 E
Bobcaygeon, Canada 102 D4 44 33N 78 33W
Böblingen, Germany 25 G5 48 40N 9 1 E
Bobo-Dioulasso, Burkina Faso 82 C4 11 8N 4 13W
Bobolice, Poland 44 E3 53 58N 16 37 E
Boboshevo, Bulgaria 40 D7 42 9N 23 0 E
Bobov Dol, Bulgaria 40 D6 42 20N 23 0 E
Bóbr →, Poland 45 F2 52 4N 15 4 E
Bobraomby, Tanjon' i, Madag. 89 A8 12 40 S 49 10 E
Bobrinets, Ukraine 47 H7 48 4N 32 5 E
Bobrov, Russia 48 E5 51 5N 40 2 E
Bobrovitsa, Ukraine 47 G6 50 45N 31 23 E
Bobruysk = Babruysk, Belarus 47 F5 53 10N 29 15 E
Boby, Pic, Madag. 85 J9 22 12 S 46 55 E
Boca do Acre, Brazil 124 E5 8 50 S 67 27W
Boca Raton, U.S.A. 109 M5 26 21N 80 5W
Bocanda, Ivory C. 82 D4 7 5N 4 31W
Bocas del Toro, Panama 120 E3 9 15N 82 20W
Boceguillas, Spain 34 D7 41 20N 3 39W
Bochnia, Poland 45 J7 49 58N 20 27 E
Bocholt, Germany 24 D2 51 50N 6 36 E
Bochum, Germany 24 D3 51 28N 7 13 E
Bockenem, Germany 24 C6 52 1N 10 8 E
Boćki, Poland 45 F10 52 39N 23 3 E
Bocognano, France 21 F13 42 5N 9 4 E
Bocoyna, Mexico 118 B3 27 52N 107 35W
Bocşa, Romania 42 E6 45 21N 21 47 E
Boda, Dalarnas, Sweden 10 C9 61 1N 15 13 E
Böda, Kalmar, Sweden 11 G11 57 15N 17 3 E
Boda, Västernorrland, Sweden 10 B10 62 52N 16 39 E
Bodafors, Sweden 11 G8 57 48N 14 23 E
Bodaybo, Russia 51 D12 57 50N 114 0 E
Boddam, U.K. 14 B7 59 56N 1 17W
Boddington, Australia 93 F2 32 50 S 116 30 E
Bode Sadu, Nigeria 83 D5 9 0N 4 47 E
Bodega Bay, U.S.A. 116 G3 38 20N 123 3W
Boden, Sweden 8 D19 65 50N 21 42 E
Bodensee, Europe 25 H5 47 35N 9 25 E
Bodenteich, Germany 24 C6 52 50N 10 42 E
Bodhan, India 66 K10 18 40N 77 44 E
Bodinga, Nigeria 83 C6 12 58N 5 10 E
Bodmin, U.K. 13 G3 50 28N 4 43W
Bodmin Moor, U.K. 13 G3 50 33N 4 36W
Bodø, Norway 8 C16 67 17N 14 24 E
Bodrog →, Hungary 42 B6 48 11N 21 22 E
Bodrum, Turkey 39 D9 37 3N 27 30 E
Bódva →, Hungary 42 B5 48 19N 20 45 E
Boën, France 21 C8 45 44N 4 1 E
Boende, Dem. Rep. of the Congo 84 E4 0 24 S 21 12 E
Boerne, U.S.A. 113 L5 29 47N 98 44W
Boesmans →, S. Africa 88 E4 33 42 S 26 39 E
Boffa, Guinea 82 C2 10 16N 14 3W
Bogalusa, U.S.A. 113 K10 30 47N 89 52W
Bogan →, Australia 95 D4 29 59 S 146 17 E
Bogan Gate, Australia 95 E4 33 7 S 147 49 E
Bogandé, Burkina Faso 83 C4 13 2N 0 8W
Bogantungan, Australia 94 C4 23 41 S 147 17 E
Bogata, U.S.A. 113 J7 33 28N 95 13W
Bogatić, Serbia, Yug. 40 B3 44 51N 19 30 E
Boğazkale, Turkey 72 B6 40 2N 34 37 E
Boğazlıyan, Turkey 72 C6 39 11N 35 14 E
Bogen, Sweden 10 D6 60 4N 12 33 E
Bogense, Denmark 11 J4 55 34N 10 5 E
Bogetići, Montenegro, Yug. 40 D2 42 41N 18 58 E
Boggabilla, Australia 95 D5 28 36 S 150 24 E
Boggabri, Australia 95 E5 30 45 S 150 5 E
Boggeragh Mts., Ireland 15 D3 52 2N 8 55W
Boglan = Solhan, Turkey 70 B4 38 57N 41 3 E
Bognor Regis, U.K. 13 G7 50 47N 0 40W
Bogo, Phil. 61 F6 11 3N 124 0 E
Bogodukhov = Bohodukhiv, Ukraine 47 G8 50 9N 35 33 E
Bogol Manya, Ethiopia 81 G5 4 32N 41 29 E
Bogong, Mt., Australia 95 F4 36 47 S 147 17 E
Bogor, Indonesia 62 F3 6 36 S 106 48 E
Bogoroditsk, Russia 46 F10 53 47N 38 8 E
Bogorodsk, Russia 48 B6 56 4N 43 30 E
Bogoso, Ghana 82 D4 5 38N 2 3W
Bogotá, Colombia 124 C4 4 34N 74 0W
Bogotol, Russia 50 D9 56 15N 89 50 E
Bogou, Togo 83 C5 10 40N 0 12 E
Bogra, Bangla. 67 G16 24 51N 89 22 E
Boguchany, Russia 51 D10 58 40N 97 30 E
Boguchar, Russia 48 F5 49 55N 40 32 E
Bogué, Mauritania 82 B2 16 45N 14 10W
Boguslav, Ukraine 47 H6 49 33N 30 56 E
Boguszów-Gorce, Poland 45 H3 50 45N 16 12 E
Bohain-en-Vermandois, France 19 C10 49 59N 3 28 E
Bohemian Forest = Böhmerwald, Germany 25 F9 49 8N 13 14 E
Bohinjska Bistrica, Slovenia 29 B11 46 17N 14 1 E
Böhmerwald, Germany 25 F9 49 8N 13 14 E
Bohmte, Germany 24 C4 52 22N 8 19 E
Bohodukhiv, Ukraine 47 G8 50 9N 35 33 E
Bohol □, Phil. 61 G6 9 50N 124 10 E
Bohol Sea, Phil. 63 C6 9 0N 124 0 E
Bohongou, Burkina Faso 83 C5 12 30N 0 40 E
Böhönye, Hungary 42 D2 46 25N 17 28 E
Bohuslän, Sweden 11 F5 58 25N 12 0 E
Boi, Nigeria 83 D6 9 35N 9 27 E
Boi, Pta. de, Brazil 127 A6 23 55 S 45 15W
Boiaçu, Brazil 124 D6 0 27 S 61 46W
Boileau, C., Australia 92 C3 17 40 S 122 7 E
Boing'o, Sudan 81 F3 9 58N 33 44 E
Boiro, Spain 34 C2 42 39N 8 54W
Boise, U.S.A. 114 E5 43 37N 116 13W
Boise City, U.S.A. 113 G3 36 44N 102 31W
Boissevain, Canada 105 D8 49 15N 100 5W
Bóite →, Italy 29 B9 46 5N 12 5 E
Boitzenburg, Germany 24 B9 53 16N 13 35 E
Boizenburg, Germany 24 B6 53 23N 10 43 E
Bojador C., W. Sahara 78 C3 26 0N 14 30W
Bojana →, Albania 40 E3 41 52N 19 22 E
Bojano, Italy 31 A7 41 29N 14 29 E
Bojanowo, Poland 45 G3 51 43N 16 42 E
Bøjden, Denmark 11 J4 55 6N 10 7 E
Bojnūrd, Iran 71 B8 37 30N 57 20 E
Bojonegoro, Indonesia 63 G14 7 11 S 111 54 E
Boju, Nigeria 83 D6 7 22N 7 55 E
Boka, Serbia, Yug. 42 E5 45 22N 20 52 E
Boka Kotorska, Montenegro, Yug. 40 D2 42 23N 18 32 E
Bokala, Ivory C. 82 D4 8 31N 4 33W
Bokani, Nigeria 83 D6 9 28N 5 10 E
Bokaro, India 69 H11 23 46N 85 55 E
Boké, Guinea 82 C2 10 56N 14 17W
Bokhara →, Australia 95 D4 29 55 S 146 42 E
Bokkos, Nigeria 83 D6 9 17N 9 1 E
Boknafjorden, Norway 9 G11 59 14N 5 40 E
Bokoro, Chad 79 F9 12 25N 17 14 E
Bokpyin, Burma 65 G2 11 18N 98 42 E
Boksitogorsk, Russia 46 C7 59 22N 33 50 E
Bol, Croatia 29 E13 43 18N 16 38 E
Bolama, Guinea-Biss. 82 C1 11 30N 15 30W
Bolan →, Pakistan 68 E2 28 38N 67 42 E
Bolan Pass, Pakistan 66 E5 29 50N 67 20 E
Bolaños →, Mexico 118 C4 21 14N 104 8W
Bolaños de Calatrava, Spain 35 G7 38 54N 3 40W
Bolayır, Turkey 41 F10 40 31N 26 45 E
Bolbec, France 18 C7 49 30N 0 30 E
Boldājī, Iran 71 D6 31 56N 51 3 E
Boldeşti-Scăeni, Romania 43 E11 45 3N 26 2 E
Bole, China 60 B3 45 11N 81 37 E
Bole, Ethiopia 81 F4 6 36N 37 20 E
Bole, Ghana 82 D4 9 3N 2 23W
Bolekhiv, Ukraine 47 H2 49 0N 23 57 E
Bolesławiec, Poland 45 G2 51 17N 15 37 E
Bolgatanga, Ghana 83 C4 10 44N 0 53W
Bolgrad = Bolhrad, Ukraine 47 K5 45 40N 28 32 E
Bolhrad, Ukraine 47 K5 45 40N 28 32 E
Bolinao, Phil. 61 C3 16 23N 119 54 E
Bolintin-Vale, Romania 43 F10 44 27N 25 46 E
Bolívar, Argentina 126 D3 36 15 S 60 53W
Bolivar, Mo., U.S.A. 113 G8 37 37N 93 25W
Bolivar, N.Y., U.S.A. 110 D6 42 4N 78 10W
Bolivar, Tenn., U.S.A. 113 H10 35 12N 89 0W
Bolivia ■, S. Amer. 124 G6 17 6 S 64 0W
Bolivian Plateau, S. Amer. 122 E4 20 0 S 67 30W
Boljevac, Serbia, Yug. 40 C5 43 51N 21 58 E
Bolkhov, Russia 46 F9 53 25N 36 0 E
Bolków, Poland 45 H3 50 55N 16 6 E
Bollebygd, Sweden 11 G6 57 40N 12 35 E
Bollène, France 21 D8 44 18N 4 45 E
Bollnäs, Sweden 10 C10 61 21N 16 24 E
Bollon, Australia 95 D4 28 2 S 147 29 E
Bollstabruk, Sweden 10 B11 62 59N 17 40 E
Bolmen, Sweden 11 H7 56 55N 13 40 E
Bolobo, Dem. Rep. of the Congo 84 E3 2 6 S 16 20 E
Bologna, Italy 29 D8 44 29N 11 20 E
Bologoye, Russia 46 D8 57 55N 34 5 E
Bolon, Ozero, Russia 60 B8 49 50N 133 0 E
Bolonchenticul, Mexico 119 D7 20 0N 89 49W
Bolótana, Italy 30 B1 40 20N 8 52 E

Bratunac

Bratunac, Bos.-H. 42 F4 44 13N 19 21 E
Braunau, Austria 26 C6 48 15N 13 3 E
Braunschweig, Germany 24 C6 52 15N 10 31 E
Braunton, U.K. 13 F3 51 7N 4 10W
Bravicea, Moldova 43 C13 47 22N 28 27 E
Bråviken, Sweden 11 F10 58 38N 16 32 E
Bravo del Norte, Rio = Grande, Rio →, U.S.A. 113 N6 25 58N 97 9W
Brawley, U.S.A. 117 N11 32 59N 115 31W
Bray, Ireland 15 C5 53 13N 6 7W
Bray, Mt., Australia 94 A1 14 0 S 134 30 E
Bray-sur-Seine, France 19 D10 48 25N 3 14 E
Brazeau →, Canada 104 C5 52 55N 115 14W
Brazil, U.S.A. 108 F2 39 32N 87 8W
Brazil ■, S. Amer. 125 F9 12 0 S 50 0W
Brazilian Highlands = Brasil, Planalto, Brazil 122 E6 18 0 S 46 30W
Brazo Sur →, S. Amer. 126 B4 25 21 S 57 42W
Brazos →, U.S.A. 113 L7 28 53N 95 23W
Brazzaville, Congo 84 E3 4 9 S 15 12 E
Brčko, Bos.-H. 42 F3 44 54N 18 46 E
Brda →, Poland 45 E5 53 8N 18 8 E
Brdy, Czech Rep. 26 B6 49 43N 13 54 E
Breaden, L., Australia 93 E4 25 51 S 125 28 E
Breaksea Sd., N.Z. 91 L1 45 35 S 166 35 E
Bream B., N.Z. 91 F5 35 56 S 174 28 E
Bream Hd., N.Z. 91 F5 35 51 S 174 36 E
Breas, Chile 126 B1 25 29 S 70 24W
Breaza, Romania 43 E10 45 11N 25 40 E
Brebes, Indonesia 63 G13 6 52 S 109 3 E
Brechin, Canada 110 B5 44 32N 79 10W
Brechin, U.K. 14 E6 56 44N 2 39W
Brecht, Belgium 17 C4 51 21N 4 38 E
Breckenridge, Colo., U.S.A. 114 G10 39 29N 106 3W
Breckenridge, Minn., U.S.A. 112 B6 46 16N 96 35W
Breckenridge, Tex., U.S.A. 113 J5 32 45N 98 54W
Breckland, U.K. 13 E8 52 30N 0 40 E
Břeclav, Czech Rep. 27 C9 48 46N 16 53 E
Brecon, U.K. 13 F4 51 57N 3 23W
Brecon Beacons, U.K. 13 F4 51 53N 3 26W
Breda, Neths. 17 C4 51 35N 4 45 E
Bredaryd, Sweden 11 G7 57 10N 13 45 E
Bredasdorp, S. Africa 88 E3 34 33 S 20 2 E
Bredebro, Denmark 11 J2 55 4N 8 50 E
Bredstedt, Germany 24 A4 54 37N 8 55 E
Bree, Belgium 17 C5 51 8N 5 35 E
Bregalnica →, Macedonia 40 E6 41 43N 22 9 E
Bregenz, Austria 26 D2 47 30N 9 45 E
Bregovo, Bulgaria 40 B6 44 9N 22 39 E
Bréhal, France 18 D5 48 53N 1 30W
Bréhat, Î. de, France 18 D4 48 51N 3 0W
Breiðafjörður, Iceland 8 D2 65 15N 23 15W
Breil-sur-Roya, France 21 E11 43 56N 7 31 E
Breisach, Germany 25 G3 48 1N 7 36 E
Brejo, Brazil 125 D10 3 41 S 42 47W
Bremen, Germany 24 B4 53 4N 8 47 E
Bremen □, Germany 24 B4 53 4N 8 50 E
Bremer Bay, Australia 93 F2 34 21 S 119 20 E
Bremer I., Australia 94 A2 12 5 S 136 45 E
Bremerhaven, Germany 24 B4 53 33N 8 36 E
Bremerton, U.S.A. 116 C4 47 34N 122 38W
Bremervörde, Germany 24 B5 53 29N 9 8 E
Brenes, Spain 35 H5 37 32N 5 54W
Brenham, U.S.A. 113 K6 30 10N 96 24W
Brenne, France 20 B5 46 44N 1 14 E
Brennerpass, Austria 26 D4 47 2N 11 30 E
Breno, Italy 28 C7 45 57N 10 18 E
Brent, U.S.A. 109 J2 32 56N 87 10W
Brenta →, Italy 29 C9 45 11N 12 18 E
Brentwood, U.K. 13 F8 51 37N 0 19 E
Brentwood, Calif., U.S.A. 116 H5 37 56N 121 42W
Brentwood, N.Y., U.S.A. 111 F11 40 47N 73 15W
Bréscia, Italy 28 C7 45 33N 10 15 E
Breskens, Neths. 17 C3 51 23N 3 33 E
Breslau = Wrocław, Poland 45 G4 51 5N 17 5 E
Bresle →, France 18 B8 50 4N 1 22 E
Bressanone, Italy 29 B8 46 43N 11 39 E
Bressay, U.K. 14 A7 60 9N 1 6W
Bresse, France 19 F12 46 50N 5 10 E
Bressuire, France 18 F6 46 51N 0 30W
Brest, Belarus 47 F2 52 10N 23 40 E
Brest, France 18 D2 48 24N 4 31W
Brest-Litovsk = Brest, Belarus 47 F2 52 10N 23 40 E
Bretagne, France 18 D3 48 10N 3 0W
Bretçu, Romania 43 D11 46 7N 26 18 E
Bretenoux, France 20 D5 44 54N 1 51 E
Breteuil, Eure, France 18 D7 48 50N 0 57 E
Breteuil, Oise, France 19 C9 49 38N 2 18 E
Breton, Canada 104 C6 53 7N 114 28W
Breton, Pertuis, France 20 B2 46 17N 1 25W
Breton Sd., U.S.A. 113 L10 29 35N 89 15W
Brett, C., N.Z. 91 F5 35 10 S 174 20 E
Bretten, Germany 25 F4 49 2N 8 42 E
Breuil-Cervínia, Italy 28 C4 45 56N 7 38 E
Brevard, U.S.A. 109 H4 35 14N 82 44W
Breves, Brazil 125 D8 1 40 S 50 29W
Brewarrina, Australia 95 E4 30 0 S 146 51 E
Brewer, U.S.A. 109 C11 44 48N 68 46W
Brewer, Mt., U.S.A. 116 J8 36 44N 118 28W
Brewerville, Liberia 82 D2 6 26N 10 47W
Brewster, N.Y., U.S.A. 111 E11 41 23N 73 37W
Brewster, Ohio, U.S.A. 110 F3 40 43N 81 36W
Brewster, Wash., U.S.A. 114 B4 48 6N 119 47W
Brewster, Kap = Kangikajik, Greenland 4 B6 70 7N 22 0W
Brewton, U.S.A. 109 K2 31 7N 87 4W
Breyten, S. Africa 89 D5 26 16 S 30 0 E
Breza, Bos.-H. 42 F3 44 2N 18 16 E
Brezhnev = Naberezhnyye Chelny, Russia 48 C11 55 42N 52 19 E
Brežice, Slovenia 29 C12 45 54N 15 35 E
Březnice, Czech Rep. 26 B6 49 32N 13 57 E
Breznik, Bulgaria 40 D6 42 44N 22 55 E
Brezno, Slovak Rep. 27 C12 48 50N 19 40 E
Brezoi, Romania 43 E9 45 21N 24 15 E
Brezovica, Kosovo, Yug. 40 D5 42 15N 21 3 E
Brezovo, Bulgaria 41 D9 42 21N 25 5 E
Briançon, France 21 D10 44 54N 6 39 E
Briare, France 19 E9 47 38N 2 45 E
Briático, Italy 31 D9 38 43N 16 2 E
Bribie I., Australia 95 D5 27 0 S 153 10 E
Bribri, Costa Rica 120 E3 9 38N 82 50W
Briceni, Moldova 43 B12 48 22N 27 6 E
Bricquebec, France 18 C5 49 28N 1 38W
Bridgehampton, U.S.A. 111 F12 40 56N 72 19W
Bridgend, U.K. 13 F4 51 30N 3 34W
Bridgend □, U.K. 13 F4 51 36N 3 36W
Bridgeport, Calif., U.S.A. 116 G7 38 15N 119 14W
Bridgeport, Conn., U.S.A. 111 E11 41 11N 73 12W
Bridgeport, Nebr., U.S.A. 112 E3 41 40N 103 6W
Bridgeport, Tex., U.S.A. 113 J6 33 13N 97 45W
Bridger, U.S.A. 114 D9 45 18N 108 55W
Bridgeton, U.S.A. 108 F8 39 26N 75 14W
Bridgetown, Australia 93 F2 33 58 S 116 7 E
Bridgetown, Barbados 121 D8 13 5N 59 30W
Bridgetown, Canada 103 D6 44 55N 65 18W
Bridgewater, Canada 103 D7 44 25N 64 31W
Bridgewater, Mass., U.S.A. 111 E14 41 59N 70 58W
Bridgewater, N.Y., U.S.A. 111 D9 42 53N 75 15W
Bridgewater, C., Australia 95 F3 38 23 S 141 23 E
Bridgewater-Gagebrook, Australia 94 G4 42 44 S 147 14 E
Bridgnorth, U.K. 13 E5 52 32N 2 25W
Bridgton, U.S.A. 111 B14 44 3N 70 42W
Bridgwater, U.K. 13 F5 51 8N 2 59W
Bridgwater B., U.K. 13 F4 51 15N 3 15W
Bridlington, U.K. 12 C7 54 5N 0 12W
Bridlington B., U.K. 12 C7 54 4N 0 10W
Bridport, Australia 94 G4 40 59 S 147 23 E
Bridport, U.K. 13 G5 50 44N 2 45W
Briec, France 18 D2 48 6N 4 0W
Brienne-le-Château, France 19 D11 48 24N 4 30 E
Brienon-sur-Armançon, France 19 E10 47 59N 3 38 E
Brienz, Switz. 25 J4 46 46N 8 2 E
Brienzersee, Switz. 25 J3 46 44N 7 53 E
Brig, Switz. 25 J3 46 18N 7 59 E
Brigg, U.K. 12 D7 53 34N 0 28W
Brigham City, U.S.A. 114 F7 41 31N 112 1W
Bright, Australia 95 F4 36 42 S 146 56 E
Brighton, Australia 95 F2 35 5 S 138 30 E
Brighton, Canada 110 B7 44 2N 77 44W
Brighton, U.K. 13 G7 50 49N 0 7W
Brighton, Colo., U.S.A. 112 F2 39 59N 104 49W
Brighton, N.Y., U.S.A. 110 C7 43 8N 77 34W
Brignogan-Plage, France 18 D2 48 40N 4 20W
Brignoles, France 21 E10 43 25N 6 5 E
Brihuega, Spain 32 E2 40 45N 2 52W
Brikama, Gambia 82 C1 13 15N 16 45W
Brilliant, U.S.A. 110 F4 40 15N 80 39W
Brilon, Germany 24 D4 51 23N 8 34 E
Bríndisi, Italy 31 B10 40 39N 17 55 E
Brinje, Croatia 29 D12 44 59N 15 9 E
Brinkley, U.S.A. 113 H9 34 53N 91 12W
Brinnon, U.S.A. 116 C4 47 41N 122 54W
Brion, I., Canada 103 C7 47 46N 61 26W
Brionne, France 18 C7 49 11N 0 43 E
Brionski, Croatia 29 D10 44 55N 13 45 E
Brioude, France 20 C7 45 18N 3 24 E
Briouze, France 18 D6 48 42N 0 23W
Brisbane, Australia 95 D5 27 25 S 153 2 E
Brisbane →, Australia 95 D5 27 24 S 153 9 E
Brisighella, Italy 29 D8 44 13N 11 46 E
Bristol, U.K. 13 F5 51 26N 2 35W
Bristol, Conn., U.S.A. 111 E12 41 40N 72 57W
Bristol, Pa., U.S.A. 111 F10 40 6N 74 51W
Bristol, R.I., U.S.A. 111 E13 41 40N 71 16W
Bristol, Tenn., U.S.A. 109 G4 36 36N 82 11W
Bristol, City of □, U.K. 13 F5 51 27N 2 36W
Bristol B., U.S.A. 100 C4 58 0N 160 0W
Bristol Channel, U.K. 13 F3 51 18N 4 30W
Bristol I., Antarctica 5 B1 58 45 S 28 0W
Bristol L., U.S.A. 115 J5 34 23N 116 50W
Bristow, U.S.A. 113 H6 35 50N 96 23W
Britain = Great Britain, Europe 6 E5 54 0N 2 15W
British Columbia □, Canada 104 C3 55 0N 125 15W
British Indian Ocean Terr. = Chagos Arch., Ind. Oc. 52 K11 6 0 S 72 0 E
British Isles, Europe 6 E5 54 0N 4 0W
Brits, S. Africa 89 D4 25 37 S 27 48 E
Britstown, S. Africa 88 E3 30 37 S 23 30 E
Britt, Canada 102 C3 45 46N 80 34W
Brittany = Bretagne, France 18 D3 48 10N 3 0W
Britton, U.S.A. 112 C6 45 48N 97 45W
Brive-la-Gaillarde, France 20 C5 45 10N 1 32 E
Briviesca, Spain 34 C7 42 32N 3 19W
Brixen = Bressanone, Italy 29 B8 46 43N 11 39 E
Brixham, U.K. 13 G4 50 23N 3 31W
Brnaze, Croatia 29 E13 43 41N 16 40 E
Brněnský □, Czech Rep. 27 B9 49 10N 16 40 E
Brno, Czech Rep. 27 B9 49 10N 16 35 E
Broad →, U.S.A. 109 J5 34 1N 81 4W
Broad Arrow, Australia 93 F3 30 23 S 121 15 E
Broad B., U.K. 14 C2 58 14N 6 18W
Broad Haven, Ireland 15 B2 54 20N 9 55W
Broad Law, U.K. 14 F5 55 30N 3 21W
Broad Sd., Australia 94 C4 22 0 S 149 45 E
Broadalbin, U.S.A. 111 C10 43 4N 74 12W
Broadback →, Canada 102 B4 51 21N 78 52W
Broadhurst Ra., Australia 92 D3 22 30 S 122 30 E
Broads, The, U.K. 12 E9 52 45N 1 30 E
Broadus, U.S.A. 112 C2 45 27N 105 25W
Broager, Denmark 11 K3 54 53N 9 40 E
Broby, Sweden 11 H8 56 15N 14 4 E
Brocēni, Latvia 44 B9 56 42N 22 32 E
Brochet, Canada 105 B8 57 53N 101 40W
Brochet, L., Canada 105 B8 58 36N 101 35W
Brocken, Germany 24 D6 51 47N 10 37 E
Brockport, U.S.A. 110 C7 43 13N 77 56W
Brockton, U.S.A. 111 D13 42 5N 71 1W
Brockville, Canada 102 D4 44 35N 75 41W
Brockway, Mont., U.S.A. 112 B2 47 18N 105 45W
Brockway, Pa., U.S.A. 110 E6 41 15N 78 47W
Brocton, U.S.A. 110 D5 42 23N 79 26W
Brod, Macedonia 40 E5 41 32N 21 17 E
Brodarevo, Serbia, Yug. 40 C3 43 14N 19 44 E
Brodeur Pen., Canada 101 A11 72 30N 88 10W
Brodhead, Mt., U.S.A. 110 E7 41 39N 77 47W
Brodick, U.K. 14 F3 55 35N 5 9W
Brodnica, Poland 45 E6 53 15N 19 25 E
Brody, Ukraine 47 G3 50 5N 25 10 E
Brogan, U.S.A. 114 D5 44 15N 117 31W
Broglie, France 18 C7 49 2N 0 30 E
Brok, Poland 45 F8 52 43N 21 52 E
Broken Arrow, U.S.A. 113 G7 36 3N 95 48W
Broken Bow, Nebr., U.S.A. 112 E5 41 24N 99 38W
Broken Bow, Okla., U.S.A. 113 H7 34 2N 94 44W
Broken Bow Lake, U.S.A. 113 H7 34 9N 94 40W
Broken Hill = Kabwe, Zambia 87 E2 14 30 S 28 29 E
Broken Hill, Australia 95 E3 31 58 S 141 29 E
Brokind, Sweden 11 F9 58 13N 15 42 E
Bromley □, U.K. 13 F8 51 24N 0 2 E
Bromölla, Sweden 11 H8 56 5N 14 28 E
Bromsgrove, U.K. 13 E5 52 21N 2 2W
Brønderslev, Denmark 11 G3 57 16N 9 57 E
Brong-Ahafo □, Ghana 82 D4 7 50N 2 0W
Broni, Italy 28 C6 45 4N 9 16 E
Bronkhorstspruit, S. Africa 89 D4 25 46 S 28 45 E
Brønnøysund, Norway 8 D15 65 28N 12 14 E
Bronte, Italy 31 E7 37 47N 14 50 E
Brook Park, U.S.A. 110 E4 41 24N 81 51W
Brookhaven, U.S.A. 113 K9 31 35N 90 26W
Brookings, Oreg., U.S.A. 114 E1 42 3N 124 17W
Brookings, S. Dak., U.S.A. 112 C6 44 19N 96 48W
Brooklin, Canada 110 C6 43 55N 78 55W
Brooklyn Park, U.S.A. 112 C8 45 6N 93 23W
Brooks, Canada 104 C6 50 35N 111 55W
Brooks Range, U.S.A. 100 B5 68 0N 152 0W
Brooksville, U.S.A. 109 L4 28 33N 82 23W
Brookton, Australia 93 F2 32 22 S 117 0 E
Brookville, U.S.A. 110 E5 41 10N 79 5W
Broom, L., U.K. 14 D3 57 55N 5 15W
Broome, Australia 92 C3 18 0 S 122 15 E
Broons, France 18 D4 48 20N 2 16W
Brora, U.K. 14 C5 58 0N 3 52W
Brora →, U.K. 14 C5 58 0N 3 51W
Brørup, Denmark 11 J2 55 29N 9 1 E
Brösarp, Sweden 11 J8 55 43N 14 6 E
Brosna →, Ireland 15 C4 53 14N 7 58W
Broşteni, Mehedinţi, Romania 42 F7 44 45N 22 59 E
Broşteni, Suceava, Romania 43 C10 47 14N 25 43 E
Brothers, U.S.A. 114 E3 43 49N 120 36W
Brou, France 18 D8 48 13N 1 11 E
Brouage, France 20 C2 45 52N 1 4W
Brough, U.K. 12 C5 54 32N 2 18W
Brough Hd., U.K. 14 B5 59 8N 3 20W
Broughton Island = Qikiqtarjuaq, Canada 101 B13 67 33N 63 0W
Broumov, Czech Rep. 27 A9 50 35N 16 20 E
Brovary, Ukraine 47 G6 50 34N 30 48 E
Brovst, Denmark 11 G3 57 6N 9 31 E
Brown, L., Australia 93 F2 31 5 S 118 15 E
Brown, Pt., Australia 95 E1 32 32 S 133 50 E
Brown City, U.S.A. 110 C2 43 13N 82 59W
Brown Willy, U.K. 13 G3 50 35N 4 37W
Brownfield, U.S.A. 113 J3 33 11N 102 17W
Browning, U.S.A. 114 B7 48 34N 113 1W
Brownsville, Oreg., U.S.A. 114 D2 44 24N 122 59W
Brownsville, Pa., U.S.A. 110 F5 40 1N 79 53W
Brownsville, Tenn., U.S.A. 113 H10 35 36N 89 16W
Brownsville, Tex., U.S.A. 113 N6 25 54N 97 30W
Brownville, U.S.A. 111 C9 44 0N 75 59W
Brownwood, U.S.A. 113 K5 31 43N 98 59W
Browse I., Australia 92 B3 14 7 S 123 33 E
Bruas, Malaysia 65 K3 4 30N 100 47 E
Bruay-la-Buissière, France 19 B9 50 29N 2 33 E
Bruce, Mt., Australia 92 D2 22 37 S 118 8 E
Bruce Pen., Canada 110 B3 45 0N 81 30W
Bruce Rock, Australia 93 F2 31 52 S 118 8 E
Bruche →, France 19 D14 48 34N 7 43 E
Bruchsal, Germany 25 F4 49 7N 8 35 E
Bruck an der Leitha, Austria 27 C9 48 1N 16 47 E
Bruck an der Mur, Austria 26 D8 47 24N 15 16 E
Brue →, U.K. 13 F5 51 13N 2 59W
Bruges = Brugge, Belgium 17 C3 51 13N 3 13 E
Brugg, Switz. 25 H4 47 29N 8 11 E
Brugge, Belgium 17 C3 51 13N 3 13 E
Bruin, U.S.A. 110 E5 41 3N 79 43W
Brûlé, Canada 104 C5 53 15N 117 58W
Brûlon, France 18 E6 47 58N 0 15W
Brumado, Brazil 125 F10 14 14 S 41 40W
Brumath, France 19 D14 48 43N 7 40 E
Brumunddal, Norway 9 F14 60 53N 10 56 E
Bruneau, U.S.A. 114 E6 42 53N 115 48W
Bruneau →, U.S.A. 114 E6 42 56N 115 57W
Bruneck = Brunico, Italy 29 B8 46 48N 11 56 E
Brunei = Bandar Seri Begawan, Brunei 62 C4 4 52N 115 0 E
Brunei ■, Asia 62 D4 4 50N 115 0 E
Brunflo, Sweden 10 A8 63 5N 14 50 E
Brunico, Italy 29 B8 46 48N 11 56 E
Brunna, Sweden 10 E11 59 52N 17 25 E
Brunnen, Switz. 25 J4 46 59N 8 37 E
Brunner, L., N.Z. 91 K3 42 37 S 171 27 E
Brunsbüttel, Germany 24 B5 53 53N 9 6 E
Brunssum, Neths. 17 D5 50 57N 5 59 E
Brunswick = Braunschweig, Germany 24 C6 52 15N 10 31 E
Brunswick, Ga., U.S.A. 109 K5 31 10N 81 30W
Brunswick, Maine, U.S.A. 109 D11 43 55N 69 58W
Brunswick, Md., U.S.A. 108 F7 39 19N 77 38W
Brunswick, Mo., U.S.A. 112 F8 39 26N 93 8W
Brunswick, Ohio, U.S.A. 110 E3 41 14N 81 51W
Brunswick, Pen. de, Chile 128 G2 53 30 S 71 30W
Brunswick B., Australia 92 C3 15 15 S 124 50 E
Brunswick Junction, Australia 93 F2 33 15 S 115 50 E
Bruntál, Czech Rep. 27 B10 49 59N 17 27 E
Bruny I., Australia 94 G4 43 20 S 147 15 E
Brus Laguna, Honduras 120 C3 15 47N 84 35W
Brusartsi, Bulgaria 40 C7 43 40N 23 5 E
Brush, U.S.A. 112 E3 40 15N 103 37W
Brushton, U.S.A. 111 B10 44 50N 74 31W
Brusio, Switz. 25 J6 46 14N 10 8 E
Brusque, Brazil 127 B6 27 5 S 49 0W
Brussel, Belgium 17 D4 50 51N 4 21 E
Brussels = Brussel, Belgium 17 D4 50 51N 4 21 E
Brussels, Canada 110 C3 43 44N 81 15W
Brusy, Poland 44 E4 53 53N 17 43 E
Bruthen, Australia 95 F4 37 42 S 147 50 E
Bruxelles = Brussel, Belgium 17 D4 50 51N 4 21 E
Bruyères, France 19 D13 48 10N 6 40 E
Bruz, France 18 D5 48 1N 1 46W
Brwinów, Poland 45 F7 52 9N 20 40 E
Bryagovo, Bulgaria 41 E9 41 58N 25 8 E
Bryan, Ohio, U.S.A. 108 E3 41 28N 84 33W
Bryan, Tex., U.S.A. 113 K6 30 40N 96 22W
Bryan, Mt., Australia 95 E2 33 30 S 139 0 E
Bryanka, Ukraine 47 H10 48 32N 38 45 E
Bryansk, Bryansk, Russia 47 F8 53 13N 34 25 E
Bryansk, Dagestan, Russia 49 H8 44 20N 47 10 E
Bryanskoye = Bryansk, Russia 49 H8 44 20N 47 10 E
Bryce Canyon National Park, U.S.A. 115 H7 37 30N 112 10W
Bryne, Norway 9 G11 58 44N 5 38 E
Bryson City, U.S.A. 109 H4 35 26N 83 27W
Bryukhovetskaya, Russia 47 K10 45 48N 39 0 E
Brza Palanka, Serbia, Yug. 40 B6 44 28N 22 27 E
Brzeg, Poland 45 H4 50 52N 17 30 E
Brzeg Dolny, Poland 45 G3 51 16N 16 41 E
Brześć Kujawski, Poland 45 F5 52 36N 18 55 E
Brzesko, Poland 45 J7 49 59N 20 34 E
Brzeziny, Poland 45 G6 51 49N 19 42 E
Brzozów, Poland 45 J9 49 41N 22 3 E
Bsharri, Lebanon 75 A5 34 15N 36 0 E
Bū Baqarah, U.A.E. 71 E8 25 35N 56 25 E
Bu Craa, W. Sahara 78 C3 26 45N 12 50W
Bū Ḥasā, U.A.E. 71 F7 23 30N 53 20 E
Bua, Sweden 11 G6 57 14N 12 7 E
Bua Yai, Thailand 64 E4 15 33N 102 26 E
Buapinang, Indonesia 63 E6 4 40 S 121 30 E
Buba, Guinea-Biss. 82 C2 11 40N 14 59W
Bubanza, Burundi 86 C2 3 6 S 29 23 E
Bubaque, Guinea-Biss. 82 C1 11 16N 15 51W
Bube, Ethiopia 81 F4 8 46N 35 48 E
Būbiyān, Kuwait 71 D6 29 45N 48 15 E
Buca, Turkey 39 C9 38 22N 27 11 E
Bucak, Turkey 39 D12 37 28N 30 36 E
Bucaramanga, Colombia 124 B4 7 0N 73 0W
Bucas Grande I., Phil. 61 G6 9 40N 125 57 E
Bucasia, Australia 94 C4 21 2 S 149 10 E
Buccaneer Arch., Australia 92 C3 16 7 S 123 20 E
Buccino, Italy 31 B8 40 38N 15 22 E
Bucecea, Romania 43 C11 47 47N 26 28 E
Buchach, Ukraine 47 H3 49 5N 25 25 E
Buchan, U.K. 14 D6 57 32N 2 21W
Buchan Ness, U.K. 14 D7 57 29N 1 46W
Buchanan, Canada 105 C8 51 40N 102 45W
Buchanan, Liberia 82 D2 5 57N 10 2W
Buchanan, L., Queens., Australia 94 C4 21 35 S 145 52 E
Buchanan, L., W. Austral., Australia 93 E3 25 33 S 123 2 E
Buchanan, L., U.S.A. 113 K5 30 45N 98 25W
Buchanan Cr. →, Australia 94 B2 19 13 S 136 33 E
Buchans, Canada 103 C8 48 50N 56 52W
Bucharest = Bucureşti, Romania 43 F11 44 27N 26 10 E
Buchen, Germany 25 F5 49 32N 9 20 E
Buchholz, Germany 24 B5 53 19N 9 52 E
Buchloe, Germany 25 G6 48 1N 10 44 E
Buchon, Pt., U.S.A. 116 K6 35 15N 120 54W
Buciumi, Romania 42 C8 47 3N 23 1 E
Buck Hill Falls, U.S.A. 111 E9 41 11N 75 16W
Bückeburg, Germany 24 C5 52 16N 9 7 E
Buckeye, U.S.A. 115 K7 33 22N 112 35W
Buckeye Lake, U.S.A. 110 G2 39 55N 82 29W
Buckhannon, U.S.A. 108 F5 39 0N 80 8W
Buckhaven, U.K. 14 E5 56 11N 3 3W
Buckhorn L., Canada 110 B6 44 29N 78 23W
Buckie, U.K. 14 D6 57 41N 2 58W
Buckingham, Canada 102 C4 45 37N 75 24W
Buckingham, U.K. 13 F7 51 59N 0 57W
Buckingham B., Australia 94 A2 12 10 S 135 40 E
Buckinghamshire □, U.K. 13 F7 51 53N 0 55W
Buckle Hd., Australia 92 B4 14 26 S 127 52 E
Buckleboo, Australia 95 E2 32 54 S 136 12 E
Buckley, U.K. 12 D4 53 10N 3 5W
Buckley →, Australia 94 C2 20 10 S 138 49 E
Bucklin, U.S.A. 113 G5 37 33N 99 38W
Bucks L., U.S.A. 116 F5 39 54N 121 12W
Bucquoy, France 19 B9 50 9N 2 43 E
Buctouche, Canada 103 C7 46 30N 64 45W
Bucureşti, Romania 43 F11 44 27N 26 10 E
Bucyrus, U.S.A. 108 E4 40 48N 82 59W
Budacu, Vf., Romania 43 C10 47 7N 25 41 E
Budalin, Burma 67 H19 22 20N 95 10 E
Budaörs, Hungary 42 C3 47 27N 18 58 E
Budapest, Hungary 42 C4 47 29N 19 5 E
Budapest □, Hungary 42 C4 47 29N 19 5 E
Budaun, India 69 E8 28 5N 79 10 E
Budd Coast, Antarctica 5 C8 68 0 S 112 0 E
Buddusò, Italy 30 B2 40 35N 9 15 E
Bude, U.K. 13 G3 50 49N 4 34W
Budennovsk, Russia 49 H7 44 50N 44 10 E
Budeşti, Romania 43 F11 44 13N 26 30 E
Budge Budge = Baj Baj, India 69 H13 22 30N 88 5 E
Budgewoi, Australia 95 E5 33 13 S 151 34 E
Budia, Spain 32 E2 40 38N 2 46W
Büdingen, Germany 25 E5 50 16N 9 7 E
Budjala, Dem. Rep. of the Congo 84 D3 2 50N 19 40 E
Budoni, Italy 30 B2 40 40N 9 45 E
Búdrio, Italy 29 D8 44 32N 11 32 E
Budva, Montenegro, Yug. 40 D2 42 17N 18 50 E
Budzyń, Poland 45 F3 52 54N 16 59 E
Buea, Cameroon 83 E6 4 10N 9 9 E
Buellton, U.S.A. 117 L6 34 37N 120 12W
Buena Esperanza, Argentina 126 C2 34 45 S 65 15W
Buena Park, U.S.A. 117 M9 33 52N 117 59W
Buena Vista, Colo., U.S.A. 115 G10 38 51N 106 8W
Buena Vista, Va., U.S.A. 108 G6 37 44N 79 21W
Buena Vista Lake Bed, U.S.A. 117 K7 35 12N 119 18W
Buenaventura, Colombia 124 C3 3 53N 77 4W
Buenaventura, Mexico 118 B3 29 50N 107 30W
Buendía, Embalse de, Spain 32 E2 40 25N 2 43W
Buenos Aires, Argentina 126 C4 34 30 S 58 20W
Buenos Aires, Costa Rica 120 E3 9 10N 83 20W
Buenos Aires □, Argentina 126 D4 36 30 S 60 0W
Buenos Aires, L., Chile 128 F2 46 35 S 72 30W
Buffalo, Mo., U.S.A. 113 G8 37 39N 93 6W
Buffalo, N.Y., U.S.A. 110 D6 42 53N 78 53W
Buffalo, Okla., U.S.A. 113 G5 36 50N 99 38W
Buffalo, S. Dak., U.S.A. 112 C3 45 35N 103 33W
Buffalo, Wyo., U.S.A. 114 D10 44 21N 106 42W
Buffalo →, Canada 104 A5 60 5N 115 5W
Buffalo →, S. Africa 89 D5 28 43 S 30 37 E
Buffalo Head Hills, Canada 104 B5 57 25N 115 55W
Buffalo L., Alta., Canada 104 C6 52 27N 112 54W
Buffalo L., N.W.T., Canada 104 A5 60 12N 115 25W
Buffalo Narrows, Canada 105 B7 55 51N 108 29W
Buffels →, S. Africa 88 D2 29 36 S 17 3 E
Buford, U.S.A. 109 H4 34 10N 84 0W
Bug = Buh →, Ukraine 47 J6 46 59N 31 58 E
Bug →, Poland 45 F8 52 31N 21 5 E
Buga, Colombia 124 C3 4 0N 76 15W
Buganda, Uganda 86 C3 0 0 31 30 E
Buganga, Uganda 86 C3 0 3 S 32 0 E
Bugasong, Phil. 61 F5 11 3N 122 4 E
Bugeat, France 20 C5 45 36N 1 55 E
Bugel, Tanjung, Indonesia 63 G14 6 26 S 111 3 E
Bugibba, Malta 36 D1 35 57N 14 25 E
Bugojno, Bos.-H. 42 F2 44 2N 17 25 E
Bugsuk, Phil. 62 C5 8 15N 117 15 E
Buguma, Nigeria 83 E6 4 42N 6 55 E
Bugun Shara, Mongolia 60 B5 49 0N 104 0 E
Buguruslan, Russia 50 D6 53 39N 52 26 E
Buh →, Ukraine 47 J6 46 59N 31 58 E
Buharkent, Turkey 39 D10 37 58N 28 44 E
Buheirat-Murrat-el-Kubra, Egypt 80 H8 30 18N 32 26 E
Buhera, Zimbabwe 89 B5 19 18 S 31 29 E
Bühl, Germany 25 G4 48 40N 8 8 E
Buhl, U.S.A. 114 E6 42 36N 114 46W
Buhuşi, Romania 43 D11 46 41N 26 45 E
Builth Wells, U.K. 13 E4 52 9N 3 25W
Buinsk, Russia 48 C9 55 0N 48 18 E
Buir Nur, Mongolia 60 B6 47 50N 117 42 E
Buis-les-Baronnies, France 21 D9 44 17N 5 16 E
Buitrago = Buitrago del Lozoya, Spain 34 E7 40 58N 3 38W
Buitrago del Lozoya, Spain 34 E7 40 58N 3 38W
Bujalance, Spain 35 H6 37 54N 4 23W
Bujanovac, Serbia, Yug. 40 D5 42 28N 21 44 E
Bujaraloz, Spain 32 D4 41 29N 0 10W
Buje, Croatia 29 C10 45 24N 13 39 E
Bujumbura, Burundi 86 C2 3 16 S 29 18 E
Bük, Hungary 42 C1 47 22N 16 45 E
Buk, Poland 45 F3 52 21N 16 30 E
Bukachacha, Russia 51 D12 52 55N 116 50 E
Bukama, Dem. Rep. of the Congo 87 D2 9 10 S 25 50 E
Bukavu, Dem. Rep. of the Congo 86 C2 2 20 S 28 52 E
Bukene, Tanzania 86 C3 4 15 S 32 48 E
Bukhara = Bukhoro, Uzbekistan 50 F7 39 48N 64 25 E
Bukhoro, Uzbekistan 50 F7 39 48N 64 25 E
Bukima, Tanzania 86 C3 1 50 S 33 25 E
Bukit Mertajam, Malaysia 65 K3 5 22N 100 28 E
Bukittinggi, Indonesia 62 E2 0 20 S 100 20 E
Bükk, Hungary 42 B5 48 0N 20 30 E
Bukoba, Tanzania 86 C3 1 20 S 31 49 E
Bukuru, Nigeria 83 D6 9 42N 8 48 E
Bukuya, Uganda 86 B3 0 40N 31 52 E
Būl, Kuh-e, Iran 71 D7 30 48N 52 45 E
Bula, Guinea-Biss. 82 C1 12 7N 15 43W
Bula, Indonesia 63 E8 3 6 S 130 30 E
Bülach, Switz. 25 H4 47 31N 8 32 E
Bulahdelah, Australia 95 E5 32 23 S 152 13 E
Bulan, Phil. 61 E5 12 40N 123 52 E
Bulancak, Turkey 73 B8 40 56N 38 14 E
Bulandshahr, India 68 E7 28 28N 77 51 E
Bulanık, Turkey 73 C10 39 4N 42 14 E
Bûlâq, Egypt 80 B3 25 10N 30 38 E
Bulawayo, Zimbabwe 87 G2 20 7 S 28 32 E
Buldan, Turkey 39 C10 38 2N 28 50 E
Bulgar, Russia 48 C9 54 57N 49 4 E
Bulgaria ■, Europe 41 D9 42 35N 25 30 E
Bulgheria, Monte, Italy 31 B8 40 4N 15 26 E
Bulgurca, Turkey 39 C9 38 9N 27 9 E
Buli, Teluk, Indonesia 63 D7 0 48N 128 25 E
Buliluyan, C., Phil. 61 G1 8 20N 117 15 E
Bulki, Ethiopia 81 F4 6 11N 36 31 E
Bulkley →, Canada 104 B3 55 15N 127 40W
Bull Shoals L., U.S.A. 113 G8 36 22N 92 35W
Bullaque →, Spain 35 G6 38 59N 4 17W
Bullas, Spain 33 G3 38 2N 1 40W
Bulle, Switz. 25 J3 46 37N 7 3 E
Bullhead City, U.S.A. 117 K12 35 8N 114 32W
Büllingen, Belgium 17 D6 50 25N 6 16 E
Bullock Creek, Australia 94 B3 17 43 S 144 31 E
Bulloo →, Australia 95 D3 28 43 S 142 30 E
Bulloo L., Australia 95 D3 28 43 S 142 25 E
Bulls, N.Z. 91 J5 40 10 S 175 24 E
Bully-les-Mines, France 19 B9 50 27N 2 44 E
Bulnes, Chile 126 D1 36 42 S 72 19W
Bulqizë, Albania 40 E4 41 30N 20 21 E
Bulsar = Valsad, India 66 J8 20 40N 72 58 E
Bultfontein, S. Africa 88 D4 28 18 S 26 10 E
Bulukumba, Indonesia 63 F6 5 33 S 120 11 E
Bulun, Russia 51 B13 70 37N 127 30 E
Bumba, Dem. Rep. of the Congo 84 D4 2 13N 22 30 E

Calvinia

Calvinia, S. Africa **88 E2** 31 28 S 19 45 E
Calvo = Calvo, Mte., Italy **29 G12** 41 44N 15 46 E
Calvo, Mte., Italy **29 G12** 41 44N 15 46 E
Calwa, U.S.A. **116 J7** 36 42N 119 46W
Calzada Almuradiel = Almuradiel, Spain **35 G7** 38 32N 3 28W
Calzada de Calatrava, Spain **35 G7** 38 42N 3 46W
Cam →, U.K. **13 E8** 52 21N 0 16 E
Cam Lam, Vietnam **65 G7** 11 54N 109 10 E
Cam Pha, Vietnam **58 G6** 21 7N 107 18 E
Cam Ranh, Vietnam **65 G7** 11 54N 109 12 E
Cam Xuyen, Vietnam **64 C6** 18 15N 106 0 E
Camabatela, Angola **84 F3** 8 20 S 15 26 E
Camacha, Madeira **37 D3** 32 41N 16 49W
Camacho, Mexico **118 C4** 24 25N 102 18W
Camacupa, Angola **85 G3** 11 58 S 17 22 E
Camagüey, Cuba **120 B4** 21 20N 78 0W
Camaiore, Italy **28 E7** 43 56N 10 18 E
Camaná, Peru **124 G4** 16 30 S 72 50W
Camanche Reservoir, U.S.A. **116 G6** 38 14N 121 1W
Camaquã, Brazil **127 C5** 30 51 S 51 49W
Camaquã →, Brazil **127 C5** 31 17 S 51 47W
Câmara de Lobos, Madeira **37 D3** 32 39N 16 59W
Camarat, C., France **21 E10** 43 12N 6 41 E
Camarès, France **20 E6** 43 49N 2 53 E
Camaret-sur-Mer, France **18 D2** 48 16N 4 37W
Camargo, Mexico **119 B5** 26 19N 98 50W
Camargue, France **21 E8** 43 34N 4 34 E
Camarillo, U.S.A. **117 L7** 34 13N 119 2W
Camariñas, Spain **34 B1** 43 8N 9 12W
Camarón, C., Honduras **120 C2** 16 0N 85 5W
Camarones, Argentina **128 E3** 44 50 S 65 40W
Camas, Spain **35 H4** 37 24N 6 2W
Camas, U.S.A. **116 E4** 45 35N 122 24W
Camas Valley, U.S.A. **114 E2** 43 2N 123 40W
Camballin, Australia **92 C3** 17 59 S 124 12 E
Cambará, Brazil **127 A5** 23 2 S 50 5W
Cambay = Khambhat, India **68 H5** 22 23N 72 33 E
Cambay, G. of = Khambhat, G. of, India **66 J8** 20 45N 72 30 E
Cambil, Spain **35 H7** 37 40N 3 33W
Cambo-les-Bains, France **20 E2** 43 22N 1 23W
Cambodia ■, Asia **64 F5** 12 15N 105 0 E
Camborne, U.K. **13 G2** 50 12N 5 19W
Cambrai, France **19 B10** 50 11N 3 14 E
Cambre, Spain **34 B2** 43 17N 8 20W
Cambria, U.S.A. **116 K5** 35 34N 121 5W
Cambrian Mts., U.K. **13 E4** 52 3N 3 57W
Cambridge, Canada **102 D3** 43 23N 80 15W
Cambridge, Jamaica **120 C4** 18 18N 77 54W
Cambridge, N.Z. **91 G5** 37 54 S 175 29 E
Cambridge, U.K. **13 E8** 52 12N 0 8 E
Cambridge, Mass., U.S.A. **111 D13** 42 22N 71 6W
Cambridge, Minn., U.S.A. **112 C8** 45 34N 93 13W
Cambridge, N.Y., U.S.A. **111 C11** 43 2N 73 22W
Cambridge, Nebr., U.S.A. **112 E4** 40 17N 100 10W
Cambridge, Ohio, U.S.A. **110 F3** 40 2N 81 35W
Cambridge Bay = Ikaluktutiak, Canada **100 B9** 69 10N 105 0W
Cambridge G., Australia **92 B4** 14 55 S 128 15 E
Cambridge Springs, U.S.A. **110 E4** 41 48N 80 4W
Cambridgeshire □, U.K. **13 E7** 52 25N 0 7W
Cambrils, Spain **32 D6** 41 8N 1 3 E
Cambuci, Brazil **127 A7** 21 35 S 41 55W
Cambundi-Catembo, Angola **84 G3** 10 10 S 17 35 E
Camden, Ala., U.S.A. **109 K2** 31 59N 87 17W
Camden, Ark., U.S.A. **113 J8** 33 35N 92 50W
Camden, Maine, U.S.A. **109 C11** 44 13N 69 4W
Camden, N.J., U.S.A. **111 G9** 39 56N 75 7W
Camden, N.Y., U.S.A. **111 C9** 43 20N 75 45W
Camden, S.C., U.S.A. **109 H5** 34 16N 80 36W
Camden Sd., Australia **92 C3** 15 27 S 124 25 E
Camdenton, U.S.A. **113 F8** 38 1N 92 45W
Çameli, Turkey **39 D11** 37 5N 29 24 E
Camenca, Moldova **43 B13** 48 3N 28 42 E
Camerino, Italy **29 E10** 43 8N 13 4 E
Cameron, Ariz., U.S.A. **115 J8** 35 53N 111 25W
Cameron, La., U.S.A. **113 L8** 29 48N 93 20W
Cameron, Mo., U.S.A. **112 F7** 39 44N 94 14W
Cameron, Tex., U.S.A. **113 K6** 30 51N 96 59W
Cameron Highlands, Malaysia **65 K3** 4 27N 101 22 E
Cameron Hills, Canada **104 B5** 59 48N 118 0W
Cameroon ■, Africa **84 C2** 6 0N 12 30 E
Camerota, Italy **31 B8** 40 2N 15 22 E
Cameroun →, Cameroon **83 E6** 4 0N 9 35 E
Cameroun, Mt., Cameroon **83 E6** 4 13N 9 10 E
Cametá, Brazil **125 D9** 2 12 S 49 30W
Çamiçi Gölü, Turkey **39 D9** 37 29N 27 28 E
Camiguin □, Phil. **61 G6** 9 11N 124 42 E
Camiguin I., Phil. **61 B4** 18 56N 121 55 E
Camiling, Phil. **61 D4** 15 42N 120 24 E
Camilla, U.S.A. **109 K3** 31 14N 84 12W
Caminha, Portugal **34 D2** 41 50N 8 50W
Camino, U.S.A. **116 G6** 38 44N 120 41W
Camira Creek, Australia **95 D5** 29 15 S 152 58 E
Cammal, U.S.A. **110 E7** 41 24N 77 28W
Cammarata, Italy **30 E6** 37 38N 13 38 E
Camocim, Brazil **125 D10** 2 55 S 40 50W
Camooweal, Australia **94 B2** 19 56 S 138 7 E
Camopi, Fr. Guiana **125 C8** 3 12N 52 17W
Camotes Is., Phil. **61 F6** 10 40N 124 24 E
Camotes Sea, Phil. **61 F6** 10 30N 124 15 E
Camp Borden, Canada **110 B5** 44 18N 79 56W
Camp Hill, U.S.A. **110 F8** 40 14N 76 55W
Camp Nelson, U.S.A. **117 J8** 36 8N 118 39W
Camp Pendleton, U.S.A. **117 M9** 33 16N 117 23W
Camp Verde, U.S.A. **115 J8** 34 34N 111 51W
Camp Wood, U.S.A. **113 L5** 29 40N 100 1W
Campagna, Italy **31 B8** 40 40N 15 6 E
Campana, Argentina **126 C4** 34 10 S 58 55W
Campana, I., Chile **128 F1** 48 20 S 75 20W
Campanário, Madeira **37 D2** 32 39N 17 2W
Campanario, Spain **35 G5** 38 52N 5 36W
Campánia □, Italy **31 B7** 41 0N 14 30 E
Campbell, S. Africa **88 D3** 28 48 S 23 44 E
Campbell, Calif., U.S.A. **116 H5** 37 17N 121 57W
Campbell, Ohio, U.S.A. **110 E4** 41 5N 80 37W
Campbell I., Pac. Oc. **96 N8** 52 30 S 169 0 E
Campbell L., Canada **105 A7** 63 14N 106 55W
Campbell River, Canada **104 C3** 50 5N 125 20W
Campbell Town, Australia **94 G4** 41 52 S 147 30 E
Campbellford, Canada **110 B7** 44 18N 77 48W
Campbellpur, Pakistan **68 C5** 33 46N 72 26 E
Campbellsville, U.S.A. **108 G3** 37 21N 85 20W
Campbellton, Canada **103 C6** 47 57N 66 43W
Campbelltown, Australia **95 E5** 34 4 S 150 49 E
Campbeltown, U.K. **14 F3** 55 26N 5 36W
Campeche, Mexico **119 D6** 19 50N 90 32W
Campeche □, Mexico **119 D6** 19 50N 90 32W
Campeche, Golfo de, Mexico **119 D6** 19 30N 93 0W
Campello, Spain **33 G4** 38 26N 0 24W
Câmpeni, Romania **42 D8** 46 22N 23 3 E
Camperdown, Australia **95 F3** 38 14 S 143 9 E
Camperville, Canada **105 C8** 51 59N 100 9W
Campi Salentina, Italy **31 B11** 40 24N 18 1 E
Câmpia Turzii, Romania **43 D8** 46 34N 23 53 E
Campidano, Italy **30 C1** 39 30N 8 47 E
Campíglia Maríttima, Italy **28 E7** 43 4N 10 37 E
Campillo de Altobuey, Spain **33 F3** 39 36N 1 49W
Campillos, Spain **35 H6** 37 4N 4 51W
Câmpina, Romania **43 E10** 45 10N 25 45 E
Campina Grande, Brazil **125 E11** 7 20 S 35 47W
Campinas, Brazil **127 A6** 22 50 S 47 0W
Campli, Italy **29 F10** 42 43N 13 41 E
Campo, Spain **32 C5** 42 25N 0 24 E
Campo de Criptana, Spain **35 F7** 39 24N 3 7W
Campo de Gibraltar, Spain **35 J5** 36 15N 5 25W
Campo Grande, Brazil **125 H8** 20 25 S 54 40W
Campo Maíor, Brazil **125 D10** 4 50 S 42 12W
Campo Maior, Portugal **35 F3** 39 2N 7 7W
Campo Mourão, Brazil **127 A5** 24 3 S 52 22W
Campo Túres, Italy **29 B8** 46 53N 11 55 E
Campobasso, Italy **31 A7** 41 34N 14 39 E
Campobello di Licata, Italy **30 E6** 37 15N 13 55 E
Campobello di Mazara, Italy **30 E5** 37 38N 12 45 E
Campofelice di Roccella, Italy **30 E6** 37 59N 13 53 E
Campomarino, Italy **29 G12** 41 57N 15 2 E
Camporeale, Italy **30 E5** 37 54N 13 6 E
Camporrobles, Spain **32 F3** 39 39N 1 24W
Campos, Brazil **127 A7** 21 50 S 41 20W
Campos Belos, Brazil **125 F9** 13 10 S 47 3W
Campos del Puerto, Spain **37 B10** 39 26N 3 1 E
Campos Novos, Brazil **127 B5** 27 21 S 51 50W
Camprodón, Spain **32 C7** 42 19N 2 23 E
Camptonville, U.S.A. **116 F5** 39 27N 121 3W
Camptown, U.S.A. **111 E8** 41 44N 76 14W
Câmpulung, Argeş, Romania **43 E10** 45 17N 25 3 E
Câmpulung, Suceava, Romania **43 C10** 47 32N 25 30 E
Câmpuri, Romania **43 D11** 46 0N 26 50 E
Camrose, Canada **104 C6** 53 0N 112 50W
Camsell Portage, Canada **105 B7** 59 37N 109 15W
Çamyuva, Turkey **39 E12** 36 30N 30 30 E
Çan, Turkey **41 F11** 40 2N 27 3 E
Can Clavo, Spain **37 C7** 38 57N 1 27 E
Can Creu, Spain **37 C7** 38 58N 1 28 E
Can Gio, Vietnam **65 G6** 10 25N 106 58 E
Can Tho, Vietnam **65 G5** 10 2N 105 46 E
Canaan, U.S.A. **111 D11** 42 2N 73 20W
Canada ■, N. Amer. **100 C10** 60 0N 100 0W
Cañada de Gómez, Argentina **126 C3** 32 40 S 61 30W
Canadian, U.S.A. **113 H4** 35 55N 100 23W
Canadian →, U.S.A. **113 H7** 35 28N 95 3W
Canajoharie, U.S.A. **111 D10** 42 54N 74 35W
Çanakkale, Turkey **41 F10** 40 8N 26 24 E
Çanakkale □, Turkey **41 F10** 40 10N 26 25 E
Çanakkale Boğazı, Turkey **41 F10** 40 17N 26 32 E
Canal Flats, Canada **104 C5** 50 10N 115 48W
Canalejas, Argentina **126 D2** 35 15 S 66 34W
Canals, Argentina **126 C3** 33 35 S 62 53W
Canals, Spain **33 G4** 38 58N 0 35W
Canandaigua, U.S.A. **110 D7** 42 54N 77 17W
Canandaigua L., U.S.A. **110 D7** 42 47N 77 19W
Cananea, Mexico **118 A2** 31 0N 110 20W
Canarias, Is., Atl. Oc. **37 F4** 28 30N 16 0W
Canarreos, Arch. de los, Cuba **120 B3** 21 35N 81 40W
Canary Is. = Canarias, Is., Atl. Oc. **37 F4** 28 30N 16 0W
Canaseraga, U.S.A. **110 D7** 42 27N 77 45W
Canatlán, Mexico **118 C4** 24 31N 104 47W
Canaveral, C., U.S.A. **109 L5** 28 27N 80 32W
Cañaveruelas, Spain **32 E2** 40 24N 2 38W
Canavieiras, Brazil **125 G11** 15 39 S 39 0W
Canberra, Australia **95 F4** 35 15 S 149 8 E
Canby, Calif., U.S.A. **114 F3** 41 27N 120 52W
Canby, Minn., U.S.A. **112 C6** 44 43N 96 16W
Canby, Oreg., U.S.A. **116 E4** 45 16N 122 42W
Cancale, France **18 D5** 48 40N 1 50W
Canche →, France **19 B8** 50 31N 1 39 E
Cancún, Mexico **119 C7** 21 8N 86 44W
Candanchu, Spain **32 C4** 42 47N 0 32W
Çandarlı, Turkey **39 C8** 38 56N 26 56 E
Çandarlı Körfezi, Turkey **39 C8** 38 52N 26 55 E
Candas, Spain **34 B5** 43 35N 5 45W
Candé, France **18 E5** 47 34N 1 2W
Candela, Italy **31 A8** 41 8N 15 31 E
Candelaria, Argentina **127 B4** 27 29 S 55 44W
Candelaria, Canary Is. **37 F3** 28 22N 16 22W
Candeleda, Spain **34 E5** 40 10N 5 14W
Candelo, Australia **95 F4** 36 47 S 149 43 E
Candia = Iráklion, Greece **36 D7** 35 20N 25 12 E
Candia, Sea of = Crete, Sea of, Greece **39 E7** 36 0N 25 0 E
Candle L., Canada **105 C7** 53 50N 105 18W
Candlemas I., Antarctica **5 B1** 57 3 S 26 40W
Cando, U.S.A. **112 A5** 48 32N 99 12W
Candon, Phil. **61 C4** 17 12N 120 27 E
Canea = Khaniá, Greece **36 D6** 35 30N 24 4 E
Canelli, Italy **28 D5** 44 43N 8 17 E
Canelones, Uruguay **127 C4** 34 32 S 56 17W
Canet-Plage, France **20 F7** 42 41N 3 2 E
Cañete, Chile **126 D1** 37 50 S 73 30W
Cañete, Peru **124 F3** 13 8 S 76 30W
Cañete, Spain **32 E3** 40 3N 1 54W
Cañete de las Torres, Spain **35 H6** 37 53N 4 19W
Cangas, Spain **34 C2** 42 16N 8 47W
Cangas de Narcea, Spain **34 B4** 43 10N 6 32W
Cangas de Onís, Spain **34 B5** 43 21N 5 8W
Cangnan, China **59 D13** 27 30N 120 23 E
Canguaretama, Brazil **125 E11** 6 20 S 35 5W
Canguçu, Brazil **127 C5** 31 22 S 52 43W
Canguçu, Serra do, Brazil **127 C5** 31 20 S 52 40W
Cangwu, China **59 F8** 23 25N 111 17 E
Cangxi, China **58 B5** 31 47N 105 59 E
Cangyuan, China **58 F2** 23 12N 99 14 E
Cangzhou, China **56 E9** 38 19N 116 52 E
Caniapiscau →, Canada **103 A6** 56 40N 69 30W
Caniapiscau, Rés. de, Canada **103 B6** 54 10N 69 55W
Canicattì, Italy **30 E6** 37 21N 13 51 E
Canicattini Bagni, Italy **31 E8** 37 2N 15 4 E
Caniles, Spain **35 H8** 37 26N 2 43W
Canim Lake, Canada **104 C4** 51 47N 120 54W
Canindeyu □, Paraguay **127 A5** 24 10 S 55 0W
Canino, Italy **29 F8** 42 28N 11 45 E
Canisteo, U.S.A. **110 D7** 42 16N 77 36W
Canisteo →, U.S.A. **110 D7** 42 7N 77 8W
Cañitas, Mexico **118 C4** 23 36N 102 43W
Cañizal, Spain **34 D5** 41 12N 5 22W
Canjáyar, Spain **35 H8** 37 1N 2 44W
Çankırı, Turkey **72 B5** 40 40N 33 37 E
Cankuzo, Burundi **86 C3** 3 10 S 30 31 E
Canmore, Canada **104 C5** 51 7N 115 18W
Cann River, Australia **95 F4** 37 35 S 149 7 E
Canna, U.K. **14 D2** 57 3N 6 33W
Cannanore, India **66 P9** 11 53N 75 27 E
Cannes, France **21 E11** 43 32N 7 1 E
Canning Town = Port Canning, India **69 H13** 22 23N 88 40 E
Cannington, Canada **110 B5** 44 20N 79 2W
Cannóbio, Italy **28 B5** 46 4N 8 42 E
Cannock, U.K. **13 E5** 52 41N 2 1W
Cannon Ball →, U.S.A. **112 B4** 46 20N 100 38W
Cannondale Mt., Australia **94 D4** 25 13 S 148 57 E
Cannonsville Reservoir, U.S.A. **111 D9** 42 4N 75 22W
Cannonvale, Australia **94 C4** 20 17 S 148 43 E
Canoas, Brazil **127 B5** 29 56 S 51 11W
Canoe L., Canada **105 B7** 55 10N 108 15W
Canon City, U.S.A. **112 F2** 38 27N 105 14W
Canora, Canada **105 C8** 51 40N 102 30W
Canosa di Púglia, Italy **31 A9** 41 13N 16 4 E
Canowindra, Australia **95 E4** 33 35 S 148 38 E
Canso, Canada **103 C7** 45 20N 61 0W
Cantabria □, Spain **34 B7** 43 10N 4 0W
Cantabria, Sierra de, Spain **32 C2** 42 40N 2 30W
Cantabrian Mts. = Cantábrica, Cordillera, Spain **34 C5** 43 0N 5 10W
Cantábrica, Cordillera, Spain **34 C5** 43 0N 5 10W
Cantal □, France **20 C6** 45 5N 2 45 E
Cantal, Plomb du, France **20 C6** 45 3N 2 45 E
Cantanhede, Portugal **34 E2** 40 20N 8 36W
Cantavieja, Spain **32 E4** 40 31N 0 25W
Čantavir, Serbia, Yug. **42 E4** 45 55N 19 46 E
Cantemir, Moldova **43 D13** 46 17N 28 14 E
Canterbury, Australia **94 D3** 25 23 S 141 53 E
Canterbury, U.K. **13 F9** 51 16N 1 6 E
Canterbury Bight, N.Z. **91 L3** 44 16 S 171 55 E
Canterbury Plains, N.Z. **91 K3** 43 55 S 171 22 E
Cantil, U.S.A. **117 K9** 35 18N 117 58W
Cantillana, Spain **35 H5** 37 36N 5 50W
Canton = Guangzhou, China **59 F9** 23 5N 113 10 E
Canton, Ga., U.S.A. **109 H3** 34 14N 84 29W
Canton, Ill., U.S.A. **112 E9** 40 33N 90 2W
Canton, Miss., U.S.A. **113 J9** 32 37N 90 2W
Canton, Mo., U.S.A. **112 E9** 40 8N 91 32W
Canton, N.Y., U.S.A. **111 B9** 44 36N 75 10W
Canton, Ohio, U.S.A. **110 F3** 40 48N 81 23W
Canton, Pa., U.S.A. **110 E8** 41 39N 76 51W
Canton, S. Dak., U.S.A. **112 D6** 43 18N 96 35W
Canton L., U.S.A. **113 G5** 36 6N 98 35W
Cantù, Italy **28 C6** 45 44N 9 8 E
Canudos, Brazil **124 E7** 7 13 S 58 5W
Canumã →, Brazil **124 D7** 3 55 S 59 10W
Canutama, Brazil **124 E6** 6 30 S 64 20W
Canutillo, U.S.A. **115 L10** 31 55N 106 36W
Canvey, U.K. **13 F8** 51 31N 0 37 E
Canyon, U.S.A. **113 H4** 34 59N 101 55W
Canyonlands National Park, U.S.A. **115 G9** 38 15N 110 0W
Canyonville, U.S.A. **114 E2** 42 56N 123 17W
Cao Bang, Vietnam **58 F6** 22 40N 106 15 E
Cao He →, China **57 D13** 40 10N 124 32 E
Cao Lanh, Vietnam **65 G5** 10 27N 105 38 E
Cao Xian, China **56 G8** 34 50N 115 35 E
Càorle, Italy **29 C9** 45 36N 12 53 E
Cap-aux-Meules, Canada **103 C7** 47 23N 61 52W
Cap-Chat, Canada **103 C6** 49 6N 66 40W
Cap-de-la-Madeleine, Canada **102 C5** 46 22N 72 31W
Cap-Haïtien, Haiti **121 C5** 19 40N 72 20W
Capac, U.S.A. **110 C2** 43 1N 82 56W
Capáccio, Italy **31 B8** 40 25N 15 5 E
Capaci, Italy **30 D6** 38 10N 13 14 E
Capanaparo →, Venezuela **124 B5** 7 1N 67 7W
Capánnori, Italy **28 E7** 43 50N 10 34 E
Capbreton, France **20 E2** 43 39N 1 26W
Capdenac, France **20 D6** 44 34N 2 5 E
Capdepera, Spain **32 F8** 39 42N 3 26 E
Cape →, Australia **94 C4** 20 59 S 146 51 E
Cape Barren I., Australia **94 G4** 40 25 S 148 15 E
Cape Breton Highlands Nat. Park, Canada **103 C7** 46 50N 60 40W
Cape Breton I., Canada **103 C7** 46 0N 60 30W
Cape Charles, U.S.A. **108 G8** 37 16N 76 1W
Cape Coast, Ghana **83 D4** 5 5N 1 15W
Cape Coral, U.S.A. **109 M5** 26 33N 81 57W
Cape Dorset, Canada **101 B12** 64 14N 76 32W
Cape Fear →, U.S.A. **109 H6** 33 53N 78 1W
Cape Girardeau, U.S.A. **113 G10** 37 19N 89 32W
Cape May, U.S.A. **108 F8** 38 56N 74 56W
Cape May Point, U.S.A. **108 F8** 38 56N 74 58W
Cape Province, S. Africa **85 L3** 32 0 S 23 0 E
Cape Tormentine, Canada **103 C7** 46 8N 63 47W
Cape Town, S. Africa **88 E2** 33 55 S 18 22 E
Cape Verde Is. ■, Atl. Oc. **77 E1** 17 10N 25 20W
Cape Vincent, U.S.A. **111 B8** 44 8N 76 20W
Cape York Peninsula, Australia **94 A3** 12 0 S 142 30 E
Capela, Brazil **125 F11** 10 30 S 37 0W
Capella, Australia **94 C4** 23 2 S 148 1 E
Capendu, France **20 E6** 43 11N 2 31 E
Capestang, France **20 E7** 43 20N 3 2 E
Capim →, Brazil **125 D9** 1 40 S 47 47W
Capistrello, Italy **29 G10** 41 57N 13 23 E
Capitan, U.S.A. **115 K11** 33 35N 105 35W
Capitol Reef National Park, U.S.A. **115 G8** 38 15N 111 10W
Capitola, U.S.A. **116 J5** 36 59N 121 57W
Capizzi, Italy **31 E7** 37 51N 14 29 E
Capoche →, Mozam. **87 F3** 15 35 S 33 0 E
Capoterra, Italy **30 C1** 39 11N 8 58 E
Cappadocia, Turkey **72 C6** 39 0N 35 0 E
Capraia, Italy **28 E6** 43 2N 9 50 E
Caprara, Pta., Italy **30 A1** 41 7N 8 19 E
Caprarola, Italy **29 F9** 42 19N 12 14 E
Capreol, Canada **102 C3** 46 43N 80 56W
Caprera, Italy **30 A2** 41 12N 9 28 E
Capri, Italy **31 B7** 40 33N 14 14 E
Capricorn Group, Australia **94 C5** 23 30 S 151 55 E
Capricorn Ra., Australia **92 D2** 23 20 S 116 50 E
Caprino Veronese, Italy **28 C7** 45 36N 10 47 E
Caprivi Strip, Namibia **88 B3** 18 0 S 23 0 E
Captain's Flat, Australia **95 F4** 35 35 S 149 27 E
Captieux, France **20 D3** 44 18N 0 16W
Caquetá →, Colombia **122 D4** 1 15 S 69 15W
Caracal, Romania **43 F9** 44 8N 24 22 E
Caracas, Venezuela **124 A5** 10 30N 66 55W
Caracol, Mato Grosso do Sul, Brazil **126 A4** 22 18 S 57 1W
Caracol, Piauí, Brazil **125 E10** 9 15 S 43 22W
Caráglio, Italy **28 D4** 44 25N 7 26 E
Carajas, Brazil **125 E8** 6 5 S 50 23W
Carajás, Serra dos, Brazil **125 E8** 6 0 S 51 30W
Carangola, Brazil **127 A7** 20 44 S 42 5W
Caransebeş, Romania **42 E7** 45 28N 22 18 E
Carantec, France **18 D3** 48 40N 3 55W
Caraquet, Canada **103 C6** 47 48N 64 57W
Caras, Peru **124 E3** 9 3 S 77 47W
Caraş Severin □, Romania **42 E7** 45 10N 22 10 E
Caraşova, Romania **42 E6** 45 11N 21 51 E
Caratasca, L., Honduras **120 C3** 15 20N 83 40W
Caratinga, Brazil **125 G10** 19 50 S 42 10W
Caraúbas, Brazil **125 E11** 5 43 S 37 33W
Caravaca = Caravaca de la Cruz, Spain **33 G3** 38 8N 1 52W
Caravaca de la Cruz, Spain **33 G3** 38 8N 1 52W
Caravággio, Italy **28 C6** 45 30N 9 38 E
Caravela, Guinea-Biss. **82 C1** 11 30N 16 30W
Caravelas, Brazil **125 G11** 17 45 S 39 15W
Caraveli, Peru **124 G4** 15 45 S 73 25W
Caràzinho, Brazil **127 B5** 28 16 S 52 46W
Carballino = O Carballiño, Spain **34 C2** 42 26N 8 5W
Carballo, Spain **34 B2** 43 13N 8 41W
Carberry, Canada **105 D9** 49 50N 99 25W
Carbó, Mexico **118 B2** 29 42N 110 58W
Carbonara, C., Italy **30 C2** 39 6N 9 31 E
Carbondale, Colo., U.S.A. **114 G10** 39 24N 107 13W
Carbondale, Ill., U.S.A. **113 G10** 37 44N 89 13W
Carbondale, Pa., U.S.A. **111 E9** 41 35N 75 30W
Carbonear, Canada **103 C9** 47 42N 53 13W
Carboneras, Spain **33 J3** 36 59N 1 53W
Carboneras de Guadazaón, Spain **32 F3** 39 54N 1 50W
Carbónia, Italy **30 C1** 39 10N 8 30 E
Carcabuey, Spain **35 H6** 37 27N 4 17W
Carcagente = Carcaixent, Spain **33 F4** 39 8N 0 28W
Carcaixent, Spain **33 F4** 39 8N 0 28W
Carcajou, Canada **104 B5** 57 47N 117 6W
Carcar, Phil. **61 F5** 10 6N 123 38 E
Carcarana →, Argentina **126 C3** 32 27 S 60 48W
Carcasse, C., Haiti **121 C5** 18 30N 74 28W
Carcassonne, France **20 E6** 43 13N 2 20 E
Carcross, Canada **104 A2** 60 13N 134 45W
Çardak, Çanakkale, Turkey **41 F10** 40 22N 26 43 E
Çardak, Denizli, Turkey **39 D11** 37 49N 29 39 E
Cardamon Hills, India **66 Q10** 9 30N 77 15 E
Cardeña, Spain **35 G6** 38 16N 4 20W
Cárdenas, Cuba **120 B3** 23 0N 81 30W
Cárdenas, San Luis Potosí, Mexico **119 C5** 22 0N 99 41W
Cárdenas, Tabasco, Mexico **119 D6** 17 59N 93 21W
Cardenete, Spain **32 F3** 39 46N 1 41W
Cardiff, U.K. **13 F4** 51 29N 3 10W
Cardiff □, U.K. **13 F4** 51 31N 3 12W
Cardiff-by-the-Sea, U.S.A. **117 M9** 33 1N 117 17W
Cardigan, U.K. **13 E3** 52 5N 4 40W
Cardigan B., U.K. **13 E3** 52 30N 4 30W
Cardinal, Canada **111 B9** 44 47N 75 23W
Cardona, Spain **32 D6** 41 56N 1 40 E
Cardona, Uruguay **126 C4** 33 53 S 57 18W
Cardoner →, Spain **32 D6** 41 41N 1 51 E
Cardoso, Ilha do, Brazil **127 B5** 25 8 S 47 58W
Cardston, Canada **104 D6** 49 15N 113 20W
Cardwell, Australia **94 B4** 18 14 S 146 2 E
Careen L., Canada **105 B7** 57 0N 108 11W
Carei, Romania **42 C7** 47 40N 22 29 E
Careme = Ciremai, Indonesia **63 G13** 6 55 S 108 27 E
Carentan, France **18 C5** 49 19N 1 15W
Carey, U.S.A. **114 E7** 43 19N 113 57W
Carey, L., Australia **93 E3** 29 0 S 122 15 E
Carey L., Canada **105 A8** 62 12N 102 55W
Careysburg, Liberia **82 D2** 6 34N 10 30W
Cargèse, France **21 F12** 42 7N 8 35 E
Carhaix-Plouguer, France **18 D3** 48 18N 3 36W
Carhué, Argentina **126 D3** 37 10 S 62 50W
Caria, Turkey **39 D10** 37 20N 28 10 E
Cariacica, Brazil **125 H10** 20 16 S 40 25W
Cariati, Italy **31 C9** 39 30N 16 57 E
Caribbean Sea, W. Indies **121 D5** 15 0N 75 0W
Cariboo Mts., Canada **104 C4** 53 0N 121 0W
Caribou, U.S.A. **109 B12** 46 52N 68 1W
Caribou →, Man., Canada **105 B10** 59 20N 94 44W
Caribou →, N.W.T., Canada **104 A3** 61 27N 125 45W
Caribou I., Canada **102 C2** 47 22N 85 49W
Caribou Is., Canada **104 A6** 61 55N 113 15W
Caribou L., Man., Canada **105 B9** 59 21N 96 10W
Caribou L., Ont., Canada **102 B2** 50 25N 89 5W
Caribou Mts., Canada **104 B5** 59 12N 115 40W
Carichic, Mexico **118 B3** 27 56N 107 3W
Carigara, Phil. **61 F6** 11 18N 124 41 E
Carignan, France **19 C12** 49 38N 5 10 E
Carignano, Italy **28 D4** 44 55N 7 40 E
Carillo, Mexico **118 B4** 26 50N 103 55W
Carinda, Australia **95 E4** 30 28 S 147 41 E
Cariñena, Spain **32 D3** 41 20N 1 13W
Carinhanha, Brazil **125 F10** 14 15 S 44 46W
Carinhanha →, Brazil **125 F10** 14 20 S 43 47W
Carini, Italy **30 D6** 38 8N 13 11 E
Cariño, Spain **34 B3** 43 45N 7 52W
Carínola, Italy **30 A6** 41 11N 13 58 E
Carinthia = Kärnten □, Austria **26 E6** 46 52N 13 30 E
Caripito, Venezuela **124 A6** 10 8N 63 6W
Carlbrod = Dimitrovgrad, Serbia, Yug. **40 C6** 43 2N 22 48 E
Carlet, Spain **33 F4** 39 14N 0 31W
Carleton, Mt., Canada **103 C6** 47 23N 66 53W
Carleton Place, Canada **102 C4** 45 8N 76 9W
Carletonville, S. Africa **88 D4** 26 23 S 27 22 E
Cârlibaba, Romania **43 C10** 47 35N 25 8 E
Carlin, U.S.A. **114 F5** 40 43N 116 7W
Carlingford L., U.K. **15 B5** 54 3N 6 9W
Carlinville, U.S.A. **112 F10** 39 17N 89 53W
Carlisle, U.K. **12 C5** 54 54N 2 56W
Carlisle, U.S.A. **110 F7** 40 12N 77 12W
Carlit, Pic, France **20 F5** 42 35N 1 55 E
Carloforte, Italy **30 C1** 39 8N 8 18 E
Carlos Casares, Argentina **126 D3** 35 32 S 61 20W
Carlos Tejedor, Argentina **126 D3** 35 25 S 62 25W
Carlow, Ireland **15 D5** 52 50N 6 56W
Carlow □, Ireland **15 D5** 52 43N 6 50W
Carlsbad, Calif., U.S.A. **117 M9** 33 10N 117 21W
Carlsbad, N. Mex., U.S.A. **113 J2** 32 25N 104 14W
Carlsbad Caverns National Park, U.S.A. **113 J2** 32 10N 104 35W
Carluke, U.K. **14 F5** 55 45N 3 50W
Carlyle, Canada **105 D8** 49 40N 102 20W
Carmacks, Canada **100 B6** 62 5N 136 16W
Carmagnola, Italy **28 D4** 44 51N 7 43 E
Carman, Canada **105 D9** 49 30N 98 0W
Carmarthen, U.K. **13 F3** 51 52N 4 19W
Carmarthen B., U.K. **13 F3** 51 40N 4 30W
Carmarthenshire □, U.K. **13 F3** 51 55N 4 13W
Carmaux, France **20 D6** 44 3N 2 10 E
Carmel, U.S.A. **111 E11** 41 26N 73 41W
Carmel-by-the-Sea, U.S.A. **116 J5** 36 33N 121 55W
Carmel Valley, U.S.A. **116 J5** 36 29N 121 43W
Carmelo, Uruguay **126 C4** 34 0 S 58 20W
Carmen, Colombia **124 B3** 9 43N 75 8W
Carmen, Paraguay **127 B4** 27 13 S 56 12W
Carmen →, Mexico **118 A3** 30 42N 106 29W
Carmen, I., Mexico **118 B2** 26 0N 111 20W
Carmen de Patagones, Argentina **128 E4** 40 50 S 63 0W
Cármenes, Spain **34 C5** 42 58N 5 34W
Carmensa, Argentina **126 D2** 35 15 S 67 40W
Carmi, Canada **104 D5** 49 36N 119 8W
Carmi, U.S.A. **108 F1** 38 5N 88 10W
Carmichael, U.S.A. **116 G5** 38 38N 121 19W
Carmila, Australia **94 C4** 21 55 S 149 24 E
Carmona, Costa Rica **120 E2** 10 0N 85 15W
Carmona, Spain **35 H5** 37 28N 5 42W
Carn Ban, U.K. **14 D4** 57 7N 4 15W
Carn Eige, U.K. **14 D3** 57 17N 5 8W
Carnamah, Australia **93 E2** 29 41 S 115 53 E
Carnarvon, Australia **93 D1** 24 51 S 113 42 E
Carnarvon, S. Africa **88 E3** 30 56 S 22 8 E
Carnarvon Ra., Queens., Australia **94 D4** 25 15 S 148 30 E
Carnarvon Ra., W. Austral., Australia **93 E3** 25 20 S 120 45 E
Carnation, U.S.A. **116 C5** 47 39N 121 55W
Carndonagh, Ireland **15 A4** 55 16N 7 15W
Carnduff, Canada **105 D8** 49 10N 101 50W
Carnegie, U.S.A. **110 F4** 40 24N 80 5W
Carnegie, L., Australia **93 E3** 26 5 S 122 30 E
Carnic Alps = Karnische Alpen, Europe **26 E6** 46 36N 13 0 E
Carniche Alpi = Karnische Alpen, Europe **26 E6** 46 36N 13 0 E
Carnot, C.A.R. **84 D3** 4 59N 15 56 E
Carnot, C., Australia **95 E2** 34 57 S 135 38 E
Carnot B., Australia **92 C3** 17 20 S 122 15 E
Carnoustie, U.K. **14 E6** 56 30N 2 42W
Carnsore Pt., Ireland **15 D5** 52 10N 6 22W
Caro, U.S.A. **108 D4** 43 29N 83 24W
Carol City, U.S.A. **109 N5** 25 56N 80 16W
Carolina, Brazil **125 E9** 7 10 S 47 30W
Carolina, Puerto Rico **121 C6** 18 23N 65 58W
Carolina, S. Africa **89 D5** 26 5 S 30 6 E
Caroline I., Kiribati **97 H12** 9 15 S 150 3W
Caroline Is., Micronesia **52 J17** 8 0N 150 0 E
Caroni →, Venezuela **124 B6** 8 21N 62 43W
Caronie = Nébrodi, Monti, Italy **31 E7** 37 54N 14 35 E
Caroona, Australia **95 E5** 31 24 S 150 26 E
Carpathians, Europe **6 F10** 49 30N 21 0 E
Carpații Meridionali, Romania **43 E9** 45 30N 25 0 E

Chāh Gay

Carpentaria, G. of, *Australia* 94 A2 14 0 S 139 0 E
Carpentras, *France* 21 D9 44 3N 5 2 E
Carpi, *Italy* 28 D7 44 47N 10 53 E
Cărpineni, *Moldova* 43 D13 46 46N 28 22 E
Carpinteria, *U.S.A.* 117 L7 34 24N 119 31W
Carpio, *Spain* 34 D5 41 13N 5 7W
Carr Boyd Ra., *Australia* 92 C4 16 15 S 128 35 E
Carrabelle, *U.S.A.* 109 L3 29 51N 84 40W
Carral, *Spain* 34 B2 43 13N 8 21W
Carranza, Presa V., *Mexico* 118 B4 27 20N 100 50W
Carrara, *Italy* 28 D7 44 5N 10 6 E
Carrascal, *Phil.* 61 G6 9 22N 125 56 E
Carrascosa del Campo, *Spain* 32 E2 40 2N 2 45W
Carrauntoohill, *Ireland* 15 D2 52 0N 9 45W
Carrick-on-Shannon, *Ireland* 15 C3 53 57N 8 5W
Carrick-on-Suir, *Ireland* 15 D4 52 21N 7 24W
Carrickfergus, *U.K.* 15 B6 54 43N 5 49W
Carrickmacross, *Ireland* 15 C5 53 59N 6 43W
Carrieton, *Australia* 95 E2 32 25 S 138 31 E
Carrington, *U.S.A.* 112 B5 47 27N 99 8W
Carrión →, *Spain* 34 D6 41 53N 4 32W
Carrión de los Condes, *Spain* 34 C6 42 20N 4 37W
Carrizal Bajo, *Chile* 126 B1 28 5 S 71 20W
Carrizalillo, *Chile* 126 B1 29 5 S 71 30W
Carrizo Cr. →, *U.S.A.* 113 G3 36 55N 103 55W
Carrizo Springs, *U.S.A.* 113 L5 28 31N 99 52W
Carrizozo, *U.S.A.* 115 K11 33 38N 105 53W
Carroll, *U.S.A.* 112 D7 42 4N 94 52W
Carrollton, *Ga., U.S.A.* 109 J3 33 35N 85 5W
Carrollton, *Ill., U.S.A.* 112 F9 39 18N 90 24W
Carrollton, *Ky., U.S.A.* 108 F3 38 41N 85 11W
Carrollton, *Mo., U.S.A.* 112 F8 39 22N 93 30W
Carrollton, *Ohio, U.S.A.* 110 F3 40 34N 81 5W
Carron →, *U.K.* 14 D4 57 53N 4 22W
Carron, L., *U.K.* 14 D3 57 22N 5 35W
Carrot →, *Canada* 105 C8 53 50N 101 17W
Carrot River, *Canada* 105 C8 53 17N 103 35W
Carrouges, *France* 18 D6 48 34N 0 10W
Carrù, *Italy* 28 D4 44 29N 7 52 E
Carruthers, *Canada* 105 C7 52 52N 109 16W
Carsa Dek, *Ethiopia* 81 F4 5 13N 39 50 E
Çarşamba, *Turkey* 72 B7 41 11N 36 44 E
Carsóli, *Italy* 29 F10 42 6N 13 5 E
Carson, *Calif., U.S.A.* 117 M8 33 48N 118 17W
Carson, *N. Dak., U.S.A.* 112 B4 46 25N 101 34W
Carson →, *U.S.A.* 116 F8 39 45N 118 40W
Carson City, *U.S.A.* 116 F7 39 10N 119 46W
Carson Sink, *U.S.A.* 114 G4 39 50N 118 25W
Cartagena, *Colombia* 124 A3 10 25N 75 33W
Cartagena, *Spain* 33 H4 37 38N 0 59W
Cartago, *Colombia* 124 C3 4 45N 75 55W
Cartago, *Costa Rica* 120 E3 9 50N 83 55W
Cártama, *Spain* 35 J6 36 43N 4 39W
Cartaxo, *Portugal* 35 F2 39 10N 8 47W
Cartaya, *Spain* 35 H3 37 16N 7 9W
Cartersville, *U.S.A.* 109 H3 34 10N 84 48W
Carterton, *N.Z.* 91 J5 41 2 S 175 31 E
Carthage, *Tunisia* 30 F3 36 50N 10 21 E
Carthage, *Ill., U.S.A.* 112 E9 40 25N 91 8W
Carthage, *Mo., U.S.A.* 113 G7 37 11N 94 19W
Carthage, *N.Y., U.S.A.* 108 D8 43 59N 75 37W
Carthage, *Tex., U.S.A.* 113 J7 32 9N 94 20W
Cartier I., *Australia* 92 B3 12 31 S 123 29 E
Cartwright, *Canada* 103 B8 53 41N 56 58W
Caruaru, *Brazil* 125 E11 8 15 S 35 55W
Carúpano, *Venezuela* 124 A6 10 39N 63 15W
Caruthersville, *U.S.A.* 113 G10 36 11N 89 39W
Carvin, *France* 19 B9 50 30N 2 57 E
Carvoeiro, *Brazil* 124 D6 1 30 S 61 59W
Carvoeiro, C., *Portugal* 35 F1 39 21N 9 24W
Cary, *U.S.A.* 109 H6 35 47N 78 46W
Casa Branca, *Portugal* 35 G2 38 29N 8 12W
Casa Grande, *U.S.A.* 115 K8 32 53N 111 45W
Casablanca, *Chile* 126 C1 33 20 S 71 25W
Casablanca, *Morocco* 78 B4 33 36N 7 36W
Casacalenda, *Italy* 29 G11 41 44N 14 51 E
Casalbordino, *Italy* 29 F11 42 9N 14 35 E
Casale Monferrato, *Italy* 28 C5 45 8N 8 27 E
Casalmaggiore, *Italy* 28 D7 44 59N 10 26 E
Casalpusterlengo, *Italy* 28 C6 45 11N 9 39 E
Casamance →, *Senegal* 82 C1 12 33N 16 46W
Casarano, *Italy* 31 B11 40 0N 18 10 E
Casares, *Spain* 35 J5 36 27N 5 16W
Casas Ibáñez, *Spain* 33 F3 39 17N 1 30W
Casasimarro, *Spain* 33 F2 39 22N 2 3W
Casatejada, *Spain* 34 F5 39 54N 5 40W
Casavieja, *Spain* 34 E6 40 17N 4 46W
Cascade, *Idaho, U.S.A.* 114 D5 44 31N 116 2W
Cascade, *Mont., U.S.A.* 114 C8 47 16N 111 42W
Cascade Locks, *U.S.A.* 116 E5 45 40N 121 54W
Cascade Ra., *U.S.A.* 116 D5 47 0N 121 30W
Cascade Reservoir, *U.S.A.* 114 D5 44 32N 116 3W
Cascais, *Portugal* 35 G1 38 41N 9 25W
Cascavel, *Brazil* 127 A5 24 57 S 53 28W
Cáscina, *Italy* 28 E7 43 41N 10 33 E
Casco B., *U.S.A.* 109 D10 43 45N 70 0W
Caselle Torinese, *Italy* 28 C4 45 10N 7 39 E
Caserta, *Italy* 31 A7 41 4N 14 20 E
Cashel, *Ireland* 15 D4 52 30N 7 53W
Casiguran, *Phil.* 61 C5 16 22N 122 7 E
Casilda, *Argentina* 126 C3 33 10 S 61 10W
Casimcea, *Romania* 43 F13 44 45N 28 23 E
Casino, *Australia* 95 D5 28 52 S 153 3 E
Casiquiare →, *Venezuela* 124 C5 2 1N 67 7W
Čáslav, *Czech Rep.* 26 B8 49 54N 15 22 E
Casma, *Peru* 124 E3 9 30 S 78 20W
Casmalia, *U.S.A.* 117 L6 34 50N 120 32W
Cásola Valsénio, *Italy* 29 D8 44 12N 11 40 E
Cásoli, *Italy* 29 F11 42 7N 14 18 E
Caspe, *Spain* 32 D4 41 14N 0 1W
Casper, *U.S.A.* 114 E10 42 51N 106 19W
Caspian Depression, *Eurasia* 49 G9 47 0N 48 0 E
Caspian Sea, *Eurasia* 50 E6 43 0N 50 0 E
Cass Lake, *U.S.A.* 112 B7 47 23N 94 37W
Cassà de la Selva, *Spain* 32 D7 41 53N 2 52 E
Cassadaga, *U.S.A.* 110 D5 42 20N 79 19W
Cassano allo Iónio, *Italy* 31 C9 39 47N 16 20 E
Casse, Grande, *France* 21 C10 45 24N 6 49 E
Cassel, *France* 19 B9 50 48N 2 30 E
Casselman, *Canada* 111 A9 45 19N 75 5W
Casselton, *U.S.A.* 112 B6 46 54N 97 13W
Cassiar, *Canada* 104 B3 59 16N 129 40W
Cassiar Mts., *Canada* 104 B2 59 30N 130 30W
Cassino, *Italy* 30 A6 41 30N 13 49 E
Cassis, *France* 21 E9 43 14N 5 32 E
Cassville, *U.S.A.* 113 G8 36 41N 93 52W
Castagneto Carducci, *Italy* 28 E7 43 9N 10 36 E
Castaic, *U.S.A.* 117 L8 34 30N 118 38W
Castalia, *U.S.A.* 110 E2 41 24N 82 49W
Castanhal, *Brazil* 125 D9 1 18 S 47 55W
Castéggio, *Italy* 28 C6 45 0N 9 7 E
Castejón de Monegros, *Spain* 32 D4 41 37N 0 15W
Castèl di Sangro, *Italy* 29 G11 41 47N 14 6 E
Castèl San Giovanni, *Italy* 28 C6 45 4N 9 26 E
Castèl San Pietro Terme, *Italy* 29 D8 44 24N 11 35 E
Castelbuono, *Italy* 31 E7 37 56N 14 5 E
Castelfidardo, *Italy* 29 E10 43 28N 13 33 E
Castelfiorentino, *Italy* 28 E7 43 36N 10 58 E
Castelfranco Emília, *Italy* 28 D8 44 37N 11 3 E
Castelfranco Véneto, *Italy* 29 C8 45 40N 11 55 E
Casteljaloux, *France* 20 D4 44 19N 0 6 E
Castellabate, *Italy* 31 B7 40 17N 14 57 E
Castellammare, G. di, *Italy* 30 D5 38 8N 12 54 E
Castellammare del Golfo, *Italy* 30 D5 38 1N 12 53 E
Castellammare di Stábia, *Italy* 31 B7 40 42N 14 29 E
Castellamonte, *Italy* 28 C4 45 23N 7 42 E
Castellane, *France* 21 E10 43 50N 6 31 E
Castellaneta, *Italy* 31 B9 40 38N 16 56 E
Castelli, *Argentina* 126 D4 36 7 S 57 47W
Castelló de la Plana, *Spain* 32 F4 39 58N 0 3W
Castellón de la Plana □, *Spain* 32 E4 40 15N 0 5W
Castellote, *Spain* 32 E4 40 48N 0 15W
Castelmáuro, *Italy* 29 G11 41 50N 14 43 E
Castelnau-de-Médoc, *France* 20 C3 45 2N 0 48W
Castelnau-Magnoac, *France* 20 E4 43 17N 0 31 E
Castelnaudary, *France* 20 E5 43 20N 1 58 E
Castelnovo ne' Monti, *Italy* 28 D7 44 26N 10 24 E
Castelnuovo di Val di Cécina, *Italy* 28 E7 43 12N 10 59 E
Castelo, *Brazil* 127 A7 20 33 S 41 14W
Castelo Branco, *Portugal* 34 F3 39 50N 7 31W
Castelo Branco □, *Portugal* 34 F3 39 52N 7 45W
Castelo de Paiva, *Portugal* 34 D2 41 2N 8 16W
Castelo de Vide, *Portugal* 35 F3 39 25N 7 27W
Castelsardo, *Italy* 30 B1 40 55N 8 43 E
Castelsarrasin, *France* 20 D5 44 2N 1 7 E
Casteltérmini, *Italy* 30 E6 37 32N 13 39 E
Castelvetrano, *Italy* 30 E5 37 41N 12 47 E
Casterton, *Australia* 95 F3 37 30 S 141 30 E
Castets, *France* 20 E2 43 52N 1 6W
Castiglion Fiorentino, *Italy* 29 E8 43 20N 11 55 E
Castiglione del Lago, *Italy* 29 E9 43 7N 12 3 E
Castiglione della Pescáia, *Italy* 28 F7 42 46N 10 53 E
Castiglione delle Stiviere, *Italy* 28 C7 45 23N 10 29 E
Castilblanco, *Spain* 35 F5 39 17N 5 5W
Castile, *U.S.A.* 110 D6 42 38N 78 3W
Castilla, Playa de, *Spain* 35 J4 37 0N 6 33W
Castilla-La Mancha □, *Spain* 6 H5 39 30N 3 30W
Castilla y Leon □, *Spain* 34 D6 42 0N 5 0W
Castillo de Locubín, *Spain* 35 H7 37 32N 3 56W
Castillon-en-Couserans, *France* 20 F5 42 56N 1 1 E
Castillonès, *France* 20 D4 44 39N 0 37 E
Castillos, *Uruguay* 127 C5 34 12 S 53 52W
Castle Dale, *U.S.A.* 114 G8 39 13N 111 1W
Castle Douglas, *U.K.* 14 G5 54 56N 3 56W
Castle Rock, *Colo., U.S.A.* 112 F2 39 22N 104 51W
Castle Rock, *Wash., U.S.A.* 116 D4 46 17N 122 54W
Castlebar, *Ireland* 15 C2 53 52N 9 18W
Castleblaney, *Ireland* 15 B5 54 7N 6 44W
Castlederg, *U.K.* 15 B4 54 42N 7 35W
Castleford, *U.K.* 12 D6 53 43N 1 21W
Castlegar, *Canada* 104 D5 49 20N 117 40W
Castlemaine, *Australia* 95 F3 37 2 S 144 12 E
Castlepollard, *Ireland* 15 C4 53 41N 7 19W
Castlerea, *Ireland* 15 C3 53 46N 8 29W
Castlereagh →, *Australia* 95 E4 30 12 S 147 32 E
Castlereagh B., *Australia* 94 A2 12 10 S 135 10 E
Castleton, *U.S.A.* 111 C11 43 37N 73 11W
Castletown, *U.K.* 12 C3 54 5N 4 38W
Castletown Bearhaven, *Ireland* 15 E2 51 39N 9 55W
Castor, *Canada* 104 C6 52 15N 111 50W
Castor →, *Canada* 102 B4 53 24N 78 58W
Castorland, *U.S.A.* 111 C9 43 53N 75 31W
Castres, *France* 20 E6 43 37N 2 13 E
Castricum, *Neths.* 17 B4 52 33N 4 40 E
Castries, *St. Lucia* 121 D7 14 2N 60 58W
Castril, *Spain* 35 H8 37 48N 2 46W
Castro, *Brazil* 127 A6 24 45 S 50 0W
Castro, *Chile* 128 E2 42 30 S 73 50W
Castro Alves, *Brazil* 125 F11 12 46 S 39 33W
Castro del Río, *Spain* 35 H6 37 41N 4 29W
Castro-Urdiales, *Spain* 34 B7 43 23N 3 11W
Castro Verde, *Portugal* 35 H2 37 41N 8 4W
Castrojeriz, *Spain* 34 C6 42 17N 4 9W
Castropol, *Spain* 34 B4 43 32N 7 0W
Castroreale, *Italy* 31 D8 38 6N 15 12 E
Castrovillari, *Italy* 31 C9 39 49N 16 12 E
Castroville, *U.S.A.* 116 J5 36 46N 121 45W
Castuera, *Spain* 35 G5 38 43N 5 37W
Çat, *Turkey* 73 C9 39 40N 41 3 E
Cat Ba, Dao, *Vietnam* 64 B6 20 50N 107 0 E
Cat I., *Bahamas* 121 B4 24 30N 75 30W
Cat L., *Canada* 102 B1 51 40N 91 50W
Cat Lake, *Canada* 102 B1 51 40N 91 50W
Čata, *Slovak Rep.* 27 D11 47 58N 18 38 E
Catacamas, *Honduras* 120 D2 14 54N 85 56W
Cataguases, *Brazil* 127 A7 21 23 S 42 39W
Çatak, *Turkey* 73 C10 38 1N 43 8 E
Catalão, *Brazil* 125 G9 18 10 S 47 57W
Çatalca, *Turkey* 41 E12 41 8N 28 27 E
Catalina, *Canada* 103 C9 48 31N 53 4W
Catalina, *Chile* 126 B2 25 13 S 69 43W
Catalina, *U.S.A.* 115 K8 32 30N 110 50W
Catalonia = Cataluña □, *Spain* 32 D6 41 40N 1 15 E
Cataluña □, *Spain* 32 D6 41 40N 1 15 E
Çatalzeytin, *Turkey* 72 B6 41 57N 34 12 E
Catamarca, *Argentina* 126 B2 28 30 S 65 50W
Catamarca □, *Argentina* 126 B2 27 0 S 65 50W
Catanauan, *Phil.* 61 E5 13 36N 122 19 E
Catanduanes □, *Phil.* 61 E6 13 50N 124 20 E
Catanduva, *Brazil* 127 A6 21 5 S 48 58W
Catánia, *Italy* 31 E8 37 30N 15 6 E
Catánia, G. di, *Italy* 31 E8 37 24N 15 9 E
Catanzaro, *Italy* 31 D9 38 54N 16 35 E
Catarman, *Phil.* 61 E6 12 28N 124 35 E
Catbalogan, *Phil.* 61 F6 11 46N 124 53 E
Cateel, *Phil.* 61 H7 7 47N 126 24 E
Catembe, *Mozam.* 89 D5 26 0 S 32 33 E
Caterham, *U.K.* 13 F7 51 15N 0 4W
Cathcart, *S. Africa* 88 E4 32 18 S 27 10 E
Cathlamet, *U.S.A.* 116 D3 46 12N 123 23W
Catio, *Guinea-Biss.* 82 C1 11 17N 15 15W
Catlettsburg, *U.S.A.* 108 F4 38 25N 82 36W
Çatma Dağı, *Turkey* 39 C11 38 25N 29 50 E
Catoche, C., *Mexico* 119 C7 21 40N 87 8W
Cátria, Mte., *Italy* 29 E9 43 28N 12 42 E
Catriló, *Argentina* 126 D3 36 26 S 63 24W
Catrimani, *Brazil* 124 C6 0 27N 61 41W
Catrimani →, *Brazil* 124 C6 0 28N 61 44W
Catskill, *U.S.A.* 111 D11 42 14N 73 52W
Catskill Mts., *U.S.A.* 111 D10 42 10N 74 25W
Catt, Mt., *Australia* 94 A1 13 49 S 134 23 E
Cattaraugus, *U.S.A.* 110 D6 42 22N 78 52W
Cattólica, *Italy* 29 E9 43 58N 12 44 E
Cattólica Eraclea, *Italy* 30 E6 37 26N 13 24 E
Catuala, *Angola* 88 B2 16 25 S 19 2 E
Catuane, *Mozam.* 89 D5 26 48 S 32 18 E
Catur, *Mozam.* 87 E4 13 45 S 35 30 E
Catwick Is., *Vietnam* 65 G7 10 0N 109 0 E
Cauca →, *Colombia* 124 B4 8 54N 74 28W
Caucaia, *Brazil* 125 D11 3 40 S 38 35W
Caucasus Mountains, *Eurasia* 49 J7 42 50N 44 0 E
Caudete, *Spain* 33 G3 38 42N 1 2W
Caudry, *France* 19 B10 50 7N 3 22 E
Caulnes, *France* 18 D4 48 18N 2 10W
Caulónia, *Italy* 31 D9 38 23N 16 24 E
Caungula, *Angola* 84 F3 8 26 S 18 38 E
Cauquenes, *Chile* 126 D1 36 0 S 72 22W
Caura →, *Venezuela* 124 B6 7 38N 64 53W
Cauresi →, *Mozam.* 87 F3 17 8 S 33 0 E
Căuşani, *Moldova* 43 D14 46 38N 29 25 E
Causapscal, *Canada* 103 C6 48 19N 67 12W
Caussade, *France* 20 D5 44 10N 1 33 E
Causse-Méjean, *France* 20 D7 44 18N 3 42 E
Cauterets, *France* 20 F3 42 52N 0 8W
Cauvery →, *India* 66 P11 11 9N 78 52 E
Caux, Pays de, *France* 18 C7 49 38N 0 35 E
Cava de' Tirreni, *Italy* 31 B7 40 42N 14 42 E
Cávado →, *Portugal* 34 D2 41 32N 8 48W
Cavaillon, *France* 21 E9 43 50N 5 2 E
Cavalaire-sur-Mer, *France* 21 E10 43 10N 6 33 E
Cavalese, *Italy* 29 B8 46 17N 11 27 E
Cavalier, *U.S.A.* 112 A6 48 48N 97 37W
Cavalla = Cavally →, *Africa* 82 E3 4 22N 7 32W
Cavalleria, C. de, *Spain* 37 A11 40 5N 4 5 E
Cavallo, I. de, *France* 21 G13 41 22N 9 16 E
Cavally →, *Africa* 82 E3 4 22N 7 32W
Cavan, *Ireland* 15 B4 54 0N 7 22W
Cavan □, *Ireland* 15 C4 54 1N 7 16W
Cavárzere, *Italy* 29 C9 45 8N 12 5 E
Çavdarhisar, *Turkey* 39 B11 39 12N 29 37 E
Çavdır, *Turkey* 39 D11 37 10N 29 42 E
Cave Creek, *U.S.A.* 115 K7 33 50N 111 57W
Cavenagh Ra., *Australia* 93 E4 26 12 S 127 55 E
Cavendish, *Australia* 95 F3 37 31 S 142 2 E
Caviana, I., *Brazil* 125 C8 0 10N 50 10W
Cavite, *Phil.* 61 D4 14 29N 120 55 E
Cavnic, *Romania* 43 C8 47 40N 23 52 E
Cavour, *Italy* 28 D4 44 47N 7 22 E
Cavtat, *Croatia* 40 D2 42 35N 18 13 E
Cawndilla L., *Australia* 95 E3 32 30 S 142 15 E
Cawnpore = Kanpur, *India* 69 F9 26 28N 80 20 E
Caxias, *Brazil* 125 D10 4 55 S 43 20W
Caxias do Sul, *Brazil* 127 B5 29 10 S 51 10W
Çay, *Turkey* 72 C4 38 35N 31 1 E
Cay Sal Bank, *Bahamas* 120 B4 23 45N 80 0W
Cayambe, *Ecuador* 124 C3 0 3N 78 8W
Çaycuma, *Turkey* 72 B5 41 25N 32 4 E
Çayeli, *Turkey* 73 B9 41 5N 40 45 E
Cayenne, *Fr. Guiana* 125 B8 5 5N 52 18W
Caygören Barajı, *Turkey* 39 B10 39 15N 28 12 E
Cayiralan, *Turkey* 72 C6 39 17N 35 38 E
Caylus, *France* 20 D5 44 15N 1 47 E
Cayman Brac, *Cayman Is.* 120 C4 19 43N 79 49W
Cayman Is. ■, *W. Indies* 120 C3 19 40N 80 30W
Cayo Romano, *Cuba* 120 B4 22 0N 78 0W
Cayres, *France* 20 D7 44 55N 3 48 E
Cayuga, *Canada* 110 D5 42 59N 79 50W
Cayuga, *U.S.A.* 111 D8 42 54N 76 44W
Cayuga L., *U.S.A.* 111 D8 42 41N 76 41W
Cazalla de la Sierra, *Spain* 35 H5 37 56N 5 45W
Căzăneşti, *Romania* 43 F12 44 36N 27 3 E
Cazaubon, *France* 20 E3 43 56N 0 3W
Cazaux et de Sanguinet, Étang de, *France* 20 D2 44 29N 1 10W
Cazenovia, *U.S.A.* 111 D9 42 56N 75 51W
Cazères, *France* 20 E5 43 13N 1 5 E
Cazin, *Bos.-H.* 29 D12 44 57N 15 57 E
Čazma, *Croatia* 29 C13 45 45N 16 39 E
Cazombo, *Angola* 85 G4 11 54 S 22 56 E
Cazorla, *Spain* 35 H7 37 55N 3 2W
Cazorla, Sierra de, *Spain* 35 G8 38 5N 2 55W
Cea →, *Spain* 34 C5 42 0N 5 36W
Ceamurlia de Jos, *Romania* 43 F13 44 43N 28 47 E
Ceanannus Mor, *Ireland* 15 C5 53 44N 6 53W
Ceará = Fortaleza, *Brazil* 125 D11 3 45 S 38 35W
Ceará □, *Brazil* 125 E11 5 0 S 40 0W
Ceará Mirim, *Brazil* 125 E11 5 38 S 35 25W
Ceauru, L., *Romania* 43 F8 44 58N 23 11 E
Cebaco, I. de, *Panama* 120 E3 7 33N 81 9W
Cebollar, *Argentina* 126 B2 29 10 S 66 35W
Cebollera, Sierra de, *Spain* 32 D2 42 0N 2 30W
Cebreros, *Spain* 34 E6 40 27N 4 28W
Cebu, *Phil.* 61 F5 10 18N 123 54 E
Čečava, *Bos.-H.* 42 F2 44 42N 17 44 E
Ceccano, *Italy* 30 A6 41 34N 13 20 E
Cece, *Hungary* 42 D3 46 46N 18 39 E
Cechi, *Ivory C.* 82 D4 6 15N 4 25W
Cecil Plains, *Australia* 95 D5 27 30 S 151 11 E
Cécina, *Italy* 28 E7 43 19N 10 31 E
Cécina →, *Italy* 28 E7 43 18N 10 29 E
Ceclavín, *Spain* 34 F4 39 50N 6 45W
Cedar →, *U.S.A.* 112 E9 41 17N 91 21W
Cedar City, *U.S.A.* 115 H7 37 41N 113 4W
Cedar Creek Reservoir, *U.S.A.* 113 J6 32 11N 96 4W
Cedar Falls, *Iowa, U.S.A.* 112 D8 42 32N 92 27W
Cedar Falls, *Wash., U.S.A.* 116 C5 47 25N 121 45W
Cedar Key, *U.S.A.* 109 L4 29 8N 83 2W
Cedar L., *Canada* 105 C9 53 10N 100 0W
Cedar Rapids, *U.S.A.* 112 E9 41 59N 91 40W
Cedartown, *U.S.A.* 109 H3 34 1N 85 15W
Cedarvale, *Canada* 104 B3 55 1N 128 22W
Cedarville, *S. Africa* 89 E4 30 23 S 29 3 E
Cedeira, *Spain* 34 B2 43 39N 8 2W
Cedral, *Mexico* 118 C4 23 50N 100 42W
Cedrino →, *Italy* 30 B2 40 11N 9 24 E
Cedro, *Brazil* 125 E11 6 34 S 39 3W
Cedros, I. de, *Mexico* 118 B1 28 10N 115 20W
Ceduna, *Australia* 95 E1 32 7 S 133 46 E
Cedynia, *Poland* 45 F1 52 53N 14 12 E
Cée, *Spain* 34 C1 42 57N 9 10W
Cefalù, *Italy* 31 D7 38 2N 14 1 E
Cega →, *Spain* 34 D6 41 33N 4 46W
Cegléd, *Hungary* 42 C4 47 11N 19 47 E
Céglie Messápico, *Italy* 31 B10 40 39N 17 31 E
Cehegín, *Spain* 33 G3 38 6N 1 48W
Ceheng, *China* 58 E5 24 58N 105 48 E
Cehu-Silvaniei, *Romania* 43 C8 47 24N 23 9 E
Ceica, *Romania* 42 D7 46 53N 22 10 E
Ceira →, *Portugal* 34 E2 40 13N 8 16W
Čelákovice, *Czech Rep.* 26 A7 50 10N 14 46 E
Celano, *Italy* 29 F10 42 5N 13 33 E
Celanova, *Spain* 34 C3 42 9N 7 58W
Celaya, *Mexico* 118 C4 20 31N 100 37W
Celebes Sea, *Indonesia* 63 D6 3 0N 123 0 E
Čelić, *Bos.-H.* 42 F3 44 43N 18 49 E
Celina, *U.S.A.* 108 E3 40 33N 84 35W
Celinac, *Bos.-H.* 42 F2 44 44N 17 22 E
Celje, *Slovenia* 29 B12 46 16N 15 18 E
Celldömölk, *Hungary* 42 C2 47 16N 17 10 E
Celle, *Germany* 24 C6 52 37N 10 4 E
Celorico da Beira, *Portugal* 34 E3 40 38N 7 24W
Çeltikçi, *Turkey* 39 D12 37 32N 30 29 E
Çemişgezek, *Turkey* 73 C8 39 3N 38 56 E
Cenderwasih, Teluk, *Indonesia* 63 E9 3 0 S 135 20 E
Cengong, *China* 58 D7 27 13N 108 44 E
Ceno →, *Italy* 28 D7 44 43N 10 5 E
Centallo, *Italy* 28 D4 44 30N 7 35 E
Centelles, *Spain* 32 D7 41 50N 2 14 E
Center, *N. Dak., U.S.A.* 112 B4 47 7N 101 18W
Center, *Tex., U.S.A.* 113 K7 31 48N 94 11W
Centerburg, *U.S.A.* 110 F2 40 18N 82 42W
Centerville, *Calif., U.S.A.* 116 J7 36 44N 119 30W
Centerville, *Iowa, U.S.A.* 112 E8 40 44N 92 52W
Centerville, *Pa., U.S.A.* 110 F5 40 3N 79 59W
Centerville, *Tenn., U.S.A.* 109 H2 35 47N 87 28W
Centerville, *Tex., U.S.A.* 113 K7 31 16N 95 59W
Cento, *Italy* 29 D8 44 43N 11 17 E
Central □, *Ghana* 83 D4 5 30N 1 0W
Central □, *Kenya* 86 C4 0 30 S 37 30 E
Central □, *Malawi* 87 E3 13 30 S 33 30 E
Central □, *Zambia* 87 E2 14 25 S 28 50 E
Central, Cordillera, *Colombia* 122 C3 5 0N 75 0W
Central, Cordillera, *Costa Rica* 120 D3 10 10N 84 5W
Central, Cordillera, *Dom. Rep.* 121 C5 19 15N 71 0W
Central, Cordillera, *Phil.* 61 C4 17 20N 120 57 E
Central African Rep. ■, *Africa* 84 C4 7 0N 20 0 E
Central America, *America* 98 H11 12 0N 85 0W
Central Butte, *Canada* 105 C7 50 48N 106 31W
Central City, *Colo., U.S.A.* 114 G11 39 48N 105 31W
Central City, *Ky., U.S.A.* 108 G2 37 18N 87 7W
Central City, *Nebr., U.S.A.* 112 E6 41 7N 98 0W
Central I., *Kenya* 86 B4 3 30N 36 0 E
Central Makran Range, *Pakistan* 66 F4 26 30N 64 15 E
Central Patricia, *Canada* 102 B1 51 30N 90 9W
Central Point, *U.S.A.* 114 E2 42 23N 122 55W
Central Russian Uplands, *Europe* 6 E13 54 0N 36 0 E
Central Siberian Plateau, *Russia* 52 C14 65 0N 105 0 E
Central Square, *U.S.A.* 111 C8 43 17N 76 9W
Centralia, *Ill., U.S.A.* 112 F10 38 32N 89 8W
Centralia, *Mo., U.S.A.* 112 F8 39 13N 92 8W
Centralia, *Wash., U.S.A.* 116 D4 46 43N 122 58W
Cenxi, *China* 59 F8 22 57N 110 57 E
Ceotina →, *Bos.-H.* 40 C2 43 36N 18 50 E
Cephalonia = Kefallinía, *Greece* 38 C2 38 20N 20 30 E
Čepin, *Croatia* 42 E3 45 32N 18 34 E
Ceprano, *Italy* 30 A6 41 33N 13 31 E
Ceptura, *Romania* 43 E11 45 1N 26 21 E
Cepu, *Indonesia* 63 G14 7 9 S 111 35 E
Ceram = Seram, *Indonesia* 63 E7 3 10 S 129 0 E
Ceram Sea = Seram Sea, *Indonesia* 63 E7 2 30 S 128 30 E
Cerbère, *France* 20 F7 42 26N 3 10 E
Cerbicales, Is., *France* 21 G13 41 33N 9 22 E
Cercal, *Portugal* 35 H2 37 48N 8 40W
Cerdaña, *Spain* 32 C6 42 22N 1 35 E
Cère →, *France* 20 D5 44 55N 1 49 E
Cerea, *Italy* 29 C8 45 12N 11 13 E
Ceredigion □, *U.K.* 13 E3 52 16N 4 15W
Ceres, *Argentina* 126 B3 29 55 S 61 55W
Ceres, *S. Africa* 88 E2 33 21 S 19 18 E
Ceres, *U.S.A.* 116 H6 37 35N 120 57W
Céret, *France* 20 F6 42 30N 2 42 E
Cergy, *France* 19 C9 49 2N 2 4 E
Cerignola, *Italy* 31 A8 41 17N 15 53 E
Cerigo = Kíthira, *Greece* 38 E5 36 8N 23 0 E
Cérilly, *France* 19 F9 46 37N 2 50 E
Cerisiers, *France* 19 D10 48 8N 3 30 E
Cerizay, *France* 18 F6 46 50N 0 40W
Çerkeş, *Turkey* 72 B5 40 49N 32 52 E
Çerkezköy, *Turkey* 41 E12 41 17N 28 0 E
Cerknica, *Slovenia* 29 C11 45 48N 14 21 E
Cerkovica, *Bulgaria* 41 C8 43 41N 24 50 E
Cermerno, *Serbia, Yug.* 40 C4 43 35N 20 25 E
Çermik, *Turkey* 73 C8 38 8N 39 26 E
Cerna, *Romania* 43 E13 45 4N 28 17 E
Cerna →, *Romania* 43 F8 44 38N 23 58 E
Cernavodă, *Romania* 43 F13 44 22N 28 3 E
Cernay, *France* 19 E14 47 44N 7 10 E
Cernik, *Croatia* 42 E2 45 17N 17 22 E
Cerralvo, I., *Mexico* 118 C3 24 20N 109 45W
Cërrik, *Albania* 40 E3 41 2N 19 58 E
Cerritos, *Mexico* 118 C4 22 27N 100 20W
Cerro Chato, *Uruguay* 127 C4 33 6 S 55 8W
Certaldo, *Italy* 28 E8 43 33N 11 2 E
Cervaro →, *Italy* 31 A8 41 30N 15 52 E
Cervati, Monte, *Italy* 31 B8 40 17N 15 29 E
Cerventes, *Australia* 93 F2 30 31 S 115 3 E
Cervera, *Spain* 32 D6 41 40N 1 16 E
Cervera de Pisuerga, *Spain* 34 C6 42 51N 4 30W
Cervera del Río Alhama, *Spain* 32 C3 42 2N 1 58W
Cervéteri, *Italy* 29 F9 42 0N 12 6 E
Cérvia, *Italy* 29 D9 44 15N 12 22 E
Cervignano del Friuli, *Italy* 29 C10 45 49N 13 20 E
Cervinara, *Italy* 31 A7 41 1N 14 37 E
Cervione, *France* 21 F13 42 20N 9 29 E
Cervo, *Spain* 34 B3 43 40N 7 24W
Cesarò, *Italy* 31 E7 37 50N 14 38 E
Cesena, *Italy* 29 D9 44 8N 12 15 E
Cesenático, *Italy* 29 D9 44 12N 12 24 E
Cēsis, *Latvia* 9 H21 57 18N 25 15 E
Česká Lípa, *Czech Rep.* 26 A7 50 45N 14 30 E
Česká Třebová, *Czech Rep.* 27 B9 49 54N 16 27 E
České Budějovice, *Czech Rep.* 26 C7 48 55N 14 25 E
České Velenice, *Czech Rep.* 26 C7 48 45N 14 57 E
Českobudějovický □, *Czech Rep.* 26 B7 49 10N 14 30 E
Českomoravská Vrchovina, *Czech Rep.* 26 B8 49 30N 15 40 E
Český Brod, *Czech Rep.* 26 A7 50 4N 14 52 E
Český Krumlov, *Czech Rep.* 26 C7 48 43N 14 21 E
Český Těšín, *Czech Rep.* 27 B11 49 45N 18 39 E
Česma →, *Croatia* 29 C13 45 35N 16 29 E
Çeşme, *Turkey* 39 C8 38 20N 26 23 E
Cessnock, *Australia* 95 E5 32 50 S 151 21 E
Cesson-Sévigné, *France* 18 D5 48 7N 1 36W
Cestas, *France* 20 D3 44 44N 0 41W
Cestos →, *Liberia* 82 D3 5 40N 9 10W
Cetate, *Romania* 42 F8 44 7N 23 2 E
Cetin Grad, *Croatia* 29 C12 45 9N 15 45 E
Cetina →, *Croatia* 29 E13 43 26N 16 42 E
Cetinje, *Montenegro, Yug.* 40 D2 42 23N 18 59 E
Cetraro, *Italy* 31 C8 39 31N 15 55 E
Ceuta, *N. Afr.* 78 A4 35 52N 5 18W
Ceva, *Italy* 28 D5 44 23N 8 2 E
Cévennes, *France* 20 D7 44 10N 3 50 E
Ceyhan, *Turkey* 70 B2 37 4N 35 47 E
Ceyhan →, *Turkey* 72 D6 36 38N 35 40 E
Ceylânpınar, *Turkey* 73 D9 36 50N 40 2 E
Ceylon = Sri Lanka ■, *Asia* 66 R12 7 30N 80 50 E
Cèze →, *France* 21 D8 44 6N 4 43 E
Cha-am, *Thailand* 64 F2 12 48N 99 58 E
Cha Pa, *Vietnam* 64 A4 22 20N 103 47 E
Chabanais, *France* 20 C4 45 52N 0 48 E
Chabeuil, *France* 21 D9 44 54N 5 3 E
Chablais, *France* 19 F13 46 20N 6 36 E
Chablis, *France* 19 E10 47 47N 3 48 E
Chacabuco, *Argentina* 126 C3 34 40 S 60 27W
Chachapoyas, *Peru* 124 E3 6 15 S 77 50W
Chachoengsao, *Thailand* 64 F3 13 42N 101 5 E
Chachran, *Pakistan* 66 E7 28 55N 70 30 E
Chachro, *Pakistan* 68 G4 25 5N 70 15 E
Chaco □, *Argentina* 126 B3 26 30 S 61 0W
Chaco □, *Paraguay* 126 B4 26 0 S 60 0W
Chaco →, *U.S.A.* 115 H9 36 46N 108 39W
Chaco Austral, *S. Amer.* 128 B4 27 0 S 61 30W
Chaco Boreal, *S. Amer.* 124 H6 22 0 S 60 0W
Chaco Central, *S. Amer.* 128 A4 24 0 S 61 0W
Chacon, C., *U.S.A.* 104 C2 54 42N 132 0W
Chad ■, *Africa* 79 F8 15 0N 17 15 E
Chad, L. = Tchad, L., *Chad* 79 F8 13 30N 14 30 E
Chadan, *Russia* 51 D10 51 17N 91 35 E
Chadileuvú →, *Argentina* 126 D2 37 46 S 66 0W
Chadiza, *Zambia* 87 E3 14 45 S 32 27 E
Chadron, *U.S.A.* 112 D3 42 50N 103 0W
Chadyr-Lunga = Ciadâr-Lunga, *Moldova* 43 D13 46 3N 28 51 E
Chae Hom, *Thailand* 64 C2 18 43N 99 35 E
Chaem →, *Thailand* 64 C2 18 11N 98 38 E
Chaeryŏng, *N. Korea* 57 E13 38 24N 125 36 E
Chagai Hills = Chāh Gay, *Afghan.* 66 E3 29 30N 64 0 E
Chagda, *Russia* 51 D14 58 45N 130 38 E
Chaghcharān, *Afghan.* 66 B4 34 31N 65 15 E
Chagny, *France* 19 F11 46 57N 4 45 E
Chagoda, *Russia* 46 C8 59 10N 35 15 E
Chagos Arch., *Ind. Oc.* 52 K11 6 0 S 72 0 E
Chagrin Falls, *U.S.A.* 110 E3 41 26N 81 24W
Chāh Ākhvor, *Iran* 71 C8 32 41N 59 40 E
Chāh Bahar, *Iran* 71 E9 25 20N 60 40 E
Chāh-e Kavīr, *Iran* 71 C8 34 29N 56 52 E
Chāh Gay, *Afghan.* 66 E3 29 30N 64 0 E

Chahar Burjak

Chahar Burjak, *Afghan.* **66 D3** 30 15N 62 0 E
Chahār Mahāll va Bakhtīarī □, *Iran* **71 C6** 32 0N 49 0 E
Chaibasa, *India* **67 H14** 22 42N 85 49 E
Chaillé-les-Marais, *France* **20 B2** 46 25N 1 2W
Chainat, *Thailand* **64 E3** 15 11N 100 8 E
Chaiya, *Thailand* **65 H2** 9 23N 99 14 E
Chaj Doab, *Pakistan* **68 C5** 32 15N 73 0 E
Chajari, *Argentina* **126 C4** 30 42 S 58 0W
Chak Amru, *Pakistan* **68 C6** 32 22N 75 11 E
Chaka, *Sudan* **81 G3** 4 49N 31 14 E
Chakar →, *Pakistan* **68 E3** 29 29N 68 2 E
Chakari, *Zimbabwe* **89 B4** 18 5 S 29 51 E
Chake Chake, *Tanzania* **86 D4** 5 15 S 39 45 E
Chakhānsūr, *Afghan.* **66 D3** 31 10N 62 0 E
Chakonipau, L., *Canada* **103 A6** 56 18N 68 30W
Chakradharpur, *India* **69 H11** 22 45N 85 40 E
Chakrata, *India* **68 D7** 30 42N 77 51 E
Chakwal, *Pakistan* **68 C5** 32 56N 72 53 E
Chala, *Peru* **124 G4** 15 48 S 74 20W
Chalais, *France* **20 C4** 45 16N 0 3 E
Chalchihuites, *Mexico* **118 C4** 23 29N 103 53W
Chalcis = Khalkís, *Greece* **38 C5** 38 27N 23 42 E
Châlette-sur-Loing, *France* **19 D9** 48 1N 2 44 E
Chaleur B., *Canada* **103 C6** 47 55N 65 30W
Chalfant, *U.S.A.* **116 H8** 37 32N 118 21W
Chalhuanca, *Peru* **124 F4** 14 15 S 73 15W
Chalindrey, *France* **19 E12** 47 43N 5 26 E
Chaling, *China* **59 D9** 26 58N 113 30 E
Chalisgaon, *India* **66 J9** 20 30N 75 10 E
Chalk River, *Canada* **102 C4** 46 1N 77 27W
Chalky Inlet, *N.Z.* **91 M1** 46 3 S 166 31 E
Challans, *France* **18 F5** 46 50N 1 52W
Challapata, *Bolivia* **124 G5** 18 53 S 66 50W
Challis, *U.S.A.* **114 D6** 44 30N 114 14W
Chalmette, *U.S.A.* **113 L10** 29 56N 89 58W
Chalon-sur-Saône, *France* **19 F11** 46 48N 4 50 E
Chalonnes-sur-Loire, *France* **18 E6** 47 20N 0 45W
Châlons-en-Champagne, *France* **19 D11** 48 58N 4 20 E
Châlus, *France* **20 C4** 45 39N 0 58 E
Chalyaphum, *Thailand* **64 E4** 15 48N 102 2 E
Cham, *Germany* **25 F8** 49 13N 12 39 E
Cham, Cu Lao, *Vietnam* **64 E7** 15 57N 108 30 E
Chama, *U.S.A.* **115 H10** 36 54N 106 35W
Chamaicó, *Argentina* **126 D3** 35 3 S 64 58W
Chaman, *Pakistan* **66 D5** 30 58N 66 25 E
Chamba, *India* **68 C7** 32 35N 76 10 E
Chamba, *Tanzania* **87 E4** 11 37 S 37 0 E
Chambal →, *India* **69 F8** 26 29N 79 15 E
Chamberlain, *U.S.A.* **112 D5** 43 49N 99 20W
Chamberlain →, *Australia* **92 C4** 15 30 S 127 54 E
Chamberlain L., *U.S.A.* **109 B11** 46 14N 69 19W
Chambers, *U.S.A.* **115 J9** 35 11N 109 26W
Chambersburg, *U.S.A.* **108 F7** 39 56N 77 40W
Chambéry, *France* **21 C9** 45 34N 5 55 E
Chambeshi →, *Zambia* **84 G6** 11 53 S 29 48 E
Chambly, *Canada* **111 A11** 45 27N 73 17W
Chambord, *Canada* **103 C5** 48 25N 72 6W
Chamboulive, *France* **20 C5** 45 26N 1 42 E
Chamchamal, *Iraq* **70 C5** 35 32N 44 50 E
Chamela, *Mexico* **118 D3** 19 32N 105 5W
Chamical, *Argentina* **126 C2** 30 22 S 66 27W
Chamkar Luong, *Cambodia* **65 G4** 11 0N 103 45 E
Chamoli, *India* **69 D8** 30 24N 79 21 E
Chamonix-Mont Blanc, *France* **21 C10** 45 55N 6 51 E
Chamouchouane →, *Canada* **102 C5** 48 37N 72 20W
Champa, *India* **69 H10** 22 2N 82 43 E
Champagne, *Canada* **104 A1** 60 49N 136 30W
Champagne, *France* **19 D11** 48 40N 4 20 E
Champagnole, *France* **19 F12** 46 45N 5 55 E
Champaign, *U.S.A.* **108 E1** 40 7N 88 15W
Champassak, *Laos* **64 E5** 14 53N 105 52 E
Champaubert, *France* **19 D10** 48 50N 3 45 E
Champawat, *India* **69 E9** 29 20N 80 6 E
Champdeniers-St-Denis, *France* **20 B3** 46 29N 0 25W
Champdoré, L., *Canada* **103 A6** 55 55N 65 49W
Champeix, *France* **20 C7** 45 37N 3 8 E
Champion, *U.S.A.* **110 E4** 41 19N 80 51W
Champlain, *U.S.A.* **111 B11** 44 59N 73 27W
Champlain, L., *U.S.A.* **111 B11** 44 40N 73 20W
Champlitte, *France* **19 E12** 47 32N 5 31 E
Champotón, *Mexico* **119 D6** 19 20N 90 50W
Champua, *India* **69 H11** 22 5N 85 40 E
Chamusca, *Portugal* **35 F2** 39 21N 8 29W
Chana, *Thailand* **65 J3** 6 55N 100 44 E
Chañaral, *Chile* **126 B1** 26 23 S 70 40W
Chanārān, *Iran* **71 B8** 36 39N 59 6 E
Chanasma, *India* **68 H5** 23 44N 72 5 E
Chanco, *Chile* **126 D1** 35 44 S 72 32W
Chand, *India* **69 J8** 21 57N 79 7 E
Chandan, *India* **69 G12** 24 38N 86 40 E
Chandan Chauki, *India* **69 E9** 28 33N 80 47 E
Chandannagar, *India* **69 H13** 22 52N 88 24 E
Chandausi, *India* **69 E8** 28 27N 78 49 E
Chandeleur Is., *U.S.A.* **113 L10** 29 55N 88 57W
Chandeleur Sd., *U.S.A.* **113 L10** 29 55N 89 0W
Chandigarh, *India* **68 D7** 30 43N 76 47 E
Chandil, *India* **69 H12** 22 58N 86 3 E
Chandler, *Australia* **95 D1** 27 0 S 133 19 E
Chandler, *Canada* **103 C7** 48 18N 64 46W
Chandler, *Ariz., U.S.A.* **115 K8** 33 18N 111 50W
Chandler, *Okla., U.S.A.* **113 H6** 35 42N 96 53W
Chandod, *India* **68 J5** 21 59N 73 28 E
Chandpur, *Bangla.* **67 H17** 23 8N 90 45 E
Chandrapur, *India* **66 K11** 19 57N 79 25 E
Chānf, *Iran* **71 E9** 26 38N 60 29 E
Chang, *Pakistan* **68 F3** 26 59N 68 30 E
Chang, Ko, *Thailand* **65 F4** 12 0N 102 23 E
Ch'ang Chiang = Chang Jiang →, *China* **59 B13** 31 48N 121 10 E
Chang Jiang →, *China* **59 B13** 31 48N 121 10 E
Changa, *India* **69 C7** 33 53N 77 35 E
Changanacheri, *India* **66 Q10** 9 25N 76 31 E
Changane →, *Mozam.* **89 C5** 24 30 S 33 30 E
Changbai, *China* **57 D15** 41 25N 128 5 E
Changbai Shan, *China* **57 C15** 42 20N 129 0 E
Changchiak'ou = Zhangjiakou, *China* **56 D8** 40 48N 114 55 E
Ch'angchou = Changzhou, *China* **59 B12** 31 47N 119 58 E
Changchun, *China* **57 C13** 43 57N 125 17 E
Changchunling, *China* **57 B13** 45 18N 125 27 E
Changde, *China* **59 C8** 29 4N 111 35 E
Changdo-ri, *N. Korea* **57 E14** 38 30N 127 40 E
Changfeng, *China* **59 A11** 32 28N 117 10 E
Changhai = Shanghai, *China* **59 B13** 31 15N 121 26 E
Changhua, *China* **59 B12** 30 12N 119 12 E
Changhua, *Taiwan* **59 E13** 24 2N 120 30 E
Changhŭng, *S. Korea* **57 G14** 34 41N 126 52 E
Changhŭngni, *N. Korea* **57 D15** 40 24N 128 19 E
Changjiang, *China* **64 C7** 19 20N 108 55 E
Changjin, *N. Korea* **57 D14** 40 23N 127 15 E
Changjin-chŏsuji, *N. Korea* **57 D14** 40 30N 127 15 E
Changle, *China* **59 E12** 25 59N 119 27 E
Changli, *China* **57 E10** 39 40N 119 13 E
Changling, *China* **57 B12** 44 20N 123 58 E
Changlun, *Malaysia* **65 J3** 6 25N 100 26 E
Changning, *Hunan, China* **59 D9** 26 28N 112 22 E
Changning, *Sichuan, China* **58 C5** 28 40N 104 56 E
Changning, *Yunnan, China* **58 E2** 24 45N 99 30 E
Changping, *China* **56 D9** 40 14N 116 12 E
Changsha, *China* **59 C9** 28 12N 113 0 E
Changshan, *China* **59 C12** 28 55N 118 27 E
Changshu, *China* **59 B13** 31 38N 120 43 E
Changshun, *China* **58 D6** 26 3N 106 25 E
Changtai, *China* **59 E11** 24 35N 117 42 E
Changting, *China* **59 E11** 25 50N 116 22 E
Changwu, *China* **56 G4** 35 10N 107 45 E
Changxing, *China* **59 B12** 31 0N 119 55 E
Changyang, *China* **59 B8** 30 30N 111 10 E
Changyi, *China* **57 F10** 36 40N 119 30 E
Changyŏn, *N. Korea* **57 E13** 38 15N 125 6 E
Changyuan, *China* **56 G8** 35 15N 114 42 E
Changzhi, *China* **56 F7** 36 10N 113 6 E
Changzhou, *China* **59 B12** 31 47N 119 58 E
Chanhanga, *Angola* **88 B1** 16 0 S 14 8 E
Chanlar = Xanlar, *Azerbaijan* **49 K8** 40 37N 46 12 E
Channapatna, *India* **66 N10** 12 40N 77 15 E
Channel Is., *U.K.* **13 H5** 49 19N 2 24W
Channel Is., *U.S.A.* **117 M7** 33 40N 119 15W
Channel Islands National Park, *U.S.A.* **117 M8** 33 30N 119 0W
Channel-Port aux Basques, *Canada* **103 C8** 47 30N 59 9W
Channel Tunnel, *Europe* **13 F9** 51 0N 1 30 E
Channing, *U.S.A.* **113 H3** 35 41N 102 20W
Chantada, *Spain* **34 C3** 42 36N 7 46W
Chanthaburi, *Thailand* **64 F4** 12 38N 102 12 E
Chantilly, *France* **19 C9** 49 12N 2 29 E
Chantonnay, *France* **18 F5** 46 40N 1 3W
Chantrey Inlet, *Canada* **100 B10** 67 48N 96 20W
Chanute, *U.S.A.* **113 G7** 37 41N 95 27W
Chanza →, *Spain* **35 H3** 37 32N 7 30W
Chao Hu, *China* **59 B11** 31 30N 117 30 E
Chao Phraya →, *Thailand* **64 F3** 13 32N 100 36 E
Chao Phraya Lowlands, *Thailand* **64 E3** 15 30N 100 0 E
Chaocheng, *China* **56 F8** 36 4N 115 37 E
Chaohu, *China* **59 B11** 31 38N 117 50 E
Chaoyang, *Guangdong, China* **59 F11** 23 17N 116 30 E
Chaoyang, *Liaoning, China* **57 D11** 41 35N 120 22 E
Chaozhou, *China* **59 F11** 23 42N 116 32 E
Chapais, *Canada* **102 C5** 49 47N 74 51W
Chapala, *Mozam.* **87 F4** 15 50 S 37 35 E
Chapala, L. de, *Mexico* **118 C4** 20 10N 103 20W
Chapayev, *Kazakhstan* **48 E10** 50 25N 51 10 E
Chapayevsk, *Russia* **48 D9** 53 0N 49 40 E
Chapecó, *Brazil* **127 B5** 27 14 S 52 41W
Chapel Hill, *U.S.A.* **109 H6** 35 55N 79 4W
Chapleau, *Canada* **102 C3** 47 50N 83 24W
Chaplin, *Canada* **105 C7** 50 28N 106 40W
Chaplin L., *Canada* **105 C7** 50 22N 106 36W
Chaplino, *Ukraine* **47 H9** 48 8N 36 15 E
Chaplygin, *Russia* **46 F11** 53 15N 40 0 E
Chappell, *U.S.A.* **112 E3** 41 6N 102 28W
Chapra = Chhapra, *India* **69 G11** 25 48N 84 44 E
Chara, *Russia* **51 D12** 56 54N 118 20 E
Charadai, *Argentina* **126 B4** 27 35 S 59 55W
Charagua, *Bolivia* **124 G6** 19 45 S 63 10W
Charambirá, Punta, *Colombia* **124 C3** 4 16N 77 32W
Charaña, *Bolivia* **124 G5** 17 30 S 69 25W
Charantsavan, *Armenia* **49 K7** 40 35N 44 41 E
Charanwala, *India* **68 F5** 27 51N 72 10 E
Charata, *Argentina* **126 B3** 27 13 S 61 14W
Charcas, *Mexico* **118 C4** 23 10N 101 20W
Chard, *U.K.* **13 G5** 50 52N 2 58W
Chardon, *U.S.A.* **110 E3** 41 35N 81 12W
Chardzhou = Chärjew, *Turkmenistan* **50 F7** 39 6N 63 34 E
Charente □, *France* **20 C4** 45 50N 0 16 E
Charente →, *France* **20 C2** 45 57N 1 5W
Charente-Maritime □, *France* **20 C3** 45 45N 0 45W
Charenton-du-Cher, *France* **19 F9** 46 44N 2 39 E
Chari →, *Chad* **79 F8** 12 58N 14 31 E
Chārīkār, *Afghan.* **66 B6** 35 0N 69 10 E
Chariton →, *U.S.A.* **112 F8** 39 19N 92 58W
Chärjew, *Turkmenistan* **50 F7** 39 6N 63 34 E
Charkhari, *India* **69 G8** 25 24N 79 45 E
Charkhi Dadri, *India* **68 E7** 28 37N 76 17 E
Charleroi, *Belgium* **17 D4** 50 24N 4 27 E
Charleroi, *U.S.A.* **110 F5** 40 9N 79 57W
Charles, C., *U.S.A.* **108 G8** 37 7N 75 58W
Charles City, *U.S.A.* **112 D8** 43 4N 92 41W
Charles L., *Canada* **105 B6** 59 50N 110 33W
Charles Town, *U.S.A.* **108 F7** 39 17N 77 52W
Charleston, *Ill., U.S.A.* **108 F1** 39 30N 88 10W
Charleston, *Miss., U.S.A.* **113 H9** 34 1N 90 4W
Charleston, *Mo., U.S.A.* **113 G10** 36 55N 89 21W
Charleston, *S.C., U.S.A.* **109 J6** 32 46N 79 56W
Charleston, *W. Va., U.S.A.* **108 F5** 38 21N 81 38W
Charleston L., *Canada* **111 B9** 44 32N 76 0W
Charleston Peak, *U.S.A.* **117 J11** 36 16N 115 42W
Charlestown, *Ireland* **15 C3** 53 58N 8 48W
Charlestown, *S. Africa* **89 D4** 27 26 S 29 53 E
Charlestown, *Ind., U.S.A.* **108 F3** 38 27N 85 40W
Charlestown, *N.H., U.S.A.* **111 C12** 43 14N 72 25W
Charleville = Rath Luirc, *Ireland* **15 D3** 52 21N 8 40W
Charleville, *Australia* **95 D4** 26 24 S 146 15 E
Charleville-Mézières, *France* **19 C11** 49 44N 4 40 E
Charlevoix, *U.S.A.* **108 C3** 45 19N 85 16W
Charlieu, *France* **19 F11** 46 10N 4 10 E
Charlotte, *Mich., U.S.A.* **108 D3** 42 34N 84 50W
Charlotte, *N.C., U.S.A.* **109 H5** 35 13N 80 51W
Charlotte, *Vt., U.S.A.* **111 B11** 44 19N 73 14W
Charlotte Amalie, *U.S. Virgin Is.* **121 C7** 18 21N 64 56W
Charlotte Harbor, *U.S.A.* **109 M4** 26 50N 82 10W
Charlotte L., *Canada* **104 C3** 52 12N 125 19W
Charlottenberg, *Sweden* **10 E6** 59 54N 12 17 E
Charlottesville, *U.S.A.* **108 F6** 38 2N 78 30W
Charlottetown, *Nfld., Canada* **103 B8** 52 46N 56 7W
Charlottetown, *P.E.I., Canada* **103 C7** 46 14N 63 8W
Charlton, *Australia* **95 F3** 36 16 S 143 24 E
Charlton, *U.S.A.* **112 E8** 40 59N 93 20W
Charlton I., *Canada* **102 B4** 52 0N 79 20W
Charmes, *France* **19 D13** 48 22N 6 17 E
Charny, *Canada* **103 C5** 46 43N 71 15W
Charolles, *France* **19 F11** 46 27N 4 16 E
Chârost, *France* **19 F9** 47 0N 2 7 E
Charre, *Mozam.* **87 F4** 17 13 S 35 10 E
Charroux, *France* **20 B4** 46 9N 0 25 E
Charsadda, *Pakistan* **68 B4** 34 7N 71 45 E
Charters Towers, *Australia* **94 C4** 20 5 S 146 13 E
Chartres, *France* **18 D8** 48 29N 1 30 E
Chascomús, *Argentina* **126 D4** 35 30 S 58 0W
Chasefu, *Zambia* **87 E3** 11 55 S 33 8 E
Chashma Barrage, *Pakistan* **68 C4** 32 27N 71 20 E
Chasseneuil-sur-Bonnieure, *France* **20 C4** 45 52N 0 29 E
Chāt, *Iran* **71 B7** 37 59N 55 16 E
Chatal Balkan = Udvoy Balkan, *Bulgaria* **41 D10** 42 50N 26 50 E
Château-Arnoux, *France* **21 D10** 44 6N 6 0 E
Château-Chinon, *France* **19 E10** 47 4N 3 56 E
Château-d'Olonne, *France* **20 B2** 46 30N 1 44W
Château-du-Loir, *France* **18 E7** 47 40N 0 25 E
Château-Gontier, *France* **18 E6** 47 50N 0 48W
Château-la-Vallière, *France* **18 E7** 47 30N 0 20 E
Château-Landon, *France* **19 D9** 48 8N 2 40 E
Château-Renault, *France* **18 E7** 47 36N 0 56 E
Château-Salins, *France* **19 D13** 48 50N 6 30 E
Château-Thierry, *France* **19 C10** 49 3N 3 20 E
Châteaubourg, *France* **18 D5** 48 7N 1 25W
Châteaubriant, *France* **18 E5** 47 43N 1 23W
Châteaudun, *France* **18 D8** 48 3N 1 20 E
Chateaugay, *U.S.A.* **111 B10** 44 56N 74 5W
Châteaugiron, *France* **18 D5** 48 3N 1 30W
Châteauguay, L., *Canada* **103 A5** 56 26N 70 3W
Châteaulin, *France* **18 D2** 48 11N 4 8W
Châteaumeillant, *France* **19 F9** 46 35N 2 12 E
Châteauneuf-du-Faou, *France* **18 D3** 48 11N 3 50W
Châteauneuf-sur-Charente, *France* **20 C3** 45 36N 0 3W
Châteauneuf-sur-Cher, *France* **19 F9** 46 52N 2 18 E
Châteauneuf-sur-Loire, *France* **19 E9** 47 52N 2 13 E
Châteaurenard, *Bouches-du-Rhône, France* **21 E8** 43 53N 4 51 E
Châteaurenard, *Loiret, France* **19 E9** 47 56N 2 55 E
Châteauroux, *France* **19 F8** 46 50N 1 40 E
Châteauvillain, *France* **19 D11** 48 2N 4 55 E
Châtelaillon-Plage, *France* **20 B2** 46 5N 1 5W
Châtelguyon, *France* **20 C7** 45 55N 3 4 E
Châtellerault, *France* **18 F7** 46 50N 0 30 E
Châtelus-Malvaleix, *France* **19 F9** 46 18N 2 1 E
Chatham = Miramichi, *Canada* **103 C6** 47 2N 65 28W
Chatham, *Canada* **102 D3** 42 24N 82 11W
Chatham, *U.K.* **13 F8** 51 22N 0 32 E
Chatham, *U.S.A.* **111 D11** 42 21N 73 36W
Chatham Is., *Pac. Oc.* **96 M10** 44 0 S 176 40W
Châtillon, *Italy* **28 C4** 45 45N 7 37 E
Châtillon-Coligny, *France* **19 E9** 47 50N 2 51 E
Châtillon-en-Diois, *France* **21 D9** 44 41N 5 29 E
Châtillon-sur-Indre, *France* **18 F8** 46 59N 1 10 E
Châtillon-sur-Loire, *France* **19 E9** 47 35N 2 44 E
Châtillon-sur-Seine, *France* **19 E11** 47 50N 4 33 E
Chatmohar, *Bangla.* **69 G13** 24 15N 89 15 E
Chatra, *India* **69 G11** 24 12N 84 56 E
Chatrapur, *India* **67 K14** 19 22N 85 2 E
Chats, L. des, *Canada* **111 A8** 45 30N 76 20W
Chatsu, *India* **68 F6** 26 36N 75 57 E
Chatsworth, *Canada* **110 B4** 44 27N 80 54W
Chatsworth, *Zimbabwe* **87 F3** 19 38 S 31 13 E
Chattahoochee, *U.S.A.* **109 K3** 30 42N 84 51W
Chattahoochee →, *U.S.A.* **109 K3** 30 54N 84 57W
Chattanooga, *U.S.A.* **109 H3** 35 3N 85 19W
Chatteris, *U.K.* **13 E8** 52 28N 0 2 E
Chaturat, *Thailand* **64 E3** 15 40N 101 51 E
Chau Doc, *Vietnam* **65 G5** 10 42N 105 7 E
Chaudes-Aigues, *France* **20 D7** 44 51N 3 1 E
Chauffailles, *France* **19 F11** 46 13N 4 20 E
Chaukan Pass, *Burma* **67 F20** 27 0N 97 15 E
Chaumont, *France* **19 D12** 48 7N 5 8 E
Chaumont, *U.S.A.* **111 B8** 44 4N 76 8W
Chaumont-en-Vexin, *France* **19 C8** 49 16N 1 53 E
Chaumont-sur-Loire, *France* **18 E8** 47 29N 1 11 E
Chaunay, *France* **20 B4** 46 13N 0 9 E
Chauny, *France* **19 C10** 49 37N 3 12 E
Chausey, Îs., *France* **18 D5** 48 52N 1 49W
Chaussin, *France* **19 F12** 46 59N 5 22 E
Chautauqua L., *U.S.A.* **110 D5** 42 10N 79 24W
Chauvigny, *France* **18 F7** 46 34N 0 39 E
Chauvin, *Canada* **105 C6** 52 45N 110 10W
Chavanges, *France* **19 D11** 48 30N 4 35 E
Chaves, *Brazil* **125 D9** 0 15 S 49 55W
Chaves, *Portugal* **34 D3** 41 45N 7 32W
Chawang, *Thailand* **65 H2** 8 25N 99 30 E
Chazelles-sur-Lyon, *France* **21 C8** 45 39N 4 22 E
Chazy, *U.S.A.* **111 B11** 44 53N 73 26W
Cheb, *Czech Rep.* **26 A5** 50 9N 12 28 E
Cheboksarskoye Vdkhr., *Russia* **48 B8** 56 13N 46 58 E
Cheboksary, *Russia* **48 B8** 56 8N 47 12 E
Cheboygan, *U.S.A.* **108 C3** 45 39N 84 29W
Chebsara, *Russia* **46 C10** 59 10N 38 59 E
Chech, Erg, *Africa* **78 D5** 25 0N 2 15W
Chechen, Ostrov, *Russia* **49 H8** 43 59N 47 40 E
Chechenia □, *Russia* **49 J7** 43 30N 45 29 E
Checheno-Ingush Republic = Chechenia □, *Russia* **49 J7** 43 30N 45 29 E
Chechnya = Chechenia □, *Russia* **49 J7** 43 30N 45 29 E
Chech'ŏn, *S. Korea* **57 F15** 37 8N 128 12 E
Chęciny, *Poland* **45 H7** 50 46N 20 28 E
Checotah, *U.S.A.* **113 H7** 35 28N 95 31W
Chedabucto B., *Canada* **103 C7** 45 25N 61 8W
Cheduba I., *Burma* **67 K18** 18 45N 93 40 E
Cheepie, *Australia* **95 D4** 26 33 S 145 1 E
Chef-Boutonne, *France* **20 B3** 46 7N 0 4W
Chegdomyn, *Russia* **51 D14** 51 7N 133 1 E
Chegga, *Mauritania* **78 C4** 25 27N 5 40W
Chegutu, *Zimbabwe* **87 F3** 18 10 S 30 14 E
Chehalis, *U.S.A.* **116 D4** 46 40N 122 58W
Chehalis →, *U.S.A.* **116 D3** 46 57N 123 50W
Cheiron, Mt., *France* **21 E10** 43 49N 6 58 E
Cheju do, *S. Korea* **57 H14** 33 29N 126 34 E
Chekalin, *Russia* **46 E9** 54 10N 36 10 E
Chekiang = Zhejiang □, *China* **59 C13** 29 0N 120 0 E
Chel = Kuru, Bahr el →, *Sudan* **81 F2** 8 10N 26 50 E
Chela, Sa. da, *Angola* **88 B1** 16 20 S 13 20 E
Chelan, *U.S.A.* **114 C4** 47 51N 120 1W
Chelan, L., *U.S.A.* **114 B3** 48 11N 120 30W
Cheleken, *Turkmenistan* **50 F6** 39 34N 53 16 E
Cheleken Yarymadasy, *Turkmenistan* **71 B7** 39 30N 53 15 E
Chelforó, *Argentina* **128 D3** 39 0 S 66 33W
Chelkar = Shalqar, *Kazakhstan* **50 E6** 47 48N 59 39 E
Chelkar Tengiz, Solonchak, *Kazakhstan* **50 E7** 48 5N 63 7 E
Chella, *Ethiopia* **81 F4** 5 0N 37 26 E
Chelles, *France* **19 D9** 48 52N 2 33 E
Chełm, *Poland* **45 G10** 51 8N 23 30 E
Chełmno, *Poland* **45 E5** 53 20N 18 30 E
Chelmsford, *U.K.* **13 F8** 51 44N 0 29 E
Chełmża, *Poland* **45 E5** 53 10N 18 39 E
Chelsea, *U.S.A.* **111 C12** 43 59N 72 27W
Cheltenham, *U.K.* **13 F5** 51 54N 2 4W
Chelva, *Spain* **32 F4** 39 45N 1 0W
Chelyabinsk, *Russia* **50 D7** 55 10N 61 24 E
Chelyuskin, C., *Russia* **52 B14** 77 30N 103 0 E
Chemainus, *Canada* **116 B3** 48 55N 123 42W
Chemba, *Mozam.* **85 H6** 17 9 S 34 53 E
Chembar = Belinskiy, *Russia* **48 D6** 53 0N 43 25 E
Chemillé, *France* **18 E6** 47 14N 0 45W
Chemnitz, *Germany* **24 E8** 50 51N 12 54 E
Chemult, *U.S.A.* **114 E3** 43 14N 121 47W
Chen, Gora, *Russia* **51 C15** 65 16N 141 50 E
Chenab →, *Pakistan* **68 D4** 30 23N 71 2 E
Chenango Forks, *U.S.A.* **111 D9** 42 15N 75 51W
Chencha, *Ethiopia* **81 F4** 6 15N 37 32 E
Chenchiang = Zhenjiang, *China* **59 A12** 32 11N 119 26 E
Cheney, *U.S.A.* **114 C5** 47 30N 117 35W
Cheng Xian, *China* **56 H3** 33 43N 105 42 E
Chengbu, *China* **59 D8** 26 18N 110 16 E
Chengcheng, *China* **56 G5** 35 8N 109 56 E
Chengchou = Zhengzhou, *China* **56 G7** 34 45N 113 34 E
Chengde, *China* **57 D9** 40 59N 117 58 E
Chengdong Hu, *China* **59 A11** 32 15N 116 20 E
Chengdu, *China* **58 B5** 30 38N 104 2 E
Chenggong, *China* **58 E4** 24 52N 102 56 E
Chenggu, *China* **56 H4** 33 10N 107 21 E
Chenghai, *China* **59 F11** 23 30N 116 42 E
Chengjiang, *China* **58 E4** 24 39N 103 0 E
Chengkou, *China* **58 B7** 31 54N 108 31 E
Ch'engmai, *China* **64 C7** 19 50N 109 58 E
Ch'engtu = Chengdu, *China* **58 B5** 30 38N 104 2 E
Chengwu, *China* **56 G8** 34 58N 115 50 E
Chengxi Hu, *China* **59 A11** 32 15N 116 10 E
Chengyang, *China* **57 F11** 36 18N 120 21 E
Chenjiagang, *China* **57 G10** 34 23N 119 47 E
Chenkán, *Mexico* **119 D6** 19 8N 90 58W
Chennai, *India* **66 N12** 13 8N 80 19 E
Chenôve, *France* **19 E12** 47 16N 5 1 E
Chenxi, *China* **59 C8** 28 2N 110 12 E
Chenzhou, *China* **59 E9** 25 47N 113 1 E
Cheo Reo, *Vietnam* **62 B3** 13 25N 108 28 E
Cheom Ksan, *Cambodia* **64 E5** 14 13N 104 56 E
Chepelare, *Bulgaria* **41 E8** 41 44N 24 40 E
Chepén, *Peru* **124 E3** 7 15 S 79 23W
Chepes, *Argentina* **126 C2** 31 20 S 66 35W
Chepo, *Panama* **120 E4** 9 10N 79 6W
Chepstow, *U.K.* **13 F5** 51 38N 2 41W
Cheptulil, Mt., *Kenya* **86 B4** 1 25N 35 35 E
Chequamegon B., *U.S.A.* **112 B9** 46 40N 90 30W
Cher □, *France* **19 E9** 47 10N 2 30 E
Cher →, *France* **18 E7** 47 21N 0 29 E
Chéradi, *Italy* **31 B10** 40 27N 17 10 E
Cherasco, *Italy* **28 D4** 44 39N 7 51 E
Cheraw, *U.S.A.* **109 H6** 34 42N 79 53W
Cherbourg, *France* **18 C5** 49 39N 1 40W
Cherdakly, *Russia* **48 C9** 54 25N 48 50 E
Cherdyn, *Russia* **50 C6** 60 24N 56 29 E
Cheremkhovo, *Russia* **51 D11** 53 8N 103 1 E
Cherepanovo, *Russia* **50 D9** 54 15N 83 30 E
Cherepovets, *Russia* **46 C9** 59 5N 37 55 E
Chergui, Chott ech, *Algeria* **78 B6** 34 21N 0 25 E
Cherikov = Cherykaw, *Belarus* **46 F6** 53 32N 31 20 E
Cherkasy, *Ukraine* **47 H7** 49 27N 32 4 E
Cherkessk, *Russia* **49 H6** 44 15N 42 5 E
Cherlak, *Russia* **50 D8** 54 15N 74 55 E
Chernaya, *Russia* **51 B9** 70 30N 89 10 E
Cherni, *Bulgaria* **40 D7** 42 35N 23 18 E
Chernigov = Chernihiv, *Ukraine* **47 G6** 51 28N 31 20 E
Chernihiv, *Ukraine* **47 G6** 51 28N 31 20 E
Chernivtsi, *Ukraine* **47 H3** 48 15N 25 52 E
Chernobyl = Chornobyl, *Ukraine* **47 G6** 51 20N 30 15 E
Chernogorsk, *Russia* **51 D10** 53 49N 91 18 E
Chernomorskoye = Chornomorske, *Ukraine* **47 K7** 45 31N 32 40 E
Chernovtsy = Chernivtsi, *Ukraine* **47 H3** 48 15N 25 52 E
Chernyakhovsk, *Russia* **9 J19** 54 36N 21 48 E
Chernyanka, *Russia* **47 G9** 50 56N 37 49 E
Chernyshevskiy, *Russia* **51 C12** 63 0N 112 30 E
Chernyye Zemli, *Russia* **49 H8** 46 10N 46 0 E
Cherokee, *Iowa, U.S.A.* **112 D7** 42 45N 95 33W
Cherokee, *Okla., U.S.A.* **113 G5** 36 45N 98 21W
Cherokee Village, *U.S.A.* **113 G9** 36 17N 91 30W
Cherokees, Grand Lake O' The, *U.S.A.* **113 G7** 36 28N 95 2W
Cherrapunji, *India* **67 G17** 25 17N 91 47 E
Cherry Valley, *Calif., U.S.A.* **117 M10** 33 59N 116 57W
Cherry Valley, *N.Y., U.S.A.* **111 D10** 42 48N 74 45W
Cherskiy, *Russia* **51 C17** 68 45N 161 18 E
Cherskogo Khrebet, *Russia* **51 C15** 65 0N 143 0 E
Chertkovo, *Russia* **47 H11** 49 25N 40 19 E
Cherven, *Belarus* **46 F5** 53 45N 28 28 E
Cherven-Bryag, *Bulgaria* **41 C8** 43 17N 24 7 E
Chervonohrad, *Ukraine* **47 G3** 50 25N 24 10 E
Cherwell →, *U.K.* **13 F6** 51 44N 1 14W
Cherykaw, *Belarus* **46 F6** 53 32N 31 20 E
Chesapeake, *U.S.A.* **108 G7** 36 50N 76 17W
Chesapeake B., *U.S.A.* **108 G7** 38 0N 76 10W
Cheshire □, *U.K.* **12 D5** 53 14N 2 30W
Cheshskaya Guba, *Russia* **50 C5** 67 20N 47 0 E
Cheshunt, *U.K.* **13 F7** 51 43N 0 1W
Chesil Beach, *U.K.* **13 G5** 50 37N 2 33W
Chesley, *Canada* **110 B3** 44 17N 81 5W
Cheste, *Spain* **33 F4** 39 30N 0 41W
Chester, *U.K.* **12 D5** 53 12N 2 53W
Chester, *Calif., U.S.A.* **114 F3** 40 19N 121 14W
Chester, *Ill., U.S.A.* **113 G10** 37 55N 89 49W
Chester, *Mont., U.S.A.* **114 B8** 48 31N 110 58W
Chester, *Pa., U.S.A.* **108 F8** 39 51N 75 22W
Chester, *S.C., U.S.A.* **109 H5** 34 43N 81 12W
Chester, *Vt., U.S.A.* **111 C12** 43 16N 72 36W
Chester, *W. Va., U.S.A.* **110 F4** 40 37N 80 34W
Chester-le-Street, *U.K.* **12 C6** 54 51N 1 34W
Chesterfield, *U.K.* **12 D6** 53 15N 1 25W
Chesterfield, Is., *N. Cal.* **96 J7** 19 52 S 158 15 E
Chesterfield Inlet, *Canada* **100 B10** 63 30N 90 45W
Chesterton Ra., *Australia* **95 D4** 25 30 S 147 27 E
Chestertown, *U.S.A.* **111 C11** 43 40N 73 48W
Chesterville, *Canada* **111 A9** 45 6N 75 14W
Chestnut Ridge, *U.S.A.* **110 F5** 40 20N 79 10W
Chesuncook L., *U.S.A.* **109 C11** 46 0N 69 21W
Chéticamp, *Canada* **103 C7** 46 37N 60 59W
Chetrosu, *Moldova* **43 B12** 48 5N 27 54 E
Chetumal, *Mexico* **119 D7** 18 30N 88 20W
Chetumal, B. de, *Mexico* **119 D7** 18 40N 88 10W
Chetwynd, *Canada* **104 B4** 55 45N 121 36W
Chevanceaux, *France* **20 C3** 45 18N 0 14W
Cheviot, The, *U.K.* **12 B5** 55 29N 2 9W
Cheviot Hills, *U.K.* **12 B5** 55 20N 2 30W
Cheviot Ra., *Australia* **94 D3** 25 20 S 143 45 E
Chew Bahir, *Ethiopia* **81 G4** 4 40N 36 50 E
Chewelah, *U.S.A.* **114 B5** 48 17N 117 43W
Cheyenne, *Okla., U.S.A.* **113 H5** 35 37N 99 40W
Cheyenne, *Wyo., U.S.A.* **112 E2** 41 8N 104 49W
Cheyenne →, *U.S.A.* **112 C4** 44 41N 101 18W
Cheyenne Wells, *U.S.A.* **112 F3** 38 49N 102 21W
Cheyne B., *Australia* **93 F2** 34 35 S 118 50 E
Chhabra, *India* **68 G7** 24 40N 76 54 E
Chhaktala, *India* **68 H6** 22 6N 74 11 E
Chhapra, *India* **69 G11** 25 48N 84 44 E
Chhata, *India* **68 F7** 27 42N 77 30 E
Chhatarpur, *Bihar, India* **69 G11** 24 23N 84 11 E
Chhatarpur, *Mad. P., India* **69 G8** 24 55N 79 35 E
Chhattisgarh □, *India* **69 J10** 22 0N 82 0 E
Chhep, *Cambodia* **64 F5** 13 45N 105 24 E
Chhindwara, *Mad. P., India* **69 H8** 23 3N 79 29 E
Chhindwara, *Mad. P., India* **69 H8** 22 2N 78 59 E
Chhlong, *Cambodia* **65 F5** 12 15N 105 58 E
Chhota Tawa →, *India* **68 H7** 22 14N 76 36 E
Chhoti Kali Sindh →, *India* **68 G6** 24 2N 75 31 E
Chhuikhadan, *India* **69 J9** 21 32N 80 59 E
Chhuk, *Cambodia* **65 G5** 10 46N 104 28 E
Chi →, *Thailand* **64 E5** 15 11N 104 43 E
Chiai, *Taiwan* **59 F13** 23 29N 120 25 E
Chiali, *Taiwan* **59 F13** 23 10N 120 11 E
Chiamboni, *Somali Rep.* **84 E8** 1 39 S 41 35 E
Chiamussu = Jiamusi, *China* **60 B8** 46 40N 130 26 E
Chianciano Terme, *Italy* **29 E8** 43 2N 11 49 E
Chiang Dao, *Thailand* **64 C2** 19 22N 98 58 E
Chiang Kham, *Thailand* **64 C3** 19 32N 100 18 E
Chiang Khan, *Thailand* **64 D3** 17 52N 101 36 E
Chiang Khong, *Thailand* **58 G3** 20 17N 100 24 E
Chiang Mai, *Thailand* **64 C2** 18 47N 98 59 E
Chiang Rai, *Thailand* **58 H2** 19 52N 99 50 E
Chiang Saen, *Thailand* **58 G3** 20 16N 100 5 E
Chiapa →, *Mexico* **119 D6** 16 42N 93 0W
Chiapa de Corzo, *Mexico* **119 D6** 16 42N 93 0W
Chiapas □, *Mexico* **119 D6** 17 0N 92 45W

Clark Fork

Clark Fork →, U.S.A. 114 B5 48 9N 116 15W
Clarkdale, U.S.A. 115 J7 34 46N 112 3W
Clarke City, Canada 103 B6 50 12N 66 38W
Clarke I., Australia 94 G4 40 32 S 148 10 E
Clarke Ra., Australia 94 C4 20 40 S 148 30 E
Clark's Fork →, U.S.A. 114 D9 45 39N 108 43W
Clark's Harbour, Canada 103 D6 43 25N 65 38W
Clarks Hill L., U.S.A. 109 J4 33 40N 82 12W
Clarks Summit, U.S.A. 111 E9 41 30N 75 42W
Clarksburg, U.S.A. 108 F5 39 17N 80 30W
Clarksdale, U.S.A. 113 H9 34 12N 90 35W
Clarksville, Ark., U.S.A. 113 H8 35 28N 93 28W
Clarksville, Tenn., U.S.A. 109 G2 36 32N 87 21W
Clarksville, Tex., U.S.A. 113 J7 33 37N 95 3W
Clatskanie, U.S.A. 116 D3 46 6N 123 12W
Claude, U.S.A. 113 H4 35 7N 101 22W
Claveria, Phil. 61 B4 18 37N 121 4 E
Clay, U.S.A. 116 G5 38 17N 121 10W
Clay Center, U.S.A. 112 F6 39 23N 97 8W
Claypool, U.S.A. 115 K8 33 25N 110 51W
Claysburg, U.S.A. 110 F6 40 17N 78 27W
Claysville, U.S.A. 110 F4 40 7N 80 25W
Clayton, N. Mex., U.S.A. 113 G3 36 27N 103 11W
Clayton, N.Y., U.S.A. 111 B8 44 14N 76 5W
Clear, C., Ireland 15 E2 51 25N 9 32W
Clear, L., Canada 110 A7 45 26N 77 12W
Clear Hills, Canada 104 B5 56 40N 119 30W
Clear I., Ireland 15 E2 51 26N 9 30W
Clear L., U.S.A. 116 F4 39 2N 122 47W
Clear Lake, Iowa, U.S.A. 112 D8 43 8N 93 23W
Clear Lake, S. Dak., U.S.A. 112 C6 44 45N 96 41W
Clear Lake Reservoir, U.S.A. 114 F3 41 56N 121 5W
Clearfield, Pa., U.S.A. 110 E6 41 2N 78 27W
Clearfield, Utah, U.S.A. 114 F8 41 7N 112 2W
Clearlake, U.S.A. 114 G2 38 57N 122 38W
Clearlake Highlands, U.S.A. 116 G4 38 57N 122 38W
Clearwater, Canada 104 C4 51 38N 120 2W
Clearwater, U.S.A. 109 M4 27 58N 82 48W
Clearwater →, Alta., Canada 104 C6 52 22N 114 57W
Clearwater →, Alta., Canada 105 B6 56 44N 111 23W
Clearwater L., Canada 105 C9 53 34N 99 49W
Clearwater Mts., U.S.A. 114 C6 46 5N 115 20W
Clearwater Prov. Park, Canada 105 C8 54 0N 101 0W
Clearwater River Prov. Park, Canada 105 B7 56 55N 109 10W
Cleburne, U.S.A. 113 J6 32 21N 97 23W
Clee Hills, U.K. 13 E5 52 26N 2 35W
Cleethorpes, U.K. 12 D7 53 33N 0 3W
Cleeve Cloud, U.K. 13 F6 51 56N 2 0W
Clelles, France 21 D9 44 50N 5 38 E
Clemson, U.S.A. 109 H4 34 41N 82 50W
Clerke Reef, Australia 92 C2 17 22 S 119 20 E
Clermont, Australia 94 C4 22 49 S 147 39 E
Clermont, France 19 C9 49 23N 2 24 E
Clermont, U.S.A. 109 L5 28 33N 81 46W
Clermont-en-Argonne, France 19 C12 49 5N 5 4 E
Clermont-Ferrand, France 20 C7 45 46N 3 4 E
Clermont-l'Hérault, France 20 E7 43 38N 3 26 E
Clerval, France 19 E13 47 25N 6 30 E
Clervaux, Lux. 17 D6 50 4N 6 2 E
Cles, Italy 28 B8 46 22N 11 2 E
Clevedon, U.K. 13 F5 51 26N 2 52W
Cleveland, Miss., U.S.A. 113 J9 33 45N 90 43W
Cleveland, Ohio, U.S.A. 110 E3 41 30N 81 42W
Cleveland, Okla., U.S.A. 113 G6 36 19N 96 28W
Cleveland, Tenn., U.S.A. 109 H3 35 10N 84 53W
Cleveland, Tex., U.S.A. 113 K7 30 21N 95 5W
Cleveland, C., Australia 94 B4 19 11 S 147 1 E
Cleveland, Mt., U.S.A. 114 B7 48 56N 113 51W
Cleveland Heights, U.S.A. 110 E3 41 30N 81 34W
Clevelândia, Brazil 127 B5 26 24 S 52 23W
Clew B., Ireland 15 C2 53 50N 9 49W
Clewiston, U.S.A. 109 M5 26 45N 80 56W
Clifden, Ireland 15 C1 53 29N 10 1W
Clifden, N.Z. 91 M1 46 1 S 167 42 E
Cliffdell, U.S.A. 116 D5 46 56N 121 5W
Cliffy Hd., Australia 93 G2 35 1 S 116 29 E
Clifton, Australia 95 D5 27 59 S 151 53 E
Clifton, Ariz., U.S.A. 115 K9 33 3N 109 18W
Clifton, Colo., U.S.A. 115 G9 39 7N 108 25W
Clifton, Tex., U.S.A. 113 K6 31 47N 97 35W
Clifton Beach, Australia 94 B4 16 46 S 145 39 E
Climax, Canada 105 D7 49 10N 108 20W
Clinch →, U.S.A. 109 H3 35 53N 84 29W
Clingmans Dome, U.S.A. 109 H4 35 34N 83 30W
Clint, U.S.A. 115 L10 31 35N 106 14W
Clinton, B.C., Canada 104 C4 51 6N 121 35W
Clinton, Ont., Canada 102 D3 43 37N 81 32W
Clinton, N.Z. 91 M2 46 12 S 169 23 E
Clinton, Ark., U.S.A. 113 H8 35 36N 92 28W
Clinton, Conn., U.S.A. 111 E12 41 17N 72 32W
Clinton, Ill., U.S.A. 112 E10 40 9N 88 57W
Clinton, Ind., U.S.A. 108 F2 39 40N 87 24W
Clinton, Iowa, U.S.A. 112 E9 41 51N 90 12W
Clinton, Mass., U.S.A. 111 D13 42 25N 71 41W
Clinton, Miss., U.S.A. 113 J9 32 20N 90 20W
Clinton, Mo., U.S.A. 112 F8 38 22N 93 46W
Clinton, N.C., U.S.A. 109 H6 35 0N 78 22W
Clinton, Okla., U.S.A. 113 H5 35 31N 98 58W
Clinton, S.C., U.S.A. 109 H5 34 29N 81 53W
Clinton, Tenn., U.S.A. 109 G3 36 6N 84 8W
Clinton, Wash., U.S.A. 116 C4 47 59N 122 21W
Clinton C., Australia 94 C5 22 30 S 150 45 E
Clinton Colden L., Canada 100 B9 63 58N 107 27W
Clintonville, U.S.A. 112 C10 44 37N 88 46W
Clipperton, I., Pac. Oc. 97 F17 10 18N 109 13W
Clisham, U.K. 14 D2 57 57N 6 49W
Clisson, France 18 E5 47 5N 1 16W
Clitheroe, U.K. 12 D5 53 53N 2 22W
Clo-oose, Canada 116 B2 48 39N 124 49W
Cloates, Pt., Australia 92 D1 22 43 S 113 40 E
Clocolan, S. Africa 89 D4 28 55 S 27 34 E
Clodomira, Argentina 126 B3 27 35 S 64 14W
Clogher Hd., Ireland 15 C5 53 48N 6 14W
Clonakilty, Ireland 15 E3 51 37N 8 53W
Clonakilty B., Ireland 15 E3 51 35N 8 51W
Cloncurry, Australia 94 C3 20 40 S 140 28 E
Cloncurry →, Australia 94 B3 18 37 S 140 40 E
Clondalkin, Ireland 15 C5 53 19N 6 25W
Clones, Ireland 15 B4 54 11N 7 15W
Clonmel, Ireland 15 D4 52 21N 7 42W
Cloppenburg, Germany 24 C4 52 51N 8 1 E
Cloquet, U.S.A. 112 B8 46 43N 92 28W
Clorinda, Argentina 126 B4 25 16 S 57 45W
Cloud Bay, Canada 102 C2 48 5N 89 26W
Cloud Peak, U.S.A. 114 D10 44 23N 107 11W
Cloudcroft, U.S.A. 115 K11 32 58N 105 45W
Cloverdale, U.S.A. 116 G4 38 48N 123 1W
Clovis, Calif., U.S.A. 116 J7 36 49N 119 42W
Clovis, N. Mex., U.S.A. 113 H3 34 24N 103 12W
Cloyes-sur-le-Loir, France 18 E8 48 0N 1 14 E
Cloyne, Canada 110 B7 44 49N 77 11W
Cluj □, Romania 43 D8 46 45N 23 30 E
Cluj-Napoca, Romania 43 D8 46 47N 23 38 E
Clunes, Australia 95 F3 37 20 S 143 45 E
Cluny, France 19 F11 46 26N 4 38 E
Cluses, France 19 F13 46 5N 6 35 E
Clusone, Italy 28 C6 45 53N 9 57 E
Clutha →, N.Z. 91 M2 46 20 S 169 49 E
Clwyd →, U.K. 12 D4 53 19N 3 31W
Clyde, Canada 104 C6 54 9N 113 39W
Clyde, N.Z. 91 L2 45 12 S 169 20 E
Clyde, U.S.A. 110 C8 43 5N 76 52W
Clyde →, U.K. 14 F4 55 55N 4 30W
Clyde, Firth of, U.K. 14 F3 55 22N 5 1W
Clyde River, Canada 101 A13 70 30N 68 30W
Clydebank, U.K. 14 F4 55 54N 4 23W
Clymer, N.Y., U.S.A. 110 D5 42 1N 79 37W
Clymer, Pa., U.S.A. 110 D5 40 40N 79 1W
Ćmielów, Poland 45 H8 50 53N 21 31 E
Côa →, Portugal 34 D3 41 5N 7 6W
Coachella, U.S.A. 117 M10 33 41N 116 10W
Coachella Canal, U.S.A. 117 N12 32 43N 114 57W
Coahoma, U.S.A. 113 J4 32 18N 101 18W
Coahuayana →, Mexico 118 D4 18 41N 103 45W
Coahuila □, Mexico 118 B4 27 0N 103 0W
Coal →, Canada 104 B3 59 39N 126 57W
Coalane, Mozam. 87 F4 17 48 S 37 2 E
Coalcomán, Mexico 118 D4 18 40N 103 10W
Coaldale, Canada 104 D6 49 45N 112 35W
Coalgate, U.S.A. 113 H6 34 32N 96 13W
Coalinga, U.S.A. 116 J6 36 9N 120 21W
Coalisland, U.K. 15 B5 54 33N 6 42W
Coalville, U.K. 12 E6 52 44N 1 23W
Coalville, U.S.A. 114 F8 40 55N 111 24W
Coari, Brazil 124 D6 4 8 S 63 7W
Coast □, Kenya 86 C4 2 40 S 39 45 E
Coast Mts., Canada 104 C3 55 0N 129 20W
Coast Ranges, U.S.A. 116 G4 39 0N 123 0W
Coatbridge, U.K. 14 F4 55 52N 4 6W
Coatepec, Mexico 119 D5 19 27N 96 58W
Coatepeque, Guatemala 120 D1 14 46N 91 55W
Coatesville, U.S.A. 108 F8 39 59N 75 50W
Coaticook, Canada 103 C5 45 10N 71 46W
Coats I., Canada 101 B11 62 30N 83 0W
Coats Land, Antarctica 5 D1 77 0 S 25 0W
Coatzacoalcos, Mexico 119 D6 18 7N 94 25W
Cobadin, Romania 43 F13 44 5N 28 13 E
Cobalt, Canada 102 C4 47 25N 79 42W
Cobán, Guatemala 120 C1 15 30N 90 21W
Çobanlar, Turkey 39 C12 38 41N 30 47 E
Cobar, Australia 95 E4 31 27 S 145 48 E
Cóbh, Ireland 15 E3 51 51N 8 17W
Cobija, Bolivia 124 F5 11 0 S 68 50W
Cobleskill, U.S.A. 111 D10 42 41N 74 29W
Coboconk, Canada 110 B6 44 39N 78 48W
Cobourg, Canada 102 D4 43 58N 78 10W
Cobourg Pen., Australia 92 B5 11 20 S 132 15 E
Cobram, Australia 95 F4 35 54 S 145 40 E
Cóbué, Mozam. 87 E3 12 0 S 34 58 E
Coburg, Germany 25 E6 50 15N 10 58 E
Coca, Spain 34 D6 41 13N 4 32W
Cocanada = Kakinada, India 67 L13 16 57N 82 11 E
Cocentaina, Spain 33 G4 38 45N 0 27W
Cochabamba, Bolivia 124 G5 17 26 S 66 10W
Cochem, Germany 25 E3 50 9N 7 9 E
Cochemane, Mozam. 87 F3 17 0 S 32 54 E
Cochin, India 66 Q10 9 59N 76 22 E
Cochin China = Nam-Phan, Vietnam 65 G6 10 30N 106 0 E
Cochran, U.S.A. 109 J4 32 23N 83 21W
Cochrane, Alta., Canada 104 C6 51 11N 114 30W
Cochrane, Ont., Canada 102 C3 49 0N 81 0W
Cochrane, Chile 128 F2 47 15 S 72 33W
Cochrane →, Canada 105 B8 59 0N 103 40W
Cochrane, L., Chile 128 F2 47 10 S 72 0W
Cochranton, U.S.A. 110 E4 41 31N 80 3W
Cockburn, Australia 95 E3 32 5 S 141 0 E
Cockburn, Canal, Chile 122 J3 54 30 S 72 0W
Cockburn I., Canada 102 C3 45 55N 83 22W
Cockburn Ra., Australia 92 C4 15 46 S 128 0 E
Cockermouth, U.K. 12 C4 54 40N 3 22W
Cocklebiddy, Australia 93 F4 32 0 S 126 3 E
Coco →, Cent. Amer. 120 D3 15 0N 83 8W
Coco, I. del, Pac. Oc. 97 G19 5 25N 87 55W
Cocoa, U.S.A. 109 L5 28 21N 80 44W
Cocobeach, Gabon 84 D1 0 59N 9 34 E
Cocora, Romania 43 F12 44 45N 27 3 E
Cocos Is., Ind. Oc. 96 J1 12 10 S 96 55 E
Cod, C., U.S.A. 108 D10 42 5N 70 10W
Codajás, Brazil 124 D6 3 55 S 62 0W
Codigoro, Italy 29 D9 44 49N 12 8 E
Codlea, Romania 43 E10 45 42N 25 27 E
Codó, Brazil 125 D10 4 30 S 43 55W
Codogno, Italy 28 C6 45 9N 9 42 E
Codróipo, Italy 29 C10 45 58N 13 0 E
Codru, Munţii, Romania 42 D7 46 30N 22 15 E
Cody, U.S.A. 114 D9 44 32N 109 3W
Coe Hill, Canada 110 B7 44 52N 77 50W
Coelemu, Chile 126 D1 36 30 S 72 48W
Coen, Australia 94 A3 13 52 S 143 12 E
Coesfeld, Germany 24 D3 51 56N 7 10 E
Cœur d'Alene, U.S.A. 114 C5 47 45N 116 51W
Cœur d'Alene L., U.S.A. 114 C5 47 32N 116 48W
Coevorden, Neths. 17 B6 52 40N 6 44 E
Cofete, Canary Is. 37 F5 28 6N 14 23W
Coffeyville, U.S.A. 113 G7 37 2N 95 37W
Coffin B., Australia 95 E2 34 38 S 135 28 E
Coffin Bay, Australia 95 E2 34 37 S 135 29 E
Coffin Bay Peninsula, Australia 95 E2 34 32 S 135 15 E
Coffs Harbour, Australia 95 E5 30 16 S 153 5 E
Cofrentes, Spain 33 F3 39 13N 1 5W
Cogalnic →, Moldova 43 E14 45 49N 29 40 E
Cogealac, Romania 43 F13 44 36N 28 36 E
Coghinas →, Italy 30 B1 40 55N 8 48 E
Coghinas, L. del, Italy 30 B2 40 46N 9 3 E
Cognac, France 20 C3 45 41N 0 20W
Cogne, Italy 28 C4 45 37N 7 21 E
Cogolin, France 21 E10 43 15N 6 32 E
Cogolludo, Spain 32 E1 40 59N 3 10W
Cohocton, U.S.A. 110 D7 42 30N 77 30W
Cohocton →, U.S.A. 110 D7 42 9N 77 6W
Cohoes, U.S.A. 111 D11 42 46N 73 42W
Cohuna, Australia 95 F3 35 45 S 144 15 E
Coiba, I., Panama 120 E3 7 30N 81 40W
Coig →, Argentina 128 G3 51 0 S 69 10W
Coigeach, Rubha, U.K. 14 C3 58 6N 5 26W
Coihaique, Chile 128 F2 45 30 S 71 45W
Coimbatore, India 66 P10 11 2N 76 59 E
Coimbra, Brazil 124 G7 19 55 S 57 48W
Coimbra, Portugal 34 E2 40 15N 8 27W
Coimbra □, Portugal 34 E2 40 12N 8 25W
Coín, Spain 35 J6 36 40N 4 48W
Coipasa, Salar de, Bolivia 124 G5 19 26 S 68 9W
Cojimies, Ecuador 124 C3 0 20N 80 0W
Cojocna, Romania 43 D8 46 45N 23 50 E
Cojutepequé, El Salv. 120 D2 13 41N 88 54W
Čoka, Serbia, Yug. 42 E5 45 57N 20 12 E
Cokeville, U.S.A. 114 E8 42 5N 110 57W
Colac, Australia 95 F3 38 21 S 143 35 E
Colatina, Brazil 125 G10 19 32 S 40 37W
Colbeck, C., Antarctica 5 D13 77 6 S 157 48W
Colborne, Canada 110 C7 44 0N 77 53W
Colby, U.S.A. 112 F4 39 24N 101 3W
Colchester, U.K. 13 F8 51 54N 0 55 E
Cold L., Canada 105 C7 54 33N 110 5W
Coldstream, Canada 104 C5 50 13N 119 11W
Coldstream, U.K. 14 F6 55 39N 2 15W
Coldwater, Canada 110 B5 44 42N 79 40W
Coldwater, Kans., U.S.A. 113 G5 37 16N 99 20W
Coldwater, Mich., U.S.A. 108 E3 41 57N 85 0W
Colebrook, U.S.A. 111 B13 44 54N 71 30W
Coleman, U.S.A. 113 K5 31 50N 99 26W
Coleman →, Australia 94 B3 15 6 S 141 38 E
Colenso, S. Africa 89 D4 28 44 S 29 50 E
Coleraine, Australia 95 F3 37 36 S 141 40 E
Coleraine, U.K. 15 A5 55 8N 6 41W
Coleridge, L., N.Z. 91 K3 43 17 S 171 30 E
Colesberg, S. Africa 88 E4 30 45 S 25 5 E
Coleville, U.S.A. 116 G7 38 34N 119 30W
Colfax, Calif., U.S.A. 116 F6 39 6N 120 57W
Colfax, La., U.S.A. 113 K8 31 31N 92 42W
Colfax, Wash., U.S.A. 114 C5 46 53N 117 22W
Colhué Huapi, L., Argentina 128 F3 45 30 S 69 0W
Colibaşi, Moldova 43 E13 45 43N 28 11 E
Colibaşi, Romania 43 F9 44 56N 24 54 E
Cólico, Italy 28 B6 46 8N 9 22 E
Coligny, France 19 F12 46 23N 5 21 E
Coligny, S. Africa 89 D4 26 17 S 26 15 E
Colima, Mexico 118 D4 19 14N 103 43W
Colima □, Mexico 118 D4 19 10N 103 40W
Colima, Nevado de, Mexico 118 D4 19 35N 103 45W
Colina, Chile 126 C1 33 13 S 70 45W
Colina do Norte, Guinea-Biss. 82 C2 12 28N 15 0W
Colinas, Brazil 125 E10 6 0 S 44 10W
Colindres, Spain 34 B7 43 24N 3 27W
Coll, U.K. 14 E2 56 39N 6 34W
Collaguasi, Chile 126 A2 21 5 S 68 45W
Collarada, Peña, Spain 32 C4 42 43N 0 29W
Collarenebri, Australia 95 D4 29 33 S 148 34 E
Colle di Val d'Elsa, Italy 28 E8 43 25N 11 7 E
Colléchio, Italy 28 D7 44 45N 10 13 E
Colleen Bawn, Zimbabwe 87 G2 21 0 S 29 12 E
College Park, U.S.A. 109 J3 33 40N 84 27W
College Station, U.S.A. 113 K6 30 37N 96 21W
Collesalvetti, Italy 28 E7 43 34N 10 27 E
Collie, Australia 93 F2 33 22 S 116 8 E
Collier B., Australia 92 C3 16 10 S 124 15 E
Collier Ra., Australia 93 D2 24 45 S 119 10 E
Collina, Passo di, Italy 28 D7 44 2N 10 56 E
Collingwood, Canada 102 D3 44 29N 80 13W
Collingwood, N.Z. 91 J4 40 41 S 172 40 E
Collins, Canada 102 B2 50 17N 89 27W
Collinsville, Australia 94 C4 20 30 S 147 56 E
Collipulli, Chile 126 D1 37 55 S 72 30W
Collooney, Ireland 15 B3 54 11N 8 29W
Colmar, France 19 D14 48 5N 7 20 E
Colmars, France 21 D10 44 11N 6 39 E
Colmenar, Spain 35 J6 36 54N 4 20W
Colmenar de Oreja, Spain 34 E7 40 6N 3 25W
Colmenar Viejo, Spain 34 E7 40 39N 3 47W
Colo →, Australia 95 E5 33 25 S 150 52 E
Cologne = Köln, Germany 24 E2 50 56N 6 57 E
Colom, I. d'en, Spain 37 B11 39 58N 4 16 E
Coloma, U.S.A. 116 G6 38 48N 120 53W
Colomb-Béchar = Béchar, Algeria 78 B5 31 38N 2 18W
Colombey-les-Belles, France 19 D12 48 32N 5 54 E
Colombey-les-Deux-Églises, France 19 D11 48 13N 4 50 E
Colombia ■, S. Amer. 124 C4 3 45N 73 0W
Colombian Basin, S. Amer. 98 H12 14 0N 76 0W
Colombo, Sri Lanka 66 R11 6 56N 79 58 E
Colomiers, France 20 E5 43 36N 1 21 E
Colón, Buenos Aires, Argentina 126 C3 33 53 S 61 7W
Colón, Entre Ríos, Argentina 126 C4 32 12 S 58 10W
Colón, Cuba 120 B3 22 42N 80 54W
Colón, Panama 120 E4 9 20N 79 54W
Colonia de Sant Jordi, Spain 37 B9 39 19N 2 59 E
Colonia del Sacramento, Uruguay 126 C4 34 25 S 57 50W
Colonia Dora, Argentina 126 B3 28 34 S 62 59W
Colonial Beach, U.S.A. 108 F7 38 15N 76 58W
Colonie, U.S.A. 111 D11 42 43N 73 50W
Colonna, C., Italy 31 C10 39 2N 17 12 E
Colonsay, Canada 105 C7 51 59N 105 52W
Colonsay, U.K. 14 E2 56 5N 6 12W
Colorado □, U.S.A. 115 G10 39 30N 105 30W
Colorado →, Argentina 128 D4 39 50 S 62 8W
Colorado →, N. Amer. 115 L6 31 45N 114 40W
Colorado →, U.S.A. 113 L7 28 36N 95 59W
Colorado City, U.S.A. 113 J4 32 24N 100 52W
Colorado Plateau, U.S.A. 115 H8 37 0N 111 0W
Colorado River Aqueduct, U.S.A. 117 L12 34 17N 114 10W
Colorado Springs, U.S.A. 112 F2 38 50N 104 49W
Colorno, Italy 28 D7 44 56N 10 23 E
Colotlán, Mexico 118 C4 22 6N 103 16W
Colstrip, U.S.A. 114 D10 45 53N 106 38W
Colton, U.S.A. 111 B10 44 33N 74 56W
Columbia, Ky., U.S.A. 108 G3 37 6N 85 18W
Columbia, La., U.S.A. 113 J8 32 6N 92 5W
Columbia, Miss., U.S.A. 113 K10 31 15N 89 50W
Columbia, Mo., U.S.A. 112 F8 38 57N 92 20W
Columbia, Pa., U.S.A. 111 F8 40 2N 76 30W
Columbia, S.C., U.S.A. 109 J5 34 0N 81 2W
Columbia, Tenn., U.S.A. 109 H2 35 37N 87 2W
Columbia →, N. Amer. 116 D2 46 15N 124 5W
Columbia, C., Canada 4 A4 83 0N 70 0W
Columbia, District of □, U.S.A. 108 F7 38 55N 77 0W
Columbia, Mt., Canada 104 C5 52 8N 117 20W
Columbia Basin, U.S.A. 114 C4 46 45N 119 5W
Columbia Falls, U.S.A. 114 B6 48 23N 114 11W
Columbia Mts., Canada 104 C5 52 0N 119 0W
Columbia Plateau, U.S.A. 114 D5 44 0N 117 30W
Columbiana, U.S.A. 110 F4 40 53N 80 42W
Columbretes, Is., Spain 32 F5 39 50N 0 50 E
Columbus, Ga., U.S.A. 109 J3 32 28N 84 59W
Columbus, Ind., U.S.A. 108 F3 39 13N 85 55W
Columbus, Kans., U.S.A. 113 G7 37 10N 94 50W
Columbus, Miss., U.S.A. 109 J1 33 30N 88 25W
Columbus, Mont., U.S.A. 114 D9 45 38N 109 15W
Columbus, N. Mex., U.S.A. 115 L10 31 50N 107 38W
Columbus, Nebr., U.S.A. 112 E6 41 26N 97 22W
Columbus, Ohio, U.S.A. 108 F4 39 58N 83 0W
Columbus, Tex., U.S.A. 113 L6 29 42N 96 33W
Colunga, Spain 34 B5 43 29N 5 16W
Colusa, U.S.A. 116 F4 39 13N 122 1W
Colville, U.S.A. 114 B5 48 33N 117 54W
Colville →, U.S.A. 100 A4 70 25N 150 30W
Colville, C., N.Z. 91 G5 36 29 S 175 21 E
Colwood, Canada 116 B3 48 26N 123 29W
Colwyn Bay, U.K. 12 D4 53 18N 3 44W
Coma, Ethiopia 81 F4 8 29N 36 53 E
Comácchio, Italy 29 D9 44 42N 12 11 E
Comalcalco, Mexico 119 D6 18 16N 93 13W
Comallo, Argentina 128 E2 41 0 S 70 5W
Comana, Romania 43 F11 44 10N 26 10 E
Comanche, U.S.A. 113 K5 31 54N 98 36W
Comăneşti, Romania 43 D11 46 25N 26 26 E
Comarnic, Romania 43 E10 45 15N 25 38 E
Comayagua, Honduras 120 D2 14 25N 87 37W
Combahee →, U.S.A. 109 J5 32 30N 80 31W
Combarbalá, Chile 126 C1 31 11 S 71 2W
Combeaufontaine, France 19 E12 47 38N 5 54 E
Comber, Canada 110 D2 42 14N 82 33W
Comber, U.K. 15 B6 54 33N 5 45W
Combermere, Canada 110 A7 45 22N 77 37W
Comblain-au-Pont, Belgium 17 D5 50 29N 5 35 E
Combourg, France 18 D5 48 25N 1 46W
Combrailles, France 19 F9 46 8N 2 8 E
Combronde, France 20 C7 45 58N 3 5 E
Comeragh Mts., Ireland 15 D4 52 18N 7 34W
Comet, Australia 94 C4 23 36 S 148 38 E
Comilla, Bangla. 67 H17 23 28N 91 10 E
Comino, Malta 36 C1 36 2N 14 20 E
Comino, C., Italy 30 B2 40 32N 9 49 E
Cómiso, Italy 31 F7 36 56N 14 36 E
Comitán, Mexico 119 D6 16 18N 92 9W
Commentry, France 19 F9 46 20N 2 46 E
Commerce, Ga., U.S.A. 109 H4 34 12N 83 28W
Commerce, Tex., U.S.A. 113 J7 33 15N 95 54W
Commercy, France 19 D12 48 43N 5 34 E
Committee B., Canada 101 B11 68 30N 86 30W
Commonwealth B., Antarctica 5 C10 67 0 S 144 0 E
Commoron Cr. →, Australia 95 D5 28 22 S 150 8 E
Communism Pk. = Kommunizma, Pik, Tajikistan 50 F8 39 0N 72 2 E
Como, Italy 28 C6 45 47N 9 5 E
Como, Lago di, Italy 28 B6 46 0N 9 11 E
Comodoro Rivadavia, Argentina 128 F3 45 50 S 67 40W
Comorâşte, Romania 42 E6 45 10N 21 35 E
Comorin, C., India 66 Q10 8 3N 77 40 E
Comoro Is. = Comoros ■, Ind. Oc. 77 H8 12 10 S 44 15 E
Comoros ■, Ind. Oc. 77 H8 12 10 S 44 15 E
Comox, Canada 104 D4 49 42N 124 55W
Compiègne, France 19 C9 49 24N 2 50 E
Comporta, Portugal 35 G2 38 22N 8 46W
Compostela, Mexico 118 C4 21 15N 104 53W
Comprida, I., Brazil 127 A6 24 50 S 47 42W
Compton, Canada 111 A13 45 14N 71 49W
Compton, U.S.A. 117 M8 33 54N 118 13W
Comrat, Moldova 43 D13 46 18N 28 40 E
Con Cuong, Vietnam 64 C5 19 2N 104 54 E
Con Son, Vietnam 65 H6 8 41N 106 37 E
Conakry, Guinea 82 D2 9 29N 13 49W
Conara, Australia 94 G4 41 50 S 147 26 E
Concarneau, France 18 E3 47 52N 3 56W
Conceição, Mozam. 87 F4 18 47 S 36 7 E
Conceição da Barra, Brazil 125 G11 18 35 S 39 45W
Conceição do Araguaia, Brazil 125 E9 8 0 S 49 2W
Concepción, Argentina 126 B2 27 20 S 65 35W
Concepción, Bolivia 124 G6 16 15 S 62 8W
Concepción, Chile 126 D1 36 50 S 73 0W
Concepción, Mexico 119 D6 18 15N 90 5W
Concepción, Paraguay 126 A4 23 22 S 57 26W
Concepción □, Chile 126 D1 37 0 S 72 30W
Concepción →, Mexico 118 A2 30 32N 113 2W
Concepción, Est. de, Chile 128 G2 50 30 S 74 55W
Concepción, L., Bolivia 124 G6 17 20 S 61 20W
Concepción, Punta, Mexico 118 B2 26 55N 111 59W
Concepción del Oro, Mexico 118 C4 24 40N 101 30W
Concepción del Uruguay, Argentina 126 C4 32 35 S 58 20W
Conception, Pt., U.S.A. 117 L6 34 27N 120 28W
Conception B., Canada 103 C9 47 45N 53 0W
Conception B., Namibia 88 C1 23 55 S 14 22 E
Conception I., Bahamas 121 B4 23 52N 75 9W
Concession, Zimbabwe 87 F3 17 27 S 30 56 E
Conchas Dam, U.S.A. 113 H2 35 22N 104 11W
Conches-en-Ouche, France 18 D7 48 58N 0 56 E
Concho, U.S.A. 115 J9 34 28N 109 36W
Concho →, U.S.A. 113 K5 31 34N 99 43W
Conchos →, Chihuahua, Mexico 118 B4 29 32N 105 0W
Conchos →, Tamaulipas, Mexico 119 B5 25 9N 98 35W
Concord, Calif., U.S.A. 116 H4 37 59N 122 2W
Concord, N.C., U.S.A. 109 H5 35 25N 80 35W
Concord, N.H., U.S.A. 111 C13 43 12N 71 32W
Concordia, Argentina 126 C4 31 20 S 58 2W
Concórdia, Brazil 124 D5 4 36 S 66 36W
Concordia, Mexico 118 C3 23 18N 106 2W
Concordia, U.S.A. 112 F6 39 34N 97 40W
Concrete, U.S.A. 114 B3 48 32N 121 45W
Condamine, Australia 95 D5 26 56 S 150 9 E
Condat, France 20 C6 45 21N 2 46 E
Conde, U.S.A. 112 C5 45 9N 98 6W
Condé-sur-Noireau, France 18 D6 48 51N 0 33W
Condeúba, Brazil 125 F10 14 52 S 42 0W
Condobolin, Australia 95 E4 33 4 S 147 6 E
Condom, France 20 E4 43 57N 0 22 E
Condon, U.S.A. 114 D3 45 14N 120 11W
Conegliano, Italy 29 C9 45 53N 12 18 E
Conejera, I. = Conills, I. des, Spain 37 B9 39 11N 2 58 E
Conejos, Mexico 118 B4 26 14N 103 53W
Confolens, France 20 B4 46 2N 0 40 E
Confuso →, Paraguay 126 B4 25 9 S 57 34W
Congaz, Moldova 43 D13 46 7N 28 36 E
Conghua, China 59 F9 23 36N 113 31 E
Congjiang, China 58 E7 25 43N 108 52 E
Congleton, U.K. 12 D5 53 10N 2 13W
Congo (Kinshasa) = Congo, Dem. Rep. of the ■, Africa 84 E4 3 0 S 23 0 E
Congo ■, Africa 84 E3 1 0 S 16 0 E
Congo →, Africa 84 F2 6 4 S 12 24 E
Congo, Dem. Rep. of the ■, Africa 84 E4 3 0 S 23 0 E
Congo Basin, Africa 84 E4 0 10 S 24 30 E
Congonhas, Brazil 127 A7 20 30 S 43 52W
Congress, U.S.A. 115 J7 34 9N 112 51W
Conil = Conil de la Frontera, Spain 35 J4 36 17N 6 10W
Conil de la Frontera, Spain 35 J4 36 17N 6 10W
Conills, I. des, Spain 37 B9 39 11N 2 58 E
Coniston, Canada 102 C3 46 29N 80 51W
Conjeeveram = Kanchipuram, India 66 N11 12 52N 79 45 E
Conklin, Canada 105 B6 55 38N 111 5W
Conklin, U.S.A. 111 D9 42 2N 75 49W
Conn, L., Ireland 15 B2 54 3N 9 15W
Connacht □, Ireland 15 C2 53 43N 9 12W
Conneaut, U.S.A. 110 E4 41 57N 80 34W
Connecticut □, U.S.A. 111 E12 41 30N 72 45W
Connecticut →, U.S.A. 111 E12 41 16N 72 20W
Connell, U.S.A. 114 C4 46 40N 118 52W
Connellsville, U.S.A. 110 F5 40 1N 79 35W
Connemara, Ireland 15 C2 53 29N 9 45W
Connemaugh →, U.S.A. 110 F5 40 28N 79 19W
Connerré, France 18 D7 48 3N 0 30 E
Connersville, U.S.A. 108 F3 39 39N 85 8W
Connors Ra., Australia 94 C4 21 40 S 149 10 E
Conques, France 20 D6 44 36N 2 23 E
Conquest, Canada 105 C7 51 32N 107 14W
Conrad, U.S.A. 114 B8 48 10N 111 57W
Conran, C., Australia 95 F4 37 49 S 148 44 E
Conroe, U.S.A. 113 K7 30 19N 95 27W
Consecon, Canada 110 C7 44 0N 77 31W
Conselheiro Lafaiete, Brazil 127 A7 20 40 S 43 48W
Conselve, Italy 29 C8 45 14N 11 52 E
Consett, U.K. 12 C6 54 51N 1 50W
Consort, Canada 105 C6 52 1N 110 46W
Constance = Konstanz, Germany 25 H5 47 40N 9 10 E
Constance, L. = Bodensee, Europe 25 H5 47 35N 9 25 E
Constanţa, Romania 43 F13 44 14N 28 38 E
Constanţa □, Romania 43 F13 44 15N 28 15 E
Constantia, U.S.A. 111 C8 43 15N 76 1W
Constantina, Spain 35 H5 37 51N 5 40W
Constantine, Algeria 78 A7 36 25N 6 42 E
Constitución, Chile 126 D1 35 20 S 72 30W
Constitución, Uruguay 126 C4 31 0 S 57 50W
Consuegra, Spain 35 F7 39 28N 3 36W
Consul, Canada 105 D7 49 20N 109 30W
Contact, U.S.A. 114 F6 41 46N 114 45W
Contai, India 69 J12 21 54N 87 46 E
Contamana, Peru 124 E4 7 19 S 74 55W
Contarina, Italy 29 C9 45 1N 12 13 E
Contas →, Brazil 125 F11 14 17 S 39 1W
Contes, France 21 E11 43 49N 7 19 E
Contoocook, U.S.A. 111 C13 43 13N 71 45W
Contra Costa, Mozam. 89 D5 25 9 S 33 30 E
Contres, France 18 E8 47 24N 1 26 E
Contrexéville, France 19 D12 48 10N 5 53 E
Contwoyto L., Canada 100 B8 65 42N 110 50W
Conversano, Italy 31 B10 40 58N 17 7 E
Conway = Conwy, U.K. 12 D4 53 17N 3 50W
Conway = Conwy →, U.K. 12 D4 53 17N 3 50W
Conway, Ark., U.S.A. 113 H8 35 5N 92 26W
Conway, N.H., U.S.A. 111 C13 43 59N 71 7W
Conway, S.C., U.S.A. 109 J6 33 51N 79 3W
Conway, L., Australia 95 D2 28 17 S 135 35 E
Conwy, U.K. 12 D4 53 17N 3 50W
Conwy □, U.K. 12 D4 53 10N 3 44W
Conwy →, U.K. 12 D4 53 17N 3 50W
Coober Pedy, Australia 95 D1 29 1 S 134 43 E
Cooch Behar = Koch Bihar, India 67 F16 26 22N 89 29 E
Cooinda, Australia 92 B5 13 15 S 130 5 E
Cook, Australia 93 F5 30 37 S 130 25 E
Cook, U.S.A. 112 B8 47 49N 92 39W
Cook, B., Chile 128 H3 55 10 S 70 0W
Cook, C., Canada 104 C3 50 8N 127 55W
Cook, Mt. = Aoraki Mount Cook, N.Z. 91 K3 43 36 S 170 9 E

Cuers

Cook Inlet, U.S.A. 100 C4 60 0N 152 0W
Cook Is., Pac. Oc. 97 J12 17 0S 160 0W
Cook Strait, N.Z. 91 J5 41 15S 174 29 E
Cookeville, U.S.A. 109 G3 36 10N 85 30W
Cookhouse, S. Africa 88 E4 32 44S 25 47 E
Cookshire, Canada 111 A13 45 25N 71 38W
Cookstown, U.K. 15 B5 54 39N 6 45W
Cooksville, Canada 110 C5 43 36N 79 35W
Cooktown, Australia 94 B4 15 30S 145 16 E
Coolabah, Australia 95 E4 31 1S 146 43 E
Cooladdi, Australia 95 D4 26 37S 145 23 E
Coolah, Australia 95 E4 31 48S 149 41 E
Coolamon, Australia 95 E4 34 46S 147 8 E
Coolgardie, Australia 93 F3 30 55S 121 8 E
Coolidge, U.S.A. 115 K8 32 59N 111 31W
Coolidge Dam, U.S.A. 115 K8 33 0N 110 20W
Cooma, Australia 95 F4 36 12S 149 8 E
Coon Rapids, U.S.A. 112 C8 45 9N 93 19W
Coonabarabran, Australia 95 E4 31 14S 149 18 E
Coonamble, Australia 95 E4 30 56S 148 27 E
Coonana, Australia 93 F3 31 0S 123 0 E
Coondapoor, India 66 N9 13 42N 74 40 E
Cooninie, L., Australia 95 D2 26 4S 139 59 E
Cooper, U.S.A. 113 J7 33 23N 95 42W
Cooper Cr. →, Australia 95 D2 28 29S 137 46 E
Cooperstown, N. Dak., U.S.A. 112 B5 47 27N 98 8W
Cooperstown, N.Y., U.S.A. 111 D10 42 42N 74 56W
Coorabie, Australia 93 F5 31 54S 132 18 E
Coorong, The, Australia 95 F2 35 50S 139 20 E
Coorow, Australia 93 E2 29 53S 116 2 E
Cooroy, Australia 95 D5 26 22S 152 54 E
Coos Bay, U.S.A. 114 E1 43 22N 124 13W
Coosa →, U.S.A. 109 J2 32 30N 86 16W
Cootamundra, Australia 95 E4 34 36S 148 1 E
Cootehill, Ireland 15 B4 54 4N 7 5W
Copahue Paso, Argentina 126 D1 37 49S 71 8W
Copainalá, Mexico 119 D6 17 8N 93 11W
Copake Falls, U.S.A. 111 D11 42 7N 73 31W
Copalnic Mănăştur, Romania 43 C8 47 30N 23 41 E
Copán, Honduras 120 D2 14 50N 89 9W
Cope, U.S.A. 112 F3 39 40N 102 51W
Cope, C., Spain 33 H3 37 26N 1 28W
Copenhagen = København, Denmark 11 J6 55 41N 12 34 E
Copenhagen, U.S.A. 111 C9 43 54N 75 41W
Copertino, Italy 31 B11 40 16N 18 3 E
Copiapó, Chile 126 B1 27 30S 70 20W
Copiapó →, Chile 126 B1 27 19S 70 56W
Coplay, U.S.A. 111 F9 40 44N 75 29W
Copp L., Canada 104 A6 60 14N 114 40W
Copparo, Italy 29 D8 44 54N 11 49 E
Coppename →, Suriname 125 B7 5 48N 55 55W
Copper Harbor, U.S.A. 108 B2 47 28N 87 53W
Copper Queen, Zimbabwe 87 F2 17 29S 29 18 E
Copperas Cove, U.S.A. 113 K6 31 8N 97 54W
Copperbelt □, Zambia 87 E2 13 15S 27 30 E
Coppermine = Kugluktuk, Canada 100 B8 67 50N 115 5W
Coppermine →, Canada 100 B8 67 49N 116 4W
Copperopolis, U.S.A. 116 H6 37 58N 120 38W
Copşa Mică, Romania 43 D9 46 7N 24 15 E
Coquet →, U.K. 12 B6 55 20N 1 32W
Coquille, U.S.A. 114 E1 43 11N 124 11W
Coquimbo, Chile 126 C1 30 0S 71 20W
Coquimbo □, Chile 126 C1 31 0S 71 0W
Corabia, Romania 43 G9 43 48N 24 30 E
Coracora, Peru 124 G4 15 5S 73 45W
Coraki, Australia 95 D5 28 59S 153 17 E
Coral, U.S.A. 110 F5 40 29N 79 10W
Coral Gables, U.S.A. 109 N5 25 45N 80 16W
Coral Harbour = Salliq, Canada 101 B11 64 8N 83 10W
Coral Sea, Pac. Oc. 96 J7 15 0S 150 0 E
Coral Springs, U.S.A. 109 M5 26 16N 80 13W
Coraopolis, U.S.A. 110 F4 40 31N 80 10W
Corato, Italy 31 A9 41 9N 16 25 E
Corbeil-Essonnes, France 19 D9 48 36N 2 26 E
Corbie, France 19 C9 49 54N 2 30 E
Corbières, France 20 F6 42 55N 2 35 E
Corbigny, France 19 E10 47 16N 3 40 E
Corbin, U.S.A. 108 G3 36 57N 84 6W
Corbones →, Spain 35 H5 37 36N 5 39W
Corbu, Romania 43 F13 44 25N 28 39 E
Corby, U.K. 13 E7 52 30N 0 41W
Corcaigh = Cork, Ireland 15 E3 51 54N 8 29W
Corcoran, U.S.A. 116 J7 36 6N 119 33W
Cordele, U.S.A. 109 K4 31 58N 83 47W
Cordell, U.S.A. 113 H5 35 17N 98 59W
Cordenòns, Italy 29 C9 45 59N 12 42 E
Cordes, France 20 D5 44 5N 1 57 E
Córdoba, Argentina 126 C3 31 20S 64 10W
Córdoba, Mexico 119 D5 18 50N 97 0W
Córdoba, Spain 35 H6 37 50N 4 50W
Córdoba □, Argentina 126 C3 31 22S 64 15W
Córdoba □, Spain 35 G6 38 5N 5 0W
Córdoba, Sierra de, Argentina 126 C3 31 10S 64 25W
Cordon, Phil. 61 C4 16 42N 121 32 E
Cordova, U.S.A. 100 B5 60 33N 145 45W
Corella, Spain 32 C3 42 7N 1 48W
Corella →, Australia 94 B3 19 34S 140 47 E
Corfield, Australia 94 C3 21 40S 143 21 E
Corfu = Kérkira, Greece 36 A3 39 38N 19 50 E
Corfu, Str. of, Greece 36 A4 39 34N 20 0 E
Corgo = O Corgo, Spain 34 C3 42 56N 7 25W
Cori, Italy 30 A5 41 39N 12 55 E
Coria, Spain 34 F4 39 58N 6 33W
Coria del Río, Spain 35 H4 37 16N 6 3W
Corigliano Cálabro, Italy 31 C9 39 36N 16 31 E
Coringa Is., Australia 94 B4 16 58S 149 58 E
Corinth = Kórinthos, Greece 38 D4 37 56N 22 55 E
Corinth, Miss., U.S.A. 109 H1 34 56N 88 31W
Corinth, N.Y., U.S.A. 111 C11 43 15N 73 49W
Corinth, G. of = Korinthiakós Kólpos, Greece 38 C4 38 16N 22 30 E
Corinth Canal, Greece 38 D4 37 58N 23 0 E
Corinto, Brazil 125 G10 18 20S 44 30W
Corinto, Nic. 120 D2 12 30N 87 10W
Cork, Ireland 15 E3 51 54N 8 29W
Cork □, Ireland 15 E3 51 57N 8 40W
Cork Harbour, Ireland 15 E3 51 47N 8 16W
Corlay, France 18 D3 48 20N 3 5W
Corleone, Italy 30 E6 37 49N 13 18 E
Corleto Perticara, Italy 31 B9 40 23N 16 2 E
Çorlu, Turkey 41 E11 41 11N 27 49 E
Cormack L., Canada 104 A4 60 56N 121 37W
Cormòns, Italy 29 C10 45 58N 13 28 E
Cormorant, Canada 105 C8 54 14N 100 35W
Cormorant L., Canada 105 C8 54 15N 100 50W
Corn Is. = Maiz, Is. del, Nic. 120 D3 12 15N 83 4W
Cornélio Procópio, Brazil 127 A5 23 7S 50 40W
Corner Brook, Canada 103 C8 48 57N 57 58W
Corneşti, Moldova 43 C13 47 21N 28 1 E
Corníglio, Italy 28 D7 44 29N 10 5 E
Corning, Ark., U.S.A. 113 G9 36 25N 90 35W
Corning, Calif., U.S.A. 114 G2 39 56N 122 11W
Corning, Iowa, U.S.A. 112 E7 40 59N 94 44W
Corning, N.Y., U.S.A. 110 D7 42 9N 77 3W
Corno Grande, Italy 29 F10 42 28N 13 34 E
Cornwall, Canada 102 C5 45 2N 74 44W
Cornwall, U.S.A. 111 F8 40 17N 76 25W
Cornwall □, U.K. 13 G3 50 26N 4 40W
Corny Pt., Australia 95 E2 34 55S 137 0 E
Coro, Venezuela 124 A5 11 25N 69 41W
Coroatá, Brazil 125 D10 4 8S 44 0W
Corocoro, Bolivia 124 G5 17 15S 68 28W
Coroico, Bolivia 124 G5 16 0S 67 50W
Coromandel, N.Z. 91 G5 36 45S 175 31 E
Coromandel Coast, India 66 N12 12 30N 81 0 E
Corona, Calif., U.S.A. 117 M9 33 53N 117 34W
Corona, N. Mex., U.S.A. 115 J11 34 15N 105 36W
Coronach, Canada 105 D7 49 7N 105 31W
Coronado, U.S.A. 117 N9 32 41N 117 11W
Coronado, B. de, Costa Rica 120 E3 9 0N 83 40W
Coronados, Is. los, U.S.A. 117 N9 32 25N 117 15W
Coronation, Canada 104 C6 52 5N 111 27W
Coronation Gulf, Canada 100 B8 68 25N 110 0W
Coronation I., Antarctica 5 C18 60 45S 46 0W
Coronation Is., Australia 92 B3 14 57S 124 55 E
Coronda, Argentina 126 C3 31 58S 60 56W
Coronel, Chile 126 D1 37 0S 73 10W
Coronel Bogado, Paraguay 126 B4 27 11S 56 18W
Coronel Dorrego, Argentina 126 D3 38 40S 61 10W
Coronel Oviedo, Paraguay 126 B4 25 24S 56 30W
Coronel Pringles, Argentina 126 D3 38 0S 61 30W
Coronel Suárez, Argentina 126 D3 37 30S 61 52W
Coronel Vidal, Argentina 126 D4 37 28S 57 45W
Coropuna, Nevado, Peru 124 G4 15 30S 72 41W
Çorovodë, Albania 40 F4 40 31N 20 14 E
Corowa, Australia 95 F4 35 58S 146 21 E
Corozal, Belize 119 D7 18 23N 88 23W
Corps, France 21 D9 44 50N 5 56 E
Corpus, Argentina 127 B4 27 10S 55 30W
Corpus Christi, U.S.A. 113 M6 27 47N 97 24W
Corpus Christi, L., U.S.A. 113 L6 28 2N 97 52W
Corral de Almaguer, Spain 34 F7 39 45N 3 10W
Corralejo, Canary Is. 37 F6 28 43N 13 53W
Corraun Pen., Ireland 15 C2 53 54N 9 54W
Corréggio, Italy 28 D7 44 46N 10 47 E
Correntes, C. das, Mozam. 89 C6 24 6S 35 34 E
Corrèze □, France 20 C5 45 20N 1 45 E
Corrèze →, France 20 C5 45 10N 1 28 E
Corrib, L., Ireland 15 C2 53 27N 9 16W
Corridónia, Italy 29 E10 43 15N 13 30 E
Corrientes, Argentina 126 B4 27 30S 58 45W
Corrientes □, Argentina 126 B4 28 0S 57 0W
Corrientes →, Argentina 126 C4 30 42S 59 38W
Corrientes →, Peru 124 D4 3 43S 74 35W
Corrientes, C., Colombia 124 B3 5 30N 77 34W
Corrientes, C., Cuba 120 B3 21 43N 84 30W
Corrientes, C., Mexico 118 C3 20 25N 105 42W
Corrigan, U.S.A. 113 K7 31 0N 94 52W
Corrigin, Australia 93 F2 32 20S 117 53 E
Corry, U.S.A. 110 E5 41 55N 79 39W
Corse, France 21 G13 42 0N 9 0 E
Corse, C., France 21 E13 43 1N 9 25 E
Corse-du-Sud □, France 21 G13 41 45N 9 0 E
Corsica = Corse, France 21 G13 42 0N 9 0 E
Corsicana, U.S.A. 113 J6 32 6N 96 28W
Corte, France 21 F13 42 19N 9 11 E
Corte Pinto, Portugal 35 H3 37 42N 7 29W
Cortegana, Spain 35 H4 37 52N 6 49W
Cortez, U.S.A. 115 H9 37 21N 108 35W
Cortina d'Ampezzo, Italy 29 B9 46 32N 12 8 E
Cortland, N.Y., U.S.A. 111 D8 42 36N 76 11W
Cortland, Ohio, U.S.A. 110 E4 41 20N 80 44W
Cortona, Italy 29 E8 43 16N 11 59 E
Corubal →, Guinea-Biss. 82 C2 11 57N 15 5W
Coruche, Portugal 35 G2 38 57N 8 30W
Çoruh →, Turkey 49 K5 41 38N 41 38 E
Çorum, Turkey 72 B6 40 30N 34 57 E
Corumbá, Brazil 124 G7 19 0S 57 30W
Corund, Romania 43 D10 46 30N 25 13 E
Corunna = A Coruña, Spain 34 B2 43 20N 8 25W
Corvallis, U.S.A. 114 D2 44 34N 123 16W
Corvette, L. de la, Canada 102 B5 53 25N 74 3W
Corydon, U.S.A. 112 E8 40 46N 93 19W
Cosalá, Mexico 118 C3 24 28N 106 40W
Cosamaloapan, Mexico 119 D5 18 23N 95 50W
Cosenza, Italy 31 C9 39 18N 16 15 E
Coşereni, Romania 43 F11 44 38N 26 35 E
Coshocton, U.S.A. 110 F3 40 16N 81 51W
Cosmo Newberry, Australia 93 E3 28 0S 122 54 E
Cosne-Cours-sur-Loire, France 19 E9 47 24N 2 54 E
Coso Junction, U.S.A. 117 J9 36 3N 117 57W
Coso Pk., U.S.A. 117 J9 36 13N 117 44W
Cospeito, Spain 34 B3 43 12N 7 34W
Cosquín, Argentina 126 C3 31 15S 64 30W
Cossato, Italy 28 C5 45 34N 8 10 E
Cossé-le-Vivien, France 18 E6 47 57N 0 54W
Cosson →, France 18 E8 47 30N 1 15 E
Costa Blanca, Spain 33 G4 38 25N 0 10W
Costa Brava, Spain 32 D8 41 30N 3 0 E
Costa del Sol, Spain 35 J6 36 30N 4 30W
Costa Dorada, Spain 32 D6 41 12N 1 15 E
Costa Mesa, U.S.A. 117 M9 33 38N 117 55W
Costa Rica ■, Cent. Amer. 120 E3 10 0N 84 0W
Costa Smeralda, Italy 30 A2 41 5N 9 35 E
Costeşti, Romania 43 F9 44 40N 24 53 E
Costigliole d'Asti, Italy 28 D5 44 47N 8 11 E
Cosumnes →, U.S.A. 116 G5 38 16N 121 26W
Coswig, Sachsen, Germany 24 D9 51 7N 13 34 E
Coswig, Sachsen-Anhalt, Germany 24 D8 51 53N 12 27 E
Cotabato, Phil. 61 H6 7 14N 124 15 E
Cotagaita, Bolivia 126 A2 20 45S 65 40W
Côte d'Azur, France 21 E11 43 25N 7 10 E
Côte-d'Ivoire = Ivory Coast ■, Africa 82 D4 7 30N 5 0W
Côte d'Or, France 19 E11 47 10N 4 50 E
Côte-d'Or □, France 19 E11 47 30N 4 50 E
Coteau des Prairies, U.S.A. 112 C6 45 20N 97 50W
Coteau du Missouri, U.S.A. 112 B4 47 0N 100 0W
Coteau Landing, Canada 111 A10 45 15N 74 13W
Cotentin, France 18 C5 49 15N 1 30W
Côtes-d'Armor □, France 18 D4 48 25N 2 40W
Côtes de Meuse, France 19 C12 49 15N 5 22 E
Côtes-du-Nord = Côtes-d'Armor □, France 18 D4 48 25N 2 40W
Cotiella, Spain 32 C5 42 31N 0 19 E
Cotillo, Canary Is. 37 F5 28 41N 14 1W
Cotiujeni, Moldova 43 C13 47 51N 28 33 E
Cotonou, Benin 83 D5 6 20N 2 25 E
Cotopaxi, Ecuador 122 D3 0 40S 78 30W
Cotronei, Italy 31 C9 39 9N 16 47 E
Cotswold Hills, U.K. 13 F5 51 42N 2 10W
Cottage Grove, U.S.A. 114 E2 43 48N 123 3W
Cottbus, Germany 24 D10 51 45N 14 20 E
Cottonwood, U.S.A. 115 J7 34 45N 112 1W
Cotulla, U.S.A. 113 L5 28 26N 99 14W
Coubre, Pte. de la, France 20 C2 45 42N 1 15W
Couches, France 19 F11 46 53N 4 30 E
Couço, Portugal 35 G2 38 59N 8 17W
Coudersport, U.S.A. 110 E6 41 46N 78 1W
Couedic, C. du, Australia 95 F2 36 5S 136 40 E
Couëron, France 18 E5 47 13N 1 44W
Couesnon →, France 18 D5 48 38N 1 32W
Couhé, France 20 B4 46 17N 0 11 E
Coulanges-sur-Yonne, France 19 E10 47 31N 3 33 E
Coulee City, U.S.A. 114 C4 47 37N 119 17W
Coulman I., Antarctica 5 D11 73 35S 170 0 E
Coulommiers, France 19 D10 48 50N 3 3 E
Coulon →, France 21 E9 43 51N 5 6 E
Coulonge →, Canada 102 C4 45 52N 76 46W
Coulonges-sur-l'Autize, France 20 B3 46 29N 0 36W
Coulounieix-Chamiers, France 20 C4 45 11N 0 42 E
Coulterville, U.S.A. 116 H6 37 43N 120 12W
Council, U.S.A. 114 D5 44 44N 116 26W
Council Bluffs, U.S.A. 112 E7 41 16N 95 52W
Council Grove, U.S.A. 112 F6 38 40N 96 29W
Coupeville, U.S.A. 116 B4 48 13N 122 41W
Courantyne →, S. Amer. 122 C5 5 55N 57 5W
Courcelles, Belgium 17 D4 50 28N 4 22 E
Courçon, France 20 B3 46 15N 0 50W
Courmayeur, Italy 28 C3 45 47N 6 58 E
Couronne, C., France 21 E9 43 19N 5 3 E
Cours-la-Ville, France 19 F11 46 7N 4 19 E
Coursan, France 20 E7 43 14N 3 4 E
Courseulles-sur-Mer, France 18 C6 49 20N 0 29W
Courtenay, Canada 104 D4 49 45N 125 0W
Courtenay, France 19 D10 48 2N 3 3 E
Courtland, U.S.A. 116 G5 38 20N 121 34W
Courtrai = Kortrijk, Belgium 17 D3 50 50N 3 17 E
Courtright, Canada 110 D2 42 49N 82 28W
Coushatta, U.S.A. 113 J8 32 1N 93 21W
Coutances, France 18 C5 49 3N 1 28W
Coutras, France 20 C3 45 3N 0 8W
Coutts Crossing, Australia 95 D5 29 49S 152 55 E
Couvin, Belgium 17 D4 50 3N 4 29 E
Covarrubias, Spain 34 C7 42 4N 3 31W
Covasna, Romania 43 E11 45 50N 26 10 E
Covasna □, Romania 43 E10 45 50N 26 0 E
Cove I., Canada 110 A3 45 17N 81 44W
Coventry, U.K. 13 E6 52 25N 1 28W
Covilhã, Portugal 34 E3 40 17N 7 31W
Covington, Ga., U.S.A. 109 J4 33 36N 83 51W
Covington, Ky., U.S.A. 108 F3 39 5N 84 31W
Covington, Okla., U.S.A. 113 G6 36 18N 97 35W
Covington, Tenn., U.S.A. 113 H10 35 34N 89 39W
Covington, Va., U.S.A. 108 G5 37 47N 79 59W
Cowal, L., Australia 95 E4 33 40S 147 25 E
Cowan, L., Australia 93 F3 31 45S 121 45 E
Cowan L., Canada 105 C7 54 0N 107 15W
Cowangie, Australia 95 F3 35 12S 141 26 E
Cowansville, Canada 102 C5 45 14N 72 46W
Coward Springs, Australia 95 D2 29 24S 136 49 E
Cowcowing Lakes, Australia 93 F2 30 55S 117 20 E
Cowdenbeath, U.K. 14 E5 56 7N 3 21W
Cowell, Australia 95 E2 33 39S 136 56 E
Cowes, U.K. 13 G6 50 45N 1 18W
Cowichan L., Canada 116 B2 48 53N 124 17W
Cowlitz →, U.S.A. 116 D4 46 6N 122 55W
Cowra, Australia 95 E4 33 49S 148 42 E
Cox, Spain 33 G4 38 8N 0 53W
Coxilha Grande, Brazil 127 B5 28 18S 51 30W
Coxim, Brazil 125 G8 18 30S 54 55W
Cox's Bazar, Bangla. 67 J17 21 26N 91 59 E
Coyote Wells, U.S.A. 117 N11 32 44N 115 58W
Coyuca de Benítez, Mexico 119 D4 17 1N 100 8W
Coyuca de Catalan, Mexico 118 D4 18 18N 100 41W
Cozad, U.S.A. 112 E5 40 52N 99 59W
Cozes, France 20 C3 45 34N 0 49W
Cozumel, Mexico 119 C7 20 31N 86 55W
Cozumel, Isla, Mexico 119 C7 20 30N 86 40W
Cracow = Kraków, Poland 45 H6 50 4N 19 57 E
Cracow, Australia 95 D5 25 17S 150 17 E
Cradock, Australia 95 E2 32 6S 138 31 E
Cradock, S. Africa 88 E4 32 8S 25 36 E
Craig, U.S.A. 114 F10 40 31N 107 33W
Craigavon, U.K. 15 B5 54 27N 6 23W
Craigmore, Zimbabwe 87 G3 20 28S 32 50 E
Craik, Canada 105 C7 51 3N 105 49W
Crailsheim, Germany 25 F6 49 8N 10 5 E
Craiova, Romania 43 F8 44 21N 23 48 E
Cramsie, Australia 94 C3 23 20S 144 15 E
Cranberry L., U.S.A. 111 B10 44 11N 74 50W
Cranberry Portage, Canada 105 C8 54 35N 101 23W
Cranbrook, Australia 93 F2 34 18S 117 33 E
Cranbrook, Canada 104 D5 49 30N 115 46W
Crandon, U.S.A. 112 C10 45 34N 88 54W
Crane, Oreg., U.S.A. 114 E4 43 25N 118 35W
Crane, Tex., U.S.A. 113 K3 31 24N 102 21W
Cranston, U.S.A. 111 E13 41 47N 71 26W
Craon, France 18 E6 47 50N 0 58W
Craonne, France 19 C10 49 27N 3 46 E
Craponne-sur-Arzon, France 20 C7 45 19N 3 51 E
Crasna, Romania 43 D12 46 32N 27 51 E
Crasna →, Romania 42 C7 47 44N 22 35 E
Crasnei, Munţii, Romania 43 C8 47 0N 23 20 E
Crater L., U.S.A. 114 E2 42 56N 122 6W
Crater Lake National Park, U.S.A. 114 E2 42 55N 122 10W
Crateús, Brazil 125 E10 5 10S 40 39W
Crati →, Italy 31 C9 39 43N 16 31 E
Crato, Brazil 125 E11 7 10S 39 25W
Crato, Portugal 35 F3 39 16N 7 39W
Craven, L., Canada 102 B4 54 20N 76 56W
Crawford, U.S.A. 112 D3 42 41N 103 25W
Crawfordsville, U.S.A. 108 E2 40 2N 86 54W
Crawley, U.K. 13 F7 51 7N 0 11W
Crazy Mts., U.S.A. 114 C8 46 12N 110 20W
Crean L., Canada 105 C7 54 5N 106 9W
Crécy-en-Ponthieu, France 19 B8 50 15N 1 53 E
Crediton, Canada 110 C3 43 17N 81 33W
Cree →, Canada 105 B7 58 57N 105 47W
Cree →, U.K. 14 G4 54 55N 4 25W
Cree L., Canada 105 B7 57 30N 106 30W
Creede, U.S.A. 115 H10 37 51N 106 56W
Creekside, U.S.A. 110 F5 40 40N 79 11W
Creel, Mexico 118 B3 27 45N 107 38W
Creemore, Canada 110 B4 44 19N 80 6W
Creighton, Canada 105 C8 54 45N 101 54W
Creighton, U.S.A. 112 D6 42 28N 97 54W
Creil, France 19 C9 49 15N 2 29 E
Crema, Italy 28 C6 45 22N 9 41 E
Cremona, Italy 28 C7 45 7N 10 2 E
Crepaja, Serbia, Yug. 42 E5 45 1N 20 38 E
Crépy, France 19 C10 49 35N 3 32 E
Crépy-en-Valois, France 19 C9 49 14N 2 54 E
Cres, Croatia 29 D11 44 58N 14 25 E
Crescent City, U.S.A. 114 F1 41 45N 124 12W
Crescentino, Italy 28 C5 45 11N 8 6 E
Crespo, Argentina 126 C3 32 2S 60 19W
Cresson, U.S.A. 110 F6 40 28N 78 36W
Crest, France 21 D9 44 44N 5 2 E
Cresta, Mt., Phil. 61 C5 17 17N 122 6 E
Crestline, Calif., U.S.A. 117 L9 34 14N 117 18W
Crestline, Ohio, U.S.A. 110 F2 40 47N 82 44W
Creston, Canada 104 D5 49 10N 116 31W
Creston, Calif., U.S.A. 116 K6 35 32N 120 33W
Creston, Iowa, U.S.A. 112 E7 41 4N 94 22W
Crestview, Calif., U.S.A. 116 H8 37 46N 118 58W
Crestview, Fla., U.S.A. 109 K2 30 46N 86 34W
Crêt de la Neige, France 19 F12 46 16N 5 58 E
Crete = Kríti, Greece 36 D7 35 15N 25 0 E
Crete, U.S.A. 112 E6 40 38N 96 58W
Crete, Sea of, Greece 39 E7 36 0N 25 0 E
Créteil, France 19 D9 48 47N 2 28 E
Creus, C. de, Spain 32 C8 42 20N 3 19 E
Creuse □, France 19 F9 46 10N 2 0 E
Creuse →, France 20 B4 47 0N 0 34 E
Creutzwald, France 19 C13 49 12N 6 42 E
Creuzburg, Germany 24 D6 51 3N 10 14 E
Crèvecœur-le-Grand, France 19 C9 49 37N 2 5 E
Crevillente, Spain 33 G4 38 12N 0 48W
Crewe, U.K. 12 D5 53 6N 2 26W
Crewkerne, U.K. 13 G5 50 53N 2 48W
Criciúma, Brazil 127 B6 28 40S 49 23W
Cricova, Moldova 43 C13 47 8N 28 52 E
Crieff, U.K. 14 E5 56 22N 3 50W
Crikvenica, Croatia 29 C11 45 11N 14 40 E
Crimea □, Ukraine 47 K8 45 30N 33 10 E
Crimean Pen. = Krymskyy Pivostriv, Ukraine 47 K8 45 0N 34 0 E
Crimmitschau, Germany 24 E8 50 48N 12 24 E
Cristuru Secuiesc, Romania 43 D10 46 17N 25 2 E
Crişul Alb →, Romania 42 D6 46 42N 21 17 E
Crişul Negru →, Romania 42 D6 46 42N 21 16 E
Crişul Repede →, Romania 42 D5 46 55N 20 59 E
Criuleni, Moldova 43 C14 47 13N 29 10 E
Crivitz, Germany 24 B7 53 34N 11 39 E
Crna →, Macedonia 40 E5 41 33N 21 59 E
Crna Gora = Montenegro □, Yugoslavia 40 D3 42 40N 19 20 E
Crna Gora, Macedonia 40 D5 42 10N 21 30 E
Crna Reka = Crna →, Macedonia 40 E5 41 33N 21 59 E
Crna Trava, Serbia, Yug. 40 D6 42 49N 22 19 E
Crni Drim →, Macedonia 40 E4 41 17N 20 40 E
Crni Timok →, Serbia, Yug. 40 C6 43 53N 22 15 E
Crnoljeva Planina, Kosovo, Yug. 40 D5 42 20N 21 0 E
Črnomelj, Slovenia 29 C12 45 33N 15 10 E
Croagh Patrick, Ireland 15 C2 53 46N 9 40W
Croatia ■, Europe 29 C13 45 20N 16 0 E
Crocker, Banjaran, Malaysia 62 C5 5 40N 116 30 E
Crockett, U.S.A. 113 K7 31 19N 95 27W
Crocodile = Krokodil →, Mozam. 89 D5 25 14S 32 18 E
Crocodile Is., Australia 94 A1 12 3S 134 58 E
Crocq, France 20 C6 45 52N 2 21 E
Crodo, Italy 28 B5 46 13N 8 19 E
Crohy Hd., Ireland 15 B3 54 55N 8 26W
Croisette, C., France 21 E9 43 14N 5 22 E
Croisic, Pte. du, France 18 E4 47 19N 2 31W
Croix, L. La, Canada 102 C1 48 20N 92 15W
Croker, C., Australia 92 B5 10 58S 132 35 E
Croker, C., Canada 110 B4 44 58N 80 59W
Croker I., Australia 92 B5 11 12S 132 32 E
Cromarty, U.K. 14 D4 57 40N 4 2W
Cromer, U.K. 12 E9 52 56N 1 17 E
Cromwell, N.Z. 91 L2 45 3S 169 14 E
Cromwell, U.S.A. 111 E12 41 36N 72 39W
Cronat, France 19 F10 46 43N 3 40 E
Crook, U.K. 12 C6 54 43N 1 45W
Crooked →, Canada 104 C4 54 50N 122 54W
Crooked →, U.S.A. 114 D3 44 32N 121 16W
Crooked I., Bahamas 121 B5 22 50N 74 10W
Crooked Island Passage, Bahamas 121 B5 23 0N 74 30W
Crookston, Minn., U.S.A. 112 B6 47 47N 96 37W
Crookston, Nebr., U.S.A. 112 D4 42 56N 100 45W
Crookwell, Australia 95 E4 34 28S 149 24 E
Crosby, U.K. 12 D4 53 30N 3 3W
Crosby, N. Dak., U.S.A. 112 A3 48 55N 103 18W
Crosby, Pa., U.S.A. 110 E6 41 45N 78 23W
Crosbyton, U.S.A. 113 J4 33 40N 101 14W
Crosía, Italy 31 C9 39 35N 16 45 E
Cross →, Nigeria 83 E6 4 42N 8 21 E
Cross City, U.S.A. 109 L4 29 38N 83 7W
Cross Fell, U.K. 12 C5 54 43N 2 28W
Cross L., Canada 105 C9 54 45N 97 30W
Cross Lake, Canada 105 C9 54 37N 97 47W
Cross River □, Nigeria 83 D6 6 0N 8 0 E
Cross Sound, U.S.A. 100 C6 58 0N 135 0W
Crossett, U.S.A. 113 J9 33 8N 91 58W
Crosshaven, Ireland 15 E3 51 47N 8 17W
Crossville, U.S.A. 109 G3 35 57N 85 2W
Croswell, U.S.A. 110 C2 43 16N 82 37W
Croton-on-Hudson, U.S.A. 111 E11 41 12N 73 55W
Crotone, Italy 31 C10 39 5N 17 8 E
Crow →, Canada 104 B4 59 41N 124 20W
Crow Agency, U.S.A. 114 D10 45 36N 107 28W
Crow Hd., Ireland 15 E1 51 35N 10 9W
Crowell, U.S.A. 113 J5 33 59N 99 43W
Crowley, U.S.A. 113 K8 30 13N 92 22W
Crowley, L., U.S.A. 116 H8 37 35N 118 42W
Crown Point, Ind., U.S.A. 108 E2 41 25N 87 22W
Crown Point, N.Y., U.S.A. 111 C11 43 57N 73 26W
Crownpoint, U.S.A. 115 J9 35 41N 108 9W
Crows Landing, U.S.A. 116 H5 37 23N 121 6W
Crows Nest, Australia 95 D5 27 16S 152 4 E
Crowsnest Pass, Canada 104 D6 49 40N 114 40W
Croydon, Australia 94 B3 18 13S 142 14 E
Croydon □, U.K. 13 F7 51 22N 0 5W
Crozet, Is., Ind. Oc. 3 G12 46 27S 52 0 E
Crozon, France 18 D2 48 15N 4 30W
Cruz, C., Cuba 120 C4 19 50N 77 50W
Cruz Alta, Brazil 127 B5 28 45S 53 40W
Cruz de Incio, Spain 34 C3 42 39N 7 21W
Cruz del Eje, Argentina 126 C3 30 45S 64 50W
Cruzeiro, Brazil 127 A7 22 33S 45 0W
Cruzeiro do Oeste, Brazil 127 A5 23 46S 53 4W
Cruzeiro do Sul, Brazil 124 E4 7 35S 72 35W
Cry L., Canada 104 B3 58 45N 129 0W
Crystal Bay, U.S.A. 116 F7 39 15N 120 0W
Crystal Brook, Australia 95 E2 33 21S 138 12 E
Crystal City, U.S.A. 113 L5 28 41N 99 50W
Crystal Falls, U.S.A. 108 B1 46 5N 88 20W
Crystal River, U.S.A. 109 L4 28 54N 82 35W
Crystal Springs, U.S.A. 113 K9 31 59N 90 21W
Csenger, Hungary 42 C7 47 50N 22 41 E
Csongrád, Hungary 42 D5 46 43N 20 12 E
Csongrád □, Hungary 42 D5 46 32N 20 15 E
Csorna, Hungary 42 C2 47 38N 17 18 E
Csurgo, Hungary 42 D2 46 16N 17 9 E
Cu Lao Hon, Vietnam 65 G7 10 54N 108 18 E
Cua Rao, Vietnam 64 C5 19 16N 104 27 E
Cuácua →, Mozam. 87 F4 17 54S 37 0 E
Cuamato, Angola 88 B2 17 2S 15 7 E
Cuamba, Mozam. 87 E4 14 45S 36 22 E
Cuando →, Angola 85 H4 17 30S 23 15 E
Cuando Cubango □, Angola 88 B3 16 25S 20 0 E
Cuangar, Angola 88 B2 17 36S 18 39 E
Cuango = Kwango →, Dem. Rep. of the Congo 84 E3 3 14S 17 22 E
Cuanza →, Angola 84 F2 9 21S 13 9 E
Cuarto →, Argentina 126 C3 33 25S 63 2W
Cuatrociénegas, Mexico 118 B4 26 59N 102 5W
Cuauhtémoc, Mexico 118 B3 28 25N 106 52W
Cuba, Portugal 35 G3 38 10N 7 54W
Cuba, N. Mex., U.S.A. 115 J10 36 1N 107 4W
Cuba, N.Y., U.S.A. 110 D6 42 13N 78 17W
Cuba ■, W. Indies 120 B4 22 0N 79 0W
Cubango →, Africa 88 B3 18 50S 22 25 E
Çubuk, Turkey 72 B5 40 14N 33 3 E
Cuchumatanes, Sierra de los, Guatemala 120 C1 15 35N 91 25W
Cuckfield, U.K. 13 F7 51 1N 0 8W
Cucuí, Brazil 124 C5 1 12N 66 50W
Cucurpe, Mexico 118 A2 30 20N 110 43W
Cúcuta, Colombia 124 B4 7 54N 72 31W
Cudalbi, Romania 43 E12 45 46N 27 41 E
Cuddalore, India 66 P11 11 46N 79 45 E
Cuddapah, India 66 M11 14 30N 78 47 E
Cuddapan, L., Australia 94 D3 25 45S 141 26 E
Cudillero, Spain 34 B4 43 33N 6 9W
Cue, Australia 93 E2 27 25S 117 54 E
Cuéllar, Spain 34 D6 41 23N 4 21W
Cuenca, Ecuador 124 D3 2 50S 79 9W
Cuenca, Spain 32 E2 40 5N 2 10W
Cuenca □, Spain 32 F3 40 0N 2 0W
Cuenca, Serranía de, Spain 32 F3 39 55N 1 50W
Cuerdo del Pozo, Embalse de la, Spain 32 D2 41 51N 2 44W
Cuernavaca, Mexico 119 D5 18 55N 99 15W
Cuero, U.S.A. 113 L6 29 6N 97 17W
Cuers, France 21 E10 43 14N 6 5 E

Dieppe

Dieppe, *France* **18 C8** 49 54N 1 4 E
Dierks, *U.S.A.* **113 H8** 34 7N 94 1W
Diest, *Belgium* **17 D5** 50 58N 5 4 E
Dietikon, *Switz.* **25 H4** 47 24N 8 24 E
Dieulefit, *France* **21 D9** 44 32N 5 4 E
Dieuze, *France* **19 D13** 48 49N 6 43 E
Dif, *Somali Rep.* **74 G3** 0 59N 0 56 E
Differdange, *Lux.* **17 E5** 49 31N 5 54 E
Dig, *India* **68 F7** 27 28N 77 20 E
Digba, *Dem. Rep. of the Congo* **86 B2** 4 25N 25 48 E
Digby, *Canada* **103 D6** 44 38N 65 50W
Diggi, *India* **68 F6** 26 22N 75 26 E
Dighinala, *Bangla.* **67 H18** 23 15N 92 5 E
Dighton, *U.S.A.* **112 F4** 38 29N 100 28W
Digna, *Mali* **82 C3** 14 48N 8 10W
Digne-les-Bains, *France* **21 D10** 44 5N 6 12 E
Digoin, *France* **19 F11** 46 29N 4 1 E
Digor, *Turkey* **73 B10** 40 22N 43 25 E
Digos, *Phil.* **61 H6** 6 45N 125 20 E
Digranes, *Iceland* **8 C6** 66 4N 14 44W
Digul →, *Indonesia* **63 F9** 7 7 S 138 42 E
Dihang →, *India* **67 F19** 27 48N 95 30 E
Dijlah, Nahr →, *Asia* **70 D5** 31 0N 47 25 E
Dijon, *France* **19 E12** 47 20N 5 3 E
Dikhil, *Djibouti* **81 E5** 11 8N 42 20 E
Dikili, *Turkey* **39 B8** 39 4N 26 53 E
Dikirnis, *Egypt* **80 H7** 31 6N 31 35 E
Dikkil = Dikhil, *Djibouti* **81 E5** 11 8N 42 20 E
Dikodougou, *Ivory C.* **82 D3** 9 4N 5 45W
Diksmuide, *Belgium* **17 C2** 51 2N 2 52 E
Dikson, *Russia* **50 B9** 73 40N 80 5 E
Dikwa, *Nigeria* **83 C7** 12 4N 13 30 E
Dila, *Ethiopia* **81 F4** 6 21N 38 22 E
Dili, *E. Timor* **63 F7** 8 39 S 125 34 E
Dilijan, *Armenia* **49 K7** 40 46N 44 57 E
Dilizhan = Dilijan, *Armenia* **49 K7** 40 46N 44 57 E
Dilj, *Croatia* **42 E3** 45 29N 18 1 E
Dillenburg, *Germany* **24 E4** 50 43N 8 17 E
Dilley, *U.S.A.* **113 L5** 28 40N 99 10W
Dilling, *Sudan* **81 E2** 12 3N 29 35 E
Dillingen, *Bayern, Germany* **25 G6** 48 36N 10 30 E
Dillingen, *Saarland, Germany* **25 F2** 49 22N 6 43 E
Dillingham, *U.S.A.* **100 C4** 59 3N 158 28W
Dillon, *Canada* **105 B7** 55 56N 108 35W
Dillon, *Mont., U.S.A.* **114 D7** 45 13N 112 38W
Dillon, *S.C., U.S.A.* **109 H6** 34 25N 79 22W
Dillon →, *Canada* **105 B7** 55 56N 108 56W
Dillsburg, *U.S.A.* **110 F7** 40 7N 77 2W
Dilly, *Mali* **82 C3** 15 1N 7 40W
Dilolo, *Dem. Rep. of the Congo* **84 G4** 10 28 S 22 18 E
Dimas, *Mexico* **118 C3** 23 43N 106 47W
Dimashq, *Syria* **75 B5** 33 30N 36 18 E
Dimashq □, *Syria* **75 B5** 33 30N 36 30 E
Dimbaza, *S. Africa* **89 E4** 32 50 S 27 14 E
Dimbokro, *Ivory C.* **82 D4** 6 45N 4 46W
Dimboola, *Australia* **95 F3** 36 28 S 142 7 E
Dîmbovița = Dâmbovița →, *Romania* **43 F11** 44 12N 26 26 E
Dimbulah, *Australia* **94 B4** 17 8 S 145 4 E
Dimitrovgrad, *Bulgaria* **41 D9** 42 5N 25 35 E
Dimitrovgrad, *Russia* **48 C9** 54 14N 49 39 E
Dimitrovgrad, *Serbia, Yug.* **40 C6** 43 2N 22 48 E
Dimitrovo = Pernik, *Bulgaria* **40 D7** 42 35N 23 2 E
Dimmitt, *U.S.A.* **113 H3** 34 33N 102 19W
Dimo, *Sudan* **81 F2** 5 19N 29 10 E
Dimona, *Israel* **75 D4** 31 2N 35 1 E
Dimovo, *Bulgaria* **40 C6** 43 43N 22 50 E
Dinagat, *Phil.* **61 F6** 10 10N 125 40 E
Dinajpur, *Bangla.* **67 G16** 25 33N 88 43 E
Dinan, *France* **18 D4** 48 28N 2 2W
Dīnān Āb, *Iran* **71 C8** 32 4N 56 49 E
Dinant, *Belgium* **17 D4** 50 16N 4 55 E
Dinapur, *India* **69 G11** 25 38N 85 5 E
Dinar, *Turkey* **39 C12** 38 5N 30 10 E
Dīnār, Kūh-e, *Iran* **71 D6** 30 42N 51 46 E
Dinara Planina, *Croatia* **29 D13** 44 0N 16 30 E
Dinard, *France* **18 D4** 48 38N 2 6W
Dinaric Alps = Dinara Planina, *Croatia* **29 D13** 44 0N 16 30 E
Dindanko, *Mali* **82 C3** 14 8N 9 30W
Dinder, Nahr ed →, *Sudan* **81 E3** 14 6N 33 40 E
Dindigul, *India* **66 P11** 10 25N 78 0 E
Dindori, *India* **69 H9** 22 57N 81 5 E
Ding Xian = Dingzhou, *China* **56 E8** 38 30N 114 59 E
Dinga, *Pakistan* **68 G2** 25 26N 67 10 E
Dingalan, *Phil.* **61 D4** 15 18N 121 25 E
Dingbian, *China* **56 F4** 37 35N 107 32 E
Dingelstädt, *Germany* **24 D6** 51 18N 10 19 E
Dingle, *Ireland* **15 D1** 52 9N 10 17W
Dingle, *Sweden* **11 F5** 58 32N 11 35 E
Dingle B., *Ireland* **15 D1** 52 3N 10 20W
Dingmans Ferry, *U.S.A.* **111 E10** 41 13N 74 55W
Dingnan, *China* **59 E10** 24 45N 115 0 E
Dingo, *Australia* **94 C4** 23 38 S 149 19 E
Dingolfing, *Germany* **25 G8** 48 37N 12 30 E
Dingtao, *China* **56 G8** 35 5N 115 35 E
Dinguira, *Mali* **82 C2** 14 11N 11 16W
Dinguiraye, *Guinea* **82 C2** 11 18N 10 49W
Dingwall, *U.K.* **14 D4** 57 36N 4 26W
Dingxi, *China* **56 G3** 35 30N 104 33 E
Dingxiang, *China* **56 E7** 38 30N 112 58 E
Dingyuan, *China* **59 A11** 32 32N 117 41 E
Dingzhou, *China* **56 E8** 38 30N 114 59 E
Dinh, Mui, *Vietnam* **65 G7** 11 22N 109 1 E
Dinh Lap, *Vietnam* **58 G6** 21 33N 107 6 E
Dinokwe, *Botswana* **88 C4** 23 29 S 26 37 E
Dinorwic, *Canada* **105 D10** 49 41N 92 30W
Dinosaur National Monument, *U.S.A.* **114 F9** 40 30N 108 45W
Dinosaur Prov. Park, *Canada* **104 C6** 50 47N 111 30W
Dinuba, *U.S.A.* **116 J7** 36 32N 119 23W
Diö, *Sweden* **11 H8** 56 37N 14 15 E
Dioïla, *Mali* **82 C3** 12 23N 6 50W
Dioka, *Mali* **82 C2** 14 57N 10 4W
Diongoï, *Mali* **82 C3** 14 38N 8 34W
Diósgyör, *Hungary* **42 B5** 48 7N 20 43 E
Diosig, *Romania* **42 C7** 47 18N 22 2 E
Diougani, *Mali* **82 C4** 14 19N 2 50W
Dioulouou, *Senegal* **82 C1** 13 5N 16 38W
Dioura, *Mali* **82 C3** 14 59N 5 12W
Diourbel, *Senegal* **82 C1** 14 39N 16 12W
Dipalpur, *Pakistan* **68 D5** 30 40N 73 39 E
Diplo, *Pakistan* **68 G3** 24 35N 69 35 E
Dipolog, *Phil.* **61 G5** 8 36N 123 20 E
Dir, *Pakistan* **66 B7** 35 8N 71 59 E
Diré, *Mali* **82 B4** 16 20N 3 25W
Dire Dawa, *Ethiopia* **81 F5** 9 35N 41 45 E
Diriamba, *Nic.* **120 D2** 11 51N 86 19W
Dirk Hartog I., *Australia* **93 E1** 25 50 S 113 5 E
Dirranbandi, *Australia* **95 D4** 28 33 S 148 17 E
Disa, *India* **68 G5** 24 18N 72 10 E
Disa, *Sudan* **81 E3** 12 5N 34 15 E
Disappointment, C., *U.S.A.* **114 C2** 46 18N 124 5W
Disappointment, L., *Australia* **92 D3** 23 20 S 122 40 E
Disaster B., *Australia* **95 F4** 37 15 S 149 58 E
Discovery B., *Australia* **95 F3** 38 10 S 140 40 E
Disentis Muster, *Switz.* **25 J4** 46 42N 8 50 E
Dishna, *Egypt* **80 B3** 26 9N 32 32 E
Disina, *Nigeria* **83 C6** 11 35N 9 50 E
Disko = Qeqertarsuaq, *Greenland* **101 B5** 69 45N 53 30W
Disko Bugt, *Greenland* **4 C5** 69 10N 52 0W
Disna = Dzisna →, *Belarus* **46 E5** 55 34N 28 12 E
Diss, *U.K.* **13 E9** 52 23N 1 7 E
Disteghil Sar, *Pakistan* **69 A6** 36 20N 75 12 E
Distrito Federal □, *Brazil* **125 G9** 15 45 S 47 45W
Distrito Federal □, *Mexico* **119 D5** 19 15N 99 10W
Disûq, *Egypt* **80 H7** 31 8N 30 35 E
Diu, *India* **68 J4** 20 45N 70 58 E
Dīvāndarreh, *Iran* **70 C5** 35 55N 47 2 E
Dives →, *France* **18 C6** 49 18N 0 7W
Dives-sur-Mer, *France* **18 C6** 49 18N 0 8W
Divichi = Däväçi, *Azerbaijan* **49 K9** 41 15N 48 57 E
Divide, *U.S.A.* **114 D7** 45 45N 112 45W
Dividing Ra., *Australia* **93 E2** 27 45 S 116 0 E
Divinópolis, *Brazil* **125 H10** 20 10 S 44 54W
Divjake, *Albania* **40 F3** 41 0N 19 32 E
Divnoye, *Russia* **49 H6** 45 55N 43 21 E
Divo, *Ivory C.* **82 D3** 5 48N 5 15W
Divriği, *Turkey* **73 C8** 39 22N 38 7 E
Dīwāl Kol, *Afghan.* **68 B2** 34 23N 67 52 E
Dixie Mt., *U.S.A.* **116 F6** 39 55N 120 16W
Dixon, *Calif., U.S.A.* **116 G5** 38 27N 121 49W
Dixon, *Ill., U.S.A.* **112 E10** 41 50N 89 29W
Dixon Entrance, *U.S.A.* **100 C6** 54 30N 132 0W
Dixville, *Canada* **111 A13** 45 4N 71 46W
Diyadin, *Turkey* **73 C10** 39 33N 43 40 E
Diyālā →, *Iraq* **70 C5** 33 14N 44 31 E
Diyarbakır, *Turkey* **70 B4** 37 55N 40 18 E
Diyodar, *India* **68 G4** 24 8N 71 50 E
Djakarta = Jakarta, *Indonesia* **62 F3** 6 9 S 106 49 E
Djamba, *Angola* **88 B1** 16 45 S 13 58 E
Djambala, *Congo* **84 E2** 2 32 S 14 30 E
Djanet, *Algeria* **78 D7** 24 35N 9 32 E
Djawa = Jawa, *Indonesia* **62 F3** 7 0 S 110 0 E
Djelfa, *Algeria* **78 B6** 34 40N 3 15 E
Djema, *C.A.R.* **86 A2** 6 3N 25 15 E
Djenné, *Mali* **82 C4** 14 0N 4 30W
Djerba, I. de, *Tunisia* **79 B8** 33 50N 10 48 E
Djerid, Chott, *Tunisia* **78 B7** 33 42N 8 30 E
Djibo, *Burkina Faso* **83 C4** 14 9N 1 35W
Djibouti, *Djibouti* **81 E5** 11 30N 43 5 E
Djibouti ■, *Africa* **81 E5** 12 0N 43 0 E
Djolu, *Dem. Rep. of the Congo* **84 D4** 0 35N 22 5 E
Djougou, *Benin* **83 D5** 9 40N 1 45 E
Djoum, *Cameroon* **84 D2** 2 41N 12 35 E
Djourab, Erg du, *Chad* **79 E9** 16 40N 18 50 E
Djugu, *Dem. Rep. of the Congo* **86 B3** 1 55N 30 35 E
Djúpivogur, *Iceland* **8 D6** 64 39N 14 17W
Djurås, *Sweden* **10 D9** 60 34N 15 8 E
Djursland, *Denmark* **11 H4** 56 27N 10 45 E
Dmitriya Lapteva, Proliv, *Russia* **51 B15** 73 0N 140 0 E
Dmitriyev Lgovskiy, *Russia* **47 F8** 52 10N 35 0 E
Dmitrov, *Russia* **46 D9** 56 25N 37 32 E
Dmitrovsk-Orlovskiy, *Russia* **47 F8** 52 29N 35 10 E
Dnepr → = Dnipro →, *Ukraine* **47 J7** 46 30N 32 18 E
Dneprodzerzhinsk = Dniprodzerzhynsk, *Ukraine* **47 H8** 48 32N 34 37 E
Dneprodzerzhinskoye Vdkhr. = Dniprodzerzhynske Vdskh., *Ukraine* **47 H8** 48 49N 34 8 E
Dnepropetrovsk = Dnipropetrovsk, *Ukraine* **47 H8** 48 30N 35 0 E
Dneprorudnoye = Dniprorudne, *Ukraine* **47 J8** 47 21N 34 58 E
Dnestr → = Dnister →, *Europe* **47 J6** 46 18N 30 17 E
Dnestrovski = Belgorod, *Russia* **47 G9** 50 35N 36 35 E
Dnieper = Dnipro →, *Ukraine* **47 J7** 46 30N 32 18 E
Dniester = Dnister →, *Europe* **47 J6** 46 18N 30 17 E
Dnipro →, *Ukraine* **47 J7** 46 30N 32 18 E
Dniprodzerzhynsk, *Ukraine* **47 H8** 48 32N 34 37 E
Dniprodzerzhynske Vdskh., *Ukraine* **47 H8** 48 49N 34 8 E
Dnipropetrovsk, *Ukraine* **47 H8** 48 30N 35 0 E
Dniprorudne, *Ukraine* **47 J8** 47 21N 34 58 E
Dnister →, *Europe* **47 J6** 46 18N 30 17 E
Dnistrovskyy Lyman, *Ukraine* **47 J6** 46 15N 30 17 E
Dno, *Russia* **46 D5** 57 50N 29 58 E
Dnyapro = Dnipro →, *Ukraine* **47 J7** 46 30N 32 18 E
Doaktown, *Canada* **103 C6** 46 33N 66 8W
Doan Hung, *Vietnam* **58 G5** 21 30N 105 10 E
Doany, *Madag.* **89 A8** 14 21 S 49 30 E
Doba, *Chad* **79 G9** 8 40N 16 50 E
Dobandi, *Pakistan* **68 D2** 31 13N 66 50 E
Dobbiaco, *Italy* **29 B9** 46 44N 12 14 E
Dobbyn, *Australia* **94 B3** 19 44 S 140 2 E
Dobczyce, *Poland* **45 J7** 49 52N 20 5 E
Dobele, *Latvia* **9 H20** 56 37N 23 16 E
Dobele □, *Latvia* **44 B10** 56 35N 23 5 E
Döbeln, *Germany* **24 D9** 51 6N 13 7 E
Doberai, Jazirah, *Indonesia* **63 E8** 1 25 S 133 0 E
Dobiegniew, *Poland* **45 F2** 52 59N 15 45 E
Doblas, *Argentina* **126 D3** 37 5 S 64 0W
Dobo, *Indonesia* **63 F8** 5 45 S 134 15 E
Doboj, *Bos.-H.* **42 F3** 44 46N 18 4 E
Dobra, *Wielkopolskie, Poland* **45 G5** 51 55N 18 37 E
Dobra, *Zachodnio-Pomorskie, Poland* **44 E2** 53 34N 15 20 E
Dobra, *Dîmbovita, Romania* **43 F10** 44 52N 25 40 E
Dobra, *Hunedoara, Romania* **42 E7** 45 54N 22 36 E
Dobre Miasto, *Poland* **44 E7** 53 58N 20 26 E
Dobrești, *Romania* **42 D7** 46 51N 22 18 E
Dobrich, *Bulgaria* **41 C11** 43 37N 27 49 E
Dobrinishta, *Bulgaria* **40 E7** 41 49N 23 34 E
Dobříš, *Czech Rep.* **26 B7** 49 46N 14 10 E
Dobrodzień, *Poland* **45 H5** 50 45N 18 25 E
Dobropole, *Ukraine* **47 H9** 48 25N 37 2 E
Dobruja, *Europe* **43 F13** 44 30N 28 15 E
Dobrush, *Belarus* **47 F6** 52 25N 31 22 E
Dobrzany, *Poland* **44 E2** 53 22N 15 25 E
Dobrzyń nad Wisłą, *Poland* **45 F6** 52 39N 19 22 E
Doc, Mui, *Vietnam* **64 D6** 17 58N 106 30 E
Docker River, *Australia* **93 D4** 24 52 S 129 5 E
Docksta, *Sweden* **10 A12** 63 3N 18 18 E
Doctor Arroyo, *Mexico* **118 C4** 23 40N 100 11W
Doda, *India* **69 C6** 33 10N 75 34 E
Doda, L., *Canada* **102 C4** 49 25N 75 13W
Dodecanese = Dhodhekánisos, *Greece* **39 E8** 36 35N 27 0 E
Dodge City, *U.S.A.* **113 G5** 37 45N 100 1W
Dodge L., *Canada* **105 B7** 59 50N 105 36W
Dodgeville, *U.S.A.* **112 D9** 42 58N 90 8W
Dodo, *Cameroon* **83 D7** 7 30N 12 3 E
Dodo, *Sudan* **81 F2** 5 10N 29 57 E
Dodola, *Ethiopia* **81 F4** 6 59N 39 11 E
Dodoma, *Tanzania* **86 D4** 6 8 S 35 45 E
Dodoma □, *Tanzania* **86 D4** 6 0 S 36 0 E
Dodona, *Greece* **38 B2** 39 40N 20 46 E
Dodsland, *Canada* **105 C7** 51 50N 108 45W
Dodson, *U.S.A.* **114 B9** 48 24N 108 15W
Dodurga, *Turkey* **39 B11** 39 49N 29 57 E
Doesburg, *Neths.* **17 B6** 52 1N 6 9 E
Doetinchem, *Neths.* **17 C6** 51 59N 6 18 E
Dog Creek, *Canada* **104 C4** 51 35N 122 14W
Dog L., *Man., Canada* **105 C9** 51 2N 98 31W
Dog L., *Ont., Canada* **102 C2** 48 48N 89 30W
Doğanşehir, *Turkey* **72 C7** 38 5N 37 53 E
Dogliani, *Italy* **28 D4** 44 32N 7 56 E
Dogondoutchi, *Niger* **83 C5** 13 38N 4 2 E
Dogran, *Pakistan* **68 D5** 31 48N 73 35 E
Doğubayazıt, *Turkey* **70 B5** 39 31N 44 5 E
Doguéraoua, *Niger* **83 C6** 14 0N 5 31 E
Doha = Ad Dawḩah, *Qatar* **71 E6** 25 15N 51 35 E
Dohazari, *Bangla.* **67 H18** 22 10N 92 5 E
Dohrighat, *India* **69 F10** 26 16N 83 31 E
Doi, *Indonesia* **63 D7** 2 14N 127 49 E
Doi Luang, *Thailand* **64 C3** 18 30N 101 0 E
Doi Saket, *Thailand* **64 C2** 18 52N 99 9 E
Dois Irmãos, Sa., *Brazil* **125 E10** 9 0 S 42 30W
Dojransko Jezero, *Macedonia* **40 E6** 41 13N 22 44 E
Dokkum, *Neths.* **17 A5** 53 20N 5 59 E
Dokri, *Pakistan* **68 F3** 27 25N 68 7 E
Dokuchayevsk, *Ukraine* **47 J9** 47 44N 37 40 E
Dol-de-Bretagne, *France* **18 D5** 48 34N 1 47W
Dolac, *Kosovo, Yug.* **40 D4** 42 36N 20 36 E
Dolak, Pulau, *Indonesia* **63 F9** 8 0 S 138 30 E
Dolbeau, *Canada* **103 C5** 48 53N 72 18W
Dole, *France* **19 E12** 47 7N 5 31 E
Doleib, Wadi →, *Sudan* **81 E3** 12 10N 33 15 E
Dolenji Logatec, *Slovenia* **29 C11** 45 56N 14 15 E
Dolgellau, *U.K.* **12 E4** 52 45N 3 53W
Dolgelley = Dolgellau, *U.K.* **12 E4** 52 45N 3 53W
Dolhasca, *Romania* **43 C11** 47 26N 26 36 E
Dolianova, *Italy* **30 C2** 39 22N 9 10 E
Dolinskaya = Dolynska, *Ukraine* **47 H7** 48 6N 32 46 E
Dolj □, *Romania* **43 F8** 44 10N 23 30 E
Dollard, *Neths.* **17 A7** 53 20N 7 10 E
Dolna Banya, *Bulgaria* **40 D7** 42 18N 23 44 E
Dolni Chiflik, *Bulgaria* **41 D11** 42 59N 27 43 E
Dolni Dŭbnik, *Bulgaria* **41 C8** 43 24N 24 26 E
Dolnośląskie □, *Poland* **45 G3** 51 10N 16 30 E
Dolný Kubín, *Slovak Rep.* **27 B12** 49 12N 19 18 E
Dolo, *Ethiopia* **81 G5** 4 11N 42 3 E
Dolo, *Italy* **29 C9** 45 25N 12 5 E
Dolomites = Dolomiti, *Italy* **29 B8** 46 23N 11 51 E
Dolomiti, *Italy* **29 B8** 46 23N 11 51 E
Dolores, *Argentina* **126 D4** 36 20 S 57 40W
Dolores, *Uruguay* **126 C4** 33 34 S 58 15W
Dolores, *U.S.A.* **115 H9** 37 28N 108 30W
Dolores →, *U.S.A.* **115 G9** 38 49N 109 17W
Dolovo, *Serbia, Yug.* **42 F5** 44 55N 20 52 E
Dolphin, C., *Falk. Is.* **128 G5** 51 10 S 59 0W
Dolphin and Union Str., *Canada* **100 B8** 69 5N 114 45W
Dolsk, *Poland* **45 G4** 51 59N 17 3 E
Dolynska, *Ukraine* **47 H7** 48 6N 32 46 E
Dolzhanskaya, *Russia* **47 J9** 46 37N 37 48 E
Dom Pedrito, *Brazil* **127 C5** 31 0 S 54 40W
Doma, *Nigeria* **83 D6** 8 25N 8 18 E
Domaniç, *Turkey* **39 B11** 39 48N 29 36 E
Domariaganj →, *India* **69 F10** 26 17N 83 44 E
Domasi, *Malawi* **87 F4** 15 15 S 35 22 E
Domažlice, *Czech Rep.* **26 B5** 49 28N 12 58 E
Dombarovskiy, *Russia* **50 D6** 50 46N 59 32 E
Dombås, *Norway* **9 E13** 62 4N 9 8 E
Dombasle-sur-Meurthe, *France* **19 D13** 48 38N 6 21 E
Dombes, *France* **21 C9** 45 58N 5 0 E
Dombóvár, *Hungary* **42 D3** 46 21N 18 9 E
Dombrád, *Hungary* **42 B6** 48 13N 21 54 E
Domel I. = Letsôk-aw Kyun, *Burma* **65 G2** 11 30N 98 25 E
Domérat, *France* **19 F9** 46 21N 2 32 E
Domeyko, *Chile* **126 B1** 29 0 S 71 0W
Domeyko, Cordillera, *Chile* **126 A2** 24 30 S 69 0W
Domfront, *France* **18 D6** 48 37N 0 40W
Dominador, *Chile* **126 A2** 24 21 S 69 20W
Dominica ■, *W. Indies* **121 C7** 15 20N 61 20W
Dominica Passage, *W. Indies* **121 C7** 15 10N 61 20W
Dominican Rep. ■, *W. Indies* **121 C5** 19 0N 70 30W
Dömitz, *Germany* **24 B7** 53 8N 11 15 E
Domme, *France* **20 D5** 44 48N 1 12 E
Domnești, *Romania* **43 E9** 45 12N 24 50 E
Domodóssola, *Italy* **28 B5** 46 7N 8 17 E
Dompaire, *France* **19 D13** 48 14N 6 14 E
Dompierre-sur-Besbre, *France* **19 F10** 46 31N 3 41 E
Dompim, *Ghana* **82 D4** 5 10N 2 5W
Domrémy-la-Pucelle, *France* **19 D12** 48 26N 5 40 E
Domville, Mt., *Australia* **95 D5** 28 1 S 151 15 E
Domvraína, *Greece* **38 C4** 38 15N 22 59 E
Domžale, *Slovenia* **29 B11** 46 9N 14 35 E
Don →, *Russia* **47 J10** 47 4N 39 18 E
Don →, *Aberds., U.K.* **14 D6** 57 11N 2 5W
Don →, *S. Yorks., U.K.* **12 D7** 53 41N 0 52W
Don, C., *Australia* **92 B5** 11 18 S 131 46 E
Don Benito, *Spain* **35 G5** 38 53N 5 51W
Dona Ana = Nhamaabué, *Mozam.* **87 F4** 17 25 S 35 5 E
Doña Mencía, *Spain* **35 H6** 37 33N 4 21W
Donaghadee, *U.K.* **15 B6** 54 39N 5 33W
Donald, *Australia* **95 F3** 36 23 S 143 0 E
Donaldsonville, *U.S.A.* **113 K9** 30 6N 90 59W
Donalsonville, *U.S.A.* **109 K3** 31 3N 84 53W
Donau = Dunărea →, *Europe* **43 E14** 45 20N 29 40 E
Donau →, *Austria* **17 D3** 48 10N 17 0 E
Donaueschingen, *Germany* **25 H4** 47 56N 8 29 E
Donauwörth, *Germany* **25 G6** 48 43N 10 47 E
Doncaster, *U.K.* **12 D6** 53 32N 1 6W
Dondo, *Mozam.* **87 F3** 19 33 S 34 46 E
Dondo, Teluk, *Indonesia* **63 D6** 0 50N 120 30 E
Dondra Head, *Sri Lanka* **66 S12** 5 55N 80 40 E
Dondușeni, *Moldova* **43 B12** 48 14N 27 36 E
Donegal, *Ireland* **15 B3** 54 39N 8 5W
Donegal □, *Ireland* **15 B4** 54 53N 8 0W
Donegal B., *Ireland* **15 B3** 54 31N 8 49W
Donets →, *Russia* **49 G5** 47 33N 40 55 E
Donetsk, *Ukraine* **47 J9** 48 0N 37 45 E
Dong Ba Thin, *Vietnam* **65 F7** 12 8N 109 13 E
Dong Dang, *Vietnam* **58 G6** 21 54N 106 42 E
Dong Giam, *Vietnam* **64 C5** 19 25N 105 31 E
Dong Ha, *Vietnam* **64 D6** 16 55N 107 8 E
Dong Hene, *Laos* **64 D5** 16 40N 105 18 E
Dong Hoi, *Vietnam* **64 D6** 17 29N 106 36 E
Dong Jiang →, *China* **59 F10** 23 6N 114 0 E
Dong Khe, *Vietnam* **64 A6** 22 26N 106 27 E
Dong Ujimqin Qi, *China* **56 B9** 45 32N 116 55 E
Dong Van, *Vietnam* **64 A5** 23 16N 105 22 E
Dong Xoai, *Vietnam* **65 G6** 11 32N 106 55 E
Donga, *Nigeria* **83 D7** 7 45N 10 2 E
Donga →, *Nigeria* **83 D7** 8 20N 9 58 E
Dong'an, *China* **59 D8** 26 23N 111 12 E
Dongara, *Australia* **93 E1** 29 14 S 114 57 E
Dongbei, *China* **57 D13** 45 0N 125 0 E
Dongchuan, *China* **58 D4** 26 8N 103 1 E
Donges, *France* **18 E4** 47 18N 2 4W
Dongfang, *China* **64 C7** 18 50N 108 33 E
Dongfeng, *China* **57 C13** 42 40N 125 34 E
Donggala, *Indonesia* **63 E5** 0 30 S 119 40 E
Donggan, *China* **58 F5** 23 22N 105 9 E
Donggou, *China* **57 E13** 39 52N 124 10 E
Dongguan, *China* **59 F9** 22 58N 113 44 E
Dongguang, *China* **56 F9** 37 50N 116 30 E
Donghai Dao, *China* **59 G8** 21 0N 110 15 E
Dongjingcheng, *China* **57 B15** 44 5N 129 10 E
Dongkou, *China* **59 D8** 27 6N 110 35 E
Donglan, *China* **58 E6** 24 30N 107 21 E
Dongliu, *China* **59 B11** 30 13N 116 55 E
Dongmen, *China* **58 F6** 22 20N 107 48 E
Dongning, *China* **57 B16** 44 2N 131 5 E
Dongnyi, *China* **58 C3** 28 3N 100 15 E
Dongola, *Sudan* **80 D3** 19 9N 30 22 E
Dongping, *China* **56 G9** 35 55N 116 20 E
Dongshan, *China* **59 F11** 23 43N 117 30 E
Dongsheng, *China* **56 E6** 39 50N 110 0 E
Dongtai, *China* **57 H11** 32 51N 120 21 E
Dongting Hu, *China* **59 C9** 29 18N 112 45 E
Dongtou, *China* **59 D13** 27 51N 121 10 E
Dongxiang, *China* **59 C11** 28 11N 116 34 E
Dongxing, *China* **58 G7** 21 34N 108 0 E
Dongyang, *China* **59 C13** 29 13N 120 15 E
Dongzhi, *China* **59 B11** 30 9N 117 0 E
Donington, C., *Australia* **95 E2** 34 45 S 136 0 E
Doniphan, *U.S.A.* **113 G9** 36 37N 90 50W
Donja Stubica, *Croatia* **29 C12** 45 59N 15 59 E
Donji Dušnik, *Serbia, Yug.* **40 C6** 43 12N 22 5 E
Donji Miholjac, *Croatia* **42 E3** 45 45N 18 10 E
Donji Milanovac, *Serbia, Yug.* **40 B6** 44 28N 22 6 E
Donji Vakuf, *Bos.-H.* **42 F2** 44 8N 17 24 E
Dønna, *Norway* **8 C15** 66 6N 12 30 E
Donna, *U.S.A.* **113 M5** 26 9N 98 4W
Donnaconna, *Canada* **103 C5** 46 41N 71 41W
Donnelly's Crossing, *N.Z.* **91 F4** 35 42 S 173 38 E
Donnybrook, *Australia* **93 F2** 33 34 S 115 48 E
Donnybrook, *S. Africa* **89 D4** 29 59 S 29 48 E
Donora, *U.S.A.* **110 F5** 40 11N 79 52W
Donostia = Donostia-San Sebastián, *Spain* **32 B3** 43 17N 1 58W
Donostia-San Sebastián, *Spain* **32 B3** 43 17N 1 58W
Donskoy, *Russia* **46 F10** 53 55N 38 15 E
Donsol, *Phil.* **61 E5** 12 54N 123 16 E
Donzère, *France* **21 D8** 44 28N 4 43 E
Donzy, *France* **19 E10** 47 20N 3 6 E
Doon →, *U.K.* **14 F4** 55 27N 4 39W
Dora, L., *Australia* **92 D3** 22 0 S 123 0 E
Dora Báltea →, *Italy* **28 C5** 45 11N 8 3 E
Dora Ripária →, *Italy* **28 C4** 45 5N 7 44 E
Doran L., *Canada* **105 A7** 61 13N 108 6W
Dorchester, *U.K.* **13 G5** 50 42N 2 27W
Dorchester, C., *Canada* **101 B12** 65 27N 77 27W
Dordabis, *Namibia* **88 C2** 22 52 S 17 38 E
Dordogne □, *France* **20 C4** 45 5N 0 40 E
Dordogne →, *France* **20 C3** 45 2N 0 36W
Dordrecht, *Neths.* **17 C4** 51 48N 4 39 E
Dordrecht, *S. Africa* **88 E4** 31 20 S 27 3 E
Dore →, *France* **20 C7** 45 50N 3 35 E
Dore, Mts., *France* **20 C6** 45 32N 2 50 E
Doré L., *Canada* **105 C7** 54 46N 107 17W
Doré Lake, *Canada* **105 C7** 54 38N 107 36W
Dorfen, *Germany* **25 G8** 48 15N 12 8 E
Dorgali, *Italy* **30 B2** 40 17N 9 35 E
Dori, *Burkina Faso* **83 C4** 14 3N 0 2W
Doring →, *S. Africa* **88 E2** 31 54 S 18 39 E
Doringbos, *S. Africa* **88 E2** 31 59 S 19 16 E
Dorion, *Canada* **111 A10** 45 23N 74 3W
Dormaa-Ahenkro, *Ghana* **82 D4** 7 15N 2 52W
Dormans, *France* **19 C10** 49 4N 3 38 E
Dormo, Ras, *Eritrea* **81 E5** 13 14N 42 35 E
Dornbirn, *Austria* **26 D2** 47 25N 9 45 E
Dornes, *France* **19 F10** 46 48N 3 18 E
Dornești, *Romania* **43 C11** 47 52N 26 1 E
Dornie, *U.K.* **14 D3** 57 17N 5 31W
Dornoch, *U.K.* **14 D4** 57 53N 4 2W
Dornoch Firth, *U.K.* **14 D4** 57 51N 4 4W
Dornogovĭ □, *Mongolia* **56 C6** 44 0N 110 0 E
Doro, *Mali* **83 B4** 16 9N 0 51W
Dorog, *Hungary* **42 C3** 47 42N 18 45 E
Dorogobuzh, *Russia* **46 E7** 54 50N 33 18 E
Dorohoi, *Romania* **43 C11** 47 56N 26 23 E
Döröö Nuur, *Mongolia* **60 B4** 48 0N 93 0 E
Dorr, *Iran* **71 C6** 33 17N 50 38 E
Dorre I., *Australia* **93 E1** 25 13 S 113 12 E
Dorrigo, *Australia* **95 E5** 30 20 S 152 44 E
Dorris, *U.S.A.* **114 F3** 41 58N 121 55W
Dorset, *Canada* **110 A6** 45 14N 78 54W
Dorset, *U.S.A.* **110 E4** 41 40N 80 40W
Dorset □, *U.K.* **13 G5** 50 45N 2 26W
Dorsten, *Germany* **24 D2** 51 40N 6 58 E
Dortmund, *Germany* **24 D3** 51 30N 7 28 E
Dortmund-Ems-Kanal →, *Germany* **24 D3** 51 50N 7 26 E
Dörtyol, *Turkey* **72 D7** 36 50N 36 13 E
Dorum, *Germany* **24 B4** 53 41N 8 34 E
Doruma, *Dem. Rep. of the Congo* **86 B2** 4 42N 27 33 E
Dorūneh, *Iran* **71 C8** 35 10N 57 18 E
Dos Bahías, C., *Argentina* **128 E3** 44 58 S 65 32W
Dos Hermanas, *Spain* **35 H5** 37 16N 5 55W
Dos Palos, *U.S.A.* **116 J6** 36 59N 120 37W
Döşemealtı, *Turkey* **39 D12** 37 4N 30 36 E
Dosso, *Niger* **83 C5** 13 0N 3 13 E
Dothan, *U.S.A.* **109 K3** 31 13N 85 24W
Doty, *U.S.A.* **116 D3** 46 38N 123 17W
Douai, *France* **19 B10** 50 21N 3 4 E
Douako, *Guinea* **82 D2** 9 45N 10 8W
Douala, *Cameroon* **83 E6** 4 0N 9 45 E
Douarnenez, *France* **18 D2** 48 6N 4 21W
Doubabougou, *Mali* **82 C3** 14 13N 7 59W
Double Island Pt., *Australia* **95 D5** 25 56 S 153 11 E
Double Mountain Fork →, *U.S.A.* **113 J4** 33 16N 100 0W
Doubrava →, *Czech Rep.* **26 A8** 50 2N 15 20 E
Doubs □, *France* **19 E13** 47 10N 6 20 E
Doubs →, *France* **19 F12** 46 53N 5 1 E
Doubtful Sd., *N.Z.* **91 L1** 45 20 S 166 49 E
Doubtless B., *N.Z.* **91 F4** 34 55 S 173 26 E
Doudeville, *France* **18 C7** 49 43N 0 47 E
Doué-la-Fontaine, *France* **18 E6** 47 11N 0 16W
Douentza, *Mali* **82 C4** 14 58N 2 48W
Douglas, *S. Africa* **88 D3** 29 4 S 23 46 E
Douglas, *U.K.* **12 C3** 54 10N 4 28W
Douglas, *Ariz., U.S.A.* **115 L9** 31 21N 109 33W
Douglas, *Ga., U.S.A.* **109 K4** 31 31N 82 51W
Douglas, *Wyo., U.S.A.* **112 D2** 42 45N 105 24W
Douglas Chan., *Canada* **104 C3** 53 40N 129 20W
Douglas Pt., *Canada* **110 B3** 44 19N 81 37W
Douglasville, *U.S.A.* **109 J3** 33 45N 84 45W
Doukáton, Ákra, *Greece* **38 C2** 38 34N 20 30 E
Doulevant-le-Château, *France* **19 D11** 48 23N 4 55 E
Doullens, *France* **19 B9** 50 10N 2 20 E
Doumen, *China* **59 F9** 22 10N 113 18 E
Douna, *Mali* **82 C3** 13 13N 6 0W
Douna, *Mali* **83 C4** 14 44N 1 38W
Dounreay, *U.K.* **14 C5** 58 35N 3 44W
Dourada, Serra, *Brazil* **125 F9** 13 10 S 48 45W
Dourados, *Brazil* **127 A5** 22 9 S 54 50W
Dourados →, *Brazil* **127 A5** 21 58 S 54 18W
Dourados, Serra dos, *Brazil* **127 A5** 23 30 S 53 30W
Dourdan, *France* **19 D9** 48 30N 2 1 E
Douro →, *Europe* **34 D2** 41 8N 8 40W
Douvaine, *France* **19 F13** 46 19N 6 16 E
Douvres-la-Délivrande, *France* **18 C6** 49 17N 0 23W
Douze →, *France* **20 E3** 43 54N 0 30W
Dove →, *U.K.* **12 E6** 52 51N 1 36W
Dove Creek, *U.S.A.* **115 H9** 37 46N 108 54W
Dover, *Australia* **94 G4** 43 18 S 147 2 E
Dover, *U.K.* **13 F9** 51 7N 1 19 E
Dover, *Del., U.S.A.* **108 F8** 39 10N 75 32W
Dover, *N.H., U.S.A.* **111 C14** 43 12N 70 56W
Dover, *N.J., U.S.A.* **111 F10** 40 53N 74 34W
Dover, *Ohio, U.S.A.* **110 F3** 40 32N 81 29W
Dover, Pt., *Australia* **93 F4** 32 32 S 125 32 E
Dover, Str. of, *Europe* **13 G9** 51 0N 1 30 E
Dover-Foxcroft, *U.S.A.* **109 C11** 45 11N 69 13W
Dover Plains, *U.S.A.* **111 E11** 41 43N 73 35W
Dovey = Dyfi →, *U.K.* **13 E3** 52 32N 4 3W
Dovrefjell, *Norway* **9 E13** 62 15N 9 33 E
Dow Rūd, *Iran* **71 C6** 33 28N 49 4 E
Dowa, *Malawi* **87 E3** 13 38 S 33 58 E
Dowagiac, *U.S.A.* **108 E2** 41 59N 86 6W
Dowerin, *Australia* **93 F2** 31 12 S 117 2 E
Dowgha'i, *Iran* **71 B8** 36 54N 58 32 E
Dowlatābād, *Iran* **71 D8** 28 20N 56 40 E
Down □, *U.K.* **15 B5** 54 23N 6 2W
Downey, *Calif., U.S.A.* **117 M8** 33 56N 118 7W
Downey, *Idaho, U.S.A.* **114 E7** 42 26N 112 7W
Downham Market, *U.K.* **13 E8** 52 37N 0 23 E
Downieville, *U.S.A.* **116 F6** 39 34N 120 50W
Downpatrick, *U.K.* **15 B6** 54 20N 5 43W
Downpatrick Hd., *Ireland* **15 B2** 54 20N 9 21W
Downsville, *U.S.A.* **111 D10** 42 5N 74 50W
Downton, Mt., *Canada* **104 C4** 52 42N 124 52W
Dowsārī, *Iran* **71 D8** 28 25N 57 59 E
Doyle, *U.S.A.* **116 E6** 40 2N 120 6W
Doylestown, *U.S.A.* **111 F9** 40 21N 75 10W
Dozois, Rés., *Canada* **102 C4** 47 30N 77 5W
Dra Khel, *Pakistan* **68 F2** 27 58N 66 45 E
Drac →, *France* **21 C9** 45 12N 5 42 E
Dračevo, *Macedonia* **40 E5** 41 56N 21 31 E
Drachten, *Neths.* **17 A6** 53 7N 6 5 E
Drăgănești, *Moldova* **43 C13** 47 43N 28 15 E

Drăgănești-Olt, *Romania* **43 F9** 44 9N 24 32 E
Drăgănești-Vlașca, *Romania* **43 F10** 44 5N 25 33 E
Dragaš, *Kosovo, Yug.* **40 D4** 42 5N 20 41 E
Drăgășani, *Romania* **43 F9** 44 39N 24 17 E
Dragichyn, *Belarus* **47 F3** 52 15N 25 8 E
Dragocvet, *Serbia, Yug.* **40 C5** 43 58N 21 15 E
Dragovishtitsa, *Bulgaria* **40 D6** 42 22N 22 39 E
Draguignan, *France* **21 E10** 43 32N 6 27 E
Drain, *U.S.A.* **114 E2** 43 40N 123 19W
Drake, *U.S.A.* **112 B4** 47 55N 100 23W
Drake Passage, *S. Ocean* **5 B17** 58 0 S 68 0W
Drakensberg, *S. Africa* **89 D4** 31 0 S 28 0 E
Dráma, *Greece* **41 E8** 41 9N 24 10 E
Dráma □, *Greece* **41 E8** 41 20N 24 0 E
Drammen, *Norway* **9 G14** 59 42N 10 12 E
Drangajökull, *Iceland* **8 C2** 66 9N 22 15W
Dranov, Ostrov, *Romania* **43 F14** 44 55N 29 30 E
Dras, *India* **69 B6** 34 25N 75 48 E
Drau = Drava →, *Croatia* **42 E3** 45 33N 18 55 E
Drava →, *Croatia* **42 E3** 45 33N 18 55 E
Dravograd, *Slovenia* **29 B12** 46 36N 15 5 E
Drawa →, *Poland* **45 F2** 52 52N 15 59 E
Drawno, *Poland* **45 E2** 53 13N 15 46 E
Drawsko Pomorskie, *Poland* **44 E2** 53 35N 15 50 E
Drayton Valley, *Canada* **104 C6** 53 12N 114 58W
Dreieich, *Germany* **25 E4** 50 1N 8 41 E
Dren, *Kosovo, Yug.* **40 C4** 43 8N 20 46 E
Drenthe □, *Neths.* **17 B6** 52 52N 6 40 E
Drepanum, C., *Cyprus* **36 E11** 34 54N 32 19 E
Dresden, *Canada* **110 D2** 42 35N 82 11W
Dresden, *Germany* **24 D9** 51 3N 13 44 E
Dreux, *France* **18 D8** 48 44N 1 23 E
Drezdenko, *Poland* **45 F2** 52 50N 15 49 E
Driffield, *U.K.* **12 C7** 54 0N 0 26W
Driftwood, *U.S.A.* **110 E6** 41 20N 78 8W
Driggs, *U.S.A.* **114 E8** 43 44N 111 6W
Drin →, *Albania* **40 D3** 42 1N 19 38 E
Drin i Zi →, *Albania* **40 E4** 41 37N 20 28 E
Drina →, *Bos.-H.* **40 B3** 44 53N 19 21 E
Drincea →, *Romania* **42 F7** 44 20N 22 55 E
Drinjača →, *Bos.-H.* **42 F4** 44 15N 19 8 E
Drissa = Vyerkhnyadzvinsk, *Belarus* **46 E4** 55 45N 27 58 E
Drniš, *Croatia* **29 E13** 43 51N 16 10 E
Drøbak, *Norway* **9 G14** 59 39N 10 39 E
Drobeta-Turnu Severin, *Romania* **42 F7** 44 39N 22 41 E
Drobin, *Poland* **45 F6** 52 42N 19 58 E
Drochia, *Moldova* **43 B12** 48 2N 27 48 E
Drogheda, *Ireland* **15 C5** 53 43N 6 22W
Drogichin = Dragichyn, *Belarus* **47 F3** 52 15N 25 8 E
Drogobych = Drohobych, *Ukraine* **47 H2** 49 20N 23 30 E
Drohiczyn, *Poland* **45 F9** 52 24N 22 39 E
Drohobych, *Ukraine* **47 H2** 49 20N 23 30 E
Droichead Atha = Drogheda, *Ireland* **15 C5** 53 43N 6 22W
Droichead Nua, *Ireland* **15 C5** 53 11N 6 48W
Droitwich, *U.K.* **13 E5** 52 16N 2 8W
Drôme □, *France* **21 D9** 44 38N 5 15 E
Drôme →, *France* **21 D8** 44 46N 4 46 E
Dromedary, C., *Australia* **95 F5** 36 17 S 150 10 E
Dromore, *U.K.* **15 B4** 54 31N 7 28W
Dromore West, *Ireland* **15 B3** 54 15N 8 52W
Dronero, *Italy* **28 D4** 44 28N 7 22 E
Dronfield, *U.K.* **12 D6** 53 19N 1 27W
Dronne →, *France* **20 C3** 45 2N 0 9W
Dronninglund, *Denmark* **11 G4** 57 10N 10 19 E
Dronten, *Neths.* **17 B5** 52 32N 5 43 E
Dropt →, *France* **20 D3** 44 35N 0 6W
Drosendorf, *Austria* **26 C8** 48 52N 15 37 E
Droué, *France* **18 D8** 48 3N 1 6 E
Drumbo, *Canada* **110 C4** 43 16N 80 35W
Drumheller, *Canada* **104 C6** 51 25N 112 40W
Drummond, *U.S.A.* **114 C7** 46 40N 113 9W
Drummond I., *U.S.A.* **108 C4** 46 1N 83 39W
Drummond Pt., *Australia* **95 E2** 34 9 S 135 16 E
Drummond Ra., *Australia* **94 C4** 23 45 S 147 10 E
Drummondville, *Canada* **102 C5** 45 55N 72 25W
Drumright, *U.S.A.* **113 H6** 35 59N 96 36W
Druskininkai, *Lithuania* **9 J20** 54 3N 23 58 E
Drut →, *Belarus* **47 F6** 53 8N 30 5 E
Druya, *Belarus* **46 E4** 55 45N 27 28 E
Druzhba, *Bulgaria* **41 C12** 43 15N 28 1 E
Druzhina, *Russia* **51 C15** 68 14N 145 18 E
Drvar, *Bos.-H.* **29 D13** 44 21N 16 23 E
Drvenik, *Croatia* **29 E13** 43 27N 16 3 E
Drwęca →, *Poland* **45 E5** 53 0N 18 42 E
Dry Tortugas, *U.S.A.* **120 B3** 24 38N 82 55W
Dryanovo, *Bulgaria* **41 D9** 42 59N 25 28 E
Dryden, *Canada* **105 D10** 49 47N 92 50W
Dryden, *U.S.A.* **111 D8** 42 30N 76 18W
Drygalski I., *Antarctica* **5 C7** 66 0 S 92 0 E
Drysdale →, *Australia* **92 B4** 13 59 S 126 51 E
Drysdale I., *Australia* **94 A2** 11 41 S 136 0 E
Drzewica, *Poland* **45 G7** 51 27N 20 29 E
Drzewiczka →, *Poland* **45 G7** 51 36N 20 36 E
Dschang, *Cameroon* **83 D7** 5 32N 10 3 E
Du Bois, *U.S.A.* **110 E6** 41 8N 78 46W
Du Gué →, *Canada* **102 A5** 57 21N 70 45W
Du He, *China* **59 A8** 32 48N 110 40 E
Du Quoin, *U.S.A.* **112 G10** 38 1N 89 14W
Du'an, *China* **58 F7** 23 59N 108 3 E
Duanesburg, *U.S.A.* **111 D10** 42 45N 74 11W
Duaringa, *Australia* **94 C4** 23 42 S 149 42 E
Ḑubā, *Si. Arabia* **70 E2** 27 10N 35 40 E
Dubai = Dubayy, *U.A.E.* **71 E7** 25 18N 55 20 E
Dubăsari, *Moldova* **43 C14** 47 15N 29 10 E
Dubăsari Vdkhr., *Moldova* **43 C13** 47 30N 29 0 E
Dubawnt →, *Canada* **105 A8** 64 33N 100 6W
Dubawnt, L., *Canada* **105 A8** 63 4N 101 42W
Dubayy, *U.A.E.* **71 E7** 25 18N 55 20 E
Dubbo, *Australia* **95 E4** 32 11 S 148 35 E
Dubele, *Dem. Rep. of the Congo* **86 B2** 2 56N 29 35 E
Dübendorf, *Switz.* **25 H4** 47 24N 8 37 E
Dubica, *Croatia* **29 C13** 45 11N 16 48 E
Dublin, *Ireland* **15 C5** 53 21N 6 15W
Dublin, *Ga., U.S.A.* **109 J4** 32 32N 82 54W
Dublin, *Tex., U.S.A.* **113 J5** 32 5N 98 21W
Dublin □, *Ireland* **15 C5** 53 24N 6 20W
Dubna, *Russia* **46 D9** 56 44N 37 10 E
Dubnica nad Váhom, *Slovak Rep.* **27 C11** 48 58N 18 11 E
Dubno, *Ukraine* **47 G3** 50 25N 25 45 E
Dubois, *U.S.A.* **114 D7** 44 10N 112 14W
Dubossary = Dubăsari, *Moldova* **43 C14** 47 15N 29 10 E
Dubossary Vdkhr. = Dubăsari Vdkhr., *Moldova* **43 C13** 47 30N 29 0 E
Dubovka, *Russia* **49 F7** 49 5N 44 50 E
Dubovskoye, *Russia* **49 G6** 47 28N 42 46 E
Dubrajpur, *India* **69 H12** 23 48N 87 25 E
Dubréka, *Guinea* **82 D2** 9 46N 13 31W
Dubrovitsa = Dubrovytsya, *Ukraine* **47 G4** 51 31N 26 35 E
Dubrovnik, *Croatia* **40 D2** 42 39N 18 6 E
Dubrovytsya, *Ukraine* **47 G4** 51 31N 26 35 E
Dubuque, *U.S.A.* **112 D9** 42 30N 90 41W
Dubysa →, *Lithuania* **44 C10** 55 5N 23 26 E
Duchang, *China* **59 C11** 29 18N 116 12 E
Duchesne, *U.S.A.* **114 F8** 40 10N 110 24W
Duchess, *Australia* **94 C2** 21 20 S 139 50 E
Ducie I., *Pac. Oc.* **97 K15** 24 40 S 124 48W
Duck →, *U.S.A.* **109 G2** 36 2N 87 52W
Duck Cr. →, *Australia* **92 D2** 22 37 S 116 53 E
Duck Lake, *Canada* **105 C7** 52 50N 106 16W
Duck Mountain Prov. Park, *Canada* **105 C8** 51 45N 101 0W
Duckwall, Mt., *U.S.A.* **116 H6** 37 58N 120 7W
Duderstadt, *Germany* **24 D6** 51 31N 10 15 E
Dudhi, *India* **67 G13** 24 15N 83 10 E
Dudinka, *Russia* **51 C9** 69 30N 86 13 E
Dudley, *U.K.* **13 E5** 52 31N 2 5W
Dudwa, *India* **69 E9** 28 30N 80 41 E
Duékoué, *Ivory C.* **82 D3** 6 40N 7 15W
Dueñas, *Spain* **34 D6** 41 52N 4 33W
Duero = Douro →, *Europe* **34 D2** 41 8N 8 40W
Dufftown, *U.K.* **14 D5** 57 27N 3 8W
Dufourspitz, *Switz.* **25 K3** 45 56N 7 52 E
Dūgī Kalā, *Afghan.* **66 C3** 32 20N 62 50 E
Dugi Otok, *Croatia* **29 D11** 44 0N 15 3 E
Dugo Selo, *Croatia* **29 C13** 45 51N 16 18 E
Duifken Pt., *Australia* **94 A3** 12 33 S 141 38 E
Duisburg, *Germany* **24 D2** 51 26N 6 45 E
Duiwelskloof, *S. Africa* **89 C5** 23 42 S 30 10 E
Dujiangyan, *China* **58 B4** 31 2N 103 38 E
Duk Fadiat, *Sudan* **81 F3** 7 45N 31 25 E
Duk Faiwil, *Sudan* **81 F3** 7 30N 31 29 E
Dukat, *Albania* **40 F3** 40 16N 19 32 E
Dūkdamīn, *Iran* **71 C8** 35 59N 57 43 E
Dukelský Průsmyk, *Slovak Rep.* **27 B14** 49 25N 21 42 E
Dukhān, *Qatar* **71 E6** 25 25N 50 50 E
Dukhovshchina, *Russia* **46 E7** 55 15N 32 27 E
Duki, *Pakistan* **66 D6** 30 14N 68 25 E
Dukla, *Poland* **45 J8** 49 30N 21 35 E
Duku, *Bauchi, Nigeria* **83 C7** 10 43N 10 43 E
Duku, *Sokoto, Nigeria* **83 C5** 11 11N 4 55 E
Dulag, *Phil.* **61 F6** 10 57N 125 2 E
Dulce, *U.S.A.* **115 H10** 36 56N 107 0W
Dulce →, *Argentina* **126 C3** 30 32 S 62 33W
Dulce, G., *Costa Rica* **120 E3** 8 40N 83 20W
Dulf, *Iraq* **70 C5** 35 7N 45 51 E
Dŭlgopol, *Bulgaria* **41 C11** 43 3N 27 22 E
Dulit, Banjaran, *Malaysia* **62 D4** 3 15N 114 30 E
Duliu, *China* **56 E9** 39 2N 116 55 E
Dullewala, *Pakistan* **68 D4** 31 50N 71 25 E
Dullstroom, *S. Africa* **89 D5** 25 27 S 30 7 E
Dülmen, *Germany* **24 D3** 51 49N 7 17 E
Dulovo, *Bulgaria* **41 C11** 43 48N 27 9 E
Dulq Maghār, *Syria* **70 B3** 36 22N 38 39 E
Duluth, *U.S.A.* **112 B8** 46 47N 92 6W
Dum Dum, *India* **69 H13** 22 39N 88 33 E
Dum Duma, *India* **67 F19** 27 40N 95 40 E
Dūmā, *Syria* **75 B5** 33 34N 36 24 E
Dumaguete, *Phil.* **61 G5** 9 17N 123 15 E
Dumai, *Indonesia* **62 D2** 1 35N 101 28 E
Dumaran, *Phil.* **61 F3** 10 33N 119 50 E
Dumas, *Ark., U.S.A.* **113 J9** 33 53N 91 29W
Dumas, *Tex., U.S.A.* **113 H4** 35 52N 101 58W
Ḑumayr, *Syria* **75 B5** 33 39N 36 42 E
Dumbarton, *U.K.* **14 F4** 55 57N 4 33W
Ďumbier, *Slovak Rep.* **27 C12** 48 56N 19 38 E
Dumbleyung, *Australia* **93 F2** 33 17 S 117 42 E
Dumboa, *Nigeria* **83 C7** 11 15N 12 55 E
Dumbrăveni, *Romania* **43 D9** 46 14N 24 34 E
Dumfries, *U.K.* **14 F5** 55 4N 3 37W
Dumfries & Galloway □, *U.K.* **14 F5** 55 9N 3 58W
Dumitrești, *Romania* **43 E11** 45 33N 26 55 E
Dumka, *India* **69 G12** 24 12N 87 15 E
Dumlupınar, *Turkey* **39 C12** 38 53N 30 0 E
Dümmer, *Germany* **24 C4** 52 31N 8 20 E
Dumoine →, *Canada* **102 C4** 46 13N 77 51W
Dumoine, L., *Canada* **102 C4** 46 55N 77 55W
Dumraon, *India* **69 G11** 25 33N 84 8 E
Dumyât, *Egypt* **80 H7** 31 24N 31 48 E
Dumyât, Masabb, *Egypt* **80 H7** 31 28N 31 51 E
Dún Dealgan = Dundalk, *Ireland* **15 B5** 54 1N 6 24W
Dún Laoghaire, *Ireland* **15 C5** 53 17N 6 8W
Dun-le-Palestel, *France* **19 F8** 46 18N 1 39 E
Dun-sur-Auron, *France* **19 F9** 46 53N 2 33 E
Dun-sur-Meuse, *France* **19 C12** 49 23N 5 11 E
Duna = Dunărea →, *Europe* **43 E14** 45 20N 29 40 E
Duna →, *Hungary* **42 E3** 45 51N 18 48 E
Duna-völgyi-főcsatorna, *Hungary* **42 D4** 46 40N 19 14 E
Dunaföldvár, *Hungary* **42 D3** 46 50N 18 57 E
Dunagiri, *India* **69 D8** 30 31N 79 52 E
Dunaj = Dunărea →, *Europe* **43 E14** 45 20N 29 40 E
Dunaj →, *Slovak Rep.* **27 D11** 47 50N 18 50 E
Dunajec →, *Poland* **45 H7** 50 15N 20 44 E
Dunajská Streda, *Slovak Rep.* **27 C10** 48 0N 17 37 E
Dunakeszi, *Hungary* **42 C4** 47 37N 19 8 E
Dunapataj, *Hungary* **42 D4** 46 39N 19 4 E
Dunărea →, *Europe* **43 E14** 45 20N 29 40 E
Dunaszekcső, *Hungary* **42 D3** 46 6N 18 45 E
Dunaújváros, *Hungary* **42 D3** 46 58N 18 57 E
Dunav = Dunărea →, *Europe* **43 E14** 45 20N 29 40 E
Dunavațu de Jos, *Romania* **43 F14** 44 59N 29 13 E
Dunavtsi, *Bulgaria* **40 C6** 43 57N 22 53 E
Dunay, *Russia* **54 C6** 42 52N 132 22 E
Dunback, *N.Z.* **91 L3** 45 23 S 170 36 E
Dunbar, *U.K.* **14 E6** 56 0N 2 31W
Dunblane, *U.K.* **14 E5** 56 11N 3 58W
Duncan, *Canada* **104 D4** 48 45N 123 40W
Duncan, *Ariz., U.S.A.* **115 K9** 32 43N 109 6W
Duncan, *Okla., U.S.A.* **113 H6** 34 30N 97 57W
Duncan, L., *Canada* **102 B4** 53 29N 77 58W
Duncan L., *Canada* **104 A6** 62 51N 113 58W
Duncan Town, *Bahamas* **120 B4** 22 15N 75 45W
Duncannon, *U.S.A.* **110 F7** 40 23N 77 2W
Duncansby Head, *U.K.* **14 C5** 58 38N 3 1W
Duncansville, *U.S.A.* **110 F6** 40 25N 78 26W
Dundaga, *Latvia* **44 A9** 57 31N 22 21 E
Dundalk, *Canada* **110 B4** 44 10N 80 24W
Dundalk, *Ireland* **15 B5** 54 1N 6 24W
Dundalk, *U.S.A.* **108 F7** 39 16N 76 32W
Dundalk Bay, *Ireland* **15 C5** 53 55N 6 15W
Dundas, *Canada* **110 C5** 43 17N 79 59W
Dundas, L., *Australia* **93 F3** 32 35 S 121 50 E
Dundas I., *Canada* **104 C2** 54 30N 130 50W
Dundas Str., *Australia* **92 B5** 11 15 S 131 35 E
Dundee, *S. Africa* **89 D5** 28 11 S 30 15 E
Dundee, *U.K.* **14 E6** 56 28N 2 59W
Dundee, *U.S.A.* **110 D8** 42 32N 76 59W
Dundee City □, *U.K.* **14 E6** 56 30N 2 58W
Dundgovĭ □, *Mongolia* **56 B4** 45 10N 106 0 E
Dundrum, *U.K.* **15 B6** 54 16N 5 52W
Dundrum B., *U.K.* **15 B6** 54 13N 5 47W
Dunedin, *N.Z.* **91 L3** 45 50 S 170 33 E
Dunedin, *U.S.A.* **109 L4** 28 1N 82 47W
Dunfermline, *U.K.* **14 E5** 56 5N 3 27W
Dungannon, *Canada* **110 C3** 43 51N 81 36W
Dungannon, *U.K.* **15 B5** 54 31N 6 46W
Dungarpur, *India* **68 H5** 23 52N 73 45 E
Dungarvan, *Ireland* **15 D4** 52 5N 7 37W
Dungarvan Harbour, *Ireland* **15 D4** 52 4N 7 35W
Dungeness, *U.K.* **13 G8** 50 54N 0 59 E
Dungo, L. do, *Angola* **88 B2** 17 15 S 19 0 E
Dungog, *Australia* **95 E5** 32 22 S 151 46 E
Dungu, *Dem. Rep. of the Congo* **86 B2** 3 40N 28 32 E
Dungun, *Malaysia* **65 K4** 4 45N 103 25 E
Dunguñâb, *Sudan* **80 C4** 21 10N 37 9 E
Dunguñâb, Khalij, *Sudan* **80 C4** 21 5N 37 12 E
Dunhua, *China* **57 C15** 43 20N 128 14 E
Dunhuang, *China* **60 B4** 40 8N 94 36 E
Dunk I., *Australia* **94 B4** 17 59 S 146 29 E
Dunkassa, *Benin* **83 C5** 10 21N 3 10 E
Dunkeld, *Australia* **95 E4** 33 25 S 149 29 E
Dunkeld, *U.K.* **14 E5** 56 34N 3 35W
Dunkerque, *France* **19 A9** 51 2N 2 20 E
Dunkery Beacon, *U.K.* **13 F4** 51 9N 3 36W
Dunkirk = Dunkerque, *France* **19 A9** 51 2N 2 20 E
Dunkirk, *U.S.A.* **110 D5** 42 29N 79 20W
Dunkuj, *Sudan* **81 E3** 12 50N 32 49 E
Dunkwa, *Central, Ghana* **82 D4** 6 0N 1 47W
Dunkwa, *Central, Ghana* **83 D4** 5 30N 1 0W
Dúnleary = Dun Laoghaire, *Ireland* **15 C5** 53 17N 6 8W
Dunleer, *Ireland* **15 C5** 53 50N 6 24W
Dunmanus B., *Ireland* **15 E2** 51 31N 9 50W
Dunmanway, *Ireland* **15 E2** 51 43N 9 6W
Dunmara, *Australia* **94 B1** 16 42 S 133 25 E
Dunmore, *U.S.A.* **111 E9** 41 25N 75 38W
Dunmore Hd., *Ireland* **15 D1** 52 10N 10 35W
Dunmore Town, *Bahamas* **120 A4** 25 30N 76 39W
Dunn, *U.S.A.* **109 H6** 35 19N 78 37W
Dunnellon, *U.S.A.* **109 L4** 29 3N 82 28W
Dunnet Hd., *U.K.* **14 C5** 58 40N 3 21W
Dunning, *U.S.A.* **112 E4** 41 50N 100 6W
Dunnville, *Canada* **110 D5** 42 54N 79 36W
Dunolly, *Australia* **95 F3** 36 51 S 143 44 E
Dunoon, *U.K.* **14 F4** 55 57N 4 56W
Dunphy, *U.S.A.* **114 F5** 40 42N 116 31W
Dunqul, *Egypt* **80 C3** 23 26N 31 37 E
Duns, *U.K.* **14 F6** 55 47N 2 20W
Dunseith, *U.S.A.* **112 A4** 48 50N 100 3W
Dunsmuir, *U.S.A.* **114 F2** 41 13N 122 16W
Dunstable, *U.K.* **13 F7** 51 53N 0 32W
Dunstan Mts., *N.Z.* **91 L2** 44 53 S 169 35 E
Dunster, *Canada* **104 C5** 53 8N 119 50W
Dunvegan L., *Canada* **105 A7** 60 8N 107 10W
Duolun, *China* **56 C9** 42 12N 116 28 E
Duong Dong, *Vietnam* **65 G4** 10 13N 103 58 E
Dupree, *U.S.A.* **112 C4** 45 4N 101 35W
Dupuyer, *U.S.A.* **114 B7** 48 13N 112 30W
Duque de Caxias, *Brazil* **127 A7** 22 45 S 43 19W
Durack →, *Australia* **92 C4** 15 33 S 127 52 E
Durack Ra., *Australia* **92 C4** 16 50 S 127 40 E
Durağan, *Turkey* **72 B6** 41 25N 35 3 E
Durak, *Turkey* **39 B10** 39 42N 28 17 E
Đurakovac, *Kosovo, Yug.* **40 D4** 42 43N 20 29 E
Durance →, *France* **21 E8** 43 55N 4 45 E
Durand, *U.S.A.* **112 C9** 44 38N 91 58W
Durango, *Mexico* **118 C4** 24 3N 104 39W
Durango, *U.S.A.* **115 H10** 37 16N 107 53W
Durango □, *Mexico* **118 C4** 25 0N 105 0W
Durankulak, *Bulgaria* **41 C12** 43 41N 28 32 E
Durant, *Miss., U.S.A.* **113 J10** 33 4N 89 51W
Durant, *Okla., U.S.A.* **113 J6** 33 59N 96 25W
Duratón →, *Spain* **34 D6** 41 37N 4 7W
Durazno, *Uruguay* **126 C4** 33 25 S 56 31W
Durazzo = Durrës, *Albania* **40 E3** 41 19N 19 28 E
Durban, *France* **20 F6** 42 59N 2 49 E
Durban, *S. Africa* **89 D5** 29 49 S 31 1 E
Durbuy, *Belgium* **17 D5** 50 21N 5 28 E
Dúrcal, *Spain* **35 J7** 36 59N 3 34W
Đurđevac, *Croatia* **42 D2** 46 2N 17 3 E
Düren, *Germany* **24 E2** 50 48N 6 29 E
Durg, *India* **67 J12** 21 15N 81 22 E
Durgapur, *India* **69 H12** 23 30N 87 20 E
Durham, *Canada* **102 D3** 44 10N 80 49W
Durham, *U.K.* **12 C6** 54 47N 1 34W
Durham, *Calif., U.S.A.* **116 F5** 39 39N 121 48W
Durham, *N.C., U.S.A.* **109 H6** 35 59N 78 54W
Durham, *N.H., U.S.A.* **111 C14** 43 8N 70 56W
Durham □, *U.K.* **12 C6** 54 42N 1 45W
Durleşti, *Moldova* **43 C13** 47 1N 28 46 E
Ḑurmā, *Si. Arabia* **70 E5** 24 37N 46 8 E
Durmitor, *Montenegro, Yug.* **40 C2** 43 10N 19 0 E
Durness, *U.K.* **14 C4** 58 34N 4 45W
Durrës, *Albania* **40 E3** 41 19N 19 28 E
Durrow, *Ireland* **15 D4** 52 51N 7 24W
Dursey I., *Ireland* **15 E1** 51 36N 10 12W
Dursunbey, *Turkey* **39 B10** 39 35N 28 37 E
Durtal, *France* **18 E6** 47 40N 0 18W
Duru, *Dem. Rep. of the Congo* **86 B2** 4 14N 28 50 E
Duru Gölü, *Turkey* **41 E12** 41 20N 28 35 E
Durusu, *Turkey* **41 E12** 41 17N 28 41 E
Durūz, Jabal ad, *Jordan* **75 C5** 32 35N 36 40 E
D'Urville, Tanjung, *Indonesia* **63 E9** 1 28 S 137 54 E
D'Urville I., *N.Z.* **91 J4** 40 50 S 173 55 E
Duryea, *U.S.A.* **111 E9** 41 20N 75 45W
Dûsh, *Egypt* **80 C3** 24 35N 30 41 E
Dushak, *Turkmenistan* **50 F7** 37 13N 60 1 E
Dushan, *China* **58 E6** 25 48N 107 30 E
Dushanbe, *Tajikistan* **50 F7** 38 33N 68 48 E
Dusheti, *Georgia* **49 J7** 42 10N 44 42 E
Dushore, *U.S.A.* **111 E8** 41 31N 76 24W
Dusky Sd., *N.Z.* **91 L1** 45 47 S 166 30 E
Dussejour, C., *Australia* **92 B4** 14 45 S 128 13 E
Düsseldorf, *Germany* **24 D2** 51 14N 6 47 E
Duszniki-Zdrój, *Poland* **45 H3** 50 24N 16 24 E
Dutch Harbor, *U.S.A.* **100 C3** 53 53N 166 32W
Dutlwe, *Botswana* **88 C3** 23 58 S 23 46 E
Dutsan Wai, *Nigeria* **83 C6** 10 50N 8 10 E
Dutton, *Canada* **110 D3** 42 39N 81 30W
Dutton →, *Australia* **94 C3** 20 44 S 143 10 E
Duved, *Sweden* **10 A6** 63 24N 12 55 E
Düvertepe, *Turkey* **39 B10** 39 14N 28 27 E
Duwayhin, Khawr, *U.A.E.* **71 E6** 24 20N 51 25 E
Duyun, *China* **58 D6** 26 18N 107 29 E
Düzağac, *Turkey* **39 C12** 38 48N 30 10 E
Düzce, *Turkey* **72 B4** 40 50N 31 10 E
Duzdab = Zāhedān, *Iran* **71 D9** 29 30N 60 50 E
Dve Mogili, *Bulgaria* **41 C9** 43 35N 25 55 E
Dvina, Severnaya →, *Russia* **50 C5** 64 32N 40 30 E
Dvinsk = Daugavpils, *Latvia* **9 J22** 55 53N 26 32 E
Dvor, *Croatia* **29 C13** 45 4N 16 22 E
Dvůr Králové nad Labem, *Czech Rep.* **26 A8** 50 27N 15 50 E
Dwarka, *India* **68 H3** 22 18N 69 8 E
Dwellingup, *Australia* **93 F2** 32 43 S 116 4 E
Dwight, *Canada* **110 A5** 45 20N 79 1W
Dwight, *U.S.A.* **108 E1** 41 5N 88 26W
Dyatkovo, *Russia* **46 F8** 53 40N 34 27 E
Dyatlovo = Dzyatlava, *Belarus* **46 F3** 53 28N 25 28 E
Dyce, *U.K.* **14 D6** 57 13N 2 12W
Dyer, C., *Canada* **101 B13** 66 40N 61 0W
Dyer Bay, *Canada* **110 A3** 45 10N 81 20W
Dyer Plateau, *Antarctica* **5 D17** 70 45 S 65 30W
Dyersburg, *U.S.A.* **113 G10** 36 3N 89 23W
Dyfi →, *U.K.* **13 E3** 52 32N 4 3W
Dyje →, *Czech Rep.* **27 C9** 48 37N 16 56 E
Dymer, *Ukraine* **47 G6** 50 47N 30 18 E
Dynów, *Poland* **45 J9** 49 50N 22 11 E
Dysart, *Australia* **94 C4** 22 32 S 148 23 E
Dzamin Üüd = Borhoyn Tal, *Mongolia* **56 C6** 43 50N 111 58 E
Dzerzhinsk, *Russia* **48 B6** 56 14N 43 30 E
Dzhalinda, *Russia* **51 D13** 53 26N 124 0 E
Dzhambul = Taraz, *Kazakhstan* **50 E8** 42 54N 71 22 E
Dzhankoy, *Ukraine* **47 K8** 45 40N 34 20 E
Dzhanybek, *Kazakhstan* **48 F8** 49 25N 46 50 E
Dzharylhach, Ostriv, *Ukraine* **47 J7** 46 2N 32 55 E
Dzhezkazgan = Zhezqazghan, *Kazakhstan* **50 E7** 47 44N 67 40 E
Dzhizak = Jizzakh, *Uzbekistan* **50 E7** 40 6N 67 50 E
Dzhugdzur, Khrebet, *Russia* **51 D14** 57 30N 138 0 E
Dzhvari = Jvari, *Georgia* **49 J6** 42 42N 42 4 E
Działdowo, *Poland* **45 E7** 53 15N 20 15 E
Działoszyce, *Poland* **45 H7** 50 22N 20 20 E
Działoszyn, *Poland* **45 G5** 51 6N 18 50 E
Dzibilchaltun, *Mexico* **119 C7** 21 5N 89 36W
Dzierzgoń, *Poland* **44 E6** 53 58N 19 20 E
Dzierżoniów, *Poland* **45 H3** 50 45N 16 39 E
Dzilam de Bravo, *Mexico* **119 C7** 21 24N 88 53W
Dzisna, *Belarus* **46 E5** 55 34N 28 12 E
Dzisna →, *Belarus* **46 E5** 55 34N 28 12 E
Dziwnów, *Poland* **44 D1** 54 2N 14 45 E
Dzungaria = Junggar Pendi, *China* **60 B3** 44 30N 86 0 E
Dzuumod, *Mongolia* **60 B5** 47 45N 106 58 E
Dzyarzhynsk, *Belarus* **46 F4** 53 40N 27 1 E
Dzyatlava, *Belarus* **46 F3** 53 28N 25 28 E

E

Eabamet L., *Canada* **102 B2** 51 30N 87 46W
Eads, *U.S.A.* **112 F3** 38 29N 102 47W
Eagar, *U.S.A.* **115 J9** 34 6N 109 17W
Eagle, *Alaska, U.S.A.* **100 B5** 64 47N 141 12W
Eagle, *Colo., U.S.A.* **114 G10** 39 39N 106 50W
Eagle →, *Canada* **103 B8** 53 36N 57 26W
Eagle Butte, *U.S.A.* **112 C4** 45 0N 101 10W
Eagle Grove, *U.S.A.* **112 D8** 42 40N 93 54W
Eagle L., *Canada* **105 D10** 49 42N 93 13W
Eagle L., *Calif., U.S.A.* **114 F3** 40 39N 120 45W
Eagle L., *Maine, U.S.A.* **109 B11** 46 20N 69 22W
Eagle Lake, *Canada* **110 A6** 45 8N 78 29W
Eagle Lake, *Maine, U.S.A.* **109 B11** 47 3N 68 36W
Eagle Lake, *Tex., U.S.A.* **113 L6** 29 35N 96 20W
Eagle Mountain, *U.S.A.* **117 M11** 33 49N 115 27W
Eagle Nest, *U.S.A.* **115 H11** 36 33N 105 16W
Eagle Pass, *U.S.A.* **113 L4** 28 43N 100 30W
Eagle Pk., *U.S.A.* **116 G7** 38 10N 119 25W
Eagle Pt., *Australia* **92 C3** 16 11 S 124 23 E
Eagle River, *Mich., U.S.A.* **108 B1** 47 24N 88 18W
Eagle River, *Wis., U.S.A.* **112 C10** 45 55N 89 15W
Eaglehawk, *Australia* **95 F3** 36 44 S 144 15 E
Eagles Mere, *U.S.A.* **111 E8** 41 25N 76 33W
Ealing □, *U.K.* **13 F7** 51 31N 0 20W
Ear Falls, *Canada* **105 C10** 50 38N 93 13W
Earle, *U.S.A.* **113 H9** 35 16N 90 28W
Earlimart, *U.S.A.* **117 K7** 35 53N 119 16W
Earn →, *U.K.* **14 E5** 56 21N 3 18W
Earn, L., *U.K.* **14 E4** 56 23N 4 13W
Earnslaw, Mt., *N.Z.* **91 L2** 44 32 S 168 27 E
Earth, *U.S.A.* **113 H3** 34 14N 102 24W
Easley, *U.S.A.* **109 H4** 34 50N 82 36W
East Anglia, *U.K.* **12 E9** 52 30N 1 0 E
East Angus, *Canada* **103 C5** 45 30N 71 40W
East Aurora, *U.S.A.* **110 D6** 42 46N 78 37W
East Ayrshire □, *U.K.* **14 F4** 55 26N 4 11W
East Bengal, *Bangla.* **67 H17** 24 0N 90 0 E
East Beskids = Vychodné Beskydy, *Europe* **27 B15** 49 20N 22 0 E
East Brady, *U.S.A.* **110 F5** 40 59N 79 36W
East C., *N.Z.* **91 G7** 37 42 S 178 35 E
East Chicago, *U.S.A.* **108 E2** 41 38N 87 27W
East China Sea, *Asia* **60 C7** 30 0N 126 0 E
East Coulee, *Canada* **104 C6** 51 23N 112 27W
East Dereham, *U.K.* **13 E8** 52 41N 0 57 E
East Dunbartonshire □, *U.K.* **14 F4** 55 57N 4 13W
East Falkland, *Falk. Is.* **122 J5** 51 30 S 58 30W
East Grand Forks, *U.S.A.* **112 B6** 47 56N 97 1W
East Greenwich, *U.S.A.* **111 E13** 41 40N 71 27W
East Grinstead, *U.K.* **13 F8** 51 7N 0 0W
East Hartford, *U.S.A.* **111 E12** 41 46N 72 39W
East Helena, *U.S.A.* **114 C8** 46 35N 111 56W
East Indies, *Asia* **52 K15** 0 0 120 0 E
East Kilbride, *U.K.* **14 F4** 55 47N 4 11W
East Lansing, *U.S.A.* **108 D3** 42 44N 84 29W
East Liverpool, *U.S.A.* **110 F4** 40 37N 80 35W
East London, *S. Africa* **89 E4** 33 0 S 27 55 E
East Lothian □, *U.K.* **14 F6** 55 58N 2 44W
East Main = Eastmain, *Canada* **102 B4** 52 10N 78 30W
East Northport, *U.S.A.* **111 F11** 40 53N 73 20W
East Orange, *U.S.A.* **111 F10** 40 46N 74 13W
East Pacific Ridge, *Pac. Oc.* **97 J17** 15 0 S 110 0W
East Palestine, *U.S.A.* **110 F4** 40 50N 80 33W
East Pine, *Canada* **104 B4** 55 48N 120 12W
East Point, *U.S.A.* **109 J3** 33 41N 84 27W
East Providence, *U.S.A.* **111 E13** 41 49N 71 23W
East Pt., *Canada* **103 C7** 46 27N 61 58W
East Renfrewshire □, *U.K.* **14 F4** 55 46N 4 21W
East Retford = Retford, *U.K.* **12 D7** 53 19N 0 56W
East Riding of Yorkshire □, *U.K.* **12 D7** 53 55N 0 30W
East Rochester, *U.S.A.* **110 C7** 43 7N 77 29W
East St. Louis, *U.S.A.* **112 F9** 38 37N 90 9W
East Schelde = Oosterschelde →, *Neths.* **17 C4** 51 33N 4 0 E
East Sea = Japan, Sea of, *Asia* **54 E7** 40 0N 135 0 E
East Siberian Sea, *Russia* **51 B17** 73 0N 160 0 E
East Stroudsburg, *U.S.A.* **111 E9** 41 1N 75 11W
East Sussex □, *U.K.* **13 G8** 50 56N 0 19 E
East Tawas, *U.S.A.* **108 C4** 44 17N 83 29W
East Timor ■, *Asia* **63 F7** 8 50 S 126 0 E
East Toorale, *Australia* **95 E4** 30 27 S 145 28 E
East Walker →, *U.S.A.* **116 G7** 38 52N 119 10W
East Windsor, *U.S.A.* **111 F10** 40 17N 74 34W
Eastbourne, *N.Z.* **91 J5** 41 19 S 174 55 E
Eastbourne, *U.K.* **13 G8** 50 46N 0 18 E
Eastend, *Canada* **105 D7** 49 32N 108 50W
Easter I. = Pascua, I. de, *Pac. Oc.* **97 K17** 27 0 S 109 0W
Eastern □, *Ghana* **83 D4** 6 30N 0 30W
Eastern □, *Kenya* **86 C4** 0 0 38 30 E
Eastern Cape □, *S. Africa* **88 E4** 32 0 S 26 0 E
Eastern Cr. →, *Australia* **94 C3** 20 40 S 141 35 E
Eastern Ghats, *India* **66 N11** 14 0N 78 50 E
Eastern Group = Lau Group, *Fiji* **91 C9** 17 0 S 178 30W
Eastern Group, *Australia* **93 F3** 33 30 S 124 30 E
Eastern Province □, *S. Leone* **82 D2** 8 15N 11 0W
Eastern Transvaal = Mpumalanga □, *S. Africa* **89 B5** 26 0 S 30 0 E
Easterville, *Canada* **105 C9** 53 8N 99 49W
Easthampton, *U.S.A.* **111 D12** 42 16N 72 40W
Eastlake, *U.S.A.* **110 E3** 41 40N 81 26W
Eastland, *U.S.A.* **113 J5** 32 24N 98 49W
Eastleigh, *U.K.* **13 G6** 50 58N 1 21W
Eastmain, *Canada* **102 B4** 52 10N 78 30W
Eastmain →, *Canada* **102 B4** 52 27N 78 26W
Eastman, *Canada* **111 A12** 45 18N 72 19W
Eastman, *U.S.A.* **109 J4** 32 12N 83 11W
Easton, *Md., U.S.A.* **108 F7** 38 47N 76 5W
Easton, *Pa., U.S.A.* **111 F9** 40 41N 75 13W
Easton, *Wash., U.S.A.* **116 C5** 47 14N 121 11W
Eastpointe, *U.S.A.* **110 D2** 42 27N 82 56W
Eastport, *U.S.A.* **109 C12** 44 56N 67 0W
Eastsound, *U.S.A.* **116 B4** 48 42N 122 55W
Eaton, *U.S.A.* **112 E2** 40 32N 104 42W
Eatonia, *Canada* **105 C7** 51 13N 109 25W
Eatonton, *U.S.A.* **109 J4** 33 20N 83 23W
Eatontown, *U.S.A.* **111 F10** 40 19N 74 4W
Eatonville, *U.S.A.* **116 D4** 46 52N 122 16W
Eau Claire, *U.S.A.* **112 C9** 44 49N 91 30W
Eau Claire, L. à l', *Canada* **102 A5** 56 10N 74 25W
Eauze, *France* **20 E4** 43 53N 0 7 E
Eban, *Nigeria* **83 D5** 9 40N 4 50 E
Ebbw Vale, *U.K.* **13 F4** 51 46N 3 12W
Ebeltoft, *Denmark* **11 H4** 56 12N 10 41 E
Ebeltoft Vig, *Denmark* **11 H4** 56 10N 10 35 E
Ebensburg, *U.S.A.* **110 F6** 40 29N 78 44W
Ebensee, *Austria* **26 D6** 47 48N 13 46 E
Eber Gölü, *Turkey* **72 C4** 38 38N 31 11 E
Eberbach, *Germany* **25 F4** 49 28N 8 59 E
Eberswalde-Finow, *Germany* **24 C9** 52 50N 13 49 E
Ebetsu, *Japan* **54 C10** 43 7N 141 34 E
Ebian, *China* **58 C4** 29 11N 103 13 E
Ebingen, *Germany* **25 G5** 48 13N 9 1 E
Éboli, *Italy* **31 B8** 40 39N 15 2 E
Ebolowa, *Cameroon* **83 E7** 2 55N 11 10 E
Ebonyi □, *Nigeria* **83 D6** 6 20N 8 0 E
Ebrach, *Germany* **25 F6** 49 51N 10 29 E
Ébrié, Lagune, *Ivory C.* **82 D4** 5 12N 4 26W
Ebro →, *Spain* **32 E5** 40 43N 0 54 E

Ebro, Embalse del

Fairfield

Empalme, *Mexico* **118 B2** 28 1N 110 49W
Empangeni, *S. Africa* . **89 D5** 28 50 S 31 52 E
Empedrado, *Argentina* **126 B4** 28 0 S 58 46W
Emperor Seamount Chain, *Pac. Oc.* .... **96 D9** 40 0N 170 0 E
Empoli, *Italy* .... **28 E7** 43 43N 10 57 E
Emporia, *Kans., U.S.A.* **112 F6** 38 25N 96 11W
Emporia, *Va., U.S.A.* . **109 G7** 36 42N 77 32W
Emporium, *U.S.A.* ... **110 E6** 41 31N 78 14W
Empress, *Canada* **105 C7** 50 57N 110 0W
Empty Quarter = Rub' al Khālī, *Si. Arabia* . **74 D4** 18 0N 48 0 E
Ems →, *Germany* .... **24 B3** 53 20N 7 12 E
Emsdale, *Canada* **110 A5** 45 32N 79 19W
Emsdetten, *Germany* . **24 C3** 52 10N 7 32 E
Emu, *China* .... **57 C15** 43 40N 128 6 E
Emu Park, *Australia* .. **94 C5** 23 13 S 150 50 E
'En 'Avrona, *Israel* ... **75 F4** 29 43N 35 0 E
En Nahud, *Sudan* .... **81 E2** 12 45N 28 25 E
En Nofalab, *Sudan* ... **81 D3** 15 52N 32 32 E
Ena, *Japan* .... **55 G8** 35 25N 137 25 E
Enana, *Namibia* ...... **88 B2** 17 30 S 16 23 E
Enånger, *Sweden* .... **10 C11** 61 30N 17 9 E
Enard B., *U.K.* **14 C3** 58 5N 5 20W
Enare = Inarijärvi, *Finland* .... **8 B22** 69 0N 28 0 E
Enarotali, *Indonesia* .. **63 E9** 3 55 S 136 21 E
Encampment, *U.S.A.* . **114 F10** 41 12N 106 47W
Encantadas, Serra, *Brazil* .... **127 C5** 30 40 S 53 0W
Encarnación, *Paraguay* **127 B4** 27 15 S 55 50W
Encarnación de Diaz, *Mexico* **118 C4** 21 30N 102 13W
Enchi, *Ghana* **82 D4** 5 53N 2 48W
Encinitas, *U.S.A.* **117 M9** 33 3N 117 17W
Encino, *U.S.A.* **115 J11** 34 39N 105 28W
Encounter B., *Australia* **95 F2** 35 45 S 138 45 E
Encs, *Hungary* .... **42 B6** 48 20N 21 8 E
Endako, *Canada* **104 C3** 54 6N 125 2W
Ende, *Indonesia* ..... **63 F6** 8 45 S 121 40 E
Endeavour Str., *Australia* .... **94 A3** 10 45 S 142 0 E
Endelave, *Denmark* .. **11 J4** 55 46N 10 18 E
Enderbury I., *Kiribati* . **96 H10** 3 8 S 171 5W
Enderby, *Canada* **104 C5** 50 35N 119 10W
Enderby I., *Australia* . **92 D2** 20 35 S 116 30 E
Enderby Land, *Antarctica* .... **5 C5** 66 0 S 53 0 E
Enderlin, *U.S.A.* **112 B6** 46 38N 97 36W
Endicott, *U.S.A.* **111 D8** 42 6N 76 4W
Endwell, *U.S.A.* **111 D8** 42 6N 76 2W
Endyalgout I., *Australia* **92 B5** 11 40 S 132 35 E
Eneabba, *Australia* ... **93 E2** 29 49 S 115 16 E
Enewetak Atoll, *Marshall Is.* .... **96 F8** 11 30N 162 15 E
Enez, *Turkey* .... **41 F10** 40 45N 26 5 E
Enfield, *Canada* **103 D7** 44 56N 63 32W
Enfield, *Conn., U.S.A.* **111 E12** 41 58N 72 36W
Enfield, *N.H., U.S.A.* . **111 C12** 43 39N 72 9W
Engadin, *Switz.* ...... **25 J6** 46 45N 10 10 E
Engaño, C., *Dom. Rep.* **121 C6** 18 30N 68 20W
Engaño, C., *Phil.* ..... **63 A6** 18 35N 122 23 E
Engaru, *Japan* .... **54 B11** 44 3N 143 31 E
Engcobo, *S. Africa* ... **89 E4** 31 37 S 28 0 E
Engelberg, *Switz.* .... **25 J4** 46 48N 8 26 E
Engels, *Russia* ...... **48 E8** 51 28N 46 6 E
Engemann L., *Canada* **105 B7** 58 0N 106 55W
Engershatu, *Eritrea* .. **81 D4** 16 7N 38 34 E
Enggano, *Indonesia* .. **62 F2** 5 20 S 102 40 E
England, *U.S.A.* **113 H9** 34 33N 91 58W
England □, *U.K.* **12 D7** 53 0N 2 0W
Englee, *Canada* **103 B8** 50 45N 56 5W
Englehart, *Canada* ... **102 C4** 47 49N 79 52W
Englewood, *U.S.A.* ... **112 F2** 39 39N 104 59W
English →, *Canada* .. **105 C10** 50 35N 93 30W
English Bazar = Ingraj Bazar, *India* ...... **69 G13** 24 58N 88 10 E
English Channel, *Europe* **13 G6** 50 0N 2 0W
English River, *Canada* **102 C1** 49 14N 91 0W
Engures ezers, *Latvia* . **44 A10** 57 16N 23 6 E
Enguri →, *Georgia* ... **49 J5** 42 27N 41 38 E
Enid, *U.S.A.* **113 G6** 36 24N 97 53W
Enipévs →, *Greece* ... **38 B4** 39 22N 22 17 E
Enkhuizen, *Neths.* ... **17 B5** 52 42N 5 17 E
Enköping, *Sweden* ... **10 E11** 59 37N 17 4 E
Enle, *China* .... **58 F3** 24 0N 101 9 E
Enna, *Italy* .... **31 E7** 37 34N 14 16 E
Ennadai, *Canada* **105 A8** 61 8N 100 53W
Ennadai L., *Canada* .. **105 A8** 61 0N 101 0W
Ennedi, *Chad* .... **79 E10** 17 15N 22 0 E
Enngonia, *Australia* .. **95 D4** 29 21 S 145 50 E
Ennigerloh, *Germany* . **24 D4** 51 50N 8 2 E
Ennis, *Ireland* **15 D3** 52 51N 8 59W
Ennis, *Mont., U.S.A.* .. **114 D8** 45 21N 111 44W
Ennis, *Tex., U.S.A.* ... **113 J6** 32 20N 96 38W
Enniscorthy, *Ireland* .. **15 D5** 52 30N 6 34W
Enniskillen, *U.K.* **15 B4** 54 21N 7 39W
Ennistimon, *Ireland* .. **15 D2** 52 57N 9 17W
Enns, *Austria* .... **26 C7** 48 12N 14 28 E
Enns →, *Austria* ..... **26 C7** 48 14N 14 32 E
Enontekiö, *Finland* ... **8 B20** 68 23N 23 37 E
Enosburg Falls, *U.S.A.* **111 B12** 44 55N 72 48W
Enping, *China* .... **59 F9** 22 16N 112 21 E
Enriquillo, L., *Dom. Rep.* **121 C5** 18 20N 72 5W
Enschede, *Neths.* .... **17 B6** 52 13N 6 53 E
Ensenada, *Argentina* . **126 C4** 34 55 S 57 55W
Ensenada, *Mexico* ... **118 A1** 31 50N 116 50W
Ensenada de los Muertos, *Mexico* ... **118 C2** 23 59N 109 50W
Enshi, *China* .... **58 B7** 30 18N 109 29 E
Ensiola, Pta. de n', *Spain* .... **37 B9** 39 7N 2 55 E
Ensisheim, *France* ... **19 E14** 47 50N 7 20 E
Entebbe, *Uganda* ..... **86 B3** 0 4N 32 28 E
Enterprise, *Canada* .. **104 A5** 60 47N 115 45W
Enterprise, *Ala., U.S.A.* **109 K3** 31 19N 85 51W
Enterprise, *Oreg., U.S.A.* **114 D5** 45 25N 117 17W
Entraygues-sur-Truyère, *France* .... **20 D6** 44 38N 2 35 E
Entre Ríos, *Bolivia* ... **126 A3** 21 30 S 64 25W
Entre Ríos □, *Argentina* .... **126 C4** 30 30 S 58 30W
Entrepeñas, Embalse de, *Spain* **32 E2** 40 34N 2 42W
Entroncamento, *Portugal* **35 F2** 39 28N 8 28W
Enugu, *Nigeria* .... **83 D6** 6 30N 7 30 E
Enugu □, *Nigeria* .... **83 D6** 6 30N 7 45 E
Enugu Ezike, *Nigeria* . **83 D6** 7 0N 7 29 E
Enumclaw, *U.S.A.* **116 C5** 47 12N 121 59W
Envermeu, *France* .... **18 C8** 49 53N 1 15 E
Enviken, *Sweden* ..... **10 D9** 60 49N 15 46 E
Enying, *Hungary* ..... **42 D3** 46 56N 18 15 E
Enza →, *Italy* .... **28 D7** 44 54N 10 31 E
Eólie, Ís., *Italy* .... **31 D7** 38 30N 14 57 E
Epanomí, *Greece* .... **40 F6** 40 25N 22 59 E
Epe, *Neths.* .... **17 B5** 52 21N 5 59 E
Epe, *Nigeria* .... **83 D5** 6 36N 3 59 E
Épernay, *France* ..... **19 C10** 49 3N 3 56 E
Épernon, *France* ..... **19 D8** 48 35N 1 40 E
Ephesus, *Turkey* ..... **39 D9** 37 55N 27 22 E
Ephraim, *U.S.A.* **114 G8** 39 22N 111 35W
Ephrata, *Pa., U.S.A.* .. **111 F8** 40 11N 76 11W
Ephrata, *Wash., U.S.A.* **114 C4** 47 19N 119 33W
Epidaurus Limera, *Greece* .... **38 E5** 36 46N 23 0 E
Épila, *Spain* **32 D3** 41 36N 1 17W
Épinac, *France* ...... **19 F11** 46 59N 4 31 E
Épinal, *France* ...... **19 D13** 48 10N 6 27 E
Episkopi, *Cyprus* .... **36 E11** 34 40N 32 54 E
Episkopí, *Greece* .... **36 D6** 35 20N 24 20 E
Episkopi Bay, *Cyprus* . **36 E11** 34 35N 32 50 E
Epitálion, *Greece* .... **38 D3** 37 37N 21 30 E
Eppan = Appiano, *Italy* **29 B8** 46 28N 11 15 E
Eppingen, *Germany* .. **25 F4** 49 8N 8 53 E
Epsom, *U.K.* **13 F7** 51 19N 0 16W
Epukiro, *Namibia* .... **88 C2** 21 40 S 19 9 E
Equatorial Guinea ■, *Africa* .... **84 D1** 2 0N 8 0 E
Er Hai, *China* .... **58 E3** 25 48N 100 11 E
Er Rachidia, *Morocco* **78 B5** 31 58N 4 20W
Er Rahad, *Sudan* .... **81 E3** 12 45N 30 32 E
Er Rif, *Morocco* **78 A5** 35 1N 4 1W
Er Rogel, *Sudan* ..... **80 D4** 18 10N 35 25 E
Er Roseires, *Sudan* .. **81 E3** 11 55N 34 30 E
Er Rua'at, *Sudan* .... **81 E3** 12 21N 32 17 E
Eraclea, *Italy* .... **29 C9** 45 35N 12 40 E
Erāwadī Myit = Irrawaddy →, *Burma* **67 M19** 15 50N 95 6 E
Erāwadī Myitwanya = Irrawaddy, Mouths of the, *Burma* .... **67 M19** 15 30N 95 0 E
Erba, *Italy* .... **28 C6** 45 48N 9 15 E
Erba, *Sudan* .... **80 D4** 19 5N 36 51 E
Erba, J., *Sudan* ..... **80 C4** 20 48N 36 47 E
Erbaa, *Turkey* .... **72 B7** 40 42N 36 36 E
Erbeskopf, *Germany* . **25 F3** 49 44N 7 2 E
Erbil = Arbīl, *Iraq* .... **70 B5** 36 15N 44 5 E
Erbu, *Ethiopia* ...... **81 E3** 6 44N 34 53 E
Erçek, *Turkey* .... **70 B4** 38 39N 43 36 E
Erciş, *Turkey* .... **73 C10** 39 2N 43 21 E
Erciyaş Dağı, *Turkey* . **70 B2** 38 30N 35 30 E
Érd, *Hungary* .... **42 C3** 47 22N 18 56 E
Erdao Jiang →, *China* **57 C14** 43 0N 127 0 E
Erdek, *Turkey* .... **41 F11** 40 23N 27 47 E
Erdemli, *Turkey* ..... **72 D6** 36 36N 34 19 E
Erdene = Ulaan-Uul, *Mongolia* .... **56 B6** 44 13N 111 10 E
Erdenetsogt, *Mongolia* **56 C4** 42 55N 106 5 E
Erding, *Germany* .... **25 G7** 48 18N 11 54 E
Erdre →, *France* **18 E5** 47 13N 1 32W
Erebus, Mt., *Antarctica* **5 D11** 77 35 S 167 0 E
Erechim, *Brazil* ..... **127 B5** 27 35 S 52 15W
Ereğli, *Konya, Turkey* **70 B2** 37 31N 34 4 E
Ereğli, *Zonguldak, Turkey* .... **72 B4** 41 15N 31 24 E
Erei, Monti, *Italy* .... **31 E7** 37 20N 14 20 E
Erenhot, *China* ...... **56 C7** 43 48N 112 2 E
Eresma →, *Spain* **34 D6** 41 26N 4 45W
Eressós, *Greece* ..... **39 B7** 39 11N 25 57 E
Erfenisdam, *S. Africa* . **88 D4** 28 30 S 26 50 E
Erftstadt, *Germany* .. **24 E2** 50 50N 6 50 E
Erft →, *Germany* .... **24 D2** 51 11N 6 44 E
Erfurt, *Germany* ..... **24 E7** 50 58N 11 2 E
Erg Iguidi, *Africa* .... **78 C4** 27 0N 7 0 E
Ergani, *Turkey* ...... **70 B3** 38 17N 39 49 E
Ergel, *Mongolia* ..... **56 C5** 43 8N 109 5 E
Ergene →, *Turkey* ... **41 E10** 41 1N 26 22 E
Ergeni Vozvyshennost, *Russia* .... **49 G7** 47 0N 44 0 E
Ērgli, *Latvia* .... **9 H21** 56 54N 25 38 E
Erhlin, *Taiwan* ...... **59 F13** 23 54N 120 22 E
Eria →, *Spain* **34 C5** 42 3N 5 44W
Eriba, *Sudan* .... **81 D4** 16 40N 36 10 E
Eriboll, L., *U.K.* **14 C4** 58 30N 4 42W
Érice, *Italy* .... **30 D5** 38 2N 12 35 E
Erie, *U.S.A.* **110 D4** 42 8N 80 5W
Erie, L., *N. Amer.* **110 D4** 42 15N 81 0W
Erie Canal, *U.S.A.* **110 C7** 43 5N 78 43W
Erieau, *Canada* **110 D3** 42 16N 81 57W
Erigavo, *Somali Rep.* . **74 E4** 10 35N 47 20 E
Erikoúsa, *Greece* .... **36 A3** 39 53N 19 34 E
Eriksdale, *Canada* ... **105 C9** 50 52N 98 7W
Erímanthos, *Greece* .. **38 D3** 37 57N 21 50 E
Erimo-misaki, *Japan* . **54 D11** 41 50N 143 15 E
Erinpura, *India* ...... **68 G5** 25 9N 73 3 E
Eriskay, *U.K.* **14 D1** 57 4N 7 18W
Erithraí, *Greece* ..... **38 C5** 38 13N 23 20 E
Eritrea ■, *Africa* ..... **81 E4** 14 0N 38 30 E
Erjas →, *Portugal* ... **34 F3** 39 40N 7 1W
Erkelenz, *Germany* .. **24 D2** 51 4N 6 19 E
Erkner, *Germany* .... **24 C9** 52 25N 13 44 E
Erlangen, *Germany* .. **25 F6** 49 36N 11 0 E
Erldunda, *Australia* .. **94 D1** 25 14 S 133 12 E
Ermelo, *Neths.* ...... **17 B5** 52 18N 5 35 E
Ermelo, *S. Africa* .... **89 D4** 26 31 S 29 59 E
Ermenek, *Turkey* .... **70 B2** 36 38N 33 0 E
Ermil, *Sudan* .... **81 E2** 13 35N 27 40 E
Ermióni, *Greece* ..... **38 D5** 37 23N 23 15 E
Ermones, *Greece* .... **36 A3** 39 37N 19 46 E
Ermoúpolis = Síros, *Greece* .... **38 D6** 37 28N 24 57 E
Ernakulam = Cochin, *India* .... **66 Q10** 9 59N 76 22 E
Erne →, *Ireland* **15 B3** 54 30N 8 16W
Erne, Lower L., *U.K.* .. **15 B4** 54 28N 7 47W
Erne, Upper L., *U.K.* .. **15 B4** 54 14N 7 32W
Ernée, *France* **18 D6** 48 18N 0 56W
Ernest Giles Ra., *Australia* .... **93 E3** 27 0 S 123 45 E
Ernstberg, *Germany* .. **25 E2** 50 13N 6 47 E
Erode, *India* .... **66 P10** 11 24N 77 45 E
Eromanga, *Australia* . **95 D3** 26 40 S 143 11 E
Erongo, *Namibia* .... **88 C2** 21 39 S 15 58 E
Erquy, *France* **18 D4** 48 38N 2 29W
Erramala Hills, *India* . **66 M11** 15 30N 78 15 E
Errer →, *Ethiopia* ... **81 F5** 7 32N 42 35 E
Errigal, *Ireland* **15 A3** 55 2N 8 6W
Erris Hd., *Ireland* **15 B1** 54 19N 10 0W
Ersekë, *Albania* ..... **40 F4** 40 22N 20 40 E
Erskine, *U.S.A.* **112 B7** 47 40N 96 0W
Erstein, *France* ...... **19 D14** 48 25N 7 38 E
Ertholmene, *Denmark* **11 J9** 55 19N 15 11 E
Ertil, *Russia* .... **48 E5** 51 55N 40 50 E
Ertis = Irtysh →, *Russia* **50 C7** 61 4N 68 52 E
Eruh, *Turkey* .... **73 D10** 37 46N 42 13 E
Eruwa, *Nigeria* ...... **83 D5** 7 33N 3 26 E
Ervy-le-Châtel, *France* **19 D10** 48 2N 3 55 E
Erwin, *U.S.A.* **109 G4** 36 9N 82 25W
Eryuan, *China* .... **58 D2** 26 7N 99 57 E
Erzgebirge, *Germany* . **24 E8** 50 27N 12 55 E
Erzin, *Russia* .... **51 D10** 50 15N 95 10 E
Erzincan, *Turkey* .... **70 B3** 39 46N 39 30 E
Erzurum, *Turkey* .... **70 B4** 39 57N 41 15 E
Es Caló, *Spain* ...... **37 C8** 38 40N 1 30 E
Es Canar, *Spain* ..... **37 B8** 39 2N 1 36 E
Es Mercadal, *Spain* .. **37 B11** 39 59N 4 5 E
Es Migjorn Gran, *Spain* **37 B11** 39 57N 4 3 E
Es Safiya, *Sudan* .... **81 D3** 15 31N 30 7 E
Es Sahrâ' Esh Sharqîya, *Egypt* .... **80 B3** 27 30N 32 30 E
Es Sînâ', *Egypt* ...... **75 F3** 29 0N 34 0 E
Es Sûkî, *Sudan* ...... **81 E3** 13 20N 33 58 E
Es Vedrà, *Spain* ..... **37 C7** 38 52N 1 12 E
Esambo, *Dem. Rep. of the Congo* .... **86 C1** 3 48 S 23 30 E
Esan-Misaki, *Japan* .. **54 D10** 41 40N 141 10 E
Esashi, *Hokkaidō, Japan* .... **54 B11** 44 56N 142 35 E
Esashi, *Hokkaidō, Japan* .... **54 D10** 41 52N 140 7 E
Esbjerg, *Denmark* ... **11 J2** 55 29N 8 29 E
Escalante, *U.S.A.* **115 H8** 37 47N 111 36W
Escalante →, *U.S.A.* . **115 H8** 37 24N 110 57W
Escalón, *Mexico* **118 B4** 26 46N 104 20W
Escambia →, *U.S.A.* .. **109 K2** 30 32N 87 11W
Escanaba, *U.S.A.* **108 C2** 45 45N 87 4W
Esch-sur-Alzette, *Lux.* **17 E6** 49 32N 6 0 E
Eschede, *Germany* ... **24 C6** 52 44N 10 14 E
Eschwege, *Germany* .. **24 D6** 51 11N 10 2 E
Eschweiler, *Germany* . **24 E2** 50 49N 6 15 E
Escondido, *U.S.A.* ... **117 M9** 33 7N 117 5W
Escravos →, *Nigeria* .. **83 D6** 5 35N 5 10 E
Escuinapa, *Mexico* ... **118 C3** 22 50N 105 50W
Escuintla, *Guatemala* **120 D1** 14 20N 90 48W
Eséka, *Cameroon* .... **83 E7** 3 41N 10 44 E
Eşen →, *Turkey* ..... **39 E11** 36 27N 29 16 E
Esenguly, *Turkmenistan* **50 F6** 37 37N 53 59 E
Esens, *Germany* ..... **24 B3** 53 38N 7 36 E
Esenyurt, *Turkey* .... **41 E12** 41 3N 28 48 E
Esera →, *Spain* ..... **32 C5** 42 6N 0 15 E
Eşfahān, *Iran* .... **71 C6** 32 39N 51 43 E
Eşfahān □, *Iran* ..... **71 C6** 32 50N 51 50 E
Esfarāyen, *Iran* ..... **71 B8** 37 4N 57 30 E
Esfideh, *Iran* .... **71 C8** 33 39N 59 46 E
Esgueva →, *Spain* ... **34 D6** 41 40N 4 43W
Esh Sham = Dimashq, *Syria* .... **75 B5** 33 30N 36 18 E
Esh Shamâlîya □, *Sudan* .... **80 D2** 19 0N 29 0 E
Esha Ness, *U.K.* **14 A7** 60 29N 1 38W
Eshan, *China* .... **58 E4** 24 11N 102 24 E
Esher, *U.K.* **13 F7** 51 21N 0 20W
Eshowe, *S. Africa* .... **89 D5** 28 50 S 31 30 E
Esiama, *Ghana* **82 E4** 4 56N 2 25W
Esigodini, *Zimbabwe* . **89 C4** 20 18 S 28 56 E
Esil = Ishim →, *Russia* **50 D8** 57 45N 71 10 E
Esino →, *Italy* ...... **29 E10** 43 39N 13 22 E
Esira, *Madag.* .... **89 C8** 24 20 S 46 42 E
Esk →, *Cumb., U.K.* .. **14 G5** 54 58N 3 2W
Esk →, *N. Yorks., U.K.* **12 C7** 54 30N 0 37W
Eskān, *Iran* .... **71 E9** 26 48N 63 9 E
Esker, *Canada* **103 B6** 53 53N 66 25W
Eskifjörður, *Iceland* .. **8 D7** 65 3N 13 55W
Eskilsäter, *Sweden* .. **11 F7** 58 57N 13 10 E
Eskilstuna, *Sweden* .. **10 E10** 59 22N 16 32 E
Eskimalatya, *Turkey* .. **73 C8** 38 24N 38 22 E
Eskimo Pt., *Canada* .. **100 B10** 61 10N 94 15W
Eskişehir, *Turkey* .... **39 B12** 39 50N 30 30 E
Eskişehir □, *Turkey* .. **39 B12** 39 40N 31 0 E
Esla →, *Spain* **34 D4** 41 29N 6 3W
Eslāmābād-e Gharb, *Iran* .... **70 C5** 34 10N 46 30 E
Eslāmshahr, *Iran* .... **71 C6** 35 40N 51 10 E
Eslöv, *Sweden* ...... **11 J7** 55 50N 13 20 E
Eşme, *Turkey* .... **39 C10** 38 23N 28 58 E
Esmeraldas, *Ecuador* . **124 C3** 1 0N 79 40W
Esnagi L., *Canada* ... **102 C3** 48 36N 84 33W
Espalion, *France* ..... **20 D6** 44 32N 2 47 E
Espanola, *Canada* ... **102 C3** 46 15N 81 46W
Espanola, *U.S.A.* **115 H10** 35 59N 106 5W
Esparreguera, *Spain* . **32 D6** 41 33N 1 52 E
Esparta, *Costa Rica* .. **120 E3** 9 59N 84 40W
Espelkamp, *Germany* . **24 C4** 52 24N 8 36 E
Esperance, *Australia* . **93 F3** 33 45 S 121 55 E
Esperance B., *Australia* **93 F3** 33 48 S 121 55 E
Esperanza, *Argentina* . **126 C3** 31 29 S 61 3W
Esperanza, *Phil.* ..... **61 G6** 8 43N 125 36 E
Espéraza, *France* .... **20 F6** 42 56N 2 14 E
Espichel, C., *Portugal* . **35 G1** 38 22N 9 16W
Espiel, *Spain* **35 G5** 38 11N 5 1W
Espigão, Serra do, *Brazil* .... **127 B5** 26 35 S 50 30W
Espinazo, Sierra del = Espinhaço, Serra do, *Brazil* .... **125 G10** 17 30 S 43 30W
Espinhaço, Serra do, *Brazil* .... **125 G10** 17 30 S 43 30W
Espinho, *Portugal* **34 D2** 41 1N 8 38W
Espinilho, Serra do, *Brazil* .... **127 B5** 28 30 S 55 0W
Espinosa de los Monteros, *Spain* **34 B7** 43 5N 3 34W
Espírito Santo □, *Brazil* **125 H10** 20 0 S 40 45W
Espíritu Santo, *Vanuatu* **96 J8** 15 15 S 166 50 E
Espíritu Santo, B. del, *Mexico* **119 D7** 19 15N 87 0W
Espíritu Santo, I., *Mexico* **118 C2** 24 30N 110 23W
Espita, *Mexico* **119 C7** 21 1N 88 19W
Espiye, *Turkey* ...... **73 B8** 40 56N 38 43 E
Espluga de Francolí, *Spain* .... **32 D6** 41 24N 1 7 E
Espoo, *Finland* ...... **9 F21** 60 12N 24 40 E
Espuña, Sierra de, *Spain* **33 H3** 37 51N 1 35W
Espungabera, *Mozam.* **89 C5** 20 29 S 32 45 E
Esquel, *Argentina* .... **128 E2** 42 55 S 71 20W
Esquimalt, *Canada* ... **104 D4** 48 26N 123 25W
Esquina, *Argentina* ... **126 C4** 30 0 S 59 30W
Essaouira, *Morocco* .. **78 B4** 31 32N 9 42W
Essebie, *Dem. Rep. of the Congo* .... **86 B3** 2 58N 30 40 E
Essen, *Belgium* ...... **17 C4** 51 28N 4 28 E
Essen, *Germany* ..... **24 D3** 51 28N 7 2 E
Essendon, Mt., *Australia* .... **93 E3** 25 0 S 120 29 E
Essequibo →, *Guyana* **122 C5** 6 50N 58 30W
Essex, *Canada* **110 D2** 42 10N 82 49W
Essex, *Calif., U.S.A.* .. **117 L11** 34 44N 115 15W
Essex, *N.Y., U.S.A.* ... **111 B11** 44 19N 73 21W
Essex □, *U.K.* .... **13 F8** 51 54N 0 27 E
Essex Junction, *U.S.A.* **111 B11** 44 29N 73 7W
Esslingen, *Germany* .. **25 G5** 48 44N 9 18 E
Essonne □, *France* ... **19 D9** 48 30N 2 20 E
Estaca de Bares, C. de, *Spain* **34 B3** 43 46N 7 42W
Estadilla, *Spain* ..... **32 C5** 42 4N 0 16 E
Estados, I. de Los, *Argentina* .... **122 J4** 54 40 S 64 30W
Estagel, *France* ..... **20 F6** 42 47N 2 40 E
Eşţahbānāt, *Iran* .... **71 D7** 29 8N 54 4 E
Estância, *Brazil* ..... **125 F11** 11 16 S 37 26W
Estancia, *U.S.A.* **115 J10** 34 46N 106 4W
Estārm, *Iran* .... **71 D8** 28 21N 58 21 E
Estarreja, *Portugal* .. **34 E2** 40 45N 8 35W
Estats, Pic d', *Spain* .. **32 C6** 42 40N 1 24 E
Estcourt, *S. Africa* ... **89 D4** 29 0 S 29 53 E
Este, *Italy* .... **29 C8** 45 14N 11 39 E
Estelí, *Nic.* **120 D2** 13 9N 86 22W
Estella, *Spain* **32 C2** 42 40N 2 2W
Estellencs, *Spain* .... **37 B9** 39 39N 2 29 E
Estena →, *Spain* **35 F6** 39 23N 4 44W
Estepa, *Spain* **35 H6** 37 17N 4 52W
Estepona, *Spain* **35 J5** 36 24N 5 7W
Esterhazy, *Canada* ... **105 C8** 50 37N 102 5W
Esternay, *France* .... **19 D10** 48 44N 3 33 E
Esterri d'Aneu, *Spain* . **32 C6** 42 38N 1 5 E
Estevan, *Canada* **105 D8** 49 10N 102 59W
Estevan Group, *Canada* **104 C3** 53 3N 129 38W
Estherville, *U.S.A.* .. **112 D7** 43 24N 94 50W
Estissac, *France* ..... **19 D10** 48 16N 3 48 E
Eston, *Canada* **105 C7** 51 8N 108 40W
Estonia ■, *Europe* ... **9 G21** 58 30N 25 30 E
Estoril, *Portugal* **35 G1** 38 42N 9 23W
Estouk, *Mali* .... **83 B5** 18 14N 1 2 E
Estreito, *Brazil* ..... **125 E9** 6 32 S 47 25W
Estrela, Serra da, *Portugal* **34 E3** 40 10N 7 45W
Estrella, *Spain* **35 G7** 38 25N 3 35W
Estremoz, *Portugal* .. **35 G3** 38 51N 7 39W
Estrondo, Serra do, *Brazil* .... **125 E9** 7 20 S 48 0W
Esztergom, *Hungary* .. **42 C3** 47 47N 18 44 E
Et Tîdra, *Mauritania* .. **82 B1** 19 45N 16 20W
Etah, *India* .... **69 F8** 27 35N 78 40 E
Étain, *France* .... **19 C12** 49 13N 5 38 E
Étampes, *France* .... **19 D9** 48 26N 2 10 E
Etanga, *Namibia* .... **88 B1** 17 55 S 13 0 E
Étaples, *France* ..... **19 B8** 50 30N 1 39 E
Etawah, *India* ...... **69 F8** 26 48N 79 6 E
Etawney L., *Canada* .. **105 B9** 57 50N 96 50W
Ete, *Nigeria* .... **83 D6** 7 2N 7 28 E
Ethel, *U.S.A.* **116 D4** 46 32N 122 46W
Ethelbert, *Canada* ... **105 C8** 51 32N 100 25W
Ethiopia ■, *Africa* ... **74 F3** 8 0N 40 0 E
Ethiopian Highlands, *Ethiopia* .... **52 J7** 10 0N 37 0 E
Etili, *Turkey* .... **41 G10** 39 59N 26 54 E
Etive, L., *U.K.* **14 E3** 56 29N 5 10W
Etna, *Italy* .... **31 E7** 37 50N 14 55 E
Etoile, *Dem. Rep. of the Congo* .... **87 E2** 11 33 S 27 30 E
Etosha Nat. Park, *Namibia* .... **88 B2** 19 0 S 16 0 E
Etosha Pan, *Namibia* . **88 B2** 18 40 S 16 30 E
Etowah, *U.S.A.* **109 H3** 35 20N 84 32W
Étréchy, *France* ..... **19 D9** 48 30N 2 12 E
Étrépagny, *France* ... **19 C8** 49 18N 1 36 E
Étretat, *France* ..... **18 C7** 49 42N 0 12 E
Etropole, *Bulgaria* ... **41 D8** 42 50N 24 0 E
Ettelbruck, *Lux.* ..... **17 E6** 49 51N 6 5 E
Ettlingen, *Germany* .. **25 G4** 48 56N 8 25 E
Ettrick Water →, *U.K.* **15 F6** 55 31N 2 55W
Etuku, *Dem. Rep. of the Congo* .... **86 C2** 3 42 S 25 45 E
Etulia, *Moldova* ..... **43 E13** 45 32N 28 27 E
Etzatlán, *Mexico* **118 C4** 20 48N 104 5W
Etzná, *Mexico* **119 D6** 19 35N 90 15W
Eu, *France* .... **18 B8** 50 3N 1 26 E
Euboea = Évvoia, *Greece* .... **38 C6** 38 30N 24 0 E
Eucla, *Australia* ..... **93 F4** 31 41 S 128 52 E
Euclid, *U.S.A.* **110 E3** 41 34N 81 32W
Eucumbene, L., *Australia* .... **95 F4** 36 2 S 148 40 E
Eudora, *U.S.A.* **113 J9** 33 7N 91 16W
Eufaula, *Ala., U.S.A.* . **109 K3** 31 54N 85 9W
Eufaula, *Okla., U.S.A.* **113 H7** 35 17N 95 35W
Eufaula L., *U.S.A.* ... **113 H7** 35 18N 95 21W
Eugene, *U.S.A.* **114 E2** 44 5N 123 4W
Eugowra, *Australia* .. **95 E4** 33 22 S 148 24 E
Eulo, *Australia* ..... **95 D4** 28 10 S 145 3 E
Eunice, *La., U.S.A.* ... **113 K8** 30 30N 92 25W
Eunice, *N. Mex., U.S.A.* **113 J3** 32 26N 103 10W
Eupen, *Belgium* ..... **17 D6** 50 37N 6 3 E
Euphrates = Furāt, Nahr al →, *Asia* .... **70 D5** 31 0N 47 25 E
Eure □, *France* ..... **18 C8** 49 10N 1 0 E
Eure →, *France* .... **18 C8** 49 18N 1 12 E
Eure-et-Loir □, *France* **18 D8** 48 22N 1 30 E
Eureka, *Canada* **4 B3** 80 0N 85 56W
Eureka, *Calif., U.S.A.* . **114 F1** 40 47N 124 9W
Eureka, *Kans., U.S.A.* **113 G6** 37 49N 96 17W
Eureka, *Mont., U.S.A.* **114 B6** 48 53N 115 3W
Eureka, *Nev., U.S.A.* .. **114 G5** 39 31N 115 58W
Eureka, *S. Dak., U.S.A.* **112 C5** 45 46N 99 38W
Eureka, Mt., *Australia* **93 E3** 26 35 S 121 35 E
Euroa, *Australia* .... **95 F4** 36 44 S 145 35 E
Europa, Île, *Ind. Oc.* .. **85 J8** 22 20 S 40 22 E
Europa, Picos de, *Spain* **34 B6** 43 10N 4 49W
Europa, Pta. de, *Gib.* . **35 J5** 36 3N 5 21W
Europe .... **6 E10** 50 0N 20 0 E
Europoort, *Neths.* .... **17 C4** 51 57N 4 10 E
Euskirchen, *Germany* . **24 E2** 50 39N 6 48 E
Eustis, *U.S.A.* **109 L5** 28 51N 81 41W
Eutin, *Germany* ..... **24 A6** 54 8N 10 36 E
Eutsuk L., *Canada* ... **104 C3** 53 20N 126 45W
Evale, *Angola* ...... **88 B2** 16 33 S 15 44 E
Evans, *U.S.A.* **112 E2** 40 23N 104 41W
Evans, L., *Canada* ... **102 B4** 50 50N 77 0W
Evans City, *U.S.A.* ... **110 F4** 40 46N 80 4W
Evans Head, *Australia* **95 D5** 29 7 S 153 27 E
Evans Mills, *U.S.A.* .. **111 B9** 44 6N 75 48W
Evansburg, *Canada* .. **104 C5** 53 36N 114 59W
Evanston, *Ill., U.S.A.* . **108 E2** 42 3N 87 41W
Evanston, *Wyo., U.S.A.* **114 F8** 41 16N 110 58W
Evansville, *U.S.A.* ... **108 G2** 37 58N 87 35W
Évaux-les-Bains, *France* **19 F9** 46 12N 2 29 E
Evaz, *Iran* .... **71 E7** 27 46N 53 59 E
Evciler, *Afyon, Turkey* **39 C11** 38 4N 29 54 E
Evciler, *Çanakkale, Turkey* .... **39 B8** 39 47N 26 44 E
Eveleth, *U.S.A.* **112 B8** 47 28N 92 32W
Evensk, *Russia* ..... **51 C16** 62 12N 159 30 E
Everard, L., *Australia* . **95 E2** 31 30 S 135 0 E
Everard Ranges, *Australia* .... **93 E5** 27 5 S 132 28 E
Everest, Mt., *Nepal* ... **69 E12** 28 5N 86 58 E
Everett, *Pa., U.S.A.* ... **110 F6** 40 1N 78 23W
Everett, *Wash., U.S.A.* **116 C4** 47 59N 122 12W
Everglades, The, *U.S.A.* **109 N5** 25 50N 81 0W
Everglades City, *U.S.A.* **109 N5** 25 52N 81 23W
Everglades National Park, *U.S.A.* **109 N5** 25 30N 81 0W
Evergreen, *Ala., U.S.A.* **109 K2** 31 26N 86 57W
Evergreen, *Mont., U.S.A.* **114 B6** 48 9N 114 13W
Everöd, *Sweden* ..... **11 J8** 55 53N 14 5 E
Evertsberg, *Sweden* .. **10 C7** 61 8N 13 58 E
Evesham, *U.K.* **13 E6** 52 6N 1 56W
Évian-les-Bains, *France* **19 F13** 46 24N 6 35 E
Évinos →, *Greece* ... **38 C3** 38 27N 21 40 E
Évisa, *France* ...... **21 F12** 42 15N 8 48 E
Evje, *Norway* .... **9 G12** 58 36N 7 51 E
Évora, *Portugal* **35 G3** 38 33N 7 57W
Évora □, *Portugal* ... **35 G3** 38 33N 7 50W
Evowghlī, *Iran* ...... **70 B5** 38 43N 45 13 E
Évreux, *France* ..... **18 C8** 49 3N 1 8 E
Evritania □, *Greece* .. **38 B3** 39 5N 21 30 E
Évron, *France* **18 D6** 48 10N 0 24W
Évros □, *Greece* .... **41 E10** 41 10N 26 0 E
Évros →, *Greece* .... **72 B2** 41 40N 26 34 E
Evrótas →, *Greece* .. **38 E4** 36 50N 22 40 E
Évry, *France* .... **19 D9** 48 38N 2 27 E
Évvoia, *Greece* ..... **38 C6** 38 30N 24 0 E
Évvoia □, *Greece* ... **38 C5** 38 40N 23 40 E
Evxinoúpolis, *Greece* . **38 B4** 39 12N 22 42 E
Ewe, L., *U.K.* **14 D3** 57 49N 5 38W
Ewing, *U.S.A.* **112 D5** 42 16N 98 21W
Ewo, *Congo* .... **84 E2** 0 48 S 14 45 E
Exaltación, *Bolivia* ... **124 F5** 13 10 S 65 20W
Excelsior Springs, *U.S.A.* **112 F7** 39 20N 94 13W
Excideuil, *France* ... **20 C5** 45 20N 1 4 E
Exe →, *U.K.* **13 G4** 50 41N 3 29W
Exeter, *Canada* **110 C3** 43 21N 81 29W
Exeter, *U.K.* **13 G4** 50 43N 3 31W
Exeter, *Calif., U.S.A.* . **116 J7** 36 18N 119 9W
Exeter, *N.H., U.S.A.* .. **111 D14** 42 59N 70 57W
Exmoor, *U.K.* **13 F4** 51 12N 3 45W
Exmouth, *Australia* .. **92 D1** 21 54 S 114 10 E
Exmouth, *U.K.* **13 G4** 50 37N 3 25W
Exmouth G., *Australia* **92 D1** 22 15 S 114 15 E
Expedition Ra., *Australia* .... **94 C4** 24 30 S 149 12 E
Extremadura □, *Spain* **35 F4** 39 30N 6 5W
Exuma Sound, *Bahamas* **120 B4** 24 30N 76 20W
Eyasi, L., *Tanzania* ... **86 C4** 3 30 S 35 0 E
Eye Pen., *U.K.* **14 C2** 58 13N 6 10W
Eyemouth, *U.K.* **14 F6** 55 52N 2 5W
Eygurande, *France* .. **19 G9** 45 40N 2 26 E
Eyjafjörður, *Iceland* .. **8 C4** 66 15N 18 30W
Eymet, *France* ..... **20 D4** 44 40N 0 25 E
Eymoutiers, *France* .. **20 C5** 45 40N 1 45 E
Eynesil, *Turkey* .... **73 B8** 41 4N 39 9 E
Eyre (North), L., *Australia* .... **95 D2** 28 30 S 137 20 E
Eyre (South), L., *Australia* .... **95 D2** 29 18 S 137 25 E
Eyre Mts., *N.Z.* ..... **91 L2** 45 25 S 168 25 E
Eyre Pen., *Australia* .. **95 E2** 33 30 S 136 17 E
Eysturoy, *Færoe Is.* .. **8 E9** 62 13N 6 54W
Eyvānkī, *Iran* ...... **71 C6** 35 24N 51 56 E
Ez Zeidab, *Sudan* ... **80 D3** 17 25N 33 55 E
Ezcaray, *Spain* **32 C1** 42 19N 3 0W
Ežerėlis, *Lithuania* .. **44 D10** 54 53N 23 37 E
Ezhou, *China* ...... **59 B10** 30 23N 114 50 E
Ezine, *Turkey* ...... **39 B8** 39 48N 26 20 E
Ezouza →, *Cyprus* .. **36 E11** 34 44N 32 27 E

F

F.Y.R.O.M. = Macedonia ■, *Europe* .... **40 E5** 41 53N 21 40 E
Fabala, *Guinea* **82 D3** 9 44N 9 5W
Fabens, *U.S.A.* **115 L10** 31 30N 106 10W
Fabero, *Spain* **34 C4** 42 46N 6 37W
Fåborg, *Denmark* ... **11 J4** 55 6N 10 15 E
Fabriano, *Italy* ...... **29 E9** 43 20N 12 54 E
Făcăeni, *Romania* ... **43 F12** 44 32N 27 53 E
Fachi, *Niger* .... **79 E8** 18 6N 11 34 E
Fada, *Chad* .... **79 E10** 17 13N 21 34 E
Fada-n-Gourma, *Burkina Faso* ...... **83 C5** 12 10N 0 30 E
Fadd, *Hungary* ..... **42 D3** 46 28N 18 49 E
Faddeyevskiy, Ostrov, *Russia* .... **51 B15** 76 0N 144 0 E
Faddor, *Sudan* ..... **81 F3** 8 7N 32 17 E
Fadghāmī, *Syria* .... **70 C4** 35 53N 40 52 E
Fadlab, *Sudan* ..... **80 D3** 17 42N 34 2 E
Faenza, *Italy* .... **29 D8** 44 17N 11 53 E
Færoe Is. = Føroyar, *Atl. Oc.* **8 F9** 62 0N 7 0W
Fafa, *Mali* .... **83 B5** 15 22N 0 48 E
Fafe, *Portugal* **34 D2** 41 27N 8 11W
Fagam, *Nigeria* ..... **83 C7** 11 1N 10 1 E
Făgăras, *Romania* ... **43 E9** 45 48N 24 58 E
Făgăras, Munţii, *Romania* .... **43 E9** 45 40N 24 40 E
Fågelmara, *Sweden* .. **11 H9** 56 16N 15 58 E
Fagerhult, *Sweden* .. **11 G9** 57 8N 15 40 E
Fagersta, *Sweden* ... **10 D9** 60 1N 15 46 E
Făget, *Romania* .... **42 E7** 45 52N 22 10 E
Făget, Munţii, *Romania* **43 C8** 47 40N 23 10 E
Fagnano, L., *Argentina* **128 G3** 54 30 S 68 0W
Fagnières, *France* ... **19 D11** 48 58N 4 20 E
Faguibine, L., *Mali* .. **82 B4** 16 45N 4 0W
Fahlīān, *Iran* ...... **71 D6** 30 11N 51 28 E
Fahraj, *Kermān, Iran* . **71 D8** 29 0N 59 0 E
Fahraj, *Yazd, Iran* .. **71 D7** 31 46N 54 36 E
Fai Tsi Long Archipelago, *Vietnam* **58 G6** 21 0N 107 30 E
Faial, *Madeira* **37 D3** 32 47N 16 53W
Fair Haven, *U.S.A.* .. **108 D9** 43 36N 73 16W
Fair Hd., *U.K.* **15 A5** 55 14N 6 9W
Fair Oaks, *U.S.A.* ... **116 G5** 38 39N 121 16W
Fairbanks, *U.S.A.* ... **100 B5** 64 51N 147 43W
Fairbury, *U.S.A.* **112 E6** 40 8N 97 11W
Fairfax, *U.S.A.* **111 B11** 44 40N 73 1W
Fairfield, *Ala., U.S.A.* . **109 J2** 33 29N 86 55W
Fairfield, *Calif., U.S.A.* **116 G4** 38 15N 122 3W
Fairfield, *Conn., U.S.A.* **111 E11** 41 9N 73 16W

Fairfield

Fairfield, *Idaho, U.S.A.* **114 E6** 43 21N 114 44W
Fairfield, *Ill., U.S.A.* **108 F1** 38 23N 88 22W
Fairfield, *Iowa, U.S.A.* **112 E9** 40 56N 91 57W
Fairfield, *Tex., U.S.A.* **113 K7** 31 44N 96 10W
Fairford, *Canada* **105 C9** 51 37N 98 38W
Fairhope, *U.S.A.* **109 K2** 30 31N 87 54W
Fairlie, *N.Z.* **91 L3** 44 5 S 170 49 E
Fairmead, *U.S.A.* **116 H6** 37 5N 120 10W
Fairmont, *Minn., U.S.A.* **112 D7** 43 39N 94 28W
Fairmont, *W. Va., U.S.A.* **108 F5** 39 29N 80 9W
Fairmont, *Calif., U.S.A.* **117 L8** 34 45N 118 26W
Fairmount, *N.Y., U.S.A.* **111 C8** 43 5N 76 12W
Fairplay, *U.S.A.* **115 G11** 39 15N 106 2W
Fairport, *U.S.A.* **110 C7** 43 6N 77 27W
Fairport Harbor, *U.S.A.* **110 E3** 41 45N 81 17W
Fairview, *Canada* **104 B5** 56 5N 118 25W
Fairview, *Mont., U.S.A.* **112 B2** 47 51N 104 3W
Fairview, *Okla., U.S.A.* **113 G5** 36 16N 98 29W
Fairweather, Mt., *U.S.A.* **104 B1** 58 55N 137 32W
Faisalabad, *Pakistan* **68 D5** 31 30N 73 5 E
Faith, *U.S.A.* **112 C3** 45 2N 102 2W
Faizabad, *India* **69 F10** 26 45N 82 10 E
Fajardo, *Puerto Rico* **121 C6** 18 20N 65 39W
Fajr, W. →, *Si. Arabia* **70 D3** 29 10N 38 10 E
Fakenham, *U.K.* **12 E8** 52 51N 0 51 E
Fåker, *Sweden* **10 A8** 63 0N 14 34 E
Fakfak, *Indonesia* **63 E8** 2 55 S 132 18 E
Fakiya, *Bulgaria* **41 D11** 42 10N 27 6 E
Fakobli, *Ivory C.* **82 D3** 7 23N 7 23W
Fakse, *Denmark* **11 J6** 55 15N 12 8 E
Fakse Bugt, *Denmark* **11 J6** 55 11N 12 15 E
Fakse Ladeplads, *Denmark* **11 J6** 55 11N 12 9 E
Faku, *China* **57 C12** 42 32N 123 21 E
Falaba, *S. Leone* **82 D2** 9 54N 11 22W
Falaise, *France* **18 D6** 48 54N 0 12W
Falaise, Mui, *Vietnam* **64 C5** 19 6N 105 45 E
Falakrón Óros, *Greece* **40 E7** 41 15N 23 58 E
Falam, *Burma* **67 H18** 23 0N 93 45 E
Falces, *Spain* **32 C3** 42 24N 1 48W
Fălciu, *Romania* **43 D13** 46 17N 28 7 E
Falcó, C. des, *Spain* **37 C7** 38 50N 1 23 E
Falcón, Presa, *Mexico* **119 B5** 26 35N 99 10W
Falcon Lake, *Canada* **105 D9** 49 42N 95 15W
Falcon Reservoir, *U.S.A.* **113 M5** 26 34N 99 10W
Falconara Maríttima, *Italy* **29 E10** 43 37N 13 24 E
Falcone, C. del, *Italy* **30 B1** 40 58N 8 12 E
Falconer, *U.S.A.* **110 D5** 42 7N 79 13W
Faléa, *Mali* **82 C2** 12 16N 11 17W
Falémé →, *Senegal* **82 C2** 14 46N 12 14W
Falerum, *Sweden* **11 F10** 58 8N 16 13 E
Faleshty = Fălești, *Moldova* **43 C12** 47 32N 27 44 E
Fălești, *Moldova* **43 C12** 47 32N 27 44 E
Falfurrias, *U.S.A.* **113 M5** 27 14N 98 9W
Falher, *Canada* **104 B5** 55 44N 117 15W
Falirakí, *Greece* **36 C10** 36 22N 28 12 E
Falkenberg, *Germany* **24 D9** 51 35N 13 14 E
Falkenberg, *Sweden* **11 H6** 56 54N 12 30 E
Falkensee, *Germany* **24 C9** 52 34N 13 4 E
Falkirk, *U.K.* **14 F5** 56 0N 3 47W
Falkirk □, *U.K.* **14 F5** 55 58N 3 49W
Falkland, *U.K.* **14 E5** 56 16N 3 12W
Falkland Is. □, *Atl. Oc.* **128 G5** 51 30 S 59 0W
Falkland Sd., *Falk. Is.* **128 G5** 52 0 S 60 0W
Falkonéra, *Greece* **38 E5** 36 50N 23 52 E
Falköping, *Sweden* **11 F7** 58 12N 13 33 E
Fall River, *U.S.A.* **111 E13** 41 43N 71 10W
Fallbrook, *U.S.A.* **117 M9** 33 23N 117 15W
Fallon, *U.S.A.* **114 G4** 39 28N 118 47W
Falls City, *U.S.A.* **112 E7** 40 3N 95 36W
Falls Creek, *U.S.A.* **110 E6** 41 9N 78 48W
Falmouth, *Jamaica* **120 C4** 18 30N 77 40W
Falmouth, *U.K.* **13 G2** 50 9N 5 5W
Falmouth, *U.S.A.* **111 E14** 41 33N 70 37W
Falsa, Pta., *Mexico* **118 B1** 27 51N 115 3W
False B., *S. Africa* **88 E2** 34 15 S 18 40 E
Falso, C., *Honduras* **120 C3** 15 12N 83 21W
Falster, *Denmark* **11 K5** 54 45N 11 55 E
Falsterbo, *Sweden* **9 J15** 55 23N 12 50 E
Fălticeni, *Romania* **43 C11** 47 21N 26 20 E
Falun, *Sweden* **10 D9** 60 37N 15 37 E
Famagusta, *Cyprus* **36 D12** 35 8N 33 55 E
Famagusta Bay, *Cyprus* **36 D13** 35 15N 34 0 E
Famalé, *Niger* **78 F6** 14 33N 1 5 E
Famatina, Sierra de, *Argentina* **126 B2** 27 30 S 68 0W
Family L., *Canada* **105 C9** 51 54N 95 27W
Famoso, *U.S.A.* **117 K7** 35 37N 119 12W
Fan Xian, *China* **56 G8** 35 55N 115 38 E
Fana, *Mali* **82 C3** 13 0N 6 56W
Fanad Hd., *Ireland* **15 A4** 55 17N 7 38W
Fanárion, *Greece* **38 B3** 39 24N 21 47 E
Fandriana, *Madag.* **89 C8** 20 14 S 47 21 E
Fang, *Thailand* **58 H2** 19 55N 99 13 E
Fang Xian, *China* **59 A8** 32 3N 110 40 E
Fangaga, *Sudan* **80 D4** 17 40N 37 50 E
Fangak, *Sudan* **81 F3** 9 4N 30 53 E
Fangchang, *China* **59 B12** 31 5N 118 4 E
Fangcheng, *China* **56 H7** 33 18N 112 59 E
Fangchenggang, *China* **58 G7** 21 42N 108 21 E
Fangliao, *Taiwan* **59 F13** 22 22N 120 38 E
Fangshan, *China* **56 E6** 38 3N 111 25 E
Fangzi, *China* **57 F10** 36 33N 119 10 E
Fani i Madh →, *Albania* **40 E4** 41 56N 20 16 E
Fanjakana, *Madag.* **89 C8** 21 10 S 46 53 E
Fanjiatun, *China* **57 C13** 43 40N 125 15 E
Fannich, L., *U.K.* **14 D4** 57 38N 4 59W
Fannūj, *Iran* **71 E8** 26 35N 59 38 E
Fanø, *Denmark* **11 J2** 55 25N 8 25 E
Fano, *Italy* **29 E10** 43 50N 13 1 E
Fanshi, *China* **56 E7** 39 12N 113 20 E
Fao = Al Fāw, *Iraq* **71 D6** 30 0N 48 30 E
Faqirwali, *Pakistan* **68 E5** 29 27N 73 0 E
Fâqûs, *Egypt* **80 H7** 30 44N 31 47 E
Fara in Sabina, *Italy* **29 F9** 42 12N 12 43 E
Faradje, *Dem. Rep. of the Congo* **86 B2** 3 50N 29 45 E
Farafangana, *Madag.* **89 C8** 22 49 S 47 50 E
Farâfra, El Wâhât el-, *Egypt* **80 B2** 27 15N 28 20 E
Farāh, *Afghan.* **66 C3** 32 20N 62 7 E
Farāh □, *Afghan.* **66 C3** 32 25N 62 10 E
Farahalana, *Madag.* **89 A9** 14 26 S 50 10 E
Faraid, Gebel, *Egypt* **80 C4** 23 33N 35 19 E
Farako, *Ivory C.* **82 D4** 10 45N 6 50W
Faramana, *Burkina Faso* **82 C4** 11 56N 4 45W
Faranah, *Guinea* **82 C2** 10 3N 10 45W
Farasān, Jazā'ir, *Si. Arabia* **74 D3** 16 45N 41 55 E
Farasan Is. = Farasān, Jazā'ir, *Si. Arabia* **74 D3** 16 45N 41 55 E
Faratsiho, *Madag.* **89 B8** 19 24 S 46 57 E
Fardes →, *Spain* **35 H7** 37 35N 3 0W
Fareham, *U.K.* **13 G6** 50 51N 1 11W
Farewell, C., *N.Z.* **91 J4** 40 29 S 172 43 E
Farewell C. = Nunap Isua, *Greenland* **101 C15** 59 48N 43 55W
Färgelanda, *Sweden* **11 F5** 58 34N 12 0 E
Farghona, *Uzbekistan* **50 E8** 40 23N 71 19 E
Fargo, *U.S.A.* **112 B6** 46 53N 96 48W
Fār'iah, W. al →, *West Bank* **75 C4** 32 12N 35 27 E
Faribault, *U.S.A.* **112 C8** 44 18N 93 16W
Faridabad, *India* **68 E6** 28 26N 77 19 E
Faridkot, *India* **68 D6** 30 44N 74 45 E
Faridpur, *Bangla.* **69 H13** 23 15N 89 55 E
Faridpur, *India* **69 E8** 28 13N 79 33 E
Färila, *Sweden* **10 C9** 61 48N 15 50 E
Farim, *Guinea-Biss.* **82 C1** 12 27N 15 9W
Farīmān, *Iran* **71 C8** 35 40N 59 49 E
Farina, *Australia* **95 E2** 30 3 S 138 15 E
Fariones, Pta., *Canary Is.* **37 E6** 29 13N 13 28W
Fârîskûr, *Egypt* **80 H7** 31 20N 31 43 E
Färjestaden, *Sweden* **11 H10** 56 39N 16 27 E
Farkadhón, *Greece* **38 B4** 39 36N 22 4 E
Farmakonisi, *Greece* **39 D9** 37 17N 27 5 E
Farmerville, *U.S.A.* **113 J8** 32 47N 92 24W
Farmingdale, *U.S.A.* **111 F10** 40 12N 74 10W
Farmington, *Canada* **104 B4** 55 54N 120 30W
Farmington, *Calif., U.S.A.* **116 H6** 37 55N 120 59W
Farmington, *Maine, U.S.A.* **109 C10** 44 40N 70 9W
Farmington, *Mo., U.S.A.* **113 G9** 37 47N 90 25W
Farmington, *N.H., U.S.A.* **111 C13** 43 24N 71 4W
Farmington, *N. Mex., U.S.A.* **115 H9** 36 44N 108 12W
Farmington, *Utah, U.S.A.* **114 F8** 41 0N 111 12W
Farmington →, *U.S.A.* **111 E12** 41 51N 72 38W
Farmville, *U.S.A.* **108 G6** 37 18N 78 24W
Färnäs, *Sweden* **10 D8** 61 0N 14 39 E
Farne Is., *U.K.* **12 B6** 55 38N 1 37W
Farnham, *Canada* **111 A12** 45 17N 72 59W
Farnham, Mt., *Canada* **104 C5** 50 29N 116 30W
Faro, *Brazil* **125 D7** 2 10 S 56 39W
Faro, *Canada* **100 B6** 62 11N 133 22W
Faro, *Portugal* **35 H3** 37 2N 7 55W
Fårö, *Sweden* **9 H18** 57 55N 19 5 E
Faro □, *Portugal* **35 H2** 37 12N 8 10W
Fårösund, *Sweden* **11 G13** 57 52N 19 2 E
Farquhar, C., *Australia* **93 D1** 23 50 S 113 36 E
Farrars Cr. →, *Australia* **94 D3** 25 35 S 140 43 E
Farrāshband, *Iran* **71 D7** 28 57N 52 5 E
Farrell, *U.S.A.* **110 E4** 41 13N 80 30W
Farrokhī, *Iran* **71 C8** 33 50N 59 31 E
Farruch, C. = Ferrutx, C., *Spain* **37 B10** 39 47N 3 21 E
Fārs □, *Iran* **71 D7** 29 30N 55 0 E
Fársala, *Greece* **38 B4** 39 17N 22 23 E
Farsø, *Denmark* **11 H3** 56 46N 9 19 E
Farson, *U.S.A.* **114 E9** 42 6N 109 27W
Farsund, *Norway* **9 G12** 58 5N 6 55 E
Fartak, Râs, *Si. Arabia* **70 D2** 28 5N 34 34 E
Fartak, Ra's, *Yemen* **74 D5** 15 38N 52 15 E
Fărțănești, *Romania* **43 E12** 45 49N 27 59 E
Fartura, Serra da, *Brazil* **127 B5** 26 21 S 52 52W
Faru, *Nigeria* **83 C6** 12 48N 6 12 E
Farūj, *Iran* **71 B8** 37 14N 58 14 E
Fårup, *Denmark* **11 H3** 56 33N 9 51 E
Farvel, Kap = Nunap Isua, *Greenland* **101 C15** 59 48N 43 55W
Farwell, *U.S.A.* **113 H3** 34 23N 103 2W
Fāryāb □, *Afghan.* **66 B4** 36 0N 65 0 E
Fasā, *Iran* **71 D7** 29 0N 53 39 E
Fasano, *Italy* **31 B10** 40 50N 17 22 E
Fashoda, *Sudan* **81 F3** 9 50N 32 2 E
Fassa, *Mali* **82 C3** 13 26N 8 15 E
Fastiv, *Ukraine* **47 G5** 50 7N 29 57 E
Fastov = Fastiv, *Ukraine* **47 G5** 50 7N 29 57 E
Fatagar, Tanjung, *Indonesia* **63 E8** 2 46 S 131 57 E
Fatehabad, *Haryana, India* **68 E6** 29 31N 75 27 E
Fatehabad, *Ut. P., India* **68 F8** 27 1N 78 19 E
Fatehgarh, *India* **69 F8** 27 25N 79 35 E
Fatehpur, *Bihar, India* **69 G11** 24 38N 85 14 E
Fatehpur, *Raj., India* **68 F6** 28 0N 74 40 E
Fatehpur, *Ut. P., India* **69 G9** 25 56N 81 13 E
Fatehpur, *Ut. P., India* **69 F9** 27 10N 81 13 E
Fatehpur Sikri, *India* **68 F6** 27 6N 77 40 E
Fatesh, *Russia* **47 F8** 52 8N 35 57 E
Fathai, *Sudan* **81 F3** 8 5N 31 48 E
Fatick, *Senegal* **82 C1** 14 19N 16 27W
Fatima, *Canada* **103 C7** 47 24N 61 53W
Fátima, *Portugal* **35 F2** 39 37N 8 39W
Fatoya, *Guinea* **82 C3** 11 37N 9 10W
Fatsa, *Turkey* **72 B7** 41 2N 37 31 E
Faucille, Col de la, *France* **19 F13** 46 22N 6 2 E
Faulkton, *U.S.A.* **112 C5** 45 2N 99 8W
Faulquemont, *France* **19 C13** 49 3N 6 36 E
Faure I., *Australia* **93 E1** 25 52 S 113 50 E
Făurei, *Romania* **43 E12** 45 6N 27 19 E
Fauresmith, *S. Africa* **88 D4** 29 44 S 25 17 E
Fauske, *Norway* **8 C16** 67 17N 15 25 E
Favara, *Italy* **30 E6** 37 19N 13 39 E
Faváritx, C. de, *Spain* **37 B11** 40 0N 4 15 E
Faverges, *France* **21 C10** 45 45N 6 17 E
Favignana, *Italy* **30 E5** 37 56N 12 20 E
Favignana, I., *Italy* **30 E5** 37 56N 12 19 E
Fawcett, Pt., *Australia* **92 B5** 11 46 S 130 2 E
Fawn →, *Canada* **102 A2** 55 20N 87 35W
Fawnskin, *U.S.A.* **117 L10** 34 16N 116 56W
Faxaflói, *Iceland* **8 D2** 64 29N 23 0W
Faxälven →, *Sweden* **10 A10** 63 13N 17 13 E
Faya-Largeau, *Chad* **79 E9** 17 58N 19 6 E
Fayd, *Si. Arabia* **70 E4** 27 1N 42 52 E
Fayence, *France* **21 E10** 43 38N 6 42 E
Fayette, *Ala., U.S.A.* **109 J2** 33 41N 87 50W
Fayette, *Mo., U.S.A.* **112 F8** 39 9N 92 41W
Fayetteville, *Ark., U.S.A.* **113 G7** 36 4N 94 10W
Fayetteville, *N.C., U.S.A.* **109 H6** 35 3N 78 53W
Fayetteville, *Tenn., U.S.A.* **109 H2** 35 9N 86 34W
Fayied, *Egypt* **80 H8** 30 18N 32 16 E
Fayón, *Spain* **32 D5** 41 15N 0 20 E
Fazilka, *India* **68 D6** 30 27N 74 2 E
Fazilpur, *Pakistan* **68 E4** 29 18N 70 29 E
Fdérik, *Mauritania* **78 D3** 22 40N 12 45W
Feale →, *Ireland* **15 D2** 52 27N 9 37W
Fear, C., *U.S.A.* **109 J7** 33 50N 77 58W
Feather →, *U.S.A.* **114 G3** 38 47N 121 36W
Feather Falls, *U.S.A.* **116 F5** 39 36N 121 16W
Featherston, *N.Z.* **91 J5** 41 6 S 175 20 E
Featherstone, *Zimbabwe* **87 F3** 18 42 S 30 55 E
Fécamp, *France* **18 C7** 49 45N 0 22 E
Fedala = Mohammedia, *Morocco* **78 B4** 33 44N 7 21W
Federación, *Argentina* **126 C4** 31 0 S 57 55W
Féderal, *Argentina* **128 C5** 30 57 S 58 48W
Federal Capital Terr. □, *Nigeria* **83 D6** 9 0N 7 10 E
Federal Way, *U.S.A.* **116 C4** 47 18N 122 19W
Fedeshkūh, *Iran* **71 D7** 28 49N 53 50 E
Fehérgyarmat, *Hungary* **42 C7** 47 58N 22 30 E
Fehmarn, *Germany* **24 A7** 54 27N 11 7 E
Fehmarn Bælt, *Europe* **11 K5** 54 35N 11 20 E
Fehmarn Belt = Fehmarn Bælt, *Europe* **11 K5** 54 35N 11 20 E
Fei Xian, *China* **57 G9** 35 18N 117 59 E
Feijó, *Brazil* **124 E4** 8 9 S 70 21W
Feilding, *N.Z.* **91 J5** 40 13 S 175 35 E
Feira de Santana, *Brazil* **125 F11** 12 15 S 38 57W
Feixi, *China* **59 B11** 31 43N 117 59 E
Feixiang, *China* **56 F8** 36 30N 114 45 E
Fejér □, *Hungary* **42 C3** 47 9N 18 30 E
Fejø, *Denmark* **11 K5** 54 55N 11 30 E
Feke, *Turkey* **72 D6** 37 48N 35 56 E
Fekete →, *Hungary* **42 E3** 45 47N 18 15 E
Felanitx, *Spain* **37 B10** 39 28N 3 9 E
Feldbach, *Austria* **26 E8** 46 57N 15 52 E
Feldberg, *Baden-W., Germany* **25 H3** 47 52N 8 0 E
Feldberg, *Mecklenburg-Vorpommern, Germany* **24 B9** 53 20N 13 25 E
Feldkirch, *Austria* **26 D2** 47 15N 9 37 E
Feldkirchen, *Austria* **26 E7** 46 44N 14 6 E
Felipe Carrillo Puerto, *Mexico* **119 D7** 19 38N 88 3W
Felixburg, *Zimbabwe* **89 B5** 19 29 S 30 51 E
Felixstowe, *U.K.* **13 F9** 51 58N 1 23 E
Felletin, *France* **20 C6** 45 53N 2 11 E
Fellingsbro, *Sweden* **10 E9** 59 26N 15 37 E
Felton, *U.S.A.* **116 H4** 37 3N 122 4W
Feltre, *Italy* **29 B8** 46 1N 11 54 E
Femer Bælt = Fehmarn Bælt, *Europe* **11 K5** 54 35N 11 20 E
Femø, *Denmark* **11 K5** 54 58N 11 35 E
Femunden, *Norway* **9 E14** 62 10N 11 53 E
Fen He →, *China* **56 G6** 35 36N 110 42 E
Fene, *Spain* **34 B2** 43 27N 8 9W
Fenelon Falls, *Canada* **110 B6** 44 32N 78 45W
Fener Burnu, *Turkey* **39 E9** 36 58N 27 18 E
Feneroa, *Ethiopia* **81 E4** 13 5N 39 3 E
Feng Xian, *Jiangsu, China* **56 G9** 34 43N 116 35 E
Feng Xian, *Shaanxi, China* **56 H4** 33 54N 106 40 E
Fengári, *Greece* **41 F9** 40 25N 25 32 E
Fengcheng, *Jiangxi, China* **59 C10** 28 12N 115 48 E
Fengcheng, *Liaoning, China* **57 D13** 40 28N 124 5 E
Fengfeng, *China* **56 F8** 36 28N 114 8 E
Fenggang, *China* **58 D6** 27 57N 107 47 E
Fenghua, *China* **59 C13** 29 40N 121 25 E
Fenghuang, *China* **58 D7** 27 57N 109 29 E
Fengkai, *China* **59 F8** 23 24N 111 30 E
Fengkang, *Taiwan* **59 F13** 22 12N 120 41 E
Fengle, *China* **59 B9** 31 29N 112 29 E
Fenglin, *Taiwan* **59 F13** 23 45N 121 26 E
Fengning, *China* **56 D9** 41 10N 116 33 E
Fengqing, *China* **58 E2** 24 38N 99 55 E
Fengqiu, *China* **56 G8** 35 2N 114 25 E
Fengrun, *China* **57 E10** 39 48N 118 8 E
Fengshan, *Guangxi Zhuangzu, China* **58 E7** 24 39N 109 15 E
Fengshan, *Guangxi Zhuangzu, China* **58 E6** 24 31N 107 3 E
Fengshan, *Taiwan* **59 F13** 22 38N 120 21 E
Fengshun, *China* **59 F11** 23 46N 116 10 E
Fengtai, *Anhui, China* **59 A11** 32 50N 116 40 E
Fengtai, *Beijing, China* **56 E9** 39 50N 116 18 E
Fengxian, *China* **59 B13** 30 55N 121 26 E
Fengxiang, *China* **56 G4** 34 29N 107 25 E
Fengxin, *China* **59 C10** 28 41N 115 18 E
Fengyang, *China* **57 H9** 32 51N 117 29 E
Fengyi, *China* **58 E3** 25 37N 100 20 E
Fengyüan, *Taiwan* **59 E13** 24 15N 120 35 E
Fengzhen, *China* **56 D7** 40 25N 113 2 E
Feno, C. de, *France* **21 G12** 41 58N 8 33 E
Fenoarivo, *Fianarantsoa, Madag.* **89 C8** 21 43 S 46 24 E
Fenoarivo, *Fianarantsoa, Madag.* **89 C8** 20 52 S 46 53 E
Fenoarivo Afovoany, *Madag.* **89 B8** 18 26 S 46 34 E
Fenoarivo Atsinanana, *Madag.* **89 B8** 17 22 S 49 25 E
Fens, The, *U.K.* **12 E7** 52 38N 0 2W
Fensmark, *Denmark* **11 J5** 55 17N 11 48 E
Fenton, *U.S.A.* **108 D4** 42 48N 83 42W
Fenxi, *China* **56 F6** 36 40N 111 31 E
Fenyang, *China* **56 F6** 37 18N 111 48 E
Fenyi, *China* **59 D10** 27 45N 114 47 E
Feodosiya, *Ukraine* **47 K8** 45 2N 35 16 E
Ferdows, *Iran* **71 C8** 33 58N 58 2 E
Fère-Champenoise, *France* **19 D10** 48 45N 3 59 E
Fère-en-Tardenois, *France* **19 C10** 49 10N 3 30 E
Ferentino, *Italy* **29 G10** 41 42N 13 15 E
Ferfer, *Somali Rep.* **74 F4** 5 4N 45 9 E
Fergana = Farghona, *Uzbekistan* **50 E8** 40 23N 71 19 E
Fergus, *Canada* **110 C4** 43 43N 80 24W
Fergus Falls, *U.S.A.* **112 B6** 46 17N 96 4W
Feričanci, *Croatia* **42 E2** 45 32N 18 0 E
Ferkéssédougou, *Ivory C.* **82 D3** 9 35N 5 6W
Ferlach, *Austria* **26 E7** 46 32N 14 18 E
Ferland, *Canada* **102 B2** 50 19N 88 27W
Ferlo, Vallée du, *Senegal* **82 B2** 15 15N 14 15W
Fermanagh □, *U.K.* **15 B4** 54 21N 7 40W
Fermo, *Italy* **29 E10** 43 9N 13 43 E
Fermont, *Canada* **103 B6** 52 47N 67 5W
Fermoselle, *Spain* **34 D4** 41 19N 6 27W
Fermoy, *Ireland* **15 D3** 52 9N 8 16W
Fernán Nuñéz, *Spain* **35 H6** 37 40N 4 44W
Fernández, *Argentina* **126 B3** 27 55 S 63 50W
Fernandina Beach, *U.S.A.* **109 K5** 30 40N 81 27W
Fernando de Noronha, *Brazil* **125 D12** 4 0 S 33 10W
Fernando Póo = Bioko, *Eq. Guin.* **83 E6** 3 30N 8 40 E
Ferndale, *U.S.A.* **116 B4** 48 51N 122 36W
Fernie, *Canada* **104 D5** 49 30N 115 5W
Fernlees, *Australia* **94 C4** 23 51 S 148 7 E
Fernley, *U.S.A.* **114 G4** 39 36N 119 15W
Ferozepore = Firozpur, *India* **68 D6** 30 55N 74 40 E
Férrai, *Greece* **41 F10** 40 53N 26 10 E
Ferrandina, *Italy* **31 B9** 40 29N 16 27 E
Ferrara, *Italy* **29 D8** 44 50N 11 35 E
Ferrato, C., *Italy* **30 C2** 39 18N 9 38 E
Ferreira do Alentejo, *Portugal* **35 G2** 38 4N 8 6W
Ferreñafe, *Peru* **124 E3** 6 42 S 79 50W
Ferrerías, *Spain* **37 B11** 39 59N 4 1 E
Ferret, C., *France* **20 D2** 44 38N 1 15W
Ferrette, *France* **19 E14** 47 30N 7 20 E
Ferriday, *U.S.A.* **113 K9** 31 38N 91 33W
Ferriere, *Italy* **28 D6** 44 40N 9 30 E
Ferrières, *France* **19 D9** 48 5N 2 48 E
Ferro, Capo, *Italy* **30 A2** 41 9N 9 31 E
Ferrol, *Spain* **34 B2** 43 29N 8 15W
Ferron, *U.S.A.* **115 G8** 39 5N 111 8W
Ferrutx, C., *Spain* **37 B10** 39 47N 3 21 E
Ferryland, *Canada* **103 C9** 47 2N 52 53W
Fertile, *U.S.A.* **112 B6** 47 32N 96 17W
Fertőszentmiklós, *Hungary* **42 C1** 47 35N 16 53 E
Fès, *Morocco* **78 B5** 34 0N 5 0W
Fessenden, *U.S.A.* **112 B5** 47 39N 99 38W
Festus, *U.S.A.* **112 F9** 38 13N 90 24W
Feté Bowé, *Senegal* **82 C2** 14 56N 13 30W
Fetești, *Romania* **43 F12** 44 22N 27 51 E
Fethiye, *Turkey* **39 E11** 36 36N 29 6 E
Fethiye Körfezi, *Turkey* **39 E10** 36 40N 28 50 E
Fetlar, *U.K.* **14 A8** 60 36N 0 52W
Feuilles →, *Canada* **101 C12** 58 47N 70 4W
Feurs, *France* **21 C8** 45 45N 4 13 E
Fez = Fès, *Morocco* **78 B5** 34 0N 5 0W
Fezzan, *Libya* **79 C8** 27 0N 13 0 E
Fiambalá, *Argentina* **126 B2** 27 45 S 67 37W
Fianarantsoa, *Madag.* **89 C8** 21 26 S 47 5 E
Fianarantsoa □, *Madag.* **89 B8** 19 30 S 47 0 E
Fiche, *Ethiopia* **81 F4** 9 50N 38 46 E
Fichtelgebirge, *Germany* **25 E7** 50 2N 11 55 E
Ficksburg, *S. Africa* **89 D4** 28 51 S 27 53 E
Fidenza, *Italy* **28 D7** 44 52N 10 3 E
Fiditi, *Nigeria* **83 D5** 7 45N 3 53 E
Field →, *Australia* **94 C2** 23 48 S 138 0 E
Field I., *Australia* **92 B5** 12 5 S 132 23 E
Fieni, *Romania* **43 E10** 45 8N 25 25 E
Fier, *Albania* **40 F3** 40 43N 19 33 E
Fierzë, *Albania* **40 D4** 42 15N 20 1 E
Fife □, *U.K.* **14 E5** 56 16N 3 1W
Fife Ness, *U.K.* **14 E6** 56 17N 2 35W
Fifth Cataract, *Sudan* **80 D3** 18 22N 33 50 E
Figari, *France* **21 G13** 41 29N 9 7 E
Figeac, *France* **20 D6** 44 37N 2 2 E
Figeholm, *Sweden* **11 G10** 57 22N 16 33 E
Figline Valdarno, *Italy* **29 E8** 43 37N 11 28 E
Figtree, *Zimbabwe* **87 G2** 20 22 S 28 20 E
Figueira Castelo Rodrigo, *Portugal* **34 E4** 40 57N 6 58W
Figueira da Foz, *Portugal* **34 E2** 40 7N 8 54W
Figueiró dos Vinhos, *Portugal* **34 F2** 39 55N 8 16W
Figueres, *Spain* **32 C7** 42 18N 2 58 E
Figuig, *Morocco* **78 B5** 32 5N 1 11W
Fihaonana, *Madag.* **89 B8** 18 36 S 47 12 E
Fiherenana, *Madag.* **89 B8** 18 29 S 48 24 E
Fiherenana →, *Madag.* **89 C7** 23 19 S 43 37 E
Fiji ■, *Pac. Oc.* **91 C8** 17 20 S 179 0 E
Fik, *Ethiopia* **81 F5** 8 10N 42 19 E
Fika, *Nigeria* **83 C7** 11 15N 11 13 E
Filabres, Sierra de los, *Spain* **35 H8** 37 13N 2 20W
Filabusi, *Zimbabwe* **89 C4** 20 34 S 29 20 E
Filadélfia, *Italy* **31 D9** 38 47N 16 17 E
Fil'akovo, *Slovak Rep.* **27 C12** 48 17N 19 50 E
Filey, *U.K.* **12 C7** 54 12N 0 18W
Filey B., *U.K.* **12 C7** 54 12N 0 15W
Filfla, *Malta* **36 D1** 35 47N 14 24 E
Filiași, *Romania* **43 F8** 44 32N 23 31 E
Filiátes, *Greece* **38 B2** 39 38N 20 16 E
Filiatrá, *Greece* **38 D3** 37 9N 21 35 E
Filicudi, *Italy* **31 D7** 38 35N 14 33 E
Filingué, *Niger* **83 C5** 14 21N 3 22 E
Filiourí →, *Greece* **41 E9** 41 15N 25 40 E
Filipstad, *Sweden* **10 E8** 59 43N 14 9 E
Filisur, *Switz.* **25 J5** 46 41N 9 40 E
Fillmore, *Calif., U.S.A.* **117 L8** 34 24N 118 55W
Fillmore, *Utah, U.S.A.* **115 G7** 38 58N 112 20W
Filótion, *Greece* **39 D7** 37 3N 25 30 E
Filottrano, *Italy* **29 E10** 43 26N 13 21 E
Filtu, *Ethiopia* **81 F5** 5 8N 40 35 E
Finale Emília, *Italy* **29 D8** 44 50N 11 18 E
Finale Lígure, *Italy* **28 D5** 44 10N 8 20 E
Fiñana, *Spain* **35 H8** 37 10N 2 50W
Finch, *Canada* **111 A9** 45 11N 75 7W
Findhorn →, *U.K.* **14 D5** 57 38N 3 38W
Findlay, *U.S.A.* **108 E4** 41 2N 83 39W
Finger L., *Canada* **102 B1** 53 33N 93 30W
Finger Lakes, *U.S.A.* **111 D8** 42 40N 76 30W
Fíngoè, *Mozam.* **87 E3** 14 55 S 31 50 E
Finike, *Turkey* **39 E12** 36 21N 30 10 E
Finike Körfezi, *Turkey* **39 E12** 36 17N 30 16 E
Finiq, *Albania* **40 G4** 39 54N 20 3 E
Finistère □, *France* **18 D3** 48 20N 4 0W
Finisterre = Fisterra, *Spain* **34 C1** 42 54N 9 16W
Finisterre, C. = Fisterra, C., *Spain* **34 C1** 42 50N 9 19W
Finke, *Australia* **94 D1** 25 34 S 134 35 E
Finland ■, *Europe* **8 E22** 63 0N 27 0 E
Finland, G. of, *Europe* **9 G21** 60 0N 26 0 E
Finlay →, *Canada* **104 B3** 57 0N 125 10W
Finley, *Australia* **95 F4** 35 38 S 145 35 E
Finley, *U.S.A.* **112 B6** 47 31N 97 50W
Finn →, *Ireland* **15 B4** 54 51N 7 28W
Finnerödja, *Sweden* **11 F8** 58 57N 14 24 E
Finnigan, Mt., *Australia* **94 B4** 15 49 S 145 17 E
Finniss, C., *Australia* **95 E1** 33 8 S 134 51 E
Finnmark, *Norway* **8 B20** 69 37N 23 57 E
Finnsnes, *Norway* **8 B18** 69 14N 18 0 E
Finspång, *Sweden* **11 F9** 58 43N 15 47 E
Finsteraarhorn, *Switz.* **25 J4** 46 31N 8 10 E
Finsterwalde, *Germany* **24 D9** 51 37N 13 42 E
Fiora →, *Italy* **29 F8** 42 20N 11 34 E
Fiorenzuola d'Arda, *Italy* **28 D6** 44 56N 9 55 E
Fīq, *Syria* **75 C4** 32 46N 35 41 E
Firat = Furāt, Nahr al →, *Asia* **70 D5** 31 0N 47 25 E
Firebag →, *Canada* **105 B6** 57 45N 111 21W
Firebaugh, *U.S.A.* **116 J6** 36 52N 120 27W
Firedrake L., *Canada* **105 A8** 61 25N 104 30W
Firenze, *Italy* **29 E8** 43 46N 11 15 E
Firenzuola, *Italy* **29 D8** 44 7N 11 23 E
Firk →, *Iraq* **70 D5** 30 59N 44 34 E
Firmi, *France* **20 D6** 44 33N 2 19 E
Firminy, *France* **21 C8** 45 23N 4 18 E
Firozabad, *India* **69 F8** 27 10N 78 25 E
Firozpur, *India* **68 D6** 30 55N 74 40 E
Firozpur-Jhirka, *India* **68 F7** 27 48N 76 57 E
Fīrūzābād, *Iran* **71 D7** 28 52N 52 35 E
Fīrūzkūh, *Iran* **71 C7** 35 50N 52 50 E
Firvale, *Canada* **104 C3** 52 27N 126 13W
Fish →, *Namibia* **88 D2** 28 7 S 17 10 E
Fish →, *S. Africa* **88 E3** 31 30 S 20 16 E
Fish River Canyon, *Namibia* **88 D2** 27 40 S 17 35 E
Fisher, *Australia* **93 F5** 30 30 S 131 0 E
Fisher B., *Canada* **105 C9** 51 35N 97 13W
Fishers I., *U.S.A.* **111 E13** 41 15N 72 0W
Fishguard, *U.K.* **13 E3** 52 0N 4 58W
Fishing L., *Canada* **105 C9** 52 10N 95 24W
Fishkill, *U.S.A.* **111 E11** 41 32N 73 53W
Fismes, *France* **19 C10** 49 20N 3 40 E
Fisterra, *Spain* **34 C1** 42 54N 9 16W
Fisterra, C., *Spain* **34 C1** 42 50N 9 19W
Fitchburg, *U.S.A.* **111 D13** 42 35N 71 48W
Fitz Roy, *Argentina* **128 F3** 47 0 S 67 0W
Fitzgerald, *Canada* **104 B6** 59 51N 111 36W
Fitzgerald, *U.S.A.* **109 K4** 31 43N 83 15W
Fitzmaurice →, *Australia* **92 B5** 14 45 S 130 5 E
Fitzroy →, *Queens., Australia* **94 C5** 23 32 S 150 52 E
Fitzroy →, *W. Austral., Australia* **92 C3** 17 31 S 123 35 E
Fitzroy, Mte., *Argentina* **128 F2** 49 17 S 73 5W
Fitzroy Crossing, *Australia* **92 C4** 18 9 S 125 38 E
Fitzwilliam I., *Canada* **110 A3** 45 30N 81 45W
Fiuggi, *Italy* **29 G10** 41 48N 13 13 E
Fiume = Rijeka, *Croatia* **29 C11** 45 20N 14 21 E
Five Points, *U.S.A.* **116 J6** 36 26N 120 6W
Fivizzano, *Italy* **28 D7** 44 14N 10 8 E
Fizi, *Dem. Rep. of the Congo* **86 C2** 4 17 S 28 55 E
Fjällbacka, *Sweden* **11 F5** 58 36N 11 17 E
Fjärdhundra, *Sweden* **10 E10** 59 47N 16 56 E
Fjellerup, *Denmark* **11 H4** 56 29N 10 34 E
Fjerritslev, *Denmark* **11 G3** 57 5N 9 15 E
Fjugesta, *Sweden* **10 E8** 59 11N 14 52 E
Flagstaff, *U.S.A.* **115 J8** 35 12N 111 39W
Flagstaff L., *U.S.A.* **109 C10** 45 12N 70 18W
Flaherty I., *Canada* **102 A4** 56 15N 79 15W
Flåm, *Norway* **9 F12** 60 50N 7 7 E
Flambeau →, *U.S.A.* **112 C9** 45 18N 91 14W
Flamborough Hd., *U.K.* **12 C7** 54 7N 0 5W
Fläming, *Germany* **24 C8** 52 6N 12 23 E
Flaming Gorge Reservoir, *U.S.A.* **114 F9** 41 10N 109 25W
Flamingo, Teluk, *Indonesia* **63 F9** 5 30 S 138 0 E
Flanders = Flandre, *Europe* **19 B9** 50 50N 2 30 E
Flandre, *Europe* **19 B9** 50 50N 2 30 E
Flandre Occidentale = West-Vlaanderen □, *Belgium* **17 D2** 51 0N 3 0 E
Flandre Orientale = Oost-Vlaanderen □, *Belgium* **17 C3** 51 5N 3 50 E
Flandreau, *U.S.A.* **112 C6** 44 3N 96 36W
Flanigan, *U.S.A.* **116 E7** 40 10N 119 53W
Flannan Is., *U.K.* **14 C1** 58 9N 7 52W
Flåsjön, *Sweden* **8 D16** 64 5N 15 40 E
Flat →, *Canada* **104 A3** 61 33N 125 18W
Flathead L., *U.S.A.* **114 C7** 47 51N 114 8W
Flattery, C., *Australia* **94 A4** 14 58 S 145 21 E
Flattery, C., *U.S.A.* **116 B2** 48 23N 124 29W
Flatwoods, *U.S.A.* **108 F4** 38 31N 82 43W
Fleetwood, *U.K.* **12 D4** 53 55N 3 1W
Fleetwood, *U.S.A.* **111 F9** 40 27N 75 49W
Flekkefjord, *Norway* **9 G12** 58 18N 6 39 E
Flemington, *U.S.A.* **110 E7** 41 7N 77 28W
Flen, *Sweden* **10 E10** 59 4N 16 35 E
Flensburg, *Germany* **24 A5** 54 47N 9 27 E
Flers, *France* **18 D6** 48 47N 0 33W
Flesherton, *Canada* **110 B4** 44 16N 80 33W
Flesko, Tanjung, *Indonesia* **63 D6** 0 29N 124 30 E
Fleurance, *France* **20 E4** 43 52N 0 40 E
Fleurier, *Switz.* **25 J2** 46 54N 6 35 E
Fleurieu Pen., *Australia* **95 F2** 35 40 S 138 5 E
Flevoland □, *Neths.* **17 B5** 52 30N 5 30 E
Flin Flon, *Canada* **105 C8** 54 46N 101 53W
Flinders →, *Australia* **94 B3** 17 36 S 140 36 E
Flinders B., *Australia* **93 F2** 34 19 S 115 19 E
Flinders Group, *Australia* **94 A3** 14 11 S 144 15 E
Flinders I., *S. Austral., Australia* **95 E1** 33 44 S 134 41 E
Flinders I., *Tas., Australia* **94 G4** 40 0 S 148 0 E
Flinders Ranges, *Australia* **95 E2** 31 30 S 138 30 E
Flinders Reefs, *Australia* **94 B4** 17 37 S 148 31 E
Flint, *U.K.* **12 D4** 53 15N 3 8W
Flint, *U.S.A.* **108 D4** 43 1N 83 41W
Flint →, *U.S.A.* **109 K3** 30 57N 84 34W
Flint I., *Kiribati* **97 J12** 11 26 S 151 48W
Flintshire □, *U.K.* **12 D4** 53 17N 3 17W
Fliseryd, *Sweden* **11 G10** 57 6N 16 15 E
Flix, *Spain* **32 D5** 41 14N 0 32 E

Fuchuan

Flixecourt, France 19 B9 50 1N 2 5 E
Floby, Sweden 11 F7 58 8N 13 20 E
Floda, Sweden 11 G6 57 49N 12 22 E
Flodden, U.K. 12 B5 55 37N 2 8W
Flogny-la-Chapelle, France 19 E10 47 57N 3 57 E
Floodwood, U.S.A. 112 B8 46 55N 92 55W
Flora, U.S.A. 108 F1 38 40N 88 29W
Florac, France 20 D7 44 20N 3 37 E
Florala, U.S.A. 109 K2 31 0N 86 20W
Florence = Firenze, Italy 29 E8 43 46N 11 15 E
Florence, Ala., U.S.A. 109 H2 34 48N 87 41W
Florence, Ariz., U.S.A. 115 K8 33 2N 111 23W
Florence, Colo., U.S.A. 112 F2 38 23N 105 8W
Florence, Oreg., U.S.A. 114 E1 43 58N 124 7W
Florence, S.C., U.S.A. 109 H6 34 12N 79 46W
Florence, L., Australia 95 D2 28 53 S 138 9 E
Florencia, Colombia 124 C3 1 36N 75 36W
Florennes, Belgium 17 D4 50 15N 4 35 E
Florensac, France 20 E7 43 23N 3 28 E
Florenville, Belgium 17 E5 49 40N 5 19 E
Flores, Guatemala 120 C2 16 59N 89 50W
Flores, Indonesia 63 F6 8 35 S 121 0 E
Flores I., Canada 104 D3 49 20N 126 10W
Flores Sea, Indonesia 63 F6 6 30 S 120 0 E
Floreşti, Moldova 43 C13 47 53N 28 17 E
Floresville, U.S.A. 113 L5 29 8N 98 10W
Floriano, Brazil 125 E10 6 50 S 43 0W
Florianópolis, Brazil 127 B6 27 30 S 48 30W
Florida, Cuba 120 B4 21 32N 78 14W
Florida, Uruguay 127 C4 34 7 S 56 10W
Florida □, U.S.A. 109 L5 28 0N 82 0W
Florida, Straits of, U.S.A. 120 B4 25 0N 80 0W
Florida B., U.S.A. 120 B3 25 0N 80 45W
Florida Keys, U.S.A. 109 N5 24 40N 81 0W
Florídia, Italy 31 E8 37 5N 15 9 E
Flórina, Greece 40 F5 40 48N 21 26 E
Flórina □, Greece 40 F5 40 45N 21 20 E
Florø, Norway 9 F11 61 35N 5 1 E
Flower Station, Canada 111 A8 45 10N 76 41W
Flowerpot I., Canada 110 A3 45 18N 81 38W
Floydada, U.S.A. 113 J4 33 59N 101 20W
Fluk, Indonesia 63 E7 1 42 S 127 44 E
Flúmen →, Spain 32 D4 41 43N 0 9W
Flumendosa →, Italy 30 C2 39 26N 9 37 E
Fluminimaggiore, Italy 30 C1 39 26N 8 30 E
Flushing = Vlissingen, Neths. 17 C3 51 26N 3 34 E
Fluvià →, Spain 32 C8 42 12N 3 7 E
Flying Fish, C., Antarctica 5 D15 72 6 S 102 29W
Foam Lake, Canada 105 C8 51 40N 103 32W
Foča, Bos.-H. 40 C2 43 31N 18 47 E
Foça, Turkey 39 C8 38 39N 26 46 E
Focşani, Romania 43 E12 45 41N 27 15 E
Fodécontéa, Guinea 82 C2 10 50N 14 22W
Fogang, China 59 F9 23 52N 113 30 E
Fóggia, Italy 31 A8 41 27N 15 34 E
Foggo, Nigeria 83 C6 11 21N 9 57 E
Foglia →, Italy 29 E9 43 55N 12 54 E
Fogo, Canada 103 C9 49 43N 54 17W
Fogo I., Canada 103 C9 49 40N 54 5W
Fohnsdorf, Austria 26 D7 47 12N 14 40 E
Föhr, Germany 24 A4 54 43N 8 30 E
Foia, Portugal 35 H2 37 19N 8 37W
Foix, France 20 E5 42 58N 1 38 E
Fojnica, Bos.-H. 42 G2 43 59N 17 51 E
Fokino, Russia 46 F8 53 30N 34 22 E
Fokís □, Greece 38 C4 38 30N 22 15 E
Fokku, Nigeria 83 C5 11 36N 4 32 E
Folda, Nord-Trøndelag, Norway 8 D14 64 32N 10 30 E
Folda, Nordland, Norway 8 C16 67 38N 14 50 E
Földeák, Hungary 42 D5 46 19N 20 30 E
Folégandros, Greece 38 E6 36 40N 24 55 E
Foley, Botswana 88 C4 21 34 S 27 21 E
Foley, U.S.A. 109 K2 30 24N 87 41W
Foleyet, Canada 102 C3 48 15N 82 25W
Folgefonni, Norway 9 F12 60 3N 6 23 E
Foligno, Italy 29 F9 42 57N 12 42 E
Folkestone, U.K. 13 F9 51 5N 1 12 E
Folkston, U.S.A. 109 K5 30 50N 82 0W
Follansbee, U.S.A. 110 F4 40 19N 80 35W
Follónica, Italy 28 F7 42 55N 10 45 E
Follónica, G. di, Italy 28 F7 42 54N 10 43 E
Folsom L., U.S.A. 116 G5 38 42N 121 9W
Folteşti, Romania 43 E13 45 45N 28 3 E
Fond-du-Lac, Canada 105 B7 59 19N 107 12W
Fond du Lac, U.S.A. 112 D10 43 47N 88 27W
Fond-du-Lac →, Canada 105 B7 59 17N 106 0W
Fonda, U.S.A. 111 D10 42 57N 74 22W
Fondi, Italy 30 A6 41 21N 13 25 E
Fonfría, Spain 34 D4 41 37N 6 9W
Fongafale, Tuvalu 96 H9 8 31 S 179 13 E
Fonni, Italy 30 B2 40 7N 9 15 E
Fonsagrada = A Fonsagrada, Spain 34 B3 43 8N 7 4W
Fonseca, G. de, Cent. Amer. 120 D2 13 10N 87 40W
Font-Romeu, France 20 F5 42 31N 2 3 E
Fontaine-Française, France 19 E12 47 32N 5 21 E
Fontainebleau, France 19 D9 48 24N 2 40 E
Fontana, U.S.A. 117 L9 34 6N 117 26W
Fontas →, Canada 104 B4 58 14N 121 48W
Fonte Boa, Brazil 124 D5 2 33 S 66 0W
Fontem, Cameroon 83 D6 5 32N 9 52 E
Fontenay-le-Comte, France 20 B3 46 28N 0 48W
Fontenelle Reservoir, U.S.A. 114 E8 42 1N 110 3W
Fontur, Iceland 8 C6 66 23N 14 32W
Fonyód, Hungary 42 D2 46 44N 17 33 E
Foochow = Fuzhou, China 59 D12 26 5N 119 16 E
Foping, China 56 H5 33 41N 108 0 E
Forbach, France 19 C13 49 10N 6 52 E
Forbes, Australia 95 E4 33 22 S 148 5 E
Forbesganj, India 69 F12 26 17N 87 18 E
Forcados, Nigeria 83 D6 5 26N 5 26 E
Forcados →, Nigeria 83 D6 5 25N 5 19 E
Forcalquier, France 21 E9 43 58N 5 47 E
Forchheim, Germany 25 F7 49 43N 11 2 E
Ford City, Calif., U.S.A. 117 K7 35 9N 119 27W
Ford City, Pa., U.S.A. 110 F5 40 46N 79 32W
Førde, Norway 9 F11 61 27N 5 53 E
Ford's Bridge, Australia 95 D4 29 41 S 145 29 E
Fordyce, U.S.A. 113 J8 33 49N 92 25W
Forécariah, Guinea 82 D2 9 28N 13 10W
Forel, Mt., Greenland 4 C6 66 52N 36 55W
Foremost, Canada 104 D6 49 26N 111 34W
Forest, Canada 110 C3 43 6N 82 0W
Forest, U.S.A. 113 J10 32 22N 89 29W
Forest City, Iowa, U.S.A. 112 D8 43 16N 93 39W
Forest City, N.C., U.S.A. 109 H5 35 20N 81 52W
Forest City, Pa., U.S.A. 111 E9 41 39N 75 28W
Forest Grove, U.S.A. 116 E3 45 31N 123 7W
Forestburg, Canada 104 C6 52 35N 112 1W
Foresthill, U.S.A. 116 F6 39 1N 120 49W
Forestier Pen., Australia 94 G4 43 0 S 148 0 E
Forestville, Canada 103 C6 48 48N 69 2W
Forestville, Calif., U.S.A. 116 G4 38 28N 122 54W
Forestville, N.Y., U.S.A. 110 D5 42 28N 79 10W
Forez, Mts. du, France 20 C7 45 40N 3 50 E
Forfar, U.K. 14 E6 56 39N 2 53W
Forks, U.S.A. 116 C2 47 57N 124 23W
Forksville, U.S.A. 111 E8 41 29N 76 35W
Forlì, Italy 29 D9 44 13N 12 3 E
Forman, U.S.A. 112 B6 46 7N 97 38W
Formazza, Italy 28 B5 46 22N 8 26 E
Formby Pt., U.K. 12 D4 53 33N 3 6W
Formentera, Spain 37 C7 38 43N 1 27 E
Formentor, C. de, Spain 37 B10 39 58N 3 13 E
Former Yugoslav Republic of Macedonia = Macedonia ■, Europe 40 E5 41 53N 21 40 E
Fórmia, Italy 30 A6 41 15N 13 37 E
Formígine, Italy 28 D7 44 37N 10 51 E
Formosa = Taiwan ■, Asia 59 F13 23 30N 121 0 E
Formosa, Argentina 126 B4 26 15 S 58 10W
Formosa, Brazil 125 G9 15 32 S 47 20W
Formosa □, Argentina 126 B4 25 0 S 60 0W
Formosa, Serra, Brazil 125 F8 12 0 S 55 0W
Formosa Bay, Kenya 86 C5 2 40 S 40 20 E
Formosa Strait = Taiwan Strait, Asia 59 E12 24 40N 120 0 E
Fornells, Spain 37 A11 40 3N 4 7 E
Fornos de Algodres, Portugal 34 E3 40 38N 7 32W
Fornovo di Taro, Italy 28 D7 44 42N 10 6 E
Føroyar, Atl. Oc. 8 F9 62 0N 7 0W
Forres, U.K. 14 D5 57 37N 3 37W
Forrest, Australia 93 F4 30 51 S 128 6 E
Forrest, Mt., Australia 93 D4 24 48 S 127 45 E
Forrest City, U.S.A. 113 H9 35 1N 90 47W
Fors, Sweden 10 D10 60 14N 16 20 E
Forsayth, Australia 94 B3 18 33 S 143 34 E
Forshaga, Sweden 10 E7 59 33N 13 29 E
Förslöv, Sweden 11 H6 56 21N 12 48 E
Forsmo, Sweden 10 A11 63 16N 17 11 E
Forssa, Finland 9 F20 60 49N 23 38 E
Forst, Germany 24 D10 51 45N 14 37 E
Forsvik, Sweden 11 F8 58 35N 14 26 E
Forsyth, U.S.A. 114 C10 46 16N 106 41W
Fort Abbas, Pakistan 68 E5 29 12N 72 52 E
Fort Albany, Canada 102 B3 52 15N 81 35W
Fort Ann, U.S.A. 111 C11 43 25N 73 30W
Fort Assiniboine, Canada 104 C6 54 20N 114 45W
Fort Augustus, U.K. 14 D4 57 9N 4 42W
Fort Beaufort, S. Africa 88 E4 32 46 S 26 40 E
Fort Benton, U.S.A. 114 C8 47 49N 110 40W
Fort Bragg, U.S.A. 114 G2 39 26N 123 48W
Fort Bridger, U.S.A. 114 F8 41 19N 110 23W
Fort Chipewyan, Canada 105 B6 58 42N 111 8W
Fort Collins, U.S.A. 112 E2 40 35N 105 5W
Fort-Coulonge, Canada 102 C4 45 50N 76 45W
Fort Covington, U.S.A. 111 B10 44 59N 74 29W
Fort Davis, U.S.A. 113 K3 30 35N 103 54W
Fort-de-France, Martinique 121 D7 14 36N 61 2W
Fort Defiance, U.S.A. 115 J9 35 45N 109 5W
Fort Dodge, U.S.A. 112 D7 42 30N 94 11W
Fort Edward, U.S.A. 111 C11 43 16N 73 35W
Fort Erie, Canada 110 D6 42 54N 78 56W
Fort Fairfield, U.S.A. 109 B12 46 46N 67 50W
Fort Frances, Canada 105 D10 48 36N 93 24W
Fort Garland, U.S.A. 115 H11 37 26N 105 26W
Fort George = Chisasibi, Canada 102 B4 53 50N 79 0W
Fort Good-Hope, Canada 100 B7 66 14N 128 40W
Fort Hancock, U.S.A. 115 L11 31 18N 105 51W
Fort Hertz = Putao, Burma 67 F20 27 28N 97 30 E
Fort Hope, Canada 102 B2 51 30N 88 0W
Fort Irwin, U.S.A. 117 K10 35 16N 116 34W
Fort Kent, U.S.A. 109 B11 47 15N 68 36W
Fort Klamath, U.S.A. 114 E3 42 42N 122 0W
Fort Laramie, U.S.A. 112 D2 42 13N 104 31W
Fort Lauderdale, U.S.A. 109 M5 26 7N 80 8W
Fort Liard, Canada 104 A4 60 14N 123 30W
Fort Liberté, Haiti 121 C5 19 42N 71 51W
Fort Lupton, U.S.A. 112 E2 40 5N 104 49W
Fort Mackay, Canada 104 B6 57 12N 111 41W
Fort Macleod, Canada 104 D6 49 45N 113 30W
Fort McMurray, Canada 104 B6 56 44N 111 7W
Fort McPherson, Canada 100 B6 67 30N 134 55W
Fort Madison, U.S.A. 112 E9 40 38N 91 27W
Fort Meade, U.S.A. 109 M5 27 45N 81 48W
Fort Morgan, U.S.A. 112 E3 40 15N 103 48W
Fort Myers, U.S.A. 109 M5 26 39N 81 52W
Fort Nelson, Canada 104 B4 58 50N 122 44W
Fort Nelson →, Canada 104 B4 59 32N 124 0W
Fort Norman = Tulita, Canada 100 B7 64 57N 125 30W
Fort Payne, U.S.A. 109 H3 34 26N 85 43W
Fort Peck, U.S.A. 114 B10 48 1N 106 27W
Fort Peck Dam, U.S.A. 114 C10 48 0N 106 26W
Fort Peck L., U.S.A. 114 C10 48 0N 106 26W
Fort Pierce, U.S.A. 109 M5 27 27N 80 20W
Fort Pierre, U.S.A. 112 C4 44 21N 100 22W
Fort Pierre Bordes = Ti-n-Zaouatene, Algeria 83 B5 19 55N 2 55 E
Fort Plain, U.S.A. 111 D10 42 56N 74 37W
Fort Portal, Uganda 86 B3 0 40N 30 20 E
Fort Providence, Canada 104 A5 61 3N 117 40W
Fort Qu'Appelle, Canada 105 C8 50 45N 103 50W
Fort Resolution, Canada 104 A6 61 10N 113 40W
Fort Rixon, Zimbabwe 87 G2 20 2 S 29 17 E
Fort Ross, U.S.A. 116 G3 38 32N 123 13W
Fort Rupert = Waskaganish, Canada 102 B4 51 30N 78 40W
Fort St. James, Canada 104 C4 54 30N 124 10W
Fort St. John, Canada 104 B4 56 15N 120 50W
Fort Saskatchewan, Canada 104 C6 53 40N 113 15W
Fort Scott, U.S.A. 113 G7 37 50N 94 42W
Fort Severn, Canada 102 A2 56 0N 87 40W
Fort Shevchenko, Kazakhstan 49 H10 44 35N 50 23 E
Fort Simpson, Canada 104 A4 61 45N 121 15W
Fort Smith, Canada 104 B6 60 0N 111 51W
Fort Smith, U.S.A. 113 H7 35 23N 94 25W
Fort Stockton, U.S.A. 113 K3 30 53N 102 53W
Fort Sumner, U.S.A. 113 H2 34 28N 104 15W
Fort Thompson, U.S.A. 112 C5 44 3N 99 26W
Fort Valley, U.S.A. 109 J4 32 33N 83 53W
Fort Vermilion, Canada 104 B5 58 24N 116 0W
Fort Walton Beach, U.S.A. 109 K2 30 25N 86 36W
Fort Wayne, U.S.A. 108 E3 41 4N 85 9W
Fort William, U.K. 14 E3 56 49N 5 7W
Fort Worth, U.S.A. 113 J6 32 45N 97 18W
Fort Yates, U.S.A. 112 B4 46 5N 100 38W
Fort Yukon, U.S.A. 100 B5 66 34N 145 16W
Fortaleza, Brazil 125 D11 3 45 S 38 35W
Forteau, Canada 103 B8 51 28N 56 58W
Fortescue →, Australia 92 D2 21 0 S 116 4 E
Forth →, U.K. 14 E5 56 9N 3 50W
Forth, Firth of, U.K. 14 E6 56 5N 2 55W
Fortore →, Italy 29 G12 41 55N 15 17 E
Fortrose, U.K. 14 D4 57 35N 4 9W
Fortuna, Spain 33 G3 38 11N 1 7W
Fortuna, Calif., U.S.A. 114 F1 40 36N 124 9W
Fortuna, N. Dak., U.S.A. 112 A3 48 55N 103 47W
Fortune, Canada 103 C8 47 4N 55 50W
Fortune B., Canada 103 C8 47 30N 55 22W
Forūr, Iran 71 E7 26 17N 54 32 E
Fos-sur-Mer, France 21 E8 43 26N 4 56 E
Foshan, China 59 F9 23 4N 113 5 E
Fosna, Norway 8 E14 63 50N 10 20 E
Fosnavåg, Norway 9 E11 62 22N 5 38 E
Foso, Ghana 83 D4 5 43N 1 15W
Fossano, Italy 28 D4 44 33N 7 43 E
Fossil, U.S.A. 114 D3 45 0N 120 9W
Fossombrone, Italy 29 E9 43 41N 12 48 E
Foster, Canada 111 A12 45 17N 72 30W
Foster →, Canada 105 B7 55 47N 105 49W
Fosters Ra., Australia 94 C1 21 35 S 133 48 E
Fostoria, U.S.A. 108 E4 41 10N 83 25W
Fotadrevo, Madag. 89 C8 24 3 S 45 1 E
Fouesnant, France 18 E2 47 53N 4 1W
Fougères, France 18 D5 48 21N 1 14W
Foul Pt., Sri Lanka 66 Q12 8 35N 81 18 E
Foula, U.K. 14 A6 60 10N 2 5W
Foulalaba, Mali 82 C3 10 40N 7 20W
Foulness I., U.K. 13 F8 51 36N 0 55 E
Foulpointe, Madag. 89 B8 17 41 S 49 31 E
Foulweather, C., U.S.A. 106 B2 44 50N 124 5W
Foumban, Cameroon 83 D7 5 45N 10 50 E
Foumbot, Cameroon 83 D7 5 31N 10 28 E
Foundiougne, Senegal 82 C1 14 5N 16 32W
Fountain, U.S.A. 112 F2 38 41N 104 42W
Fountain Springs, U.S.A. 117 K8 35 54N 118 51W
Fourchambault, France 19 E10 47 2N 3 3 E
Fouriesburg, S. Africa 88 D4 28 38 S 28 14 E
Fourmies, France 19 B11 50 1N 4 2 E
Fournás, Greece 38 B3 39 3N 21 52 E
Foúrnoi, Greece 39 D8 37 36N 26 32 E
Fours, France 19 F10 46 50N 3 42 E
Fourth Cataract, Sudan 80 D3 18 47N 32 3 E
Fouta Djalon, Guinea 82 C2 11 20N 12 10W
Foux, Cap-à-, Haiti 121 C5 19 43N 73 27W
Foveaux Str., N.Z. 91 M2 46 42 S 168 10 E
Fowey, U.K. 13 G3 50 20N 4 39W
Fowler, Calif., U.S.A. 116 J7 36 38N 119 41W
Fowler, Colo., U.S.A. 112 F3 38 8N 104 2W
Fowlers B., Australia 93 F5 31 59 S 132 34 E
Fowman, Iran 71 B6 37 13N 49 19 E
Fox →, Canada 105 B10 56 3N 93 18W
Fox Creek, Canada 104 C5 54 24N 116 48W
Fox Lake, Canada 104 B6 58 28N 114 31W
Fox Valley, Canada 105 C7 50 30N 109 25W
Foxboro, U.S.A. 111 D13 42 4N 71 16W
Foxe Basin, Canada 101 B12 66 0N 77 0W
Foxe Chan., Canada 101 B11 65 0N 80 0W
Foxe Pen., Canada 101 B12 65 0N 76 0W
Foxen, Sweden 10 E5 59 25N 11 55 E
Foxton, N.Z. 91 J5 40 29 S 175 18 E
Foyle, Lough, U.K. 15 A4 55 7N 7 4W
Foynes, Ireland 15 D2 52 37N 9 7W
Foz, Spain 34 B3 43 33N 7 20W
Foz do Cunene, Angola 88 B1 17 15 S 11 48 E
Foz do Iguaçu, Brazil 127 B5 25 30 S 54 30W
Frackville, U.S.A. 111 F8 40 47N 76 14W
Fraga, Spain 32 D5 41 32N 0 21 E
Fraile Muerto, Uruguay 127 C5 32 31 S 54 32W
Framingham, U.S.A. 111 D13 42 17N 71 25W
Frampol, Poland 45 H9 50 41N 22 40 E
Franca, Brazil 125 H9 20 33 S 47 30W
Francavilla al Mare, Italy 29 F11 42 25N 14 17 E
Francavilla Fontana, Italy 31 B10 40 32N 17 35 E
France ■, Europe 7 F6 47 0N 3 0 E
Frances, Australia 95 F3 36 41 S 140 55 E
Frances →, Canada 104 A3 60 16N 129 10W
Frances L., Canada 104 A3 61 23N 129 30W
Franceville, Gabon 84 E2 1 40 S 13 32 E
Franche-Comté, France 19 F12 46 50N 5 55 E
Francis Case, L., U.S.A. 112 D5 43 4N 98 34W
Francisco Beltrão, Brazil 127 B5 26 5 S 53 4W
Francisco I. Madero, Coahuila, Mexico 118 B4 25 48N 103 18W
Francisco I. Madero, Durango, Mexico 118 C4 24 32N 104 22W
Francistown, Botswana 89 C4 21 7 S 27 33 E
Francofonte, Italy 31 E7 37 14N 14 53 E
François, Canada 103 C8 47 35N 56 45W
François L., Canada 104 C3 54 0N 125 30W
Franeker, Neths. 17 A5 53 12N 5 33 E
Frankado, Djibouti 81 E5 12 30N 43 12 E
Frankenberg, Germany 24 D4 51 3N 8 48 E
Frankenwald, Germany 25 E7 50 20N 11 30 E
Frankford, Canada 110 B7 44 12N 77 36W
Frankfort, S. Africa 89 D4 27 17 S 28 30 E
Frankfort, Ind., U.S.A. 108 E2 40 17N 86 31W
Frankfort, Kans., U.S.A. 112 F6 39 42N 96 25W
Frankfort, Ky., U.S.A. 108 F3 38 12N 84 52W
Frankfort, N.Y., U.S.A. 111 C9 43 2N 75 4W
Frankfurt, Brandenburg, Germany 24 C10 52 20N 14 32 E
Frankfurt, Hessen, Germany 25 E4 50 7N 8 41 E
Fränkische Alb, Germany 25 F7 49 10N 11 23 E
Fränkische Rezat →, Germany 25 F7 49 11N 11 1 E
Fränkische Saale →, Germany 25 E5 50 3N 9 42 E
Fränkische Schweiz, Germany 25 F7 49 50N 11 16 E
Frankland →, Australia 93 G2 35 0 S 116 48 E
Franklin, Ky., U.S.A. 109 G2 36 43N 86 35W
Franklin, La., U.S.A. 113 L9 29 48N 91 30W
Franklin, Mass., U.S.A. 111 D13 42 5N 71 24W
Franklin, N.H., U.S.A. 111 C13 43 27N 71 39W
Franklin, Nebr., U.S.A. 112 E5 40 6N 98 57W
Franklin, Pa., U.S.A. 110 E5 41 24N 79 50W
Franklin, Va., U.S.A. 109 G7 36 41N 76 56W
Franklin, W. Va., U.S.A. 108 F6 38 39N 79 20W
Franklin B., Canada 100 B7 69 45N 126 0W
Franklin D. Roosevelt L., U.S.A. 114 B4 48 18N 118 9W
Franklin I., Antarctica 5 D11 76 10 S 168 30 E
Franklin L., U.S.A. 114 F6 40 25N 115 22W
Franklin Mts., Canada 100 B7 65 0N 125 0W
Franklin Str., Canada 100 A10 72 0N 96 0W
Franklinton, U.S.A. 113 K9 30 51N 90 9W
Franklinville, U.S.A. 110 D6 42 20N 78 27W
Franks Pk., U.S.A. 114 E9 43 58N 109 18W
Frankston, Australia 95 F4 38 8 S 145 8 E
Frånö, Sweden 10 B11 62 55N 17 50 E
Fransfontein, Namibia 88 C2 20 12 S 15 1 E
Fränsta, Sweden 10 B10 62 30N 16 11 E
Frantsa Iosifa, Zemlya, Russia 50 A6 82 0N 55 0 E
Franz, Canada 102 C3 48 25N 84 30W
Franz Josef Land = Frantsa Iosifa, Zemlya, Russia 50 A6 82 0N 55 0 E
Franzburg, Germany 24 A8 54 11N 12 51 E
Frascati, Italy 29 G9 41 48N 12 41 E
Fraser, U.S.A. 110 D2 42 32N 82 57W
Fraser →, B.C., Canada 104 D4 49 7N 123 11W
Fraser →, Nfld., Canada 103 A7 56 39N 62 10W
Fraser, Mt., Australia 93 E2 25 35 S 118 20 E
Fraser I., Australia 95 D5 25 15 S 153 10 E
Fraser Lake, Canada 104 C4 54 0N 124 50W
Fraserburg, S. Africa 88 E3 31 55 S 21 30 E
Fraserburgh, U.K. 14 D6 57 42N 2 1W
Fraserdale, Canada 102 C3 49 55N 81 37W
Frashër, Albania 40 F4 40 23N 20 30 E
Frasne, France 19 F13 46 50N 6 10 E
Frăteşti, Romania 43 G10 43 58N 25 58 E
Frauenfeld, Switz. 25 H4 47 34N 8 54 E
Fray Bentos, Uruguay 126 C4 33 10 S 58 15W
Frechilla, Spain 34 C6 42 8N 4 50W
Fredericia, Denmark 11 J3 55 34N 9 45 E
Frederick, Md., U.S.A. 108 F7 39 25N 77 25W
Frederick, Okla., U.S.A. 113 H5 34 23N 99 1W
Frederick, S. Dak., U.S.A. 112 C5 45 50N 98 31W
Fredericksburg, Pa., U.S.A. 111 F8 40 27N 76 26W
Fredericksburg, Tex., U.S.A. 113 K5 30 16N 98 52W
Fredericksburg, Va., U.S.A. 108 F7 38 18N 77 28W
Fredericktown, Mo., U.S.A. 113 G9 37 34N 90 18W
Fredericktown, Ohio, U.S.A. 110 F2 40 29N 82 33W
Frederico I. Madero, Presa, Mexico 118 B3 28 7N 105 40W
Frederico Westphalen, Brazil 127 B5 27 22 S 53 24W
Fredericton, Canada 103 C6 45 57N 66 40W
Fredericton Junction, Canada 103 C6 45 41N 66 40W
Frederiksborg Amtskommune □, Denmark 11 J6 55 50N 12 10 E
Frederikshåb = Paamiut, Greenland 4 C5 62 0N 49 43W
Frederikshavn, Denmark 11 G4 57 28N 10 31 E
Frederikssund, Denmark 11 J6 55 50N 12 3 E
Frederiksted, U.S. Virgin Is. 121 C7 17 43N 64 53W
Frederiksværk, Denmark 11 J6 55 58N 12 4 E
Fredonia, Ariz., U.S.A. 115 H7 36 57N 112 32W
Fredonia, Kans., U.S.A. 113 G7 37 32N 95 49W
Fredonia, N.Y., U.S.A. 110 D5 42 26N 79 20W
Fredriksberg, Sweden 10 D8 60 8N 14 23 E
Fredrikstad, Norway 9 G14 59 13N 10 57 E
Free State □, S. Africa 88 D4 28 30 S 27 0 E
Freehold, U.S.A. 111 F10 40 16N 74 17W
Freel Peak, U.S.A. 116 G7 38 52N 119 54W
Freeland, U.S.A. 111 E9 41 1N 75 54W
Freels, C., Canada 103 C9 49 15N 53 30W
Freeman, Calif., U.S.A. 117 K9 35 35N 117 53W
Freeman, S. Dak., U.S.A. 112 D6 43 21N 97 26W
Freeport, Bahamas 120 A4 26 30N 78 47W
Freeport, Ill., U.S.A. 112 D10 42 17N 89 36W
Freeport, N.Y., U.S.A. 111 F11 40 39N 73 35W
Freeport, Ohio, U.S.A. 110 F3 40 12N 81 15W
Freeport, Pa., U.S.A. 110 F5 40 41N 79 41W
Freeport, Tex., U.S.A. 113 L7 28 57N 95 21W
Freetown, S. Leone 82 D2 8 30N 13 17W
Frégate, L., Canada 102 B5 53 15N 74 45W
Fregenal de la Sierra, Spain 35 G4 38 10N 6 39W
Fregene, Italy 29 G9 41 51N 12 12 E
Fréhel, C., France 18 D4 48 40N 2 20W
Freiberg, Germany 24 E9 50 55N 13 20 E
Freibourg = Fribourg, Switz. 25 J3 46 49N 7 9 E
Freiburg, Baden-W., Germany 25 H3 47 59N 7 51 E
Freiburg, Niedersachsen, Germany 24 B5 53 49N 9 16 E
Freilassing, Germany 25 H8 47 50N 12 58 E
Freire, Chile 128 D2 38 54 S 72 38W
Freirina, Chile 126 B1 28 30 S 71 10W
Freising, Germany 25 G7 48 24N 11 45 E
Freistadt, Austria 26 C7 48 30N 14 30 E
Freital, Germany 24 D9 51 1N 13 39 E
Fréjus, France 21 E10 43 25N 6 44 E
Fremantle, Australia 93 F2 32 7 S 115 47 E
Fremont, Calif., U.S.A. 116 H4 37 32N 121 57W
Fremont, Mich., U.S.A. 108 D3 43 28N 85 57W
Fremont, Nebr., U.S.A. 112 E6 41 26N 96 30W
Fremont, Ohio, U.S.A. 108 E4 41 21N 83 7W
Fremont →, U.S.A. 115 G8 38 24N 110 42W
French Camp, U.S.A. 116 H5 37 53N 121 16W
French Creek →, U.S.A. 110 E5 41 24N 79 50W
French Guiana ■, S. Amer. 125 C8 4 0N 53 0W
French Polynesia ■, Pac. Oc. 97 K13 20 0 S 145 0W
Frenchman Cr. →, N. Amer. 114 B10 48 31N 107 10W
Frenchman Cr. →, U.S.A. 112 E4 40 14N 100 50W
Frenštát pod Radhoštěm, Czech Rep. 27 B11 49 33N 18 13 E
Fresco, Ivory C. 82 D3 5 3N 5 31W
Fresco →, Brazil 125 E8 7 15 S 51 30W
Freshfield, C., Antarctica 5 C10 68 25 S 151 10 E
Fresnay-sur-Sarthe, France 18 D7 48 17N 0 1 E
Fresnillo, Mexico 118 C4 23 10N 103 0W
Fresno, U.S.A. 116 J7 36 44N 119 47W
Fresno Alhandiga, Spain 34 E5 40 42N 5 37W
Fresno Reservoir, U.S.A. 114 B9 48 36N 109 57W
Freudenstadt, Germany 25 G4 48 27N 8 24 E
Frévent, France 19 B9 50 15N 2 17 E
Frew →, Australia 94 C2 20 0 S 135 38 E
Frewsburg, U.S.A. 110 D5 42 3N 79 10W
Freycinet Pen., Australia 94 G4 42 10 S 148 25 E
Freyming-Merlebach, France 19 C13 49 8N 6 48 E
Freyung, Germany 25 G9 48 48N 13 31 E
Fria, Guinea 82 C2 10 27N 13 38W
Fria, C., Namibia 88 B1 18 0 S 12 0 E
Friant, U.S.A. 116 J7 36 59N 119 43W
Frías, Argentina 126 B2 28 40 S 65 5W
Fribourg, Switz. 25 J3 46 49N 7 9 E
Fribourg □, Switz. 25 J3 46 40N 7 0 E
Fridafors, Sweden 11 H8 56 25N 14 39 E
Friday Harbor, U.S.A. 116 B3 48 32N 123 1W
Friedberg, Bayern, Germany 25 G6 48 21N 10 59 E
Friedberg, Hessen, Germany 25 E4 50 19N 8 45 E
Friedens, U.S.A. 110 F6 40 3N 78 59W
Friedland, Germany 24 B9 53 40N 13 33 E
Friedrichshafen, Germany 25 H5 47 39N 9 30 E
Friedrichskoog, Germany 24 A4 54 1N 8 53 E
Friedrichstadt, Germany 24 A5 54 23N 9 6 E
Friendly Is. = Tonga ■, Pac. Oc. 91 D11 19 50 S 174 30W
Friendship, U.S.A. 110 D6 42 12N 78 8W
Friesach, Austria 26 E7 46 57N 14 24 E
Friesack, Germany 24 C8 52 44N 12 34 E
Friesland □, Neths. 17 A5 53 5N 5 50 E
Friesoythe, Germany 24 B3 53 1N 7 51 E
Friggesund, Sweden 10 C10 61 54N 16 33 E
Frillesås, Sweden 11 G6 57 20N 12 12 E
Frinnaryd, Sweden 11 G8 57 55N 14 50 E
Frio →, U.S.A. 113 L5 28 26N 98 11W
Frio, C., Brazil 122 F6 22 50 S 41 50W
Friol, Spain 34 B3 43 2N 7 47W
Friona, U.S.A. 113 H3 34 38N 102 43W
Fristad, Sweden 11 G6 57 50N 13 0 E
Fritch, U.S.A. 113 H4 35 38N 101 36W
Fritsla, Sweden 11 G6 57 33N 12 47 E
Fritzlar, Germany 24 D5 51 7N 9 16 E
Friuli-Venézia Giulia □, Italy 29 B9 46 0N 13 0 E
Frobisher B., Canada 101 B13 62 30N 66 0W
Frobisher Bay = Iqaluit, Canada 101 B13 63 44N 68 31W
Frobisher L., Canada 105 B7 56 20N 108 15W
Frohavet, Norway 8 E13 64 0N 9 30 E
Frohnleiten, Austria 26 D8 47 16N 15 19 E
Frolovo, Russia 48 F6 49 45N 43 40 E
Frombork, Poland 44 D6 54 21N 19 41 E
Frome, U.K. 13 F5 51 14N 2 19W
Frome →, U.K. 13 G5 50 41N 2 6W
Frome, L., Australia 95 E2 30 45 S 139 45 E
Frómista, Spain 34 C6 42 16N 4 25W
Front Range, U.S.A. 106 C5 40 25N 105 45W
Front Royal, U.S.A. 108 F6 38 55N 78 12W
Fronteira, Portugal 35 F3 39 3N 7 39W
Frontera, Canary Is. 37 G2 27 47N 17 59W
Frontera, Mexico 119 D6 18 30N 92 40W
Fronteras, Mexico 118 A3 30 56N 109 31W
Frontignan, France 20 E7 43 27N 3 45 E
Frosinone, Italy 30 A6 41 38N 13 19 E
Frostburg, U.S.A. 108 F6 39 39N 78 56W
Frostisen, Norway 8 B17 68 14N 17 10 E
Frouard, France 19 D13 48 47N 6 8 E
Frövi, Sweden 10 E9 59 28N 15 24 E
Frøya, Norway 8 E13 63 43N 8 40 E
Frumoasa, Romania 43 D10 46 28N 25 48 E
Frunze = Bishkek, Kyrgyzstan 50 E8 42 54N 74 46 E
Fruška Gora, Serbia, Yug. 42 E4 45 7N 19 30 E
Frutal, Brazil 125 H9 20 0 S 49 0W
Frutigen, Switz. 25 J3 46 35N 7 38 E
Frýdek-Místek, Czech Rep. 27 B11 49 40N 18 20 E
Frýdlant, Czech Rep. 26 A8 50 56N 15 9 E
Fryeburg, U.S.A. 111 B14 44 1N 70 59W
Fryvaldov = Jeseník, Czech Rep. 27 A10 50 14N 17 8 E
Fthiótis □, Greece 38 C4 38 50N 22 25 E
Fu Jiang →, China 58 C6 30 0N 106 16 E
Fu Xian = Wafangdian, China 57 E11 39 38N 121 58 E
Fu Xian, China 56 G5 36 0N 109 20 E
Fu'an, China 59 D12 27 11N 119 36 E
Fubian, China 58 B4 31 17N 102 22 E
Fucécchio, Italy 28 E7 43 44N 10 48 E
Fucheng, China 56 F9 37 50N 116 10 E
Fuchou = Fuzhou, China 59 D12 26 5N 119 16 E
Fuchū, Japan 55 G6 34 34N 133 14 E
Fuchuan, China 59 E8 24 50N 111 5 E

G

Glorieuses, Is.

Gaya, Niger 83 C5 11 52N 3 28 E
Gaya, Nigeria 83 C6 11 57N 9 0 E
Gayéri, Burkina Faso 83 C5 12 39N 0 29 E
Gaylord, U.S.A. 108 C3 45 2N 84 41W
Gayndah, Australia 95 D5 25 35 S 151 32 E
Gaysin = Haysyn, Ukraine 47 H5 48 57N 29 25 E
Gayvoron = Hayvoron, Ukraine 47 H5 48 22N 29 52 E
Gaza, Gaza Strip 75 D3 31 30N 34 28 E
Gaza □, Mozam. 89 C5 23 10 S 32 45 E
Gaza Strip □, Asia 75 D3 31 29N 34 25 E
Gazanjyk, Turkmenistan 71 B7 39 16N 55 32 E
Gazaoua, Niger 83 C6 13 32N 7 55 E
Gāzbor, Iran 71 D8 28 5N 58 51 E
Gazi, Dem. Rep. of the Congo 86 B1 1 3N 24 30 E
Gaziantep, Turkey 70 B3 37 6N 37 23 E
Gazipaşa, Turkey 72 D5 36 16N 32 18 E
Gbarnga, Liberia 82 D3 7 19N 9 13W
Gbekebo, Nigeria 83 D5 6 20N 4 56 E
Gboko, Nigeria 83 D6 7 17N 9 4 E
Gbongan, Nigeria 83 D5 7 28N 4 20 E
Gcoverega, Botswana 88 B3 19 8 S 24 18 E
Gcuwa, S. Africa 89 E4 32 20 S 28 11 E
Gdańsk, Poland 44 D5 54 22N 18 40 E
Gdańska, Zatoka, Poland 44 D6 54 30N 19 20 E
Gdov, Russia 9 G22 58 48N 27 55 E
Gdynia, Poland 44 D5 54 35N 18 33 E
Geba →, Guinea-Biss. 82 C1 11 46N 15 36W
Gebe, Indonesia 63 D7 0 5N 129 25 E
Gebeciler, Turkey 39 C12 38 46N 30 46 E
Gebeit Mine, Sudan 80 C4 21 3N 36 29 E
Gebel Abyad, Sudan 80 D2 19 0N 28 0 E
Gebel Iweibid, Egypt 80 H8 30 8N 32 13 E
Gebze, Turkey 41 F13 40 47N 29 25 E
Gecha, Ethiopia 81 F4 7 30N 35 18 E
Gedaref, Sudan 81 E4 14 2N 35 28 E
Gedaref □, Sudan 81 E4 14 0N 35 0 E
Gediz, Turkey 39 B11 39 1N 29 24 E
Gediz →, Turkey 39 C8 38 35N 26 48 E
Gedo, Ethiopia 81 F4 9 2N 37 25 E
Gèdre, France 20 F4 42 47N 0 2 E
Gedser, Denmark 11 K5 54 35N 11 55 E
Geegully Cr. →, Australia 92 C3 18 32 S 123 41 E
Geel, Belgium 17 C4 51 10N 4 59 E
Geelong, Australia 95 F3 38 10 S 144 22 E
Geelvink B. = Cenderwasih, Teluk, Indonesia 63 E9 3 0 S 135 20 E
Geelvink Chan., Australia 93 E1 28 30 S 114 0 E
Geesthacht, Germany 24 B6 53 26N 10 22 E
Geidam, Nigeria 83 C7 12 57N 11 57 E
Geikie →, Canada 105 B8 57 45N 103 52W
Geilenkirchen, Germany 24 E2 50 57N 6 8 E
Geili, Sudan 81 D3 16 1N 32 37 E
Geisingen, Germany 25 H4 47 54N 8 38 E
Geislingen, Germany 25 G5 48 37N 9 50 E
Geistown, U.S.A. 110 F6 40 18N 78 52W
Geita, Tanzania 86 C3 2 48 S 32 12 E
Gejiu, China 58 F4 23 20N 103 10 E
Gel →, Sudan 81 F2 7 5N 29 10 E
Gel, Meydān-e, Iran 71 D7 29 4N 54 50 E
Gel River, Sudan 81 F2 7 5N 29 10 E
Gela, Italy 31 E7 37 4N 14 15 E
Gela, G. di, Italy 31 F7 37 0N 14 20 E
Gelahun, Liberia 82 D2 7 55N 10 28W
Gelderland □, Neths. 17 B6 52 5N 6 10 E
Geldern, Germany 24 D2 51 31N 6 20 E
Geldrop, Neths. 17 C5 51 25N 5 32 E
Geleen, Neths. 17 D5 50 57N 5 49 E
Gelehun, S. Leone 82 D2 8 20N 11 40W
Gelembe, Turkey 39 B9 39 10N 27 50 E
Gelemso, Ethiopia 81 F5 8 49N 40 31 E
Gelendost, Turkey 72 C4 38 7N 31 1 E
Gelendzhik, Russia 47 K10 44 33N 38 10 E
Gelibolu, Turkey 41 F10 40 28N 26 43 E
Gelibolu Yarımadası, Turkey 41 F10 40 20N 26 30 E
Gelidonya Burnu, Turkey 72 D4 36 12N 30 24 E
Gelnhausen, Germany 25 E5 50 11N 9 11 E
Gelnica, Slovak Rep. 27 C13 48 51N 20 55 E
Gelsenkirchen, Germany 24 D3 51 32N 7 6 E
Gelting, Germany 24 A5 54 45N 9 53 E
Gemas, Malaysia 65 L4 2 37N 102 36 E
Gembloux, Belgium 17 D4 50 34N 4 43 E
Gembu, Nigeria 83 D7 6 42N 11 10 E
Gemena, Dem. Rep. of the Congo 84 D3 3 13N 19 48 E
Gemerek, Turkey 70 B3 39 15N 36 10 E
Gemla, Sweden 11 H8 56 52N 14 39 E
Gemlik, Turkey 41 F13 40 26N 29 9 E
Gemlik Körfezi, Turkey 41 F12 40 25N 28 55 E
Gemona del Friuli, Italy 29 B10 46 16N 13 9 E
Gemsa, Egypt 80 B3 27 39N 33 35 E
Gemünden, Germany 25 E5 50 3N 9 42 E
Genale →, Ethiopia 81 F4 6 2N 39 1 E
Genç, Turkey 73 C9 38 44N 40 34 E
Gençay, France 20 B4 46 23N 0 23 E
Geneina, Gebel, Egypt 80 B3 29 2N 33 55 E
General Acha, Argentina 126 D3 37 20 S 64 38W
General Alvear, Buenos Aires, Argentina 126 D4 36 0 S 60 0W
General Alvear, Mendoza, Argentina 126 D2 35 0 S 67 40W
General Artigas, Paraguay 126 B4 26 52 S 56 16W
General Belgrano, Argentina 126 D4 36 35 S 58 47W
General Cabrera, Argentina 126 C3 32 53 S 63 52W
General Cepeda, Mexico 118 B4 25 23N 101 27W
General Guido, Argentina 126 D4 36 40 S 57 50W
General Juan Madariaga, Argentina 126 D4 37 0 S 57 0W
General La Madrid, Argentina 126 D3 37 17 S 61 20W
General MacArthur, Phil. 61 F6 11 18N 125 28 E
General Martin Miguel de Güemes, Argentina 126 A3 24 50 S 65 0W
General Paz, Argentina 126 B4 27 45 S 57 36W
General Pico, Argentina 126 D3 35 45 S 63 50W
General Pinedo, Argentina 126 B3 27 15 S 61 20W
General Pinto, Argentina 126 C3 34 45 S 61 50W
General Roca, Argentina 128 D3 39 2 S 67 35W
General Santos, Phil. 61 H6 6 5N 125 14 E
General Toshevo, Bulgaria 41 C12 43 42N 28 6 E
General Trevino, Mexico 119 B5 26 14N 99 29W
General Trías, Mexico 118 B3 28 21N 106 22W
General Viamonte, Argentina 126 D3 35 1 S 61 3W
General Villegas, Argentina 126 D3 35 5 S 63 0W
Genesee, Idaho, U.S.A. 114 C5 46 33N 116 56W
Genesee, Pa., U.S.A. 110 E7 41 59N 77 54W
Genesee →, U.S.A. 110 C7 43 16N 77 36W
Geneseo, Ill., U.S.A. 112 E9 41 27N 90 9W
Geneseo, N.Y., U.S.A. 110 D7 42 48N 77 49W
Geneva = Genève, Switz. 25 J2 46 12N 6 9 E
Geneva, Ala., U.S.A. 109 K3 31 2N 85 52W
Geneva, N.Y., U.S.A. 110 D8 42 52N 76 59W
Geneva, Nebr., U.S.A. 112 E6 40 32N 97 36W
Geneva, Ohio, U.S.A. 110 E4 41 48N 80 57W
Geneva, L. = Léman, L., Europe 19 F13 46 26N 6 30 E
Geneva, L., U.S.A. 108 D1 42 38N 88 30W
Genève, Switz. 25 J2 46 12N 6 9 E
Gengenbach, Germany 25 G4 48 24N 8 1 E
Gengma, China 58 F2 23 32N 99 20 E
Genichesk = Henichesk, Ukraine 47 J8 46 12N 34 50 E
Genil →, Spain 35 H5 37 42N 5 19W
Genk, Belgium 17 D5 50 58N 5 32 E
Genlis, France 19 E12 47 11N 5 12 E
Gennargentu, Mti. del, Italy 30 B2 40 1N 9 19 E
Gennes, France 18 E6 47 20N 0 17W
Genoa = Génova, Italy 28 D5 44 25N 8 57 E
Genoa, Australia 95 F4 37 29 S 149 35 E
Genoa, N.Y., U.S.A. 111 D8 42 40N 76 32W
Genoa, Nebr., U.S.A. 112 E6 41 27N 97 44W
Genoa, Nev., U.S.A. 116 F7 39 2N 119 50W
Génova, Italy 28 D5 44 25N 8 57 E
Génova, G. di, Italy 28 E6 44 0N 9 0 E
Genriyetty, Ostrov, Russia 51 B16 77 6N 156 30 E
Gent, Belgium 17 C3 51 2N 3 42 E
Genteng, Indonesia 63 G12 7 22 S 106 24 E
Genthin, Germany 24 C8 52 25N 12 9 E
Genyem, Indonesia 63 E10 2 46 S 140 12 E
Genzano di Lucánia, Italy 31 B9 40 51N 16 2 E
Genzano di Roma, Italy 29 G9 41 42N 12 41 E
Geoagiu, Romania 43 E8 45 55N 23 12 E
Geographe B., Australia 93 F2 33 30 S 115 15 E
Geographe Chan., Australia 93 D1 24 30 S 113 0 E
Geokchay = Göyçay, Azerbaijan 49 K8 40 42N 47 43 E
Georga, Zemlya, Russia 50 A5 80 30N 49 0 E
George, S. Africa 88 E3 33 58 S 22 29 E
George →, Canada 103 A6 58 49N 66 10W
George, L., N.S.W., Australia 95 F4 35 10 S 149 25 E
George, L., S. Austral., Australia 95 F3 37 25 S 140 0 E
George, L., W. Austral., Australia 92 D3 22 45 S 123 40 E
George, L., Uganda 86 B3 0 5N 30 10 E
George, L., Fla., U.S.A. 109 L5 29 17N 81 36W
George, L., N.Y., U.S.A. 111 C11 43 37N 73 33W
George Gill Ra., Australia 92 D5 24 22 S 131 45 E
George River = Kangiqsualujjuaq, Canada 101 C13 58 30N 65 59W
George Sound, N.Z. 91 L1 44 52 S 167 25 E
George Town, Australia 94 G4 41 6 S 146 49 E
George Town, Bahamas 120 B4 23 33N 75 47W
George Town, Cayman Is. 120 C3 19 20N 81 24W
George Town, Malaysia 65 K3 5 25N 100 15 E
George V Land, Antarctica 5 C10 69 0 S 148 0 E
George VI Sound, Antarctica 5 D17 71 0 S 68 0W
George West, U.S.A. 113 L5 28 20N 98 7W
Georgetown, Australia 94 B3 18 17 S 143 33 E
Georgetown, Ont., Canada 102 D4 43 40N 79 56W
Georgetown, P.E.I., Canada 103 C7 46 13N 62 24W
Georgetown, Gambia 82 C2 13 30N 14 47W
Georgetown, Guyana 124 B7 6 50N 58 12W
Georgetown, Calif., U.S.A. 116 G6 38 54N 120 50W
Georgetown, Colo., U.S.A. 114 G11 39 42N 105 42W
Georgetown, Ky., U.S.A. 108 F3 38 13N 84 33W
Georgetown, N.Y., U.S.A. 111 D9 42 46N 75 44W
Georgetown, Ohio, U.S.A. 108 F4 38 52N 83 54W
Georgetown, S.C., U.S.A. 109 J6 33 23N 79 17W
Georgetown, Tex., U.S.A. 113 K6 30 38N 97 41W
Georgia □, U.S.A. 109 K5 32 50N 83 15W
Georgia ■, Asia 49 J6 42 0N 43 0 E
Georgia, Str. of, Canada 104 D4 49 25N 124 0W
Georgian B., Canada 102 C3 45 15N 81 0W
Georgina →, Australia 94 C2 23 30 S 139 47 E
Georgina I., Canada 110 B5 44 22N 79 17W
Georgiu-Dezh = Liski, Russia 47 G10 51 3N 39 30 E
Georgiyevsk, Russia 49 H6 44 12N 43 28 E
Georgsmarienhütte, Germany 24 C4 52 13N 8 3 E
Gera, Germany 24 E8 50 53N 12 4 E
Geraardsbergen, Belgium 17 D3 50 45N 3 53 E
Geral, Serra, Brazil 127 B6 26 25 S 50 0W
Geral de Goiás, Serra, Brazil 125 F9 12 0 S 46 0W
Geraldine, U.S.A. 114 C8 47 36N 110 16W
Geraldton, Australia 93 E1 28 48 S 114 32 E
Geraldton, Canada 102 C2 49 44N 86 59W
Gérardmer, France 19 D13 48 3N 6 50 E
Gercüş, Turkey 73 D9 37 34N 41 23 E
Gerede, Turkey 72 B5 40 45N 32 10 E
Gerês, Sierra do, Portugal 34 D3 41 48N 8 0W
Gereshk, Afghan. 66 D4 31 47N 64 35 E
Geretsried, Germany 25 H7 47 51N 11 28 E
Gérgal, Spain 33 H2 37 7N 2 31W
Gerik, Malaysia 65 K3 5 50N 101 15 E
Gering, U.S.A. 112 E3 41 50N 103 40W
Gerlach, U.S.A. 114 F4 40 39N 119 21W
Gerlachovský štit, Slovak Rep. 27 B13 49 11N 20 7 E
German Planina, Macedonia 40 D6 42 20N 22 0 E
Germansen Landing, Canada 104 B4 55 43N 124 40W
Germantown, U.S.A. 113 M10 35 5N 89 49W
Germany ■, Europe 24 E6 51 0N 10 0 E
Germencik, Turkey 39 D9 37 52N 27 37 E
Germering, Germany 25 G7 48 8N 11 22 E
Germersheim, Germany 25 F4 49 12N 8 22 E
Germī, Iran 71 B6 39 1N 48 3 E
Germiston, S. Africa 89 D4 26 15 S 28 10 E
Gernika-Lumo, Spain 32 B2 43 19N 2 40W
Gernsheim, Germany 25 F4 49 45N 8 30 E
Gero, Japan 55 G8 35 48N 137 14 E
Gerolzhofen, Germany 25 F6 49 54N 10 21 E
Gerona = Girona, Spain 32 D7 41 58N 2 46 E
Gerrard, Canada 104 C5 50 30N 117 17W
Gers □, France 20 E4 43 35N 0 30 E
Gers →, France 20 D4 44 9N 0 39 E
Gersfeld, Germany 24 E5 50 27N 9 56 E
Gersthofen, Germany 25 G6 48 25N 10 53 E
Gerzat, France 20 C7 45 48N 3 8 E
Gerze, Turkey 72 B6 41 48N 35 12 E
Geseke, Germany 24 D4 51 38N 8 31 E
Geser, Indonesia 63 E8 3 50 S 130 54 E
Gesso →, Italy 28 D4 44 24N 7 33 E
Gestro, Wabi →, Ethiopia 81 G5 4 12N 42 2 E
Getafe, Spain 34 E7 40 18N 3 44W
Getinge, Sweden 11 H6 56 49N 12 44 E
Gettysburg, Pa., U.S.A. 108 F7 39 50N 77 14W
Gettysburg, S. Dak., U.S.A. 112 C5 45 1N 99 57W
Getxo, Spain 32 B2 43 21N 2 59W
Getz Ice Shelf, Antarctica 5 D14 75 0 S 130 0W
Gevaş, Turkey 73 C10 38 15N 43 6 E
Gévaudan, France 20 D7 44 40N 3 40 E
Gevgelija, Macedonia 40 E6 41 9N 22 30 E
Gévora →, Spain 35 G4 38 53N 6 57W
Gewani, Ethiopia 81 E5 10 12N 40 40 E
Gex, France 19 F13 46 21N 6 3 E
Geyikli, Turkey 39 B8 39 48N 26 12 E
Geyser, U.S.A. 114 C8 47 16N 110 30W
Geyserville, U.S.A. 116 G4 38 42N 122 54W
Geyve, Turkey 72 B4 40 30N 30 18 E
Ghâbat el Arab = Wang Kai, Sudan 81 F2 9 3N 29 23 E
Ghabeish, Sudan 81 E2 12 9N 27 21 E
Ghaggar →, India 68 E6 29 30N 74 53 E
Ghaghara →, India 69 G11 25 45N 84 40 E
Ghaghat →, Bangla. 69 G13 25 19N 89 38 E
Ghagra, India 69 H11 23 17N 84 33 E
Ghagra →, India 69 F9 27 29N 81 9 E
Ghalla, Wadi el →, Sudan 81 E2 10 25N 27 32 E
Ghana ■, W. Afr. 83 D4 8 0N 1 0W
Ghansor, India 69 H9 22 39N 80 1 E
Ghanzi, Botswana 88 C3 21 50 S 21 34 E
Gharb el Istiwa'iya □, Sudan 81 G3 5 0N 30 0 E
Gharb Kordofân, Sudan 81 E2 12 10N 28 0 E
Gharbîya, Es Sahrâ el, Egypt 80 B2 27 40N 26 30 E
Ghardaïa, Algeria 78 B6 32 20N 3 37 E
Ghârib, G., Egypt 80 B3 28 6N 32 54 E
Gharig, Sudan 81 E2 10 47N 27 33 E
Gharyān, Libya 79 B8 32 10N 13 0 E
Ghat, Libya 79 D8 24 59N 10 11 E
Ghatal, India 69 H12 22 40N 87 46 E
Ghatampur, India 69 F9 26 8N 80 13 E
Ghatsila, India 69 H12 22 36N 86 29 E
Ghaṭṭī, Si. Arabia 70 D3 31 16N 37 31 E
Ghawdex = Gozo, Malta 36 C1 36 3N 14 13 E
Ghazal, Bahr el →, Chad 79 F9 13 0N 15 47 E
Ghazâl, Bahr el →, Sudan 81 F3 9 31N 30 25 E
Ghaziabad, India 68 E7 28 42N 77 26 E
Ghazipur, India 69 G10 25 38N 83 35 E
Ghaznī, Afghan. 68 C3 33 30N 68 28 E
Ghaznī □, Afghan. 66 C6 32 10N 68 20 E
Ghedi, Italy 28 C7 45 24N 10 16 E
Ghelari, Romania 42 E7 45 38N 22 45 E
Ghent = Gent, Belgium 17 C3 51 2N 3 42 E
Gheorghe Gheorghiu-Dej = Oneşti, Romania 43 D11 46 17N 26 47 E
Gheorgheni, Romania 43 D10 46 43N 25 41 E
Gherla, Romania 43 C8 47 2N 23 57 E
Ghidigeni, Romania 43 D12 46 3N 27 30 E
Ghilarza, Italy 30 B1 40 7N 8 50 E
Ghimeş-Făget, Romania 43 D11 46 35N 26 2 E
Ghīnah, Wādī al →, Si. Arabia 70 D3 30 27N 38 14 E
Ghisonaccia, France 21 F13 42 1N 9 26 E
Ghisoni, France 21 F13 42 7N 9 12 E
Ghizao, Afghan. 68 C1 33 20N 65 44 E
Ghizar →, Pakistan 69 A5 36 15N 73 43 E
Ghot Ogrein, Egypt 80 A2 31 10N 25 20 E
Ghotaru, India 68 F4 27 20N 70 1 E
Ghotki, Pakistan 68 E3 28 5N 69 21 E
Ghowr □, Afghan. 66 C4 34 0N 64 20 E
Ghudaf, W. al →, Iraq 70 C4 32 56N 43 30 E
Ghudāmis, Libya 77 C4 30 11N 9 29 E
Ghughri, India 69 H9 22 39N 80 41 E
Ghugus, India 66 K11 19 58N 79 12 E
Ghulam Mohammad Barrage, Pakistan 68 G3 25 30N 68 20 E
Ghūrīān, Afghan. 66 B2 34 17N 61 25 E
Gia Dinh, Vietnam 65 G6 10 49N 106 42 E
Gia Lai = Plei Ku, Vietnam 64 F7 13 57N 108 0 E
Gia Nghia, Vietnam 65 G6 11 58N 107 42 E
Gia Ngoc, Vietnam 64 E7 14 50N 108 58 E
Gia Vuc, Vietnam 64 E7 14 42N 108 34 E
Giannutri, Italy 28 F8 42 15N 11 6 E
Giant Forest, U.S.A. 116 J8 36 36N 118 43W
Giant Mts. = Krkonoše, Czech Rep. 26 A8 50 50N 15 35 E
Giants Causeway, U.K. 15 A5 55 16N 6 29W
Giarabub = Al Jaghbūb, Libya 79 C10 29 42N 24 38 E
Giarre, Italy 31 E8 37 43N 15 11 E
Giaveno, Italy 28 C4 45 2N 7 21 E
Gibara, Cuba 120 B4 21 9N 76 11W
Gibb River, Australia 92 C4 16 26 S 126 26 E
Gibbon, U.S.A. 112 E5 40 45N 98 51W
Gibe →, Ethiopia 81 F4 7 20N 37 36 E
Gibellina Nuova, Italy 30 E5 37 47N 12 58 E
Gibeon, Namibia 88 D2 25 9 S 17 43 E
Gibraleón, Spain 35 H4 37 23N 6 58W
Gibraltar ■, Europe 35 J5 36 7N 5 22W
Gibraltar, Str. of, Medit. S. 35 K5 35 55N 5 40W
Gibson Desert, Australia 92 D4 24 0 S 126 0 E
Gibsons, Canada 104 D4 49 24N 123 32W
Gibsonville, U.S.A. 116 F6 39 46N 120 54W
Giddings, U.S.A. 113 K6 30 11N 96 56W
Gidole, Ethiopia 81 F4 5 40N 37 25 E
Giebnegáisi = Kebnekaise, Sweden 8 C18 67 53N 18 33 E
Gien, France 19 E9 47 40N 2 36 E
Giengen, Germany 25 G6 48 37N 10 14 E
Giessen, Germany 24 E4 50 34N 8 41 E
Gīfān, Iran 71 B8 37 54N 57 28 E
Gifatin, Geziret, Egypt 80 B3 27 10N 33 50 E
Gifhorn, Germany 24 C6 52 30N 10 33 E
Gift Lake, Canada 104 B5 55 53N 115 49W
Gifu, Japan 55 G8 35 30N 136 45 E
Gifu □, Japan 55 G8 35 40N 137 0 E
Gigant, Russia 49 G5 46 28N 41 20 E
Giganta, Sa. de la, Mexico 118 B2 25 30N 111 30W
Gigen, Bulgaria 41 C8 43 40N 24 28 E
Gigha, U.K. 14 F3 55 42N 5 44W
Gíglio, Italy 28 F7 42 20N 10 52 E
Gignac, France 20 E7 43 39N 3 32 E
Gigüela →, Spain 35 F7 39 8N 3 44W
Gijón, Spain 34 B5 43 32N 5 42W
Gil I., Canada 104 C3 53 12N 129 15W
Gila →, U.S.A. 115 K6 32 43N 114 33W
Gila Bend, U.S.A. 115 K7 32 57N 112 43W
Gila Bend Mts., U.S.A. 115 K7 33 10N 113 0W
Gīlān □, Iran 71 B6 37 0N 50 0 E
Gilău, Romania 43 D8 46 45N 23 23 E
Gilbert →, Australia 94 B3 16 35 S 141 15 E
Gilbert Is., Kiribati 96 G9 1 0N 172 0 E
Gilbert River, Australia 94 B3 18 9 S 142 52 E
Gilead, U.S.A. 111 B14 44 24N 70 59W
Gilf el Kebîr, Hadabat el, Egypt 80 C2 23 50N 25 50 E
Gilford I., Canada 104 C3 50 40N 126 30W
Gilgandra, Australia 95 E4 31 43 S 148 39 E
Gilgil, Kenya 86 C4 0 30 S 36 20 E
Gilgit, India 69 B6 35 50N 74 15 E
Gilgit →, Pakistan 69 B6 35 44N 74 37 E
Giljeva Planina, Serbia, Yug. 40 C3 43 9N 20 0 E
Gillam, Canada 105 B10 56 20N 94 40W
Gilleleje, Denmark 11 H6 56 8N 12 19 E
Gillen, L., Australia 93 E3 26 11 S 124 38 E
Gilles, L., Australia 95 E2 32 50 S 136 45 E
Gillette, U.S.A. 112 C2 44 18N 105 30W
Gilliat, Australia 94 C3 20 40 S 141 28 E
Gillingham, U.K. 13 F8 51 23N 0 33 E
Gilmer, U.S.A. 113 J7 32 44N 94 57W
Gilmore, L., Australia 93 F3 32 29 S 121 37 E
Gilo →, Ethiopia 81 F3 8 10N 33 15 E
Gilort →, Romania 43 F8 44 38N 23 32 E
Gilroy, U.S.A. 116 H5 37 1N 121 34W
Gimbi, Ethiopia 81 F4 9 3N 35 42 E
Gimli, Canada 105 C9 50 40N 97 0W
Gimo, Sweden 10 D12 60 11N 18 12 E
Gimone →, France 20 E5 44 0N 1 6 E
Gimont, France 20 E4 43 38N 0 52 E
Gin Gin, Australia 95 D5 25 0 S 151 58 E
Ginâh, Egypt 80 B3 25 21N 30 30 E
Gineifa, Egypt 80 H8 30 12N 32 25 E
Gingin, Australia 93 F2 31 22 S 115 54 E
Gingindlovu, S. Africa 89 D5 29 2 S 31 30 E
Ginir, Ethiopia 81 F5 7 6N 40 40 E
Ginosa, Italy 31 B9 40 35N 16 45 E
Ginzo de Limia = Xinzo de Limia, Spain 34 C3 42 3N 7 47W
Gióia, G. di, Italy 31 D8 38 30N 15 45 E
Gióia del Colle, Italy 31 B9 40 48N 16 55 E
Gióia Táuro, Italy 31 D8 38 25N 15 54 E
Gioiosa Iónica, Italy 31 D9 38 20N 16 18 E
Gioiosa Marea, Italy 31 D7 38 10N 14 54 E
Gióna, Óros, Greece 38 C4 38 38N 22 14 E
Giovi, Passo dei, Italy 28 D5 44 33N 8 57 E
Giovinazzo, Italy 31 A9 41 11N 16 40 E
Gir Hills, India 68 J4 21 0N 71 0 E
Girab, India 68 F4 26 2N 70 38 E
Girâfi, W. →, Egypt 75 F3 29 58N 34 39 E
Giraltovce, Slovak Rep. 27 B14 49 7N 21 32 E
Girard, Kans., U.S.A. 113 G7 37 31N 94 51W
Girard, Ohio, U.S.A. 110 E4 41 9N 80 42W
Girard, Pa., U.S.A. 110 E4 42 0N 80 19W
Girdle Ness, U.K. 14 D6 57 9N 2 3W
Giresun, Turkey 73 B8 40 55N 38 30 E
Girga, Egypt 80 B3 26 17N 31 55 E
Giri →, India 68 D7 30 28N 77 41 E
Giridih, India 69 G12 24 10N 86 21 E
Girifalco, Italy 31 D9 38 49N 16 25 E
Girne = Kyrenia, Cyprus 36 D12 35 20N 33 20 E
Giro, Nigeria 83 C5 11 7N 4 42 E
Giromagny, France 19 E13 47 45N 6 50 E
Girona, Spain 32 D7 41 58N 2 46 E
Girona □, Spain 32 C7 42 11N 2 30 E
Gironde □, France 20 D3 44 45N 0 30W
Gironde →, France 20 C2 45 32N 1 7W
Gironella, Spain 32 C6 42 2N 1 53 E
Giru, Australia 94 B4 19 30 S 147 5 E
Girvan, U.K. 14 F4 55 14N 4 51W
Gisborne, N.Z. 91 H7 38 39 S 178 5 E
Gisenyi, Rwanda 86 C2 1 41 S 29 15 E
Gislaved, Sweden 11 G7 57 19N 13 32 E
Gisors, France 19 C8 49 15N 1 47 E
Gitega, Burundi 86 C2 3 26 S 29 56 E
Giuba →, Somali Rep. 74 G3 1 30N 42 35 E
Giugliano in Campania, Italy 31 B7 40 56N 14 12 E
Giulianova, Italy 29 F10 42 45N 13 57 E
Giurgeni, Romania 43 F12 44 45N 27 48 E
Giurgiu, Romania 43 G10 43 52N 25 57 E
Giurgiu □, Romania 43 F10 44 20N 26 0 E
Giurgiuleşti, Moldova 43 E13 45 29N 28 12 E
Give, Denmark 11 J3 55 51N 9 13 E
Givet, France 19 B11 50 8N 4 49 E
Givors, France 21 C8 45 35N 4 45 E
Givry, France 19 F11 46 41N 4 46 E
Giyon, Ethiopia 81 F4 8 33N 38 1 E
Giza = El Gîza, Egypt 80 J7 30 0N 31 10 E
Gizhiga, Russia 51 C17 62 3N 160 30 E
Gizhiginskaya Guba, Russia 51 C16 61 0N 158 0 E
Giżycko, Poland 44 D8 54 2N 21 48 E
Gizzeria, Italy 31 D9 38 59N 16 12 E
Gjalicë e Lumës, Mal., Albania 40 D4 42 2N 20 25 E
Gjegjan, Albania 40 E4 41 58N 20 3 E
Gjirokastër, Albania 40 F4 40 7N 20 10 E
Gjoa Haven, Canada 100 B10 68 20N 96 8W
Gjøvik, Norway 9 F14 60 47N 10 43 E
Gjuhës, Kep i, Albania 40 F3 40 28N 19 15 E
Glace Bay, Canada 103 C8 46 11N 59 58W
Glacier Bay National Park and Preserve, U.S.A. 104 B1 58 45N 136 30W
Glacier National Park, Canada 104 C5 51 15N 117 30W
Glacier National Park, U.S.A. 114 B7 48 30N 113 18W
Glacier Peak, U.S.A. 114 B3 48 7N 121 7W
Gladewater, U.S.A. 113 J7 32 33N 94 56W
Gladstone, Queens., Australia 94 C5 23 52 S 151 16 E
Gladstone, S. Austral., Australia 95 E2 33 15 S 138 22 E
Gladstone, Canada 105 C9 50 13N 98 57W
Gladstone, U.S.A. 108 C2 45 51N 87 1W
Gladwin, U.S.A. 108 D3 43 59N 84 29W
Glafsfjorden, Sweden 10 E6 59 30N 12 37 E
Głagów Małapolski, Poland 45 H8 50 10N 21 56 E
Glåma = Glomma →, Norway 9 G14 59 12N 10 57 E
Gláma, Iceland 8 D2 65 48N 23 0W
Glamis, U.S.A. 117 N11 32 55N 115 5W
Glamoč, Bos.-H. 29 D13 44 3N 16 51 E
Glamsbjerg, Denmark 11 J4 55 17N 10 6 E
Glarus, Switz. 25 H5 47 3N 9 4 E
Glarus □, Switz. 25 J5 47 0N 9 5 E
Glasco, Kans., U.S.A. 112 F6 39 22N 97 50W
Glasco, N.Y., U.S.A. 111 D11 42 3N 73 57W
Glasgow, U.K. 14 F4 55 51N 4 15W
Glasgow, Ky., U.S.A. 108 G3 37 0N 85 55W
Glasgow, Mont., U.S.A. 114 B10 48 12N 106 38W
Glasgow, City of □, U.K. 14 F4 55 51N 4 12W
Glaslyn, Canada 105 C7 53 22N 108 21W
Glastonbury, U.K. 13 F5 51 9N 2 43W
Glastonbury, U.S.A. 111 E12 41 43N 72 37W
Glauchau, Germany 24 E8 50 49N 12 31 E
Glava, Sweden 10 E6 59 33N 12 35 E
Glavice, Croatia 29 E13 43 43N 16 41 E
Glazov, Russia 48 A11 58 9N 52 40 E
Gleichen, Canada 104 C6 50 52N 113 3W
Gleisdorf, Austria 26 D8 47 6N 15 44 E
Gleiwitz = Gliwice, Poland 45 H5 50 22N 18 41 E
Glen, U.S.A. 111 B13 44 7N 71 11W
Glen Affric, U.K. 14 D3 57 17N 5 1W
Glen Canyon, U.S.A. 115 H8 37 30N 110 40W
Glen Canyon Dam, U.S.A. 115 H8 36 57N 111 29W
Glen Canyon National Recreation Area, U.S.A. 115 H8 37 15N 111 0W
Glen Coe, U.K. 14 E3 56 40N 5 0W
Glen Cove, U.S.A. 111 F11 40 52N 73 38W
Glen Garry, U.K. 14 D3 57 3N 5 7W
Glen Innes, Australia 95 D5 29 44 S 151 44 E
Glen Lyon, U.S.A. 111 E8 41 10N 76 5W
Glen Mor, U.K. 14 D4 57 9N 4 37W
Glen Moriston, U.K. 14 D4 57 11N 4 52W
Glen Robertson, Canada 111 A10 45 22N 74 30W
Glen Spean, U.K. 14 E4 56 53N 4 40W
Glen Ullin, U.S.A. 112 B4 46 49N 101 50W
Glénan, Îs. de, France 18 E3 47 42N 4 0W
Glencoe, Canada 110 D3 42 45N 81 43W
Glencoe, S. Africa 89 D5 28 11 S 30 11 E
Glencoe, U.S.A. 112 C7 44 46N 94 9W
Glendale, Ariz., U.S.A. 115 K7 33 32N 112 11W
Glendale, Calif., U.S.A. 117 L8 34 9N 118 15W
Glendale, Zimbabwe 87 F3 17 22 S 31 5 E
Glendive, U.S.A. 112 B2 47 7N 104 43W
Glendo, U.S.A. 112 D2 42 30N 105 2W
Glenelg →, Australia 95 F3 38 4 S 140 59 E
Glenfield, U.S.A. 111 C9 43 43N 75 24W
Glengarriff, Ireland 15 E2 51 45N 9 34W
Glenmont, U.S.A. 110 F2 40 31N 82 6W
Glenmorgan, Australia 95 D4 27 14 S 149 42 E
Glenn, U.S.A. 116 F4 39 31N 122 1W
Glennallen, U.S.A. 100 B5 62 7N 145 33W
Glennamaddy, Ireland 15 C3 53 37N 8 33W
Glenns Ferry, U.S.A. 114 E6 42 57N 115 18W
Glenore, Australia 94 B3 17 50 S 141 12 E
Glenreagh, Australia 95 E5 30 2 S 153 1 E
Glenrock, U.S.A. 114 E11 42 52N 105 52W
Glenrothes, U.K. 14 E5 56 12N 3 10W
Glens Falls, U.S.A. 111 C11 43 19N 73 39W
Glenside, U.S.A. 111 F9 40 6N 75 9W
Glenties, Ireland 15 B3 54 49N 8 16W
Glenville, U.S.A. 108 F5 38 56N 80 50W
Glenwood, Canada 103 C9 49 0N 54 58W
Glenwood, Ark., U.S.A. 113 H8 34 20N 93 33W
Glenwood, Iowa, U.S.A. 112 E7 41 3N 95 45W
Glenwood, Minn., U.S.A. 112 C7 45 39N 95 23W
Glenwood, Wash., U.S.A. 116 D5 46 1N 121 17W
Glenwood Springs, U.S.A. 114 G10 39 33N 107 19W
Glettinganes, Iceland 8 D7 65 30N 13 37W
Glifádha, Greece 38 D5 37 52N 23 45 E
Glimåkra, Sweden 11 H8 56 19N 14 7 E
Glina, Croatia 29 C13 45 20N 16 6 E
Glinojeck, Poland 45 F7 52 49N 20 21 E
Gliwice, Poland 45 H5 50 22N 18 41 E
Globe, U.S.A. 115 K8 33 24N 110 47W
Glodeanu Siliştea, Romania 43 F11 44 50N 26 48 E
Glodeni, Moldova 43 C12 47 45N 27 31 E
Glödnitz, Austria 26 E7 46 53N 14 7 E
Gloggnitz, Austria 26 D8 47 41N 15 56 E
Głogów, Poland 45 G3 51 37N 16 5 E
Głogówek, Poland 45 H4 50 21N 17 53 E
Glomma →, Norway 9 G14 59 12N 10 57 E
Glorieuses, Is., Ind. Oc. 89 A8 11 30 S 47 20 E

Glóssa

Glóssa, Greece 38 B5 39 10N 23 45 E
Glossop, U.K. 12 D6 53 27N 1 56W
Gloucester, Australia 95 E5 32 0 S 151 59 E
Gloucester, U.K. 13 F5 51 53N 2 15W
Gloucester, U.S.A. 111 D14 42 37N 70 40W
Gloucester I., Australia 94 C4 20 0 S 148 30 E
Gloucester Point, U.S.A. 108 G7 37 15N 76 29W
Gloucestershire □, U.K. 13 F5 51 46N 2 15W
Gloversville, U.S.A. 111 C10 43 3N 74 21W
Glovertown, Canada 103 C9 48 40N 54 3W
Głowno, Poland 45 G6 51 59N 19 42 E
Głubczyce, Poland 45 H4 50 13N 17 52 E
Glubokiy, Russia 49 F5 48 35N 40 25 E
Glubokoye = Hlybokaye, Belarus 46 E4 55 10N 27 45 E
Głuchołazy, Poland 45 H4 50 19N 17 24 E
Glücksburg, Germany 24 A5 54 50N 9 33 E
Glückstadt, Germany 24 B5 53 45N 9 25 E
Glukhov = Hlukhiv, Ukraine 47 G7 51 40N 33 58 E
Glusk, Belarus 47 F5 52 53N 28 41 E
Głuszyca, Poland 45 H3 50 41N 16 23 E
Glyngøre, Denmark 11 H2 56 46N 8 52 E
Gmünd, Kärnten, Austria 26 E6 46 54N 13 31 E
Gmünd, Niederösterreich, Austria 26 C8 48 45N 15 0 E
Gmunden, Austria 26 D6 47 55N 13 48 E
Gnarp, Sweden 10 B11 62 3N 17 16 E
Gnesta, Sweden 10 E11 59 3N 17 17 E
Gniew, Poland 44 E5 53 50N 18 50 E
Gniewkowo, Poland 45 F5 52 54N 18 25 E
Gniezno, Poland 45 F4 52 30N 17 35 E
Gnjilane, Kosovo, Yug. 40 D5 42 28N 21 29 E
Gnoien, Germany 24 B8 53 58N 12 41 E
Gnosjö, Sweden 11 G7 57 22N 13 43 E
Gnowangerup, Australia 93 F2 33 58 S 117 59 E
Go Cong, Vietnam 65 G6 10 22N 106 40 E
Gō-no-ura, Japan 55 H4 33 44N 129 40 E
Goa, India 66 M8 15 33N 73 59 E
Goa □, India 66 M8 15 33N 73 59 E
Goalen Hd., Australia 95 F5 36 33 S 150 4 E
Goalpara, India 67 F17 26 10N 90 40 E
Goaltor, India 69 H12 22 43N 87 10 E
Goalundo Ghat, Bangla. 69 H13 23 50N 89 47 E
Goaso, Ghana 82 D4 6 48N 2 30W
Goat Fell, U.K. 14 F3 55 38N 5 11W
Goba, Ethiopia 81 F4 7 1N 39 59 E
Goba, Mozam. 89 D5 26 15 S 32 13 E
Gobabis, Namibia 88 C2 22 30 S 19 0 E
Göbel, Turkey 41 F12 40 0N 28 9 E
Gobi, Asia 56 C6 44 0N 110 0 E
Gobō, Japan 55 H7 33 53N 135 10 E
Gobo, Sudan 81 F3 5 40N 31 10 E
Göçbeyli, Turkey 39 B9 39 13N 27 25 E
Goch, Germany 24 D2 51 41N 6 9 E
Gochas, Namibia 88 C2 24 59 S 18 55 E
Godavari →, India 67 L13 16 25N 82 18 E
Godavari Pt., India 67 L13 17 0N 82 20 E
Godbout, Canada 103 C6 49 20N 67 38W
Godda, India 69 G12 24 50N 87 13 E
Godech, Bulgaria 40 C7 43 1N 23 4 E
Goderich, Canada 102 D3 43 45N 81 41W
Goderville, France 18 C7 49 38N 0 22 E
Godfrey Ra., Australia 93 D2 24 0 S 117 0 E
Godhavn = Qeqertarsuaq, Greenland 4 C5 69 15N 53 38W
Godhra, India 68 H5 22 49N 73 40 E
Gödöllő, Hungary 42 C4 47 38N 19 25 E
Godoy Cruz, Argentina 126 C2 32 56 S 68 52W
Gods →, Canada 102 A1 56 22N 92 51W
Gods L., Canada 102 B1 54 40N 94 15W
Gods River, Canada 105 C10 54 50N 94 5W
Godthåb = Nuuk, Greenland 101 B14 64 10N 51 35W
Godwin Austen = K2, Pakistan 69 B7 35 58N 76 32 E
Goeie Hoop, Kaap die = Good Hope, C. of, S. Africa 88 E2 34 24 S 18 30 E
Goéland, L. au, Canada 102 C4 49 50N 76 48W
Goeree, Neths. 17 C3 51 50N 4 0 E
Goes, Neths. 17 C3 51 30N 3 55 E
Goffstown, U.S.A. 111 C13 43 1N 71 36W
Gogama, Canada 102 C3 47 35N 81 43W
Gogebic, L., U.S.A. 112 B10 46 30N 89 35W
Goggetti, Ethiopia 81 F4 8 11N 38 35 E
Gogolin, Poland 45 H5 50 30N 18 0 E
Gogonou, Benin 83 C5 10 50N 2 50 E
Gogra = Ghaghara →, India 69 G11 25 45N 84 40 E
Gogriâl, Sudan 81 F2 8 30N 28 8 E
Gogti, Ethiopia 81 E5 10 7N 42 51 E
Gohana, India 68 E7 29 8N 76 42 E
Goharganj, India 68 H7 23 1N 77 41 E
Goi →, India 68 H6 22 4N 74 46 E
Goiânia, Brazil 125 G9 16 43 S 49 20W
Goiás, Brazil 125 G8 15 55 S 50 10W
Goiás □, Brazil 125 F9 12 10 S 48 0W
Goio-Erê, Brazil 127 A5 24 12 S 53 1W
Góis, Portugal 34 E2 40 10N 8 6W
Gojam □, Ethiopia 81 E4 10 55N 36 30 E
Gojeb, Wabi →, Ethiopia 81 F4 7 12N 36 40 E
Gojō, Japan 55 G7 34 21N 135 42 E
Gojra, Pakistan 68 D5 31 10N 72 40 E
Gökçeada, Turkey 41 F9 40 10N 25 50 E
Gökçedağ, Turkey 39 B10 39 33N 28 56 E
Gökçen, Turkey 39 C9 38 7N 27 53 E
Gökçeören, Turkey 39 C10 38 37N 28 35 E
Gökçeyazı, Turkey 39 B9 39 40N 27 40 E
Gökırmak →, Turkey 72 B6 41 25N 35 8 E
Gökova, Turkey 39 D10 37 1N 28 17 E
Gökova Körfezi, Turkey 39 E9 36 55N 27 50 E
Göksu →, Turkey 72 D6 36 19N 34 5 E
Göksun, Turkey 72 C7 38 2N 36 30 E
Gokteik, Burma 67 H20 22 26N 97 0 E
Göktepe, Turkey 39 D10 37 25N 28 34 E
Gokurt, Pakistan 68 E2 29 40N 67 26 E
Gokwe, Zimbabwe 89 B4 18 7 S 28 58 E
Gola, India 69 E9 28 3N 80 32 E
Golakganj, India 69 F13 26 8N 89 52 E
Golan Heights = Hagolan, Syria 75 C4 33 0N 35 45 E
Gołańcz, Poland 45 F4 52 57N 17 18 E
Golāshkerd, Iran 71 E8 27 59N 57 16 E
Golaya Pristen = Hola Pristan, Ukraine 47 J7 46 29N 32 32 E
Gölbaşı, Adiyaman, Turkey 72 D7 37 43N 37 25 E
Gölbaşı, Ankara, Turkey 72 C5 39 47N 32 49 E
Golchikha, Russia 4 B12 71 45N 83 30 E
Golconda, U.S.A. 114 F5 40 58N 117 30W
Gölcük, Kocaeli, Turkey 41 F13 40 42N 29 48 E
Gölcük, Niğde, Turkey 72 C6 38 14N 34 47 E
Gold, U.S.A. 110 E7 41 52N 77 50W
Gold Beach, U.S.A. 114 E1 42 25N 124 25W
Gold Coast, W. Afr. 83 E4 4 0N 1 40W
Gold Hill, U.S.A. 114 E2 42 26N 123 3W
Gold River, Canada 104 D3 49 46N 126 3W
Gołdap, Poland 44 D9 54 19N 22 18 E
Goldberg, Germany 24 B8 53 35N 12 4 E
Golden, Canada 104 C5 51 20N 116 59W
Golden B., N.Z. 91 J4 40 40 S 172 50 E
Golden Gate, U.S.A. 114 H2 37 54N 122 30W
Golden Hinde, Canada 104 D3 49 40N 125 44W
Golden Lake, Canada 110 A7 45 34N 77 21W
Golden Vale, Ireland 15 D3 52 33N 8 17W
Goldendale, U.S.A. 114 D3 45 49N 120 50W
Goldfield, U.S.A. 115 H5 37 42N 117 14W
Goldsand L., Canada 105 B8 57 2N 101 8W
Goldsboro, U.S.A. 109 H7 35 23N 77 59W
Goldsmith, U.S.A. 113 K3 31 59N 102 37W
Goldsworthy, Australia 92 D2 20 21 S 119 30 E
Goldthwaite, U.S.A. 113 K5 31 27N 98 34W
Golegã, Portugal 35 F2 39 24N 8 29W
Goleniów, Poland 44 E1 53 35N 14 50 E
Golestānak, Iran 71 D7 30 36N 54 14 E
Goleta, U.S.A. 117 L7 34 27N 119 50W
Golfito, Costa Rica 120 E3 8 41N 83 5W
Golfo Aranci, Italy 30 B2 40 59N 9 38 E
Gölgeli Dağları, Turkey 39 D10 37 10N 28 55 E
Gölhisar, Turkey 39 D11 37 8N 29 31 E
Goliad, U.S.A. 113 L6 28 40N 97 23W
Golija, Montenegro, Yug. 40 C2 43 5N 18 45 E
Golija, Serbia, Yug. 40 C4 43 22N 20 15 E
Golina, Poland 45 F5 52 15N 18 4 E
Gölköy, Turkey 72 B7 40 41N 37 37 E
Göllersdorf, Austria 26 C9 48 29N 16 7 E
Gölmarmara, Turkey 39 C9 38 42N 27 55 E
Golo →, France 21 F13 42 31N 9 32 E
Gölova, Turkey 39 E12 36 48N 30 5 E
Golpāyegān, Iran 71 C6 33 27N 50 18 E
Gölpazarı, Turkey 72 B4 40 16N 30 18 E
Golra, Pakistan 68 C5 33 37N 72 56 E
Golspie, U.K. 14 D5 57 58N 3 59W
Golub-Dobrzyń, Poland 45 E6 53 7N 19 2 E
Golubac, Serbia, Yug. 40 B5 44 38N 21 38 E
Golyam Perelik, Bulgaria 41 E8 41 36N 24 33 E
Golyama Kamchiya →, Bulgaria 41 C11 43 10N 27 55 E
Goma, Dem. Rep. of the Congo 86 C2 1 37 S 29 10 E
Gomal Pass, Pakistan 68 D3 31 56N 69 20 E
Gomati →, India 69 G10 25 32N 83 11 E
Gombari, Dem. Rep. of the Congo 86 B2 2 45N 29 3 E
Gombe, Nigeria 83 C7 10 19N 11 2 E
Gömbe, Turkey 39 E11 36 33N 29 38 E
Gombe □, Nigeria 83 C7 10 0N 11 10 E
Gombe →, Tanzania 86 C3 4 38 S 31 40 E
Gombi, Nigeria 83 C7 10 12N 12 30 E
Gomel = Homyel, Belarus 47 F6 52 28N 31 0 E
Gomera, Canary Is. 37 F2 28 7N 17 14W
Gómez Palacio, Mexico 118 B4 25 40N 104 0W
Gomīshān, Iran 71 B7 37 4N 54 6 E
Gommern, Germany 24 C7 52 4N 11 50 E
Gomogomo, Indonesia 63 F8 6 39 S 134 43 E
Gomoh, India 67 H15 23 52N 86 10 E
Gomotartsi, Bulgaria 40 B6 44 6N 22 57 E
Gompa = Ganta, Liberia 82 D3 7 15N 8 59W
Gomphi, Greece 38 B3 39 26N 21 36 E
Gonābād, Iran 71 C8 34 15N 58 45 E
Gonaïves, Haiti 121 C5 19 20N 72 42W
Gonâve, G. de la, Haiti 121 C5 19 29N 72 42W
Gonâve, I. de la, Haiti 121 C5 18 45N 73 0W
Gonbad-e Kāvūs, Iran 71 B7 37 20N 55 25 E
Gönc, Hungary 42 B6 48 28N 21 14 E
Gonda, India 69 F9 27 9N 81 58 E
Gondal, India 68 J4 21 58N 70 52 E
Gonder, Ethiopia 81 E4 12 39N 37 30 E
Gonder □, Ethiopia 81 E4 12 55N 37 30 E
Gondia, India 66 J12 21 23N 80 10 E
Gondola, Mozam. 87 F3 19 10 S 33 37 E
Gondomar, Portugal 34 D2 41 10N 8 35W
Gondrecourt-le-Château, France 19 D12 48 31N 5 30 E
Gönen, Balıkesir, Turkey 41 F11 40 6N 27 39 E
Gönen, Isparta, Turkey 39 D12 37 57N 30 31 E
Gönen →, Turkey 41 F11 40 6N 27 39 E
Gong Xian, China 58 C5 28 23N 104 47 E
Gong'an, China 59 B9 30 7N 112 12 E
Gongcheng, China 59 E8 24 50N 110 49 E
Gongga Shan, China 58 C3 29 40N 101 55 E
Gongguan, China 58 G7 21 48N 109 36 E
Gonghe, China 60 C5 36 18N 100 32 E
Gongola →, Nigeria 83 D7 9 30N 12 4 E
Gongolgon, Australia 95 E4 30 21 S 146 54 E
Gongshan, China 58 D2 27 43N 98 29 E
Gongtan, China 58 C7 28 55N 108 20 E
Gongzhuling, China 57 C13 43 30N 124 40 E
Goniadz, Poland 44 E9 53 30N 22 44 E
Goniri, Nigeria 83 C7 11 30N 12 15 E
Gonjo, China 58 B2 30 52N 98 17 E
Gonnesa, Italy 30 C1 39 16N 8 28 E
Gónnos, Greece 38 B4 39 52N 22 29 E
Gonnosfanadiga, Italy 30 C1 39 29N 8 39 E
Gonzaga, Phil. 61 B5 18 16N 122 0 E
Gonzales, Calif., U.S.A. 116 J5 36 30N 121 26W
Gonzales, Tex., U.S.A. 113 L6 29 30N 97 27W
González Chaves, Argentina 126 D3 38 2 S 60 5W
Good Hope, C. of, S. Africa 88 E2 34 24 S 18 30 E
Gooderham, Canada 110 B6 44 54N 78 21W
Goodhouse, S. Africa 88 D2 28 57 S 18 13 E
Gooding, U.S.A. 114 E6 42 56N 114 43W
Goodland, U.S.A. 112 F4 39 21N 101 43W
Goodlow, Canada 104 B4 56 20N 120 8W
Goodooga, Australia 95 D4 29 3 S 147 28 E
Goodsprings, U.S.A. 117 K11 35 49N 115 27W
Goole, U.K. 12 D7 53 42N 0 53W
Goolgowi, Australia 95 E4 33 58 S 145 41 E
Goomalling, Australia 93 F2 31 15 S 116 49 E
Goomeri, Australia 95 D5 26 12 S 152 6 E
Goonda, Mozam. 87 F3 19 48 S 33 57 E
Goondiwindi, Australia 95 D5 28 30 S 150 21 E
Goongarrie, L., Australia 93 F3 30 3 S 121 9 E
Goonyella, Australia 94 C4 21 47 S 147 58 E
Goose →, Canada 103 B7 53 20N 60 35W
Goose Creek, U.S.A. 109 J5 32 59N 80 2W
Goose L., U.S.A. 114 F3 41 56N 120 26W
Gop, India 66 H6 22 5N 69 50 E
Gopalganj, India 69 F11 26 28N 84 30 E
Göppingen, Germany 25 G5 48 42N 9 39 E
Gor, Spain 35 H8 37 23N 2 58W
Góra, Dolnośląskie, Poland 45 G3 51 40N 16 31 E
Góra, Mazowieckie, Poland 45 F7 52 39N 20 6 E
Góra Kalwaria, Poland 45 G8 51 59N 21 14 E
Gorakhpur, India 69 F10 26 47N 83 23 E
Goražde, Bos.-H. 42 G3 43 38N 18 58 E
Gorbatov, Russia 48 B6 56 12N 43 2 E
Gorbea, Peña, Spain 32 B2 43 1N 2 50W
Gorda, U.S.A. 116 K5 35 53N 121 26W
Gorda, Pta., Canary Is. 37 F2 28 45N 18 0W
Gorda, Pta., Nic. 120 D3 14 20N 83 10W
Gordan B., Australia 92 B5 11 35 S 130 10 E
Gördes, Turkey 39 C10 38 54N 28 17 E
Gordon, U.S.A. 112 D3 42 48N 102 12W
Gordon →, Australia 94 G4 42 27 S 145 30 E
Gordon L., Alta., Canada 105 B6 56 30N 110 25W
Gordon L., N.W.T., Canada 104 A6 63 5N 113 11W
Gordonvale, Australia 94 B4 17 5 S 145 50 E
Gore, Ethiopia 81 F4 8 12N 35 32 E
Gore, N.Z. 91 M2 46 5 S 168 58 E
Gore Bay, Canada 102 C3 45 57N 82 28W
Görele, Turkey 73 B8 41 2N 39 0 E
Goreme, Turkey 72 C6 38 35N 34 52 E
Gorey, Ireland 15 D5 52 41N 6 18W
Gorg, Iran 71 D8 29 29N 59 43 E
Gorgān, Iran 71 B7 36 50N 54 29 E
Gorgona, Italy 28 E6 43 26N 9 54 E
Gorgona, I., Colombia 124 C3 3 0N 78 10W
Gorgora, Ethiopia 81 E4 12 15N 37 17 E
Gorgoram, Nigeria 83 C7 12 40N 10 45 E
Gorham, U.S.A. 111 B13 44 23N 71 10W
Gori, Georgia 49 J7 42 0N 44 7 E
Goriganga →, India 69 E9 29 45N 80 23 E
Gorinchem, Neths. 17 C4 51 50N 4 59 E
Goris, Armenia 73 C12 39 31N 46 22 E
Goritsy, Russia 46 D9 57 4N 36 43 E
Gorízia, Italy 29 C10 45 56N 13 37 E
Gorj □, Romania 43 E8 45 5N 23 25 E
Gorki = Horki, Belarus 46 E6 54 17N 30 59 E
Gorki = Nizhniy Novgorod, Russia 48 B7 56 20N 44 0 E
Gorkiy = Nizhniy Novgorod, Russia 48 B7 56 20N 44 0 E
Gorkovskoye Vdkhr., Russia 48 B6 57 2N 43 4 E
Gorlice, Poland 45 J8 49 35N 21 11 E
Görlitz, Germany 24 D10 51 9N 14 58 E
Gorlovka = Horlivka, Ukraine 47 H10 48 19N 38 5 E
Gorman, U.S.A. 117 L8 34 47N 118 51W
Gorna Dzhumayo = Blagoevgrad, Bulgaria 40 D7 42 2N 23 5 E
Gorna Oryakhovitsa, Bulgaria 41 C9 43 7N 25 40 E
Gornja Radgona, Slovenia 29 B13 46 40N 16 2 E
Gornja Tuzla, Bos.-H. 42 F3 44 35N 18 46 E
Gornji Grad, Slovenia 29 B11 46 20N 14 52 E
Gornji Milanovac, Serbia, Yug. 40 B4 44 3N 20 29 E
Gornji Vakuf, Bos.-H. 42 G2 43 57N 17 34 E
Gorno Ablanovo, Bulgaria 41 C9 43 37N 25 43 E
Gorno-Altay □, Russia 50 D9 51 0N 86 0 E
Gorno-Altaysk, Russia 50 D9 51 50N 86 5 E
Gornyatskiy, Russia 49 F5 48 18N 40 56 E
Gornyy, Saratov, Russia 48 E9 51 50N 48 30 E
Gornyy, Sib., Russia 54 B6 44 57N 133 59 E
Gorodenka = Horodenka, Ukraine 47 H3 48 41N 25 29 E
Gorodets, Russia 48 B6 56 38N 43 28 E
Gorodishche = Horodyshche, Ukraine 47 H6 49 17N 31 27 E
Gorodishche, Russia 48 D7 53 13N 45 40 E
Gorodnya = Horodnya, Ukraine 47 G6 51 55N 31 33 E
Gorodok = Haradok, Belarus 46 E6 55 30N 30 3 E
Gorodok = Horodok, Ukraine 47 H2 49 46N 23 32 E
Gorodovikovsk, Russia 49 G5 46 8N 41 58 E
Gorokhov = Horokhiv, Ukraine 47 G3 50 30N 24 45 E
Gorokhovets, Russia 48 B6 56 13N 42 39 E
Gorom Gorom, Burkina Faso 83 C4 14 26N 0 14W
Goromonzi, Zimbabwe 87 F3 17 52 S 31 22 E
Gorong, Kepulauan, Indonesia 63 E8 3 59 S 131 25 E
Gorongose →, Mozam. 89 C5 20 30 S 34 40 E
Gorongoza, Mozam. 87 F3 18 44 S 34 2 E
Gorongoza, Sa. da, Mozam. 87 F3 18 27 S 34 2 E
Gorontalo, Indonesia 63 D6 0 35N 123 5 E
Goronyo, Nigeria 83 C6 13 29N 5 39 E
Górowo Iławeckie, Poland 44 D7 54 17N 20 30 E
Gorron, France 18 D6 48 25N 0 50W
Gorshechnoye, Russia 47 G10 51 31N 38 2 E
Gort, Ireland 15 C3 53 3N 8 49W
Gortis, Greece 36 D6 35 4N 24 58 E
Góry Bystrzyckie, Poland 45 H3 50 16N 16 33 E
Goryachiy Klyuch, Russia 49 H4 44 38N 39 8 E
Gorzkowice, Poland 45 G6 51 13N 19 36 E
Górzno, Poland 45 E6 53 12N 19 38 E
Gorzów Śląski, Poland 45 G5 51 3N 18 22 E
Gorzów Wielkopolski, Poland 45 F2 52 43N 15 15 E
Gosford, Australia 95 E5 33 23 S 151 18 E
Goshen, Calif., U.S.A. 116 J7 36 21N 119 25W
Goshen, Ind., U.S.A. 108 E3 41 35N 85 50W
Goshen, N.Y., U.S.A. 111 E10 41 24N 74 20W
Goshogawara, Japan 54 D10 40 48N 140 27 E
Goslar, Germany 24 D6 51 54N 10 25 E
Gospić, Croatia 29 D12 44 35N 15 23 E
Gosport, U.K. 13 G6 50 48N 1 9W
Gossas, Senegal 82 C1 14 28N 16 0W
Gosse →, Australia 94 B1 19 32 S 134 37 E
Gossi, Mali 83 B4 15 48N 1 20W
Gossinga, Sudan 81 F2 8 36N 25 59 E
Gostivar, Macedonia 40 E4 41 48N 20 57 E
Gostyń, Poland 45 G4 51 50N 17 3 E
Gostynin, Poland 45 F6 52 26N 19 29 E
Göta älv →, Sweden 11 G5 57 42N 11 54 E
Göta kanal, Sweden 11 F9 58 30N 15 58 E
Götaland, Sweden 11 G8 57 30N 14 30 E
Göteborg, Sweden 11 G5 57 43N 11 59 E
Götene, Sweden 11 F7 58 32N 13 30 E
Goteşti, Moldova 43 D13 46 9N 28 10 E
Gotha, Germany 24 E6 50 56N 10 42 E
Gothenburg = Göteborg, Sweden 11 G5 57 43N 11 59 E
Gothenburg, U.S.A. 112 E4 40 56N 100 10W
Gothèye, Niger 83 C5 13 52N 1 34 E
Gotland, Sweden 11 G12 57 30N 18 33 E
Gotlands län □, Sweden 11 G12 57 15N 18 30 E
Gotō-Rettō, Japan 55 H4 32 55N 129 5 E
Gotse Delchev, Bulgaria 40 E7 41 36N 23 46 E
Gotska Sandön, Sweden 9 G18 58 24N 19 15 E
Gōtsu, Japan 55 G6 35 0N 132 14 E
Gott Pk., Canada 104 C4 50 18N 122 16W
Góttero, Monte, Italy 28 D6 44 22N 9 42 E
Göttingen, Germany 24 D5 51 31N 9 55 E
Gottwald = Zmiyev, Ukraine 47 H9 49 39N 36 27 E
Gottwaldov = Zlín, Czech Rep. 27 B10 49 14N 17 40 E
Goubangzi, China 57 D11 41 20N 121 52 E
Gouda, Neths. 17 B4 52 1N 4 42 E
Goúdhoura, Ákra, Greece 36 E8 34 59N 26 6 E
Goudiry, Senegal 82 C2 14 15N 12 45W
Goudoumaria, Niger 83 C7 13 40N 11 10 E
Gouéké, Guinea 82 D3 8 2N 8 43W
Gough I., Atl. Oc. 2 G9 40 10 S 9 45W
Gouin, Rés., Canada 102 C5 48 35N 74 40W
Gouitafla, Ivory C. 82 D3 7 30N 5 53W
Goulburn, Australia 95 E4 34 44 S 149 44 E
Goulburn Is., Australia 94 A1 11 40 S 133 20 E
Goulia, Ivory C. 82 C3 10 1N 7 11W
Goulimine, Morocco 78 C3 28 56N 10 0W
Goumbou, Mali 82 B3 15 2N 7 25W
Gouménissa, Greece 40 F6 40 56N 22 37 E
Goundam, Mali 82 B4 16 27N 3 40W
Goúra, Greece 38 D4 37 56N 22 20 E
Gourbassi, Mali 82 C2 13 24N 11 38W
Gourdon, France 20 D5 44 44N 1 23 E
Gouré, Niger 83 C7 14 0N 10 10 E
Gourin, France 18 D3 48 8N 3 37W
Gourits →, S. Africa 88 E3 34 21 S 21 52 E
Gourma-Rharous, Mali 83 B4 16 55N 1 50W
Goúrnais, Greece 36 D7 35 19N 25 16 E
Gournay-en-Bray, France 19 C8 49 29N 1 44 E
Gourssi, Burkina Faso 82 C4 12 42N 2 37W
Gouverneur, U.S.A. 111 B9 44 20N 75 28W
Gouviá, Greece 36 A3 39 39N 19 50 E
Gouzon, France 19 F9 46 12N 2 14 E
Governador Valadares, Brazil 125 G10 18 15 S 41 57W
Governor's Harbour, Bahamas 120 A4 25 10N 76 14W
Govindgarh, India 69 G9 24 23N 81 18 E
Gowan Ra., Australia 94 D4 25 0 S 145 0 E
Gowanda, U.S.A. 110 D6 42 28N 78 56W
Gower, U.K. 13 F3 51 35N 4 10W
Gowna, L., Ireland 15 C4 53 51N 7 34W
Goya, Argentina 126 B4 29 10 S 59 10W
Göyçay, Azerbaijan 49 K8 40 42N 47 43 E
Goyder Lagoon, Australia 95 D2 27 3 S 138 58 E
Goyllarisquisga, Peru 124 F3 10 31 S 76 24W
Göynük, Antalya, Turkey 39 E12 36 41N 30 33 E
Göynük, Bolu, Turkey 72 B4 40 24N 30 48 E
Goz Beïda, Chad 79 F10 12 10N 21 20 E
Goz Regeb, Sudan 81 D4 16 3N 35 33 E
Gozdnica, Poland 45 G2 51 28N 15 4 E
Gozo, Malta 36 C1 36 3N 14 13 E
Graaff-Reinet, S. Africa 88 E3 32 13 S 24 32 E
Grabo, Ivory C. 82 D3 4 57N 7 30W
Grabow, Germany 24 B7 53 17N 11 34 E
Grabów nad Prosną, Poland 45 G5 51 31N 18 7 E
Gračac, Croatia 29 D12 44 18N 15 57 E
Gračanica, Bos.-H. 42 F3 44 43N 18 18 E
Graçay, France 19 E8 47 10N 1 50 E
Gracias a Dios, C., Honduras 120 D3 15 0N 83 10W
Graciosa, I., Canary Is. 37 E6 29 15N 13 32W
Grad Sofiya □, Bulgaria 40 D7 42 45N 23 20 E
Gradac, Montenegro, Yug. 40 C3 43 23N 19 9 E
Gradačac, Bos.-H. 42 F3 44 52N 18 26 E
Gradeška Planina, Macedonia 40 E6 41 30N 22 15 E
Gradets, Bulgaria 41 D10 42 46N 26 30 E
Gradišče, Slovenia 29 B12 46 37N 15 50 E
Grădiştea de Munte, Romania 43 E8 45 37N 23 13 E
Grado, Italy 29 C10 45 40N 13 23 E
Grado, Spain 34 B4 43 23N 6 4W
Grady, U.S.A. 113 H3 34 49N 103 19W
Graeca, Lacul, Romania 43 F11 44 5N 26 10 E
Grafenau, Germany 25 G9 48 51N 13 22 E
Gräfenberg, Germany 25 F7 49 39N 11 14 E
Grafham Water, U.K. 13 E7 52 19N 0 18W
Grafton, Australia 95 D5 29 38 S 152 58 E
Grafton, N. Dak., U.S.A. 112 A6 48 25N 97 25W
Grafton, W. Va., U.S.A. 108 F5 39 21N 80 2W
Graham, Canada 102 C1 49 20N 90 30W
Graham, U.S.A. 113 J5 33 6N 98 35W
Graham, Mt., U.S.A. 115 K9 32 42N 109 52W
Graham Bell, Ostrov = Greem-Bell, Ostrov, Russia 50 A7 81 0N 62 0 E
Graham I., Canada 104 C2 53 40N 132 30W
Graham Land, Antarctica 5 C17 65 0 S 64 0W
Grahamstown, S. Africa 88 E4 33 19 S 26 31 E
Grahamsville, U.S.A. 111 E10 41 51N 74 33W
Grahovo, Montenegro, Yug. 40 D2 42 40N 18 40 E
Graie, Alpi, Europe 21 C11 45 30N 7 10 E
Grain Coast, W. Afr. 82 E3 4 20N 10 0W
Grajaú, Brazil 125 E9 5 50 S 46 4W
Grajaú →, Brazil 125 D10 3 41 S 44 48W
Grajewo, Poland 44 E9 53 39N 22 30 E
Gramada, Bulgaria 40 C6 43 49N 22 39 E
Gramat, France 20 D5 44 48N 1 43 E
Grammichele, Italy 31 E7 37 13N 14 38 E
Grámmos, Óros, Greece 40 F4 40 18N 20 47 E
Grampian, U.S.A. 110 F6 40 58N 78 37W
Grampian Highlands = Grampian Mts., U.K. 14 E5 56 50N 4 0W
Grampian Mts., U.K. 14 E5 56 50N 4 0W
Grampians, The, Australia 95 F3 37 0 S 142 20 E
Gramsh, Albania 40 F4 40 52N 20 12 E
Gran Canaria, Canary Is. 37 G4 27 55N 15 35W
Gran Chaco, S. Amer. 126 B3 25 0 S 61 0W
Gran Paradiso, Italy 28 C4 45 33N 7 17 E
Gran Sasso d'Itália, Italy 29 F10 42 27N 13 42 E
Granada, Nic. 120 D2 11 58N 86 0W
Granada, Spain 35 H7 37 10N 3 35W
Granada, U.S.A. 113 F3 38 4N 102 19W
Granada □, Spain 35 H7 37 18N 3 0W
Granadilla de Abona, Canary Is. 37 F3 28 7N 16 33W
Granard, Ireland 15 C4 53 47N 7 30W
Granbury, U.S.A. 113 J6 32 27N 97 47W
Granby, Canada 102 C5 45 25N 72 45W
Granby, U.S.A. 114 F11 40 5N 105 56W
Grand →, Canada 110 D5 42 51N 79 34W
Grand →, Mo., U.S.A. 112 F8 39 23N 93 7W
Grand →, S. Dak., U.S.A. 112 C4 45 40N 100 45W
Grand Bahama, Bahamas 120 A4 26 40N 78 30W
Grand Bank, Canada 103 C8 47 6N 55 48W
Grand Bassam, Ivory C. 82 D4 5 10N 3 49W
Grand Béréby, Ivory C. 82 E3 4 38N 6 55W
Grand-Bourg, Guadeloupe 121 C7 15 53N 61 19W
Grand Canal = Yun Ho →, China 57 E9 39 10N 117 10 E
Grand Canyon, U.S.A. 115 H7 36 3N 112 9W
Grand Canyon National Park, U.S.A. 115 H7 36 15N 112 30W
Grand Cayman, Cayman Is. 120 C3 19 20N 81 20W
Grand Centre, Canada 105 C6 54 25N 110 13W
Grand Cess, Liberia 82 E3 4 40N 8 12W
Grand Coulee, U.S.A. 114 C4 47 57N 119 0W
Grand Coulee Dam, U.S.A. 114 C4 47 57N 118 59W
Grand Erg Occidental, Algeria 78 B6 30 20N 1 0 E
Grand Erg Oriental, Algeria 78 B7 30 0N 6 30 E
Grand Falls, Canada 103 C6 47 3N 67 44W
Grand Falls-Windsor, Canada 103 C8 48 56N 55 40W
Grand Forks, Canada 104 D5 49 0N 118 30W
Grand Forks, U.S.A. 112 B6 47 55N 97 3W
Grand Gorge, U.S.A. 111 D10 42 21N 74 29W
Grand Haven, U.S.A. 108 D2 43 4N 86 13W
Grand I., Mich., U.S.A. 108 B2 46 31N 86 40W
Grand I., N.Y., U.S.A. 110 D6 43 0N 78 58W
Grand Island, U.S.A. 112 E5 40 55N 98 21W
Grand Isle, La., U.S.A. 113 L9 29 14N 90 0W
Grand Isle, Vt., U.S.A. 111 B11 44 43N 73 18W
Grand Junction, U.S.A. 115 G9 39 4N 108 33W
Grand L., N.B., Canada 103 C6 45 57N 66 7W
Grand L., Nfld., Canada 103 C8 49 0N 57 30W
Grand L., Nfld., Canada 103 B7 53 40N 60 30W
Grand L., U.S.A. 113 L8 29 55N 92 47W
Grand Lahou, Ivory C. 82 D3 5 10N 5 5W
Grand Lake, U.S.A. 114 F11 40 15N 105 49W
Grand-Lieu, L. de, France 18 E5 47 6N 1 40W
Grand Manan I., Canada 103 D6 44 45N 66 52W
Grand Marais, Canada 112 B9 47 45N 90 25W
Grand Marais, U.S.A. 108 B3 46 40N 85 59W
Grand-Mère, Canada 102 C5 46 36N 72 40W
Grand Popo, Benin 83 D5 6 15N 1 57 E
Grand Portage, U.S.A. 112 B10 47 58N 89 41W
Grand Prairie, U.S.A. 113 J6 32 47N 97 0W
Grand Rapids, Canada 105 C9 53 12N 99 19W
Grand Rapids, Mich., U.S.A. 108 D2 42 58N 85 40W
Grand Rapids, Minn., U.S.A. 112 B8 47 14N 93 31W
Grand St-Bernard, Col du, Europe 25 K3 45 50N 7 10 E
Grand Teton, U.S.A. 114 E8 43 54N 111 50W
Grand Teton National Park, U.S.A. 114 D8 43 50N 110 50W
Grand Union Canal, U.K. 13 E7 52 7N 0 53W
Grand View, Canada 105 C8 51 10N 100 42W
Grandas de Salime, Spain 34 B4 43 13N 6 53W
Grande →, Jujuy, Argentina 126 A2 24 20 S 65 2W
Grande →, Mendoza, Argentina 126 D2 36 52 S 69 45W
Grande →, Bolivia 124 G6 15 51 S 64 39W
Grande →, Bahia, Brazil 125 F10 11 30 S 44 30W
Grande →, Minas Gerais, Brazil 125 H8 20 6 S 51 4W
Grande, B., Argentina 128 G3 50 30 S 68 20W
Grande, Rio →, U.S.A. 113 N6 25 58N 97 9W
Grande Baleine, R. de la →, Canada 102 A4 55 16N 77 47W
Grande Cache, Canada 104 C5 53 53N 119 8W
Grande-Entrée, Canada 103 C7 47 30N 61 40W
Grande Prairie, Canada 104 B5 55 10N 118 50W
Grande-Rivière, Canada 103 C7 48 26N 64 30W
Grande-Vallée, Canada 103 C6 49 14N 65 8W
Grandfalls, U.S.A. 113 K3 31 20N 102 51W
Grândola, Portugal 35 G2 38 12N 8 35W
Grandpré, France 19 C11 49 20N 4 50 E
Grandview, U.S.A. 114 C4 46 15N 119 54W
Grandvilliers, France 19 C8 49 40N 1 57 E
Graneros, Chile 126 C1 34 5 S 70 45W
Grangemouth, U.K. 14 E5 56 1N 3 42W
Granger, U.S.A. 114 F9 41 35N 109 58W
Grängesberg, Sweden 10 D9 60 6N 15 1 E
Grangeville, U.S.A. 114 D5 45 56N 116 7W
Granisle, Canada 104 C3 54 53N 126 13W
Granite City, U.S.A. 112 F9 38 42N 90 9W
Granite Falls, U.S.A. 112 C7 44 49N 95 33W
Granite L., Canada 103 C8 48 8N 57 5W
Granite Mt., U.S.A. 117 M10 33 5N 116 28W

Herreid

Hannibal, *N.Y., U.S.A.* **111 C8** 43 19N 76 35W
Hannik, *Sudan* **80 D3** 18 12N 32 20 E
Hannover, *Germany* **24 C5** 52 22N 9 46 E
Hanö, *Sweden* **11 H8** 56 1N 14 50 E
Hanöbukten, *Sweden* **11 J8** 55 35N 14 30 E
Hanoi, *Vietnam* **58 G5** 21 5N 105 55 E
Hanover = Hannover, *Germany* **24 C5** 52 22N 9 46 E
Hanover, *Canada* **102 D3** 44 9N 81 2W
Hanover, *S. Africa* **88 E3** 31 4 S 24 29 E
Hanover, *N.H., U.S.A.* **111 C12** 43 42N 72 17W
Hanover, *Ohio, U.S.A.* **110 F2** 40 4N 82 16W
Hanover, *Pa., U.S.A.* **108 F7** 39 48N 76 59W
Hanover, I., *Chile* **128 G2** 51 0 S 74 50W
Hansdiha, *India* **69 G12** 24 36N 87 5 E
Hanshou, *China* **59 C8** 28 56N 111 50 E
Hansi, *India* **68 E6** 29 10N 75 57 E
Hanson, L., *Australia* **95 E2** 31 0 S 136 15 E
Hanstholm, *Denmark* **11 G2** 57 7N 8 36 E
Hantsavichy, *Belarus* **47 F4** 52 49N 26 30 E
Hanumangarh, *India* **68 E6** 29 35N 74 19 E
Hanyin, *China* **58 A7** 32 54N 108 28 E
Hanyuan, *China* **58 C4** 29 21N 102 40 E
Hanzhong, *China* **56 H4** 33 10N 107 1 E
Hanzhuang, *China* **57 G9** 34 33N 117 23 E
Haora, *India* **69 H13** 22 37N 88 20 E
Haoxue, *China* **59 B9** 30 3N 112 24 E
Haparanda, *Sweden* **8 D21** 65 52N 24 8 E
Happy, *U.S.A.* **113 H4** 34 45N 101 52W
Happy Camp, *U.S.A.* **114 F2** 41 48N 123 23W
Happy Valley-Goose Bay, *Canada* **103 B7** 53 15N 60 20W
Hapsu, *N. Korea* **57 D15** 41 13N 128 51 E
Hapur, *India* **68 E7** 28 45N 77 45 E
Ḥaql, *Si. Arabia* **75 F3** 29 10N 34 58 E
Har, *Indonesia* **63 F8** 5 16 S 133 14 E
Har-Ayrag, *Mongolia* **56 B5** 45 47N 109 16 E
Har Hu, *China* **60 C4** 38 20N 97 38 E
Har Us Nuur, *Mongolia* **60 B4** 48 0N 92 0 E
Har Yehuda, *Israel* **75 D3** 31 35N 34 57 E
Ḥaraḍ, *Si. Arabia* **74 C4** 24 22N 49 0 E
Haradok, *Belarus* **46 E6** 55 30N 30 3 E
Häradsbäck, *Sweden* **11 H8** 56 32N 14 26 E
Haranomachi, *Japan* **54 F10** 37 38N 140 58 E
Harare, *Zimbabwe* **87 F3** 17 43 S 31 2 E
Harat, *Eritrea* **81 D4** 16 5N 39 26 E
Harbin, *China* **57 B14** 45 48N 126 40 E
Harbiye, *Turkey* **72 D7** 36 10N 36 8 E
Harbo, *Sweden* **10 D11** 60 7N 17 12 E
Harboør, *Denmark* **11 H2** 56 38N 8 10 E
Harbor Beach, *U.S.A.* **110 C2** 43 51N 82 39W
Harbour Breton, *Canada* **103 C8** 47 29N 55 50W
Harbour Deep, *Canada* **103 B8** 50 25N 56 32W
Harburg, *Germany* **24 B5** 53 27N 9 58 E
Hårby, *Denmark* **11 J4** 55 13N 10 7 E
Harda, *India* **68 H7** 22 27N 77 5 E
Hardangerfjorden, *Norway* **9 F12** 60 5N 6 0 E
Hardangervidda, *Norway* **9 F12** 60 7N 7 20 E
Hardap Dam, *Namibia* **88 C2** 24 32 S 17 50 E
Hardenberg, *Neths.* **17 B6** 52 34N 6 37 E
Harderwijk, *Neths.* **17 B5** 52 21N 5 38 E
Hardey →, *Australia* **92 D2** 22 45 S 116 8 E
Hardin, *U.S.A.* **114 D10** 45 44N 107 37W
Harding, *S. Africa* **89 E4** 30 35 S 29 55 E
Harding Ra., *Australia* **92 C3** 16 17 S 124 55 E
Hardisty, *Canada* **104 C6** 52 40N 111 18W
Hardoi, *India* **69 F9** 27 26N 80 6 E
Hardwar = Haridwar, *India* **68 E8** 29 58N 78 9 E
Hardwick, *U.S.A.* **111 B12** 44 30N 72 22W
Hardy, Pen., *Chile* **128 H3** 55 30 S 68 20W
Hare B., *Canada* **103 B8** 51 15N 55 45W
Hareid, *Norway* **9 E12** 62 22N 6 1 E
Haren, *Germany* **24 C3** 52 47N 7 13 E
Harer, *Ethiopia* **81 F5** 9 20N 42 8 E
Harerge ☐, *Ethiopia* **81 F5** 7 12N 42 0 E
Hareto, *Ethiopia* **81 F4** 9 23N 37 6 E
Harfleur, *France* **18 C7** 49 30N 0 10 E
Hargeisa, *Somali Rep.* **74 F3** 9 30N 44 2 E
Harghita ☐, *Romania* **43 D10** 46 30N 25 30 E
Harghita, Munţii, *Romania* **43 D10** 46 25N 25 35 E
Hargshamn, *Sweden* **10 D12** 60 12N 18 30 E
Hari →, *Indonesia* **62 E2** 1 16 S 104 5 E
Haria, *Canary Is.* **37 E6** 29 8N 13 32W
Haridwar, *India* **68 E8** 29 58N 78 9 E
Harim, Jabal al, *Oman* **71 E8** 25 58N 56 14 E
Haringhata →, *Bangla.* **67 J16** 22 0N 89 58 E
Harīrūd →, *Asia* **66 A2** 37 24N 60 38 E
Härjedalen, *Sweden* **10 B7** 62 22N 13 5 E
Harlan, *Iowa, U.S.A.* **112 E7** 41 39N 95 19W
Harlan, *Ky., U.S.A.* **109 G4** 36 51N 83 19W
Hârlău, *Romania* **43 C11** 47 23N 26 55 E
Harlech, *U.K.* **12 E3** 52 52N 4 6W
Harlem, *U.S.A.* **114 B9** 48 32N 108 47W
Hårlev, *Denmark* **11 J6** 55 21N 12 14 E
Harlingen, *Neths.* **17 A5** 53 11N 5 25 E
Harlingen, *U.S.A.* **113 M6** 26 12N 97 42W
Harlow, *U.K.* **13 F8** 51 46N 0 8 E
Harlowton, *U.S.A.* **114 C9** 46 26N 109 50W
Harmancık, *Turkey* **39 B11** 39 41N 29 9 E
Harmånger, *Sweden* **10 C11** 61 55N 17 20 E
Harmil, *Eritrea* **81 D5** 16 30N 40 10 E
Harnai, *Pakistan* **68 D2** 30 6N 67 56 E
Harney Basin, *U.S.A.* **114 E4** 43 30N 119 0W
Harney L., *U.S.A.* **114 E4** 43 14N 119 8W
Harney Peak, *U.S.A.* **112 D3** 43 52N 103 32W
Härnön, *Sweden* **10 B12** 62 36N 18 0 E
Härnösand, *Sweden* **10 B11** 62 38N 17 55 E
Haro, *Spain* **32 C2** 42 35N 2 55W
Haroldswick, *U.K.* **14 A8** 60 48N 0 50W
Harp L., *Canada* **103 A7** 55 5N 61 50W
Harper, *Liberia* **82 E3** 4 25N 7 43W
Harplinge, *Sweden* **11 H6** 56 45N 12 45 E
Harr, *Mauritania* **82 B2** 15 20N 12 28W
Harrai, *India* **69 H8** 22 37N 79 13 E
Harrand, *Pakistan* **68 E4** 29 28N 70 3 E
Ḥarrat Khaybar, *Si. Arabia* **80 B5** 25 30N 39 45 E
Ḥarrat Nawāṣīf, *Si. Arabia* **80 C5** 21 20N 42 10 E
Harricana →, *Canada* **102 B4** 50 56N 79 32W
Harriman, *U.S.A.* **109 H3** 35 56N 84 33W
Harrington Harbour, *Canada* **103 B8** 50 31N 59 30W
Harris, *U.K.* **14 D2** 57 50N 6 55W
Harris, Sd. of, *U.K.* **14 D1** 57 44N 7 6W
Harris L., *Australia* **95 E2** 31 10 S 135 10 E
Harris Pt., *Canada* **110 C2** 43 6N 82 9W
Harrisburg, *Ill., U.S.A.* **113 G10** 37 44N 88 32W
Harrisburg, *Nebr., U.S.A.* **112 E3** 41 33N 103 44W
Harrisburg, *Pa., U.S.A.* **110 F8** 40 16N 76 53W
Harrismith, *S. Africa* **89 D4** 28 15 S 29 8 E
Harrison, *Ark., U.S.A.* **113 G8** 36 14N 93 7W
Harrison, *Maine, U.S.A.* **111 B14** 44 7N 70 39W
Harrison, *Nebr., U.S.A.* **112 D3** 42 41N 103 53W
Harrison, C., *Canada* **103 B8** 54 55N 57 55W
Harrison L., *Canada* **104 D4** 49 33N 121 50W
Harrisonburg, *U.S.A.* **108 F6** 38 27N 78 52W
Harrisonville, *U.S.A.* **112 F7** 38 39N 94 21W
Harriston, *Canada* **110 C4** 43 57N 80 53W
Harrisville, *Mich., U.S.A.* **110 B1** 44 39N 83 17W
Harrisville, *N.Y., U.S.A.* **111 B9** 44 9N 75 19W
Harrisville, *Pa., U.S.A.* **110 E5** 41 8N 80 0W
Harrodsburg, *U.S.A.* **108 G3** 37 46N 84 51W
Harrogate, *U.K.* **12 C6** 54 0N 1 33W
Harrow ☐, *U.K.* **13 F7** 51 35N 0 21W
Harrowsmith, *Canada* **111 B8** 44 24N 76 40W
Harry S. Truman Reservoir, *U.S.A.* **112 F7** 38 16N 93 24W
Harsefeld, *Germany* **24 B5** 53 27N 9 30 E
Harsewinkel, *Germany* **24 D4** 51 56N 8 14 E
Harsīn, *Iran* **70 C5** 34 18N 47 33 E
Hârşova, *Romania* **43 F12** 44 40N 27 59 E
Harstad, *Norway* **8 B17** 68 48N 16 30 E
Harsud, *India* **68 H7** 22 6N 76 44 E
Hart, *U.S.A.* **108 D2** 43 42N 86 22W
Hart, L., *Australia* **95 E2** 31 10 S 136 25 E
Hartbees →, *S. Africa* **88 D3** 28 45 S 20 32 E
Hartberg, *Austria* **26 D8** 47 17N 15 58 E
Hartford, *Conn., U.S.A.* **111 E12** 41 46N 72 41W
Hartford, *Ky., U.S.A.* **108 G2** 37 27N 86 55W
Hartford, *S. Dak., U.S.A.* **112 D6** 43 38N 96 57W
Hartford, *Wis., U.S.A.* **112 D10** 43 19N 88 22W
Hartford City, *U.S.A.* **108 E3** 40 27N 85 22W
Hartland, *Canada* **103 C6** 46 20N 67 32W
Hartland Pt., *U.K.* **13 F3** 51 1N 4 32W
Hartlepool, *U.K.* **12 C6** 54 42N 1 13W
Hartlepool ☐, *U.K.* **12 C6** 54 42N 1 17W
Hartley Bay, *Canada* **104 C3** 53 25N 129 15W
Hartmannberge, *Namibia* **88 B1** 17 0 S 13 0 E
Hartney, *Canada* **105 D8** 49 30N 100 35W
Hârtop, *Moldova* **43 D13** 46 39N 28 40 E
Harts →, *S. Africa* **88 D3** 28 24 S 24 17 E
Hartselle, *U.S.A.* **109 H2** 34 27N 86 56W
Hartshorne, *U.S.A.* **113 H7** 34 51N 95 34W
Hartstown, *U.S.A.* **110 E4** 41 33N 80 23W
Hartsville, *U.S.A.* **109 H5** 34 23N 80 4W
Hartswater, *S. Africa* **88 D3** 27 34 S 24 43 E
Hartwell, *U.S.A.* **109 H4** 34 21N 82 56W
Harunabad, *Pakistan* **68 E5** 29 35N 73 8 E
Harvand, *Iran* **71 D7** 28 25N 55 43 E
Harvey, *Australia* **93 F2** 33 5 S 115 54 E
Harvey, *Ill., U.S.A.* **108 E2** 41 36N 87 50W
Harvey, *N. Dak., U.S.A.* **112 B5** 47 47N 99 56W
Harwich, *U.K.* **13 F9** 51 56N 1 17 E
Haryana ☐, *India* **68 E7** 29 0N 76 10 E
Haryn →, *Belarus* **47 F4** 52 7N 27 17 E
Harz, *Germany* **24 D6** 51 38N 10 44 E
Harzgerode, *Germany* **24 D7** 51 38N 11 8 E
Hasa ☐, *Si. Arabia* **71 E6** 25 50N 49 0 E
Hasaheisa, *Sudan* **81 E3** 14 44N 33 20 E
Ḥasanābād, *Iran* **71 C7** 32 8N 52 44 E
Hasdo →, *India* **69 J10** 21 44N 82 44 E
Haselünne, *Germany* **24 C3** 52 40N 7 29 E
Hashimoto, *Japan* **55 G7** 34 19N 135 37 E
Hashtjerd, *Iran* **71 C6** 35 52N 50 40 E
Haskell, *U.S.A.* **113 J5** 33 10N 99 44W
Hasköy, *Turkey* **41 E10** 41 38N 26 52 E
Haslach, *Germany* **25 G4** 48 16N 8 5 E
Hasle, *Denmark* **11 J8** 55 11N 14 44 E
Haslemere, *U.K.* **13 F7** 51 5N 0 43W
Haslev, *Denmark* **11 J5** 55 18N 11 57 E
Hasparren, *France* **20 E2** 43 24N 1 18W
Hassa, *Turkey* **72 D7** 36 48N 36 29 E
Hassela, *Sweden* **10 B10** 62 7N 16 42 E
Hasselt, *Belgium* **17 D5** 50 56N 5 21 E
Hassfurt, *Germany* **25 E6** 50 2N 10 30 E
Hassi Messaoud, *Algeria* **78 B7** 31 51N 6 1 E
Hässleholm, *Sweden* **11 H7** 56 10N 13 46 E
Hassloch, *Germany* **25 F4** 49 22N 8 16 E
Hästholmen, *Sweden* **11 F8** 58 17N 14 38 E
Hastings, *N.Z.* **91 H6** 39 39 S 176 52 E
Hastings, *U.K.* **13 G8** 50 51N 0 35 E
Hastings, *Mich., U.S.A.* **108 D3** 42 39N 85 17W
Hastings, *Minn., U.S.A.* **112 C8** 44 44N 92 51W
Hastings, *Nebr., U.S.A.* **112 E5** 40 35N 98 23W
Hastings Ra., *Australia* **95 E5** 31 15 S 152 14 E
Hästveda, *Sweden* **11 H7** 56 17N 13 55 E
Hat Yai, *Thailand* **65 J3** 7 1N 100 27 E
Hatanbulag = Ergel, *Mongolia* **56 C5** 43 8N 109 5 E
Hatay = Antalya, *Turkey* **72 D4** 36 52N 30 45 E
Hatch, *U.S.A.* **115 K10** 32 40N 107 9W
Hatchet L., *Canada* **105 B8** 58 36N 103 40W
Haţeg, *Romania* **42 E7** 45 36N 22 55 E
Hateruma-Shima, *Japan* **55 M1** 24 3N 123 47 E
Hatfield P.O., *Australia* **95 E3** 33 54 S 143 49 E
Hatgal, *Mongolia* **60 A5** 50 26N 100 9 E
Hathras, *India* **68 F8** 27 36N 78 6 E
Hatia, *Bangla.* **67 H17** 22 30N 91 5 E
Ḥāṭibah, Ra's, *Si. Arabia* **80 C4** 21 55N 38 57 E
Hato Mayor, *Dom. Rep.* **121 C6** 18 46N 69 15W
Hatta, *India* **69 G8** 24 7N 79 36 E
Hattah, *Australia* **95 E3** 34 48 S 142 17 E
Hatteras, C., *U.S.A.* **109 H8** 35 14N 75 32W
Hattiesburg, *U.S.A.* **113 K10** 31 20N 89 17W
Hatvan, *Hungary* **42 C4** 47 40N 19 45 E
Hau Bon = Cheo Reo, *Vietnam* **62 B3** 13 25N 108 28 E
Hau Duc, *Vietnam* **64 E7** 15 20N 108 13 E
Haugesund, *Norway* **9 G11** 59 23N 5 13 E
Haukipudas, *Finland* **8 D21** 65 12N 25 20 E
Haultain →, *Canada* **105 B7** 55 51N 106 46W
Hauraki G., *N.Z.* **91 G5** 36 35 S 175 5 E
Hausruck, *Austria* **26 C6** 48 6N 13 30 E
Haut Atlas, *Morocco* **78 B4** 32 30N 5 0W
Haut-Rhin ☐, *France* **19 E14** 48 0N 7 15 E
Haut-Zaïre = Orientale ☐, *Dem. Rep. of the Congo* **86 B2** 2 20N 26 0 E
Haute-Corse ☐, *France* **21 F13** 42 30N 9 30 E
Haute-Garonne ☐, *France* **20 E5** 43 30N 1 30 E
Haute-Loire ☐, *France* **20 C7** 45 5N 3 50 E
Haute-Marne ☐, *France* **19 D12** 48 10N 5 20 E
Haute-Normandie ☐, *France* **18 C7** 49 20N 1 0 E
Haute-Saône ☐, *France* **19 E13** 47 45N 6 10 E
Haute-Savoie ☐, *France* **21 C10** 46 0N 6 20 E
Haute-Vienne ☐, *France* **20 C5** 45 50N 1 10 E
Hautes-Alpes ☐, *France* **21 D10** 44 42N 6 20 E
Hautes Fagnes = Hohe Venn, *Belgium* **17 D6** 50 30N 6 5 E
Hautes-Pyrénées ☐, *France* **20 F4** 43 0N 0 10 E
Hauteville-Lompnès, *France* **21 C9** 45 58N 5 36 E
Hautmont, *France* **19 B10** 50 15N 3 55 E
Hauts-de-Seine ☐, *France* **19 D9** 48 52N 2 15 E
Hauts Plateaux, *Algeria* **76 C4** 35 0N 1 0 E
Hauzenberg, *Germany* **25 G9** 48 40N 13 37 E
Havana = La Habana, *Cuba* **120 B3** 23 8N 82 22W
Havana, *U.S.A.* **112 E9** 40 18N 90 4W
Havant, *U.K.* **13 G7** 50 51N 0 58W
Havârna, *Romania* **43 B11** 48 4N 26 43 E
Havasu, L., *U.S.A.* **117 L12** 34 18N 114 28W
Havdhem, *Sweden* **11 G12** 57 10N 18 20 E
Havel →, *Germany* **24 C8** 52 50N 12 3 E
Havelian, *Pakistan* **68 B5** 34 2N 73 10 E
Havelock, *Canada* **102 D4** 44 26N 77 53W
Havelock, *N.Z.* **91 J4** 41 17 S 173 48 E
Havelock, *U.S.A.* **109 H7** 34 53N 76 54W
Haverfordwest, *U.K.* **13 F3** 51 48N 4 58W
Haverhill, *U.S.A.* **111 D13** 42 47N 71 5W
Haverstraw, *U.S.A.* **111 E11** 41 12N 73 58W
Håverud, *Sweden* **11 F6** 58 50N 12 28 E
Havirga, *Mongolia* **56 B7** 45 41N 113 5 E
Havířov, *Czech Rep.* **27 B11** 49 46N 18 20 E
Havlíčkův Brod, *Czech Rep.* **26 B8** 49 36N 15 33 E
Havneby, *Denmark* **11 J2** 55 5N 8 34 E
Havran, *Turkey* **39 B9** 39 33N 27 6 E
Havre, *U.S.A.* **114 B9** 48 33N 109 41W
Havre-Aubert, *Canada* **103 C7** 47 12N 61 56W
Havre-St.-Pierre, *Canada* **103 B7** 50 18N 63 33W
Havsa, *Turkey* **41 E10** 41 31N 26 48 E
Havza, *Turkey* **72 B6** 41 0N 35 35 E
Haw →, *U.S.A.* **109 H6** 35 36N 79 3W
Hawaii ☐, *U.S.A.* **106 H16** 19 30N 156 30W
Hawaii I., *Pac. Oc.* **106 J17** 20 0N 155 0W
Hawaiian Is., *Pac. Oc.* **106 H17** 20 30N 156 0W
Hawaiian Ridge, *Pac. Oc.* **97 E11** 24 0N 165 0W
Hawarden, *U.S.A.* **112 D6** 43 0N 96 29W
Hawea, L., *N.Z.* **91 L2** 44 28 S 169 19 E
Hawera, *N.Z.* **91 H5** 39 35 S 174 19 E
Hawick, *U.K.* **14 F6** 55 26N 2 47W
Hawk Junction, *Canada* **102 C3** 48 5N 84 38W
Hawke B., *N.Z.* **91 H6** 39 25 S 177 20 E
Hawker, *Australia* **95 E2** 31 59 S 138 22 E
Hawkesbury, *Canada* **102 C5** 45 37N 74 37W
Hawkesbury I., *Canada* **104 C3** 53 37N 129 3W
Hawkesbury Pt., *Australia* **94 A1** 11 55 S 134 5 E
Hawkinsville, *U.S.A.* **109 J4** 32 17N 83 28W
Hawley, *Minn., U.S.A.* **112 B6** 46 53N 96 19W
Hawley, *Pa., U.S.A.* **111 E9** 41 28N 75 11W
Ḥawrān, W. →, *Iraq* **70 C4** 33 58N 42 34 E
Hawsh Müssá, *Lebanon* **75 B4** 33 45N 35 55 E
Hawthorne, *U.S.A.* **114 G4** 38 32N 118 38W
Hay, *Australia* **95 E3** 34 30 S 144 51 E
Hay →, *Australia* **94 C2** 24 50 S 138 0 E
Hay →, *Canada* **104 A5** 60 50N 116 26W
Hay, C., *Australia* **92 B4** 14 5 S 129 29 E
Hay I., *Canada* **110 B4** 44 53N 80 58W
Hay L., *Canada* **104 B5** 58 50N 118 50W
Hay-on-Wye, *U.K.* **13 E4** 52 5N 3 8W
Hay River, *Canada* **104 A5** 60 51N 115 44W
Hay Springs, *U.S.A.* **112 D3** 42 41N 102 41W
Haya = Tehoru, *Indonesia* **63 E7** 3 23 S 129 30 E
Hayachine-San, *Japan* **54 E10** 39 34N 141 29 E
Hayange, *France* **19 C13** 49 20N 6 2 E
Haydarlı, *Turkey* **39 C12** 38 16N 30 23 E
Hayden, *U.S.A.* **114 F10** 40 30N 107 16W
Haydon, *Australia* **94 B3** 18 0 S 141 30 E
Hayes, *U.S.A.* **112 C4** 44 23N 101 1W
Hayes →, *Canada* **102 A1** 57 3N 92 12W
Hayes Creek, *Australia* **92 B5** 13 43 S 131 22 E
Hayle, *U.K.* **13 G2** 50 11N 5 26W
Hayling I., *U.K.* **13 G7** 50 48N 0 59W
Haymana, *Turkey* **72 C5** 39 26N 32 31 E
Hayrabolu, *Turkey* **41 E11** 41 12N 27 5 E
Hays, *Canada* **104 C6** 50 6N 111 48W
Hays, *U.S.A.* **112 F5** 38 53N 99 20W
Haysyn, *Ukraine* **47 H5** 48 57N 29 25 E
Hayvoron, *Ukraine* **47 H5** 48 22N 29 52 E
Hayward, *Calif., U.S.A.* **116 H4** 37 40N 122 5W
Hayward, *Wis., U.S.A.* **112 B9** 46 1N 91 29W
Haywards Heath, *U.K.* **13 G7** 51 0N 0 5W
Haẓafon ☐, *Israel* **75 C4** 32 40N 35 20 E
Hazārān, Kūh-e, *Iran* **71 D8** 29 35N 57 20 E
Hazard, *U.S.A.* **108 G4** 37 15N 83 12W
Hazaribag, *India* **69 H11** 23 58N 85 26 E
Hazaribag Road, *India* **69 G11** 24 12N 85 57 E
Hazebrouck, *France* **19 B9** 50 42N 2 31 E
Hazelton, *Canada* **104 B3** 55 20N 127 42W
Hazelton, *U.S.A.* **112 B4** 46 29N 100 17W
Hazen, *U.S.A.* **112 B4** 47 18N 101 38W
Hazlehurst, *Ga., U.S.A.* **109 K4** 31 52N 82 36W
Hazlehurst, *Miss., U.S.A.* **113 K9** 31 52N 90 24W
Hazlet, *U.S.A.* **111 F10** 40 25N 74 12W
Hazleton, *U.S.A.* **111 F9** 40 57N 75 59W
Hazlett, L., *Australia* **92 D4** 21 30 S 128 48 E
Hazro, *Turkey* **70 B4** 38 15N 40 47 E
He Xian, *Anhui, China* **59 B12** 31 45N 118 20 E
He Xian, *Guangxi Zhuangzu, China* **59 E8** 24 27N 111 30 E
Head of Bight, *Australia* **93 F5** 31 30 S 131 25 E
Headlands, *Zimbabwe* **87 F3** 18 15 S 32 2 E
Healdsburg, *U.S.A.* **116 G4** 38 37N 122 52W
Healdton, *U.S.A.* **113 H6** 34 14N 97 29W
Healesville, *Australia* **95 F4** 37 35 S 145 30 E
Heany Junction, *Zimbabwe* **89 C4** 20 6 S 28 54 E
Heard I., *Ind. Oc.* **3 G13** 53 0 S 74 0 E
Hearne, *U.S.A.* **113 K6** 30 53N 96 36W
Hearst, *Canada* **102 C3** 49 40N 83 41W
Heart →, *U.S.A.* **112 B4** 46 46N 100 50W
Heart's Content, *Canada* **103 C9** 47 54N 53 27W
Heath Pt., *Canada* **103 C7** 49 8N 61 40W
Heavener, *U.S.A.* **113 H7** 34 53N 94 36W
Hebbronville, *U.S.A.* **113 M5** 27 18N 98 41W
Hebei ☐, *China* **56 E9** 39 0N 116 0 E
Hebel, *Australia* **95 D4** 28 58 S 147 47 E
Heber, *U.S.A.* **117 N11** 32 44N 115 32W
Heber City, *U.S.A.* **114 F8** 40 31N 111 25W
Heber Springs, *U.S.A.* **113 H9** 35 30N 92 2W
Hebert, *Canada* **105 C7** 50 30N 107 10W
Hebgen L., *U.S.A.* **114 D8** 44 52N 111 20W
Hebi, *China* **56 G8** 35 57N 114 7 E
Hebrides, *U.K.* **6 D4** 57 30N 7 0W
Hebrides, Sea of the, *U.K.* **14 D2** 57 5N 7 0W
Hebron = Al Khalīl, *West Bank* **75 D4** 31 32N 35 6 E
Hebron, *Canada* **101 C13** 58 5N 62 30W
Hebron, *N. Dak., U.S.A.* **112 B3** 46 54N 102 3W
Hebron, *Nebr., U.S.A.* **112 E6** 40 10N 97 35W
Heby, *Sweden* **10 E10** 59 56N 16 53 E
Hecate Str., *Canada* **104 C2** 53 10N 130 30W
Heceta I., *U.S.A.* **104 B2** 55 46N 133 40W
Hechi, *China* **58 E7** 24 40N 108 2 E
Hechingen, *Germany* **25 G4** 48 21N 8 57 E
Hechuan, *China* **58 B6** 30 2N 106 12 E
Hecla, *U.S.A.* **112 C5** 45 53N 98 9W
Hecla I., *Canada* **105 C9** 51 10N 96 43W
Hédé, *France* **18 D5** 48 18N 1 49W
Hede, *Sweden* **10 B7** 62 23N 13 30 E
Hedemora, *Sweden* **10 D9** 60 18N 15 58 E
Hedensted, *Denmark* **11 J3** 55 46N 9 42 E
Hedesunda, *Sweden* **10 D10** 60 24N 17 0 E
Heerde, *Neths.* **17 B6** 52 24N 6 2 E
Heerenveen, *Neths.* **17 B5** 52 57N 5 55 E
Heerhugowaard, *Neths.* **17 B4** 52 40N 4 51 E
Heerlen, *Neths.* **17 D5** 50 55N 5 58 E
Ḥefa, *Israel* **75 C4** 32 46N 35 0 E
Ḥefa ☐, *Israel* **75 C4** 32 40N 35 0 E
Hefei, *China* **59 B11** 31 52N 117 18 E
Hefeng, *China* **59 C8** 29 55N 109 52 E
Hegalig, *Sudan* **81 E3** 14 36N 31 54 E
Hegang, *China* **60 B8** 47 20N 130 19 E
Heiban, *Sudan* **81 E3** 11 13N 30 31 E
Heichengzhen, *China* **56 F4** 36 24N 106 3 E
Heide, *Germany* **24 A5** 54 11N 9 6 E
Heidelberg, *Germany* **25 F4** 49 24N 8 42 E
Heidelberg, *S. Africa* **88 E3** 34 6 S 20 59 E
Heidenau, *Germany* **24 E9** 50 57N 13 52 E
Heidenheim, *Germany* **25 G6** 48 41N 10 9 E
Heijing, *China* **58 E3** 25 22N 101 44 E
Heilbad Heiligenstadt, *Germany* **24 D6** 51 22N 10 8 E
Heilbron, *S. Africa* **89 D4** 27 16 S 27 59 E
Heilbronn, *Germany* **25 F5** 49 9N 9 13 E
Heiligenblut, *Austria* **26 D5** 47 2N 12 51 E
Heiligenhafen, *Germany* **24 A6** 54 22N 10 59 E
Heilongjiang ☐, *China* **60 B7** 48 0N 126 0 E
Heilunkiang = Heilongjiang ☐, *China* **60 B7** 48 0N 126 0 E
Heimaey, *Iceland* **8 E3** 63 26N 20 17W
Heinola, *Finland* **9 F22** 61 13N 26 2 E
Heinsberg, *Germany* **24 D2** 51 3N 6 5 E
Heinze Kyun, *Burma* **64 E1** 14 25N 97 45 E
Heishan, *China* **57 D12** 41 40N 122 5 E
Heishui, *Liaoning, China* **57 C10** 42 8N 119 30 E
Heishui, *Sichuan, China* **58 A4** 32 4N 103 2 E
Hejaz = Ḥijāz ☐, *Si. Arabia* **70 E3** 24 0N 40 0 E
Hejian, *China* **56 E9** 38 25N 116 5 E
Hejiang, *China* **58 C5** 28 43N 105 46 E
Hejin, *China* **56 G6** 35 35N 110 42 E
Hekimhan, *Turkey* **70 B3** 38 50N 37 55 E
Hekla, *Iceland* **8 E4** 63 56N 19 35W
Hekou, *Guangdong, China* **59 F9** 23 13N 112 45 E
Hekou, *Yunnan, China* **58 F4** 22 30N 103 59 E
Hel, *Poland* **44 D5** 54 37N 18 47 E
Helagsfjället, *Sweden* **10 B6** 62 54N 12 25 E
Helan Shan, *China* **56 E3** 38 30N 105 55 E
Helechosa, *Spain* **35 F6** 39 22N 4 53W
Helen Atoll, *Pac. Oc.* **63 D8** 2 40N 132 0 E
Helena, *Ark., U.S.A.* **113 H9** 34 32N 90 36W
Helena, *Mont., U.S.A.* **114 C7** 46 36N 112 2W
Helendale, *U.S.A.* **117 L9** 34 44N 117 19W
Helensburgh, *U.K.* **14 E4** 56 1N 4 43W
Helensville, *N.Z.* **91 G5** 36 41 S 174 29 E
Helenvale, *Australia* **94 B4** 15 43 S 145 14 E
Helgasjön, *Sweden* **11 H8** 56 55N 14 50 E
Helgeland, *Norway* **8 C15** 66 7N 13 29 E
Helgoland, *Germany* **24 A3** 54 10N 7 53 E
Heligoland = Helgoland, *Germany* **24 A3** 54 10N 7 53 E
Heligoland B. = Deutsche Bucht, *Germany* **24 A4** 54 15N 8 0 E
Heliopolis, *Egypt* **80 H7** 30 6N 31 17 E
Hella, *Iceland* **8 E3** 63 50N 20 24W
Hellertown, *U.S.A.* **111 F9** 40 35N 75 21W
Hellespont = Çanakkale Boğazı, *Turkey* **41 F10** 40 17N 26 32 E
Hellevoetsluis, *Neths.* **17 C4** 51 50N 4 8 E
Hellín, *Spain* **33 G3** 38 31N 1 40W
Helmand ☐, *Afghan.* **66 D4** 31 20N 64 0 E
Helmand →, *Afghan.* **66 D2** 31 12N 61 34 E
Helme →, *Germany* **24 D7** 51 20N 11 21 E
Helmeringhausen, *Namibia* **88 D2** 25 54 S 16 57 E
Helmond, *Neths.* **17 C5** 51 29N 5 41 E
Helmsdale, *U.K.* **14 C5** 58 7N 3 39W
Helmsdale →, *U.K.* **14 C5** 58 7N 3 40W
Helmstedt, *Germany* **24 C7** 52 12N 11 0 E
Helong, *China* **57 C15** 42 40N 129 0 E
Helper, *U.S.A.* **114 G8** 39 41N 110 51W
Helsingborg, *Sweden* **11 H6** 56 3N 12 42 E
Helsinge, *Denmark* **11 H6** 56 2N 12 12 E
Helsingfors = Helsinki, *Finland* **9 F21** 60 15N 25 3 E
Helsingør, *Denmark* **11 H6** 56 2N 12 35 E
Helsinki, *Finland* **9 F21** 60 15N 25 3 E
Helska, Mierzeja, *Poland* **44 D5** 54 45N 18 40 E
Helston, *U.K.* **13 G2** 50 6N 5 17W
Helvellyn, *U.K.* **12 C4** 54 32N 3 1W
Helwân, *Egypt* **80 J7** 29 50N 31 20 E
Hemel Hempstead, *U.K.* **13 F7** 51 44N 0 28W
Hemet, *U.S.A.* **117 M10** 33 45N 116 58W
Hemingford, *U.S.A.* **112 D3** 42 19N 103 4W
Hemmingford, *Canada* **111 A11** 45 3N 73 35W
Hempstead, *U.S.A.* **113 K6** 30 6N 96 5W
Hemse, *Sweden* **11 G12** 57 15N 18 22 E
Hemsön, *Sweden* **10 B12** 62 42N 18 5 E
Henån, *Sweden* **11 F5** 58 14N 11 40 E
Henan ☐, *China* **56 H8** 34 0N 114 0 E
Henares →, *Spain* **34 E7** 40 24N 3 30W
Henashi-Misaki, *Japan* **54 D9** 40 37N 139 51 E
Hendaye, *France* **20 E2** 43 23N 1 47W
Hendek, *Turkey* **72 B4** 40 48N 30 44 E
Henderson, *Argentina* **126 D3** 36 18 S 61 43W
Henderson, *Ky., U.S.A.* **108 G2** 37 50N 87 35W
Henderson, *N.C., U.S.A.* **109 G6** 36 20N 78 25W
Henderson, *Nev., U.S.A.* **117 J12** 36 2N 114 59W
Henderson, *Tenn., U.S.A.* **109 H1** 35 26N 88 38W
Henderson, *Tex., U.S.A.* **113 J7** 32 9N 94 48W
Hendersonville, *N.C., U.S.A.* **109 H4** 35 19N 82 28W
Hendersonville, *Tenn., U.S.A.* **109 G2** 36 18N 86 37W
Hendījān, *Iran* **71 D6** 30 14N 49 43 E
Hendorābī, *Iran* **71 E7** 26 40N 53 37 E
Heng Jiang, *China* **58 C5** 28 40N 104 25 E
Heng Xian, *China* **58 F7** 22 40N 109 17 E
Hengcheng, *China* **56 E4** 38 18N 106 28 E
Hëngchun, *Taiwan* **59 F13** 22 0N 120 44 E
Hengdaohezi, *China* **57 B15** 44 52N 129 0 E
Hengelo, *Neths.* **17 B6** 52 16N 6 48 E
Hengfeng, *China* **59 C10** 28 12N 115 48 E
Hengshan, *Hunan, China* **59 D9** 27 16N 112 45 E
Hengshan, *Shaanxi, China* **56 F5** 37 58N 109 5 E
Hengshui, *China* **56 F8** 37 41N 115 40 E
Hengyang, *China* **59 D9** 26 59N 112 22 E
Henichesk, *Ukraine* **47 J8** 46 12N 34 50 E
Hénin-Beaumont, *France* **19 B9** 50 25N 2 58 E
Henlopen, C., *U.S.A.* **108 F8** 38 48N 75 6W
Hennan, *Sweden* **10 B9** 62 2N 15 54 E
Hennebont, *France* **18 E3** 47 49N 3 19W
Hennenman, *S. Africa* **88 D4** 27 59 S 27 1 E
Hennessey, *U.S.A.* **113 G6** 36 6N 97 54W
Hennigsdorf, *Germany* **24 C9** 52 38N 13 12 E
Henrietta, *U.S.A.* **113 J5** 33 49N 98 12W
Henrietta, Ostrov = Genriyetty, Ostrov, *Russia* **51 B16** 77 6N 156 30 E
Henrietta Maria, C., *Canada* **102 A3** 55 9N 82 20W
Henry, *U.S.A.* **112 E10** 41 7N 89 22W
Henryetta, *U.S.A.* **113 H7** 35 27N 95 59W
Henryville, *Canada* **111 A11** 45 8N 73 11W
Hensall, *Canada* **110 C3** 43 26N 81 30W
Henstedt-Ulzburg, *Germany* **24 B6** 53 47N 10 0 E
Hentiesbaai, *Namibia* **88 C1** 22 8 S 14 18 E
Hentiyn Nuruu, *Mongolia* **60 B5** 48 30N 108 30 E
Henty, *Australia* **95 F4** 35 30 S 147 0 E
Henzada, *Burma* **67 L19** 17 38N 95 26 E
Hephaestia, *Greece* **39 B7** 39 55N 25 14 E
Heping, *China* **59 E10** 24 29N 115 0 E
Heppner, *U.S.A.* **114 D4** 45 21N 119 33W
Hepu, *China* **58 G7** 21 40N 109 12 E
Hepworth, *Canada* **110 B3** 44 37N 81 9W
Heqing, *China* **58 D3** 26 37N 100 11 E
Hequ, *China* **56 E6** 39 20N 111 15 E
Héraðsflói, *Iceland* **8 D6** 65 42N 14 12W
Héraðsvötn →, *Iceland* **8 D4** 65 45N 19 25W
Herald Cays, *Australia* **94 B4** 16 58 S 149 9 E
Herāt, *Afghan.* **66 B3** 34 20N 62 7 E
Herāt ☐, *Afghan.* **66 B3** 35 0N 62 0 E
Hérault ☐, *France* **20 E7** 43 34N 3 15 E
Hérault →, *France* **20 E7** 43 17N 3 26 E
Herbault, *France* **18 E8** 47 36N 1 8 E
Herbert →, *Australia* **94 B4** 18 31 S 146 17 E
Herberton, *Australia* **94 B4** 17 20 S 145 25 E
Herbertsdale, *S. Africa* **88 E3** 34 1 S 21 46 E
Herbignac, *France* **18 E4** 47 27N 2 18W
Herborn, *Germany* **24 E4** 50 40N 8 18 E
Herby, *Poland* **45 H5** 50 45N 18 50 E
Herceg-Novi, *Montenegro, Yug.* **40 D2** 42 30N 18 33 E
Herchmer, *Canada* **105 B10** 57 22N 94 10W
Herðubreið, *Iceland* **8 D5** 65 11N 16 21W
Hereford, *U.K.* **13 E5** 52 4N 2 43W
Hereford, *U.S.A.* **113 H3** 34 49N 102 24W
Herefordshire ☐, *U.K.* **13 E5** 52 8N 2 40W
Hereke, *Turkey* **41 F13** 40 47N 29 38 E
Herencia, *Spain* **35 F7** 39 21N 3 22W
Herentals, *Belgium* **17 C4** 51 12N 4 51 E
Herford, *Germany* **24 C4** 52 7N 8 39 E
Héricourt, *France* **19 E13** 47 32N 6 45 E
Herington, *U.S.A.* **112 F6** 38 40N 96 57W
Herisau, *Switz.* **25 H5** 47 22N 9 17 E
Hérisson, *France* **19 F9** 46 32N 2 42 E
Herkimer, *U.S.A.* **111 D10** 43 0N 74 59W
Herlong, *U.S.A.* **116 E6** 40 8N 120 8W
Herm, *U.K.* **13 H5** 49 30N 2 28W
Hermann, *U.S.A.* **112 F9** 38 42N 91 27W
Hermannsburg, *Australia* **92 D5** 23 57 S 132 45 E
Hermannsburg, *Germany* **24 C6** 52 50N 10 5 E
Hermanus, *S. Africa* **88 E2** 34 27 S 19 12 E
Herment, *France* **20 C6** 45 45N 2 24 E
Hermidale, *Australia* **95 E4** 31 30 S 146 42 E
Hermiston, *U.S.A.* **114 D4** 45 51N 119 17W
Hermite, I., *Chile* **128 H3** 55 50 S 68 0W
Hermon, *U.S.A.* **111 B9** 44 28N 75 14W
Hermon, Mt. = Shaykh, J. ash, *Lebanon* **75 B4** 33 25N 35 50 E
Hermosillo, *Mexico* **118 B2** 29 10N 111 0W
Hernád →, *Hungary* **42 C6** 47 56N 21 8 E
Hernandarias, *Paraguay* **127 B5** 25 20 S 54 40W
Hernandez, *U.S.A.* **116 J6** 36 24N 120 46W
Hernando, *Argentina* **126 C3** 32 28 S 63 40W
Hernando, *U.S.A.* **113 H10** 34 50N 90 0W
Hernani, *Spain* **32 B3** 43 16N 1 58W
Herndon, *U.S.A.* **110 F8** 40 43N 76 51W
Herne, *Germany* **17 C7** 51 32N 7 14 E
Herne Bay, *U.K.* **13 F9** 51 21N 1 8 E
Herning, *Denmark* **11 H2** 56 8N 8 58 E
Heroica = Caborca, *Mexico* **118 A2** 30 40N 112 10W
Heroica Nogales = Nogales, *Mexico* **118 A2** 31 20N 110 56W
Heron Bay, *Canada* **102 C2** 48 40N 86 25W
Herradura, Pta. de la, *Canary Is.* **37 F5** 28 26N 14 8W
Herreid, *U.S.A.* **112 C4** 45 50N 100 4W

Herrenberg

Herrenberg, *Germany* **25 G4** 48 35N 8 52 E
Herrera, *Spain* **35 H6** 37 26N 4 55W
Herrera de Alcántara, *Spain* **35 F3** 39 39N 7 25W
Herrera de Pisuerga, *Spain* **34 C6** 42 35N 4 20W
Herrera del Duque, *Spain* **35 F5** 39 10N 5 3W
Herrestad, *Sweden* **11 F5** 58 21N 11 50 E
Herrin, *U.S.A.* **113 G10** 37 48N 89 2W
Herriot, *Canada* **105 B8** 56 22N 101 16W
Herrljunga, *Sweden* **11 F7** 58 5N 13 1 E
Hersbruck, *Germany* **25 F7** 49 30N 11 26 E
Hershey, *U.S.A.* **111 F8** 40 17N 76 39W
Hersonissos, *Greece* **36 D7** 35 18N 25 22 E
Herstal, *Belgium* **17 D5** 50 40N 5 38 E
Hertford, *U.K.* **13 F7** 51 48N 0 4W
Hertfordshire □, *U.K.* **13 F7** 51 51N 0 5W
's-Hertogenbosch, *Neths.* **17 C5** 51 42N 5 17 E
Hertzogville, *S. Africa* **88 D4** 28 9 S 25 30 E
Hervás, *Spain* **34 E5** 40 16N 5 52W
Hervey B., *Australia* **94 C5** 25 0 S 152 52 E
Herzberg, *Brandenburg, Germany* **24 D9** 51 41N 13 14 E
Herzberg, *Niedersachsen, Germany* **24 D6** 51 38N 10 20 E
Herzliyya, *Israel* **75 C3** 32 10N 34 50 E
Herzogenburg, *Austria* **26 C8** 48 17N 15 41 E
Ḩeşār, *Fārs, Iran* **71 D6** 29 52N 50 16 E
Ḩeşār, *Markazī, Iran* **71 C6** 35 50N 49 12 E
Hesdin, *France* **19 B9** 50 21N 2 2 E
Heshan, *China* **58 F7** 23 50N 108 53 E
Heshui, *China* **56 G5** 35 48N 108 0 E
Heshun, *China* **56 F7** 37 22N 113 32 E
Hesperia, *U.S.A.* **117 L9** 34 25N 117 18W
Hesse = Hessen □, *Germany* **24 E4** 50 30N 9 0 E
Hessen □, *Germany* **24 E4** 50 30N 9 0 E
Hestra, *Sweden* **11 G7** 57 26N 13 35 E
Hetch Hetchy Aqueduct, *U.S.A.* **116 H5** 37 29N 122 19W
Hettinger, *U.S.A.* **112 C3** 46 0N 102 42W
Hettstedt, *Germany* **24 D7** 51 39N 11 31 E
Heuvelton, *U.S.A.* **111 B9** 44 37N 75 25W
Heves, *Hungary* **42 C5** 47 36N 20 17 E
Heves □, *Hungary* **42 C5** 47 50N 20 0 E
Hewitt, *U.S.A.* **113 K6** 31 27N 97 11W
Hexham, *U.K.* **12 C5** 54 58N 2 4W
Hexi, *Yunnan, China* **58 E4** 24 9N 102 38 E
Hexi, *Zhejiang, China* **59 D12** 27 58N 119 38 E
Hexigten Qi, *China* **57 C9** 43 18N 117 30 E
Ḩeydarābād, *Iran* **71 D7** 30 33N 55 38 E
Heysham, *U.K.* **12 C5** 54 3N 2 53W
Heyuan, *China* **59 F10** 23 39N 114 40 E
Heywood, *Australia* **95 F3** 38 8 S 141 37 E
Heze, *China* **56 G8** 35 14N 115 20 E
Hezhang, *China* **58 D5** 27 8N 104 41 E
Hi Vista, *U.S.A.* **117 L9** 34 45N 117 46W
Hialeah, *U.S.A.* **109 N5** 25 50N 80 17W
Hiawatha, *U.S.A.* **112 F7** 39 51N 95 32W
Hibbing, *U.S.A.* **112 B8** 47 25N 92 56W
Hibbs B., *Australia* **94 G4** 42 35 S 145 15 E
Hibernia Reef, *Australia* **92 B3** 12 0 S 123 23 E
Hickman, *U.S.A.* **113 G10** 36 34N 89 11W
Hickory, *U.S.A.* **109 H5** 35 44N 81 21W
Hicks, Pt., *Australia* **95 F4** 37 49 S 149 17 E
Hicks L., *Canada* **105 A9** 61 25N 100 0W
Hicksville, *U.S.A.* **111 F11** 40 46N 73 32W
Hida, *Romania* **43 C8** 47 10N 23 19 E
Hida-Gawa →, *Japan* **55 G8** 35 26N 137 3 E
Hida-Sammyaku, *Japan* **55 F8** 36 30N 137 40 E
Hidaka-Sammyaku, *Japan* **54 C11** 42 35N 142 45 E
Hidalgo, *Mexico* **119 C5** 24 15N 99 26W
Hidalgo □, *Mexico* **119 C5** 20 30N 99 10W
Hidalgo, Presa M., *Mexico* **118 B3** 26 30N 108 35W
Hidalgo, Pta. del, *Canary Is.* **37 F3** 28 33N 16 19W
Hidalgo del Parral, *Mexico* **118 B3** 26 58N 105 40W
Hiddensee, *Germany* **24 A9** 54 32N 13 6 E
Hieflau, *Austria* **26 D7** 47 36N 14 46 E
Hiendelaencina, *Spain* **32 D2** 41 5N 3 0W
Hierro, *Canary Is.* **37 G1** 27 44N 18 0W
Higashiajima-San, *Japan* **54 F10** 37 40N 140 10 E
Higashiōsaka, *Japan* **55 G7** 34 40N 135 37 E
Higgins, *U.S.A.* **113 G4** 36 7N 100 2W
Higgins Corner, *U.S.A.* **116 F5** 39 2N 121 5W
High Atlas = Haut Atlas, *Morocco* **78 B4** 32 30N 5 0W
High Bridge, *U.S.A.* **111 F10** 40 40N 74 54W
High Level, *Canada* **104 B5** 58 31N 117 8W
High Point, *U.S.A.* **109 H6** 35 57N 80 0W
High Prairie, *Canada* **104 B5** 55 30N 116 30W
High River, *Canada* **104 C6** 50 30N 113 50W
High Tatra = Tatry, *Slovak Rep.* **27 B13** 49 20N 20 0 E
High Veld, *Africa* **76 J6** 27 0 S 27 0 E
High Wycombe, *U.K.* **13 F7** 51 37N 0 45W
Highland □, *U.K.* **14 D4** 57 17N 4 21W
Highland Park, *U.S.A.* **108 D2** 42 11N 87 48W
Highmore, *U.S.A.* **112 C5** 44 31N 99 27W
Highrock L., *Man., Canada* **105 B8** 55 45N 100 30W
Highrock L., *Sask., Canada* **105 B7** 57 5N 105 32W
Higüey, *Dom. Rep.* **121 C6** 18 37N 68 42W
Hihya, *Egypt* **80 H7** 30 40N 31 36 E
Hiiumaa, *Estonia* **9 G20** 58 50N 22 45 E
Híjar, *Spain* **32 D4** 41 10N 0 27W
Ḩijāz □, *Si. Arabia* **70 E3** 24 0N 40 0 E
Hijo = Tagum, *Phil.* **61 H6** 7 33N 125 53 E
Hikari, *Japan* **55 H5** 33 58N 131 58 E
Hikmak, Ras el, *Egypt* **80 A2** 31 15N 27 51 E
Hiko, *U.S.A.* **116 H11** 37 32N 115 14W
Hikone, *Japan* **55 G8** 35 15N 136 10 E
Hikurangi, *N.Z.* **91 F5** 35 36 S 174 17 E
Hikurangi, Mt., *N.Z.* **91 H6** 37 55 S 178 4 E
Hildburghausen, *Germany* **24 E6** 50 25N 10 42 E
Hildesheim, *Germany* **24 C5** 52 9N 9 56 E
Hill →, *Australia* **93 F2** 30 23 S 115 3 E
Hill City, *Idaho, U.S.A.* **114 E6** 43 18N 115 3W
Hill City, *Kans., U.S.A.* **112 F5** 39 22N 99 51W
Hill City, *S. Dak., U.S.A.* **112 D3** 43 56N 103 35W
Hill Island L., *Canada* **105 A7** 60 30N 109 50W
Hillared, *Sweden* **11 G7** 57 37N 13 10 E
Hillcrest Center, *U.S.A.* **117 K8** 35 23N 118 57W
Hillegom, *Neths.* **17 B4** 52 18N 4 35 E
Hillerød, *Denmark* **11 J6** 55 56N 12 19 E
Hillerstorp, *Sweden* **11 G7** 57 20N 13 52 E
Hillsboro, *Kans., U.S.A.* **112 F6** 38 21N 97 12W
Hillsboro, *N. Dak., U.S.A.* **112 B6** 47 26N 97 3W
Hillsboro, *N.H., U.S.A.* **111 C13** 43 7N 71 54W
Hillsboro, *Ohio, U.S.A.* **108 F4** 39 12N 83 37W
Hillsboro, *Oreg., U.S.A.* **116 E4** 45 31N 122 59W
Hillsboro, *Tex., U.S.A.* **113 J6** 32 1N 97 8W
Hillsborough, *Grenada* **121 D7** 12 28N 61 28W
Hillsdale, *Mich., U.S.A.* **108 E3** 41 56N 84 38W
Hillsdale, *N.Y., U.S.A.* **111 D11** 42 11N 73 30W
Hillsport, *Canada* **102 C2** 49 27N 85 34W
Hillston, *Australia* **95 E4** 33 30 S 145 31 E
Hilo, *U.S.A.* **106 J17** 19 44N 155 5W
Hilton, *U.S.A.* **110 C7** 43 17N 77 48W
Hilton Head Island, *U.S.A.* **109 J5** 32 13N 80 45W
Hilvan, *Turkey* **73 D8** 37 34N 38 58 E
Hilversum, *Neths.* **17 B5** 52 14N 5 10 E
Himachal Pradesh □, *India* **68 D7** 31 30N 77 0 E
Himalaya, *Asia* **69 E11** 29 0N 84 0 E
Himamaylan, *Phil.* **61 F5** 10 6N 122 52 E
Himarë, *Albania* **40 F3** 40 8N 19 43 E
Himatnagar, *India* **66 H8** 23 37N 72 57 E
Himeji, *Japan* **55 G7** 34 50N 134 40 E
Himi, *Japan* **55 F8** 36 50N 136 55 E
Himmerland, *Denmark* **11 H3** 56 45N 9 30 E
Ḩimş, *Syria* **75 A5** 34 40N 36 45 E
Ḩimş □, *Syria* **75 A6** 34 30N 37 0 E
Hinche, *Haiti* **121 C5** 19 9N 72 1W
Hinchinbrook I., *Australia* **94 B4** 18 20 S 146 15 E
Hinckley, *U.K.* **13 E6** 52 33N 1 22W
Hinckley, *U.S.A.* **112 B8** 46 1N 92 56W
Hindaun, *India* **68 F7** 26 44N 77 5 E
Hindmarsh, L., *Australia* **95 F3** 36 5 S 141 55 E
Hindsholm, *Denmark* **11 J4** 55 30N 10 40 E
Hindu Bagh, *Pakistan* **68 D2** 30 56N 67 50 E
Hindu Kush, *Asia* **66 B7** 36 0N 71 0 E
Hindubagh, *Pakistan* **66 D5** 30 56N 67 57 E
Hindupur, *India* **66 N10** 13 49N 77 32 E
Hines Creek, *Canada* **104 B5** 56 20N 118 40W
Hinesville, *U.S.A.* **109 K5** 31 51N 81 36W
Hinganghat, *India* **66 J11** 20 30N 78 52 E
Hingham, *U.S.A.* **114 B8** 48 33N 110 25W
Hingir, *India* **69 J10** 21 57N 83 41 E
Hingoli, *India* **66 K10** 19 41N 77 15 E
Hinigaran, *Phil.* **61 F5** 10 16N 122 50 E
Hinis, *Turkey* **73 C9** 39 22N 41 43 E
Hinna = Imi, *Ethiopia* **81 F5** 6 28N 42 10 E
Hinna, *Nigeria* **83 C7** 10 25N 11 35 E
Hinnerup, *Denmark* **11 H4** 56 16N 10 4 E
Hinnøya, *Norway* **8 B16** 68 35N 15 50 E
Hinojosa del Duque, *Spain* **35 G5** 38 30N 5 9W
Hinsdale, *U.S.A.* **111 D12** 42 47N 72 29W
Hinterrhein →, *Switz.* **25 J5** 46 40N 9 25 E
Hinton, *Canada* **104 C5** 53 26N 117 34W
Hinton, *U.S.A.* **108 G5** 37 40N 80 54W
Hınzır Burnu, *Turkey* **72 D6** 36 19N 35 46 E
Hirado, *Japan* **55 H4** 33 22N 129 33 E
Hirakud Dam, *India* **67 J13** 21 32N 83 45 E
Hiran →, *India* **69 H8** 23 6N 79 21 E
Hirapur, *India* **69 G8** 24 22N 79 13 E
Hiratsuka, *Japan* **55 G9** 35 19N 139 21 E
Hirfanlı Barajı, *Turkey* **72 C5** 39 18N 33 31 E
Hiroo, *Japan* **54 C11** 42 17N 143 19 E
Hirosaki, *Japan* **54 D10** 40 34N 140 28 E
Hiroshima, *Japan* **55 G6** 34 24N 132 30 E
Hiroshima □, *Japan* **55 G6** 34 50N 133 0 E
Hirson, *France* **19 C11** 49 55N 4 4 E
Hirtshals, *Denmark* **11 G3** 57 36N 9 57 E
Hisar, *India* **68 E6** 29 12N 75 45 E
Hisarcık, *Turkey* **39 B11** 39 15N 29 14 E
Hisaria, *Bulgaria* **41 D8** 42 30N 24 44 E
Hisb →, *Iraq* **70 D5** 31 45N 44 17 E
Ḩismá, *Si. Arabia* **70 D3** 28 30N 36 0 E
Hispaniola, *W. Indies* **121 C5** 19 0N 71 0W
Hīt, *Iraq* **70 C4** 33 38N 42 49 E
Hita, *Japan* **55 H5** 33 20N 130 58 E
Hitachi, *Japan* **55 F10** 36 36N 140 39 E
Hitchin, *U.K.* **13 F7** 51 58N 0 16W
Hitoyoshi, *Japan* **55 H5** 32 13N 130 45 E
Hitra, *Norway* **8 E13** 63 30N 8 45 E
Hitzacker, *Germany* **24 B7** 53 9N 11 2 E
Hixon, *Canada* **104 C4** 53 25N 122 35W
Ḩiyyon, N. →, *Israel* **75 E4** 30 25N 35 10 E
Hjalmar L., *Canada* **105 A7** 61 33N 109 25W
Hjälmaren, *Sweden* **10 E9** 59 18N 15 40 E
Hjältevad, *Sweden* **11 G9** 57 38N 15 20 E
Hjo, *Sweden* **11 F8** 58 22N 14 17 E
Hjørring, *Denmark* **11 G3** 57 29N 9 59 E
Hjortkvarn, *Sweden* **11 F9** 58 54N 15 26 E
Hkakabo Razi, *Burma* **67 E20** 28 25N 97 23 E
Hlinsko, *Czech Rep.* **26 B8** 49 45N 15 54 E
Hlobane, *S. Africa* **89 D5** 27 42 S 31 0 E
Hlohovec, *Slovak Rep.* **27 C10** 48 26N 17 49 E
Hlučín, *Czech Rep.* **27 B11** 49 54N 18 11 E
Hluhluwe, *S. Africa* **89 D5** 28 1 S 32 15 E
Hlukhiv, *Ukraine* **47 G7** 51 40N 33 58 E
Hlyboka, *Ukraine* **47 H3** 48 5N 25 56 E
Hlybokaye, *Belarus* **46 E4** 55 10N 27 45 E
Hnúšťa, *Slovak Rep.* **27 C12** 48 35N 19 58 E
Ho, *Ghana* **83 D5** 6 37N 0 27 E
Ho Chi Minh City = Thanh Pho Ho Chi Minh, *Vietnam* **65 G6** 10 58N 106 40 E
Ho Thuong, *Vietnam* **64 C5** 19 32N 105 48 E
Hoa Binh, *Vietnam* **58 G5** 20 50N 105 20 E
Hoa Da, *Vietnam* **65 G7** 11 16N 108 40 E
Hoa Hiep, *Vietnam* **65 G5** 11 34N 105 51 E
Hoai Nhon, *Vietnam* **64 E7** 14 28N 109 1 E
Hoang Lien Son, *Vietnam* **58 F4** 22 0N 104 0 E
Hoanib →, *Namibia* **88 B2** 19 27 S 12 46 E
Hoare B., *Canada* **101 B13** 65 17N 62 30W
Hoarusib →, *Namibia* **88 B2** 19 3 S 12 36 E
Hobart, *Australia* **94 G4** 42 50 S 147 21 E
Hobart, *U.S.A.* **113 H5** 35 1N 99 6W
Hobbs, *U.S.A.* **113 J3** 32 42N 103 8W
Hobbs Coast, *Antarctica* **5 D14** 74 50 S 131 0W
Hobe Sound, *U.S.A.* **109 M5** 27 4N 80 8W
Hoboken, *U.S.A.* **111 F10** 40 45N 74 4W
Hobro, *Denmark* **11 H3** 56 39N 9 46 E
Hoburgen, *Sweden* **11 H12** 56 55N 18 7 E
Hocalar, *Turkey* **39 C11** 38 36N 30 0 E
Hochfeld, *Namibia* **88 C2** 21 28 S 17 58 E
Hochschwab, *Austria* **26 D8** 47 35N 15 0 E
Höchstadt, *Germany* **25 F6** 49 42N 10 47 E
Hockenheim, *Germany* **25 F4** 49 18N 8 32 E
Hodaka-Dake, *Japan* **55 F8** 36 17N 137 39 E
Hodgeville, *Canada* **105 C7** 50 7N 106 58W
Hodgson, *Canada* **105 C9** 51 13N 97 36W
Hódmezővásárhely, *Hungary* **42 D5** 46 28N 20 22 E
Hodna, Chott el, *Algeria* **78 A6** 35 26N 4 43 E
Hodonín, *Czech Rep.* **27 C10** 48 50N 17 10 E
Hoeamdong, *N. Korea* **57 C16** 42 30N 130 16 E
Hœdic, Î. de, *France* **18 E4** 47 20N 2 53W
Hoek van Holland, *Neths.* **17 C4** 52 0N 4 7 E
Hoengsŏng, *S. Korea* **57 F14** 37 29N 127 59 E
Hoeryong, *N. Korea* **57 C15** 42 30N 129 45 E
Hoeyang, *N. Korea* **57 E14** 38 43N 127 36 E
Hof, *Germany* **25 E7** 50 19N 11 55 E
Hofgeismar, *Germany* **24 D5** 51 29N 9 23 E
Hofheim, *Germany* **25 E4** 50 5N 8 26 E
Hofmeyr, *S. Africa* **88 E4** 31 39 S 25 50 E
Höfn, *Iceland* **8 D6** 64 15N 15 13W
Hofors, *Sweden* **10 D10** 60 31N 16 15 E
Hofsjökull, *Iceland* **8 D4** 64 49N 18 48W
Hōfu, *Japan* **55 G5** 34 3N 131 34 E
Hogan Group, *Australia* **95 F4** 39 13 S 147 1 E
Höganäs, *Sweden* **11 H6** 56 12N 12 33 E
Hogarth, Mt., *Australia* **94 C2** 21 48 S 136 58 E
Hoggar = Ahaggar, *Algeria* **78 D7** 23 0N 6 30 E
Högsäter, *Sweden* **11 F6** 58 38N 12 5 E
Högsby, *Sweden* **11 G10** 57 10N 16 1 E
Högsjö, *Sweden* **10 E9** 59 4N 15 44 E
Hogsty Reef, *Bahamas* **121 B5** 21 41N 73 48W
Hoh →, *U.S.A.* **116 C2** 47 45N 124 29W
Hohe Acht, *Germany* **25 E3** 50 22N 7 0 E
Hohe Tauern, *Austria* **26 D5** 47 11N 12 40 E
Hohe Venn, *Belgium* **17 D6** 50 30N 6 5 E
Hohenau, *Austria* **27 C9** 48 36N 16 55 E
Hohenems, *Austria* **26 D2** 47 22N 9 42 E
Hohenloher Ebene, *Germany* **25 F5** 49 14N 9 36 E
Hohenwald, *U.S.A.* **109 H2** 35 33N 87 33W
Hohenwestedt, *Germany* **24 A5** 54 5N 9 40 E
Hoher Rhön = Rhön, *Germany* **24 E5** 50 24N 9 58 E
Hohhot, *China* **56 D6** 40 52N 111 40 E
Hóhlakas, *Greece* **36 D9** 35 57N 27 53 E
Hohoe, *Ghana* **83 D5** 7 8N 0 32 E
Hoi An, *Vietnam* **64 E7** 15 30N 108 19 E
Hoi Xuan, *Vietnam* **58 G5** 20 25N 105 9 E
Hoisington, *U.S.A.* **112 F5** 38 31N 98 47W
Højer, *Denmark* **11 K2** 54 58N 8 42 E
Hōjō, *Japan* **55 H6** 33 58N 132 46 E
Hok, *Sweden* **11 G8** 57 31N 14 16 E
Hökensås, *Sweden* **11 G8** 58 0N 14 5 E
Hökerum, *Sweden* **11 G7** 57 51N 13 16 E
Hokianga Harbour, *N.Z.* **91 F4** 35 31 S 173 22 E
Hokitika, *N.Z.* **91 K3** 42 42 S 171 0 E
Hokkaidō □, *Japan* **54 C11** 43 30N 143 0 E
Hol-Hol, *Djibouti* **81 E5** 11 20N 42 50 E
Hola Pristan, *Ukraine* **47 J7** 46 29N 32 32 E
Holbæk, *Denmark* **11 J5** 55 43N 11 43 E
Holbrook, *Australia* **95 F4** 35 42 S 147 18 E
Holbrook, *U.S.A.* **115 J8** 34 54N 110 10W
Holden, *U.S.A.* **114 G7** 39 6N 112 16W
Holdenville, *U.S.A.* **113 H6** 35 5N 96 24W
Holdrege, *U.S.A.* **112 E5** 40 26N 99 23W
Holešov, *Czech Rep.* **27 B10** 49 20N 17 35 E
Holguín, *Cuba* **120 B4** 20 50N 76 20W
Holíč, *Slovak Rep.* **27 C10** 48 49N 17 10 E
Holice, *Czech Rep.* **26 A8** 50 5N 16 0 E
Höljes, *Sweden* **10 D6** 60 50N 12 35 E
Hollabrunn, *Austria* **26 C9** 48 34N 16 5 E
Hollams Bird I., *Namibia* **88 C1** 24 40 S 14 30 E
Holland, *Mich., U.S.A.* **108 D2** 42 47N 86 7W
Holland, *N.Y., U.S.A.* **110 D6** 42 38N 78 32W
Hollandale, *U.S.A.* **113 J9** 33 10N 90 51W
Hollandia = Jayapura, *Indonesia* **63 E10** 2 28 S 140 38 E
Holley, *U.S.A.* **110 C6** 43 14N 78 2W
Hollfeld, *Germany* **25 F7** 49 56N 11 18 E
Hollidaysburg, *U.S.A.* **110 F6** 40 26N 78 24W
Hollis, *U.S.A.* **113 H5** 34 41N 99 55W
Hollister, *Calif., U.S.A.* **116 J5** 36 51N 121 24W
Hollister, *Idaho, U.S.A.* **114 E6** 42 21N 114 35W
Höllviken = Höllviksnäs, *Sweden* **11 J6** 55 26N 12 58 E
Höllviksnäs, *Sweden* **11 J6** 55 26N 12 58 E
Holly Hill, *U.S.A.* **109 L5** 29 16N 81 3W
Holly Springs, *U.S.A.* **113 H10** 34 46N 89 27W
Hollywood, *U.S.A.* **109 N5** 26 1N 80 9W
Holman, *Canada* **100 A8** 70 44N 117 44W
Hólmavík, *Iceland* **8 D3** 65 42N 21 40W
Holmen, *U.S.A.* **112 D9** 43 58N 91 15W
Holmes Reefs, *Australia* **94 B4** 16 27 S 148 0 E
Holmsjö, *Sweden* **11 H9** 56 25N 15 32 E
Holmsjön, *Västernorrland, Sweden* **10 B10** 62 41N 16 33 E
Holmsjön, *Västernorrland, Sweden* **10 B9** 62 26N 15 20 E
Holmsland Klit, *Denmark* **11 J2** 56 0N 8 5 E
Holmsund, *Sweden* **8 E19** 63 41N 20 20 E
Holod, *Romania* **42 D7** 46 49N 22 8 E
Holroyd →, *Australia* **94 A3** 14 10 S 141 36 E
Holstebro, *Denmark* **11 H2** 56 22N 8 37 E
Holsworthy, *U.K.* **13 G3** 50 48N 4 22W
Holton, *Canada* **103 B8** 54 31N 57 12W
Holton, *U.S.A.* **112 F7** 39 28N 95 44W
Holtville, *U.S.A.* **117 N11** 32 49N 115 23W
Holwerd, *Neths.* **17 A5** 53 22N 5 54 E
Holy I., *Angl., U.K.* **12 D3** 53 17N 4 37W
Holy I., *Northumb., U.K.* **12 B6** 55 40N 1 47W
Holyhead, *U.K.* **12 D3** 53 18N 4 38W
Holyoke, *Colo., U.S.A.* **112 E3** 40 35N 102 18W
Holyoke, *Mass., U.S.A.* **111 D12** 42 12N 72 37W
Holyrood, *Canada* **103 C9** 47 27N 53 8W
Holzkirchen, *Germany* **25 H7** 47 52N 11 42 E
Holzminden, *Germany* **24 D5** 51 50N 9 28 E
Homa Bay, *Kenya* **86 C3** 0 36 S 34 30 E
Homalin, *Burma* **67 G19** 24 55N 95 0 E
Homand, *Iran* **71 C8** 32 28N 59 37 E
Homathko →, *Canada* **104 C4** 51 0N 124 56W
Homberg, *Germany* **24 D5** 51 2N 9 25 E
Hombori, *Mali* **83 B4** 15 20N 1 38W
Homburg, *Germany* **25 F3** 49 28N 7 18 E
Home B., *Canada* **101 B13** 68 40N 67 10W
Home Hill, *Australia* **94 B4** 19 43 S 147 25 E
Homedale, *U.S.A.* **114 E5** 43 37N 116 56W
Homer, *Alaska, U.S.A.* **100 C4** 59 39N 151 33W
Homer, *La., U.S.A.* **113 J8** 32 48N 93 4W
Homer City, *U.S.A.* **110 F5** 40 32N 79 10W
Homestead, *Australia* **94 C4** 20 20 S 145 40 E
Homestead, *U.S.A.* **109 N5** 25 28N 80 29W
Homewood, *U.S.A.* **116 F6** 39 4N 120 8W
Homoine, *Mozam.* **89 C6** 23 55 S 35 8 E
Homoljske Planina, *Serbia, Yug.* **40 B5** 44 10N 21 45 E
Homorod, *Romania* **43 D10** 46 5N 25 15 E
Homs = Ḩimş, *Syria* **75 A5** 34 40N 36 45 E
Homyel, *Belarus* **47 F6** 52 28N 31 0 E
Hon Chong, *Vietnam* **65 G5** 10 25N 104 30 E
Hon Me, *Vietnam* **64 C5** 19 23N 105 56 E
Honan = Henan □, *China* **56 H8** 34 0N 114 0 E
Honaz, *Turkey* **39 D11** 37 46N 29 18 E
Honbetsu, *Japan* **54 C11** 43 7N 143 37 E
Honcut, *U.S.A.* **116 F5** 39 20N 121 32W
Honda Bay, *Phil.* **61 G3** 9 53N 118 49 E
Hondarribia, *Spain* **32 B3** 43 22N 1 47W
Hondeklipbaai, *S. Africa* **88 E2** 30 19 S 17 17 E
Hondo, *Japan* **55 H5** 32 27N 130 12 E
Hondo, *U.S.A.* **113 L5** 29 21N 99 9W
Hondo →, *Belize* **119 D7** 18 25N 88 21W
Honduras ■, *Cent. Amer.* **120 D2** 14 40N 86 30W
Honduras, G. de, *Caribbean* **120 C2** 16 50N 87 0W
Hønefoss, *Norway* **9 F14** 60 10N 10 18 E
Honesdale, *U.S.A.* **111 E9** 41 34N 75 16W
Honey L., *U.S.A.* **116 E6** 40 15N 120 19W
Honfleur, *France* **18 C7** 49 25N 0 13 E
Høng, *Denmark* **11 J5** 55 31N 11 18 E
Hong →, *Vietnam* **58 F5** 22 0N 104 0 E
Hong Gai, *Vietnam* **58 G6** 20 57N 107 5 E
Hong He →, *China* **56 H8** 32 25N 115 35 E
Hong Hu, *China* **59 C9** 29 54N 113 24 E
Hong Kong □, *China* **59 F10** 22 11N 114 14 E
Hong'an, *China* **59 B10** 31 20N 114 40 E
Hongch'ŏn, *S. Korea* **57 F14** 37 44N 127 53 E
Honghai Wan, *China* **59 F10** 22 40N 115 0 E
Honghe, *China* **58 F4** 23 25N 102 25 E
Honghu, *China* **59 C9** 29 50N 113 30 E
Hongjiang, *China* **58 D7** 27 7N 109 59 E
Hongliu He →, *China* **56 F5** 38 0N 109 50 E
Hongor, *Mongolia* **56 B7** 45 45N 112 50 E
Hongsa, *Laos* **64 C3** 19 43N 101 20 E
Hongshui He →, *China* **58 F7** 23 48N 109 30 E
Hongsŏng, *S. Korea* **57 F14** 36 37N 126 38 E
Hongtong, *China* **56 F6** 36 16N 111 40 E
Honguedo, Détroit d', *Canada* **103 C7** 49 15N 64 0W
Hongwon, *N. Korea* **57 E14** 40 0N 127 56 E
Hongya, *China* **58 C4** 29 57N 103 22 E
Hongyuan, *China* **58 A4** 32 51N 102 40 E
Hongze Hu, *China* **57 H10** 33 15N 118 35 E
Honiara, *Solomon Is.* **96 H7** 9 27 S 159 57 E
Honiton, *U.K.* **13 G4** 50 47N 3 11W
Honjō, *Japan* **54 E10** 39 23N 140 3 E
Honkorâb, Ras, *Egypt* **80 C4** 24 35N 35 10 E
Honningsvåg, *Norway* **8 A21** 70 59N 25 59 E
Hönö, *Sweden* **11 G5** 57 41N 11 39 E
Honolulu, *U.S.A.* **106 H16** 21 19N 157 52W
Hontoria del Pinar, *Spain* **32 D1** 41 50N 3 10W
Hood, Mt., *U.S.A.* **114 D3** 45 23N 121 42W
Hood, Pt., *Australia* **93 F2** 34 23 S 119 34 E
Hood River, *U.S.A.* **114 D3** 45 43N 121 31W
Hoodsport, *U.S.A.* **116 C3** 47 24N 123 9W
Hooge, *Germany* **24 A4** 54 34N 8 33 E
Hoogeveen, *Neths.* **17 B6** 52 44N 6 28 E
Hoogezand-Sappemeer, *Neths.* **17 A6** 53 9N 6 45 E
Hooghly = Hugli →, *India* **69 J13** 21 56N 88 4 E
Hooghly-Chinsura = Chunchura, *India* **69 H13** 22 53N 88 27 E
Hook Hd., *Ireland* **15 D5** 52 7N 6 56W
Hook I., *Australia* **94 C4** 20 4 S 149 0 E
Hook of Holland = Hoek van Holland, *Neths.* **17 C4** 52 0N 4 7 E
Hooker, *U.S.A.* **113 G4** 36 52N 101 13W
Hooker Creek, *Australia* **92 C5** 18 23 S 130 38 E
Hoonah, *U.S.A.* **104 B1** 58 7N 135 27W
Hooper Bay, *U.S.A.* **100 B3** 61 32N 166 6W
Hoopeston, *U.S.A.* **108 E2** 40 28N 87 40W
Hoopstad, *S. Africa* **88 D4** 27 50 S 25 55 E
Höör, *Sweden* **11 J7** 55 56N 13 33 E
Hoorn, *Neths.* **17 B5** 52 38N 5 4 E
Hoover, *U.S.A.* **109 J2** 33 20N 86 11W
Hoover Dam, *U.S.A.* **117 K12** 36 1N 114 44W
Hooversville, *U.S.A.* **110 F6** 40 9N 78 55W
Hop Bottom, *U.S.A.* **111 E9** 41 42N 75 46W
Hopa, *Turkey* **73 B9** 41 28N 41 30 E
Hope, *Canada* **104 D4** 49 25N 121 25W
Hope, *Ariz., U.S.A.* **117 M13** 33 43N 113 42W
Hope, *Ark., U.S.A.* **113 J8** 33 40N 93 36W
Hope, L., *S. Austral., Australia* **95 D2** 28 24 S 139 18 E
Hope, L., *W. Austral., Australia* **93 F3** 32 35 S 120 15 E
Hope I., *Canada* **110 B4** 44 55N 80 11W
Hope Town, *Bahamas* **120 A4** 26 35N 76 57W
Hopedale, *Canada* **103 A7** 55 28N 60 13W
Hopedale, *U.S.A.* **111 D13** 42 8N 71 33W
Hopefield, *S. Africa* **88 E2** 33 3 S 18 22 E
Hopei = Hebei □, *China* **56 E9** 39 0N 116 0 E
Hopelchén, *Mexico* **119 D7** 19 46N 89 50W
Hopetoun, *Vic., Australia* **95 F3** 35 42 S 142 22 E
Hopetoun, *W. Austral., Australia* **93 F3** 33 57 S 120 7 E
Hopetown, *S. Africa* **88 D3** 29 34 S 24 3 E
Hopevale, *Australia* **94 B4** 15 16 S 145 20 E
Hopewell, *U.S.A.* **108 G7** 37 18N 77 17W
Hopfgarten, *Austria* **26 D5** 47 27N 12 10 E
Hopkins, L., *Australia* **92 D4** 24 15 S 128 35 E
Hopkinsville, *U.S.A.* **109 G2** 36 52N 87 29W
Hopland, *U.S.A.* **116 G3** 38 58N 123 7W
Hoquiam, *U.S.A.* **116 D3** 46 59N 123 53W
Horasan, *Turkey* **73 B10** 40 3N 42 11 E
Horažďovice, *Czech Rep.* **26 B6** 49 19N 13 42 E
Horb, *Germany* **25 G4** 48 26N 8 47 E
Hörby, *Sweden* **11 J7** 55 51N 13 40 E
Horcajo de Santiago, *Spain* **32 F1** 39 50N 3 1W
Horden Hills, *Australia* **92 D5** 20 15 S 130 0 E
Horezu, *Romania* **43 E8** 45 6N 24 0 E
Horgen, *Switz.* **25 H4** 47 15N 8 35 E
Horgoš, *Serbia, Yug.* **42 D4** 46 10N 20 0 E
Hořice, *Czech Rep.* **26 A8** 50 21N 15 39 E
Horinger, *China* **56 D6** 40 28N 111 48 E
Horki, *Belarus* **46 E6** 54 17N 30 59 E
Horlick Mts., *Antarctica* **5 E15** 84 0 S 102 0W
Horlivka, *Ukraine* **47 H10** 48 19N 38 5 E
Hormak, *Iran* **71 D9** 29 58N 60 51 E
Hormoz, *Iran* **71 E7** 27 35N 55 0 E
Hormoz, Jaz.-ye, *Iran* **71 E8** 27 8N 56 28 E
Hormozgān □, *Iran* **71 E8** 27 30N 56 0 E
Hormuz, Kūh-e, *Iran* **71 E7** 27 27N 55 10 E
Hormuz, Str. of, *The Gulf* **71 E8** 26 30N 56 30 E
Horn, *Austria* **26 C8** 48 39N 15 40 E
Horn, *Iceland* **8 C2** 66 28N 22 28W
Horn, *Sweden* **11 G9** 57 54N 15 51 E
Horn →, *Canada* **104 A5** 61 30N 118 1W
Horn, Cape = Hornos, C. de, *Chile* **122 J4** 55 50 S 67 30W
Horn Head, *Ireland* **15 A3** 55 14N 8 0W
Horn I., *Australia* **94 A3** 10 37 S 142 17 E
Horn Mts., *Canada* **104 A5** 62 15N 119 15W
Hornachuelos, *Spain* **35 H5** 37 50N 5 14W
Hornavan, *Sweden* **8 C17** 66 15N 17 30 E
Hornbeck, *U.S.A.* **113 K8** 31 20N 93 24W
Hornbrook, *U.S.A.* **114 F2** 41 55N 122 33W
Hornburg, *Germany* **24 C6** 52 2N 10 37 E
Horncastle, *U.K.* **12 D7** 53 13N 0 7W
Horndal, *Sweden* **10 D10** 60 18N 16 23 E
Hornell, *U.S.A.* **110 D7** 42 20N 77 40W
Hornell L., *Canada* **104 A5** 62 20N 119 25W
Hornepayne, *Canada* **102 C3** 49 14N 84 48W
Horní Planá, *Czech Rep.* **26 C7** 48 46N 14 2 E
Hornings Mills, *Canada* **110 B4** 44 9N 80 12W
Hornitos, *U.S.A.* **116 H6** 37 30N 120 14W
Hornos, C. de, *Chile* **122 J4** 55 50 S 67 30W
Hornoy-le-Bourg, *France* **19 C8** 49 50N 1 54 E
Hornsea, *U.K.* **12 D7** 53 55N 0 11W
Hornslandet, *Sweden* **10 C11** 61 35N 17 37 E
Hörnum, *Germany* **24 A4** 54 45N 8 17 E
Horobetsu, *Japan* **54 C10** 42 24N 141 6 E
Horodenka, *Ukraine* **47 H3** 48 41N 25 29 E
Horodnya, *Ukraine* **47 G6** 51 55N 31 33 E
Horodok, *Khmelnytskyy, Ukraine* **47 H4** 49 10N 26 34 E
Horodok, *Lviv, Ukraine* **47 H2** 49 46N 23 32 E
Horodyshche, *Ukraine* **47 H6** 49 17N 31 27 E
Horokhiv, *Ukraine* **47 G3** 50 30N 24 45 E
Horovice, *Czech Rep.* **26 B6** 49 48N 13 53 E
Horqin Youyi Qianqi, *China* **57 A12** 46 5N 122 3 E
Horqueta, *Paraguay* **126 A4** 23 15 S 56 55W
Horred, *Sweden* **11 G6** 57 22N 12 28 E
Horse Creek, *U.S.A.* **112 E3** 41 57N 105 10W
Horse Is., *Canada* **103 B8** 50 15N 55 50W
Horsefly L., *Canada* **104 C4** 52 25N 121 0W
Horseheads, *U.S.A.* **110 D8** 42 10N 76 49W
Horsens, *Denmark* **11 J3** 55 52N 9 51 E
Horsham, *Australia* **95 F3** 36 44 S 142 13 E
Horsham, *U.K.* **13 F7** 51 4N 0 20W
Horšovský Týn, *Czech Rep.* **26 B5** 49 31N 12 58 E
Horten, *Norway* **9 G14** 59 25N 10 32 E
Hortobágy →, *Hungary* **42 C6** 47 30N 21 6 E
Horton, *U.S.A.* **112 F7** 39 40N 95 32W
Horton →, *Canada* **100 B7** 69 56N 126 52W
Horwood L., *Canada* **102 C3** 48 5N 82 20W
Hosaina, *Ethiopia* **81 F4** 7 30N 37 47 E
Hose, Gunung-Gunung, *Malaysia* **62 D4** 2 5N 114 6 E
Ḩoseynābād, *Khuzestān, Iran* **71 C6** 32 45N 48 20 E
Ḩoseynābād, *Kordestān, Iran* **70 C5** 35 33N 47 8 E
Hoshangabad, *India* **68 H7** 22 45N 77 45 E
Hoshiarpur, *India* **68 D6** 31 30N 75 58 E
Hospet, *India* **66 M10** 15 15N 76 20 E
Hoste, I., *Chile* **128 H3** 55 0 S 69 0W
Hostens, *France* **20 D3** 44 30N 0 40W
Hot, *Thailand* **64 C2** 18 8N 98 29 E
Hot Creek Range, *U.S.A.* **114 G6** 38 40N 116 20W
Hot Springs, *Ark., U.S.A.* **113 H8** 34 31N 93 3W
Hot Springs, *S. Dak., U.S.A.* **112 D3** 43 26N 103 29W
Hotagen, *Sweden* **8 E16** 63 50N 14 30 E
Hotan, *China* **60 C2** 37 25N 79 55 E
Hotazel, *S. Africa* **88 D3** 27 17 S 22 58 E
Hotchkiss, *U.S.A.* **115 G10** 38 48N 107 43W
Hotham, C., *Australia* **92 B5** 12 2 S 131 18 E
Hoting, *Sweden* **8 D17** 64 8N 16 15 E
Hotolisht, *Albania* **40 E4** 41 10N 20 25 E
Hotte, Massif de la, *Haiti* **121 C5** 18 30N 73 45W
Hottentotsbaai, *Namibia* **88 D1** 26 8 S 14 59 E
Houat, Î. de, *France* **18 E4** 47 24N 2 58W
Houdan, *France* **19 D8** 48 48N 1 35 E
Houei Sai, *Laos* **58 G3** 20 18N 100 26 E
Houeillès, *France* **20 D4** 44 12N 0 2 E
Houffalize, *Belgium* **17 D5** 50 8N 5 48 E
Houghton, *Mich., U.S.A.* **112 B10** 47 7N 88 34W
Houghton, *N.Y., U.S.A.* **110 D6** 42 25N 78 10W
Houghton L., *U.S.A.* **108 C3** 44 21N 84 44W
Houhora Heads, *N.Z.* **91 F4** 34 49 S 173 9 E
Houlton, *U.S.A.* **109 B12** 46 8N 67 51W
Houma, *U.S.A.* **113 L9** 29 36N 90 43W
Houndé, *Burkina Faso* **82 C4** 11 34N 3 31W
Hourtin, *France* **20 C2** 45 11N 1 4W
Hourtin-Carcans, Étang d', *France* **20 C2** 45 10N 1 6W
Housatonic →, *U.S.A.* **111 E11** 41 10N 73 7W
Houston, *Canada* **104 C3** 54 25N 126 39W
Houston, *Mo., U.S.A.* **113 G9** 37 22N 91 58W
Houston, *Tex., U.S.A.* **113 L7** 29 46N 95 22W
Hout →, *S. Africa* **89 C4** 23 4 S 29 36 E
Houtkraal, *S. Africa* **88 E3** 30 23 S 24 5 E
Houtman Abrolhos, *Australia* **93 E1** 28 43 S 113 48 E
Hovd, *Mongolia* **60 B4** 48 2N 91 37 E
Hove, *U.K.* **13 G7** 50 50N 0 10W
Hoveyzeh, *Iran* **71 D6** 31 27N 48 4 E
Hovmantorp, *Sweden* **11 H9** 56 47N 15 7 E
Hövsgöl, *Mongolia* **56 C5** 43 37N 109 39 E

Illampu

Hövsgöl Nuur, Mongolia 60 A5 51 0N 100 30 E
Hovsta, Sweden 10 E9 59 22N 15 15 E
Howakil, Eritrea 81 D5 15 10N 40 16 E
Howar, Wadi →, Sudan 81 D2 17 30N 27 8 E
Howard, Australia 95 D5 25 16 S 152 32 E
Howard, Pa., U.S.A. 110 F7 41 1N 77 40W
Howard, S. Dak., U.S.A. 112 C6 44 1N 97 32W
Howe, U.S.A. 114 E7 43 48N 113 0W
Howe, C., Australia 95 F5 37 30 S 150 0 E
Howe I., Canada 111 B8 44 16N 76 17W
Howell, U.S.A. 108 D4 42 36N 83 56W
Howick, Canada 111 A11 45 11N 73 51W
Howick, S. Africa 89 D5 29 28 S 30 14 E
Howick Group, Australia 94 A4 14 20 S 145 30 E
Howitt, L., Australia 95 D2 27 40 S 138 40 E
Howland I., Pac. Oc. 96 G10 0 48N 176 38W
Howrah = Haora, India 69 H13 22 37N 88 20 E
Howth Hd., Ireland 15 C5 53 22N 6 3W
Höxter, Germany 24 D5 51 46N 9 22 E
Hoy, U.K. 14 C5 58 50N 3 15W
Hoya, Germany 24 C5 52 49N 9 8 E
Høyanger, Norway 9 F12 61 13N 6 4 E
Hoyerswerda, Germany 24 D10 51 26N 14 14 E
Hoylake, U.K. 12 D4 53 24N 3 10W
Hoyos, Spain 34 E4 40 9N 6 45W
Hpa-an = Pa-an, Burma 67 L20 16 51N 97 40 E
Hpungan Pass, Burma 67 F20 27 30N 96 55 E
Hradec Králové, Czech Rep. 26 A8 50 15N 15 50 E
Hrádek, Czech Rep. 27 C9 48 46N 16 16 E
Hranice, Czech Rep. 27 B10 49 34N 17 45 E
Hrazdan, Armenia 49 K7 40 30N 44 46 E
Hrebenka, Ukraine 47 G7 50 9N 32 22 E
Hrodna, Belarus 46 F2 53 42N 23 52 E
Hrodzyanka, Belarus 46 F5 53 31N 28 42 E
Hron →, Slovak Rep. 27 D11 47 49N 18 45 E
Hrubieszów, Poland 45 H10 50 49N 23 51 E
Hrubý Jeseník, Czech Rep. 27 A10 50 5N 17 10 E
Hrvatska = Croatia ■, Europe 29 C13 45 20N 16 0 E
Hrymayliv, Ukraine 47 H4 49 20N 26 5 E
Hsenwi, Burma 67 H20 23 22N 97 55 E
Hsiamen = Xiamen, China 59 E12 24 25N 118 4 E
Hsian = Xi'an, China 56 G5 34 15N 109 0 E
Hsinchu, Taiwan 59 E13 24 48N 120 58 E
Hsinhailien = Lianyungang, China 57 G10 34 40N 119 11 E
Hsinying, Taiwan 59 F13 23 18N 120 19 E
Hsopket, Burma 58 F2 23 11N 98 26 E
Hsüchou = Xuzhou, China 57 G9 34 18N 117 10 E
Hu Xian, China 56 G5 34 8N 108 42 E
Hua Hin, Thailand 64 F2 12 34N 99 58 E
Hua Xian, Henan, China 56 G8 35 30N 114 30 E
Hua Xian, Shaanxi, China 56 G5 34 30N 109 48 E
Hua'an, China 59 E11 25 1N 117 32 E
Huab →, Namibia 88 B2 20 52 S 13 25 E
Huacheng, China 59 E10 24 4N 115 37 E
Huachinera, Mexico 118 A3 30 9N 108 55W
Huacho, Peru 124 F3 11 10 S 77 35W
Huade, China 56 D7 41 55N 113 59 E
Huadian, China 57 C14 43 0N 126 40 E
Huadu, China 59 F9 23 22N 113 12 E
Huai He →, China 59 A12 33 0N 118 30 E
Huai Yot, Thailand 65 J2 7 45N 99 37 E
Huai'an, Hebei, China 56 D8 40 30N 114 20 E
Huai'an, Jiangsu, China 57 H10 33 30N 119 10 E
Huaibei, China 56 G9 34 0N 116 48 E
Huaibin, China 59 A10 32 32N 115 27 E
Huaide = Gongzhuling, China 57 C13 43 30N 124 40 E
Huaidezhen, China 57 C13 43 48N 124 50 E
Huaihua, China 58 D7 27 32N 109 57 E
Huaiji, China 59 F9 23 55N 112 12 E
Huainan, China 59 A11 32 38N 116 58 E
Huaining, China 59 B11 30 24N 116 40 E
Huairen, China 56 E7 39 48N 113 20 E
Huairou, China 56 D9 40 20N 116 35 E
Huaiyang, China 56 H8 33 40N 114 52 E
Huaiyin, China 57 H10 33 30N 119 2 E
Huaiyuan, Anhui, China 57 H9 32 55N 117 10 E
Huaiyuan, Guangxi Zhuangzu, China 58 E7 24 31N 108 22 E
Huajianzi, China 57 D13 41 23N 125 20 E
Huajuapan de Leon, Mexico 119 D5 17 50N 97 48W
Hualapai Peak, U.S.A. 115 J7 35 5N 113 54W
Hualien, Taiwan 59 E13 24 0N 121 30 E
Huallaga →, Peru 124 E3 5 15 S 75 30W
Huambo, Angola 85 G3 12 42 S 15 54 E
Huan Jiang →, China 56 G5 34 28N 109 0 E
Huan Xian, China 56 F4 36 33N 107 7 E
Huancabamba, Peru 124 E3 5 10 S 79 15W
Huancane, Peru 124 G5 15 10 S 69 44W
Huancavelica, Peru 124 F3 12 50 S 75 5W
Huancayo, Peru 124 F3 12 5 S 75 12W
Huanchaca, Bolivia 124 H5 20 15 S 66 40W
Huang Hai = Yellow Sea, China 57 G12 35 0N 123 0 E
Huang He →, China 57 F10 37 55N 118 50 E
Huang Xian, China 57 F11 37 38N 120 30 E
Huangchuan, China 59 A10 32 15N 115 10 E
Huanggang, China 59 B10 30 29N 114 52 E
Huangguoshu, China 58 E5 26 0N 105 40 E
Huangling, China 56 G5 35 34N 109 15 E
Huanglong, China 56 G5 35 30N 109 59 E
Huanglongtan, China 59 A8 32 40N 110 33 E
Huangmei, China 59 B10 30 5N 115 56 E
Huangpi, China 59 B10 30 50N 114 22 E
Huangping, China 58 D6 26 52N 107 54 E
Huangshan, China 59 C12 29 42N 118 25 E
Huangshi, China 59 B10 30 10N 115 3 E
Huangsongdian, China 57 C14 43 45N 127 25 E
Huangyan, China 59 C13 28 38N 121 19 E
Huangyangsi, China 59 D8 26 33N 111 39 E
Huaning, China 58 E4 24 17N 102 56 E
Huanjiang, China 58 E7 24 50N 108 18 E
Huantai, China 57 F9 36 58N 117 56 E
Huánuco, Peru 124 E3 9 55 S 76 15W
Huaping, China 58 D3 26 46N 101 25 E
Huaraz, Peru 124 E3 9 30 S 77 32W
Huarmey, Peru 124 F3 10 5 S 78 5W
Huarong, China 59 C9 29 29N 112 30 E
Huascarán, Peru 122 D3 9 8 S 77 36W
Huasco, Chile 126 B1 28 30 S 71 15W
Huasco →, Chile 126 B1 28 27 S 71 13W
Huasna, U.S.A. 117 K6 35 6N 120 24W
Huatabampo, Mexico 118 B3 26 50N 109 50W
Huauchinango, Mexico 119 C5 20 11N 98 3W
Huautla de Jiménez, Mexico 119 D5 18 8N 96 51W
Huaxi, China 58 D6 26 25N 106 40 E
Huay Namota, Mexico 118 C4 21 56N 104 30W
Huayin, China 56 G6 34 35N 110 5 E
Huayuan, China 58 C7 28 37N 109 29 E
Huayun, China 58 B6 30 14N 106 40 E
Huazhou, China 59 G8 21 33N 110 33 E
Hubbard, Ohio, U.S.A. 110 E4 41 9N 80 34W
Hubbard, Tex., U.S.A. 113 K6 31 51N 96 48W
Hubbart Pt., Canada 105 B10 59 21N 94 41W
Hubei □, China 59 B9 31 0N 112 0 E
Huch'ang, N. Korea 57 D14 41 25N 127 2 E
Hucknall, U.K. 12 D6 53 3N 1 13W
Huddersfield, U.K. 12 D6 53 39N 1 47W
Hude, Germany 24 B4 53 7N 8 26 E
Hudi, Sudan 80 D3 17 43N 34 18 E
Hudiksvall, Sweden 10 C11 61 43N 17 10 E
Hudson, Canada 102 B1 50 6N 92 9W
Hudson, Mass., U.S.A. 111 D13 42 23N 71 34W
Hudson, N.Y., U.S.A. 111 D11 42 15N 73 46W
Hudson, Wis., U.S.A. 112 C8 44 58N 92 45W
Hudson, Wyo., U.S.A. 114 E9 42 54N 108 35W
Hudson →, U.S.A. 111 F10 40 42N 74 2W
Hudson Bay, Nunavut, Canada 101 C11 60 0N 86 0W
Hudson Bay, Sask., Canada 105 C8 52 51N 102 23W
Hudson Falls, U.S.A. 111 C11 43 18N 73 35W
Hudson Mts., Antarctica 5 D16 74 32 S 99 20W
Hudson Str., Canada 101 B13 62 0N 70 0W
Hudson's Hope, Canada 104 B4 56 0N 121 54W
Hue, Vietnam 64 D6 16 30N 107 35 E
Huebra →, Spain 34 D4 41 2N 6 48W
Huedin, Romania 42 D8 46 52N 23 2 E
Huehuetenango, Guatemala 120 C1 15 20N 91 28W
Huejúcar, Mexico 118 C4 22 21N 103 13W
Huélamo, Spain 32 E3 40 17N 1 48W
Huelgoat, France 18 D3 48 22N 3 46W
Huelma, Spain 35 H7 37 39N 3 28W
Huelva, Spain 35 H4 37 18N 6 57W
Huelva □, Spain 35 H4 37 40N 7 0W
Huelva →, Spain 35 H5 37 27N 6 0W
Huentelauquén, Chile 126 C1 31 38 S 71 33W
Huércal-Overa, Spain 33 H3 37 23N 1 57W
Huerta, Sa. de la, Argentina 126 C2 31 10 S 67 30W
Huertas, C. de las, Spain 33 G4 38 21N 0 24W
Huerva →, Spain 32 D4 41 39N 0 52W
Huesca, Spain 32 C4 42 8N 0 25W
Huesca □, Spain 32 C5 42 20N 0 1 E
Huéscar, Spain 33 H2 37 44N 2 35W
Huetamo, Mexico 118 D4 18 36N 100 54W
Huete, Spain 32 E2 40 10N 2 43W
Hugh →, Australia 94 D1 25 1 S 134 1 E
Hughenden, Australia 94 C3 20 52 S 144 10 E
Hughes, Australia 93 F4 30 42 S 129 31 E
Hughesville, U.S.A. 111 E8 41 14N 76 44W
Hugli →, India 69 J13 21 56N 88 4 E
Hugo, Colo., U.S.A. 112 F3 39 8N 103 28W
Hugo, Okla., U.S.A. 113 H7 34 1N 95 31W
Hugoton, U.S.A. 113 G4 37 11N 101 21W
Hui Xian = Huixian, China 56 G7 35 27N 113 12 E
Hui Xian, China 56 H4 33 50N 106 4 E
Hui'an, China 59 E12 25 1N 118 43 E
Hui'anbu, China 56 F4 37 28N 106 38 E
Huichang, China 59 E10 25 32N 115 45 E
Huichapán, Mexico 119 C5 20 24N 99 40W
Huidong, Guangdong, China 59 F10 22 58N 114 43 E
Huidong, Sichuan, China 58 D4 26 34N 102 35 E
Huifa He →, China 57 C14 43 0N 127 50 E
Huila, Nevado del, Colombia 124 C3 3 0N 76 0W
Huilai, China 59 F11 23 0N 116 18 E
Huili, China 58 D4 26 35N 102 17 E
Huimin, China 57 F9 37 27N 117 28 E
Huinan, China 57 C14 42 40N 126 2 E
Huinca Renancó, Argentina 126 C3 34 51 S 64 22W
Huining, China 56 G3 35 38N 105 0 E
Huinong, China 56 E4 39 5N 106 35 E
Huisache, Mexico 118 C4 22 55N 100 25W
Huishui, China 58 D6 26 7N 106 38 E
Huisne →, France 18 E7 47 59N 0 11 E
Huiting, China 56 G9 34 5N 116 5 E
Huitong, China 58 D7 26 51N 109 45 E
Huixian, China 56 G7 35 27N 113 12 E
Huixtla, Mexico 119 D6 15 9N 92 28W
Huize, China 58 D4 26 24N 103 15 E
Huizhou, China 59 F10 23 0N 114 23 E
Hukawng Valley, Burma 67 F20 26 30N 96 30 E
Hukou, China 59 C11 29 45N 116 21 E
Hukuntsi, Botswana 88 C3 23 58 S 21 45 E
Ḥulayfā', Si. Arabia 70 E4 25 58N 40 45 E
Huld = Ulaanjirem, Mongolia 56 B3 45 5N 105 30 E
Hulin He →, China 57 B12 45 0N 122 10 E
Hull = Kingston upon Hull, U.K. 12 D7 53 45N 0 21W
Hull, Canada 102 C4 45 25N 75 44W
Hull →, U.K. 12 D7 53 44N 0 20W
Hulst, Neths. 17 C4 51 17N 4 2 E
Hultsfred, Sweden 11 G9 57 30N 15 52 E
Hulun Nur, China 60 B6 49 0N 117 30 E
Hulyaypole, Ukraine 47 J9 47 45N 36 21 E
Humahuaca, Argentina 126 A2 23 10 S 65 25W
Humaitá, Brazil 124 E6 7 35 S 63 1W
Humaitá, Paraguay 126 B4 27 2 S 58 31W
Humansdorp, S. Africa 88 E3 34 2 S 24 46 E
Humara, J., Sudan 81 D3 16 16N 30 59 E
Humbe, Angola 88 B1 16 40 S 14 55 E
Humber →, U.K. 12 D7 53 42N 0 27W
Humboldt, Canada 105 C7 52 15N 105 9W
Humboldt, Iowa, U.S.A. 112 D7 42 44N 94 13W
Humboldt, Tenn., U.S.A. 113 H10 35 50N 88 55W
Humboldt →, U.S.A. 114 F4 39 59N 118 36W
Humboldt Gletscher, Greenland 4 B4 79 30N 62 0W
Hume, U.S.A. 116 J8 36 48N 118 54W
Hume, L., Australia 95 F4 36 0 S 147 5 E
Humenné, Slovak Rep. 27 C14 48 55N 21 50 E
Hummelsta, Sweden 10 E10 59 34N 16 58 E
Humphreys, Mt., U.S.A. 116 H8 37 17N 118 40W
Humphreys Peak, U.S.A. 115 J8 35 21N 111 41W
Humpolec, Czech Rep. 26 B8 49 31N 15 20 E
Humptulips, U.S.A. 116 C3 47 14N 123 57W
Hūn, Libya 79 C9 29 2N 16 0 E
Hun Jiang →, China 57 D13 40 50N 125 38 E
Húnaflói, Iceland 8 D3 65 50N 20 50W
Hunan □, China 59 D9 27 30N 112 0 E
Hunchun, China 57 C16 42 52N 130 28 E
Hundested, Denmark 11 J5 55 58N 11 52 E
Hundewali, Pakistan 68 D5 31 55N 72 38 E
Hundred Mile House, Canada 104 C4 51 38N 121 18W
Hunedoara, Romania 42 E7 45 40N 22 50 E
Hunedoara □, Romania 42 E7 45 50N 22 54 E
Hünfeld, Germany 24 E5 50 39N 9 46 E
Hung Yen, Vietnam 58 G6 20 39N 106 4 E
Hungary ■, Europe 27 D12 47 20N 19 20 E
Hungary, Plain of, Europe 6 F10 47 0N 20 0 E
Hungerford, Australia 95 D3 28 58 S 144 24 E
Hŭngnam, N. Korea 57 E14 39 49N 127 45 E
Hungt'ou Hsü, Taiwan 59 G13 22 0N 121 30 E
Huni Valley, Ghana 82 D4 5 33N 1 56W
Hunneberg, Sweden 11 F6 58 18N 12 30 E
Hunnebostrand, Sweden 11 F5 58 27N 11 18 E
Hunsberge, Namibia 88 D2 27 45 S 17 12 E
Hunsrück, Germany 25 F3 49 56N 7 27 E
Hunstanton, U.K. 12 E8 52 56N 0 29 E
Hunte →, Germany 24 B4 53 14N 8 28 E
Hunter, U.S.A. 111 D10 42 13N 74 13W
Hunter I., Australia 94 G3 40 30 S 144 45 E
Hunter I., Canada 104 C3 51 55N 128 0W
Hunter Ra., Australia 95 E5 32 45 S 150 15 E
Hunters Road, Zimbabwe 87 F2 19 9 S 29 49 E
Hunterville, N.Z. 91 H5 39 56 S 175 35 E
Huntingburg, U.S.A. 108 F2 38 18N 86 57W
Huntingdon, Canada 102 C5 45 6N 74 10W
Huntingdon, U.K. 13 E7 52 20N 0 11W
Huntingdon, U.S.A. 110 F6 40 30N 78 1W
Huntington, Ind., U.S.A. 108 E3 40 53N 85 30W
Huntington, Oreg., U.S.A. 114 D5 44 21N 117 16W
Huntington, Utah, U.S.A. 114 G8 39 20N 110 58W
Huntington, W. Va., U.S.A. 108 F4 38 25N 82 27W
Huntington Beach, U.S.A. 117 M9 33 40N 118 5W
Huntington Station, U.S.A. 111 F11 40 52N 73 26W
Huntly, N.Z. 91 G5 37 34 S 175 11 E
Huntly, U.K. 14 D6 57 27N 2 47W
Huntsville, Canada 102 C4 45 20N 79 14W
Huntsville, Ala., U.S.A. 109 H2 34 44N 86 35W
Huntsville, Tex., U.S.A. 113 K7 30 43N 95 33W
Hunyani →, Zimbabwe 87 F3 15 57 S 30 39 E
Hunyuan, China 56 E7 39 42N 113 42 E
Hunza →, India 69 B6 35 54N 74 20 E
Huo Xian = Huozhou, China 56 F6 36 36N 111 42 E
Huong Hoa, Vietnam 64 D6 16 37N 106 45 E
Huong Khe, Vietnam 64 C5 18 13N 105 41 E
Huonville, Australia 94 G4 43 0 S 147 5 E
Huoqiu, China 59 A11 32 20N 116 12 E
Huoshan, Anhui, China 59 A12 32 28N 118 30 E
Huoshan, Anhui, China 59 B11 31 25N 116 20 E
Huoshao Dao = Lü-Tao, Taiwan 59 F13 22 40N 121 30 E
Huozhou, China 56 F6 36 36N 111 42 E
Hupeh = Hubei □, China 59 B9 31 0N 112 0 E
Ḥūr, Iran 71 D8 30 50N 57 7 E
Hurbanovo, Slovak Rep. 27 D11 47 51N 18 11 E
Hurd, C., Canada 110 A3 45 13N 81 44W
Hure Qi, China 57 C11 42 45N 121 45 E
Hurezani, Romania 43 F8 44 49N 23 40 E
Hurghada, Egypt 80 B3 27 15N 33 50 E
Hurley, N. Mex., U.S.A. 115 K9 32 42N 108 8W
Hurley, Wis., U.S.A. 112 B9 46 27N 90 11W
Huron, Calif., U.S.A. 116 J6 36 12N 120 6W
Huron, Ohio, U.S.A. 110 E2 41 24N 82 33W
Huron, S. Dak., U.S.A. 112 C5 44 22N 98 13W
Huron, L., U.S.A. 110 B2 44 30N 82 40W
Hurricane, U.S.A. 115 H7 37 11N 113 17W
Hurso, Ethiopia 81 F5 9 35N 41 33 E
Hurunui →, N.Z. 91 K4 42 54 S 173 18 E
Hurup, Denmark 11 H2 56 46N 8 25 E
Húsavík, Iceland 8 C5 66 3N 17 21W
Huşi, Romania 43 D13 46 41N 28 7 E
Huskvarna, Sweden 11 G8 57 47N 14 15 E
Hustadvika, Norway 8 E12 63 0N 7 0 E
Hustontown, U.S.A. 110 F6 40 3N 78 2W
Hustopeče, Czech Rep. 27 C9 48 57N 16 43 E
Husum, Germany 24 A5 54 28N 9 4 E
Husum, Sweden 10 A13 63 21N 19 12 E
Hutchinson, Kans., U.S.A. 113 F6 38 5N 97 56W
Hutchinson, Minn., U.S.A. 112 C7 44 54N 94 22W
Hutte Sauvage, L. de la, Canada 103 A7 56 15N 64 45W
Hüttenberg, Austria 26 E7 46 56N 14 33 E
Hutton, Mt., Australia 95 D4 25 51 S 148 20 E
Huwun, Ethiopia 81 G5 4 23N 40 6 E
Huy, Belgium 17 D5 50 31N 5 15 E
Huzhou, China 59 B13 30 51N 120 8 E
Hvalpsund, Denmark 11 H3 56 42N 9 11 E
Hvammstangi, Iceland 8 D3 65 24N 20 57W
Hvar, Croatia 29 E13 43 11N 16 28 E
Hvarski Kanal, Croatia 29 E13 43 15N 16 35 E
Hvítá →, Iceland 8 D3 64 30N 21 58W
Hwachŏn-chŏsuji, S. Korea 57 E14 38 5N 127 50 E
Hwang Ho = Huang He →, China 57 F10 37 55N 118 50 E
Hwange, Zimbabwe 87 F2 18 18 S 26 30 E
Hwange Nat. Park, Zimbabwe 88 B4 19 0 S 26 30 E
Hyannis, Mass., U.S.A. 108 E10 41 39N 70 17W
Hyannis, Nebr., U.S.A. 112 E4 42 0N 101 46W
Hyargas Nuur, Mongolia 60 B4 49 0N 93 0 E
Hybo, Sweden 10 C10 61 49N 16 15 E
Hydaburg, U.S.A. 104 B2 55 15N 132 50W
Hyde Park, U.S.A. 111 E11 41 47N 73 56W
Hyden, Australia 93 F2 32 24 S 118 53 E
Hyder, U.S.A. 104 B2 55 55N 130 5W
Hyderabad, India 66 L11 17 22N 78 29 E
Hyderabad, Pakistan 68 G3 25 23N 68 24 E
Hyères, France 21 E10 43 8N 6 9 E
Hyères, Îs. d', France 21 F10 43 0N 6 20 E
Hyesan, N. Korea 57 D15 41 20N 128 10 E
Hyland →, Canada 104 B3 59 52N 128 12W
Hyltebruk, Sweden 11 H7 56 59N 13 15 E
Hymia, India 69 C8 33 40N 78 2 E
Hyndman Peak, U.S.A. 114 E6 43 45N 114 8W
Hyōgo □, Japan 55 G7 35 15N 134 50 E
Hyrum, U.S.A. 114 F8 41 38N 111 51W
Hysham, U.S.A. 114 C10 46 18N 107 14W
Hythe, U.K. 13 F9 51 4N 1 5 E
Hyūga, Japan 55 H5 32 25N 131 35 E
Hyvinge = Hyvinkää, Finland 9 F21 60 38N 24 50 E
Hyvinkää, Finland 9 F21 60 38N 24 50 E

I

I-n-Gall, Niger 83 B6 16 51N 7 1 E
I-n-Oudad, Algeria 83 A5 20 17N 4 38 E
I-n-Ouzzal, Algeria 83 A5 20 40N 2 35 E
I-n-Tadreft, Niger 83 B6 19 5N 6 38 E
Iablaniţa, Romania 42 F7 44 57N 22 19 E
Iaco →, Brazil 124 E5 9 3 S 68 34W
Iacobeni, Romania 43 C10 47 25N 25 20 E
Iakora, Madag. 89 C8 23 6 S 46 40 E
Ialomiţa □, Romania 43 F12 44 30N 27 30 E
Ialomiţa →, Romania 43 F12 44 42N 27 51 E
Ialoveni, Moldova 43 D13 46 56N 28 47 E
Ialpug →, Moldova 43 E13 45 41N 28 35 E
Ianca, Romania 43 E12 45 6N 27 29 E
Iara, Romania 43 D8 46 31N 23 35 E
Iarda, Ethiopia 81 E4 11 9N 35 53 E
Iargara, Moldova 43 D13 46 24N 28 23 E
Iaşi, Romania 43 C12 47 10N 27 40 E
Iaşi □, Romania 43 C12 47 20N 27 0 E
Íasmos, Greece 41 E9 41 8N 25 11 E
Ib →, India 69 J10 21 34N 83 48 E
Iba, Phil. 61 D3 15 22N 120 0 E
Ibadan, Nigeria 83 D5 7 22N 3 58 E
Ibagué, Colombia 124 C3 4 20N 75 20W
Iballë, Albania 40 D4 42 12N 20 2 E
Ibăneşti, Botoşani, Romania 43 B11 48 4N 26 22 E
Ibăneşti, Mureş, Romania 43 D9 46 45N 24 57 E
Ibar →, Serbia, Yug. 40 C4 43 43N 20 45 E
Ibaraki □, Japan 55 F10 36 10N 140 10 E
Ibarra, Ecuador 124 C3 0 21N 78 7W
Ibba, Sudan 81 G2 4 49N 29 2 E
Ibba, Bahr el →, Sudan 81 F2 5 30N 28 55 E
Ibbenbüren, Germany 24 C3 52 16N 7 43 E
Ibembo, Dem. Rep. of the Congo 86 B1 2 35N 23 35 E
Ibera, L., Argentina 126 B4 28 30 S 57 9W
Iberian Peninsula, Europe 6 H5 40 0N 5 0W
Iberville, Canada 102 C5 45 19N 73 17W
Iberville, Lac d', Canada 102 A5 55 55N 73 15W
Ibi, Nigeria 83 D6 8 15N 9 44 E
Ibi, Spain 33 G4 38 38N 0 34W
Ibiá, Brazil 125 G9 19 30 S 46 30W
Ibiapaba, Sa. da, Brazil 125 D10 4 0 S 41 30W
Ibicuí →, Brazil 127 B4 29 25 S 56 47W
Ibicuy, Argentina 126 C4 33 55 S 59 10W
Ibiza = Eivissa, Spain 37 C7 38 54N 1 26 E
Íblei, Monti, Italy 31 E7 37 15N 14 45 E
Ibo, Mozam. 87 E5 12 22 S 40 40 E
Ibonma, Indonesia 63 E8 3 29 S 133 31 E
Ibotirama, Brazil 125 F10 12 13 S 43 12W
Ibrāhīm →, Lebanon 75 A4 34 4N 35 38 E
'Ibrī, Oman 71 F8 23 14N 56 30 E
İbriktepe, Turkey 41 E10 41 0N 26 30 E
Ibshawâi, Egypt 80 J7 29 21N 30 40 E
Ibu, Indonesia 63 D7 1 35N 127 33 E
Ibusuki, Japan 55 J5 31 12N 130 40 E
Ica, Peru 124 F3 14 0 S 75 48W
Iça →, Brazil 124 D5 2 55 S 67 58W
Içana, Brazil 124 C5 0 21N 67 19W
Içana →, Brazil 124 C5 0 26N 67 19W
İçel = Mersin, Turkey 70 B2 36 51N 34 36 E
Iceland ■, Europe 8 D4 64 45N 19 0W
Ich'ang = Yichang, China 59 B8 30 40N 111 20 E
Ichchapuram, India 67 K14 19 10N 84 40 E
Ichhawar, India 68 H7 23 1N 77 1 E
Ichihara, Japan 55 G10 35 28N 140 5 E
Ichikawa, Japan 55 G9 35 44N 139 55 E
Ichilo →, Bolivia 124 G6 15 57 S 64 50W
Ichinohe, Japan 54 D10 40 13N 141 17 E
Ichinomiya, Japan 55 G8 35 18N 136 48 E
Ichinoseki, Japan 54 E10 38 55N 141 8 E
Ichnya, Ukraine 47 G7 50 52N 32 24 E
Icod, Canary Is. 37 F3 28 22N 16 43W
Ida Grove, U.S.A. 112 D7 42 21N 95 28W
Idabel, U.S.A. 113 J7 33 54N 94 50W
Idaga Hamus, Ethiopia 81 E4 14 13N 39 48 E
Idah, Nigeria 83 D6 7 5N 6 40 E
Idaho □, U.S.A. 114 D7 45 0N 115 0W
Idaho City, U.S.A. 114 E6 43 50N 115 50W
Idaho Falls, U.S.A. 114 E7 43 30N 112 2W
Idanha-a-Nova, Portugal 34 F3 39 50N 7 15W
Idar-Oberstein, Germany 25 F3 49 43N 7 16 E
Idfû, Egypt 80 C3 24 55N 32 49 E
Ídhi Óros, Greece 36 D6 35 15N 24 45 E
Ídhra, Greece 38 D5 37 20N 23 28 E
Idi, Indonesia 62 C1 5 2N 97 37 E
Idiofa, Dem. Rep. of the Congo 84 E3 4 55 S 19 42 E
Idkerberget, Sweden 10 D9 60 22N 15 15 E
Idku, Bahra el, Egypt 80 H7 31 18N 30 18 E
Idlib, Syria 70 C3 35 55N 36 36 E
Idre, Sweden 10 C6 61 52N 12 42 E
Idria, U.S.A. 116 J6 36 25N 120 41W
Idrija, Slovenia 29 C11 46 0N 14 5 E
Idritsa, Russia 46 D5 56 17N 28 53 E
Idutywa, S. Africa 89 E4 32 8 S 28 18 E
Ieper, Belgium 17 D2 50 51N 2 53 E
Ierápetra, Greece 36 E7 35 1N 25 44 E
Ierissós, Greece 40 F7 40 22N 23 52 E
Ierissóu Kólpos, Greece 40 F7 40 27N 23 57 E
Iernut, Romania 43 D9 46 27N 24 15 E
Iesi, Italy 29 E10 43 31N 13 14 E
Iésolo, Italy 29 C9 45 32N 12 38 E
Ifach, Peñón de, Spain 33 G5 38 38N 0 5 E
Ifakara, Tanzania 84 F7 8 8 S 36 41 E
'Ifāl, W. al →, Si. Arabia 70 D2 28 7N 35 3 E
Ifanadiana, Madag. 89 C8 21 19 S 47 39 E
Ife, Nigeria 83 D5 7 30N 4 31 E
Iférouâne, Niger 83 B6 19 5N 8 24 E
Iffley, Australia 94 B3 18 53 S 141 12 E
Ifon, Nigeria 83 D6 6 58N 5 40 E
Iforas, Adrar des, Africa 83 B5 19 40N 1 40 E
Ifould, L., Australia 93 F5 30 52 S 132 6 E
Iganga, Uganda 86 B3 0 37N 33 28 E
Igarapava, Brazil 125 H9 20 3 S 47 47W
Igarka, Russia 50 C9 67 30N 86 33 E
Igatimi, Paraguay 127 A4 24 5 S 55 40W
Igbetti, Nigeria 83 D5 8 44N 4 8 E
Igbo-Ora, Nigeria 83 D5 7 29N 3 15 E
Igboho, Nigeria 83 D5 8 53N 3 50 E
Igbor, Nigeria 83 D6 7 27N 8 34 E
Iğdır, Turkey 73 C11 39 55N 44 2 E
Igelfors, Sweden 11 F9 58 52N 15 41 E
Iggesund, Sweden 10 C11 61 39N 17 10 E
Iglésias, Italy 30 C1 39 19N 8 32 E
Igloolik, Canada 101 B11 69 20N 81 49W
Igluligaarjuk, Canada 101 B10 63 21N 90 42W
Iglulik = Igloolik, Canada 101 B11 69 20N 81 49W
'Igma, Gebel el, Egypt 80 B3 28 55N 34 0 E
Ignace, Canada 102 C1 49 30N 91 40W
İğneada, Turkey 41 E11 41 52N 27 59 E
İğneada Burnu, Turkey 41 E12 41 53N 28 2 E
Igoumenítsa, Greece 38 B2 39 32N 20 18 E
Igra, Russia 48 B11 57 33N 53 7 E
Iguaçu →, Brazil 127 B5 25 36 S 54 36W
Iguaçu, Cat. del, Brazil 127 B5 25 41 S 54 26W
Iguaçu Falls = Iguaçu, Cat. del, Brazil 127 B5 25 41 S 54 26W
Iguala, Mexico 119 D5 18 20N 99 40W
Igualada, Spain 32 D6 41 37N 1 37 E
Iguassu = Iguaçu →, Brazil 127 B5 25 36 S 54 36W
Iguatu, Brazil 125 E11 6 20 S 39 18W
Iharana, Madag. 89 A9 13 25 S 50 0 E
Ihbulag, Mongolia 56 C4 43 11N 107 10 E
Iheya-Shima, Japan 55 L3 27 4N 127 58 E
Ihiala, Nigeria 83 D6 5 51N 6 55 E
Ihosy, Madag. 89 C8 22 24 S 46 8 E
Ihotry, Farihy, Madag. 89 C7 21 56 S 43 41 E
Ihugh, Nigeria 83 D6 7 2N 9 0 E
Ii, Finland 8 D21 65 19N 25 22 E
Ii-Shima, Japan 55 L3 26 43N 127 47 E
Iida, Japan 55 G8 35 35N 137 50 E
Iijoki →, Finland 8 D21 65 20N 25 20 E
Iisalmi, Finland 8 E22 63 32N 27 10 E
Iiyama, Japan 55 F9 36 51N 138 22 E
Iizuka, Japan 55 H5 33 38N 130 42 E
Ijebu-Igbo, Nigeria 83 D5 6 56N 4 1 E
Ijebu-Ode, Nigeria 83 D5 6 47N 3 58 E
IJmuiden, Neths. 17 B4 52 28N 4 35 E
IJssel →, Neths. 17 B5 52 35N 5 50 E
IJsselmeer, Neths. 17 B5 52 45N 5 20 E
Ijuí, Brazil 127 B5 28 23 S 53 55W
Ijuí →, Brazil 127 B4 27 58 S 55 20W
Ikalamavony, Madag. 89 C8 21 9 S 46 35 E
Ikale, Nigeria 83 D6 7 40N 5 37 E
Ikaluktutiak, Canada 100 B9 69 10N 105 0W
Ikang, Nigeria 83 E6 4 49N 8 30 E
Ikara, Nigeria 83 C6 11 12N 8 15 E
Ikare, Nigeria 83 D6 7 32N 5 40 E
Ikaría, Greece 39 D8 37 35N 26 10 E
Ikast, Denmark 11 H3 56 8N 9 10 E
Ikeda, Japan 55 G6 34 1N 133 48 E
Ikeja, Nigeria 83 D5 6 36N 3 23 E
Ikela, Dem. Rep. of the Congo 84 E4 1 6 S 23 6 E
Ikerre-Ekiti, Nigeria 83 D6 7 25N 5 19 E
Ikhtiman, Bulgaria 40 D7 42 27N 23 48 E
Iki, Japan 55 H4 33 45N 129 42 E
Ikimba L., Tanzania 86 C3 1 30 S 31 20 E
Ikire, Nigeria 83 D5 7 23N 4 15 E
Ikizdere, Turkey 73 B9 40 46N 40 32 E
Ikom, Nigeria 83 D6 6 0N 8 42 E
Ikongo, Madag. 89 C8 21 52 S 47 27 E
Ikopa →, Madag. 89 B8 16 45 S 46 40 E
Ikot Ekpene, Nigeria 83 D6 5 12N 7 40 E
Ikungu, Tanzania 86 C3 1 33 S 33 42 E
Ikurun, Nigeria 83 D5 7 54N 4 40 E
Ila, Nigeria 83 D5 8 0N 4 39 E
Ilagan, Phil. 61 C4 17 7N 121 53 E
Ilaka, Madag. 89 B8 19 33 S 48 52 E
Īlām, Iran 70 C5 33 36N 46 36 E
Ilam, Nepal 69 F12 26 58N 87 58 E
Īlām □, Iran 70 C5 33 0N 47 0 E
Ilan, Taiwan 59 E13 24 45N 121 44 E
Ilanskiy, Russia 51 D10 56 14N 96 3 E
Ilaro, Nigeria 83 D5 6 53N 3 3 E
Ilatane, Niger 83 B5 16 30N 4 45 E
Iława, Poland 44 E6 53 36N 19 34 E
Ile →, Kazakhstan 50 E8 45 53N 77 10 E
Ile-à-la-Crosse, Canada 105 B7 55 27N 107 53W
Ile-à-la-Crosse, Lac, Canada 105 B7 55 40N 107 45W
Île-de-France □, France 19 D9 49 0N 2 20 E
Ileanda, Romania 43 C8 47 20N 23 38 E
Ilebo, Dem. Rep. of the Congo 84 E4 4 17 S 20 55 E
Ilek, Russia 50 D6 51 32N 53 21 E
Ilero, Nigeria 83 D5 8 0N 3 20 E
Ilesha, Kwara, Nigeria 83 D5 8 57N 3 28 E
Ilesha, Oyo, Nigeria 83 D5 7 37N 4 40 E
Ilford, Canada 105 B9 56 4N 95 35W
Ilfracombe, Australia 94 C3 23 30 S 144 30 E
Ilfracombe, U.K. 13 F3 51 12N 4 8W
Ilgaz, Turkey 72 B5 40 55N 33 37 E
Ilgaz Dağları, Turkey 72 B5 41 10N 33 50 E
Ilgın, Turkey 72 C4 38 16N 31 55 E
Ílhavo, Portugal 34 E2 40 33N 8 43W
Ilhéus, Brazil 125 F11 14 49 S 39 2W
Ili = Ile →, Kazakhstan 50 E8 45 53N 77 10 E
Ilia, Romania 42 E7 45 57N 22 40 E
Ilia □, Greece 38 D3 37 45N 21 35 E
Iliamna L., U.S.A. 100 C4 59 30N 155 0W
Iliç, Turkey 73 C8 39 27N 38 33 E
Ilica, Turkey 39 B9 39 52N 27 46 E
Ilichevsk, Azerbaijan 73 C11 39 22N 45 5 E
Iligan, Phil. 61 G6 8 12N 124 13 E
Iligan Bay, Phil. 61 G6 8 25N 124 5 E
Ilíki, L., Greece 38 C5 38 24N 23 15 E
Ilin I., Phil. 61 E4 12 14N 121 5 E
Iliodhrómia, Greece 38 B5 39 12N 23 50 E
Ilion, U.S.A. 111 D9 43 1N 75 2W
Ilirska-Bistrica, Slovenia 29 C11 45 34N 14 14 E
Ilkeston, U.K. 12 E6 52 58N 1 19W
Ilkley, U.K. 12 D6 53 56N 1 48W
Illampu = Ancohuma, Nevada, Bolivia 122 E4 16 0 S 68 50W

Illana B.

Illana B., *Phil.* **61 H5** 7 35N 123 45 E
Illapel, *Chile* **126 C1** 32 0 S 71 10W
Ille-et-Vilaine □, *France* **18 D5** 48 10N 1 30W
Ille-sur-Têt, *France* **20 F6** 42 40N 2 38 E
Illéla, *Niger* **83 C6** 14 32N 5 20 E
Iller →, *Germany* **25 G5** 48 23N 9 58 E
Illertissen, *Germany* **25 G6** 48 12N 10 7 E
Illescas, *Spain* **34 E7** 40 8N 3 51W
Illetas, *Spain* **37 B9** 39 32N 2 35 E
Illichivsk, *Ukraine* **47 J6** 46 20N 30 35 E
Illiers-Combray, *France* **18 D8** 48 18N 1 15 E
Illimani, Nevado, *Bolivia* **124 G5** 16 30 S 67 50W
Illinois □, *U.S.A.* **112 E10** 40 15N 89 30W
Illinois →, *U.S.A.* **107 C8** 38 58N 90 28W
Illium = Troy, *Turkey* **39 B8** 39 57N 26 12 E
Illizi, *Algeria* **78 C7** 26 31N 8 32 E
Illkirch-Graffenstaden, *France* **19 D14** 48 34N 7 42 E
Íllora, *Spain* **35 H7** 37 17N 3 53W
Ilm →, *Germany* **24 D7** 51 6N 11 40 E
Ilmajoki, *Finland* **9 E20** 62 44N 22 34 E
Ilmen, Ozero, *Russia* **46 C6** 58 15N 31 10 E
Ilmenau, *Germany* **24 E6** 50 41N 10 54 E
Ilo, *Peru* **124 G4** 17 40 S 71 20W
Ilobu, *Nigeria* **83 D5** 7 45N 4 25 E
Iloilo, *Phil.* **61 F5** 10 45N 122 33 E
Ilora, *Nigeria* **83 D5** 7 45N 3 50 E
Ilorin, *Nigeria* **83 D5** 8 30N 4 35 E
Ilovatka, *Russia* **48 E7** 50 30N 45 50 E
Ilovlya, *Russia* **49 F7** 49 15N 44 2 E
Ilovlya →, *Russia* **49 F7** 49 14N 44 0 E
Iłowa, *Poland* **45 G2** 51 30N 15 10 E
Ilubabor □, *Ethiopia* **81 F4** 7 25N 35 0 E
Ilva Mică, *Romania* **43 C9** 47 17N 24 40 E
Ilwaco, *U.S.A.* **116 D2** 46 19N 124 3W
Ilwaki, *Indonesia* **63 F7** 7 55 S 126 30 E
Ilyichevsk = Illichivsk, *Ukraine* **47 J6** 46 20N 30 35 E
Iłża, *Poland* **45 G8** 51 10N 21 15 E
Iłżanka →, *Poland* **45 G8** 51 14N 21 48 E
Imabari, *Japan* **55 G6** 34 4N 133 0 E
Imaloto →, *Madag.* **89 C8** 23 27 S 45 13 E
İmamoğlu, *Turkey* **72 D6** 37 15N 35 38 E
Imandra, Ozero, *Russia* **50 C4** 67 30N 33 0 E
Imanombo, *Madag.* **89 C8** 24 26 S 45 49 E
Imari, *Japan* **55 H4** 33 15N 129 52 E
Imasa, *Sudan* **80 D4** 18 0N 36 12 E
Imathía □, *Greece* **40 F6** 40 30N 22 15 E
Imatra, *Finland* **46 B5** 61 12N 28 48 E
Imbil, *Australia* **95 D5** 26 22 S 152 32 E
Iménas, *Mali* **83 B5** 16 20N 0 40 E
imeni 26 Bakinskikh Komissarov = Neftçala, *Azerbaijan* **71 B6** 39 19N 49 12 E
imeni 26 Bakinskikh Komissarov, *Turkmenistan* **71 B7** 39 22N 54 10 E
Imeri, Serra, *Brazil* **124 C5** 0 50N 65 25W
Imerimandroso, *Madag.* **89 B8** 17 26 S 48 35 E
Imi, *Ethiopia* **81 F5** 6 28N 42 10 E
Imishly = Imişli, *Azerbaijan* **49 L9** 39 55N 48 4 E
Imişli, *Azerbaijan* **49 L9** 39 55N 48 4 E
Imlay, *U.S.A.* **114 F4** 40 40N 118 9W
Imlay City, *U.S.A.* **110 D1** 43 2N 83 5W
Immaseri, *Sudan* **81 D2** 15 40N 25 31 E
Immenstadt, *Germany* **25 H6** 47 33N 10 13 E
Immingham, *U.K.* **12 D7** 53 37N 0 13W
Immokalee, *U.S.A.* **109 M5** 26 25N 81 25W
Imo □, *Nigeria* **83 D6** 5 30N 7 10 E
Imo →, *Nigeria* **83 E6** 4 36N 7 35 E
Ímola, *Italy* **29 D8** 44 20N 11 42 E
Imotski, *Croatia* **29 E14** 43 27N 17 12 E
Imperatriz, *Brazil* **125 E9** 5 30 S 47 29W
Impéria, *Italy* **28 E5** 43 53N 8 3 E
Imperial, *Canada* **105 C7** 51 21N 105 28W
Imperial, *Calif., U.S.A.* **117 N11** 32 51N 115 34W
Imperial, *Nebr., U.S.A.* **112 E4** 40 31N 101 39W
Imperial Beach, *U.S.A.* **117 N9** 32 35N 117 8W
Imperial Dam, *U.S.A.* **117 N12** 32 55N 114 25W
Imperial Reservoir, *U.S.A.* **117 N12** 32 53N 114 28W
Imperial Valley, *U.S.A.* **117 N11** 33 0N 115 30W
Imperieuse Reef, *Australia* **92 C2** 17 36 S 118 50 E
Impfondo, *Congo* **84 D3** 1 40N 18 0 E
Imphal, *India* **67 G18** 24 48N 93 56 E
Imphy, *France* **19 F10** 46 55N 3 16 E
Imranlı, *Turkey* **73 C8** 39 54N 38 7 E
İmroz = Gökçeada, *Turkey* **41 F9** 40 10N 25 50 E
İmroz, *Turkey* **41 F9** 40 10N 25 55 E
Imst, *Austria* **26 D3** 47 15N 10 44 E
Imuris, *Mexico* **118 A2** 30 47N 110 52W
Imuruan B., *Phil.* **63 B5** 10 40N 119 10 E
In Akhmed, *Mali* **83 B4** 19 49N 0 56W
In Aleï, *Mali* **82 B4** 17 42N 2 30W
In Delimane, *Mali* **83 B5** 15 52N 1 31 E
In Guezzam, *Algeria* **83 B6** 19 37N 5 52 E
In Koufi, *Mali* **83 B5** 19 11N 1 25 E
In Salah, *Algeria* **78 C6** 27 10N 2 32 E
In Tallak, *Mali* **83 B5** 16 19N 3 15 E
In Tebezas, *Mali* **83 B5** 17 49N 1 53 E
Ina, *Japan* **55 G8** 35 50N 137 55 E
Inangahua, *N.Z.* **91 J3** 41 52 S 171 59 E
Inanwatan, *Indonesia* **63 E8** 2 8 S 132 10 E
Iñapari, *Peru* **124 F5** 11 0 S 69 40W
Inari, *Finland* **8 B22** 68 54N 27 5 E
Inarijärvi, *Finland* **8 B22** 69 0N 28 0 E
Inawashiro-Ko, *Japan* **54 F10** 37 29N 140 6 E
Inca, *Spain* **37 B9** 39 43N 2 54 E
Inca de Oro, *Chile* **126 B2** 26 45 S 69 54W
Incaguasi, *Chile* **126 B1** 29 12 S 71 5W
İnce Burun, *Turkey* **72 A6** 42 7N 34 56 E
İncekum Burnu, *Turkey* **72 D5** 36 13N 33 57 E
İncesu, *Turkey* **70 B2** 38 38N 35 11 E
Inch'ŏn, *S. Korea* **57 F14** 37 27N 126 40 E
Incio = Cruz de Incio, *Spain* **34 C3** 42 39N 7 21W
İncirliova, *Turkey* **39 D9** 37 50N 27 41 E
Incline Village, *U.S.A.* **114 G4** 39 10N 119 58W
Incomáti →, *Mozam.* **89 D5** 25 46 S 32 43 E
Inda Silase, *Ethiopia* **81 E4** 14 10N 38 15 E
Indal, *Sweden* **10 B11** 62 36N 17 5 E
Indalsälven →, *Sweden* **10 B11** 62 36N 17 30 E
Indaw, *Burma* **67 G20** 24 15N 96 5 E
Indbir, *Ethiopia* **81 F4** 8 7N 37 52 E
Independence, *Calif., U.S.A.* **116 J8** 36 48N 118 12W
Independence, *Iowa, U.S.A.* **112 D9** 42 28N 91 54W
Independence, *Kans., U.S.A.* **113 G7** 37 14N 95 42W
Independence, *Ky., U.S.A.* **108 F3** 38 57N 84 33W
Independence, *Mo., U.S.A.* **112 F7** 39 6N 94 25W
Independence Fjord, *Greenland* **4 A6** 82 10N 29 0W
Independence Mts., *U.S.A.* **114 F5** 41 20N 116 0W
Independenţa, *Romania* **43 E12** 45 25N 27 42 E
Index, *U.S.A.* **116 C5** 47 50N 121 33W
India ■, *Asia* **66 K11** 20 0N 78 0 E
Indian →, *U.S.A.* **109 M5** 27 59N 80 34W
Indian Cabins, *Canada* **104 B5** 59 52N 117 40W
Indian Harbour, *Canada* **103 B8** 54 27N 57 13W
Indian Head, *Canada* **105 C8** 50 30N 103 41W
Indian Lake, *U.S.A.* **111 C10** 43 47N 74 16W
Indian Ocean **52 K11** 5 0 S 75 0 E
Indian Springs, *U.S.A.* **117 J11** 36 35N 115 40W
Indiana, *U.S.A.* **110 F5** 40 37N 79 9W
Indiana □, *U.S.A.* **108 F3** 40 0N 86 0W
Indianapolis, *U.S.A.* **108 F2** 39 46N 86 9W
Indianola, *Iowa, U.S.A.* **112 E8** 41 22N 93 34W
Indianola, *Miss., U.S.A.* **113 J9** 33 27N 90 39W
Indigirka →, *Russia* **51 B15** 70 48N 148 54 E
Inđija, *Serbia, Yug.* **42 E5** 45 6N 20 7 E
Indio, *U.S.A.* **117 M10** 33 43N 116 13W
Indo-China, *Asia* **52 H14** 15 0N 102 0 E
Indonesia ■, *Asia* **62 F5** 5 0 S 115 0 E
Indore, *India* **68 H6** 22 42N 75 53 E
Indramayu, *Indonesia* **63 G13** 6 20 S 108 19 E
Indravati →, *India* **67 K12** 19 20N 80 20 E
Indre □, *France* **19 F8** 46 50N 1 39 E
Indre →, *France* **18 E7** 47 16N 0 11 E
Indre-et-Loire □, *France* **18 E7** 47 20N 0 40 E
Indulkana, *Australia* **95 D1** 26 58 S 133 5 E
Indus →, *Pakistan* **68 G2** 24 20N 67 47 E
Indus, Mouth of the, *Pakistan* **68 H3** 24 0N 68 0 E
İnebolu, *Turkey* **72 B5** 41 55N 33 40 E
İnecik, *Turkey* **41 F11** 40 56N 27 16 E
İnegöl, *Turkey* **41 F13** 40 5N 29 31 E
Ineu, *Romania* **42 D6** 46 26N 21 51 E
Infantes = Villanueva de los Infantes, *Spain* **35 G7** 38 43N 3 1W
Infiernillo, Presa del, *Mexico* **118 D4** 18 9N 102 0W
Infiesto, *Spain* **34 B5** 43 21N 5 21W
Ingelstad, *Sweden* **11 H8** 56 45N 14 56 E
Ingenio, *Canary Is.* **37 G4** 27 55N 15 26W
Ingenio Santa Ana, *Argentina* **126 B2** 27 25 S 65 40W
Ingersoll, *Canada* **102 D3** 43 4N 80 55W
Ingham, *Australia* **94 B4** 18 43 S 146 10 E
Ingleborough, *U.K.* **12 C5** 54 10N 2 22W
Inglewood, *Queens., Australia* **95 D5** 28 25 S 151 2 E
Inglewood, *Vic., Australia* **95 F3** 36 29 S 143 53 E
Inglewood, *N.Z.* **91 H5** 39 9 S 174 14 E
Inglewood, *U.S.A.* **117 M8** 33 58N 118 21W
Ingólfshöfði, *Iceland* **8 E5** 63 48N 16 39W
Ingolstadt, *Germany* **25 G7** 48 46N 11 26 E
Ingomar, *U.S.A.* **114 C10** 46 35N 107 23W
Ingonish, *Canada* **103 C7** 46 42N 60 18W
Ingore, *Guinea-Biss.* **82 C1** 12 24N 15 48W
Ingraj Bazar, *India* **69 G13** 24 58N 88 10 E
Ingrid Christensen Coast, *Antarctica* **5 C6** 69 30 S 76 0 E
Ingul → = Inhul →, *Ukraine* **47 J7** 46 50N 32 0 E
Ingulec = Inhulec, *Ukraine* **47 J7** 47 42N 33 14 E
Ingulets → = Inhulets →, *Ukraine* **47 J7** 46 46N 32 47 E
Inguri → = Enguri →, *Georgia* **49 J5** 42 27N 41 38 E
Ingushetia □, *Russia* **49 J7** 43 20N 44 50 E
Ingwavuma, *S. Africa* **89 D5** 27 9 S 31 59 E
Inhaca, *Mozam.* **89 D5** 26 1 S 32 57 E
Inhafenga, *Mozam.* **89 C5** 20 36 S 33 53 E
Inhambane, *Mozam.* **89 C6** 23 54 S 35 30 E
Inhambane □, *Mozam.* **89 C5** 22 30 S 34 20 E
Inhaminga, *Mozam.* **87 F4** 18 26 S 35 0 E
Inharrime, *Mozam.* **89 C6** 24 30 S 35 0 E
Inharrime →, *Mozam.* **89 C6** 24 30 S 35 0 E
Inhisar, *Turkey* **39 A12** 40 3N 30 23 E
Inhul →, *Ukraine* **47 J7** 46 50N 32 0 E
Inhulec, *Ukraine* **47 J7** 47 42N 33 14 E
Inhulets →, *Ukraine* **47 J7** 46 46N 32 47 E
Iniesta, *Spain* **33 F3** 39 27N 1 45W
Ining = Yining, *China* **50 E9** 43 58N 81 10 E
Inírida →, *Colombia* **124 C5** 3 55N 67 52W
Inishbofin, *Ireland* **15 C1** 53 37N 10 13W
Inisheer, *Ireland* **15 C2** 53 3N 9 32W
Inishfree B., *Ireland* **15 A3** 55 4N 8 23W
Inishkea North, *Ireland* **15 B1** 54 9N 10 11W
Inishkea South, *Ireland* **15 B1** 54 7N 10 12W
Inishmaan, *Ireland* **15 C2** 53 5N 9 35W
Inishmore, *Ireland* **15 C2** 53 8N 9 45W
Inishowen Pen., *Ireland* **15 A4** 55 14N 7 15W
Inishshark, *Ireland* **15 C1** 53 37N 10 16W
Inishturk, *Ireland* **15 C1** 53 42N 10 7W
Inishvickillane, *Ireland* **15 D1** 52 3N 10 37W
Injibara, *Ethiopia* **81 E4** 10 59N 37 0 E
Injune, *Australia* **95 D4** 25 53 S 148 32 E
Inklin →, *Canada* **104 B2** 58 50N 133 10W
Inland Sea = Setonaikai, *Japan* **55 G6** 34 20N 133 30 E
Inle L., *Burma* **67 J20** 20 30N 96 58 E
Inlet, *U.S.A.* **111 C10** 43 45N 74 48W
Inn →, *Austria* **26 C6** 48 35N 13 28 E
Innamincka, *Australia* **95 D3** 27 44 S 140 46 E
Inner Hebrides, *U.K.* **14 E2** 57 0N 6 30W
Inner Mongolia = Nei Monggol Zizhiqu □, *China* **56 D7** 42 0N 112 0 E
Inner Sound, *U.K.* **14 D3** 57 30N 5 55W
Innerkip, *Canada* **110 C4** 43 13N 80 42W
Innetalling I., *Canada* **102 A4** 56 0N 79 0W
Innisfail, *Australia* **94 B4** 17 33 S 146 5 E
Innisfail, *Canada* **104 C6** 52 0N 113 57W
In'noshima, *Japan* **55 G6** 34 19N 133 10 E
Innsbruck, *Austria* **26 D4** 47 16N 11 23 E
Innviertel, *Austria* **26 C6** 48 15N 13 15 E
Inny →, *Ireland* **15 C4** 53 30N 7 50W
Inongo, *Dem. Rep. of the Congo* **84 E3** 1 55 S 18 30 E
İnönü, *Turkey* **39 B12** 39 48N 30 9 E
Inoucdjouac = Inukjuak, *Canada* **101 C12** 58 25N 78 15W
Inowrocław, *Poland* **45 F5** 52 50N 18 12 E
Inpundong, *N. Korea* **57 D14** 41 25N 126 34 E
Inscription, C., *Australia* **93 E1** 25 29 S 112 59 E
Insein, *Burma* **67 L20** 16 50N 96 5 E
Insjön, *Sweden* **10 D9** 60 41N 15 6 E
Ińsko, *Poland* **44 E2** 53 25N 15 32 E
Însurăţei, *Romania* **43 F12** 44 50N 27 40 E
Inta, *Russia* **50 C6** 66 5N 60 8 E
Intendente Alvear, *Argentina* **126 D3** 35 12 S 63 32W
Intepe, *Turkey* **39 A8** 40 1N 26 20 E
Interlaken, *Switz.* **25 J3** 46 41N 7 50 E
Interlaken, *U.S.A.* **111 D8** 42 37N 76 44W
International Falls, *U.S.A.* **112 A8** 48 36N 93 25W
Intiyaco, *Argentina* **126 B3** 28 43 S 60 5W
Întorsura Buzăului, *Romania* **43 E11** 45 41N 26 2 E
Inukjuak, *Canada* **101 C12** 58 25N 78 15W
Inútil, B., *Chile* **128 G2** 53 30 S 70 15W
Inuvik, *Canada* **100 B6** 68 16N 133 40W
Inveraray, *U.K.* **14 E3** 56 14N 5 5W
Inverbervie, *U.K.* **14 E6** 56 51N 2 17W
Invercargill, *N.Z.* **91 M2** 46 24 S 168 24 E
Inverclyde □, *U.K.* **14 F4** 55 55N 4 49W
Inverell, *Australia* **95 D5** 29 45 S 151 8 E
Invergordon, *U.K.* **14 D4** 57 41N 4 10W
Inverloch, *Australia* **95 F4** 38 38 S 145 45 E
Invermere, *Canada* **104 C5** 50 30N 116 2W
Inverness, *Canada* **103 C7** 46 15N 61 19W
Inverness, *U.K.* **14 D4** 57 29N 4 13W
Inverness, *U.S.A.* **109 L4** 28 50N 82 20W
Inverurie, *U.K.* **14 D6** 57 17N 2 23W
Investigator Group, *Australia* **95 E1** 34 45 S 134 20 E
Investigator Str., *Australia* **95 F2** 35 30 S 137 0 E
Inya, *Russia* **50 D9** 50 28N 86 37 E
Inyanga, *Zimbabwe* **87 F3** 18 12 S 32 40 E
Inyangani, *Zimbabwe* **87 F3** 18 5 S 32 50 E
Inyantue, *Zimbabwe* **88 B4** 18 33 S 26 39 E
Inyo Mts., *U.S.A.* **116 J9** 36 40N 118 0W
Inyokern, *U.S.A.* **117 K9** 35 39N 117 49W
Inza, *Russia* **48 D8** 53 55N 46 25 E
Inzhavino, *Russia* **48 D6** 52 22N 42 30 E
Iō-Jima, *Japan* **55 J5** 30 48N 130 18 E
Ioánnina, *Greece* **38 B2** 39 42N 20 47 E
Ioánnina □, *Greece* **38 B2** 39 39N 20 57 E
Iola, *U.S.A.* **113 G7** 37 55N 95 24W
Ion Corvin, *Romania* **43 F12** 44 7N 27 50 E
Iona, *U.K.* **14 E2** 56 20N 6 25W
Ione, *U.S.A.* **116 G6** 38 21N 120 56W
Ionia, *U.S.A.* **108 D3** 42 59N 85 4W
Ionian Is. = Iónioi Nísoi, *Greece* **38 C2** 38 40N 20 0 E
Ionian Sea, *Medit. S.* **6 H9** 37 30N 17 30 E
Iónioi Nísoi, *Greece* **38 C2** 38 40N 20 0 E
Iónioi Nísoi □, *Greece* **38 C2** 38 40N 20 0 E
Íos, *Greece* **39 E7** 36 41N 25 20 E
Iowa □, *U.S.A.* **112 D8** 42 18N 93 30W
Iowa →, *U.S.A.* **112 E9** 41 10N 91 1W
Iowa City, *U.S.A.* **112 E9** 41 40N 91 32W
Iowa Falls, *U.S.A.* **112 D8** 42 31N 93 16W
Iowa Park, *U.S.A.* **113 J5** 33 57N 98 40W
Ipala, *Tanzania* **86 C3** 4 30 S 32 52 E
Ipameri, *Brazil* **125 G9** 17 44 S 48 9W
Ipáti, *Greece* **38 C4** 38 52N 22 14 E
Ipatinga, *Brazil* **125 G10** 19 32 S 42 30W
Ipatovo, *Russia* **49 H6** 45 45N 42 50 E
Ipel' →, *Europe* **27 D11** 47 48N 18 53 E
Ipiales, *Colombia* **124 C3** 0 50N 77 37W
Ipin = Yibin, *China* **58 C5** 28 45N 104 32 E
Ípiros □, *Greece* **38 B2** 39 30N 20 30 E
Ipixuna, *Brazil* **124 E4** 7 0 S 71 40W
Ipoh, *Malaysia* **65 K3** 4 35N 101 5 E
Ippy, *C.A.R.* **84 C4** 6 5N 21 7 E
İpsala, *Turkey* **41 F10** 40 55N 26 23 E
Ipsárion, Óros, *Greece* **41 F8** 40 40N 24 40 E
Ipswich, *Australia* **95 D5** 27 35 S 152 40 E
Ipswich, *U.K.* **13 E9** 52 4N 1 10 E
Ipswich, *Mass., U.S.A.* **111 D14** 42 41N 70 50W
Ipswich, *S. Dak., U.S.A.* **112 C5** 45 27N 99 2W
Ipu, *Brazil* **125 D10** 4 23 S 40 44W
Iqaluit, *Canada* **101 B13** 63 44N 68 31W
Iquique, *Chile* **124 H4** 20 19 S 70 5W
Iquitos, *Peru* **124 D4** 3 45 S 73 10W
Irabu-Jima, *Japan* **55 M2** 24 50N 125 10 E
Iracoubo, *Fr. Guiana* **125 B8** 5 30N 53 10W
Īrafshān, *Iran* **71 E9** 26 42N 61 56 E
Irahuan, *Phil.* **61 G3** 9 48N 118 41 E
Iráklia, *Kikládhes, Greece* **39 E7** 36 50N 25 28 E
Iráklia, *Sérrai, Greece* **40 E7** 41 10N 23 16 E
Iráklion, *Greece* **36 D7** 35 20N 25 12 E
Iráklion □, *Greece* **36 D7** 35 10N 25 10 E
Irala, *Paraguay* **127 B5** 25 55 S 54 35W
Iran ■, *Asia* **71 C7** 33 0N 53 0 E
Iran, Gunung-Gunung, *Malaysia* **62 D4** 2 20N 114 50 E
Iran, Plateau of, *Asia* **52 F9** 32 0N 55 0 E
Iran Ra. = Iran, Gunung-Gunung, *Malaysia* **62 D4** 2 20N 114 50 E
Īrānshahr, *Iran* **71 E9** 27 15N 60 40 E
Irapuato, *Mexico* **118 C4** 20 40N 101 30W
Iraq ■, *Asia* **70 C5** 33 0N 44 0 E
Irati, *Brazil* **127 B5** 25 25 S 50 38W
Irbes saurums, *Latvia* **44 A9** 57 45N 22 5 E
Irbid, *Jordan* **75 C4** 32 35N 35 48 E
Irbid □, *Jordan* **75 C5** 32 15N 36 35 E
Iregua →, *Spain* **32 C7** 42 27N 2 24 E
Ireland ■, *Europe* **15 C4** 53 50N 7 52W
Irele, *Nigeria* **83 D6** 7 40N 5 40 E
Irgiz, Bolshaya →, *Russia* **48 D9** 52 10N 49 10 E
Irhyangdong, *N. Korea* **57 D15** 41 15N 129 30 E
Iri, *S. Korea* **57 G14** 35 59N 127 0 E
Irian Jaya □, *Indonesia* **63 E9** 4 0 S 137 0 E
Irié, *Guinea* **82 D3** 8 15N 9 10W
Iriga, *Phil.* **61 E5** 13 25N 123 25 E
Iringa, *Tanzania* **86 D4** 7 48 S 35 43 E
Iringa □, *Tanzania* **86 D4** 7 48 S 35 43 E
Iriomote-Jima, *Japan* **55 M1** 24 19N 123 48 E
Iriona, *Honduras* **120 C2** 15 57N 85 11W
Iriri →, *Brazil* **125 D8** 3 52 S 52 37W
Irish Republic ■, *Europe* **15 C3** 53 0N 8 0W
Irish Sea, *U.K.* **12 D3** 53 38N 4 48W
Irkutsk, *Russia* **51 D11** 52 18N 104 20 E
Irlıganlı, *Turkey* **39 D11** 37 53N 29 12 E
Irma, *Canada* **105 C6** 52 55N 111 14W
Irō-Zaki, *Japan* **55 G9** 34 36N 138 51 E
Iroise, Mer d', *France* **18 D2** 48 15N 4 45W
Iron Baron, *Australia* **95 E2** 32 58 S 137 11 E
Iron Gate = Portile de Fier, *Europe* **42 F7** 44 44N 22 30 E
Iron Knob, *Australia* **95 E2** 32 46 S 137 8 E
Iron Mountain, *U.S.A.* **108 C1** 45 49N 88 4W
Iron River, *U.S.A.* **112 B10** 46 6N 88 39W
Irondequoit, *U.S.A.* **110 C7** 43 13N 77 35W
Ironton, *Mo., U.S.A.* **113 G9** 37 36N 90 38W
Ironton, *Ohio, U.S.A.* **108 F4** 38 32N 82 41W
Ironwood, *U.S.A.* **112 B9** 46 27N 90 9W
Iroquois, *Canada* **111 B9** 44 51N 75 19W
Iroquois Falls, *Canada* **102 C3** 48 46N 80 41W
Irosin, *Phil.* **61 E6** 12 42N 124 2 E
Irpin, *Ukraine* **47 G6** 50 30N 30 15 E
Irrara Cr. →, *Australia* **95 D4** 29 35 S 145 31 E
Irrawaddy □, *Burma* **67 L19** 17 0N 95 0 E
Irrawaddy →, *Burma* **67 M19** 15 50N 95 6 E
Irrawaddy, Mouths of the, *Burma* **67 M19** 15 30N 95 0 E
Irricana, *Canada* **104 C6** 51 19N 113 37W
Irsina, *Italy* **31 B9** 40 45N 16 14 E
Irtysh →, *Russia* **50 C7** 61 4N 68 52 E
Irumu, *Dem. Rep. of the Congo* **86 B2** 1 32N 29 53 E
Irún, *Spain* **32 B3** 43 20N 1 52W
Irunea = Pamplona, *Spain* **32 C3** 42 48N 1 38W
Irurzun, *Spain* **32 C3** 42 55N 1 50W
Irvine, *U.K.* **14 F4** 55 37N 4 41W
Irvine, *Calif., U.S.A.* **117 M9** 33 41N 117 46W
Irvine, *Ky., U.S.A.* **108 G4** 37 42N 83 58W
Irvinestown, *U.K.* **15 B4** 54 28N 7 39W
Irving, *U.S.A.* **113 J6** 32 49N 96 56W
Irvona, *U.S.A.* **110 F6** 40 46N 78 33W
Irwin →, *Australia* **93 E1** 29 15 S 114 54 E
Irymple, *Australia* **95 E3** 34 14 S 142 8 E
Is, Jebel, *Sudan* **80 C4** 22 3N 35 28 E
Is-sur-Tille, *France* **19 E12** 47 30N 5 8 E
Isa, *Nigeria* **83 C6** 13 14N 6 24 E
Isa Khel, *Pakistan* **68 C4** 32 41N 71 17 E
Isaac →, *Australia* **94 C4** 22 55 S 149 20 E
Isabel, *U.S.A.* **112 C4** 45 24N 101 26W
Isabela, *Phil.* **61 H5** 6 40N 122 10 E
Isabela, I., *Mexico* **118 C3** 21 51N 105 55W
Isabelia, Cord., *Nic.* **120 D2** 13 30N 85 25W
Isabella Ra., *Australia* **92 D3** 21 0 S 121 4 E
Isaccea, *Romania* **43 E13** 45 16N 28 28 E
Ísafjarðardjúp, *Iceland* **8 C2** 66 10N 23 0W
Ísafjörður, *Iceland* **8 C2** 66 5N 23 9W
Isagarh, *India* **68 G7** 24 48N 77 51 E
Isahaya, *Japan* **55 H5** 32 52N 130 2 E
Isaka, *Tanzania* **86 C3** 3 56 S 32 59 E
Isakly, *Russia* **48 C10** 54 8N 51 32 E
Işalniţa, *Romania* **43 F8** 44 24N 23 44 E
Isan →, *India* **69 F9** 26 51N 80 7 E
Isana = Içana →, *Brazil* **124 C5** 0 26N 67 19W
Isanlu Makutu, *Nigeria* **83 D6** 8 20N 5 50 E
Isar →, *Germany* **25 G8** 48 48N 12 57 E
Isarco →, *Italy* **29 B8** 46 27N 11 18 E
Ísari, *Greece* **38 D3** 37 22N 22 0 E
Íscar, *Spain* **34 D6** 41 22N 4 32W
Iscehisar, *Turkey* **39 C12** 38 51N 30 45 E
Íschia, *Italy* **30 B6** 40 44N 13 57 E
Isdell →, *Australia* **92 C3** 16 27 S 124 51 E
Ise, *Japan* **55 G8** 34 25N 136 45 E
Ise-Wan, *Japan* **55 G8** 34 43N 136 43 E
Isefjord, *Denmark* **11 J5** 55 53N 11 50 E
Isel →, *Austria* **26 E5** 46 50N 12 47 E
Iseo, *Italy* **28 C7** 45 39N 10 3 E
Iseo, L. d', *Italy* **28 C7** 45 43N 10 4 E
Iseramagazi, *Tanzania* **86 C3** 4 37 S 32 10 E
Isère □, *France* **21 C9** 45 15N 5 40 E
Isère →, *France* **21 D8** 44 59N 4 51 E
Iserlohn, *Germany* **24 D3** 51 22N 7 41 E
Isérnia, *Italy* **31 A7** 41 36N 14 14 E
Iseyin, *Nigeria* **83 D5** 8 0N 3 36 E
Isfahan = Eşfahān, *Iran* **71 C6** 32 39N 51 43 E
Ishëm, *Albania* **40 E3** 41 33N 19 34 E
Ishigaki-Shima, *Japan* **55 M2** 24 20N 124 10 E
Ishikari-Gawa →, *Japan* **54 C10** 43 15N 141 23 E
Ishikari-Sammyaku, *Japan* **54 C11** 43 30N 143 0 E
Ishikari-Wan, *Japan* **54 C10** 43 25N 141 1 E
Ishikawa □, *Japan* **55 F8** 36 30N 136 30 E
Ishim, *Russia* **50 D7** 56 10N 69 30 E
Ishim →, *Russia* **50 D8** 57 45N 71 10 E
Ishinomaki, *Japan* **54 E10** 38 32N 141 20 E
Ishioka, *Japan* **55 F10** 36 11N 140 16 E
Ishkuman, *Pakistan* **69 A5** 36 30N 73 50 E
Ishpeming, *U.S.A.* **108 B2** 46 29N 87 40W
Isigny-sur-Mer, *France* **18 C5** 49 19N 1 6W
Isıklar Dağı, *Turkey* **41 F11** 40 45N 27 15 E
Işıklı, *Turkey* **39 C11** 38 19N 29 51 E
Isil Kul, *Russia* **50 D8** 54 55N 71 16 E
Ísili, *Italy* **30 C2** 39 44N 9 6 E
Isiolo, *Kenya* **86 B4** 0 24N 37 33 E
Isiro, *Dem. Rep. of the Congo* **86 B2** 2 53N 27 40 E
Isisford, *Australia* **94 C3** 24 15 S 144 21 E
İskenderun, *Turkey* **70 B3** 36 32N 36 10 E
İskenderun Körfezi, *Turkey* **72 D6** 36 40N 35 50 E
İskilip, *Turkey* **72 B6** 40 45N 34 29 E
Iskŭr →, *Bulgaria* **41 C8** 43 45N 24 25 E
Iskŭr, Yazovir, *Bulgaria* **40 D7** 42 23N 23 30 E
Iskut →, *Canada* **104 B2** 56 45N 131 49W
Isla →, *U.K.* **14 E5** 56 32N 3 20W
Isla Cristina, *Spain* **35 H3** 37 13N 7 17W
Isla Vista, *U.S.A.* **117 L7** 34 25N 119 53W
İslâhiye, *Turkey* **72 D7** 37 0N 36 35 E
Islam Headworks, *Pakistan* **68 E5** 29 49N 72 33 E
Islamabad, *Pakistan* **68 C5** 33 40N 73 10 E
Islamgarh, *Pakistan* **68 F4** 27 51N 70 48 E
Islamkot, *Pakistan* **68 G4** 24 42N 70 13 E
Islampur, *India* **69 G11** 25 9N 85 12 E
Island L., *Canada* **105 C10** 53 47N 94 25W
Island Lagoon, *Australia* **95 E2** 31 30 S 136 40 E
Island Pond, *U.S.A.* **111 B13** 44 49N 71 53W
Islands, B. of, *Canada* **103 C8** 49 11N 58 15W
Islands, B. of, *N.Z.* **91 F5** 35 15 S 174 6 E
Islay, *U.K.* **14 F2** 55 46N 6 10W
Isle →, *France* **20 D3** 44 55N 0 15W
Isle aux Morts, *Canada* **103 C8** 47 35N 59 0W
Isle of Wight □, *U.K.* **13 G6** 50 41N 1 17W
Isle Royale, *U.S.A.* **112 B10** 48 0N 88 54W
Isle Royale National Park, *U.S.A.* **112 B10** 48 0N 88 55W
Isleton, *U.S.A.* **116 G5** 38 10N 121 37W
Ismail = Izmayil, *Ukraine* **47 K5** 45 22N 28 46 E
Ismâ'ilîya, *Egypt* **80 H8** 30 37N 32 18 E
Ismaning, *Germany* **25 G7** 48 13N 11 40 E
Isna, *Egypt* **80 B3** 25 17N 32 30 E
Isoanala, *Madag.* **89 C8** 23 50 S 45 44 E
Isogstalo, *India* **69 B8** 34 15N 78 46 E
Ísola del Liri, *Italy* **29 G10** 41 41N 13 34 E
Ísola della Scala, *Italy* **28 C7** 45 16N 11 0 E
Ísola di Capo Rizzuto, *Italy* **31 D10** 38 58N 17 6 E
Isparta, *Turkey* **39 D12** 37 47N 30 30 E
Isperikh, *Bulgaria* **41 C10** 43 43N 26 50 E
Íspica, *Italy* **31 F7** 36 47N 14 55 E
Israel ■, *Asia* **75 D3** 32 0N 34 50 E
Isratu, *Eritrea* **81 D4** 16 20N 39 53 E
Issia, *Ivory C.* **82 D3** 6 33N 6 33W
Issoire, *France* **20 C7** 45 32N 3 15 E
Issoudun, *France* **19 F8** 46 57N 1 59 E
Issyk-Kul, Ozero = Ysyk-Köl, *Kyrgyzstan* **50 E8** 42 25N 77 15 E
Ist, *Croatia* **29 D11** 44 17N 14 47 E
Istállós-kő, *Hungary* **42 B5** 48 4N 20 26 E
Istanbul, *Turkey* **41 E12** 41 0N 29 0 E
Istanbul □, *Turkey* **41 E12** 41 0N 29 0 E
Istanbul Boğazi, *Turkey* **41 E13** 41 10N 29 10 E
Istiaía, *Greece* **38 C5** 38 57N 23 9 E
Istok, *Kosovo, Yug.* **40 D4** 42 45N 20 24 E
Istokpoga, L., *U.S.A.* **109 M5** 27 23N 81 17W
Istra, *Croatia* **29 C10** 45 10N 14 0 E
Istres, *France* **21 E8** 43 31N 4 59 E
Istria = Istra, *Croatia* **29 C10** 45 10N 14 0 E
Itá, *Paraguay* **126 B4** 25 29 S 57 21W
Itaberaba, *Brazil* **125 F10** 12 32 S 40 18W
Itabira, *Brazil* **125 G10** 19 37 S 43 13W
Itabirito, *Brazil* **127 A7** 20 15 S 43 48W
Itabuna, *Brazil* **125 F11** 14 48 S 39 16W
Itacaunas →, *Brazil* **125 E9** 5 21 S 49 8W
Itacoatiara, *Brazil* **124 D7** 3 8 S 58 25W
Itaipú, Represa de, *Brazil* **127 B5** 25 30 S 54 30W
Itaituba, *Brazil* **125 D7** 4 10 S 55 50W
Itajaí, *Brazil* **127 B6** 27 50 S 48 39W
Itajubá, *Brazil* **127 A6** 22 24 S 45 30W
Itaka, *Tanzania* **87 D3** 8 50 S 32 49 E
Italy ■, *Europe* **7 G8** 42 0N 13 0 E
Itamaraju, *Brazil* **125 G11** 17 5 S 39 31W
Itampolo, *Madag.* **89 C7** 24 41 S 43 57 E
Itandrano, *Madag.* **89 C8** 21 47 S 45 17 E
Itapecuru-Mirim, *Brazil* **125 D10** 3 24 S 44 20W
Itaperuna, *Brazil* **127 A7** 21 10 S 41 54W
Itapetininga, *Brazil* **127 A6** 23 36 S 48 7W
Itapeva, *Brazil* **127 A6** 23 59 S 48 59W
Itapicuru →, *Bahia, Brazil* **125 F11** 11 47 S 37 32W
Itapicuru →, *Maranhão, Brazil* **125 D10** 2 52 S 44 12W
Itapipoca, *Brazil* **125 D11** 3 30 S 39 35W
Itapuá □, *Paraguay* **127 B4** 26 40 S 55 40W
Itaquari, *Brazil* **127 A7** 20 20 S 40 25W
Itaquí, *Brazil* **126 B4** 29 8 S 56 30W
Itararé, *Brazil* **127 A6** 24 6 S 49 23W
Itarsi, *India* **68 H7** 22 36N 77 51 E
Itatí, *Argentina* **126 B4** 27 16 S 58 15W
Itbayat, *Phil.* **61 A4** 20 47N 121 51 E
Itchen →, *U.K.* **13 G6** 50 55N 1 22W
Itéa, *Greece* **38 C4** 38 25N 22 25 E
Itezhi Tezhi, L., *Zambia* **87 F2** 15 30 S 25 30 E
Ithaca = Itháki, *Greece* **38 C2** 38 25N 20 40 E
Ithaca, *U.S.A.* **111 D8** 42 27N 76 30W
Itháki, *Greece* **38 C2** 38 25N 20 40 E
Itiquira →, *Brazil* **125 G7** 17 18 S 56 44W
Itō, *Japan* **55 G9** 34 58N 139 5 E
Itoigawa, *Japan* **55 F8** 37 2N 137 51 E
Iton →, *France* **18 C8** 49 9N 1 12 E
Itonamas →, *Bolivia* **124 F6** 12 28 S 64 24W
Itri, *Italy* **30 A6** 41 17N 13 32 E
Itsa, *Egypt* **80 J7** 29 15N 30 47 E
Íttiri, *Italy* **30 B1** 40 36N 8 34 E
Ittoqqortoormiit, *Greenland* **4 B6** 70 20N 23 0W
Itu, *Brazil* **127 A6** 23 17 S 47 15W
Itu, *Nigeria* **83 D6** 5 10N 7 58 E
Itu Aba I., *S. China Sea* **62 B4** 10 23N 114 21 E
Ituiutaba, *Brazil* **125 G9** 19 0 S 49 25W
Itumbiara, *Brazil* **125 G9** 18 20 S 49 10W
Ituna, *Canada* **105 C8** 51 10N 103 24W
Itunge Port, *Tanzania* **87 D3** 9 40 S 33 55 E
Iturbe, *Argentina* **126 A2** 23 0 S 65 25W
Ituri →, *Dem. Rep. of the Congo* **86 B2** 1 40N 27 1 E
Iturup, Ostrov, *Russia* **51 E15** 45 0N 148 0 E
Ituxi →, *Brazil* **124 E6** 7 18 S 64 51W
Ituyuro →, *Argentina* **126 A3** 22 40 S 63 50W
Itzehoe, *Germany* **24 B5** 53 55N 9 31 E
Ivahona, *Madag.* **89 C8** 23 27 S 46 10 E
Ivaí →, *Brazil* **127 A5** 23 18 S 53 42W
Ivalo, *Finland* **8 B22** 68 38N 27 35 E
Ivalojoki →, *Finland* **8 B22** 68 40N 27 40 E
Ivanava, *Belarus* **47 F3** 52 7N 25 29 E
Ivančice, *Czech Rep.* **27 B9** 49 6N 16 23 E
Ivăneşti, *Romania* **43 D12** 46 39N 27 27 E
Ivangorod, *Russia* **46 C5** 59 27N 28 13 E
Ivanhoe, *Australia* **95 E3** 32 56 S 144 20 E
Ivanhoe, *Calif., U.S.A.* **116 J7** 36 23N 119 13W
Ivanhoe, *Minn., U.S.A.* **112 C6** 44 28N 96 15W
Ivanić Grad, *Croatia* **29 C13** 45 41N 16 25 E
Ivanjica, *Serbia, Yug.* **40 C4** 43 35N 20 12 E
Ivanjska, *Bos.-H.* **42 F2** 44 55N 17 4 E
Ivankoyskoye Vdkhr., *Russia* **46 D9** 56 37N 36 32 E
Ivano-Frankivsk, *Ukraine* **47 H3** 48 40N 24 40 E
Ivano-Frankovsk = Ivano-Frankivsk, *Ukraine* **47 H3** 48 40N 24 40 E
Ivanovo = Ivanava, *Belarus* **47 F3** 52 7N 25 29 E
Ivanovo, *Russia* **46 D11** 57 5N 41 0 E
Ivanšćica, *Croatia* **29 B13** 46 12N 16 13 E
Ivato, *Madag.* **89 C8** 20 37 S 47 10 E
Ivatsevichy, *Belarus* **47 F3** 52 43N 25 21 E
Ivaylovgrad, *Bulgaria* **41 E10** 41 32N 26 8 E
Ivinheima →, *Brazil* **127 A5** 23 14 S 53 42W
Ivinhema, *Brazil* **127 A5** 22 10 S 53 37W
Ivohibe, *Madag.* **89 C8** 22 31 S 46 57 E
Ivory Coast, *W. Afr.* **82 E4** 4 20N 5 0W
Ivory Coast ■, *Africa* **82 D4** 7 30N 5 0W
Ivösjön, *Sweden* **11 H8** 56 8N 14 25 E
Ivrea, *Italy* **28 C4** 45 28N 7 52 E
Ivrindi, *Turkey* **39 B9** 39 34N 27 30 E
Ivujivik, *Canada* **101 B12** 62 24N 77 55W
Ivybridge, *U.K.* **13 G4** 50 23N 3 56W
Iwaizumi, *Japan* **54 E10** 39 50N 141 45 E
Iwaki, *Japan* **55 F10** 37 3N 140 55 E
Iwakuni, *Japan* **55 G6** 34 15N 132 8 E

Kalimpong, India 69 F13 27 4N 88 35 E
Kalinin = Tver, Russia 46 D8 56 55N 35 55 E
Kaliningrad, Russia 9 J19 54 42N 20 32 E
Kalininsk, Russia 48 E7 51 30N 44 40 E
Kalinkavichy, Belarus 47 F5 52 12N 29 20 E
Kalinkovichi = Kalinkavichy, Belarus 47 F5 52 12N 29 20 E
Kalinovik, Bos.-H. 40 C2 43 31N 18 25 E
Kalipetrovo, Bulgaria 41 B11 44 5N 27 14 E
Kaliro, Uganda 86 B3 0 56N 33 30 E
Kalirrákhi, Greece 41 F8 40 40N 24 35 E
Kalispell, U.S.A. 114 B6 48 12N 114 19W
Kalisz, Poland 45 G5 51 45N 18 8 E
Kalisz Pomorski, Poland 45 E2 53 17N 15 55 E
Kaliua, Tanzania 86 D3 5 5 S 31 48 E
Kalívia Thorikoú, Greece 38 D5 37 50N 23 55 E
Kalix, Sweden 8 D20 65 53N 23 12 E
Kalix →, Sweden 8 D20 65 50N 23 11 E
Kalka, India 68 D7 30 46N 76 57 E
Kalkan, Turkey 39 E11 36 15N 29 23 E
Kalkarindji, Australia 92 C5 17 30 S 130 47 E
Kalkaska, U.S.A. 108 C3 44 44N 85 11W
Kalkfeld, Namibia 88 C2 20 57 S 16 14 E
Kalkfontein, Botswana 88 C3 22 4 S 20 57 E
Kalkım, Turkey 39 B9 39 48N 27 13 E
Kalkrand, Namibia 88 C2 24 1 S 17 35 E
Kållandsö, Sweden 11 F7 58 40N 13 5 E
Kallavesi, Finland 8 E22 62 58N 27 30 E
Källby, Sweden 11 F7 58 30N 13 8 E
Kållered, Sweden 11 G6 57 32N 12 4 E
Kallimasiá, Greece 39 C8 38 18N 26 6 E
Kallinge, Sweden 11 H9 56 15N 15 18 E
Kallithéa, Greece 38 D5 37 55N 23 41 E
Kallmet, Albania 40 E3 41 51N 19 41 E
Kalloní, Greece 39 B8 39 14N 26 12 E
Kallonís, Kólpos, Greece 39 B8 39 10N 26 10 E
Kallsjön, Sweden 8 E15 63 38N 13 0 E
Kalmalo, Nigeria 83 C6 13 40N 5 20 E
Kalmar, Sweden 11 H10 56 40N 16 20 E
Kalmar län □, Sweden 11 G10 57 25N 16 0 E
Kalmar sund, Sweden 11 H10 56 40N 16 25 E
Kalmyk Republic = Kalmykia □, Russia 49 G8 46 5N 46 1 E
Kalmykia □, Russia 49 G8 46 5N 46 1 E
Kalmykovo, Kazakhstan 50 E6 49 0N 51 47 E
Kalna, India 69 H13 23 13N 88 25 E
Kalnai, India 69 H10 22 46N 83 30 E
Kalocsa, Hungary 42 D4 46 32N 19 0 E
Kalofer, Bulgaria 41 D8 42 37N 24 59 E
Kalokhorio, Cyprus 36 E12 34 51N 33 2 E
Kaloko, Dem. Rep. of the Congo 86 D2 6 47 S 25 48 E
Kalol, Gujarat, India 68 H5 22 37N 73 31 E
Kalol, Gujarat, India 68 H5 23 15N 72 33 E
Kalolímnos, Greece 39 D9 37 4N 27 5 E
Kalomo, Zambia 87 F2 17 0 S 26 30 E
Kalonerón, Greece 38 D3 37 20N 21 38 E
Kalpi, India 69 F8 26 8N 79 47 E
Kaltern = Caldaro, Italy 29 B8 46 25N 11 14 E
Kaltungo, Nigeria 83 D7 9 48N 11 19 E
Kalu, Pakistan 68 G2 25 5N 67 39 E
Kaluga, Russia 46 E9 54 35N 36 10 E
Kalulushi, Zambia 87 E2 12 50 S 28 3 E
Kalundborg, Denmark 11 J5 55 41N 11 5 E
Kalush, Ukraine 47 H3 49 3N 24 23 E
Kałuszyn, Poland 45 F8 52 13N 21 52 E
Kalutara, Sri Lanka 66 R12 6 35N 80 0 E
Kalvarija, Lithuania 44 D10 54 24N 23 14 E
Kalyazin, Russia 46 D9 57 15N 37 55 E
Kam, Albania 40 D4 42 17N 20 18 E
Kam →, Nigeria 83 D7 8 15N 1 10 E
Kama, Dem. Rep. of the Congo 86 C2 3 30 S 27 5 E
Kama →, Russia 50 D6 55 45N 52 0 E
Kamachumu, Tanzania 86 C3 1 37 S 31 37 E
Kamaishi, Japan 54 E10 39 16N 141 53 E
Kamalia, Pakistan 68 D5 30 44N 72 42 E
Kaman, India 68 F6 27 39N 77 16 E
Kaman, Turkey 72 C5 39 22N 33 44 E
Kamanjab, Namibia 88 B2 19 35 S 14 51 E
Kamapanda, Zambia 87 E1 12 5 S 24 0 E
Kamaran, Yemen 74 D3 15 21N 42 35 E
Kamativi, Zimbabwe 88 B4 18 20 S 27 6 E
Kamba, Nigeria 83 C5 11 50N 3 45 E
Kambalda, Australia 93 F3 31 10 S 121 37 E
Kambar, Pakistan 68 F3 27 37N 68 1 E
Kambia, S. Leone 82 D2 9 3N 12 53W
Kambolé, Togo 83 D5 8 43N 1 39 E
Kambolé, Zambia 87 D3 8 47 S 30 48 E
Kambos, Cyprus 36 D11 35 2N 32 44 E
Kambove, Dem. Rep. of the Congo 87 E2 10 51 S 26 33 E
Kamchatka, Poluostrov, Russia 51 D16 57 0N 160 0 E
Kamchatka Pen. = Kamchatka, Poluostrov, Russia 51 D16 57 0N 160 0 E
Kamchiya →, Bulgaria 41 C11 43 4N 27 44 E
Kamen, Russia 50 D9 53 50N 81 30 E
Kamen-Rybolov, Russia 54 B6 44 46N 132 2 E
Kamenica, Serbia, Yug. 40 C6 43 27N 22 27 E
Kamenica, Serbia, Yug. 40 B3 44 25N 19 45 E
Kamenice nad Lipou, Czech Rep. 26 B8 49 18N 15 2 E
Kamenjak, Rt, Croatia 29 D10 44 47N 13 55 E
Kamenka = Kaminka, Ukraine 47 H7 49 3N 32 6 E
Kamenka, Kazakhstan 48 E10 51 7N 50 19 E
Kamenka, Penza, Russia 48 D6 53 10N 44 5 E
Kamenka, Voronezh, Russia 47 G10 50 47N 39 20 E
Kamenka Bugskaya = Kamyanka-Buzka, Ukraine 47 G3 50 8N 24 16 E
Kamenka Dneprovskaya = Kamyanka-Dniprovska, Ukraine 47 J8 47 29N 34 28 E
Kamennomostskiy, Russia 49 H5 44 18N 40 13 E
Kameno, Bulgaria 41 D11 42 34N 27 18 E
Kamenolomini, Russia 49 G5 47 40N 40 14 E
Kamensk-Shakhtinskiy, Russia 49 F5 48 23N 40 20 E
Kamensk Uralskiy, Russia 50 D7 56 25N 62 2 E
Kamenskiy, Russia 48 E7 50 48N 45 25 E
Kamenskoye, Russia 51 C17 62 45N 165 30 E
Kamenyak, Bulgaria 41 C10 43 24N 26 57 E
Kamenz, Germany 24 D10 51 15N 14 5 E
Kameoka, Japan 55 G7 35 0N 135 35 E
Kamiah, U.S.A. 114 C5 46 14N 116 2W
Kamień Krajeński, Poland 44 E4 53 32N 17 32 E
Kamień Pomorski, Poland 44 E1 53 57N 14 43 E
Kamienna →, Poland 45 G8 51 6N 21 47 E
Kamienna Góra, Poland 45 H3 50 47N 16 2 E
Kamieńsk, Poland 45 G6 51 12N 19 29 E
Kamieskroon, S. Africa 88 E2 30 9 S 17 56 E
Kamilukuak, L., Canada 105 A8 62 22N 101 40W
Kamin-Kashyrskyy, Ukraine 47 G3 51 39N 24 56 E
Kamina, Dem. Rep. of the Congo 87 D2 8 45 S 25 0 E
Kaminak L., Canada 105 A10 62 10N 95 0W
Kaministiquia, Canada 102 C1 48 32N 89 35W
Kaminka, Ukraine 47 H7 49 3N 32 6 E
Kaminoyama, Japan 54 E10 38 9N 140 17 E
Kamiros, Greece 36 C9 36 20N 27 56 E
Kamituga, Dem. Rep. of the Congo 86 C2 3 2 S 28 10 E
Kamla →, India 69 G12 25 35N 86 36 E
Kamloops, Canada 104 C4 50 40N 120 20W
Kamnik, Slovenia 29 B11 46 14N 14 37 E
Kamo, Armenia 49 K7 40 21N 45 7 E
Kamo, Japan 54 F9 37 39N 139 3 E
Kamoke, Pakistan 68 C6 32 4N 74 4 E
Kamp →, Austria 26 C8 48 23N 15 42 E
Kampala, Uganda 86 B3 0 20N 32 30 E
Kampang Chhnang, Cambodia 65 F5 12 20N 104 35 E
Kampar, Malaysia 65 K3 4 18N 101 9 E
Kampar →, Indonesia 62 D2 0 30N 103 8 E
Kampen, Neths. 17 B5 52 33N 5 53 E
Kampene, Dem. Rep. of the Congo 84 E5 3 36 S 26 40 E
Kamphaeng Phet, Thailand 64 D2 16 28N 99 30 E
Kampolombo, L., Zambia 87 E2 11 37 S 29 42 E
Kampong Saom, Cambodia 65 G4 10 38N 103 30 E
Kampong Saom, Chaak, Cambodia 65 G4 10 50N 103 32 E
Kampong To, Thailand 65 J3 6 3N 101 13 E
Kampot, Cambodia 65 G5 10 36N 104 10 E
Kampti, Burkina Faso 82 C4 10 7N 3 25W
Kampuchea = Cambodia ■, Asia 64 F5 12 15N 105 0 E
Kampung Air Putih, Malaysia 65 K4 4 15N 103 10 E
Kampung Jerangau, Malaysia 65 K4 4 50N 103 10 E
Kampung Raja, Malaysia 65 K4 5 45N 102 35 E
Kampungbaru = Tolitoli, Indonesia 63 D6 1 5N 120 50 E
Kamrau, Teluk, Indonesia 63 E8 3 30 S 133 36 E
Kamsack, Canada 105 C8 51 34N 101 54W
Kamsai, Guinea 82 C2 10 40N 14 36W
Kamskoye Ustye, Russia 48 C9 55 10N 49 20 E
Kamuchawie L., Canada 105 B8 56 18N 101 59W
Kamui-Misaki, Japan 54 C10 43 20N 140 21 E
Kamyanets-Podilskyy, Ukraine 47 H4 48 45N 26 40 E
Kamyanka-Buzka, Ukraine 47 G3 50 8N 24 16 E
Kamyanka-Dniprovska, Ukraine 47 J8 47 29N 34 28 E
Kāmyārān, Iran 70 C5 34 47N 46 56 E
Kamyshin, Russia 48 E7 50 10N 45 24 E
Kamyzyak, Russia 49 G9 46 4N 48 10 E
Kan, Sudan 81 F3 9 1N 31 47 E
Kanaaupscow, Canada 102 B4 54 2N 76 30W
Kanaaupscow →, Canada 101 C12 53 39N 77 9W
Kanab, U.S.A. 115 H7 37 3N 112 32W
Kanab →, U.S.A. 115 H7 36 24N 112 38W
Kanagi, Japan 54 D10 40 54N 140 27 E
Kanairiktok →, Canada 103 A7 55 2N 60 18W
Kanália, Greece 38 B4 39 30N 22 53 E
Kananga, Dem. Rep. of the Congo 84 F4 5 55 S 22 18 E
Kanash, Russia 48 C8 55 30N 47 32 E
Kanaskat, U.S.A. 116 C5 47 19N 121 54W
Kanastraíon, Ákra = Palioúrion, Ákra, Greece 40 G7 39 57N 23 45 E
Kanawha →, U.S.A. 108 F4 38 50N 82 9W
Kanazawa, Japan 55 F8 36 30N 136 38 E
Kanchanaburi, Thailand 64 E2 14 2N 99 31 E
Kanchenjunga, Nepal 69 F13 27 50N 88 10 E
Kanchipuram, India 66 N11 12 52N 79 45 E
Kańczuga, Poland 45 J9 49 59N 22 25 E
Kandaghat, India 68 D7 30 59N 77 7 E
Kandahar = Qandahār, Afghan. 66 D4 31 32N 65 30 E
Kandalaksha, Russia 50 C4 67 9N 32 30 E
Kandangan, Indonesia 62 E5 2 50 S 115 20 E
Kandanghaur, Indonesia 63 G13 6 21 S 108 6 E
Kandanos, Greece 36 D5 35 19N 23 44 E
Kandava, Latvia 44 A9 57 2N 22 46 E
Kandavu, Fiji 91 D8 19 0 S 178 15 E
Kandhíla, Greece 38 D4 37 46N 22 22 E
Kandhkot, Pakistan 68 E3 28 16N 69 8 E
Kandhla, India 68 E7 29 18N 77 19 E
Kandi, Benin 83 C5 11 7N 2 55 E
Kandi, India 69 H13 23 58N 88 5 E
Kandiaro, Pakistan 68 F3 27 4N 68 13 E
Kandıra, Turkey 72 B4 41 4N 30 9 E
Kandla, India 68 H4 23 0N 70 10 E
Kandos, Australia 95 E4 32 45 S 149 58 E
Kandreho, Madag. 89 B8 17 29 S 46 6 E
Kandy, Sri Lanka 66 R12 7 18N 80 43 E
Kane, U.S.A. 110 E6 41 40N 78 49W
Kane Basin, Greenland 4 B4 79 1N 70 0W
Kanel, Senegal 82 B2 15 30N 13 18W
Kaneohe, U.S.A. 106 H16 21 25N 157 48W
Kanevskaya, Russia 49 G4 46 3N 38 57 E
Kanfanar, Croatia 29 C10 45 7N 13 50 E
Kang, Botswana 88 C3 23 41 S 22 50 E
Kangaba, Mali 82 C3 11 56N 8 25W
Kangal, Turkey 72 C7 39 14N 37 23 E
Kangān, Fārs, Iran 71 E7 27 50N 52 3 E
Kangān, Hormozgān, Iran 71 E8 25 48N 57 28 E
Kangar, Malaysia 65 J3 6 27N 100 12 E
Kangaré, Mali 82 C3 11 36N 8 4W
Kangaroo I., Australia 95 F2 35 45 S 137 0 E
Kangaroo Mts., Australia 94 C3 23 29 S 141 51 E
Kangasala, Finland 9 F21 61 28N 24 4 E
Kangāvar, Iran 71 C6 34 40N 48 0 E
Kangding, China 58 B3 30 2N 101 57 E
Kangdong, N. Korea 57 E14 39 9N 126 5 E
Kangean, Kepulauan, Indonesia 62 F5 6 55 S 115 23 E
Kangean Is. = Kangean, Kepulauan, Indonesia 62 F5 6 55 S 115 23 E
Kangen →, Sudan 81 F3 6 47N 33 9 E
Kanggye, N. Korea 57 D14 41 0N 126 35 E
Kanggyŏng, S. Korea 57 F14 36 10N 127 0 E
Kanghwa, S. Korea 57 F14 37 45N 126 30 E
Kangikajik, Greenland 4 B6 70 7N 22 0W
Kangiqsliniq = Rankin Inlet, Canada 100 B10 62 30N 93 0W
Kangiqsualujjuaq, Canada 101 C13 58 30N 65 59W
Kangiqsujuaq, Canada 101 B12 61 30N 72 0W
Kangiqtugaapik = Clyde River, Canada 101 A13 70 30N 68 30W
Kangirsuk, Canada 101 B13 60 0N 70 0W
Kangnŭng, S. Korea 57 F15 37 45N 128 54 E
Kangping, China 57 C12 42 43N 123 18 E
Kangra, India 68 C7 32 6N 76 16 E
Kangto, India 67 F18 27 50N 92 35 E
Kanhar →, India 69 G10 24 28N 83 8 E
Kani, Ivory C. 82 D3 8 29N 6 36W
Kaniama, Dem. Rep. of the Congo 86 D1 7 30 S 24 12 E
Kaniapiskau = Caniapiscau →, Canada 103 A6 56 40N 69 30W
Kaniapiskau, Res. = Caniapiscau, Rés. de, Canada 103 B6 54 10N 69 55W
Kanin, Poluostrov, Russia 50 C5 68 0N 45 0 E
Kanin Nos, Mys, Russia 50 C5 68 39N 43 32 E
Kanin Pen. = Kanin, Poluostrov, Russia 50 C5 68 0N 45 0 E
Kaninë, Albania 40 F3 40 23N 19 30 E
Kaniva, Australia 95 F3 36 22 S 141 18 E
Kanjiža, Serbia, Yug. 42 D5 46 3N 20 4 E
Kanjut Sar, Pakistan 69 A6 36 7N 75 25 E
Kankaanpää, Finland 9 F20 61 44N 22 50 E
Kankakee, U.S.A. 108 E2 41 7N 87 52W
Kankakee →, U.S.A. 108 E1 41 23N 88 15W
Kankan, Guinea 82 C3 10 23N 9 15W
Kankendy = Xankändi, Azerbaijan 70 B5 39 52N 46 49 E
Kanker, India 67 J12 20 10N 81 40 E
Kankossa, Mauritania 82 B2 15 54N 11 31W
Kankroli, India 68 G5 25 4N 73 53 E
Kannapolis, U.S.A. 109 H5 35 30N 80 37W
Kannauj, India 69 F8 27 3N 79 56 E
Kannod, India 66 H10 22 45N 76 40 E
Kano, Nigeria 83 C6 12 2N 8 30 E
Kano □, Nigeria 83 C6 11 30N 8 30 E
Kan'onji, Japan 55 G6 34 7N 133 39 E
Kanoroba, Ivory C. 82 D3 9 7N 6 8W
Kanowit, Malaysia 62 D4 2 14N 112 20 E
Kanoya, Japan 55 J5 31 25N 130 50 E
Kanpetlet, Burma 67 J18 21 10N 93 59 E
Kanpur, India 69 F9 26 28N 80 20 E
Kansas □, U.S.A. 112 F6 38 30N 99 0W
Kansas →, U.S.A. 112 F7 39 7N 94 37W
Kansas City, Kans., U.S.A. 112 F7 39 7N 94 38W
Kansas City, Mo., U.S.A. 112 F7 39 6N 94 35W
Kansenia, Dem. Rep. of the Congo 87 E2 10 20 S 26 0 E
Kansk, Russia 51 D10 56 20N 95 37 E
Kansŏng, S. Korea 57 E15 38 24N 128 30 E
Kansu = Gansu □, China 56 G3 36 0N 104 0 E
Kantaphor, India 68 H7 22 35N 76 34 E
Kantchari, Burkina Faso 83 C5 12 37N 1 37 E
Kantché, Niger 83 C6 13 31N 8 30 E
Kanté, Togo 83 D5 9 57N 1 3 E
Kantemirovka, Russia 47 H10 49 43N 39 55 E
Kantharalak, Thailand 64 E5 14 39N 104 39 E
Kantli →, India 68 E6 28 20N 75 30 E
Kantō □, Japan 55 F9 36 15N 139 30 E
Kantō-Sanchi, Japan 55 G9 35 59N 138 50 E
Kanturk, Ireland 15 D3 52 11N 8 54W
Kanuma, Japan 55 F9 36 34N 139 42 E
Kanus, Namibia 88 D2 27 50 S 18 39 E
Kanye, Botswana 88 C4 24 55 S 25 28 E
Kanzenze, Dem. Rep. of the Congo 87 E2 10 30 S 25 12 E
Kanzi, Ras, Tanzania 86 D4 7 1 S 39 33 E
Kaohsiung, Taiwan 59 F13 22 35N 120 16 E
Kaokoveld, Namibia 88 B1 19 15 S 14 30 E
Kaolack, Senegal 82 C1 14 5N 16 8W
Kaoshan, China 57 B13 44 38N 124 50 E
Kapaa, U.S.A. 106 G15 22 5N 159 19W
Kapadvanj, India 68 H5 23 5N 73 0 E
Kapaklı, Turkey 41 E11 41 19N 27 59 E
Kapan, Armenia 70 B5 39 18N 46 27 E
Kapanga, Dem. Rep. of the Congo 84 F4 8 30 S 22 40 E
Kapchagai = Qapshaghay, Kazakhstan 50 E8 43 51N 77 14 E
Kapela = Velika Kapela, Croatia 29 C12 45 10N 15 5 E
Kapéllo, Ákra, Greece 38 E5 36 9N 23 3 E
Kapema, Dem. Rep. of the Congo 87 E2 10 45 S 28 22 E
Kapfenberg, Austria 26 D8 47 26N 15 18 E
Kapı Dağı, Turkey 41 F11 40 28N 27 50 E
Kapiri Mposhi, Zambia 87 E2 13 59 S 28 43 E
Kāpīsā □, Afghan. 66 B6 35 0N 69 20 E
Kapiskau →, Canada 102 B3 52 47N 81 55W
Kapit, Malaysia 62 D4 2 0N 112 55 E
Kapiti I., N.Z. 91 J5 40 50 S 174 56 E
Kaplan, U.S.A. 113 K8 30 0N 92 17W
Kaplice, Czech Rep. 26 C7 48 42N 14 30 E
Kapoe, Thailand 65 H2 9 34N 98 32 E
Kapoeta, Sudan 81 G3 4 50N 33 35 E
Kápolnásnyék, Hungary 42 C3 47 16N 18 41 E
Kapos →, Hungary 42 D3 46 44N 18 30 E
Kaposvár, Hungary 42 D2 46 25N 17 47 E
Kapowsin, U.S.A. 116 D4 46 59N 122 13W
Kappeln, Germany 24 A5 54 40N 9 55 E
Kappelshamn, Sweden 11 G12 57 52N 18 47 E
Kaprije, Croatia 29 E12 43 42N 15 43 E
Kaps, Namibia 88 C2 22 32 S 17 18 E
Kapsan, N. Korea 57 D15 41 4N 128 19 E
Kapsukas = Marijampolė, Lithuania 9 J20 54 33N 23 19 E
Kapuas →, Indonesia 62 E3 0 25 S 109 20 E
Kapuas Hulu, Pegunungan, Malaysia 62 D4 1 30N 113 30 E
Kapuas Hulu Ra. = Kapuas Hulu, Pegunungan, Malaysia 62 D4 1 30N 113 30 E
Kapulo, Dem. Rep. of the Congo 87 D2 8 18 S 29 15 E
Kapunda, Australia 95 E2 34 20 S 138 56 E
Kapuni, N.Z. 91 H5 39 29 S 174 8 E
Kapurthala, India 68 D6 31 23N 75 25 E
Kapuskasing, Canada 102 C3 49 25N 82 30W
Kapuskasing →, Canada 102 C3 49 49N 82 0W
Kapustin Yar, Russia 49 F7 48 37N 45 40 E
Kaputar, Australia 95 E5 30 15 S 150 10 E
Kaputir, Kenya 86 B4 2 5N 35 28 E
Kapuvár, Hungary 42 C2 47 36N 17 1 E
Kara, Russia 50 C7 69 10N 65 0 E
Karā, W. →, Si. Arabia 80 C5 20 45N 41 42 E
Kara Ada, Turkey 39 E9 36 58N 27 28 E
Kara Bogaz Gol, Zaliv = Garabogazköl Aylagy, Turkmenistan 50 E6 41 0N 53 30 E
Kara Burun, Turkey 39 E9 36 32N 27 58 E
Kara Kalpak Republic = Qoraqalpoghistan □, Uzbekistan 50 E6 43 0N 58 0 E
Kara Kum, Turkmenistan 50 F6 39 30N 60 0 E
Kara Sea, Russia 50 B7 75 0N 70 0 E
Karaadilli, Turkey 39 C12 38 18N 30 37 E
Karabiğa, Turkey 41 F11 40 23N 27 17 E
Karabük, Turkey 72 B5 41 12N 32 37 E
Karaburun, Albania 40 F3 40 25N 19 20 E
Karaburun, Turkey 39 C8 38 41N 26 28 E
Karabutak = Qarabutaq, Kazakhstan 50 E7 49 59N 60 14 E
Karacabey, Turkey 41 F12 40 12N 28 21 E
Karacakılavuz, Turkey 41 E11 41 8N 27 21 E
Karacaköy, Turkey 41 E12 41 24N 28 22 E
Karacasu, Turkey 39 D10 37 43N 28 35 E
Karachala = Qaraçala, Azerbaijan 49 L9 39 45N 48 53 E
Karachayevsk, Russia 49 J5 43 50N 41 55 E
Karachev, Russia 47 F8 53 10N 35 5 E
Karachey-Cherkessia □, Russia 49 J5 43 40N 41 30 E
Karachi, Pakistan 68 G2 24 53N 67 0 E
Karad, India 66 L9 17 15N 74 10 E
Karadirek, Turkey 39 C12 38 34N 30 11 E
Karaga, Ghana 83 D4 9 58N 0 28W
Karaganda = Qaraghandy, Kazakhstan 50 E8 49 50N 73 10 E
Karagayly, Kazakhstan 50 E8 49 26N 76 0 E
Karaginskiy, Ostrov, Russia 51 D17 58 45N 164 0 E
Karagola Road, India 69 G12 25 29N 87 23 E
Karagüney Dağları, Turkey 72 B6 40 30N 34 40 E
Karahallı, Turkey 39 C11 38 21N 29 33 E
Karaikal, India 66 P11 10 59N 79 50 E
Karaikkudi, India 66 P11 10 5N 78 45 E
Karaisali, Turkey 72 D6 37 16N 35 2 E
Karaj, Iran 71 C6 35 48N 51 0 E
Karak, Malaysia 65 L4 3 25N 102 2 E
Karakalpakstan = Qoraqalpoghistan □, Uzbekistan 50 E6 43 0N 58 0 E
Karakelong, Indonesia 63 D7 4 35N 126 50 E
Karakitang, Indonesia 63 D7 3 14N 125 28 E
Karaklis = Vanadzor, Armenia 49 K7 40 48N 44 30 E
Karakoçan, Turkey 73 C9 38 57N 40 2 E
Karakol, Kyrgyzstan 50 E8 42 30N 78 20 E
Karakoram Pass, Pakistan 69 B7 35 33N 77 50 E
Karakoram Ra., Pakistan 69 B7 35 30N 77 0 E
Karakurt, Turkey 73 B10 40 10N 42 37 E
Karakuwisa, Namibia 88 B2 18 56 S 19 40 E
Karalon, Russia 51 D12 57 5N 115 50 E
Karama, Jordan 75 D4 31 57N 35 35 E
Karaman, Balıkesir, Turkey 39 B9 39 39N 28 0 E
Karaman, Konya, Turkey 70 B2 37 14N 33 13 E
Karamanlı, Turkey 39 D11 37 23N 29 47 E
Karamay, China 60 B3 45 30N 84 58 E
Karambu, Indonesia 62 E5 3 53 S 116 6 E
Karamea Bight, N.Z. 91 J3 41 22 S 171 40 E
Karamnasa →, India 69 G10 25 31N 83 52 E
Karamürsel, Turkey 41 F13 40 41N 29 36 E
Karand, Iran 70 C5 34 16N 46 15 E
Karangana, Mali 82 C3 12 15N 5 4W
Karanganyar, Indonesia 63 G13 7 38 S 109 37 E
Karanjia, India 69 J11 21 47N 85 58 E
Karankasso, Burkina Faso 82 C4 10 50N 3 53W
Karaova, Turkey 39 D9 37 5N 27 40 E
Karapınar, Turkey 72 D5 37 41N 33 30 E
Karasburg, Namibia 88 D2 28 0 S 18 44 E
Karasino, Russia 50 C9 66 50N 86 50 E
Karasjok, Norway 8 B21 69 27N 25 30 E
Karasu, Turkey 72 B4 41 4N 30 46 E
Karasu →, Turkey 39 E12 36 18N 30 10 E
Karasuk, Russia 50 D8 53 44N 78 2 E
Karasuyama, Japan 55 F10 36 39N 140 9 E
Karataş, Adana, Turkey 72 D6 36 36N 35 21 E
Karataş, Manisa, Turkey 39 C10 38 35N 28 16 E
Karataş Burnu, Turkey 72 D6 36 32N 35 24 E
Karatau, Khrebet = Qarataū, Kazakhstan 50 E7 43 30N 69 30 E
Karatoprak, Turkey 39 D9 37 2N 27 15 E
Karatsu, Japan 55 H5 33 26N 129 58 E
Karaul, Russia 50 B9 70 6N 82 15 E
Karauli, India 68 F7 26 30N 77 4 E
Karavastasë, L. e, Albania 40 F3 40 55N 19 30 E
Karávi, Greece 38 E5 36 49N 23 37 E
Karavostasi, Cyprus 36 D11 35 8N 32 50 E
Karawang, Indonesia 63 G12 6 30 S 107 15 E
Karawanken, Europe 26 E7 46 30N 14 40 E
Karayazı, Turkey 73 C10 39 41N 42 9 E
Karazhal, Kazakhstan 50 E8 48 2N 70 49 E
Karbalā', Iraq 70 C5 32 36N 44 3 E
Kårböle, Sweden 10 C9 61 59N 15 22 E
Karcag, Hungary 42 C5 47 19N 20 57 E
Karcha →, Pakistan 69 B7 34 45N 76 10 E
Karchana, India 69 G9 25 17N 81 56 E
Karczew, Poland 45 F8 52 5N 21 15 E
Kardam, Bulgaria 41 C12 43 45N 28 6 E
Kardeljovo = Ploče, Croatia 29 E14 43 4N 17 26 E
Kardhámila, Greece 39 C8 38 35N 26 5 E
Kardhamíli, Greece 38 E4 36 53N 22 13 E
Kardhítsa, Greece 38 B3 39 23N 21 54 E
Kardhítsa □, Greece 38 B3 39 15N 21 50 E
Kärdla, Estonia 9 G20 58 50N 22 40 E
Kareeberge, S. Africa 88 E3 30 59 S 21 50 E
Kareha →, India 69 G12 25 44N 86 21 E
Kareima, Sudan 80 D3 18 30N 31 49 E
Karelia □, Russia 50 C4 65 30N 32 30 E
Karelian Republic = Karelia □, Russia 50 C4 65 30N 32 30 E
Karera, India 68 G8 25 32N 78 9 E
Kārevāndar, Iran 71 E9 27 53N 60 44 E
Kargasok, Russia 50 D9 59 3N 80 53 E
Kargat, Russia 50 D9 55 10N 80 15 E
Kargı, Turkey 72 B6 41 11N 34 30 E
Kargil, India 69 B7 34 32N 76 12 E
Kargopol, Russia 46 B10 61 30N 38 58 E
Kargowa, Poland 45 F2 52 5N 15 51 E
Karguéri, Niger 83 C7 13 27N 10 30 E
Karhal, India 69 F8 27 1N 78 57 E
Kariá, Greece 38 C2 38 45N 20 39 E
Kariaí, Greece 41 F8 40 14N 24 19 E
Karīān, Iran 71 E8 26 57N 57 14 E
Karianga, Madag. 89 C8 22 25 S 47 22 E
Kariba, Zimbabwe 87 F2 16 28 S 28 50 E
Kariba, L., Zimbabwe 87 F2 16 40 S 28 25 E
Kariba Dam, Zimbabwe 87 F2 16 30 S 28 35 E
Kariba Gorge, Zambia 87 F2 16 30 S 28 50 E
Karibib, Namibia 88 C2 22 0 S 15 56 E
Karimata, Kepulauan, Indonesia 62 E3 1 25 S 109 0 E
Karimata, Selat, Indonesia 62 E3 2 0 S 108 40 E
Karimata Is. = Karimata, Kepulauan, Indonesia 62 E3 1 25 S 109 0 E
Karimnagar, India 66 K11 18 26N 79 10 E
Karimunjawa, Kepulauan, Indonesia 62 F4 5 50 S 110 30 E
Karin, Somali Rep. 74 E4 10 50N 45 52 E
Káristos, Greece 38 C6 38 1N 24 29 E
Karīt, Iran 71 C8 33 29N 56 55 E
Kariya, Japan 55 G8 34 58N 137 1 E
Kariyangwe, Zimbabwe 89 B4 18 0 S 27 38 E
Karjala, Finland 46 A5 62 0N 30 25 E
Karkaralinsk = Qarqaraly, Kazakhstan 50 E8 49 26N 75 30 E
Karkheh →, Iran 70 D5 31 2N 47 29 E
Karkinitska Zatoka, Ukraine 47 K7 45 56N 33 0 E
Karkinitskiy Zaliv = Karkinitska Zatoka, Ukraine 47 K7 45 56N 33 0 E
Karkur Tohl, Egypt 80 C2 22 5N 25 5 E
Karl Liebknecht, Russia 47 G8 51 40N 35 35 E
Karl-Marx-Stadt = Chemnitz, Germany 24 E8 50 51N 12 54 E
Karlholmsbruk, Sweden 10 D11 60 31N 17 37 E
Karlino, Poland 44 D2 54 3N 15 53 E
Karlivka, Ukraine 47 H8 49 29N 35 8 E
Karlobag, Croatia 29 D12 44 32N 15 5 E
Karlovac, Croatia 29 C12 45 31N 15 36 E
Karlovarský □, Czech Rep. 26 A5 50 10N 12 50 E
Karlovka = Karlivka, Ukraine 47 H8 49 29N 35 8 E
Karlovo, Bulgaria 41 D8 42 38N 24 47 E
Karlovy Vary, Czech Rep. 26 A5 50 13N 12 51 E
Karlsbad = Karlovy Vary, Czech Rep. 26 A5 50 13N 12 51 E
Karlsborg, Sweden 11 F8 58 33N 14 33 E
Karlshamn, Sweden 11 H8 56 10N 14 51 E
Karlskoga, Sweden 10 E8 59 28N 14 33 E
Karlskrona, Sweden 11 H9 56 10N 15 35 E
Karlsruhe, Germany 25 F4 49 0N 8 23 E
Karlstad, Sweden 10 E7 59 23N 13 30 E
Karlstad, U.S.A. 112 A6 48 35N 96 31W
Karlstadt, Germany 25 F5 49 57N 9 47 E
Karma, Niger 83 C5 13 38N 1 52 E
Karmėlava, Lithuania 44 D11 54 58N 24 4 E
Karmi'el, Israel 75 C4 32 55N 35 18 E
Karnak, Egypt 79 C12 25 43N 32 39 E
Karnal, India 68 E7 29 42N 77 2 E
Karnali →, Nepal 69 E9 28 45N 81 16 E
Karnaphuli Res., Bangla. 67 H18 22 40N 92 20 E
Karnaprayag, India 69 D8 30 16N 79 15 E
Karnataka □, India 66 N10 13 15N 77 0 E
Karnes City, U.S.A. 113 L6 28 53N 97 54W
Karnische Alpen, Europe 26 E6 46 36N 13 0 E
Karnobat, Bulgaria 41 D10 42 39N 26 59 E
Kärnten □, Austria 26 E6 46 52N 13 30 E
Karo, Mali 82 C4 12 16N 3 18W
Karoi, Zimbabwe 87 F2 16 48 S 29 45 E
Karonga, Malawi 87 D3 9 57 S 33 55 E
Karoonda, Australia 95 F2 35 1 S 139 59 E
Karor, Pakistan 68 D4 31 15N 70 59 E
Karora, Sudan 80 D4 17 44N 38 15 E
Káros, Greece 39 E7 36 54N 25 40 E
Karounga, Mali 82 B3 15 20N 7 35W
Karousádhes, Greece 38 B1 39 47N 19 45 E
Karpacz, Poland 45 H2 50 46N 15 46 E
Karpasia □, Cyprus 36 D13 35 32N 34 15 E
Kárpathos, Greece 39 F9 35 37N 27 10 E
Kárpathos, Stenón, Greece 39 F9 36 0N 27 30 E
Karpenísion, Greece 38 C3 38 55N 21 40 E
Karpuz Burnu = Apostolos Andreas, C., Cyprus 36 D13 35 42N 34 35 E
Karpuzlu, Turkey 39 D9 37 33N 27 51 E
Karratha, Australia 92 D2 20 53 S 116 40 E
Kars, Turkey 73 B10 40 40N 43 5 E

Kitaibaraki

Khān Abū Shāmat, Syria 75 B5 33 39N 36 53 E
Khān Azād, Iraq 70 C5 33 7N 44 22 E
Khān Mujiddah, Iraq 70 C4 32 21N 43 48 E
Khān Shaykhūn, Syria 70 C3 35 26N 36 38 E
Khān Yūnis, Gaza Strip 75 D3 31 21N 34 18 E
Khanai, Pakistan 68 D2 30 30N 67 8 E
Khānaqīn, Iraq 70 C5 34 23N 45 25 E
Khānbāghī, Iran 71 B7 36 10N 55 25 E
Khandrá, Greece 39 F8 35 3N 26 8 E
Khandwa, India 66 J10 21 49N 76 22 E
Khandyga, Russia 51 C14 62 42N 135 35 E
Khāneh, Iran 70 B5 36 41N 45 8 E
Khanewal, Pakistan 68 D4 30 20N 71 55 E
Khangah Dogran, Pakistan 68 D5 31 50N 73 37 E
Khanh Duong, Vietnam 64 F7 12 44N 108 44 E
Khaniá, Greece 36 D6 35 30N 24 4 E
Khaniá □, Greece 36 D6 35 30N 24 0 E
Khaniadhana, India 68 G8 25 1N 78 8 E
Khaníon, Kólpos, Greece 36 D5 35 33N 23 55 E
Khanka, L., Asia 51 E14 45 0N 132 24 E
Khankendy = Xankändi, Azerbaijan 70 B5 39 52N 46 49 E
Khanna, India 68 D7 30 42N 76 16 E
Khanozai, Pakistan 68 D2 30 37N 67 19 E
Khanpur, Pakistan 68 E4 28 42N 70 35 E
Khanty-Mansiysk, Russia 50 C7 61 0N 69 0 E
Khapalu, Pakistan 69 B7 35 10N 76 20 E
Khapcheranga, Russia 51 E12 49 42N 112 24 E
Kharabali, Russia 49 G8 47 25N 47 15 E
Kharaghoda, India 68 H4 23 11N 71 46 E
Kharagpur, India 69 H12 22 20N 87 25 E
Khárakas, Greece 36 D7 35 1N 25 7 E
Kharan Kalat, Pakistan 66 E4 28 34N 65 21 E
Kharānaq, Iran 71 C7 32 20N 54 45 E
Kharda, India 66 K9 18 40N 75 34 E
Khardung La, India 69 B7 34 20N 77 43 E
Khârga, El Wâhât-el, Egypt 80 B3 25 10N 30 35 E
Khargon, India 66 J9 21 45N 75 40 E
Khari →, India 68 G6 25 54N 74 31 E
Kharian, Pakistan 68 C5 32 49N 73 52 E
Kharit, Wadi el →, Egypt 80 C3 24 26N 33 3 E
Khārk, Jazīreh-ye, Iran 71 D6 29 15N 50 28 E
Kharkiv, Ukraine 47 H9 49 58N 36 20 E
Kharkov = Kharkiv, Ukraine 47 H9 49 58N 36 20 E
Kharmanli, Bulgaria 41 E9 41 55N 25 55 E
Kharovsk, Russia 46 C11 59 56N 40 13 E
Kharsawangarh, India 69 H11 22 48N 85 50 E
Kharta, Turkey 72 B3 40 55N 29 7 E
Khartoum = El Khartûm, Sudan 81 D3 15 31N 32 35 E
Khasan, Russia 54 C5 42 25N 130 40 E
Khasavyurt, Russia 49 J8 43 16N 46 40 E
Khāsh, Iran 66 E2 28 15N 61 15 E
Khashm el Girba, Sudan 81 E4 14 59N 35 58 E
Khashum, Sudan 81 E2 12 27N 28 2 E
Khashuri, Georgia 49 J6 42 3N 43 35 E
Khaskovo, Bulgaria 41 E9 41 56N 25 30 E
Khaskovo □, Bulgaria 41 E9 42 0N 25 40 E
Khatanga, Russia 51 B11 72 0N 102 20 E
Khatanga →, Russia 51 B11 72 55N 106 0 E
Khatauli, India 68 E7 29 17N 77 43 E
Khatra, India 69 H12 22 59N 86 51 E
Khātūnābād, Iran 71 D7 30 1N 55 25 E
Khatyrka, Russia 51 C18 62 3N 175 15 E
Khavda, India 68 H3 23 51N 69 43 E
Khaybar, Ḥarrat, Si. Arabia 70 E4 25 45N 40 0 E
Khayelitsha, S. Africa 85 L3 34 5S 18 42 E
Khāzimiyah, Iraq 70 C4 34 46N 43 37 E
Khazzān Jabal al Awliyā, Sudan 81 D3 15 24N 32 20 E
Khe Bo, Vietnam 64 C5 19 8N 104 41 E
Khe Long, Vietnam 64 B5 21 29N 104 46 E
Khed Brahma, India 66 G8 24 7N 73 5 E
Khekra, India 68 E7 28 52N 77 20 E
Khemarak Phouminville, Cambodia 65 G4 11 37N 102 59 E
Khemisset, Morocco 78 B4 33 50N 6 1W
Khemmarat, Thailand 64 D5 16 10N 105 15 E
Khenāmān, Iran 71 D8 30 27N 56 29 E
Khenchela, Algeria 78 A7 35 28N 7 11 E
Khersān →, Iran 71 D6 31 33N 50 22 E
Khérson, Greece 40 E6 41 5N 22 47 E
Kherson, Ukraine 47 J7 46 35N 32 35 E
Khersónisos Akrotíri, Greece 36 D6 35 30N 24 10 E
Kheta →, Russia 51 B11 71 54N 102 6 E
Khewari, Pakistan 68 F3 26 36N 68 52 E
Khilchipur, India 68 G7 24 2N 76 34 E
Khiliomódhion, Greece 38 D4 37 48N 22 51 E
Khilok, Russia 51 D12 51 30N 110 45 E
Khimki, Russia 46 E9 55 50N 37 20 E
Khíos, Greece 39 C8 38 27N 26 9 E
Khíos □, Greece 39 C8 38 27N 26 9 E
Khirsadoh, India 69 H8 22 11N 78 47 E
Khiuma = Hiiumaa, Estonia 9 G20 58 50N 22 45 E
Khiva, Uzbekistan 50 E7 41 30N 60 18 E
Khīyāv, Iran 70 B5 38 30N 47 45 E
Khlebarovo, Bulgaria 41 C10 43 37N 26 15 E
Khlong Khlung, Thailand 64 D2 16 12N 99 43 E
Khmelnik, Ukraine 47 H4 49 33N 27 58 E
Khmelnitskiy = Khmelnytskyy, Ukraine 47 H4 49 23N 27 0 E
Khmelnytskyy, Ukraine 47 H4 49 23N 27 0 E
Khmer Rep. = Cambodia ■, Asia 64 F5 12 15N 105 0 E
Khoai, Hon, Vietnam 65 H5 8 26N 104 50 E
Khodoriv, Ukraine 47 H3 49 24N 24 19 E
Khodzent = Khŭjand, Tajikistan 50 E7 40 17N 69 37 E
Khojak Pass, Afghan. 68 D2 30 51N 66 34 E
Khok Kloi, Thailand 65 H2 8 17N 98 19 E
Khok Pho, Thailand 65 J3 6 43N 101 6 E
Kholm, Russia 46 D6 57 10N 31 15 E
Kholmsk, Russia 51 E15 47 40N 142 5 E
Khomas Hochland, Namibia 88 C2 22 40S 16 0 E
Khombole, Senegal 82 C1 14 43N 16 42W
Khomeyn, Iran 71 C6 33 40N 50 7 E
Khomeynī Shahr, Iran 71 C6 32 41N 51 31 E
Khomodino, Botswana 88 C3 22 46S 23 52 E
Khon Kaen, Thailand 64 D4 16 30N 102 47 E
Khong →, Cambodia 64 F5 13 32N 105 58 E
Khong Sedone, Laos 64 E5 15 34N 105 49 E
Khonuu, Russia 51 C15 66 30N 143 12 E
Khoper →, Russia 48 F6 49 30N 42 20 E
Khor el 'Atash, Sudan 81 E3 13 20N 34 15 E
Khóra, Greece 38 D3 37 3N 21 42 E
Khóra Sfakíon, Greece 36 D6 35 15N 24 9 E
Khorāsān □, Iran 71 C8 34 0N 58 0 E
Khorat = Nakhon Ratchasima, Thailand 64 E4 14 59N 102 12 E
Khorat, Cao Nguyen, Thailand 64 E4 15 30N 102 50 E
Khorixas, Namibia 88 C1 20 16S 14 59 E
Khorol, Ukraine 47 H7 49 48N 33 15 E
Khorramābād, Khorāsān, Iran 71 C8 35 6N 57 57 E
Khorramābād, Lorestān, Iran 71 C6 33 30N 48 25 E
Khorrāmshahr, Iran 71 D6 30 29N 48 15 E
Khorugh, Tajikistan 50 F8 37 30N 71 36 E
Khosravī, Iran 71 D6 30 48N 51 28 E
Khosrowābād, Khuzestān, Iran 71 D6 30 10N 48 25 E
Khosrowābād, Kordestān, Iran 70 C5 35 31N 47 38 E
Khost, Pakistan 68 D2 30 13N 67 35 E
Khosūyeh, Iran 71 D7 28 32N 54 26 E
Khotyn, Ukraine 47 H4 48 31N 26 27 E
Khouribga, Morocco 78 B4 32 58N 6 57W
Khowst, Afghan. 68 C3 33 22N 69 58 E
Khowst □, Afghan. 66 C6 33 20N 70 0 E
Khoyniki, Belarus 47 G5 51 54N 29 55 E
Khrami →, Georgia 49 K7 41 25N 45 0 E
Khrenovoye, Russia 48 E5 51 4N 40 16 E
Khrisoúpolis, Greece 41 F8 40 58N 24 42 E
Khristianá, Greece 39 E7 36 14N 25 13 E
Khrysokhou B., Cyprus 36 D11 35 6N 32 25 E
Khtapodhiá, Greece 39 D7 37 24N 25 34 E
Khu Khan, Thailand 64 E5 14 42N 104 12 E
Khudzhand = Khŭjand, Tajikistan 50 E7 40 17N 69 37 E
Khuff, Si. Arabia 70 E5 24 55N 44 53 E
Khūgīānī, Afghan. 68 D2 31 28N 65 14 E
Khuis, Botswana 88 D3 26 40S 21 49 E
Khuiyala, India 68 F4 27 9N 70 25 E
Khŭjand, Tajikistan 50 E7 40 17N 69 37 E
Khujner, India 68 H7 23 47N 76 36 E
Khulna, Bangla. 67 H16 22 45N 89 34 E
Khulna □, Bangla. 67 H16 22 25N 89 35 E
Khulo, Georgia 49 K6 41 33N 42 19 E
Khumago, Botswana 88 C3 20 26S 24 32 E
Khūnsorkh, Iran 71 E8 27 9N 56 7 E
Khunti, India 69 H11 23 5N 85 17 E
Khūr, Iran 71 C8 32 55N 58 18 E
Khurai, India 68 G8 24 3N 78 23 E
Khurayṣ, Si. Arabia 71 E6 25 6N 48 2 E
Khureit, Sudan 81 E2 13 59N 26 3 E
Khurīyā Murīyā, Jazā'ir, Oman 74 D6 17 30N 55 58 E
Khurja, India 68 E7 28 15N 77 58 E
Khūrmāl, Iraq 70 C5 35 18N 46 2 E
Khurr, Wādī al, Iraq 70 C4 32 3N 43 52 E
Khūsf, Iran 71 C8 32 46N 58 53 E
Khush, Afghan. 66 C3 32 55N 62 10 E
Khushab, Pakistan 68 C5 32 20N 72 20 E
Khust, Ukraine 47 H2 48 10N 23 18 E
Khuzdar, Pakistan 68 F2 27 52N 66 30 E
Khūzestān □, Iran 71 D6 31 0N 49 0 E
Khvāf, Iran 71 C9 34 33N 60 8 E
Khvājeh, Iran 70 B5 38 9N 46 35 E
Khvalynsk, Russia 48 D9 52 30N 48 2 E
Khvānsār, Iran 71 D7 29 56N 54 8 E
Khvatovka, Russia 48 D8 52 24N 46 32 E
Khvor, Iran 71 C7 33 45N 55 0 E
Khvorgū, Iran 71 E8 27 34N 56 27 E
Khvormūj, Iran 71 D6 28 40N 51 30 E
Khvoy, Iran 70 B5 38 35N 45 0 E
Khvoynaya, Russia 46 C8 58 58N 34 28 E
Khyber Pass, Afghan. 68 B4 34 10N 71 8 E
Kiabukwa, Dem. Rep. of the Congo 87 D1 8 40S 24 48 E
Kiama, Australia 95 E5 34 40S 150 50 E
Kiamba, Phil. 61 H6 6 2N 124 46 E
Kiambi, Dem. Rep. of the Congo 86 D2 7 15S 28 0 E
Kiambu, Kenya 86 C4 1 8S 36 50 E
Kiangara, Madag. 89 B8 17 58S 47 2 E
Kiangsi = Jiangxi □, China 59 D11 27 30N 116 0 E
Kiangsu = Jiangsu □, China 57 H11 33 0N 120 0 E
Kiáton, Greece 38 C4 38 1N 22 45 E
Kibæk, Denmark 11 H2 56 2N 8 51 E
Kibanga Port, Uganda 86 B3 0 10N 32 58 E
Kibara, Tanzania 86 C3 2 8S 33 30 E
Kibare, Mts., Dem. Rep. of the Congo 86 D2 8 25S 27 10 E
Kibombo, Dem. Rep. of the Congo 86 C2 3 57S 25 53 E
Kibondo, Tanzania 86 C3 3 35S 30 45 E
Kibre Mengist, Ethiopia 81 F4 5 54N 38 59 E
Kibumbu, Burundi 86 C2 3 32S 29 45 E
Kibungo, Rwanda 86 C3 2 10S 30 32 E
Kibuye, Burundi 86 C2 3 39S 29 59 E
Kibuye, Rwanda 86 C2 2 3S 29 21 E
Kibwesa, Tanzania 86 D2 6 30S 29 58 E
Kibwezi, Kenya 86 C4 2 27S 37 57 E
Kicasalih, Turkey 41 E10 41 23N 26 48 E
Kičevo, Macedonia 40 E4 41 34N 20 59 E
Kichha, India 69 E8 28 53N 79 30 E
Kichha →, India 69 E8 28 41N 79 18 E
Kicking Horse Pass, Canada 104 C5 51 28N 116 16W
Kidal, Mali 83 B5 18 26N 1 22 E
Kidderminster, U.K. 13 E5 52 24N 2 15W
Kidete, Tanzania 86 D4 6 25S 37 17 E
Kidira, Senegal 82 C2 14 28N 12 13W
Kidnappers, C., N.Z. 91 H6 39 38S 177 5 E
Kidsgrove, U.K. 12 D5 53 5N 2 14W
Kidston, Australia 94 B3 18 52S 144 8 E
Kidugallo, Tanzania 86 D4 6 49S 38 15 E
Kiel, Germany 24 A6 54 19N 10 8 E
Kiel Canal = Nord-Ostsee-Kanal, Germany 24 A5 54 12N 9 32 E
Kielce, Poland 45 H7 50 52N 20 42 E
Kielder Water, U.K. 12 B5 55 11N 2 31W
Kieler Bucht, Germany 24 A6 54 35N 10 25 E
Kiembara, Burkina Faso 82 C4 13 15N 2 44W
Kien Binh, Vietnam 65 H5 9 55N 105 19 E
Kien Tan, Vietnam 65 G5 10 7N 105 17 E
Kienge, Dem. Rep. of the Congo 87 E2 10 30S 27 30 E
Kiessé, Niger 83 C5 13 29N 4 1 E
Kiev = Kyyiv, Ukraine 47 G6 50 30N 30 28 E
Kifaya, Guinea 82 C2 12 10N 13 4W
Kiffa, Mauritania 82 B2 16 37N 11 24W
Kifisiá, Greece 38 C5 38 4N 23 49 E
Kifissós →, Greece 38 C5 38 35N 23 20 E
Kifrī, Iraq 70 C5 34 45N 45 0 E
Kigali, Rwanda 86 C3 1 59S 30 4 E
Kigarama, Tanzania 86 C3 1 1S 31 50 E
Kigelle, Sudan 81 F3 8 40N 34 2 E
Kigoma □, Tanzania 86 D3 5 0S 30 0 E
Kigoma-Ujiji, Tanzania 86 C2 4 55S 29 36 E
Kigomasha, Ras, Tanzania 86 C4 4 58S 38 58 E
Kığzı, Turkey 70 B4 38 18N 43 25 E
Kihei, U.S.A. 106 H16 20 47N 156 28W
Kihnu, Estonia 9 G21 58 9N 24 1 E
Kii-Sanchi, Japan 55 G8 34 20N 136 0 E
Kii-Suidō, Japan 55 H7 33 40N 134 45 E
Kikaiga-Shima, Japan 55 K4 28 19N 129 59 E
Kikinda, Serbia, Yug. 42 E5 45 50N 20 30 E
Kikládhes, Greece 38 E6 37 0N 24 30 E
Kikládhes □, Greece 38 D6 37 0N 25 0 E
Kikwit, Dem. Rep. of the Congo 84 E3 5 0S 18 45 E
Kil, Sweden 10 E7 59 30N 13 20 E
Kilafors, Sweden 10 C10 61 14N 16 36 E
Kilar, India 68 C7 33 6N 76 25 E
Kilauea Crater, U.S.A. 106 J17 19 25N 155 17W
Kilbrannan Sd., U.K. 14 F3 55 37N 5 26W
Kilchu, N. Korea 57 D15 40 57N 129 25 E
Kilcoy, Australia 95 D5 26 59S 152 30 E
Kildare, Ireland 15 C5 53 9N 6 55W
Kildare □, Ireland 15 C5 53 10N 6 50W
Kileikli, Sudan 81 E2 11 25N 25 31 E
Kilfinnane, Ireland 15 D3 52 21N 8 28W
Kilgore, U.S.A. 113 J7 32 23N 94 53W
Kilibo, Benin 83 D5 8 32N 2 38 E
Kilifi, Kenya 86 C4 3 40S 39 48 E
Kilimanjaro, Tanzania 86 C4 3 7S 37 20 E
Kilimanjaro □, Tanzania 86 C4 4 0S 38 0 E
Kilimli, Turkey 72 B4 41 28N 31 50 E
Kilindini, Kenya 86 C4 4 4S 39 40 E
Kilis, Turkey 70 B3 36 42N 37 6 E
Kiliya, Ukraine 47 K5 45 28N 29 16 E
Kilkee, Ireland 15 D2 52 41N 9 39W
Kilkeel, U.K. 15 B5 54 4N 6 0W
Kilkenny, Ireland 15 D4 52 39N 7 15W
Kilkenny □, Ireland 15 D4 52 35N 7 15W
Kilkieran B., Ireland 15 C2 53 20N 9 41W
Kilkís, Greece 40 F6 40 58N 22 57 E
Kilkís □, Greece 40 E6 41 5N 22 50 E
Killala, Ireland 15 B2 54 13N 9 12W
Killala B., Ireland 15 B2 54 16N 9 8W
Killaloe, Ireland 15 D3 52 48N 8 28W
Killaloe Station, Canada 110 A7 45 33N 77 25W
Killarney, Australia 95 D5 28 20S 152 18 E
Killarney, Canada 105 D9 49 10N 99 40W
Killarney, Ireland 15 D2 52 4N 9 30W
Killary Harbour, Ireland 15 C2 53 38N 9 52W
Killdeer, U.S.A. 112 B3 47 26N 102 48W
Killeberg, Sweden 11 H8 56 29N 14 5 E
Killeen, U.S.A. 113 K6 31 7N 97 44W
Killin, U.K. 14 E4 56 28N 4 19W
Killíni, Ilía, Greece 38 D3 37 55N 21 8 E
Killíni, Korinthía, Greece 38 D4 37 54N 22 25 E
Killorglin, Ireland 15 D2 52 6N 9 47W
Killybegs, Ireland 15 B3 54 38N 8 26W
Kilmarnock, U.K. 14 F4 55 37N 4 29W
Kilmez, Russia 48 B10 56 58N 50 55 E
Kilmez →, Russia 48 B10 56 58N 50 28 E
Kilmore, Australia 95 F3 37 25S 144 53 E
Kilondo, Tanzania 87 D3 9 45S 34 20 E
Kilosa, Tanzania 86 D4 6 48S 37 0 E
Kilrush, Ireland 15 D2 52 38N 9 29W
Kilwa Kisiwani, Tanzania 87 D4 8 58S 39 32 E
Kilwa Kivinje, Tanzania 87 D4 8 45S 39 25 E
Kilwa Masoko, Tanzania 87 D4 8 55S 39 30 E
Kilwinning, U.K. 14 F4 55 39N 4 43W
Kim, U.S.A. 113 G3 37 15N 103 21W
Kim →, Cameroon 83 D7 5 28N 11 7 E
Kimaam, Indonesia 63 F9 7 58S 138 53 E
Kimamba, Tanzania 86 D4 6 45S 37 10 E
Kimba, Australia 95 E2 33 8S 136 23 E
Kimball, Nebr., U.S.A. 112 E3 41 14N 103 40W
Kimball, S. Dak., U.S.A. 112 D5 43 45N 98 57W
Kimberley, Australia 92 C4 16 20S 127 0 E
Kimberley, Canada 104 D5 49 40N 115 59W
Kimberley, S. Africa 88 D3 28 43S 24 46 E
Kimberly, U.S.A. 114 E6 42 32N 114 22W
Kimch'aek, N. Korea 57 D15 40 40N 129 10 E
Kimch'ŏn, S. Korea 57 F15 36 11N 128 4 E
Kími, Greece 38 C6 38 38N 24 6 E
Kimje, S. Korea 57 G14 35 48N 126 45 E
Kimmirut, Canada 101 B13 62 50N 69 50W
Kímolos, Greece 38 E6 36 48N 24 37 E
Kimovsk, Moskva, Russia 46 E9 55 21N 37 28 E
Kimovsk, Tula, Russia 46 E10 54 0N 38 29 E
Kimparana, Mali 82 C4 12 48N 5 0W
Kimpese, Dem. Rep. of the Congo 84 F2 5 35S 14 26 E
Kimry, Russia 46 D9 56 55N 37 15 E
Kimstad, Sweden 11 F9 58 35N 15 58 E
Kinabalu, Gunong, Malaysia 62 C5 6 3N 116 14 E
Kínaros, Greece 39 E8 36 59N 26 15 E
Kinaskan L., Canada 104 B2 57 38N 130 8W
Kinbasket L., Canada 104 C5 52 0N 118 10W
Kincardine, Canada 102 D3 44 10N 81 40W
Kincolith, Canada 104 B3 55 0N 129 57W
Kinda, Dem. Rep. of the Congo 87 D2 9 18S 25 4 E
Kindberg, Austria 26 D8 47 30N 15 27 E
Kinde, U.S.A. 110 C2 43 56N 83 0W
Kinder Scout, U.K. 12 D6 53 24N 1 52W
Kindersley, Canada 105 C7 51 30N 109 10W
Kindia, Guinea 82 D2 10 0N 12 52W
Kindu, Dem. Rep. of the Congo 86 C2 2 55S 25 50 E
Kinel, Russia 48 D10 53 15N 50 40 E
Kineshma, Russia 48 B6 57 30N 42 5 E
Kinesi, Tanzania 86 C3 1 25S 33 50 E
King, L., Australia 93 F2 33 10S 119 35 E
King, Mt., Australia 94 D4 25 10S 147 30 E
King City, U.S.A. 116 J5 36 13N 121 8W
King Cr. →, Australia 94 C2 24 35S 139 30 E
King Edward →, Australia 92 B4 14 14S 126 35 E
King Frederick VI Land = Kong Frederik VI Kyst, Greenland 4 C5 63 0N 43 0W
King George B., Falk. Is. 128 G4 51 30S 60 30W
King George I., Antarctica 5 C18 60 0S 60 0W
King George Is., Canada 101 C11 57 20N 80 30W
King I. = Kadan Kyun, Burma 64 F2 12 30N 98 20 E
King I., Australia 94 F3 39 50S 144 0 E
King I., Canada 104 C3 52 10N 127 40W
King Leopold Ranges, Australia 92 C4 17 30S 125 45 E
King of Prussia, U.S.A. 111 F9 40 5N 75 23W
King Sd., Australia 92 C3 16 50S 123 20 E
King William I., Canada 100 B10 69 10N 97 25W
King William's Town, S. Africa 88 E4 32 51S 27 22 E
Kingaok = Bathurst Inlet, Canada 100 B9 66 50N 108 1W
Kingaroy, Australia 95 D5 26 32S 151 51 E
Kingfisher, U.S.A. 113 H6 35 52N 97 56W
Kingirbān, Iraq 70 C5 34 40N 44 54 E
Kingisepp = Kuressaare, Estonia 9 G20 58 15N 22 30 E
Kingisepp, Russia 46 C5 59 25N 28 40 E
Kingman, Ariz., U.S.A. 117 K12 35 12N 114 4W
Kingman, Kans., U.S.A. 113 G5 37 39N 98 7W
Kingoonya, Australia 95 E2 30 55S 135 19 E
Kingri, Pakistan 68 D3 30 27N 69 49 E
Kings →, U.S.A. 116 J7 36 3N 119 50W
Kings Canyon National Park, U.S.A. 116 J8 36 50N 118 40W
King's Lynn, U.K. 12 E8 52 45N 0 24 E
Kings Mountain, U.S.A. 109 H5 35 15N 81 20W
Kings Park, U.S.A. 111 F11 40 53N 73 16W
King's Peak, U.S.A. 114 F8 40 46N 110 27W
Kingsbridge, U.K. 13 G4 50 17N 3 47W
Kingsburg, U.S.A. 116 J7 36 31N 119 33W
Kingscote, Australia 95 F2 35 40S 137 38 E
Kingscourt, Ireland 15 C5 53 55N 6 48W
Kingsford, U.S.A. 108 C1 45 48N 88 4W
Kingsland, U.S.A. 109 K5 30 48N 81 41W
Kingsley, U.S.A. 112 D7 42 35N 95 58W
Kingsport, U.S.A. 109 G4 36 33N 82 33W
Kingston, Canada 102 D4 44 14N 76 30W
Kingston, Jamaica 120 C4 18 0N 76 50W
Kingston, N.Z. 91 L2 45 20S 168 43 E
Kingston, N.H., U.S.A. 111 D13 42 56N 71 3W
Kingston, N.Y., U.S.A. 111 E11 41 56N 73 59W
Kingston, Pa., U.S.A. 111 E9 41 16N 75 54W
Kingston, R.I., U.S.A. 111 E13 41 29N 71 30W
Kingston Pk., U.S.A. 117 K11 35 45N 115 54W
Kingston South East, Australia 95 F2 36 51S 139 55 E
Kingston upon Hull, U.K. 12 D7 53 45N 0 21W
Kingston upon Hull □, U.K. 12 D7 53 45N 0 21W
Kingston-upon-Thames □, U.K. 13 F7 51 24N 0 17W
Kingstown, St. Vincent 121 D7 13 10N 61 10W
Kingstree, U.S.A. 109 J6 33 40N 79 50W
Kingsville, Canada 102 D3 42 2N 82 45W
Kingsville, U.S.A. 113 M6 27 31N 97 52W
Kingussie, U.K. 14 D4 57 6N 4 2W
Kingwood, U.S.A. 113 K7 29 54N 95 18W
Kınık, Antalya, Turkey 39 E11 36 20N 29 20 E
Kınık, İzmir, Turkey 39 B9 39 6N 27 24 E
Kinistino, Canada 105 C7 52 57N 105 2W
Kinkala, Congo 84 E2 4 18S 14 49 E
Kinki □, Japan 55 H8 33 45N 136 0 E
Kinleith, N.Z. 91 H5 38 20S 175 56 E
Kinmount, Canada 110 B6 44 48N 78 45W
Kinna, Sweden 11 G6 57 32N 12 42 E
Kinnairds Hd., U.K. 14 D6 57 43N 2 1W
Kinnared, Sweden 11 G7 57 2N 13 7 E
Kinnarodden, Norway 6 A11 71 8N 27 40 E
Kinnarp, Sweden 11 F7 58 5N 13 32 E
Kinneviken, Sweden 11 F7 58 35N 13 15 E
Kinngait = Cape Dorset, Canada 101 B12 64 14N 76 32W
Kino, Mexico 118 B2 28 45N 111 59W
Kinoje →, Canada 102 B3 52 8N 81 25W
Kinomoto, Japan 55 G8 35 30N 136 13 E
Kinoni, Uganda 86 C3 0 41S 30 28 E
Kinoosao, Canada 105 B8 57 5N 102 1W
Kinross, U.K. 14 E5 56 13N 3 25W
Kinsale, Ireland 15 E3 51 42N 8 31W
Kinsale, Old Hd. of, Ireland 15 E3 51 37N 8 33W
Kinsha = Chang Jiang →, China 59 B13 31 48N 121 10 E
Kinshasa, Dem. Rep. of the Congo 84 E3 4 20S 15 15 E
Kinsley, U.S.A. 113 G5 37 55N 99 25W
Kinsman, U.S.A. 110 E4 41 26N 80 35W
Kinston, U.S.A. 109 H7 35 16N 77 35W
Kintampo, Ghana 83 D4 8 5N 1 41W
Kintore Ra., Australia 92 D4 23 15S 128 47 E
Kintyre, U.K. 14 F3 55 30N 5 35W
Kintyre, Mull of, U.K. 14 F3 55 17N 5 47W
Kinushseo →, Canada 102 A3 55 15N 83 45W
Kinuso, Canada 104 B5 55 20N 115 25W
Kinyangiri, Tanzania 86 C3 4 25S 34 37 E
Kinyeti, Sudan 81 G3 3 57N 32 54 E
Kinzig →, Germany 25 G3 48 36N 7 49 E
Kinzua, U.S.A. 110 E6 41 52N 78 58W
Kinzua Dam, U.S.A. 110 E6 41 53N 79 0W
Kióni, Greece 38 C2 38 27N 20 41 E
Kiosk, Canada 102 C4 46 6N 78 53W
Kiowa, Kans., U.S.A. 113 G5 37 1N 98 29W
Kiowa, Okla., U.S.A. 113 H7 34 43N 95 54W
Kipahigan L., Canada 105 B8 55 20N 101 55W
Kipanga, Tanzania 86 D4 6 15S 35 20 E
Kiparissía, Greece 38 D3 37 15N 21 40 E
Kiparissiakós Kólpos, Greece 38 D3 37 25N 21 25 E
Kipawa, L., Canada 102 C4 46 50N 79 0W
Kipembawe, Tanzania 86 D3 7 38S 33 27 E
Kipengere Ra., Tanzania 87 D3 9 12S 34 15 E
Kipili, Tanzania 86 D3 7 28S 30 32 E
Kipini, Kenya 86 C5 2 30S 40 32 E
Kipling, Canada 105 C8 50 6N 102 38W
Kippure, Ireland 15 C5 53 11N 6 21W
Kipushi, Dem. Rep. of the Congo 87 E2 11 48S 27 12 E
Kirane, Mali 82 B2 15 20N 10 20W
Kiranomena, Madag. 89 B8 18 17S 46 2 E
Kiraz, Turkey 39 C10 38 14N 28 13 E
Kirazlı, Turkey 41 F10 40 2N 26 41 E
Kirchhain, Germany 24 E4 50 47N 8 56 E
Kirchheim, Germany 25 G5 48 39N 9 27 E
Kirchheimbolanden, Germany 25 F3 49 40N 8 0 E
Kirchschlag, Austria 27 D9 47 30N 16 19 E
Kireç, Turkey 39 B10 39 33N 28 22 E
Kirensk, Russia 51 D11 57 50N 107 55 E
Kirghizia = Kyrgyzstan ■, Asia 50 E8 42 0N 75 0 E
Kirghizstan = Kyrgyzstan ■, Asia 50 E8 42 0N 75 0 E
Kiribati ■, Pac. Oc. 96 H10 5 0S 180 0 E
Kırıkhan, Turkey 72 D7 36 31N 36 21 E
Kırıkkale, Turkey 72 C5 39 51N 33 32 E
Kirillov, Russia 46 C10 59 49N 38 24 E
Kirin = Jilin, China 57 C14 43 44N 126 30 E
Kirishi, Russia 46 C7 59 28N 31 59 E
Kiritimati, Kiribati 97 G12 1 58N 157 27W
Kırka, Turkey 39 B12 39 17N 30 33 E
Kırkağaç, Turkey 39 B9 39 8N 27 40 E
Kirkby, U.K. 12 D5 53 30N 2 54W
Kirkby Lonsdale, U.K. 12 C5 54 12N 2 36W
Kirkcaldy, U.K. 14 E5 56 7N 3 9W
Kirkcudbright, U.K. 14 G4 54 50N 4 2W
Kirkee, India 66 K8 18 34N 73 56 E
Kirkenes, Norway 8 B23 69 40N 30 5 E
Kirkfield, Canada 110 B6 44 34N 78 59W
Kirkjubæjarklaustur, Iceland 8 E4 63 47N 18 4W
Kirkkonummi, Finland 9 F21 60 8N 24 26 E
Kirkland Lake, Canada 102 C3 48 9N 80 2W
Kırklareli, Turkey 41 E11 41 44N 27 15 E
Kırklareli □, Turkey 41 E11 41 45N 27 15 E
Kirksville, U.S.A. 112 E8 40 12N 92 35W
Kirkūk, Iraq 70 C5 35 30N 44 21 E
Kirkwall, U.K. 14 C6 58 59N 2 58W
Kirkwood, S. Africa 88 E4 33 22S 25 15 E
Kirn, Germany 25 F3 49 47N 7 26 E
Kirov, Kaluga, Russia 46 E8 54 3N 34 20 E
Kirov, Kirov, Russia 50 D5 58 35N 49 40 E
Kirovabad = Gäncä, Azerbaijan 49 K8 40 45N 46 20 E
Kirovakan = Vanadzor, Armenia 49 K7 40 48N 44 30 E
Kirovograd = Kirovohrad, Ukraine 47 H7 48 35N 32 20 E
Kirovohrad, Ukraine 47 H7 48 35N 32 20 E
Kirovsk = Babadayhan, Turkmenistan 50 F7 37 42N 60 23 E
Kirovskiy, Astrakhan, Russia 49 H9 45 51N 48 11 E
Kirovskiy, Kamchatka, Russia 51 D16 54 27N 155 42 E
Kirovskiy, Primorsk, Russia 54 B6 45 7N 133 30 E
Kirriemuir, U.K. 14 E5 56 41N 3 1W
Kirsanov, Russia 48 D6 52 35N 42 40 E
Kırşehir, Turkey 70 B2 39 14N 34 5 E
Kirtachi, Niger 83 C5 12 52N 2 30 E
Kirthar Range, Pakistan 68 F2 27 0N 67 0 E
Kirtland, U.S.A. 115 H9 36 44N 108 21W
Kiruna, Sweden 8 C19 67 52N 20 15 E
Kirundu, Dem. Rep. of the Congo 86 C2 0 50S 25 35 E
Kirya, Russia 48 C8 55 8N 46 55 E
Kiryū, Japan 55 F9 36 24N 139 20 E
Kisa, Sweden 11 G9 58 0N 15 39 E
Kisaga, Tanzania 86 C3 4 30S 34 23 E
Kisalaya, Nic. 120 D3 14 40N 84 3W
Kisalföld, Hungary 42 C2 47 30N 17 0 E
Kisámou, Kólpos, Greece 36 D5 35 30N 23 38 E
Kisanga, Dem. Rep. of the Congo 86 B2 2 30N 26 35 E
Kisangani, Dem. Rep. of the Congo 86 B2 0 35N 25 15 E
Kisar, Indonesia 63 F7 8 5S 127 10 E
Kisarawe, Tanzania 86 D4 6 53S 39 0 E
Kisarazu, Japan 55 G9 35 23N 139 55 E
Kisbér, Hungary 42 C3 47 30N 18 2 E
Kishanganga →, Pakistan 69 B5 34 18N 73 28 E
Kishanganj, India 69 F13 26 3N 88 14 E
Kishangarh, Raj., India 68 F6 26 34N 74 52 E
Kishangarh, Raj., India 68 F4 27 50N 70 30 E
Kishi, Nigeria 83 D5 9 1N 3 52 E
Kishinev = Chişinău, Moldova 43 C13 47 2N 28 50 E
Kishiwada, Japan 55 G7 34 28N 135 22 E
Kishtwar, India 69 C6 33 20N 75 48 E
Kisielice, Poland 44 E6 53 36N 19 16 E
Kisii, Kenya 86 C3 0 40S 34 45 E
Kisiju, Tanzania 86 D4 7 23S 39 19 E
Kisir, Turkey 73 B10 41 0N 43 5 E
Kisizi, Uganda 86 C2 1 0S 29 58 E
Kiskomárom = Zalakomár, Hungary 42 D2 46 33N 17 10 E
Kiskőrei-víztároló, Hungary 42 C5 47 31N 20 36 E
Kiskőrös, Hungary 42 D4 46 37N 19 20 E
Kiskundorozsma, Hungary 42 D5 46 16N 20 5 E
Kiskunfélegyháza, Hungary 42 D4 46 42N 19 53 E
Kiskunhalas, Hungary 42 D4 46 28N 19 37 E
Kiskunmajsa, Hungary 42 D4 46 30N 19 48 E
Kislovodsk, Russia 49 J6 43 50N 42 45 E
Kismayu = Chisimaio, Somali Rep. 77 G8 0 22S 42 32 E
Kiso-Gawa →, Japan 55 G8 35 20N 136 45 E
Kiso-Sammyaku, Japan 55 G8 35 45N 137 45 E
Kisofukushima, Japan 55 G8 35 52N 137 43 E
Kisoro, Uganda 86 C2 1 17S 29 48 E
Kissidougou, Guinea 82 D2 9 5N 10 5W
Kissimmee, U.S.A. 109 L5 28 18N 81 24W
Kissimmee →, U.S.A. 109 M5 27 9N 80 52W
Kississing L., Canada 105 B8 55 10N 101 20W
Kissónerga, Cyprus 36 E11 34 49N 32 24 E
Kissu, J., Sudan 80 C2 21 37N 25 10 E
Kistanje, Croatia 29 E12 43 58N 15 55 E
Kisújszállás, Hungary 42 C5 47 12N 20 50 E
Kisumu, Kenya 86 C3 0 3S 34 45 E
Kisvárda, Hungary 42 B7 48 14N 22 4 E
Kiswani, Tanzania 86 C4 4 5S 37 57 E
Kiswere, Tanzania 87 D4 9 27S 39 30 E
Kit Carson, U.S.A. 112 F3 38 46N 102 48W
Kita, Mali 82 C3 13 5N 9 25W
Kitaibaraki, Japan 55 F10 36 50N 140 45 E

Kitakami

Kitakami, Japan 54 E10 39 20N 141 10 E
Kitakami-Gawa →, Japan 54 E10 38 25N 141 19 E
Kitakami-Sammyaku, Japan 54 E10 39 30N 141 30 E
Kitakata, Japan 54 F9 37 39N 139 52 E
Kitakyūshū, Japan 55 H5 33 50N 130 50 E
Kitale, Kenya 86 B4 1 0N 35 0 E
Kitami, Japan 54 C11 43 48N 143 54 E
Kitami-Sammyaku, Japan 54 B11 44 22N 142 43 E
Kitangiri, L., Tanzania 86 C3 4 5 S 34 20 E
Kitaya, Tanzania 87 E5 10 38 S 40 8 E
Kitchener, Canada 102 D3 43 27N 80 29W
Kitee, Finland 46 A6 62 5N 30 8 E
Kitega = Gitega, Burundi 86 C2 3 26 S 29 56 E
Kitengo, Dem. Rep. of the Congo 86 D1 7 26 S 24 8 E
Kitgum, Uganda 86 B3 3 17N 32 52 E
Kíthira, Greece 38 E5 36 8N 23 0 E
Kíthnos, Greece 38 D6 37 26N 24 27 E
Kiti, Cyprus 36 E12 34 50N 33 34 E
Kiti, C., Cyprus 36 E12 34 48N 33 36 E
Kitimat, Canada 104 C3 54 3N 128 38W
Kitinen →, Finland 8 C22 67 14N 27 27 E
Kitiyab, Sudan 81 D3 17 13N 33 35 E
Kítros, Greece 40 F6 40 22N 22 34 E
Kitsuki, Japan 55 H5 33 25N 131 37 E
Kittakittaooloo, L., Australia 95 D2 28 3 S 138 14 E
Kittanning, U.S.A. 110 F5 40 49N 79 31W
Kittatinny Mts., U.S.A. 111 F10 41 0N 75 0W
Kittery, U.S.A. 109 D10 43 5N 70 45W
Kittilä, Finland 8 C21 67 40N 24 51 E
Kitui, Kenya 86 C4 1 17 S 38 0 E
Kitwanga, Canada 104 B3 55 6N 128 4W
Kitwe, Zambia 87 E2 12 54 S 28 13 E
Kitzbühel, Austria 26 D5 47 27N 12 24 E
Kitzbühler Alpen, Austria 26 D5 47 20N 12 20 E
Kitzingen, Germany 25 F6 49 44N 10 9 E
Kivarli, India 68 G5 24 33N 72 46 E
Kivertsi, Ukraine 47 G3 50 50N 25 28 E
Kividhes, Cyprus 36 E11 34 46N 32 51 E
Kivik, Sweden 11 J8 55 41N 14 13 E
Kivotós, Greece 40 F5 40 13N 21 26 E
Kivu, L., Dem. Rep. of the Congo 86 C2 1 48 S 29 0 E
Kiyev = Kyyiv, Ukraine 47 G6 50 30N 30 28 E
Kiyevskoye Vdkhr. = Kyyivske Vdskh., Ukraine 47 G6 51 0N 30 25 E
Kıyıköy, Turkey 41 E12 41 38N 28 5 E
Kiziguru, Rwanda 86 C3 1 46 S 30 23 E
Kızıl Adalar, Turkey 41 F13 40 52N 29 5 E
Kızıl Irmak →, Turkey 72 B6 41 44N 35 58 E
Kizil Jilga, India 69 B8 35 26N 78 50 E
Kizil Yurt, Russia 49 J8 43 13N 46 54 E
Kızılcabölük, Turkey 39 D11 37 37N 29 1 E
Kızılcadağ, Turkey 39 D11 37 1N 29 58 E
Kızılcahamam, Turkey 72 B5 40 30N 32 30 E
Kızılhisar, Turkey 72 D3 37 32N 29 17 E
Kızılırmak, Turkey 72 B5 40 21N 33 59 E
Kızılkaya, Turkey 39 D12 37 18N 30 27 E
Kızılören, Turkey 39 C12 38 15N 30 10 E
Kızıltepe, Turkey 70 B4 37 12N 40 35 E
Kizimkazi, Tanzania 86 D4 6 28 S 39 30 E
Kizlyar, Russia 49 J8 43 51N 46 40 E
Kizyl-Arvat = Gyzylarbat, Turkmenistan 50 F6 39 4N 56 23 E
Kjellerup, Denmark 11 H3 56 17N 9 25 E
Kjölur, Iceland 8 D4 64 50N 19 25W
Kladanj, Bos.-H. 42 F3 44 14N 18 42 E
Kladnica, Serbia, Yug. 40 C4 43 23N 20 2 E
Kladno, Czech Rep. 26 A7 50 10N 14 7 E
Kladovo, Serbia, Yug. 40 B6 44 36N 22 33 E
Klaeng, Thailand 64 F3 12 47N 101 39 E
Klagenfurt, Austria 26 E7 46 38N 14 20 E
Klaipeda, Lithuania 9 J19 55 43N 21 10 E
Klaipėda □, Lithuania 44 C8 55 43N 21 7 E
Klaksvík, Færoe Is. 8 E9 62 14N 6 35W
Klamath →, U.S.A. 114 F1 41 33N 124 5W
Klamath Falls, U.S.A. 114 E3 42 13N 121 46W
Klamath Mts., U.S.A. 114 F2 41 20N 123 0W
Klamono, Indonesia 63 E8 1 8 S 131 30 E
Klanjec, Croatia 29 B12 46 3N 15 45 E
Klappan →, Canada 104 B3 58 0N 129 43W
Klarälven →, Sweden 10 E7 59 23N 13 32 E
Klässbol, Sweden 10 E6 59 33N 12 45 E
Klatovy, Czech Rep. 26 B6 49 23N 13 18 E
Klawer, S. Africa 88 E2 31 44 S 18 36 E
Klazienaveen, Neths. 17 B6 52 44N 7 0 E
Klé, Mali 82 C3 12 0N 6 28W
Klecko, Poland 45 F4 52 38N 17 25 E
Kleczew, Poland 45 F5 52 22N 18 9 E
Kleena Kleene, Canada 104 C4 52 0N 124 59W
Klein-Karas, Namibia 88 D2 27 33 S 18 7 E
Klekovača, Bos.-H. 29 D13 44 25N 16 32 E
Klenoec, Macedonia 40 E4 41 32N 20 49 E
Klenovec, Slovak Rep. 27 C12 48 36N 19 54 E
Klerksdorp, S. Africa 88 D4 26 53 S 26 38 E
Kleszczele, Poland 45 F10 52 35N 23 19 E
Kletnya, Russia 46 F7 53 23N 33 12 E
Kletsk = Klyetsk, Belarus 47 F4 53 5N 26 45 E
Kletskiy, Russia 49 F6 49 16N 43 11 E
Kleve, Germany 24 D2 51 47N 6 7 E
Klickitat, U.S.A. 114 D3 45 49N 121 9W
Klickitat →, U.S.A. 116 E5 45 42N 121 17W
Klidhes, Cyprus 36 D13 35 42N 34 36 E
Klimovichi, Belarus 46 F6 53 36N 32 0 E
Klin, Russia 46 D9 56 20N 36 48 E
Klina, Kosovo, Yug. 40 D4 42 37N 20 35 E
Klinaklini →, Canada 104 C3 51 21N 125 40W
Klintehamn, Sweden 11 G12 57 24N 18 12 E
Klintsy, Russia 47 F7 52 50N 32 10 E
Klip →, S. Africa 89 D4 27 3 S 29 3 E
Klipdale, S. Africa 88 E2 34 19 S 19 57 E
Klippan, Sweden 11 H7 56 8N 13 10 E
Klipplaat, S. Africa 88 E3 33 1 S 24 22 E
Klisura, Bulgaria 41 D8 42 40N 24 28 E
Kljajićevo, Serbia, Yug. 42 E4 45 45N 19 17 E
Ključ, Bos.-H. 29 D13 44 32N 16 48 E
Kłobuck, Poland 45 H5 50 55N 18 55 E
Klockestrand, Sweden 10 B11 62 53N 17 55 E
Kłodawa, Poland 45 F5 52 15N 18 55 E
Kłodzko, Poland 45 H3 50 28N 16 38 E
Klos, Albania 40 E4 41 28N 20 10 E
Klosterneuburg, Austria 27 C9 48 18N 16 19 E
Klosters, Switz. 25 J5 46 52N 9 52 E
Klötze, Germany 24 C7 52 37N 11 10 E
Klouto, Togo 83 D5 6 57N 0 44 E
Kluane L., Canada 100 B6 61 15N 138 40W
Kluane Nat. Park, Canada 104 A1 60 45N 139 30W
Kluczbork, Poland 45 H5 50 58N 18 12 E
Klukwan, U.S.A. 104 B1 59 24N 135 54W
Klyetsk, Belarus 47 F4 53 5N 26 45 E
Klyuchevskaya, Gora, Russia 51 D17 55 50N 160 30 E
Knäred, Sweden 11 H7 56 31N 13 19 E
Knaresborough, U.K. 12 C6 54 1N 1 28W
Knee L., Man., Canada 102 A1 55 3N 94 45W
Knee L., Sask., Canada 105 B7 55 51N 107 0W
Knezha, Bulgaria 41 C8 43 30N 24 5 E
Knić, Serbia, Yug. 40 C4 43 53N 20 42 E
Knight Inlet, Canada 104 C3 50 45N 125 40W
Knighton, U.K. 13 E4 52 21N 3 3W
Knights Ferry, U.S.A. 116 H6 37 50N 120 40W
Knights Landing, U.S.A. 116 G5 38 48N 121 43W
Knin, Croatia 29 D13 44 3N 16 17 E
Knislinge, Sweden 11 H8 56 12N 14 5 E
Knittelfeld, Austria 26 D7 47 13N 14 51 E
Knivsta, Sweden 10 E11 59 43N 17 48 E
Knjaževac, Serbia, Yug. 40 C6 43 35N 22 18 E
Knob, C., Australia 93 F2 34 32 S 119 16 E
Knock, Ireland 15 C3 53 48N 8 55W
Knockmealdown Mts., Ireland 15 D4 52 14N 7 56W
Knokke-Heist, Belgium 17 C3 51 21N 3 17 E
Knossós, Greece 36 D7 35 16N 25 10 E
Knowlton, Canada 111 A12 45 13N 72 31W
Knox, U.S.A. 108 E2 41 18N 86 37W
Knox Coast, Antarctica 5 C8 66 30 S 108 0 E
Knoxville, Iowa, U.S.A. 112 E8 41 19N 93 6W
Knoxville, Pa., U.S.A. 110 E7 41 57N 77 27W
Knoxville, Tenn., U.S.A. 109 H4 35 58N 83 55W
Knysna, S. Africa 88 E3 34 2 S 23 2 E
Knyszyn, Poland 44 E9 53 20N 22 56 E
Ko Kha, Thailand 64 C2 18 11N 99 24 E
Koartac = Quaqtaq, Canada 101 B13 60 55N 69 40W
Koba, Indonesia 63 F8 6 37 S 134 37 E
Kobarid, Slovenia 29 B10 46 15N 13 30 E
Kobayashi, Japan 55 J5 31 56N 130 59 E
Kobdo = Hovd, Mongolia 60 B4 48 2N 91 37 E
Kōbe, Japan 55 G7 34 45N 135 10 E
Kobelyaky, Ukraine 47 H8 49 11N 34 9 E
København, Denmark 11 J6 55 41N 12 34 E
Københavns Amtskommune □, Denmark 11 J6 55 42N 12 21 E
Kobenni, Mauritania 82 B3 15 58N 9 24W
Kōbi-Sho, Japan 55 M1 25 56N 123 41 E
Koblenz, Germany 25 E3 50 21N 7 36 E
Kobo, Ethiopia 81 E4 12 2N 39 56 E
Kobryn, Belarus 47 F3 52 15N 24 22 E
Kobuleti, Georgia 49 K5 41 55N 41 45 E
Kobylin, Poland 45 G4 51 43N 17 12 E
Kobyłka, Poland 45 F8 52 21N 21 10 E
Kobylkino, Russia 48 C6 54 8N 43 56 E
Koca →, Turkey 41 F11 40 8N 27 57 E
Kocabaş, Turkey 39 D11 37 49N 29 20 E
Kocaeli, Turkey 41 F13 40 45N 29 50 E
Kocaeli □, Turkey 41 F13 40 45N 29 55 E
Kočane, Serbia, Yug. 40 C5 43 12N 21 52 E
Kočani, Macedonia 40 E6 41 55N 22 25 E
Koçarlı, Turkey 39 D9 37 45N 27 43 E
Koceljevo, Serbia, Yug. 40 B3 44 28N 19 50 E
Kočevje, Slovenia 29 C11 45 39N 14 50 E
Koch Bihar, India 67 F16 26 22N 89 29 E
Kochang, S. Korea 57 G14 35 41N 127 55 E
Kochas, India 69 G10 25 15N 83 56 E
Kocher →, Germany 25 F5 49 13N 9 12 E
Kochi = Cochin, India 66 Q10 9 59N 76 22 E
Kōchi, Japan 55 H6 33 30N 133 35 E
Kōchi □, Japan 55 H6 33 40N 133 30 E
Kochiu = Gejiu, China 58 F4 23 20N 103 10 E
Kock, Poland 45 G9 51 38N 22 27 E
Kodarma, India 69 G11 24 28N 85 36 E
Kode, Sweden 11 G5 57 57N 11 51 E
Kodiak, U.S.A. 100 C4 57 47N 152 24W
Kodiak I., U.S.A. 100 C4 57 30N 152 45W
Kodinar, India 68 J4 20 46N 70 46 E
Kodok, Sudan 81 F3 9 53N 32 7 E
Kodori →, Georgia 49 J5 42 47N 41 10 E
Koedoesberge, S. Africa 88 E3 32 40 S 20 11 E
Koes, Namibia 88 D2 26 0 S 19 15 E
Kofçaz, Turkey 41 E11 41 58N 27 12 E
Koffiefontein, S. Africa 88 D4 29 30 S 25 0 E
Kofiau, Indonesia 63 E7 1 11 S 129 50 E
Köflach, Austria 26 D8 47 4N 15 5 E
Koforidua, Ghana 83 D4 6 3N 0 17W
Kōfu, Japan 55 G9 35 40N 138 30 E
Koga, Japan 55 F9 36 11N 139 43 E
Kogaluk →, Canada 103 A7 56 12N 61 44W
Køge, Denmark 11 J6 55 27N 12 11 E
Køge Bugt, Denmark 11 J6 55 30N 12 20 E
Kogi □, Nigeria 83 D6 7 45N 6 45 E
Kogin Baba, Nigeria 83 D7 7 55N 11 35 E
Koh-i-Khurd, Afghan. 68 C1 33 30N 65 59 E
Koh-i-Maran, Pakistan 68 E2 29 18N 66 50 E
Kohat, Pakistan 68 C4 33 40N 71 29 E
Kohima, India 67 G19 25 35N 94 10 E
Kohkīlūyeh va Būyer Aḥmadi □, Iran 71 D6 31 30N 50 30 E
Kohler Ra., Antarctica 5 D15 77 0 S 110 0W
Kohlu, Pakistan 68 E3 29 54N 69 15 E
Kohtla-Järve, Estonia 9 G22 59 20N 27 20 E
Koillismaa, Finland 8 D23 65 44N 28 36 E
Koin-dong, N. Korea 57 D14 40 28N 126 18 E
Koinare, Bulgaria 41 C8 43 21N 24 8 E
Koindu, S. Leone 82 D2 8 26N 10 19W
Kojetín, Czech Rep. 27 B10 49 21N 17 20 E
Kojō, N. Korea 57 E14 38 58N 127 58 E
Kojonup, Australia 93 F2 33 48 S 117 10 E
Kojūr, Iran 71 B6 36 23N 51 43 E
Koka, Sudan 80 C3 20 5N 30 35 E
Kokand = Qŭqon, Uzbekistan 50 E8 40 30N 70 57 E
Kokas, Indonesia 63 E8 2 42 S 132 26 E
Kokava, Slovak Rep. 27 C12 48 35N 19 50 E
Kokchetav = Kökshetaū, Kazakhstan 50 D7 53 20N 69 25 E
Kokemäenjoki →, Finland 9 F19 61 32N 21 44 E
Kokhma, Russia 48 B5 56 57N 41 8 E
Koki, Senegal 82 B1 15 30N 15 59W
Kokkola, Finland 8 E20 63 50N 23 8 E
Koko, Nigeria 83 C5 11 28N 4 29 E
Koko Kyunzu, Burma 67 M18 14 10N 93 25 E
Kokolopozo, Ivory C. 82 D3 5 8N 6 5W
Kokomo, U.S.A. 108 E2 40 29N 86 8W
Kokoro, Niger 83 C5 14 12N 0 55 E
Koksan, N. Korea 57 E14 38 46N 126 40 E
Kökshetaū, Kazakhstan 50 D7 53 20N 69 25 E
Koksoak →, Canada 101 C13 58 30N 68 10W
Kokstad, S. Africa 89 E4 30 32 S 29 29 E
Kokubu, Japan 55 J5 31 44N 130 46 E
Kola, Indonesia 63 F8 5 35 S 134 30 E
Kola Pen. = Kolskiy Poluostrov, Russia 50 C4 67 30N 38 0 E
Kolachi →, Pakistan 68 F2 27 8N 67 2 E
Kolahoi, India 69 B6 34 12N 75 22 E
Kolahun, Liberia 82 D2 8 15N 10 4W
Kolaka, Indonesia 63 E6 4 3 S 121 46 E
Kolar, India 66 N11 13 12N 78 15 E
Kolar Gold Fields, India 66 N11 12 58N 78 16 E
Kolaras, India 68 G6 25 14N 77 36 E
Kolari, Finland 8 C20 67 20N 23 48 E
Kolárovo, Slovak Rep. 27 D10 47 54N 18 0 E
Kolašin, Montenegro, Yug. 40 D3 42 50N 19 31 E
Kolayat, India 66 F8 27 50N 72 50 E
Kolbäck, Sweden 10 E10 59 34N 16 15 E
Kolbäcksån →, Sweden 10 E10 59 36N 16 16 E
Kolbermoor, Germany 25 H8 47 51N 12 4 E
Kolbuszowa, Poland 45 H8 50 15N 21 46 E
Kolchugino = Leninsk-Kuznetskiy, Russia 50 D9 54 44N 86 10 E
Kolchugino, Russia 46 D10 56 17N 39 22 E
Kolda, Senegal 82 C2 12 55N 14 57W
Koldegi, Sudan 81 E3 12 3N 30 16 E
Kolding, Denmark 11 J3 55 30N 9 29 E
Kolepom = Dolak, Pulau, Indonesia 63 F9 8 0 S 138 30 E
Kolguyev, Ostrov, Russia 50 C5 69 20N 48 30 E
Kolhapur, India 66 L9 16 43N 74 15 E
Kolia, Ivory C. 82 D3 9 46N 6 28W
Kolín, Czech Rep. 26 A8 50 2N 15 9 E
Kolind, Denmark 11 H4 56 21N 10 34 E
Kolkas rags, Latvia 9 H20 57 46N 22 37 E
Kolkata, India 69 H13 22 36N 88 24 E
Kollam = Quilon, India 66 Q10 8 50N 76 38 E
Kölleda, Germany 24 D7 51 11N 11 15 E
Kollum, Neths. 17 A6 53 17N 6 10 E
Kolmanskop, Namibia 88 D2 26 45 S 15 14 E
Köln, Germany 24 E2 50 56N 6 57 E
Kolno, Poland 44 E8 53 25N 21 56 E
Koło, Poland 45 F5 52 14N 18 40 E
Kołobrzeg, Poland 44 D2 54 10N 15 35 E
Kolokani, Mali 82 C3 13 35N 7 45W
Koloko, Burkina Faso 82 C3 11 5N 5 19W
Kololo, Ethiopia 81 F5 7 29N 41 58 E
Kolomna, Russia 46 E10 55 8N 38 45 E
Kolomyya, Ukraine 47 H3 48 31N 25 2 E
Kolondiéba, Mali 82 C3 11 5N 6 54W
Kolonodale, Indonesia 63 E6 2 0 S 121 19 E
Kolonowskie, Poland 45 H5 50 39N 18 22 E
Kolosib, India 67 G18 24 15N 92 45 E
Kolpashevo, Russia 50 D9 58 20N 83 5 E
Kolpino, Russia 46 C6 59 44N 30 39 E
Kolpny, Russia 47 F9 52 17N 37 1 E
Kolskiy Poluostrov, Russia 50 C4 67 30N 38 0 E
Kolsva, Sweden 10 E9 59 36N 15 51 E
Kolubara →, Serbia, Yug. 40 B4 44 35N 20 15 E
Kołuszki, Poland 45 G6 51 45N 19 46 E
Kolwezi, Dem. Rep. of the Congo 87 E2 10 40 S 25 25 E
Kolyma →, Russia 51 C17 69 30N 161 0 E
Kolymskoye Nagorye, Russia 51 C16 63 0N 157 0 E
Kôm Hamâda, Egypt 80 H7 30 46N 30 41 E
Kôm Ombo, Egypt 80 C3 24 25N 32 52 E
Komadugu Gana →, Nigeria 83 C7 13 5N 12 24 E
Komandorskiye Is. = Komandorskiye Ostrova, Russia 51 D17 55 0N 167 0 E
Komandorskiye Ostrova, Russia 51 D17 55 0N 167 0 E
Komárno, Slovak Rep. 27 D11 47 49N 18 5 E
Komárom, Hungary 42 C3 47 43N 18 7 E
Komárom-Esztergom □, Hungary 42 C3 47 35N 18 20 E
Komatipoort, S. Africa 89 D5 25 25 S 31 55 E
Komatou Yialou, Cyprus 36 D13 35 25N 34 8 E
Komatsu, Japan 55 F8 36 25N 136 30 E
Komatsushima, Japan 55 H7 34 0N 134 35 E
Kombissiri, Burkina Faso 83 C4 12 4N 1 20W
Kombori, Burkina Faso 82 C4 13 26N 3 56W
Kombóti, Greece 38 B3 39 6N 21 5 E
Komen, Slovenia 29 C10 45 49N 13 45 E
Komenda, Ghana 83 D4 5 4N 1 28W
Komi □, Russia 50 C6 64 0N 55 0 E
Komiža, Croatia 29 E13 43 3N 16 11 E
Komló, Hungary 42 D3 46 15N 18 16 E
Kommunarsk = Alchevsk, Ukraine 47 H10 48 30N 38 45 E
Kommunizma, Pik, Tajikistan 50 F8 39 0N 72 2 E
Komodo, Indonesia 63 F5 8 37 S 119 20 E
Komoé →, Ivory C. 82 D4 5 12N 3 44W
Komoran, Pulau, Indonesia 63 F9 8 18 S 138 45 E
Komoro, Japan 55 F9 36 19N 138 26 E
Komotini, Greece 41 E9 41 9N 25 26 E
Komovi, Montenegro, Yug. 40 D3 42 41N 19 39 E
Kompasberg, S. Africa 88 E3 31 45 S 24 32 E
Kompong Bang, Cambodia 65 F5 12 24N 104 40 E
Kompong Cham, Cambodia 65 F5 12 0N 105 30 E
Kompong Chhnang = Kampang Chhnang, Cambodia 65 F5 12 20N 104 35 E
Kompong Chikreng, Cambodia 64 F5 13 5N 104 18 E
Kompong Kleang, Cambodia 64 F5 13 6N 104 8 E
Kompong Luong, Cambodia 65 G5 11 49N 104 48 E
Kompong Pranak, Cambodia 64 F5 13 35N 104 55 E
Kompong Som = Kampong Saom, Cambodia 65 G4 10 38N 103 30 E
Kompong Som, Chhung = Kampong Saom, Chaak, Cambodia 65 G4 10 50N 103 32 E
Kompong Speu, Cambodia 65 G5 11 26N 104 32 E
Kompong Sralao, Cambodia 64 E5 14 5N 105 46 E
Kompong Thom, Cambodia 64 F5 12 35N 104 51 E
Kompong Trabeck, Cambodia 64 F5 13 6N 105 14 E
Kompong Trabeck, Cambodia 65 G5 11 9N 105 28 E
Kompong Trach, Cambodia 65 G5 11 25N 105 48 E
Kompong Tralach, Cambodia 65 G5 11 54N 104 47 E
Komrat = Comrat, Moldova 43 D13 46 18N 28 40 E
Komsberg, S. Africa 88 E3 32 40 S 20 45 E
Komsomolets, Ostrov, Russia 51 A10 80 30N 95 0 E
Komsomolsk, Amur, Russia 51 D14 50 30N 137 0 E
Komsomolsk, Ivanovo, Russia 46 D11 57 2N 40 20 E
Komsomolskiy, Russia 48 C7 54 27N 45 33 E
Kömür Burnu, Turkey 39 C8 38 39N 26 12 E
Kon Tum, Vietnam 64 E7 14 24N 108 0 E
Kon Tum, Plateau du, Vietnam 64 E7 14 30N 108 30 E
Kona, Mali 82 C4 14 57N 3 53W
Konakovo, Russia 46 D9 56 40N 36 51 E
Konarhā □, Afghan. 66 B7 34 30N 71 3 E
Konārī, Iran 71 D6 28 13N 51 36 E
Konch, India 69 G8 26 0N 79 10 E
Konde, Tanzania 86 C4 4 57 S 39 45 E
Kondiá, Greece 39 B7 39 49N 25 10 E
Kondinin, Australia 93 F2 32 34 S 118 8 E
Kondoa, Tanzania 86 C4 4 55 S 35 50 E
Kondókali, Greece 36 A3 39 38N 19 51 E
Kondopaga, Russia 46 A8 62 12N 34 17 E
Kondratyevo, Russia 51 D10 57 22N 98 15 E
Kondrovo, Russia 46 E8 54 48N 35 56 E
Konduga, Nigeria 83 C7 11 35N 13 26 E
Köneürgench, Turkmenistan 50 E6 42 19N 59 10 E
Konevo, Russia 46 A10 62 8N 39 20 E
Kong = Khong →, Cambodia 64 F5 13 32N 105 58 E
Kong, Ivory C. 82 D4 8 54N 4 36W
Kong, Koh, Cambodia 65 G4 11 20N 103 0 E
Kong Christian IX Land, Greenland 4 C6 68 0N 36 0W
Kong Christian X Land, Greenland 4 B6 74 0N 29 0W
Kong Frederik IX Land, Greenland 4 C5 67 0N 52 0W
Kong Frederik VI Kyst, Greenland 4 C5 63 0N 43 0W
Kong Frederik VIII Land, Greenland 4 B6 78 30N 26 0W
Kong Oscar Fjord, Greenland 4 B6 72 20N 24 0W
Kongeå →, Denmark 11 J2 55 23N 8 39 E
Kongerslev, Denmark 11 H4 56 54N 10 6 E
Kongju, S. Korea 57 F14 36 30N 127 0 E
Konglu, Burma 67 F20 27 13N 97 57 E
Kongola, Namibia 88 B3 17 45 S 23 20 E
Kongolo, Kasai-Or., Dem. Rep. of the Congo 86 D1 5 26 S 24 49 E
Kongolo, Katanga, Dem. Rep. of the Congo 86 D2 5 22 S 27 0 E
Kongor, Sudan 81 F3 7 1N 31 27 E
Kongoussi, Burkina Faso 83 C4 13 19N 1 32W
Kongsberg, Norway 9 G13 59 39N 9 39 E
Kongsvinger, Norway 9 F15 60 12N 12 2 E
Kongwa, Tanzania 86 D4 6 11 S 36 26 E
Koni, Dem. Rep. of the Congo 87 E2 10 40 S 27 11 E
Koni, Mts., Dem. Rep. of the Congo 87 E2 10 36 S 27 10 E
Koniakari, Mali 82 C2 14 35N 10 50W
Koniecpol, Poland 45 H6 50 46N 19 40 E
Königs Wusterhausen, Germany 24 C9 52 19N 13 38 E
Königsberg = Kaliningrad, Russia 9 J19 54 42N 20 32 E
Königsbrunn, Germany 25 G6 48 16N 10 54 E
Königslutter, Germany 24 C6 52 15N 10 49 E
Konin, Poland 45 F5 52 12N 18 15 E
Konispol, Albania 40 G4 39 42N 20 10 E
Kónitsa, Greece 38 A2 40 5N 20 48 E
Konjic, Bos.-H. 42 G2 43 42N 17 58 E
Konkiep, Namibia 88 D2 26 49 S 17 15 E
Konkouré →, Guinea 82 D2 9 50N 13 42W
Könnern, Germany 24 D7 51 41N 11 47 E
Kono, S. Leone 82 D2 8 30N 11 5W
Konongo, Ghana 83 D4 6 40N 1 15W
Konosha, Russia 46 B11 61 0N 40 5 E
Kōnosu, Japan 55 F9 36 3N 139 31 E
Konotop, Ukraine 47 G7 51 12N 33 7 E
Konsankoro, Guinea 82 D3 9 2N 9 0W
Końskie, Poland 45 G7 51 15N 20 23 E
Konstancin-Jeziorna, Poland 45 F8 52 5N 21 7 E
Konstantinovka = Kostyantynivka, Ukraine 47 H9 48 32N 37 39 E
Konstantinovsk, Russia 49 G5 47 33N 41 10 E
Konstantynów Łódźki, Poland 45 G6 51 45N 19 20 E
Konstanz, Germany 25 H5 47 40N 9 10 E
Kont, Iran 71 E9 26 55N 61 50 E
Kontagora, Nigeria 83 C6 10 23N 5 27 E
Kontcha, Cameroon 83 D7 7 59N 12 15 E
Konya, Turkey 70 B2 37 52N 32 35 E
Konya Ovası, Turkey 72 C5 38 30N 33 5 E
Konz, Germany 25 F2 49 42N 6 34 E
Konza, Kenya 86 C4 1 45 S 37 7 E
Koocanusa, L., Canada 114 B6 49 20N 115 15W
Kookynie, Australia 93 E3 29 17 S 121 22 E
Koolyanobbing, Australia 93 F2 30 48 S 119 36 E
Koonibba, Australia 95 E1 31 54 S 133 25 E
Koorawatha, Australia 95 E4 34 2 S 148 33 E
Koorda, Australia 93 F2 30 48 S 117 35 E
Kooskia, U.S.A. 114 C6 46 9N 115 59W
Kootenay →, U.S.A. 104 D5 49 19N 117 39W
Kootenay L., Canada 104 D5 49 45N 116 50W
Kootenay Nat. Park, Canada 104 C5 51 0N 116 0W
Kootjieskolk, S. Africa 88 E3 31 15 S 20 21 E
Kopanovka, Russia 49 G8 47 28N 46 50 E
Kopaonik, Yugoslavia 40 C4 43 10N 20 50 E
Kópavogur, Iceland 8 D3 64 6N 21 55W
Koper, Slovenia 29 C10 45 31N 13 44 E
Kopervik, Norway 9 G11 59 17N 5 17 E
Kopet Dagh, Asia 71 B8 38 0N 58 0 E
Kopi, Australia 95 E2 33 24 S 135 40 E
Köping, Sweden 10 E10 59 31N 16 3 E
Köpingsvik, Sweden 11 H10 56 53N 16 43 E
Kopište, Croatia 29 F13 42 48N 16 42 E
Koplik, Albania 40 D3 42 15N 19 25 E
Köpmanholmen, Sweden 10 A12 63 10N 18 35 E
Kopparberg, Sweden 10 E9 59 52N 15 0 E
Koppeh Dāgh = Kopet Dagh, Asia 71 B8 38 0N 58 0 E
Koppies, S. Africa 89 D4 27 20 S 27 30 E
Koppom, Sweden 10 E6 59 43N 12 10 E
Koprivlen, Bulgaria 40 E7 41 31N 23 53 E
Koprivnica, Croatia 29 B13 46 12N 16 45 E
Kopřivnice, Czech Rep. 27 B11 49 36N 18 9 E
Koprivshtitsa, Bulgaria 41 D8 42 40N 24 19 E
Köprübaşı, Turkey 39 C10 38 43N 28 23 E
Kopychyntsi, Ukraine 47 H3 49 7N 25 58 E
Korab, Macedonia 40 E4 41 44N 20 40 E
Korakiána, Greece 36 A3 39 42N 19 45 E
Koral, India 68 J5 21 50N 73 12 E
Korarou, L., Mali 82 B4 15 15N 3 15W
Korba, India 69 H10 22 20N 82 45 E
Korbach, Germany 24 D4 51 16N 8 52 E
Korbu, G., Malaysia 65 K3 4 41N 101 18 E
Korce = Korçë, Albania 40 F4 40 37N 20 50 E
Korçë, Albania 40 F4 40 37N 20 50 E
Korčula, Croatia 29 F13 42 56N 16 57 E
Korčulanski Kanal, Croatia 29 E13 43 3N 16 40 E
Kord Kūy, Iran 71 B7 36 48N 54 7 E
Kord Sheykh, Iran 71 D7 28 31N 52 53 E
Kordestān □, Iran 70 C5 36 0N 47 0 E
Kordofân, Sudan 79 F11 13 0N 29 0 E
Koré Mayroua, Niger 83 C5 13 18N 3 55 E
Korea, North ■, Asia 57 E14 40 0N 127 0 E
Korea, South ■, Asia 57 G15 36 0N 128 0 E
Korea Bay, Korea 57 E13 39 0N 124 0 E
Korea Strait, Asia 57 H15 34 0N 129 30 E
Korem, Ethiopia 81 E4 12 30N 39 32 E
Korenevo, Russia 47 G8 51 27N 34 55 E
Korenovsk, Russia 49 H4 45 30N 39 22 E
Korets, Ukraine 47 G4 50 40N 27 5 E
Korfantów, Poland 45 H4 50 29N 17 36 E
Korgan, Turkey 72 B7 40 44N 37 13 E
Korgus, Sudan 80 D3 19 16N 33 29 E
Korhogo, Ivory C. 82 D3 9 29N 5 28W
Koribundu, S. Leone 82 D2 7 41N 11 46W
Korienzé, Mali 82 B4 15 22N 3 50W
Korinthía □, Greece 38 D4 37 50N 22 35 E
Korinthiakós Kólpos, Greece 38 C4 38 16N 22 30 E
Kórinthos, Greece 38 D4 37 56N 22 55 E
Korioumé, Mali 82 B4 16 35N 3 0W
Koríssa, Límni, Greece 36 B3 39 27N 19 53 E
Kōriyama, Japan 54 F10 37 24N 140 23 E
Korkuteli, Turkey 39 D12 37 4N 30 13 E
Kormakiti, C., Cyprus 36 D11 35 23N 32 56 E
Körmend, Hungary 42 C1 47 5N 16 35 E
Kornat, Croatia 29 E12 43 50N 15 20 E
Korneshty = Cornești, Moldova 43 C13 47 21N 28 1 E
Korneuburg, Austria 27 C9 48 20N 16 20 E
Kórnik, Poland 45 F4 52 15N 17 6 E
Koro, Fiji 91 C8 17 19 S 179 23 E
Koro, Ivory C. 82 D3 8 32N 7 30W
Koro, Mali 82 C4 14 1N 2 58W
Koro Sea, Fiji 91 C9 17 30 S 179 45W
Korocha, Russia 47 G9 50 54N 37 19 E
Köroğlu Dağları, Turkey 72 B5 40 38N 33 0 E
Korogwe, Tanzania 86 D4 5 5 S 38 25 E
Koronadal, Phil. 61 H6 6 12N 125 1 E
Koróni, Greece 38 E3 36 48N 21 57 E
Korónia, Limni, Greece 40 F7 40 47N 23 10 E
Koronís, Greece 39 D7 37 12N 25 35 E
Koronowo, Poland 45 E4 53 19N 17 55 E
Koror, Palau 63 C8 7 20N 134 28 E
Körös →, Hungary 42 D5 46 43N 20 12 E
Köröstarcsa, Hungary 42 D6 46 53N 21 3 E
Korosten, Ukraine 47 G5 50 54N 28 36 E
Korostyshev, Ukraine 47 G5 50 19N 29 4 E
Korotoyak, Russia 47 G10 51 1N 39 2 E
Korraraika, Helodranon' i, Madag. 89 B7 17 45 S 43 57 E
Korsakov, Russia 51 E15 46 36N 142 42 E
Korsberga, Sweden 11 G9 57 19N 15 7 E
Korshunovo, Russia 51 D12 58 37N 110 10 E
Korsør, Denmark 11 J5 55 20N 11 9 E
Korsun Shevchenkovskiy, Ukraine 47 H6 49 26N 31 16 E
Korsze, Poland 44 D8 54 11N 21 9 E
Korti, Sudan 80 D3 18 6N 31 33 E
Kortrijk, Belgium 17 D3 50 50N 3 17 E
Korucu, Turkey 39 B9 39 28N 27 22 E
Korwai, India 68 G8 24 7N 78 5 E
Koryakskoye Nagorye, Russia 51 C18 61 0N 171 0 E
Koryŏng, S. Korea 57 G15 35 44N 128 15 E
Koryukovka, Ukraine 47 G7 51 46N 32 16 E
Kos, Greece 39 E9 36 50N 27 15 E
Kosa, Ethiopia 81 F4 7 50N 36 50 E
Kosaya Gora, Russia 46 E9 54 10N 37 30 E
Kościan, Poland 45 F3 52 5N 16 40 E
Kościerzyna, Poland 44 D4 54 8N 17 59 E
Kosciusko, U.S.A. 113 J10 33 4N 89 35W
Kosciuszko, Mt., Australia 95 F4 36 27 S 148 16 E
Kösély →, Hungary 42 C6 47 25N 21 5 E
Kosha, Sudan 80 C3 20 50N 30 30 E
Koshava, Bulgaria 40 B7 44 4N 23 2 E
K'oshih = Kashi, China 60 C2 39 30N 76 2 E
Koshiki-Rettō, Japan 55 J4 31 45N 129 49 E
Kosi, India 68 F7 27 48N 77 29 E
Kosi →, India 69 E8 28 41N 78 57 E
Košice, Slovak Rep. 27 C14 48 42N 21 15 E
Košický □, Slovak Rep. 27 C14 48 45N 21 0 E
Kosjerić, Serbia, Yug. 40 B3 44 0N 19 55 E
Köşk, Turkey 39 D10 37 50N 28 3 E
Koskhinoú, Greece 36 C10 36 23N 28 13 E
Koslan, Russia 50 C5 63 34N 49 14 E
Kosŏng, N. Korea 57 E15 38 40N 128 22 E
Kosovo □, Yugoslavia 40 D4 42 30N 21 0 E

Kuressaare

Kuressaare, *Estonia* .. **9 G20** 58 15N 22 30 E
Kurgan, *Russia* ...... **50 D7** 55 26N 65 18 E
Kurganinsk, *Russia* .. **49 H5** 44 54N 40 34 E
Kurgannaya =
Kurganinsk, *Russia* . **49 H5** 44 54N 40 34 E
Kuri, *India* .... **68 F4** 26 37N 70 43 E
Kuria Maria Is. =
Khuriyā Muriyā,
Jazā'ir, *Oman* ...... **74 D6** 17 30N 55 58 E
Kuridala, *Australia* ... **94 C3** 21 16 S 140 29 E
Kurigram, *Bangla.* .... **67 G16** 25 49N 89 39 E
Kurikka, *Finland* ..... **9 E20** 62 36N 22 24 E
Kuril Is. = Kurilskiye
Ostrova, *Russia* .... **51 E15** 45 0N 150 0 E
Kuril Trench, *Pac. Oc.* **52 E19** 44 0N 153 0 E
Kurilsk, *Russia* ...... **51 E15** 45 14N 147 53 E
Kurilskiye Ostrova,
Russia .... **51 E15** 45 0N 150 0 E
Kurino, *Japan* .... **55 J5** 31 57N 130 43 E
Kurinskaya Kosa = Kür
Dili, *Azerbaijan* .... **71 B6** 39 3N 49 13 E
Kurkur, *Egypt* .... **80 C3** 23 50N 32 0 E
Kurlovskiy, *Russia* ... **48 C5** 55 25N 40 40 E
Kurmuk, *Sudan* ...... **81 E3** 10 33N 34 21 E
Kurnool, *India* .... **66 M11** 15 45N 78 0 E
Kuro-Shima,
Kagoshima, Japan .. **55 J4** 30 50N 129 57 E
Kuro-Shima, *Okinawa,*
Japan .... **55 M2** 24 14N 124 1 E
Kuror, J., *Sudan* ..... **80 C3** 20 27N 31 30 E
Kurow, *N.Z.* .... **91 L3** 44 44 S 170 29 E
Kurów, *Poland* .... **45 G9** 51 23N 22 12 E
Kurram →, *Pakistan* . **68 C4** 32 36N 71 20 E
Kurri Kurri, *Australia* . **95 E5** 32 50 S 151 28 E
Kurrimine, *Australia* .. **94 B4** 17 47 S 146 6 E
Kursavka, *Russia* .... **49 H6** 44 29N 42 32 E
Kurshskiy Zaliv, *Russia* **9 J19** 55 9N 21 6 E
Kursk, *Russia* .... **47 G9** 51 42N 36 11 E
Kuršumlija,
Serbia, Yug. .... **40 C5** 43 9N 21 19 E
Kuršumlijska Banja,
Serbia, Yug. .... **40 C5** 43 3N 21 11 E
Kurşunlu, *Bursa,*
Turkey .... **41 F13** 40 3N 29 40 E
Kurşunlu, *Çankırı,*
Turkey .... **72 B5** 40 51N 33 15 E
Kurtalan, *Turkey* ..... **73 D9** 37 56N 41 44 E
Kurtbey, *Turkey* ...... **41 E10** 41 9N 26 35 E
Kuru, *Sudan* .... **81 F2** 7 43N 26 31 E
Kuru, Bahr el →,
Sudan .... **81 F2** 8 10N 26 50 E
Kurucaşile, *Turkey* ... **72 B5** 41 49N 32 42 E
Kuruçay, *Turkey* ..... **70 B3** 39 39N 38 29 E
Kuruktag, *China* ..... **60 B3** 41 0N 89 0 E
Kuruman, *S. Africa* ... **88 D3** 27 28 S 23 28 E
Kuruman →, *S. Africa* **88 D3** 26 56 S 20 39 E
Kurume, *Japan* ...... **55 H5** 33 15N 130 30 E
Kurun →, *Sudan* ..... **81 F3** 5 30N 34 17 E
Kurunegala, *Sri Lanka* **66 R12** 7 30N 80 23 E
Kurya, *Russia* .... **50 C6** 61 42N 57 9 E
Kus Gölü, *Turkey* .... **41 F11** 40 10N 27 55 E
Kuşadası, *Turkey* .... **72 D2** 37 52N 27 15 E
Kuşadası Körfezi,
Turkey .... **39 D8** 37 56N 27 0 E
Kusatsu, *Japan* ...... **55 F9** 36 37N 138 36 E
Kusawa L., *Canada* .. **104 A1** 60 20N 136 13W
Kusel, *Germany* ..... **25 F3** 49 32N 7 24 E
Kushaka, *Nigeria* .... **83 C6** 10 32N 6 48 E
Kushalgarh, *India* .... **68 H6** 23 10N 74 27 E
Kushchevskaya, *Russia* **49 G4** 46 33N 39 35 E
Kusheriki, *Nigeria* ... **83 C6** 10 33N 6 28 E
Kushikino, *Japan* .... **55 J5** 31 44N 130 16 E
Kushima, *Japan* ..... **55 J5** 31 29N 131 14 E
Kushimoto, *Japan* ... **55 H7** 33 28N 135 47 E
Kushiro, *Japan* ...... **54 C12** 43 0N 144 25 E
Kushiro-Gawa →,
Japan .... **54 C12** 42 59N 144 23 E
Kūshk, *Iran* .... **71 D8** 28 46N 56 51 E
Kushka = Gushgy,
Turkmenistan ...... **50 F7** 35 20N 62 18 E
Kūshkī, *Iran* .... **70 C5** 33 31N 47 13 E
Kushol, *India* .... **69 C7** 33 40N 76 36 E
Kushtia, *Bangla.* ..... **67 H16** 23 55N 89 5 E
Kushum →,
Kazakhstan .... **48 F10** 49 20N 50 30 E
Kuskokwim B., *U.S.A.* **100 C3** 59 45N 162 25W
Kusmi, *India* .... **69 H10** 23 17N 83 55 E
Kussharo-Ko, *Japan* .. **54 C12** 43 38N 144 21 E
Kustanay = Qostanay,
Kazakhstan .... **50 D7** 53 10N 63 35 E
Kut, Ko, *Thailand* .... **65 G4** 11 40N 102 35 E
Kütahya, *Turkey* ..... **39 B12** 39 30N 30 2 E
Kütahya □, *Turkey* ... **39 B11** 39 10N 29 30 E
Kutaisi, *Georgia* ..... **49 J6** 42 19N 42 40 E
Kutaraja = Banda
Aceh, *Indonesia* .... **62 C1** 5 35N 95 20 E
Kutch, Gulf of =
Kachchh, Gulf of,
India .... **68 H3** 22 50N 69 15 E
Kutch, Rann of =
Kachchh, Rann of,
India .... **68 H4** 24 0N 70 0 E
Kutina, *Croatia* ...... **29 C13** 45 29N 16 48 E
Kutiyana, *India* ...... **68 J4** 21 36N 70 2 E
Kutjevo, *Croatia* ..... **42 E2** 45 23N 17 55 E
Kutkashen, *Azerbaijan* **49 K8** 40 58N 47 47 E
Kutná Hora,
Czech Rep. .... **26 B8** 49 57N 15 16 E
Kutno, *Poland* .... **45 F6** 52 15N 19 23 E
Kutse, *Botswana* ..... **88 C3** 21 7 S 22 16 E
Kutu, *Dem. Rep. of*
the Congo .... **84 E3** 2 40 S 18 11 E
Kutum, *Sudan* .... **81 E1** 14 10N 24 40 E
Küty, *Slovak Rep.* .... **27 C10** 48 40N 17 3 E
Kuujjuaq, *Canada* **101 C13** 58 6N 68 15W
Kuujjuarapik, *Canada* **102 A4** 55 20N 77 35W
Kuŭp-tong, *N. Korea* . **57 D14** 40 45N 126 1 E
Kuusamo, *Finland* .... **8 D23** 65 57N 29 8 E
Kuusankoski, *Finland* . **9 F22** 60 55N 26 38 E
Kuvshinovo, *Russia* .. **46 D8** 57 2N 34 11 E
Kuwait = Al Kuwayt,
Kuwait .... **70 D5** 29 30N 48 0 E
Kuwait ■, *Asia* ...... **70 D5** 29 30N 47 30 E
Kuwana, *Japan* ...... **55 G8** 35 5N 136 43 E
Kuwana →, *India* .... **69 F10** 26 25N 83 15 E
Kuybyshev = Samara,
Russia .... **48 D10** 53 8N 50 6 E
Kuybyshev, *Russia* ... **50 D8** 55 27N 78 19 E
Kuybyshevo, *Ukraine* . **47 J9** 47 25N 36 40 E
Kuybyshevskoye
Vdkhr., *Russia* ..... **48 C9** 55 2N 49 30 E
Kuye He →, *China* ... **56 E6** 38 23N 110 46 E
Küyeh, *Iran* .... **70 B5** 38 45N 47 57 E
Küysanjaq, *Iraq* ..... **70 B5** 36 5N 44 38 E
Kuyucak, *Turkey* ..... **39 D10** 37 55N 28 28 E
Kuyumba, *Russia* .... **51 C10** 60 58N 96 59 E
Kuzey Anadolu
Dağları, *Turkey* .... **72 B7** 41 30N 35 0 E
Kuzmin, *Serbia, Yug.* . **42 E4** 45 2N 19 25 E
Kuznetsk, *Russia* .... **48 D8** 53 12N 46 40 E
Kuzomen, *Russia* .... **50 C4** 66 22N 36 50 E
Kvænangen, *Norway* .. **8 A19** 70 5N 21 15 E
Kværndrup, *Denmark* . **11 J4** 55 10N 10 31 E
Kvaløy, *Norway* ...... **8 B18** 69 40N 18 30 E
Kvänum, *Sweden* .... **11 F7** 58 18N 13 11 E
Kvareli = Qvareli,
Georgia .... **49 K7** 41 57N 45 47 E
Kvarner, *Croatia* ..... **29 D11** 44 50N 14 10 E
Kvarnerič, *Croatia* ... **29 D11** 44 43N 14 37 E
Kvicksund, *Sweden* ... **10 E10** 59 27N 16 19 E
Kvillsfors, *Sweden* ... **11 G9** 57 24N 15 29 E
Kvismare kanal,
Sweden .... **10 E9** 59 11N 15 35 E
Kvissleby, *Sweden* ... **10 B11** 62 18N 17 22 E
Kwa-Nobuhle, *S. Africa* **85 L5** 33 50 S 25 22 E
Kwabhaca, *S. Africa* .. **89 E4** 30 51 S 29 0 E
Kwakhanai, *Botswana* . **88 C3** 21 39 S 21 16 E
Kwakoegron, *Suriname* **125 B7** 5 12N 55 25W
Kwale, *Kenya* .... **86 C4** 4 15 S 39 31 E
Kwale, *Nigeria* ...... **83 D6** 5 46N 6 26 E
KwaMashu, *S. Africa* . **89 D5** 29 45 S 30 58 E
Kwando →, *Africa* ... **88 B3** 18 27 S 23 32 E
Kwangdaeri, *N. Korea* **57 D14** 40 31N 127 32 E
Kwangju, *S. Korea* ... **57 G14** 35 9N 126 54 E
Kwango →, *Dem. Rep.*
of the Congo ...... **84 E3** 3 14 S 17 22 E
Kwangsi-Chuang =
Guangxi Zhuangzu
Zizhiqu □, *China* .. **58 F7** 24 0N 109 0 E
Kwangtung =
Guangdong □, *China* **59 F9** 23 0N 113 0 E
Kwara □, *Nigeria* .... **83 D6** 8 45N 4 30 E
Kwataboahegan →,
Canada **102 B3** 51 9N 80 50W
Kwatisore, *Indonesia* . **63 E8** 3 18 S 134 50 E
KwaZulu Natal □,
S. Africa .... **89 D5** 29 0 S 30 0 E
Kweichow =
Guizhou □, *China* .. **58 D6** 27 0N 107 0 E
Kwekwe, *Zimbabwe* .. **87 F2** 18 58 S 29 48 E
Kwidzyn, *Poland* ..... **44 E5** 53 44N 18 55 E
Kwiha, *Ethiopia* ..... **81 E4** 13 29N 39 32 E
Kwinana New Town,
Australia .... **93 F2** 32 15 S 115 47 E
Kwisa →, *Poland* .... **45 G2** 51 34N 15 24 E
Kwoka, *Indonesia* .... **63 E8** 0 31 S 132 27 E
Kwolla, *Nigeria* ...... **83 D6** 9 0N 9 15 E
Kyabra Cr. →,
Australia .... **95 D3** 25 36 S 142 55 E
Kyabram, *Australia* ... **95 F4** 36 19 S 145 4 E
Kyaikto, *Burma* ...... **64 D1** 17 20N 97 3 E
Kyakhta, *Russia* ..... **51 D11** 50 30N 106 25 E
Kyancutta, *Australia* .. **95 E2** 33 8 S 135 33 E
Kyaukpadaung, *Burma* **67 J19** 20 52N 95 8 E
Kyaukpyu, *Burma* .... **67 K18** 19 28N 93 30 E
Kyaukse, *Burma* ..... **67 J20** 21 36N 96 10 E
Kybartai, *Lithuania* ... **44 D9** 54 39N 22 45 E
Kyburz, *U.S.A.* **116 G6** 38 47N 120 18W
Kyelang, *India* .... **68 C7** 32 35N 77 2 E
Kyenjojo, *Uganda* .... **86 B3** 0 40N 30 37 E
Kyjov, *Czech Rep.* .... **27 B10** 49 1N 17 7 E
Kyle, *Canada* **105 C7** 50 50N 108 2W
Kyle Dam, *Zimbabwe* . **87 G3** 20 15 S 31 0 E
Kyle of Lochalsh, *U.K.* **14 D3** 57 17N 5 44W
Kyll →, *Germany* .... **25 F2** 49 48N 6 41 E
Kyllburg, *Germany* ... **25 E2** 50 2N 6 34 E
Kymijoki →, *Finland* . **9 F22** 60 30N 26 55 E
Kyneton, *Australia* ... **95 F3** 37 10 S 144 29 E
Kynuna, *Australia* .... **94 C3** 21 37 S 141 55 E
Kyō-ga-Saki, *Japan* .. **55 G7** 35 45N 135 15 E
Kyoga, L., *Uganda* ... **86 B3** 1 35N 33 0 E
Kyogle, *Australia* .... **95 D5** 28 40 S 153 0 E
Kyom →, *Sudan* ..... **81 F2** 8 58N 28 13 E
Kyongju, *S. Korea* ... **57 G15** 35 51N 129 14 E
Kyongpyaw, *Burma* ... **67 L19** 17 12N 95 10 E
Kyŏngsŏng, *N. Korea* . **57 D15** 41 35N 129 36 E
Kyōto, *Japan* .... **55 G7** 35 0N 135 45 E
Kyōto □, *Japan* ..... **55 G7** 35 15N 135 45 E
Kyparissovouno,
Cyprus .... **36 D12** 35 19N 33 10 E
Kyperounda, *Cyprus* .. **36 E11** 34 56N 32 58 E
Kyrenia, *Cyprus* ..... **36 D12** 35 20N 33 20 E
Kyrgyzstan ■, *Asia* ... **50 E8** 42 0N 75 0 E
Kyritz, *Germany* ..... **24 C8** 52 56N 12 24 E
Kyrkhult, *Sweden* .... **11 H8** 56 22N 14 34 E
Kyrönjoki →, *Finland* **8 E19** 63 14N 21 45 E
Kystatyam, *Russia* ... **51 C13** 67 20N 123 10 E
Kysucké Nové Mesto,
Slovak Rep. .... **27 B11** 49 18N 18 47 E
Kythréa, *Cyprus* ..... **36 D12** 35 15N 33 29 E
Kyunhla, *Burma* ..... **67 H19** 23 25N 95 15 E
Kyuquot Sound,
Canada **104 D3** 50 2N 127 22W
Kyurdamir = Kürdämir,
Azerbaijan .... **49 K9** 40 25N 48 3 E
Kyūshū, *Japan* ...... **55 H5** 33 0N 131 0 E
Kyūshū □, *Japan* .... **55 H5** 33 0N 131 0 E
Kyūshū-Sanchi, *Japan* **55 H5** 32 35N 131 17 E
Kyustendil, *Bulgaria* .. **40 D6** 42 16N 22 41 E
Kyusyur, *Russia* ..... **51 B13** 70 19N 127 30 E
Kyyiv, *Ukraine* ...... **47 G6** 50 30N 30 28 E
Kyyivske Vdskh.,
Ukraine .... **47 G6** 51 0N 30 25 E
Kyzyl, *Russia* .... **51 D10** 51 50N 94 30 E
Kyzyl Kum, *Uzbekistan* **50 E7** 42 30N 65 0 E
Kyzyl-Kyya, *Kyrgyzstan* **50 E8** 40 16N 72 8 E
Kzyl-Orda = Qyzylorda,
Kazakhstan .... **50 E7** 44 48N 65 28 E

L

La Albuera, *Spain* **35 G4** 38 45N 6 49W
La Alcarria, *Spain* **32 E2** 40 31N 2 45W
La Almarcha, *Spain* .. **32 F2** 39 41N 2 24W
La Almunia de Doña
Godina, *Spain* **32 D3** 41 29N 1 23W
La Asunción, *Venezuela* **124 A6** 11 2N 63 53W
La Baie, *Canada* **103 C5** 48 19N 70 53W
La Banda, *Argentina* .. **126 B3** 27 45 S 64 10W
La Bañeza, *Spain* **34 C5** 42 17N 5 54W
La Barca, *Mexico* **118 C4** 20 20N 102 40W
La Barge, *U.S.A.* **114 E8** 42 16N 110 12W
La Bastide-Puylaurent,
France .... **20 D7** 44 35N 3 55 E
La Baule-Escoubiac,
France **18 E4** 47 17N 2 24W
La Belle, *U.S.A.* **109 M5** 26 46N 81 26W
La Biche →, *Canada* . **104 B4** 59 57N 123 50W
La Biche, L., *Canada* . **104 C6** 54 50N 112 5W
La Bisbal d'Empordà,
Spain .... **32 D8** 41 58N 3 2 E
La Bomba, *Mexico* ... **118 A1** 31 53N 115 2W
La Brède, *France* **20 D3** 44 41N 0 32W
La Bresse, *France* ... **19 D13** 48 2N 6 53 E
La Bureba, *Spain* **34 C7** 42 36N 3 24W
La Calera, *Chile* ..... **126 C1** 32 50 S 71 10W
La Campiña, *Spain* ... **35 H6** 37 45N 4 45W
La Canal = Sa Canal,
Spain .... **37 C7** 38 51N 1 23 E
La Cañiza = A Cañiza,
Spain **34 C2** 42 13N 8 16W
La Canourgue, *France* **20 D7** 44 26N 3 13 E
La Capelle, *France* ... **19 C10** 49 59N 3 50 E
La Carlota, *Argentina* . **126 C3** 33 30 S 63 20W
La Carlota, *Phil.* ..... **61 F5** 10 25N 122 55 E
La Carlota, *Spain* **35 H6** 37 40N 4 56W
La Carolina, *Spain* ... **35 G7** 38 17N 3 38W
La Cavalerie, *France* .. **20 D7** 44 1N 3 10 E
La Ceiba, *Honduras* .. **120 C2** 15 40N 86 50W
La Chaise-Dieu, *France* **20 C7** 45 18N 3 42 E
La Chapelle d'Angillon,
France .... **19 E9** 47 21N 2 25 E
La Chapelle-St-Luc,
France .... **19 D11** 48 20N 4 3 E
La Chapelle-sur-Erdre,
France **18 E5** 47 18N 1 34W
La Charité-sur-Loire,
France .... **19 E10** 47 10N 3 1 E
La Chartre-sur-le-Loir,
France .... **18 E7** 47 44N 0 34 E
La Châtaigneraie,
France **20 B3** 46 39N 0 44W
La Châtre, *France* .... **19 F9** 46 35N 2 0 E
La Chaux-de-Fonds,
Switz. .... **25 H2** 47 7N 6 50 E
La Chorrera, *Panama* . **120 E4** 8 53N 79 47W
La Ciotat, *France* .... **21 E9** 43 10N 5 37 E
La Clayette, *France* .. **19 F11** 46 17N 4 19 E
La Cocha, *Argentina* .. **126 B2** 27 50 S 65 40W
La Concepción = Ri-
Aba, *Eq. Guin.* .... **83 E6** 3 28N 8 40 E
La Concepción,
Panama **120 E3** 8 31N 82 37W
La Concordia, *Mexico* **119 D6** 16 8N 92 38W
La Coruña = A Coruña,
Spain **34 B2** 43 20N 8 25W
La Coruña □, *Spain* .. **34 B2** 43 10N 8 30W
La Côte-St-André,
France .... **21 C9** 45 24N 5 15 E
La Courtine-le-Trucq,
France .... **20 C6** 45 41N 2 15 E
La Crau,
Bouches-du-Rhône,
France .... **21 E8** 43 32N 4 40 E
La Crau, *Var, France* . **21 E10** 43 9N 6 4 E
La Crescent, *U.S.A.* .. **112 D9** 43 50N 91 18W
La Crete, *Canada* **104 B5** 58 11N 116 24W
La Crosse, *Kans.,*
U.S.A. **112 F5** 38 32N 99 18W
La Crosse, *Wis., U.S.A.* **112 D9** 43 48N 91 15W
La Cruz, *Costa Rica* .. **120 D2** 11 4N 85 39W
La Cruz, *Mexico* **118 C3** 23 55N 106 54W
La Désirade,
Guadeloupe **121 C7** 16 18N 61 3W
La Escondida, *Mexico* **118 C5** 24 6N 99 55W
La Esmeralda,
Paraguay .... **126 A3** 22 16 S 62 33W
La Esperanza, *Cuba* .. **120 B3** 22 46N 83 44W
La Esperanza,
Honduras **120 D2** 14 15N 88 10W
La Estrada = A
Estrada, *Spain* **34 C2** 42 43N 8 27W
La Faouët, *France* ... **18 D3** 48 2N 3 30W
La Fayette, *U.S.A.* .. **109 H3** 34 42N 85 17W
La Fé, *Cuba* **120 B3** 22 2N 84 15W
La Fère, *France* ..... **19 C10** 49 39N 3 21 E
La Ferté-Bernard,
France .... **18 D7** 48 10N 0 40 E
La Ferté-Gaucher,
France .... **19 D10** 48 47N 3 19 E
La Ferté-Macé, *France* **18 D6** 48 35N 0 22W
La Ferté-St-Aubin,
France .... **19 E8** 47 42N 1 57 E
La Ferté-sous-Jouarre,
France .... **19 D10** 48 56N 3 8 E
La Ferté-Vidame,
France .... **18 D7** 48 37N 0 53 E
La Flèche, *France* ... **18 E6** 47 42N 0 4W
La Follette, *U.S.A.* .. **109 G3** 36 23N 84 7W
La Fregeneda, *Spain* . **34 E4** 40 58N 6 54W
La Fuente de San
Esteban, *Spain* **34 E4** 40 49N 6 15W
La Gacilly, *France* ... **18 E4** 47 45N 2 8W
La Gineta, *Spain* **33 F2** 39 8N 2 1W
La Grand-Combe,
France .... **21 D8** 44 13N 4 2 E
La Grande, *U.S.A.* ... **114 D4** 45 20N 118 5W
La Grande →, *Canada* **102 B5** 53 50N 79 0W
La Grande Deux, Rés.,
Canada **102 B4** 53 40N 76 55W
La Grande-Motte,
France .... **21 E8** 43 23N 4 5 E
La Grande Quatre,
Rés., *Canada* **102 B5** 54 0N 73 15W
La Grande Trois, Rés.,
Canada **102 B4** 53 40N 75 10W
La Grange, *Calif.,*
U.S.A. **116 H6** 37 42N 120 27W
La Grange, *Ga., U.S.A.* **109 J3** 33 2N 85 2W
La Grange, *Ky., U.S.A.* **108 F3** 38 25N 85 23W
La Grange, *Tex., U.S.A.* **113 L6** 29 54N 96 52W
La Grave, *France* .... **21 C10** 45 3N 6 18 E
La Guaira, *Venezuela* . **124 A5** 10 36N 66 56W
La Guardia = A
Guarda, *Spain* **34 D2** 41 56N 8 52W
La Gudiña = A Gudiña,
Spain **34 C3** 42 4N 7 8W
La Guerche-de-
Bretagne, *France* .. **18 E5** 47 57N 1 16W
La Guerche-sur-
l'Aubois, *France* ... **19 F9** 46 58N 2 56 E
La Habana, *Cuba* **120 B3** 23 8N 82 22W
La Haye-du-Puits,
France **18 C5** 49 17N 1 33W
La Horra, *Spain* **34 D7** 41 44N 3 53W
La Independencia,
Mexico **119 D6** 16 31N 91 47W
La Isabela, *Dom. Rep.* **121 C5** 19 58N 71 2W
La Jonquera, *Spain* .. **32 C7** 42 25N 2 53 E
La Junta, *U.S.A.* **113 F3** 37 59N 103 33W
La Laguna, *Canary Is.* **37 F3** 28 28N 16 18W
La Libertad, *Guatemala* **120 C1** 16 47N 90 7W
La Libertad, *Mexico* .. **118 B2** 29 55N 112 41W
La Ligua, *Chile* ...... **126 C1** 32 30 S 71 16W
La Línea de la
Concepción, *Spain* . **35 J5** 36 15N 5 23W
La Loche, *Canada* **105 B7** 56 29N 109 26W
La Londe-les-Maures,
France .... **21 E10** 43 8N 6 14 E
La Lora, *Spain* **34 C7** 42 45N 4 0W
La Loupe, *France* .... **18 D8** 48 29N 1 0 E
La Louvière, *Belgium* . **17 D4** 50 27N 4 10 E
La Machine, *France* .. **19 F10** 46 54N 3 27 E
La Maddalena, *Italy* .. **30 A2** 41 13N 9 24 E
La Malbaie, *Canada* .. **103 C5** 47 40N 70 10W
La Mancha, *Spain* ... **33 F2** 39 10N 2 54W
La Mariña, *Spain* **34 B3** 43 30N 7 40W
La Martre, L., *Canada* **104 A5** 63 15N 117 55W
La Mesa, *U.S.A.* **117 N9** 32 46N 117 3W
La Misión, *Mexico* ... **118 A1** 32 5N 116 50W
La Mothe-Achard,
France **18 F5** 46 37N 1 40W
La Motte, *France* .... **21 D10** 44 20N 6 3 E
La Motte-Chalançon,
France .... **21 D9** 44 30N 5 21 E
La Motte-Servolex,
France .... **21 C9** 45 35N 5 53 E
La Moure, *U.S.A.* **112 B5** 46 21N 98 18W
La Muela, *Spain* **32 D3** 41 36N 1 7W
La Mure, *France* ..... **21 D9** 44 55N 5 48 E
La Negra, *Chile* ..... **126 A1** 23 46 S 70 18W
La Oliva, *Canary Is.* .. **37 F6** 28 36N 13 57W
La Orotava, *Canary Is.* **37 F3** 28 22N 16 31W
La Oroya, *Peru* ...... **124 F3** 11 32 S 75 54W
La Pacaudière, *France* **19 F10** 46 11N 3 52 E
La Palma, *Canary Is.* . **37 F2** 28 40N 17 50W
La Palma, *Panama* ... **120 E4** 8 15N 78 0W
La Palma del Condado,
Spain **35 H4** 37 21N 6 38W
La Paloma, *Chile* .... **126 C1** 30 35 S 71 0W
La Pampa □, *Argentina* **126 D2** 36 50 S 66 0W
La Paragua, *Venezuela* **124 B6** 6 50N 63 20W
La Paz, *Entre Ríos,*
Argentina .... **126 C4** 30 50 S 59 45W
La Paz, *San Luis,*
Argentina .... **126 C2** 33 30 S 67 20W
La Paz, *Bolivia* ...... **124 G5** 16 20 S 68 10W
La Paz, *Honduras* **120 D2** 14 20N 87 47W
La Paz, *Mexico* **118 C2** 24 10N 110 20W
La Paz, *Phil.* .... **61 D4** 15 26N 120 45 E
La Paz Centro, *Nic.* .. **120 D2** 12 20N 86 41W
La Pedrera, *Colombia* **124 D5** 1 18 S 69 43W
La Pérade, *Canada* ... **103 C5** 46 35N 72 12W
La Perouse Str., *Asia* . **54 B11** 45 40N 142 0 E
La Pesca, *Mexico* **119 C5** 23 46N 97 47W
La Piedad, *Mexico* ... **118 C4** 20 20N 102 1W
La Pine, *U.S.A.* **114 E3** 43 40N 121 30W
La Plata, *Argentina* .. **126 D4** 35 0 S 57 55W
La Pobla de Lillet,
Spain .... **32 C6** 42 16N 1 59 E
La Pocatière, *Canada* . **103 C5** 47 22N 70 2W
La Pola de Gordón,
Spain **34 C5** 42 51N 5 41W
La Porta, *France* .... **21 F13** 42 25N 9 21 E
La Porte, *Ind., U.S.A.* **108 E2** 41 36N 86 43W
La Porte, *Tex., U.S.A.* **113 L7** 29 39N 95 1W
La Presanella, *Italy* .. **28 B7** 46 13N 10 40 E
La Puebla = Sa Pobla,
Spain .... **32 F8** 39 46N 3 1 E
La Puebla de Cazalla,
Spain **35 H5** 37 10N 5 20W
La Puebla de los
Infantes, *Spain* **35 H5** 37 47N 5 24W
La Puebla de
Montalbán, *Spain* .. **34 F6** 39 52N 4 22W
La Puebla del Río,
Spain **35 H4** 37 16N 6 3W
La Puerta de Segura,
Spain **35 G8** 38 22N 2 45W
La Purísima, *Mexico* . **118 B2** 26 10N 112 4W
La Push, *U.S.A.* **116 C2** 47 55N 124 38W
La Quiaca, *Argentina* . **126 A2** 22 5 S 65 35W
La Réole, *France* **20 D3** 44 35N 0 1W
La Restinga, *Canary Is.* **37 G2** 27 38N 17 59W
La Rioja, *Argentina* .. **126 B2** 29 20 S 67 0W
La Rioja □, *Argentina* **126 B2** 29 30 S 67 0W
La Rioja □, *Spain* ... **32 C2** 42 20N 2 20W
La Robla, *Spain* **34 C5** 42 50N 5 41W
La Roche-Bernard,
France **18 E4** 47 31N 2 19W
La Roche-Canillac,
France .... **20 C5** 45 12N 1 57 E
La Roche-en-Ardenne,
Belgium .... **17 D5** 50 11N 5 35 E
La Roche-sur-Foron,
France .... **19 F13** 46 4N 6 19 E
La Roche-sur-Yon,
France **18 F5** 46 40N 1 25W
La Rochefoucauld,
France .... **20 C4** 45 44N 0 24 E
La Rochelle, *France* .. **20 B2** 46 10N 1 9W
La Roda, *Spain* **33 F2** 39 13N 2 15W
La Roda de Andalucía,
Spain **35 H6** 37 12N 4 46W
La Romana, *Dom. Rep.* **121 C6** 18 27N 68 57W
La Ronge, *Canada* ... **105 B7** 55 5N 105 20W
La Rumorosa, *Mexico* **117 N10** 32 33N 116 4W
La Sabina = Sa Savina,
Spain .... **37 C7** 38 44N 1 25 E
La Sagra, *Spain* **33 H2** 37 57N 2 35W
La Salle, *U.S.A.* **112 E10** 41 20N 89 6W
La Sanabria, *Spain* ... **34 C4** 42 0N 6 30W
La Santa, *Canary Is.* .. **37 E6** 29 5N 13 40W
La Sarre, *Canada* **102 C4** 48 45N 79 15W
La Scie, *Canada* **103 C8** 49 57N 55 36W
La Selva, *Spain* ..... **32 C7** 42 0N 2 45 E
La Selva Beach, *U.S.A.* **116 J5** 36 56N 121 51W
La Selva del Camp,
Spain .... **32 D6** 41 13N 1 8 E
La Serena, *Chile* .... **126 B1** 29 55 S 71 10W
La Serena, *Spain* **35 G5** 38 45N 5 40W
La Seu d'Urgell, *Spain* **32 C6** 42 22N 1 23 E
La Seyne-sur-Mer,
France .... **21 E9** 43 7N 5 52 E
La Sila, *Italy* .... **31 C9** 39 15N 16 35 E
La Solana, *Spain* **35 G7** 38 59N 3 14W
La Soufrière,
St. Vincent **121 D7** 13 20N 61 11W
La Souterraine, *France* **19 F8** 46 15N 1 30 E
La Spézia, *Italy* ..... **28 D6** 44 7N 9 50 E
La Suze-sur-Sarthe,
France .... **18 E7** 47 53N 0 2 E
La Tagua, *Colombia* .. **124 C4** 0 3N 74 40W
La Teste, *France* **20 D2** 44 37N 1 8W
La Tortuga, *Venezuela* **121 D6** 11 0N 65 22W
La Tour-du-Pin, *France* **21 C9** 45 33N 5 27 E
La Tranche-sur-Mer,
France **18 F5** 46 20N 1 27W
La Tremblade, *France* **20 C2** 45 46N 1 8W
La Tuque, *Canada* ... **102 C5** 47 30N 72 50W
La Unión, *Chile* ..... **128 E2** 40 10 S 73 0W
La Unión, *El Salv.* ... **120 D2** 13 20N 87 50W
La Unión, *Mexico* **118 D4** 17 58N 101 49W
La Unión, *Spain* **33 H4** 37 38N 0 53W
La Urbana, *Venezuela* **124 B5** 7 8N 66 56W
La Vall d'Uixó, *Spain* . **32 F4** 39 49N 0 15W
La Vecilla de Curveño,
Spain **34 C5** 42 51N 5 27W
La Vega, *Dom. Rep.* .. **121 C5** 19 20N 70 30W
La Vela de Coro,
Venezuela **124 A5** 11 27N 69 34W
La Veleta, *Spain* **35 H7** 37 1N 3 22W
La Venta, *Mexico* **119 D6** 18 8N 94 3W
La Ventura, *Mexico* .. **118 C4** 24 38N 100 54W
La Voulte-sur-Rhône,
France .... **21 D8** 44 48N 4 46 E
Laa an der Thaya,
Austria .... **27 C9** 48 43N 16 23 E
Laaber, Grosse →,
Germany .... **25 G8** 48 55N 12 30 E
Laage, *Germany* ..... **24 B8** 53 55N 12 21 E
Laatzen, *Germany* ... **24 C5** 52 19N 9 48 E
Laba →, *Russia* ..... **49 H4** 45 11N 39 42 E
Labasa, *Fiji* .... **91 C8** 16 30 S 179 10 E
Labason, *Phil.* ...... **61 G5** 8 4N 122 31 E
Labastide-Murat,
France .... **20 D5** 44 39N 1 33 E
Labastide-Rouairoux,
France .... **20 E6** 43 28N 2 39 E
Labbézenga, *Mali* ... **83 B5** 15 2N 0 48 E
Labe = Elbe →, *Europe* **24 B4** 53 50N 9 0 E
Labé, *Guinea* **82 C2** 11 24N 12 16W
Laberge, L., *Canada* .. **104 A1** 61 11N 135 12W
Labin, *Croatia* ...... **29 C11** 45 5N 14 8 E
Labinsk, *Russia* ..... **49 H5** 44 40N 40 48 E
Labis, *Malaysia* ..... **65 L4** 2 22N 103 2 E
Łabiszyn, *Poland* .... **45 F4** 52 57N 17 54 E
Labo, *Phil.* .... **61 D5** 14 9N 122 51 E
Laboe, *Germany* .... **24 A6** 54 24N 10 13 E
Laborec →,
Slovak Rep. .... **27 C14** 48 37N 21 58 E
Labouheyre, *France* .. **20 D3** 44 13N 0 55W
Laboulaye, *Argentina* . **126 C3** 34 10 S 63 30W
Labrador, *Canada* ... **103 B7** 53 20N 61 0W
Labrador City, *Canada* **103 B6** 52 57N 66 55W
Labrador Sea, *Atl. Oc.* **101 C14** 57 0N 54 0W
Lábrea, *Brazil* .... **124 E6** 7 15 S 64 51W
Labruguière, *France* .. **20 E6** 43 31N 2 16 E
Labuan, *Malaysia* .... **62 C5** 5 20N 115 14 E
Labuan, Pulau,
Malaysia .... **62 C5** 5 21N 115 13 E
Labuha, *Indonesia* ... **63 E7** 0 30 S 127 30 E
Labuhan, *Indonesia* .. **63 G11** 6 22 S 105 50 E
Labuhanbajo, *Indonesia* **63 F6** 8 28 S 119 54 E
Labuk, Telok, *Malaysia* **62 C5** 6 10N 117 50 E
Labyrinth, L., *Australia* **95 E2** 30 40 S 135 11 E
Labytnangi, *Russia* ... **50 C7** 66 39N 66 21 E
Laç, *Albania* .... **40 E3** 41 38N 19 43 E
Lac Bouchette, *Canada* **103 C5** 48 16N 72 11W
Lac Édouard, *Canada* . **103 C5** 47 40N 72 16W
Lac La Biche, *Canada* **104 C6** 54 45N 111 58W
Lac la Martre = Wha Ti,
Canada **100 B8** 63 8N 117 16W
Lac La Ronge Prov.
Park, *Canada* **105 B7** 55 9N 104 41W
Lac-Mégantic, *Canada* **103 C5** 45 35N 70 53W
Lac Thien, *Vietnam* .. **64 F7** 12 25N 108 11 E
Lacanau, *France* **20 D2** 44 58N 1 5W
Lacanau, Étang de,
France **20 D2** 44 58N 1 7W
Lacantúm →, *Mexico* . **119 D6** 16 36N 90 40W
Lacara →, *Spain* **35 G4** 38 55N 6 25W
Lacaune, *France* .... **20 E6** 43 43N 2 40 E
Lacaune, Mts. de,
France .... **20 E6** 43 43N 2 50 E
Laccadive Is. =
Lakshadweep Is.,
India .... **52 H11** 10 0N 72 30 E
Lacepede B., *Australia* **95 F2** 36 40 S 139 40 E
Lacepede Is., *Australia* **92 C3** 16 55 S 122 0 E
Lacerdónia, *Mozam.* .. **87 F4** 18 3 S 35 35 E
Lacey, *U.S.A.* **116 C4** 47 7N 122 49W
Lachhmangarh, *India* . **68 F6** 27 50N 75 4 E
Lachi, *Pakistan* ..... **68 C4** 33 25N 71 20 E
Lachine, *Canada* **102 C5** 45 30N 73 40W
Lachlan →, *Australia* . **95 E3** 34 22 S 143 55 E
Lachute, *Canada* **102 C5** 45 39N 74 21W
Lackawanna, *U.S.A.* .. **110 D6** 42 50N 78 50W
Lackawaxen, *U.S.A.* .. **111 E10** 41 29N 74 59W
Lacolle, *Canada* **111 A11** 45 5N 73 22W
Lacombe, *Canada* ... **104 C6** 52 30N 113 44W
Lacona, *U.S.A.* **111 C8** 43 39N 76 10W
Láconi, *Italy* .... **30 C2** 39 54N 9 4 E
Laconia, *U.S.A.* **111 C13** 43 32N 71 28W
Lacq, *France* **20 E3** 43 25N 0 35W
Ladakh Ra., *India* ... **69 C8** 34 0N 78 0 E
Lądek-Zdrój, *Poland* . **45 H3** 50 21N 16 53 E
Lādhon →, *Greece* .. **38 D3** 37 40N 21 50 E
Ladik, *Turkey* .... **72 B6** 40 57N 35 58 E
Ladismith, *S. Africa* .. **88 E3** 33 28 S 21 15 E
Ladíspoli, *Italy* ..... **29 G9** 41 56N 12 5 E
Lādīz, *Iran* .... **71 D9** 28 55N 61 15 E
Ladnun, *India* ...... **68 F6** 27 38N 74 25 E
Ladoga, L. =
Ladozhskoye Ozero,
Russia .... **46 B6** 61 15N 30 30 E
Ladozhskoye Ozero,
Russia .... **46 B6** 61 15N 30 30 E
Lady Elliott I.,
Australia .... **94 C5** 24 7 S 152 42 E
Lady Grey, *S. Africa* .. **88 E4** 30 43 S 27 13 E
Ladybrand, *S. Africa* . **88 D4** 29 9 S 27 29 E
Ladysmith, *Canada* .. **104 D4** 49 0N 123 49W
Ladysmith, *S. Africa* . **89 D4** 28 32 S 29 46 E
Ladysmith, *U.S.A.* ... **112 C9** 45 28N 91 12W
Lae, *Papua N. G.* .... **96 H6** 6 40 S 147 2 E
Laem Ngop, *Thailand* . **65 F4** 12 10N 102 26 E
Laem Pho, *Thailand* .. **65 J3** 6 55N 101 19 E
Læsø, *Denmark* ..... **11 G5** 57 15N 11 5 E
Læsø Rende, *Denmark* **11 G5** 57 20N 10 45 E
Lafayette, *Colo., U.S.A.* **112 F2** 39 58N 105 12W
Lafayette, *Ind., U.S.A.* **108 E2** 40 25N 86 54W
Lafayette, *La., U.S.A.* . **113 K9** 30 14N 92 1W
Lafayette, *Tenn., U.S.A.* **109 G2** 36 31N 86 2W
Laferte →, *Canada* ... **104 A5** 61 53N 117 44W
Lafia, *Nigeria* .... **83 D6** 8 30N 8 34 E
Lafiagi, *Nigeria* ..... **83 D6** 8 52N 5 20 E
Lafleche, *Canada* **105 D7** 49 45N 106 40W

Lafon, *Sudan* **81 F3** 5 5N 32 29 E
Lagan, *Sweden* **11 H7** 56 56N 13 58 E
Lagan →, *Sweden* **11 H6** 56 30N 12 58 E
Lagan →, *U.K.* **15 B6** 54 36N 5 55W
Lagarfljót →, *Iceland* **8 D6** 65 40N 14 18W
Lage, *Germany* **24 D4** 51 59N 8 48 E
Lågen →, *Oppland, Norway* **9 F14** 61 8N 10 25 E
Lågen →, *Vestfold, Norway* **9 G14** 59 3N 10 3 E
Lägerdorf, *Germany* **24 B5** 53 53N 9 34 E
Laghouat, *Algeria* **78 B6** 33 50N 2 59 E
Lagnieu, *France* **21 C9** 45 55N 5 20 E
Lagny-sur-Marne, *France* **19 D9** 48 52N 2 44 E
Lago, *Italy* **31 C9** 39 10N 16 9 E
Lagôa, *Portugal* **35 H2** 37 8N 8 27W
Lagoa Vermelha, *Brazil* **127 B5** 28 13 S 51 32W
Lagoaça, *Portugal* **34 D4** 41 11N 6 44W
Lagodekhi, *Georgia* **49 K8** 41 50N 46 22 E
Lagónegro, *Italy* **31 B8** 40 8N 15 45 E
Lagonoy G., *Phil.* **61 E5** 13 35N 123 50 E
Lagos, *Nigeria* **83 D5** 6 25N 3 27 E
Lagos, *Portugal* **35 H2** 37 5N 8 41W
Lagos □, *Nigeria* **83 D5** 6 28N 3 25 E
Lagos de Moreno, *Mexico* **118 C4** 21 21N 101 55W
Lagrange, *Australia* **92 C3** 18 45 S 121 43 E
Lagrange B., *Australia* **92 C3** 18 38 S 121 42 E
Laguardia, *Spain* **32 C2** 42 33N 2 35W
Laguépie, *France* **20 D5** 44 8N 1 57 E
Laguna, *Brazil* **127 B6** 28 30 S 48 50W
Laguna, *U.S.A.* **115 J10** 35 2N 107 25W
Laguna Beach, *U.S.A.* **117 M9** 33 33N 117 47W
Laguna de Duera, *Spain* **34 D6** 41 35N 4 43W
Laguna Limpia, *Argentina* **126 B4** 26 32 S 59 45W
Lagunas, *Chile* **126 A2** 21 0 S 69 45W
Lagunas, *Peru* **124 E3** 5 10 S 75 35W
Lahad Datu, *Malaysia* **63 C5** 5 0N 118 20 E
Lahad Datu, Teluk, *Malaysia* **63 D5** 4 50N 118 20 E
Lahan Sai, *Thailand* **64 E4** 14 25N 102 52 E
Lahanam, *Laos* **64 D5** 16 16N 105 16 E
Lahar, *India* **69 F8** 26 12N 78 57 E
Laharpur, *India* **69 F9** 27 43N 80 56 E
Lahat, *Indonesia* **62 E2** 3 45 S 103 30 E
Lahewa, *Indonesia* **62 D1** 1 22N 97 12 E
Lāhījān, *Iran* **71 B6** 37 10N 50 6 E
Lahn →, *Germany* **25 E3** 50 19N 7 37 E
Lahnstein, *Germany* **25 E3** 50 19N 7 37 E
Laholm, *Sweden* **11 H7** 56 30N 13 2 E
Laholmsbukten, *Sweden* **11 H6** 56 30N 12 45 E
Lahore, *Pakistan* **68 D6** 31 32N 74 22 E
Lahr, *Germany* **25 G3** 48 20N 7 53 E
Lahri, *Pakistan* **68 E3** 29 11N 68 13 E
Lahti, *Finland* **9 F21** 60 58N 25 40 E
Lahtis = Lahti, *Finland* **9 F21** 60 58N 25 40 E
Laï, *Chad* **79 G9** 9 25N 16 18 E
Lai Chau, *Vietnam* **58 F4** 22 5N 103 3 E
Lai'an, *China* **59 A12** 32 28N 118 30 E
Laibin, *China* **58 F7** 23 42N 109 14 E
Laifeng, *China* **58 C7** 29 27N 109 20 E
L'Aigle, *France* **18 D7** 48 46N 0 38 E
Laignes, *France* **19 E11** 47 50N 4 20 E
L'Aiguillon-sur-Mer, *France* **20 B2** 46 20N 1 18W
Laila = Laylá, *Si. Arabia* **74 C4** 22 10N 46 40 E
Laingsburg, *S. Africa* **88 E3** 33 9 S 20 52 E
Lainio älv →, *Sweden* **8 C20** 67 35N 22 40 E
Lairg, *U.K.* **14 C4** 58 2N 4 24W
Laishui, *China* **56 E8** 39 23N 115 45 E
Laissac, *France* **20 D6** 44 23N 2 50 E
Láives, *Italy* **29 B8** 46 26N 11 20 E
Laiwu, *China* **57 F9** 36 15N 117 40 E
Laixi, *China* **57 F11** 36 50N 120 31 E
Laiyang, *China* **57 F11** 36 59N 120 45 E
Laiyuan, *China* **56 E8** 39 20N 114 40 E
Laizhou, *China* **57 F10** 37 8N 119 57 E
Laizhou Wan, *China* **57 F10** 37 30N 119 30 E
Laja →, *Mexico* **118 C4** 20 55N 100 46W
Lajere, *Nigeria* **83 C7** 12 10N 11 25 E
Lajes, *Brazil* **127 B5** 27 48 S 50 20W
Lajkovac, *Serbia, Yug.* **40 B4** 44 27N 20 14 E
Lajosmizse, *Hungary* **42 C4** 47 3N 19 32 E
Lak Sao, *Laos* **64 C5** 18 11N 104 59 E
Lakaband, *Pakistan* **68 D3** 31 2N 69 15 E
Lakamané, *Mali* **82 C3** 14 35N 9 44W
Lake Alpine, *U.S.A.* **116 G7** 38 29N 120 0W
Lake Andes, *U.S.A.* **112 D5** 43 9N 98 32W
Lake Arthur, *U.S.A.* **113 K8** 30 5N 92 41W
Lake Cargelligo, *Australia* **95 E4** 33 15 S 146 22 E
Lake Charles, *U.S.A.* **113 K8** 30 14N 93 13W
Lake City, *Colo., U.S.A.* **115 G10** 38 2N 107 19W
Lake City, *Fla., U.S.A.* **109 K4** 30 11N 82 38W
Lake City, *Mich., U.S.A.* **108 C3** 44 20N 85 13W
Lake City, *Minn., U.S.A.* **112 C8** 44 27N 92 16W
Lake City, *Pa., U.S.A.* **110 D4** 42 1N 80 21W
Lake City, *S.C., U.S.A.* **109 J6** 33 52N 79 45W
Lake Cowichan, *Canada* **104 D4** 48 49N 124 3W
Lake District, *U.K.* **12 C4** 54 35N 3 20 E
Lake Elsinore, *U.S.A.* **117 M9** 33 38N 117 20W
Lake George, *U.S.A.* **111 C11** 43 26N 73 43W
Lake Grace, *Australia* **93 F2** 33 7 S 118 28 E
Lake Harbour = Kimmirut, *Canada* **101 B13** 62 50N 69 50W
Lake Havasu City, *U.S.A.* **117 L12** 34 27N 114 22W
Lake Hughes, *U.S.A.* **117 L8** 34 41N 118 26W
Lake Isabella, *U.S.A.* **117 K8** 35 38N 118 28W
Lake Jackson, *U.S.A.* **113 L7** 29 3N 95 27W
Lake Junction, *U.S.A.* **114 D8** 44 35N 110 28W
Lake King, *Australia* **93 F2** 33 5 S 119 45 E
Lake Lenore, *Canada* **105 C8** 52 24N 104 59W
Lake Louise, *Canada* **104 C5** 51 30N 116 10W
Lake Mead National Recreation Area, *U.S.A.* **117 K12** 36 15N 114 30W
Lake Mills, *U.S.A.* **112 D8** 43 25N 93 32W
Lake Placid, *U.S.A.* **111 B11** 44 17N 73 59W
Lake Pleasant, *U.S.A.* **111 C10** 43 28N 74 25W
Lake Providence, *U.S.A.* **113 J9** 32 48N 91 10W
Lake St. Peter, *Canada* **110 A6** 45 18N 78 2W
Lake Superior Prov. Park, *Canada* **102 C3** 47 45N 84 45W
Lake Village, *U.S.A.* **113 J9** 33 20N 91 17W
Lake Wales, *U.S.A.* **109 M5** 27 54N 81 35W
Lake Worth, *U.S.A.* **109 M5** 26 37N 80 3W
Lakeba, *Fiji* **91 D9** 18 13 S 178 47W
Lakefield, *Canada* **102 D4** 44 25N 78 16W
Lakehurst, *U.S.A.* **111 F10** 40 1N 74 19W
Lakeland, *Australia* **94 B3** 15 49 S 144 57 E
Lakeland, *U.S.A.* **109 M5** 28 3N 81 57W
Lakeport, *Calif., U.S.A.* **116 F4** 39 3N 122 55W
Lakeport, *Mich., U.S.A.* **110 C2** 43 7N 82 30W
Lakes Entrance, *Australia* **95 F4** 37 50 S 148 0 E
Lakeside, *Ariz., U.S.A.* **115 J9** 34 9N 109 58W
Lakeside, *Calif., U.S.A.* **117 N10** 32 52N 116 55W
Lakeside, *Nebr., U.S.A.* **112 D3** 42 3N 102 26W
Lakeside, *Ohio, U.S.A.* **110 E2** 41 32N 82 46W
Lakeview, *U.S.A.* **114 E3** 42 11N 120 21W
Lakeville, *U.S.A.* **112 C8** 44 39N 93 14W
Lakewood, *Colo., U.S.A.* **112 F2** 39 44N 105 5W
Lakewood, *N.J., U.S.A.* **111 F10** 40 6N 74 13W
Lakewood, *N.Y., U.S.A.* **110 D5** 42 6N 79 19W
Lakewood, *Ohio, U.S.A.* **110 E3** 41 29N 81 48W
Lakewood, *Wash., U.S.A.* **116 C4** 47 11N 122 32W
Lakha, *India* **68 F4** 26 9N 70 54 E
Lakhaniá, *Greece* **36 D9** 35 58N 27 54 E
Lakhimpur, *India* **69 F9** 27 57N 80 46 E
Lakhnadon, *India* **69 H8** 22 36N 79 36 E
Lakhonpheng, *Laos* **64 E5** 15 54N 105 34 E
Lakhpat, *India* **68 H3** 23 48N 68 47 E
Läki, *Azerbaijan* **49 K8** 40 34N 47 22 E
Lakin, *U.S.A.* **113 G4** 37 57N 101 15W
Lakitusaki →, *Canada* **102 B3** 54 21N 82 25W
Lakki, *Pakistan* **68 C4** 32 36N 70 55 E
Lákkoi, *Greece* **36 D5** 35 24N 23 57 E
Lakonía □, *Greece* **38 E4** 36 55N 22 30 E
Lakonikós Kólpos, *Greece* **38 E4** 36 40N 22 40 E
Lakor, *Indonesia* **63 F7** 8 15 S 128 17 E
Lakota, *Ivory C.* **82 D3** 5 50N 5 30W
Lakota, *U.S.A.* **112 A5** 48 2N 98 21W
Laksar, *India* **68 E8** 29 46N 78 3 E
Laksefjorden, *Norway* **8 A22** 70 45N 26 50 E
Lakselv, *Norway* **8 A21** 70 2N 25 0 E
Lakshadweep Is., *India* **52 H11** 10 0N 72 30 E
Lakshmanpur, *India* **69 H10** 22 58N 83 3 E
Lakshmikantapur, *India* **69 H13** 22 5N 88 20 E
Lala Ghat, *India* **67 G18** 24 30N 92 40 E
Lala Musa, *Pakistan* **68 C5** 32 40N 73 57 E
Lalago, *Tanzania* **86 C3** 3 28 S 33 58 E
Lalapanzi, *Zimbabwe* **87 F3** 19 20 S 30 15 E
Lalapaşa, *Turkey* **41 E10** 41 49N 26 44 E
Lalbenque, *France* **20 D5** 44 19N 1 34 E
L'Albufera, *Spain* **33 F4** 39 20N 0 27W
Lalganj, *India* **69 G11** 25 52N 85 13 E
Lalgola, *India* **69 G13** 24 25N 88 15 E
Lālī, *Iran* **71 C6** 32 21N 49 6 E
Lalibela, *Ethiopia* **81 E4** 12 2N 39 2 E
Lalin, *China* **57 B14** 45 12N 127 0 E
Lalín, *Spain* **34 C2** 42 40N 8 5W
Lalin He →, *China* **57 B13** 45 32N 125 40 E
Lalinde, *France* **20 D4** 44 50N 0 44 E
Lalitapur, *India* **69 G8** 24 42N 78 28 E
Lalkua, *India* **69 E8** 29 5N 79 31 E
Lalsot, *India* **68 F7** 26 34N 76 20 E
Lam, *Vietnam* **64 B6** 21 21N 106 31 E
Lam Pao Res., *Thailand* **64 D4** 16 50N 103 15 E
Lama Kara, *Togo* **83 D5** 9 30N 1 15 E
Lamaing, *Burma* **67 M20** 15 25N 97 53 E
Lamar, *Colo., U.S.A.* **112 F3** 38 5N 102 37W
Lamar, *Mo., U.S.A.* **113 G7** 37 30N 94 16W
Lamas, *Peru* **124 E3** 6 28 S 76 31W
Lamastre, *France* **21 D8** 44 59N 4 35 E
Lambach, *Austria* **26 C6** 48 6N 13 51 E
Lamballe, *France* **18 D4** 48 29N 2 31W
Lambaréné, *Gabon* **84 E2** 0 41 S 10 12 E
Lambay I., *Ireland* **15 C5** 53 29N 6 1W
Lambert Glacier, *Antarctica* **5 D6** 71 0 S 70 0 E
Lambert's Bay, *S. Africa* **88 E2** 32 5 S 18 17 E
Lambesc, *France* **21 E9** 43 39N 5 16 E
Lambeth, *Canada* **110 D3** 42 54N 81 18W
Lámbia, *Greece* **38 D3** 37 52N 21 53 E
Lambomakondro, *Madag.* **89 C7** 22 41 S 44 44 E
Lambro →, *Italy* **28 C6** 45 8N 9 32 E
Lame, *Nigeria* **83 C6** 10 30N 9 20 E
Lame Deer, *U.S.A.* **114 D10** 45 37N 106 40W
Lamego, *Portugal* **34 D3** 41 5N 7 52W
Lamèque, *Canada* **103 C7** 47 45N 64 38W
Lameroo, *Australia* **95 F3** 35 19 S 140 33 E
Lamesa, *U.S.A.* **113 J4** 32 44N 101 58W
Lamía, *Greece* **38 C4** 38 55N 22 26 E
Lamitan, *Phil.* **61 H5** 6 39N 122 8 E
Lammermuir Hills, *U.K.* **14 F6** 55 50N 2 40W
Lammhult, *Sweden* **11 G8** 57 10N 14 35 E
Lamoille →, *U.S.A.* **111 B11** 44 38N 73 13W
Lamon B., *Phil.* **61 D5** 14 30N 122 20 E
Lamont, *Canada* **104 C6** 53 46N 112 50W
Lamont, *Calif., U.S.A.* **117 K8** 35 15N 118 55W
Lamont, *Wyo., U.S.A.* **114 E10** 42 13N 107 29W
Lamotte-Beuvron, *France* **19 E9** 47 36N 2 2 E
Lampa, *Peru* **124 G4** 15 22 S 70 22W
Lampang, *Thailand* **64 C2** 18 16N 99 32 E
Lampasas, *U.S.A.* **113 K5** 31 4N 98 11W
Lampazos de Naranjo, *Mexico* **118 B4** 27 2N 100 32W
Lampertheim, *Germany* **25 F4** 49 35N 8 27 E
Lampeter, *U.K.* **13 E3** 52 7N 4 4W
Lampman, *Canada* **105 D8** 49 25N 102 50W
Lamprechtshausen, *Austria* **26 D5** 48 0N 12 58 E
Lampung □, *Indonesia* **62 F2** 5 30 S 104 30 E
Lamta, *India* **69 H9** 22 8N 80 7 E
Lamu, *Kenya* **86 C5** 2 16 S 40 55 E
Lamy, *U.S.A.* **115 J11** 35 29N 105 53W
Lan Xian, *China* **56 E6** 38 15N 111 35 E
Lan Yu = Hungt'ou Hsü, *Taiwan* **59 G13** 22 0N 121 30 E
Lanak La, *India* **69 B8** 34 27N 79 32 E
Lanak'o Shank'ou = Lanak La, *India* **69 B8** 34 27N 79 32 E
Lanao, L., *Phil.* **61 H6** 7 52N 124 15 E
Lanark, *Canada* **111 A8** 45 1N 76 22W
Lanark, *U.K.* **14 F5** 55 40N 3 47W
Lanbi Kyun, *Burma* **65 G2** 10 50N 98 20 E
Lancang, *China* **58 F2** 22 36N 99 58 E
Lancang Jiang →, *China* **58 G3** 21 40N 101 10 E
Lancashire □, *U.K.* **12 D5** 53 50N 2 48W
Lancaster, *Canada* **111 A10** 45 10N 74 30W
Lancaster, *U.K.* **12 C5** 54 3N 2 48W
Lancaster, *Calif., U.S.A.* **117 L8** 34 42N 118 8W
Lancaster, *Ky., U.S.A.* **108 G3** 37 37N 84 35W
Lancaster, *N.H., U.S.A.* **111 B13** 44 29N 71 34W
Lancaster, *N.Y., U.S.A.* **110 D6** 42 54N 78 40W
Lancaster, *Ohio, U.S.A.* **108 F4** 39 43N 82 36W
Lancaster, *Pa., U.S.A.* **111 F8** 40 2N 76 19W
Lancaster, *S.C., U.S.A.* **109 H5** 34 43N 80 46W
Lancaster, *Wis., U.S.A.* **112 D9** 42 51N 90 43W
Lancaster Sd., *Canada* **101 A11** 74 13N 84 0W
Lancelin, *Australia* **93 F2** 31 0 S 115 18 E
Lanchow = Lanzhou, *China* **56 F2** 36 1N 103 52 E
Lanciano, *Italy* **29 F11** 42 14N 14 23 E
Lancun, *China* **57 F11** 36 25N 120 10 E
Łańcut, *Poland* **45 H9** 50 10N 22 13 E
Landau, *Bayern, Germany* **25 G8** 48 40N 12 41 E
Landau, *Rhld-Pfz., Germany* **25 F4** 49 12N 8 6 E
Landeck, *Austria* **26 D3** 47 9N 10 34 E
Lander, *U.S.A.* **114 E9** 42 50N 108 44W
Lander →, *Australia* **92 D5** 22 0 S 132 0 E
Landerneau, *France* **18 D2** 48 28N 4 17W
Landeryd, *Sweden* **11 G7** 57 7N 13 15 E
Landes, *France* **20 D2** 44 0N 1 0W
Landes □, *France* **20 E3** 43 57N 0 48W
Landete, *Spain* **32 F3** 39 56N 1 25W
Landi Kotal, *Pakistan* **68 B4** 34 7N 71 6 E
Landisburg, *U.S.A.* **110 F7** 40 21N 77 19W
Landivisiau, *France* **18 D2** 48 31N 4 6W
Landquart, *Switz.* **25 J5** 46 58N 9 32 E
Landrecies, *France* **19 B10** 50 7N 3 40 E
Land's End, *U.K.* **13 G2** 50 4N 5 44W
Landsberg, *Germany* **25 G6** 48 2N 10 53 E
Landsborough Cr. →, *Australia* **94 C3** 22 28 S 144 35 E
Landsbro, *Sweden* **11 G8** 57 24N 14 56 E
Landshut, *Germany* **25 G8** 48 34N 12 8 E
Landskrona, *Sweden* **11 J6** 55 53N 12 50 E
Landstuhl, *Germany* **25 F3** 49 24N 7 33 E
Landvetter, *Sweden* **11 G6** 57 41N 12 17 E
Lanesboro, *U.S.A.* **111 E9** 41 57N 75 34W
Lanester, *France* **18 E3** 47 46N 3 22W
Lanett, *U.S.A.* **109 J3** 32 52N 85 12W
Lang Qua, *Vietnam* **64 A5** 22 16N 104 27 E
Lang Shan, *China* **56 D4** 41 0N 106 30 E
Lang Son, *Vietnam* **58 G6** 21 52N 106 42 E
Lang Suan, *Thailand* **65 H2** 9 57N 99 4 E
Langå, *Denmark* **11 H3** 56 23N 9 54 E
La'nga Co, *China* **67 D12** 30 45N 81 15 E
Langádhas, *Greece* **40 F7** 40 46N 23 6 E
Langádhia, *Greece* **38 D4** 37 43N 22 1 E
Långan →, *Sweden* **10 A8** 63 19N 14 44 E
Langano, L., *Ethiopia* **81 F4** 7 36N 38 43 E
Langar, *Iran* **71 C9** 35 23N 60 25 E
Langara I., *Canada* **104 C2** 54 14N 133 1W
Långås, *Sweden* **11 H6** 56 58N 12 26 E
Langdai, *China* **58 D5** 26 6N 105 21 E
Langdon, *U.S.A.* **112 A5** 48 45N 98 22W
Långe Jan = Ölands södra udde, *Sweden* **11 H10** 56 12N 16 23 E
Langeac, *France* **20 C7** 45 7N 3 29 E
Langeais, *France* **18 E7** 47 20N 0 24 E
Langeb Baraka →, *Sudan* **80 D4** 17 28N 36 50 E
Langeberg, *S. Africa* **88 E3** 33 55 S 21 0 E
Langeberge, *S. Africa* **88 D3** 28 15 S 22 33 E
Langeland, *Denmark* **11 K4** 54 56N 10 48 E
Langelands Bælt, *Denmark* **11 K4** 54 50N 10 55 E
Langen, *Hessen, Germany* **25 F4** 49 59N 8 40 E
Langen, *Niedersachsen, Germany* **24 B4** 53 36N 8 36 E
Langenburg, *Canada* **105 C8** 50 51N 101 43W
Langeneß, *Germany* **24 A4** 54 38N 8 36 E
Langenlois, *Austria* **26 C8** 48 29N 15 40 E
Langeoog, *Germany* **24 B3** 53 45N 7 32 E
Langeskov, *Denmark* **11 J4** 55 22N 10 35 E
Länghem, *Sweden* **11 G7** 57 36N 13 14 E
Langhirano, *Italy* **28 D7** 44 37N 10 16 E
Langholm, *U.K.* **14 F5** 55 9N 3 0W
Langjökull, *Iceland* **8 D3** 64 39N 20 12W
Langkawi, Pulau, *Malaysia* **65 J2** 6 25N 99 45 E
Langklip, *S. Africa* **88 D3** 28 12 S 20 20 E
Langkon, *Malaysia* **62 C5** 6 30N 116 40 E
Langlade, *St- P. & M.* **103 C8** 46 50N 56 20W
Langley, *Canada* **116 A4** 49 7N 122 39W
Langnau, *Switz.* **25 J3** 46 56N 7 47 E
Langogne, *France* **20 D7** 44 43N 3 50 E
Langon, *France* **20 D3** 44 33N 0 16W
Langøya, *Norway* **8 B16** 68 45N 14 50 E
Langreo, *Spain* **34 B5** 43 18N 5 40W
Langres, *France* **19 E12** 47 52N 5 20 E
Langres, Plateau de, *France* **19 E12** 47 45N 5 3 E
Langsa, *Indonesia* **62 D1** 4 30N 97 57 E
Långsele, *Sweden* **10 A11** 63 12N 17 4 E
Långshyttan, *Sweden* **10 D10** 60 27N 16 2 E
Langtry, *U.S.A.* **113 L4** 29 49N 101 34W
Langu, *Thailand* **65 J2** 6 53N 99 47 E
Languedoc, *France* **20 E7** 43 58N 3 55 E
Languedoc-Roussillon □, *France* **20 E6** 43 25N 3 0 E
Langxi, *China* **59 B12** 31 10N 119 12 E
Langxiangzhen, *China* **56 E9** 39 43N 116 8 E
Langzhong, *China* **58 B5** 31 38N 105 58 E
Lanigan, *Canada* **105 C7** 51 51N 105 2W
Lankao, *China* **56 G8** 34 48N 114 50 E
Länkäran, *Azerbaijan* **71 B6** 38 48N 48 52 E
Lanmeur, *France* **18 D3** 48 39N 3 43W
Lannemezan, *France* **20 E4** 43 8N 0 23 E
Lannilis, *France* **18 D2** 48 35N 4 32W
Lannion, *France* **18 D3** 48 46N 3 29W
L'Annonciation, *Canada* **102 C5** 46 25N 74 55W
Lanouaille, *France* **20 C5** 45 24N 1 9 E
Lanping, *China* **58 D2** 26 28N 99 15 E
Lansdale, *U.S.A.* **111 F9** 40 14N 75 17W
Lansdowne, *Australia* **95 E5** 31 48 S 152 30 E
Lansdowne, *Canada* **111 B8** 44 24N 76 1W
Lansdowne, *India* **69 E8** 29 50N 78 41 E
Lansdowne House, *Canada* **102 B2** 52 14N 87 53W
L'Anse, *U.S.A.* **108 B1** 46 45N 88 27W
L'Anse au Loup, *Canada* **103 B8** 51 32N 56 50W
L'Anse aux Meadows, *Canada* **103 B8** 51 36N 55 32W
Lansford, *U.S.A.* **111 F9** 40 50N 75 53W
Lanshan, *China* **59 E9** 25 24N 112 10 E
Lansing, *U.S.A.* **108 D3** 42 44N 84 33W
Lanslebourg-Mont-Cenis, *France* **21 C10** 45 17N 6 52 E
Lanta Yai, Ko, *Thailand* **65 J2** 7 35N 99 3 E
Lantewa, *Nigeria* **83 C7** 12 16N 11 44 E
Lantian, *China* **56 G5** 34 11N 109 20 E
Lanus, *Argentina* **126 C4** 34 44 S 58 27W
Lanusei, *Italy* **30 C2** 39 52N 9 34 E
Lanuza, *Phil.* **61 G7** 9 14N 126 4 E
Lanxi, *China* **59 C12** 29 13N 119 28 E
Lanzarote, *Canary Is.* **37 F6** 29 0N 13 40W
Lanzhou, *China* **56 F2** 36 1N 103 52 E
Lanzo Torinese, *Italy* **28 C4** 45 16N 7 28 E
Lao →, *Italy* **31 C8** 39 47N 15 48 E
Lao Bao, *Laos* **64 D6** 16 35N 106 30 E
Lao Cai, *Vietnam* **58 F4** 22 30N 103 57 E
Laoag, *Phil.* **61 B4** 18 7N 120 34 E
Laoang, *Phil.* **61 E6** 12 32N 125 8 E
Laoha He →, *China* **57 C11** 43 25N 120 35 E
Laohekou, *China* **59 A8** 32 22N 111 38 E
Laois □, *Ireland* **15 D4** 52 57N 7 36W
Laon, *France* **19 C10** 49 33N 3 35 E
Laona, *U.S.A.* **108 C1** 45 34N 88 40W
Laos ■, *Asia* **64 D5** 17 45N 105 0 E
Lapa, *Brazil* **127 B6** 25 46 S 49 44W
Lapai, *Nigeria* **83 D6** 9 5N 6 32 E
Lapalisse, *France* **19 F10** 46 15N 3 38 E
Lapeer, *U.S.A.* **108 D4** 43 3N 83 19W
Lapeyrade, *France* **20 D3** 44 4N 0 3W
Lapithos, *Cyprus* **36 D12** 35 21N 33 11 E
Lapland = Lappland, *Europe* **8 B21** 68 7N 24 0 E
Laporte, *U.S.A.* **111 E8** 41 25N 76 30W
Lapovo, *Serbia, Yug.* **40 B5** 44 10N 21 7 E
Lappeenranta, *Finland* **9 F23** 61 3N 28 12 E
Lappland, *Europe* **8 B21** 68 7N 24 0 E
Laprida, *Argentina* **126 D3** 37 34 S 60 45W
Lapseki, *Turkey* **41 F10** 40 20N 26 41 E
Laptev Sea, *Russia* **51 B13** 76 0N 125 0 E
Lapua, *Finland* **8 E20** 62 58N 23 0 E
Lăpuş →, *Romania* **43 C8** 47 25N 23 40 E
Lapuş, Munţii, *Romania* **43 C8** 47 20N 23 50 E
Lăpuşna, *Moldova* **43 D13** 46 53N 28 25 E
Łapy, *Poland* **45 F9** 52 59N 22 52 E
Laqiya Arba'in, *Sudan* **80 C2** 20 1N 28 1 E
Laqiya Umran, *Sudan* **80 D2** 19 55N 28 18 E
L'Áquila, *Italy* **29 F10** 42 22N 13 22 E
Lār, Āzarbājān-e Sharqī, *Iran* **70 B5** 38 30N 47 52 E
Lār, *Fārs, Iran* **71 E7** 27 40N 54 14 E
Larabanga, *Ghana* **82 D4** 9 16N 1 56W
Laragne-Montéglin, *France* **21 D9** 44 18N 5 49 E
Laramie, *U.S.A.* **112 E2** 41 19N 105 35W
Laramie →, *U.S.A.* **114 F11** 42 13N 104 33W
Laramie Mts., *U.S.A.* **112 E2** 42 0N 105 30W
Laranjeiras do Sul, *Brazil* **127 B5** 25 23 S 52 23W
Larantuka, *Indonesia* **63 F6** 8 21 S 122 55 E
Larat, *Indonesia* **63 F8** 7 0 S 132 0 E
L'Arbresle, *France* **21 C8** 45 50N 4 36 E
Lärbro, *Sweden* **11 G12** 57 47N 18 50 E
Larde, *Mozam.* **87 F4** 16 28 S 39 43 E
Larder Lake, *Canada* **102 C4** 48 5N 79 40W
Lardhos, Ákra = Líndhos, Ákra, *Greece* **36 C10** 36 4N 28 10 E
Lardhos, Órmos, *Greece* **36 C10** 36 4N 28 2 E
Laredo, *Spain* **34 B7** 43 26N 3 28W
Laredo, *U.S.A.* **113 M5** 27 30N 99 30W
Laredo Sd., *Canada* **104 C3** 52 30N 128 53W
Largentière, *France* **21 D8** 44 34N 4 18 E
L'Argentière-la-Bessée, *France* **21 D10** 44 47N 6 33 E
Largo, *U.S.A.* **109 M4** 27 55N 82 47W
Largs, *U.K.* **14 F4** 55 47N 4 52W
Lari, *Italy* **28 E7** 43 34N 10 35 E
Lariang, *Indonesia* **63 E5** 1 26 S 119 17 E
Larimore, *U.S.A.* **112 B6** 47 54N 97 38W
Lārīn, *Iran* **71 C7** 35 55N 52 19 E
Larino, *Italy* **29 G11** 41 48N 14 54 E
Lárisa, *Greece* **38 B4** 39 36N 22 27 E
Lárisa □, *Greece* **38 B4** 39 39N 22 24 E
Larkana, *Pakistan* **68 F3** 27 32N 68 18 E
Larnaca, *Cyprus* **36 E12** 34 55N 33 38 E
Larnaca Bay, *Cyprus* **36 E12** 34 53N 33 45 E
Larne, *U.K.* **15 B6** 54 51N 5 51W
Larned, *U.S.A.* **112 F5** 38 11N 99 6W
Laroquebrou, *France* **20 D6** 44 58N 2 12 E
Larose, *U.S.A.* **113 L9** 29 34N 90 23W
Larrimah, *Australia* **92 C5** 15 35 S 133 12 E
Larsen Ice Shelf, *Antarctica* **5 C17** 67 0 S 62 0W
Laruns, *France* **20 F3** 43 0N 0 26W
Larvik, *Norway* **9 G14** 59 4N 10 2 E
Larzac, Causse du, *France* **20 E7** 43 50N 3 17 E
Las Alpujarras, *Spain* **33 J1** 36 55N 3 20W
Las Animas, *U.S.A.* **112 F3** 38 4N 103 13W
Las Anod, *Somali Rep.* **74 F4** 8 26N 47 19 E
Las Arenas, *Spain* **34 B6** 43 17N 4 50W
Las Aves, Is., *W. Indies* **121 C7** 15 45N 63 55W
Las Brenãs, *Argentina* **126 B3** 27 5 S 61 7W
Las Cabezas de San Juan, *Spain* **35 J5** 36 57N 5 58W
Las Cejas, *Argentina* **128 B4** 26 53 S 64 44W
Las Chimeneas, *Mexico* **117 N10** 32 8N 116 5W
Las Cruces, *U.S.A.* **115 K10** 32 19N 106 47W
Las Flores, *Argentina* **126 D4** 36 10 S 59 7W
Las Heras, *Argentina* **126 C2** 32 51 S 68 49W
Las Lajas, *Argentina* **128 D2** 38 30 S 70 25W
Las Lomitas, *Argentina* **126 A3** 24 43 S 60 35W
Las Marismas, *Spain* **35 H4** 37 5N 6 20W
Las Minas, *Spain* **33 G3** 38 20N 1 41W
Las Navas de la Concepción, *Spain* **35 H5** 37 56N 5 30W
Las Navas del Marqués, *Spain* **34 E6** 40 36N 4 20W
Las Palmas, *Argentina* **126 B4** 27 8 S 58 45W
Las Palmas, *Canary Is.* **37 F4** 28 7N 15 26W
Las Palmas →, *Mexico* **117 N10** 32 26N 116 54W
Las Pedroñas, *Spain* **33 F2** 39 26N 2 40W
Las Piedras, *Uruguay* **127 C4** 34 44 S 56 14W
Las Pipinas, *Argentina* **126 D4** 35 30 S 57 19W
Las Plumas, *Argentina* **128 E3** 43 40 S 67 15W
Las Rosas, *Argentina* **126 C3** 32 30 S 61 35W
Las Rozas, *Spain* **34 E7** 40 29N 3 52W
Las Tablas, *Panama* **120 E3** 7 49N 80 14W
Las Termas, *Argentina* **126 B3** 27 29 S 64 52W
Las Toscas, *Argentina* **126 B4** 28 21 S 59 18W
Las Truchas, *Mexico* **118 D4** 17 57N 102 13W
Las Varillas, *Argentina* **126 C3** 31 50 S 62 50W
Las Vegas, *N. Mex., U.S.A.* **115 J11** 35 36N 105 13W
Las Vegas, *Nev., U.S.A.* **117 J11** 36 10N 115 9W
Lasarte, *Spain* **32 B2** 43 16N 2 1W
Lascano, *Uruguay* **127 C5** 33 35 S 54 12W
Lash-e Joveyn, *Afghan.* **66 D2** 31 45N 61 30 E
Lashburn, *Canada* **105 C7** 53 10N 109 40W
Lashio, *Burma* **67 H20** 22 56N 97 45 E
Lashkar, *India* **68 F8** 26 10N 78 10 E
Łasin, *Poland* **44 E6** 53 30N 19 2 E
Lasíthi, *Greece* **36 D7** 35 11N 25 31 E
Lasíthi □, *Greece* **36 D7** 35 5N 25 50 E
Läsjerd, *Iran* **71 C7** 35 24N 53 4 E
Lask, *Poland* **45 G6** 51 34N 19 8 E
Łaskarzew, *Poland* **45 G8** 51 48N 21 36 E
Laško, *Slovenia* **29 B12** 46 10N 15 16 E
Lassay-les-Châteaux, *France* **18 D6** 48 27N 0 30W
Lassen Pk., *U.S.A.* **114 F3** 40 29N 121 31W
Lassen Volcanic National Park, *U.S.A.* **114 F3** 40 30N 121 20W
Last Mountain L., *Canada* **105 C7** 51 5N 105 14W
Lastchance Cr. →, *U.S.A.* **116 E5** 40 2N 121 15W
Lastoursville, *Gabon* **84 E2** 0 55 S 12 38 E
Lastovo, *Croatia* **29 F13** 42 46N 16 55 E
Lastovski Kanal, *Croatia* **29 F14** 42 50N 17 0 E
Lat Yao, *Thailand* **64 E2** 15 45N 99 48 E
Latacunga, *Ecuador* **124 D3** 0 50 S 78 35W
Latakia = Al Lādhiqīyah, *Syria* **70 C2** 35 30N 35 45 E
Latchford, *Canada* **102 C4** 47 20N 79 50W
Latehar, *India* **69 H11** 23 45N 84 30 E
Laterza, *Italy* **31 B9** 40 37N 16 48 E
Latham, *Australia* **93 E2** 29 44 S 116 20 E
Lathen, *Germany* **24 C3** 52 52N 7 19 E
Lathi, *India* **68 F4** 27 43N 71 23 E
Lathrop Wells, *U.S.A.* **117 J10** 36 39N 116 24W
Latiano, *Italy* **31 B10** 40 33N 17 43 E
Latina, *Italy* **30 A5** 41 28N 12 52 E
Latisana, *Italy* **29 C10** 45 47N 13 0 E
Latium = Lazio □, *Italy* **29 F9** 42 10N 12 30 E
Laton, *U.S.A.* **116 J7** 36 26N 119 41W
Latorytsya →, *Slovak Rep.* **27 C14** 48 28N 21 50 E
Latouche Treville, C., *Australia* **92 C3** 18 27 S 121 49 E
Latrobe, *Australia* **94 G4** 41 14 S 146 30 E
Latrobe, *U.S.A.* **110 F5** 40 19N 79 23W
Latrónico, *Italy* **31 B9** 40 5N 16 1 E
Latvia ■, *Europe* **9 H20** 56 50N 24 0 E
Lau, *Nigeria* **83 D7** 9 11N 11 19 E
Lau Group, *Fiji* **91 C9** 17 0 S 178 30W
Lauchhammer, *Germany* **24 D9** 51 29N 13 47 E
Lauda-Königshofen, *Germany* **25 F5** 49 33N 9 42 E
Lauenburg, *Germany* **24 B6** 53 22N 10 32 E
Lauf, *Germany* **25 F7** 49 30N 11 16 E
Laughlin, *U.S.A.* **115 J6** 35 8N 114 35W
Laujar de Andarax, *Spain* **33 H2** 37 0N 2 54W
Laukaa, *Finland* **9 E21** 62 24N 25 56 E
Launceston, *Australia* **94 G4** 41 24 S 147 8 E
Launceston, *U.K.* **13 G3** 50 38N 4 22W
Laune →, *Ireland* **15 D2** 52 7N 9 47W
Launglon Bok, *Burma* **64 F1** 13 50N 97 54 E
Laupheim, *Germany* **25 G5** 48 14N 9 52 E
Laura, *Australia* **94 B3** 15 32 S 144 32 E
Laureana di Borrello, *Italy* **31 D9** 38 30N 16 5 E
Laurel, *Miss., U.S.A.* **113 K10** 31 41N 89 8W
Laurel, *Mont., U.S.A.* **114 D9** 45 40N 108 46W
Laurencekirk, *U.K.* **14 E6** 56 50N 2 28W
Laurens, *U.S.A.* **109 H4** 34 30N 82 1W
Laurentian Plateau, *Canada* **103 B6** 52 0N 70 0W
Lauria, *Italy* **31 B8** 40 2N 15 50 E
Laurie L., *Canada* **105 B8** 56 35N 101 57W
Laurinburg, *U.S.A.* **109 H6** 34 47N 79 28W
Laurium, *U.S.A.* **108 B1** 47 14N 88 27W
Lausanne, *Switz.* **25 J2** 46 32N 6 38 E
Laut, *Indonesia* **65 K6** 4 45N 108 0 E
Laut, Pulau, *Indonesia* **62 E5** 3 40 S 116 10 E
Laut Kecil, Kepulauan, *Indonesia* **62 E5** 4 45 S 115 40 E
Lauterbach, *Germany* **24 E5** 50 37N 9 24 E
Lauterecken, *Germany* **25 F3** 49 38N 7 35 E
Lautoka, *Fiji* **91 C7** 17 37 S 177 27 E
Lauzès, *France* **20 D5** 44 34N 1 35 E
Lavagh More, *Ireland* **15 B3** 54 46N 8 6W
Lavagna, *Italy* **28 D6** 44 18N 9 20 E
Laval, *France* **18 D6** 48 4N 0 48W
Lavalle, *Argentina* **126 B2** 28 15 S 65 15W
Lavant Station, *Canada* **111 A8** 45 3N 76 42W
Lāvar Meydān, *Iran* **71 D7** 30 20N 54 30 E
Lávara, *Greece* **41 E10** 41 19N 26 22 E
Lavardac, *France* **20 D4** 44 12N 0 20 E
Lavaur, *France* **20 E5** 43 40N 1 49 E
Lavelanet, *France* **20 F5** 42 57N 1 51 E
Lavello, *Italy* **31 A8** 41 3N 15 48 E
Laverton, *Australia* **93 E3** 28 44 S 122 29 E
Lavis, *Italy* **28 B8** 46 8N 11 7 E
Lávkos, *Greece* **38 B5** 39 9N 23 14 E
Lavos, *Portugal* **34 E2** 40 6N 8 49W
Lavradio, *Portugal* **35 G1** 38 40N 9 3W
Lavras, *Brazil* **127 A7** 21 20 S 45 0W
Lavre, *Portugal* **35 G2** 38 46N 8 22W
Lávrion, *Greece* **38 D6** 37 40N 24 4 E
Lávris, *Greece* **36 D6** 35 25N 24 40 E
Lavumisa, *Swaziland* **89 D5** 27 20 S 31 55 E
Lawas, *Malaysia* **62 D5** 4 55N 115 25 E
Lawele, *Indonesia* **63 F6** 5 13 S 122 57 E
Lawng Pit, *Burma* **67 G20** 25 30N 97 25 E
Lawqah, *Si. Arabia* **70 D4** 29 49N 42 45 E
Lawra, *Ghana* **82 C4** 10 39N 2 51W
Lawrence, *N.Z.* **91 L2** 45 55 S 169 41 E
Lawrence, *Kans., U.S.A.* **112 F7** 38 58N 95 14W
Lawrence, *Mass., U.S.A.* **111 D13** 42 43N 71 10W
Lawrenceburg, *Ind., U.S.A.* **108 F3** 39 6N 84 52W
Lawrenceburg, *Tenn., U.S.A.* **109 H2** 35 14N 87 20W
Lawrenceville, *Ga., U.S.A.* **109 J4** 33 57N 83 59W
Lawrenceville, *Pa., U.S.A.* **110 E7** 41 59N 77 8W
Laws, *U.S.A.* **116 H8** 37 24N 118 20W

Mahmudia

Luoyuan, China 59 D12 26 28N 119 30 E
Luozigou, China 57 C16 43 42N 130 18 E
Lupanshui, China 58 D5 26 38N 104 48 E
Lupeni, Romania 43 E8 45 21N 23 13 E
Lupilichi, Mozam. 87 E4 11 47 S 35 13 E
Łupków, Poland 45 J9 49 15N 22 4 E
Lupoing, China 58 E5 24 53N 104 21 E
Luquan, China 58 E4 25 35N 102 25 E
Luque, Paraguay 126 B4 25 19 S 57 25W
Lúras, Italy 30 B2 40 56N 9 10 E
Luray, U.S.A. 108 F6 38 40N 78 28W
Lure, France 19 E13 47 40N 6 30 E
Lurgan, U.K. 15 B5 54 28N 6 19W
Lusaka, Zambia 87 F2 15 28 S 28 16 E
Lusambo, Dem. Rep. of the Congo 86 C1 4 58 S 23 28 E
Lusangaye, Dem. Rep. of the Congo 86 C2 4 54 S 26 0 E
Luseland, Canada 105 C7 52 5N 109 24W
Lushan, Henan, China 56 H7 33 45N 112 55 E
Lushan, Sichuan, China 58 B4 30 12N 102 52 E
Lushi, China 56 G6 34 3N 111 3 E
Lushnjë, Albania 40 F3 40 55N 19 41 E
Lushoto, Tanzania 86 C4 4 47 S 38 20 E
Lushui, China 58 E2 25 58N 98 44 E
Lüshun, China 57 E11 38 45N 121 15 E
Lusignan, France 20 B4 46 26N 0 8 E
Lusigny-sur-Barse, France 19 D11 48 16N 4 15 E
Lusk, U.S.A. 112 D2 42 46N 104 27W
Lussac-les-Châteaux, France 20 B4 46 24N 0 43 E
Lustenau, Austria 26 D2 47 26N 9 39 E
Lūt, Dasht-e, Iran 71 D8 31 30N 58 0 E
Luta = Dalian, China 57 E11 38 50N 121 40 E
Lutherstadt Wittenberg, Germany 24 D8 51 53N 12 39 E
Luton, U.K. 13 F7 51 53N 0 24W
Luton □, U.K. 13 F7 51 53N 0 24W
Lutselke, Canada 105 A6 62 24N 110 44W
Lutsk, Ukraine 47 G3 50 50N 25 15 E
Lützow Holmbukta, Antarctica 5 C4 69 10 S 37 30 E
Lutzputs, S. Africa 88 D3 28 3 S 20 40 E
Luverne, Ala., U.S.A. 109 K2 31 43N 86 16W
Luverne, Minn., U.S.A. 112 D6 43 39N 96 13W
Luvua, Dem. Rep. of the Congo 87 D2 8 48 S 25 17 E
Luvua →, Dem. Rep. of the Congo 86 D2 6 50 S 27 30 E
Luvuvhu →, S. Africa 89 C5 22 25 S 31 18 E
Luwegu →, Tanzania 87 D4 8 31 S 37 23 E
Luwuk, Indonesia 63 E6 0 56 S 122 47 E
Luxembourg, Lux. 17 E6 49 37N 6 9 E
Luxembourg □, Belgium 17 E5 49 58N 5 30 E
Luxembourg ■, Europe 7 F7 49 45N 6 0 E
Luxeuil-les-Bains, France 19 E13 47 49N 6 24 E
Luxi, Hunan, China 59 C8 28 20N 110 7 E
Luxi, Yunnan, China 58 E4 24 40N 103 55 E
Luxi, Yunnan, China 58 E2 24 27N 98 36 E
Luxor = El Uqsur, Egypt 80 B3 25 41N 32 38 E
Luy-de-Béarn →, France 20 E3 43 39N 0 48W
Luy-de-France →, France 20 E3 43 39N 0 48W
Luyi, China 56 H8 33 50N 115 35 E
Luz-St-Sauveur, France 20 F4 42 53N 0 0W
Luzern, Switz. 25 H4 47 3N 8 18 E
Luzern □, Switz. 25 H3 47 2N 7 55 E
Luzhai, China 58 E7 24 29N 109 42 E
Luzhi, China 58 D5 26 21N 105 16 E
Luzhou, China 58 C5 28 52N 105 20 E
Luziânia, Brazil 125 G9 16 20 S 48 0W
Lužnice →, Czech Rep. 26 B7 49 14N 14 23 E
Luzon, Phil. 61 D4 16 0N 121 0 E
Luzy, France 19 F10 46 47N 3 58 E
Luzzi, Italy 31 C9 39 27N 16 17 E
Lviv, Ukraine 47 H3 49 50N 24 0 E
Lvov = Lviv, Ukraine 47 H3 49 50N 24 0 E
Lwówek, Poland 45 F3 52 28N 16 10 E
Lwówek Śląski, Poland 45 G2 51 7N 15 38 E
Lyakhavichy, Belarus 47 F4 53 2N 26 32 E
Lyakhovskiye, Ostrova, Russia 51 B15 73 40N 141 0 E
Lyaki = Läki, Azerbaijan 49 K8 40 34N 47 22 E
Lyal I., Canada 110 B3 44 57N 81 24W
Lyallpur = Faisalabad, Pakistan 68 D5 31 30N 73 5 E
Lyaskovets, Bulgaria 41 C9 43 6N 25 44 E
Lybster, U.K. 14 C5 58 18N 3 15W
Lycaonia, Turkey 72 D5 38 0N 33 0 E
Lychen, Germany 24 B9 53 12N 13 18 E
Lychkova, Russia 46 D7 57 55N 32 24 E
Lycia, Turkey 39 E11 36 30N 29 30 E
Lyckebyån →, Sweden 11 H9 56 12N 15 39 E
Lycksele, Sweden 8 D18 64 38N 18 40 E
Lycosura, Greece 38 D4 37 20N 22 3 E
Lydda = Lod, Israel 75 D3 31 57N 34 54 E
Lydenburg, S. Africa 89 D5 25 10 S 30 29 E
Lydia, Turkey 39 C10 38 48N 28 19 E
Łydynia →, Poland 45 F7 52 43N 20 26 E
Lyell, N.Z. 91 J4 41 48 S 172 4 E
Lyell I., Canada 104 C2 52 40N 131 35W
Lyepyel, Belarus 46 E5 54 50N 28 40 E
Lygnern, Sweden 11 G6 57 30N 12 15 E
Lykens, U.S.A. 111 F8 40 34N 76 42W
Lyman, U.S.A. 114 F8 41 20N 110 18W
Lyme B., U.K. 13 G4 50 42N 2 53W
Lyme Regis, U.K. 13 G5 50 43N 2 57W
Lymington, U.K. 13 G6 50 45N 1 32W
Łyna →, Poland 9 J19 54 37N 21 14 E
Lynchburg, U.S.A. 108 G6 37 25N 79 9W
Lynd →, Australia 94 B3 16 28 S 143 18 E
Lynd Ra., Australia 95 D4 25 30 S 149 20 E
Lynden, Canada 110 C4 43 14N 80 9W
Lynden, U.S.A. 116 B4 48 57N 122 27W
Lyndhurst, Australia 95 E2 30 15 S 138 18 E
Lyndon →, Australia 93 D1 23 29 S 114 6 E
Lyndonville, N.Y., U.S.A. 110 C6 43 20N 78 23W
Lyndonville, Vt., U.S.A. 111 B12 44 31N 72 1W
Lyngen, Norway 8 B19 69 45N 20 30 E
Lynher Reef, Australia 92 C3 15 27 S 121 55 E
Lynn, U.S.A. 111 D14 42 28N 70 57W
Lynn Lake, Canada 105 B8 56 51N 101 3W
Lynnwood, U.S.A. 116 C4 47 49N 122 19W
Lynton, U.K. 13 F4 51 13N 3 50W
Lyntupy, Belarus 9 J22 55 4N 26 23 E
Lynx L., Canada 105 A7 62 25N 106 15W
Lyon, France 21 C8 45 46N 4 50 E
Lyonnais, France 21 C8 45 45N 4 15 E
Lyons = Lyon, France 21 C8 45 46N 4 50 E
Lyons, Ga., U.S.A. 109 J4 32 12N 82 19W
Lyons, Kans., U.S.A. 112 F5 38 21N 98 12W
Lyons, N.Y., U.S.A. 110 C8 43 5N 77 0W
Lyons →, Australia 93 E2 25 2 S 115 9 E
Lyons Falls, U.S.A. 111 C9 43 37N 75 22W
Lyozna, Belarus 46 E6 55 0N 30 50 E
Lys = Leie →, Belgium 17 C3 51 2N 3 45 E
Lysá nad Labem, Czech Rep. 26 A7 50 11N 14 51 E
Lysekil, Sweden 11 F5 58 17N 11 26 E
Lyskovo, Russia 48 B7 56 0N 45 3 E
Lystrup, Denmark 11 H4 56 14N 10 14 E
Lysvik, Sweden 10 D7 60 1N 13 9 E
Lysychansk, Ukraine 47 H10 48 55N 38 30 E
Lytham St. Anne's, U.K. 12 D4 53 45N 3 0W
Lyttelton, N.Z. 91 K4 43 35 S 172 44 E
Lytton, Canada 104 C4 50 13N 121 31W
Lyuban, Russia 46 C6 59 16N 31 18 E
Lyubertsy, Russia 46 E9 55 39N 37 50 E
Lyubim, Russia 46 C11 58 20N 40 39 E
Lyubimets, Bulgaria 41 E10 41 50N 26 5 E
Lyuboml, Ukraine 47 G3 51 11N 24 4 E
Lyubotyn, Ukraine 47 H8 50 0N 36 0 E
Lyubytino, Russia 46 C7 58 50N 33 16 E
Lyudinovo, Russia 46 F8 53 52N 34 28 E

M

M.R. Gomez, Presa, Mexico 119 B5 26 10N 99 0W
Ma →, Vietnam 58 H5 19 47N 105 56 E
Ma'adaba, Jordan 75 E4 30 43N 35 47 E
Maamba, Zambia 88 B4 17 17 S 26 28 E
Ma'ān, Jordan 75 E4 30 12N 35 44 E
Ma'ān □, Jordan 75 F5 30 0N 36 0 E
Maanselkä, Finland 8 C23 63 52N 28 32 E
Ma'anshan, China 59 B12 31 44N 118 29 E
Maarianhamina, Finland 9 F18 60 5N 19 55 E
Ma'arrat an Nu'mān, Syria 70 C3 35 43N 36 43 E
Maas →, Neths. 17 C4 51 45N 4 32 E
Maaseik, Belgium 17 C5 51 6N 5 45 E
Maasin, Phil. 63 B6 10 8N 124 50 E
Maastricht, Neths. 17 D5 50 50N 5 40 E
Maave, Mozam. 89 C5 21 4 S 34 47 E
Mababe Depression, Botswana 88 B3 18 50 S 24 15 E
Mabalane, Mozam. 89 C5 23 37 S 32 31 E
Mabel L., Canada 104 C5 50 35N 118 43W
Mabenge, Dem. Rep. of the Congo 86 B1 4 15N 24 12 E
Maberly, Canada 111 B8 44 50N 76 32W
Mabian, China 58 C4 28 47N 103 37 E
Mabil, Ethiopia 81 E4 10 26N 36 52 E
Mablethorpe, U.K. 12 D8 53 20N 0 15 E
Mably, France 19 F11 46 5N 4 4 E
Maboma, Dem. Rep. of the Congo 86 B2 2 30N 28 10 E
Mabonto, S. Leone 82 D2 8 53N 11 50W
Mabrouk, Mali 83 B4 19 29N 1 15W
Mac Bac, Vietnam 65 H6 9 46N 106 7 E
Macachín, Argentina 126 D3 37 10 S 63 43W
Macaé, Brazil 127 A7 22 20 S 41 43W
Macael, Spain 33 H2 37 20N 2 18W
McAlester, U.S.A. 113 H7 34 56N 95 46W
McAllen, U.S.A. 113 M5 26 12N 98 14W
MacAlpine L., Canada 100 B9 66 40N 102 50W
Macamic, Canada 102 C4 48 45N 79 0W
Macao = Macau □, China 59 F9 22 16N 113 35 E
Macão, Portugal 35 F3 39 35N 7 59W
Macapá, Brazil 125 C8 0 5N 51 4W
McArthur →, Australia 94 B2 15 54 S 136 40 E
McArthur, Port, Australia 94 B2 16 4 S 136 23 E
Macau, Brazil 125 E11 5 15 S 36 40W
Macau □, China 59 F9 22 16N 113 35 E
McBride, Canada 104 C4 53 20N 120 19W
McCall, U.S.A. 114 D5 44 55N 116 6W
McCamey, U.S.A. 113 K3 31 8N 102 14W
McCammon, U.S.A. 114 E7 42 39N 112 12W
McCauley I., Canada 104 C2 53 40N 130 15W
McCleary, U.S.A. 116 C3 47 3N 123 16W
Macclenny, U.S.A. 109 K4 30 17N 82 7W
Macclesfield, U.K. 12 D5 53 15N 2 8W
M'Clintock Chan., Canada 100 A9 72 0N 102 0W
McClintock Ra., Australia 92 C4 18 44 S 127 38 E
McCloud, U.S.A. 114 F2 41 15N 122 8W
McCluer I., Australia 92 B5 11 5 S 133 0 E
McClure, U.S.A. 110 F7 40 42N 77 19W
McClure, L., U.S.A. 116 H6 37 35N 120 16W
M'Clure Str., Canada 4 B2 75 0N 119 0W
McClusky, U.S.A. 112 B4 47 29N 100 27W
McComb, U.S.A. 113 K9 31 15N 90 27W
McConaughy, L., U.S.A. 112 E4 41 14N 101 40W
McCook, U.S.A. 112 E4 40 12N 100 38W
McCreary, Canada 105 C9 50 47N 99 29W
McCullough Mt., U.S.A. 117 K11 35 35N 115 13W
McCusker →, Canada 105 B7 55 32N 108 39W
McDame, Canada 104 B3 59 44N 128 59W
McDermitt, U.S.A. 114 F5 41 59N 117 43W
McDonald, U.S.A. 110 F4 40 22N 80 14W
Macdonald, L., Australia 92 D4 23 30 S 129 0 E
McDonald Is., Ind. Oc. 3 G13 53 0 S 73 0 E
MacDonnell Ranges, Australia 92 D5 23 40 S 133 0 E
MacDowell L., Canada 102 B1 52 15N 92 45W
Macduff, U.K. 14 D6 57 40N 2 31W
Maceda, Spain 34 C3 42 16N 7 39W
Macedonia, U.S.A. 110 E3 41 19N 81 31W
Macedonia □, Greece 40 F6 40 39N 22 0 E
Macedonia ■, Europe 40 E5 41 53N 21 40 E
Maceió, Brazil 125 E11 9 40 S 35 41W
Maceira, Portugal 34 F2 39 41N 8 55W
Macenta, Guinea 82 D3 8 35N 9 32W
Macerata, Italy 29 E10 43 18N 13 27 E
McFarland, U.S.A. 117 K7 35 41N 119 14W
McFarlane →, Canada 105 B7 59 12N 107 58W
Macfarlane, L., Australia 95 E2 32 0 S 136 40 E
McGehee, U.S.A. 113 J9 33 38N 91 24W
McGill, U.S.A. 114 G6 39 23N 114 47W
Macgillycuddy's Reeks, Ireland 15 E2 51 58N 9 45W
McGraw, U.S.A. 111 D8 42 36N 76 8W
McGregor, U.S.A. 112 D9 43 1N 91 11W
McGregor Ra., Australia 95 D3 27 0 S 142 45 E
Mach, Pakistan 66 E5 29 50N 67 20 E
Māch Kowr, Iran 71 E9 25 48N 61 28 E
Machado = Jiparaná →, Brazil 124 E6 8 3 S 62 52W
Machagai, Argentina 126 B3 26 56 S 60 2W
Machakos, Kenya 86 C4 1 30 S 37 15 E
Machala, Ecuador 124 D3 3 20 S 79 57W
Machanga, Mozam. 89 C6 20 59 S 35 0 E
Machattie, L., Australia 94 C2 24 50 S 139 48 E
Machault, France 19 C11 49 21N 4 29 E
Machava, Mozam. 89 D5 25 54 S 32 28 E
Machece, Mozam. 87 F4 19 15 S 35 32 E
Machecoul, France 18 F5 47 0N 1 49W
Macheke, Zimbabwe 89 B5 18 5 S 31 51 E
Macheng, China 59 B10 31 12N 115 2 E
Machero, Spain 35 F6 39 21N 4 20W
Machhu →, India 68 H4 23 6N 70 46 E
Machias, Maine, U.S.A. 109 C12 44 43N 67 28W
Machias, N.Y., U.S.A. 110 D6 42 25N 78 30W
Machichi →, Canada 105 B10 57 3N 92 6W
Machico, Madeira 37 D3 32 43N 16 44W
Machilipatnam, India 67 L12 16 12N 81 8 E
Machiques, Venezuela 124 A4 10 4N 72 34W
Machupicchu, Peru 124 F4 13 8 S 72 30W
Machynlleth, U.K. 13 E4 52 35N 3 50W
Macia, Mozam. 89 D5 25 2 S 33 8 E
Maciejowice, Poland 45 G8 51 36N 21 26 E
McIlwraith Ra., Australia 94 A3 13 50 S 143 20 E
Măcin, Romania 43 E13 45 16N 28 8 E
Macina, Mali 82 C4 14 50N 5 0W
McInnes L., Canada 105 C10 52 13N 93 45W
McIntosh, U.S.A. 112 C4 45 55N 101 21W
McIntosh L., Canada 105 B8 55 45N 105 0W
Macintosh Ra., Australia 93 E4 27 39 S 125 32 E
Macintyre →, Australia 95 D5 28 37 S 150 47 E
Macizo Galaico, Spain 34 C3 42 30N 7 30W
Mackay, Australia 94 C4 21 8 S 149 11 E
Mackay, U.S.A. 114 E7 43 55N 113 37W
MacKay →, Canada 104 B6 57 10N 111 38W
Mackay, L., Australia 92 D4 22 30 S 129 0 E
McKay Ra., Australia 92 D3 23 0 S 122 30 E
McKeesport, U.S.A. 110 F5 40 21N 79 52W
McKellar, Canada 110 A5 45 30N 79 55W
McKenna, U.S.A. 116 D4 46 56N 122 33W
Mackenzie, Canada 104 B4 55 20N 123 5W
McKenzie, U.S.A. 109 G1 36 8N 88 31W
Mackenzie →, Australia 94 C4 23 38 S 149 46 E
Mackenzie →, Canada 100 B6 69 10N 134 20W
McKenzie →, U.S.A. 114 D2 44 7N 123 6W
Mackenzie Bay, Canada 4 B1 69 0N 137 30W
Mackenzie City = Linden, Guyana 124 B7 6 0N 58 10W
Mackenzie Mts., Canada 100 B6 64 0N 130 0W
Mackinaw City, U.S.A. 108 C3 45 47N 84 44W
McKinlay, Australia 94 C3 21 16 S 141 18 E
McKinlay →, Australia 94 C3 20 50 S 141 28 E
McKinley, Mt., U.S.A. 100 B4 63 4N 151 0W
McKinley Sea, Arctic 4 A7 82 0N 0 0W
McKinney, U.S.A. 113 J6 33 12N 96 37W
Mackinnon Road, Kenya 86 C4 3 40 S 39 1 E
McKittrick, U.S.A. 117 K7 35 18N 119 37W
Macklin, Canada 105 C7 52 20N 109 56W
Macksville, Australia 95 E5 30 40 S 152 56 E
McLaughlin, U.S.A. 112 C4 45 49N 100 49W
Maclean, Australia 95 D5 29 26 S 153 16 E
McLean, U.S.A. 113 H4 35 14N 100 36W
McLeansboro, U.S.A. 112 F10 38 6N 88 32W
Maclear, S. Africa 89 E4 31 2 S 28 23 E
Macleay →, Australia 95 E5 30 56 S 153 0 E
McLennan, Canada 104 B5 55 42N 116 50W
McLeod →, Canada 104 C5 54 9N 115 44W
MacLeod, B., Canada 105 A7 62 53N 110 0W
McLeod, L., Australia 93 D1 24 9 S 113 47 E
MacLeod Lake, Canada 104 C4 54 58N 123 0W
McLoughlin, Mt., U.S.A. 114 E2 42 27N 122 19W
McMechen, U.S.A. 110 G4 39 57N 80 44W
McMinnville, Oreg., U.S.A. 114 D2 45 13N 123 12W
McMinnville, Tenn., U.S.A. 109 H3 35 41N 85 46W
McMurdo Sd., Antarctica 5 D11 77 0 S 170 0 E
McMurray = Fort McMurray, Canada 104 B6 56 44N 111 7W
McMurray, U.S.A. 116 B4 48 19N 122 14W
Macodoene, Mozam. 89 C6 23 32 S 35 5 E
Macomb, U.S.A. 112 E9 40 27N 90 40W
Macomer, Italy 30 B1 40 16N 8 47 E
Mâcon, France 19 F11 46 19N 4 50 E
Macon, Ga., U.S.A. 109 J4 32 51N 83 38W
Macon, Miss., U.S.A. 109 J1 33 7N 88 34W
Macon, Mo., U.S.A. 112 F8 39 44N 92 28W
Macossa, Mozam. 87 F3 17 55 S 33 56 E
Macoun L., Canada 105 B8 56 32N 103 40W
Macovane, Mozam. 89 C6 21 30 S 35 2 E
McPherson, U.S.A. 112 F6 38 22N 97 40W
McPherson Pk., U.S.A. 117 L7 34 53N 119 53W
McPherson Ra., Australia 95 D5 28 15 S 153 15 E
Macquarie →, Australia 95 E4 30 5 S 147 30 E
Macquarie Harbour, Australia 94 G4 42 15 S 145 23 E
Macquarie Is., Pac. Oc. 96 N7 54 36 S 158 55 E
MacRobertson Land, Antarctica 5 D6 71 0 S 64 0 E
Macroom, Ireland 15 E3 51 54N 8 57W
MacTier, Canada 110 A5 45 9N 79 46W
Macubela, Mozam. 87 F4 16 53 S 37 49 E
Macugnaga, Italy 28 C4 45 58N 7 58 E
Macuiza, Mozam. 87 F3 18 7 S 34 29 E
Macusani, Peru 124 F4 14 4 S 70 29W
Macuse, Mozam. 87 F4 17 45 S 37 10 E
Macuspana, Mexico 119 D6 17 46N 92 36W
Macusse, Angola 88 B3 17 48 S 20 23 E
Mada →, Nigeria 83 D6 7 59N 7 55 E
Madadeni, S. Africa 89 D5 27 43 S 30 3 E
Madagali, Nigeria 83 C7 10 56N 13 33 E
Madagascar ■, Africa 89 C8 20 0 S 47 0 E
Madā'in Sālih, Si. Arabia 70 E3 26 46N 37 57 E
Madama, Niger 79 D8 22 0N 13 40 E
Madame I., Canada 103 C7 45 30N 60 58W
Madan, Bulgaria 41 E8 41 30N 24 57 E
Madaoua, Niger 83 C6 14 5N 6 27 E
Madara, Nigeria 83 C7 11 45N 10 35 E
Madaripur, Bangla. 67 H17 23 19N 90 15 E
Madauk, Burma 67 L20 17 56N 96 52 E
Madawaska, Canada 110 A7 45 30N 78 0W
Madawaska →, Canada 102 C4 45 27N 76 21W
Madaya, Burma 67 H20 22 12N 96 10 E
Madbar, Sudan 81 F3 6 17N 30 45 E
Maddalena, Italy 30 A2 41 16N 9 23 E
Maddaloni, Italy 31 A7 41 2N 14 23 E
Madeira, Atl. Oc. 37 D3 32 50N 17 0W
Madeira →, Brazil 122 D5 3 22 S 58 45W
Madeleine, Îs. de la, Canada 103 C7 47 30N 61 40W
Maden, Turkey 73 C8 38 23N 39 40 E
Madera, Mexico 118 B3 29 12N 108 7W
Madera, Calif., U.S.A. 116 J6 36 57N 120 3W
Madera, Pa., U.S.A. 110 F6 40 49N 78 26W
Madha, India 66 L9 18 0N 75 30 E
Madhavpur, India 68 J3 21 15N 69 58 E
Madhepura, India 69 F12 26 11N 86 23 E
Madhubani, India 69 F12 26 21N 86 7 E
Madhupur, India 69 G12 24 16N 86 39 E
Madhya Pradesh □, India 68 J8 22 50N 78 0 E
Madidi →, Bolivia 124 F5 12 32 S 66 52W
Madikeri, India 66 N9 12 30N 75 45 E
Madill, U.S.A. 113 H6 34 6N 96 46W
Madimba, Dem. Rep. of the Congo 84 E3 4 58 S 15 5 E
Ma'din, Syria 70 C3 35 45N 39 36 E
Madina, Mali 82 C3 13 25N 8 50W
Madinani, Ivory C. 82 D3 9 37N 6 57W
Madingou, Congo 84 E2 4 10 S 13 33 E
Madirovalo, Madag. 89 B8 16 26 S 46 32 E
Madison, Calif., U.S.A. 116 G5 38 41N 121 59W
Madison, Fla., U.S.A. 109 K4 30 28N 83 25W
Madison, Ind., U.S.A. 108 F3 38 44N 85 23W
Madison, Nebr., U.S.A. 112 E6 41 50N 97 27W
Madison, Ohio, U.S.A. 110 E3 41 46N 81 3W
Madison, S. Dak., U.S.A. 112 D6 44 0N 97 7W
Madison, Wis., U.S.A. 112 D10 43 4N 89 24W
Madison →, U.S.A. 114 D8 45 56N 111 31W
Madison Heights, U.S.A. 108 G6 37 25N 79 8W
Madisonville, Ky., U.S.A. 108 G2 37 20N 87 30W
Madisonville, Tex., U.S.A. 113 K7 30 57N 95 55W
Madista, Botswana 88 C4 21 15 S 25 6 E
Madiun, Indonesia 62 F4 7 38 S 111 32 E
Madoc, Canada 110 B7 44 30N 77 28W
Madol, Sudan 81 F2 9 3N 27 45 E
Madon →, France 19 D13 48 36N 6 6 E
Madona, Latvia 9 H22 56 53N 26 5 E
Madonie, Italy 30 E6 37 50N 13 50 E
Madonna di Campíglio, Italy 28 B7 46 14N 10 49 E
Madra Dağı, Turkey 39 B9 39 23N 27 12 E
Madrakah, Ra's al, Oman 74 D6 19 0N 57 50 E
Madras = Chennai, India 66 N12 13 8N 80 19 E
Madras = Tamil Nadu □, India 66 P10 11 0N 77 0 E
Madras, U.S.A. 114 D3 44 38N 121 8W
Madre, Laguna, U.S.A. 113 M6 27 0N 97 30W
Madre, Sierra, Phil. 61 C5 17 0N 122 0 E
Madre de Dios →, Bolivia 122 E4 10 59 S 66 8W
Madre de Dios, I., Chile 122 J3 50 20 S 75 10W
Madre del Sur, Sierra, Mexico 119 D5 17 30N 100 0W
Madre Occidental, Sierra, Mexico 118 B3 27 0N 107 0W
Madre Oriental, Sierra, Mexico 118 C5 25 0N 100 0W
Madri, India 68 G5 24 16N 73 32 E
Madrid, Spain 34 E7 40 25N 3 45W
Madrid, U.S.A. 111 B9 44 45N 75 8W
Madrid □, Spain 34 E7 40 30N 3 45W
Madridejos, Spain 35 F7 39 28N 3 33W
Madrigal de las Altas Torres, Spain 34 D6 41 5N 5 0W
Madrona, Sierra, Spain 35 G6 38 27N 4 16W
Madroñera, Spain 35 F5 39 26N 5 42W
Madu, Sudan 81 E2 14 37N 26 4 E
Madura, Australia 93 F4 31 55 S 127 0 E
Madura, Indonesia 63 G15 7 30 S 114 0 E
Madura, Selat, Indonesia 63 G15 7 30 S 113 20 E
Madurai, India 66 Q11 9 55N 78 10 E
Madurantakam, India 66 N11 12 30N 79 50 E
Madzhalis, Russia 49 J8 42 9N 47 47 E
Mae Chan, Thailand 64 B2 20 9N 99 52 E
Mae Hong Son, Thailand 64 C2 19 16N 97 56 E
Mae Khlong →, Thailand 64 F3 13 24N 100 0 E
Mae Phrik, Thailand 64 D2 17 27N 99 7 E
Mae Ramat, Thailand 64 D2 16 58N 98 31 E
Mae Rim, Thailand 64 C2 18 54N 98 57 E
Mae Sot, Thailand 64 D2 16 43N 98 34 E
Mae Suai, Thailand 58 H2 19 39N 99 33 E
Mae Tha, Thailand 64 C2 18 28N 99 8 E
Maebashi, Japan 55 F9 36 24N 139 4 E
Maella, Spain 32 D5 41 8N 0 7 E
Maesteg, U.K. 13 F4 51 36N 3 40W
Maestra, Sierra, Cuba 120 B4 20 15N 77 0W
Maevatanana, Madag. 89 B8 16 56 S 46 49 E
Mafeking = Mafikeng, S. Africa 88 D4 25 50 S 25 38 E
Mafeking, Canada 105 C8 52 40N 101 10W
Maféré, Ivory C. 82 D4 5 30N 3 2W
Mafeteng, Lesotho 88 D4 29 51 S 27 15 E
Maffra, Australia 95 F4 37 53 S 146 58 E
Mafia I., Tanzania 86 D4 7 45 S 39 50 E
Mafikeng, S. Africa 88 D4 25 50 S 25 38 E
Mafra, Brazil 127 B6 26 10 S 49 55W
Mafra, Portugal 35 G1 38 55N 9 20W
Mafungabusi Plateau, Zimbabwe 87 F2 18 30 S 29 8 E
Magadan, Russia 51 D16 59 38N 150 50 E
Magadi, Kenya 86 C4 1 54 S 36 19 E
Magadi, L., Kenya 86 C4 1 54 S 36 19 E
Magaliesburg, S. Africa 89 D4 26 0 S 27 32 E
Magallanes, Estrecho de, Chile 122 J3 52 30 S 75 0W
Magaluf, Spain 33 F7 39 29N 2 32 E
Magangué, Colombia 124 B4 9 14N 74 45W
Magaria, Niger 83 C6 13 4N 9 5 E
Magburaka, S. Leone 82 D2 8 47N 12 0W
Magdalen Is. = Madeleine, Îs. de la, Canada 103 C7 47 30N 61 40W
Magdalena, Argentina 126 D4 35 5 S 57 30W
Magdalena, Bolivia 124 F6 13 13 S 63 57W
Magdalena, Mexico 118 A2 30 50N 112 0W
Magdalena, U.S.A. 115 J10 34 7N 107 15W
Magdalena →, Colombia 122 B3 11 6N 74 51W
Magdalena →, Mexico 118 A2 30 40N 112 25W
Magdalena, B., Mexico 118 C2 24 30N 112 10W
Magdalena, Llano de la, Mexico 118 C2 25 0N 111 30W
Magdeburg, Germany 24 C7 52 7N 11 38 E
Magdelaine Cays, Australia 94 B5 16 33 S 150 18 E
Magdub, Sudan 81 E2 13 42N 25 5 E
Magee, U.S.A. 113 K10 31 52N 89 44W
Magelang, Indonesia 62 F4 7 29 S 110 13 E
Magellan's Str. = Magallanes, Estrecho de, Chile 122 J3 52 30 S 75 0W
Magenta, Italy 28 C5 45 28N 8 53 E
Magenta, L., Australia 93 F2 33 30 S 119 2 E
Magerøya, Norway 8 A21 71 3N 25 40 E
Maggia →, Switz. 25 J4 46 18N 8 36 E
Maggiorasca, Mte., Italy 28 D6 44 33N 9 29 E
Maggiore, Lago, Italy 28 C5 45 57N 8 39 E
Maghâgha, Egypt 80 B3 28 38N 30 50 E
Maghama, Mauritania 82 B2 15 32N 12 57W
Magherafelt, U.K. 15 B5 54 45N 6 37W
Maghreb, N. Afr. 78 B5 32 0N 4 0W
Magione, Italy 29 E9 43 8N 12 12 E
Magistralnyy, Russia 51 D11 56 16N 107 36 E
Maglaj, Bos.-H. 42 F3 44 33N 18 7 E
Magliano in Toscana, Italy 29 F8 42 36N 11 17 E
Máglie, Italy 31 B11 40 7N 18 18 E
Magnac-Laval, France 20 B5 46 13N 1 11 E
Magnetic Pole (North) = North Magnetic Pole, Canada 4 B2 77 58N 102 8W
Magnetic Pole (South) = South Magnetic Pole, Antarctica 5 C9 64 8 S 138 8 E
Magnisía □, Greece 38 B5 39 15N 23 0 E
Magnitogorsk, Russia 50 D6 53 27N 59 4 E
Magnolia, Ark., U.S.A. 113 J8 33 16N 93 14W
Magnolia, Miss., U.S.A. 113 K9 31 9N 90 28W
Magny-en-Vexin, France 19 C8 49 9N 1 47 E
Magog, Canada 103 C5 45 18N 72 9W
Magoro, Uganda 86 B3 1 45N 34 12 E
Magosa = Famagusta, Cyprus 36 D12 35 8N 33 55 E
Magouládhes, Greece 36 A3 39 45N 19 42 E
Magoye, Zambia 87 F2 16 1 S 27 30 E
Magozal, Mexico 119 C5 21 34N 97 59W
Magpie, L., Canada 103 B7 51 0N 64 41W
Magrath, Canada 104 D6 49 25N 112 50W
Magre →, Spain 33 F4 39 11N 0 25W
Magrur, Sudan 81 E3 14 1N 30 27 E
Magrur, Wadi →, Sudan 81 D2 16 5N 26 30 E
Magta Lahjar, Mauritania 82 B2 17 28N 13 17W
Maguan, China 58 F5 23 0N 104 21 E
Maguarinho, C., Brazil 125 D9 0 15 S 48 30W
Mague, Mozam. 89 D5 25 2 S 32 40 E
Mağusa = Famagusta, Cyprus 36 D12 35 8N 33 55 E
Maguse L., Canada 105 A9 61 40N 95 10W
Maguse Pt., Canada 105 A10 61 20N 93 50W
Magvana, India 68 H3 23 13N 69 22 E
Magwe, Burma 67 J19 20 10N 95 0 E
Magwe, Sudan 81 G3 4 8N 32 17 E
Maha Sarakham, Thailand 64 D4 16 12N 103 16 E
Mahābād, Iran 70 B5 36 50N 45 45 E
Mahabharat Lekh, Nepal 69 E10 28 30N 82 0 E
Mahabo, Madag. 89 C7 20 23 S 44 40 E
Mahadeo Hills, India 69 H8 22 20N 78 30 E
Mahaffey, U.S.A. 110 F6 40 53N 78 44W
Mahagi, Dem. Rep. of the Congo 86 B3 2 20N 31 0 E
Mahajamba →, Madag. 89 B8 15 33 S 47 8 E
Mahajamba, Helodranon' i, Madag. 89 B8 15 24 S 47 5 E
Mahajan, India 68 E5 28 48N 73 56 E
Mahajanga, Madag. 89 B8 15 40 S 46 25 E
Mahajanga □, Madag. 89 B8 17 0 S 47 0 E
Mahajilo →, Madag. 89 B8 19 42 S 45 22 E
Mahakam →, Indonesia 62 E5 0 35 S 117 17 E
Mahalapye, Botswana 88 C4 23 1 S 26 51 E
Maḩallāt, Iran 71 C6 33 55N 50 30 E
Māhān, Iran 71 D8 30 5N 57 18 E
Mahan →, India 69 H10 23 30N 82 50 E
Mahanadi →, India 67 J15 20 20N 86 25 E
Mahananda →, India 69 G12 25 12N 87 52 E
Mahanoro, Madag. 89 B8 19 54 S 48 48 E
Mahanoy City, U.S.A. 111 F8 40 49N 76 9W
Maharashtra □, India 66 J9 20 30N 75 30 E
Mahari Mts., Tanzania 86 D3 6 20 S 30 0 E
Mahasham, W. →, Egypt 75 E3 30 15N 34 10 E
Mahasoa, Madag. 89 C8 22 12 S 46 6 E
Mahasolo, Madag. 89 B8 19 7 S 46 22 E
Mahattat ash Shīdīyah, Jordan 75 F4 29 55N 35 55 E
Mahattat 'Unayzah, Jordan 75 E4 30 30N 35 47 E
Mahavavy →, Madag. 89 B8 15 57 S 45 54 E
Mahaxay, Laos 64 D5 17 22N 105 12 E
Mahbubnagar, India 66 L10 16 45N 77 59 E
Maḩḑah, Oman 71 E7 24 24N 55 59 E
Mahdia, Tunisia 79 A8 35 28N 11 0 E
Mahe, India 69 C8 33 10N 78 32 E
Mahendragarh, India 68 E7 28 17N 76 14 E
Mahenge, Tanzania 87 D4 8 45 S 36 41 E
Maheno, N.Z. 91 L3 45 10 S 170 50 E
Mahesana, India 68 H5 23 39N 72 26 E
Maheshwar, India 68 H6 22 11N 75 35 E
Mahgawan, India 69 F8 26 29N 78 37 E
Mahi →, India 68 H5 22 15N 72 55 E
Mahia Pen., N.Z. 91 H6 39 9 S 177 55 E
Mahilyow, Belarus 46 F6 53 55N 30 18 E
Mahmiya, Sudan 81 D3 17 12N 33 43 E
Mahmud Kot, Pakistan 68 D4 30 16N 71 0 E
Mahmudia, Romania 43 E14 45 5N 29 5 E

Mahmudiye

Mahmudiye, *Turkey* **39 B12** 39 48N 30 15 E
Mahmutbey, *Turkey* **41 E12** 41 3N 28 49 E
Mahnomen, *U.S.A.* **112 B7** 47 19N 95 58W
Mahoba, *India* **69 G8** 25 15N 79 55 E
Mahón = Maó, *Spain* **37 B11** 39 53N 4 16 E
Mahone Bay, *Canada* **103 D7** 44 30N 64 20W
Mahopac, *U.S.A.* **111 E11** 41 22N 73 45W
Mahuta, *Nigeria* **83 C5** 11 32N 4 58 E
Mahuva, *India* **68 J4** 21 5N 71 48 E
Mahya Daği, *Turkey* **41 E11** 41 47N 27 36 E
Mai-Ndombe, L., *Dem. Rep. of the Congo* **84 E3** 2 0 S 18 20 E
Mai-Sai, *Thailand* **58 G2** 20 20N 99 55 E
Maia, *Portugal* **34 D2** 41 14N 8 37W
Maia, *Spain* **32 B3** 43 12N 1 29W
Maials, *Spain* **32 D5** 41 22N 0 30 E
Maîche, *France* **19 E13** 47 16N 6 48 E
Maicurú →, *Brazil* **125 D8** 2 14 S 54 17W
Máida, *Italy* **31 D9** 38 51N 16 22 E
Maidan Khula, *Afghan.* **68 C3** 33 36N 69 50 E
Maidenhead, *U.K.* **13 F7** 51 31N 0 42W
Maidstone, *Canada* **105 C7** 53 5N 109 20W
Maidstone, *U.K.* **13 F8** 51 16N 0 32 E
Maiduguri, *Nigeria* **83 C7** 12 0N 13 20 E
Măieruş, *Romania* **43 E10** 45 53N 25 31 E
Maigatari, *Nigeria* **83 C6** 12 46N 9 27 E
Maignelay Montigny, *France* **19 C9** 49 32N 2 30 E
Maigo, *Phil.* **61 G5** 8 10N 123 57 E
Maigudo, *Ethiopia* **81 F4** 7 30N 37 8 E
Maihar, *India* **69 G9** 24 16N 80 45 E
Maijdi, *Bangla.* **67 H17** 22 48N 91 10 E
Maikala Ra., *India* **67 J12** 22 0N 81 0 E
Mailani, *India* **69 E9** 28 17N 80 21 E
Maillezais, *France* **20 B3** 46 22N 0 45W
Mailsi, *Pakistan* **68 E5** 29 48N 72 15 E
Main →, *Germany* **25 F4** 50 0N 8 18 E
Main →, *U.K.* **15 B5** 54 48N 6 18W
Mainburg, *Germany* **25 G7** 48 38N 11 47 E
Maine, *France* **18 D6** 48 20N 0 15W
Maine □, *U.S.A.* **109 C11** 45 20N 69 0W
Maine →, *Ireland* **15 D2** 52 9N 9 45W
Maine-et-Loire □, *France* **18 E6** 47 31N 0 30W
Maïne-Soroa, *Niger* **83 C7** 13 13N 12 2 E
Maingkwan, *Burma* **67 F20** 26 15N 96 37 E
Mainit, L., *Phil.* **61 G6** 9 31N 125 30 E
Mainland, *Orkney, U.K.* **14 C5** 58 59N 3 8W
Mainland, *Shet., U.K.* **14 A7** 60 15N 1 22W
Mainoru, *Australia* **94 A1** 14 0 S 134 6 E
Mainpuri, *India* **69 F8** 27 18N 79 4 E
Maintal, *Germany* **25 E4** 50 7N 8 52 E
Maintenon, *France* **19 D8** 48 35N 1 35 E
Maintirano, *Madag.* **89 B7** 18 3 S 44 1 E
Mainz, *Germany* **25 E4** 50 1N 8 14 E
Maipú, *Argentina* **126 D4** 36 52 S 57 50W
Maiquetía, *Venezuela* **124 A5** 10 36N 66 57W
Máira →, *Italy* **28 D4** 44 49N 7 38 E
Mairabari, *India* **67 F18** 26 30N 92 22 E
Maisí, *Cuba* **121 B5** 20 17N 74 9W
Maisí, Pta. de, *Cuba* **121 B5** 20 10N 74 10W
Maitland, *N.S.W., Australia* **95 E5** 32 33 S 151 36 E
Maitland, *S. Austral., Australia* **95 E2** 34 23 S 137 40 E
Maitland →, *Canada* **110 C3** 43 45N 81 43W
Maiyema, *Nigeria* **83 C5** 12 5N 4 25 E
Maiyuan, *China* **59 E11** 25 34N 117 28 E
Maiz, Is. del, *Nic.* **120 D3** 12 15N 83 4W
Maizuru, *Japan* **55 G7** 35 25N 135 22 E
Majalengka, *Indonesia* **63 G13** 6 50 S 108 13 E
Majene, *Indonesia* **63 E5** 3 38 S 118 57 E
Majevica, *Bos.-H.* **42 F3** 44 45N 18 50 E
Maji, *Ethiopia* **81 F4** 6 12N 35 30 E
Majiang, *China* **58 D6** 26 28N 107 32 E
Majorca = Mallorca, *Spain* **37 B10** 39 30N 3 0 E
Maka, *Senegal* **82 C2** 13 40N 14 10W
Makaha, *Zimbabwe* **89 B5** 17 20 S 32 39 E
Makak, *Cameroon* **83 E7** 3 36N 11 0 E
Makalamabedi, *Botswana* **88 C3** 20 19 S 23 51 E
Makale, *Indonesia* **63 E5** 3 6 S 119 51 E
Makamba, *Burundi* **86 C2** 4 8 S 29 49 E
Makari, *Cameroon* **83 C7** 12 35N 10 27 E
Makarikari = Makgadikgadi Salt Pans, *Botswana* **88 C4** 20 40 S 25 45 E
Makarovo, *Russia* **51 D11** 57 40N 107 45 E
Makarska, *Croatia* **29 E14** 43 20N 17 2 E
Makaryev, *Russia* **48 B6** 57 52N 43 50 E
Makasar = Ujung Pandang, *Indonesia* **63 F5** 5 10 S 119 20 E
Makasar, Selat, *Indonesia* **63 E5** 1 0 S 118 20 E
Makasar, Str. of = Makasar, Selat, *Indonesia* **63 E5** 1 0 S 118 20 E
Makat, *Kazakhstan* **50 E6** 47 39N 53 19 E
Makedonija = Macedonia ■, *Europe* **40 E5** 41 53N 21 40 E
Makeni, *S. Leone* **82 D2** 8 55N 12 5W
Makeyevka = Makiyivka, *Ukraine* **47 H9** 48 0N 38 0 E
Makgadikgadi Salt Pans, *Botswana* **88 C4** 20 40 S 25 45 E
Makhachkala, *Russia* **49 J8** 43 0N 47 30 E
Makharadze = Ozurgeti, *Georgia* **49 K5** 41 55N 42 2 E
Makhmūr, *Iraq* **70 C4** 35 46N 43 35 E
Makian, *Indonesia* **63 D7** 0 20N 127 20 E
Makindu, *Kenya* **86 C4** 2 18 S 37 50 E
Makinsk, *Kazakhstan* **50 D8** 52 37N 70 26 E
Makiyivka, *Ukraine* **47 H9** 48 0N 38 0 E
Makkah, *Si. Arabia* **74 C2** 21 30N 39 54 E
Makkovik, *Canada* **103 A8** 55 10N 59 10W
Makó, *Hungary* **42 D5** 46 14N 20 33 E
Mako, *Senegal* **82 C2** 12 52N 12 20W
Makokou, *Gabon* **84 D2** 0 40N 12 50 E
Makongo, *Dem. Rep. of the Congo* **86 B2** 3 25N 26 17 E
Makoro, *Dem. Rep. of the Congo* **86 B2** 3 10N 29 59 E
Maków Mazowiecki, *Poland* **45 F8** 52 52N 21 6 E
Maków Podhalański, *Poland* **45 J6** 49 43N 19 45 E
Makrá, *Greece* **39 E7** 36 15N 25 54 E
Makrai, *India* **66 H10** 22 2N 77 0 E
Makran Coast Range, *Pakistan* **66 G4** 25 40N 64 0 E
Makrana, *India* **68 F6** 27 2N 74 46 E
Mákri, *Greece* **41 F9** 40 52N 25 40 E
Makriyialos, *Greece* **36 D7** 35 2N 25 59 E
Mākū, *Iran* **70 B5** 39 15N 44 31 E
Makunda, *Botswana* **88 C3** 22 30 S 20 7 E
Makung, *Taiwan* **59 F12** 23 34N 119 34 E
Makurazaki, *Japan* **55 J5** 31 15N 130 20 E
Makurdi, *Nigeria* **83 D6** 7 43N 8 35 E
Makūyeh, *Iran* **71 D7** 28 7N 53 9 E
Makwassie, *S. Africa* **88 D4** 27 17 S 26 0 E
Makwiro, *Zimbabwe* **89 B5** 17 58 S 30 25 E
Mâl, *Mauritania* **82 B2** 16 58N 13 23W
Mal B., *Ireland* **15 D2** 52 50N 9 30W
Mala, Pta., *Panama* **120 E3** 7 28N 80 2W
Mala Belozërka, *Ukraine* **47 J8** 47 12N 34 56 E
Mala Kapela, *Croatia* **29 D12** 44 45N 15 30 E
Mała Panew →, *Poland* **45 H4** 50 43N 17 54 E
Mala Vyska, *Ukraine* **47 H6** 48 39N 31 36 E
Malabang, *Phil.* **61 H6** 7 36N 124 3 E
Malabar Coast, *India* **66 P9** 11 0N 75 0 E
Malabo = Rey Malabo, *Eq. Guin.* **83 E6** 3 45N 8 50 E
Malabon, *Phil.* **61 D4** 14 21N 121 0 E
Malabu, *Nigeria* **83 D7** 9 32N 12 48 E
Malacca, Str. of, *Indonesia* **65 L3** 3 0N 101 0 E
Malacky, *Slovak Rep.* **27 C10** 48 27N 17 0 E
Malad City, *U.S.A.* **114 E7** 42 12N 112 15W
Maladeta, *Spain* **32 C5** 42 39N 0 39 E
Maladzyechna, *Belarus* **46 E4** 54 20N 26 50 E
Málaga, *Spain* **35 J6** 36 43N 4 23W
Málaga □, *Spain* **35 J6** 36 38N 4 58W
Malagarasi, *Tanzania* **86 D3** 5 5 S 30 50 E
Malagarasi →, *Tanzania* **86 D2** 5 12 S 29 47 E
Malagasy Rep. = Madagascar ■, *Africa* **89 C8** 20 0 S 47 0 E
Malagón, *Spain* **35 F7** 39 11N 3 52W
Malagón →, *Spain* **35 H3** 37 35N 7 29W
Malahide, *Ireland* **15 C5** 53 26N 6 9W
Malaimbandy, *Madag.* **89 C8** 20 20 S 45 36 E
Malakâl, *Sudan* **81 F3** 9 33N 31 40 E
Malakand, *Pakistan* **68 B4** 34 40N 71 55 E
Malakwal, *Pakistan* **68 C5** 32 34N 73 13 E
Malamala, *Indonesia* **63 E6** 3 21 S 120 55 E
Malanda, *Australia* **94 B4** 17 22 S 145 35 E
Malang, *Indonesia* **62 F4** 7 59 S 112 45 E
Malangen, *Norway* **8 B18** 69 24N 18 37 E
Malanje, *Angola* **84 F3** 9 36 S 16 17 E
Mälaren, *Sweden* **10 E11** 59 30N 17 10 E
Malargüe, *Argentina* **126 D2** 35 32 S 69 30W
Malartic, *Canada* **102 C4** 48 9N 78 9W
Malaryta, *Belarus* **47 G3** 51 50N 24 3 E
Malatya, *Turkey* **70 B3** 38 25N 38 20 E
Malawi ■, *Africa* **87 E3** 11 55 S 34 0 E
Malawi, L. = Nyasa, L., *Africa* **87 E3** 12 30 S 34 30 E
Malay Pen., *Asia* **65 J3** 7 25N 100 0 E
Malaya Belozërka = Mala Belozërka, *Ukraine* **47 J8** 47 12N 34 56 E
Malaya Vishera, *Russia* **46 C7** 58 55N 32 25 E
Malaya Viska = Mala Vyska, *Ukraine* **47 H6** 48 39N 31 36 E
Malaybalay, *Phil.* **61 G6** 8 5N 125 7 E
Malāyer, *Iran* **71 C6** 34 19N 48 51 E
Malaysia ■, *Asia* **65 K4** 5 0N 110 0 E
Malazgirt, *Turkey* **70 B4** 39 10N 42 33 E
Malbaza, *Niger* **83 C6** 13 59N 5 38 E
Malbon, *Australia* **94 C3** 21 5 S 140 17 E
Malbooma, *Australia* **95 E1** 30 41 S 134 11 E
Malbork, *Poland* **44 D6** 54 3N 19 1 E
Malcésine, *Italy* **28 C7** 45 46N 10 48 E
Malchin, *Germany* **24 B8** 53 44N 12 44 E
Malchow, *Germany* **24 B8** 53 28N 12 25 E
Malcolm, *Australia* **93 E3** 28 51 S 121 25 E
Malcolm, Pt., *Australia* **93 F3** 33 48 S 123 45 E
Malczyce, *Poland* **45 G3** 51 14N 16 29 E
Maldah, *India* **69 G13** 25 2N 88 9 E
Maldegem, *Belgium* **17 C3** 51 14N 3 26 E
Malden, *Mass., U.S.A.* **111 D13** 42 26N 71 4W
Malden, *Mo., U.S.A.* **113 G10** 36 34N 89 57W
Malden I., *Kiribati* **97 H12** 4 3 S 155 1W
Maldives ■, *Ind. Oc.* **52 J11** 5 0N 73 0 E
Maldonado, *Uruguay* **127 C5** 34 59 S 55 0W
Maldonado, Punta, *Mexico* **119 D5** 16 19N 98 35W
Malè, *Italy* **28 B7** 46 21N 10 55 E
Malé, *Maldives* **53 J11** 4 0N 73 28 E
Malé Karpaty, *Slovak Rep.* **27 C10** 48 30N 17 20 E
Maléa, Ákra, *Greece* **38 E5** 36 28N 23 7 E
Malegaon, *India* **66 J9** 20 30N 74 38 E
Malei, *Mozam.* **87 F4** 17 12 S 36 58 E
Malek, *Sudan* **81 F3** 6 4N 31 36 E
Malek Kandī, *Iran* **70 B5** 37 9N 46 6 E
Malela, *Dem. Rep. of the Congo* **86 C2** 4 22 S 26 8 E
Malema, *Mozam.* **87 E4** 14 57 S 37 20 E
Máleme, *Greece* **36 D5** 35 31N 23 49 E
Maleny, *Australia* **95 D5** 26 45 S 152 52 E
Målerås, *Sweden* **11 H9** 56 54N 15 34 E
Malerkotla, *India* **68 D6** 30 32N 75 58 E
Máles, *Greece* **36 D7** 35 6N 25 35 E
Malesherbes, *France* **19 D9** 48 15N 2 24 E
Maleshevska Planina, *Europe* **40 E7** 41 38N 23 7 E
Malesína, *Greece* **38 C5** 38 37N 23 14 E
Malestroit, *France* **18 E4** 47 49N 2 25W
Malfa, *Italy* **31 D7** 38 35N 14 50 E
Malgobek, *Russia* **49 J7** 43 30N 44 34 E
Malgomaj, *Sweden* **8 D17** 64 40N 16 30 E
Malgrat = Malgrat de Mar, *Spain* **32 D7** 41 39N 2 46 E
Malgrat de Mar, *Spain* **32 D7** 41 39N 2 46 E
Malha, *Sudan* **81 D2** 15 8N 25 10 E
Malhargarh, *India* **68 G6** 24 17N 74 59 E
Malheur →, *U.S.A.* **114 D5** 44 4N 116 59W
Malheur L., *U.S.A.* **114 E4** 43 20N 118 48W
Mali, *Guinea* **82 C2** 12 10N 12 20W
Mali ■, *Africa* **82 B4** 17 0N 3 0W
Mali →, *Burma* **67 G20** 25 40N 97 40 E
Mali Kanal, *Serbia, Yug.* **42 E4** 45 36N 19 24 E
Mali Kyun, *Burma* **64 F2** 13 0N 98 20 E
Malibu, *U.S.A.* **117 L8** 34 2N 118 41W
Maliku, *Indonesia* **63 E6** 0 39 S 123 16 E
Malili, *Indonesia* **63 E6** 2 42 S 121 6 E
Målilla, *Sweden* **11 G9** 57 23N 15 48 E
Malimba, Mts., *Dem. Rep. of the Congo* **86 D2** 7 30 S 29 30 E
Malin Hd., *Ireland* **15 A4** 55 23N 7 23W
Malin Pen., *Ireland* **15 A4** 55 20N 7 17W
Malindi, *Kenya* **86 C5** 3 12 S 40 5 E
Malines = Mechelen, *Belgium* **17 C4** 51 2N 4 29 E
Malino, *Indonesia* **63 D6** 1 0N 121 0 E
Malinyi, *Tanzania* **87 D4** 8 56 S 36 0 E
Malipo, *China* **58 F5** 23 7N 104 42 E
Maliq, *Albania* **40 F4** 40 45N 20 48 E
Malita, *Phil.* **63 C7** 6 19N 125 39 E
Maliwun, *Burma* **62 B1** 10 17N 98 40 E
Maliya, *India* **68 H4** 23 5N 70 46 E
Maljenik, *Serbia, Yug.* **40 C5** 43 54N 21 43 E
Malkara, *Turkey* **41 F10** 40 53N 26 53 E
Małkinia Górna, *Poland* **45 F9** 52 42N 22 5 E
Malko Tŭrnovo, *Bulgaria* **41 E11** 41 59N 27 31 E
Mallacoota Inlet, *Australia* **95 F4** 37 34 S 149 40 E
Mallaig, *U.K.* **14 D3** 57 0N 5 50W
Mallaoua, *Niger* **83 C6** 13 2N 9 36 E
Mallawan, *India* **69 F9** 27 4N 80 12 E
Mallawi, *Egypt* **80 B3** 27 44N 30 44 E
Mallemort, *France* **21 E9** 43 43N 5 11 E
Málles Venosta, *Italy* **28 B7** 46 41N 10 32 E
Mállia, *Greece* **36 D7** 35 17N 25 32 E
Mallión, Kólpos, *Greece* **36 D7** 35 19N 25 27 E
Mallorca, *Spain* **37 B10** 39 30N 3 0 E
Mallorytown, *Canada* **111 B9** 44 29N 75 53W
Mallow, *Ireland* **15 D3** 52 8N 8 39W
Malmbäck, *Sweden* **11 G8** 57 34N 14 28 E
Malmberget, *Sweden* **8 C19** 67 11N 20 40 E
Malmédy, *Belgium* **17 D6** 50 25N 6 2 E
Malmesbury, *S. Africa* **88 E2** 33 28 S 18 41 E
Malmköping, *Sweden* **10 E10** 59 8N 16 44 E
Malmö, *Sweden* **11 J6** 55 36N 12 59 E
Malmslätt, *Sweden* **11 F9** 58 27N 15 33 E
Malmyzh, *Russia* **48 B10** 56 31N 50 41 E
Malnaş, *Romania* **43 D10** 46 2N 25 49 E
Malo Konare, *Bulgaria* **41 D8** 42 12N 24 24 E
Maloarkhangelsk, *Russia* **47 F9** 52 28N 36 30 E
Malolos, *Phil.* **63 B6** 14 50N 120 49 E
Malombe L., *Malawi* **87 E4** 14 40 S 35 15 E
Małomice, *Poland* **45 G2** 51 34N 15 29 E
Malomir, *Bulgaria* **41 D10** 42 16N 26 32 E
Malone, *U.S.A.* **111 B10** 44 51N 74 18W
Malong, *China* **58 E4** 25 24N 103 34 E
Małopolskie □, *Poland* **45 J7** 49 50N 20 20 E
Malorad, *Bulgaria* **40 C7** 43 28N 23 41 E
Måløy, *Norway* **9 F11** 61 57N 5 6 E
Maloyaroslovets, *Russia* **46 E9** 55 2N 36 20 E
Malpartida, *Spain* **35 F4** 39 26N 6 30W
Malpaso, *Canary Is.* **37 G1** 27 43N 18 3W
Malpelo, I. de, *Colombia* **124 C2** 4 3N 81 35W
Malpica de Bergantiños, *Spain* **34 B2** 43 19N 8 50W
Malpur, *India* **68 H5** 23 21N 73 27 E
Malpura, *India* **68 F6** 26 17N 75 23 E
Mals = Málles Venosta, *Italy* **28 B7** 46 41N 10 32 E
Malta, *Idaho, U.S.A.* **114 E7** 42 18N 113 22W
Malta, *Mont., U.S.A.* **114 B10** 48 21N 107 52W
Malta ■, *Europe* **36 D2** 35 50N 14 30 E
Maltahöhe, *Namibia* **88 C2** 24 55 S 17 0 E
Maltepe, *Turkey* **41 F13** 40 55N 29 8 E
Malton, *Canada* **110 C5** 43 42N 79 38W
Malton, *U.K.* **12 C7** 54 8N 0 49W
Maluku, *Indonesia* **63 E7** 1 0 S 127 0 E
Maluku □, *Indonesia* **63 E7** 3 0 S 128 0 E
Maluku Sea = Molucca Sea, *Indonesia* **63 E6** 0 0 125 0 E
Malumfashi, *Nigeria* **83 C6** 11 48N 7 39 E
Malung, *Sweden* **10 D7** 60 42N 13 44 E
Malungsfors, *Sweden* **10 D7** 60 44N 13 33 E
Maluwe, *Ghana* **82 D4** 8 40N 2 17W
Malvan, *India* **66 L8** 16 2N 73 30 E
Malvern, *U.S.A.* **113 H8** 34 22N 92 49W
Malvern Hills, *U.K.* **13 E5** 52 0N 2 19W
Malvinas, Is. = Falkland Is. □, *Atl. Oc.* **128 G5** 51 30 S 59 0W
Malý Dunaj →, *Slovak Rep.* **27 D11** 47 45N 18 9 E
Malya, *Tanzania* **86 C3** 3 5 S 33 38 E
Malyn, *Ukraine* **47 G5** 50 46N 29 3 E
Malyy Lyakhovskiy, Ostrov, *Russia* **51 B15** 74 7N 140 36 E
Mama, *Russia* **51 D12** 58 18N 112 54 E
Mamadysh, *Russia* **48 C10** 55 44N 51 23 E
Mamanguape, *Brazil* **125 E11** 6 50 S 35 4W
Mamarr Mitlā, *Egypt* **75 E1** 30 2N 32 54 E
Mamasa, *Indonesia* **63 E5** 2 55 S 119 20 E
Mambasa, *Dem. Rep. of the Congo* **86 B2** 1 22N 29 3 E
Mamberamo →, *Indonesia* **63 E9** 2 0 S 137 50 E
Mambilima Falls, *Zambia* **87 E2** 10 31 S 28 45 E
Mambirima, *Dem. Rep. of the Congo* **87 E2** 11 25 S 27 33 E
Mambo, *Tanzania* **86 C4** 4 52 S 38 22 E
Mambrui, *Kenya* **86 C5** 3 5 S 40 5 E
Mamburao, *Phil.* **61 E4** 13 13N 120 39 E
Mameigwess L., *Canada* **102 B2** 52 35N 87 50W
Mamers, *France* **18 D7** 48 21N 0 22 E
Mamfé, *Cameroon* **83 D6** 5 50N 9 15 E
Mammoth, *U.S.A.* **115 K8** 32 43N 110 39W
Mammoth Cave National Park, *U.S.A.* **108 G3** 37 8N 86 13W
Mamoré →, *Bolivia* **122 E4** 10 23 S 65 53W
Mamou, *Guinea* **82 C2** 10 15N 12 0W
Mampatá, *Guinea-Biss.* **82 C2** 11 54N 14 53W
Mampikony, *Madag.* **89 B8** 16 6 S 47 38 E
Mampong, *Ghana* **83 D4** 7 6N 1 26W
Mamry, Jezioro, *Poland* **44 D8** 54 5N 21 50 E
Mamuju, *Indonesia* **63 E5** 2 41 S 118 50 E
Mamuno, *Botswana* **88 C3** 22 16 S 20 1 E
Mamuras, *Albania* **40 E3** 41 34N 19 41 E
Man, *Ivory C.* **82 D3** 7 30N 7 40W
Man, I. of, *U.K.* **12 C3** 54 15N 4 30W
Man-Bazar, *India* **69 H12** 23 4N 86 39 E
Man Na, *Burma* **67 H20** 23 27N 97 19 E
Mana →, *Fr. Guiana* **125 B8** 5 45N 53 55W
Manaar, G. of = Mannar, G. of, *Asia* **66 Q11** 8 30N 79 0 E
Manacapuru, *Brazil* **124 D6** 3 16 S 60 37W
Manacor, *Spain* **37 B10** 39 34N 3 13 E
Manado, *Indonesia* **63 D6** 1 29N 124 51 E
Managua, *Nic.* **120 D2** 12 6N 86 20W
Managua, L. de, *Nic.* **120 D2** 12 20N 86 30W
Manakara, *Madag.* **89 C8** 22 8 S 48 1 E
Manali, *India* **68 C7** 32 16N 77 10 E
Manama = Al Manāmah, *Bahrain* **71 E6** 26 10N 50 30 E
Manambao →, *Madag.* **89 B7** 17 35 S 44 0 E
Manambato, *Madag.* **89 A8** 13 43 S 49 7 E
Manambolo →, *Madag.* **89 B7** 19 18 S 44 22 E
Manambolosy, *Madag.* **89 B8** 16 2 S 49 40 E
Mananara, *Madag.* **89 B8** 16 10 S 49 46 E
Mananara →, *Madag.* **89 C8** 23 21 S 47 42 E
Mananjary, *Madag.* **89 C8** 21 13 S 48 20 E
Manankoro, *Mali* **82 C3** 10 28N 7 25W
Manantenina, *Madag.* **89 C8** 24 17 S 47 19 E
Manaos = Manaus, *Brazil* **124 D7** 3 0 S 60 0W
Manapire →, *Venezuela* **124 B5** 7 42N 66 7W
Manapouri, *N.Z.* **91 L1** 45 34 S 167 39 E
Manapouri, L., *N.Z.* **91 L1** 45 32 S 167 32 E
Manaqil, *Sudan* **81 E3** 14 15N 32 59 E
Manār, Jabal, *Yemen* **74 E3** 14 2N 44 17 E
Manaravolo, *Madag.* **89 C8** 23 59 S 45 39 E
Manas, *China* **60 B3** 44 17N 85 56 E
Manas →, *India* **67 F17** 26 12N 90 40 E
Manaslu, *Nepal* **69 E11** 28 33N 84 33 E
Manasquan, *U.S.A.* **111 F10** 40 8N 74 3W
Manassa, *U.S.A.* **115 H11** 37 11N 105 56W
Manaung, *Burma* **67 K18** 18 45N 93 40 E
Manaus, *Brazil* **124 D7** 3 0 S 60 0W
Manavgat, *Turkey* **72 D4** 36 47N 31 26 E
Manawan L., *Canada* **105 B8** 55 24N 103 14W
Manay, *Phil.* **61 H7** 7 17N 126 33 E
Manbij, *Syria* **70 B3** 36 31N 37 57 E
Mancha Real, *Spain* **35 H7** 37 48N 3 39W
Manche □, *France* **18 C5** 49 10N 1 20W
Manchegorsk, *Russia* **50 C4** 67 54N 32 58 E
Manchester, *U.K.* **12 D5** 53 29N 2 12W
Manchester, *Calif., U.S.A.* **116 G3** 38 58N 123 41W
Manchester, *Conn., U.S.A.* **111 E12** 41 47N 72 31W
Manchester, *Ga., U.S.A.* **109 J3** 32 51N 84 37W
Manchester, *Iowa, U.S.A.* **112 D9** 42 29N 91 27W
Manchester, *Ky., U.S.A.* **108 G4** 37 9N 83 46W
Manchester, *N.H., U.S.A.* **111 D13** 42 59N 71 28W
Manchester, *N.Y., U.S.A.* **110 D7** 42 56N 77 16W
Manchester, *Pa., U.S.A.* **111 F8** 40 4N 76 43W
Manchester, *Tenn., U.S.A.* **109 H2** 35 29N 86 5W
Manchester, *Vt., U.S.A.* **111 C11** 43 10N 73 5W
Manchester L., *Canada* **105 A7** 61 28N 107 29W
Manchhar L., *Pakistan* **68 F2** 26 25N 67 39 E
Manchuria = Dongbei, *China* **57 D13** 45 0N 125 0 E
Manchurian Plain, *China* **52 E16** 47 0N 124 0 E
Manciano, *Italy* **29 F8** 42 35N 11 31 E
Mancifa, *Ethiopia* **81 F5** 6 53N 41 50 E
Mand →, *India* **69 J10** 21 42N 83 15 E
Mand →, *Iran* **71 D7** 28 20N 52 30 E
Manda, *Ludewe, Tanzania* **87 E3** 10 30 S 34 40 E
Manda, *Mbeya, Tanzania* **86 D3** 7 58 S 32 29 E
Manda, *Mbeya, Tanzania* **87 D3** 8 30 S 32 49 E
Mandabé, *Madag.* **89 C7** 21 0 S 44 55 E
Mandaguari, *Brazil* **127 A5** 23 32 S 51 42W
Mandah = Töhöm, *Mongolia* **56 B5** 44 27N 108 2 E
Mandal, *Norway* **9 G12** 58 2N 7 25 E
Mandala, Puncak, *Indonesia* **63 E10** 4 44 S 140 20 E
Mandalay, *Burma* **67 J20** 22 0N 96 4 E
Mandale = Mandalay, *Burma* **67 J20** 22 0N 96 4 E
Mandalgarh, *India* **68 G6** 25 12N 75 6 E
Mandalgovi, *Mongolia* **56 B4** 45 45N 106 10 E
Mandalī, *Iraq* **70 C5** 33 43N 45 28 E
Mandan, *U.S.A.* **112 B4** 46 50N 100 54W
Mandaon, *Phil.* **61 E5** 12 13N 123 17 E
Mandar, Teluk, *Indonesia* **63 E5** 3 35 S 119 15 E
Mándas, *Italy* **30 C2** 39 40N 9 8 E
Mandaue, *Phil.* **61 F5** 10 20N 123 56 E
Mandelieu-la-Napoule, *France* **21 E10** 43 34N 6 57 E
Mandera, *Kenya* **86 B5** 3 55N 41 53 E
Mandi, *India* **68 D7** 31 39N 76 58 E
Mandi Dabwali, *India* **68 E6** 29 58N 74 42 E
Mandiana, *Guinea* **82 C3** 10 37N 8 39W
Mandimba, *Mozam.* **87 E4** 14 20 S 35 40 E
Mandioli, *Indonesia* **63 E7** 0 40 S 127 20 E
Mandla, *India* **69 H9** 22 39N 80 30 E
Mandø, *Denmark* **11 J2** 55 18N 8 33 E
Mandorah, *Australia* **92 B5** 12 32 S 130 42 E
Mandoto, *Madag.* **89 B8** 19 34 S 46 17 E
Mandoúdhion, *Greece* **38 C5** 38 48N 23 29 E
Mándra, *Greece* **38 C5** 38 4N 23 30 E
Mandra, *Pakistan* **68 C5** 33 23N 73 12 E
Mandrákhi, *Greece* **39 E9** 36 36N 27 11 E
Mandrare →, *Madag.* **89 D8** 25 10 S 46 30 E
Mandritsara, *Madag.* **89 B8** 15 50 S 48 49 E
Mandronarivo, *Madag.* **89 C8** 21 7 S 45 38 E
Mandsaur, *India* **68 G6** 24 3N 75 8 E
Mandurah, *Australia* **93 F2** 32 36 S 115 48 E
Mandúria, *Italy* **31 B10** 40 24N 17 38 E
Mandvi, *India* **68 H3** 22 51N 69 22 E
Mandya, *India* **66 N10** 12 30N 77 0 E
Mandzai, *Pakistan* **68 D2** 30 55N 67 6 E
Mané, *Burkina Faso* **83 C4** 12 59N 1 21W
Maneh, *Iran* **71 B8** 37 39N 57 7 E
Manengouba, Mts., *Cameroon* **83 E6** 5 0N 9 50 E
Manera, *Madag.* **89 C7** 22 55 S 44 20 E
Manérbio, *Italy* **28 C7** 45 21N 10 8 E
Maneroo Cr. →, *Australia* **94 C3** 23 21 S 143 53 E
Manfalût, *Egypt* **80 B3** 27 20N 30 52 E
Manfredónia, *Italy* **29 G12** 41 38N 15 55 E
Manfredónia, G. di, *Italy* **29 G13** 41 35N 16 5 E
Manga, *Burkina Faso* **83 C4** 11 40N 1 4W
Manga, *Niger* **83 C7** 15 0N 14 0 E
Mangabeiras, Chapada das, *Brazil* **125 F9** 10 0 S 46 30W
Mangalia, *Romania* **43 G13** 43 50N 28 35 E
Mangalore, *India* **66 N9** 12 55N 74 47 E
Mangan, *India* **69 F13** 27 31N 88 32 E
Mangaung, *S. Africa* **85 K5** 29 10 S 26 25 E
Mangawan, *India* **69 G9** 24 41N 81 33 E
Mangaweka, *N.Z.* **91 H5** 39 48 S 175 47 E
Manggar, *Indonesia* **62 E3** 2 50 S 108 10 E
Manggawitu, *Indonesia* **63 E8** 4 8 S 133 32 E
Mangindrano, *Madag.* **89 A8** 14 17 S 48 58 E
Mangkalihat, Tanjung, *Indonesia* **63 D5** 1 2N 118 59 E
Mangla, *Pakistan* **68 C5** 33 7N 73 39 E
Mangla Dam, *Pakistan* **69 C5** 33 9N 73 44 E
Manglaur, *India* **68 E7** 29 44N 77 49 E
Mangnai, *China* **60 C4** 37 52N 91 43 E
Mango, *Togo* **83 C5** 10 20N 0 30 E
Mangoche, *Malawi* **87 E4** 14 25 S 35 16 E
Mangoky →, *Madag.* **89 C7** 21 29 S 43 41 E
Mangole, *Indonesia* **63 E6** 1 50 S 125 55 E
Mangombe, *Dem. Rep. of the Congo* **86 C2** 1 20 S 26 48 E
Mangonui, *N.Z.* **91 F4** 35 1 S 173 32 E
Mangoro →, *Madag.* **89 B8** 20 0 S 48 45 E
Mangrol, *Mad. P., India* **68 J4** 21 7N 70 7 E
Mangrol, *Raj., India* **68 G6** 25 20N 76 31 E
Mangualde, *Portugal* **34 E3** 40 38N 7 48W
Mangueira, L. da, *Brazil* **127 C5** 33 0 S 52 50W
Mangum, *U.S.A.* **113 H5** 34 53N 99 30W
Mangyshlak Poluostrov, *Kazakhstan* **50 E6** 44 30N 52 30 E
Manhattan, *U.S.A.* **112 F6** 39 11N 96 35W
Manhiça, *Mozam.* **89 D5** 25 23 S 32 49 E
Mania →, *Madag.* **89 B8** 19 42 S 45 22 E
Maniago, *Italy* **29 B9** 46 10N 12 43 E
Manica, *Mozam.* **89 B5** 18 58 S 32 59 E
Manica □, *Mozam.* **89 B5** 19 10 S 33 45 E
Manicaland □, *Zimbabwe* **87 F3** 19 0 S 32 30 E
Manicoré, *Brazil* **124 E6** 5 48 S 61 16W
Manicouagan →, *Canada* **103 C6** 49 30N 68 30W
Manicouagan, Rés., *Canada* **103 B6** 51 5N 68 40W
Maniema □, *Dem. Rep. of the Congo* **86 C2** 3 0 S 26 0 E
Manīfah, *Si. Arabia* **71 E6** 27 44N 49 0 E
Manifold, C., *Australia* **94 C5** 22 41 S 150 50 E
Maniganggo, *China* **58 B2** 31 56N 99 10 E
Manigotagan, *Canada* **105 C9** 51 6N 96 18W
Manigotagan →, *Canada* **105 C9** 51 7N 96 20W
Manihari, *India* **69 G12** 25 21N 87 38 E
Manihiki, *Cook Is.* **97 J11** 10 24 S 161 1W
Manika, Plateau de la, *Dem. Rep. of the Congo* **87 E2** 10 0 S 25 5 E
Manikpur, *India* **69 G9** 25 4N 81 7 E
Manila, *Phil.* **61 D4** 14 40N 121 3 E
Manila, *U.S.A.* **114 F9** 40 59N 109 43W
Manila B., *Phil.* **61 D4** 14 40N 120 35 E
Manilla, *Australia* **95 E5** 30 45 S 150 43 E
Manimpé, *Mali* **82 C3** 14 11N 5 28W
Maningrida, *Australia* **94 A1** 12 3 S 134 13 E
Maninian, *Ivory C.* **82 C3** 10 3N 7 52W
Manipur □, *India* **67 G19** 25 0N 94 0 E
Manipur →, *Burma* **67 H19** 23 45N 94 20 E
Manisa, *Turkey* **39 C9** 38 38N 27 30 E
Manisa □, *Turkey* **39 C9** 38 40N 28 0 E
Manistee, *U.S.A.* **108 C2** 44 15N 86 19W
Manistee →, *U.S.A.* **108 C2** 44 15N 86 21W
Manistique, *U.S.A.* **108 C2** 45 57N 86 15W
Manito L., *Canada* **105 C7** 52 43N 109 43W
Manitoba □, *Canada* **105 B9** 55 30N 97 0W
Manitoba, L., *Canada* **105 C9** 51 0N 98 45W
Manitou, *Canada* **105 D9** 49 15N 98 32W
Manitou, L., *Canada* **103 B6** 50 55N 65 17W
Manitou Is., *U.S.A.* **108 C3** 45 8N 86 0W
Manitou Springs, *U.S.A.* **112 F2** 38 52N 104 55W
Manitoulin I., *Canada* **102 C3** 45 40N 82 30W
Manitouwadge, *Canada* **102 C2** 49 8N 85 48W
Manitowoc, *U.S.A.* **108 C2** 44 5N 87 40W
Manizales, *Colombia* **124 B3** 5 5N 75 32W
Manja, *Madag.* **89 C7** 21 26 S 44 20 E
Manjacaze, *Mozam.* **89 C5** 24 45 S 34 0 E
Manjakandriana, *Madag.* **89 B8** 18 55 S 47 47 E
Manjhand, *Pakistan* **68 G3** 25 50N 68 10 E
Manjil, *Iran* **71 B6** 36 46N 49 30 E
Manjimup, *Australia* **93 F2** 34 15 S 116 6 E
Manjra →, *India* **66 K10** 18 49N 77 52 E
Mankato, *Kans., U.S.A.* **112 F5** 39 47N 98 13W
Mankato, *Minn., U.S.A.* **112 C8** 44 10N 94 0W
Mankayane, *Swaziland* **89 D5** 26 40 S 31 4 E
Mankera, *Pakistan* **68 D4** 31 23N 71 26 E
Mankim, *Cameroon* **83 D7** 5 6N 12 3 E
Mankono, *Ivory C.* **82 D3** 8 1N 6 10W
Mankota, *Canada* **105 D7** 49 25N 107 5W
Manlay = Üydzin, *Mongolia* **56 B4** 44 9N 107 0 E
Manlleu, *Spain* **32 C7** 42 2N 2 17 E
Manmad, *India* **66 J9** 20 18N 74 28 E
Mann Ranges, *Australia* **93 E5** 26 6 S 130 5 E
Manna, *Indonesia* **62 E2** 4 25 S 102 55 E
Mannahill, *Australia* **95 E3** 32 25 S 140 0 E
Mannar, *Sri Lanka* **66 Q11** 9 1N 79 54 E
Mannar, G. of, *Asia* **66 Q11** 8 30N 79 0 E
Mannar I., *Sri Lanka* **66 Q11** 9 5N 79 45 E
Mannheim, *Germany* **25 F4** 49 29N 8 29 E
Manning, *Canada* **104 B5** 56 53N 117 39W
Manning, *Oreg., U.S.A.* **116 E3** 45 45N 123 13W
Manning, *S.C., U.S.A.* **109 J5** 33 42N 80 13W
Manning Prov. Park, *Canada* **104 D4** 49 5N 120 45W
Mannu →, *Italy* **30 C2** 39 16N 9 0 E
Mannu, C., *Italy* **30 B1** 40 3N 8 21 E
Mannum, *Australia* **95 E2** 34 50 S 139 20 E
Mano, *S. Leone* **82 D2** 8 3N 12 2W
Mano →, *Liberia* **82 D2** 6 56N 11 30W
Mano River, *Liberia* **82 D2** 7 20N 11 6W
Manoharpur, *India* **69 H11** 22 23N 85 12 E
Manokwari, *Indonesia* **63 E8** 0 54 S 134 0 E
Manolás, *Greece* **38 C3** 38 4N 21 21 E
Manombo, *Madag.* **89 C7** 22 57 S 43 28 E
Manono, *Dem. Rep. of the Congo* **86 D2** 7 15 S 27 25 E
Manoppello, *Italy* **29 F11** 42 15N 14 3 E
Manosque, *France* **21 E9** 43 49N 5 47 E
Manotick, *Canada* **111 A9** 45 13N 75 41W
Manouane →, *Canada* **103 C5** 49 30N 71 10W
Manouane, L., *Canada* **103 B5** 50 45N 70 45W
Manp'o, *N. Korea* **57 D14** 41 6N 126 24 E
Manpojin = Manp'o, *N. Korea* **57 D14** 41 6N 126 24 E
Manpur, *Mad. P., India* **68 H6** 22 26N 75 37 E
Manpur, *Mad. P., India* **69 H10** 23 17N 83 35 E
Manresa, *Spain* **32 D6** 41 48N 1 50 E
Mansa, *Gujarat, India* **68 H5** 23 27N 72 45 E
Mansa, *Punjab, India* **68 E6** 30 0N 75 27 E
Mansa, *Zambia* **87 E2** 11 13 S 28 55 E
Månsåsen, *Sweden* **10 A8** 63 5N 14 18 E
Mansehra, *Pakistan* **68 B5** 34 20N 73 15 E

Mintabie

Mintabie, *Australia* **95 D1** 27 15 S 133 7 E
Mintaka Pass, *Pakistan* **69 A6** 37 0N 74 58 E
Minto, *Canada* **103 C6** 46 5N 66 5W
Minto, L., *Canada* **102 A5** 57 13N 75 0W
Minton, *Canada* **105 D8** 49 10N 104 35W
Minturn, *U.S.A.* **114 G10** 39 35N 106 26W
Minturno, *Italy* **30 A6** 41 15N 13 45 E
Minûf, *Egypt* **80 H7** 30 26N 30 52 E
Minusinsk, *Russia* **51 D10** 53 43N 91 20 E
Minutang, *India* **67 E20** 28 15N 96 30 E
Minya el Qamh, *Egypt* **80 H7** 30 31N 31 21 E
Mionica, *Bos.-H.* **42 F3** 44 51N 18 29 E
Mionica, *Serbia, Yug.* **40 B4** 44 14N 20 6 E
Miquelon, *Canada* **102 C4** 49 25N 76 27W
Miquelon, *St- P. & M.* **103 C8** 47 8N 56 22W
Mir, *Niger* **83 C7** 14 5N 11 59 E
Mīr Kūh, *Iran* **71 E8** 26 22N 58 55 E
Mīr Shahdād, *Iran* **71 E8** 26 15N 58 29 E
Mira, *Italy* **29 C9** 45 26N 12 8 E
Mira, *Portugal* **34 E2** 40 26N 8 44W
Mira →, *Portugal* **35 H2** 37 43N 8 47W
Mira por vos Cay, *Bahamas* **121 B5** 22 9N 74 30W
Mirabella Eclano, *Italy* **31 A7** 41 2N 14 59 E
Miraj, *India* **66 L9** 16 50N 74 45 E
Miram Shah, *Pakistan* **68 C4** 33 0N 70 2 E
Miramar, *Argentina* **126 D4** 38 15 S 57 50W
Miramar, *Mozam.* **89 C6** 23 50 S 35 35 E
Miramas, *France* **21 E8** 43 33N 4 59 E
Mirambeau, *France* **20 C3** 45 23N 0 35W
Miramichi, *Canada* **103 C6** 47 2N 65 28W
Miramichi B., *Canada* **103 C7** 47 15N 65 0W
Miramont-de-Guyenne, *France* **20 D4** 44 37N 0 21 E
Miranda, *Brazil* **125 H7** 20 10 S 56 15W
Miranda →, *Brazil* **124 G7** 19 25 S 57 20W
Miranda de Ebro, *Spain* **32 C2** 42 41N 2 57W
Miranda do Corvo, *Portugal* **34 E2** 40 6N 8 20W
Miranda do Douro, *Portugal* **34 D4** 41 30N 6 16W
Mirande, *France* **20 E4** 43 31N 0 25 E
Mirandela, *Portugal* **34 D3** 41 32N 7 10W
Mirándola, *Italy* **28 D8** 44 53N 11 4 E
Mirandópolis, *Brazil* **127 A5** 21 9 S 51 6W
Mirango, *Malawi* **87 E3** 13 32 S 34 58 E
Mirano, *Italy* **29 C9** 45 30N 12 7 E
Miras, *Albania* **40 F4** 40 30N 20 56 E
Mirassol, *Brazil* **127 A6** 20 46 S 49 28W
Mirbāţ, *Oman* **74 D5** 17 0N 54 45 E
Mirear, *Egypt* **80 C4** 23 15N 35 41 E
Mirebeau, *Côte-d'Or, France* **19 E12** 47 25N 5 20 E
Mirebeau, *Vienne, France* **18 F7** 46 49N 0 10 E
Mirecourt, *France* **19 D13** 48 20N 6 10 E
Mirgorod = Myrhorod, *Ukraine* **47 H7** 49 58N 33 37 E
Miri, *Malaysia* **62 D4** 4 23N 113 59 E
Miriam Vale, *Australia* **94 C5** 24 20 S 151 33 E
Miribel, *France* **19 G11** 45 50N 4 57 E
Mirim, L., *S. Amer.* **127 C5** 32 45 S 52 50W
Mirnyy, *Russia* **51 C12** 62 33N 113 53 E
Miroč, *Serbia, Yug.* **40 B6** 44 32N 22 16 E
Mirokhan, *Pakistan* **68 F3** 27 46N 68 6 E
Mirond L., *Canada* **105 B8** 55 6N 102 47W
Mirosławiec, *Poland* **44 E3** 53 20N 16 5 E
Mirpur, *Pakistan* **69 C5** 33 32N 73 56 E
Mirpur Batoro, *Pakistan* **68 G3** 24 44N 68 16 E
Mirpur Bibiwari, *Pakistan* **68 E2** 28 33N 67 44 E
Mirpur Khas, *Pakistan* **68 G3** 25 30N 69 0 E
Mirpur Sakro, *Pakistan* **68 G2** 24 33N 67 41 E
Mirria, *Niger* **83 C6** 13 43N 9 7 E
Mirsk, *Poland* **45 H2** 50 58N 15 23 E
Mirtağ, *Turkey* **70 B4** 38 23N 41 56 E
Miryang, *S. Korea* **57 G15** 35 31N 128 44 E
Mirzaani, *Georgia* **49 K8** 41 24N 46 5 E
Mirzapur, *India* **69 G10** 25 10N 82 34 E
Mirzapur-cum-Vindhyachal = Mirzapur, *India* **69 G10** 25 10N 82 34 E
Misantla, *Mexico* **119 D5** 19 56N 96 50W
Misawa, *Japan* **54 D10** 40 41N 141 24 E
Miscou I., *Canada* **103 C7** 47 57N 64 31W
Mish'āb, Ra's al, *Si. Arabia* **71 D6** 28 15N 48 43 E
Mishan, *China* **60 B8** 45 37N 131 48 E
Mishawaka, *U.S.A.* **108 E2** 41 40N 86 11W
Mishbih, Gebel, *Egypt* **80 C3** 22 38N 34 44 E
Mishima, *Japan* **55 G9** 35 10N 138 52 E
Misión, *Mexico* **117 N10** 32 6N 116 53W
Misiones □, *Argentina* **127 B5** 27 0 S 55 0W
Misiones □, *Paraguay* **126 B4** 27 0 S 56 0W
Miskah, *Si. Arabia* **70 E4** 24 49N 42 56 E
Miskitos, Cayos, *Nic.* **120 D3** 14 26N 82 50W
Miskolc, *Hungary* **42 B5** 48 7N 20 50 E
Misoke, *Dem. Rep. of the Congo* **86 C2** 0 42 S 28 2 E
Misool, *Indonesia* **63 E8** 1 52 S 130 10 E
Mişrātah, *Libya* **79 B9** 32 24N 15 3 E
Missanabie, *Canada* **102 C3** 48 20N 84 6W
Missinaibi →, *Canada* **102 B3** 50 43N 81 29W
Missinaibi L., *Canada* **102 C3** 48 23N 83 40W
Mission, *Canada* **104 D4** 49 10N 122 15W
Mission, *S. Dak., U.S.A.* **112 D4** 43 18N 100 39W
Mission, *Tex., U.S.A.* **113 M5** 26 13N 98 20W
Mission Beach, *Australia* **94 B4** 17 53 S 146 6 E
Mission Viejo, *U.S.A.* **117 M9** 33 36N 117 40W
Missirah, *Senegal* **82 C1** 13 40N 16 30W
Missisa L., *Canada* **102 B2** 52 20N 85 7W
Missisicabi →, *Canada* **102 B4** 51 14N 79 31W
Mississagi →, *Canada* **102 C3** 46 15N 83 9W
Mississauga, *Canada* **110 C5** 43 32N 79 35W
Mississippi □, *U.S.A.* **113 J10** 33 0N 90 0W
Mississippi →, *U.S.A.* **113 L10** 29 9N 89 15W
Mississippi L., *Canada* **111 A8** 45 5N 76 10W
Mississippi River Delta, *U.S.A.* **113 L9** 29 10N 89 15W
Mississippi Sd., *U.S.A.* **113 K10** 30 20N 89 0W
Missoula, *U.S.A.* **114 C7** 46 52N 114 1W
Missouri □, *U.S.A.* **112 F8** 38 25N 92 30W
Missouri →, *U.S.A.* **112 F9** 38 49N 90 7W
Missouri City, *U.S.A.* **113 L7** 29 37N 95 32W
Missouri Valley, *U.S.A.* **112 E7** 41 34N 95 53W
Mist, *U.S.A.* **116 E3** 45 59N 123 15W
Mistassibi →, *Canada* **103 B5** 48 53N 72 13W
Mistassini, *Canada* **103 C5** 48 53N 72 12W
Mistassini →, *Canada* **103 C5** 48 42N 72 20W
Mistassini, L., *Canada* **102 B5** 51 0N 73 30W
Mistastin L., *Canada* **103 A7** 55 57N 63 20W
Mistelbach, *Austria* **27 C9** 48 34N 16 34 E
Misterbianco, *Italy* **31 E8** 37 31N 15 1 E
Mistinibi, L., *Canada* **103 A7** 55 56N 64 17W
Mistretta, *Italy* **31 E7** 37 56N 14 22 E
Misty L., *Canada* **105 B8** 58 53N 101 40W
Misurata = Mişrātah, *Libya* **79 B9** 32 24N 15 3 E
Mît Ghamr, *Egypt* **80 H7** 30 42N 31 12 E
Mitatib, *Sudan* **81 D4** 15 59N 36 12 E
Mitchell, *Australia* **95 D4** 26 29 S 147 58 E
Mitchell, *Canada* **110 C3** 43 28N 81 12W
Mitchell, *Nebr., U.S.A.* **112 E3** 41 57N 103 49W
Mitchell, *Oreg., U.S.A.* **114 D3** 44 34N 120 9W
Mitchell, *S. Dak., U.S.A.* **112 D6** 43 43N 98 2W
Mitchell →, *Australia* **94 B3** 15 12 S 141 35 E
Mitchell, Mt., *U.S.A.* **109 H4** 35 46N 82 16W
Mitchell Ranges, *Australia* **94 A2** 12 49 S 135 36 E
Mitchelstown, *Ireland* **15 D3** 52 15N 8 16W
Mitha Tiwana, *Pakistan* **68 C5** 32 13N 72 6 E
Mithi, *Pakistan* **68 G3** 24 44N 69 48 E
Míthimna, *Greece* **39 B8** 39 20N 26 12 E
Mithrao, *Pakistan* **68 F3** 27 28N 69 40 E
Mitilíni, *Greece* **39 B8** 39 6N 26 35 E
Mitilinoí, *Greece* **39 D8** 37 42N 26 56 E
Mito, *Japan* **55 F10** 36 20N 140 30 E
Mitrofanovka, *Russia* **47 H10** 49 58N 39 42 E
Mitrovica = Kosovska Mitrovica, *Kosovo, Yug.* **40 D4** 42 54N 20 52 E
Mitsinjo, *Madag.* **89 B8** 16 1 S 45 52 E
Mitsiwa, *Eritrea* **81 D4** 15 35N 39 25 E
Mitsiwa Channel, *Eritrea* **81 D5** 15 30N 40 0 E
Mitsukaidō, *Japan* **55 F9** 36 1N 139 59 E
Mittagong, *Australia* **95 E5** 34 28 S 150 29 E
Mittelberg, *Austria* **26 D3** 47 20N 10 10 E
Mittelfranken □, *Germany* **25 F6** 49 25N 10 40 E
Mittellandkanal →, *Germany* **24 C4** 52 20N 8 28 E
Mittenwalde, *Germany* **24 C9** 52 15N 13 31 E
Mittersill, *Austria* **26 D5** 47 16N 12 29 E
Mitterteich, *Germany* **25 F8** 49 57N 12 14 E
Mittimatalik = Pond Inlet, *Canada* **101 A12** 72 40N 77 0W
Mittweida, *Germany* **24 E8** 50 59N 12 59 E
Mitú, *Colombia* **124 C4** 1 15N 70 13W
Mitumba, *Tanzania* **86 D3** 7 8 S 31 2 E
Mitumba, Mts., *Dem. Rep. of the Congo* **86 D2** 7 0 S 27 30 E
Mitwaba, *Dem. Rep. of the Congo* **87 D2** 8 2 S 27 17 E
Mityana, *Uganda* **86 B3** 0 23N 32 2 E
Mixteco →, *Mexico* **119 D5** 18 11N 98 30W
Miyagi □, *Japan* **54 E10** 38 15N 140 45 E
Miyāh, W. el →, *Egypt* **80 C3** 25 0N 33 23 E
Miyāh, W. el →, *Syria* **70 C3** 34 44N 39 57 E
Miyake-Jima, *Japan* **55 G9** 34 5N 139 30 E
Miyako, *Japan* **54 E10** 39 40N 141 59 E
Miyako-Jima, *Japan* **55 M2** 24 45N 125 20 E
Miyako-Rettō, *Japan* **55 M2** 24 24N 125 0 E
Miyakonojō, *Japan* **55 J5** 31 40N 131 5 E
Miyani, *India* **68 J3** 21 50N 69 26 E
Miyanoura-Dake, *Japan* **55 J5** 30 20N 130 31 E
Miyazaki, *Japan* **55 J5** 31 56N 131 30 E
Miyazaki □, *Japan* **55 H5** 32 30N 131 30 E
Miyazu, *Japan* **55 G7** 35 35N 135 10 E
Miyet, Bahr el = Dead Sea, *Asia* **75 D4** 31 30N 35 30 E
Miyi, *China* **58 D4** 26 47N 102 9 E
Miyoshi, *Japan* **55 G6** 34 48N 132 51 E
Miyun, *China* **56 D9** 40 28N 116 50 E
Miyun Shuiku, *China* **57 D9** 40 30N 117 0 E
Mizan Teferi, *Ethiopia* **81 F4** 6 57N 35 3 E
Mizdah, *Libya* **79 B8** 31 30N 13 0 E
Mizen Hd., *Cork, Ireland* **15 E2** 51 27N 9 50W
Mizen Hd., *Wick., Ireland* **15 D5** 52 51N 6 4W
Mizhi, *China* **56 F6** 37 47N 110 12 E
Mizil, *Romania* **43 F11** 44 59N 26 29 E
Mizoram □, *India* **67 H18** 23 30N 92 40 E
Mizpe Ramon, *Israel* **75 E3** 30 34N 34 49 E
Mizusawa, *Japan* **54 E10** 39 8N 141 8 E
Mjällby, *Sweden* **11 H8** 56 3N 14 40 E
Mjöbäck, *Sweden* **11 G6** 57 28N 12 53 E
Mjölby, *Sweden* **11 F9** 58 20N 15 10 E
Mjörn, *Sweden* **11 G6** 57 55N 12 25 E
Mjøsa, *Norway* **9 F14** 60 40N 11 0 E
Mkata, *Tanzania* **86 D4** 5 45 S 38 20 E
Mkokotoni, *Tanzania* **86 D4** 5 55 S 39 15 E
Mkomazi, *Tanzania* **86 C4** 4 40 S 38 7 E
Mkomazi →, *S. Africa* **89 E5** 30 12 S 30 50 E
Mkulwe, *Tanzania* **87 D3** 8 37 S 32 20 E
Mkumbi, Ras, *Tanzania* **86 D4** 7 38 S 39 55 E
Mkushi, *Zambia* **87 E2** 14 25 S 29 15 E
Mkushi River, *Zambia* **87 E2** 13 32 S 29 45 E
Mkuze, *S. Africa* **89 D5** 27 10 S 32 0 E
Mladá Boleslav, *Czech Rep.* **26 A7** 50 27N 14 53 E
Mladenovac, *Serbia, Yug.* **40 B4** 44 28N 20 44 E
Mlala Hills, *Tanzania* **86 D3** 6 50 S 31 40 E
Mlange = Mulanje, *Malawi* **87 F4** 16 2 S 35 33 E
Mlanje, Pic, *Malawi* **85 H7** 15 57 S 35 38 E
Mlava →, *Serbia, Yug.* **40 B5** 44 45N 21 13 E
Mława, *Poland* **45 E7** 53 9N 20 25 E
Mlinište, *Bos.-H.* **29 D13** 44 15N 16 50 E
Mljet, *Croatia* **29 F14** 42 43N 17 30 E
Mljetski Kanal, *Croatia* **29 F14** 42 48N 17 35 E
Młynary, *Poland* **44 D6** 54 12N 19 46 E
Mmabatho, *S. Africa* **88 D4** 25 49 S 25 30 E
Mme, *Cameroon* **83 D7** 6 18N 10 14 E
Mnichovo Hradiště, *Czech Rep.* **26 A7** 50 32N 14 59 E
Mo i Rana, *Norway* **8 C16** 66 20N 14 7 E
Moa, *Cuba* **121 B4** 20 40N 74 56W
Moa, *Indonesia* **63 F7** 8 0 S 128 0 E
Moa →, *S. Leone* **82 D2** 6 59N 11 36W
Moab, *U.S.A.* **115 G9** 38 35N 109 33W
Moala, *Fiji* **91 D8** 18 36 S 179 53 E
Moama, *Australia* **95 F3** 36 7 S 144 46 E
Moamba, *Mozam.* **89 D5** 25 36 S 32 15 E
Moapa, *U.S.A.* **117 J12** 36 40N 114 37W
Moate, *Ireland* **15 C4** 53 24N 7 44W
Moba, *Dem. Rep. of the Congo* **86 D2** 7 0 S 29 48 E
Mobārakābād, *Iran* **71 D7** 28 24N 53 20 E
Mobaye, *C.A.R.* **84 D4** 4 25N 21 5 E
Mobayi, *Dem. Rep. of the Congo* **84 D4** 4 15N 21 8 E
Moberley Lake, *Canada* **104 B4** 55 50N 121 44W
Moberly, *U.S.A.* **112 F8** 39 25N 92 26W
Mobile, *U.S.A.* **109 K1** 30 41N 88 3W
Mobile B., *U.S.A.* **109 K2** 30 30N 88 0W
Mobridge, *U.S.A.* **112 C4** 45 32N 100 26W
Mobutu Sese Seko, L. = Albert, L., *Africa* **86 B3** 1 30N 31 0 E
Moc Chau, *Vietnam* **64 B5** 20 50N 104 38 E
Moc Hoa, *Vietnam* **65 G5** 10 46N 105 56 E
Mocabe Kasari, *Dem. Rep. of the Congo* **87 D2** 9 58 S 26 12 E
Moçambique, *Mozam.* **87 F5** 15 3 S 40 42 E
Moçâmedes = Namibe, *Angola* **85 H2** 15 7 S 12 11 E
Mocanaqua, *U.S.A.* **111 E8** 41 9N 76 8W
Mochudi, *Botswana* **88 C4** 24 27 S 26 7 E
Mocimboa da Praia, *Mozam.* **87 E5** 11 25 S 40 20 E
Mociu, *Romania* **43 D9** 46 46N 24 3 E
Möckeln, *Sweden* **11 H8** 56 40N 14 15 E
Mockfjärd, *Sweden* **10 D8** 60 30N 14 57 E
Moclips, *U.S.A.* **116 C2** 47 14N 124 13W
Mocoa, *Colombia* **124 C3** 1 7N 76 35W
Mococa, *Brazil* **127 A6** 21 28 S 47 0W
Mocorito, *Mexico* **118 B3** 25 30N 107 53W
Moctezuma, *Mexico* **118 B3** 29 50N 109 0W
Moctezuma →, *Mexico* **119 C5** 21 59N 98 34W
Mocuba, *Mozam.* **87 F4** 16 54 S 36 57 E
Mocúzari, Presa, *Mexico* **118 B3** 27 10N 109 10W
Modane, *France* **21 C10** 45 12N 6 40 E
Modasa, *India* **68 H5** 23 30N 73 21 E
Modder →, *S. Africa* **88 D3** 29 2 S 24 37 E
Modderrivier, *S. Africa* **88 D3** 29 2 S 24 38 E
Módena, *Italy* **28 D7** 44 40N 10 55 E
Modena, *U.S.A.* **115 H7** 37 48N 113 56W
Modesto, *U.S.A.* **116 H6** 37 39N 121 0W
Módica, *Italy* **31 F7** 36 52N 14 46 E
Mödling, *Austria* **27 C9** 48 5N 16 17 E
Modo, *Sudan* **81 F3** 5 31N 30 33 E
Modra, *Slovak Rep.* **27 C10** 48 19N 17 20 E
Modriča, *Bos.-H.* **42 F3** 44 57N 18 17 E
Moe, *Australia* **95 F4** 38 12 S 146 19 E
Moebase, *Mozam.* **87 F4** 17 3 S 38 41 E
Moëlan-sur-Mer, *France* **18 E3** 47 49N 3 38W
Moengo, *Suriname* **125 B8** 5 45N 54 20W
Moffat, *U.K.* **14 F5** 55 21N 3 27W
Moga, *India* **68 D6** 30 48N 75 8 E
Mogadishu = Muqdisho, *Somali Rep.* **74 G4** 2 2N 45 25 E
Mogador = Essaouira, *Morocco* **78 B4** 31 32N 9 42W
Mogadouro, *Portugal* **34 D4** 41 22N 6 47W
Mogalakwena →, *S. Africa* **89 C4** 22 38 S 28 40 E
Mogami-Gawa →, *Japan* **54 E10** 38 45N 140 0 E
Mogán, *Canary Is.* **37 G4** 27 53N 15 43W
Mogaung, *Burma* **67 G20** 25 20N 97 0 E
Mogente = Moixent, *Spain* **33 G4** 38 52N 0 45W
Mogho, *Ethiopia* **81 G5** 4 54N 40 16 E
Mogi das Cruzes, *Brazil* **127 A6** 23 31 S 46 11W
Mogi-Guaçu →, *Brazil* **127 A6** 20 53 S 48 10W
Mogi-Mirim, *Brazil* **127 A6** 22 29 S 47 0W
Mogielnica, *Poland* **45 G7** 51 42N 20 41 E
Mogige, *Ethiopia* **81 F4** 5 24N 36 14 E
Mogilev = Mahilyow, *Belarus* **46 F6** 53 55N 30 18 E
Mogilev-Podolskiy = Mohyliv-Podilskyy, *Ukraine* **47 H4** 48 26N 27 48 E
Mogilno, *Poland* **45 F4** 52 39N 17 55 E
Mogincual, *Mozam.* **87 F5** 15 35 S 40 25 E
Mogliano Véneto, *Italy* **29 C9** 45 33N 12 14 E
Mogocha, *Russia* **51 D12** 53 40N 119 50 E
Mogok, *Burma* **67 H20** 23 0N 96 40 E
Mogollon Rim, *U.S.A.* **115 J8** 34 10N 110 50W
Mógoro, *Italy* **30 C1** 39 41N 8 47 E
Mograt, *Sudan* **80 D3** 19 28N 33 16 E
Moguer, *Spain* **35 H4** 37 15N 6 52W
Mogumber, *Australia* **93 F2** 31 2 S 116 3 E
Mohács, *Hungary* **42 E3** 45 58N 18 41 E
Mohales Hoek, *Lesotho* **88 E4** 30 7 S 27 26 E
Mohall, *U.S.A.* **112 A4** 48 46N 101 31W
Moḥammadābād, *Iran* **71 B8** 37 52N 59 5 E
Mohammedia, *Morocco* **78 B4** 33 44N 7 21W
Mohana →, *India* **69 G11** 24 43N 85 0 E
Mohanlalganj, *India* **69 F9** 26 41N 80 58 E
Mohave, L., *U.S.A.* **117 K12** 35 12N 114 34W
Mohawk →, *U.S.A.* **111 D11** 42 47N 73 41W
Moheda, *Sweden* **11 G8** 57 1N 14 35 E
Mohenjodaro, *Pakistan* **68 F3** 27 19N 68 7 E
Mohicanville Reservoir, *U.S.A.* **110 F3** 40 45N 82 0W
Möhne →, *Germany* **24 D3** 51 29N 7 57 E
Mohoro, *Tanzania* **86 D4** 8 6 S 39 8 E
Mohyliv-Podilskyy, *Ukraine* **47 H4** 48 26N 27 48 E
Moia, *Sudan* **81 F2** 5 3N 28 2 E
Moidart, L., *U.K.* **14 E3** 56 47N 5 52W
Moinești, *Romania* **43 D11** 46 28N 26 31 E
Moira →, *Canada* **110 B7** 44 21N 77 24W
Moirans, *France* **21 C9** 45 20N 5 33 E
Moirans-en-Montagne, *France* **19 F12** 46 26N 5 43 E
Moíres, *Greece* **36 D6** 35 4N 24 56 E
Moisaküla, *Estonia* **9 G21** 58 3N 25 12 E
Moisie, *Canada* **103 B6** 50 12N 66 1W
Moisie →, *Canada* **103 B6** 50 14N 66 5W
Moissac, *France* **20 D5** 44 7N 1 5 E
Moita, *Portugal* **35 G2** 38 38N 8 58W
Moixent, *Spain* **33 G4** 38 52N 0 45W
Möja, *Sweden* **10 E12** 59 26N 18 55 E
Mojácar, *Spain* **33 H3** 37 6N 1 55W
Mojados, *Spain* **34 D6** 41 26N 4 40W
Mojave, *U.S.A.* **117 K8** 35 3N 118 10W
Mojave Desert, *U.S.A.* **117 L10** 35 0N 116 30W
Mojiang, *China* **58 F3** 23 37N 101 35 E
Mojjo →, *Ethiopia* **81 F5** 7 55N 42 0 E
Mojkovac, *Montenegro, Yug.* **40 D3** 42 58N 19 35 E
Mojo, *Bolivia* **126 A2** 21 48 S 65 33W
Mojo, *Ethiopia* **81 F4** 8 35N 39 5 E
Mojokerto, *Indonesia* **63 G15** 7 28 S 112 26 E
Mokai, *N.Z.* **91 H5** 38 32 S 175 56 E
Mokambo, *Dem. Rep. of the Congo* **87 E2** 12 25 S 28 20 E
Mokameh, *India* **69 G11** 25 24N 85 55 E
Mokau, *N.Z.* **91 H5** 38 42 S 174 39 E
Mokelumne →, *U.S.A.* **116 G5** 38 13N 121 28W
Mokelumne Hill, *U.S.A.* **116 G6** 38 18N 120 43W
Mokhós, *Greece* **36 D7** 35 16N 25 27 E
Mokhotlong, *Lesotho* **89 D4** 29 22 S 29 2 E
Möklinta, *Sweden* **10 D10** 60 4N 16 33 E
Mokokchung, *India* **67 F19** 26 15N 94 30 E
Mokolo, *Cameroon* **83 C7** 10 50N 13 55 E
Mokolo →, *S. Africa* **89 C4** 23 14 S 27 43 E
Mokp'o, *S. Korea* **57 G14** 34 50N 126 25 E
Mokra Gora, *Yugoslavia* **40 D4** 42 50N 20 30 E
Mokronog, *Slovenia* **29 C12** 45 57N 15 9 E
Moksha →, *Russia* **48 C6** 54 45N 41 53 E
Mokshan, *Russia* **48 D7** 53 25N 44 35 E
Mokwa, *Nigeria* **83 D6** 9 19N 5 0 E
Mol, *Belgium* **17 C5** 51 11N 5 5 E
Mola di Bari, *Italy* **31 A10** 41 4N 17 5 E
Molale, *Ethiopia* **81 E4** 10 10N 39 41 E
Moláoi, *Greece* **38 E4** 36 49N 22 56 E
Molara, *Italy* **30 B2** 40 52N 9 43 E
Molat, *Croatia* **29 D11** 44 15N 14 50 E
Molchanovo, *Russia* **50 D9** 57 40N 83 50 E
Mold, *U.K.* **12 D4** 53 9N 3 8W
Moldava nad Bodvou, *Slovak Rep.* **27 C14** 48 38N 21 0 E
Moldavia = Moldova ■, *Europe* **43 C13** 47 0N 28 0 E
Moldavia, *Romania* **43 D12** 46 30N 27 0 E
Molde, *Norway* **8 E12** 62 45N 7 9 E
Moldova ■, *Europe* **43 C13** 47 0N 28 0 E
Moldova Nouă, *Romania* **42 F6** 44 45N 21 41 E
Moldoveanu, Vf., *Romania* **43 E9** 45 36N 24 45 E
Moldoviţa, *Romania* **43 C10** 47 41N 25 32 E
Mole →, *U.K.* **13 F7** 51 24N 0 21W
Mole Creek, *Australia* **94 G4** 41 34 S 146 24 E
Molepolole, *Botswana* **88 C4** 24 28 S 25 28 E
Molfetta, *Italy* **31 A9** 41 12N 16 36 E
Molina de Aragón, *Spain* **32 E3** 40 46N 1 52W
Molina de Segura, *Spain* **33 G3** 38 3N 1 12W
Moline, *U.S.A.* **112 E9** 41 30N 90 31W
Molinella, *Italy* **29 D8** 44 37N 11 40 E
Molinos, *Argentina* **126 B2** 25 28 S 66 15W
Moliro, *Dem. Rep. of the Congo* **86 D3** 8 12 S 30 30 E
Moliterno, *Italy* **31 B8** 40 14N 15 52 E
Molkom, *Sweden* **10 E7** 59 37N 13 44 E
Mölle, *Sweden* **11 H6** 56 17N 12 31 E
Molledo, *Spain* **34 B6** 43 8N 4 6W
Mollendo, *Peru* **124 G4** 17 0 S 72 0W
Mollerin, L., *Australia* **93 F2** 30 30 S 117 35 E
Mollerussa, *Spain* **32 D5** 41 37N 0 54 E
Mollina, *Spain* **35 H6** 37 8N 4 38W
Mölln, *Germany* **24 B6** 53 39N 10 32 E
Mölltorp, *Sweden* **11 F8** 58 30N 14 26 E
Mölnlycke, *Sweden* **11 G6** 57 40N 12 8 E
Molochansk, *Ukraine* **47 J8** 47 15N 35 35 E
Molochnoye, Ozero, *Ukraine* **47 J8** 46 30N 35 20 E
Molodechno = Maladzyechna, *Belarus* **46 E4** 54 20N 26 50 E
Molokai, *U.S.A.* **106 H16** 21 8N 157 0W
Molong, *Australia* **95 E4** 33 5 S 148 54 E
Molopo →, *Africa* **88 D3** 27 30 S 20 13 E
Mólos, *Greece* **38 C4** 38 47N 22 37 E
Molotov = Perm, *Russia* **50 D6** 58 0N 56 10 E
Molsheim, *France* **19 D14** 48 33N 7 29 E
Molson L., *Canada* **105 C9** 54 22N 96 40W
Molteno, *S. Africa* **88 E4** 31 22 S 26 22 E
Molu, *Indonesia* **63 F8** 6 45 S 131 40 E
Molucca Sea, *Indonesia* **63 E6** 0 0 125 0 E
Moluccas = Maluku, *Indonesia* **63 E7** 1 0 S 127 0 E
Moma, *Dem. Rep. of the Congo* **86 C1** 1 35 S 23 52 E
Moma, *Mozam.* **87 F4** 16 47 S 39 4 E
Mombasa, *Kenya* **86 C4** 4 2 S 39 43 E
Mombetsu, *Japan* **54 B11** 44 21N 143 22 E
Mombuey, *Spain* **34 C4** 42 3N 6 20W
Momchilgrad, *Bulgaria* **41 E9** 41 33N 25 23 E
Momi, *Dem. Rep. of the Congo* **86 C2** 1 42 S 27 0 E
Mompós, *Colombia* **124 B4** 9 14N 74 26W
Møn, *Denmark* **11 K6** 54 57N 12 20 E
Mon □, *Burma* **67 L20** 16 0N 97 30 E
Mona, Canal de la, *W. Indies* **121 C6** 18 30N 67 45W
Mona, Isla, *Puerto Rico* **121 C6** 18 5N 67 54W
Mona, Pta., *Costa Rica* **120 E3** 9 37N 82 36W
Monaca, *U.S.A.* **110 F4** 40 41N 80 17W
Monaco ■, *Europe* **21 E11** 43 46N 7 23 E
Monadhliath Mts., *U.K.* **14 D4** 57 10N 4 4W
Monadnock, Mt., *U.S.A.* **111 D12** 42 52N 72 7W
Monaghan, *Ireland* **15 B5** 54 15N 6 57W
Monaghan □, *Ireland* **15 B5** 54 11N 6 56W
Monahans, *U.S.A.* **113 K3** 31 36N 102 54W
Monapo, *Mozam.* **87 E5** 14 56 S 40 19 E
Monar, L., *U.K.* **14 D3** 57 26N 5 8W
Monarch Mt., *Canada* **104 C3** 51 55N 125 57W
Monashee Mts., *Canada* **104 C5** 51 0N 118 43W
Monasterevin, *Ireland* **15 C4** 53 8N 7 4W
Monastir = Bitola, *Macedonia* **40 E5** 41 1N 21 20 E
Moncada, *Phil.* **61 D4** 15 44N 120 34 E
Moncalieri, *Italy* **28 D4** 45 0N 7 41 E
Moncalvo, *Italy* **28 C5** 45 3N 8 16 E
Monção, *Portugal* **34 C2** 42 4N 8 27W
Moncarapacho, *Portugal* **35 H3** 37 5N 7 46W
Moncayo, Sierra del, *Spain* **32 D3** 41 48N 1 50W
Mönchengladbach, *Germany* **24 D2** 51 11N 6 27 E
Monchique, *Portugal* **35 H2** 37 19N 8 38W
Moncks Corner, *U.S.A.* **109 J5** 33 12N 80 1W
Monclova, *Mexico* **118 B4** 26 50N 101 30W
Moncontour, *France* **18 D4** 48 22N 2 38W
Moncton, *Canada* **103 C7** 46 7N 64 51W
Mondariz, *Spain* **34 C2** 42 14N 8 27W
Mondego →, *Portugal* **34 E2** 40 9N 8 52W
Mondego, C., *Portugal* **34 E2** 40 11N 8 54W
Mondeodo, *Indonesia* **63 E6** 3 34 S 122 9 E
Mondeville, *France* **18 C6** 49 10N 0 18W
Mondolfo, *Italy* **29 E10** 43 45N 13 6 E
Mondoñedo, *Spain* **34 B3** 43 25N 7 23W
Mondovì, *Italy* **28 D4** 44 23N 7 49 E
Mondragon, *Phil.* **61 E6** 12 31N 124 45 E
Mondragone, *Italy* **30 A6** 41 7N 13 53 E
Mondrain I., *Australia* **93 F3** 34 9 S 122 14 E
Monemvasía, *Greece* **38 E5** 36 41N 23 3 E
Monessen, *U.S.A.* **110 F5** 40 9N 79 54W
Monesterio, *Spain* **35 G4** 38 6N 6 15W
Monestier-de-Clermont, *France* **21 D9** 44 55N 5 38 E
Monett, *U.S.A.* **113 G8** 36 55N 93 55W
Moneymore, *U.K.* **15 B5** 54 41N 6 40W
Monfalcone, *Italy* **29 C10** 45 49N 13 32 E
Monflanquin, *France* **20 D4** 44 32N 0 47 E
Monforte, *Portugal* **35 F3** 39 6N 7 25W
Monforte de Lemos, *Spain* **34 C3** 42 31N 7 33W
Mong Hsu, *Burma* **58 G2** 21 54N 98 30 E
Mong Kung, *Burma* **67 J20** 21 35N 97 35 E
Mong Nai, *Burma* **67 J20** 20 32N 97 46 E
Mong Pawk, *Burma* **67 H21** 22 4N 99 16 E
Mong Ping, *Burma* **58 G2** 21 22N 99 2 E
Mong Ton, *Burma* **67 J21** 20 17N 98 45 E
Mong Wa, *Burma* **67 J22** 21 26N 100 27 E
Mong Yai, *Burma* **67 H21** 22 21N 98 3 E
Mongalla, *Sudan* **81 F3** 5 8N 31 42 E
Mongers, L., *Australia* **93 E2** 29 25 S 117 5 E
Monghyr = Munger, *India* **69 G12** 25 23N 86 30 E
Mongibello = Etna, *Italy* **31 E7** 37 50N 14 55 E
Mongo, *Chad* **79 F9** 12 14N 18 43 E
Mongo →, *S. Leone* **82 D2** 9 35N 12 10W
Mongolia ■, *Asia* **51 E10** 47 0N 103 0 E
Mongonu, *Nigeria* **83 C7** 12 40N 13 32 E
Mongu, *Zambia* **85 H4** 15 16 S 23 12 E
Môngua, *Angola* **88 B2** 16 43 S 15 20 E
Monifieth, *U.K.* **14 E6** 56 30N 2 48W
Monistrol-sur-Loire, *France* **21 C8** 45 17N 4 11 E
Monkey Bay, *Malawi* **87 E4** 14 7 S 35 1 E
Monkey Mia, *Australia* **93 E1** 25 48 S 113 43 E
Monkey River, *Belize* **119 D7** 16 22N 88 29W
Mońki, *Poland* **44 E9** 53 23N 22 48 E
Monkoto, *Dem. Rep. of the Congo* **84 E4** 1 38 S 20 35 E
Monkton, *Canada* **110 C3** 43 35N 81 5W
Monmouth, *U.K.* **13 F5** 51 48N 2 42W
Monmouth, *Ill., U.S.A.* **112 E9** 40 55N 90 39W
Monmouth, *Oreg., U.S.A.* **114 D2** 44 51N 123 14W
Monmouthshire □, *U.K.* **13 F5** 51 48N 2 54W
Mono L., *U.S.A.* **116 H7** 38 1N 119 1W
Monolith, *U.S.A.* **117 K8** 35 7N 118 22W
Monólithos, *Greece* **36 C9** 36 7N 27 45 E
Monongahela, *U.S.A.* **110 F5** 40 12N 79 56W
Monópoli, *Italy* **31 B10** 40 57N 17 18 E
Monor, *Hungary* **42 C4** 47 21N 19 27 E
Monóvar, *Spain* **33 G4** 38 28N 0 53W
Monreal del Campo, *Spain* **32 E3** 40 47N 1 20W
Monreale, *Italy* **30 D6** 38 5N 13 17 E
Monroe, *Ga., U.S.A.* **109 J4** 33 47N 83 43W
Monroe, *La., U.S.A.* **113 J8** 32 30N 92 7W
Monroe, *Mich., U.S.A.* **108 E4** 41 55N 83 24W
Monroe, *N.C., U.S.A.* **109 H5** 34 59N 80 33W
Monroe, *N.Y., U.S.A.* **111 E10** 41 20N 74 11W
Monroe, *Utah, U.S.A.* **115 G7** 38 38N 112 7W
Monroe, *Wash., U.S.A.* **116 C5** 47 51N 121 58W
Monroe, *Wis., U.S.A.* **112 D10** 42 36N 89 38W
Monroe City, *U.S.A.* **112 F9** 39 39N 91 44W
Monroeton, *U.S.A.* **111 E8** 41 43N 76 29W
Monroeville, *Ala., U.S.A.* **109 K2** 31 31N 87 20W
Monroeville, *Pa., U.S.A.* **110 F5** 40 26N 79 45W
Monrovia, *Liberia* **82 D2** 6 18N 10 47W
Mons, *Belgium* **17 D3** 50 27N 3 58 E
Møns Klint, *Denmark* **11 K6** 54 57N 12 33 E
Monsaraz, *Portugal* **35 G3** 38 28N 7 22W
Monse, *Indonesia* **63 E6** 4 7 S 123 15 E
Monségur, *France* **20 D4** 44 38N 0 4 E
Monsélice, *Italy* **29 C8** 45 14N 11 45 E
Mönsterås, *Sweden* **11 G10** 57 3N 16 26 E
Mont Cenis, Col du, *France* **21 C10** 45 15N 6 55 E
Mont-de-Marsan, *France* **20 E3** 43 54N 0 31W
Mont-Joli, *Canada* **103 C6** 48 37N 68 10W
Mont-Laurier, *Canada* **102 C4** 46 35N 75 30W
Mont-Louis, *Canada* **103 C6** 49 15N 65 44W
Mont-roig del Camp, *Spain* **32 D5** 41 5N 0 58 E
Mont-St-Michel, Le = Le Mont-St-Michel, *France* **18 D5** 48 40N 1 30W
Mont Tremblant, Parc Recr. du, *Canada* **102 C5** 46 30N 74 30W
Montabaur, *Germany* **24 E3** 50 25N 7 50 E
Montagnac, *France* **20 E7** 43 29N 3 28 E
Montagnana, *Italy* **29 C8** 45 14N 11 28 E
Montagu, *S. Africa* **88 E3** 33 45 S 20 8 E
Montagu I., *Antarctica* **5 B1** 58 25 S 26 20W
Montague, *Canada* **103 C7** 46 10N 62 39W
Montague, I., *Mexico* **118 A2** 31 40N 114 56W
Montague Ra., *Australia* **93 E2** 27 15 S 119 30 E
Montague Sd., *Australia* **92 B4** 14 28 S 125 20 E
Montaigu, *France* **18 F5** 46 59N 1 18W
Montalbán, *Spain* **32 E4** 40 50N 0 45W
Montalbano Iónico, *Italy* **31 B9** 40 17N 16 34 E
Montalbo, *Spain* **32 F2** 39 53N 2 42W
Montalcino, *Italy* **29 E8** 43 3N 11 29 E
Montalegre, *Portugal* **34 D3** 41 49N 7 47W
Montalto, *Italy* **31 D8** 38 10N 15 55 E
Montalto di Castro, *Italy* **29 F8** 42 21N 11 37 E
Montalto Uffugo, *Italy* **31 C9** 39 24N 16 9 E
Montalvo, *U.S.A.* **117 L7** 34 15N 119 12W
Montamarta, *Spain* **34 D5** 41 39N 5 49W
Montana, *Bulgaria* **40 C7** 43 27N 23 16 E
Montaña, *Peru* **124 E4** 6 0 S 73 0W
Montana □, *Bulgaria* **40 C7** 43 30N 23 20 E
Montana □, *U.S.A.* **114 C9** 47 0N 110 0W
Montaña Clara, I., *Canary Is.* **37 E6** 29 17N 13 33W
Montánchez, *Spain* **35 F4** 39 15N 6 8W
Montargil, *Portugal* **35 F2** 39 5N 8 10W
Montargis, *France* **19 E9** 47 59N 2 43 E
Montauban, *France* **20 D5** 44 2N 1 21 E
Montauk, *U.S.A.* **111 E13** 41 3N 71 57W
Montauk Pt., *U.S.A.* **111 E13** 41 4N 71 52W
Montbard, *France* **19 E11** 47 38N 4 20 E
Montbarrey, *France* **19 E13** 47 1N 5 39 E
Montbéliard, *France* **19 E13** 47 31N 6 48 E

Mount Robson Prov. Park

Mount Robson Prov. Park, Canada 104 C5 53 0N 119 0W
Mount Selinda, Zimbabwe 89 C5 20 24 S 32 43 E
Mount Shasta, U.S.A. 114 F2 41 19N 122 19W
Mount Signal, U.S.A. 117 N11 32 39N 115 37W
Mount Sterling, Ill., U.S.A. 112 F9 39 59N 90 45W
Mount Sterling, Ky., U.S.A. 108 F4 38 4N 83 56W
Mount Surprise, Australia 94 B3 18 10 S 144 17 E
Mount Union, U.S.A. 110 F7 40 23N 77 53W
Mount Upton, U.S.A. 111 D9 42 26N 75 23W
Mount Vernon, Ill., U.S.A. 108 F1 38 19N 88 55W
Mount Vernon, Ind., U.S.A. 112 F10 38 17N 88 57W
Mount Vernon, N.Y., U.S.A. 111 F11 40 55N 73 50W
Mount Vernon, Ohio, U.S.A. 110 F2 40 23N 82 29W
Mount Vernon, Wash., U.S.A. 116 B4 48 25N 122 20W
Mountain Ash, U.K. 13 F4 51 40N 3 23W
Mountain Center, U.S.A. 117 M10 33 42N 116 44W
Mountain City, Nev., U.S.A. 114 F6 41 50N 115 58W
Mountain City, Tenn., U.S.A. 109 G5 36 29N 81 48W
Mountain Dale, U.S.A. 111 E10 41 41N 74 32W
Mountain Grove, U.S.A. 113 G8 37 8N 92 16W
Mountain Home, Ark., U.S.A. 113 G8 36 20N 92 23W
Mountain Home, Idaho, U.S.A. 114 E6 43 8N 115 41W
Mountain Iron, U.S.A. 112 B8 47 32N 92 37W
Mountain Pass, U.S.A. 117 K11 35 29N 115 35W
Mountain View, Ark., U.S.A. 113 H8 35 52N 92 7W
Mountain View, Calif., U.S.A. 116 H4 37 23N 122 5W
Mountain View, Hawaii, U.S.A. 106 J17 19 33N 155 7W
Mountainair, U.S.A. 115 J10 34 31N 106 15W
Mountlake Terrace, U.S.A. 116 C4 47 47N 122 19W
Mountmellick, Ireland 15 C4 53 7N 7 20W
Mountrath, Ireland 15 D4 53 0N 7 28W
Moura, Australia 94 C4 24 35 S 149 58 E
Moura, Brazil 124 D6 1 32 S 61 38W
Moura, Portugal 35 G3 38 7N 7 30W
Mourão, Portugal 35 G3 38 22N 7 22W
Mourdi, Dépression du, Chad 79 E10 18 10N 23 0 E
Mourdiah, Mali 82 C3 14 35N 7 25W
Mourenx, France 20 E3 43 22N 0 38W
Mouri, Ghana 83 D4 5 6N 1 14W
Mourilyan, Australia 94 B4 17 35 S 146 3 E
Mourmelon-le-Grand, France 19 C11 49 8N 4 22 E
Mourne →, U.K. 15 B4 54 52N 7 26W
Mourne Mts., U.K. 15 B5 54 10N 6 0W
Mourniaí, Greece 36 D6 35 29N 24 1 E
Mournies = Mourniaí, Greece 36 D6 35 29N 24 1 E
Mouscron, Belgium 17 D3 50 45N 3 12 E
Moussoro, Chad 79 F9 13 41N 16 35 E
Mouthe, France 19 F13 46 44N 6 12 E
Moutier, Switz. 25 H3 47 16N 7 21 E
Moûtiers, France 21 C10 45 29N 6 32 E
Moutong, Indonesia 63 D6 0 28N 121 13 E
Mouy, France 19 C9 49 18N 2 20 E
Mouzáki, Greece 38 B3 39 25N 21 37 E
Mouzon, France 19 C12 49 36N 5 3 E
Movas, Mexico 118 B3 28 10N 109 25W
Moville, Ireland 15 A4 55 11N 7 3W
Mowandjum, Australia 92 C3 17 22 S 123 40 E
Moy →, Ireland 15 B2 54 8N 9 8W
Moyale, Kenya 81 G4 3 30N 39 0 E
Moyamba, S. Leone 82 D2 8 4N 12 30W
Moyen Atlas, Morocco 78 B4 33 0N 5 0W
Moyne, L. le, Canada 103 A6 56 45N 68 47W
Moyo, Indonesia 62 F5 8 10 S 117 40 E
Moyobamba, Peru 124 E3 6 0 S 77 0W
Moyyero →, Russia 51 C11 68 44N 103 42 E
Moyynty, Kazakhstan 50 E8 47 10N 73 18 E
Mozambique = Moçambique, Mozam. 87 F5 15 3 S 40 42 E
Mozambique ■, Africa 87 F4 19 0 S 35 0 E
Mozambique Chan., Africa 89 B7 17 30 S 42 30 E
Mozdok, Russia 49 J7 43 45N 44 48 E
Mozdūrān, Iran 71 B9 36 9N 60 35 E
Mozhaysk, Russia 46 E9 55 30N 36 2 E
Mozhga, Russia 48 B11 56 26N 52 15 E
Mozhnābād, Iran 71 C9 34 7N 60 6 E
Mozirje, Slovenia 29 B11 46 22N 14 58 E
Mozyr = Mazyr, Belarus 47 F5 51 59N 29 15 E
Mpanda, Tanzania 86 D3 6 23 S 31 1 E
Mpésoba, Mali 82 C3 12 31N 5 39W
Mphoengs, Zimbabwe 89 C4 21 10 S 27 51 E
Mpika, Zambia 87 E3 11 51 S 31 25 E
Mpulungu, Zambia 87 D3 8 51 S 31 5 E
Mpumalanga, S. Africa 89 D5 29 50 S 30 33 E
Mpumalanga □, S. Africa 89 B5 26 0 S 30 0 E
Mpwapwa, Tanzania 86 D4 6 23 S 36 30 E
Mqanduli, S. Africa 89 E4 31 49 S 28 45 E
Mqinvartsveri = Kazbek, Russia 49 J7 42 42N 44 30 E
Mrągowo, Poland 44 E8 53 52N 21 18 E
Mramor, Serbia, Yug. 40 C5 43 20N 21 45 E
Mrkonjić Grad, Bos.-H. 42 F2 44 26N 17 4 E
Mrkopalj, Croatia 29 C11 45 21N 14 52 E
Mrocza, Poland 45 E4 53 16N 17 35 E
Msambansovu, Zimbabwe 87 F3 15 50 S 30 3 E
M'sila →, Algeria 78 A6 35 30N 4 29 E
Msoro, Zambia 87 E3 13 35 S 31 50 E
Msta →, Russia 46 C6 58 25N 31 20 E
Mstislavl = Mstsislaw, Belarus 46 E6 54 0N 31 50 E
Mstsislaw, Belarus 46 E6 54 0N 31 50 E
Mszana Dolna, Poland 45 J7 49 41N 20 5 E
Mszczonów, Poland 45 G7 51 58N 20 33 E
Mtama, Tanzania 87 E4 10 17 S 39 21 E
Mtamvuna →, S. Africa 89 E5 31 6S 30 12 E
Mtilikwe →, Zimbabwe 87 G3 21 9S 31 30 E
Mtsensk, Russia 46 F9 53 17N 36 36 E
Mtskheta, Georgia 49 K7 41 52N 44 45 E
Mtubatuba, S. Africa 89 D5 28 30 S 32 8 E
Mtwalume, S. Africa 89 E5 30 30 S 30 38 E
Mtwara-Mikindani, Tanzania 87 E5 10 20 S 40 20 E
Mu Gia, Deo, Vietnam 64 D5 17 40N 105 47 E
Mu Us Shamo, China 56 E5 39 0N 109 0 E
Muang Chiang Rai = Chiang Rai, Thailand 58 H2 19 52N 99 50 E
Muang Khong, Laos 64 E5 14 7N 105 51 E
Muang Lamphun, Thailand 64 C2 18 40N 99 2 E
Muang Pak Beng, Laos 58 H3 19 54N 101 8 E
Muar, Malaysia 65 L4 2 3N 102 34 E
Muarabungo, Indonesia 62 E2 1 28 S 102 52 E
Muaraenim, Indonesia 62 E2 3 40 S 103 50 E
Muarajuloi, Indonesia 62 E4 0 12 S 114 3 E
Muarakaman, Indonesia 62 E5 0 2 S 116 45 E
Muaratebo, Indonesia 62 E2 1 30 S 102 26 E
Muaratembesi, Indonesia 62 E2 1 42 S 103 8 E
Muaratewe, Indonesia 62 E4 0 58 S 114 52 E
Mubarakpur, India 69 F10 26 6N 83 18 E
Mubarraz = Al Mubarraz, Si. Arabia 71 E6 25 30N 49 40 E
Mubende, Uganda 86 B3 0 33N 31 22 E
Mubi, Nigeria 83 C7 10 18N 13 16 E
Mubur, Pulau, Indonesia 65 L6 3 20N 106 12 E
Mucajaí →, Brazil 124 C6 2 25N 60 52W
Muchachos, Roque de los, Canary Is. 37 F2 28 44N 17 52W
Mücheln, Germany 24 D7 51 17N 11 47 E
Muchinga Mts., Zambia 87 E3 11 30 S 31 30 E
Muchkapskiy, Russia 48 E6 51 52N 42 28 E
Muchuan, China 58 C5 28 57N 103 55 E
Muck, U.K. 14 E2 56 50N 6 15W
Muckadilla, Australia 95 D4 26 35 S 148 23 E
Mucur, Turkey 72 C6 39 3N 34 22 E
Mucuri, Brazil 125 G11 18 0 S 39 36W
Mucusso, Angola 88 B3 18 1 S 21 25 E
Muda, Canary Is. 37 F6 28 34N 13 57W
Mudanjiang, China 57 B15 44 38N 129 30 E
Mudanya, Turkey 41 F12 40 25N 28 50 E
Muddy Cr. →, U.S.A. 115 H8 38 24N 110 42W
Mudgee, Australia 95 E4 32 32 S 149 31 E
Mudjatik →, Canada 105 B7 56 1N 107 36W
Mudurnu, Turkey 72 B4 40 27N 31 12 E
Muecate, Mozam. 87 E4 14 55 S 39 40 E
Mueda, Mozam. 87 E4 11 36 S 39 28 E
Mueller Ra., Australia 92 C4 18 18 S 126 46 E
Muende, Mozam. 87 E3 14 28 S 33 0 E
Muerto, Mar, Mexico 119 D6 16 10N 94 10W
Mufu Shan, China 59 C10 29 20N 114 30 E
Mufulira, Zambia 87 E2 12 32 S 28 15 E
Mufumbiro Range, Africa 86 C2 1 25 S 29 30 E
Mugardos, Spain 34 B2 43 27N 8 15W
Muge →, Portugal 35 F2 39 8N 8 44W
Múggia, Italy 29 C10 45 36N 13 46 E
Mughal Sarai, India 69 G10 25 18N 83 7 E
Mughayrā', Si. Arabia 70 D3 29 17N 37 41 E
Mugi, Japan 55 H7 33 40N 134 25 E
Mugia = Muxía, Spain 34 B1 43 3N 9 10W
Mugila, Mts., Dem. Rep. of the Congo 86 D2 7 0 S 28 50 E
Muğla, Turkey 39 D10 37 15N 28 22 E
Muğla □, Turkey 39 D10 37 15N 28 0 E
Muglad, Sudan 81 E2 11 1N 27 50 E
Mŭglizh, Bulgaria 41 D9 42 37N 25 32 E
Mugu, Nepal 69 E10 29 45N 82 30 E
Muhammad, Ras, Egypt 70 E2 27 44N 34 16 E
Muhammad Qol, Sudan 80 C4 20 53N 37 9 E
Muhammadabad, India 69 F10 26 4N 83 25 E
Muhesi →, Tanzania 86 D4 7 0 S 35 20 E
Mühlacker, Germany 25 G4 48 57N 8 51 E
Mühldorf, Germany 25 G8 48 14N 12 32 E
Mühlhausen, Germany 24 D6 51 12N 10 27 E
Mühlig Hofmann fjell, Antarctica 5 D3 72 30 S 5 0 E
Mühlviertel, Austria 26 C7 48 30N 14 10 E
Muhos, Finland 8 D22 64 47N 25 59 E
Muhu, Estonia 9 G20 58 36N 23 11 E
Muhutwe, Tanzania 86 C3 1 35 S 31 45 E
Muine Bheag, Ireland 15 D5 52 42N 6 58W
Muir, L., Australia 93 F2 34 30 S 116 40 E
Mujnak = Muynak, Uzbekistan 50 E6 43 44N 59 10 E
Mukacheve, Ukraine 47 H2 48 27N 22 45 E
Mukachevo = Mukacheve, Ukraine 47 H2 48 27N 22 45 E
Mukah, Malaysia 62 D4 2 55N 112 5 E
Mukandwara, India 68 G6 24 49N 75 59 E
Mukawwa, Geziret, Egypt 80 C4 23 55N 35 53 E
Mukawwar, Sudan 80 C4 20 50N 37 17 E
Mukdahan, Thailand 64 D5 16 32N 104 43 E
Mukden = Shenyang, China 57 D12 41 48N 123 27 E
Mukerian, India 68 D6 31 57N 75 37 E
Mukhtolovo, Russia 48 C6 55 29N 43 15 E
Mukhtuya = Lensk, Russia 51 C12 60 48N 114 55 E
Mukinbudin, Australia 93 F2 30 55 S 118 5 E
Mukishi, Dem. Rep. of the Congo 87 D1 8 30 S 24 44 E
Mukomuko, Indonesia 62 E2 2 30 S 101 10 E
Mukomwenze, Dem. Rep. of the Congo 86 D2 6 49 S 27 15 E
Muktsar, India 68 D6 30 30N 74 30 E
Mukur = Moqor, Afghan. 68 C2 32 50N 67 42 E
Mukutawa →, Canada 105 C9 53 10N 97 24W
Mukwela, Zambia 87 F2 17 0 S 26 40 E
Mula, Spain 33 G3 38 3N 1 33W
Mula →, Pakistan 68 F2 27 57N 67 36 E
Mulange, Dem. Rep. of the Congo 86 C2 3 40 S 27 10 E
Mulanje, Malawi 87 F4 16 2 S 35 33 E
Mulchén, Chile 126 D1 37 45 S 72 20W
Mulde →, Germany 24 D8 51 53N 12 15 E
Mule Creek Junction, U.S.A. 112 D2 43 19N 104 8W
Muleba, Tanzania 86 C3 1 50 S 31 37 E
Mulejé, Mexico 118 B2 26 53N 112 1W
Muleshoe, U.S.A. 113 H3 34 13N 102 43W
Muletta, Gara, Ethiopia 81 F5 9 15N 41 44 E
Mulgrave, Canada 103 C7 45 38N 61 31W
Mulhacén, Spain 35 H7 37 4N 3 20W
Mülheim, Germany 24 D2 51 25N 6 54 E
Mulhouse, France 19 E14 47 40N 7 20 E
Muli, China 58 D3 27 52N 101 8 E
Muling, China 57 B16 44 35N 130 10 E
Mull, U.K. 14 E3 56 25N 5 56W
Mull, Sound of, U.K. 14 E3 56 30N 5 50W
Mullaittivu, Sri Lanka 66 Q12 9 15N 80 49 E
Mullen, U.S.A. 112 D4 42 3N 101 1W
Mullens, U.S.A. 108 G5 37 35N 81 23W
Muller, Pegunungan, Indonesia 62 D4 0 30N 113 30 E
Mullet Pen., Ireland 15 B1 54 13N 10 2W
Mullewa, Australia 93 E2 28 29 S 115 30 E
Müllheim, Germany 25 H3 47 47N 7 36 E
Mulligan →, Australia 94 D2 25 0 S 139 0 E
Mullingar, Ireland 15 C4 53 31N 7 21W
Mullins, U.S.A. 109 H6 34 12N 79 15W
Mullsjö, Sweden 11 G7 57 56N 13 55 E
Mullumbimby, Australia 95 D5 28 30 S 153 30 E
Mulobezi, Zambia 87 F2 16 45 S 25 7 E
Mulroy B., Ireland 15 A4 55 15N 7 46W
Multan, Pakistan 68 D4 30 15N 71 36 E
Mulumbe, Mts., Dem. Rep. of the Congo 87 D2 8 40 S 27 30 E
Mulungushi Dam, Zambia 87 E2 14 48 S 28 48 E
Mulvane, U.S.A. 113 G6 37 29N 97 15W
Mulwad, Sudan 80 D3 18 45N 30 39 E
Mumbai, India 66 K8 18 55N 72 50 E
Mumbwa, Zambia 87 F2 15 0 S 27 0 E
Mumra, Russia 49 H8 45 45N 47 41 E
Mun →, Thailand 64 E5 15 19N 105 30 E
Muna, Indonesia 63 F6 5 0 S 122 30 E
Munabao, India 68 G4 25 45N 70 17 E
Munamagi, Estonia 9 H22 57 43N 27 4 E
Münchberg, Germany 25 E7 50 11N 11 47 E
Müncheberg, Germany 24 C10 52 30N 14 9 E
München, Germany 25 G7 48 8N 11 34 E
Munchen-Gladbach = Mönchengladbach, Germany 24 D2 51 11N 6 27 E
Muncho Lake, Canada 104 B3 59 0N 125 50W
Munch'ŏn, N. Korea 57 E14 39 14N 127 19 E
Muncie, U.S.A. 108 E3 40 12N 85 23W
Muncoonie, L., Australia 94 D2 25 12 S 138 40 E
Mundabbera, Australia 95 D5 25 36 S 151 18 E
Munday, U.S.A. 113 J5 33 27N 99 38W
Münden, Germany 24 D5 51 25N 9 38 E
Mundiwindi, Australia 92 D3 23 47 S 120 9 E
Mundo →, Spain 33 G2 38 30N 2 15W
Mundo Novo, Brazil 125 F10 11 50 S 40 29W
Mundra, India 68 H3 22 54N 69 48 E
Mundrabilla, Australia 93 F4 31 52 S 127 51 E
Munera, Spain 33 F2 39 2N 2 29W
Mungallala, Australia 95 D4 26 28 S 147 34 E
Mungallala Cr. →, Australia 95 D4 28 53 S 147 5 E
Mungana, Australia 94 B3 17 8 S 144 27 E
Mungaoli, India 68 G8 24 24N 78 7 E
Mungari, Mozam. 87 F3 17 12 S 33 30 E
Mungbere, Dem. Rep. of the Congo 86 B2 2 36N 28 28 E
Mungeli, India 69 H9 22 4N 81 41 E
Munger, India 69 G12 25 23N 86 30 E
Munich = München, Germany 25 G7 48 8N 11 34 E
Munising, U.S.A. 108 B2 46 25N 86 40W
Munka-Ljungby, Sweden 11 H6 56 16N 12 58 E
Munkebo, Denmark 11 J4 55 27N 10 34 E
Munkedal, Sweden 11 F5 58 28N 11 40 E
Munkfors, Sweden 10 E7 59 47N 13 30 E
Munku-Sardyk, Russia 51 D11 51 45N 100 20 E
Münnerstadt, Germany 25 E6 50 14N 10 12 E
Muñoz Gamero, Pen., Chile 128 G2 52 30 S 73 5W
Munroe L., Canada 105 B9 59 13N 98 35W
Munsan, S. Korea 57 F14 37 51N 126 48 E
Munster, France 19 D14 48 2N 7 8 E
Munster, Niedersachsen, Germany 24 C6 52 58N 10 5 E
Münster, Nordrhein-Westfalen, Germany 24 D3 51 58N 7 37 E
Munster □, Ireland 15 D3 52 18N 8 44W
Muntadgin, Australia 93 F2 31 45 S 118 33 E
Muntele Mare, Vf., Romania 43 D8 46 30N 23 12 E
Muntok, Indonesia 62 E3 2 5 S 105 10 E
Munyama, Zambia 87 F2 16 5 S 28 31 E
Munzur Dağları, Turkey 73 C8 39 30N 39 10 E
Muong Beng, Laos 58 G3 20 23N 101 46 E
Muong Boum, Vietnam 58 F4 22 24N 102 49 E
Muong Et, Laos 64 B5 20 49N 104 1 E
Muong Hai, Laos 58 G3 21 3N 101 49 E
Muong Hiem, Laos 64 B4 20 5N 103 22 E
Muong Houn, Laos 58 G3 20 8N 101 23 E
Muong Hung, Vietnam 58 G4 20 56N 103 53 E
Muong Kau, Laos 64 E5 15 6N 105 47 E
Muong Khao, Laos 64 C4 19 38N 103 32 E
Muong Khoua, Laos 58 G4 21 5N 102 31 E
Muong Liep, Laos 64 C3 18 29N 101 40 E
Muong May, Laos 64 E6 14 49N 106 56 E
Muong Ngeun, Laos 58 G3 20 36N 101 3 E
Muong Ngoi, Laos 58 G4 20 43N 102 41 E
Muong Nhie, Vietnam 58 F4 22 12N 102 28 E
Muong Nong, Laos 64 D6 16 22N 106 30 E
Muong Ou Tay, Laos 58 F3 22 7N 101 48 E
Muong Oua, Laos 64 C3 18 18N 101 20 E
Muong Peun, Laos 58 G4 20 13N 103 52 E
Muong Phalane, Laos 64 D5 16 39N 105 34 E
Muong Phieng, Laos 64 C3 19 6N 101 32 E
Muong Phine, Laos 64 D6 16 32N 106 2 E
Muong Sai, Laos 58 G3 20 42N 101 59 E
Muong Saiapoun, Laos 64 C3 18 24N 101 31 E
Muong Sen, Vietnam 64 C5 19 24N 104 8 E
Muong Sing, Laos 58 G3 21 11N 101 9 E
Muong Son, Laos 58 G4 20 27N 103 19 E
Muong Soui, Laos 64 C4 19 33N 102 52 E
Muong Va, Laos 58 G4 21 53N 102 19 E
Muong Xia, Vietnam 64 B5 20 19N 104 50 E
Muonio, Finland 8 C20 67 57N 23 40 E
Muonionjoki →, Finland 8 C20 67 11N 23 34 E
Muping, China 57 F11 37 22N 121 36 E
Mupoi, Sudan 81 F2 5 28N 27 40 E
Muqaddam, Wadi →, Sudan 80 D3 18 4N 31 30 E
Muqdisho, Somali Rep. 74 G4 2 2N 45 25 E
Mur →, Austria 27 E9 46 18N 16 52 E
Mur-de-Bretagne, France 18 D4 48 12N 3 0W
Muradiye, Manisa, Turkey 39 C9 38 39N 27 21 E
Muradiye, Van, Turkey 73 C10 39 0N 43 44 E
Murakami, Japan 54 E9 38 14N 139 29 E
Murallón, Cerro, Chile 128 F2 49 48 S 73 30W
Muranda, Rwanda 86 C2 1 52 S 29 20 E
Murang'a, Kenya 86 C4 0 45 S 37 9 E
Murashi, Russia 50 D5 59 30N 49 0 E
Murat, France 20 C6 45 7N 2 53 E
Murat →, Turkey 73 C9 38 46N 40 0 E
Murat Dağı, Turkey 39 C11 38 55N 29 43 E
Muratlı, Turkey 41 E11 41 10N 27 29 E
Murato, France 21 F13 42 35N 9 20 E
Murau, Austria 26 D7 47 6N 14 10 E
Muravera, Italy 30 C2 39 25N 9 34 E
Murayama, Japan 54 E10 38 30N 140 25 E
Murça, Portugal 34 D3 41 24N 7 28W
Murchison →, Australia 93 E1 27 45 S 114 0 E
Murchison, Mt., Antarctica 5 D11 73 0 S 168 0 E
Murchison Falls, Uganda 86 B3 2 15N 31 30 E
Murchison Ra., Australia 94 C1 20 0 S 134 10 E
Murchison Rapids, Malawi 87 F3 15 55 S 34 35 E
Murcia, Spain 33 G3 38 5N 1 10W
Murcia □, Spain 33 H3 37 50N 1 30W
Murdo, U.S.A. 112 D4 43 53N 100 43W
Murdoch Pt., Australia 94 A3 14 37 S 144 55 E
Mürefte, Turkey 41 F11 40 40N 27 14 E
Mureş □, Romania 43 D9 46 45N 24 40 E
Mureş →, Romania 42 D5 46 15N 20 13 E
Mureşul = Mureş →, Romania 42 D5 46 15N 20 13 E
Muret, France 20 E5 43 30N 1 20 E
Murewa, Zimbabwe 89 B5 17 39 S 31 47 E
Murfreesboro, N.C., U.S.A. 109 G7 36 27N 77 6W
Murfreesboro, Tenn., U.S.A. 109 H2 35 51N 86 24W
Murgab = Murghob, Tajikistan 50 F8 38 10N 74 2 E
Murgab →, Turkmenistan 71 B9 38 18N 61 12 E
Murgenella, Australia 92 B5 11 34 S 132 56 E
Murgeni, Romania 43 D13 46 12N 28 1 E
Murgha Kibzai, Pakistan 68 D3 30 44N 69 25 E
Murghob, Tajikistan 50 F8 38 10N 74 2 E
Murgon, Australia 95 D5 26 15 S 151 54 E
Muri, India 69 H11 23 22N 85 52 E
Muria, Indonesia 63 G14 6 36 S 110 53 E
Muriaé, Brazil 127 A7 21 8 S 42 23W
Murias de Paredes, Spain 34 C4 42 52N 6 11W
Muriel Mine, Zimbabwe 87 F3 17 14 S 30 40 E
Müritz, Germany 24 B8 53 25N 12 42 E
Murka, Kenya 86 C4 3 27 S 38 0 E
Murliganj, India 69 G12 25 54N 86 59 E
Murmansk, Russia 50 C4 68 57N 33 10 E
Murnau, Germany 25 H7 47 40N 11 12 E
Muro, France 21 F12 42 34N 8 54 E
Muro, Spain 37 B10 39 44N 3 3 E
Muro, C. de, France 21 G12 41 44N 8 37 E
Muro de Alcoy, Spain 33 G4 38 46N 0 26W
Muro Lucano, Italy 31 B8 40 45N 15 29 E
Murom, Russia 48 C6 55 35N 42 3 E
Muroran, Japan 54 C10 42 25N 141 0 E
Muros, Spain 34 C1 42 45N 9 5W
Muros y de Noya, Ría de, Spain 34 C1 42 45N 9 0W
Muroto, Japan 55 H7 33 18N 134 9 E
Muroto-Misaki, Japan 55 H7 33 15N 134 10 E
Murowana Goślina, Poland 45 F3 52 35N 17 0 E
Murphy, U.S.A. 114 E5 43 13N 116 33W
Murphys, U.S.A. 116 G6 38 8N 120 28W
Murrat, Sudan 80 D2 18 51N 29 33 E
Murrat Wells, Sudan 80 C3 21 3N 32 55 E
Murray, Ky., U.S.A. 109 G1 36 37N 88 19W
Murray, Utah, U.S.A. 114 F8 40 40N 111 53W
Murray →, Australia 95 F2 35 20 S 139 22 E
Murray, L., U.S.A. 109 H5 34 3N 81 13W
Murray Bridge, Australia 95 F2 35 6 S 139 14 E
Murray Harbour, Canada 103 C7 46 0N 62 28W
Murraysburg, S. Africa 88 E3 31 58 S 23 47 E
Murree, Pakistan 68 C5 33 56N 73 28 E
Murrieta, U.S.A. 117 M9 33 33N 117 13W
Murro di Porco, Capo, Italy 31 F8 37 0N 15 20 E
Murrumbidgee →, Australia 95 E3 34 43 S 143 12 E
Murrumburrah, Australia 95 E4 34 32 S 148 22 E
Murrurundi, Australia 95 E5 31 42 S 150 51 E
Murshid, Sudan 80 C3 21 40N 31 10 E
Murshidabad, India 69 G13 24 11N 88 19 E
Murska Sobota, Slovenia 29 B13 46 39N 16 12 E
Murtle L., Canada 104 C5 52 8N 119 38W
Murtoa, Australia 95 F3 36 35 S 142 28 E
Murtosa, Portugal 34 E2 40 44N 8 40W
Murungu, Tanzania 86 C3 4 12 S 31 10 E
Mururoa, Pac. Oc. 97 K14 21 52 S 138 55W
Murwara, India 69 H9 23 46N 80 28 E
Murwillumbah, Australia 95 D5 28 18 S 153 27 E
Mürz →, Austria 26 D8 47 30N 15 25 E
Mürzzuschlag, Austria 26 D8 47 36N 15 41 E
Muş, Turkey 70 B4 38 45N 41 30 E
Mûsa, Gebel, Egypt 70 D2 28 33N 33 59 E
Musa Khel, Pakistan 68 D3 30 59N 69 52 E
Mūsa Qal'eh, Afghan. 66 C4 32 20N 64 50 E
Musafirkhana, India 69 F9 26 22N 81 48 E
Musala, Bulgaria 40 D7 42 13N 23 37 E
Musala, Indonesia 62 D1 1 41N 98 28 E
Musan, N. Korea 57 C15 42 12N 129 12 E
Musangu, Dem. Rep. of the Congo 87 E1 10 28 S 23 55 E
Musasa, Tanzania 86 C3 3 25 S 31 30 E
Musay'īd, Qatar 71 E6 25 0N 51 33 E
Muscat = Masqat, Oman 74 C6 23 37N 58 36 E
Muscat & Oman = Oman ■, Asia 74 C6 23 0N 58 0 E
Muscatine, U.S.A. 112 E9 41 25N 91 3W
Musgrave Harbour, Canada 103 C9 49 27N 53 58W
Musgrave Ranges, Australia 93 E5 26 0 S 132 0 E
Mushie, Dem. Rep. of the Congo 84 E3 2 56 S 16 55 E
Mushin, Nigeria 83 D5 6 32N 3 21 E
Musi →, Indonesia 62 E2 2 20 S 104 56 E
Muskeg →, Canada 104 A4 60 20N 123 20W
Muskegon, U.S.A. 108 D2 43 14N 86 16W
Muskegon →, U.S.A. 108 D2 43 14N 86 21W
Muskegon Heights, U.S.A. 108 D2 43 12N 86 16W
Muskogee, U.S.A. 113 H7 35 45N 95 22W
Muskoka, L., Canada 110 B5 45 0N 79 25W
Muskwa →, Canada 104 B4 58 47N 122 48W
Muslīmiyah, Syria 70 B3 36 19N 37 12 E
Musmar, Sudan 80 D4 18 13N 35 40 E
Musofu, Zambia 87 E2 13 30 S 29 0 E
Musoma, Tanzania 86 C3 1 30 S 33 48 E
Musquaro, L., Canada 103 B7 50 38N 61 5W
Musquodoboit Harbour, Canada 103 D7 44 50N 63 9W
Musselburgh, U.K. 14 F5 55 57N 3 2W
Musselshell →, U.S.A. 114 C10 47 21N 107 57W
Mussidan, France 20 C4 45 2N 0 22 E
Mussomeli, Italy 30 E6 37 35N 13 45 E
Mussoorie, India 68 D8 30 27N 78 6 E
Mussuco, Angola 88 B2 17 2S 19 3 E
Mustafakemalpaşa, Turkey 41 F12 40 2N 28 24 E
Mustang, Nepal 69 E10 29 10N 83 55 E
Musters, L., Argentina 128 F3 45 20 S 69 25W
Musudan, N. Korea 57 D15 40 50N 129 43 E
Muswellbrook, Australia 95 E5 32 16 S 150 56 E
Muszyna, Poland 45 J7 49 22N 20 55 E
Mût, Egypt 80 B2 25 28N 28 58 E
Mut, Turkey 70 B2 36 40N 33 28 E
Mutanda, Mozam. 89 C5 21 0 S 33 34 E
Mutanda, Zambia 87 E2 12 24 S 26 13 E
Mutare, Zimbabwe 87 F3 18 58 S 32 38 E
Muting, Indonesia 63 F10 7 23 S 140 20 E
Mutoko, Zimbabwe 89 B5 17 24 S 32 13 E
Mutoray, Russia 51 C11 60 56N 101 0 E
Mutshatsha, Dem. Rep. of the Congo 87 E1 10 35 S 24 20 E
Mutsu, Japan 54 D10 41 5N 140 55 E
Mutsu-Wan, Japan 54 D10 41 5N 140 55 E
Muttaburra, Australia 94 C3 22 38 S 144 29 E
Muttalip, Turkey 39 B12 39 50N 30 32 E
Mutton I., Ireland 15 D2 52 49N 9 32W
Mutuáli, Mozam. 87 E4 14 55 S 37 0 E
Mutum Biyu, Nigeria 83 D7 8 40N 10 50 E
Muweilih, Egypt 75 E3 30 42N 34 19 E
Muxía, Spain 34 B1 43 3N 9 10W
Muy Muy, Nic. 120 D2 12 39N 85 36W
Muyinga, Burundi 86 C3 3 14 S 30 33 E
Muynak, Uzbekistan 50 E6 43 44N 59 10 E
Muzaffarabad, Pakistan 69 B5 34 25N 73 30 E
Muzaffargarh, Pakistan 68 D4 30 5N 71 14 E
Muzaffarnagar, India 68 E7 29 26N 77 40 E
Muzaffarpur, India 69 F11 26 7N 85 23 E
Muzafirpur, Pakistan 68 D3 30 58N 69 9 E
Muzhi, Russia 50 C7 65 25N 64 40 E
Muzillac, France 18 E4 47 35N 2 30W
Muzūra, Egypt 80 J7 28 53N 30 48 E
Mvôlô, Sudan 81 F2 6 2N 29 53 E
Mvuma, Zimbabwe 87 F3 19 16 S 30 30 E
Mvurwi, Zimbabwe 87 F3 17 0 S 30 57 E
Mwadui, Tanzania 86 C3 3 26 S 33 32 E
Mwambo, Tanzania 87 E5 10 30 S 40 22 E
Mwandi, Zambia 87 F1 17 30 S 24 51 E
Mwanza, Dem. Rep. of the Congo 86 D2 7 55 S 26 43 E
Mwanza, Tanzania 86 C3 2 30 S 32 58 E
Mwanza, Zambia 87 F1 16 58 S 24 28 E
Mwanza □, Tanzania 86 C3 2 0 S 33 0 E
Mwaya, Tanzania 87 D3 9 32 S 33 55 E
Mweelrea, Ireland 15 C2 53 39N 9 49W
Mweka, Dem. Rep. of the Congo 84 E4 4 50 S 21 34 E
Mwenezi, Zimbabwe 87 G3 21 15 S 30 48 E
Mwenezi →, Mozam. 87 G3 22 40 S 31 50 E
Mwenga, Dem. Rep. of the Congo 86 C2 3 1 S 28 28 E
Mweru, L., Zambia 87 D2 9 0 S 28 40 E
Mweza Range, Zimbabwe 87 G3 21 0 S 30 0 E
Mwilambwe, Dem. Rep. of the Congo 86 D2 8 7 S 25 5 E
Mwimbi, Tanzania 87 D3 8 38 S 31 39 E
Mwinilunga, Zambia 87 E1 11 43 S 24 25 E
My Tho, Vietnam 65 G6 10 29N 106 23 E
Myajlar, India 68 F4 26 15N 70 20 E
Myanaung, Burma 67 K19 18 18N 95 22 E
Myanmar = Burma ■, Asia 67 J20 21 0N 96 30 E
Myaungmya, Burma 67 L19 16 30N 94 40 E
Myeik Kyunzu, Burma 65 G1 11 30N 97 30 E
Myers Chuck, U.S.A. 104 B2 55 44N 132 11W
Myerstown, U.S.A. 111 F8 40 22N 76 19W
Myingyan, Burma 67 J19 21 30N 95 20 E
Myitkyina, Burma 67 G20 25 24N 97 26 E
Myjava, Slovak Rep. 27 C10 48 41N 17 37 E
Mykhaylivka, Ukraine 47 J8 47 12N 35 15 E
Mykines, Færoe Is. 8 E9 62 7N 7 35W
Mykolayiv, Ukraine 47 J7 46 58N 32 0 E
Mymensingh, Bangla. 67 G17 24 45N 90 24 E
Mynydd Du, U.K. 13 F4 51 52N 3 50W
Mýrdalsjökull, Iceland 8 E4 63 40N 19 6W
Myrhorod, Ukraine 47 H7 49 58N 33 37 E
Myrtle Beach, U.S.A. 109 J6 33 42N 78 53W
Myrtle Creek, U.S.A. 114 E2 43 1N 123 17W
Myrtle Point, U.S.A. 114 E1 43 4N 124 8W
Myrtou, Cyprus 36 D12 35 18N 33 4 E
Mysia, Turkey 41 G11 39 50N 27 0 E
Myślenice, Poland 45 J6 49 51N 19 57 E
Myślibórz, Poland 45 F1 52 55N 14 50 E
Mysłowice, Poland 45 H6 50 15N 19 12 E
Mysore = Karnataka □, India 66 N10 13 15N 77 0 E
Mysore, India 66 N10 12 17N 76 41 E
Mystic, U.S.A. 111 E13 41 21N 71 58W
Myszków, Poland 45 H6 50 45N 19 22 E
Myszyniec, Poland 44 E8 53 23N 21 21 E
Mytishchi, Russia 46 E9 55 50N 37 50 E
Mývatn, Iceland 8 D5 65 36N 17 0W
Mže →, Czech Rep. 26 B6 49 46N 13 24 E
Mzimba, Malawi 87 E3 11 55 S 33 39 E
Mzimkulu →, S. Africa 89 E5 30 44 S 30 28 E
Mzimvubu →, S. Africa 89 E4 31 38 S 29 33 E
Mzuzu, Malawi 87 E3 11 30 S 33 55 E

Nduguti

N

Na Hearadh = Harris, *U.K.* **14 D2** 57 50N 6 55W
Na Noi, *Thailand* **64 C3** 18 19N 100 43 E
Na Phao, *Laos* **64 D5** 17 35N 105 44 E
Na Sam, *Vietnam* **58 F6** 22 3N 106 37 E
Na San, *Vietnam* **64 B5** 21 12N 104 2 E
Naab →, *Germany* **25 F8** 49 1N 12 2 E
Na'am, *Sudan* **81 F2** 9 42N 28 27 E
Na'am →, *Sudan* **81 F2** 6 48N 29 57 E
Naantali, *Finland* **9 F19** 60 29N 22 2 E
Naas, *Ireland* **15 C5** 53 12N 6 40W
Nababeep, *S. Africa* **88 D2** 29 36 S 17 46 E
Nabadwip = Navadwip, *India* **69 H13** 23 34N 88 20 E
Nabari, *Japan* **55 G8** 34 37N 136 5 E
Nabawa, *Australia* **93 E1** 28 30 S 114 48 E
Nabberu, L., *Australia* **93 E3** 25 50 S 120 30 E
Nabburg, *Germany* **25 F8** 49 27N 12 11 E
Naberezhnyye Chelny, *Russia* **48 C11** 55 42N 52 19 E
Nabeul, *Tunisia* **79 A8** 36 30N 10 44 E
Nabha, *India* **68 D7** 30 26N 76 14 E
Nabīd, *Iran* **71 D8** 29 40N 57 38 E
Nabire, *Indonesia* **63 E9** 3 15 S 135 26 E
Nabisar, *Pakistan* **68 G3** 25 8N 69 40 E
Nabisipi →, *Canada* **103 B7** 50 14N 62 13W
Nabiswera, *Uganda* **86 B3** 1 27N 32 15 E
Nablus = Nābulus, *West Bank* **75 C4** 32 14N 35 15 E
Naboomspruit, *S. Africa* **89 C4** 24 32 S 28 40 E
Nabou, *Burkina Faso* **82 C4** 11 25N 2 50W
Nabua, *Phil.* **61 E5** 13 24N 123 22 E
Nābulus, *West Bank* **75 C4** 32 14N 35 15 E
Nacala, *Mozam.* **87 E5** 14 31 S 40 34 E
Nacala-Velha, *Mozam.* **87 E5** 14 32 S 40 34 E
Nacaome, *Honduras* **120 D2** 13 31N 87 30W
Nacaroa, *Mozam.* **87 E4** 14 22 S 39 56 E
Naches, *U.S.A.* **114 C3** 46 44N 120 42W
Naches →, *U.S.A.* **116 D6** 46 38N 120 31W
Nachicapau, L., *Canada* **103 A6** 56 40N 68 5W
Nachingwea, *Tanzania* **87 E4** 10 23 S 38 49 E
Nachna, *India* **68 F4** 27 34N 71 41 E
Náchod, *Czech Rep.* **26 A9** 50 25N 16 8 E
Nacimiento L., *U.S.A.* **116 K6** 35 46N 120 53W
Naco, *Mexico* **118 A3** 31 20N 109 56W
Nacogdoches, *U.S.A.* **113 K7** 31 36N 94 39W
Nácori Chico, *Mexico* **118 B3** 29 39N 109 1W
Nacozari, *Mexico* **118 A3** 30 24N 109 39W
Nadi, *Sudan* **80 D3** 18 40N 33 41 E
Nadiad, *India* **68 H5** 22 41N 72 56 E
Nădlac, *Romania* **42 D5** 46 10N 20 50 E
Nador, *Morocco* **78 B5** 35 14N 2 58W
Nadur, *Malta* **36 C1** 36 2N 14 17 E
Nadūshan, *Iran* **71 C7** 32 2N 53 35 E
Nadvirna, *Ukraine* **47 H3** 48 37N 24 30 E
Nadvornaya = Nadvirna, *Ukraine* **47 H3** 48 37N 24 30 E
Nadym, *Russia* **50 C8** 65 35N 72 42 E
Nadym →, *Russia* **50 C8** 66 12N 72 0 E
Nærbø, *Norway* **9 G11** 58 40N 5 39 E
Næstved, *Denmark* **11 J5** 55 13N 11 44 E
Nafada, *Nigeria* **83 C7** 11 8N 11 20 E
Naft-e Safīd, *Iran* **71 D6** 31 40N 49 17 E
Naftshahr, *Iran* **70 C5** 34 0N 45 30 E
Nafud Desert = An Nafūd, *Si. Arabia* **70 D4** 28 15N 41 0 E
Nag Hammâdi, *Egypt* **80 B3** 26 2N 32 18 E
Naga, *Phil.* **61 E5** 13 38N 123 15 E
Nagahama, *Japan* **55 G8** 35 23N 136 16 E
Nagai, *Japan* **54 E10** 38 6N 140 2 E
Nagaland □, *India* **67 G19** 26 0N 94 30 E
Nagano, *Japan* **55 F9** 36 40N 138 10 E
Nagano □, *Japan* **55 F9** 36 15N 138 0 E
Nagaoka, *Japan* **55 F9** 37 27N 138 51 E
Nagappattinam, *India* **66 P11** 10 46N 79 51 E
Nagar →, *Bangla.* **69 G13** 24 27N 89 12 E
Nagar Parkar, *Pakistan* **68 G4** 24 28N 70 46 E
Nagasaki, *Japan* **55 H4** 32 47N 129 50 E
Nagasaki □, *Japan* **55 H4** 32 50N 129 40 E
Nagato, *Japan* **55 G5** 34 19N 131 5 E
Nagaur, *India* **68 F5** 27 15N 73 45 E
Nagda, *India* **68 H6** 23 27N 75 25 E
Nagercoil, *India* **66 Q10** 8 12N 77 26 E
Nagina, *India* **69 E8** 29 30N 78 30 E
Nagīneh, *Iran* **71 C8** 34 20N 57 15 E
Nagir, *Pakistan* **69 A6** 36 12N 74 42 E
Naglarby, *Sweden* **10 D9** 60 25N 15 34 E
Nagod, *India* **69 G9** 24 34N 80 36 E
Nagold, *Germany* **25 G4** 48 32N 8 43 E
Nagold →, *Germany* **25 G4** 48 52N 8 42 E
Nagoorin, *Australia* **94 C5** 24 17 S 151 15 E
Nagorno-Karabakh, *Azerbaijan* **70 B5** 39 55N 46 45 E
Nagornyy, *Russia* **51 D13** 55 58N 124 57 E
Nagoya, *Japan* **55 G8** 35 10N 136 50 E
Nagpur, *India* **66 J11** 21 8N 79 10 E
Nagua, *Dom. Rep.* **121 C6** 19 23N 69 50W
Nagyatád, *Hungary* **42 D2** 46 14N 17 22 E
Nagyecsed, *Hungary* **42 C7** 47 53N 22 24 E
Nagykálló, *Hungary* **42 C6** 47 53N 21 51 E
Nagykanizsa, *Hungary* **42 D2** 46 28N 17 0 E
Nagykáta, *Hungary* **42 C4** 47 25N 19 45 E
Nagykőrös, *Hungary* **42 C4** 47 5N 19 48 E
Naha, *Japan* **55 L3** 26 13N 127 42 E
Nahan, *India* **68 D7** 30 33N 77 18 E
Nahanni Butte, *Canada* **104 A4** 61 2N 123 31W
Nahanni Nat. Park, *Canada* **104 A4** 61 15N 125 0W
Nahargarh, *Mad. P., India* **68 G6** 24 10N 75 14 E
Nahargarh, *Raj., India* **68 G7** 24 55N 76 50 E
Nahariyya, *Israel* **70 C2** 33 1N 35 5 E
Nahāvand, *Iran* **71 C6** 34 10N 48 22 E
Nahe →, *Germany* **25 F3** 49 58N 7 54 E
Nahîya, W. →, *Egypt* **80 B3** 28 55N 31 0 E
Naicá, *Mexico* **118 B3** 27 53N 105 31W
Naicam, *Canada* **105 C8** 52 30N 104 30W
Naikoon Prov. Park, *Canada* **104 C2** 53 55N 131 55W
Naila, *Germany* **25 E7** 50 19N 11 42 E
Naimisharanya, *India* **69 F9** 27 21N 80 30 E
Nain, *Canada* **103 A7** 56 34N 61 40W
Nā'īn, *Iran* **71 C7** 32 54N 53 0 E
Naini Tal, *India* **69 E8** 29 30N 79 30 E
Nainpur, *India* **66 H12** 22 30N 80 10 E
Naintré, *France* **18 F7** 46 46N 0 29 E
Nainwa, *India* **68 G6** 25 46N 75 51 E
Naipu, *Romania* **43 F10** 44 12N 25 47 E
Nairn, *U.K.* **14 D5** 57 35N 3 53W
Nairobi, *Kenya* **86 C4** 1 17 S 36 48 E
Naissaar, *Estonia* **9 G21** 59 34N 24 29 E
Naita, Mt., *Ethiopia* **81 F4** 5 30N 35 18 E
Naivasha, *Kenya* **86 C4** 0 40 S 36 30 E
Naivasha, L., *Kenya* **86 C4** 0 48 S 36 20 E
Najac, *France* **20 D5** 44 14N 1 58 E
Najafābād, *Iran* **71 C6** 32 40N 51 15 E
Najd, *Si. Arabia* **74 B3** 26 30N 42 0 E
Nájera, *Spain* **32 C2** 42 26N 2 48W
Najerilla →, *Spain* **32 C2** 42 32N 2 48W
Najibabad, *India* **68 E8** 29 40N 78 20 E
Najin, *N. Korea* **57 C16** 42 12N 130 15 E
Najmah, *Si. Arabia* **71 E6** 26 42N 50 6 E
Naju, *S. Korea* **57 G14** 35 3N 126 43 E
Nakadōri-Shima, *Japan* **55 H4** 32 57N 129 4 E
Nakalagba, *Dem. Rep. of the Congo* **86 B2** 2 50N 27 58 E
Nakaminato, *Japan* **55 F10** 36 21N 140 36 E
Nakamura, *Japan* **55 H6** 32 59N 132 56 E
Nakano, *Japan* **55 F9** 36 45N 138 22 E
Nakano-Shima, *Japan* **55 K4** 29 51N 129 52 E
Nakashibetsu, *Japan* **54 C12** 43 33N 144 59 E
Nakfa, *Eritrea* **81 D4** 16 40N 38 32 E
Nakhfar al Buşayyah, *Iraq* **70 D5** 30 0N 46 10 E
Nakhichevan = Naxçıvan, *Azerbaijan* **70 B5** 39 12N 45 15 E
Nakhichevan Republic = Naxçıvan □, *Azerbaijan* **50 F5** 39 25N 45 26 E
Nakhl, *Egypt* **75 F2** 29 55N 33 43 E
Nakhl-e Taqī, *Iran* **71 E7** 27 28N 52 36 E
Nakhodka, *Russia* **51 E14** 42 53N 132 54 E
Nakhon Nayok, *Thailand* **64 E3** 14 12N 101 13 E
Nakhon Pathom, *Thailand* **64 F3** 13 49N 100 3 E
Nakhon Phanom, *Thailand* **64 D5** 17 23N 104 43 E
Nakhon Ratchasima, *Thailand* **64 E4** 14 59N 102 12 E
Nakhon Sawan, *Thailand* **64 E3** 15 35N 100 10 E
Nakhon Si Thammarat, *Thailand* **65 H3** 8 29N 100 0 E
Nakhon Thai, *Thailand* **64 D3** 17 5N 100 44 E
Nakhtarana, *India* **68 H3** 23 20N 69 15 E
Nakina, *Canada* **102 B2** 50 10N 86 40W
Nakło nad Notecią, *Poland* **45 E4** 53 9N 17 38 E
Nako, *Burkina Faso* **82 C4** 10 40N 3 4W
Nakodar, *India* **68 D6** 31 8N 75 31 E
Nakskov, *Denmark* **11 K5** 54 50N 11 8 E
Naktong →, *S. Korea* **57 G15** 35 7N 128 57 E
Nakuru, *Kenya* **86 C4** 0 15 S 36 4 E
Nakuru, L., *Kenya* **86 C4** 0 23 S 36 5 E
Nakusp, *Canada* **104 C5** 50 20N 117 45W
Nal, *Pakistan* **68 F2** 27 40N 66 12 E
Nal →, *Pakistan* **68 G1** 25 20N 65 30 E
Nalázi, *Mozam.* **89 C5** 24 3 S 33 20 E
Nalchik, *Russia* **49 J6** 43 30N 43 33 E
Nałęczów, *Poland* **45 G9** 51 17N 22 9 E
Nalerigu, *Ghana* **83 C4** 10 35N 0 25W
Nalgonda, *India* **66 L11** 17 6N 79 15 E
Nalhati, *India* **69 G12** 24 17N 87 52 E
Naliya, *India* **68 H3** 23 16N 68 50 E
Nallamalai Hills, *India* **66 M11** 15 30N 78 50 E
Nallıhan, *Turkey* **72 B4** 40 11N 31 20 E
Nalón →, *Spain* **34 B4** 43 32N 6 4W
Nam Can, *Vietnam* **65 H5** 8 46N 104 59 E
Nam-ch'on, *N. Korea* **57 E14** 38 15N 126 26 E
Nam Co, *China* **60 C4** 30 30N 90 45 E
Nam Dinh, *Vietnam* **58 G6** 20 25N 106 5 E
Nam Du, Hon, *Vietnam* **65 H5** 9 41N 104 21 E
Nam Ngum Dam, *Laos* **64 C4** 18 35N 102 34 E
Nam-Phan, *Vietnam* **65 G6** 10 30N 106 0 E
Nam Phong, *Thailand* **64 D4** 16 42N 102 52 E
Nam Tha, *Laos* **58 G3** 20 58N 101 30 E
Nam Tok, *Thailand* **64 E2** 14 21N 99 4 E
Namacunde, *Angola* **88 B2** 17 18 S 15 50 E
Namacurra, *Mozam.* **89 B6** 17 30 S 36 50 E
Namak, Daryācheh-ye, *Iran* **71 C7** 34 30N 52 0 E
Namak, Kavir-e, *Iran* **71 C8** 34 30N 57 30 E
Namakzār, Daryācheh-ye, *Iran* **71 C9** 34 0N 60 30 E
Namaland, *Namibia* **88 C2** 26 0 S 17 0 E
Namangan, *Uzbekistan* **50 E8** 41 0N 71 40 E
Namapa, *Mozam.* **87 E4** 13 43 S 39 50 E
Namaqualand, *S. Africa* **88 E2** 30 0 S 17 25 E
Namasagali, *Uganda* **86 B3** 1 2N 33 0 E
Namber, *Indonesia* **63 E8** 1 2 S 134 49 E
Nambour, *Australia* **95 D5** 26 32 S 152 58 E
Nambucca Heads, *Australia* **95 E5** 30 37 S 153 0 E
Namche Bazar, *Nepal* **69 F12** 27 51N 86 47 E
Namchonjŏm = Nam-ch'on, *N. Korea* **57 E14** 38 15N 126 26 E
Namecunda, *Mozam.* **87 E4** 14 54 S 37 37 E
Nameponda, *Mozam.* **87 F4** 15 50 S 39 50 E
Náměšť nad Oslavou, *Czech Rep.* **27 B9** 49 12N 16 10 E
Námestovo, *Slovak Rep.* **27 B12** 49 24N 19 25 E
Nametil, *Mozam.* **87 F4** 15 40 S 39 21 E
Namew L., *Canada* **105 C8** 54 14N 101 56W
Namgia, *India* **69 D8** 31 48N 78 40 E
Namhkam, *Burma* **58 E1** 23 50N 97 41 E
Namib Desert, *Namibia* **88 C2** 22 30 S 15 0 E
Namibe, *Angola* **85 H2** 15 7 S 12 11 E
Namibe □, *Angola* **88 B1** 16 35 S 12 30 E
Namibia ■, *Africa* **88 C2** 22 0 S 18 9 E
Namibwoestyn = Namib Desert, *Namibia* **88 C2** 22 30 S 15 0 E
Namīn, *Iran* **73 C13** 38 25N 48 30 E
Namlea, *Indonesia* **63 E7** 3 18 S 127 5 E
Namoi →, *Australia* **95 E4** 30 12 S 149 30 E
Nampa, *U.S.A.* **114 E5** 43 34N 116 34W
Nampala, *Mali* **82 B3** 15 20N 5 30W
Namp'o, *N. Korea* **57 E13** 38 52N 125 10 E
Nampō-Shotō, *Japan* **55 J10** 32 0N 140 0 E
Nampula, *Mozam.* **87 F4** 15 6 S 39 15 E
Namrole, *Indonesia* **63 E7** 3 46 S 126 46 E
Namse Shankou, *China* **67 E13** 30 0N 82 25 E
Namsen →, *Norway* **8 D14** 64 28N 11 37 E
Namsos, *Norway* **8 D14** 64 29N 11 30 E
Namtsy, *Russia* **51 C13** 62 43N 129 37 E
Namtu, *Burma* **67 H20** 23 5N 97 28 E
Namtumbo, *Tanzania* **87 E4** 10 30 S 36 4 E
Namu, *Canada* **104 C3** 51 52N 127 50W
Namur, *Belgium* **17 D4** 50 27N 4 52 E
Namur □, *Belgium* **17 D4** 50 17N 5 0 E
Namutoni, *Namibia* **88 B2** 18 49 S 16 55 E
Namwala, *Zambia* **87 F2** 15 44 S 26 30 E
Namwŏn, *S. Korea* **57 G14** 35 23N 127 23 E
Namysłów, *Poland* **45 G4** 51 6N 17 42 E
Nan, *Thailand* **64 C3** 18 48N 100 46 E
Nan →, *Thailand* **64 E3** 15 42N 100 9 E
Nan-ch'ang = Nanchang, *China* **59 C10** 28 42N 115 55 E
Nan Ling, *China* **59 E8** 25 0N 112 30 E
Nan Xian, *China* **59 C9** 29 20N 112 22 E
Nana, *Romania* **43 F11** 44 17N 26 34 E
Nana Kru, *Liberia* **82 E3** 4 55N 8 45W
Nanaimo, *Canada* **104 D4** 49 10N 124 0W
Nanam, *N. Korea* **57 D15** 41 44N 129 40 E
Nanan, *China* **59 E12** 24 59N 118 21 E
Nanango, *Australia* **95 D5** 26 40 S 152 0 E
Nan'ao, *China* **59 F11** 23 28N 117 5 E
Nanao, *Japan* **55 F8** 37 0N 137 0 E
Nanbu, *China* **58 B6** 31 18N 106 3 E
Nanchang, *Jiangxi, China* **59 C10** 28 42N 115 55 E
Nanchang, *Kiangsi, China* **59 C10** 28 34N 115 48 E
Nancheng, *China* **59 D11** 27 33N 116 35 E
Nanching = Nanjing, *China* **59 A12** 32 2N 118 47 E
Nanchong, *China* **58 B6** 30 43N 106 2 E
Nanchuan, *China* **58 C6** 29 9N 107 6 E
Nancy, *France* **19 D13** 48 42N 6 12 E
Nanda Devi, *India* **69 D8** 30 23N 79 59 E
Nanda Kot, *India* **69 D9** 30 17N 80 5 E
Nandan, *China* **58 E6** 24 58N 107 29 E
Nandan, *Japan* **55 G7** 34 10N 134 42 E
Nanded, *India* **66 K10** 19 10N 77 20 E
Nandewar Ra., *Australia* **95 E5** 30 15 S 150 35 E
Nandi, *Fiji* **91 C7** 17 42 S 177 20 E
Nandigram, *India* **69 H12** 22 1N 87 58 E
Nandurbar, *India* **66 J9** 21 20N 74 15 E
Nandyal, *India* **66 M11** 15 30N 78 30 E
Nanfeng, *Guangdong, China* **59 F8** 23 45N 111 47 E
Nanfeng, *Jiangxi, China* **59 D11** 27 12N 116 28 E
Nanga-Eboko, *Cameroon* **83 E7** 4 41N 12 22 E
Nanga Parbat, *Pakistan* **69 B6** 35 10N 74 35 E
Nangade, *Mozam.* **87 E4** 11 5 S 39 36 E
Nangapinoh, *Indonesia* **62 E4** 0 20 S 111 44 E
Nangarhār □, *Afghan.* **66 B7** 34 20N 70 0 E
Nangatayap, *Indonesia* **62 E4** 1 32 S 110 34 E
Nangeya Mts., *Uganda* **86 B3** 3 30N 33 30 E
Nangis, *France* **19 D10** 48 33N 3 1 E
Nangong, *China* **56 F8** 37 23N 115 22 E
Nanhua, *China* **58 E3** 25 13N 101 21 E
Nanhuang, *China* **57 F11** 36 58N 121 48 E
Nanhui, *China* **59 B13** 31 5N 121 44 E
Nanjeko, *Zambia* **87 F1** 15 31 S 23 30 E
Nanji Shan, *China* **59 D13** 27 27N 121 4 E
Nanjian, *China* **58 E3** 25 2N 100 25 E
Nanjiang, *China* **58 A6** 32 28N 106 51 E
Nanjing, *Fujian, China* **59 E11** 24 25N 117 20 E
Nanjing, *Jiangsu, China* **59 A12** 32 2N 118 47 E
Nanjirinji, *Tanzania* **87 D4** 9 41 S 39 5 E
Nankana Sahib, *Pakistan* **68 D5** 31 27N 73 38 E
Nankang, *China* **59 E10** 25 40N 114 45 E
Nanking = Nanjing, *China* **59 A12** 32 2N 118 47 E
Nankoku, *Japan* **55 H6** 33 39N 133 44 E
Nanling, *China* **59 B12** 30 55N 118 20 E
Nanning, *China* **58 F7** 22 48N 108 20 E
Nannup, *Australia* **93 F2** 33 59 S 115 48 E
Nanpan Jiang →, *China* **58 E6** 25 10N 106 5 E
Nanpara, *India* **69 F9** 27 52N 81 33 E
Nanpi, *China* **56 E9** 38 2N 116 45 E
Nanping, *Fujian, China* **59 D12** 26 38N 118 10 E
Nanping, *Henan, China* **59 C9** 29 55N 112 3 E
Nanri Dao, *China* **59 E12** 25 15N 119 25 E
Nanripe, *Mozam.* **87 E4** 13 52 S 38 52 E
Nansei-Shotō = Ryūkyū-rettō, *Japan* **55 M3** 26 0N 126 0 E
Nansen Sd., *Canada* **4 A3** 81 0N 91 0W
Nanshan I., *S. China Sea* **62 B5** 10 45N 115 49 E
Nansio, *Tanzania* **86 C3** 2 3 S 33 4 E
Nant, *France* **20 D7** 44 1N 3 18 E
Nanterre, *France* **19 D9** 48 53N 2 13 E
Nantes, *France* **18 E5** 47 12N 1 33W
Nantiat, *France* **20 B5** 46 1N 1 11 E
Nanticoke, *U.S.A.* **111 E8** 41 12N 76 0W
Nanton, *Canada* **104 C6** 50 21N 113 46W
Nantong, *China* **59 A13** 32 1N 120 52 E
Nantou, *Taiwan* **59 F13** 23 57N 120 35 E
Nantua, *France* **19 F12** 46 10N 5 35 E
Nantucket I., *U.S.A.* **108 E10** 41 16N 70 5W
Nantwich, *U.K.* **12 D5** 53 4N 2 31W
Nanty Glo, *U.S.A.* **110 F6** 40 28N 78 50W
Nanuque, *Brazil* **125 G10** 17 50 S 40 21W
Nanusa, Kepulauan, *Indonesia* **63 D7** 4 45N 127 1 E
Nanutarra Roadhouse, *Australia* **92 D2** 22 32 S 115 30 E
Nanxi, *China* **58 C5** 28 54N 104 59 E
Nanxiong, *China* **59 E10** 25 6N 114 15 E
Nanyang, *China* **56 H7** 33 11N 112 30 E
Nanyi Hu, *China* **59 B12** 31 5N 119 0 E
Nanyuki, *Kenya* **86 B4** 0 2N 37 4 E
Nanzhang, *China* **59 B8** 31 45N 111 50 E
Nao, C. de la, *Spain* **33 G5** 38 44N 0 14 E
Naococane, L., *Canada* **103 B5** 52 50N 70 45W
Náousa, *Imathía, Greece* **40 F6** 40 42N 22 9 E
Náousa, *Kikládhes, Greece* **39 D7** 37 7N 25 14 E
Naozhou Dao, *China* **59 G8** 20 55N 110 20 E
Napa, *U.S.A.* **116 G4** 38 18N 122 17W
Napa →, *U.S.A.* **116 G4** 38 10N 122 19W
Napanee, *Canada* **102 D4** 44 15N 77 0W
Napanoch, *U.S.A.* **111 E10** 41 44N 74 22W
Nape, *Laos* **64 C5** 18 18N 105 6 E
Nape Pass = Keo Neua, Deo, *Vietnam* **64 C5** 18 23N 105 10 E
Napier, *N.Z.* **91 H6** 39 30 S 176 56 E
Napier Broome B., *Australia* **92 B4** 14 2 S 126 37 E
Napier Pen., *Australia* **94 A2** 12 4 S 135 43 E
Napierville, *Canada* **111 A11** 45 11N 73 25W
Naples = Nápoli, *Italy* **31 B7** 40 50N 14 15 E
Naples, *U.S.A.* **109 M5** 26 8N 81 48W
Napo, *China* **58 F5** 23 22N 105 50 E
Napo →, *Peru* **122 D3** 3 20 S 72 40W
Napoleon, *N. Dak., U.S.A.* **112 B5** 46 30N 99 46W
Napoleon, *Ohio, U.S.A.* **108 E3** 41 23N 84 8W
Nápoli, *Italy* **31 B7** 40 50N 14 15 E
Nápoli, G. di, *Italy* **31 B7** 40 43N 14 10 E
Napopo, *Dem. Rep. of the Congo* **86 B2** 4 15N 28 0 E
Naqâda, *Egypt* **80 B3** 25 53N 32 42 E
Naqadeh, *Iran* **73 D11** 36 57N 45 23 E
Naqb, Ra's an, *Jordan* **75 F4** 30 0N 35 29 E
Naqqāsh, *Iran* **71 C6** 35 40N 49 6 E
Nara, *Japan* **55 G7** 34 40N 135 49 E
Nara, *Mali* **82 B3** 15 10N 7 20W
Nara □, *Japan* **55 G8** 34 30N 136 0 E
Nara Canal, *Pakistan* **68 G3** 24 30N 69 20 E
Nara Visa, *U.S.A.* **113 H3** 35 37N 103 6W
Naracoorte, *Australia* **95 F3** 36 58 S 140 45 E
Naradhan, *Australia* **95 E4** 33 34 S 146 17 E
Naraini, *India* **69 G9** 25 11N 80 29 E
Narasapur, *India* **67 L12** 16 26N 81 40 E
Narathiwat, *Thailand* **65 J3** 6 30N 101 48 E
Narayanganj, *Bangla.* **67 H17** 23 40N 90 33 E
Narayanpet, *India* **66 L10** 16 45N 77 30 E
Narbonne, *France* **20 E7** 43 11N 3 0 E
Narcea →, *Spain* **34 B4** 43 33N 6 44W
Nardīn, *Iran* **71 B7** 37 3N 55 59 E
Nardò, *Italy* **31 B11** 40 11N 18 2 E
Narembeen, *Australia* **93 F2** 32 7 S 118 24 E
Narendranagar, *India* **68 D8** 30 10N 78 18 E
Nares Str., *Arctic* **98 A13** 80 0N 70 0W
Naretha, *Australia* **93 F3** 31 0 S 124 45 E
Narew →, *Poland* **45 F7** 52 26N 20 41 E
Nari →, *Pakistan* **68 F2** 28 0N 67 40 E
Narin, *Afghan.* **66 A6** 36 5N 69 0 E
Narindra, Helodranon' i, *Madag.* **89 A8** 14 55 S 47 30 E
Narita, *Japan* **55 G10** 35 47N 140 19 E
Närke, *Sweden* **10 E8** 59 10N 15 0 E
Narmada →, *India* **68 J5** 21 38N 72 36 E
Narman, *Turkey* **73 B9** 40 26N 41 57 E
Narmland, *Sweden* **9 F15** 60 0N 13 30 E
Narnaul, *India* **68 E7** 28 5N 76 11 E
Narni, *Italy* **29 F9** 42 30N 12 30 E
Naro, *Ghana* **82 C4** 10 22N 2 27W
Naro Fominsk, *Russia* **46 E9** 55 23N 36 43 E
Narodnaya, *Russia* **6 B17** 65 5N 59 58 E
Narok, *Kenya* **86 C4** 1 55 S 35 52 E
Narón, *Spain* **34 B2** 43 32N 8 9W
Narooma, *Australia* **95 F5** 36 14 S 150 4 E
Narowal, *Pakistan* **68 C6** 32 6N 74 52 E
Narrabri, *Australia* **95 E4** 30 19 S 149 46 E
Narran →, *Australia* **95 D4** 28 37 S 148 12 E
Narrandera, *Australia* **95 E4** 34 42 S 146 31 E
Narrogin, *Australia* **93 F2** 32 58 S 117 14 E
Narromine, *Australia* **95 E4** 32 12 S 148 12 E
Narrow Hills Prov. Park, *Canada* **105 C8** 54 0N 104 37W
Narsimhapur, *India* **69 H8** 22 54N 79 14 E
Narsinghgarh, *India* **68 H7** 23 45N 76 40 E
Nartes, L. e, *Albania* **40 F3** 40 32N 19 25 E
Nartkala, *Russia* **49 J6** 43 33N 43 51 E
Naruto, *Japan* **55 G7** 34 11N 134 37 E
Narva, *Estonia* **46 C5** 59 23N 28 12 E
Narva →, *Russia* **9 G22** 59 27N 28 2 E
Narva Bay, *Estonia* **9 G19** 59 35N 27 35 E
Narvik, *Norway* **8 B17** 68 28N 17 26 E
Narvskoye Vdkhr., *Russia* **46 C5** 59 18N 28 14 E
Narwana, *India* **68 E7** 29 39N 76 6 E
Naryan-Mar, *Russia* **50 C6** 67 42N 53 12 E
Narym, *Russia* **50 D9** 59 0N 81 30 E
Naryn, *Kyrgyzstan* **50 E8** 41 26N 75 58 E
Nasa, *Norway* **8 C16** 66 29N 15 23 E
Nasarawa, *Nigeria* **83 D6** 8 32N 7 41 E
Năsăud, *Romania* **43 C9** 47 19N 24 29 E
Naseby, *N.Z.* **91 L3** 45 1 S 170 10 E
Naselle, *U.S.A.* **116 D3** 46 22N 123 49W
Naser, Buheirat en, *Egypt* **80 C3** 23 0N 32 30 E
Nashua, *Mont., U.S.A.* **114 B10** 48 8N 106 22W
Nashua, *N.H., U.S.A.* **111 D13** 42 45N 71 28W
Nashville, *Ark., U.S.A.* **113 J8** 33 57N 93 51W
Nashville, *Ga., U.S.A.* **109 K4** 31 12N 83 15W
Nashville, *Tenn., U.S.A.* **109 G2** 36 10N 86 47W
Našice, *Croatia* **42 E3** 45 32N 18 4 E
Nasielsk, *Poland* **45 F7** 52 35N 20 50 E
Nasik, *India* **66 K8** 19 58N 73 50 E
Nasipit, *Phil.* **61 G6** 8 57N 125 19 E
Nasir, *Sudan* **81 F3** 8 36N 33 4 E
Nasirabad, *India* **68 F6** 26 15N 74 45 E
Nasirabad, *Pakistan* **68 E3** 28 23N 68 24 E
Naskaupi →, *Canada* **103 B7** 53 47N 60 51W
Naso, *Italy* **31 D7** 38 7N 14 47 E
Naşrābād, *Iran* **71 C6** 34 8N 51 26 E
Naşriān-e Pā'īn, *Iran* **70 C5** 32 52N 46 52 E
Nass →, *Canada* **104 C3** 55 0N 129 40W
Nassarawa □, *Nigeria* **83 D6** 8 30N 8 20 E
Nassau, *Bahamas* **120 A4** 25 5N 77 20W
Nassau, *U.S.A.* **111 D11** 42 31N 73 37W
Nassau, B., *Chile* **128 H3** 55 20 S 68 0W
Nasser, L. = Naser, Buheirat en, *Egypt* **80 C3** 23 0N 32 30 E
Nasser City = Kôm Ombo, *Egypt* **80 C3** 24 25N 32 52 E
Nassian, *Ivory C.* **82 D4** 8 28N 3 28W
Nässjö, *Sweden* **11 G8** 57 39N 14 42 E
Nastapoka →, *Canada* **102 A4** 56 55N 76 33W
Nastapoka, Is., *Canada* **102 A4** 56 55N 76 50W
Nasugbu, *Phil.* **61 D4** 14 5N 120 38 E
Näsum, *Sweden* **11 H8** 56 10N 14 29 E
Näsviken, *Sweden* **10 C10** 61 46N 16 52 E
Nata, *Botswana* **88 C4** 20 12 S 26 12 E
Nata →, *Botswana* **88 C4** 20 14 S 26 10 E
Natal, *Brazil* **125 E11** 5 47 S 35 13W
Natal, *Indonesia* **62 D1** 0 35N 99 7 E
Natal, *S. Africa* **85 K6** 28 30 S 30 30 E
Natalinci, *Serbia, Yug.* **42 F5** 44 15N 20 49 E
Naţanz, *Iran* **71 C6** 33 30N 51 55 E
Natashquan, *Canada* **103 B7** 50 14N 61 46W
Natashquan →, *Canada* **103 B7** 50 7N 61 50W
Natchez, *U.S.A.* **113 K9** 31 34N 91 24W
Natchitoches, *U.S.A.* **113 K8** 31 46N 93 5W
Nathalia, *Australia* **95 F4** 36 1 S 145 13 E
Nathdwara, *India* **68 G5** 24 55N 73 50 E
Nati, Pta., *Spain* **37 A10** 40 3N 3 50 E
Natimuk, *Australia* **95 F3** 36 42 S 142 0 E
Nation →, *Canada* **104 B4** 55 30N 123 32W
National City, *U.S.A.* **117 N9** 32 41N 117 6W
Natitingou, *Benin* **83 C5** 10 20N 1 26 E
Natividad, I., *Mexico* **118 B1** 27 50N 115 10W
Natkyizin, *Burma* **64 E1** 14 57N 97 59 E
Natron, L., *Tanzania* **86 C4** 2 20 S 36 0 E
Natrona Heights, *U.S.A.* **110 F5** 40 37N 79 44W
Natrûn, W. el →, *Egypt* **80 H7** 30 25N 30 13 E
Nättraby, *Sweden* **11 H9** 56 13N 15 31 E
Natukanaoka Pan, *Namibia* **88 B2** 18 40 S 15 45 E
Natuna Besar, Kepulauan, *Indonesia* **65 L7** 4 0N 108 15 E
Natuna Is. = Natuna Besar, Kepulauan, *Indonesia* **65 L7** 4 0N 108 15 E
Natuna Selatan, Kepulauan, *Indonesia* **65 L7** 2 45N 109 0 E
Natural Bridge, *U.S.A.* **111 B9** 44 5N 75 30W
Naturaliste, C., *Australia* **94 G4** 40 50 S 148 15 E
Nau Qala, *Afghan.* **68 B3** 34 5N 68 5 E
Naucelle, *France* **20 D6** 44 13N 2 20 E
Nauders, *Austria* **26 E3** 46 54N 10 30 E
Nauen, *Germany* **24 C8** 52 36N 12 52 E
Naugatuck, *U.S.A.* **111 E11** 41 30N 73 3W
Naujaat = Repulse Bay, *Canada* **101 B11** 66 30N 86 30W
Naujoji Akmenė, *Lithuania* **44 B9** 56 19N 22 54 E
Naumburg, *Germany* **24 D7** 51 9N 11 47 E
Nā'ūr at Tunayb, *Jordan* **75 D4** 31 48N 35 57 E
Nauru ■, *Pac. Oc.* **96 H8** 1 0 S 166 0 E
Naushahra = Nowshera, *Pakistan* **66 C8** 34 0N 72 0 E
Naushahro, *Pakistan* **68 F3** 26 50N 68 7 E
Naushon I., *U.S.A.* **111 E14** 41 29N 70 45W
Nauta, *Peru* **124 D4** 4 31 S 73 35W
Nautanwa, *India* **67 F13** 27 20N 83 25 E
Nautla, *Mexico* **119 C5** 20 20N 96 50W
Nava, *Mexico* **118 B4** 28 25N 100 46W
Nava, *Spain* **34 B5** 43 21N 5 31W
Nava del Rey, *Spain* **34 D5** 41 22N 5 6W
Navadwip, *India* **69 H13** 23 34N 88 20 E
Navahermosa, *Spain* **35 F6** 39 41N 4 28W
Navahrudak, *Belarus* **46 F3** 53 40N 25 50 E
Navajo Reservoir, *U.S.A.* **115 H10** 36 48N 107 36W
Navalcarnero, *Spain* **34 E6** 40 17N 4 5W
Navalmoral de la Mata, *Spain* **34 F5** 39 52N 5 33W
Navalvillar de Pela, *Spain* **35 F5** 39 9N 5 24W
Navan = An Uaimh, *Ireland* **15 C5** 53 39N 6 41W
Navapolatsk, *Belarus* **46 E5** 55 32N 28 37 E
Navarino, I., *Chile* **128 H3** 55 0 S 67 40W
Navarra □, *Spain* **32 C3** 42 40N 1 40W
Navarre, *U.S.A.* **110 F3** 40 43N 81 31W
Navarro →, *U.S.A.* **116 F3** 39 11N 123 45W
Navas de San Juan, *Spain* **35 G7** 38 30N 3 19W
Navasota, *U.S.A.* **113 K6** 30 23N 96 5W
Navassa I., *W. Indies* **121 C5** 18 30N 75 0W
Nävekvarn, *Sweden* **11 F10** 58 38N 16 49 E
Naver →, *U.K.* **14 C4** 58 32N 4 14W
Navia, *Spain* **34 B4** 43 35N 6 42W
Navia →, *Spain* **34 B4** 43 15N 6 50W
Navia de Suarna, *Spain* **34 C3** 42 58N 7 3W
Navibandar, *India* **68 J3** 21 26N 69 48 E
Navidad, *Chile* **126 C1** 33 57 S 71 50W
Naviraí, *Brazil* **127 A5** 23 8 S 54 13W
Navlakhi, *India* **68 H4** 22 58N 70 28 E
Navlya, *Russia* **47 F8** 52 53N 34 30 E
Năvodari, *Romania* **43 F13** 44 19N 28 36 E
Navoi = Nawoiy, *Uzbekistan* **50 E7** 40 9N 65 22 E
Navojoa, *Mexico* **118 B3** 27 0N 109 30W
Navolato, *Mexico* **118 C3** 24 47N 107 42W
Návpaktos, *Greece* **38 C3** 38 24N 21 50 E
Návplion, *Greece* **38 D4** 37 33N 22 50 E
Navrongo, *Ghana* **83 C4** 10 51N 1 3W
Navsari, *India* **66 J8** 20 57N 72 59 E
Nawa Kot, *Pakistan* **68 E4** 28 21N 71 24 E
Nawab Khan, *Pakistan* **68 D3** 30 17N 69 12 E
Nawabganj, *Ut. P., India* **69 F9** 26 56N 81 14 E
Nawabganj, *Ut. P., India* **69 E8** 28 32N 79 40 E
Nawabshah, *Pakistan* **68 F3** 26 15N 68 25 E
Nawada, *India* **69 G11** 24 50N 85 33 E
Nawakot, *Nepal* **69 F11** 27 55N 85 10 E
Nawalgarh, *India* **68 F6** 27 50N 75 15 E
Nawanshahr, *India* **69 C6** 32 33N 74 48 E
Nawar, Dasht-i-, *Afghan.* **68 C3** 33 52N 68 0 E
Nawi, *Sudan* **80 D3** 18 32N 30 50 E
Nawoiy, *Uzbekistan* **50 E7** 40 9N 65 22 E
Naxçıvan, *Azerbaijan* **70 B5** 39 12N 45 15 E
Naxçıvan □, *Azerbaijan* **50 F5** 39 25N 45 26 E
Náxos, *Greece* **39 D7** 37 8N 25 25 E
Nay, *France* **20 E3** 43 10N 0 18W
Nay, Mui, *Vietnam* **62 B3** 12 55N 109 23 E
Nāy Band, *Būshehr, Iran* **71 E7** 27 20N 52 40 E
Nāy Band, *Khorāsān, Iran* **71 C8** 32 20N 57 34 E
Nayakhan, *Russia* **51 C16** 61 56N 159 0 E
Nayarit □, *Mexico* **118 C4** 22 0N 105 0W
Nayé, *Senegal* **82 C2** 14 28N 12 12W
Nayong, *China* **58 D5** 26 50N 105 20 E
Nayoro, *Japan* **54 B11** 44 21N 142 28 E
Nayyāl, W. →, *Si. Arabia* **70 D3** 28 35N 39 4 E
Nazaré, *Brazil* **125 F11** 13 2 S 39 0W
Nazaré, *Portugal* **35 F1** 39 36N 9 4W
Nazareth = Naẕerat, *Israel* **75 C4** 32 42N 35 17 E
Nazareth, *U.S.A.* **111 F9** 40 44N 75 19W
Nazas, *Mexico* **118 B4** 25 10N 104 6W
Nazas →, *Mexico* **118 B4** 25 35N 103 25W
Nazca, *Peru* **124 F4** 14 50 S 74 57W
Naze, The, *U.K.* **13 F9** 51 53N 1 18 E
Naẕerat, *Israel* **75 C4** 32 42N 35 17 E
Nāzīk, *Iran* **70 B5** 39 1N 45 4 E
Nazilli, *Turkey* **39 D10** 37 55N 28 15 E
Nazko, *Canada* **104 C4** 53 1N 123 37W
Nazko →, *Canada* **104 C4** 53 7N 123 34W
Nazret, *Ethiopia* **81 F4** 8 32N 39 22 E
Nazwá, *Oman* **74 C6** 22 56N 57 32 E
Nchanga, *Zambia* **87 E2** 12 30 S 27 49 E
Ncheu, *Malawi* **87 E3** 14 50 S 34 47 E
Ndala, *Tanzania* **86 C3** 4 45 S 33 15 E
Ndalatando, *Angola* **84 F2** 9 12 S 14 48 E
Ndali, *Benin* **83 D5** 9 50N 2 46 E
Ndareda, *Tanzania* **86 C4** 4 12 S 35 30 E
Ndélé, *C.A.R.* **84 C4** 8 25N 20 36 E
Ndikinimeki, *Cameroon* **83 E7** 4 46N 10 50 E
N'Dioum, *Senegal* **82 B2** 16 31N 14 39W
Ndjamena, *Chad* **79 F8** 12 10N 14 59 E
Ndola, *Zambia* **87 E2** 13 0 S 28 34 E
Ndoto Mts., *Kenya* **86 B4** 2 0N 37 0 E
Nduguti, *Tanzania* **86 C3** 4 18 S 34 41 E

Néa Alikarnassós

Néa Alikarnassós, *Greece* **39 F7** 35 18N 25 13 E
Néa Ankhíalos, *Greece* **38 B4** 39 16N 22 49 E
Néa Epídhavros, *Greece* **38 D5** 37 40N 23 7 E
Néa Flippiás, *Greece* **38 B2** 39 12N 20 53 E
Néa Ionia, *Greece* **38 B4** 39 21N 22 56 E
Néa Kallikrátia, *Greece* **40 F7** 40 21N 23 3 E
Néa Mákri, *Greece* **38 C5** 38 5N 23 59 E
Néa Moudhaniá, *Greece* **40 F7** 40 15N 23 17 E
Néa Péramos, *Attikí, Greece* **38 C5** 38 0N 23 26 E
Néa Péramos, *Kavála, Greece* **41 F8** 40 50N 24 18 E
Néa Víssi, *Greece* **41 E10** 41 34N 26 33 E
Néa Zíkhna, *Greece* **40 E7** 41 2N 23 49 E
Neagh, Lough, *U.K.* **15 B5** 54 37N 6 25W
Neah Bay, *U.S.A.* **116 B2** 48 22N 124 37W
Neale, L., *Australia* **92 D5** 24 15 S 130 0 E
Neamţ ☐, *Romania* **43 C11** 47 0N 26 20 E
Neápolis, *Kozáni, Greece* **40 F5** 40 20N 21 24 E
Neápolis, *Kríti, Greece* **36 D7** 35 15N 25 37 E
Neápolis, *Lakonía, Greece* **38 E5** 36 27N 23 8 E
Near Is., *U.S.A.* **100 C1** 52 30N 174 0 E
Neath, *U.K.* **13 F4** 51 39N 3 48W
Neath Port Talbot ☐, *U.K.* **13 F4** 51 42N 3 45W
Nebbou, *Burkina Faso* **83 C4** 11 9N 1 51W
Nebelat el Hagana, *Sudan* **81 E2** 13 13N 29 2 E
Nebine Cr. →, *Australia* **95 D4** 29 27 S 146 56 E
Nebitdag, *Turkmenistan* **50 F6** 39 30N 54 22 E
Nebo, *Australia* **94 C4** 21 42 S 148 42 E
Nebolchy, *Russia* **46 C7** 59 8N 33 18 E
Nebraska ☐, *U.S.A.* **112 E5** 41 30N 99 30W
Nebraska City, *U.S.A.* **112 E7** 40 41N 95 52W
Nébrodi, Monti, *Italy* **31 E7** 37 54N 14 35 E
Necedah, *U.S.A.* **112 C9** 44 2N 90 4W
Nechako →, *Canada* **104 C4** 53 30N 122 44W
Neches →, *U.S.A.* **113 L8** 29 58N 93 51W
Neckar →, *Germany* **25 F4** 49 27N 8 29 E
Necochea, *Argentina* **126 D4** 38 30 S 58 50W
Neda, *Spain* **34 B2** 43 30N 8 9W
Nedelino, *Bulgaria* **41 E9** 41 27N 25 3 E
Nedelišće, *Croatia* **29 B13** 46 23N 16 22 E
Nédha →, *Greece* **38 D3** 37 25N 21 45 E
Needles, *Canada* **104 D5** 49 53N 118 7W
Needles, *U.S.A.* **117 L12** 34 51N 114 37W
Needles, The, *U.K.* **13 G6** 50 39N 1 35W
Ñeembucú ☐, *Paraguay* **126 B4** 27 0 S 58 0W
Neemuch = Nimach, *India* **68 G6** 24 30N 74 56 E
Neenah, *U.S.A.* **108 C1** 44 11N 88 28W
Neepawa, *Canada* **105 C9** 50 15N 99 30W
Neftçala, *Azerbaijan* **71 B6** 39 19N 49 12 E
Neftegorsk, *Russia* **49 H4** 44 25N 39 45 E
Neftekumsk, *Russia* **49 H7** 44 46N 44 50 E
Nefyn, *U.K.* **12 E3** 52 56N 4 31W
Négala, *Mali* **82 C3** 12 52N 8 30W
Negapatam = Nagappattinam, *India* **66 P11** 10 46N 79 51 E
Negaunee, *U.S.A.* **108 B2** 46 30N 87 36W
Negele, *Ethiopia* **81 F4** 5 20N 39 36 E
Negev Desert = Hanegev, *Israel* **75 E4** 30 50N 35 0 E
Negoiul, Vf., *Romania* **43 E9** 45 38N 24 35 E
Negombo, *Sri Lanka* **66 R11** 7 12N 79 50 E
Negotin, *Serbia, Yug.* **40 B6** 44 16N 22 37 E
Negotino, *Macedonia* **40 E6** 41 29N 22 7 E
Negra, Peña, *Spain* **34 C4** 42 11N 6 30W
Negra, Pta., *Peru* **122 D2** 6 6 S 81 10W
Negrais, C. = Maudin Sun, *Burma* **67 M19** 16 0N 94 30 E
Negreşti, *Romania* **43 D12** 46 50N 27 30 E
Negreşti-Oaş, *Romania* **43 C8** 47 52N 23 26 E
Negril, *Jamaica* **120 C4** 18 22N 78 20W
Negro →, *Argentina* **122 H4** 41 2 S 62 47W
Negro →, *Brazil* **122 D4** 3 0 S 60 0W
Negro →, *Uruguay* **127 C4** 33 24 S 58 22W
Negros, *Phil.* **61 G5** 9 30N 122 40 E
Negru Vodă, *Romania* **43 G13** 43 47N 28 21 E
Neguac, *Canada* **103 C6** 47 15N 65 5W
Nehalem →, *U.S.A.* **116 E3** 45 40N 123 56W
Nehāvand, *Iran* **71 C6** 35 56N 49 31 E
Nehbandān, *Iran* **71 D9** 31 35N 60 5 E
Nehoiu, *Romania* **43 E11** 45 24N 26 20 E
Nei Monggol Zizhiqu ☐, *China* **56 D7** 42 0N 112 0 E
Neijiang, *China* **58 C5** 29 35N 104 55 E
Neillsville, *U.S.A.* **112 C9** 44 34N 90 36W
Neilton, *U.S.A.* **114 C2** 47 25N 123 53W
Neiqiu, *China* **56 F8** 37 15N 114 30 E
Neiva, *Colombia* **124 C3** 2 56N 75 18W
Neixiang, *China* **56 H6** 33 10N 111 52 E
Nejanilini L., *Canada* **105 B9** 59 33N 97 48W
Nejd = Najd, *Si. Arabia* **74 B3** 26 30N 42 0 E
Nejo, *Ethiopia* **81 F4** 9 30N 35 28 E
Nekā, *Iran* **71 B7** 36 39N 53 19 E
Nekemte, *Ethiopia* **81 F4** 9 4N 36 30 E
Nêkheb, *Egypt* **80 B3** 25 10N 32 48 E
Neksø, *Denmark* **11 J9** 55 4N 15 8 E
Nelas, *Portugal* **34 E3** 40 32N 7 52W
Nelia, *Australia* **94 C3** 20 39 S 142 12 E
Nelidovo, *Russia* **46 D7** 56 13N 32 49 E
Neligh, *U.S.A.* **112 D5** 42 8N 98 2W
Nelkan, *Russia* **51 D14** 57 40N 136 4 E
Nellore, *India* **66 M11** 14 27N 79 59 E
Nelson, *Canada* **104 D5** 49 30N 117 20W
Nelson, *N.Z.* **91 J4** 41 18 S 173 16 E
Nelson, *U.K.* **12 D5** 53 50N 2 13W
Nelson, *Ariz., U.S.A.* **115 J7** 35 31N 113 19W
Nelson, *Nev., U.S.A.* **117 K12** 35 42N 114 50W
Nelson →, *Canada* **105 C9** 54 33N 98 2W
Nelson, C., *Australia* **95 F3** 38 26 S 141 32 E
Nelson, Estrecho, *Chile* **128 G2** 51 30 S 75 0W
Nelson Forks, *Canada* **104 B4** 59 30N 124 0W
Nelson House, *Canada* **105 B9** 55 47N 98 51W
Nelson L., *Canada* **105 B8** 55 48N 100 7W
Nelspoort, *S. Africa* **88 E3** 32 7 S 23 0 E
Nelspruit, *S. Africa* **89 D5** 25 29 S 30 59 E
Néma, *Mauritania* **82 B3** 16 40N 7 15W
Neman, *Russia* **9 J20** 55 2N 22 2 E
Neman →, *Lithuania* **9 J19** 55 25N 21 10 E
Neméa, *Greece* **38 D4** 37 49N 22 40 E
Nemeiben L., *Canada* **105 B7** 55 20N 105 20W
Nemërçkë, Mal, *Albania* **40 F4** 40 15N 20 15 E
Nemira, Vf., *Romania* **43 D11** 46 17N 26 19 E
Némiscau, *Canada* **102 B4** 51 18N 76 54W
Némiscau, L., *Canada* **102 B4** 51 25N 76 40W
Nemours, *France* **19 D9** 48 16N 2 40 E
Nemšová, *Slovak Rep.* **27 C11** 48 58N 18 7 E
Nemunas = Neman →, *Lithuania* **9 J19** 55 25N 21 10 E
Nemuro, *Japan* **54 C12** 43 20N 145 35 E
Nemuro-Kaikyō, *Japan* **54 C12** 43 30N 145 30 E
Nen Jiang →, *China* **57 B13** 45 28N 124 30 E
Nenagh, *Ireland* **15 D3** 52 52N 8 11W
Nenasi, *Malaysia* **65 L4** 3 9N 103 23 E
Nene →, *U.K.* **13 E8** 52 49N 0 11 E
Nénita, *Greece* **39 C8** 38 14N 26 6 E
Nenjiang, *China* **60 B7** 49 10N 125 10 E
Neno, *Malawi* **87 F3** 15 25 S 34 40 E
Neodesha, *U.S.A.* **113 G7** 37 25N 95 41W
Neokhórion, *Aitolía kai Akarnanía, Greece* **38 C3** 38 25N 21 17 E
Neokhórion, *Árta, Greece* **38 B2** 39 4N 21 0 E
Néon Karlovásion, *Greece* **39 D8** 37 45N 26 42 E
Néon Petrítsi, *Greece* **40 E7** 41 16N 23 15 E
Neosho, *U.S.A.* **113 G7** 36 52N 94 22W
Neosho →, *U.S.A.* **113 H7** 36 48N 95 18W
Nepal ■, *Asia* **69 F11** 28 0N 84 30 E
Nepalganj, *Nepal* **69 E9** 28 5N 81 40 E
Nepalganj Road, *India* **69 E9** 28 1N 81 41 E
Nephi, *U.S.A.* **114 G8** 39 43N 111 50W
Nephin, *Ireland* **15 B2** 54 1N 9 22W
Nepi, *Italy* **29 F9** 42 14N 12 21 E
Nepomuk, *Czech Rep.* **26 B6** 49 29N 13 35 E
Neptune, *U.S.A.* **111 F10** 40 13N 74 2W
Nera →, *Italy* **29 F9** 42 26N 12 24 E
Nera →, *Romania* **42 F6** 44 48N 21 25 E
Nérac, *France* **20 D4** 44 8N 0 21 E
Nerang, *Australia* **95 D5** 27 58 S 153 20 E
Neratovice, *Czech Rep.* **26 A7** 50 16N 14 31 E
Nerchinsk, *Russia* **51 D12** 52 0N 116 39 E
Nereju, *Romania* **43 E11** 45 43N 26 43 E
Nerekhta, *Russia* **46 D11** 57 26N 40 38 E
Néret, L., *Canada* **103 B5** 54 45N 70 44W
Neretvanski Kanal, *Croatia* **29 E14** 43 7N 17 10 E
Neringa, *Lithuania* **9 J19** 55 20N 21 5 E
Nerja, *Spain* **35 J7** 36 43N 3 55W
Nerl →, *Russia* **46 D11** 56 11N 40 34 E
Nerpio, *Spain* **33 G2** 38 11N 2 16W
Nerva, *Spain* **35 H4** 37 42N 6 30W
Nervi, *Italy* **28 D6** 44 23N 9 2 E
Neryungri, *Russia* **51 D13** 57 38N 124 28 E
Nescopeck, *U.S.A.* **111 E8** 41 3N 76 12W
Nesebūr, *Bulgaria* **41 D11** 42 41N 27 46 E
Ness, L., *U.K.* **14 D4** 57 15N 4 32W
Ness City, *U.S.A.* **112 F5** 38 27N 99 54W
Nesterov, *Poland* **47 G2** 50 4N 23 58 E
Nestórion, *Greece* **40 F5** 40 24N 21 5 E
Néstos →, *Greece* **41 E8** 41 20N 24 35 E
Nesvady, *Slovak Rep.* **27 D11** 47 56N 18 7 E
Nesvizh = Nyasvizh, *Belarus* **47 F4** 53 14N 26 38 E
Netanya, *Israel* **75 C3** 32 20N 34 51 E
Netarhat, *India* **69 H11** 23 29N 84 16 E
Nete →, *Belgium* **17 C4** 51 7N 4 14 E
Netherdale, *Australia* **94 C4** 21 10 S 148 33 E
Netherlands ■, *Europe* **17 C5** 52 0N 5 30 E
Netherlands Antilles ■, *W. Indies* **124 A5** 12 15N 69 0W
Neto →, *Italy* **31 C10** 39 12N 17 9 E
Netrang, *India* **68 J5** 21 39N 73 21 E
Nettancourt, *France* **19 D11** 48 51N 4 57 E
Nettetal, *Germany* **24 D2** 51 19N 6 12 E
Nettilling L., *Canada* **101 B12** 66 30N 71 0W
Nettuno, *Italy* **30 A5** 41 27N 12 39 E
Netzahualcoyotl, Presa, *Mexico* **119 D6** 17 10N 93 30W
Neu-Isenburg, *Germany* **25 E4** 50 3N 8 42 E
Neu-Ulm, *Germany* **25 G6** 48 22N 10 0 E
Neubrandenburg, *Germany* **24 B9** 53 33N 13 15 E
Neubukow, *Germany* **24 A7** 54 2N 11 39 E
Neuburg, *Germany* **25 G7** 48 44N 11 11 E
Neuchâtel, *Switz.* **25 J2** 47 0N 6 55 E
Neuchâtel ☐, *Switz.* **25 J2** 47 0N 6 55 E
Neuchâtel, Lac de, *Switz.* **25 J2** 46 53N 6 50 E
Neudau, *Austria* **26 D9** 47 11N 16 6 E
Neuenhagen, *Germany* **24 C9** 52 30N 13 38 E
Neuenhaus, *Germany* **24 C2** 52 30N 6 58 E
Neuf-Brisach, *France* **19 D14** 48 1N 7 30 E
Neufahrn, *Bayern, Germany* **25 G8** 48 41N 12 11 E
Neufahrn, *Bayern, Germany* **25 G7** 48 18N 11 40 E
Neufchâteau, *Belgium* **17 E5** 49 50N 5 25 E
Neufchâteau, *France* **19 D12** 48 21N 5 40 E
Neufchâtel-en-Bray, *France* **18 C8** 49 44N 1 26 E
Neufchâtel-sur-Aisne, *France* **19 C11** 49 26N 4 1 E
Neuhaus, *Germany* **24 B6** 53 17N 10 56 E
Neuillé-Pont-Pierre, *France* **18 E7** 47 33N 0 33 E
Neuilly-St-Front, *France* **19 C10** 49 10N 3 15 E
Neukalen, *Germany* **24 B8** 53 49N 12 46 E
Neumarkt, *Germany* **25 F7** 49 26N 11 27 E
Neumünster, *Germany* **24 A5** 54 4N 9 58 E
Neung-sur-Beuvron, *France* **19 E8** 47 30N 1 50 E
Neunkirchen, *Austria* **26 D9** 47 43N 16 4 E
Neunkirchen, *Germany* **25 F3** 49 20N 7 9 E
Neuquén, *Argentina* **128 D3** 38 55 S 68 0W
Neuquén ☐, *Argentina* **126 D2** 38 0 S 69 50W
Neuruppin, *Germany* **24 C8** 52 55N 12 48 E
Neusäss, *Germany* **25 G6** 48 24N 10 50 E
Neuse →, *U.S.A.* **109 H7** 35 6N 76 29W
Neusiedl, *Austria* **27 D9** 47 57N 16 50 E
Neusiedler See, *Austria* **27 D9** 47 50N 16 47 E
Neuss, *Germany* **24 D2** 51 11N 6 42 E
Neussargues-Moissac, *France* **20 C7** 45 9N 3 0 E
Neustadt, *Bayern, Germany* **25 F8** 49 44N 12 10 E
Neustadt, *Bayern, Germany* **25 G7** 48 48N 11 46 E
Neustadt, *Bayern, Germany* **25 F6** 49 34N 10 37 E
Neustadt, *Bayern, Germany* **25 E7** 50 19N 11 7 E
Neustadt, *Brandenburg, Germany* **24 C8** 52 50N 12 27 E
Neustadt, *Hessen, Germany* **24 E5** 50 51N 9 9 E
Neustadt, *Niedersachsen, Germany* **24 C5** 52 30N 9 30 E
Neustadt, *Rhld-Pfz., Germany* **25 F4** 49 21N 8 10 E
Neustadt, *Sachsen, Germany* **24 D10** 51 2N 14 12 E
Neustadt, *Schleswig-Holstein, Germany* **24 A6** 54 6N 10 49 E
Neustadt, *Thüringen, Germany* **24 E7** 50 45N 11 43 E
Neustrelitz, *Germany* **24 B9** 53 21N 13 4 E
Neuvic, *France* **20 C6** 45 23N 2 16 E
Neuville-sur-Saône, *France* **21 C8** 45 52N 4 51 E
Neuvy-le-Roi, *France* **18 E7** 47 36N 0 36 E
Neuvy-St-Sépulchre, *France* **19 F8** 46 35N 1 48 E
Neuvy-sur-Barangeon, *France* **19 E9** 47 20N 2 15 E
Neuwerk, *Germany* **24 B4** 53 55N 8 30 E
Neuwied, *Germany* **24 E3** 50 26N 7 29 E
Neva →, *Russia* **46 C6** 59 50N 30 30 E
Nevada, *Iowa, U.S.A.* **112 D8** 42 1N 93 27W
Nevada, *Mo., U.S.A.* **113 G7** 37 51N 94 22W
Nevada ☐, *U.S.A.* **114 G5** 39 0N 117 0W
Nevada City, *U.S.A.* **116 F6** 39 16N 121 1W
Nevado, Cerro, *Argentina* **126 D2** 35 30 S 68 32W
Nevel, *Russia* **46 D5** 56 0N 29 55 E
Nevers, *France* **19 F10** 47 0N 3 9 E
Nevertire, *Australia* **95 E4** 31 50 S 147 44 E
Nevesinje, *Bos.-H.* **40 C2** 43 14N 18 6 E
Neville, *Canada* **105 D7** 49 58N 107 39W
Nevinnomyssk, *Russia* **49 H6** 44 40N 42 0 E
Nevis, *St. Kitts & Nevis* **121 C7** 17 0N 62 30W
Nevrokop = Gotse Delchev, *Bulgaria* **40 E7** 41 36N 23 46 E
Nevşehir, *Turkey* **70 B2** 38 33N 34 40 E
New →, *U.S.A.* **108 F5** 38 10N 81 12W
New Aiyansh, *Canada* **104 B3** 55 12N 129 4W
New Albany, *Ind., U.S.A.* **108 F3** 38 18N 85 49W
New Albany, *Miss., U.S.A.* **113 H10** 34 29N 89 0W
New Albany, *Pa., U.S.A.* **111 E8** 41 36N 76 27W
New Amsterdam, *Guyana* **124 B7** 6 15N 57 36W
New Angledool, *Australia* **95 D4** 29 5 S 147 55 E
New Baltimore, *U.S.A.* **110 D2** 42 41N 82 44W
New Bedford, *U.S.A.* **111 E14** 41 38N 70 56W
New Berlin, *N.Y., U.S.A.* **111 D9** 42 37N 75 20W
New Berlin, *Pa., U.S.A.* **110 F8** 40 50N 76 57W
New Bern, *U.S.A.* **109 H7** 35 7N 77 3W
New Bethlehem, *U.S.A.* **110 F5** 41 0N 79 20W
New Bloomfield, *U.S.A.* **110 F7** 40 25N 77 11W
New Boston, *U.S.A.* **113 J7** 33 28N 94 25W
New Braunfels, *U.S.A.* **113 L5** 29 42N 98 8W
New Brighton, *N.Z.* **91 K4** 43 29 S 172 43 E
New Brighton, *U.S.A.* **110 F4** 40 42N 80 19W
New Britain, *Papua N. G.* **96 H7** 5 50 S 150 20 E
New Britain, *U.S.A.* **111 E12** 41 40N 72 47W
New Brunswick, *U.S.A.* **111 F10** 40 30N 74 27W
New Brunswick ☐, *Canada* **103 C6** 46 50N 66 30W
New Bussa, *Nigeria* **83 D5** 9 53N 4 31 E
New Caledonia ■, *Pac. Oc.* **96 K8** 21 0 S 165 0 E
New Castile = Castilla-La Mancha ☐, *Spain* **6 H5** 39 30N 3 30W
New Castle, *Ind., U.S.A.* **108 F3** 39 55N 85 22W
New Castle, *Pa., U.S.A.* **110 F4** 41 0N 80 21W
New City, *U.S.A.* **111 E11** 41 9N 73 59W
New Concord, *U.S.A.* **110 G3** 39 59N 81 54W
New Cumberland, *U.S.A.* **110 F4** 40 30N 80 36W
New Cuyama, *U.S.A.* **117 L7** 34 57N 119 38W
New Delhi, *India* **68 E7** 28 37N 77 13 E
New Denver, *Canada* **104 D5** 50 0N 117 25W
New Don Pedro Reservoir, *U.S.A.* **116 H6** 37 43N 120 24W
New England, *U.S.A.* **112 B3** 46 32N 102 52W
New England Ra., *Australia* **95 E5** 30 20 S 151 45 E
New Forest, *U.K.* **13 G6** 50 53N 1 34W
New Galloway, *U.K.* **14 F4** 55 5N 4 9W
New Glasgow, *Canada* **103 C7** 45 35N 62 36W
New Guinea, *Oceania* **52 K17** 4 0 S 136 0 E
New Hamburg, *Canada* **110 C4** 43 23N 80 42W
New Hampshire ☐, *U.S.A.* **111 C13** 44 0N 71 30W
New Hampton, *U.S.A.* **112 D8** 43 3N 92 19W
New Hanover, *S. Africa* **89 D5** 29 22 S 30 31 E
New Hartford, *U.S.A.* **111 C9** 43 4N 75 18W
New Haven, *Conn., U.S.A.* **111 E12** 41 18N 72 55W
New Haven, *Mich., U.S.A.* **110 D2** 42 44N 82 48W
New Hazelton, *Canada* **104 B3** 55 20N 127 30W
New Hebrides = Vanuatu ■, *Pac. Oc.* **96 J8** 15 0 S 168 0 E
New Holland, *U.S.A.* **111 F8** 40 6N 76 5W
New Iberia, *U.S.A.* **113 K9** 30 1N 91 49W
New Ireland, *Papua N. G.* **96 H7** 3 20 S 151 50 E
New Jersey ☐, *U.S.A.* **108 E8** 40 0N 74 30W
New Kensington, *U.S.A.* **110 F5** 40 34N 79 46W
New Lexington, *U.S.A.* **108 F4** 39 43N 82 13W
New Liskeard, *Canada* **102 C4** 47 31N 79 41W
New London, *Conn., U.S.A.* **111 E12** 41 22N 72 6W
New London, *Ohio, U.S.A.* **110 E2** 41 5N 82 24W
New London, *Wis., U.S.A.* **112 C10** 44 23N 88 45W
New Madrid, *U.S.A.* **113 G10** 36 36N 89 32W
New Martinsville, *U.S.A.* **108 F5** 39 39N 80 52W
New Meadows, *U.S.A.* **114 D5** 44 58N 116 18W
New Melones L., *U.S.A.* **116 H6** 37 57N 120 31W
New Mexico ☐, *U.S.A.* **115 J10** 34 30N 106 0W
New Milford, *Conn., U.S.A.* **111 E11** 41 35N 73 25W
New Milford, *Pa., U.S.A.* **111 E9** 41 52N 75 44W
New Norcia, *Australia* **93 F2** 30 57 S 116 13 E
New Norfolk, *Australia* **94 G4** 42 46 S 147 2 E
New Orleans, *U.S.A.* **113 L9** 29 58N 90 4W
New Philadelphia, *U.S.A.* **110 F3** 40 30N 81 27W
New Plymouth, *N.Z.* **91 H5** 39 4 S 174 5 E
New Plymouth, *U.S.A.* **114 E5** 43 58N 116 49W
New Port Richey, *U.S.A.* **109 L4** 28 16N 82 43W
New Providence, *Bahamas* **120 A4** 25 25N 78 35W
New Quay, *U.K.* **13 E3** 52 13N 4 21W
New Radnor, *U.K.* **13 E4** 52 15N 3 9W
New Richmond, *Canada* **103 C6** 48 15N 65 45W
New Richmond, *U.S.A.* **112 C8** 45 7N 92 32W
New Roads, *U.S.A.* **113 K9** 30 42N 91 26W
New Rochelle, *U.S.A.* **111 F11** 40 55N 73 47W
New Rockford, *U.S.A.* **112 B5** 47 41N 99 8W
New Romney, *U.K.* **13 G8** 50 59N 0 57 E
New Ross, *Ireland* **15 D5** 52 23N 6 57W
New Salem, *U.S.A.* **112 B4** 46 51N 101 25W
New Scone, *U.K.* **14 E5** 56 25N 3 24W
New Siberian I. = Novaya Sibir, Ostrov, *Russia* **51 B16** 75 10N 150 0 E
New Siberian Is. = Novosibirskiye Ostrova, *Russia* **51 B15** 75 0N 142 0 E
New Smyrna Beach, *U.S.A.* **109 L5** 29 1N 80 56W
New South Wales ☐, *Australia* **95 E4** 33 0 S 146 0 E
New Town, *U.S.A.* **112 B3** 47 59N 102 30W
New Tredegar, *U.K.* **13 F4** 51 44N 3 16W
New Ulm, *U.S.A.* **112 C7** 44 19N 94 28W
New Waterford, *Canada* **103 C7** 46 13N 60 4W
New Westminster, *Canada* **116 A4** 49 13N 122 55W
New York, *U.S.A.* **111 F11** 40 45N 74 0W
New York ☐, *U.S.A.* **111 D9** 43 0N 75 0W
New York Mts., *U.S.A.* **115 J6** 35 0N 115 20W
New Zealand ■, *Oceania* **91 J6** 40 0 S 176 0 E
Newaj →, *India* **68 G7** 24 24N 76 49 E
Newala, *Tanzania* **87 E4** 10 58 S 39 18 E
Newark, *Del., U.S.A.* **108 F8** 39 41N 75 46W
Newark, *N.J., U.S.A.* **111 F10** 40 44N 74 10W
Newark, *N.Y., U.S.A.* **110 C7** 43 3N 77 6W
Newark, *Ohio, U.S.A.* **110 F2** 40 3N 82 24W
Newark-on-Trent, *U.K.* **12 D7** 53 5N 0 48W
Newark Valley, *U.S.A.* **111 D8** 42 14N 76 11W
Newberg, *U.S.A.* **114 D2** 45 18N 122 58W
Newberry, *Mich., U.S.A.* **108 B3** 46 21N 85 30W
Newberry, *S.C., U.S.A.* **109 H5** 34 17N 81 37W
Newberry Springs, *U.S.A.* **117 L10** 34 50N 116 41W
Newboro L., *Canada* **111 B8** 44 38N 76 20W
Newbridge = Droichead Nua, *Ireland* **15 C5** 53 11N 6 48W
Newburgh, *Canada* **110 B8** 44 19N 76 52W
Newburgh, *U.S.A.* **111 E10** 41 30N 74 1W
Newbury, *U.K.* **13 F6** 51 24N 1 20W
Newbury, *N.H., U.S.A.* **111 B12** 43 19N 72 3W
Newbury, *Vt., U.S.A.* **111 B12** 44 5N 72 4W
Newburyport, *U.S.A.* **109 D10** 42 49N 70 53W
Newcastle, *Australia* **95 E5** 33 0 S 151 46 E
Newcastle, *N.B., Canada* **103 C6** 47 1N 65 38W
Newcastle, *Ont., Canada* **102 D4** 43 55N 78 35W
Newcastle, *S. Africa* **89 D4** 27 45 S 29 58 E
Newcastle, *U.K.* **15 B6** 54 13N 5 54W
Newcastle, *Calif., U.S.A.* **116 G5** 38 53N 121 8W
Newcastle, *Wyo., U.S.A.* **112 D2** 43 50N 104 11W
Newcastle Emlyn, *U.K.* **13 E3** 52 2N 4 28W
Newcastle Ra., *Australia* **92 C5** 15 45 S 130 15 E
Newcastle-under-Lyme, *U.K.* **12 D5** 53 1N 2 14W
Newcastle-upon-Tyne, *U.K.* **12 C6** 54 58N 1 36W
Newcastle Waters, *Australia* **94 B1** 17 30 S 133 28 E
Newcastle West, *Ireland* **15 D2** 52 27N 9 3W
Newcomb, *U.S.A.* **111 C10** 43 58N 74 10W
Newcomerstown, *U.S.A.* **110 F3** 40 16N 81 36W
Newdegate, *Australia* **93 F2** 33 6 S 119 0 E
Newell, *Australia* **94 B4** 16 20 S 145 16 E
Newell, *U.S.A.* **112 C3** 44 43N 103 25W
Newfane, *U.S.A.* **110 C6** 43 17N 78 43W
Newfield, *U.S.A.* **111 D8** 42 18N 76 33W
Newfound L., *U.S.A.* **111 C13** 43 40N 71 47W
Newfoundland, *Canada* **98 E14** 49 0N 55 0W
Newfoundland, *U.S.A.* **111 E9** 41 18N 75 19W
Newfoundland ☐, *Canada* **103 B8** 53 0N 58 0W
Newhall, *U.S.A.* **117 L8** 34 23N 118 32W
Newhaven, *U.K.* **13 G8** 50 47N 0 3 E
Newkirk, *U.S.A.* **113 G6** 36 53N 97 3W
Newlyn, *U.K.* **13 G2** 50 6N 5 34W
Newman, *Australia* **92 D2** 23 18 S 119 45 E
Newman, *U.S.A.* **116 H5** 37 19N 121 1W
Newmarket, *Canada* **110 B5** 44 3N 79 28W
Newmarket, *Ireland* **15 D2** 52 13N 9 0W
Newmarket, *U.K.* **13 E8** 52 15N 0 25 E
Newmarket, *U.S.A.* **111 C14** 43 4N 70 56W
Newnan, *U.S.A.* **109 J3** 33 23N 84 48W
Newport, *Ireland* **15 C2** 53 53N 9 33W
Newport, *I. of W., U.K.* **13 G6** 50 42N 1 17W
Newport, *Newp., U.K.* **13 F5** 51 35N 3 0W
Newport, *Ark., U.S.A.* **113 H9** 35 37N 91 16W
Newport, *Ky., U.S.A.* **108 F3** 39 5N 84 30W
Newport, *N.H., U.S.A.* **111 C12** 43 22N 72 10W
Newport, *N.Y., U.S.A.* **111 C9** 43 11N 75 1W
Newport, *Oreg., U.S.A.* **114 D1** 44 39N 124 3W
Newport, *Pa., U.S.A.* **110 F7** 40 29N 77 8W
Newport, *R.I., U.S.A.* **111 E13** 41 29N 71 19W
Newport, *Tenn., U.S.A.* **109 H4** 35 58N 83 11W
Newport, *Vt., U.S.A.* **111 B12** 44 56N 72 13W
Newport, *Wash., U.S.A.* **114 B5** 48 11N 117 3W
Newport ☐, *U.K.* **13 F4** 51 33N 3 1W
Newport Beach, *U.S.A.* **117 M9** 33 37N 117 56W
Newport News, *U.S.A.* **108 G7** 36 59N 76 25W
Newport Pagnell, *U.K.* **13 E7** 52 5N 0 43W
Newquay, *U.K.* **13 G2** 50 25N 5 6W
Newry, *U.K.* **15 B5** 54 11N 6 21W
Newton, *Ill., U.S.A.* **112 F10** 38 59N 88 10W
Newton, *Iowa, U.S.A.* **112 E8** 41 42N 93 3W
Newton, *Kans., U.S.A.* **113 F6** 38 3N 97 21W
Newton, *Mass., U.S.A.* **111 D13** 42 21N 71 12W
Newton, *Miss., U.S.A.* **113 J10** 32 19N 89 10W
Newton, *N.C., U.S.A.* **109 H5** 35 40N 81 13W
Newton, *N.J., U.S.A.* **111 E10** 41 3N 74 45W
Newton, *Tex., U.S.A.* **113 K8** 30 51N 93 46W
Newton Abbot, *U.K.* **13 G4** 50 32N 3 37W
Newton Aycliffe, *U.K.* **12 C6** 54 37N 1 34W
Newton Falls, *U.S.A.* **110 E4** 41 11N 80 59W
Newton Stewart, *U.K.* **14 G4** 54 57N 4 30W
Newtonmore, *U.K.* **14 D4** 57 4N 4 8W
Newtown, *U.K.* **13 E4** 52 31N 3 19W
Newtownabbey, *U.K.* **15 B6** 54 40N 5 56W
Newtownards, *U.K.* **15 B6** 54 36N 5 42W
Newtownbarry = Bunclody, *Ireland* **15 D5** 52 39N 6 40W
Newtownstewart, *U.K.* **15 B4** 54 43N 7 23W
Newville, *U.S.A.* **110 F7** 40 10N 77 24W
Nexon, *France* **20 C5** 45 41N 1 11 E
Neya, *Russia* **48 A6** 58 21N 43 49 E
Neyrīz, *Iran* **71 D7** 29 15N 54 19 E
Neyshābūr, *Iran* **71 B8** 36 10N 58 50 E
Nezhin = Nizhyn, *Ukraine* **47 G6** 51 5N 31 55 E
Nezperce, *U.S.A.* **114 C5** 46 14N 116 14W
Ngabang, *Indonesia* **62 D3** 0 23N 109 55 E
Ngabordamlu, Tanjung, *Indonesia* **63 F8** 6 56 S 134 11 E
N'Gage, *Angola* **84 F3** 7 46 S 15 16 E
Ngala, *Nigeria* **83 C7** 12 20N 14 11 E
Ngambé, *Cameroon* **83 D7** 5 48N 11 29 E
Ngambé, *Cameroon* **83 E7** 4 21N 10 40 E
Ngami Depression, *Botswana* **88 C3** 20 30 S 22 46 E
Ngamo, *Zimbabwe* **87 F2** 19 3 S 27 32 E
Ngangala, *Sudan* **81 G3** 4 42N 31 55 E
Nganglong Kangri, *China* **67 C12** 33 0N 81 0 E
Ngao, *Thailand* **64 C2** 18 46N 99 59 E
Ngaoundéré, *Cameroon* **84 C2** 7 15N 13 35 E
Ngapara, *N.Z.* **91 L3** 44 57 S 170 46 E
Ngara, *Tanzania* **86 C3** 2 29 S 30 40 E
Ngawi, *Indonesia* **63 G14** 7 24 S 111 26 E
Nghia Lo, *Vietnam* **58 G5** 21 33N 104 28 E
Ngoboli, *Sudan* **81 G3** 4 57N 32 37 E
Ngoma, *Malawi* **87 E3** 13 8 S 33 45 E
Ngomahura, *Zimbabwe* **87 G3** 20 26 S 30 43 E
Ngomba, *Tanzania* **87 D3** 8 20 S 32 53 E
Ngop, *Sudan* **81 F3** 6 17N 30 9 E
Ngoring Hu, *China* **60 C4** 34 55N 97 5 E
Ngorkou, *Mali* **82 B4** 15 40N 3 41W
Ngorongoro, *Tanzania* **86 C4** 3 11 S 35 32 E
Ngozi, *Burundi* **86 C2** 2 54 S 29 50 E
Ngudu, *Tanzania* **86 C3** 2 58 S 33 25 E
Nguigmi, *Niger* **79 F8** 14 20N 13 20 E
Nguila, *Cameroon* **83 E7** 4 41N 11 43 E
Nguiu, *Australia* **92 B5** 11 46 S 130 38 E
Ngukurr, *Australia* **94 A1** 14 44 S 134 44 E
Ngulu Atoll, *Pac. Oc.* **63 C9** 8 0N 137 30 E
Ngunga, *Tanzania* **86 C3** 3 37 S 33 37 E
Nguru, *Nigeria* **83 C7** 12 56N 10 29 E
Nguru Mts., *Tanzania* **86 D4** 6 0 S 37 30 E
Nguyen Binh, *Vietnam* **58 F5** 22 39N 105 56 E
Nha Trang, *Vietnam* **65 F7** 12 16N 109 10 E
Nhacoongo, *Mozam.* **89 C6** 24 18 S 35 14 E
Nhamaabué, *Mozam.* **87 F4** 17 25 S 35 5 E
Nhamundá →, *Brazil* **125 D7** 2 12 S 56 41W
Nhangulaze, L., *Mozam.* **89 C5** 24 0 S 34 30 E
Nhill, *Australia* **95 F3** 36 18 S 141 40 E
Nho Quan, *Vietnam* **58 G5** 20 18N 105 45 E
Nhulunbuy, *Australia* **94 A2** 12 10 S 137 20 E
Nia-nia, *Dem. Rep. of the Congo* **86 B2** 1 30N 27 40 E
Niafounké, *Mali* **82 B4** 16 0N 4 5W
Niagara Falls, *Canada* **102 D4** 43 7N 79 5W
Niagara Falls, *U.S.A.* **110 C6** 43 5N 79 4W
Niagara-on-the-Lake, *Canada* **110 C5** 43 15N 79 4W
Niah, *Malaysia* **62 D4** 3 58N 113 46 E
Niamey, *Niger* **83 C5** 13 27N 2 6 E
Niandan-Koro, *Guinea* **82 C3** 11 5N 9 15W
Nianforando, *Guinea* **82 D2** 9 37N 10 36W
Niangara, *Dem. Rep. of the Congo* **86 B2** 3 42N 27 50 E
Niangbo, *Ivory C.* **82 D3** 8 49N 5 10W
Niangoloko, *Burkina Faso* **82 C4** 10 15N 4 55W
Niantic, *U.S.A.* **111 E12** 41 20N 72 11W
Niaro, *Sudan* **81 E3** 10 38N 31 31 E
Nias, *Indonesia* **62 D1** 1 0N 97 30 E
Niassa ☐, *Mozam.* **87 E4** 13 30 S 36 0 E
Nībāk, *Si. Arabia* **71 E7** 24 25N 50 50 E
Nibe, *Denmark* **11 H3** 56 59N 9 38 E
Nicaragua ■, *Cent. Amer.* **120 D2** 11 40N 85 30W
Nicaragua, L. de, *Nic.* **120 D2** 12 0N 85 30W
Nicastro, *Italy* **31 D9** 38 59N 16 19 E
Nice, *France* **21 E11** 43 42N 7 14 E
Niceville, *U.S.A.* **109 K2** 30 31N 86 30W
Nichicun, L., *Canada* **103 B5** 53 5N 71 0W
Nichinan, *Japan* **55 J5** 31 38N 131 23 E
Nicholás, Canal, *W. Indies* **120 B3** 23 30N 80 5W
Nicholasville, *U.S.A.* **108 G3** 37 53N 84 34W
Nichols, *U.S.A.* **111 D8** 42 1N 76 22W
Nicholson, *Australia* **92 C4** 18 2 S 128 54 E
Nicholson, *U.S.A.* **111 E9** 41 37N 75 47W
Nicholson →, *Australia* **94 B2** 17 31 S 139 36 E
Nicholson L., *Canada* **105 A8** 62 40N 102 40W
Nicholson Ra., *Australia* **93 E2** 27 15 S 116 45 E
Nicholville, *U.S.A.* **111 B10** 44 41N 74 39W
Nicobar Is., *Ind. Oc.* **52 J13** 9 0N 93 0 E
Nicola, *Canada* **104 C4** 50 12N 120 40W
Nicolls Town, *Bahamas* **120 A4** 25 8N 78 0W
Nicopolis, *Greece* **38 B2** 39 2N 20 37 E
Nicosia, *Cyprus* **36 D12** 35 10N 33 25 E
Nicosia, *Italy* **31 E7** 37 45N 14 24 E
Nicótera, *Italy* **31 D8** 38 33N 15 56 E
Nicoya, *Costa Rica* **120 D2** 10 9N 85 27W
Nicoya, G. de, *Costa Rica* **120 E3** 10 0N 85 0W
Nicoya, Pen. de, *Costa Rica* **120 E2** 9 45N 85 40W
Nidd →, *U.K.* **12 D6** 53 59N 1 23W
Nidda, *Germany* **25 E5** 50 23N 9 1 E
Nidda →, *Germany* **25 E4** 50 17N 8 48 E
Nidwalden ☐, *Switz.* **25 J4** 46 50N 8 25 E
Nidzica, *Poland* **45 E7** 53 25N 20 28 E
Niebüll, *Germany* **24 A4** 54 46N 8 48 E
Nied →, *Germany* **19 C13** 49 23N 6 40 E
Niederaula, *Germany* **24 E5** 50 47N 9 36 E
Niederbayern ☐, *Germany* **25 G8** 48 40N 12 50 E
Niederbronn-les-Bains, *France* **19 D14** 48 57N 7 39 E
Niedere Tauern, *Austria* **26 D7** 47 20N 14 0 E
Niederlausitz, *Germany* **24 D9** 51 42N 13 59 E

Norwich

Niederösterreich □, Austria 26 C8 48 25N 15 40 E
Niedersachsen □, Germany 24 C4 52 50N 9 0 E
Niekerkshoop, S. Africa 88 D3 29 19 S 22 51 E
Niellé, Ivory C. 82 C3 10 5N 5 38W
Niemba, Dem. Rep. of the Congo 86 D2 5 58 S 28 24 E
Niemen = Neman →, Lithuania 9 J19 55 25N 21 10 E
Niemodlin, Poland 45 H4 50 38N 17 38 E
Nienburg, Germany 24 C5 52 39N 9 13 E
Niepołomice, Poland 45 H7 50 3N 20 13 E
Niers →, Germany 24 D1 51 43N 5 57 E
Niesky, Germany 24 D10 51 17N 14 49 E
Nieszawa, Poland 45 F5 52 52N 18 50 E
Nieu Bethesda, S. Africa 88 E3 31 51 S 24 34 E
Nieuw Amsterdam, Suriname 125 B7 5 53N 55 5W
Nieuw Nickerie, Suriname 125 B7 6 0N 56 59W
Nieuwoudtville, S. Africa 88 E2 31 23 S 19 7 E
Nieuwpoort, Belgium 17 C2 51 8N 2 45 E
Nieves, Pico de las, Canary Is. 37 G4 27 57N 15 35W
Nièvre □, France 19 E10 47 10N 3 40 E
Niga, Mali 82 C3 13 38N 5 27W
Niğde, Turkey 70 B2 37 58N 34 40 E
Nigel, S. Africa 89 D4 26 27 S 28 25 E
Niger □, Nigeria 83 D6 10 0N 5 30 E
Niger ■, W. Afr. 83 B7 17 30N 10 0 E
Niger →, W. Afr. 83 D6 5 33N 6 33 E
Niger Delta, Africa 83 E6 5 0N 6 0 E
Nigeria ■, W. Afr. 83 D6 8 30N 8 0 E
Nighasin, India 69 E9 28 14N 80 52 E
Nightcaps, N.Z. 91 L2 45 57 S 168 2 E
Nigrita, Greece 40 F7 40 56N 23 29 E
Nii-Jima, Japan 55 G9 34 20N 139 15 E
Niigata, Japan 54 F9 37 58N 139 0 E
Niigata □, Japan 55 F9 37 15N 138 45 E
Niihama, Japan 55 H6 33 55N 133 16 E
Niihau, U.S.A. 106 H14 21 54N 160 9W
Niimi, Japan 55 G6 34 59N 133 28 E
Niitsu, Japan 54 F9 37 48N 139 7 E
Níjar, Spain 33 J2 36 53N 2 15W
Nijil, Jordan 75 E4 30 32N 35 33 E
Nijkerk, Neths. 17 B5 52 13N 5 30 E
Nijmegen, Neths. 17 C5 51 50N 5 52 E
Nijverdal, Neths. 17 B6 52 22N 6 28 E
Nīk Pey, Iran 71 B6 36 50N 48 10 E
Nike, Nigeria 83 D6 6 26N 7 29 E
Nikiniki, Indonesia 63 F6 9 49 S 124 30 E
Nikísiani, Greece 41 F8 40 57N 24 9 E
Níkitas, Greece 40 F7 40 13N 23 43 E
Nikki, Benin 83 D5 9 58N 3 12 E
Nikkō, Japan 55 F9 36 45N 139 35 E
Nikolayev = Mykolayiv, Ukraine 47 J7 46 58N 32 0 E
Nikolayevsk, Russia 48 E7 50 0N 45 35 E
Nikolayevsk-na-Amur, Russia 51 D15 53 8N 140 44 E
Nikolsk, Russia 48 D8 53 49N 46 4 E
Nikolskoye, Russia 51 D17 55 12N 166 0 E
Nikopol, Bulgaria 41 C8 43 43N 24 54 E
Nikopol, Ukraine 47 J8 47 35N 34 25 E
Niksar, Turkey 72 B7 40 31N 37 2 E
Nīkshahr, Iran 71 E9 26 15N 60 10 E
Nikšić, Montenegro, Yug. 40 D2 42 50N 18 57 E
Nîl, Nahr en →, Africa 80 H7 30 10N 31 6 E
Nîl el Abyad →, Sudan 81 D3 15 38N 32 31 E
Nîl el Azraq →, Sudan 81 D3 15 38N 32 31 E
Nila, Indonesia 63 F7 6 44 S 129 31 E
Niland, U.S.A. 117 M11 33 14N 115 31W
Nile = Nîl, Nahr en →, Africa 80 H7 30 10N 31 6 E
Niles, Mich., U.S.A. 108 E2 41 50N 86 15W
Niles, Ohio, U.S.A. 110 E4 41 11N 80 46W
Nilüfer →, Turkey 41 F12 40 18N 28 27 E
Nim Ka Thana, India 68 F6 27 44N 75 48 E
Nimach, India 68 G6 24 30N 74 56 E
Nimbahera, India 68 G6 24 37N 74 45 E
Nîmes, France 21 E8 43 50N 4 23 E
Nimfaíon, Ákra = Pínnes, Ákra, Greece 41 F8 40 5N 24 20 E
Nimmitabel, Australia 95 F4 36 29 S 149 15 E
Nimule, Sudan 81 G3 3 32N 32 3 E
Nin, Croatia 29 D12 44 16N 15 12 E
Nīnawá, Iraq 70 B4 36 25N 43 10 E
Nindigully, Australia 95 D4 28 21 S 148 50 E
Nineveh = Nīnawá, Iraq 70 B4 36 25N 43 10 E
Ning Xian, China 56 G4 35 30N 107 58 E
Ning'an, China 57 B15 44 22N 129 20 E
Ningbo, China 59 C13 29 51N 121 28 E
Ningcheng, China 57 D10 41 32N 119 53 E
Ningde, China 59 D12 26 38N 119 23 E
Ningdu, China 59 D10 26 25N 115 59 E
Ninggang, China 59 D9 26 42N 113 55 E
Ningguo, China 59 B12 30 35N 119 0 E
Ninghai, China 59 C13 29 15N 121 27 E
Ninghua, China 59 D11 26 14N 116 45 E
Ningi, Nigeria 83 C6 10 55N 9 30 E
Ningjin, China 56 F8 37 35N 114 57 E
Ningjing Shan, China 58 C2 30 0N 98 20 E
Ninglang, China 58 D3 27 20N 100 55 E
Ningling, China 56 G8 34 25N 115 22 E
Ningming, China 58 F6 22 8N 107 4 E
Ningnan, China 58 D4 27 5N 102 36 E
Ningpo = Ningbo, China 59 C13 29 51N 121 28 E
Ningqiang, China 56 H4 32 47N 106 15 E
Ningshan, China 56 H5 33 21N 108 21 E
Ningsia Hui A.R. = Ningxia Huizu Zizhiqu □, China 56 F4 38 0N 106 0 E
Ningwu, China 56 E7 39 0N 112 18 E
Ningxia Huizu Zizhiqu □, China 56 F4 38 0N 106 0 E
Ningxiang, China 59 C9 28 15N 112 30 E
Ningyang, China 56 G9 35 47N 116 45 E
Ningyuan, China 59 E8 25 37N 111 57 E
Ninh Binh, Vietnam 58 G5 20 15N 105 55 E
Ninh Giang, Vietnam 64 B6 20 44N 106 24 E
Ninh Hoa, Vietnam 64 F7 12 30N 109 7 E
Ninh Ma, Vietnam 64 F7 12 48N 109 21 E
Ninove, Belgium 17 D4 50 51N 4 2 E
Nioaque, Brazil 127 A4 21 5 S 55 50W
Niobrara, U.S.A. 112 D6 42 45N 98 2W
Niobrara →, U.S.A. 112 D6 42 46N 98 3W
Niono, Mali 82 C3 14 15N 6 0W
Nionsamoridougou, Guinea 82 D3 8 45N 8 50W
Nioro du Rip, Senegal 82 C1 13 40N 15 50W
Nioro du Sahel, Mali 82 B3 15 15N 9 30W
Niort, France 20 B3 46 19N 0 29W
Nipawin, Canada 105 C8 53 20N 104 0W
Nipfjället, Sweden 10 C6 61 59N 12 50 E
Nipigon, Canada 102 C2 49 0N 88 17W
Nipigon, L., Canada 102 C2 49 50N 88 30W
Nipishish L., Canada 103 B7 54 12N 60 45W
Nipissing, L., Canada 102 C4 46 20N 80 0W
Nipomo, U.S.A. 117 K6 35 3N 120 29W
Nipton, U.S.A. 117 K11 35 28N 115 16W
Niquelândia, Brazil 125 F9 14 33 S 48 23W
Nīr, Iran 70 B5 38 2N 47 59 E
Nirasaki, Japan 55 G9 35 42N 138 27 E
Nirmal, India 66 K11 19 3N 78 20 E
Nirmali, India 69 F12 26 20N 86 35 E
Niš, Serbia, Yug. 40 C5 43 19N 21 58 E
Nisa, Portugal 35 F3 39 30N 7 41W
Nişāb, Si. Arabia 70 D5 29 11N 44 43 E
Nişāb, Yemen 74 E4 14 25N 46 29 E
Nišava →, Serbia, Yug. 40 C5 43 20N 21 46 E
Niscemi, Italy 31 E7 37 9N 14 23 E
Nishinomiya, Japan 55 G7 34 45N 135 20 E
Nishino'omote, Japan 55 J5 30 43N 130 59 E
Nishiwaki, Japan 55 G7 34 59N 134 58 E
Nísíros, Greece 39 E9 36 35N 27 12 E
Niška Banja, Serbia, Yug. 40 C6 43 18N 22 1 E
Niskibi →, Canada 102 A2 56 29N 88 9W
Nisko, Poland 45 H9 50 35N 22 7 E
Nisporeni, Moldova 43 C13 47 4N 28 10 E
Nisqually →, U.S.A. 116 C4 47 6N 122 42W
Nissáki, Greece 36 A3 39 43N 19 52 E
Nissan →, Sweden 11 H6 56 40N 12 51 E
Nissum Bredning, Denmark 11 H2 56 40N 8 20 E
Nissum Fjord, Denmark 11 H2 56 20N 8 11 E
Nistru = Dnister →, Europe 47 J6 46 18N 30 17 E
Nisutlin →, Canada 104 A2 60 14N 132 34W
Nitchequon, Canada 103 B5 53 10N 70 58W
Niterói, Brazil 127 A7 22 52 S 43 0W
Nith →, Canada 110 C4 43 12N 80 23W
Nith →, U.K. 14 F5 55 14N 3 33W
Nitra, Slovak Rep. 27 C11 48 19N 18 4 E
Nitra →, Slovak Rep. 27 D11 47 46N 18 10 E
Nitriansky □, Slovak Rep. 27 C11 48 10N 18 30 E
Nittenau, Germany 25 F8 49 12N 12 16 E
Niuafo'ou, Tonga 91 B11 15 30 S 175 58W
Niue, Cook Is. 97 J11 19 2 S 169 54W
Niulan Jiang →, China 58 D4 27 30N 103 5 E
Niut, Indonesia 62 D4 0 55N 110 6 E
Niutou Shan, China 59 C13 29 5N 121 59 E
Niuzhuang, China 57 D12 40 58N 122 28 E
Nivala, Finland 8 E21 63 56N 24 57 E
Nivelles, Belgium 17 D4 50 35N 4 20 E
Nivernais, France 19 E10 47 15N 3 30 E
Niwas, India 69 H9 23 3N 80 26 E
Nixon, U.S.A. 113 L6 29 16N 97 46W
Nizamabad, India 66 K11 18 45N 78 7 E
Nizamghat, India 67 E19 28 20N 95 45 E
Nizhne Kolymsk, Russia 51 C17 68 34N 160 55 E
Nizhnegorskiy = Nyzhnohirskyy, Ukraine 47 K8 45 27N 34 38 E
Nizhnekamsk, Russia 48 C10 55 38N 51 49 E
Nizhneudinsk, Russia 51 D10 54 54N 99 3 E
Nizhnevartovsk, Russia 50 C8 60 56N 76 38 E
Nizhniy Chir, Russia 49 F6 48 22N 43 5 E
Nizhniy Lomov, Russia 48 D6 53 34N 43 38 E
Nizhniy Novgorod, Russia 48 B7 56 20N 44 0 E
Nizhniy Tagil, Russia 50 D6 57 55N 59 57 E
Nizhyn, Ukraine 47 G6 51 5N 31 55 E
Nizina Mazowiecka, Poland 45 F8 52 30N 21 0 E
Nizip, Turkey 70 B3 37 5N 37 50 E
Nízké Tatry, Slovak Rep. 27 C12 48 55N 19 30 E
Nízký Jeseník, Czech Rep. 27 B10 49 50N 17 30 E
Nizza Monferrato, Italy 28 D5 44 46N 8 21 E
Njakwa, Malawi 87 E3 11 1 S 33 56 E
Njanji, Zambia 87 E3 14 25 S 31 46 E
Njegoš, Montenegro, Yug. 40 D2 42 53N 18 45 E
Njinjo, Tanzania 87 D4 8 48 S 38 54 E
Njombe, Tanzania 87 D3 9 20 S 34 50 E
Njombe →, Tanzania 86 D4 6 56 S 35 6 E
Njurundabommen, Sweden 10 B11 62 15N 17 25 E
Nkambe, Cameroon 83 D7 6 35N 10 40 E
Nkana, Zambia 87 E2 12 50 S 28 8 E
Nkandla, S. Africa 89 D5 28 37 S 31 5 E
Nkawkaw, Ghana 83 D4 6 36N 0 49W
Nkayi, Zimbabwe 87 F2 19 41 S 29 20 E
Nkhotakota, Malawi 87 E3 12 56 S 34 15 E
Nkongsamba, Cameroon 83 E6 4 55N 9 55 E
Nkurenkuru, Namibia 88 B2 17 42 S 18 32 E
Nkwanta, Ghana 82 D4 6 10N 2 10W
Nmai →, Burma 58 F2 25 30N 97 25 E
Noakhali = Maijdi, Bangla. 67 H17 22 48N 91 10 E
Nobel, Canada 110 A4 45 25N 80 6W
Nobeoka, Japan 55 H5 32 36N 131 41 E
Noblejas, Spain 34 F7 39 58N 3 26W
Noblesville, U.S.A. 108 E3 40 3N 86 1W
Noce →, Italy 28 B8 46 9N 11 4 E
Nocera Inferiore, Italy 31 B7 40 44N 14 38 E
Nocera Umbra, Italy 29 E9 43 5N 12 47 E
Noci, Italy 31 B10 40 48N 17 7 E
Nocona, U.S.A. 113 J6 33 47N 97 44W
Nocrich, Romania 43 E9 45 55N 24 26 E
Noda, Japan 55 G9 35 56N 139 52 E
Nogales, Mexico 118 A2 31 20N 110 56W
Nogales, U.S.A. 115 L8 31 20N 110 56W
Nogaro, France 20 E3 43 45N 0 2W
Nogat →, Poland 44 D6 54 17N 19 17 E
Nōgata, Japan 55 H5 33 48N 130 44 E
Nogent, France 19 D12 48 1N 5 20 E
Nogent-le-Rotrou, France 18 D7 48 20N 0 50 E
Nogent-sur-Seine, France 19 D10 48 30N 3 30 E
Noggerup, Australia 93 F2 33 32 S 116 5 E
Noginsk, Moskva, Russia 46 E10 55 50N 38 25 E
Noginsk, Tunguska, Russia 51 C10 64 30N 90 50 E
Nogoa →, Australia 94 C4 23 40 S 147 55 E
Nogoyá, Argentina 126 C4 32 24 S 59 48W
Nógrád □, Hungary 42 C4 48 0N 19 30 E
Noguera Pallaresa →, Spain 32 D5 41 55N 0 55 E
Noguera Ribagorzana →, Spain 32 D5 41 40N 0 43 E
Nohar, India 68 E6 29 11N 74 49 E
Nohfelden, Germany 25 F3 49 35N 7 7 E
Nohta, India 69 H8 23 40N 79 34 E
Noia, Spain 34 C2 42 48N 8 53W
Noire, Montagne, France 20 E6 43 28N 2 18 E
Noires, Mts., France 18 D3 48 11N 3 40W
Noirétable, France 20 C7 45 48N 3 46 E
Noirmoutier, Î. de, France 18 F4 46 58N 2 10W
Noirmoutier-en-l'Île, France 18 F4 47 0N 2 14W
Nojane, Botswana 88 C3 23 15 S 20 14 E
Nojima-Zaki, Japan 55 G9 34 54N 139 53 E
Nok Kundi, Pakistan 66 E3 28 50N 62 45 E
Nokaneng, Botswana 88 B3 19 40 S 22 17 E
Nokia, Finland 9 F20 61 30N 23 30 E
Nokomis, Canada 105 C8 51 35N 105 0W
Nokomis L., Canada 105 B8 57 0N 103 0W
Nol, Sweden 11 G6 57 56N 12 5 E
Nola, C.A.R. 84 D3 3 35N 16 4 E
Nola, Italy 31 B7 40 55N 14 33 E
Nolay, France 19 F11 46 58N 4 35 E
Noli, C. di, Italy 28 D5 44 12N 8 25 E
Nolinsk, Russia 48 B9 57 28N 49 57 E
Noma Omuramba →, Namibia 88 B3 18 52 S 20 53 E
Nombre de Dios, Panama 120 E4 9 34N 79 28W
Nome, U.S.A. 100 B3 64 30N 165 25W
Nomo-Zaki, Japan 55 H4 32 35N 129 44 E
Nonacho L., Canada 105 A7 61 42N 109 40W
Nonancourt, France 18 D8 48 47N 1 11 E
Nonda, Australia 94 C3 20 40 S 142 28 E
None, Italy 28 D4 44 56N 7 32 E
Nong Chang, Thailand 64 E2 15 23N 99 51 E
Nong Het, Laos 64 C4 19 29N 103 59 E
Nong Khai, Thailand 64 D4 17 50N 102 46 E
Nong'an, China 57 B13 44 25N 125 5 E
Nongoma, S. Africa 89 D5 27 58 S 31 35 E
Nonoava, Mexico 118 B3 27 28N 106 44W
Nonoava →, Mexico 118 B3 27 29N 106 45W
Nonthaburi, Thailand 64 F3 13 51N 100 34 E
Nontron, France 20 C4 45 31N 0 40 E
Nonza, France 21 F13 42 47N 9 21 E
Noonamah, Australia 92 B5 12 40 S 131 4 E
Noord Brabant □, Neths. 17 C5 51 40N 5 0 E
Noord Holland □, Neths. 17 B4 52 30N 4 45 E
Noordbeveland, Neths. 17 C3 51 35N 3 50 E
Noordoostpolder, Neths. 17 B5 52 45N 5 45 E
Noordwijk, Neths. 17 B4 52 14N 4 26 E
Nootka I., Canada 104 D3 49 32N 126 42W
Nopiming Prov. Park, Canada 105 C9 50 30N 95 37W
Nora, Eritrea 81 D5 16 6N 40 4 E
Nora, Sweden 10 E9 59 32N 15 2 E
Noralee, Canada 104 C3 53 59N 126 26W
Noranda = Rouyn-Noranda, Canada 102 C4 48 20N 79 0W
Norberg, Sweden 10 D9 60 4N 15 56 E
Nórcia, Italy 29 F10 42 48N 13 5 E
Norco, U.S.A. 117 M9 33 56N 117 33W
Nord □, France 19 B10 50 15N 3 30 E
Nord-Kivu □, Dem. Rep. of the Congo 86 C2 1 0 S 29 0 E
Nord-Ostsee-Kanal, Germany 24 A5 54 12N 9 32 E
Nord-Pas-de-Calais □, France 19 B9 50 30N 2 50 E
Nordaustlandet, Svalbard 4 B9 79 14N 23 0 E
Nordborg, Denmark 11 J3 55 5N 9 50 E
Nordby, Denmark 11 J2 55 27N 8 24 E
Norddeich, Germany 24 B3 53 36N 7 9 E
Nordegg, Canada 104 C5 52 29N 116 5W
Norden, Germany 24 B3 53 35N 7 12 E
Nordenham, Germany 24 B4 53 30N 8 30 E
Norderney, Germany 24 B3 53 42N 7 9 E
Norderstedt, Germany 24 B6 53 42N 10 1 E
Nordfjord, Norway 9 F11 61 55N 5 30 E
Nordfriesische Inseln, Germany 24 A4 54 40N 8 20 E
Nordhausen, Germany 24 D6 51 30N 10 47 E
Nordhorn, Germany 24 C3 52 26N 7 4 E
Norðoyar, Færoe Is. 8 E9 62 17N 6 35W
Nordingrå, Sweden 10 B12 62 56N 18 17 E
Nordjyllands Amtskommune □, Denmark 11 G4 57 20N 10 0 E
Nordkapp, Norway 8 A21 71 10N 25 50 E
Nordkapp, Svalbard 4 A9 80 31N 20 0 E
Nordkinn = Kinnarodden, Norway 6 A11 71 8N 27 40 E
Nordkinn-halvøya, Norway 8 A22 70 55N 27 40 E
Nördlingen, Germany 25 G6 48 48N 10 30 E
Nordrhein-Westfalen □, Germany 24 D3 51 45N 7 30 E
Nordstrand, Germany 24 A4 54 30N 8 52 E
Nordvik, Russia 51 B12 74 2N 111 32 E
Nore →, Ireland 15 D4 52 25N 6 58W
Norfolk, Nebr., U.S.A. 112 D6 42 2N 97 25W
Norfolk, Va., U.S.A. 108 G7 36 51N 76 17W
Norfolk □, U.K. 13 E8 52 39N 0 54 E
Norfolk I., Pac. Oc. 96 K8 28 58 S 168 3 E
Norfork L., U.S.A. 113 G8 36 15N 92 14W
Norilsk, Russia 51 C9 69 20N 88 6 E
Norma, Mt., Australia 94 C3 20 55 S 140 42 E
Normal, U.S.A. 112 E10 40 31N 88 59W
Norman, U.S.A. 113 H6 35 13N 97 26W
Norman →, Australia 94 B3 19 18 S 141 51 E
Norman Wells, Canada 100 B7 65 17N 126 51W
Normanby →, Australia 94 A3 14 23 S 144 10 E
Normandin, Canada 102 C5 48 49N 72 31W
Normanhurst, Mt., Australia 93 E3 25 4 S 122 30 E
Normanton, Australia 94 B3 17 40 S 141 10 E
Normétal, Canada 102 C4 49 0N 79 22W
Norquay, Canada 105 C8 51 53N 102 5W
Norquinco, Argentina 128 E2 41 51 S 70 55W
Norra Dellen, Sweden 10 C10 61 53N 16 43 E
Norra Ulvön, Sweden 10 A12 63 3N 18 40 E
Norrahammar, Sweden 11 G8 57 43N 14 7 E
Norrbotten □, Sweden 8 C19 66 30N 22 30 E
Nørre Åby, Denmark 11 J3 55 27N 9 52 E
Nørre Alslev, Denmark 11 K5 54 54N 11 52 E
Nørresundby, Denmark 11 G3 57 5N 9 52 E
Norrhult, Sweden 11 G9 57 7N 15 10 E
Norris Point, Canada 103 C8 49 31N 57 53W
Norristown, U.S.A. 111 F9 40 7N 75 21W
Norrköping, Sweden 11 F10 58 37N 16 11 E
Norrland, Sweden 9 E16 62 15N 15 45 E
Norrsundet, Sweden 10 D11 60 56N 17 8 E
Norrtälje, Sweden 10 E12 59 46N 18 42 E
Norseman, Australia 93 F3 32 8 S 121 43 E
Norsk, Russia 51 D14 52 30N 130 5 E
Norte, Pta. del, Canary Is. 37 G2 27 51N 17 57W
Norte, Serra do, Brazil 124 F7 11 20 S 59 0W
North, C., Canada 103 C7 47 2N 60 20W
North Adams, U.S.A. 111 D11 42 42N 73 7W
North Arm, Canada 104 A5 62 0N 114 30W
North Augusta, U.S.A. 109 J5 33 30N 81 59W
North Ayrshire □, U.K. 14 F4 55 45N 4 44W
North Bass I., U.S.A. 110 E2 41 43N 82 49W
North Battleford, Canada 105 C7 52 50N 108 17W
North Bay, Canada 102 C4 46 20N 79 30W
North Belcher Is., Canada 102 A4 56 50N 79 50W
North Bend, Oreg., U.S.A. 114 E1 43 24N 124 14W
North Bend, Pa., U.S.A. 110 E7 41 20N 77 42W
North Bend, Wash., U.S.A. 116 C5 47 30N 121 47W
North Bennington, U.S.A. 111 D11 42 56N 73 15W
North Berwick, U.K. 14 E6 56 4N 2 42W
North Berwick, U.S.A. 111 C14 43 18N 70 44W
North C., Canada 103 C7 47 5N 64 0W
North C., N.Z. 91 F4 34 23 S 173 4 E
North Canadian →, U.S.A. 113 H7 35 16N 95 31W
North Canton, U.S.A. 110 F3 40 53N 81 24W
North Cape = Nordkapp, Norway 8 A21 71 10N 25 50 E
North Cape = Nordkapp, Svalbard 4 A9 80 31N 20 0 E
North Caribou L., Canada 102 B1 52 50N 90 40W
North Carolina □, U.S.A. 109 H6 35 30N 80 0W
North Cascades National Park, U.S.A. 114 B3 48 45N 121 10W
North Channel, Canada 102 C3 46 0N 83 0W
North Channel, U.K. 14 F3 55 13N 5 52W
North Charleston, U.S.A. 109 J6 32 53N 79 58W
North Chicago, U.S.A. 108 D2 42 19N 87 51W
North Creek, U.S.A. 111 C11 43 41N 73 59W
North Dakota □, U.S.A. 112 B5 47 30N 100 15W
North Downs, U.K. 13 F8 51 19N 0 21 E
North East, U.S.A. 110 D5 42 13N 79 50W
North East Frontier Agency = Arunachal Pradesh □, India 67 F19 28 0N 95 0 E
North East Lincolnshire □, U.K. 12 D7 53 34N 0 2W
North Eastern □, Kenya 86 B5 1 30N 40 0 E
North Esk →, U.K. 14 E6 56 46N 2 24W
North European Plain, Europe 6 E10 55 0N 25 0 E
North Foreland, U.K. 13 F9 51 22N 1 28 E
North Fork, U.S.A. 116 H7 37 14N 119 21W
North Fork American →, U.S.A. 116 G5 38 57N 120 59W
North Fork Feather →, U.S.A. 116 F5 38 33N 121 30W
North Fork Grand →, U.S.A. 112 C3 45 47N 102 16W
North Fork Red →, U.S.A. 113 H5 34 24N 99 14W
North Frisian Is. = Nordfriesische Inseln, Germany 24 A4 54 40N 8 20 E
North Gower, Canada 111 A9 45 8N 75 43W
North Hd., Australia 93 F1 30 14 S 114 59 E
North Henik L., Canada 105 A9 61 45N 97 40W
North Highlands, U.S.A. 116 G5 38 40N 121 23W
North Horr, Kenya 86 B4 3 20N 37 8 E
North I., Kenya 86 B4 4 5N 36 5 E
North I., N.Z. 91 H5 38 0 S 175 0 E
North Kingsville, U.S.A. 110 E4 41 54N 80 42W
North Knife →, Canada 105 B10 58 53N 94 45W
North Koel →, India 69 G10 24 45N 83 50 E
North Korea ■, Asia 57 E14 40 0N 127 0 E
North Lakhimpur, India 67 F19 27 14N 94 7 E
North Lanarkshire □, U.K. 14 F5 55 52N 3 56W
North Las Vegas, U.S.A. 117 J11 36 12N 115 7W
North Lincolnshire □, U.K. 12 D7 53 36N 0 30W
North Little Rock, U.S.A. 113 H8 34 45N 92 16W
North Loup →, U.S.A. 112 E5 41 17N 98 24W
North Magnetic Pole, Canada 4 B2 77 58N 102 8W
North Minch, U.K. 14 C3 58 5N 5 55W
North Moose L., Canada 105 C8 54 11N 100 6W
North Myrtle Beach, U.S.A. 109 J6 33 48N 78 42W
North Nahanni →, Canada 104 A4 62 15N 123 20W
North Olmsted, U.S.A. 110 E3 41 25N 81 56W
North Ossetia □, Russia 49 J7 43 30N 44 30 E
North Pagai, I. = Pagai Utara, Pulau, Indonesia 62 E2 2 35 S 100 0 E
North Palisade, U.S.A. 116 H8 37 6N 118 31W
North Platte, U.S.A. 112 E4 41 8N 100 46W
North Platte →, U.S.A. 112 E4 41 7N 100 42W
North Pole, Arctic 4 A 90 0N 0 0W
North Portal, Canada 105 D8 49 0N 102 33W
North Powder, U.S.A. 114 D5 45 2N 117 55W
North Pt., U.S.A. 110 A1 45 2N 83 16W
North Rhine Westphalia = Nordrhein-Westfalen □, Germany 24 D3 51 45N 7 30 E
North River, Canada 103 B8 53 49N 57 6W
North Ronaldsay, U.K. 14 B6 59 22N 2 26W
North Saskatchewan →, Canada 105 C7 53 15N 105 5W
North Sea, Europe 6 D6 56 0N 4 0 E
North Seal →, Canada 105 B9 58 50N 98 7W
North Somerset □, U.K. 13 F5 51 24N 2 45W
North Sporades = Vóriai Sporádhes, Greece 38 B5 39 15N 23 30 E
North Sydney, Canada 103 C7 46 12N 60 15W
North Syracuse, U.S.A. 111 C8 43 8N 76 7W
North Taranaki Bight, N.Z. 91 H5 38 50 S 174 15 E
North Thompson →, Canada 104 C4 50 40N 120 20W
North Tonawanda, U.S.A. 110 C6 43 2N 78 53W
North Troy, U.S.A. 111 B12 45 0N 72 24W
North Truchas Pk., U.S.A. 115 J11 36 0N 105 30W
North Twin I., Canada 102 B4 53 20N 80 0W
North Tyne →, U.K. 12 B5 55 0N 2 8W
North Uist, U.K. 14 D1 57 40N 7 15W
North Vancouver, Canada 104 D4 49 19N 123 4W
North Vernon, U.S.A. 108 F3 39 0N 85 38W
North Wabasca L., Canada 104 B6 56 0N 113 55W
North Walsham, U.K. 12 E9 52 50N 1 22 E
North-West □, S. Africa 88 D4 27 0 S 25 0 E
North West C., Australia 92 D1 21 45 S 114 9 E
North West Christmas I. Ridge, Pac. Oc. 97 G11 6 30N 165 0W
North West Frontier □, Pakistan 68 C4 34 0N 72 0 E
North West Highlands, U.K. 14 D4 57 33N 4 58W
North West River, Canada 103 B7 53 30N 60 10W
North Western □, Zambia 87 E2 13 30 S 25 30 E
North Wildwood, U.S.A. 108 F8 39 0N 74 48W
North York Moors, U.K. 12 C7 54 23N 0 53W
North Yorkshire □, U.K. 12 C6 54 15N 1 25W
Northallerton, U.K. 12 C6 54 20N 1 26W
Northam, Australia 93 F2 31 35 S 116 42 E
Northam, S. Africa 88 C4 24 56 S 27 18 E
Northampton, Australia 93 E1 28 27 S 114 33 E
Northampton, U.K. 13 E7 52 15N 0 53W
Northampton, Mass., U.S.A. 111 D12 42 19N 72 38W
Northampton, Pa., U.S.A. 111 F9 40 41N 75 30W
Northamptonshire □, U.K. 13 E7 52 16N 0 55W
Northbridge, U.S.A. 111 D13 42 9N 71 39W
Northcliffe, Australia 93 F2 34 39 S 116 7 E
Northeast Providence Chan., W. Indies 120 A4 26 0N 76 0W
Northeim, Germany 24 D6 51 42N 10 0 E
Northern □, Ghana 83 D4 9 30N 1 0W
Northern □, Malawi 87 E3 11 0 S 34 0 E
Northern □, Zambia 87 E3 10 30 S 31 0 E
Northern Areas □, Pakistan 69 A5 36 0N 73 0 E
Northern Cape □, S. Africa 88 D3 30 0 S 20 0 E
Northern Circars, India 67 L13 17 30N 82 30 E
Northern Indian L., Canada 105 B9 57 20N 97 20W
Northern Ireland □, U.K. 15 B5 54 45N 7 0W
Northern Light L., Canada 102 C1 48 15N 90 39W
Northern Marianas ■, Pac. Oc. 96 F6 17 0N 145 0 E
Northern Province □, S. Leone 82 D2 9 15N 11 30W
Northern Province □, S. Africa 89 C4 24 0 S 29 0 E
Northern Territory □, Australia 92 D5 20 0 S 133 0 E
Northfield, Minn., U.S.A. 112 C8 44 27N 93 9W
Northfield, Vt., U.S.A. 111 B12 44 9N 72 40W
Northland □, N.Z. 91 F4 35 30 S 173 30 E
Northome, U.S.A. 112 B7 47 52N 94 17W
Northport, Ala., U.S.A. 109 J2 33 14N 87 35W
Northport, Wash., U.S.A. 114 B5 48 55N 117 48W
Northumberland □, U.K. 12 B6 55 12N 2 0W
Northumberland, C., Australia 95 F3 38 5 S 140 40 E
Northumberland Is., Australia 94 C4 21 30 S 149 50 E
Northumberland Str., Canada 103 C7 46 20N 64 0W
Northville, U.S.A. 111 C10 43 13N 74 11W
Northwest Providence Channel, W. Indies 120 A4 26 0N 78 0W
Northwest Territories □, Canada 100 B9 63 0N 118 0W
Northwood, Iowa, U.S.A. 112 D8 43 27N 93 13W
Northwood, N. Dak., U.S.A. 112 B6 47 44N 97 34W
Norton, U.S.A. 112 F5 39 50N 99 53W
Norton, Zimbabwe 87 F3 17 52 S 30 40 E
Norton Sd., U.S.A. 100 B3 63 50N 164 0W
Nortorf, Germany 24 A5 54 10N 9 50 E
Norwalk, Calif., U.S.A. 117 M8 33 54N 118 5W
Norwalk, Conn., U.S.A. 111 E11 41 7N 73 22W
Norwalk, Iowa, U.S.A. 112 E8 41 29N 93 41W
Norwalk, Ohio, U.S.A. 110 E2 41 15N 82 37W
Norway, Maine, U.S.A. 109 C10 44 13N 70 32W
Norway, Mich., U.S.A. 108 C2 45 47N 87 55W
Norway ■, Europe 8 E14 63 0N 11 0 E
Norway House, Canada 105 C9 53 59N 97 50W
Norwegian Sea, Atl. Oc. 4 C8 66 0N 1 0 E
Norwich, Canada 110 D4 42 59N 80 36W
Norwich, U.K. 13 E9 52 38N 1 18 E

Norwich

Norwich, *Conn., U.S.A.* **111 E12** 41 31N 72 5W
Norwich, *N.Y., U.S.A.* **111 D9** 42 32N 75 32W
Norwood, *Canada* **110 B7** 44 23N 77 59W
Norwood, *U.S.A.* **111 B10** 44 45N 75 0W
Noshiro, *Japan* **54 D10** 40 12N 140 0 E
Nosivka, *Ukraine* **47 G6** 50 50N 31 37 E
Nosovka = Nosivka, *Ukraine* **47 G6** 50 50N 31 37 E
Noşratābād, *Iran* **71 D8** 29 55N 60 0 E
Noss Hd., *U.K.* **14 C5** 58 28N 3 3W
Nossebro, *Sweden* **11 F6** 58 12N 12 43 E
Nossob →, *S. Africa* **88 D3** 26 55 S 20 45 E
Nossombougou, *Mali* **82 C3** 13 5N 7 55W
Nosy Barren, *Madag.* **85 H8** 18 25 S 43 40 E
Nosy Be, *Madag.* **85 G9** 13 25 S 48 15 E
Nosy Boraha, *Madag.* **89 B8** 16 50 S 49 55 E
Nosy Lava, *Madag.* **89 A8** 14 33 S 47 36 E
Nosy Varika, *Madag.* **89 C8** 20 35 S 48 32 E
Noteć →, *Poland* **45 F2** 52 44N 15 26 E
Notikewin →, *Canada* **104 B5** 57 2N 117 38W
Notio Aigaio = Notios Aiyaíon □ **39 E7** 36 52N 25 34 E
Notios Aiyaíon □ **39 E7** 36 52N 25 34 E
Notios Evvoïkos Kólpos, *Greece* **38 C5** 38 20N 24 0 E
Noto, *Italy* **31 F8** 36 53N 15 4 E
Noto, G. di, *Italy* **31 F8** 36 50N 15 12 E
Notodden, *Norway* **9 G13** 59 35N 9 17 E
Notre Dame B., *Canada* **103 C8** 49 45N 55 30W
Notre Dame de Koartac = Quaqtaq, *Canada* **101 B13** 60 55N 69 40W
Notre-Dame-des-Bois, *Canada* **111 A13** 45 24N 71 4W
Notre Dame d'Ivugivic = Ivujivik, *Canada* **101 B12** 62 24N 77 55W
Notre-Dame-du-Nord, *Canada* **102 C4** 47 36N 79 30W
Notsé, *Togo* **83 D5** 7 0N 1 17 E
Nottawasaga B., *Canada* **110 B4** 44 35N 80 15W
Nottaway →, *Canada* **102 B4** 51 22N 78 55W
Nottingham, *U.K.* **12 E6** 52 58N 1 10W
Nottingham, City of □, *U.K.* **12 E6** 52 58N 1 10W
Nottingham I., *Canada* **101 B12** 63 20N 77 55W
Nottinghamshire □, *U.K.* **12 D6** 53 10N 1 3W
Nottoway →, *U.S.A.* **108 G7** 36 33N 76 55W
Notwane →, *Botswana* **88 C4** 23 35 S 26 58 E
Nouâdhibou, *Mauritania* **78 D2** 20 54N 17 0W
Nouâdhibou, Ras, *Mauritania* **78 D2** 20 50N 17 0W
Nouakchott, *Mauritania* **82 B1** 18 9N 15 58W
Nouâmghâr, *Mauritania* **82 B1** 19 20N 16 20W
Nouméa, *N. Cal.* **96 K8** 22 17 S 166 30 E
Nouna, *Burkina Faso* **82 C4** 12 45N 3 52W
Noupoort, *S. Africa* **88 E3** 31 10 S 24 57 E
Nouveau Comptoir = Wemindji, *Canada* **102 B4** 53 0N 78 49W
Nouvelle-Amsterdam, I., *Ind. Oc.* **3 F13** 38 30 S 77 30 E
Nouvelle-Calédonie = New Caledonia ■, *Pac. Oc.* **96 K8** 21 0 S 165 0 E
Nouzonville, *France* **19 C11** 49 48N 4 44 E
Nová Baňa, *Slovak Rep.* **27 C11** 48 28N 18 39 E
Nová Bystřice, *Czech Rep.* **26 B8** 49 2N 15 8 E
Nova Casa Nova, *Brazil* **125 E10** 9 25 S 41 5W
Nova Esperança, *Brazil* **127 A5** 23 8 S 52 24W
Nova Friburgo, *Brazil* **127 A7** 22 16 S 42 30W
Nova Gaia = Cambundi-Catembo, *Angola* **84 G3** 10 10 S 17 35 E
Nova Gorica, *Slovenia* **29 C10** 45 57N 13 39 E
Nova Gradiška, *Croatia* **42 E2** 45 17N 17 28 E
Nova Iguaçu, *Brazil* **127 A7** 22 45 S 43 28W
Nova Iorque, *Brazil* **125 E10** 7 0 S 44 5W
Nova Kakhovka, *Ukraine* **47 J7** 46 42N 33 27 E
Nova Lamego, *Guinea-Biss.* **82 C2** 12 19N 14 11W
Nova Lima, *Brazil* **127 A7** 19 59 S 43 51W
Nova Lisboa = Huambo, *Angola* **85 G3** 12 42 S 15 54 E
Nova Lusitânia, *Mozam.* **87 F3** 19 50 S 34 34 E
Nova Mambone, *Mozam.* **89 C6** 21 0 S 35 3 E
Nova Odesa, *Ukraine* **47 J6** 47 19N 31 47 E
Nová Paka, *Czech Rep.* **26 A8** 50 29N 15 30 E
Nova Pavova, *Serbia, Yug.* **42 F5** 44 56N 20 14 E
Nova Scotia □, *Canada* **103 C7** 45 10N 63 0W
Nova Siri, *Italy* **31 B9** 40 10N 16 35 E
Nova Sofala, *Mozam.* **89 C5** 20 7 S 34 42 E
Nova Varoš, *Serbia, Yug.* **40 C3** 43 29N 19 48 E
Nova Venécia, *Brazil* **125 G10** 18 45 S 40 24W
Nova Zagora, *Bulgaria* **41 D10** 42 32N 26 1 E
Novaci, *Macedonia* **40 E5** 41 5N 21 29 E
Novaci, *Romania* **43 E8** 45 10N 23 42 E
Novaféltria, *Italy* **29 E9** 43 53N 12 17 E
Novaleksandrovskaya = Novoaleksandrovsk, *Russia* **49 H5** 45 29N 41 17 E
Novannenskiy = Novoannenskiy, *Russia* **48 E6** 50 32N 42 39 E
Novar, *Canada* **110 A5** 45 27N 79 15W
Novara, *Italy* **28 C5** 45 28N 8 38 E
Novato, *U.S.A.* **116 G4** 38 6N 122 35W
Novaya Kakhovka = Nova Kakhovka, *Ukraine* **47 J7** 46 42N 33 27 E
Novaya Kazanka, *Kazakhstan* **49 F9** 48 56N 49 36 E
Novaya Ladoga, *Russia* **46 B7** 60 7N 32 16 E
Novaya Lyalya, *Russia* **50 D7** 59 4N 60 45 E
Novaya Sibir, Ostrov, *Russia* **51 B16** 75 10N 150 0 E
Novaya Zemlya, *Russia* **50 B6** 75 0N 56 0 E
Nové Město, *Slovak Rep.* **27 C10** 48 45N 17 50 E
Nové Město na Moravě, *Czech Rep.* **26 B9** 49 34N 16 5 E
Nové Město nad Metují, *Czech Rep.* **27 A9** 50 20N 16 10 E
Nové Zámky, *Slovak Rep.* **27 C11** 48 2N 18 8 E
Novelda, *Spain* **33 G4** 38 24N 0 45W
Novellara, *Italy* **28 D7** 44 51N 10 44 E
Noventa Vicentina, *Italy* **29 C8** 45 17N 11 32 E
Novgorod, *Russia* **46 C6** 58 30N 31 25 E
Novgorod-Severskiy = Novhorod-Siverskyy, *Ukraine* **47 G7** 52 2N 33 10 E
Novhorod-Siverskyy, *Ukraine* **47 G7** 52 2N 33 10 E
Novi Bečej, *Serbia, Yug.* **42 E5** 45 36N 20 10 E
Novi Iskar, *Bulgaria* **40 D7** 42 48N 23 21 E
Novi Kneževac, *Serbia, Yug.* **42 D5** 46 4N 20 8 E
Novi Lígure, *Italy* **28 D5** 44 46N 8 47 E
Novi Pazar, *Bulgaria* **41 C11** 43 25N 27 15 E
Novi Pazar, *Serbia, Yug.* **40 C4** 43 12N 20 28 E
Novi Sad, *Serbia, Yug.* **42 E4** 45 18N 19 52 E
Novi Slankamen, *Serbia, Yug.* **42 E5** 45 8N 20 15 E
Novi Travnik, *Bos.-H.* **42 F2** 44 10N 17 40 E
Novi Vinodolski, *Croatia* **29 C11** 45 10N 14 48 E
Novigrad, *Istra, Croatia* **29 C10** 45 19N 13 33 E
Novigrad, *Zadar, Croatia* **29 D12** 44 10N 15 32 E
Novigradsko More, *Croatia* **29 D12** 44 12N 15 33 E
Nôvo Hamburgo, *Brazil* **127 B5** 29 37 S 51 7W
Novo Mesto, *Slovenia* **29 C12** 45 47N 15 12 E
Novo Miloševo, *Serbia, Yug.* **42 E5** 45 42N 20 20 E
Novo Remanso, *Brazil* **125 E10** 9 41 S 42 4W
Novoaleksandrovsk, *Russia* **49 H5** 45 29N 41 17 E
Novoannenskiy, *Russia* **48 E6** 50 32N 42 39 E
Novoataysk, *Russia* **50 D9** 53 30N 84 0 E
Novoazovsk, *Ukraine* **47 J10** 47 15N 38 4 E
Novocheboksarsk, *Russia* **48 B8** 56 5N 47 27 E
Novocherkassk, *Russia* **49 G5** 47 27N 40 15 E
Novodevichye, *Russia* **48 D9** 53 37N 48 50 E
Novogrudok = Navahrudak, *Belarus* **46 F3** 53 40N 25 50 E
Novohrad-Volynskyy, *Ukraine* **47 G4** 50 34N 27 35 E
Novokachalinsk, *Russia* **54 B6** 45 5N 132 0 E
Novokazalinsk = Zhangaqazaly, *Kazakhstan* **50 E7** 45 48N 62 6 E
Novokhopersk, *Russia* **48 E5** 51 5N 41 39 E
Novokuybyshevsk, *Russia* **48 D9** 53 7N 49 58 E
Novokuznetsk, *Russia* **50 D9** 53 45N 87 10 E
Novomirgorod, *Ukraine* **47 H6** 48 45N 31 33 E
Novomoskovsk, *Russia* **46 E10** 54 5N 38 15 E
Novomoskovsk, *Ukraine* **47 H8** 48 33N 35 17 E
Novopolotsk = Navapolatsk, *Belarus* **46 E5** 55 32N 28 37 E
Novorossiysk, *Russia* **47 K9** 44 43N 37 46 E
Novorybnoye, *Russia* **51 B11** 72 50N 105 50 E
Novorzhev, *Russia* **46 D5** 57 3N 29 25 E
Novosej, *Albania* **40 E4** 41 56N 20 35 E
Novoselytsya, *Ukraine* **47 H4** 48 14N 26 15 E
Novoshakhtinsk, *Russia* **47 J10** 47 46N 39 58 E
Novosibirsk, *Russia* **50 D9** 55 0N 83 5 E
Novosibirskiye Ostrova, *Russia* **51 B15** 75 0N 142 0 E
Novosil, *Russia* **47 F9** 52 59N 37 2 E
Novosokolniki, *Russia* **46 D6** 56 20N 30 2 E
Novotitarovskaya, *Russia* **49 H4** 45 17N 39 2 E
Novotroitsk, *Russia* **50 D6** 51 10N 58 15 E
Novoukrayinka, *Ukraine* **47 H6** 48 25N 31 30 E
Novouljanovsk, *Russia* **48 C9** 54 8N 48 24 E
Novouzensk, *Russia* **48 E9** 50 32N 48 17 E
Novovolynsk, *Ukraine* **47 G3** 50 45N 24 4 E
Novovoronezhskiy, *Russia* **47 G10** 51 19N 39 13 E
Novozybkov, *Russia* **47 F6** 52 30N 32 0 E
Novska, *Croatia* **29 C14** 45 19N 17 0 E
Novyy Urengoy, *Russia* **50 C8** 65 48N 76 52 E
Nový Bor, *Czech Rep.* **26 A7** 50 46N 14 35 E
Novy Bug = Novyy Buh, *Ukraine* **47 J7** 47 34N 32 29 E
Nový Bydžov, *Czech Rep.* **26 A8** 50 14N 15 29 E
Novy Dwór Mazowiecki, *Poland* **45 F7** 52 26N 20 44 E
Nový Jičín, *Czech Rep.* **27 B11** 49 30N 18 2 E
Novyy Afon, *Georgia* **49 J5** 43 7N 40 50 E
Novyy Buh, *Ukraine* **47 J7** 47 34N 32 29 E
Novyy Oskol, *Russia* **47 G9** 50 44N 37 55 E
Novyy Port, *Russia* **50 C8** 67 40N 72 30 E
Now Shahr, *Iran* **71 B6** 36 40N 51 30 E
Nowa Deba, *Poland* **45 H8** 50 26N 21 41 E
Nowa Ruda, *Poland* **45 H3** 50 35N 16 30 E
Nowa Sarzyna, *Poland* **45 H9** 50 21N 22 21 E
Nowa Sól, *Poland* **45 G2** 51 48N 15 44 E
Nowata, *U.S.A.* **113 G7** 36 42N 95 38W
Nowbarān, *Iran* **71 C6** 35 8N 49 42 E
Nowe, *Poland* **44 E5** 53 41N 18 44 E
Nowe Miasteczko, *Poland* **45 G2** 51 42N 15 42 E
Nowe Miasto, *Poland* **45 G7** 51 38N 20 34 E
Nowe Miasto Lubawskie, *Poland* **44 E6** 53 27N 19 33 E
Nowe Skalmierzyce, *Poland* **45 G4** 51 43N 18 0 E
Nowe Warpno, *Poland* **44 E1** 53 42N 14 18 E
Nowghāb, *Iran* **71 C8** 33 53N 59 4 E
Nowgong, *Assam, India* **67 F18** 26 20N 92 50 E
Nowgong, *Mad. P., India* **69 G8** 25 4N 79 27 E
Nowogard, *Poland* **44 E2** 53 41N 15 10 E
Nowogród, *Poland* **45 E8** 53 14N 21 53 E
Nowogród Bobrzanski, *Poland* **45 G2** 51 48N 15 15 E
Nowogrodziec, *Poland* **45 G2** 51 12N 15 24 E
Nowra, *Australia* **95 E5** 34 53 S 150 35 E
Nowshera, *Pakistan* **66 C8** 34 0N 72 0 E
Nowy Dwór Gdański, *Poland* **44 D6** 54 13N 19 7 E
Nowy Sącz, *Poland* **45 J7** 49 40N 20 41 E
Nowy Staw, *Poland* **44 D6** 54 13N 19 2 E
Nowy Targ, *Poland* **45 J7** 49 29N 20 2 E
Nowy Tomyśl, *Poland* **45 F3** 52 19N 16 10 E
Nowy Wiśnicz, *Poland* **45 J7** 49 55N 20 28 E
Noxen, *U.S.A.* **111 E8** 41 25N 76 4W
Noxon, *U.S.A.* **114 C6** 48 0N 115 43W
Noyabr'sk, *Russia* **50 C8** 64 34N 76 21 E
Noyant, *France* **18 E7** 47 30N 0 6 E
Noyers, *France* **19 E10** 47 40N 4 0 E
Noyon, *France* **19 C9** 49 34N 2 59 E
Noyon, *Mongolia* **56 C2** 43 2N 102 4 E
Nozay, *France* **18 E5** 47 34N 1 38W
Nqutu, *S. Africa* **89 D5** 28 13 S 30 32 E
Nsanje, *Malawi* **87 F4** 16 55 S 35 12 E
Nsawam, *Ghana* **83 D4** 5 50N 0 24W
Nsomba, *Zambia* **87 E2** 10 45 S 29 51 E
Nsukka, *Nigeria* **83 D6** 6 51N 7 29 E
Ntui, *Cameroon* **83 E7** 4 27N 11 38 E
Nu Jiang →, *China* **58 E2** 29 58N 97 25 E
Nu Shan, *China* **58 E2** 26 0N 99 20 E
Nuba Mts. = Nubah, Jibalan, *Sudan* **81 E3** 12 0N 31 0 E
Nubah, Jibalan, *Sudan* **81 E3** 12 0N 31 0 E
Nubia, *Africa* **76 D7** 21 0N 32 0 E
Nubian Desert = Nûbîya, Es Sahrâ en, *Sudan* **80 C3** 21 30N 33 30 E
Nûbîya, Es Sahrâ en, *Sudan* **80 C3** 21 30N 33 30 E
Nubledo, *Spain* **34 B5** 43 31N 5 52W
Nuboai, *Indonesia* **63 E9** 2 10 S 136 30 E
Nubra →, *India* **69 B7** 34 35N 77 35 E
Nucet, *Romania* **42 D7** 46 28N 22 35 E
Nueces →, *U.S.A.* **113 M6** 27 51N 97 30W
Nueltin L., *Canada* **105 A9** 60 30N 99 30W
Nueva Asunción □, *Paraguay* **126 A3** 21 0 S 61 0W
Nueva Carteya, *Spain* **35 H6** 37 35N 4 28W
Nueva Gerona, *Cuba* **120 B3** 21 53N 82 49W
Nueva Palmira, *Uruguay* **126 C4** 33 52 S 58 20W
Nueva Rosita, *Mexico* **118 B4** 28 0N 101 11W
Nueva San Salvador, *El Salv.* **120 D2** 13 40N 89 18W
Nueva Tabarca, *Spain* **33 G4** 38 17N 0 30W
Nuéve de Julio, *Argentina* **126 D3** 35 30 S 61 0W
Nuevitas, *Cuba* **120 B4** 21 30N 77 20W
Nuevo, G., *Argentina* **128 E4** 43 0 S 64 30W
Nuevo Casas Grandes, *Mexico* **118 A3** 30 22N 108 0W
Nuevo Guerrero, *Mexico* **119 B5** 26 34N 99 15W
Nuevo Laredo, *Mexico* **119 B5** 27 30N 99 30W
Nuevo León □, *Mexico* **118 C5** 25 0N 100 0W
Nuevo Rocafuerte, *Ecuador* **124 D3** 0 55 S 75 27W
Nugget Pt., *N.Z.* **91 M2** 46 27 S 169 50 E
Nugrus, Gebel, *Egypt* **80 C3** 24 47N 34 35 E
Nuhaka, *N.Z.* **91 H6** 39 3 S 177 45 E
Nuits-St-Georges, *France* **19 E11** 47 10N 4 56 E
Nukey Bluff, *Australia* **95 E2** 32 26 S 135 29 E
Nukheila, *Sudan* **80 D2** 19 1N 26 21 E
Nukhuyb, *Iraq* **70 C4** 32 4N 42 3 E
Nuku'alofa, *Tonga* **91 E12** 21 10 S 174 0W
Nukus, *Uzbekistan* **50 E6** 42 27N 59 41 E
Nules, *Spain* **32 F4** 39 51N 0 9W
Nullagine, *Australia* **92 D3** 21 53 S 120 7 E
Nullagine →, *Australia* **92 D3** 21 20 S 120 20 E
Nullarbor, *Australia* **93 F5** 31 28 S 130 55 E
Nullarbor Plain, *Australia* **93 F4** 31 10 S 129 0 E
Numalla, L., *Australia* **95 D3** 28 43 S 144 20 E
Numan, *Nigeria* **83 D7** 9 29N 12 3 E
Numata, *Japan* **55 F9** 36 45N 139 4 E
Numatinna →, *Sudan* **81 F2** 7 38N 27 20 E
Numazu, *Japan* **55 G9** 35 7N 138 51 E
Numbulwar, *Australia* **94 A2** 14 15 S 135 45 E
Numfoor, *Indonesia* **63 E8** 1 0 S 134 50 E
Numurkah, *Australia* **95 F4** 36 5 S 145 26 E
Nunaksaluk I., *Canada* **103 A7** 55 49N 60 20W
Nunap Isua, *Greenland* **101 C15** 59 48N 43 55W
Nunavut □, *Canada* **101 B11** 66 0N 85 0W
Nunda, *U.S.A.* **110 D7** 42 35N 77 56W
Nungarin, *Australia* **93 F2** 31 12 S 118 6 E
Nungo, *Mozam.* **87 E4** 13 23 S 37 43 E
Nungwe, *Tanzania* **86 C3** 2 48 S 32 2 E
Nunivak I., *U.S.A.* **100 B3** 60 10N 166 30W
Nunkun, *India* **69 C7** 33 57N 76 2 E
Nùoro, *Italy* **30 B2** 40 20N 9 20 E
Nūrābād, *Iran* **71 E8** 27 47N 57 12 E
Nure →, *Italy* **28 C6** 45 3N 9 49 E
Nuremberg = Nürnberg, *Germany* **25 F7** 49 27N 11 3 E
Nuri, *Mexico* **118 B3** 28 2N 109 22W
Nuriootpa, *Australia* **95 E2** 34 27 S 139 0 E
Nuristān □, *Afghan.* **66 B7** 35 20N 71 0 E
Nurlat, *Russia* **48 C10** 54 29N 50 45 E
Nurmes, *Finland* **8 E23** 63 33N 29 10 E
Nürnberg, *Germany* **25 F7** 49 27N 11 3 E
Nurpur, *Pakistan* **68 D4** 31 53N 71 54 E
Nurra, La, *Italy* **30 B1** 40 45N 8 15 E
Nurran, L. = Terewah, L., *Australia* **95 D4** 29 52 S 147 35 E
Nurrari Lakes, *Australia* **93 E5** 29 1 S 130 5 E
Nurri, *Italy* **30 C2** 39 43N 9 14 E
Nürtingen, *Germany* **25 G5** 48 37N 9 19 E
Nurzec →, *Poland* **45 F9** 52 37N 22 25 E
Nus, *Italy* **28 C4** 45 45N 7 28 E
Nusa Barung, *Indonesia* **63 H15** 8 30 S 113 30 E
Nusa Kambangan, *Indonesia* **63 G13** 7 40 S 108 10 E
Nusa Tenggara Barat □, *Indonesia* **62 F5** 8 50 S 117 30 E
Nusa Tenggara Timur □, *Indonesia* **63 F6** 9 30 S 122 0 E
Nusaybin, *Turkey* **73 D9** 37 3N 41 10 E
Nushki, *Pakistan* **68 E2** 29 35N 66 0 E
Nuuk, *Greenland* **101 B14** 64 10N 51 35W
Nuwakot, *Nepal* **69 E10** 28 10N 83 55 E
Nuweiba', *Egypt* **70 D2** 28 59N 34 39 E
Nuwerus, *S. Africa* **88 E2** 31 8 S 18 24 E
Nuweveldberge, *S. Africa* **88 E3** 32 10 S 21 45 E
Nuyts, C., *Australia* **93 F5** 32 2 S 132 21 E
Nuyts, Pt., *Australia* **93 G2** 35 4 S 116 38 E
Nuyts Arch., *Australia* **95 E1** 32 35 S 133 20 E
Nxau-Nxau, *Botswana* **88 B3** 18 57 S 21 4 E
Nyaake, *Liberia* **82 E3** 4 52N 7 37W
Nyabing, *Australia* **93 F2** 33 33 S 118 9 E
Nyack, *U.S.A.* **111 E11** 41 5N 73 55W
Nyagan, *Russia* **50 C7** 62 30N 65 38 E
Nyahanga, *Tanzania* **86 C3** 2 20 S 33 37 E
Nyahua, *Tanzania* **86 D3** 5 25 S 33 23 E
Nyahururu, *Kenya* **86 B4** 0 2N 36 27 E
Nyainqentanglha Shan, *China* **60 C4** 30 0N 90 0 E
Nyakanazi, *Tanzania* **86 C3** 3 2 S 31 10 E
Nyakrom, *Ghana* **83 D4** 5 40N 0 50W
Nyâlâ, *Sudan* **81 E1** 12 2N 24 58 E
Nyamandhlovu, *Zimbabwe* **87 F2** 19 55 S 28 16 E
Nyambiti, *Tanzania* **86 C3** 2 48 S 33 27 E
Nyamlell, *Sudan* **81 F2** 9 7N 26 59 E
Nyamwaga, *Tanzania* **86 C3** 1 27 S 34 33 E
Nyandekwa, *Tanzania* **86 C3** 3 57 S 32 32 E
Nyanding →, *Sudan* **81 F3** 8 40N 32 41 E
Nyandoma, *Russia* **46 B11** 61 40N 40 12 E
Nyangana, *Namibia* **88 B3** 18 0 S 20 40 E
Nyanguge, *Tanzania* **86 C3** 2 30 S 33 12 E
Nyankpala, *Ghana* **83 D4** 9 21N 0 58W
Nyanza, *Rwanda* **86 C2** 2 20 S 29 42 E
Nyanza □, *Kenya* **86 C3** 0 10 S 34 15 E
Nyanza-Lac, *Burundi* **86 C2** 4 21 S 29 36 E
Nyaponges, *Sudan* **81 F3** 5 5N 33 45 E
Nyasa, L., *Africa* **87 E3** 12 30 S 34 30 E
Nyasvizh, *Belarus* **47 F4** 53 14N 26 38 E
Nyazura, *Zimbabwe* **87 F3** 18 40 S 32 16 E
Nyazwidzi →, *Zimbabwe* **87 G3** 20 0 S 31 17 E
Nyborg, *Denmark* **11 J4** 55 18N 10 47 E
Nybro, *Sweden* **11 H9** 56 44N 15 55 E
Nyda, *Russia* **50 C8** 66 40N 72 58 E
Nyeri, *Kenya* **86 C4** 0 23 S 36 56 E
Nyerol, *Sudan* **81 F3** 8 41N 32 1 E
Nyhammar, *Sweden* **10 D8** 60 17N 14 58 E
Nyinahin, *Ghana* **82 D4** 6 43N 2 3W
Nyíradony, *Hungary* **42 C6** 47 41N 21 55 E
Nyirbátor, *Hungary* **42 C7** 47 49N 22 9 E
Nyíregyháza, *Hungary* **42 C6** 47 58N 21 47 E
Nykøbing, *Storstrøm, Denmark* **11 K5** 54 56N 11 52 E
Nykøbing, *Vestsjælland, Denmark* **11 J5** 55 55N 11 40 E
Nykøbing, *Viborg, Denmark* **11 H2** 56 48N 8 51 E
Nyköping, *Sweden* **11 F11** 58 45N 17 1 E
Nykroppa, *Sweden* **10 E8** 59 37N 14 18 E
Nykvarn, *Sweden* **10 E11** 59 11N 17 25 E
Nyland, *Sweden* **10 A11** 63 1N 17 45 E
Nylstroom, *S. Africa* **89 C4** 24 42 S 28 22 E
Nymagee, *Australia* **95 E4** 32 7 S 146 20 E
Nymburk, *Czech Rep.* **26 A8** 50 10N 15 1 E
Nynäshamn, *Sweden* **11 F11** 58 54N 17 57 E
Nyngan, *Australia* **95 E4** 31 30 S 147 8 E
Nyoma Rap, *India* **69 C8** 33 10N 78 40 E
Nyoman = Neman →, *Lithuania* **9 J19** 55 25N 21 10 E
Nyon, *Switz.* **25 J2** 46 23N 6 14 E
Nyong →, *Cameroon* **83 E6** 3 17N 9 54 E
Nyons, *France* **21 D9** 44 22N 5 10 E
Nyou, *Burkina Faso* **83 C4** 12 42N 2 1W
Nýrsko, *Czech Rep.* **26 B6** 49 18N 13 9 E
Nysa, *Poland* **45 H4** 50 30N 17 22 E
Nysa →, *Europe* **24 C10** 52 4N 14 46 E
Nysa Kłodzka →, *Poland* **45 H4** 50 49N 17 40 E
Nysäter, *Sweden* **10 E6** 59 17N 12 47 E
Nyssa, *U.S.A.* **114 E5** 43 53N 117 0W
Nysted, *Denmark* **11 K5** 54 40N 11 44 E
Nyunzu, *Dem. Rep. of the Congo* **86 D2** 5 57 S 27 58 E
Nyurba, *Russia* **51 C12** 63 17N 118 28 E
Nyzhnohirskyy, *Ukraine* **47 K8** 45 27N 34 38 E
Nzébéla, *Guinea* **82 D3** 8 9N 9 7W
Nzega, *Tanzania* **86 C3** 4 10 S 33 12 E
Nzérékoré, *Guinea* **82 D3** 7 49N 8 48W
Nzeto, *Angola* **84 F2** 7 10 S 12 52 E
Nzilo, Chutes de, *Dem. Rep. of the Congo* **87 E2** 10 18 S 25 27 E
Nzo →, *Ivory C.* **82 D3** 6 15N 7 3W
Nzubuka, *Tanzania* **86 C3** 4 45 S 32 50 E

O

O Barco, *Spain* **34 C4** 42 23N 6 58W
O Carballiño, *Spain* **34 C2** 42 26N 8 5W
O Corgo, *Spain* **34 C3** 42 56N 7 25W
O Pino, *Spain* **34 C2** 42 56N 8 20W
O Porriño, *Spain* **34 C2** 42 10N 8 37W
Ō-Shima, *Japan* **55 G9** 34 44N 139 24 E
Oa, Mull of, *U.K.* **14 F2** 55 35N 6 20W
Oacoma, *U.S.A.* **112 D5** 43 48N 99 24W
Oahe, L., *U.S.A.* **112 C4** 44 27N 100 24W
Oahe Dam, *U.S.A.* **112 C4** 44 27N 100 24W
Oahu, *U.S.A.* **106 H16** 21 28N 157 58W
Oak Harbor, *U.S.A.* **116 B4** 48 18N 122 39W
Oak Hill, *U.S.A.* **108 G5** 37 59N 81 9W
Oak Ridge, *U.S.A.* **109 G3** 36 1N 84 16W
Oak View, *U.S.A.* **117 L7** 34 24N 119 18W
Oakan-Dake, *Japan* **54 C12** 43 27N 144 10 E
Oakdale, *Calif., U.S.A.* **116 H6** 37 46N 120 51W
Oakdale, *La., U.S.A.* **113 K8** 30 49N 92 40W
Oakes, *U.S.A.* **112 B5** 46 8N 98 6W
Oakesdale, *U.S.A.* **114 C5** 47 8N 117 15W
Oakey, *Australia* **95 D5** 27 25 S 151 43 E
Oakfield, *U.S.A.* **110 C6** 43 4N 78 16W
Oakham, *U.K.* **13 E7** 52 40N 0 43W
Oakhurst, *U.S.A.* **116 H7** 37 19N 119 40W
Oakland, *U.S.A.* **116 H4** 37 49N 122 16W
Oakley, *Idaho, U.S.A.* **114 E7** 42 15N 113 53W
Oakley, *Kans., U.S.A.* **112 F4** 39 8N 100 51W
Oakover →, *Australia* **92 D3** 21 0 S 120 40 E
Oakridge, *U.S.A.* **114 E2** 43 45N 122 28W
Oakville, *Canada* **110 C5** 43 27N 79 41W
Oakville, *U.S.A.* **116 D3** 46 51N 123 14W
Oamaru, *N.Z.* **91 L3** 45 5 S 170 59 E
Oancea, *Romania* **43 E12** 45 21N 27 42 E
Oasis, *Calif., U.S.A.* **117 M10** 33 28N 116 6W
Oasis, *Nev., U.S.A.* **116 H9** 37 29N 117 55W
Oates Land, *Antarctica* **5 C11** 69 0 S 160 0 E
Oatlands, *Australia* **94 G4** 42 17 S 147 21 E
Oatman, *U.S.A.* **117 K12** 35 1N 114 19W
Oaxaca, *Mexico* **119 D5** 17 2N 96 40W
Oaxaca □, *Mexico* **119 D5** 17 0N 97 0W
Ob →, *Russia* **50 C7** 66 45N 69 30 E
Oba, *Canada* **102 C3** 49 4N 84 7W
Obala, *Cameroon* **83 E7** 4 9N 11 32 E
Obama, *Japan* **55 G7** 35 30N 135 45 E
Oban, *Nigeria* **83 D6** 5 17N 8 33 E
Oban, *U.K.* **14 E3** 56 25N 5 29W
Obbia, *Somali Rep.* **74 F4** 5 25N 48 30 E
Obera, *Argentina* **127 B4** 27 21 S 55 2W
Oberammergau, *Germany* **25 H7** 47 36N 11 4 E
Oberasbach, *Germany* **25 F6** 49 25N 10 57 E
Oberbayern □, *Germany* **25 G7** 48 5N 11 50 E
Oberdrauburg, *Austria* **26 E5** 46 44N 12 58 E
Oberfranken □, *Germany* **25 E7** 50 10N 11 20 E
Oberhausen, *Germany* **24 D2** 51 28N 6 51 E
Oberkirch, *Germany* **25 G4** 48 31N 8 4 E
Oberlausitz, *Germany* **24 D10** 51 16N 14 18 E
Oberlin, *Kans., U.S.A.* **112 F4** 39 49N 100 32W
Oberlin, *La., U.S.A.* **113 K8** 30 37N 92 46W
Oberlin, *Ohio, U.S.A.* **110 E2** 41 18N 82 13W
Obernai, *France* **19 D14** 48 28N 7 30 E
Oberndorf, *Germany* **25 G4** 48 17N 8 34 E
Oberon, *Australia* **95 E4** 33 45 S 149 52 E
Oberösterreich □, *Austria* **26 C7** 48 10N 14 0 E
Oberpfalz □, *Germany* **25 F8** 49 20N 12 10 E
Oberpfälzer Wald, *Germany* **25 F8** 49 30N 12 30 E
Oberstdorf, *Germany* **25 H6** 47 24N 10 15 E
Oberursel, *Germany* **25 E4** 50 11N 8 35 E
Oberwart, *Austria* **27 D9** 47 17N 16 12 E
Obi, Kepulauan, *Indonesia* **63 E7** 1 23 S 127 45 E
Obi Is. = Obi, Kepulauan, *Indonesia* **63 E7** 1 23 S 127 45 E
Obiaruku, *Nigeria* **83 D6** 5 51N 6 9 E
Óbidos, *Brazil* **125 D7** 1 50 S 55 30W
Óbidos, *Portugal* **35 F1** 39 19N 9 10W
Obihiro, *Japan* **54 C11** 42 56N 143 12 E
Obilatu, *Indonesia* **63 E7** 1 25 S 127 20 E
Obilnoye, *Russia* **49 G7** 47 32N 44 30 E
Obing, *Germany* **25 G8** 48 0N 12 24 E
Objat, *France* **20 C5** 45 16N 1 24 E
Obluchye, *Russia* **51 E14** 49 1N 131 4 E
Obninsk, *Russia* **46 E9** 55 8N 36 37 E
Obo, *C.A.R.* **86 A2** 5 20N 26 32 E
Oboa, Mt., *Uganda* **86 B3** 1 45N 34 45 E
Obock, *Djibouti* **81 E5** 12 0N 43 20 E
Oborniki, *Poland* **45 F3** 52 39N 16 50 E
Oborniki Śląskie, *Poland* **45 G3** 51 17N 16 53 E
Oboyan, *Russia* **47 G9** 51 15N 36 21 E
Obozerskaya = Obozerskiy, *Russia* **50 C5** 63 34N 40 21 E
Obozerskiy, *Russia* **50 C5** 63 34N 40 21 E
Obrenovac, *Serbia, Yug.* **40 B4** 44 40N 20 11 E
Obrovac, *Croatia* **29 D12** 44 11N 15 41 E
Obruk, *Turkey* **72 C5** 38 7N 33 12 E
Obrzycko, *Poland* **45 F3** 52 42N 16 32 E
Observatory Inlet, *Canada* **104 B3** 55 10N 129 54W
Obshchi Syrt, *Russia* **6 E16** 52 0N 53 0 E
Obskaya Guba, *Russia* **50 C8** 69 0N 73 0 E
Obuasi, *Ghana* **83 D4** 6 17N 1 40W
Obubra, *Nigeria* **83 D6** 6 8N 8 20 E
Obudu, *Nigeria* **83 D6** 6 38N 9 5 E
Obwalden □, *Switz.* **25 J4** 46 55N 8 15 E
Obzor, *Bulgaria* **41 D11** 42 50N 27 52 E
Ocala, *U.S.A.* **109 L4** 29 11N 82 8W
Ocampo, *Chihuahua, Mexico* **118 B3** 28 9N 108 24W
Ocampo, *Tamaulipas, Mexico* **119 C5** 22 50N 99 20W
Ocaña, *Spain* **34 F7** 39 55N 3 30W
Ocanomowoc, *U.S.A.* **112 D10** 43 7N 88 30W
Occidental, Cordillera, *Colombia* **122 C3** 5 0N 76 0W
Ocean City, *Md., U.S.A.* **108 F8** 38 20N 75 5W
Ocean City, *N.J., U.S.A.* **108 F8** 39 17N 74 35W
Ocean City, *Wash., U.S.A.* **116 C2** 47 4N 124 10W
Ocean Falls, *Canada* **104 C3** 52 18N 127 48W
Ocean I. = Banaba, *Kiribati* **96 H8** 0 45 S 169 50 E
Ocean Park, *U.S.A.* **116 D2** 46 30N 124 3W
Oceano, *U.S.A.* **117 K6** 35 6N 120 37W
Oceanport, *U.S.A.* **111 F10** 40 19N 74 3W
Oceanside, *U.S.A.* **117 M9** 33 12N 117 23W
Ochagavía, *Spain* **32 C3** 42 55N 1 5W
Ochakiv, *Ukraine* **47 J6** 46 37N 31 33 E
Ochamchira, *Georgia* **49 J5** 42 46N 41 32 E
Ochil Hills, *U.K.* **14 E5** 56 14N 3 40W
Ochsenfurt, *Germany* **25 F6** 49 40N 10 4 E
Ochsenhausen, *Germany* **25 G5** 48 4N 9 57 E
Ocilla, *U.S.A.* **109 K4** 31 36N 83 15W
Ockelbo, *Sweden* **10 D10** 60 54N 16 45 E
Ocmulgee →, *U.S.A.* **109 K4** 31 58N 82 33W
Ocna Mureş, *Romania* **43 D8** 46 23N 23 55 E
Ocna Sibiului, *Romania* **43 E9** 45 52N 24 2 E
Ocnele Mari, *Romania* **43 E9** 45 8N 24 18 E
Ocniţa, *Moldova* **43 B12** 48 25N 27 30 E
Oconee →, *U.S.A.* **109 K4** 31 58N 82 33W
Oconto, *U.S.A.* **108 C2** 44 53N 87 52W
Oconto Falls, *U.S.A.* **108 C1** 44 52N 88 9W
Ocosingo, *Mexico* **119 D6** 17 10N 92 15W
Ocotal, *Nic.* **120 D2** 13 41N 86 31W
Ocotlán, *Mexico* **118 C4** 20 21N 102 42W
Ocotlán de Morelos, *Mexico* **119 D5** 16 48N 96 40W
Ocreza →, *Portugal* **35 F3** 39 32N 7 50W
Ócsa, *Hungary* **42 C4** 47 17N 19 15 E
Octeville, *France* **18 C5** 49 38N 1 40W
Oda, *Ghana* **83 D4** 5 50N 0 51W
Ōda, *Japan* **55 G6** 35 11N 132 30 E
Oda, J., *Sudan* **80 C4** 20 21N 36 39 E
Ódáðahraun, *Iceland* **8 D5** 65 5N 17 0W
Ödåkra, *Sweden* **11 H6** 56 7N 12 45 E
Odate, *Japan* **54 D10** 40 16N 140 34 E
Odawara, *Japan* **55 G9** 35 20N 139 6 E
Odda, *Norway* **9 F12** 60 3N 6 35 E
Odder, *Denmark* **11 J4** 55 58N 10 10 E
Odei →, *Canada* **105 B9** 56 6N 96 54W
Odemira, *Portugal* **35 H2** 37 35N 8 40W
Ödemiş, *Turkey* **39 C9** 38 15N 28 0 E
Odendaalsrus, *S. Africa* **88 D4** 27 48 S 26 45 E
Odensbacken, *Sweden* **10 E9** 59 10N 15 32 E
Odense, *Denmark* **11 J4** 55 22N 10 23 E
Odenwald, *Germany* **25 F5** 49 35N 9 0 E
Oder →, *Europe* **24 B10** 53 33N 14 38 E
Oder-Havel Kanal, *Germany* **24 C10** 52 52N 14 2 E
Oderzo, *Italy* **29 C9** 45 47N 12 29 E
Odesa, *Ukraine* **47 J6** 46 30N 30 45 E
Ödeshög, *Sweden* **11 F8** 58 14N 14 39 E
Odessa = Odesa, *Ukraine* **47 J6** 46 30N 30 45 E
Odessa, *Canada* **111 B8** 44 17N 76 43W
Odessa, *Tex., U.S.A.* **113 K3** 31 52N 102 23W
Odessa, *Wash., U.S.A.* **114 C4** 47 20N 118 41W
Odiakwe, *Botswana* **88 C4** 20 12 S 25 17 E
Odiel →, *Spain* **35 H4** 37 10N 6 55W
Odienné, *Ivory C.* **82 D3** 9 30N 7 34W
Odintsovo, *Russia* **46 E9** 55 39N 37 15 E
Odiongan, *Phil.* **61 E4** 12 24N 121 59 E

Orillia

Odobeşti, *Romania* **43 E12** 45 43N 27 4 E
Odolanów, *Poland* **45 G4** 51 34N 17 40 E
O'Donnell, *U.S.A.* **113 J4** 32 58N 101 50W
Odorheiu Secuiesc, *Romania* **43 D10** 46 21N 25 21 E
Odoyevo, *Russia* **46 F9** 53 56N 36 42 E
Odra = Oder →, *Europe* **24 B10** 53 33N 14 38 E
Odra →, *Spain* **34 C6** 42 14N 4 17W
Odžaci, *Serbia, Yug.* **42 E4** 45 30N 19 17 E
Odžak, *Bos.-H.* **42 E3** 45 3N 18 18 E
Odzi, *Zimbabwe* **89 B5** 19 0S 32 20 E
Odzi →, *Zimbabwe* **89 B5** 19 45S 32 23 E
Oebisfelde, *Germany* **24 C6** 52 27N 10 57 E
Oeiras, *Brazil* **125 E10** 7 0S 42 8W
Oeiras, *Portugal* **35 G1** 38 41N 9 18W
Oelrichs, *U.S.A.* **112 D3** 43 11N 103 14W
Oelsnitz, *Germany* **25 E8** 50 24N 12 10 E
Oelwein, *U.S.A.* **112 D9** 42 41N 91 55W
Oenpelli, *Australia* **92 B5** 12 20S 133 4 E
Oetz, *Austria* **26 D3** 47 13N 10 53 E
Of, *Turkey* **73 B9** 40 59N 40 23 E
Ofanto →, *Italy* **31 A9** 41 22N 16 13 E
Offa, *Nigeria* **83 D5** 8 13N 4 42 E
Offaly □, *Ireland* **15 C4** 53 15N 7 30W
Offenbach, *Germany* **25 E4** 50 6N 8 44 E
Offenburg, *Germany* **25 G3** 48 28N 7 56 E
Offida, *Italy* **29 F10** 42 56N 13 41 E
Ofidhousa, *Greece* **39 E8** 36 33N 26 8 E
Ofotfjorden, *Norway* **8 B17** 68 27N 17 0 E
Ōfunato, *Japan* **54 E10** 39 4N 141 43 E
Oga, *Japan* **54 E9** 39 55N 139 50 E
Oga-Hantō, *Japan* **54 E9** 39 58N 139 47 E
Ogaden, *Ethiopia* **74 F3** 7 30N 45 30 E
Ōgaki, *Japan* **55 G8** 35 21N 136 37 E
Ogallala, *U.S.A.* **112 E4** 41 8N 101 43W
Ogasawara Gunto, *Pac. Oc.* **52 G18** 27 0N 142 0 E
Ogbomosho, *Nigeria* **83 D5** 8 1N 4 11 E
Ogden, *U.S.A.* **114 F7** 41 13N 111 58W
Ogdensburg, *U.S.A.* **111 B9** 44 42N 75 30W
Ogeechee →, *U.S.A.* **109 K5** 31 50N 81 3W
Ogilby, *U.S.A.* **117 N12** 32 49N 114 50W
Oglio →, *Italy* **28 C7** 45 2N 10 39 E
Ogmore, *Australia* **94 C4** 22 37S 149 35 E
Ognon →, *France* **19 E12** 47 16N 5 28 E
Ogoja, *Nigeria* **83 D6** 6 38N 8 39 E
Ogoki, *Canada* **102 B2** 51 38N 85 58W
Ogoki →, *Canada* **102 B2** 51 38N 85 57W
Ogoki L., *Canada* **102 B2** 50 50N 87 10W
Ogoki Res., *Canada* **102 B2** 50 45N 88 15W
Ogooué →, *Gabon* **84 E1** 1 0S 9 0 E
Ogosta →, *Bulgaria* **40 C7** 43 48N 23 55 E
Ogowe = Ogooué →, *Gabon* **84 E1** 1 0S 9 0 E
Ogr = Sharafa, *Sudan* **81 E2** 11 59N 27 7 E
Ograźden, *Macedonia* **40 E6** 41 30N 22 50 E
Ogre, *Latvia* **9 H21** 56 49N 24 36 E
Ogrein, *Sudan* **80 D3** 17 55N 34 50 E
Ogulin, *Croatia* **29 C12** 45 16N 15 16 E
Ogun □, *Nigeria* **83 D5** 7 0N 3 0 E
Ogurchinskiy, Ostrov, *Turkmenistan* **71 B7** 38 55N 53 2 E
Oguta, *Nigeria* **83 D6** 5 44N 6 44 E
Ogwashi-Uku, *Nigeria* **83 D6** 6 15N 6 30 E
Ogwe, *Nigeria* **83 E6** 5 0N 7 14 E
Ohai, *N.Z.* **91 L2** 45 55S 168 0 E
Ohakune, *N.Z.* **91 H5** 39 24S 175 24 E
Ohata, *Japan* **54 D10** 41 24N 141 10 E
Ohau, L., *N.Z.* **91 L2** 44 15S 169 53 E
Ohio □, *U.S.A.* **110 F2** 40 15N 82 45W
Ohio →, *U.S.A.* **108 G1** 36 59N 89 8W
Ohře →, *Czech Rep.* **26 A7** 50 30N 14 10 E
Ohre →, *Germany* **24 C7** 52 18N 11 46 E
Ohrid, *Macedonia* **40 E4** 41 8N 20 52 E
Ohridsko Jezero, *Macedonia* **40 E4** 41 8N 20 52 E
Ohrigstad, *S. Africa* **89 C5** 24 39S 30 36 E
Öhringen, *Germany* **25 F5** 49 12N 9 31 E
Oi Qu, *China* **58 C2** 28 37N 98 16 E
Oiapoque, *Brazil* **125** 3 50N 51 50W
Oikou, *China* **57 E9** 38 35N 117 42 E
Oil City, *U.S.A.* **110 E5** 41 26N 79 42W
Oil Springs, *Canada* **110 D2** 42 47N 82 7W
Oildale, *U.S.A.* **117 K7** 35 25N 119 1W
Oinousa, *Greece* **39 C8** 38 33N 26 14 E
Oise □, *France* **19 C9** 49 28N 2 30 E
Oise →, *France* **19 C9** 49 0N 2 4 E
Ōita, *Japan* **55 H5** 33 14N 131 36 E
Ōita □, *Japan* **55 H5** 33 15N 131 30 E
Oiticica, *Brazil* **125 E10** 5 3S 41 5W
Ojacaliente, *Mexico* **118 C4** 22 34N 102 15W
Ojai, *U.S.A.* **117 L7** 34 27N 119 15W
Ojinaga, *Mexico* **118 B4** 29 34N 104 25W
Ojiya, *Japan* **55 F9** 37 18N 138 48 E
Ojos del Salado, Cerro, *Argentina* **126 B2** 27 0S 68 40W
Oka →, *Russia* **48 B7** 56 20N 43 59 E
Okaba, *Indonesia* **63 F9** 8 6S 139 42 E
Okahandja, *Namibia* **88 C2** 22 0S 16 59 E
Okanagan L., *Canada* **104 D5** 50 0N 119 30W
Okanogan, *U.S.A.* **114 B4** 48 22N 119 35W
Okanogan →, *U.S.A.* **114 B4** 48 6N 119 44W
Okány, *Hungary* **42 D6** 46 52N 21 21 E
Okaputa, *Namibia* **88 C2** 20 5S 17 0 E
Okara, *Pakistan* **68 D5** 30 50N 73 31 E
Okaukuejo, *Namibia* **88 B2** 19 10S 16 0 E
Okavango Swamps, *Botswana* **88 B3** 18 45S 22 45 E
Okaya, *Japan* **55 F9** 36 5N 138 10 E
Okayama, *Japan* **55 G6** 34 40N 133 54 E
Okayama □, *Japan* **55 G6** 35 0N 133 50 E
Okazaki, *Japan* **55 G8** 34 57N 137 10 E
Oke-Iho, *Nigeria* **83 D5** 8 1N 3 18 E
Okeechobee, *U.S.A.* **109 M5** 27 15N 80 50W
Okeechobee, L., *U.S.A.* **109 M5** 27 0N 80 50W
Okefenokee Swamp, *U.S.A.* **109 K4** 30 40N 82 20W
Okehampton, *U.K.* **13 G4** 50 44N 4 0W
Okene, *Nigeria* **83 D6** 7 32N 6 11 E
Oker →, *Germany* **24 C6** 52 32N 10 22 E
Okha, *India* **68 H3** 22 27N 69 4 E
Okha, *Russia* **51 D15** 53 40N 143 0 E
Ókhi Óros, *Greece* **38 C6** 38 5N 24 25 E
Okhotsk, *Russia* **51 D15** 59 20N 143 10 E
Okhotsk, Sea of, *Asia* **51 D15** 55 0N 145 0 E
Okhotskiy Perevoz, *Russia* **51 C14** 61 52N 135 35 E
Okhtyrka, *Ukraine* **47 G8** 50 25N 35 0 E
Oki-Shotō, *Japan* **55 F6** 36 5N 133 15 E
Okiep, *S. Africa* **88 D2** 29 39S 17 53 E
Okigwi, *Nigeria* **83 D6** 5 52N 7 20 E
Okija, *Nigeria* **83 D6** 5 54N 6 55 E
Okinawa □, *Japan* **55 L4** 26 40N 128 0 E
Okinawa-Guntō, *Japan* **55 L4** 26 40N 128 0 E
Okinawa-Jima, *Japan* **55 L4** 26 32N 128 0 E
Okino-erabu-Shima, *Japan* **55 L4** 27 21N 128 33 E
Okitipupa, *Nigeria* **83 D5** 6 31N 4 50 E
Oklahoma □, *U.S.A.* **113 H6** 35 20N 97 30W
Oklahoma City, *U.S.A.* **113 H6** 35 30N 97 30W
Okmulgee, *U.S.A.* **113 H7** 35 37N 95 58W
Oknitsa = Ocniţa, *Moldova* **43 B12** 48 25N 27 30 E
Oko, W. →, *Sudan* **80 C4** 21 15N 35 56 E
Okolo, *Uganda* **86 B3** 2 37N 31 8 E
Okolona, *U.S.A.* **113 J10** 34 0N 88 45W
Okombahe, *Namibia* **88 C2** 21 23S 15 22 E
Okonek, *Poland* **44 E3** 53 32N 16 51 E
Okotoks, *Canada* **104 C6** 50 43N 113 58W
Okrika, *Nigeria* **83 E6** 4 40N 7 10 E
Oksibil, *Indonesia* **63 E10** 4 59S 140 35 E
Oktabrsk = Oktyabrsk, *Kazakhstan* **50 E6** 49 28N 57 25 E
Oktyabrsk, *Kazakhstan* **50 E6** 49 28N 57 25 E
Oktyabrsk, *Russia* **48 D9** 53 11N 48 40 E
Oktyabrskiy = Aktsyabrski, *Belarus* **47 F5** 52 38N 28 53 E
Oktyabrskiy, *Russia* **49 G5** 47 30N 40 4 E
Oktyabrskoy Revolyutsii, Ostrov, *Russia* **51 B10** 79 30N 97 0 E
Oktyabrskoye = Zhovtneve, *Ukraine* **47 J7** 46 54N 32 3 E
Okulovka, *Russia* **46 C7** 58 25N 33 19 E
Okuru, *N.Z.* **91 K2** 43 55S 168 55 E
Okushiri-Tō, *Japan* **54 C9** 42 15N 139 30 E
Okuta, *Nigeria* **83 D5** 9 14N 3 12 E
Okwa →, *Botswana* **88 C3** 22 30S 23 0 E
Ola, *U.S.A.* **113 H8** 35 2N 93 13W
Ólafsfjörður, *Iceland* **8 C4** 66 4N 18 39W
Ólafsvík, *Iceland* **8 D2** 64 53N 23 43W
Olaine, *Latvia* **44 B10** 56 48N 23 59 E
Olancha, *U.S.A.* **117 J8** 36 17N 118 1W
Olancha Pk., *U.S.A.* **117 J8** 36 15N 118 7W
Olanchito, *Honduras* **120 C2** 15 30N 86 30W
Öland, *Sweden* **11 H10** 56 45N 16 38 E
Ölands norra udde, *Sweden* **11 G11** 57 22N 17 5 E
Ölands södra udde, *Sweden* **11 H10** 56 12N 16 23 E
Olargues, *France* **20 E6** 43 34N 2 53 E
Olary, *Australia* **95 E3** 32 18S 140 19 E
Olascoaga, *Argentina* **126 D3** 35 15S 60 39W
Olathe, *U.S.A.* **112 F7** 38 53N 94 49W
Olavarría, *Argentina* **126 D3** 36 55S 60 20W
Oława, *Poland* **45 H4** 50 57N 17 20 E
Olbernhau, *Germany* **24 E9** 50 40N 13 19 E
Ólbia, *Italy* **30 B2** 40 55N 9 31 E
Ólbia, G. di, *Italy* **30 B2** 40 55N 9 39 E
Olching, *Germany* **25 G7** 48 12N 11 21 E
Olcott, *U.S.A.* **110 C6** 43 20N 78 42W
Old Bahama Chan. = Bahama, Canal Viejo de, *W. Indies* **120 B4** 22 10N 77 30W
Old Baldy Pk. = San Antonio, Mt., *U.S.A.* **117 L9** 34 17N 117 38W
Old Castile = Castilla y Leon □, *Spain* **34 D6** 42 0N 5 0W
Old Crow, *Canada* **100 B6** 67 30N 139 55W
Old Dale, *U.S.A.* **117 L11** 34 8N 115 47W
Old Dongola, *Sudan* **80 D3** 18 11N 30 44 E
Old Forge, *N.Y., U.S.A.* **111 C10** 43 43N 74 58W
Old Forge, *Pa., U.S.A.* **111 E9** 41 22N 75 45W
Old Perlican, *Canada* **103 C9** 48 5N 53 1W
Old Shinyanga, *Tanzania* **86 C3** 3 33S 33 27 E
Old Speck Mt., *U.S.A.* **111 B14** 44 34N 70 57W
Old Town, *U.S.A.* **109 C11** 44 56N 68 39W
Old Washington, *U.S.A.* **110 F3** 40 2N 81 27W
Old Wives L., *Canada* **105 C7** 50 5N 106 0W
Oldbury, *U.K.* **13 F5** 51 38N 2 33W
Oldcastle, *Ireland* **15 C4** 53 46N 7 10W
Oldeani, *Tanzania* **86 C4** 3 22S 35 35 E
Oldenburg, *Niedersachsen, Germany* **24 B4** 53 9N 8 13 E
Oldenburg, *Schleswig-Holstein, Germany* **24 A6** 54 17N 10 52 E
Oldenzaal, *Neths.* **17 B6** 52 19N 6 53 E
Oldham, *U.K.* **12 D5** 53 33N 2 7W
Oldman →, *Canada* **104 D6** 49 57N 111 42W
Oldmeldrum, *U.K.* **14 D6** 57 20N 2 19W
Olds, *Canada* **104 C6** 51 50N 114 10W
Oldziyt, *Mongolia* **56 B5** 44 40N 109 1 E
Olean, *U.S.A.* **110 D6** 42 5N 78 26W
Olecko, *Poland* **44 D9** 54 2N 22 31 E
Oléggio, *Italy* **28 C5** 45 36N 8 38 E
Oleiros, *Portugal* **34 F3** 39 56N 7 56W
Oleiros, *Spain* **34 B2** 43 20N 8 19W
Olekma →, *Russia* **51 C13** 60 22N 120 42 E
Olekminsk, *Russia* **51 C13** 60 25N 120 30 E
Oleksandriya, *Kirovohrad, Ukraine* **47 H7** 48 42N 33 3 E
Oleksandriya, *Rivne, Ukraine* **47 G4** 50 37N 26 19 E
Oleksandrovka, *Ukraine* **47 H7** 48 55N 32 20 E
Olema, *U.S.A.* **116 G4** 38 3N 122 47W
Olenek, *Russia* **51 C12** 68 28N 112 18 E
Olenek →, *Russia* **51 B13** 73 0N 120 10 E
Olenino, *Russia* **46 D7** 56 15N 33 30 E
Oléron, Î. d', *France* **20 C2** 45 55N 1 15W
Oleśnica, *Poland* **45 G4** 51 13N 17 22 E
Olesno, *Poland* **45 H5** 50 51N 18 26 E
Olevsk, *Ukraine* **47 G4** 51 12N 27 39 E
Olga, *Russia* **51 E14** 43 50N 135 14 E
Olga, L., *Canada* **102 C4** 49 47N 77 15W
Olga, Mt., *Australia* **93 E5** 25 20S 130 50 E
Ølgod, *Denmark* **11 J2** 55 49N 8 36 E
Olhão, *Portugal* **35 H3** 37 3N 7 48W
Olib, *Croatia* **29 D11** 44 23N 14 44 E
Oliena, *Italy* **30 B2** 40 16N 9 24 E
Oliete, *Spain* **32 D4** 41 1N 0 41W
Olifants →, *Africa* **89 C5** 23 57S 31 58 E
Olifants →, *Namibia* **88 C2** 25 30S 19 30 E
Olifantshoek, *S. Africa* **88 D3** 27 57S 22 42 E
Ólimbos, *Greece* **39 F9** 35 44N 27 11 E
Ólimbos, Óros, *Greece* **40 F6** 40 6N 22 23 E
Olímpia, *Brazil* **127 A6** 20 44S 48 54W
Olinda, *Brazil* **125 E12** 8 1S 34 51W
Olite, *Spain* **32 C3** 42 29N 1 40W
Oliva, *Argentina* **126 C3** 32 0S 63 38W
Oliva, *Spain* **33 G4** 38 58N 0 9W
Oliva, Punta del, *Spain* **34 B5** 43 37N 5 28W
Oliva de la Frontera, *Spain* **35 G4** 38 17N 6 54W
Olivares, *Spain* **32 F2** 39 46N 2 20W
Olivehurst, *U.S.A.* **116 F5** 39 6N 121 34W
Oliveira de Azeméis, *Portugal* **34 E2** 40 49N 8 29W
Oliveira do Douro, *Portugal* **34 D2** 41 5N 8 2W
Olivenza, *Spain* **35 G3** 38 41N 7 9W
Oliver, *Canada* **104 D5** 49 13N 119 37W
Oliver L., *Canada* **105 B8** 56 56N 103 22W
Olivet, *France* **19 E8** 47 51N 1 55 E
Olkhovka, *Russia* **48 F7** 49 48N 44 32 E
Olkusz, *Poland* **45 H6** 50 18N 19 33 E
Ollagüe, *Chile* **126 A2** 21 15S 68 10W
Olmedo, *Spain* **34 D6** 41 20N 4 43W
Olmeto, *France* **21 G12** 41 43N 8 55 E
Olney, *Ill., U.S.A.* **108 F1** 38 44N 88 5W
Olney, *Tex., U.S.A.* **113 J5** 33 22N 98 45W
Olofström, *Sweden* **11 H8** 56 17N 14 32 E
Oloma, *Cameroon* **83 E7** 3 29N 11 19 E
Olomane →, *Canada* **103 B7** 50 14N 60 37W
Olomouc, *Czech Rep.* **27 B10** 49 38N 17 12 E
Olomoucký □, *Czech Rep.* **27 B10** 49 45N 17 5 E
Olonets, *Russia* **46 B7** 61 0N 32 54 E
Olongapo, *Phil.* **61 D4** 14 50N 120 18 E
Olonne-sur-Mer, *France* **20 B2** 46 32N 1 47W
Oloron, Gave d' →, *France* **20 E2** 43 33N 1 5W
Oloron-Ste-Marie, *France* **20 E3** 43 11N 0 38W
Olot, *Spain* **32 C7** 42 11N 2 30 E
Olovo, *Bos.-H.* **42 F3** 44 8N 18 35 E
Olovyannaya, *Russia* **51 D12** 50 58N 115 35 E
Oloy →, *Russia* **51 C16** 66 29N 159 29 E
Olsberg, *Germany* **24 D4** 51 21N 8 31 E
Olshammar, *Sweden* **11 F8** 58 45N 14 48 E
Olshanka, *Ukraine* **47 H6** 48 16N 30 58 E
Olshany, *Ukraine* **47 G8** 50 3N 35 53 E
Olsztyn, *Poland* **44 E7** 53 48N 20 29 E
Olsztynek, *Poland* **44 E7** 53 34N 20 19 E
Olt □, *Romania* **43 F9** 44 20N 24 30 E
Olt →, *Romania* **43 G9** 43 43N 24 51 E
Olten, *Switz.* **25 H3** 47 21N 7 53 E
Olteniţa, *Romania* **43 F11** 44 7N 26 42 E
Olton, *U.S.A.* **113 H3** 34 11N 102 8W
Oltu, *Turkey* **73 B9** 40 35N 41 58 E
Oluanpi, *Taiwan* **59 G13** 21 54N 120 51 E
Olula del Río, *Spain* **33 H2** 37 21N 2 18W
Olur, *Turkey* **73 B10** 40 49N 42 8 E
Olutanga, *Phil.* **61 H5** 7 26N 122 54 E
Olvega, *Spain* **32 D2** 41 47N 2 0W
Olvera, *Spain* **35 J5** 36 55N 5 18W
Olymbos, *Cyprus* **36 D12** 35 21N 33 45 E
Olympia, *Greece* **38 D3** 37 39N 21 39 E
Olympia, *U.S.A.* **116 D4** 47 3N 122 53W
Olympic Dam, *Australia* **95 E2** 30 30S 136 55 E
Olympic Mts., *U.S.A.* **116 C3** 47 55N 123 45W
Olympic Nat. Park, *U.S.A.* **116 C3** 47 48N 123 30W
Olympus, *Cyprus* **36 E11** 34 56N 32 52 E
Olympus, Mt. = Ólimbos, Óros, *Greece* **40 F6** 40 6N 22 23 E
Olympus, Mt. = Uludağ, *Turkey* **41 F13** 40 4N 29 13 E
Olympus, Mt., *U.S.A.* **116 C3** 47 48N 123 43W
Olyphant, *U.S.A.* **111 E9** 41 27N 75 36W
Om →, *Russia* **50 D8** 54 59N 73 22 E
Om Hajer, *Eritrea* **81 E4** 14 20N 36 41 E
Om Koi, *Thailand* **64 D2** 17 48N 98 22 E
Ōma, *Japan* **54 D10** 41 45N 141 5 E
Ōmachi, *Japan* **55 F8** 36 30N 137 50 E
Omae-Zaki, *Japan* **55 G9** 34 36N 138 14 E
Ōmagari, *Japan* **54 E10** 39 27N 140 29 E
Omagh, *U.K.* **15 B4** 54 36N 7 19W
Omagh □, *U.K.* **15 B4** 54 35N 7 15W
Omaha, *U.S.A.* **112 E7** 41 17N 95 58W
Omak, *U.S.A.* **114 B4** 48 25N 119 31W
Omalos, *Greece* **36 D5** 35 19N 23 55 E
Oman ■, *Asia* **74 C6** 23 0N 58 0 E
Oman, G. of, *Asia* **71 E8** 24 30N 58 30 E
Omaruru, *Namibia* **88 C2** 21 26S 16 0 E
Omaruru →, *Namibia* **88 C1** 22 7S 14 15 E
Omate, *Peru* **124 G4** 16 45S 71 0W
Ombai, Selat, *Indonesia* **63 F6** 8 30S 124 50 E
Omboué, *Gabon* **84 E1** 1 35S 9 15 E
Ombrone →, *Italy* **28 F8** 42 42N 11 5 E
Omdurmân, *Sudan* **81 D3** 15 40N 32 28 E
Omegna, *Italy* **28 C5** 45 53N 8 24 E
Omemee, *Canada* **110 B6** 44 18N 78 33W
Omeonga, *Dem. Rep. of the Congo* **86 C1** 3 40S 24 22 E
Ometepe, I. de, *Nic.* **120 D2** 11 32N 85 35W
Ometepec, *Mexico* **119 D5** 16 39N 98 23W
Ominato, *Japan* **54 D10** 41 17N 141 10 E
Omineca →, *Canada* **104 B4** 56 3N 124 16W
Omiš, *Croatia* **29 E13** 43 28N 16 40 E
Omišalj, *Croatia* **29 C11** 45 13N 14 32 E
Omitara, *Namibia* **88 C2** 22 16S 18 2 E
Ōmiya, *Japan* **55 G9** 35 54N 139 38 E
Omme Å →, *Denmark* **11 J2** 55 56N 8 32 E
Ommen, *Neths.* **17 B6** 52 31N 6 26 E
Ömnögovĭ □, *Mongolia* **56 C3** 43 15N 104 0 E
Omo →, *Ethiopia* **81 F4** 6 25N 36 10 E
Omodeo, L., *Italy* **30 B1** 40 8N 8 56 E
Omodhos, *Cyprus* **36 E11** 34 51N 32 48 E
Omoko, *Nigeria* **83 D6** 5 19N 6 40 E
Omolon →, *Russia* **51 C16** 68 42N 158 36 E
Omono-Gawa →, *Japan* **54 E10** 39 46N 140 3 E
Omsk, *Russia* **50 D8** 55 0N 73 12 E
Omsukchan, *Russia* **51 C16** 62 32N 155 48 E
Ōmu, *Japan* **54 B11** 44 34N 142 58 E
Omul, Vf., *Romania* **43 E10** 45 27N 25 29 E
Omulew →, *Poland* **45 E8** 53 5N 21 33 E
Ōmura, *Japan* **55 H4** 32 56N 129 57 E
Omuramba Omatako →, *Namibia* **88 B2** 17 45S 20 25 E
Omuramba Ovambo →, *Namibia* **88 B2** 18 45S 16 59 E
Omurtag, *Bulgaria* **41 C10** 43 8N 26 26 E
Ōmuta, *Japan* **55 H5** 33 5N 130 26 E
Oña, *Spain* **34 C7** 42 43N 3 25W
Onaga, *U.S.A.* **112 F6** 39 29N 96 10W
Onalaska, *U.S.A.* **112 D9** 43 53N 91 14W
Onancock, *U.S.A.* **108 G8** 37 43N 75 45W
Onang, *Indonesia* **63 E5** 3 2S 118 49 E
Onaping L., *Canada* **102 C3** 47 3N 81 30W
Oñati, *Spain* **32 B2** 43 3N 2 25W
Onavas, *Mexico* **118 B3** 28 28N 109 30W
Onawa, *U.S.A.* **112 D6** 42 2N 96 6W
Oncócua, *Angola* **88 B1** 16 30S 13 25 E
Onda, *Spain* **32 F4** 39 55N 0 17W
Ondaejin, *N. Korea* **57 D15** 41 34N 129 40 E
Ondangwa, *Namibia* **88 B2** 17 57S 16 4 E
Ondarroa, *Spain* **32 B2** 43 19N 2 25W
Ondava →, *Slovak Rep.* **27 C14** 48 27N 21 48 E
Ondjiva, *Angola* **88 B2** 16 48S 15 50 E
Ondo, *Nigeria* **83 D5** 7 4N 4 47 E
Ondo □, *Nigeria* **83 D6** 6 45N 5 0 E
Öndörshil, *Mongolia* **56 B5** 45 13N 108 5 E
Öndverðarnes, *Iceland* **8 D1** 64 52N 24 0W
One Tree, *Australia* **95 E3** 34 11S 144 43 E
Onega, *Russia* **50 C4** 64 0N 38 10 E
Onega →, *Russia* **6 C13** 63 58N 38 2 E
Onega, L. = Onezhskoye Ozero, *Russia* **46 B8** 61 44N 35 22 E
Oneida, *U.S.A.* **111 C9** 43 6N 75 39W
Oneida L., *U.S.A.* **111 C9** 43 12N 75 54W
O'Neill, *U.S.A.* **112 D5** 42 27N 98 39W
Onekotan, Ostrov, *Russia* **51 E16** 49 25N 154 45 E
Onema, *Dem. Rep. of the Congo* **86 C1** 4 35S 24 30 E
Oneonta, *U.S.A.* **111 D9** 42 27N 75 4W
Oneşti, *Romania* **43 D11** 46 17N 26 47 E
Onezhskoye Ozero, *Russia* **46 B8** 61 44N 35 22 E
Ongarue, *N.Z.* **91 H5** 38 42S 175 19 E
Ongers →, *S. Africa* **88 E3** 31 4S 23 13 E
Ongerup, *Australia* **93 F2** 33 58S 118 28 E
Ongjin, *N. Korea* **57 F13** 37 56N 125 21 E
Ongkharak, *Thailand* **64 E3** 14 8N 101 1 E
Ongniud Qi, *China* **57 C10** 43 0N 118 38 E
Ongoka, *Dem. Rep. of the Congo* **86 C2** 1 20S 26 0 E
Ongole, *India* **66 M12** 15 33N 80 2 E
Ongon = Havirga, *Mongolia* **56 B7** 45 41N 113 5 E
Oni, *Georgia* **49 J6** 42 33N 43 26 E
Onida, *U.S.A.* **112 C4** 44 42N 100 4W
Onilahy →, *Madag.* **89 C7** 23 34S 43 45 E
Onitsha, *Nigeria* **83 D6** 6 6N 6 42 E
Onoda, *Japan* **55 G5** 33 59N 131 11 E
Onpyŏng-ni, *S. Korea* **57 H14** 33 25N 126 55 E
Ons, I. de, *Spain* **34 C2** 42 23N 8 55W
Onslow, *Australia* **92 D2** 21 40S 115 12 E
Onslow B., *U.S.A.* **109 H7** 34 20N 77 15W
Ontake-San, *Japan* **55 G8** 35 53N 137 29 E
Ontario, *Calif., U.S.A.* **117 L9** 34 4N 117 39W
Ontario, *Oreg., U.S.A.* **114 D5** 44 2N 116 58W
Ontario □, *Canada* **102 B2** 48 0N 83 0W
Ontario, L., *N. Amer.* **110 C7** 43 20N 78 0W
Ontinyent, *Spain* **33 G4** 38 50N 0 35W
Ontonagon, *U.S.A.* **112 B10** 46 52N 89 19W
Ontur, *Spain* **33 G3** 38 38N 1 29W
Onyx, *U.S.A.* **117 K8** 35 41N 118 14W
Oodnadatta, *Australia* **95 D2** 27 33S 135 30 E
Ooldea, *Australia* **93 F5** 30 27S 131 50 E
Oombulgurri, *Australia* **92 C4** 15 15S 127 45 E
Oorindi, *Australia* **94 C3** 20 40S 141 1 E
Oost-Vlaanderen □, *Belgium* **17 C3** 51 5N 3 50 E
Oostende, *Belgium* **17 C2** 51 15N 2 54 E
Oosterhout, *Neths.* **17 C4** 51 39N 4 47 E
Oosterschelde →, *Neths.* **17 C4** 51 33N 4 0 E
Oosterwolde, *Neths.* **17 B6** 53 0N 6 17 E
Ootacamund = Udagamandalam, *India* **66 P10** 11 30N 76 44 E
Ootsa L., *Canada* **104 C3** 53 50N 126 2W
Opaka, *Bulgaria* **41 C10** 43 28N 26 10 E
Opala, *Dem. Rep. of the Congo* **86 C1** 0 40S 24 20 E
Opalenica, *Poland* **45 F3** 52 18N 16 24 E
Opan, *Bulgaria* **41 D9** 42 13N 25 41 E
Opanake, *Sri Lanka* **66 R12** 6 35N 80 40 E
Opasatika, *Canada* **102 C3** 49 30N 82 50W
Opasquia Prov. Park, *Canada* **102 B1** 53 33N 93 5W
Opatija, *Croatia* **29 C11** 45 21N 14 17 E
Opatów, *Poland* **45 H8** 50 50N 21 27 E
Opava, *Czech Rep.* **27 B10** 49 57N 17 58 E
Opelika, *U.S.A.* **109 J3** 32 39N 85 23W
Opelousas, *U.S.A.* **113 K8** 30 32N 92 5W
Opémisca, L., *Canada* **102 C5** 49 56N 74 52W
Opheim, *U.S.A.* **114 B10** 48 51N 106 24W
Ophthalmia Ra., *Australia* **92 D2** 23 15S 119 30 E
Opi, *Nigeria* **83 D6** 6 36N 7 28 E
Opinaca →, *Canada* **102 B4** 52 15N 78 2W
Opinaca, Rés., *Canada* **102 B4** 52 39N 76 20W
Opinnagau →, *Canada* **102 B3** 54 12N 82 25W
Opiscoteo, L., *Canada* **103 B6** 53 10N 68 10W
Opobo, *Nigeria* **83 E6** 4 35N 7 34 E
Opochka, *Russia* **46 D5** 56 42N 28 45 E
Opoczno, *Poland* **45 G7** 51 22N 20 18 E
Opol, *Phil.* **61 G6** 8 31N 124 34 E
Opole, *Poland* **45 H4** 50 42N 17 58 E
Opole Lubelskie, *Poland* **45 G8** 51 9N 21 58 E
Opolskie □, *Poland* **45 H5** 50 30N 18 0 E
Oponono L., *Namibia* **88 B2** 18 8S 15 45 E
Oporto = Porto, *Portugal* **34 D2** 41 8N 8 40W
Opotiki, *N.Z.* **91 H6** 38 1S 177 19 E
Opp, *U.S.A.* **109 K2** 31 17N 86 16W
Oppdal, *Norway* **9 E13** 62 35N 9 41 E
Óppido Mamertina, *Italy* **31 D8** 38 16N 15 59 E
Opportunity, *U.S.A.* **114 C5** 47 39N 117 15W
Oprişor, *Romania* **42 F8** 44 17N 23 5 E
Oprtalj, *Croatia* **29 C10** 45 23N 13 50 E
Opua, *N.Z.* **91 F5** 35 19S 174 9 E
Opunake, *N.Z.* **91 H4** 39 26S 173 52 E
Opuwo, *Namibia* **88 B1** 18 3S 13 45 E
Opuzen, *Croatia* **29 E14** 43 1N 17 34 E
Ora, *Cyprus* **36 E12** 34 51N 33 12 E
Oracle, *U.S.A.* **115 K8** 32 37N 110 46W
Oradea, *Romania* **42 C6** 47 2N 21 58 E
Öræfajökull, *Iceland* **8 D5** 64 2N 16 39W
Orahovac, *Kosovo, Yug.* **40 D4** 42 24N 20 40 E
Orahovica, *Croatia* **42 E2** 45 35N 17 52 E
Orai, *India* **69 G8** 25 58N 79 30 E
Oraison, *France* **21 E9** 43 55N 5 55 E
Oral = Zhayyq →, *Kazakhstan* **50 E6** 47 0N 51 48 E
Oral, *Kazakhstan* **48 E10** 51 20N 51 20 E
Oran, *Algeria* **78 A5** 35 45N 0 39W
Orange, *Australia* **95 E4** 33 15S 149 7 E
Orange, *France* **21 D8** 44 8N 4 47 E
Orange, *Calif., U.S.A.* **117 M9** 33 47N 117 51W
Orange, *Mass., U.S.A.* **111 D12** 42 35N 72 19W
Orange, *Tex., U.S.A.* **113 K8** 30 6N 93 44W
Orange, *Va., U.S.A.* **108 F6** 38 15N 78 7W
Orange →, *S. Africa* **88 D2** 28 41S 16 28 E
Orange, C., *Brazil* **122 C5** 4 20N 51 30W
Orange Cove, *U.S.A.* **116 J7** 36 38N 119 19W
Orange Free State = Free State □, *S. Africa* **88 D4** 28 30S 27 0 E
Orange Grove, *U.S.A.* **113 M6** 27 58N 97 56W
Orange Walk, *Belize* **119 D7** 18 6N 88 33W
Orangeburg, *U.S.A.* **109 J5** 33 30N 80 52W
Orangeville, *Canada* **102 D3** 43 55N 80 5W
Orango, *Guinea-Biss.* **82 C1** 11 5N 16 0W
Orani, *Phil.* **61 D4** 14 49N 120 32 E
Oranienburg, *Germany* **24 C9** 52 45N 13 14 E
Oranje = Orange →, *S. Africa* **88 D2** 28 41S 16 28 E
Oranje Vrystaat = Free State □, *S. Africa* **88 D4** 28 30S 27 0 E
Oranjemund, *Namibia* **88 D2** 28 38S 16 29 E
Oranjerivier, *S. Africa* **88 D3** 29 40S 24 12 E
Orapa, *Botswana* **85 J5** 21 15S 25 30 E
Orarak, *Sudan* **81 F3** 6 15N 32 23 E
Oras, *Phil.* **61 E6** 12 9N 125 28 E
Orašje, *Bos.-H.* **42 E3** 45 1N 18 42 E
Orăştie, *Romania* **43 E8** 45 50N 23 10 E
Oraşul Stalin = Braşov, *Romania* **43 E10** 45 38N 25 35 E
Orava →, *Slovak Rep.* **27 B12** 49 9N 19 8 E
Orava, Vodna nádrž, *Slovak Rep.* **27 B12** 49 25N 19 35 E
Oraviţa, *Romania* **42 E6** 45 2N 21 43 E
Orb →, *France* **20 E7** 43 15N 3 18 E
Orba →, *Italy* **28 D5** 44 53N 8 37 E
Ørbæk, *Denmark* **11 J4** 55 17N 10 39 E
Orbe, *Switz.* **25 J2** 46 43N 6 32 E
Orbec, *France* **18 C7** 49 1N 0 23 E
Orbetello, *Italy* **29 F8** 42 27N 11 13 E
Órbigo →, *Spain* **34 C5** 42 5N 5 42W
Orbisonia, *U.S.A.* **110 F7** 40 15N 77 54W
Orbost, *Australia* **95 F4** 37 40S 148 29 E
Orbyhus, *Sweden* **10 D11** 60 15N 17 43 E
Orcas I., *U.S.A.* **116 B4** 48 42N 122 56W
Orce, *Spain* **33 H2** 37 44N 2 28W
Orce →, *Spain* **33 H2** 37 44N 2 28W
Orchard City, *U.S.A.* **115 G10** 38 50N 107 58W
Orchies, *France* **19 B10** 50 28N 3 14 E
Orchila, I., *Venezuela* **121 D6** 11 48N 66 10W
Órcia →, *Italy* **29 F8** 42 58N 11 21 E
Orco →, *Italy* **28 C4** 45 10N 7 52 E
Orcutt, *U.S.A.* **117 L6** 34 52N 120 27W
Ord, *U.S.A.* **112 E5** 41 36N 98 56W
Ord →, *Australia* **92 C4** 15 33S 128 15 E
Ord, Mt., *Australia* **92 C4** 17 20S 125 34 E
Ordenes = Ordes, *Spain* **34 B2** 43 5N 8 29W
Orderville, *U.S.A.* **115 H7** 37 17N 112 38W
Ordes, *Spain* **34 B2** 43 5N 8 29W
Ording = St-Peter-Ording, *Germany* **24 A4** 54 20N 8 36 E
Ordos = Mu Us Shamo, *China* **56 E5** 39 0N 109 0 E
Ordu, *Turkey* **72 B7** 40 55N 37 53 E
Ordubad, *Azerbaijan* **73 C12** 38 54N 46 1 E
Orduña, *Álava, Spain* **32 C2** 42 58N 2 58W
Orduña, *Granada, Spain* **35 H7** 37 20N 3 30W
Ordway, *U.S.A.* **112 F3** 38 13N 103 46W
Ordzhonikidze = Vladikavkaz, *Russia* **49 J7** 43 0N 44 35 E
Ordzhonikidze, *Ukraine* **47 J8** 47 39N 34 3 E
Ore, *Dem. Rep. of the Congo* **86 B2** 3 17N 29 30 E
Ore Mts. = Erzgebirge, *Germany* **24 E8** 50 27N 12 55 E
Orebić, *Croatia* **29 F14** 43 0N 17 11 E
Örebro, *Sweden* **10 E9** 59 20N 15 18 E
Örebro län □, *Sweden* **10 E8** 59 27N 15 0 E
Oregon, *U.S.A.* **112 D10** 42 1N 89 20W
Oregon □, *U.S.A.* **114 E3** 44 0N 121 0W
Oregon City, *U.S.A.* **116 E4** 45 21N 122 36W
Öregrund, *Sweden* **10 D12** 60 21N 18 30 E
Öregrundsgrepen, *Sweden* **10 D12** 60 25N 18 15 E
Orekhov = Orikhiv, *Ukraine* **47 J8** 47 30N 35 48 E
Orekhovo-Zuyevo, *Russia* **46 E10** 55 50N 38 55 E
Orel, *Russia* **47 F9** 52 57N 36 3 E
Orel →, *Ukraine* **47 H8** 48 40N 34 39 E
Orellana, *Spain* **35 F5** 39 1N 5 32W
Orellana, Canal de, *Spain* **35 F5** 39 2N 6 0W
Orellana, Embalse de, *Spain* **35 F5** 39 5N 5 10W
Orem, *U.S.A.* **114 F8** 40 19N 111 42W
Ören, *Turkey* **39 D9** 37 3N 27 57 E
Orenburg, *Russia* **50 D6** 51 45N 55 6 E
Örencik, *Turkey* **39 B11** 39 16N 29 33 E
Orense = Ourense, *Spain* **34 C3** 42 19N 7 55W
Orense □, *Spain* **34 C3** 42 15N 7 51W
Orepuki, *N.Z.* **91 M1** 46 19S 167 46 E
Orestiás, *Greece* **41 E10** 41 30N 26 33 E
Orestos Pereyra, *Mexico* **118 B3** 26 31N 105 40W
Øresund, *Europe* **11 J6** 55 45N 12 45 E
Orford Ness, *U.K.* **13 E9** 52 5N 1 35 E
Orgañà = Organyà, *Spain* **32 C6** 42 13N 1 20 E
Organos, Pta. de los, *Canary Is.* **37 F2** 28 12N 17 17W
Organyà, *Spain* **32 C6** 42 13N 1 20 E
Orgaz, *Spain* **35 F7** 39 39N 3 53W
Orgeyev = Orhei, *Moldova* **43 C13** 47 24N 28 50 E
Orhaneli, *Turkey* **41 G12** 39 54N 28 59 E
Orhaneli →, *Turkey* **41 G12** 39 50N 28 55 E
Orhangazi, *Turkey* **41 F13** 40 29N 29 18 E
Orhei, *Moldova* **43 C13** 47 24N 28 50 E
Orhon Gol →, *Mongolia* **60 A5** 50 21N 106 0 E
Ória, *Italy* **31 B10** 40 30N 17 38 E
Oriental, Cordillera, *Colombia* **122 C3** 6 0N 73 0W
Orientale □, *Dem. Rep. of the Congo* **86 B2** 2 20N 26 0 E
Oriente, *Argentina* **126 D3** 38 44S 60 37W
Orihuela, *Spain* **33 G4** 38 7N 0 55W
Orihuela del Tremedal, *Spain* **32 E3** 40 33N 1 39W
Orikhiv, *Ukraine* **47 J8** 47 30N 35 48 E
Orikum, *Albania* **40 F3** 40 20N 19 26 E
Orillia, *Canada* **102 D4** 44 40N 79 24W

Orinoco →, Venezuela 122 C4 9 15N 61 30W
Orion, Canada 105 D6 49 27N 110 49W
Oriskany, U.S.A. 111 C9 43 10N 75 20W
Orissa □, India 67 K14 20 0N 84 0 E
Orissaare, Estonia 9 G20 58 34N 23 5 E
Oristano, Italy 30 C1 39 54N 8 36 E
Oristano, G. di, Italy 30 C1 39 50N 8 29 E
Orizaba, Mexico 119 D5 18 51N 97 6W
Orizare, Bulgaria 41 D11 42 44N 27 39 E
Orjen, Bos.-H. 40 D2 42 35N 18 34 E
Orjiva, Spain 35 J7 36 53N 3 24W
Orkanger, Norway 8 E13 63 18N 9 52 E
Örkelljunga, Sweden 11 H7 56 17N 13 17 E
Örken, Sweden 11 G9 57 6N 15 1 E
Örkény, Hungary 42 C4 47 9N 19 26 E
Orkla →, Norway 8 E13 63 18N 9 51 E
Orkney, S. Africa 88 D4 26 58 S 26 40 E
Orkney □, U.K. 14 B5 59 2N 3 13W
Orkney Is., U.K. 14 B6 59 0N 3 0W
Orland, U.S.A. 116 F4 39 45N 122 12W
Orlando, U.S.A. 109 L5 28 33N 81 23W
Orlando, C. d', Italy 31 D7 38 10N 14 43 E
Orléanais, France 19 E9 48 0N 2 0 E
Orléans, France 19 E8 47 54N 1 52 E
Orleans, U.S.A. 111 B12 44 49N 72 12W
Orléans, I. d', Canada 103 C5 46 54N 70 58W
Orlice →, Czech Rep. 26 A8 50 13N 15 50 E
Orlov, Slovak Rep. 27 B13 49 17N 20 51 E
Orlov Gay, Russia 48 E9 50 56N 48 19 E
Orlová, Czech Rep. 27 B11 49 51N 18 26 E
Orlovat, Serbia, Yug. 42 E5 45 14N 20 33 E
Ormara, Pakistan 66 G4 25 16N 64 33 E
Ormea, Italy 28 D4 44 9N 7 54 E
Ormília, Greece 40 F7 40 16N 23 39 E
Ormoc, Phil. 61 F6 11 0N 124 37 E
Ormond, N.Z. 91 H6 38 33 S 177 56 E
Ormond Beach, U.S.A. 109 L5 29 17N 81 3W
Ormož, Slovenia 29 B13 46 25N 16 10 E
Ormskirk, U.K. 12 D5 53 35N 2 54W
Ormstown, Canada 111 A11 45 8N 74 0W
Ornans, France 19 E13 47 7N 6 10 E
Orne □, France 18 D7 48 40N 0 5 E
Orne →, France 18 C6 49 18N 0 15W
Orneta, Poland 44 D7 54 8N 20 9 E
Ornö, Sweden 10 E12 59 4N 18 24 E
Örnsköldsvik, Sweden 10 A12 63 17N 18 40 E
Oro, N. Korea 57 D14 40 1N 127 27 E
Oro →, Mexico 118 B3 25 35N 105 2W
Oro Grande, U.S.A. 117 L9 34 36N 117 20W
Oro Valley, U.S.A. 115 K8 32 26N 110 58W
Orobie, Alpi, Italy 28 B6 46 7N 10 0 E
Orocué, Colombia 124 C4 4 48N 71 20W
Orodara, Burkina Faso 82 C4 11 0N 4 55W
Orodo, Nigeria 83 D6 5 34N 7 4 E
Orofino, U.S.A. 114 C5 46 29N 116 15W
Orol Dengizi = Aral Sea, Asia 50 E7 44 30N 60 0 E
Oromocto, Canada 103 C6 45 54N 66 29W
Oron, Nigeria 83 E6 4 48N 8 14 E
Orono, Canada 110 C6 43 59N 78 37W
Orono, U.S.A. 109 C11 44 53N 68 40W
Oronsay, U.K. 14 E2 56 1N 6 15W
Oropesa, Spain 34 F5 39 57N 5 10W
Oroquieta, Phil. 61 G5 8 32N 123 44 E
Orosei, Italy 30 B2 40 23N 9 42 E
Orosei, G. di, Italy 30 B2 40 15N 9 44 E
Orosháza, Hungary 42 D5 46 32N 20 42 E
Oroszlány, Hungary 42 C3 47 29N 18 19 E
Orotukan, Russia 51 C16 62 16N 151 42 E
Oroville, Calif., U.S.A. 116 F5 39 31N 121 33W
Oroville, Wash., U.S.A. 114 B4 48 56N 119 26W
Oroville, L., U.S.A. 116 F5 39 33N 121 29W
Orrefors, Sweden 11 H9 56 50N 15 45 E
Orroroo, Australia 95 E2 32 43 S 138 38 E
Orrviken, Sweden 10 A8 63 6N 14 26 E
Orrville, U.S.A. 110 F3 40 50N 81 46W
Orsa, Sweden 10 C8 61 7N 14 37 E
Orsara di Púglia, Italy 31 A8 41 17N 15 16 E
Orsasjön, Sweden 10 C8 61 7N 14 37 E
Orsha, Belarus 46 E6 54 30N 30 25 E
Örsjö, Sweden 11 H9 56 42N 15 45 E
Orsk, Russia 50 D6 51 12N 58 34 E
Orşova, Romania 42 F7 44 41N 22 25 E
Ørsted, Denmark 11 H4 56 30N 10 20 E
Örsundsbro, Sweden 10 E11 59 44N 17 18 E
Orta, L. d', Italy 28 C5 45 49N 8 24 E
Orta Nova, Italy 31 A8 41 19N 15 42 E
Ortaca, Turkey 39 E10 36 49N 28 45 E
Ortakent, Turkey 39 D9 37 5N 27 21 E
Ortaklar, Turkey 39 D9 37 53N 27 30 E
Ortaköy, Çorum, Turkey 72 B6 40 16N 35 15 E
Ortaköy, Niğde, Turkey 72 C6 38 44N 34 3 E
Orte, Italy 29 F9 42 27N 12 23 E
Ortegal, C., Spain 34 B3 43 43N 7 52W
Orthez, France 20 E3 43 29N 0 48W
Ortigueira, Spain 34 B3 43 40N 7 50W
Orting, U.S.A. 116 C4 47 6N 122 12W
Ortisei, Italy 29 B8 46 34N 11 40 E
Ortles, Italy 28 B7 46 31N 10 33 E
Ortón →, Bolivia 124 F5 10 50 S 67 0W
Ortona, Italy 29 F11 42 21N 14 24 E
Ortonville, U.S.A. 112 C6 45 19N 96 27W
Orūmīyeh, Iran 70 B5 37 40N 45 0 E
Orūmīyeh, Daryācheh-ye, Iran 70 B5 37 50N 45 30 E
Orune, Italy 30 B2 40 24N 9 22 E
Oruro, Bolivia 124 G5 18 0 S 67 9W
Orust, Sweden 11 F5 58 10N 11 40 E
Oruzgān □, Afghan. 66 C5 33 30N 66 0 E
Orvault, France 18 E5 47 17N 1 38W
Orvieto, Italy 29 F9 42 43N 12 7 E
Orwell, N.Y., U.S.A. 111 C9 43 35N 75 50W
Orwell, Ohio, U.S.A. 110 E4 41 32N 80 52W
Orwell →, U.K. 13 F9 51 59N 1 18 E
Orwigsburg, U.S.A. 111 F8 40 38N 76 6W
Oryakhovo, Bulgaria 40 C7 43 40N 23 57 E
Orzinuovi, Italy 28 C6 45 24N 9 55 E
Orzyc →, Poland 45 F8 52 46N 21 14 E
Orzysz, Poland 44 E8 53 50N 21 58 E
Osa →, Poland 44 E5 53 33N 18 46 E
Osa, Pen. de, Costa Rica 120 E3 8 0N 84 0W
Osage, U.S.A. 112 D8 43 17N 92 49W
Osage →, U.S.A. 112 F9 38 35N 91 57W
Osage City, U.S.A. 112 F7 38 38N 95 50W
Ōsaka, Japan 55 G7 34 40N 135 30 E
Osan, S. Korea 57 F14 37 11N 127 4 E
Osawatomie, U.S.A. 112 F7 38 31N 94 57W
Osborne, U.S.A. 112 F5 39 26N 98 42W
Osby, Sweden 11 H7 56 23N 13 59 E
Osceola, Ark., U.S.A. 113 H10 35 42N 89 58W
Osceola, Iowa, U.S.A. 112 E8 41 2N 93 46W
Oschatz, Germany 24 D9 51 17N 13 6 E
Oschersleben, Germany 24 C7 52 2N 11 14 E
Ōschiri, Italy 30 B2 40 43N 9 6 E
Oscoda, U.S.A. 110 B1 44 26N 83 20W
Osečina, Serbia, Yug. 40 B3 44 23N 19 34 E
Ösel = Saaremaa, Estonia 9 G20 58 30N 22 30 E
Osery, Russia 46 E10 54 52N 38 28 E
Osgoode, Canada 111 A9 45 8N 75 36W
Osh, Kyrgyzstan 50 E8 40 37N 72 49 E
Oshakati, Namibia 85 H3 17 45 S 15 40 E
Oshawa, Canada 102 D4 43 50N 78 50W
Oshigambo, Namibia 88 B2 17 45 S 16 5 E
Oshkosh, Nebr., U.S.A. 112 E3 41 24N 102 21W
Oshkosh, Wis., U.S.A. 112 C10 44 1N 88 33W
Oshmyany = Ashmyany, Belarus 9 J21 54 26N 25 52 E
Oshnovīyeh, Iran 70 B5 37 2N 45 6 E
Oshogbo, Nigeria 83 D5 7 48N 4 37 E
Oshtorīnān, Iran 71 C6 34 1N 48 38 E
Oshwe, Dem. Rep. of the Congo 84 E3 3 25 S 19 28 E
Osi, Nigeria 83 D6 8 8N 5 14 E
Osieczna, Poland 45 G3 51 55N 16 40 E
Osijek, Croatia 42 E3 45 34N 18 41 E
Ósilo, Italy 30 B1 40 45N 8 40 E
Ósimo, Italy 29 E10 43 28N 13 30 E
Osintorf, Belarus 46 E6 54 40N 30 39 E
Osipenko = Berdyansk, Ukraine 47 J9 46 45N 36 50 E
Osipovichi = Asipovichy, Belarus 46 F5 53 19N 28 33 E
Osiyan, India 68 F5 26 43N 72 55 E
Osizweni, S. Africa 89 D5 27 49 S 30 7 E
Oskaloosa, U.S.A. 112 E8 41 18N 92 39W
Oskarshamn, Sweden 11 G10 57 15N 16 27 E
Oskarström, Sweden 11 H6 56 48N 12 58 E
Oskélanéo, Canada 102 C4 48 5N 75 15W
Öskemen, Kazakhstan 50 E9 50 0N 82 36 E
Oskol →, Ukraine 47 H9 49 6N 37 25 E
Oslo, Norway 9 G14 59 55N 10 45 E
Oslob, Phil. 61 G5 9 31N 123 26 E
Oslofjorden, Norway 9 G14 59 20N 10 35 E
Osmanabad, India 66 K10 18 5N 76 10 E
Osmancık, Turkey 72 B6 40 58N 34 47 E
Osmaniye, Turkey 70 B3 37 5N 36 10 E
Osmanlı, Turkey 41 E10 41 35N 26 51 E
Ösmo, Sweden 10 F11 58 58N 17 55 E
Osnabrück, Germany 24 C4 52 17N 8 3 E
Ośno Lubuskie, Poland 45 F1 52 28N 14 51 E
Osoblaha, Czech Rep. 27 A10 50 17N 17 44 E
Osogovska Planina, Macedonia 40 D6 42 10N 22 30 E
Osor, Italy 29 D11 44 42N 14 24 E
Osorio, Brazil 127 B5 29 53 S 50 17W
Osorno, Chile 128 E2 40 25 S 73 0W
Osorno, Spain 34 C6 42 24N 4 22W
Osoyoos, Canada 104 D5 49 0N 119 30W
Osøyro, Norway 9 F11 60 9N 5 30 E
Ospika →, Canada 104 B4 56 20N 124 0W
Osprey Reef, Australia 94 A4 13 52 S 146 36 E
Oss, Neths. 17 C5 51 46N 5 32 E
Ossa, Mt., Australia 94 G4 41 52 S 146 3 E
Óssa, Óros, Greece 38 B4 39 47N 22 42 E
Ossa de Montiel, Spain 33 G2 38 58N 2 45W
Ossabaw I., U.S.A. 109 K5 31 50N 81 5W
Osse →, France 20 D4 44 7N 0 17 E
Osse →, Nigeria 83 D6 6 10N 5 20 E
Ossi, Italy 30 B1 40 40N 8 35 E
Ossining, U.S.A. 111 E11 41 10N 73 55W
Ossipee, U.S.A. 111 C13 43 41N 71 7W
Ossokmanuan L., Canada 103 B7 53 25N 65 0W
Ossora, Russia 51 D17 59 20N 163 13 E
Ostashkov, Russia 46 D7 57 4N 33 2 E
Östavall, Sweden 10 B9 62 26N 15 29 E
Oste →, Germany 24 B5 53 49N 9 2 E
Ostend = Oostende, Belgium 17 C2 51 15N 2 54 E
Oster, Ukraine 47 G6 50 57N 30 53 E
Osterburg, Germany 24 C7 52 47N 11 45 E
Osterburg, U.S.A. 110 F6 40 16N 78 31W
Osterburken, Germany 25 F5 49 25N 9 26 E
Österbybruk, Sweden 10 D11 60 13N 17 55 E
Österbymo, Sweden 11 G9 57 49N 15 15 E
Österdalälven, Sweden 10 C7 61 30N 13 45 E
Østerdalen, Norway 9 F14 61 40N 10 50 E
Österfärnebo, Sweden 10 D10 60 19N 16 48 E
Österforse, Sweden 10 A11 63 9N 17 3 E
Östergötlands län □, Sweden 11 F9 58 35N 15 45 E
Osterholz-Scharmbeck, Germany 24 B4 53 13N 8 47 E
Østerild, Denmark 11 G2 57 2N 8 51 E
Osterode, Germany 24 D6 51 43N 10 15 E
Östersund, Sweden 10 A8 63 10N 14 38 E
Östervåla, Sweden 10 D11 60 11N 17 11 E
Ostfriesische Inseln, Germany 24 B3 53 42N 7 0 E
Ostfriesland, Germany 24 B3 53 20N 7 30 E
Östhammar, Sweden 10 D12 60 16N 18 22 E
Óstia, Lido di, Italy 29 G9 41 43N 12 17 E
Ostíglia, Italy 29 C8 45 4N 11 8 E
Östmark, Sweden 10 D6 60 17N 12 45 E
Östra Husby, Sweden 11 F10 58 35N 16 33 E
Ostrava, Czech Rep. 27 B11 49 51N 18 18 E
Ostravský □, Czech Rep. 27 B10 49 55N 17 58 E
Ostróda, Poland 44 E6 53 42N 19 58 E
Ostrogozhsk, Russia 47 G10 50 55N 39 7 E
Ostroh, Ukraine 47 G4 50 20N 26 30 E
Ostrołęka, Poland 45 E8 53 4N 21 32 E
Ostrov, Bulgaria 41 C8 43 40N 24 9 E
Ostrov, Czech Rep. 26 A5 50 18N 12 57 E
Ostrov, Romania 43 F12 44 6N 27 24 E
Ostrov, Russia 46 D5 57 25N 28 20 E
Ostrów Lubelski, Poland 45 G9 51 29N 22 51 E
Ostrów Mazowiecka, Poland 45 F8 52 50N 21 51 E
Ostrów Wielkopolski, Poland 45 G4 51 36N 17 44 E
Ostrowiec-Świętokrzyski, Poland 45 H8 50 55N 21 22 E
Ostrožac, Bos.-H. 42 G2 43 43N 17 49 E
Ostrzeszów, Poland 45 G4 51 25N 17 52 E
Ostseebad Kühlungsborn, Germany 24 A7 54 8N 11 44 E
Osttirol □, Austria 26 E5 46 50N 12 30 E
Ostuni, Italy 31 B10 40 44N 17 35 E
Osum →, Albania 40 F4 40 40N 20 10 E
Osüm →, Bulgaria 41 C8 43 40N 24 50 E
Ōsumi-Kaikyō, Japan 55 J5 30 55N 131 0 E
Ōsumi-Shotō, Japan 55 J5 30 30N 130 0 E
Osun □, Nigeria 83 D5 7 30N 4 30 E
Osuna, Spain 35 H5 37 14N 5 8W
Oswegatchie →, U.S.A. 111 B9 44 42N 75 30W
Oswego, U.S.A. 111 C8 43 27N 76 31W
Oswego →, U.S.A. 111 C8 43 27N 76 30W
Oswestry, U.K. 12 E4 52 52N 3 3W
Oświęcim, Poland 45 H6 50 2N 19 11 E
Otaci, Moldova 43 B12 48 27N 27 47 E
Otago □, N.Z. 91 L2 45 15 S 170 0 E
Otago Harbour, N.Z. 91 L3 45 47 S 170 42 E
Ōtake, Japan 55 G6 34 12N 132 13 E
Otaki, N.Z. 91 J5 40 45 S 175 10 E
Otaru, Japan 54 C10 43 10N 141 0 E
Otaru-Wan = Ishikari-Wan, Japan 54 C10 43 25N 141 1 E
Otava →, Czech Rep. 26 B7 49 26N 14 12 E
Otavalo, Ecuador 124 C3 0 13N 78 20W
Otavi, Namibia 88 B2 19 40 S 17 24 E
Otchinjau, Angola 88 B1 16 30 S 13 56 E
Otelec, Romania 42 E5 45 36N 20 50 E
Otelnuk L., Canada 103 A6 56 9N 68 12W
Oţelu Roşu, Romania 42 E7 45 32N 22 22 E
Otero de Rey = Outeiro de Rei, Spain 34 B3 43 6N 7 36W
Othello, U.S.A. 114 C4 46 50N 119 10W
Othonoí, Greece 38 B1 39 52N 19 22 E
Óthris, Óros, Greece 38 B4 39 2N 22 37 E
Otjiwarongo, Namibia 88 C2 20 30 S 16 33 E
Otmuchów, Poland 45 H4 50 28N 17 10 E
Otočac, Croatia 29 D12 44 53N 15 12 E
Otoineppu, Japan 54 B11 44 44N 142 16 E
Otok, Croatia 29 E13 43 42N 16 44 E
Otorohanga, N.Z. 91 H5 38 12 S 175 14 E
Otoskwin →, Canada 102 B2 52 13N 88 6W
Otra →, Norway 9 G13 58 9N 8 1 E
Otradnyy, Russia 48 D10 53 22N 51 21 E
Otranto, Italy 31 B11 40 9N 18 28 E
Otranto, C. d', Italy 31 B11 40 7N 18 30 E
Otranto, Str. of, Italy 31 B11 40 15N 18 40 E
Otrokovice, Czech Rep. 27 B10 49 12N 17 32 E
Otse, S. Africa 88 D4 25 2 S 25 45 E
Ōtsu, Japan 55 G7 35 0N 135 50 E
Ōtsuki, Japan 55 G9 35 36N 138 57 E
Ottawa = Outaouais →, Canada 102 C5 45 27N 74 8W
Ottawa, Canada 102 C4 45 27N 75 42W
Ottawa, Ill., U.S.A. 112 E10 41 21N 88 51W
Ottawa, Kans., U.S.A. 112 F7 38 37N 95 16W
Ottawa Is., Canada 101 C11 59 35N 80 10W
Ottélé, Cameroon 83 E7 3 38N 11 19 E
Ottensheim, Austria 26 C7 48 21N 14 12 E
Otter Cr. →, U.S.A. 111 B11 44 13N 73 17W
Otter L., Canada 105 B8 55 35N 104 39W
Otterndorf, Germany 24 B4 53 48N 8 53 E
Otterup, Denmark 11 J4 55 30N 10 22 E
Otterville, Canada 110 D4 42 55N 80 36W
Ottery St. Mary, U.K. 13 G4 50 44N 3 17W
Otto Beit Bridge, Zimbabwe 87 F2 15 59 S 28 56 E
Ottosdal, S. Africa 88 D4 26 46 S 25 59 E
Ottumwa, U.S.A. 112 E8 41 1N 92 25W
Otu, Nigeria 83 D5 8 14N 3 22 E
Otukpa, Nigeria 83 D6 7 9N 7 41 E
Oturkpo, Nigeria 83 D6 7 16N 8 8 E
Otway, B., Chile 128 G2 53 30 S 74 0W
Otway, C., Australia 95 F3 38 52 S 143 30 E
Otwock, Poland 45 F8 52 5N 21 20 E
Ötztaler Ache →, Austria 26 D3 47 14N 10 50 E
Ötztaler Alpen, Austria 26 E3 46 56N 11 0 E
Ou →, Laos 64 B4 20 4N 102 13 E
Ou Neua, Laos 58 F3 22 18N 101 48 E
Ou-Sammyaku, Japan 54 E10 39 20N 140 35 E
Ouachita →, U.S.A. 113 K9 31 38N 91 49W
Ouachita, L., U.S.A. 113 H8 34 34N 93 12W
Ouachita Mts., U.S.A. 113 H7 34 40N 94 25W
Ouagadougou, Burkina Faso 83 C4 12 25N 1 30W
Ouahigouya, Burkina Faso 82 C4 13 31N 2 25W
Ouahran = Oran, Algeria 78 A5 35 45N 0 39W
Oualâta, Mauritania 82 B3 17 20N 6 55W
Ouallam, Niger 83 C5 14 23N 2 10 E
Ouallene, Algeria 78 D6 24 41N 1 11 E
Ouargaye, Burkina Faso 83 C5 11 40N 0 5 E
Ouargla, Algeria 78 B7 31 59N 5 16 E
Ouarkoye, Burkina Faso 82 C4 12 5N 3 40W
Ouarzazate, Morocco 78 B4 30 55N 6 50W
Ouassouas, Mali 83 B5 16 10N 1 23 E
Ouatagouna, Mali 83 B5 15 11N 0 43 E
Oubangi →, Dem. Rep. of the Congo 84 E3 0 30 S 17 50 E
Ouche →, France 19 E12 47 6N 5 16 E
Ouddorp, Neths. 17 C3 51 50N 3 57 E
Oude Rijn →, Neths. 17 B4 52 12N 4 24 E
Oudeïka, Mali 83 B4 17 30N 1 40W
Oudenaarde, Belgium 17 D3 50 50N 3 37 E
Oudon →, France 18 E6 47 41N 0 53W
Oudtshoorn, S. Africa 88 E3 33 35 S 22 14 E
Ouellé, Ivory C. 82 D4 7 26N 4 1W
Ouémé →, Benin 83 D5 6 30N 2 30 E
Ouessa, Burkina Faso 82 C4 11 4N 2 47W
Ouessant, Î. d', France 18 D1 48 28N 5 6W
Ouesso, Congo 84 D3 1 37N 16 5 E
Ouest, Pte. de l', Canada 103 C7 49 52N 64 40W
Ouezzane, Morocco 78 B4 34 51N 5 35W
Ougarou, Burkina Faso 83 C5 12 10N 0 58 E
Oughterard, Ireland 15 C2 53 26N 9 18W
Ouidah, Benin 83 D5 6 25N 2 0 E
Ouidi, Niger 83 C7 14 10N 13 0 E
Ouistreham, France 18 C6 49 17N 0 18W
Oujda, Morocco 78 B5 34 41N 1 55W
Oujeft, Mauritania 82 A2 20 2N 13 0W
Oulainen, Finland 8 D21 64 17N 24 47 E
Ould Yenjé, Mauritania 82 B2 15 38N 12 16W
Oullins, France 21 C8 45 43N 4 49 E
Oulu, Finland 8 D21 65 1N 25 29 E
Oulujärvi, Finland 8 D22 64 25N 27 15 E
Oulujoki →, Finland 8 D21 65 1N 25 30 E
Oulx, Italy 28 C3 45 2N 6 50 E
Oum Chalouba, Chad 79 E10 15 48N 20 46 E
Oum Hadjer, Chad 79 F9 13 18N 19 41 E
Oumé, Ivory C. 82 D3 6 21N 5 27W
Ounasjoki →, Finland 8 C21 66 31N 25 40 E
Ounguati, Namibia 88 C2 22 0 S 15 46 E
Ounianga Sérir, Chad 79 E10 18 54N 20 51 E
Our →, Lux. 17 E6 49 55N 6 5 E
Ouranópolis, Greece 40 F7 40 20N 23 59 E
Ourârene, Niger 83 B6 19 30N 7 10 E
Ouray, U.S.A. 115 G10 38 1N 107 40W
Ourcq →, France 19 C10 49 1N 3 1 E
Ourense, Spain 34 C3 42 19N 7 55W
Ouricuri, Brazil 125 E10 7 53 S 40 5W
Ourinhos, Brazil 127 A6 23 0 S 49 54W
Ourique, Portugal 35 H2 37 38N 8 16W
Ouro Fino, Brazil 127 A6 22 16 S 46 25W
Ouro-Ndia, Mali 82 B4 15 8N 4 35W
Ouro Prêto, Brazil 127 A7 20 20 S 43 30W
Ouro Sogui, Senegal 82 B2 15 36N 13 19W
Oursi, Burkina Faso 83 C4 14 41N 0 27W
Ourthe →, Belgium 17 D5 50 29N 5 35 E
Ouse →, E. Susx., U.K. 13 G8 50 47N 0 4 E
Ouse →, N. Yorks., U.K. 12 D7 53 44N 0 55W
Oust, France 20 F5 42 52N 1 13 E
Oust →, France 18 E4 47 35N 2 6W
Outaouais →, Canada 102 C5 45 27N 74 8W
Outardes →, Canada 103 C6 49 24N 69 30W
Outeiro de Rei, Spain 34 B3 43 6N 7 36W
Outer Hebrides, U.K. 14 D1 57 30N 7 40W
Outes = Serra de Outes, Spain 34 C2 42 52N 8 55W
Outjo, Namibia 88 C2 20 5 S 16 7 E
Outlook, Canada 105 C7 51 30N 107 0W
Outokumpu, Finland 8 E23 62 43N 29 1 E
Outreau, France 19 B8 50 40N 1 36 E
Ouvèze →, France 21 E8 43 59N 4 51 E
Ouyen, Australia 95 F3 35 1 S 142 22 E
Ouzouer-le-Marché, France 19 E8 47 54N 1 32 E
Ovada, Italy 28 D5 44 38N 8 38 E
Ovalau, Fiji 91 C8 17 40 S 178 48 E
Ovalle, Chile 126 C1 30 33 S 71 18W
Ovamboland, Namibia 88 B2 18 30 S 16 0 E
Ovar, Portugal 34 E2 40 51N 8 40W
Overath, Germany 24 E3 50 56N 7 17 E
Overflakkee, Neths. 17 C4 51 44N 4 10 E
Overijssel □, Neths. 17 B6 52 25N 6 35 E
Overland Park, U.S.A. 112 F7 38 55N 94 50W
Overton, U.S.A. 117 J12 36 33N 114 27W
Övertorneå, Sweden 8 C20 66 23N 23 38 E
Överum, Sweden 11 F10 58 0N 16 20 E
Ovid, U.S.A. 111 D8 42 41N 76 49W
Ovidiopol, Ukraine 47 J6 46 15N 30 30 E
Ovidiu, Romania 43 F13 44 16N 28 34 E
Oviedo, Spain 34 B5 43 25N 5 50W
Oviksfjällen, Sweden 10 A7 63 0N 13 49 E
Oviši, Latvia 9 H19 57 33N 21 44 E
Ovoot, Mongolia 56 B7 45 21N 113 45 E
Övör Hangay □, Mongolia 56 B2 45 0N 102 30 E
Ovoro, Nigeria 83 D6 5 26N 7 16 E
Øvre Årdal, Norway 9 F12 61 19N 7 48 E
Övre Fryken, Sweden 10 E7 60 0N 13 7 E
Ovruch, Ukraine 47 G5 51 25N 28 45 E
Owaka, N.Z. 91 M2 46 27 S 169 40 E
Owambo = Ovamboland, Namibia 88 B2 18 30 S 16 0 E
Owasco L., U.S.A. 111 D8 42 50N 76 31W
Owase, Japan 55 G8 34 7N 136 12 E
Owatonna, U.S.A. 112 C8 44 5N 93 14W
Owbeh, Afghan. 66 B3 34 28N 63 10 E
Owego, U.S.A. 111 D8 42 6N 76 16W
Owen Falls Dam, Uganda 86 B3 0 30N 33 5 E
Owen Sound, Canada 102 D3 44 35N 80 55W
Owens →, U.S.A. 116 J9 36 32N 117 59W
Owens L., U.S.A. 117 J9 36 26N 117 57W
Owensboro, U.S.A. 108 G2 37 46N 87 7W
Owerri, Nigeria 83 D6 5 29N 7 0 E
Owl →, Canada 105 B10 57 51N 92 44W
Owo, Nigeria 83 D6 7 10N 5 39 E
Owosso, U.S.A. 108 D3 43 0N 84 10W
Owyhee, U.S.A. 114 F5 41 57N 116 6W
Owyhee →, U.S.A. 114 E5 43 49N 117 2W
Owyhee, L., U.S.A. 114 E5 43 38N 117 14W
Ox Mts. = Slieve Gamph, Ireland 15 B3 54 6N 9 0W
Öxarfjörður, Iceland 8 C5 66 15N 16 45W
Oxbow, Canada 105 D8 49 14N 102 10W
Oxelösund, Sweden 11 F11 58 43N 17 5 E
Oxford, N.Z. 91 K4 43 18 S 172 11 E
Oxford, U.K. 13 F6 51 46N 1 15W
Oxford, Mass., U.S.A. 111 D13 42 7N 71 52W
Oxford, Miss., U.S.A. 113 H10 34 22N 89 31W
Oxford, N.C., U.S.A. 109 G6 36 19N 78 35W
Oxford, N.Y., U.S.A. 111 D9 42 27N 75 36W
Oxford, Ohio, U.S.A. 108 F3 39 31N 84 45W
Oxford L., Canada 105 C9 54 51N 95 37W
Oxfordshire □, U.K. 13 F6 51 48N 1 16W
Oxía, Greece 38 C3 38 16N 21 5 E
Oxie, Sweden 11 J7 55 33N 13 6 E
Oxílithos, Greece 38 C6 38 35N 24 7 E
Oxnard, U.S.A. 117 L7 34 12N 119 11W
Oxsjövålen, Sweden 10 B7 62 34N 13 57 E
Oxus = Amudarya →, Uzbekistan 50 E6 43 58N 59 34 E
Oya, Malaysia 62 D4 2 55N 111 55 E
Oyama, Japan 55 F9 36 18N 139 48 E
Oyem, Gabon 84 D2 1 34N 11 31 E
Oyen, Canada 105 C6 51 22N 110 28W
Oykel →, U.K. 14 D4 57 56N 4 26W
Oymyakon, Russia 51 C15 63 25N 142 44 E
Oyo, Nigeria 83 D5 7 46N 3 56 E
Oyo □, Nigeria 83 D5 8 15N 3 30 E
Oyonnax, France 19 F12 46 16N 5 40 E
Oyster Bay, U.S.A. 111 F11 40 52N 73 32W
Ōyūbari, Japan 54 C11 43 1N 142 5 E
Özalp, Turkey 73 C10 38 39N 43 59 E
Ozamiz, Phil. 61 G5 8 15N 123 50 E
Ozark, Ala., U.S.A. 109 K3 31 28N 85 39W
Ozark, Ark., U.S.A. 113 H8 35 29N 93 50W
Ozark, Mo., U.S.A. 113 G8 37 1N 93 12W
Ozark Plateau, U.S.A. 113 G9 37 20N 91 40W
Ozarks, L. of the, U.S.A. 112 F8 38 12N 92 38W
Ożarów, Poland 45 H8 50 53N 21 40 E
Ózd, Hungary 42 B5 48 14N 20 15 E
Ozernoye, Russia 48 E10 51 46N 51 28 E
Ozette L., U.S.A. 116 B2 48 6N 124 38W
Ozieri, Italy 30 B2 40 35N 9 0 E
Ozimek, Poland 45 H5 50 41N 18 11 E
Ozinki, Russia 48 E9 51 12N 49 44 E
Ozona, U.S.A. 113 K4 30 43N 101 12W
Ozorków, Poland 45 G6 51 57N 19 16 E
Ozren, Bos.-H. 42 G3 43 55N 18 29 E
Ozuluama, Mexico 119 C5 21 40N 97 50W
Ozun, Romania 43 E10 45 47N 25 50 E
Ozurgeti, Georgia 49 K5 41 55N 42 2 E

P

Pa, Burkina Faso 82 C4 11 33N 3 19W
Pa-an, Burma 67 L20 16 51N 97 40 E
Pa Mong Dam, Thailand 64 D4 18 0N 102 22 E
Pa Sak →, Thailand 62 B2 15 30N 101 0 E
Paamiut, Greenland 4 C5 62 0N 49 43W
Paar →, Germany 25 G7 48 46N 11 36 E
Paarl, S. Africa 88 E2 33 45 S 18 56 E
Pab Hills, Pakistan 68 F2 26 30N 66 45 E
Pabbay, U.K. 14 D1 57 46N 7 14W
Pabianice, Poland 45 G6 51 40N 19 20 E
Pabna, Bangla. 67 G16 24 1N 89 18 E
Pabo, Uganda 86 B3 3 1N 32 10 E
Pacaja →, Brazil 125 D8 1 56 S 50 50W
Pacaraima, Sa., S. Amer. 122 C4 4 0N 62 30W
Pacasmayo, Peru 124 E3 7 20 S 79 35W
Paceco, Italy 30 E5 37 59N 12 33 E
Pachhar, India 68 G7 24 40N 77 42 E
Pachino, Italy 31 F8 36 43N 15 5 E
Pachitea →, Peru 124 E4 8 46 S 74 33W
Pachmarhi, India 69 H8 22 28N 78 26 E
Pachpadra, India 66 G8 25 58N 72 10 E
Pachuca, Mexico 119 C5 20 10N 98 40W
Pacific, Canada 104 C3 54 48N 128 28W
Pacific-Antarctic Ridge, Pac. Oc. 97 M16 43 0 S 115 0W
Pacific Grove, U.S.A. 116 J5 36 38N 121 56W
Pacific Ocean, Pac. Oc. 97 G14 10 0N 140 0W
Pacific Rim Nat. Park, Canada 116 B2 48 40N 124 45W
Pacifica, U.S.A. 116 H4 37 36N 122 30W
Pacitan, Indonesia 63 H14 8 12 S 111 7 E
Packwood, U.S.A. 116 D5 46 36N 121 40W
Pacov, Czech Rep. 26 B8 49 27N 15 0 E
Pacy-sur-Eure, France 18 C8 49 1N 1 23 E
Padaido, Kepulauan, Indonesia 63 E9 1 15 S 136 30 E
Padang, Indonesia 62 E2 1 0 S 100 20 E
Padang Endau, Malaysia 65 L4 2 40N 103 38 E
Padangpanjang, Indonesia 62 E2 0 40 S 100 20 E
Padangsidempuan, Indonesia 62 D1 1 30N 99 15 E
Padborg, Denmark 11 K3 54 49N 9 21 E
Paddle Prairie, Canada 104 B5 57 57N 117 29W
Paddockwood, Canada 105 C7 53 30N 105 30W
Paderborn, Germany 24 D4 51 42N 8 45 E
Padeş, Vf., Romania 42 E7 45 40N 22 22 E
Padina, Romania 43 F12 44 50N 27 8 E
Padma, India 69 G11 24 12N 85 22 E
Pádova, Italy 29 C8 45 25N 11 53 E
Padra, India 68 H5 22 15N 73 7 E
Padrauna, India 69 F10 26 54N 83 59 E
Padre I., U.S.A. 113 M6 27 10N 97 25W
Padrón, Spain 34 C2 42 41N 8 39W
Padstow, U.K. 13 G3 50 33N 4 58W
Padua = Pádova, Italy 29 C8 45 25N 11 53 E
Paducah, Ky., U.S.A. 108 G1 37 5N 88 37W
Paducah, Tex., U.S.A. 113 H4 34 1N 100 18W
Padul, Spain 35 H7 37 1N 3 38W
Paengnyŏng-do, S. Korea 57 F13 37 57N 124 40 E
Paeroa, N.Z. 91 G5 37 23 S 175 41 E
Paesana, Italy 28 D4 44 41N 7 16 E
Pafúri, Mozam. 89 C5 22 28 S 31 17 E
Pag, Croatia 29 D12 44 25N 15 3 E
Paga, Ghana 83 C4 11 1N 1 8W
Pagadian, Phil. 61 H5 7 55N 123 30 E
Pagai Selatan, Pulau, Indonesia 62 E2 3 0 S 100 15 E
Pagai Utara, Pulau, Indonesia 62 E2 2 35 S 100 0 E
Pagalu = Annobón, Atl. Oc. 77 G4 1 25 S 5 36 E
Pagara, India 69 G9 24 22N 80 1 E
Pagastikós Kólpos, Greece 38 B5 39 15N 23 0 E
Pagatan, Indonesia 62 E5 3 33 S 115 59 E
Page, U.S.A. 115 H8 36 57N 111 27W
Pagėgiai, Lithuania 44 C8 55 9N 21 54 E
Pago Pago, Amer. Samoa 91 B13 14 16 S 170 43W
Pagosa Springs, U.S.A. 115 H10 37 16N 107 1W
Pagwa River, Canada 102 B2 50 2N 85 14W
Pahala, U.S.A. 106 J17 19 12N 155 29W
Pahang →, Malaysia 65 L4 3 30N 103 9 E
Pahiatua, N.Z. 91 J5 40 27 S 175 50 E
Pahokee, U.S.A. 109 M5 26 50N 80 40W
Pahrump, U.S.A. 117 J11 36 12N 115 59W
Pahute Mesa, U.S.A. 116 H10 37 20N 116 45W
Pai, Thailand 64 C2 19 19N 98 27 E
Paicines, U.S.A. 116 J5 36 44N 121 17W
Paide, Estonia 9 G21 58 57N 25 31 E
Paignton, U.K. 13 G4 50 26N 3 35W
Paiho, Taiwan 59 F13 23 21N 120 25 E
Päijänne, Finland 9 F21 61 30N 25 30 E
Pailani, India 69 G9 25 45N 80 26 E
Pailin, Cambodia 64 F4 12 46N 102 36 E
Paimpol, France 18 D3 48 48N 3 4W
Painan, Indonesia 62 E2 1 21 S 100 34 E
Painesville, U.S.A. 110 E3 41 43N 81 15W
Paint Hills = Wemindji, Canada 102 B4 53 0N 78 49W
Paint L., Canada 105 B9 55 28N 97 57W
Painted Desert, U.S.A. 115 J8 36 0N 111 0W
Paintsville, U.S.A. 108 G4 37 49N 82 48W
País Vasco □, Spain 32 C2 42 50N 2 45W
Paisley, Canada 110 B3 44 18N 81 16W
Paisley, U.K. 14 F4 55 50N 4 25W
Paisley, U.S.A. 114 E3 42 42N 120 32W
Paita, Peru 124 E2 5 11 S 81 9W
Paiva →, Portugal 34 D2 41 4N 8 16W
Paizhou, China 59 B9 30 12N 113 55 E
Pajares, Spain 34 B5 43 1N 5 46W
Pajares, Puerto de, Spain 34 C5 42 58N 5 46W
Pajęczno, Poland 45 G5 51 10N 19 0 E
Pak Lay, Laos 64 C3 18 15N 101 27 E
Pak Phanang, Thailand 65 H3 8 21N 100 12 E
Pak Sane, Laos 64 C4 18 22N 103 39 E
Pak Song, Laos 64 E6 15 11N 106 14 E
Pak Suong, Laos 58 H4 19 58N 102 15 E
Pakaur, India 69 G12 24 38N 87 51 E
Pakenham, Canada 111 A8 45 18N 76 18W
Pákhnes, Greece 36 D6 35 16N 24 4 E
Pakhuis, S. Africa 88 E2 32 9 S 19 5 E
Pakistan ■, Asia 68 E4 30 0N 70 0 E
Pakkading, Laos 64 C4 18 19N 103 59 E
Pakokku, Burma 67 J19 21 20N 95 0 E

Pāveh

Pakość, Poland **45 F5** 52 48N 18 6 E
Pakowki L., Canada **105 D6** 49 20N 111 0W
Pakpattan, Pakistan **68 D5** 30 25N 73 27 E
Pakrac, Croatia **42 E2** 45 27N 17 12 E
Pakruojis, Lithuania **44 C10** 55 58N 23 52 E
Paks, Hungary **42 D3** 46 38N 18 55 E
Paktīā □, Afghan. **66 C6** 33 30N 69 15 E
Paktīkā □, Afghan. **66 C6** 32 30N 69 0 E
Pakwach, Uganda **86 B3** 2 28N 31 27 E
Pakxe, Laos **64 E5** 15 5N 105 52 E
Pal Lahara, India **69 J11** 21 27N 85 11 E
Pala, Chad **79 G9** 9 25N 15 5 E
Pala, Dem. Rep. of the Congo **86 D2** 6 45 S 29 30 E
Pala, U.S.A. **117 M9** 33 22N 117 5W
Palabek, Uganda **86 B3** 3 22N 32 33 E
Palacios, U.S.A. **113 L6** 28 42N 96 13W
Palafrugell, Spain **32 D8** 41 55N 3 10 E
Palagiano, Italy **31 B10** 40 35N 17 2 E
Palagonía, Italy **31 E7** 37 19N 14 45 E
Palagruža, Croatia **29 F13** 42 24N 16 15 E
Palaiókastron, Greece **36 D8** 35 12N 26 15 E
Palaiokhóra, Greece **36 D5** 35 16N 23 39 E
Pálairos, Greece **38 C2** 38 45N 20 51 E
Palaiseau, France **19 D9** 48 43N 2 15 E
Palam, India **66 K10** 19 0N 77 0 E
Palamás, Greece **38 B4** 39 26N 22 4 E
Palamós, Spain **32 D8** 41 50N 3 10 E
Palampur, India **68 C7** 32 10N 76 30 E
Palamut, Turkey **39 C9** 38 59N 27 41 E
Palana, Australia **94 F4** 39 45 S 147 55 E
Palana, Russia **51 D16** 59 10N 159 59 E
Palanan, Phil. **61 C5** 17 8N 122 29 E
Palanan Pt., Phil. **61 C5** 17 17N 122 30 E
Palandri, Pakistan **69 C5** 33 42N 73 40 E
Palanga, Lithuania **9 J19** 55 58N 21 3 E
Palangkaraya, Indonesia **62 E4** 2 16 S 113 56 E
Palani Hills, India **66 P10** 10 14N 77 33 E
Palanpur, India **68 G5** 24 10N 72 25 E
Palapye, Botswana **88 C4** 22 30 S 27 7 E
Palas, Pakistan **69 B5** 35 4N 73 14 E
Palas de Rei, Spain **34 C3** 42 52N 7 52W
Palashi, India **69 H13** 23 47N 88 15 E
Palasponga, India **69 J11** 21 47N 85 34 E
Palatka, Russia **51 C16** 60 6N 150 54 E
Palatka, U.S.A. **109 L5** 29 39N 81 38W
Palau, Italy **30 A2** 41 11N 9 23 E
Palau ■, Pac. Oc. **52 J17** 7 30N 134 30 E
Palauk, Burma **64 F2** 13 10N 98 40 E
Palawan, Phil. **61 G3** 9 30N 118 30 E
Palayankottai, India **66 Q10** 8 45N 77 45 E
Palazzo, Pte., France **21 F12** 42 28N 8 30 E
Palazzo San Gervásio, Italy **31 B8** 40 56N 15 59 E
Palazzolo Acréide, Italy **31 E7** 37 4N 14 54 E
Paldiski, Estonia **9 G21** 59 23N 24 9 E
Pale, Bos.-H. **42 G3** 43 50N 18 38 E
Paleleh, Indonesia **63 D6** 1 10N 121 50 E
Palembang, Indonesia **62 E2** 3 0 S 104 50 E
Palencia, Spain **34 C6** 42 1N 4 34W
Palencia □, Spain **34 C6** 42 31N 4 33W
Palenque, Mexico **119 D6** 17 31N 91 58W
Paleokastrítsa, Greece **36 A3** 39 40N 19 41 E
Paleometokho, Cyprus **36 D12** 35 7N 33 11 E
Palermo, Italy **30 D6** 38 7N 13 22 E
Palermo, U.S.A. **114 G3** 39 26N 121 33W
Palestina, Chile **128 A3** 23 50 S 69 47W
Palestine, Asia **75 D4** 32 0N 35 0 E
Palestine, U.S.A. **113 K7** 31 46N 95 38W
Palestrina, Italy **29 G9** 41 50N 12 53 E
Paletwa, Burma **67 J18** 21 10N 92 50 E
Palghat, India **66 P10** 10 46N 76 42 E
Palgrave, Mt., Australia **92 D2** 23 22 S 115 58 E
Pali, India **68 G5** 25 50N 73 20 E
Palikir, Micronesia **96 G7** 6 55N 158 9 E
Palinuro, Italy **31 B8** 40 2N 15 17 E
Palinuro, C., Italy **31 B8** 40 2N 15 16 E
Palioúrion, Ákra, Greece **40 G7** 39 57N 23 45 E
Palisades Reservoir, U.S.A. **114 E8** 43 20N 111 12W
Paliseul, Belgium **17 E5** 49 54N 5 8 E
Palitana, India **68 J4** 21 32N 71 49 E
Palizada, Mexico **119 D6** 18 18N 92 8W
Palk Bay, Asia **66 Q11** 9 30N 79 15 E
Palk Strait, Asia **66 Q11** 10 0N 79 45 E
Palkānah, Iraq **70 C5** 35 49N 44 26 E
Palkot, India **69 H11** 22 53N 84 39 E
Palla Road = Dinokwe, Botswana **88 C4** 23 29 S 26 37 E
Pallanza = Verbánia, Italy **28 C5** 45 56N 8 33 E
Pallarenda, Australia **94 B4** 19 12 S 146 46 E
Pallasovka, Russia **48 E8** 50 4N 47 0 E
Pallës, Bishti i, Albania **40 E3** 41 24N 19 24 E
Pallinup →, Australia **93 F2** 34 27 S 118 50 E
Pallisa, Uganda **86 B3** 1 12N 33 43 E
Pallu, India **68 E6** 28 59N 74 14 E
Palm Bay, U.S.A. **109 L5** 28 2N 80 35W
Palm Beach, U.S.A. **109 M6** 26 43N 80 2W
Palm Coast, U.S.A. **109 L5** 29 32N 81 10W
Palm Desert, U.S.A. **117 M10** 33 43N 116 22W
Palm Is., Australia **94 B4** 18 40 S 146 35 E
Palm Springs, U.S.A. **117 M10** 33 50N 116 33W
Palma, Mozam. **87 E5** 10 46 S 40 29 E
Palma, B. de, Spain **37 B9** 39 30N 2 39 E
Palma de Mallorca, Spain **37 B9** 39 35N 2 39 E
Palma del Río, Spain **35 H5** 37 43N 5 17W
Palma di Montechiaro, Italy **30 E6** 37 11N 13 46 E
Palma Soriano, Cuba **120 B4** 20 15N 76 0W
Palmares, Brazil **125 E11** 8 41 S 35 28W
Palmarola, Italy **30 B5** 40 56N 12 51 E
Palmas, Brazil **127 B5** 26 29 S 52 0W
Palmas, C., Liberia **82 E3** 4 27N 7 46W
Pálmas, G. di, Italy **30 D1** 39 0N 8 30 E
Palmdale, U.S.A. **117 L8** 34 35N 118 7W
Palmeira das Missões, Brazil **127 B5** 27 55 S 53 17W
Palmeira dos Índios, Brazil **125 E11** 9 25 S 36 37W
Palmela, Portugal **35 G2** 38 32N 8 57W
Palmer, U.S.A. **100 B5** 61 36N 149 7W
Palmer →, Australia **94 B3** 16 0 S 142 26 E
Palmer Arch., Antarctica **5 C17** 64 15 S 65 0W
Palmer Lake, U.S.A. **112 F2** 39 7N 104 55W
Palmer Land, Antarctica **5 D18** 73 0 S 63 0W
Palmerston, Canada **110 C4** 43 50N 80 51W
Palmerston, N.Z. **91 L3** 45 29 S 170 43 E
Palmerston North, N.Z. **91 J5** 40 21 S 175 39 E
Palmerton, U.S.A. **111 F9** 40 48N 75 37W
Palmetto, U.S.A. **109 M4** 27 31N 82 34W
Palmi, Italy **31 D8** 38 21N 15 51 E
Palmira, Argentina **126 C2** 32 59 S 68 34W
Palmira, Colombia **124 C3** 3 32N 76 16W
Palmyra = Tudmur, Syria **70 C3** 34 36N 38 15 E
Palmyra, Mo., U.S.A. **112 F9** 39 48N 91 32W
Palmyra, N.J., U.S.A. **111 F9** 40 1N 75 1W
Palmyra, N.Y., U.S.A. **110 C7** 43 5N 77 18W
Palmyra, Pa., U.S.A. **111 F8** 40 18N 76 36W
Palmyra Is., Pac. Oc. **97 G11** 5 52N 162 5W
Palo Alto, U.S.A. **116 H4** 37 27N 122 10W
Palo Verde, U.S.A. **117 M12** 33 26N 114 44W
Paloich, Sudan **81 E3** 10 28N 32 32 E
Palompon, Phil. **61 F6** 11 3N 124 23 E
Palopo, Indonesia **63 E6** 3 0 S 120 16 E
Palos, C. de, Spain **33 H4** 37 38N 0 40W
Palos de la Frontera, Spain **35 H4** 37 14N 6 53W
Palos Verdes, U.S.A. **117 M8** 33 48N 118 23W
Palos Verdes, Pt., U.S.A. **117 M8** 33 43N 118 26W
Pålsboda, Sweden **10 E9** 59 3N 15 22 E
Palu, Indonesia **63 E5** 1 0 S 119 52 E
Palu, Turkey **70 B3** 38 45N 40 0 E
Paluke, Liberia **82 D3** 5 2N 8 5W
Paluzza, Italy **29 B10** 46 32N 13 1 E
Palwal, India **68 E7** 28 8N 77 19 E
Pama, Burkina Faso **83 C5** 11 19N 0 44 E
Pamanukan, Indonesia **63 G12** 6 16 S 107 49 E
Pamiers, France **20 E5** 43 7N 1 39 E
Pamir, Tajikistan **50 F8** 37 40N 73 0 E
Pamlico →, U.S.A. **109 H7** 35 20N 76 28W
Pamlico Sd., U.S.A. **109 H8** 35 20N 76 0W
Pampa, U.S.A. **113 H4** 35 32N 100 58W
Pampa de las Salinas, Argentina **126 C2** 32 1 S 66 58W
Pampanua, Indonesia **63 E6** 4 16 S 120 8 E
Pampas, Argentina **126 D3** 35 0 S 63 0W
Pampas, Peru **124 F4** 12 20 S 74 50W
Pamphylia, Turkey **72 D4** 37 0N 31 20 E
Pamplona, Colombia **124 B4** 7 23N 72 39W
Pamplona, Spain **32 C3** 42 48N 1 38W
Pampoenpoort, S. Africa **88 E3** 31 3 S 22 40 E
Pamukçu, Turkey **39 B9** 39 30N 27 54 E
Pamukkale, Turkey **39 D11** 37 55N 29 8 E
Pan Xian, China **58 E5** 25 46N 104 38 E
Pana, U.S.A. **112 F10** 39 23N 89 5W
Panabo, Phil. **61 H6** 7 19N 125 42 E
Panaca, U.S.A. **115 H6** 37 47N 114 23W
Panagyurishte, Bulgaria **41 D8** 42 30N 24 15 E
Panaitan, Indonesia **63 G11** 6 36 S 105 12 E
Panaji, India **66 M8** 15 25N 73 50 E
Panamá, Panama **120 E4** 9 0N 79 25W
Panama ■, Cent. Amer. **120 E4** 8 48N 79 55W
Panamá, G. de, Panama **120 E4** 8 4N 79 20W
Panama Canal, Panama **120 E4** 9 10N 79 37W
Panama City, U.S.A. **109 K3** 30 10N 85 40W
Panamint Range, U.S.A. **117 J9** 36 20N 117 20W
Panamint Springs, U.S.A. **117 J9** 36 20N 117 28W
Panão, Peru **124 E3** 9 55 S 75 55W
Panaon I., Phil. **61 F6** 10 3N 125 13 E
Panare, Thailand **65 J3** 6 51N 101 30 E
Panarea, Italy **31 D8** 38 38N 15 4 E
Panaro →, Italy **29 D8** 44 55N 11 25 E
Panay, Phil. **61 F5** 11 10N 122 30 E
Panay, G., Phil. **63 B6** 11 0N 122 30 E
Pančevo, Serbia, Yug. **42 F5** 44 52N 20 41 E
Panch'iao, Taiwan **59 E13** 25 1N 121 27 E
Panciu, Romania **43 E12** 45 54N 27 8 E
Pancorbo, Desfiladero, Spain **34 C7** 42 32N 3 5W
Pâncota, Romania **42 D6** 46 20N 21 45 E
Panda, Mozam. **89 C5** 24 2 S 34 45 E
Pandan, Antique, Phil. **61 F5** 11 45N 122 10 E
Pandan, Catanduanes, Phil. **61 D6** 14 3N 124 10 E
Pandegelang, Indonesia **63 G12** 6 25 S 106 5 E
Pandhana, India **68 J7** 21 42N 76 13 E
Pandharpur, India **66 L9** 17 41N 75 20 E
Pando, Uruguay **127 C4** 34 44 S 56 0W
Pando, L. = Hope, L., Australia **95 D2** 28 24 S 139 18 E
Pandokrátor, Greece **36 A3** 39 45N 19 50 E
Pandora, Costa Rica **120 E3** 9 43N 83 3W
Pandrup, Denmark **11 G3** 57 14N 9 40 E
Panevėžys, Lithuania **9 J21** 55 42N 24 25 E
Panfilov, Kazakhstan **50 E8** 44 10N 80 0 E
Panfilovo, Russia **48 E6** 50 25N 42 46 E
Pang-Long, Burma **67 H21** 23 11N 98 45 E
Pang-Yang, Burma **67 H21** 22 7N 98 48 E
Panga, Dem. Rep. of the Congo **86 B2** 1 52N 26 18 E
Pangaíon Óros, Greece **41 F8** 40 50N 24 0 E
Pangalanes, Canal des = Ampangalana, Lakandranon', Madag. **89 C8** 22 48 S 47 50 E
Pangani, Tanzania **86 D4** 5 25 S 38 58 E
Pangani →, Tanzania **86 D4** 5 26 S 38 58 E
Pangfou = Bengbu, China **57 H9** 32 58N 117 20 E
Pangil, Dem. Rep. of the Congo **86 C2** 3 10 S 26 35 E
Pangkah, Tanjung, Indonesia **63 G15** 6 51 S 112 33 E
Pangkajene, Indonesia **63 E5** 4 46 S 119 34 E
Pangkalanbrandan, Indonesia **62 D1** 4 1N 98 20 E
Pangkalanbuun, Indonesia **62 E4** 2 41 S 111 37 E
Pangkalpinang, Indonesia **62 E3** 2 0 S 106 0 E
Pangnirtung, Canada **101 B13** 66 8N 65 54W
Pangong Tso, India **68 B8** 34 40N 78 40 E
Panguitch, U.S.A. **115 H7** 37 50N 112 26W
Pangutaran Group, Phil. **61 H4** 6 18N 120 34 E
Panhandle, U.S.A. **113 H4** 35 21N 101 23W
Pani Mines, India **68 H5** 22 29N 73 50 E
Pania-Mutombo, Dem. Rep. of the Congo **86 D1** 5 11 S 23 51 E
Panikota I., India **68 J4** 20 46N 71 21 E
Panipat, India **68 E7** 29 25N 77 2 E
Panjal Range, India **68 C7** 32 30N 76 50 E
Panjang, Hon, Vietnam **65 H4** 9 20N 103 28 E
Panjgur, Pakistan **66 F4** 27 0N 64 5 E
Panjim = Panaji, India **66 M8** 15 25N 73 50 E
Panjin, China **57 D12** 41 3N 122 2 E
Panjinad Barrage, Pakistan **66 E7** 29 22N 71 15 E
Panjnad →, Pakistan **68 E4** 28 57N 70 30 E
Panjwai, Afghan. **68 D1** 31 26N 65 27 E
Pankshin, Nigeria **83 D6** 9 16N 9 25 E
Panmunjŏm, N. Korea **57 F14** 37 59N 126 38 E
Panna, India **69 G9** 24 40N 80 15 E
Panna Hills, India **69 G9** 24 40N 81 15 E
Pannawonica, Australia **92 D2** 21 39 S 116 19 E
Pannirtuuq = Pangnirtung, Canada **101 B13** 66 8N 65 54W
Pano Akil, Pakistan **68 F3** 27 51N 69 7 E
Pano Lefkara, Cyprus **36 E12** 34 53N 33 20 E
Pano Panayia, Cyprus **36 E11** 34 55N 32 38 E
Panorama, Brazil **127 A5** 21 21 S 51 51W
Pánormon, Greece **36 D6** 35 25N 24 41 E
Pansemal, India **68 J6** 21 39N 74 42 E
Panshan = Panjin, China **57 D12** 41 3N 122 2 E
Panshi, China **57 C14** 42 58N 126 5 E
Pantanal, Brazil **124 H7** 17 30 S 57 40W
Pantar, Indonesia **63 F6** 8 28 S 124 10 E
Pante Macassar, E. Timor **63 F6** 9 30 S 123 58 E
Pante Makasar = Pante Macassar, E. Timor **63 F6** 9 30 S 123 58 E
Pantelleria, Italy **30 F4** 36 50N 11 57 E
Pantón, Spain **34 C3** 42 31N 7 37W
Pánuco, Mexico **119 C5** 22 0N 98 15W
Panyam, Nigeria **83 D6** 9 27N 9 8 E
Panyu, China **59 F9** 22 51N 113 20 E
Panzhihua, China **58 D3** 26 33N 101 44 E
Páola, Italy **31 C9** 39 21N 16 2 E
Paola, Malta **36 D2** 35 52N 14 30 E
Paola, U.S.A. **112 F7** 38 35N 94 53W
Paonia, U.S.A. **115 G10** 38 52N 107 36W
Paoting = Baoding, China **56 E8** 38 50N 115 28 E
Paot'ou = Baotou, China **56 D6** 40 32N 110 2 E
Paoua, C.A.R. **84 C3** 7 9N 16 20 E
Pápa, Hungary **42 C2** 47 22N 17 30 E
Papa Stour, U.K. **14 A7** 60 20N 1 42W
Papa Westray, U.K. **14 B6** 59 20N 2 55W
Papagayo →, Mexico **119 D5** 16 36N 99 43W
Papagayo, G. de, Costa Rica **120 D2** 10 30N 85 50W
Papakura, N.Z. **91 G5** 37 4 S 174 59 E
Papantla, Mexico **119 C5** 20 30N 97 30W
Papar, Malaysia **62 C5** 5 45N 116 0 E
Pápas, Ákra, Greece **38 C3** 38 13N 21 20 E
Papeete, Tahiti **97 J13** 17 32 S 149 34W
Papenburg, Germany **24 B3** 53 5N 7 23 E
Paphlagonia, Turkey **72 B5** 41 30N 33 0 E
Paphos, Cyprus **36 E11** 34 46N 32 25 E
Papien Chiang = Da →, Vietnam **58 G5** 21 15N 105 20 E
Papigochic →, Mexico **118 B3** 29 9N 109 40W
Paposo, Chile **126 B1** 25 0 S 70 30W
Papoutsa, Cyprus **36 E12** 34 54N 33 4 E
Papua New Guinea ■, Oceania **96 H6** 8 0 S 145 0 E
Papudo, Chile **126 C1** 32 29 S 71 27W
Papuk, Croatia **42 E2** 45 30N 17 30 E
Papun, Burma **67 K20** 18 2N 97 30 E
Papunya, Australia **92 D5** 23 15 S 131 54 E
Pará = Belém, Brazil **125 D9** 1 20 S 48 30W
Pará □, Brazil **125 D8** 3 20 S 52 0W
Paraburdoo, Australia **92 D2** 23 14 S 117 32 E
Paracale, Phil. **61 D5** 14 17N 122 48 E
Paracatu, Brazil **125 G9** 17 10 S 46 50W
Paracel Is., S. China Sea **62 A4** 15 50N 112 0 E
Parachilna, Australia **95 E2** 31 10 S 138 21 E
Parachinar, Pakistan **68 C4** 33 55N 70 5 E
Paraćin, Serbia, Yug. **40 C5** 43 54N 21 27 E
Paradas, Spain **35 H5** 37 18N 5 29W
Paradela, Spain **34 C3** 42 44N 7 37W
Paradhísi, Greece **36 C10** 36 18N 28 7 E
Paradip, India **67 J15** 20 15N 86 35 E
Paradise, Calif., U.S.A. **116 F5** 39 46N 121 37W
Paradise, Nev., U.S.A. **117 J11** 36 9N 115 10W
Paradise →, Canada **103 B8** 53 27N 57 19W
Paradise Hill, Canada **105 C7** 53 32N 109 28W
Paradise River, Canada **103 B8** 53 27N 57 17W
Paradise Valley, U.S.A. **114 F5** 41 30N 117 32W
Parado, Indonesia **63 F5** 8 42 S 118 30 E
Paragould, U.S.A. **113 G9** 36 3N 90 29W
Paragua →, Venezuela **124 B6** 6 55N 62 55W
Paraguaçu →, Brazil **125 F11** 12 45 S 38 54W
Paraguaçu Paulista, Brazil **127 A5** 22 22 S 50 35W
Paraguaná, Pen. de, Venezuela **124 A5** 12 0N 70 0W
Paraguarí, Paraguay **126 B4** 25 36 S 57 0W
Paraguarí □, Paraguay **126 B4** 26 0 S 57 10W
Paraguay ■, S. Amer. **126 A4** 23 0 S 57 0W
Paraguay →, Paraguay **126 B4** 27 18 S 58 38W
Paraíba = João Pessoa, Brazil **125 E12** 7 10 S 34 52W
Paraíba □, Brazil **125 E11** 7 0 S 36 0W
Paraíba do Sul →, Brazil **127 A7** 21 37 S 41 3W
Parainen, Finland **9 F20** 60 18N 22 18 E
Paraiso, Mexico **119 D6** 18 24N 93 14W
Parak, Iran **71 E7** 27 38N 52 25 E
Parakhino Paddubye, Russia **46 C7** 58 26N 33 10 E
Parakou, Benin **83 D5** 9 25N 2 40 E
Paralimni, Cyprus **36 D12** 35 2N 33 58 E
Parálion-Astrous, Greece **38 D4** 37 25N 22 45 E
Paramaribo, Suriname **125 B7** 5 50N 55 10W
Paramithiá, Greece **38 B2** 39 30N 20 35 E
Paramushir, Ostrov, Russia **51 D16** 50 24N 156 0 E
Paran →, Israel **75 E4** 30 20N 35 10 E
Paraná, Argentina **126 C3** 31 45 S 60 30W
Paraná, Brazil **125 F9** 12 30 S 47 48W
Paraná □, Brazil **127 A5** 24 30 S 51 0W
Paraná →, Argentina **126 C4** 33 43 S 59 15W
Paranaguá, Brazil **127 B6** 25 30 S 48 30W
Paranaíba, Brazil **125 G8** 19 40 S 51 11W
Paranaíba →, Brazil **125 H8** 20 6 S 51 4W
Paranapanema →, Brazil **127 A5** 22 40 S 53 9W
Paranapiacaba, Serra do, Brazil **127 A6** 24 31 S 48 35W
Paranas, Phil. **61 F6** 11 42N 125 2 E
Paranavaí, Brazil **127 A5** 23 4 S 52 56W
Parang, Maguindanao, Phil. **63 C6** 7 23N 124 16 E
Parang, Sulu, Phil. **61 J4** 5 55N 120 54 E
Parângul Mare, Vf., Romania **43 E8** 45 20N 23 37 E
Paraparaumu, N.Z. **91 J5** 40 57 S 175 3 E
Parapóla, Greece **38 E5** 36 55N 23 27 E
Paraspóri, Ákra, Greece **39 F9** 35 55N 27 15 E
Paray-le-Monial, France **19 F11** 46 27N 4 7 E
Parbati →, Mad. P., India **68 G7** 25 50N 76 30 E
Parbati →, Raj., India **68 F7** 26 54N 77 53 E
Parbhani, India **66 K10** 19 8N 76 52 E
Parchim, Germany **24 B7** 53 26N 11 52 E
Parczew, Poland **45 G9** 51 40N 22 52 E
Pardes Hanna-Karkur, Israel **75 C3** 32 28N 34 57 E
Pardilla, Spain **34 D7** 41 33N 3 43W
Pardo →, Bahia, Brazil **125 G11** 15 40 S 39 0W
Pardo →, Mato Grosso, Brazil **127 A5** 21 46 S 52 9W
Pardubice, Czech Rep. **26 A8** 50 3N 15 45 E
Pardubický □, Czech Rep. **26 B8** 49 50N 16 0 E
Pare, Indonesia **63 G15** 7 43 S 112 12 E
Pare Mts., Tanzania **86 C4** 4 0 S 37 45 E
Parecis, Serra dos, Brazil **124 F7** 13 0 S 60 0W
Paredes de Nava, Spain **34 C6** 42 9N 4 42W
Paren, Russia **51 C17** 62 30N 163 15 E
Parent, Canada **102 C5** 47 55N 74 35W
Parent, L., Canada **102 C4** 48 31N 77 1W
Parentis-en-Born, France **20 D2** 44 21N 1 4W
Parepare, Indonesia **63 E5** 4 0 S 119 40 E
Parfino, Russia **46 D6** 57 59N 31 34 E
Párga, Greece **38 B2** 39 15N 20 29 E
Pargo, Pta. do, Madeira **37 D2** 32 49N 17 17W
Pariaguán, Venezuela **124 B6** 8 51N 64 34W
Paricutín, Cerro, Mexico **118 D4** 19 28N 102 15W
Parigi, Indonesia **63 E6** 0 50 S 120 5 E
Parika, Guyana **124 B7** 6 50N 58 20W
Parikkala, Finland **46 B5** 61 33N 29 31 E
Parima, Serra, Brazil **124 C6** 2 30N 64 0W
Parinari, Peru **124 D4** 4 35 S 74 25W
Pariñas, Pta., S. Amer. **122 D2** 4 30 S 82 0W
Parincea, Romania **43 D12** 46 27N 27 9 E
Parintins, Brazil **125 D7** 2 40 S 56 50W
Pariparit Kyun, Burma **67 M18** 14 55N 93 45 E
Paris, Canada **110 C4** 43 12N 80 25W
Paris, France **19 D9** 48 50N 2 20 E
Paris, Idaho, U.S.A. **114 E8** 42 14N 111 24W
Paris, Ky., U.S.A. **108 F3** 38 13N 84 15W
Paris, Tenn., U.S.A. **109 G1** 36 18N 88 19W
Paris, Tex., U.S.A. **113 J7** 33 40N 95 33W
Paris, Ville de □, France **19 D9** 48 50N 2 20 E
Parish, U.S.A. **111 C8** 43 25N 76 8W
Parishville, U.S.A. **111 B10** 44 38N 74 49W
Park, U.S.A. **116 B4** 48 45N 122 18W
Park City, U.S.A. **113 G6** 37 48N 97 20W
Park Falls, U.S.A. **112 C9** 45 56N 90 27W
Park Head, Canada **110 B3** 44 36N 81 9W
Park Hills, U.S.A. **113 G9** 37 53N 90 28W
Park Range, U.S.A. **114 G10** 40 0N 106 30W
Park Rapids, U.S.A. **112 B7** 46 55N 95 4W
Park River, U.S.A. **112 A6** 48 24N 97 45W
Park Rynie, S. Africa **89 E5** 30 25 S 30 45 E
Parkā Bandar, Iran **71 E8** 25 55N 59 35 E
Parkano, Finland **9 E20** 62 1N 23 0 E
Parker, Ariz., U.S.A. **117 L12** 34 9N 114 17W
Parker, Pa., U.S.A. **110 E5** 41 5N 79 41W
Parker Dam, U.S.A. **117 L12** 34 18N 114 8W
Parkersburg, U.S.A. **108 F5** 39 16N 81 34W
Parkes, Australia **95 E4** 33 9 S 148 11 E
Parkfield, U.S.A. **116 K6** 35 54N 120 26W
Parkhill, Canada **110 C3** 43 15N 81 38W
Parkland, U.S.A. **116 C4** 47 9N 122 26W
Parkston, U.S.A. **112 D6** 43 24N 97 59W
Parksville, Canada **104 D4** 49 20N 124 21W
Parla, Spain **34 E7** 40 14N 3 46W
Pârliţa, Moldova **43 C12** 47 19N 27 52 E
Parma, Italy **28 D7** 44 48N 10 20 E
Parma, Idaho, U.S.A. **114 E5** 43 47N 116 57W
Parma, Ohio, U.S.A. **110 E3** 41 23N 81 43W
Parma →, Italy **28 D7** 44 56N 10 26 E
Parnaguá, Brazil **125 F10** 10 10 S 44 38W
Parnaíba, Brazil **125 D10** 2 54 S 41 47W
Parnaíba →, Brazil **122 D6** 3 0 S 41 50W
Parnassós, Greece **38 C4** 38 35N 22 30 E
Párnis, Greece **38 C5** 38 14N 23 45 E
Párnon Óros, Greece **38 D4** 37 15N 22 45 E
Pärnu, Estonia **9 G21** 58 28N 24 33 E
Paroo →, Australia **95 E3** 31 28 S 143 32 E
Páros, Greece **39 D7** 37 5N 25 12 E
Parowan, U.S.A. **115 H7** 37 51N 112 50W
Parpaillon, France **21 D10** 44 30N 6 40 E
Parral, Chile **126 D1** 36 10 S 71 52W
Parras, Mexico **118 B4** 25 30N 102 20W
Parrett →, U.K. **13 F4** 51 12N 3 1W
Parris I., U.S.A. **109 J5** 32 20N 80 41W
Parrsboro, Canada **103 C7** 45 30N 64 25W
Parry I., Canada **110 A4** 45 18N 80 10W
Parry Is., Canada **4 B2** 77 0N 110 0W
Parry Sound, Canada **102 C4** 45 20N 80 0W
Parsberg, Germany **25 F7** 49 10N 11 43 E
Parsęta →, Poland **44 D2** 54 11N 15 34 E
Parsnip →, Canada **104 B4** 55 10N 123 2W
Parsons, U.S.A. **113 G7** 37 20N 95 16W
Parsons Ra., Australia **94 A2** 13 30 S 135 15 E
Partanna, Italy **30 E5** 37 43N 12 53 E
Parthenay, France **18 F6** 46 38N 0 16W
Partinico, Italy **30 D6** 38 3N 13 7 E
Partizánske, Slovak Rep. **27 C11** 48 38N 18 23 E
Partridge I., Canada **102 A2** 55 59N 87 37W
Paru →, Brazil **125 D8** 1 33 S 52 38W
Parvān □, Afghan. **66 B6** 35 0N 69 0 E
Parvatipuram, India **67 K13** 18 50N 83 25 E
Parvatsar, India **68 F6** 26 52N 74 49 E
Påryd, Sweden **11 H9** 56 34N 15 55 E
Parys, S. Africa **88 D4** 26 52 S 27 29 E
Pas, Pta. des, Spain **37 C7** 38 46N 1 26 E
Pas-de-Calais □, France **19 B9** 50 30N 2 10 E
Pasada, Spain **34 B5** 43 23N 5 40W
Pasadena, Canada **103 C8** 49 1N 57 36W
Pasadena, Calif., U.S.A. **117 L8** 34 9N 118 9W
Pasadena, Tex., U.S.A. **113 L7** 29 43N 95 13W
Pasaje →, Argentina **126 B3** 25 39 S 63 56W
Paşalimani, Turkey **41 F11** 40 29N 27 36 E
Pasay, Phil. **61 D4** 14 33N 121 0 E
Pascagoula, U.S.A. **113 K10** 30 21N 88 33W
Pascagoula →, U.S.A. **113 K10** 30 23N 88 37W
Paşcani, Romania **43 C11** 47 14N 26 45 E
Pasco, U.S.A. **114 C4** 46 14N 119 6W
Pasco, Cerro de, Peru **124 F3** 10 45 S 76 10W
Pasco I., Australia **92 D2** 20 57 S 115 20 E
Pascoag, U.S.A. **111 E13** 41 57N 71 42W
Pascua, I. de, Pac. Oc. **97 K17** 27 0 S 109 0W
Pasewalk, Germany **24 B9** 53 30N 13 58 E
Pasfield L., Canada **105 B7** 58 24N 105 20W
Pasha →, Russia **46 B7** 60 29N 32 55 E
Pashmakli = Smolyan, Bulgaria **41 E8** 41 36N 24 38 E
Pasinler, Turkey **73 C9** 39 59N 41 41 E
Pasir Mas, Malaysia **65 J4** 6 2N 102 8 E
Pasir Putih, Malaysia **65 K4** 5 50N 102 24 E
Pasirian, Indonesia **63 H15** 8 13 S 113 8 E
Pasirkuning, Indonesia **62 E2** 0 30 S 104 33 E
Påskallavik, Sweden **11 G10** 57 10N 16 26 E
Paskūh, Iran **71 E9** 27 34N 61 39 E
Pasłęk, Poland **44 D6** 54 3N 19 41 E
Pasłęka →, Poland **44 D6** 54 26N 19 46 E
Pasley, C., Australia **93 F3** 33 52 S 123 35 E
Pašman, Croatia **29 E12** 43 58N 15 20 E
Pasni, Pakistan **66 G3** 25 15N 63 27 E
Paso Cantinela, Mexico **117 N11** 32 33N 115 47W
Paso de Indios, Argentina **128 E3** 43 55 S 69 0W
Paso de los Libres, Argentina **126 B4** 29 44 S 57 10W
Paso de los Toros, Uruguay **126 C4** 32 45 S 56 30W
Paso Robles, U.S.A. **115 J3** 35 38N 120 41W
Paspébiac, Canada **103 C6** 48 3N 65 17W
Pasrur, Pakistan **68 C6** 32 16N 74 43 E
Passage West, Ireland **15 E3** 51 52N 8 21W
Passaic, U.S.A. **111 F10** 40 51N 74 7W
Passau, Germany **25 G9** 48 34N 13 28 E
Passero, C., Italy **31 F8** 36 41N 15 10 E
Passo Fundo, Brazil **127 B5** 28 10 S 52 20W
Passos, Brazil **125 H9** 20 45 S 46 37W
Passow, Germany **24 B10** 53 8N 14 6 E
Passy, France **21 C10** 45 55N 6 41 E
Pastavy, Belarus **9 J22** 55 4N 26 50 E
Pastaza →, Peru **124 D3** 4 50 S 76 52W
Pasto, Colombia **124 C3** 1 13N 77 17W
Pastrana, Spain **32 E2** 40 27N 2 53W
Pasuruan, Indonesia **63 G15** 7 40 S 112 44 E
Pasym, Poland **44 E7** 53 48N 20 49 E
Pásztó, Hungary **42 C4** 47 52N 19 43 E
Patagonia, Argentina **122 H4** 45 0 S 69 0W
Patagonia, U.S.A. **115 L8** 31 33N 110 45W
Patambar, Iran **71 D9** 29 45N 60 17 E
Patan, Gujarat, India **66 H8** 23 54N 72 14 E
Patan, Maharashtra, India **68 H5** 23 54N 72 14 E
Patani, Indonesia **63 D7** 0 20N 128 50 E
Pătârlagele, Romania **43 E11** 45 19N 26 21 E
Pataudi, India **68 E7** 28 18N 76 48 E
Patchewollock, Australia **95 F3** 35 22 S 142 12 E
Patchogue, U.S.A. **111 F11** 40 46N 73 1W
Patea, N.Z. **91 H5** 39 45 S 174 30 E
Pategi, Nigeria **83 D6** 8 50N 5 45 E
Patensie, S. Africa **88 E3** 33 46 S 24 49 E
Paterna, Spain **33 F4** 39 30N 0 26W
Paternion, Austria **26 E6** 46 43N 13 38 E
Paternò, Italy **31 E7** 37 34N 14 54 E
Pateros, U.S.A. **114 B4** 48 3N 119 54W
Paterson, U.S.A. **111 F10** 40 55N 74 11W
Paterson Ra., Australia **92 D3** 21 45 S 122 10 E
Pathankot, India **68 C6** 32 18N 75 45 E
Pathfinder Reservoir, U.S.A. **114 E10** 42 28N 106 51W
Pathiu, Thailand **65 G2** 10 42N 99 19 E
Pathum Thani, Thailand **64 E3** 14 1N 100 32 E
Pati, Indonesia **63 G14** 6 45 S 111 1 E
Patía →, Colombia **124 C3** 2 13N 78 40W
Patiala, Punjab, India **68 D7** 30 23N 76 26 E
Patiala, Ut. P., India **69 F8** 27 43N 79 1 E
Patine Kouka, Senegal **82 C2** 12 45N 13 45W
Patitírion, Greece **38 B5** 39 8N 23 50 E
Patkai Bum, India **67 F19** 27 0N 95 30 E
Pátmos, Greece **39 D8** 37 21N 26 36 E
Patna, India **69 G11** 25 35N 85 12 E
Patnos, Turkey **73 C10** 39 13N 42 51 E
Pato Branco, Brazil **127 B5** 26 13 S 52 40W
Patonga, Uganda **86 B3** 2 45N 33 15 E
Patos, Albania **40 F3** 40 42N 19 38 E
Patos, Brazil **125 E11** 6 55 S 37 16W
Patos, L. dos, Brazil **127 C5** 31 20 S 51 0W
Patos, Río de los →, Argentina **126 C2** 31 18 S 69 25W
Patos de Minas, Brazil **125 G9** 18 35 S 46 32W
Patquía, Argentina **126 C2** 30 2 S 66 55W
Pátrai, Greece **38 C3** 38 14N 21 47 E
Pátraikós Kólpos, Greece **38 C3** 38 17N 21 30 E
Patras = Pátrai, Greece **38 C3** 38 14N 21 47 E
Patrocínio, Brazil **125 G9** 18 57 S 47 0W
Patta, Kenya **86 C5** 2 10 S 41 0 E
Pattada, Italy **30 B2** 40 35N 9 6 E
Pattani, Thailand **65 J3** 6 48N 101 15 E
Pattaya, Thailand **62 B2** 12 52N 100 55 E
Patten, U.S.A. **109 C11** 46 0N 68 38W
Patterson, Calif., U.S.A. **116 H5** 37 28N 121 8W
Patterson, La., U.S.A. **113 L9** 29 42N 91 18W
Patterson, Mt., U.S.A. **116 G7** 38 29N 119 20W
Patti, Punjab, India **68 D6** 31 17N 74 54 E
Patti, Ut. P., India **69 G10** 25 55N 82 12 E
Patti, Italy **31 D7** 38 8N 14 58 E
Pattoki, Pakistan **68 D5** 31 5N 73 52 E
Patton, U.S.A. **110 F6** 40 38N 78 39W
Patuakhali, Bangla. **67 H17** 22 20N 90 25 E
Patuanak, Canada **105 B7** 55 55N 107 43W
Patuca →, Honduras **120 C3** 15 50N 84 18W
Patuca, Punta, Honduras **120 C3** 15 49N 84 14W
Pătulele, Romania **42 F7** 44 21N 22 47 E
Pátzcuaro, Mexico **118 D4** 19 30N 101 40W
Pau, France **20 E3** 43 19N 0 25W
Pau, Gave de →, France **20 E2** 43 33N 1 12W
Pauillac, France **20 C3** 45 11N 0 46W
Pauk, Burma **67 J19** 21 27N 94 30 E
Paul I., Canada **103 A7** 56 30N 61 20W
Paul Smiths, U.S.A. **111 B10** 44 26N 74 15W
Paulatuk, Canada **100 B7** 69 25N 124 0W
Paulhan, France **20 E7** 43 33N 3 28 E
Paulis = Isiro, Dem. Rep. of the Congo **86 B2** 2 53N 27 40 E
Paulistana, Brazil **125 E10** 8 9 S 41 9W
Paulo Afonso, Brazil **125 E11** 9 21 S 38 15W
Paulpietersburg, S. Africa **89 D5** 27 23 S 30 50 E
Pauls Valley, U.S.A. **113 H6** 34 44N 97 13W
Pauma Valley, U.S.A. **117 M10** 33 16N 116 58W
Pauri, India **69 D8** 30 9N 78 47 E
Pāveh, Iran **70 C5** 35 3N 46 22 E

Pavelets

Podu Iloaiei

Philipstown = Daingean, *Ireland* 15 C4 53 18N 7 17W
Philipstown, *S. Africa* 88 E3 30 28 S 24 30 E
Phillip I., *Australia* 95 F4 38 30 S 145 12 E
Phillips, *U.S.A.* 112 C9 45 42N 90 24W
Phillipsburg, *Kans., U.S.A.* 112 F5 39 45N 99 19W
Phillipsburg, *N.J., U.S.A.* 111 F9 40 42N 75 12W
Philmont, *U.S.A.* 111 D11 42 15N 73 39W
Philomath, *U.S.A.* 114 D2 44 32N 123 22W
Phimai, *Thailand* 64 E4 15 13N 102 30 E
Phitsanulok, *Thailand* 64 D3 16 50N 100 12 E
Phnom Dangrek, *Thailand* 62 B2 14 20N 104 0 E
Phnom Penh, *Cambodia* 65 G5 11 33N 104 55 E
Phnum Penh = Phnom Penh, *Cambodia* 65 G5 11 33N 104 55 E
Phoenicia, *U.S.A.* 111 D10 42 5N 74 14W
Phoenix, *Ariz., U.S.A.* 115 K7 33 27N 112 4W
Phoenix, *N.Y., U.S.A.* 111 C8 43 14N 76 18W
Phoenix Is., *Kiribati* 96 H10 3 30 S 172 0W
Phoenixville, *U.S.A.* 111 F9 40 8N 75 31W
Phon, *Thailand* 64 E4 15 49N 102 36 E
Phon Tiou, *Laos* 64 D5 17 53N 104 37 E
Phong →, *Thailand* 64 D4 16 23N 102 56 E
Phong Saly, *Laos* 58 G4 21 42N 102 9 E
Phong Tho, *Vietnam* 64 A4 22 32N 103 21 E
Phonhong, *Laos* 64 C4 18 30N 102 25 E
Phonum, *Thailand* 65 H2 8 49N 98 48 E
Phosphate Hill, *Australia* 94 C2 21 53 S 139 58 E
Photharam, *Thailand* 64 F2 13 41N 99 51 E
Phra Nakhon Si Ayutthaya, *Thailand* 64 E3 14 25N 100 30 E
Phra Thong, Ko, *Thailand* 65 H2 9 5N 98 17 E
Phrae, *Thailand* 64 C3 18 7N 100 9 E
Phrom Phiram, *Thailand* 64 D3 17 2N 100 12 E
Phrygia, *Turkey* 72 C4 38 40N 30 0 E
Phu Dien, *Vietnam* 64 C5 18 58N 105 31 E
Phu Loi, *Laos* 64 B4 20 14N 103 14 E
Phu Ly, *Vietnam* 58 G5 20 35N 105 50 E
Phu Quoc, Dao, *Vietnam* 65 G4 10 20N 104 0 E
Phu Tho, *Vietnam* 58 G5 21 24N 105 13 E
Phuc Yen, *Vietnam* 58 G5 21 16N 105 45 E
Phuket, *Thailand* 65 J2 7 52N 98 22 E
Phuket, Ko, *Thailand* 65 J2 8 0N 98 22 E
Phul, *India* 68 D6 30 19N 75 14 E
Phulad, *India* 68 G5 25 38N 73 49 E
Phulchari, *Bangla.* 69 G13 25 11N 89 37 E
Phulera, *India* 68 F6 26 52N 75 16 E
Phulpur, *India* 69 G10 25 31N 82 49 E
Phun Phin, *Thailand* 65 H2 9 7N 99 12 E
Piacenza, *Italy* 28 C6 45 1N 9 40 E
Pian Cr. →, *Australia* 95 E4 30 2 S 148 12 E
Piana, *France* 21 F12 42 15N 8 34 E
Pianella, *Italy* 29 F11 42 24N 14 2 E
Pianosa, *Puglia, Italy* 29 F12 42 12N 15 44 E
Pianosa, *Toscana, Italy* 28 F7 42 35N 10 5 E
Piapot, *Canada* 105 D7 49 59N 109 8W
Pias, *Portugal* 35 G3 38 1N 7 29W
Piaseczno, *Poland* 45 F8 52 5N 21 2 E
Piaski, *Poland* 45 G9 51 8N 22 52 E
Piastów, *Poland* 45 F7 52 12N 20 48 E
Piatra, *Romania* 43 G10 43 51N 25 9 E
Piatra Neamţ, *Romania* 43 D11 46 56N 26 21 E
Piatra Olt, *Romania* 43 F9 44 22N 24 16 E
Piauí □, *Brazil* 125 E10 7 0 S 43 0W
Piauí →, *Brazil* 125 E10 6 38 S 42 42W
Piave →, *Italy* 29 C9 45 32N 12 44 E
Piazza Ármerina, *Italy* 31 E7 37 21N 14 20 E
Pibor →, *Sudan* 81 F3 7 35N 33 0 E
Pibor Post, *Sudan* 81 F3 6 47N 33 3 E
Picardie, *France* 19 C10 49 50N 3 0 E
Picardie, Plaine de, *France* 19 C9 50 0N 2 0 E
Picardy = Picardie, *France* 19 C10 49 50N 3 0 E
Picayune, *U.S.A.* 113 K10 30 32N 89 41W
Picerno, *Italy* 31 B8 40 38N 15 38 E
Pichhor, *India* 69 G8 25 58N 78 20 E
Pichilemu, *Chile* 126 C1 34 22 S 72 0W
Pichor, *India* 68 G8 25 11N 78 11 E
Pickerel L., *Canada* 102 C1 48 40N 91 25W
Pickering, *U.K.* 12 C7 54 15N 0 46W
Pickering, Vale of, *U.K.* 12 C7 54 14N 0 45W
Pickle Lake, *Canada* 102 B1 51 30N 90 12W
Pickwick L., *U.S.A.* 109 H1 35 4N 88 15W
Pico Truncado, *Argentina* 128 F3 46 40 S 68 0W
Picos, *Brazil* 125 E10 7 5 S 41 28W
Picton, *Australia* 95 E5 34 12 S 150 34 E
Picton, *Canada* 102 D4 44 1N 77 9W
Picton, *N.Z.* 91 J5 41 18 S 174 3 E
Pictou, *Canada* 103 C7 45 41N 62 42W
Picture Butte, *Canada* 104 D6 49 55N 112 45W
Picún Leufú, *Argentina* 128 D3 39 30 S 69 5W
Pidurutalagala, *Sri Lanka* 66 R12 7 10N 80 50 E
Piechowice, *Poland* 45 H2 50 51N 15 36 E
Piedmont = Piemonte □, *Italy* 28 D5 45 0N 8 0 E
Piedmont, *Ala., U.S.A.* 109 J3 33 55N 85 37W
Piedmont, *S.C., U.S.A.* 107 D10 34 0N 81 30W
Piedmonte Matese, *Italy* 31 A7 41 22N 14 22 E
Piedra →, *Spain* 32 D3 41 18N 1 47W
Piedrabuena, *Spain* 35 G6 39 0N 4 10W
Piedrahita, *Spain* 34 E5 40 28N 5 23W
Piedralaves, *Spain* 34 E6 40 19N 4 42W
Piedras Blancas, *Spain* 34 B5 43 33N 5 58W
Piedras Negras, *Mexico* 118 B4 28 42N 100 31W
Piekary Śląskie, *Poland* 45 H5 50 24N 18 57 E
Pieksämäki, *Finland* 9 E22 62 18N 27 10 E
Piemonte □, *Italy* 28 D5 45 0N 8 0 E
Pienaarsrivier, *S. Africa* 89 D4 25 15 S 28 18 E
Pieniężno, *Poland* 44 D7 54 14N 20 8 E
Pieńsk, *Poland* 45 G2 51 16N 15 2 E
Piercefield, *U.S.A.* 111 B10 44 13N 74 35W
Pierceland, *Canada* 105 C7 54 20N 109 46W
Piería □, *Greece* 40 F6 40 13N 22 25 E
Pierpont, *U.S.A.* 110 E4 41 45N 80 34W
Pierre, *U.S.A.* 112 C4 44 22N 100 21W
Pierre-Buffière, *France* 20 C5 45 41N 1 22 E
Pierre-de-Bresse, *France* 19 F12 46 54N 5 13 E
Pierre E. Trudeau, Mt. = Logan, Mt., *Canada* 100 B5 60 31N 140 22W
Pierrefontaine-les-Varans, *France* 19 E13 47 14N 6 32 E
Pierrefort, *France* 20 D6 44 55N 2 50 E
Pierrelatte, *France* 21 D8 44 23N 4 43 E
Pieštany, *Slovak Rep.* 27 C10 48 38N 17 55 E
Piesting →, *Austria* 27 C9 48 6N 16 40 E
Pieszyce, *Poland* 45 H3 50 43N 16 33 E
Piet Retief, *S. Africa* 89 D5 27 1 S 30 50 E
Pietarsaari, *Finland* 8 E20 63 40N 22 43 E
Pietermaritzburg, *S. Africa* 89 D5 29 35 S 30 25 E
Pietersburg, *S. Africa* 89 C4 23 54 S 29 25 E
Pietragalla, *Italy* 31 B8 40 45N 15 53 E
Pietrasanta, *Italy* 28 E7 43 57N 10 14 E
Pietroşiţa, *Romania* 43 E10 45 11N 25 26 E
Pietrosul, Vf., *Maramureş, Romania* 43 C9 47 35N 24 43 E
Pietrosul, Vf., *Suceava, Romania* 43 C10 47 12N 25 18 E
Pieve di Cadore, *Italy* 29 B9 46 26N 12 22 E
Pieve di Teco, *Italy* 28 D4 44 3N 7 56 E
Pievepélago, *Italy* 28 D7 44 12N 10 37 E
Pigadhítsa, *Greece* 40 G5 39 59N 21 23 E
Pigeon L., *Canada* 110 B6 44 27N 78 30W
Piggott, *U.S.A.* 113 G9 36 23N 90 11W
Pigna, *Italy* 28 E4 43 56N 7 40 E
Pigüe, *Argentina* 126 D3 37 36 S 62 25W
Pihani, *India* 69 F9 27 36N 80 15 E
Pihlajavesi, *Finland* 9 F23 61 45N 28 45 E
Pijijiapan, *Mexico* 119 D6 15 42N 93 14W
Pikalevo, *Russia* 46 C8 59 37N 34 9 E
Pikangikum Berens, *Canada* 105 C10 51 49N 94 0W
Pikes Peak, *U.S.A.* 112 F2 38 50N 105 3W
Piketberg, *S. Africa* 88 E2 32 55 S 18 40 E
Pikeville, *U.S.A.* 108 G4 37 29N 82 31W
Pikou, *China* 57 E12 39 18N 122 22 E
Pikwitonei, *Canada* 105 B9 55 35N 97 9W
Piła, *Poland* 45 E3 53 10N 16 48 E
Pila, *Spain* 33 G3 38 16N 1 11W
Pilaía, *Greece* 40 F6 40 32N 22 59 E
Pilani, *India* 68 E6 28 22N 75 33 E
Pilar, *Paraguay* 126 B4 26 50 S 58 20W
Pilar de la Horadada, *Spain* 33 H4 37 52N 0 47W
Pilawa, *Poland* 45 G8 51 57N 21 32 E
Pilaya →, *Bolivia* 124 H6 20 55 S 64 4W
Pilbara, *Australia* 92 D2 23 35 S 117 25 E
Pilcomayo →, *Paraguay* 126 B4 25 21 S 57 42W
Pilgrim's Rest, *S. Africa* 89 C5 24 55 S 30 44 E
Pilgrimstad, *Sweden* 10 B9 62 57N 15 2 E
Píli, *Greece* 39 E9 36 50N 27 15 E
Pilibhit, *India* 69 E8 28 40N 79 50 E
Pilica →, *Poland* 45 G8 51 52N 21 17 E
Pilion, *Greece* 38 B5 39 27N 23 7 E
Pilis, *Hungary* 42 C4 47 17N 19 35 E
Pilisvörösvár, *Hungary* 42 C3 47 38N 18 56 E
Pilkhawa, *India* 68 E7 28 43N 77 42 E
Pilliga, *Australia* 95 E4 30 21 S 148 54 E
Pílos, *Greece* 38 E3 36 55N 21 42 E
Pilot Mound, *Canada* 105 D9 49 15N 98 54W
Pilot Point, *U.S.A.* 113 J6 33 24N 96 58W
Pilot Rock, *U.S.A.* 114 D4 45 29N 118 50W
Pilsen = Plzeň, *Czech Rep.* 26 B6 49 45N 13 22 E
Pilštanj, *Slovenia* 29 B12 46 8N 15 39 E
Piltene, *Latvia* 44 A8 57 13N 21 40 E
Pilzno, *Poland* 45 J8 49 58N 21 16 E
Pima, *U.S.A.* 115 K9 32 54N 109 50W
Pimba, *Australia* 95 E2 31 18 S 136 46 E
Pimenta Bueno, *Brazil* 124 F6 11 35 S 61 10W
Pimentel, *Peru* 124 E3 6 45 S 79 55W
Pina de Ebro, *Spain* 32 D4 41 29N 0 33W
Pinamalayan, *Phil.* 61 E4 13 2N 121 29 E
Pinang, *Malaysia* 65 K3 5 25N 100 15 E
Pinar, C. des, *Spain* 37 B10 39 53N 3 12 E
Pinar del Río, *Cuba* 120 B3 22 26N 83 40W
Pınarbaşı, *Çanakkale, Turkey* 39 B8 39 53N 26 15 E
Pınarbaşı, *Kayseri, Turkey* 72 C7 38 43N 36 23 E
Pınarhisar, *Turkey* 41 E11 41 37N 27 30 E
Pinatubo, Mt., *Phil.* 61 D3 15 8N 120 21 E
Pincehely, *Hungary* 42 D3 46 41N 18 27 E
Pinchang, *China* 58 B6 31 36N 107 3 E
Pincher Creek, *Canada* 104 D6 49 30N 113 57W
Pinchi L., *Canada* 104 C4 54 38N 124 30W
Pinckneyville, *U.S.A.* 112 F10 38 5N 89 23W
Pińczów, *Poland* 45 H7 50 32N 20 32 E
Pindar, *Australia* 93 E2 28 30 S 115 47 E
Pindi Gheb, *Pakistan* 68 C5 33 14N 72 21 E
Pindiga, *Nigeria* 83 D7 9 58N 10 53 E
Pindos Óros, *Greece* 38 B3 40 0N 21 0 E
Pindus Mts. = Pindos Óros, *Greece* 38 B3 40 0N 21 0 E
Pine →, *B.C., Canada* 104 B4 56 8N 120 43W
Pine →, *Sask., Canada* 105 B7 58 50N 105 38W
Pine, C., *Canada* 103 C9 46 37N 53 32W
Pine Bluff, *U.S.A.* 113 H9 34 13N 92 1W
Pine Bluffs, *U.S.A.* 112 E2 41 11N 104 4W
Pine City, *U.S.A.* 112 C8 45 50N 92 59W
Pine Cr. →, *U.S.A.* 110 E7 41 10N 77 16W
Pine Creek, *Australia* 92 B5 13 50 S 131 50 E
Pine Falls, *Canada* 105 C9 50 34N 96 11W
Pine Flat Res., *U.S.A.* 116 J7 36 50N 119 20W
Pine Grove, *U.S.A.* 111 F8 40 33N 76 23W
Pine Pass, *Canada* 104 B4 55 25N 122 42W
Pine Point, *Canada* 104 A6 60 50N 114 28W
Pine Ridge, *U.S.A.* 112 D3 43 2N 102 33W
Pine River, *Canada* 105 C8 51 45N 100 30W
Pine River, *U.S.A.* 112 B7 46 43N 94 24W
Pine Valley, *U.S.A.* 117 N10 32 50N 116 32W
Pinecrest, *U.S.A.* 116 G6 38 12N 120 1W
Pineda de Mar, *Spain* 32 D7 41 37N 2 42 E
Pinedale, *Calif., U.S.A.* 116 J7 36 50N 119 48W
Pinedale, *Wyo., U.S.A.* 114 E9 42 52N 109 52W
Pinega →, *Russia* 50 C5 64 30N 44 19 E
Pinehill, *Australia* 94 C4 23 38 S 146 57 E
Pinehouse L., *Canada* 105 B7 55 32N 106 35W
Pineimuta →, *Canada* 102 B1 52 8N 88 33W
Pinerolo, *Italy* 28 D4 44 53N 7 21 E
Pineto, *Italy* 29 F11 42 36N 14 4 E
Pinetop, *U.S.A.* 115 J9 34 8N 109 56W
Pinetown, *S. Africa* 89 D5 29 48 S 30 54 E
Pineville, *U.S.A.* 113 K8 31 19N 92 26W
Piney, *France* 19 D11 48 22N 4 21 E
Ping →, *Thailand* 64 E3 15 42N 100 9 E
Pingaring, *Australia* 93 F2 32 40 S 118 32 E
Pingba, *China* 58 D6 26 23N 106 12 E
Pingbian, *China* 58 F4 23 0N 103 45 E
Pingchuan, *China* 58 D3 27 35N 101 55 E
Pingding, *China* 56 F7 37 47N 113 38 E
Pingdingshan, *China* 56 H7 33 43N 113 27 E
Pingdong, *Taiwan* 59 F13 22 39N 120 30 E
Pingdu, *China* 57 F10 36 42N 119 59 E
Pingelly, *Australia* 93 F2 32 32 S 117 5 E
Pingguo, *China* 58 F6 23 19N 107 36 E
Pinghe, *China* 59 E11 24 17N 117 21 E
Pinghu, *China* 59 B13 30 40N 121 2 E
Pingjiang, *China* 59 C9 28 45N 113 36 E
Pingle, *China* 59 E8 24 40N 110 40 E
Pingli, *China* 58 A7 32 27N 109 22 E
Pingliang, *China* 56 G4 35 35N 106 31 E
Pinglu, *China* 56 E7 39 31N 112 30 E
Pingluo, *China* 56 E4 38 52N 106 30 E
Pingnan, *Fujian, China* 59 D12 26 55N 119 0 E
Pingnan, *Guangxi Zhuangzu, China* 59 F8 23 33N 110 22 E
Pingquan, *China* 57 D10 41 1N 118 37 E
Pingrup, *Australia* 93 F2 33 32 S 118 29 E
Pingshan, *China* 58 C5 28 39N 104 3 E
Pingtan, *China* 59 E12 25 31N 119 47 E
Pingtang, *China* 58 E6 25 49N 107 17 E
P'ingtung, *Taiwan* 59 F13 22 38N 120 30 E
Pingwu, *China* 56 H3 32 25N 104 30 E
Pingxiang, *Guangxi Zhuangzu, China* 58 F6 22 6N 106 46 E
Pingxiang, *Jiangxi, China* 59 D9 27 43N 113 48 E
Pingyao, *China* 56 F7 37 12N 112 10 E
Pingyi, *China* 57 G9 35 30N 117 35 E
Pingyin, *China* 56 F9 36 20N 116 25 E
Pingyuan, *Guangdong, China* 59 E10 24 37N 115 57 E
Pingyuan, *Shandong, China* 56 F9 37 10N 116 22 E
Pingyuanjie, *China* 58 F4 23 45N 103 48 E
Pinhal, *Brazil* 127 A6 22 10 S 46 46W
Pinhal Novo, *Portugal* 35 G2 38 38N 8 55W
Pinheiro, *Brazil* 125 D9 2 31 S 45 5W
Pinheiro Machado, *Brazil* 127 C5 31 34 S 53 23W
Pinhel, *Portugal* 34 E3 40 50N 7 1W
Pini, *Indonesia* 62 D1 0 10N 98 40 E
Piniós →, *Ilía, Greece* 38 D3 37 48N 21 20 E
Piniós →, *Tríkkala, Greece* 38 B4 39 55N 22 41 E
Pinjarra, *Australia* 93 F2 32 37 S 115 52 E
Pink Mountain, *Canada* 104 B4 57 3N 122 52W
Pinkafeld, *Austria* 27 D9 47 22N 16 9 E
Pinnacles, *U.S.A.* 116 J5 36 33N 121 19W
Pinnaroo, *Australia* 95 F3 35 17 S 140 53 E
Pinneberg, *Germany* 24 B5 53 40N 9 48 E
Pínnes, Ákra, *Greece* 41 F8 40 5N 24 20 E
Pinon Hills, *U.S.A.* 117 L9 34 26N 117 39W
Pinos, *Mexico* 118 C4 22 20N 101 40W
Pinos, Mt., *U.S.A.* 117 L7 34 49N 119 8W
Pinos Pt., *U.S.A.* 115 H3 36 38N 121 57W
Pinos Puente, *Spain* 35 H7 37 15N 3 45W
Pinotepa Nacional, *Mexico* 119 D5 16 19N 98 3W
Pinrang, *Indonesia* 63 E5 3 46 S 119 41 E
Pins, Pte. aux, *Canada* 110 D3 42 15N 81 51W
Pinsk, *Belarus* 47 F4 52 10N 26 1 E
Pintados, *Chile* 124 H5 20 35 S 69 40W
Pinyang, *China* 59 D13 27 42N 120 31 E
Pinyug, *Russia* 50 C5 60 5N 48 0 E
Pioche, *U.S.A.* 115 H6 37 56N 114 27W
Piombino, *Italy* 28 F7 42 55N 10 32 E
Piombino, Canale di, *Italy* 28 F7 42 53N 10 30 E
Pioner, Ostrov, *Russia* 51 B10 79 50N 92 0 E
Pionki, *Poland* 45 G8 51 29N 21 28 E
Piorini, L., *Brazil* 124 D6 3 15 S 62 35W
Piotrków Trybunalski, *Poland* 45 G6 51 23N 19 43 E
Piove di Sacco, *Italy* 29 C9 45 18N 12 2 E
Pīp, *Iran* 71 E9 26 45N 60 10 E
Pipar, *India* 68 F5 26 25N 73 31 E
Pipar Road, *India* 68 F5 26 27N 73 27 E
Piparia, *Mad. P., India* 68 H8 22 45N 78 23 E
Piparia, *Mad. P., India* 68 J7 21 49N 77 37 E
Pipéri, *Greece* 38 B6 39 20N 24 19 E
Pipestone, *U.S.A.* 112 D6 44 0N 96 19W
Pipestone →, *Canada* 102 B2 52 53N 89 23W
Pipestone Cr. →, *Canada* 105 D8 49 38N 100 15W
Piplan, *Pakistan* 68 C4 32 17N 71 21 E
Piploda, *India* 68 H6 23 37N 74 56 E
Pipmuacan, Rés., *Canada* 103 C5 49 45N 70 30W
Pippingarra, *Australia* 92 D2 20 27 S 118 42 E
Pipriac, *France* 18 E5 47 49N 1 58W
Piqua, *U.S.A.* 108 E3 40 9N 84 15W
Piquiri →, *Brazil* 127 A5 24 3 S 54 14W
Pīr Sohrāb, *Iran* 71 E9 25 44N 60 54 E
Pira, *Benin* 83 D5 8 28N 1 48 E
Piracicaba, *Brazil* 127 A6 22 45 S 47 40W
Piracuruca, *Brazil* 125 D10 3 50 S 41 50W
Piræus = Piraiévs, *Greece* 38 D5 37 57N 23 42 E
Piraiévs, *Greece* 38 D5 37 57N 23 42 E
Pirajuí, *Brazil* 127 A6 21 59 S 49 29W
Piram I., *India* 68 J5 21 36N 72 21 E
Piran, *Slovenia* 29 C10 45 31N 13 33 E
Pirané, *Argentina* 126 B4 25 42 S 59 6W
Pirano = Piran, *Slovenia* 29 C10 45 31N 13 33 E
Pirapora, *Brazil* 125 G10 17 20 S 44 56W
Pirawa, *India* 68 G7 24 10N 76 2 E
Pirdop, *Bulgaria* 41 D8 42 40N 24 10 E
Pírgos, *Ilía, Greece* 38 D3 37 40N 21 27 E
Pírgos, *Kríti, Greece* 39 F7 35 0N 25 9 E
Pirgovo, *Bulgaria* 41 C9 43 44N 25 43 E
Piribebuy, *Paraguay* 126 B4 25 26 S 57 2W
Pirimapun, *Indonesia* 63 F9 6 20 S 138 24 E
Pirin Planina, *Bulgaria* 40 E7 41 40N 23 30 E
Píríneos = Pyrénées, *Europe* 20 F4 42 45N 0 18 E
Piripiri, *Brazil* 125 D10 4 15 S 41 46W
Pirmasens, *Germany* 25 F3 49 12N 7 36 E
Pirna, *Germany* 24 E9 50 57N 13 56 E
Pirot, *Serbia, Yug.* 40 C6 43 9N 22 33 E
Piru, *Indonesia* 63 E7 3 4 S 128 12 E
Piru, *U.S.A.* 117 L8 34 25N 118 48W
Piryatin = Pyryatyn, *Ukraine* 47 G7 50 15N 32 25 E
Piryí, *Greece* 39 C7 38 13N 25 59 E
Pisa, *Italy* 28 E7 43 43N 10 23 E
Pisa →, *Poland* 45 E8 53 14N 21 52 E
Pisagne, *Italy* 28 C7 45 45N 10 10 E
Pisagua, *Chile* 124 G4 19 40 S 70 15W
Pisarovina, *Croatia* 29 C12 45 35N 15 50 E
Pisco, *Peru* 124 F3 13 50 S 76 12W
Piscu, *Romania* 43 E12 45 30N 27 43 E
Písek, *Czech Rep.* 26 B7 49 19N 14 10 E
Pishan, *China* 60 C2 37 30N 78 33 E
Pīshīn, *Iran* 71 E9 26 6N 61 47 E
Pishin, *Pakistan* 68 D2 30 35N 67 0 E
Pishin Lora →, *Pakistan* 68 E1 29 9N 64 5 E
Pisidia, *Turkey* 72 D4 37 30N 31 40 E
Pising, *Indonesia* 63 F6 5 8 S 121 53 E
Pismo Beach, *U.S.A.* 117 K6 35 9N 120 38W
Piso, L., *Liberia* 82 D2 6 50N 11 15W
Pissila, *Burkina Faso* 83 C4 13 7N 0 50W
Pissis, Cerro, *Argentina* 126 B2 27 45 S 68 48W
Pissos, *France* 20 D3 44 19N 0 49W
Pissouri, *Cyprus* 36 E11 34 40N 32 42 E
Pisticci, *Italy* 31 B9 40 23N 16 33 E
Pistóia, *Italy* 28 E7 43 55N 10 54 E
Pistol B., *Canada* 105 A10 62 25N 92 37W
Pisuerga →, *Spain* 34 D6 41 33N 4 52W
Pisz, *Poland* 44 E8 53 38N 21 49 E
Pit →, *U.S.A.* 114 F2 40 47N 122 6W
Pita, *Guinea* 82 C2 11 5N 12 15W
Pitarpunga, L., *Australia* 95 E3 34 24 S 143 30 E
Pitcairn I., *Pac. Oc.* 97 K14 25 5 S 130 5W
Pite älv →, *Sweden* 8 D19 65 20N 21 25 E
Piteå, *Sweden* 8 D19 65 20N 21 25 E
Piterka, *Russia* 48 E8 50 41N 47 29 E
Piteşti, *Romania* 43 F9 44 52N 24 54 E
Pithapuram, *India* 67 L13 17 10N 82 15 E
Pithara, *Australia* 93 F2 30 20 S 116 35 E
Píthion, *Greece* 41 E10 41 24N 26 40 E
Pithiviers, *France* 19 D9 48 10N 2 13 E
Pithoragarh, *India* 69 E9 29 35N 80 13 E
Pithoro, *Pakistan* 68 G3 25 31N 69 23 E
Pitigliano, *Italy* 29 F8 42 38N 11 40 E
Pitkyaranta, *Russia* 46 B6 61 34N 31 37 E
Pitlochry, *U.K.* 14 E5 56 42N 3 44W
Pitsilia □, *Cyprus* 36 E12 34 55N 33 0 E
Pitt I., *Canada* 104 C3 53 30N 129 50W
Pittsburg, *Calif., U.S.A.* 116 G5 38 2N 121 53W
Pittsburg, *Kans., U.S.A.* 113 G7 37 25N 94 42W
Pittsburg, *Tex., U.S.A.* 113 J7 33 0N 94 59W
Pittsburgh, *U.S.A.* 110 F5 40 26N 80 1W
Pittsfield, *Ill., U.S.A.* 112 F9 39 36N 90 49W
Pittsfield, *Maine, U.S.A.* 109 C11 44 47N 69 23W
Pittsfield, *Mass., U.S.A.* 111 D11 42 27N 73 15W
Pittsfield, *N.H., U.S.A.* 111 C13 43 18N 71 20W
Pittston, *U.S.A.* 111 E9 41 19N 75 47W
Pittsworth, *Australia* 95 D5 27 41 S 151 37 E
Pituri →, *Australia* 94 C2 22 35 S 138 30 E
Piura, *Peru* 124 E2 5 15 S 80 38W
Piva →, *Montenegro, Yug.* 40 C2 43 20N 18 50 E
Piwniczna, *Poland* 45 J7 49 27N 20 42 E
Pixley, *U.S.A.* 116 K7 35 58N 119 18W
Piyai, *Greece* 38 B3 39 17N 21 25 E
Pizarra, *Spain* 35 J6 36 36N 4 42W
Pizhou, *China* 56 G9 34 44N 116 55 E
Pizzo, *Italy* 31 D9 38 44N 16 10 E
Placentia, *Canada* 103 C9 47 20N 54 0W
Placentia B., *Canada* 103 C9 47 0N 54 40W
Placer, *Masbate, Phil.* 61 F5 11 52N 123 55 E
Placer, *Surigao N., Phil.* 61 G6 9 36N 125 38 E
Placerville, *U.S.A.* 116 G6 38 44N 120 48W
Placetas, *Cuba* 120 B4 22 15N 79 44W
Plačkovica, *Macedonia* 40 E6 41 45N 22 30 E
Plainfield, *N.J., U.S.A.* 111 F10 40 37N 74 25W
Plainfield, *Ohio, U.S.A.* 110 F3 40 13N 81 43W
Plainfield, *Vt., U.S.A.* 111 B12 44 17N 72 26W
Plains, *Mont., U.S.A.* 114 C6 47 28N 114 53W
Plains, *Tex., U.S.A.* 113 J3 33 11N 102 50W
Plainview, *Nebr., U.S.A.* 112 D6 42 21N 97 47W
Plainview, *Tex., U.S.A.* 113 H4 34 11N 101 43W
Plainwell, *U.S.A.* 108 D3 42 27N 85 38W
Plaisance, *France* 20 E4 43 36N 0 3 E
Plaistow, *U.S.A.* 111 D13 42 50N 71 6W
Pláka, *Greece* 39 B7 40 0N 25 24 E
Pláka, Ákra, *Greece* 36 D8 35 11N 26 19 E
Plakenska Planina, *Macedonia* 40 E5 41 14N 21 2 E
Planá, *Czech Rep.* 26 B5 49 50N 12 44 E
Plana Cays, *Bahamas* 121 B5 22 38N 73 30W
Planada, *U.S.A.* 116 H6 37 16N 120 19W
Plancoët, *France* 18 D4 48 32N 2 13W
Plandište, *Serbia, Yug.* 42 E6 45 16N 21 10 E
Plano, *U.S.A.* 113 J6 33 1N 96 42W
Plant City, *U.S.A.* 109 M4 28 1N 82 7W
Plaquemine, *U.S.A.* 113 K9 30 17N 91 14W
Plasencia, *Spain* 34 E4 40 3N 6 8W
Plaški, *Croatia* 29 C12 45 4N 15 22 E
Plaster City, *U.S.A.* 117 N11 32 47N 115 51W
Plaster Rock, *Canada* 103 C6 46 53N 67 22W
Plastun, *Russia* 54 B8 44 45N 136 19 E
Plasy, *Czech Rep.* 26 B6 49 56N 13 24 E
Plata, Río de la, *S. Amer.* 126 C4 34 45 S 57 30W
Plátani →, *Italy* 30 E6 37 23N 13 16 E
Plátanos, *Greece* 36 D5 35 28N 23 33 E
Plateau □, *Nigeria* 83 D6 8 30N 9 0 E
Platí, Ákra, *Greece* 41 F8 40 27N 24 0 E
Platte, *U.S.A.* 112 D5 43 23N 98 51W
Platte →, *Mo., U.S.A.* 112 F7 39 16N 94 50W
Platte →, *Nebr., U.S.A.* 112 E7 41 4N 95 53W
Platteville, *U.S.A.* 112 D9 42 44N 90 29W
Plattling, *Germany* 25 G8 48 46N 12 53 E
Plattsburgh, *U.S.A.* 111 B11 44 42N 73 28W
Plattsmouth, *U.S.A.* 112 E7 41 1N 95 53W
Plau, *Germany* 24 B8 53 27N 12 15 E
Plauen, *Germany* 24 E8 50 30N 12 8 E
Plauer See, *Germany* 24 B8 53 28N 12 17 E
Plav, *Montenegro, Yug.* 40 D3 42 38N 19 57 E
Plavinas, *Latvia* 9 H21 56 35N 25 46 E
Plavnica, *Montenegro, Yug.* 40 D3 42 20N 19 13 E
Plavno, *Croatia* 29 D13 44 9N 16 10 E
Plavsk, *Russia* 46 F9 53 40N 37 18 E
Playa Blanca, *Canary Is.* 37 F6 28 55N 13 37W
Playa Blanca Sur, *Canary Is.* 37 F6 28 51N 13 50W
Playa de las Americas, *Canary Is.* 37 F3 28 5N 16 43W
Playa de Mogán, *Canary Is.* 37 G4 27 48N 15 47W
Playa del Inglés, *Canary Is.* 37 G4 27 45N 15 33W
Playa Esmerelda, *Canary Is.* 37 F5 28 8N 14 16W
Playgreen L., *Canada* 105 C9 54 0N 98 15W
Pleasant Bay, *Canada* 103 C7 46 51N 60 48W
Pleasant Hill, *U.S.A.* 116 H4 37 57N 122 4W
Pleasant Mount, *U.S.A.* 111 E9 41 44N 75 26W
Pleasanton, *Calif., U.S.A.* 116 H5 37 39N 121 52W
Pleasanton, *Tex., U.S.A.* 113 L5 28 58N 98 29W
Pleasantville, *N.J., U.S.A.* 108 F8 39 24N 74 32W
Pleasantville, *Pa., U.S.A.* 110 E5 41 35N 79 34W
Pléaux, *France* 20 C6 45 8N 2 13 E
Plei Ku, *Vietnam* 64 F7 13 57N 108 0 E
Plélan-le-Grand, *France* 18 D4 48 0N 2 7W
Pléneuf-Val-André, *France* 18 D4 48 35N 2 32W
Pleniţa, *Romania* 43 F8 44 14N 23 10 E
Plenty →, *Australia* 94 C2 23 25 S 136 31 E
Plenty, B. of, *N.Z.* 91 G6 37 45 S 177 0 E
Plentywood, *U.S.A.* 112 A2 48 47N 104 34W
Plérin, *France* 18 D4 48 32N 2 46W
Plessisville, *Canada* 103 C5 46 14N 71 47W
Plestin-les-Grèves, *France* 18 D3 48 40N 3 39W
Pleszew, *Poland* 45 G4 51 53N 17 47 E
Pleternica, *Croatia* 42 E2 45 17N 17 48 E
Plétipi, L., *Canada* 103 B5 51 44N 70 6W
Pleven, *Bulgaria* 41 C8 43 26N 24 37 E
Plevlja, *Montenegro, Yug.* 40 C3 43 21N 19 21 E
Plevna, *Canada* 110 B8 44 58N 76 59W
Plješevica, *Croatia* 29 D12 44 45N 15 45 E
Ploaghe, *Italy* 30 B1 40 40N 8 45 E
Ploče, *Croatia* 29 E14 43 4N 17 26 E
Płock, *Poland* 45 F6 52 32N 19 40 E
Plöckenpass, *Italy* 29 B9 46 37N 12 57 E
Plöckenstein, *Germany* 25 G9 48 46N 13 51 E
Ploemeur, *France* 18 E3 47 44N 3 26W
Ploërmel, *France* 18 E4 47 55N 2 26W
Ploieşti, *Romania* 43 F11 44 57N 26 5 E
Plomárion, *Greece* 39 C8 38 59N 26 22 E
Plombières-les-Bains, *France* 19 E13 47 58N 6 27 E
Plomin, *Croatia* 29 C11 45 8N 14 10 E
Plön, *Germany* 24 A6 54 9N 10 24 E
Plonge, Lac la, *Canada* 105 B7 55 8N 107 20W
Płońsk, *Poland* 45 F7 52 37N 20 21 E
Plopeni, *Romania* 43 E10 45 4N 25 59 E
Plopişului, Munţii, *Romania* 42 C7 47 5N 22 30 E
Płoty, *Poland* 44 E2 53 48N 15 18 E
Plouaret, *France* 18 D3 48 37N 3 28W
Plouay, *France* 18 E3 47 55N 3 21W
Ploučnice →, *Czech Rep.* 26 A7 50 46N 14 13 E
Ploudalmézeau, *France* 18 D2 48 34N 4 41W
Plouescat, *France* 18 D2 48 39N 4 10W
Plougasnou, *France* 18 D3 48 42N 3 49W
Plougastel-Daoulas, *France* 18 D2 48 22N 4 17W
Plouguerneau, *France* 18 D2 48 36N 4 30W
Plouha, *France* 18 D4 48 41N 2 57W
Plouhinec, *France* 18 E2 48 0N 4 29W
Plovdiv, *Bulgaria* 41 D8 42 8N 24 44 E
Plovdiv □, *Bulgaria* 41 D8 42 15N 24 30 E
Plum, *U.S.A.* 110 F5 40 29N 79 47W
Plum I., *U.S.A.* 111 E12 41 11N 72 12W
Plumas, *U.S.A.* 116 F7 39 45N 120 4W
Plummer, *U.S.A.* 114 C5 47 20N 116 53W
Plumtree, *Zimbabwe* 87 G2 20 27 S 27 55 E
Plungė, *Lithuania* 9 J19 55 53N 21 59 E
Pluvigner, *France* 18 E3 47 46N 3 1W
Plymouth, *U.K.* 13 G3 50 22N 4 10W
Plymouth, *Calif., U.S.A.* 116 G6 38 29N 120 51W
Plymouth, *Ind., U.S.A.* 108 E2 41 21N 86 19W
Plymouth, *Mass., U.S.A.* 111 E14 41 57N 70 40W
Plymouth, *N.C., U.S.A.* 109 H7 35 52N 76 43W
Plymouth, *N.H., U.S.A.* 111 C13 43 46N 71 41W
Plymouth, *Pa., U.S.A.* 111 E9 41 14N 75 57W
Plymouth, *Wis., U.S.A.* 108 D2 43 45N 87 59W
Plynlimon = Pumlumon Fawr, *U.K.* 13 E4 52 28N 3 46W
Plyusa, *Russia* 46 C5 58 28N 29 27 E
Plyusa →, *Russia* 46 C5 59 4N 28 6 E
Plyussa = Plyusa, *Russia* 46 C5 58 28N 29 27 E
Plyussa → = Plyusa →, *Russia* 46 C5 59 4N 28 6 E
Plzeň, *Czech Rep.* 26 B6 49 45N 13 22 E
Plzeňský □, *Czech Rep.* 26 B6 49 35N 13 0 E
Pniewy, *Poland* 45 F3 52 31N 16 16 E
Pô, *Burkina Faso* 83 C4 11 14N 1 5W
Po →, *Italy* 29 D9 44 57N 12 4 E
Po, Foci del, *Italy* 29 D9 44 55N 12 30 E
Po Hai = Bo Hai, *China* 57 E10 39 0N 119 0 E
Pobé, *Benin* 83 D5 7 0N 2 56 E
Pobé, *Burkina Faso* 83 C4 13 53N 1 42W
Pobeda, *Russia* 51 C15 65 12N 146 12 E
Pobedy, Pik, *Kyrgyzstan* 50 E8 42 0N 79 58 E
Pobiedziska, *Poland* 45 F4 52 29N 17 11 E
Pobla de Segur, *Spain* 32 C5 42 15N 0 58 E
Pobladura del Valle, *Spain* 34 C5 42 6N 5 44W
Pobra de Trives, *Spain* 34 C3 42 20N 7 10W
Pocahontas, *Ark., U.S.A.* 113 G9 36 16N 90 58W
Pocahontas, *Iowa, U.S.A.* 112 D7 42 44N 94 40W
Pocatello, *U.S.A.* 114 E7 42 52N 112 27W
Počátky, *Czech Rep.* 26 B8 49 15N 15 14 E
Pochep, *Russia* 47 F7 52 58N 33 29 E
Pochinki, *Russia* 48 C7 54 41N 44 59 E
Pochinok, *Russia* 46 E7 54 28N 32 29 E
Pöchlarn, *Austria* 26 C8 48 12N 15 12 E
Pochutla, *Mexico* 119 D5 15 50N 96 31W
Pocito Casas, *Mexico* 118 B2 28 32N 111 6W
Pocking, *Germany* 25 G9 48 23N 13 19 E
Pocomoke City, *U.S.A.* 108 F8 38 5N 75 34W
Poços de Caldas, *Brazil* 127 A6 21 50 S 46 33W
Podbořany, *Czech Rep.* 26 A6 50 14N 13 25 E
Podębice, *Poland* 45 G5 51 54N 18 58 E
Poděbrady, *Czech Rep.* 26 A8 50 9N 15 8 E
Podensac, *France* 20 D3 44 40N 0 22W
Podenzano, *Italy* 28 D6 44 57N 9 41 E
Podgorač, *Croatia* 42 E3 45 27N 18 13 E
Podgorica, *Montenegro, Yug.* 40 D3 42 30N 19 19 E
Podgorie, *Albania* 40 F4 40 49N 20 48 E
Podilska Vysochyna, *Ukraine* 47 H4 49 0N 28 0 E
Podkarpackie □, *Poland* 45 H9 50 0N 22 10 E
Podkova, *Bulgaria* 41 E9 41 24N 25 24 E
Podlapača, *Croatia* 29 D12 44 37N 15 47 E
Podlaskie □, *Poland* 45 E10 53 10N 23 0 E
Podoleni, *Romania* 43 D11 46 46N 26 39 E
Podolínec, *Slovak Rep.* 27 B13 49 16N 20 31 E
Podolsk, *Russia* 46 E9 55 25N 37 30 E
Podor, *Senegal* 82 B1 16 40N 15 2W
Podporozhye, *Russia* 46 B8 60 55N 34 2 E
Podu Iloaiei, *Romania* 43 C12 47 13N 27 16 E

Podu Turcului

Podu Turcului, *Romania* **43 D12** 46 11N 27 25 E
Podujevo, *Kosovo, Yug.* **40 D5** 42 54N 21 10 E
Poel, *Germany* **24 B6** 54 0N 11 25 E
Pofadder, *S. Africa* **88 D2** 29 10 S 19 22 E
Poggiardo, *Italy* **31 B11** 40 3N 18 23 E
Poggibonsi, *Italy* **28 E8** 43 28N 11 9 E
Póggio Mirteto, *Italy* **29 F9** 42 16N 12 41 E
Pogoanele, *Romania* **43 F12** 44 55N 27 0 E
Pogorzela, *Poland* **45 G4** 51 50N 17 12 E
Pogradec, *Albania* **40 F4** 40 54N 20 37 E
Pogranitšnyi, *Russia* **54 B5** 44 25N 131 24 E
Poh, *Indonesia* **63 E6** 0 46 S 122 51 E
P'ohang, *S. Korea* **57 F15** 36 1N 129 23 E
Pohjanmaa, *Finland* **8 E20** 62 58N 22 50 E
Pohnpei, *Micronesia* **96 G7** 6 55N 158 10 E
Pohořelá, *Slovak Rep.* **27 C13** 48 50N 20 2 E
Pohořelice, *Czech Rep.* **27 C9** 48 59N 16 31 E
Pohorje, *Slovenia* **29 B12** 46 30N 15 20 E
Pohri, *India* **68 G6** 25 32N 77 22 E
Poiana Mare, *Romania* **42 G8** 43 57N 23 5 E
Poiana Ruscăi, Munţii, *Romania* **42 E7** 45 45N 22 25 E
Poiana Stampei, *Romania* **43 C10** 47 19N 25 8 E
Poinsett, C., *Antarctica* **5 C8** 65 42 S 113 18 E
Point Arena, *U.S.A.* **116 G3** 38 55N 123 41W
Point Baker, *U.S.A.* **104 B2** 56 21N 133 37W
Point Edward, *Canada* **102 D3** 43 0N 82 30W
Point Hope, *U.S.A.* **100 B3** 68 21N 166 47W
Point L., *Canada* **100 B8** 65 15N 113 4W
Point Pedro, *Sri Lanka* **66 Q12** 9 50N 80 15 E
Point Pleasant, *N.J., U.S.A.* **111 F10** 40 5N 74 4W
Point Pleasant, *W. Va., U.S.A.* **108 F4** 38 51N 82 8W
Pointe-à-Pitre, *Guadeloupe* **121 C7** 16 10N 61 30W
Pointe-Claire, *Canada* **111 A11** 45 26N 73 50W
Pointe-Gatineau, *Canada* **111 A9** 45 28N 75 42W
Pointe-Noire, *Congo* **84 E2** 4 48 S 11 53 E
Poio, *Spain* **34 C2** 42 28N 8 41W
Poirino, *Italy* **28 D4** 44 56N 7 48 E
Poisonbush Ra., *Australia* **92 D3** 22 30 S 121 30 E
Poissonnier Pt., *Australia* **92 C2** 19 57 S 119 10 E
Poitiers, *France* **18 F7** 46 35N 0 20 E
Poitou, *France* **20 B3** 46 40N 0 10W
Poitou-Charentes □, *France* **20 B4** 46 10N 0 15 E
Poix-de-Picardie, *France* **19 C8** 49 47N 1 58 E
Poix-Terron, *France* **19 C11** 49 38N 4 38 E
Pojoaque, *U.S.A.* **115 J11** 35 54N 106 1W
Pokaran, *India* **66 F7** 27 0N 71 50 E
Pokataroo, *Australia* **95 D4** 29 30 S 148 36 E
Pokhara, *Nepal* **69 E10** 28 14N 83 58 E
Pokhvistnevo, *Russia* **48 D11** 53 36N 52 0 E
Poko, *Dem. Rep. of the Congo* **86 B2** 3 7N 26 52 E
Poko, *Sudan* **81 F3** 5 41N 31 55 E
Pokrov, *Russia* **46 E10** 55 55N 39 7 E
Pokrovsk = Engels, *Russia* **48 E8** 51 28N 46 6 E
Pokrovsk, *Russia* **51 C13** 61 29N 129 0 E
Pokrovskoye, *Russia* **47 J10** 47 25N 38 54 E
Pola = Pula, *Croatia* **29 D10** 44 54N 13 57 E
Pola, *Russia* **46 D7** 57 55N 32 0 E
Pola de Allande, *Spain* **34 B4** 43 16N 6 37W
Pola de Lena, *Spain* **34 B5** 43 10N 5 49W
Pola de Siero, *Spain* **34 B5** 43 24N 5 39W
Pola de Somiedo, *Spain* **34 B4** 43 5N 6 15W
Polacca, *U.S.A.* **115 J8** 35 50N 110 23W
Polan, *Iran* **71 E9** 25 30N 61 10 E
Pol'ana, *Slovak Rep.* **27 C12** 48 38N 19 29 E
Poland ■, *Europe* **45 G3** 52 0N 20 0 E
Polanica-Zdrój, *Poland* **45 H3** 50 24N 16 32 E
Połaniec, *Poland* **45 H8** 50 26N 21 17 E
Polanów, *Poland* **44 D3** 54 7N 16 41 E
Polar Bear Prov. Park, *Canada* **102 A2** 55 0N 83 45W
Polatlı, *Turkey* **72 C5** 39 36N 32 9 E
Polatsk, *Belarus* **46 E5** 55 30N 28 50 E
Polcura, *Chile* **126 D1** 37 17 S 71 43W
Połczyn-Zdrój, *Poland* **44 E3** 53 47N 16 5 E
Polessk, *Russia* **9 J19** 54 50N 21 8 E
Polesye = Pripet Marshes, *Europe* **47 F5** 52 10N 28 10 E
Polgar, *Hungary* **42 C6** 47 54N 21 6 E
Pŏlgyo-ri, *S. Korea* **57 G14** 34 51N 127 21 E
Poli, *Cameroon* **83 C7** 8 34N 13 15 E
Políaigos, *Greece* **38 E6** 36 45N 24 38 E
Policastro, G. di, *Italy* **31 C8** 40 0N 15 35 E
Police, *Poland* **44 E1** 53 33N 14 33 E
Polička, *Czech Rep.* **27 B9** 49 43N 16 15 E
Policoro, *Italy* **31 B9** 40 13N 16 41 E
Polignano a Mare, *Italy* **31 A9** 41 0N 17 13 E
Poligny, *France* **19 F12** 46 50N 5 42 E
Políkhnitas, *Greece* **39 B8** 39 6N 26 10 E
Polillo Is., *Phil.* **61 D4** 14 56N 122 0 E
Polillo Strait, *Phil.* **61 D4** 14 44N 121 51 E
Polis, *Cyprus* **36 D11** 35 2N 32 26 E
Polístena, *Italy* **31 D9** 38 24N 16 4 E
Políyiros, *Greece* **40 F7** 40 23N 23 25 E
Polk, *U.S.A.* **110 E5** 41 22N 79 56W
Polkowice, *Poland* **45 G3** 51 29N 16 3 E
Polla, *Italy* **31 B8** 40 31N 15 29 E
Pollachi, *India* **66 P10** 10 35N 77 0 E
Pollença, *Spain* **37 B10** 39 54N 3 1 E
Pollença, B. de, *Spain* **37 B10** 39 53N 3 8 E
Póllica, *Italy* **31 B8** 40 11N 15 3 E
Pollino, Mte., *Italy* **31 C9** 39 55N 16 11 E
Polna, *Russia* **46 C5** 58 31N 28 5 E
Polnovat, *Russia* **50 C7** 63 50N 65 54 E
Pology, *Ukraine* **47 J9** 47 29N 36 15 E
Polonne, *Ukraine* **47 G4** 50 6N 27 30 E
Polonnoye = Polonne, *Ukraine* **47 G4** 50 6N 27 30 E
Polski Trŭmbesh, *Bulgaria* **41 C9** 43 20N 25 38 E
Polsko Kosovo, *Bulgaria* **41 C9** 43 23N 25 38 E
Polson, *U.S.A.* **114 C6** 47 41N 114 9W
Poltár, *Slovak Rep.* **27 C12** 48 26N 19 48 E
Poltava, *Ukraine* **47 H8** 49 35N 34 35 E
Põltsamaa, *Estonia* **9 G21** 58 41N 25 58 E
Polunochnoye, *Russia* **50 C7** 60 52N 60 25 E
Põlva, *Estonia* **9 G22** 58 3N 27 3 E
Polynesia, *Pac. Oc.* **97 J11** 10 0 S 162 0W
Polynésie française = French Polynesia ■, *Pac. Oc.* **97 K13** 20 0 S 145 0W
Pomarance, *Italy* **28 E7** 43 18N 10 52 E
Pomaro, *Mexico* **118 D4** 18 20N 103 18W
Pombal, *Portugal* **34 F2** 39 55N 8 40W
Pómbia, *Greece* **36 E6** 35 0N 24 51 E
Pomene, *Mozam.* **89 C6** 22 53 S 35 33 E
Pomeroy, *Ohio, U.S.A.* **108 F4** 39 2N 82 2W
Pomeroy, *Wash., U.S.A.* **114 C5** 46 28N 117 36W
Pomézia, *Italy* **30 A5** 41 40N 12 30 E
Pomichna, *Ukraine* **47 H6** 48 13N 31 36 E
Pomona, *Australia* **95 D5** 26 22 S 152 52 E
Pomona, *U.S.A.* **117 L9** 34 4N 117 45W
Pomorie, *Bulgaria* **41 D11** 42 32N 27 41 E
Pomorskie □, *Poland* **44 D5** 54 30N 18 0 E
Pomorskie, Pojezierze, *Poland* **44 E3** 53 40N 16 37 E
Pomos, *Cyprus* **36 D11** 35 9N 32 33 E
Pomos, C., *Cyprus* **36 D11** 35 10N 32 33 E
Pompano Beach, *U.S.A.* **109 M5** 26 14N 80 8W
Pompei, *Italy* **31 B7** 40 45N 14 30 E
Pompey, *France* **19 D13** 48 46N 6 6 E
Pompeys Pillar, *U.S.A.* **114 D10** 45 59N 107 57W
Pompton Lakes, *U.S.A.* **111 F10** 41 0N 74 17W
Ponape = Pohnpei, *Micronesia* **96 G7** 6 55N 158 10 E
Ponask L., *Canada* **102 B1** 54 0N 92 41W
Ponca, *U.S.A.* **112 D6** 42 34N 96 43W
Ponca City, *U.S.A.* **113 G6** 36 42N 97 5W
Ponce, *Puerto Rico* **121 C6** 18 1N 66 37W
Ponchatoula, *U.S.A.* **113 K9** 30 26N 90 26W
Poncheville, L., *Canada* **102 B4** 50 10N 76 55W
Pond, *U.S.A.* **117 K7** 35 43N 119 20W
Pond Inlet, *Canada* **101 A12** 72 40N 77 0W
Pondicherry, *India* **66 P11** 11 59N 79 50 E
Ponds, I. of, *Canada* **103 B8** 53 27N 55 52W
Ponferrada, *Spain* **34 C4** 42 32N 6 35W
Pongo, Wadi →, *Sudan* **81 F2** 8 42N 27 40 E
Poniatowa, *Poland* **45 G9** 51 11N 22 3 E
Poniec, *Poland* **45 G3** 51 48N 16 50 E
Ponikva, *Slovenia* **29 B12** 46 16N 15 26 E
Ponnani, *India* **66 P9** 10 45N 75 59 E
Ponoka, *Canada* **104 C6** 52 42N 113 40W
Ponorogo, *Indonesia* **63 G14** 7 52 S 111 27 E
Pons = Ponts, *Spain* **32 D6** 41 55N 1 12 E
Pons, *France* **20 C3** 45 35N 0 34W
Ponsul →, *Portugal* **34 F3** 39 40N 7 31W
Pont-à-Mousson, *France* **19 D13** 48 54N 6 1 E
Pont-Audemer, *France* **18 C7** 49 21N 0 30 E
Pont-Aven, *France* **18 E3** 47 51N 3 47W
Pont Canavese, *Italy* **28 C4** 45 25N 7 36 E
Pont-d'Ain, *France* **19 F12** 46 3N 5 21 E
Pont-de-Roide, *France* **19 E13** 47 23N 6 45 E
Pont-de-Salars, *France* **20 D6** 44 18N 2 44 E
Pont-de-Vaux, *France* **19 F11** 46 26N 4 56 E
Pont-de-Veyle, *France* **19 F11** 46 17N 4 53 E
Pont-du-Château, *France* **19 G10** 45 47N 3 15 E
Pont-l'Abbé, *France* **18 E2** 47 52N 4 15W
Pont-l'Évêque, *France* **18 C7** 49 18N 0 11 E
Pont-St-Esprit, *France* **21 D8** 44 16N 4 40 E
Pont-St-Martin, *Italy* **28 C4** 45 36N 7 48 E
Pont-Ste-Maxence, *France* **19 C9** 49 18N 2 35 E
Pont-sur-Yonne, *France* **19 D10** 48 18N 3 10 E
Ponta do Sol, *Madeira* **37 D2** 32 42N 17 7W
Ponta Grossa, *Brazil* **127 B5** 25 7 S 50 10W
Ponta Pora, *Brazil* **127 A4** 22 20 S 55 35W
Pontacq, *France* **20 E3** 43 11N 0 8W
Pontailler-sur-Saône, *France* **19 E12** 47 13N 5 25 E
Pontarlier, *France* **19 F13** 46 54N 6 20 E
Pontassieve, *Italy* **29 E8** 43 46N 11 26 E
Pontaumur, *France* **20 C6** 45 52N 2 40 E
Pontcharra, *France* **21 C10** 45 26N 6 1 E
Pontchartrain L., *U.S.A.* **113 K10** 30 5N 90 5W
Pontchâteau, *France* **18 E4** 47 25N 2 5W
Ponte da Barca, *Portugal* **34 D2** 41 48N 8 25W
Ponte de Sor, *Portugal* **35 F2** 39 17N 8 1W
Ponte dell'Ólio, *Italy* **28 D6** 44 52N 9 39 E
Ponte di Legno, *Italy* **28 B7** 46 16N 10 31 E
Ponte do Lima, *Portugal* **34 D2** 41 46N 8 35W
Ponte do Pungué, *Mozam.* **87 F3** 19 30 S 34 33 E
Ponte-Leccia, *France* **21 F13** 42 28N 9 13 E
Ponte nelle Alpi, *Italy* **29 B9** 46 11N 12 16 E
Ponte Nova, *Brazil* **127 A7** 20 25 S 42 54W
Ponteareas, *Spain* **34 C2** 42 10N 8 28W
Pontebba, *Italy* **29 B10** 46 30N 13 18 E
Ponteceso, *Spain* **34 B2** 43 15N 8 54W
Pontecorvo, *Italy* **30 A6** 41 27N 13 40 E
Pontedeume, *Spain* **34 B2** 43 24N 8 10W
Ponteix, *Canada* **105 D7** 49 46N 107 29W
Pontevedra, *Spain* **34 C2** 42 26N 8 40W
Pontevedra □, *Spain* **34 C2** 42 25N 8 39W
Pontevedra, R. de →, *Spain* **34 C2** 42 22N 8 45W
Pontevico, *Italy* **28 C7** 45 16N 10 5 E
Pontiac, *Ill., U.S.A.* **112 E10** 40 53N 88 38W
Pontiac, *Mich., U.S.A.* **108 D4** 42 38N 83 18W
Pontian Kecil, *Malaysia* **65 M4** 1 29N 103 23 E
Pontianak, *Indonesia* **62 E3** 0 3 S 109 15 E
Pontine Is. = Ponziane, Ísole, *Italy* **30 B5** 40 55N 12 57 E
Pontine Mts. = Kuzey Anadolu Dağları, *Turkey* **72 B7** 41 30N 35 0 E
Pontínia, *Italy* **30 A6** 41 25N 13 2 E
Pontivy, *France* **18 D4** 48 5N 2 58W
Pontoise, *France* **19 C9** 49 3N 2 5 E
Ponton →, *Canada* **104 B5** 58 27N 116 11W
Pontorson, *France* **18 D5** 48 34N 1 30W
Pontrémoli, *Italy* **28 D6** 44 22N 9 53 E
Pontrieux, *France* **18 D3** 48 42N 3 10W
Ponts, *Spain* **32 D6** 41 55N 1 12 E
Pontypool, *Canada* **110 B6** 44 6N 78 38W
Pontypool, *U.K.* **13 F4** 51 42N 3 2W
Ponza, *Italy* **30 B5** 40 54N 12 58 E
Ponziane, Ísole, *Italy* **30 B5** 40 55N 12 57 E
Poochera, *Australia* **95 E1** 32 43 S 134 51 E
Poole, *U.K.* **13 G6** 50 43N 1 59W
Poole □, *U.K.* **13 G6** 50 43N 1 59W
Poona = Pune, *India* **66 K8** 18 29N 73 57 E
Pooncarie, *Australia* **95 E3** 33 22 S 142 31 E
Poopelloe L., *Australia* **95 E3** 31 40 S 144 0 E
Poopó, L. de, *Bolivia* **122 E4** 18 30 S 67 35W
Popayán, *Colombia* **124 C3** 2 27N 76 36W
Poperinge, *Belgium* **17 D2** 50 51N 2 42 E
Popilta L., *Australia* **95 E3** 33 10 S 141 42 E
Popina, *Bulgaria* **41 B10** 44 7N 26 57 E
Popio L., *Australia* **95 E3** 33 10 S 141 52 E
Poplar, *U.S.A.* **112 A2** 48 7N 105 12W
Poplar →, *Canada* **105 C9** 53 0N 97 19W
Poplar Bluff, *U.S.A.* **113 G9** 36 46N 90 24W
Poplarville, *U.S.A.* **113 K10** 30 51N 89 32W
Popocatépetl, Volcán, *Mexico* **119 D5** 19 2N 98 38W
Popokabaka, *Dem. Rep. of the Congo* **84 F3** 5 41 S 16 40 E
Pópoli, *Italy* **29 F10** 42 10N 13 50 E
Popovača, *Croatia* **29 C13** 45 30N 16 41 E
Popovo, *Bulgaria* **41 C10** 43 21N 26 18 E
Poppberg, *Germany* **25 F7** 49 26N 11 37 E
Poppi, *Italy* **29 E8** 43 43N 11 46 E
Poprad, *Slovak Rep.* **27 B13** 49 3N 20 18 E
Poprad →, *Slovak Rep.* **27 B13** 49 38N 20 42 E
Porali →, *Pakistan* **68 G2** 25 58N 66 26 E
Porbandar, *India* **66 J6** 21 44N 69 43 E
Porcher I., *Canada* **104 C2** 53 50N 130 30W
Porcuna, *Spain* **35 H6** 37 52N 4 11W
Porcupine →, *Canada* **105 B8** 59 11N 104 46W
Porcupine →, *U.S.A.* **100 B5** 66 34N 145 19W
Pordenone, *Italy* **29 C9** 45 57N 12 39 E
Pordim, *Bulgaria* **41 C8** 43 23N 24 51 E
Poreč, *Croatia* **29 C10** 45 14N 13 36 E
Poretskoye, *Russia* **48 C8** 55 9N 46 21 E
Pori, *Finland* **9 F19** 61 29N 21 48 E
Porí, *Greece* **38 F5** 35 58N 23 13 E
Porkhov, *Russia* **46 D5** 57 45N 29 38 E
Porlamar, *Venezuela* **124 A6** 10 57N 63 51W
Porlezza, *Italy* **28 B6** 46 2N 9 7 E
Porma →, *Spain* **34 C5** 42 49N 5 28W
Pornic, *France* **18 E4** 47 7N 2 5W
Poronaysk, *Russia* **51 E15** 49 13N 143 0 E
Póros, *Greece* **38 D5** 37 30N 23 30 E
Poroshiri-Dake, *Japan* **54 C11** 42 41N 142 52 E
Poroszló, *Hungary* **42 C5** 47 39N 20 40 E
Poroto Mts., *Tanzania* **87 D3** 9 0 S 33 30 E
Porpoise B., *Antarctica* **5 C9** 66 0 S 127 0 E
Porquerolles, Î. de, *France* **21 F10** 43 0N 6 13 E
Porrentruy, *Switz.* **25 H3** 47 25N 7 6 E
Porreres, *Spain* **37 B10** 39 31N 3 2 E
Porsangen, *Norway* **8 A21** 70 40N 25 40 E
Porsgrunn, *Norway* **9 G13** 59 10N 9 40 E
Port Alberni, *Canada* **104 D4** 49 14N 124 50W
Port Alfred, *S. Africa* **88 E4** 33 36 S 26 55 E
Port Alice, *Canada* **104 C3** 50 20N 127 25W
Port Allegany, *U.S.A.* **110 E6** 41 48N 78 17W
Port Allen, *U.S.A.* **113 K9** 30 27N 91 12W
Port Alma, *Australia* **94 C5** 23 38 S 150 53 E
Port Angeles, *U.S.A.* **116 B3** 48 7N 123 27W
Port Antonio, *Jamaica* **120 C4** 18 10N 76 30W
Port Aransas, *U.S.A.* **113 M6** 27 50N 97 4W
Port Arthur = Lüshun, *China* **57 E11** 38 45N 121 15 E
Port Arthur, *Australia* **94 G4** 43 7 S 147 50 E
Port Arthur, *U.S.A.* **113 L8** 29 54N 93 56W
Port au Choix, *Canada* **103 B8** 50 43N 57 22W
Port au Port B., *Canada* **103 C8** 48 40N 58 50W
Port-au-Prince, *Haiti* **121 C5** 18 40N 72 20W
Port Augusta, *Australia* **95 E2** 32 30 S 137 50 E
Port Austin, *U.S.A.* **110 B2** 44 3N 83 1W
Port Bell, *Uganda* **86 B3** 0 18N 32 35 E
Port Bergé Vaovao, *Madag.* **89 B8** 15 33 S 47 40 E
Port Blandford, *Canada* **103 C9** 48 20N 54 10W
Port-Bouët, *Ivory C.* **82 D4** 5 16N 3 57W
Port Bradshaw, *Australia* **94 A2** 12 30 S 137 20 E
Port Broughton, *Australia* **95 E2** 33 37 S 137 56 E
Port Burwell, *Canada* **110 D4** 42 40N 80 48W
Port Canning, *India* **69 H13** 22 23N 88 40 E
Port-Cartier, *Canada* **103 B6** 50 2N 66 50W
Port Chalmers, *N.Z.* **91 L3** 45 49 S 170 30 E
Port Charlotte, *U.S.A.* **109 M4** 26 59N 82 6W
Port Chester, *U.S.A.* **111 F11** 41 0N 73 40W
Port Clements, *Canada* **104 C2** 53 40N 132 10W
Port Clinton, *U.S.A.* **108 E4** 41 31N 82 56W
Port Colborne, *Canada* **102 D4** 42 50N 79 10W
Port Coquitlam, *Canada* **104 D4** 49 15N 122 45W
Port Credit, *Canada* **110 C5** 43 33N 79 35W
Port Curtis, *Australia* **94 C5** 23 57 S 151 20 E
Port d'Alcúdia, *Spain* **37 B10** 39 50N 3 7 E
Port Dalhousie, *Canada* **110 C5** 43 13N 79 16W
Port Darwin, *Australia* **92 B5** 12 24 S 130 45 E
Port Darwin, *Falk. Is.* **128 G5** 51 50 S 59 0W
Port Davey, *Australia* **94 G4** 43 16 S 145 55 E
Port-de-Bouc, *France* **21 E8** 43 24N 4 59 E
Port-de-Paix, *Haiti* **121 C5** 19 50N 72 50W
Port de Pollença, *Spain* **37 B10** 39 54N 3 4 E
Port de Sóller, *Spain* **37 B9** 39 48N 2 42 E
Port Dickson, *Malaysia* **65 L3** 2 30N 101 49 E
Port Douglas, *Australia* **94 B4** 16 30 S 145 30 E
Port Dover, *Canada* **110 D4** 42 47N 80 12W
Port Edward, *Canada* **104 C2** 54 12N 130 10W
Port Elgin, *Canada* **102 D3** 44 25N 81 25W
Port Elizabeth, *S. Africa* **88 E4** 33 58 S 25 40 E
Port Ellen, *U.K.* **14 F2** 55 38N 6 11W
Port-en-Bessin, *France* **18 C6** 49 21N 0 45W
Port Erin, *U.K.* **12 C3** 54 5N 4 45W
Port Essington, *Australia* **92 B5** 11 15 S 132 10 E
Port Etienne = Nouâdhibou, *Mauritania* **78 D2** 20 54N 17 0W
Port Ewen, *U.S.A.* **111 E11** 41 54N 73 59W
Port Fairy, *Australia* **95 F3** 38 22 S 142 12 E
Port Fouâd = Bûr Fuad, *Egypt* **80 H8** 31 15N 32 20 E
Port Gamble, *U.S.A.* **116 C4** 47 51N 122 35W
Port-Gentil, *Gabon* **84 E1** 0 40 S 8 50 E
Port Germein, *Australia* **95 E2** 33 1 S 138 1 E
Port Gibson, *U.S.A.* **113 K9** 31 58N 90 59W
Port Glasgow, *U.K.* **14 F4** 55 56N 4 41W
Port Harcourt, *Nigeria* **83 E6** 4 40N 7 10 E
Port Hardy, *Canada* **104 C3** 50 41N 127 30W
Port Harrison = Inukjuak, *Canada* **101 C12** 58 25N 78 15W
Port Hawkesbury, *Canada* **103 C7** 45 36N 61 22W
Port Hedland, *Australia* **92 D2** 20 25 S 118 35 E
Port Henry, *U.S.A.* **111 B11** 44 3N 73 28W
Port Hood, *Canada* **103 C7** 46 0N 61 32W
Port Hope, *Canada* **102 D4** 43 56N 78 20W
Port Hope, *U.S.A.* **110 C2** 43 57N 82 43W
Port Hope Simpson, *Canada* **103 B8** 52 33N 56 18W
Port Hueneme, *U.S.A.* **117 L7** 34 7N 119 12W
Port Huron, *U.S.A.* **110 D2** 42 58N 82 26W
Port Iliç, *Azerbaijan* **73 C13** 38 53N 48 47 E
Port Jefferson, *U.S.A.* **111 F11** 40 57N 73 3W
Port Jervis, *U.S.A.* **111 E10** 41 22N 74 41W
Port-Joinville, *France* **18 F4** 46 45N 2 23W
Port Katon, *Russia* **47 J10** 46 52N 38 46 E
Port Kelang = Pelabuhan Kelang, *Malaysia* **65 L3** 3 0N 101 23 E
Port Kenny, *Australia* **95 E1** 33 10 S 134 41 E
Port-la-Nouvelle, *France* **20 E7** 43 1N 3 3 E
Port Lairge = Waterford, *Ireland* **15 D4** 52 15N 7 8W
Port Laoise, *Ireland* **15 C4** 53 2N 7 18W
Port Lavaca, *U.S.A.* **113 L6** 28 37N 96 38W
Port Leyden, *U.S.A.* **111 C9** 43 35N 75 21W
Port Lincoln, *Australia* **95 E2** 34 42 S 135 52 E
Port Loko, *S. Leone* **82 D2** 8 48N 12 46W
Port Louis, *France* **18 E3** 47 42N 3 22W
Port Louis, *Mauritius* **77 H9** 20 10 S 57 30 E
Port Lyautey = Kenitra, *Morocco* **78 B4** 34 15N 6 40W
Port MacDonnell, *Australia* **95 F3** 38 5 S 140 48 E
Port McNeill, *Canada* **104 C3** 50 35N 127 6W
Port Macquarie, *Australia* **95 E5** 31 25 S 152 25 E
Port Maria, *Jamaica* **120 C4** 18 25N 76 55W
Port Matilda, *U.S.A.* **110 F6** 40 48N 78 3W
Port Mellon, *Canada* **104 D4** 49 32N 123 31W
Port-Menier, *Canada* **103 C7** 49 51N 64 15W
Port Moody, *Canada* **116 A4** 49 17N 122 51W
Port Morant, *Jamaica* **120 C4** 17 54N 76 19W
Port Moresby, *Papua N. G.* **96 H6** 9 24 S 147 8 E
Port Musgrave, *Australia* **94 A3** 11 55 S 141 50 E
Port-Navalo, *France* **18 E4** 47 34N 2 54W
Port Neches, *U.S.A.* **113 L8** 30 0N 93 59W
Port Nolloth, *S. Africa* **88 D2** 29 17 S 16 52 E
Port Nouveau-Québec = Kangiqsualujjuaq, *Canada* **101 C13** 58 30N 65 59W
Port of Spain, *Trin. & Tob.* **121 D7** 10 40N 61 31W
Port Orange, *U.S.A.* **109 L5** 29 9N 80 59W
Port Orchard, *U.S.A.* **116 C4** 47 32N 122 38W
Port Orford, *U.S.A.* **114 E1** 42 45N 124 30W
Port Pegasus, *N.Z.* **91 M1** 47 12 S 167 41 E
Port Perry, *Canada* **102 D4** 44 6N 78 56W
Port Phillip B., *Australia* **95 F3** 38 10 S 144 50 E
Port Pirie, *Australia* **95 E2** 33 10 S 138 1 E
Port Radium = Echo Bay, *Canada* **100 B8** 66 5N 117 55W
Port Renfrew, *Canada* **104 D4** 48 30N 124 20W
Port Roper, *Australia* **94 A2** 14 45 S 135 25 E
Port Rowan, *Canada* **110 D4** 42 40N 80 30W
Port Safaga = Bûr Safâga, *Egypt* **70 E2** 26 43N 33 57 E
Port Said = Bûr Sa'îd, *Egypt* **80 H8** 31 16N 32 18 E
Port St. Joe, *U.S.A.* **109 L3** 29 49N 85 18W
Port St. Johns = Umzimvubu, *S. Africa* **89 E4** 31 38 S 29 33 E
Port-St-Louis-du-Rhône, *France* **21 E8** 43 23N 4 49 E
Port St. Lucie, *U.S.A.* **109 M5** 27 20N 80 20W
Port-Ste-Marie, *France* **20 D4** 44 15N 0 25 E
Port Sanilac, *U.S.A.* **110 C2** 43 26N 82 33W
Port Severn, *Canada* **110 B5** 44 48N 79 43W
Port Shepstone, *S. Africa* **89 E5** 30 44 S 30 28 E
Port Simpson, *Canada* **104 C2** 54 30N 130 20W
Port Stanley = Stanley, *Falk. Is.* **128 G5** 51 40 S 59 51W
Port Stanley, *Canada* **102 D3** 42 40N 81 10W
Port Sudan = Bûr Sûdân, *Sudan* **80 D4** 19 32N 37 9 E
Port Sulphur, *U.S.A.* **113 L10** 29 29N 89 42W
Port-sur-Saône, *France* **19 E13** 47 42N 6 2 E
Port Talbot, *U.K.* **13 F4** 51 35N 3 47W
Port Taufiq = Bûr Taufiq, *Egypt* **80 J8** 29 54N 32 32 E
Port Townsend, *U.S.A.* **116 B4** 48 7N 122 45W
Port-Vendres, *France* **20 F7** 42 32N 3 8 E
Port Vila, *Vanuatu* **96 J8** 17 45 S 168 18 E
Port Wakefield, *Australia* **95 E2** 34 12 S 138 10 E
Port Washington, *U.S.A.* **108 D2** 43 23N 87 53W
Port Weld = Kuala Sepetang, *Malaysia* **65 K3** 4 49N 100 28 E
Portadown, *U.K.* **15 B5** 54 25N 6 27W
Portaferry, *U.K.* **15 B6** 54 23N 5 33W
Portage, *Pa., U.S.A.* **110 F6** 40 23N 78 41W
Portage, *Wis., U.S.A.* **112 D10** 43 33N 89 28W
Portage La Prairie, *Canada* **105 D9** 49 58N 98 18W
Portageville, *U.S.A.* **113 G10** 36 26N 89 42W
Portalegre, *Portugal* **35 F3** 39 19N 7 25W
Portalegre □, *Portugal* **35 F3** 39 20N 7 40W
Portales, *U.S.A.* **113 H3** 34 11N 103 20W
Portarlington, *Ireland* **15 C4** 53 9N 7 14W
Portbou, *Spain* **32 C8** 42 25N 3 9 E
Portel, *Portugal* **35 G3** 38 19N 7 41W
Porter L., *N.W.T., Canada* **105 A7** 61 41N 108 5W
Porter L., *Sask., Canada* **105 B7** 56 20N 107 20W
Porterville, *S. Africa* **88 E2** 33 0 S 19 0 E
Porterville, *U.S.A.* **116 J8** 36 4N 119 1W
Portes-lès-Valence, *France* **21 D8** 44 52N 4 54 E
Porthcawl, *U.K.* **13 F4** 51 29N 3 42W
Porthill, *U.S.A.* **114 B5** 48 59N 116 30W
Porthmadog, *U.K.* **12 E3** 52 55N 4 8W
Portile de Fier, *Europe* **42 F7** 44 44N 22 30 E
Portimão, *Portugal* **35 H2** 37 8N 8 32W
Portishead, *U.K.* **13 F5** 51 29N 2 46W
Portiţei, Gura, *Romania* **43 F14** 44 41N 29 0 E
Portknockie, *U.K.* **14 D6** 57 42N 2 51W
Portland, *N.S.W., Australia* **95 E5** 33 20 S 150 0 E
Portland, *Vic., Australia* **95 F3** 38 20 S 141 35 E
Portland, *Canada* **111 B8** 44 42N 76 12W
Portland, *Conn., U.S.A.* **111 E12** 41 34N 72 38W
Portland, *Maine, U.S.A.* **101 D12** 43 39N 70 16W
Portland, *Mich., U.S.A.* **108 D3** 42 52N 84 54W
Portland, *Oreg., U.S.A.* **116 E4** 45 32N 122 37W
Portland, *Pa., U.S.A.* **111 F9** 40 55N 75 6W
Portland, *Tex., U.S.A.* **113 M6** 27 53N 97 20W
Portland, I. of, *U.K.* **13 G5** 50 33N 2 26W
Portland B., *Australia* **95 F3** 38 15 S 141 45 E
Portland Bill, *U.K.* **13 G5** 50 31N 2 28W
Portland Canal, *U.S.A.* **104 B2** 55 56N 130 0W
Portmadoc = Porthmadog, *U.K.* **12 E3** 52 55N 4 8W
Porto, *France* **21 F12** 42 16N 8 42 E
Porto, *Portugal* **34 D2** 41 8N 8 40W
Porto □, *Portugal* **34 D2** 41 8N 8 20W
Porto, G. de, *France* **21 F12** 42 17N 8 34 E
Pôrto Alegre, *Brazil* **127 C5** 30 5 S 51 10W
Porto Amboim = Gunza, *Angola* **84 G2** 10 50 S 13 50 E
Porto Azzurro, *Italy* **28 F7** 42 46N 10 24 E
Porto Cristo, *Spain* **37 B10** 39 33N 3 20 E
Pôrto de Móz, *Brazil* **125 D8** 1 41 S 52 13W
Porto Empédocle, *Italy* **30 E6** 37 17N 13 32 E
Pôrto Esperança, *Brazil* **124 G7** 19 37 S 57 29W
Pôrto Franco, *Brazil* **125 E9** 6 20 S 47 24W
Pôrto Lágos, *Greece* **41 E9** 41 1N 25 6 E
Pôrto Mendes, *Brazil* **127 A5** 24 30 S 54 15W
Porto Moniz, *Madeira* **37 D2** 32 52N 17 11W
Pôrto Murtinho, *Brazil* **124 H7** 21 45 S 57 55W
Pôrto Nacional, *Brazil* **125 F9** 10 40 S 48 30W
Porto-Novo, *Benin* **83 D5** 6 23N 2 42 E
Porto Petro, *Spain* **37 B10** 39 22N 3 13 E
Porto San Giórgio, *Italy* **29 E10** 43 11N 13 48 E
Porto Sant' Elpídio, *Italy* **29 E10** 43 15N 13 43 E
Porto Santo, I. de, *Madeira* **78 B2** 33 45N 16 25W
Porto Santo Stéfano, *Italy* **28 F8** 42 26N 11 7 E
Pôrto São José, *Brazil* **127 A5** 22 43 S 53 10W
Pôrto Seguro, *Brazil* **125 G11** 16 26 S 39 5W
Porto Tolle, *Italy* **29 D9** 44 56N 12 22 E
Porto Tórres, *Italy* **30 B1** 40 50N 8 24 E
Pôrto União, *Brazil* **127 B5** 26 10 S 51 10W
Pôrto Válter, *Brazil* **124 E4** 8 15 S 72 40W
Porto-Vecchio, *France* **21 G13** 41 35N 9 16 E
Pôrto Velho, *Brazil* **124 E6** 8 46 S 63 54W
Portobelo, *Panama* **120 E4** 9 35N 79 42W
Portoferráio, *Italy* **28 F7** 42 48N 10 20 E
Portogruaro, *Italy* **29 C9** 45 47N 12 50 E
Portola, *U.S.A.* **116 F6** 39 49N 120 28W
Portomaggiore, *Italy* **29 D8** 44 42N 11 48 E
Portoscuso, *Italy* **30 C1** 39 12N 8 24 E
Portovénere, *Italy* **28 D6** 44 3N 9 51 E
Portoviejo, *Ecuador* **124 D2** 1 7 S 80 28W
Portpatrick, *U.K.* **14 G3** 54 51N 5 7W
Portree, *U.K.* **14 D2** 57 25N 6 12W
Portrush, *U.K.* **15 A5** 55 12N 6 40W
Portsmouth, *Domin.* **121 C7** 15 34N 61 27W
Portsmouth, *U.K.* **13 G6** 50 48N 1 6W
Portsmouth, *N.H., U.S.A.* **109 D10** 43 5N 70 45W
Portsmouth, *Ohio, U.S.A.* **108 F4** 38 44N 82 57W
Portsmouth, *R.I., U.S.A.* **111 E13** 41 36N 71 15W
Portsmouth, *Va., U.S.A.* **108 G7** 36 50N 76 18W
Portsmouth □, *U.K.* **13 G6** 50 48N 1 6W
Portsoy, *U.K.* **14 D6** 57 41N 2 41W
Portstewart, *U.K.* **15 A5** 55 11N 6 43W
Porttipahtan tekojärvi, *Finland* **8 B22** 68 5N 26 40 E
Portugal ■, *Europe* **34 F3** 40 0N 8 0W
Portugalete, *Spain* **32 B1** 43 19N 3 4W
Portumna, *Ireland* **15 C3** 53 6N 8 14W
Portville, *U.S.A.* **110 D6** 42 3N 78 20W
Porvenir, *Chile* **128 G2** 53 10 S 70 16W
Porvoo, *Finland* **9 F21** 60 24N 25 40 E
Porzuna, *Spain* **35 F6** 39 9N 4 9W
Posada, *Italy* **30 B2** 40 38N 9 43 E
Posada →, *Italy* **30 B2** 40 39N 9 45 E
Posadas, *Argentina* **127 B4** 27 30 S 55 50W
Posadas, *Spain* **35 H5** 37 47N 5 11W
Poschiavo, *Switz.* **25 J6** 46 19N 10 4 E
Posets, *Spain* **32 C5** 42 39N 0 25 E
Poshan = Boshan, *China* **57 F9** 36 28N 117 49 E
Posht-e-Badam, *Iran* **71 C7** 33 2N 55 23 E
Posídhion, Ákra, *Greece* **40 G7** 39 57N 23 30 E
Posidium, *Greece* **39 F9** 35 30N 27 10 E
Poso, *Indonesia* **63 E6** 1 20 S 120 55 E
Posong, *S. Korea* **57 G14** 34 46N 127 5 E
Posse, *Brazil* **125 F9** 14 4 S 46 18W
Possession I., *Antarctica* **5 D11** 72 4 S 172 0 E
Pössneck, *Germany* **24 E7** 50 42N 11 35 E
Possum Kingdom L., *U.S.A.* **113 J5** 32 52N 98 26W
Post, *U.S.A.* **113 J4** 33 12N 101 23W
Post Falls, *U.S.A.* **114 C5** 47 43N 116 57W
Postavy = Pastavy, *Belarus* **9 J22** 55 4N 26 50 E
Poste-de-la-Baleine = Kuujjuarapik, *Canada* **102 A4** 55 20N 77 35W
Postmasburg, *S. Africa* **88 D3** 28 18 S 23 5 E
Postojna, *Slovenia* **29 C11** 45 46N 14 12 E
Poston, *U.S.A.* **117 M12** 34 0N 114 24W
Postville, *Canada* **103 B8** 54 54N 59 47W
Potamós, *Andikíthira, Greece* **38 F5** 35 52N 23 15 E
Potamós, *Kíthira, Greece* **38 E4** 36 15N 22 58 E
Potchefstroom, *S. Africa* **88 D4** 26 41 S 27 7 E
Potcoava, *Romania* **43 F9** 44 30N 24 39 E
Poteau, *U.S.A.* **113 H7** 35 3N 94 37W
Poteet, *U.S.A.* **113 L5** 29 2N 98 35W
Potenza, *Italy* **31 B8** 40 38N 15 48 E
Potenza →, *Italy* **29 E10** 43 25N 13 40 E
Potenza Picena, *Italy* **29 E10** 43 22N 13 37 E
Poteriteri, L., *N.Z.* **91 M1** 46 5 S 167 10 E
Potgietersrus, *S. Africa* **89 C4** 24 10 S 28 55 E
Poti, *Georgia* **49 J5** 42 10N 41 38 E
Potiskum, *Nigeria* **83 C7** 11 39N 11 2 E
Potlogi, *Romania* **43 F10** 44 34N 25 34 E
Potomac →, *U.S.A.* **108 G7** 38 0N 76 23W
Potosí, *Bolivia* **124 G5** 19 38 S 65 50W
Potosi Mt., *U.S.A.* **117 K11** 35 57N 115 29W
Pototan, *Phil.* **61 F5** 10 54N 122 38 E
Potrerillos, *Chile* **126 B2** 26 30 S 69 30W
Potsdam, *Germany* **24 C9** 52 25N 13 4 E
Potsdam, *U.S.A.* **111 B10** 44 40N 74 59W
Pottenstein, *Germany* **25 F7** 49 46N 11 24 E
Pottersville, *U.S.A.* **111 C11** 43 43N 73 50W
Pottery Hill = Abu Ballas, *Egypt* **80 C2** 24 26N 27 36 E
Pottstown, *U.S.A.* **111 F9** 40 15N 75 39W
Pottsville, *U.S.A.* **111 F8** 40 41N 76 12W
Pottuvil, *Sri Lanka* **66 R12** 6 55N 81 50 E
P'otzu, *Taiwan* **59 F13** 23 30N 120 25 E
Pouancé, *France* **18 E5** 47 44N 1 10W
Pouce Coupé, *Canada* **104 B4** 55 40N 120 10W
Poughkeepsie, *U.S.A.* **111 E11** 41 42N 73 56W

Rakata, Pulau, *Indonesia* . . . . **62 F3** 6 10 S 105 20 E
Rakhiv, *Ukraine* . . . . . **47 H3** 48 3N 24 12 E
Rakhni, *Pakistan* . . . . . **68 D3** 30 4N 69 56 E
Rakhni →, *Pakistan* . . **68 E3** 29 31N 69 36 E
Rakitnoye, *Russia* . . . . **54 B7** 45 36N 134 17 E
Rakitovo, *Bulgaria* . . . . **41 E8** 41 59N 24 5 E
Rakoniewice, *Poland* . . **45 F3** 52 10N 16 16 E
Rakops, *Botswana* . . . . **88 C3** 21 1 S 24 28 E
Rakovica, *Croatia* . . . . **29 D12** 44 59N 15 38 E
Rakovník, *Czech Rep.* . . **26 A6** 50 6N 13 42 E
Rakovski, *Bulgaria* . . . . **41 D8** 42 21N 24 57 E
Rakvere, *Estonia* . . . . . **9 G22** 59 20N 26 25 E
Raleigh, *U.S.A.* **109 H6** 35 47N 78 39W
Ralja, *Serbia, Yug.* . . . **40 B4** 44 33N 20 34 E
Ralls, *U.S.A.* **113 J4** 33 41N 101 24W
Ralston, *U.S.A.* **110 E8** 41 30N 76 57W
Ram →, *Canada* **104 A4** 62 1N 123 41W
Rām Allāh, *West Bank* **75 D4** 31 55N 35 10 E
Rama, *Nic.* **120 D3** 12 9N 84 15W
Ramacca, *Italy* . . . . . . **31 E7** 37 23N 14 42 E
Ramakona, *India* . . . . **69 J8** 21 43N 78 50 E
Ramales de la Victoria, *Spain* **34 B7** 43 15N 3 28W
Raman, *Thailand* . . . . **65 J3** 6 29N 101 18 E
Ramanathapuram, *India* . . . . **66 Q11** 9 25N 78 55 E
Ramanetaka, B. de, *Madag.* . . . . **89 A8** 14 13 S 47 52 E
Ramanujganj, *India* . . **69 H10** 23 48N 83 42 E
Ramat Gan, *Israel* . . . . **75 C3** 32 4N 34 48 E
Ramatlhabama, *S. Africa* . . . . **88 D4** 25 37 S 25 33 E
Ramban, *India* . . . . **69 C6** 33 14N 75 12 E
Rambervillers, *France* . **19 D13** 48 20N 6 38 E
Rambipuji, *Indonesia* . . **63 H15** 8 12 S 113 37 E
Rambouillet, *France* . . . **19 D8** 48 39N 1 50 E
Rame Hd., *Australia* . . **95 F4** 37 47 S 149 30 E
Ramechhap, *Nepal* . . . **69 F12** 27 25N 86 10 E
Ramenskoye, *Russia* . . **46 E10** 55 32N 38 15 E
Ramganga →, *India* . . **69 F8** 27 5N 79 58 E
Ramgarh, *Bihar, India* **69 H11** 23 40N 85 35 E
Ramgarh, *Raj., India* . **68 F6** 27 16N 75 14 E
Ramgarh, *Raj., India* . **68 F4** 27 30N 70 36 E
Rāmhormoz, *Iran* . . . . **71 D6** 31 15N 49 35 E
Ramīān, *Iran* . . . . **71 B7** 37 3N 55 16 E
Ramingining, *Australia* **94 A2** 12 19 S 135 3 E
Ramla, *Israel* . . . . **75 D3** 31 55N 34 52 E
Ramlu, *Eritrea* . . . . **81 E5** 13 32N 41 40 E
Râmna →, *Romania* . . **43 E12** 45 36N 27 3 E
Ramnad = Ramanathapuram, *India* . . . . **66 Q11** 9 25N 78 55 E
Ramnagar, *Jammu & Kashmir, India* . . . . **69 C6** 32 47N 75 18 E
Ramnagar, *Ut. P., India* **69 E8** 29 24N 79 7 E
Ramnäs, *Sweden* . . . . . **10 E10** 59 46N 16 12 E
Râmnicu Sărat, *Romania* . . . . **43 E12** 45 26N 27 3 E
Râmnicu Vâlcea, *Romania* . . . . **43 E9** 45 9N 24 21 E
Ramon, *Russia* . . . . **47 G10** 51 55N 39 21 E
Ramona, *U.S.A.* **117 M10** 33 2N 116 52W
Ramonville-St-Agne, *France* . . . . **20 E5** 43 33N 1 28 E
Ramore, *Canada* **102 C3** 48 30N 80 25W
Ramos →, *Nigeria* . . . **83 D6** 5 8N 5 22 E
Ramotswa, *Botswana* . . **88 C4** 24 50 S 25 52 E
Rampur, *H.P., India* . . . **68 D7** 31 26N 77 43 E
Rampur, *Mad. P., India* **68 H5** 23 25N 73 53 E
Rampur, *Ut. P., India* . **69 E8** 28 50N 79 5 E
Rampur Hat, *India* . . . . **69 G12** 24 10N 87 50 E
Rampura, *India* . . . . **68 G6** 24 30N 75 27 E
Ramrama Tola, *India* . . **69 J8** 21 52N 79 55 E
Ramree I., *Burma* . . . . **67 K19** 19 0N 94 0 E
Rāmsar, *Iran* . . . . **71 B6** 36 53N 50 41 E
Ramsey, *U.K.* **12 C3** 54 20N 4 22W
Ramsey, *U.S.A.* **111 E10** 41 4N 74 9W
Ramsey L., *Canada* . . . **102 C3** 47 13N 82 15W
Ramsgate, *U.K.* . . . . . . **13 F9** 51 20N 1 25 E
Ramsjö, *Sweden* . . . . . **10 B9** 62 11N 15 37 E
Ramstein, *Germany* . . . **25 F3** 49 27N 7 32 E
Ramtek, *India* . . . . **66 J11** 21 20N 79 15 E
Ramvik, *Sweden* . . . . . **10 B11** 62 49N 17 51 E
Rana Pratap Sagar Dam, *India* . . . . **68 G6** 24 58N 75 38 E
Ranaghat, *India* . . . . . **69 H13** 23 15N 88 35 E
Ranahu, *Pakistan* . . . . **68 G3** 25 55N 69 45 E
Ranau, *Malaysia* . . . . . **62 C5** 6 2N 116 40 E
Rancagua, *Chile* . . . . . **126 C1** 34 10 S 70 50W
Rance →, *France* **18 D5** 48 34N 1 59W
Rancheria →, *Canada* . **104 A3** 60 13N 129 7W
Ranchester, *U.S.A.* . . . **114 D10** 44 54N 107 10W
Ranchi, *India* . . . . **69 H11** 23 19N 85 27 E
Rancho Cucamonga, *U.S.A.* **117 L9** 34 10N 117 30W
Randalstown, *U.K.* **15 B5** 54 45N 6 19W
Randan, *France* . . . . . . **19 F10** 46 2N 3 21 E
Randazzo, *Italy* . . . . . . **31 E7** 37 53N 14 57 E
Randers, *Denmark* . . . . **11 H4** 56 29N 10 1 E
Randers Fjord, *Denmark* . . . . **11 H4** 56 37N 10 20 E
Randfontein, *S. Africa* **89 D4** 26 8 S 27 45 E
Randle, *U.S.A.* **116 D5** 46 32N 121 57W
Randolph, *Mass., U.S.A.* **111 D13** 42 10N 71 2W
Randolph, *N.Y., U.S.A.* **110 D6** 42 10N 78 59W
Randolph, *Utah, U.S.A.* **114 F8** 41 40N 111 11W
Randolph, *Vt., U.S.A.* . **111 C12** 43 55N 72 40W
Randsburg, *U.S.A.* **117 K9** 35 22N 117 39W
Råne älv →, *Sweden* . . **8 D20** 65 50N 22 20 E
Rangae, *Thailand* . . . . **65 J3** 6 19N 101 44 E
Rangaunu B., *N.Z.* . . . . **91 F4** 34 51 S 173 15 E
Rangeley, *U.S.A.* **111 B14** 44 58N 70 39W
Rangeley L., *U.S.A.* . . . **111 B14** 44 55N 70 43W
Rangely, *U.S.A.* **114 F9** 40 5N 108 48W
Ranger, *U.S.A.* **113 J5** 32 28N 98 41W
Rangia, *India* . . . . **67 F17** 26 28N 91 38 E
Rangiora, *N.Z.* . . . . **91 K4** 43 19 S 172 36 E
Rangitaiki →, *N.Z.* . . . **91 G6** 37 54 S 176 49 E
Rangitata →, *N.Z.* . . . **91 K3** 43 45 S 171 15 E
Rangkasbitung, *Indonesia* . . . . **63 G12** 6 21 S 106 15 E
Rangon →, *Burma* . . . **67 L20** 16 28N 96 40 E
Rangoon, *Burma* . . . . . **67 L20** 16 45N 96 20 E
Rangpur, *Bangla.* . . . . **67 G16** 25 42N 89 22 E
Rangsit, *Thailand* . . . . **64 F3** 13 59N 100 37 E
Ranibennur, *India* . . . . **66 M9** 14 35N 75 30 E
Raniganj, *Ut. P., India* **69 F9** 27 3N 82 13 E
Raniganj, *W. Bengal, India* . . . . **67 H15** 23 40N 87 5 E
Ranikhet, *India* . . . . . . **69 E8** 29 39N 79 25 E
Raniwara, *India* . . . . . . **66 G8** 24 50N 72 10 E
Rāniyah, *Iraq* . . . . **70 B5** 36 15N 44 53 E
Ranka, *India* . . . . **69 H10** 23 59N 83 47 E
Ranken →, *Australia* . **94 C2** 20 31 S 137 36 E
Rankin, *U.S.A.* **113 K4** 31 13N 101 56W
Rankin Inlet, *Canada* . **100 B10** 62 30N 93 0W
Rankins Springs, *Australia* . . . . **95 E4** 33 49 S 146 14 E
Rankweil, *Austria* . . . . **26 D2** 47 17N 9 39 E
Rannoch, L., *U.K.* **14 E4** 56 41N 4 20W
Rannoch Moor, *U.K.* . . **14 E4** 56 38N 4 48W
Ranobe, Helodranon' i, *Madag.* . . . . **89 C7** 23 3 S 43 33 E
Ranohira, *Madag.* . . . . **89 C8** 22 29 S 45 24 E
Ranomafana, *Toamasina, Madag.* . **89 B8** 18 57 S 48 50 E
Ranomafana, *Toliara, Madag.* . . . . **89 C8** 24 34 S 47 0 E
Ranomena, *Madag.* . . . . **89 C8** 23 25 S 47 17 E
Ranong, *Thailand* . . . . **65 H2** 9 56N 98 40 E
Ranotsara Nord, *Madag.* . . . . **89 C8** 22 48 S 46 36 E
Rānsa, *Iran* . . . . **71 C6** 33 39N 48 18 E
Ransiki, *Indonesia* . . . . **63 E8** 1 30 S 134 10 E
Rantabe, *Madag.* . . . . . **89 B8** 15 42 S 49 39 E
Rantauprapat, *Indonesia* . . . . **62 D1** 2 15N 99 50 E
Rantemario, *Indonesia* **63 E5** 3 15 S 119 57 E
Rantoul, *U.S.A.* **108 E1** 40 19N 88 9W
Ranum, *Denmark* . . . . . **11 H3** 56 54N 9 14 E
Ranyah, W. →, *Si. Arabia* . . . . **80 C5** 21 18N 43 20 E
Raon l'Étape, *France* . **19 D13** 48 24N 6 50 E
Raoping, *China* . . . . . . **59 F11** 23 42N 117 1 E
Raoyang, *China* . . . . . . **56 E8** 38 15N 115 45 E
Rapa, *Pac. Oc.* . . . . **97 K13** 27 35 S 144 20W
Rapallo, *Italy* . . . . **28 D6** 44 21N 9 14 E
Rapar, *India* . . . . **68 H4** 23 34N 70 38 E
Rāpch, *Iran* . . . . **71 E8** 25 40N 59 15 E
Raper, C., *Canada* **101 B13** 69 44N 67 6W
Rapid City, *U.S.A.* **112 D3** 44 5N 103 14W
Rapid River, *U.S.A.* . . . **108 C2** 45 55N 86 58W
Rapla, *Estonia* . . . . **9 G21** 59 1N 24 52 E
Rapti →, *India* . . . . . . **69 F10** 26 18N 83 41 E
Rapu Rapu I., *Phil.* . . . . **61 E6** 13 12N 124 9 E
Raqaba ez Zarqa →, *Sudan* . . . . **81 F2** 9 14N 29 44 E
Raquette →, *U.S.A.* . . . **111 B10** 45 0N 74 42W
Raquette Lake, *U.S.A.* . **111 C10** 43 49N 74 40W
Rarotonga, *Cook Is.* . . . **97 K12** 21 30 S 160 0W
Ra's al 'Ayn, *Syria* . . . **70 B4** 36 45N 40 12 E
Ra's al Khaymah, *U.A.E.* . . . . **71 E7** 25 50N 55 59 E
Râs el Mâ, *Mali* **82 B4** 16 35N 4 30W
Ras Ghârib, *Egypt* . . . . **80 B3** 28 6N 33 18 E
Ras Mallap, *Egypt* . . . . **80 B3** 29 18N 32 50 E
Rasca, Pta. de la, *Canary Is.* **37 G3** 27 59N 16 41W
Râşcani, *Moldova* . . . . **43 C12** 47 58N 27 33 E
Raseiniai, *Lithuania* . . . **9 J20** 55 25N 23 5 E
Rashad, *Sudan* . . . . **81 E3** 11 55N 31 0 E
Rashîd, *Egypt* . . . . **80 H7** 31 21N 30 22 E
Rashîd, Masabb, *Egypt* **80 H7** 31 22N 30 17 E
Rashmi, *India* . . . . **68 G6** 25 4N 74 22 E
Rasht, *Iran* . . . . **71 B6** 37 20N 49 40 E
Rasi Salai, *Thailand* . . **64 E5** 15 20N 104 9 E
Raška, *Serbia, Yug.* . . . **40 C4** 43 19N 20 39 E
Râsnov, *Romania* . . . . **43 E10** 45 35N 25 27 E
Rason L., *Australia* . . . **93 E3** 28 45 S 124 25 E
Raşova, *Romania* . . . . . **43 F12** 44 15N 27 55 E
Rasovo, *Bulgaria* . . . . . **40 C7** 43 42N 23 17 E
Rasra, *India* . . . . **69 G10** 25 50N 83 50 E
Rasskazovo, *Russia* . . . **48 D5** 52 35N 41 50 E
Rast, *Romania* . . . . **43 G8** 43 53N 23 16 E
Rastatt, *Germany* . . . . . **25 G4** 48 50N 8 11 E
Rastede, *Germany* . . . . **24 B4** 53 15N 8 12 E
Răstolita, *Romania* . . . **43 D9** 46 59N 24 58 E
Rasul, *Pakistan* . . . . . . **68 C5** 32 42N 73 34 E
Raszków, *Poland* . . . . . **45 G4** 51 43N 17 40 E
Rat Buri, *Thailand* . . . . **64 F2** 13 30N 99 54 E
Rat Islands, *U.S.A.* . . . **100 C1** 52 0N 178 0 E
Rat L., *Canada* **105 B9** 56 10N 99 40W
Ratangarh, *India* . . . . . **68 E6** 28 5N 74 35 E
Rätansbyn, *Sweden* . . . **10 B8** 62 29N 14 33 E
Raṭāwī, *Iraq* . . . . **70 D5** 30 38N 47 13 E
Rath, *India* . . . . **69 G8** 25 36N 79 37 E
Rath Luirc, *Ireland* . . . **15 D3** 52 21N 8 40W
Rathdrum, *Ireland* **15 D5** 52 56N 6 14W
Rathenow, *Germany* . . **24 C8** 52 37N 12 19 E
Rathkeale, *Ireland* . . . **15 D3** 52 32N 8 56W
Rathlin I., *U.K.* **15 A5** 55 18N 6 14W
Rathmelton, *Ireland* . . **15 A4** 55 2N 7 38W
Ratibor = Racibórz, *Poland* . . . . **45 H5** 50 7N 18 18 E
Rätikon, *Austria* . . . . . **26 D2** 47 0N 9 55 E
Ratingen, *Germany* . . . **24 D2** 51 18N 6 52 E
Ratlam, *India* . . . . **68 H6** 23 20N 75 0 E
Ratnagiri, *India* . . . . . . **66 L8** 16 57N 73 18 E
Ratodero, *Pakistan* . . . **68 F3** 27 48N 68 18 E
Raton, *U.S.A.* **113 G2** 36 54N 104 24W
Rattaphum, *Thailand* . . **65 J3** 7 8N 100 16 E
Ratten, *Austria* . . . . . . **26 D8** 47 28N 15 44 E
Rattray Hd., *U.K.* **14 D7** 57 38N 1 50W
Rättvik, *Sweden* . . . . . **10 D9** 60 52N 15 7 E
Ratz, Mt., *Canada* **104 B2** 57 23N 132 12W
Ratzeburg, *Germany* . . **24 B6** 53 40N 10 46 E
Raub, *Malaysia* . . . . . . **65 L3** 3 47N 101 52 E
Rauch, *Argentina* . . . . . **126 D4** 36 45 S 59 5W
Raudales de Malpaso, *Mexico* **119 D6** 17 30N 23 30W
Raufarhöfn, *Iceland* . . . **8 C6** 66 27N 15 57W
Raufoss, *Norway* . . . . . **9 F14** 60 44N 10 37 E
Raukumara Ra., *N.Z.* . . **91 H6** 38 5 S 177 55 E
Rauma, *Finland* . . . . . . **9 F19** 61 10N 21 30 E
Raurkela, *India* . . . . . . **69 H11** 22 14N 84 50 E
Rausu-Dake, *Japan* . . . **54 B12** 44 4N 145 7 E
Răut →, *Moldova* . . . . **43 C14** 47 15N 29 9 E
Rava-Ruska, *Poland* . . . **47 G2** 50 15N 23 42 E
Rava Russkaya = Rava-Ruska, *Poland* . . . . **47 G2** 50 15N 23 42 E
Ravalli, *U.S.A.* **114 C6** 47 17N 114 11W
Ravānsar, *Iran* . . . . **70 C5** 34 43N 46 40 E
Ravanusa, *Italy* . . . . . . **30 E6** 37 16N 13 58 E
Rāvar, *Iran* . . . . **71 D8** 31 20N 56 51 E
Ravena, *U.S.A.* **111 D11** 42 28N 73 49W
Ravenna, *Italy* . . . . **29 D9** 44 25N 12 12 E
Ravenna, *Nebr., U.S.A.* **112 E5** 41 1N 98 55W
Ravenna, *Ohio, U.S.A.* **110 E3** 41 9N 81 15W
Ravensburg, *Germany* . **25 H5** 47 46N 9 36 E
Ravenshoe, *Australia* . **94 B4** 17 37 S 145 29 E
Ravensthorpe, *Australia* . . . . **93 F3** 33 35 S 120 2 E
Ravenswood, *Australia* **94 C4** 20 6 S 146 54 E
Ravenswood, *U.S.A.* . . **108 F5** 38 57N 81 46W
Ravi →, *Pakistan* . . . . **68 D4** 30 35N 71 49 E
Ravna Gora, *Croatia* . . **29 C11** 45 24N 14 50 E
Ravna Reka, *Serbia, Yug.* . . . . **40 B5** 44 1N 21 35 E
Ravne na Koroškem, *Slovenia* . . . . **29 B11** 46 36N 14 59 E
Rawa Mazowiecka, *Poland* . . . . **45 G7** 51 46N 20 12 E
Rawalpindi, *Pakistan* . **68 C5** 33 38N 73 8 E
Rawāndūz, *Iraq* . . . . . . **70 B5** 36 40N 44 30 E
Rawang, *Malaysia* . . . . **65 L3** 3 20N 101 35 E
Rawene, *N.Z.* . . . . **91 F4** 35 25 S 173 32 E
Rawicz, *Poland* . . . . . . **45 G3** 51 36N 16 52 E
Rawka →, *Poland* . . . . **45 F7** 52 9N 20 8 E
Rawlinna, *Australia* . . . **93 F4** 30 58 S 125 28 E
Rawlins, *U.S.A.* **114 F10** 41 47N 107 14W
Rawlinson Ra., *Australia* . . . . **93 D4** 24 40 S 128 30 E
Rawson, *Argentina* . . . . **128 E3** 43 15 S 65 5W
Raxaul, *India* . . . . **69 F11** 26 59N 84 51 E
Ray, *U.S.A.* **112 A3** 48 21N 103 10W
Ray, C., *Canada* **103 C8** 47 33N 59 15W
Rayadurg, *India* . . . . . . **66 M10** 14 40N 76 50 E
Rayagada, *India* . . . . . . **67 K13** 19 15N 83 20 E
Raychikhinsk, *Russia* . . **51 E13** 49 46N 129 25 E
Rāyen, *Iran* . . . . **71 D8** 29 34N 57 26 E
Rayleigh, *U.K.* . . . . **13 F8** 51 36N 0 37 E
Raymond, *Canada* **104 D6** 49 30N 112 35W
Raymond, *Calif., U.S.A.* **116 H7** 37 13N 119 54W
Raymond, *N.H., U.S.A.* **111 C13** 43 2N 71 11W
Raymond, *Wash., U.S.A.* **116 D3** 46 41N 123 44W
Raymondville, *U.S.A.* . . **113 M6** 26 29N 97 47W
Raymore, *Canada* **105 C8** 51 25N 104 31W
Rayón, *Mexico* **118 B2** 29 43N 110 35W
Rayong, *Thailand* . . . . . **64 F3** 12 40N 101 20 E
Rayville, *U.S.A.* **113 J9** 32 29N 91 46W
Raz, Pte. du, *France* . . **18 D2** 48 2N 4 47W
Razan, *Iran* . . . . **71 C6** 35 23N 49 2 E
Ražana, *Serbia, Yug.* . . **40 B3** 44 6N 19 55 E
Ražanj, *Serbia, Yug.* . . **40 C5** 43 40N 21 31 E
Razdelna, *Bulgaria* . . . **41 C11** 43 13N 27 41 E
Razdel'naya = Rozdilna, *Ukraine* . . **47 J6** 46 50N 30 2 E
Razdolnoye, *Russia* . . . **54 C5** 43 30N 131 52 E
Razdolnoye, *Ukraine* . . **47 K7** 45 46N 33 29 E
Razeh, *Iran* . . . . **71 C6** 32 47N 48 9 E
Razgrad, *Bulgaria* . . . . **41 C10** 43 33N 26 34 E
Razim, Lacul, *Romania* **43 F14** 44 50N 29 0 E
Razlog, *Bulgaria* . . . . . **40 E7** 41 53N 23 28 E
Razmak, *Pakistan* . . . . **68 C3** 32 45N 69 50 E
Ré, Î. de, *France* **20 B2** 46 12N 1 30W
Reading, *U.K.* **13 F7** 51 27N 0 58W
Reading, *U.S.A.* **111 F9** 40 20N 75 56W
Reading □, *U.K.* **13 F7** 51 27N 0 58W
Realicó, *Argentina* . . . **126 D3** 35 0 S 64 15W
Réalmont, *France* . . . . **20 E6** 43 48N 2 10 E
Ream, *Cambodia* . . . . . **65 G4** 10 34N 103 39 E
Reata, *Mexico* **118 B4** 26 8N 101 5W
Reay Forest, *U.K.* **14 C4** 58 22N 4 55W
Rebais, *France* . . . . **19 D10** 48 50N 3 10 E
Rebi, *Indonesia* . . . . . . **63 F8** 6 23 S 134 7 E
Rebiana, *Libya* . . . . **79 D10** 24 12N 22 10 E
Rebun-Tō, *Japan* . . . . **54 B10** 45 23N 141 2 E
Recanati, *Italy* . . . . . . **29 E10** 43 24N 13 32 E
Recaş, *Romania* . . . . . **42 E6** 45 46N 21 30 E
Recco, *Italy* . . . . **28 D6** 44 22N 9 9 E
Recherche, Arch. of the, *Australia* . . . . **93 F3** 34 15 S 122 50 E
Rechna Doab, *Pakistan* **68 D5** 31 35N 73 30 E
Rechytsa, *Belarus* . . . . **47 F6** 52 21N 30 24 E
Recife, *Brazil* . . . . **125 E12** 8 0 S 35 0W
Recklinghausen, *Germany* . . . . **17 C7** 51 37N 7 12 E
Reconquista, *Argentina* **126 B4** 29 10 S 59 45W
Recreo, *Argentina* . . . . **126 B2** 29 25 S 65 10W
Recz, *Poland* . . . . **45 E2** 53 16N 15 31 E
Red →, *La., U.S.A.* . . . **113 K9** 31 1N 91 45W
Red →, *N. Dak., U.S.A.* **100 C10** 49 0N 97 15W
Red Bank, *U.S.A.* **111 F10** 40 21N 74 5W
Red Bay, *Canada* **103 B8** 51 44N 56 25W
Red Bluff, *U.S.A.* **114 F2** 40 11N 122 15W
Red Bluff L., *U.S.A.* . . . **113 K3** 31 54N 103 55W
Red Cliffs, *Australia* . . **95 E3** 34 19 S 142 11 E
Red Cloud, *U.S.A.* **112 E5** 40 5N 98 32W
Red Creek, *U.S.A.* **111 C8** 43 14N 76 45W
Red Deer, *Canada* **104 C6** 52 20N 113 50W
Red Deer →, *Alta., Canada* **105 C7** 50 58N 110 0W
Red Deer →, *Man., Canada* **105 C8** 52 53N 101 1W
Red Deer L., *Canada* . . **105 C8** 52 55N 101 20W
Red Hook, *U.S.A.* **111 E11** 41 55N 73 53W
Red Indian L., *Canada* . **103 C8** 48 35N 57 0W
Red L., *Canada* **105 C10** 51 3N 93 49W
Red Lake, *Canada* **105 C10** 51 3N 93 49W
Red Lake Falls, *U.S.A.* . **112 B6** 47 53N 96 16W
Red Lake Road, *Canada* **105 C10** 49 59N 93 25W
Red Lodge, *U.S.A.* **114 D9** 45 11N 109 15W
Red Mountain, *U.S.A.* . **117 K9** 35 37N 117 38W
Red Oak, *U.S.A.* **112 E7** 41 1N 95 14W
Red Rock, *Canada* **102 C2** 48 55N 88 15W
Red Rock, L., *U.S.A.* . . **112 E8** 41 22N 92 59W
Red Rocks Pt., *Australia* . . . . **93 F4** 32 13 S 127 32 E
Red Sea, *Asia* . . . . **74 C2** 25 0N 36 0 E
Red Slate Mt., *U.S.A.* . **116 H8** 37 31N 118 52W
Red Sucker L., *Canada* **102 B1** 54 9N 93 40W
Red Tower Pass = Turnu Roşu, P., *Romania* . . . . **43 E9** 45 33N 24 17 E
Red Wing, *U.S.A.* **112 C8** 44 34N 92 31W
Reda, *Poland* . . . . **44 D5** 54 40N 18 19 E
Redang, *Malaysia* . . . . **62 C2** 5 49N 103 2 E
Redange, *Lux.* . . . . **17 E5** 49 46N 5 52 E
Redcar, *U.K.* **12 C6** 54 37N 1 4W
Redcar & Cleveland □, *U.K.* **12 C7** 54 29N 1 0W
Redcliff, *Canada* **105 C6** 50 10N 110 50W
Redcliffe, *Australia* . . . **95 D5** 27 12 S 153 0 E
Redcliffe, Mt., *Australia* **93 E3** 28 30 S 121 30 E
Reddersburg, *S. Africa* **88 D4** 29 41 S 26 10 E
Redding, *U.S.A.* **114 F2** 40 35N 122 24W
Redditch, *U.K.* **13 E6** 52 18N 1 55W
Redfield, *U.S.A.* **112 C5** 44 53N 98 31W
Redford, *U.S.A.* **111 B11** 44 38N 73 48W
Redkino, *Russia* . . . . . . **46 D9** 56 39N 36 16 E
Redlands, *U.S.A.* **117 M9** 34 4N 117 11W
Redmond, *Oreg., U.S.A.* **114 D3** 44 17N 121 11W
Redmond, *Wash., U.S.A.* **116 C4** 47 41N 122 7W
Redon, *France* **18 E4** 47 40N 2 6W
Redonda, *Antigua* **121 C7** 16 58N 62 19W
Redondela, *Spain* **34 C2** 42 15N 8 38W
Redondo, *Portugal* **35 G3** 38 39N 7 37W
Redondo Beach, *U.S.A.* **117 M8** 33 50N 118 23W
Redruth, *U.K.* **13 G2** 50 14N 5 14W
Redvers, *Canada* **105 D8** 49 35N 101 40W
Redwater, *Canada* **104 C6** 53 55N 113 6W
Redwood, *U.S.A.* **111 B9** 44 18N 75 48W
Redwood City, *U.S.A.* . **116 H4** 37 30N 122 15W
Redwood Falls, *U.S.A.* . **112 C7** 44 32N 95 7W
Redwood National Park, *U.S.A.* **114 F1** 41 40N 124 5W
Ree, L., *Ireland* **15 C3** 53 35N 8 0W
Reed, L., *Canada* **105 C8** 54 38N 100 30W
Reed City, *U.S.A.* **108 D3** 43 53N 85 31W
Reedley, *U.S.A.* **116 J7** 36 36N 119 27W
Reedsburg, *U.S.A.* **112 D9** 43 32N 90 0W
Reedsport, *U.S.A.* **114 E1** 43 42N 124 6W
Reedsville, *U.S.A.* **110 F7** 40 39N 77 35W
Reefton, *N.Z.* . . . . **91 K3** 42 6 S 171 51 E
Rees, *Germany* . . . . . . **24 D2** 51 46N 6 24 E
Reese →, *U.S.A.* **114 F5** 40 48N 117 4W
Refahiye, *Turkey* . . . . . **73 C8** 39 54N 38 47 E
Reftele, *Sweden* . . . . . . **11 G7** 57 11N 13 35 E
Refugio, *U.S.A.* **113 L6** 28 18N 97 17W
Rega →, *Poland* . . . . . **44 D2** 54 10N 15 18 E
Regalbuto, *Italy* . . . . . . **31 E7** 37 39N 14 38 E
Regen, *Germany* . . . . . **25 G9** 48 58N 13 8 E
Regen →, *Germany* . . . **25 F8** 49 1N 12 6 E
Regensburg, *Germany* . **25 F8** 49 1N 12 6 E
Regenstauf, *Germany* . . **25 F8** 49 7N 12 8 E
Reggâne = Zaouiet Reggâne, *Algeria* . . . **78 C6** 26 32N 0 3 E
Reggello, *Italy* . . . . **29 E8** 43 41N 11 32 E
Réggio di Calábria, *Italy* . . . . **31 D8** 38 6N 15 39 E
Réggio nell'Emília, *Italy* . . . . **28 D7** 44 43N 10 36 E
Reghin, *Romania* . . . . . **43 D9** 46 46N 24 42 E
Regina, *Canada* **105 C8** 50 27N 104 35W
Regina Beach, *Canada* **105 C8** 50 47N 105 0W
Registro, *Brazil* . . . . . . **127 A6** 24 29 S 47 49W
Reguengos de Monsaraz, *Portugal* . **35 G3** 38 25N 7 32W
Rehar →, *India* . . . . . . **69 H10** 23 55N 82 40 E
Rehli, *India* . . . . **69 H8** 23 38N 79 5 E
Rehoboth, *Namibia* . . . **88 C2** 23 15 S 17 4 E
Rehovot, *Israel* . . . . . . **75 D3** 31 54N 34 48 E
Reichenbach, *Germany* **24 E8** 50 37N 12 17 E
Reid, *Australia* . . . . . . **93 F4** 30 49 S 128 26 E
Reidsville, *U.S.A.* **109 G6** 36 21N 79 40W
Reigate, *U.K.* **13 F7** 51 14N 0 12W
Reillo, *Spain* **32 F3** 39 54N 1 53W
Reims, *France* . . . . **19 C11** 49 15N 4 1 E
Reina Adelaida, Arch., *Chile* . . . . **128 G2** 52 20 S 74 0W
Reinbek, *Germany* . . . . **24 B6** 53 30N 10 16 E
Reindeer →, *Canada* . . **105 B8** 55 36N 103 11W
Reindeer I., *Canada* . . . **105 C9** 52 30N 98 0W
Reindeer L., *Canada* . . **105 B8** 57 15N 102 15W
Reinga, C., *N.Z.* . . . . . . **91 F4** 34 25 S 172 43 E
Reinosa, *Spain* **34 B6** 43 2N 4 15W
Reitz, *S. Africa* . . . . . . **89 D4** 27 48 S 28 29 E
Reivilo, *S. Africa* . . . . . **88 D3** 27 36 S 24 8 E
Rejaf, *Sudan* . . . . **81 G3** 4 45N 31 35 E
Rejmyre, *Sweden* . . . . . **11 F9** 58 50N 15 55 E
Rejowiec Fabryczny, *Poland* . . . . **45 G10** 51 5N 23 17 E
Reka →, *Slovenia* . . . . **29 C11** 45 40N 14 0 E
Rekovac, *Serbia, Yug.* . **40 C5** 43 51N 21 3 E
Reliance, *Canada* **105 A7** 63 0N 109 20W
Rémalard, *France* . . . . . **18 D7** 48 26N 0 47 E
Remarkable, Mt., *Australia* . . . . **95 E2** 32 48 S 138 10 E
Rembang, *Indonesia* . . **63 G14** 6 42 S 111 21 E
Remedios, *Panama* . . . **120 E3** 8 15N 81 50W
Remeshk, *Iran* . . . . **71 E8** 26 55N 58 50 E
Remetea, *Romania* . . . . **43 D10** 46 45N 25 29 E
Remich, *Lux.* . . . . **17 E6** 49 32N 6 22 E
Remiremont, *France* . . **19 D13** 48 2N 6 36 E
Remo, *Ethiopia* . . . . . . **81 F5** 6 48N 41 20 E
Remontnoye, *Russia* . . **49 G6** 46 34N 43 37 E
Remoulins, *France* . . . . **21 E8** 43 55N 4 35 E
Remscheid, *Germany* . . **17 C7** 51 11N 7 12 E
Ren Xian, *China* . . . . . . **56 F8** 37 8N 114 40 E
Rende, *Italy* . . . . **31 C9** 39 20N 16 11 E
Rendína, *Greece* . . . . . **38 B3** 39 4N 21 58 E
Rendsburg, *Germany* . . **24 A5** 54 17N 9 39 E
Renfrew, *Canada* **102 C4** 45 30N 76 40W
Renfrewshire □, *U.K.* . . **14 F4** 55 49N 4 38W
Rengat, *Indonesia* . . . . **62 E2** 0 30 S 102 45 E
Rengo, *Chile* . . . . **126 C1** 34 24 S 70 50W
Renhua, *China* . . . . **59 E9** 25 5N 113 40 E
Renhuai, *China* . . . . **58 D6** 27 48N 106 24 E
Reni, *Ukraine* . . . . **47 K5** 45 28N 28 15 E
Renk, *Sudan* . . . . **81 E3** 11 50N 32 50 E
Renmark, *Australia* . . . **95 E3** 34 11 S 140 43 E
Rennell Sd., *Canada* . . **104 C2** 53 23N 132 35W
Renner Springs, *Australia* . . . . **94 B1** 18 20 S 133 47 E
Rennes, *France* **18 D5** 48 7N 1 41W
Rennie L., *Canada* **105 A7** 61 32N 105 35W
Reno, *U.S.A.* **116 F7** 39 31N 119 48W
Reno →, *Italy* . . . . **29 D9** 44 38N 12 16 E
Renovo, *U.S.A.* **110 E7** 41 20N 77 45W
Renqiu, *China* . . . . **56 E9** 38 43N 116 5 E
Rens, *Denmark* . . . . . . **11 K3** 54 54N 9 5 E
Renshou, *China* . . . . . . **58 C5** 30 3N 104 9 E
Rensselaer, *Ind., U.S.A.* **108 E2** 40 57N 87 9W
Rensselaer, *N.Y., U.S.A.* **111 D11** 42 38N 73 45W
Rentería, *Spain* **32 B3** 43 19N 1 54W
Renton, *U.S.A.* **116 C4** 47 29N 122 12W
Réo, *Burkina Faso* **82 C4** 12 28N 2 35W
Reocín, *Spain* **34 B6** 43 21N 4 5W
Reotipur, *India* . . . . . . **69 G10** 25 33N 83 45 E
Répcelak, *Hungary* . . . . **42 C2** 47 24N 17 1 E
Republic, *Mo., U.S.A.* . **113 G8** 37 7N 93 29W
Republic, *Wash., U.S.A.* **114 B4** 48 39N 118 44W
Republican →, *U.S.A.* . **112 F6** 39 4N 96 48W
Repulse Bay, *Canada* . **101 B11** 66 30N 86 30W
Requena, *Peru* . . . . **124 E4** 5 5 S 73 52W
Requena, *Spain* **33 F3** 39 30N 1 4W
Réquista, *France* . . . . . **20 D6** 44 1N 2 32 E
Reşadiye = Datça, *Turkey* . . . . **39 E9** 36 46N 27 40 E
Reşadiye, *Turkey* . . . . . **72 B7** 40 23N 37 20 E
Reşadiye Yarımadası, *Turkey* . . . . **39 E9** 36 40N 27 45 E
Resavica, *Serbia, Yug.* . **40 B5** 44 4N 21 31 E
Resen, *Macedonia* . . . . **40 E5** 41 5N 21 0 E
Reserve, *U.S.A.* **115 K9** 33 43N 108 45W
Resht = Rasht, *Iran* . . . **71 B6** 37 20N 49 40 E
Resistencia, *Argentina* **126 B4** 27 30 S 59 0W
Reşiţa, *Romania* . . . . . **42 E6** 45 18N 21 53 E
Resko, *Poland* . . . . **44 E2** 53 47N 15 25 E
Resolution I., *Canada* . **101 B13** 61 30N 65 0W
Resolution I., *N.Z.* . . . **91 L1** 45 40 S 166 40 E
Ressano Garcia, *Mozam.* . . . . **89 D5** 25 25 S 32 0 E
Reston, *Canada* **105 D8** 49 33N 101 6W
Reszel, *Poland* . . . . **44 D8** 54 4N 21 10 E
Retalhuleu, *Guatemala* **120 D1** 14 33N 91 46W
Retenue, L. de, *Dem. Rep. of the Congo* . . . . **87 E2** 11 0 S 27 0 E
Retezat, Munţii, *Romania* . . . . **42 E8** 45 25N 23 0 E
Retford, *U.K.* **12 D7** 53 19N 0 56W
Rethel, *France* . . . . **19 C11** 49 30N 4 20 E
Rethem, *Germany* . . . . **24 C5** 52 47N 9 22 E
Réthimnon, *Greece* . . . **36 D6** 35 18N 24 30 E
Réthimnon □, *Greece* . **36 D6** 35 23N 24 28 E
Reti, *Pakistan* . . . . **68 E3** 28 5N 69 48 E
Retiche, Alpi, *Switz.* . . **25 J6** 46 30N 10 0 E
Retiers, *France* **18 E5** 47 55N 1 23W
Retortillo, *Spain* **34 E4** 40 48N 6 21W
Retournac, *France* . . . . **21 C8** 45 12N 4 2 E
Rétság, *Hungary* . . . . . **42 C4** 47 58N 19 10 E
Réunion ■, *Ind. Oc.* . . **77 J9** 21 0 S 56 0 E
Reus, *Spain* . . . . **32 D6** 41 10N 1 5 E
Reuterstadt Stavenhagen, *Germany* . . . . **24 B8** 53 42N 12 54 E
Reutlingen, *Germany* . . **25 G5** 48 29N 9 12 E
Reutte, *Austria* . . . . . . **26 D3** 47 29N 10 42 E
Reval = Tallinn, *Estonia* **9 G21** 59 22N 24 48 E
Revel, *France* . . . . **20 E6** 43 28N 2 1 E
Revelganj, *India* . . . . . **69 G11** 25 50N 84 40 E
Revelstoke, *Canada* . . **104 C5** 51 0N 118 10W
Reventazón, *Peru* . . . . **124 E2** 6 10 S 80 58W
Revigny-sur-Ornain, *France* . . . . **19 D11** 48 49N 4 59 E
Revillagigedo, Is. de, *Pac. Oc.* **118 D2** 18 40N 112 0W
Revin, *France* . . . . **19 C11** 49 55N 4 39 E
Revúca, *Slovak Rep.* . . **27 C13** 48 41N 20 7 E
Revuè →, *Mozam.* . . . . **87 F3** 19 50 S 34 0 E
Rewa, *India* . . . . **69 G9** 24 33N 81 25 E
Rewari, *India* . . . . **68 E7** 28 15N 76 40 E
Rexburg, *U.S.A.* **114 E8** 43 49N 111 47W
Rey, *Iran* . . . . **71 C6** 35 35N 51 25 E
Rey, I. del, *Panama* . . . **120 E4** 8 20N 78 30W
Rey Malabo, *Eq. Guin.* . **83 E6** 3 45N 8 50 E
Reyðarfjörður, *Iceland* **8 D6** 65 2N 14 13W
Reyes, Pt., *U.S.A.* **116 H3** 38 0N 123 0W
Reyhanlı, *Turkey* . . . . . **72 D7** 36 16N 36 35 E
Reykjahlið, *Iceland* . . . **8 D5** 65 40N 16 55W
Reykjanes, *Iceland* **8 E2** 63 48N 22 40W
Reykjavík, *Iceland* **8 D3** 64 10N 21 57W
Reynolds Ra., *Australia* **92 D5** 22 30 S 133 0 E
Reynoldsville, *U.S.A.* . . **110 E6** 41 5N 78 58W
Reynosa, *Mexico* **119 B5** 26 5N 98 18W
Rēzekne, *Latvia* . . . . . . **9 H22** 56 30N 27 17 E
Rezina, *Moldova* . . . . . **43 C13** 47 45N 28 58 E
Rezovo, *Bulgaria* . . . . . **41 D12** 42 0N 28 0 E
Rezvān, *Iran* . . . . **71 E8** 27 34N 56 6 E
Rgotina, *Serbia, Yug.* . . **40 B6** 44 1N 22 17 E
Rhamnus, *Greece* . . . . **38 C6** 38 12N 24 3 E
Rhayader, *U.K.* **13 E4** 52 18N 3 29W
Rheda-Wiedenbrück, *Germany* . . . . **24 D4** 51 50N 8 20 E
Rhede, *Germany* . . . . . **24 D2** 51 50N 6 42 E
Rhein →, *Europe* . . . . **17 C6** 51 52N 6 2 E
Rhein-Main-Donau-Kanal, *Germany* . . . **25 F7** 49 1N 11 27 E
Rheinbach, *Germany* . . **24 E2** 50 38N 6 57 E
Rheine, *Germany* . . . . . **24 C3** 52 17N 7 26 E
Rheinfelden, *Germany* . **25 H3** 47 33N 7 47 E
Rheinhessen-Pfalz □, *Germany* . . . . **25 F3** 49 20N 8 0 E
Rheinland-Pfalz □, *Germany* . . . . **25 E2** 50 0N 7 0 E
Rheinsberg, *Germany* . . **24 B8** 53 6N 12 54 E
Rhin = Rhein →, *Europe* . . . . **17 C6** 51 52N 6 2 E
Rhine = Rhein →, *Europe* . . . . **17 C6** 51 52N 6 2 E
Rhinebeck, *U.S.A.* **111 E11** 41 56N 73 55W
Rhineland-Palatinate = Rheinland-Pfalz □, *Germany* . . . . **25 E2** 50 0N 7 0 E
Rhinelander, *U.S.A.* . . **112 C10** 45 38N 89 25W
Rhinns Pt., *U.K.* **14 F2** 55 40N 6 29W
Rhino Camp, *Uganda* . . **86 B3** 3 0N 31 22 E
Rhir, Cap, *Morocco* . . . **78 B4** 30 38N 9 54W
Rho, *Italy* . . . . **28 C6** 45 32N 9 2 E
Rhode Island □, *U.S.A.* **111 E13** 41 40N 71 30W
Rhodes = Ródhos, *Greece* . . . . **36 C10** 36 15N 28 10 E
Rhodesia = Zimbabwe ■, *Africa* **87 F3** 19 0 S 30 0 E
Rhodope Mts. = Rhodopi Planina, *Bulgaria* . . . . **41 E8** 41 40N 24 20 E
Rhodopi Planina, *Bulgaria* . . . . **41 E8** 41 40N 24 20 E
Rhön, *Germany* . . . . . . **24 E5** 50 24N 9 58 E
Rhondda, *U.K.* **13 F4** 51 39N 3 31W
Rhondda Cynon Taff □, *U.K.* **13 F4** 51 42N 3 27W
Rhône □, *France* . . . . . **21 C8** 45 54N 4 35 E
Rhône →, *France* . . . . **21 E8** 43 28N 4 42 E
Rhône-Alpes □, *France* **21 C9** 45 40N 6 0 E
Rhum, *U.K.* **14 E2** 57 0N 6 20W
Rhyl, *U.K.* **12 D4** 53 20N 3 29W
Ri-Aba, *Eq. Guin.* . . . . . **83 E6** 3 28N 8 40 E
Riachão, *Brazil* . . . . . . **125 E9** 7 20 S 46 37W
Riangnom, *Sudan* . . . . . **81 F3** 9 55N 30 1 E
Riaño, *Spain* **34 C6** 42 59N 4 59W
Rians, *France* . . . . **21 E9** 43 37N 5 44 E
Riansáres →, *Spain* . . **35 F7** 39 32N 3 18W
Riasi, *India* . . . . **69 C6** 33 10N 74 50 E
Riau □, *Indonesia* . . . . **62 D2** 0 0 102 35 E
Riau, Kepulauan, *Indonesia* . . . . **62 D2** 0 30N 104 20 E
Riau Arch. = Riau, Kepulauan, *Indonesia* **62 D2** 0 30N 104 20 E
Riaza, *Spain* **34 D7** 41 18N 3 30W
Riaza →, *Spain* **34 D7** 41 42N 3 55W
Riba de Saelices, *Spain* **32 E2** 40 55N 2 17W
Riba-Roja de Turia, *Spain* **33 F4** 39 33N 0 34W
Ribadavia, *Spain* **34 C2** 42 17N 8 8W
Ribadeo, *Spain* **34 B3** 43 35N 7 5W
Ribadesella, *Spain* **34 B5** 43 30N 5 7W
Ribado, *Nigeria* . . . . . . **83 D7** 9 16N 12 47 E
Ribao, *Cameroon* . . . . . **83 D7** 6 32N 11 30 E

Ribas

Ribas = Ribes de Freser, Spain 32 C7 42 19N 2 15 E
Ribas do Rio Pardo, Brazil 125 H8 20 27 S 53 46W
Ribble →, U.K. 12 D5 53 52N 2 25W
Ribe, Denmark 11 J2 55 19N 8 44 E
Ribe Amtskommune □, Denmark 11 J2 55 35N 8 45 E
Ribeauvillé, France 19 D14 48 10N 7 20 E
Ribécourt-Dreslincourt, France 19 C9 49 30N 2 55 E
Ribeira = Santa Uxía, Spain 34 C2 42 36N 8 58W
Ribeira Brava, Madeira 37 D2 32 41N 17 4W
Ribeirão Prêto, Brazil 127 A6 21 10 S 47 50W
Ribemont, France 19 C10 49 47N 3 27 E
Ribera, Italy 30 E6 37 30N 13 16 E
Ribérac, France 20 C4 45 15N 0 20 E
Riberalta, Bolivia 124 F5 11 0 S 66 0W
Ribes de Freser, Spain 32 C7 42 19N 2 15 E
Ribnica, Slovenia 29 C11 45 45N 14 45 E
Ribnitz-Damgarten, Germany 24 A8 54 15N 12 27 E
Říčany, Czech Rep. 26 B7 50 0N 14 40 E
Riccarton, N.Z. 91 K4 43 32 S 172 37 E
Ríccia, Italy 31 A7 41 30N 14 50 E
Riccione, Italy 29 E9 43 59N 12 39 E
Rice, U.S.A. 117 L12 34 5N 114 51W
Rice L., Canada 110 B6 44 12N 78 10W
Rice Lake, U.S.A. 112 C9 45 30N 91 44W
Rich, C., Canada 110 B4 44 43N 80 38W
Richard Toll, Senegal 82 B1 16 25N 15 42W
Richards Bay, S. Africa 89 D5 28 48 S 32 6 E
Richardson →, Canada 105 B6 58 25N 111 14W
Richardson Lakes, U.S.A. 108 C10 44 46N 70 58W
Richardson Springs, U.S.A. 116 F5 39 51N 121 46W
Riche, C., Australia 93 F2 34 36 S 118 47 E
Richelieu, France 18 E7 47 1N 0 20 E
Richey, U.S.A. 112 B2 47 39N 105 4W
Richfield, U.S.A. 115 G8 38 46N 112 5W
Richfield Springs, U.S.A. 111 D10 42 51N 74 59W
Richford, U.S.A. 111 B12 45 0N 72 40W
Richibucto, Canada 103 C7 46 42N 64 54W
Richland, Ga., U.S.A. 109 J3 32 5N 84 40W
Richland, Wash., U.S.A. 114 C4 46 17N 119 18W
Richland Center, U.S.A. 112 D9 43 21N 90 23W
Richlands, U.S.A. 108 G5 37 6N 81 48W
Richmond, Australia 94 C3 20 43 S 143 8 E
Richmond, N.Z. 91 J4 41 20 S 173 12 E
Richmond, U.K. 12 C6 54 25N 1 43W
Richmond, Calif., U.S.A. 116 H4 37 56N 122 21W
Richmond, Ind., U.S.A. 108 F3 39 50N 84 53W
Richmond, Ky., U.S.A. 108 G3 37 45N 84 18W
Richmond, Mich., U.S.A. 110 D2 42 49N 82 45W
Richmond, Mo., U.S.A. 112 F8 39 17N 93 58W
Richmond, Tex., U.S.A. 113 L7 29 35N 95 46W
Richmond, Utah, U.S.A. 114 F8 41 56N 111 48W
Richmond, Va., U.S.A. 108 G7 37 33N 77 27W
Richmond, Vt., U.S.A. 111 B12 44 24N 72 59W
Richmond Hill, Canada 110 C5 43 52N 79 27W
Richmond Ra., Australia 95 D5 29 0 S 152 45 E
Richwood, U.S.A. 108 F5 38 14N 80 32W
Ricla, Spain 32 D3 41 31N 1 24W
Ridder = Leninogorsk, Kazakhstan 50 D9 50 20N 83 30 E
Riddlesburg, U.S.A. 110 F6 40 9N 78 15W
Ridgecrest, U.S.A. 117 K9 35 38N 117 40W
Ridgefield, Conn., U.S.A. 111 E11 41 17N 73 30W
Ridgefield, Wash., U.S.A. 116 E4 45 49N 122 45W
Ridgeland, U.S.A. 109 J5 32 29N 80 59W
Ridgetown, Canada 102 D3 42 26N 81 52W
Ridgewood, U.S.A. 111 F10 40 59N 74 7W
Ridgway, U.S.A. 110 E6 41 25N 78 44W
Riding Mountain Nat. Park, Canada 105 C9 50 50N 100 0W
Ridley, Mt., Australia 93 F3 33 12 S 122 7 E
Riebeek-Oos, S. Africa 88 E4 33 10 S 26 10 E
Ried, Austria 26 C6 48 14N 13 30 E
Riedlingen, Germany 25 G5 48 9N 9 28 E
Riedstadt, Germany 25 F4 49 45N 8 30 E
Rienza →, Italy 29 B8 46 49N 11 47 E
Riesa, Germany 24 D9 51 17N 13 17 E
Riesi, Italy 31 E7 37 17N 14 5 E
Riet →, S. Africa 88 D3 29 0 S 23 54 E
Rietavas, Lithuania 44 C8 55 44N 21 56 E
Rietbron, S. Africa 88 E3 32 54 S 23 10 E
Rietfontein, Namibia 88 C3 21 58 S 20 58 E
Rieti, Italy 29 F9 42 24N 12 51 E
Rieupeyroux, France 20 D6 44 19N 2 12 E
Riez, France 21 E10 43 49N 6 6 E
Riffe L., U.S.A. 116 D4 46 32N 122 26W
Rifle, U.S.A. 114 G10 39 32N 107 47W
Rift Valley □, Kenya 86 B4 0 20N 36 0 E
Rīga, Latvia 9 H21 56 53N 24 8 E
Riga, G. of, Latvia 9 H20 57 40N 23 45 E
Rigacikun, Nigeria 83 C6 10 40N 7 28 E
Rīgān, Iran 71 D8 28 37N 58 58 E
Rīgas Jūras Līcis = Riga, G. of, Latvia 9 H20 57 40N 23 45 E
Rigaud, Canada 111 A10 45 29N 74 18W
Rigby, U.S.A. 114 E8 43 40N 111 55W
Rīgestān, Afghan. 66 D4 30 15N 65 0 E
Riggins, U.S.A. 114 D5 45 25N 116 19W
Rignac, France 20 D6 44 25N 2 16 E
Rigolet, Canada 103 B8 54 10N 58 23W
Rihand Dam, India 69 G10 24 9N 83 2 E
Riihimäki, Finland 9 F21 60 45N 24 48 E
Riiser-Larsen-halvøya, Antarctica 5 C4 68 0 S 35 0 E
Rijau, Nigeria 83 C6 11 8N 5 17 E
Rijeka, Croatia 29 C11 45 20N 14 21 E
Rijeka Crnojevića, Montenegro, Yug. 40 D3 42 24N 19 1 E
Rijssen, Neths. 17 B6 52 19N 6 31 E
Rike, Ethiopia 81 E4 10 50N 39 53 E
Rikuzentakada, Japan 54 E10 39 0N 141 40 E
Rila, Bulgaria 40 D7 42 7N 23 7 E
Rila Planina, Bulgaria 40 D7 42 10N 23 20 E
Riley, U.S.A. 114 E4 43 32N 119 28W
Rima →, Nigeria 83 C6 13 4N 5 10 E
Rimah, Wadi ar →, Si. Arabia 70 E4 26 5N 41 30 E
Rimavská Sobota, Slovak Rep. 27 C13 48 22N 20 2 E
Rimbey, Canada 104 C6 52 35N 114 15W
Rimbo, Sweden 10 E12 59 44N 18 21 E
Rimersburg, U.S.A. 110 E5 41 3N 79 30W
Rimforsa, Sweden 11 F9 58 6N 15 43 E
Rimi, Nigeria 83 C6 12 58N 7 43 E
Rímini, Italy 29 D9 44 3N 12 33 E
Rimouski, Canada 103 C6 48 27N 68 30W
Rimrock, U.S.A. 116 D5 46 38N 121 10W
Rinca, Indonesia 63 F5 8 45 S 119 35 E
Rincón de la Victoria, Spain 35 J6 36 43N 4 18W
Rincón de Romos, Mexico 118 C4 22 14N 102 18W
Rinconada, Argentina 126 A2 22 26 S 66 10W
Rind →, India 69 G9 25 53N 80 33 E
Ringarum, Sweden 11 F10 58 21N 16 26 E
Ringas, India 68 F6 27 21N 75 34 E
Ringe, Denmark 11 J4 55 13N 10 28 E
Ringim, Nigeria 83 C6 12 13N 9 10 E
Ringkøbing, Denmark 11 H2 56 5N 8 15 E
Ringkøbing Amtskommune □, Denmark 11 H2 56 10N 8 45 E
Ringkøbing Fjord, Denmark 11 H2 56 0N 8 15 E
Ringsjön, Sweden 11 J7 55 55N 13 30 E
Ringsted, Denmark 11 J5 55 25N 11 46 E
Ringvassøy, Norway 8 B18 69 56N 19 15 E
Ringwood, U.S.A. 111 E10 41 7N 74 15W
Rinía, Greece 39 D7 37 23N 25 13 E
Rinjani, Indonesia 62 F5 8 24 S 116 28 E
Rinteln, Germany 24 C5 52 10N 9 8 E
Río, Punta del, Spain 33 J2 36 49N 2 24W
Rio Branco, Brazil 124 E5 9 58 S 67 49W
Río Branco, Uruguay 127 C5 32 40 S 53 40W
Río Bravo del Norte →, Mexico 119 B5 25 57N 97 9W
Rio Brilhante, Brazil 127 A5 21 48 S 54 33W
Rio Claro, Brazil 127 A6 22 19 S 47 35W
Rio Claro, Trin. & Tob. 121 D7 10 20N 61 25W
Río Colorado, Argentina 128 D4 39 0 S 64 0W
Río Cuarto, Argentina 126 C3 33 10 S 64 25W
Rio das Pedras, Mozam. 89 C6 23 8 S 35 28 E
Rio de Janeiro, Brazil 127 A7 23 0 S 43 12W
Rio de Janeiro □, Brazil 127 A7 22 50 S 43 0W
Rio do Sul, Brazil 127 B6 27 13 S 49 37W
Río Gallegos, Argentina 128 G3 51 35 S 69 15W
Rio Grande = Grande, Rio →, U.S.A. 113 N6 25 58N 97 9W
Río Grande, Argentina 128 G3 53 50 S 67 45W
Rio Grande, Brazil 127 C5 32 0 S 52 20W
Río Grande, Mexico 118 C4 23 50N 103 2W
Río Grande, Nic. 120 D3 12 54N 83 33W
Rio Grande City, U.S.A. 113 M5 26 23N 98 49W
Río Grande de Santiago →, Mexico 118 C3 21 36N 105 26W
Rio Grande do Norte □, Brazil 125 E11 5 40 S 36 0W
Rio Grande do Sul □, Brazil 127 C5 30 0 S 53 0W
Río Hato, Panama 120 E3 8 22N 80 10W
Río Lagartos, Mexico 119 C7 21 36N 88 10W
Rio Largo, Brazil 125 E11 9 28 S 35 50W
Rio Maior, Portugal 35 F2 39 19N 8 57W
Rio Marina, Italy 28 F7 42 49N 10 25 E
Río Mulatos, Bolivia 124 G5 19 40 S 66 50W
Río Muni = Mbini □, Eq. Guin. 84 D2 1 30N 10 0 E
Rio Negro, Brazil 127 B6 26 0 S 49 55W
Rio Pardo, Brazil 127 C5 30 0 S 52 30W
Rio Rancho, U.S.A. 115 J10 35 14N 106 38W
Río Segundo, Argentina 126 C3 31 40 S 63 59W
Río Tercero, Argentina 126 C3 32 15 S 64 8W
Rio Tinto, Portugal 34 D2 41 11N 8 34W
Rio Verde, Brazil 125 G8 17 50 S 51 0W
Río Verde, Mexico 119 C5 21 56N 99 59W
Rio Vista, U.S.A. 116 G5 38 10N 121 42W
Ríobamba, Ecuador 124 D3 1 50 S 78 45W
Ríohacha, Colombia 124 A4 11 33N 72 55W
Riom, France 20 C7 45 54N 3 7 E
Riom-ès-Montagnes, France 20 C6 45 17N 2 39 E
Rion-des-Landes, France 20 E3 43 55N 0 56W
Rionero in Vúlture, Italy 31 B8 40 55N 15 40 E
Rioni →, Georgia 49 J5 42 14N 41 44 E
Riós, Spain 34 D3 41 58N 7 16W
Ríosucio, Colombia 124 B3 7 27N 77 7W
Riou L., Canada 105 B7 59 7N 106 25W
Rioz, France 19 E13 47 26N 6 5 E
Ripatransone, Italy 29 F10 42 59N 13 46 E
Ripley, Canada 110 B3 44 4N 81 35W
Ripley, Calif., U.S.A. 117 M12 33 32N 114 39W
Ripley, N.Y., U.S.A. 110 D5 42 16N 79 43W
Ripley, Tenn., U.S.A. 113 H10 35 45N 89 32W
Ripley, W. Va., U.S.A. 108 F5 38 49N 81 43W
Ripoll, Spain 32 C7 42 15N 2 13 E
Ripon, U.K. 12 C6 54 9N 1 31W
Ripon, Calif., U.S.A. 116 H5 37 44N 121 7W
Ripon, Wis., U.S.A. 108 D1 43 51N 88 50W
Riposto, Italy 31 E8 37 44N 15 12 E
Risan, Montenegro, Yug. 40 D2 42 32N 18 42 E
Riscle, France 20 E3 43 39N 0 5W
Rishā', W. ar →, Si. Arabia 70 E5 25 33N 44 5 E
Rishiri-Tō, Japan 54 B10 45 11N 141 15 E
Rishon le Ẓiyyon, Israel 75 D3 31 58N 34 48 E
Risle →, France 18 C7 49 26N 0 23 E
Rison, U.S.A. 113 J8 33 58N 92 11W
Risør, Norway 9 G13 58 43N 9 13 E
Rita Blanca Cr. →, U.S.A. 113 H3 35 40N 102 29W
Riti, Nigeria 83 D6 7 57N 9 41 E
Ritter, Mt., U.S.A. 116 H7 37 41N 119 12W
Rittman, U.S.A. 110 F3 40 58N 81 47W
Ritzville, U.S.A. 114 C4 47 8N 118 23W
Riva del Garda, Italy 28 C7 45 53N 10 50 E
Riva Lígure, Italy 28 E4 43 50N 7 50 E
Rivadavia, Buenos Aires, Argentina 126 D3 35 29 S 62 59W
Rivadavia, Mendoza, Argentina 126 C2 33 13 S 68 30W
Rivadavia, Salta, Argentina 126 A3 24 5 S 62 54W
Rivadavia, Chile 126 B1 29 57 S 70 35W
Rivarolo Canavese, Italy 28 C4 45 19N 7 43 E
Rivas, Nic. 120 D2 11 30N 85 50W
Rive-de-Gier, France 21 C8 45 32N 4 37 E
River Cess, Liberia 82 D3 5 30N 9 32W
River Jordan, Canada 116 B2 48 26N 124 3W
Rivera, Argentina 126 D3 37 12 S 63 14W
Rivera, Uruguay 127 C4 31 0 S 55 50W
Riverbank, U.S.A. 116 H6 37 44N 120 56W
Riverdale, U.S.A. 116 J7 36 26N 119 52W
Riverhead, U.S.A. 111 F12 40 55N 72 40W
Riverhurst, Canada 105 C7 50 55N 106 50W
Rivers, Canada 105 C8 50 2N 100 14W
Rivers □, Nigeria 83 E6 4 30N 7 10 E
Rivers Inlet, Canada 104 C3 51 42N 127 15W
Riversdale, S. Africa 88 E3 34 7 S 21 15 E
Riverside, U.S.A. 117 M9 33 59N 117 22W
Riverton, Australia 95 E2 34 10 S 138 46 E
Riverton, Canada 105 C9 51 1N 97 0W
Riverton, N.Z. 91 M2 46 21 S 168 0 E
Riverton, U.S.A. 114 E9 43 2N 108 23W
Riverton Heights, U.S.A. 116 C4 47 28N 122 17W
Rives, France 21 C9 45 21N 5 31 E
Rivesaltes, France 20 F6 42 47N 2 50 E
Riviera, U.S.A. 117 K12 35 4N 114 35W
Riviera di Levante, Italy 28 D6 44 15N 9 30 E
Riviera di Ponente, Italy 28 D5 44 10N 8 20 E
Rivière-au-Renard, Canada 103 C7 48 59N 64 23W
Rivière-du-Loup, Canada 103 C6 47 50N 69 30W
Rivière-Pentecôte, Canada 103 C6 49 57N 67 1W
Rivière-Pilote, Martinique 121 D7 14 26N 60 53W
Rivière St. Paul, Canada 103 B8 51 28N 57 45W
Rivne, Ukraine 47 G4 50 40N 26 10 E
Rívoli, Italy 28 C4 45 3N 7 31 E
Rivoli B., Australia 95 F3 37 32 S 140 3 E
Rixheim, France 19 E14 47 40N 7 24 E
Riyadh = Ar Riyāḍ, Si. Arabia 70 E5 24 41N 46 42 E
Rize, Turkey 73 B9 41 0N 40 30 E
Rizhao, China 57 G10 35 25N 119 30 E
Rizokarpaso, Cyprus 36 D13 35 36N 34 23 E
Rizzuto, C., Italy 31 D10 38 53N 17 5 E
Rjukan, Norway 9 G13 59 54N 8 33 E
Ro, Greece 39 E11 36 9N 29 33 E
Roa, Spain 34 D7 41 41N 3 56W
Road Town, Br. Virgin Is. 121 C7 18 27N 64 37W
Roan Plateau, U.S.A. 114 G9 39 20N 109 20W
Roanne, France 19 F11 46 3N 4 4 E
Roanoke, Ala., U.S.A. 109 J3 33 9N 85 22W
Roanoke, Va., U.S.A. 108 G6 37 16N 79 56W
Roanoke →, U.S.A. 109 H7 35 57N 76 42W
Roanoke I., U.S.A. 109 H8 35 55N 75 40W
Roanoke Rapids, U.S.A. 109 G7 36 28N 77 40W
Roatán, Honduras 120 C2 16 18N 86 35W
Robāt Sang, Iran 71 C8 35 35N 59 10 E
Robbins I., Australia 94 G4 40 42 S 145 0 E
Róbbio, Italy 28 C5 45 17N 8 35 E
Robe →, Australia 92 D2 21 42 S 116 15 E
Röbel, Germany 24 B8 53 22N 12 35 E
Robert Lee, U.S.A. 113 K4 31 54N 100 29W
Robertsdale, U.S.A. 110 F6 40 11N 78 6W
Robertsganj, India 69 G10 24 44N 83 4 E
Robertson, S. Africa 88 E2 33 46 S 19 50 E
Robertson I., Antarctica 5 C18 65 15 S 59 30W
Robertson Ra., Australia 92 D3 23 15 S 121 0 E
Robertsport, Liberia 82 D2 6 45N 11 26W
Robertstown, Australia 95 E2 33 58 S 139 5 E
Roberval, Canada 103 C5 48 32N 72 15W
Robeson Chan., Greenland 4 A4 82 0N 61 30W
Robesonia, U.S.A. 111 F8 40 21N 76 8W
Robi, Ethiopia 81 F4 7 52N 39 38 E
Robinson, U.S.A. 108 F2 39 0N 87 44W
Robinson →, Australia 94 B2 16 3 S 137 16 E
Robinson Ra., Australia 93 E2 25 40 S 119 0 E
Robinvale, Australia 95 E3 34 40 S 142 45 E
Robledo, Spain 33 G2 38 46N 2 26W
Roblin, Canada 105 C8 51 14N 101 21W
Roboré, Bolivia 124 G7 18 10 S 59 45W
Robson, Canada 104 D5 49 20N 117 41W
Robson, Mt., Canada 104 C5 53 10N 119 10W
Robstown, U.S.A. 113 M6 27 47N 97 40W
Roca, C. da, Portugal 35 G1 38 40N 9 31W
Roca Partida, I., Mexico 118 D2 19 1N 112 2W
Rocamadour, France 20 D5 44 48N 1 37 E
Rocas, I., Brazil 125 D12 4 0 S 34 1W
Rocca San Casciano, Italy 29 D8 44 3N 11 50 E
Roccadáspide, Italy 31 B8 40 27N 15 10 E
Roccastrada, Italy 29 F8 43 0N 11 10 E
Roccella Iónica, Italy 31 D9 38 19N 16 24 E
Rocha, Uruguay 127 C5 34 30 S 54 25W
Rochdale, U.K. 12 D5 53 38N 2 9W
Rochechouart, France 20 C4 45 50N 0 49 E
Rochefort, Belgium 17 D5 50 9N 5 12 E
Rochefort, France 20 C3 45 56N 0 57W
Rochefort-en-Terre, France 18 E4 47 42N 2 22W
Rochelle, U.S.A. 112 E10 41 56N 89 4W
Rocher River, Canada 104 A6 61 23N 112 44W
Rocheservière, France 18 F5 46 57N 1 30W
Rochester, U.K. 13 F8 51 23N 0 31 E
Rochester, Ind., U.S.A. 108 E2 41 4N 86 13W
Rochester, Minn., U.S.A. 112 C8 44 1N 92 28W
Rochester, N.H., U.S.A. 111 C14 43 18N 70 59W
Rochester, N.Y., U.S.A. 110 C7 43 10N 77 37W
Rociu, Romania 43 F10 44 43N 25 2 E
Rock →, Canada 104 A3 60 7N 127 7W
Rock Creek, U.S.A. 110 E4 41 40N 80 52W
Rock Falls, U.S.A. 112 E10 41 47N 89 41W
Rock Hill, U.S.A. 109 H5 34 56N 81 1W
Rock Island, U.S.A. 112 E9 41 30N 90 34W
Rock Rapids, U.S.A. 112 D6 43 26N 96 10W
Rock Sound, Bahamas 120 B4 24 54N 76 12W
Rock Springs, Mont., U.S.A. 114 C10 46 49N 106 15W
Rock Springs, Wyo., U.S.A. 114 F9 41 35N 109 14W
Rock Valley, U.S.A. 112 D6 43 12N 96 18W
Rockall, Atl. Oc. 6 D3 57 37N 13 42W
Rockdale, Tex., U.S.A. 113 K6 30 39N 97 0W
Rockdale, Wash., U.S.A. 116 C5 47 22N 121 28W
Rockefeller Plateau, Antarctica 5 E14 80 0 S 140 0W
Rockford, U.S.A. 112 D10 42 16N 89 6W
Rockglen, Canada 105 D7 49 11N 105 57W
Rockhampton, Australia 94 C5 23 22 S 150 32 E
Rockingham, Australia 93 F2 32 15 S 115 38 E
Rockingham, U.S.A. 109 H6 34 57N 79 46W
Rockingham B., Australia 94 B4 18 5 S 146 10 E
Rocklake, U.S.A. 112 A5 48 47N 99 15W
Rockland, Canada 111 A9 45 33N 75 17W
Rockland, Idaho, U.S.A. 114 E7 42 34N 112 53W
Rockland, Maine, U.S.A. 109 C11 44 6N 69 7W
Rockland, Mich., U.S.A. 112 B10 46 44N 89 11W
Rocklin, U.S.A. 116 G5 38 48N 121 14W
Rockmart, U.S.A. 109 H3 34 0N 85 3W
Rockport, Mass., U.S.A. 111 D14 42 39N 70 37W
Rockport, Mo., U.S.A. 112 E7 40 25N 95 31W
Rockport, Tex., U.S.A. 113 L6 28 2N 97 3W
Rocksprings, U.S.A. 113 K4 30 1N 100 13W
Rockville, Conn., U.S.A. 111 E12 41 52N 72 28W
Rockville, Md., U.S.A. 108 F7 39 5N 77 9W
Rockwall, U.S.A. 113 J6 32 56N 96 28W
Rockwell City, U.S.A. 112 D7 42 24N 94 38W
Rockwood, Canada 110 C4 43 37N 80 8W
Rockwood, Maine, U.S.A. 109 C11 45 41N 69 45W
Rockwood, Tenn., U.S.A. 109 H3 35 52N 84 41W
Rocky Ford, U.S.A. 112 F3 38 3N 103 43W
Rocky Gully, Australia 93 F2 34 30 S 116 57 E
Rocky Harbour, Canada 103 C8 49 36N 57 55W
Rocky Island L., Canada 102 C3 46 55N 83 0W
Rocky Lane, Canada 104 B5 58 31N 116 22W
Rocky Mount, U.S.A. 109 H7 35 57N 77 48W
Rocky Mountain House, Canada 104 C6 52 22N 114 55W
Rocky Mountain National Park, U.S.A. 114 F11 40 25N 105 45W
Rocky Mts., N. Amer. 114 G10 49 0N 115 0W
Rocky Point, Namibia 88 B2 19 3 S 12 30 E
Rocroi, France 19 C11 49 55N 4 30 E
Rod, Pakistan 66 E3 28 10N 63 5 E
Rødby, Denmark 11 K5 54 41N 11 23 E
Rødbyhavn, Denmark 11 K5 54 39N 11 22 E
Roddickton, Canada 103 B8 50 51N 56 8W
Rødding, Denmark 11 J3 55 23N 9 3 E
Rödeby, Sweden 11 H9 56 15N 15 37 E
Rødekro, Denmark 11 J3 55 4N 9 20 E
Rodenkirchen, Germany 24 B4 53 23N 8 26 E
Rodez, France 20 D6 44 21N 2 33 E
Rodholívas, Greece 40 F7 40 55N 24 0 E
Rodhópi □, Greece 41 E9 41 5N 25 30 E
Rodhopoú, Greece 36 D5 35 34N 23 45 E
Ródhos, Greece 36 C10 36 15N 28 10 E
Rodi Gargánico, Italy 29 G12 41 55N 15 53 E
Rodna, Romania 43 C9 47 25N 24 50 E
Rodnei, Munţii, Romania 43 C9 47 35N 24 35 E
Rodney, Canada 110 D3 42 34N 81 41W
Rodney, C., N.Z. 91 G5 36 17 S 174 50 E
Rodniki, Russia 48 B5 57 7N 41 47 E
Rodonit, Kepi i, Albania 40 E3 41 35N 19 27 E
Rodriguez, Ind. Oc. 3 E13 19 45 S 63 20 E
Roe →, U.K. 15 A5 55 6N 6 59W
Roebling, U.S.A. 111 F10 40 7N 74 47W
Roebourne, Australia 92 D2 20 44 S 117 9 E
Roebuck B., Australia 92 C3 18 5 S 122 20 E
Roermond, Neths. 17 C6 51 12N 6 0 E
Roes Welcome Sd., Canada 101 B11 65 0N 87 0W
Roeselare, Belgium 17 D3 50 57N 3 7 E
Rogachev = Ragachow, Belarus 47 F6 53 8N 30 5 E
Rogačica, Serbia, Yug. 40 B3 44 4N 19 40 E
Rogagua, L., Bolivia 124 F5 13 43 S 66 50W
Rogaška Slatina, Slovenia 29 B12 46 15N 15 42 E
Rogatec, Slovenia 29 B12 46 15N 15 46 E
Rogatica, Bos.-H. 42 G4 43 47N 19 0 E
Rogatyn, Ukraine 47 H3 49 24N 24 36 E
Rogdhia, Greece 36 D7 35 22N 25 1 E
Rogers, U.S.A. 113 G7 36 20N 94 7W
Rogers City, U.S.A. 108 C4 45 25N 83 49W
Rogersville, Canada 103 C6 46 44N 65 26W
Roggan →, Canada 102 B4 54 24N 79 25W
Roggan L., Canada 102 B4 54 8N 77 50W
Roggeveldberge, S. Africa 88 E3 32 10 S 20 10 E
Roggiano Gravina, Italy 31 C9 39 37N 16 9 E
Rogliano, France 21 F13 42 57N 9 30 E
Rogliano, Italy 31 C9 39 10N 16 19 E
Rogoaguado, L., Bolivia 124 F5 13 0 S 65 30W
Rogoźno, Poland 45 F3 52 45N 16 59 E
Rogue →, U.S.A. 114 E1 42 26N 124 26W
Rohan, France 18 D4 48 4N 2 45W
Róhda, Greece 36 A3 39 48N 19 46 E
Rohnert Park, U.S.A. 116 G4 38 16N 122 40W
Rohri, Pakistan 68 F3 27 45N 68 51 E
Rohri Canal, Pakistan 68 F3 26 15N 68 27 E
Rohtak, India 68 E7 28 55N 76 43 E
Roi Et, Thailand 64 D4 16 4N 103 40 E
Roja, Latvia 9 H20 57 29N 22 43 E
Rojas, Argentina 126 C3 34 10 S 60 45W
Rojište, Romania 43 F8 44 4N 23 53 E
Rojo, C., Mexico 119 C5 21 33N 97 20W
Rokan →, Indonesia 62 D2 2 0N 100 50 E
Rokel →, S. Leone 82 D2 8 30N 12 48W
Rokiškis, Lithuania 9 J21 55 55N 25 35 E
Rokitno, Russia 47 G8 50 57N 35 56 E
Rokycany, Czech Rep. 26 B6 49 43N 13 35 E
Rolândia, Brazil 127 A5 23 18 S 51 23W
Rolla, U.S.A. 113 G9 37 57N 91 46W
Rolleston, Australia 94 C4 24 28 S 148 35 E
Rollingstone, Australia 94 B4 19 2 S 146 24 E
Rom, Sudan 81 F3 9 54N 32 16 E
Roma, Australia 95 D4 26 32 S 148 49 E
Roma, Italy 29 G9 41 54N 12 29 E
Roma, Sweden 11 G12 57 32N 18 26 E
Roma, U.S.A. 113 M5 26 25N 99 1W
Romain C., U.S.A. 109 J6 33 0N 79 22W
Romaine, Canada 103 B7 50 13N 60 40W
Romaine →, Canada 103 B7 50 18N 63 47W
Roman, Bulgaria 40 C7 43 8N 23 57 E
Roman, Romania 43 D11 46 57N 26 55 E
Roman-Kosh, Gora, Ukraine 47 K8 44 37N 34 15 E
Romanche →, France 21 C9 45 5N 5 43 E
Romang, Indonesia 63 F7 7 30 S 127 20 E
Românî, Egypt 75 E1 30 59N 32 38 E
Romania ■, Europe 43 D10 46 0N 25 0 E
Romanija, Bos.-H. 42 G3 43 50N 18 45 E
Romano, Cayo, Cuba 120 B4 22 0N 77 30W
Romanovka = Basarabeasca, Moldova 43 D13 46 21N 28 58 E
Romans-sur-Isère, France 21 C9 45 3N 5 3 E
Romanshorn, Switz. 25 H5 47 33N 9 22 E
Rombari, Sudan 81 G3 4 33N 31 2 E
Romblon, Phil. 61 E5 12 33N 122 17 E
Rome = Roma, Italy 29 G9 41 54N 12 29 E
Rome, Ga., U.S.A. 109 H3 34 15N 85 10W
Rome, N.Y., U.S.A. 111 C9 43 13N 75 27W
Rome, Pa., U.S.A. 111 E8 41 51N 76 21W
Rometta, Italy 31 D8 38 10N 15 25 E
Romilly-sur-Seine, France 19 D10 48 31N 3 44 E
Romney, U.S.A. 108 F6 39 21N 78 45W
Romney Marsh, U.K. 13 F8 51 2N 0 54 E
Romny, Ukraine 47 G7 50 48N 33 28 E
Rømø, Denmark 11 J2 55 10N 8 30 E
Romodan, Ukraine 47 G7 49 55N 33 15 E
Romodanovo, Russia 48 C7 54 26N 45 23 E
Romont, Switz. 25 J2 46 42N 6 54 E
Romorantin-Lanthenay, France 19 E8 47 21N 1 45 E
Romsdalen, Norway 9 E12 62 25N 7 52 E
Romsey, U.K. 13 G6 51 0N 1 29W
Ron, Vietnam 64 D6 17 53N 106 27 E
Rona, U.K. 14 D3 57 34N 5 59W
Ronan, U.S.A. 114 C6 47 32N 114 6W
Roncador, Cayos, Caribbean 120 D3 13 32N 80 4W
Roncador, Serra do, Brazil 125 F8 12 30 S 52 30W
Ronciglione, Italy 29 F9 42 17N 12 13 E
Ronco →, Italy 29 D9 44 24N 12 12 E
Ronda, Spain 35 J5 36 46N 5 12W
Ronda, Serranía de, Spain 35 J5 36 44N 5 3W
Rondane, Norway 9 F13 61 57N 9 50 E
Rondônia □, Brazil 124 F6 11 0 S 63 0W
Rondonópolis, Brazil 125 G8 16 28 S 54 38W
Rong, Koh, Cambodia 65 G4 10 45N 103 15 E
Rong Jiang →, China 58 E7 24 35N 109 20 E
Rong Xian, Guangxi Zhuangzu, China 59 F8 22 50N 110 31 E
Rong Xian, Sichuan, China 58 C5 29 23N 104 22 E
Rong'an, China 58 E7 25 14N 109 22 E
Rongchang, China 58 C5 29 20N 105 32 E
Ronge, L. la, Canada 105 B7 55 6N 105 17W
Rongjiang, China 58 E7 25 57N 108 28 E
Rongshui, China 58 E7 25 5N 109 12 E
Rønne, Denmark 11 J8 55 6N 14 43 E
Ronne Ice Shelf, Antarctica 5 D18 78 0 S 60 0W
Ronneby, Sweden 11 H9 56 12N 15 17 E
Ronnebyån →, Sweden 11 H9 56 11N 15 18 E
Rönneshytta, Sweden 11 F9 58 56N 15 2 E
Ronsard, C., Australia 93 D1 24 46 S 113 10 E
Ronse, Belgium 17 D3 50 45N 3 35 E
Roodepoort, S. Africa 89 D4 26 11 S 27 54 E
Roof Butte, U.S.A. 115 H9 36 28N 109 5W
Rooiboklaagte →, Namibia 88 C3 20 50 S 21 0 E
Roorkee, India 68 E7 29 52N 77 59 E
Roosendaal, Neths. 17 C4 51 32N 4 29 E
Roosevelt, U.S.A. 114 F8 40 18N 109 59W
Roosevelt →, Brazil 122 D4 7 35 S 60 20W
Roosevelt, Mt., Canada 104 B3 58 26N 125 20W
Roosevelt I., Antarctica 5 D12 79 30 S 162 0W
Ropczyce, Poland 45 H8 50 4N 21 38 E
Roper →, Australia 94 A2 14 43 S 135 27 E
Roper Bar, Australia 94 A1 14 44 S 134 44 E
Roque Pérez, Argentina 126 D4 35 25 S 59 24W
Roquefort, France 20 D3 44 2N 0 20W
Roquemaure, France 21 D8 44 3N 4 48 E
Roquetas de Mar, Spain 33 J2 36 46N 2 36W
Roquetes, Spain 32 E5 40 50N 0 30 E
Roquevaire, France 21 E9 43 20N 5 36 E
Roraima □, Brazil 124 C6 2 0N 61 30W
Roraima, Mt., Venezuela 122 C4 5 10N 60 40W
Røros, Norway 9 E14 62 35N 11 23 E
Rorschach, Switz. 25 H5 47 28N 9 28 E
Rosa, Zambia 87 D3 9 33 S 31 15 E
Rosa, L., Bahamas 121 B5 21 0N 73 30W
Rosa, Monte, Italy 28 C4 45 55N 7 53 E
Rosal de la Frontera, Spain 35 H3 37 59N 7 13W
Rosalia, U.S.A. 114 C5 47 14N 117 22W
Rosamond, U.S.A. 117 L8 34 52N 118 10W
Rosans, France 21 D9 44 24N 5 29 E
Rosario, Argentina 126 C3 33 0 S 60 40W
Rosário, Brazil 125 D10 3 0 S 44 15W
Rosario, Baja Calif., Mexico 118 B1 30 0N 115 50W
Rosario, Sinaloa, Mexico 118 C3 23 0N 105 52W
Rosario, Paraguay 126 A4 24 30 S 57 35W
Rosario de la Frontera, Argentina 126 B3 25 50 S 65 0W
Rosario de Lerma, Argentina 126 A2 24 59 S 65 35W
Rosario del Tala, Argentina 126 C4 32 20 S 59 10W
Rosário do Sul, Brazil 127 C5 30 15 S 54 55W
Rosarito, Mexico 117 N9 32 18N 117 4W
Rosarno, Italy 31 D8 38 29N 15 58 E
Rosas = Roses, Spain 32 C8 42 19N 3 10 E
Roscoe, U.S.A. 111 E10 41 56N 74 55W
Roscoff, France 18 D3 48 44N 3 58W
Roscommon, Ireland 15 C3 53 38N 8 11W
Roscommon □, Ireland 15 C3 53 49N 8 23W
Roscrea, Ireland 15 D4 52 57N 7 49W
Rose →, Australia 94 A2 14 16 S 135 45 E
Rose Blanche, Canada 103 C8 47 38N 58 45W
Rose Pt., Canada 104 C2 54 11N 131 39W
Rose Valley, Canada 105 C8 52 19N 103 49W
Roseau, Domin. 121 C7 15 20N 61 24W
Roseau, U.S.A. 112 A7 48 51N 95 46W
Rosebery, Australia 94 G4 41 46 S 145 33 E
Rosebud, S. Dak., U.S.A. 112 D4 43 14N 100 51W
Rosebud, Tex., U.S.A. 113 K6 31 4N 96 59W
Roseburg, U.S.A. 114 E2 43 13N 123 20W

San Pedro Mixtepec

Salka, Nigeria 83 C5 10 20N 4 58 E
Şalkhad, Syria 75 C5 32 29N 36 43 E
Salla, Finland 8 C23 66 50N 28 49 E
Sallanches, France 21 C10 45 55N 6 38 E
Sallent, Spain 32 D6 41 49N 1 54 E
Salles, France 20 D3 44 33N 0 52W
Salles-Curan, France 20 D6 44 11N 2 48 E
Salling, Denmark 11 H2 56 40N 8 55 E
Salliq, Canada 101 B11 64 8N 83 10W
Sallisaw, U.S.A. 113 H7 35 28N 94 47W
Sallom Junction, Sudan 80 D4 19 17N 37 6 E
Salluit, Canada 101 B12 62 14N 75 38W
Salmās, Iran 70 B5 38 11N 44 47 E
Salmerón, Spain 32 E2 40 33N 2 29W
Salmo, Canada 104 D5 49 10N 117 20W
Salmon, U.S.A. 114 D7 45 11N 113 54W
Salmon →, Canada 104 C4 54 3N 122 40W
Salmon →, U.S.A. 114 D5 45 51N 116 47W
Salmon Arm, Canada 104 C5 50 40N 119 15W
Salmon Gums, Australia 93 F3 32 59 S 121 38 E
Salmon River Mts., U.S.A. 114 D6 45 0N 114 30W
Salo, Finland 9 F20 60 22N 23 10 E
Salò, Italy 28 C7 45 36N 10 31 E
Salobreña, Spain 35 J7 36 44N 3 35W
Salome, U.S.A. 117 M13 33 47N 113 37W
Salon, India 69 F9 26 2N 81 27 E
Salon-de-Provence, France 21 E9 43 39N 5 6 E
Salonica = Thessaloníki, Greece 40 F6 40 38N 22 58 E
Salonta, Romania 42 D6 46 49N 21 42 E
Salor →, Spain 35 F3 39 39N 7 3W
Salou, Spain 32 D6 41 4N 1 8 E
Salou, C. de, Spain 32 D6 41 3N 1 10 E
Saloum →, Senegal 82 C1 13 50N 16 45W
Salpausselkä, Finland 9 F22 61 0N 27 0 E
Salsacate, Argentina 126 C2 31 20 S 65 5W
Salses, France 20 F6 42 50N 2 55 E
Salsk, Russia 49 G5 46 28N 41 30 E
Salso →, Italy 30 E6 37 6N 13 57 E
Salsomaggiore Terme, Italy 28 D6 44 49N 9 59 E
Salt, Spain 32 D7 41 59N 2 47 E
Salt →, Canada 104 B6 60 0N 112 25W
Salt →, U.S.A. 115 K7 33 23N 112 19W
Salt Lake City, U.S.A. 114 F8 40 45N 111 53W
Salt Range, Pakistan 68 C5 32 30N 72 25 E
Salta, Argentina 126 A2 24 57 S 65 25W
Salta □, Argentina 126 A2 24 48 S 65 30W
Saltara, Italy 29 E9 43 45N 12 50 E
Saltash, U.K. 13 G3 50 24N 4 14W
Saltburn by the Sea, U.K. 12 C7 54 35N 0 58W
Saltcoats, U.K. 14 F4 55 38N 4 47W
Saltee Is., Ireland 15 D5 52 7N 6 37W
Saltfjellet, Norway 8 C16 66 40N 15 15 E
Saltfjorden, Norway 8 C16 67 15N 14 10 E
Saltholm, Denmark 11 J6 55 38N 12 43 E
Saltillo, Mexico 118 B4 25 25N 101 0W
Salto, Argentina 126 C3 34 20 S 60 15W
Salto, Uruguay 126 C4 31 27 S 57 50W
Salto del Guaíra, Paraguay 127 A5 24 3 S 54 17W
Salton City, U.S.A. 117 M11 33 29N 115 51W
Salton Sea, U.S.A. 117 M11 33 15N 115 45W
Saltpond, Ghana 83 D4 5 15N 1 3W
Saltsburg, U.S.A. 110 F5 40 29N 79 27W
Saltsjöbaden, Sweden 10 E12 59 15N 18 20 E
Saluda →, U.S.A. 109 J5 34 1N 81 4W
Salûm, Egypt 80 A2 31 31N 25 7 E
Salûm, Khâlig el, Egypt 80 A2 31 35N 25 24 E
Salur, India 67 K13 18 27N 83 18 E
Saluzzo, Italy 28 D4 44 39N 7 29 E
Salvador, Brazil 125 F11 13 0 S 38 30W
Salvador, Canada 105 C7 52 10N 109 32W
Salvador, L., U.S.A. 113 L9 29 43N 90 15W
Salvaterra de Magos, Portugal 35 F2 39 1N 8 47W
Sálvora, I. de, Spain 34 C2 42 30N 8 58W
Salween →, Burma 67 L20 16 31N 97 37 E
Salyan, Azerbaijan 50 F5 39 33N 48 59 E
Salza →, Austria 26 D7 47 40N 14 43 E
Salzach →, Austria 26 C5 48 12N 12 56 E
Salzburg, Austria 26 D6 47 48N 13 2 E
Salzburg □, Austria 26 D6 47 15N 13 0 E
Salzgitter, Germany 24 C6 52 9N 10 19 E
Salzkotten, Germany 24 D4 51 40N 8 37 E
Salzwedel, Germany 24 C7 52 52N 11 10 E
Sam, India 68 F4 26 50N 70 31 E
Sam Neua, Laos 58 G5 20 29N 104 5 E
Sam Ngao, Thailand 64 D2 17 18N 99 0 E
Sam Rayburn Reservoir, U.S.A. 113 K7 31 4N 94 5W
Sam Son, Vietnam 64 C5 19 44N 105 54 E
Sam Teu, Laos 64 C5 19 59N 104 38 E
Sama de Langreo = Langreo, Spain 34 B5 43 18N 5 40W
Samagaltay, Russia 51 D10 50 36N 95 3 E
Samales Group, Phil. 61 J4 6 0N 122 0 E
Samâlût, Egypt 80 B3 28 20N 30 42 E
Samana, India 68 D7 30 10N 76 13 E
Samana Cay, Bahamas 121 B5 23 3N 73 45W
Samandağı, Turkey 72 D6 36 5N 35 59 E
Samandıra, Turkey 41 F13 40 59N 29 13 E
Samanga, Tanzania 87 D4 8 20 S 39 13 E
Samangān □, Afghan. 66 B5 36 15N 68 3 E
Samangwa, Dem. Rep. of the Congo 86 C1 4 23 S 24 10 E
Samani, Japan 54 C11 42 7N 142 56 E
Samanli Dağları, Turkey 41 F13 40 32N 29 10 E
Samar, Phil. 61 F6 12 0N 125 0 E
Samara, Russia 48 D10 53 8N 50 6 E
Samara →, Russia 48 D10 53 10N 50 4 E
Samara →, Ukraine 47 H8 48 28N 35 7 E
Samaria = Shōmrōn, West Bank 75 C4 32 15N 35 13 E
Samariá, Greece 36 D5 35 17N 23 58 E
Samarinda, Indonesia 62 E5 0 30 S 117 9 E
Samarkand = Samarqand, Uzbekistan 50 F7 39 40N 66 55 E
Samarqand, Uzbekistan 50 F7 39 40N 66 55 E
Sāmarrā, Iraq 70 C4 34 12N 43 52 E
Samastipur, India 69 G11 25 50N 85 50 E
Şamaxi, Azerbaijan 49 K9 40 38N 48 37 E
Samba, Dem. Rep. of the Congo 86 C2 4 38 S 26 22 E
Samba, India 69 C6 32 32N 75 10 E
Sambalpur, India 67 J14 21 28N 84 4 E
Sambar, Tanjung, Indonesia 62 E4 2 59 S 110 19 E
Sambas, Indonesia 62 D3 1 20N 109 20 E
Sambava, Madag. 89 A9 14 16 S 50 10 E
Sambawizi, Zimbabwe 87 F2 18 24 S 26 13 E
Sambhal, India 69 E8 28 35N 78 37 E
Sambhar, India 68 F6 26 52N 75 6 E
Sambhar L., India 68 F6 26 55N 75 12 E
Sambiase, Italy 31 D9 38 58N 16 17 E
Sambir, Ukraine 47 H2 49 30N 23 10 E
Sambor, Cambodia 64 F6 12 46N 106 0 E
Samborombón, B., Argentina 126 D4 36 5 S 57 20W
Sambuca di Sicília, Italy 30 E6 37 39N 13 7 E
Samch'ŏk, S. Korea 57 F15 37 30N 129 10 E
Samch'onp'o, S. Korea 57 G15 35 0N 128 6 E
Same, Tanzania 86 C4 4 2 S 37 38 E
Samer, France 19 B8 50 38N 1 44 E
Samfya, Zambia 87 E2 11 22 S 29 31 E
Sámi, Greece 38 C2 38 15N 20 39 E
Şämkir, Azerbaijan 49 K8 40 50N 46 0 E
Şamlı, Turkey 39 B9 39 48N 27 51 E
Samnah, Si. Arabia 70 E3 25 10N 37 15 E
Samo Alto, Chile 126 C1 30 22 S 71 0W
Samoa ■, Pac. Oc. 91 B13 14 0 S 172 0W
Samobor, Croatia 29 C12 45 47N 15 44 E
Samoëns, France 19 F13 46 5N 6 45 E
Samokov, Bulgaria 40 D7 42 18N 23 35 E
Šamorín, Slovak Rep. 27 C10 48 2N 17 19 E
Samorogouan, Burkina Faso 82 C4 11 21N 4 57W
Sámos, Greece 39 D8 37 45N 26 50 E
Samoš, Serbia, Yug. 42 E5 45 13N 20 46 E
Samos, Spain 34 C3 42 44N 7 20W
Sámos □, Greece 39 D8 37 45N 26 50 E
Samothráki = Mathráki, Greece 36 A3 39 48N 19 31 E
Samothráki, Évros, Greece 41 F9 40 28N 25 28 E
Samothráki, Évros, Greece 41 F9 40 28N 25 28 E
Samoylovka, Russia 48 E6 51 12N 43 43 E
Sampa, Ghana 82 D4 8 0N 2 36W
Sampacho, Argentina 126 C3 33 20 S 64 50W
Sampang, Indonesia 63 G15 7 11 S 113 13 E
Samper de Calanda, Spain 32 D4 41 11N 0 28W
Sampéyre, Italy 28 D4 44 34N 7 11 E
Sampit, Indonesia 62 E4 2 34 S 113 0 E
Sampit, Teluk, Indonesia 62 E4 3 5 S 113 3 E
Samrong, Cambodia 64 E4 14 15N 103 30 E
Samrong, Thailand 64 E3 15 10N 100 40 E
Samsø, Denmark 11 J4 55 50N 10 35 E
Samsø Bælt, Denmark 11 J4 55 45N 10 45 E
Samsun, Turkey 72 B7 41 15N 36 22 E
Samtredia, Georgia 49 J6 42 7N 42 24 E
Samui, Ko, Thailand 65 H3 9 30N 100 0 E
Samur →, Russia 49 K9 41 53N 48 32 E
Samurskiy Khrebet, Russia 49 K8 41 55N 47 11 E
Samusole, Dem. Rep. of the Congo 87 E1 10 2 S 24 0 E
Samut Prakan, Thailand 64 F3 13 32N 100 40 E
Samut Songkhram →, Thailand 62 B1 13 24N 100 1 E
Samwari, Pakistan 68 E2 28 30N 66 46 E
San, Mali 82 C4 13 15N 4 57W
San →, Cambodia 64 F5 13 32N 105 57 E
San →, Poland 45 H8 50 45N 21 51 E
San Adrián, Spain 32 C3 42 20N 1 56W
San Adrián, C. de, Spain 34 B2 43 21N 8 50W
San Agustin, C., Phil. 61 H7 6 20N 126 13 E
San Agustín de Valle Fértil, Argentina 126 C2 30 35 S 67 30W
San Ambrosio, Pac. Oc. 122 F3 26 28 S 79 53W
San Andreas, U.S.A. 116 G6 38 12N 120 41W
San Andres, Phil. 61 E6 13 36N 124 6 E
San Andrés, I. de, Caribbean 120 D3 12 42N 81 46W
San Andrês del Rabanedo, Spain 34 C5 42 37N 5 36W
San Andres Mts., U.S.A. 115 K10 33 0N 106 30W
San Andrés Tuxtla, Mexico 119 D5 18 30N 95 20W
San Angelo, U.S.A. 113 K4 31 28N 100 26W
San Anselmo, U.S.A. 116 H4 37 59N 122 34W
San Antonio, Belize 119 D7 16 15N 89 2W
San Antonio, Chile 126 C1 33 40 S 71 40W
San Antonio, Phil. 61 D4 14 57N 120 5 E
San Antonio, N. Mex., U.S.A. 115 K10 33 55N 106 52W
San Antonio, Tex., U.S.A. 113 L5 29 25N 98 30W
San Antonio →, U.S.A. 113 L6 28 30N 96 54W
San Antonio, C., Argentina 126 D4 36 15 S 56 40W
San Antonio, C., Cuba 120 B3 21 50N 84 57W
San Antonio, C. de, Spain 33 G5 38 48N 0 12 E
San Antonio, Mt., U.S.A. 117 L9 34 17N 117 38W
San Antonio de los Baños, Cuba 120 B3 22 54N 82 31W
San Antonio de los Cobres, Argentina 126 A2 24 10 S 66 17W
San Antonio Oeste, Argentina 128 E4 40 40 S 65 0W
San Arcángelo, Italy 31 B9 40 14N 16 14 E
San Ardo, U.S.A. 116 J6 36 1N 120 54W
San Augustín, Canary Is. 37 G4 27 47N 15 32W
San Augustine, U.S.A. 113 K7 31 30N 94 7W
San Bartolomé, Canary Is. 37 F6 28 59N 13 37W
San Bartolomé de Tirajana, Canary Is. 37 G4 27 54N 15 34W
San Bartolomeo in Galdo, Italy 31 A8 41 24N 15 1 E
San Benedetto del Tronto, Italy 29 F10 42 57N 13 53 E
San Benedetto Po, Italy 28 C7 45 2N 10 55 E
San Benedicto, I., Mexico 118 D2 19 18N 110 49W
San Benito, U.S.A. 113 M6 26 8N 97 38W
San Benito →, U.S.A. 116 J5 36 53N 121 34W
San Benito Mt., U.S.A. 116 J6 36 22N 120 37W
San Bernardino, U.S.A. 117 L9 34 7N 117 19W
San Bernardino Mts., U.S.A. 117 L10 34 10N 116 45W
San Bernardino Str., Phil. 61 E6 13 0N 125 0 E
San Bernardo, Chile 126 C1 33 40 S 70 50W
San Bernardo, I. de, Colombia 124 B3 9 45N 75 50W
San Blas, Mexico 118 B3 26 4N 108 46W
San Blas, Arch. de, Panama 120 E4 9 50N 78 31W
San Blas, C., U.S.A. 109 L3 29 40N 85 21W
San Bonifacio, Italy 29 C8 45 24N 11 16 E
San Borja, Bolivia 124 F5 14 50 S 66 52W
San Buenaventura, Mexico 118 B4 27 5N 101 32W
San Carlos = Butuku-Luba, Eq. Guin. 83 E6 3 29N 8 33 E
San Carlos = Sant Carles, Spain 37 B8 39 3N 1 34 E
San Carlos, Argentina 126 C2 33 50 S 69 0W
San Carlos, Chile 126 D1 36 10 S 72 0W
San Carlos, Baja Calif. S., Mexico 118 C2 24 47N 112 6W
San Carlos, Coahuila, Mexico 118 B4 29 0N 100 54W
San Carlos, Nic. 120 D3 11 12N 84 50W
San Carlos, Neg. Occ., Phil. 61 F5 10 29N 123 25 E
San Carlos, Pangasinan, Phil. 61 D4 15 55N 120 20 E
San Carlos, Uruguay 127 C5 34 46 S 54 58W
San Carlos, U.S.A. 115 K8 33 21N 110 27W
San Carlos, Venezuela 124 B5 9 40N 68 36W
San Carlos de Bariloche, Argentina 128 E2 41 10 S 71 25W
San Carlos de Bolívar, Argentina 128 D4 36 15 S 61 6W
San Carlos de la Rápita = Sant Carles de la Ràpita, Spain 32 E5 40 37N 0 35 E
San Carlos del Zulia, Venezuela 124 B4 9 1N 71 55W
San Carlos L., U.S.A. 115 K8 33 11N 110 32W
San Cataldo, Italy 30 E6 37 29N 13 59 E
San Celoni = Sant Celoni, Spain 32 D7 41 42N 2 30 E
San Clemente, Chile 126 D1 35 30 S 71 29W
San Clemente, Spain 33 F2 39 24N 2 25W
San Clemente, U.S.A. 117 M9 33 26N 117 37W
San Clemente I., U.S.A. 117 N8 32 53N 118 29W
San Cristóbal = Es Migjorn Gran, Spain 37 B11 39 57N 4 3 E
San Cristóbal, Argentina 126 C3 30 20 S 61 10W
San Cristóbal, Dom. Rep. 121 C5 18 25N 70 6W
San Cristóbal, Venezuela 124 B4 7 46N 72 14W
San Cristóbal de la Casas, Mexico 119 D6 16 50N 92 33W
San Damiano d'Asti, Italy 28 D5 44 50N 8 4 E
San Daniele del Friuli, Italy 29 B10 46 9N 13 1 E
San Diego, Calif., U.S.A. 117 N9 32 43N 117 9W
San Diego, Tex., U.S.A. 113 M5 27 46N 98 14W
San Diego, C., Argentina 128 G3 54 40 S 65 10W
San Diego de la Unión, Mexico 118 C4 21 28N 100 52W
San Dimitri, Ras, Malta 36 C1 36 4N 14 11 E
San Donà di Piave, Italy 29 C9 45 38N 12 34 E
San Estanislao, Paraguay 126 A4 24 39 S 56 26W
San Esteban de Gormaz, Spain 32 D1 41 34N 3 13W
San Felice Circeo, Italy 30 A6 41 14N 13 5 E
San Felice sul Panaro, Italy 29 D8 44 51N 11 8 E
San Felipe, Chile 126 C1 32 43 S 70 42W
San Felipe, Mexico 118 A2 31 0N 114 52W
San Felipe, Venezuela 124 A5 10 20N 68 44W
San Felipe →, U.S.A. 117 M11 33 12N 115 49W
San Felix, Chile 126 B1 28 56 S 70 28W
San Félix, Pac. Oc. 122 F2 26 23 S 80 0W
San Fernando = Sant Ferran, Spain 37 C7 38 42N 1 28 E
San Fernando, Chile 126 C1 34 30 S 71 0W
San Fernando, Baja Calif., Mexico 118 B1 29 55N 115 10W
San Fernando, Tamaulipas, Mexico 119 C5 24 51N 98 10W
San Fernando, La Union, Phil. 61 C4 16 40N 120 23 E
San Fernando, Pampanga, Phil. 61 D4 15 5N 120 37 E
San Fernando, Spain 35 J4 36 28N 6 17W
San Fernando, Trin. & Tob. 121 D7 10 20N 61 30W
San Fernando, U.S.A. 117 L8 34 17N 118 26W
San Fernando de Apure, Venezuela 124 B5 7 54N 67 15W
San Fernando de Atabapo, Venezuela 124 C5 4 3N 67 42W
San Fernando di Púglia, Italy 31 A9 41 18N 16 5 E
San Francisco, Argentina 126 C3 31 30 S 62 5W
San Francisco, U.S.A. 116 H4 37 47N 122 25W
San Francisco →, U.S.A. 115 K9 32 59N 109 22W
San Francisco, Paso de, S. Amer. 126 B2 27 0 S 68 0W
San Francisco de Macorís, Dom. Rep. 121 C5 19 19N 70 15W
San Francisco del Monte de Oro, Argentina 126 C2 32 36 S 66 8W
San Francisco del Oro, Mexico 118 B3 26 52N 105 50W
San Francisco Javier = Sant Francesc de Formentera, Spain 37 C7 38 42N 1 26 E
San Francisco Solano, Pta., Colombia 122 C3 6 18N 77 29W
San Fratello, Italy 31 D7 38 1N 14 36 E
San Gabriel, Chile 126 C1 33 47 S 70 15W
San Gabriel Mts., U.S.A. 117 L9 34 20N 118 0W
San Gavino Monreale, Italy 30 C1 39 33N 8 47 E
San Gimignano, Italy 28 E8 43 28N 11 2 E
San Giórgio di Nogaro, Italy 29 C10 45 50N 13 13 E
San Giórgio Iónico, Italy 31 B10 40 27N 17 23 E
San Giovanni Bianco, Italy 28 C6 45 52N 9 39 E
San Giovanni in Fiore, Italy 31 C9 39 15N 16 42 E
San Giovanni in Persiceto, Italy 29 D8 44 38N 11 11 E
San Giovanni Rotondo, Italy 29 G12 41 42N 15 44 E
San Giovanni Valdarno, Italy 29 E8 43 34N 11 32 E
San Giuliano Terme, Italy 28 E7 43 46N 10 26 E
San Gorgonio Mt., U.S.A. 117 L10 34 7N 116 51W
San Gottardo, P. del, Switz. 25 J4 46 33N 8 33 E
San Gregorio, Uruguay 127 C4 32 37 S 55 40W
San Gregorio, U.S.A. 116 H4 37 20N 122 23W
San Guiseppe Jato, Italy 30 E6 37 57N 13 11 E
San Ignacio, Belize 119 D7 17 10N 89 0W
San Ignacio, Bolivia 124 G6 16 20 S 60 55W
San Ignacio, Mexico 118 B2 27 27N 113 0W
San Ignacio, Paraguay 120 C2 26 52 S 57 3W
San Ignacio, L., Mexico 118 B2 26 50N 113 11W
San Ildefonso, C., Phil. 61 C5 16 0N 122 1 E
San Isidro, Argentina 126 C4 34 29 S 58 31W
San Isidro, Phil. 61 H7 6 50N 126 5 E
San Jacinto, U.S.A. 117 M10 33 47N 116 57W
San Jaime = Sant Jaume, Spain 37 B11 39 54N 4 4 E
San Javier, Misiones, Argentina 127 B4 27 55 S 55 5W
San Javier, Santa Fe, Argentina 126 C4 30 40 S 59 55W
San Javier, Bolivia 124 G6 16 18 S 62 30W
San Javier, Chile 126 D1 35 40 S 71 45W
San Javier, Spain 33 H4 37 49N 0 50W
San Jeronimo Taviche, Mexico 119 D5 16 38N 96 32W
San Joaquin, U.S.A. 116 J6 36 36N 120 11W
San Joaquin →, U.S.A. 116 G5 38 4N 121 51W
San Joaquin Valley, U.S.A. 116 J6 37 20N 121 0W
San Jon, U.S.A. 113 H3 35 6N 103 20W
San Jordi = Sant Jordi, Spain 37 B9 39 33N 2 46 E
San Jorge, Argentina 126 C3 31 54 S 61 50W
San Jorge, Spain 37 C7 38 54N 1 24 E
San Jorge, B. de, Mexico 118 A2 31 20N 113 20W
San Jorge, G., Argentina 128 F3 46 0 S 66 0W
San Jorge, G. of, Argentina 122 H4 46 0 S 66 0W
San José = San Josep, Spain 37 C7 38 55N 1 18 E
San José, Costa Rica 120 E3 9 55N 84 2W
San José, Guatemala 120 D1 14 0N 90 50W
San José, Mexico 118 C2 25 0N 110 50W
San Jose, Mind. Occ., Phil. 61 E4 12 27N 121 4 E
San Jose, Nueva Ecija, Phil. 61 D4 15 45N 120 55 E
San Jose, U.S.A. 116 H5 37 20N 121 53W
San Jose →, U.S.A. 115 J10 34 25N 106 45W
San Jose de Buenavista, Phil. 63 B6 10 45N 121 56 E
San José de Chiquitos, Bolivia 124 G6 17 53 S 60 50W
San José de Feliciano, Argentina 126 C4 30 26 S 58 46W
San José de Jáchal, Argentina 126 C2 30 15 S 68 46W
San José de Mayo, Uruguay 126 C4 34 27 S 56 40W
San José del Cabo, Mexico 118 C3 23 0N 109 40W
San José del Guaviare, Colombia 124 C4 2 35N 72 38W
San Josep, Spain 37 C7 38 55N 1 18 E
San Juan, Argentina 126 C2 31 30 S 68 30W
San Juan, Mexico 118 C4 21 20N 102 50W
San Juan, Phil. 61 F6 10 16N 125 10 E
San Juan, Puerto Rico 121 C6 18 28N 66 7W
San Juan □, Argentina 126 C2 31 9 S 69 0W
San Juan →, Argentina 126 C2 32 20 S 67 25W
San Juan →, Nic. 120 D3 10 56N 83 42W
San Juan →, U.S.A. 115 H8 37 16N 110 26W
San Juan Bautista = Sant Joan Baptista, Spain 37 B8 39 5N 1 31 E
San Juan Bautista, Paraguay 126 B4 26 37 S 57 6W
San Juan Bautista, U.S.A. 116 J5 36 51N 121 32W
San Juan Bautista Valle Nacional, Mexico 119 D5 17 47N 96 19W
San Juan Capistrano, U.S.A. 117 M9 33 30N 117 40W
San Juan Cr. →, U.S.A. 116 J5 35 40N 120 22W
San Juan de Alicante, Spain 33 G4 38 24N 0 26W
San Juan de Guadalupe, Mexico 118 C4 24 38N 102 44W
San Juan de la Costa, Mexico 118 C2 24 23N 110 45W
San Juan de los Morros, Venezuela 124 B5 9 55N 67 21W
San Juan del Norte, Nic. 120 D3 10 58N 83 40W
San Juan del Norte, B. de, Nic. 120 D3 11 0N 83 40W
San Juan del Río, Mexico 119 C5 20 25N 100 0W
San Juan del Sur, Nic. 120 D2 11 20N 85 51W
San Juan I., U.S.A. 116 B3 48 32N 123 5W
San Juan Mts., U.S.A. 115 H10 37 30N 107 0W
San Just, Sierra de, Spain 32 E4 40 45N 0 49W
San Justo, Argentina 126 C3 30 47 S 60 30W
San Kamphaeng, Thailand 64 C2 18 45N 99 8 E
San Lázaro, C., Mexico 118 C2 24 50N 112 18W
San Lázaro, Sa., Mexico 118 C3 23 25N 110 0W
San Leandro, U.S.A. 116 H4 37 44N 122 9W
San Leonardo de Yagüe, Spain 32 D1 41 51N 3 5W
San Lorenzo = Sant Llorenç des Cardassar, Spain 37 B10 39 37N 3 17 E
San Lorenzo, Argentina 126 C3 32 45 S 60 45W
San Lorenzo, Ecuador 124 C3 1 15N 78 50W
San Lorenzo, Paraguay 126 B4 25 20 S 57 32W
San Lorenzo →, Mexico 118 C3 24 15N 107 24W
San Lorenzo, I., Mexico 118 B2 28 35N 112 50W
San Lorenzo, Mte., Argentina 128 F2 47 40 S 72 20W
San Lorenzo de la Parrilla, Spain 32 F2 39 51N 2 22W
San Lorenzo de Morunys = Sant Llorenç de Morunys, Spain 32 C6 42 8N 1 35 E
San Lucas, Bolivia 124 H5 20 5 S 65 7W
San Lucas, Baja Calif. S., Mexico 118 C3 22 53N 109 54W
San Lucas, Baja Calif. S., Mexico 118 B2 27 10N 112 14W
San Lucas, U.S.A. 116 J5 36 8N 121 1W
San Lucas, C., Mexico 118 C3 22 50N 110 0W
San Lúcido, Italy 31 C9 39 18N 16 3 E
San Luis, Argentina 126 C2 33 20 S 66 20W
San Luis, Cuba 120 B3 22 17N 83 46W
San Luis, Guatemala 120 C2 16 14N 89 27W
San Luis, Ariz., U.S.A. 115 K6 32 29N 114 47W
San Luis, Colo., U.S.A. 115 H11 37 12N 105 25W
San Luis □, Argentina 126 C2 34 0 S 66 0W
San Luis, I., Mexico 118 B2 29 58N 114 26W
San Luis, Sierra de, Argentina 126 C2 32 30 S 66 10W
San Luis de la Paz, Mexico 118 C4 21 19N 100 32W
San Luis Obispo, U.S.A. 117 K6 35 17N 120 40W
San Luis Potosí, Mexico 118 C4 22 9N 100 59W
San Luis Potosí □, Mexico 118 C4 22 10N 101 0W
San Luis Reservoir, U.S.A. 116 H5 37 4N 121 5W
San Luis Río Colorado, Mexico 118 A2 32 29N 114 58W
San Manuel, U.S.A. 115 K8 32 36N 110 38W
San Marco, C., Italy 30 C1 39 51N 8 26 E
San Marco Argentano, Italy 31 C9 39 33N 16 7 E
San Marco in Lámis, Italy 29 G12 41 43N 15 38 E
San Marcos, Guatemala 120 D1 14 59N 91 52W
San Marcos, Mexico 118 B2 27 13N 112 6W
San Marcos, Calif., U.S.A. 117 M9 33 9N 117 10W
San Marcos, Tex., U.S.A. 113 L6 29 53N 97 56W
San Marino, San Marino 29 E9 43 55N 12 30 E
San Marino ■, Europe 29 E9 43 56N 12 25 E
San Martín, Argentina 126 C2 33 5 S 68 28W
San Martín →, Bolivia 124 F6 13 8 S 63 43W
San Martín, L., Argentina 128 F2 48 50 S 72 50W
San Martín de la Vega, Spain 34 E7 40 13N 3 34W
San Martin de los Andes, Argentina 128 E2 40 10 S 71 20W
San Martín de Valdeiglesias, Spain 34 E6 40 21N 4 24W
San Mateo = Sant Mateu, Baleares, Spain 37 B7 39 3N 1 23 E
San Mateo = Sant Mateu, Valencia, Spain 32 E5 40 28N 0 10 E
San Mateo, Phil. 61 C4 16 54N 121 33 E
San Mateo, U.S.A. 116 H4 37 34N 122 19W
San Matías, Bolivia 124 G7 16 25 S 58 20W
San Matías, G., Argentina 122 H4 41 30 S 64 0W
San Miguel = Sant Miquel, Spain 37 B7 39 3N 1 26 E
San Miguel, El Salv. 120 D2 13 30N 88 12W
San Miguel, Panama 120 E4 8 27N 78 55W
San Miguel, U.S.A. 116 K6 35 45N 120 42W
San Miguel →, Bolivia 124 F6 13 52 S 63 56W
San Miguel de Tucumán, Argentina 126 B2 26 50 S 65 20W
San Miguel del Monte, Argentina 126 D4 35 23 S 58 50W
San Miguel I., U.S.A. 117 L6 34 2N 120 23W
San Miniato, Italy 28 E7 43 41N 10 51 E
San Nicolás, Canary Is. 37 G4 27 58N 15 47W
San Nicolas, Phil. 61 B4 18 10N 120 36 E
San Nicolás de los Arroyas, Argentina 126 C3 33 25 S 60 10W
San Nicolas I., U.S.A. 117 M7 33 15N 119 30W
San Onofre, U.S.A. 117 M9 33 22N 117 34W
San Pablo, Bolivia 126 A2 21 43 S 66 38W
San Pablo, Phil. 61 D4 14 11N 121 31 E
San Pablo, U.S.A. 116 H4 37 58N 122 21W
San Páolo di Civitate, Italy 29 G12 41 44N 15 15 E
San Pedro, Buenos Aires, Argentina 126 C4 33 40 S 59 40W
San Pedro, Misiones, Argentina 127 B5 26 30 S 54 10W
San Pedro, Chile 126 C1 33 54 S 71 28W
San Pédro, Ivory C. 82 E3 4 50N 6 33W
San Pedro, Mexico 118 C2 23 55N 110 17W
San Pedro □, Paraguay 126 A4 24 0 S 57 0W
San Pedro →, Chihuahua, Mexico 118 B3 28 20N 106 10W
San Pedro →, Nayarit, Mexico 118 C3 21 45N 105 30W
San Pedro →, U.S.A. 115 K8 32 59N 110 47W
San Pedro, Pta., Chile 126 B1 25 30 S 70 38W
San Pedro, Sierra de, Spain 35 F4 39 18N 6 40W
San Pedro Channel, U.S.A. 117 M8 33 30N 118 25W
San Pedro de Atacama, Chile 126 A2 22 55 S 68 15W
San Pedro de Jujuy, Argentina 126 A3 24 12 S 64 55W
San Pedro de las Colonias, Mexico 118 B4 25 50N 102 59W
San Pedro de Macorís, Dom. Rep. 121 C6 18 30N 69 18W
San Pedro del Norte, Nic. 120 D3 13 4N 84 33W
San Pedro del Paraná, Paraguay 126 B4 26 43 S 56 13W
San Pedro del Pinatar, Spain 33 H4 37 50N 0 50W
San Pedro Mártir, Sierra, Mexico 118 A1 31 0N 115 30W
San Pedro Mixtepec, Mexico 119 D5 16 2N 97 7W

Sretensk

Solapur, *India* **66 L9** 17 43N 75 56 E
Solca, *Romania* **43 C10** 47 40N 25 50 E
Solda Gölü, *Turkey* **39 D11** 37 33N 29 42 E
Soldănești, *Moldova* **43 C13** 47 49N 28 48 E
Soldotna, *U.S.A.* **100 B4** 60 29N 151 3W
Soléa □, *Cyprus* **36 D12** 35 5N 33 4 E
Solec Kujawski, *Poland* **45 E5** 53 5N 18 14 E
Soledad, *Colombia* **124 A4** 10 55N 74 46W
Soledad, *U.S.A.* **116 J5** 36 26N 121 20W
Soledad, *Venezuela* **124 B6** 8 10N 63 34W
Solent, The, *U.K.* **13 G6** 50 45N 1 25W
Solenzara, *France* **21 G13** 41 53N 9 23 E
Solesmes, *France* **19 B10** 50 10N 3 30 E
Solfonn, *Norway* **9 F12** 60 2N 6 57 E
Solhan, *Turkey* **70 B4** 38 57N 41 3 E
Soligorsk = Salihorsk, *Belarus* **47 F4** 52 51N 27 27 E
Solihull, *U.K.* **13 E6** 52 26N 1 47W
Solikamsk, *Russia* **50 D6** 59 38N 56 50 E
Solila, *Madag.* **89 C8** 21 25 S 46 37 E
Solimões = Amazonas →, *S. Amer.* **122 D5** 0 5 S 50 0W
Solin, *Croatia* **29 E13** 43 33N 16 30 E
Solingen, *Germany* **24 D3** 51 10N 7 5 E
Sollebrunn, *Sweden* **11 F6** 58 8N 12 32 E
Sollefteå, *Sweden* **10 A11** 63 12N 17 20 E
Sollentuna, *Sweden* **10 E11** 59 26N 17 56 E
Sóller, *Spain* **37 B9** 39 46N 2 43 E
Sollerön, *Sweden* **10 D8** 60 55N 14 37 E
Solling, *Germany* **24 D5** 51 42N 9 38 E
Solnechnogorsk, *Russia* **46 D9** 56 10N 36 57 E
Solo →, *Indonesia* **63 G15** 6 47 S 112 22 E
Solofra, *Italy* **31 B7** 40 50N 14 51 E
Sologne, *France* **19 E8** 47 40N 1 45 E
Solok, *Indonesia* **62 E2** 0 45 S 100 40 E
Sololá, *Guatemala* **120 D1** 14 49N 91 10W
Solomon, N. Fork →, *U.S.A.* **112 F5** 39 29N 98 26W
Solomon, S. Fork →, *U.S.A.* **112 F5** 39 25N 99 12W
Solomon Is. ■, *Pac. Oc.* **96 H7** 6 0 S 155 0 E
Solon, *China* **60 B7** 46 32N 121 10 E
Solon Springs, *U.S.A.* **112 B9** 46 22N 91 49W
Solor, *Indonesia* **63 F6** 8 27 S 123 0 E
Solotcha, *Russia* **46 E10** 54 48N 39 53 E
Solothurn, *Switz.* **25 H3** 47 13N 7 32 E
Solothurn □, *Switz.* **25 H3** 47 18N 7 40 E
Solsona, *Spain* **32 C6** 42 0N 1 31 E
Solt, *Hungary* **42 D4** 46 45N 19 1 E
Šolta, *Croatia* **29 E13** 43 24N 16 15 E
Solṭānābād, *Khorāsān, Iran* **71 C8** 34 13N 59 58 E
Solṭānābād, *Khorāsān, Iran* **71 B8** 36 29N 58 5 E
Soltau, *Germany* **24 C5** 52 59N 9 50 E
Soltsy, *Russia* **46 C6** 58 10N 30 30 E
Solunska Glava, *Macedonia* **40 E5** 41 44N 21 31 E
Solvang, *U.S.A.* **117 L6** 34 36N 120 8W
Solvay, *U.S.A.* **111 C8** 43 3N 76 13W
Sölvesborg, *Sweden* **11 H8** 56 5N 14 35 E
Solway Firth, *U.K.* **12 C4** 54 49N 3 35W
Solwezi, *Zambia* **87 E2** 12 11 S 26 21 E
Sōma, *Japan* **54 F10** 37 40N 140 50 E
Soma, *Turkey* **39 B9** 39 10N 27 35 E
Somabhula, *Zimbabwe* **89 B4** 19 42 S 29 40 E
Somali Pen., *Africa* **76 F8** 7 0N 46 0 E
Somali Rep. ■, *Africa* **74 F4** 7 0N 47 0 E
Somalia = Somali Rep. ■, *Africa* **74 F4** 7 0N 47 0 E
Sombernon, *France* **19 E11** 47 20N 4 40 E
Sombor, *Serbia, Yug.* **42 E4** 45 46N 19 9 E
Sombra, *Canada* **110 D2** 42 43N 82 29W
Sombrerete, *Mexico* **118 C4** 23 40N 103 40W
Sombrero, *Anguilla* **121 C7** 18 37N 63 30W
Şomcuta Mare, *Romania* **43 C8** 47 31N 23 28 E
Somdari, *India* **68 G5** 25 47N 72 38 E
Somers, *U.S.A.* **114 B6** 48 5N 114 13W
Somerset, *Ky., U.S.A.* **108 G3** 37 5N 84 36W
Somerset, *Mass., U.S.A.* **111 E13** 41 47N 71 8W
Somerset, *Pa., U.S.A.* **110 F5** 40 1N 79 5W
Somerset □, *U.K.* **13 F5** 51 9N 3 0W
Somerset East, *S. Africa* **88 E4** 32 42 S 25 35 E
Somerset I., *Canada* **100 A10** 73 30N 93 0W
Somerset West, *S. Africa* **88 E2** 34 8 S 18 50 E
Somersworth, *U.S.A.* **111 C14** 43 16N 70 52W
Somerton, *U.S.A.* **115 K6** 32 36N 114 43W
Somerville, *U.S.A.* **111 F10** 40 35N 74 38W
Someș →, *Romania* **42 C7** 47 49N 22 43 E
Someșul Mare →, *Romania* **43 C8** 47 9N 23 55 E
Somme □, *France* **19 C9** 49 57N 2 20 E
Somme →, *France* **19 B8** 50 11N 1 38 E
Somme, B. de la, *France* **18 B8** 50 14N 1 33 E
Sommen, *Jönköping, Sweden* **11 F8** 58 12N 14 58 E
Sommen, *Östergötland, Sweden* **11 F9** 58 0N 15 15 E
Sommepy-Tahure, *France* **19 C11** 49 15N 4 31 E
Sömmerda, *Germany* **24 D7** 51 9N 11 7 E
Sommesous, *France* **19 D11** 48 44N 4 12 E
Sommières, *France* **21 E8** 43 47N 4 6 E
Somnath, *India* **68 J4** 20 53N 70 22 E
Somogy □, *Hungary* **42 D2** 46 19N 17 30 E
Somogyszob, *Hungary* **42 D2** 46 18N 17 20 E
Somoto, *Nic.* **120 D2** 13 28N 86 37W
Sompolno, *Poland* **45 F5** 52 26N 18 30 E
Somport, Puerto de, *Spain* **32 C4** 42 48N 0 31W
Son →, *India* **69 G11** 25 42N 84 52 E
Son Ha, *Vietnam* **64 E7** 15 3N 108 34 E
Son Hoa, *Vietnam* **64 F7** 13 2N 108 58 E
Son La, *Vietnam* **58 G4** 21 20N 103 50 E
Son Serra, *Spain* **37 B10** 39 43N 3 13 E
Son Servera, *Spain* **32 F8** 39 37N 3 21 E
Son Tay, *Vietnam* **58 G5** 21 8N 105 30 E
Soná, *Panama* **120 E3** 8 0N 81 20W
Sonamarg, *India* **69 B6** 34 18N 75 21 E
Sonamukhi, *India* **69 H12** 23 18N 87 27 E
Sonar →, *India* **69 G8** 24 24N 79 56 E
Sŏnch'ŏn, *N. Korea* **57 E13** 39 48N 124 55 E
Sondags →, *S. Africa* **88 E4** 33 44 S 25 51 E
Sóndalo, *Italy* **28 B7** 46 20N 10 19 E
Sondar, *India* **69 C6** 33 28N 75 56 E
Sønder Felding, *Denmark* **11 J2** 55 57N 8 47 E
Sønder Omme, *Denmark* **11 J2** 55 50N 8 54 E
Sønderborg, *Denmark* **11 K3** 54 55N 9 49 E
Sønderjyllands Amtskommune □, *Denmark* **11 J3** 55 10N 9 10 E
Sondershausen, *Germany* **24 D6** 51 22N 10 51 E
Sóndrio, *Italy* **28 B6** 46 10N 9 52 E
Sone, *Mozam.* **87 F3** 17 23 S 34 55 E
Sonepur, *India* **67 J13** 20 55N 83 50 E
Song, *Nigeria* **83 D7** 9 49N 12 39 E
Song, *Thailand* **64 C3** 18 28N 100 11 E
Song Cau, *Vietnam* **64 F7** 13 27N 109 18 E
Song Xian, *China* **56 G7** 34 12N 112 8 E
Songch'ŏn, *N. Korea* **57 E14** 39 12N 126 15 E
Songea, *Tanzania* **87 E4** 10 40 S 35 40 E
Songeons, *France* **19 C8** 49 32N 1 50 E
Songhua Hu, *China* **57 C14** 43 35N 126 50 E
Songhua Jiang →, *China* **60 B8** 47 45N 132 30 E
Songjiang, *China* **59 B13** 31 1N 121 12 E
Songjin, *N. Korea* **57 D15** 40 40N 129 10 E
Songjŏng-ni, *S. Korea* **57 G14** 35 8N 126 47 E
Songkan, *China* **58 C6** 28 35N 106 52 E
Songkhla, *Thailand* **65 J3** 7 13N 100 37 E
Songming, *China* **58 E4** 25 12N 103 2 E
Songnim, *N. Korea* **57 E13** 38 45N 125 39 E
Songo, *Mozam.* **85 H6** 15 34 S 32 38 E
Songo, *Sudan* **79 G10** 9 47N 24 21 E
Songpan, *China* **58 A4** 32 40N 103 30 E
Songtao, *China* **58 C7** 28 11N 109 10 E
Songwe, *Dem. Rep. of the Congo* **86 C2** 3 20 S 26 16 E
Songwe →, *Africa* **87 D3** 9 44 S 33 58 E
Songxi, *China* **59 D12** 27 31N 118 44 E
Songzi, *China* **59 B8** 30 12N 111 45 E
Sonhat, *India* **69 H10** 23 29N 82 31 E
Sonid Youqi, *China* **56 C7** 42 45N 112 48 E
Sonipat, *India* **68 E7** 29 0N 77 5 E
Sonkach, *India* **68 H7** 22 59N 76 21 E
Sonkovo, *Russia* **46 D9** 57 50N 37 5 E
Sonmiani, *Pakistan* **68 G2** 25 25N 66 40 E
Sonmiani B., *Pakistan* **68 G2** 25 15N 66 30 E
Sonnino, *Italy* **30 A6** 41 25N 13 14 E
Sono →, *Brazil* **125 E9** 9 58 S 48 11W
Sonoma, *U.S.A.* **116 G4** 38 18N 122 28W
Sonora, *Calif., U.S.A.* **116 H6** 37 59N 120 23W
Sonora, *Tex., U.S.A.* **113 K4** 30 34N 100 39W
Sonora □, *Mexico* **118 B2** 29 0N 111 0W
Sonora →, *Mexico* **118 B2** 28 50N 111 33W
Sonoran Desert, *U.S.A.* **117 L12** 33 40N 114 15W
Sonoyta, *Mexico* **118 A2** 31 51N 112 50W
Sonqor, *Iran* **73 E12** 34 47N 47 36 E
Sŏnsan, *S. Korea* **57 F15** 36 14N 128 17 E
Sonseca, *Spain* **35 F7** 39 42N 3 57W
Sonsonate, *El Salv.* **120 D2** 13 43N 89 44W
Sonsorol Is., *Pac. Oc.* **63 C8** 5 30N 132 15 E
Sonstorp, *Sweden* **11 F9** 58 44N 15 38 E
Sonthofen, *Germany* **25 H6** 47 30N 10 16 E
Soochow = Suzhou, *China* **59 B13** 31 19N 120 38 E
Sooke, *Canada* **116 B3** 48 13N 123 43W
Sop Hao, *Laos* **58 G5** 20 33N 104 27 E
Sop Prap, *Thailand* **64 D2** 17 53N 99 20 E
Sopelana, *Spain* **32 B2** 43 23N 2 58W
Sopi, *Indonesia* **63 D7** 2 34N 128 28 E
Sopo, Nahr →, *Sudan* **81 F2** 8 40N 26 30 E
Sopot, *Bulgaria* **41 D8** 42 39N 24 45 E
Sopot, *Poland* **44 D5** 54 27N 18 31 E
Sopot, *Serbia, Yug.* **40 B4** 44 29N 20 36 E
Sopotnica, *Macedonia* **40 E5** 41 18N 21 13 E
Sopron, *Hungary* **42 C1** 47 45N 16 32 E
Sopur, *India* **69 B6** 34 18N 74 27 E
Sør-Rondane, *Antarctica* **5 D4** 72 0 S 25 0 E
Sora, *Italy* **29 G10** 41 43N 13 37 E
Sorah, *Pakistan* **68 F3** 27 13N 68 56 E
Soråker, *Sweden* **10 B11** 62 30N 17 32 E
Sorano, *Italy* **29 F8** 42 41N 11 43 E
Soraon, *India* **69 G9** 25 37N 81 51 E
Sorbas, *Spain* **33 H2** 37 6N 2 7W
Sörbygden, *Sweden* **10 B10** 62 48N 16 12 E
Sore, *France* **20 D3** 44 18N 0 35W
Sorel, *Canada* **102 C5** 46 0N 73 10W
Soresina, *Italy* **28 C6** 45 17N 9 51 E
Sörforsa, *Sweden* **10 C10** 61 43N 16 58 E
Sórgono, *Italy* **30 B2** 40 1N 9 6 E
Sorgues, *France* **21 D8** 44 1N 4 53 E
Sorgun, *Turkey* **72 C6** 39 46N 35 11 E
Soria, *Spain* **32 D2** 41 43N 2 32W
Soria □, *Spain* **32 D2** 41 46N 2 28W
Soriano, *Uruguay* **126 C4** 33 24 S 58 19W
Soriano nel Cimino, *Italy* **29 F9** 42 25N 12 14 E
Sorkh, Kuh-e, *Iran* **71 C8** 35 40N 58 30 E
Sorø, *Denmark* **11 J5** 55 26N 11 32 E
Soro, *Guinea* **82 C3** 10 9N 9 48W
Soroca, *Moldova* **43 B13** 48 8N 28 12 E
Sorocaba, *Brazil* **127 A6** 23 31 S 47 27W
Soroki = Soroca, *Moldova* **43 B13** 48 8N 28 12 E
Sorol Atoll, *Pac. Oc.* **63 C10** 7 45N 140 45 E
Sorong, *Indonesia* **63 E8** 0 55 S 131 15 E
Soroní, *Greece* **36 C10** 36 21N 28 1 E
Soroti, *Uganda* **86 B3** 1 43N 33 35 E
Sørøya, *Norway* **8 A20** 70 40N 22 30 E
Sørøysundet, *Norway* **8 A20** 70 25N 23 0 E
Sorraia →, *Portugal* **35 G2** 38 55N 8 53W
Sorrell, *Australia* **94 G4** 42 47 S 147 34 E
Sorrento, *Italy* **31 B7** 40 37N 14 22 E
Sorsele, *Sweden* **8 D17** 65 31N 17 30 E
Sörsjön, *Sweden* **10 C7** 61 24N 13 5 E
Sorso, *Italy* **30 B1** 40 48N 8 34 E
Sorsogon, *Phil.* **61 E6** 13 0N 124 0 E
Sortavala, *Russia* **46 B6** 61 42N 30 41 E
Sortino, *Italy* **31 E8** 37 9N 15 2 E
Sortland, *Norway* **8 B16** 68 42N 15 25 E
Sorvizhi, *Russia* **48 B9** 57 52N 48 32 E
Sos = Sos del Rey Católico, *Spain* **32 C3** 42 30N 1 13W
Sos del Rey Católico, *Spain* **32 C3** 42 30N 1 13W
Sŏsan, *S. Korea* **57 F14** 36 47N 126 27 E
Soscumica, L., *Canada* **102 B4** 50 15N 77 27W
Sösdala, *Sweden* **11 H7** 56 2N 13 41 E
Sosna →, *Russia* **47 F10** 52 42N 38 55 E
Sosnovka, *Kirov, Russia* **48 B10** 56 17N 51 17 E
Sosnovka, *Tambov, Russia* **48 D5** 53 13N 41 24 E
Sosnovyy Bor, *Russia* **46 C5** 59 55N 29 6 E
Sosnowiec, *Poland* **45 H6** 50 20N 19 10 E
Sospel, *France* **21 E11** 43 52N 7 27 E
Sossus Vlei, *Namibia* **88 C2** 24 40 S 15 23 E
Šoštanj, *Slovenia* **29 B12** 46 23N 15 4 E
Sŏsura, *N. Korea* **57 C16** 42 16N 130 36 E
Sot →, *India* **69 F8** 27 27N 79 37 E
Sotkamo, *Finland* **8 D23** 64 8N 28 23 E
Soto del Barco, *Spain* **34 B4** 43 32N 6 4W
Soto la Marina →, *Mexico* **119 C5** 23 40N 97 40W
Soto y Amío, *Spain* **34 C5** 42 46N 5 53W
Sotrondio, *Spain* **34 B5** 43 17N 5 36W
Sotuta, *Mexico* **119 C7** 20 29N 89 43W
Souanké, *Congo* **84 D2** 2 10N 14 3 E
Soubré, *Ivory C.* **82 D3** 5 50N 6 35W
Souderton, *U.S.A.* **111 F9** 40 19N 75 19W
Soúdha, *Greece* **36 D6** 35 29N 24 4 E
Soúdhas, Kólpos, *Greece* **36 D6** 35 25N 24 10 E
Souflíon, *Greece* **41 E10** 41 12N 26 18 E
Soufrière, *St. Lucia* **121 D7** 13 51N 61 3W
Souillac, *France* **20 D5** 44 53N 1 29 E
Souilly, *France* **19 C12** 49 3N 5 17 E
Soukhouma, *Laos* **64 E5** 14 38N 105 48 E
Sŏul, *S. Korea* **57 F14** 37 31N 126 58 E
Soulac-sur-Mer, *France* **20 C2** 45 30N 1 7W
Soulougou, *Burkina Faso* **83 C5** 13 1N 0 25 E
Soultz-sous-Forêts, *France* **19 D14** 48 57N 7 52 E
Sound, The = Øresund, *Europe* **11 J6** 55 45N 12 45 E
Sound, The, *U.K.* **13 G3** 50 20N 4 10W
Soúnion, Ákra, *Greece* **38 D6** 37 37N 24 1 E
Sources, Mt. aux, *Lesotho* **89 D4** 28 45 S 28 50 E
Soure, *Brazil* **125 D9** 0 35 S 48 30W
Soure, *Portugal* **34 E2** 40 4N 8 38W
Souris, *Man., Canada* **105 D8** 49 40N 100 20W
Souris, *P.E.I., Canada* **103 C7** 46 21N 62 15W
Souris →, *Canada* **112 A5** 49 40N 99 34W
Sourou →, *Africa* **82 C4** 12 45N 3 25W
Soúrpi, *Greece* **38 B4** 39 6N 22 54 E
Sousa, *Brazil* **125 E11** 6 45 S 38 10W
Sousel, *Portugal* **35 G3** 38 57N 7 40W
Sousse, *Tunisia* **79 A8** 35 50N 10 38 E
Soustons, *France* **20 E2** 43 45N 1 19W
Sout →, *S. Africa* **88 E2** 31 35 S 18 24 E
South Africa ■, *Africa* **88 E3** 32 0 S 23 0 E
South America **122 E5** 10 0 S 60 0W
South Atlantic Ocean **122 H7** 20 0 S 10 0W
South Aulatsivik I., *Canada* **103 A7** 56 45N 61 30W
South Australia □, *Australia* **95 E2** 32 0 S 139 0 E
South Ayrshire □, *U.K.* **14 F4** 55 18N 4 41W
South Baldy, *U.S.A.* **115 J10** 33 59N 107 11W
South Bass I., *U.S.A.* **110 E2** 41 39N 82 49W
South Bend, *Ind., U.S.A.* **108 E2** 41 41N 86 15W
South Bend, *Wash., U.S.A.* **116 D3** 46 40N 123 48W
South Boston, *U.S.A.* **109 G6** 36 42N 78 54W
South Branch, *Canada* **103 C8** 47 55N 59 2W
South Brook, *Canada* **103 C8** 49 26N 56 5W
South Carolina □, *U.S.A.* **109 J5** 34 0N 81 0W
South Charleston, *U.S.A.* **108 F5** 38 22N 81 44W
South China Sea, *Asia* **62 C4** 10 0N 113 0 E
South Dakota □, *U.S.A.* **112 C5** 44 15N 100 0W
South Deerfield, *U.S.A.* **111 D12** 42 29N 72 37W
South Downs, *U.K.* **13 G7** 50 52N 0 25W
South East C., *Australia* **94 G4** 43 40 S 146 50 E
South East Is., *Australia* **93 F3** 34 17 S 123 30 E
South Esk →, *U.K.* **14 E6** 56 43N 2 31W
South Foreland, *U.K.* **13 F9** 51 8N 1 24 E
South Fork American →, *U.S.A.* **116 G5** 38 45N 121 5W
South Fork Feather →, *U.S.A.* **116 F5** 39 17N 121 36W
South Fork Grand →, *U.S.A.* **112 C3** 45 43N 102 17W
South Fork Republican →, *U.S.A.* **112 E4** 40 3N 101 31W
South Georgia, *Antarctica* **122 J7** 54 30 S 37 0W
South Gloucestershire □, *U.K.* **13 F5** 51 32N 2 28W
South Hadley, *U.S.A.* **111 D12** 42 16N 72 35W
South Haven, *U.S.A.* **108 D2** 42 24N 86 16W
South Henik, L., *Canada* **105 A9** 61 30N 97 30W
South Honshu Ridge, *Pac. Oc.* **96 E6** 23 0N 143 0 E
South Horr, *Kenya* **86 B4** 2 12N 36 56 E
South I., *Kenya* **86 B4** 2 35N 36 35 E
South I., *N.Z.* **91 L3** 44 0 S 170 0 E
South Indian Lake, *Canada* **105 B9** 56 47N 98 56W
South Invercargill, *N.Z.* **91 M2** 46 26 S 168 23 E
South Knife →, *Canada* **105 B10** 58 55N 94 37W
South Koel →, *India* **69 H11** 22 32N 85 14 E
South Korea ■, *Asia* **57 G15** 36 0N 128 0 E
South Lake Tahoe, *U.S.A.* **116 G6** 38 57N 119 59W
South Lanarkshire □, *U.K.* **14 F5** 55 37N 3 53W
South Loup →, *U.S.A.* **112 E5** 41 4N 98 39W
South Magnetic Pole, *Antarctica* **5 C9** 64 8 S 138 8 E
South Milwaukee, *U.S.A.* **108 D2** 42 55N 87 52W
South Molton, *U.K.* **13 F4** 51 1N 3 51W
South Moose L., *Canada* **105 C8** 53 46N 100 8W
South Nahanni →, *Canada* **104 A4** 61 3N 123 21W
South Nation →, *Canada* **111 A9** 45 34N 75 6W
South Natuna Is. = Natuna Selatan, Kepulauan, *Indonesia* **65 L7** 2 45N 109 0 E
South Negril Pt., *Jamaica* **120 C4** 18 14N 78 30W
South Orkney Is., *Antarctica* **5 C18** 63 0 S 45 0W
South Ossetia □, *Georgia* **49 J7** 42 21N 44 2 E
South Pagai, I. = Pagai Selatan, Pulau, *Indonesia* **62 E2** 3 0 S 100 15 E
South Paris, *U.S.A.* **111 B14** 44 14N 70 31W
South Pittsburg, *U.S.A.* **109 H3** 35 1N 85 42W
South Platte →, *U.S.A.* **112 E4** 41 7N 100 42W
South Pole, *Antarctica* **5 E** 90 0 S 0 0W
South Porcupine, *Canada* **102 C3** 48 30N 81 12W
South Portland, *U.S.A.* **109 D10** 43 38N 70 15W
South Pt., *U.S.A.* **110 B1** 44 52N 83 19W
South River, *Canada* **102 C4** 45 52N 79 23W
South River, *U.S.A.* **111 F10** 40 27N 74 23W
South Ronaldsay, *U.K.* **14 C6** 58 48N 2 58W
South Sandwich Is., *Antarctica* **5 B1** 57 0 S 27 0W
South Saskatchewan →, *Canada* **105 C7** 53 15N 105 5W
South Seal →, *Canada* **105 B9** 58 48N 98 8W
South Shetland Is., *Antarctica* **5 C18** 62 0 S 59 0W
South Shields, *U.K.* **12 C6** 55 0N 1 25W
South Sioux City, *U.S.A.* **112 D6** 42 28N 96 24W
South Taranaki Bight, *N.Z.* **91 H5** 39 40 S 174 5 E
South Thompson →, *Canada* **104 C4** 50 40N 120 20W
South Twin I., *Canada* **102 B4** 53 7N 79 52W
South Tyne →, *U.K.* **12 C5** 54 59N 2 8W
South Uist, *U.K.* **14 D1** 57 20N 7 15W
South West Africa = Namibia ■, *Africa* **88 C2** 22 0 S 18 9 E
South West C., *Australia* **94 G4** 43 34 S 146 3 E
South Williamsport, *U.S.A.* **110 E8** 41 13N 77 0W
South Yorkshire □, *U.K.* **12 D6** 53 27N 1 36W
Southampton, *Canada* **102 D3** 44 30N 81 25W
Southampton, *U.K.* **13 G6** 50 54N 1 23W
Southampton, *U.S.A.* **111 F12** 40 53N 72 23W
Southampton □, *U.K.* **13 G6** 50 54N 1 23W
Southampton I., *Canada* **101 B11** 64 30N 84 0W
Southaven, *U.S.A.* **113 H9** 34 59N 90 2W
Southbank, *Canada* **104 C3** 54 2N 125 46W
Southbridge, *N.Z.* **91 K4** 43 48 S 172 16 E
Southbridge, *U.S.A.* **111 D12** 42 5N 72 2W
Southend, *Canada* **105 B8** 56 19N 103 22W
Southend-on-Sea, *U.K.* **13 F8** 51 32N 0 44 E
Southend-on-Sea □, *U.K.* **13 F8** 51 32N 0 44 E
Southern □, *Malawi* **87 F4** 15 0 S 35 0 E
Southern □, *S. Leone* **82 D2** 8 0N 12 30W
Southern □, *Zambia* **87 F2** 16 20 S 26 20 E
Southern Alps, *N.Z.* **91 K3** 43 41 S 170 11 E
Southern Cross, *Australia* **93 F2** 31 12 S 119 15 E
Southern Indian L., *Canada* **105 B9** 57 10N 98 30W
Southern Ocean, *Antarctica* **5 C6** 62 0 S 60 0 E
Southern Pines, *U.S.A.* **109 H6** 35 11N 79 24W
Southern Uplands, *U.K.* **14 F5** 55 28N 3 52W
Southington, *U.S.A.* **111 E12** 41 36N 72 53W
Southland □, *N.Z.* **91 L1** 45 30 S 168 0 E
Southold, *U.S.A.* **111 E12** 41 4N 72 26W
Southport, *Australia* **95 D5** 27 58 S 153 25 E
Southport, *U.K.* **12 D4** 53 39N 3 0W
Southport, *Fla., U.S.A.* **109 K3** 30 17N 85 38W
Southport, *N.Y., U.S.A.* **110 D8** 42 3N 76 49W
Southwest C., *N.Z.* **91 M1** 47 17 S 167 28 E
Southwold, *U.K.* **13 E9** 52 20N 1 41 E
Soutpansberg, *S. Africa* **89 C4** 23 0 S 29 30 E
Souvigny, *France* **19 F10** 46 33N 3 10 E
Sovata, *Romania* **43 D10** 46 35N 25 3 E
Soverato, *Italy* **31 D9** 38 41N 16 33 E
Sovetsk, *Kaliningd., Russia* **9 J19** 55 6N 21 50 E
Sovetsk, *Kirov, Russia* **48 B9** 57 38N 48 53 E
Sovetskaya Gavan = Vanino, *Russia* **51 E15** 48 50N 140 5 E
Sovicille, *Italy* **29 E8** 43 17N 11 13 E
Soweto, *S. Africa* **89 D4** 26 14 S 27 54 E
Sōya-Kaikyō = La Perouse Str., *Asia* **54 B11** 45 40N 142 0 E
Sōya-Misaki, *Japan* **54 B10** 45 30N 141 55 E
Soyaux, *France* **20 C4** 45 39N 0 12 E
Sozh →, *Belarus* **47 F6** 51 57N 30 48 E
Sozopol, *Bulgaria* **41 D11** 42 23N 27 42 E
Spa, *Belgium* **17 D5** 50 29N 5 53 E
Spain ■, *Europe* **7 H5** 39 0N 4 0W
Spalding, *Australia* **95 E2** 33 30 S 138 37 E
Spalding, *U.K.* **12 E7** 52 48N 0 9W
Spangler, *U.S.A.* **110 F6** 40 39N 78 48W
Spanish, *Canada* **102 C3** 46 12N 82 20W
Spanish Fork, *U.S.A.* **114 F8** 40 7N 111 39W
Spanish Town, *Jamaica* **120 C4** 18 0N 76 57W
Sparks, *U.S.A.* **116 F7** 39 32N 119 45W
Sparreholm, *Sweden* **10 E10** 59 4N 16 49 E
Sparta = Spárti, *Greece* **38 D4** 37 5N 22 25 E
Sparta, *Mich., U.S.A.* **108 D3** 43 10N 85 42W
Sparta, *N.J., U.S.A.* **111 E10** 41 2N 74 38W
Sparta, *Wis., U.S.A.* **112 D9** 43 56N 90 49W
Spartanburg, *U.S.A.* **109 H5** 34 56N 81 57W
Spartansburg, *U.S.A.* **110 E5** 41 49N 79 41W
Spárti, *Greece* **38 D4** 37 5N 22 25 E
Spartivento, C., *Calabria, Italy* **31 E9** 37 55N 16 4 E
Spartivento, C., *Sard., Italy* **30 D1** 38 53N 8 50 E
Sparwood, *Canada* **104 D6** 49 44N 114 53W
Spas-Demensk, *Russia* **46 E7** 54 20N 34 0 E
Spas-Klepiki, *Russia* **46 E11** 55 10N 40 10 E
Spassk Dalniy, *Russia* **51 E14** 44 40N 132 48 E
Spassk-Ryazanskiy, *Russia* **46 E11** 54 24N 40 25 E
Spátha, Ákra, *Greece* **36 D5** 35 42N 23 43 E
Spatsizi →, *Canada* **104 B3** 57 42N 128 7W
Spatsizi Plateau Wilderness Park, *Canada* **104 B3** 57 40N 128 0W
Spean →, *U.K.* **14 E4** 56 55N 4 59W
Spearfish, *U.S.A.* **112 C3** 44 30N 103 52W
Spearman, *U.S.A.* **113 G4** 36 12N 101 12W
Speculator, *U.S.A.* **111 C10** 43 30N 74 25W
Speia, *Moldova* **43 D14** 46 59N 29 19 E
Speightstown, *Barbados* **121 D8** 13 15N 59 39W
Speke Gulf, *Tanzania* **86 C3** 2 20 S 32 50 E
Spello, *Italy* **29 F9** 42 59N 12 40 E
Spencer, *Idaho, U.S.A.* **114 D7** 44 22N 112 11W
Spencer, *Iowa, U.S.A.* **112 D7** 43 9N 95 9W
Spencer, *N.Y., U.S.A.* **111 D8** 42 13N 76 30W
Spencer, *Nebr., U.S.A.* **112 D5** 42 53N 98 42W
Spencer, C., *Australia* **95 F2** 35 20 S 136 53 E
Spencer B., *Namibia* **88 D1** 25 30 S 14 47 E
Spencer G., *Australia* **95 E2** 34 0 S 137 20 E
Spencerville, *Canada* **111 B9** 44 51N 75 33W
Spences Bridge, *Canada* **104 C4** 50 25N 121 20W
Spennymoor, *U.K.* **12 C6** 54 42N 1 36W
Spenser Mts., *N.Z.* **91 K4** 42 15 S 172 45 E
Spentrup, *Denmark* **11 H4** 56 33N 10 2 E
Sperkhiós →, *Greece* **38 C4** 38 57N 22 3 E
Sperrin Mts., *U.K.* **15 B5** 54 50N 7 0W
Spessart, *Germany* **25 F5** 49 56N 9 18 E
Spétsai, *Greece* **38 D5** 37 15N 23 10 E
Spey →, *U.K.* **14 D5** 57 40N 3 6W
Speyer, *Germany* **25 F4** 49 29N 8 25 E
Spezand, *Pakistan* **68 E2** 29 59N 67 0 E
Spezzano Albanese, *Italy* **31 C9** 39 40N 16 19 E
Spiekeroog, *Germany* **24 B3** 53 46N 7 42 E
Spiez, *Switz.* **25 J3** 46 40N 7 40 E
Spíli, *Greece* **36 D6** 35 13N 24 31 E
Spilimbergo, *Italy* **29 B9** 46 7N 12 54 E
Spīn Búldak, *Afghan.* **68 D2** 31 1N 66 25 E
Spinalónga, *Greece* **36 D7** 35 18N 25 44 E
Spinazzola, *Italy* **31 B9** 40 58N 16 5 E
Spineni, *Romania* **43 F9** 44 43N 24 37 E
Spirit Lake, *U.S.A.* **116 D4** 46 15N 122 9W
Spirit River, *Canada* **104 B5** 55 45N 118 50W
Spiritwood, *Canada* **105 C7** 53 24N 107 33W
Spišská Nová Ves, *Slovak Rep.* **27 C13** 48 58N 20 34 E
Spišské Podhradie, *Slovak Rep.* **27 B13** 49 0N 20 48 E
Spital, *Austria* **26 D7** 47 42N 14 18 E
Spithead, *U.K.* **13 G6** 50 45N 1 10W
Spittal an der Drau, *Austria* **26 E6** 46 48N 13 31 E
Spitzbergen = Svalbard, *Arctic* **4 B8** 78 0N 17 0 E
Spjelkavik, *Norway* **9 E12** 62 28N 6 22 E
Split, *Croatia* **29 E13** 43 31N 16 26 E
Split L., *Canada* **105 B9** 56 8N 96 15W
Split Lake, *Canada* **105 B9** 56 8N 96 15W
Splitski Kanal, *Croatia* **29 E13** 43 31N 16 20 E
Splügenpass, *Switz.* **25 J5** 46 30N 9 20 E
Spofford, *U.S.A.* **113 L4** 29 10N 100 25W
Spokane, *U.S.A.* **114 C5** 47 40N 117 24W
Spoleto, *Italy* **29 F9** 42 44N 12 44 E
Spooner, *U.S.A.* **112 C9** 45 50N 91 53W
Sporyy Navolok, Mys, *Russia* **50 B7** 75 50N 68 40 E
Sprague, *U.S.A.* **114 C5** 47 18N 117 59W
Spratly I., *S. China Sea* **62 C4** 8 38N 111 55 E
Spratly Is., *S. China Sea* **62 C4** 8 20N 112 0 E
Spray, *U.S.A.* **114 D4** 44 50N 119 48W
Spreča →, *Bos.-H.* **42 F3** 44 44N 18 6 E
Spree →, *Germany* **24 C9** 52 32N 13 13 E
Spreewald, *Germany* **24 D9** 51 58N 13 51 E
Spremberg, *Germany* **24 D10** 51 34N 14 22 E
Sprengisandur, *Iceland* **8 D5** 64 52N 18 7W
Spring City, *U.S.A.* **111 F9** 40 11N 75 33W
Spring Creek, *U.S.A.* **114 F6** 40 45N 115 38W
Spring Garden, *U.S.A.* **116 F6** 39 52N 120 47W
Spring Hill, *U.S.A.* **109 L4** 28 27N 82 41W
Spring Mts., *U.S.A.* **115 H6** 36 0N 115 45W
Spring Valley, *U.S.A.* **117 N10** 32 45N 117 5W
Springbok, *S. Africa* **88 D2** 29 42 S 17 54 E
Springboro, *U.S.A.* **110 E4** 41 48N 80 22W
Springdale, *Canada* **103 C8** 49 30N 56 6W
Springdale, *U.S.A.* **113 G7** 36 11N 94 8W
Springe, *Germany* **24 C5** 52 13N 9 33 E
Springer, *U.S.A.* **113 G2** 36 22N 104 36W
Springerville, *U.S.A.* **115 J9** 34 8N 109 17W
Springfield, *Canada* **110 D4** 42 50N 80 56W
Springfield, *N.Z.* **91 K3** 43 19 S 171 56 E
Springfield, *Colo., U.S.A.* **113 G3** 37 24N 102 37W
Springfield, *Ill., U.S.A.* **112 F10** 39 48N 89 39W
Springfield, *Mass., U.S.A.* **111 D12** 42 6N 72 35W
Springfield, *Mo., U.S.A.* **113 G8** 37 13N 93 17W
Springfield, *Ohio, U.S.A.* **108 F4** 39 55N 83 49W
Springfield, *Oreg., U.S.A.* **114 D2** 44 3N 123 1W
Springfield, *Tenn., U.S.A.* **109 G2** 36 31N 86 53W
Springfield, *Vt., U.S.A.* **111 C12** 43 18N 72 29W
Springfontein, *S. Africa* **88 E4** 30 15 S 25 40 E
Springhill, *Canada* **103 C7** 45 40N 64 4W
Springhill, *U.S.A.* **113 J8** 33 0N 93 28W
Springhouse, *Canada* **104 C4** 51 56N 122 7W
Springs, *S. Africa* **89 D4** 26 13 S 28 25 E
Springsure, *Australia* **94 C4** 24 8 S 148 6 E
Springvale, *U.S.A.* **111 C14** 43 28N 70 48W
Springville, *Calif., U.S.A.* **116 J8** 36 8N 118 49W
Springville, *N.Y., U.S.A.* **110 D6** 42 31N 78 40W
Springville, *Utah, U.S.A.* **114 F8** 40 10N 111 37W
Springwater, *U.S.A.* **110 D7** 42 38N 77 35W
Spruce-Creek, *U.S.A.* **110 F6** 40 36N 78 9W
Spruce Mt., *U.S.A.* **111 B12** 44 12N 72 19W
Spur, *U.S.A.* **113 J4** 33 28N 100 52W
Spurn Hd., *U.K.* **12 D8** 53 35N 0 8 E
Spuž, *Montenegro, Yug.* **40 D3** 42 32N 19 10 E
Spuzzum, *Canada* **104 D4** 49 37N 121 23W
Squam L., *U.S.A.* **111 C13** 43 45N 71 32W
Squamish, *Canada* **104 D4** 49 45N 123 10W
Square Islands, *Canada* **103 B8** 52 47N 55 47W
Squillace, G. di, *Italy* **31 D9** 38 45N 16 50 E
Squinzano, *Italy* **31 B11** 40 26N 18 2 E
Squires, Mt., *Australia* **93 E4** 26 14 S 127 28 E
Srbac, *Bos.-H.* **42 E2** 45 7N 17 30 E
Srbica, *Kosovo, Yug.* **40 D4** 42 45N 20 47 E
Srbija = Serbia □, *Yugoslavia* **40 C5** 43 30N 21 0 E
Srbobran, *Serbia, Yug.* **42 E4** 45 32N 19 48 E
Sre Ambel, *Cambodia* **65 G4** 11 8N 103 46 E
Sre Khtum, *Cambodia* **65 F6** 12 10N 106 52 E
Sre Umbell = Sre Ambel, *Cambodia* **65 G4** 11 8N 103 46 E
Srebrenica, *Bos.-H.* **42 F4** 44 6N 19 18 E
Sredinny Ra. = Sredinnyy Khrebet, *Russia* **51 D16** 57 0N 160 0 E
Sredinnyy Khrebet, *Russia* **51 D16** 57 0N 160 0 E
Središče, *Slovenia* **29 B13** 46 24N 16 17 E
Sredna Gora, *Bulgaria* **41 D8** 42 40N 24 20 E
Srednekolymsk, *Russia* **51 C16** 67 27N 153 40 E
Sredni Rodopi, *Bulgaria* **41 E8** 41 40N 24 45 E
Srednogorie, *Bulgaria* **41 D8** 42 43N 24 10 E
Śrem, *Poland* **45 F4** 52 6N 17 2 E
Sremska Mitrovica, *Serbia, Yug.* **42 F4** 44 59N 19 38 E
Sremski Karlovci, *Serbia, Yug.* **42 E4** 45 12N 19 56 E
Srepok →, *Cambodia* **64 F6** 13 33N 106 16 E
Sretensk, *Russia* **51 D12** 52 10N 117 40 E

Tai'an

Tai'an, China 57 F9 36 12N 117 8 E
Taibei = T'aipei, Taiwan 59 E13 25 2N 121 30 E
Taibique, Canary Is. 37 G2 27 42N 17 58W
Taibus Qi, China 56 D8 41 54N 115 22 E
Taicang, China 59 B13 31 30N 121 5 E
T'aichung, Taiwan 59 E13 24 9N 120 37 E
Taieri →, N.Z. 91 M3 46 3 S 170 12 E
Taigu, China 56 F7 37 28N 112 30 E
Taihang Shan, China 56 G7 36 0N 113 30 E
Taihape, N.Z. 91 H5 39 41 S 175 48 E
Taihe, Anhui, China 56 H8 33 20N 115 42 E
Taihe, Jiangxi, China 59 D10 26 47N 114 52 E
Taihu, China 59 B11 30 22N 116 20 E
Taijiang, China 58 D7 26 39N 108 21 E
Taikang, China 56 G8 34 5N 114 50 E
Tailem Bend, Australia 95 F2 35 12 S 139 29 E
Tailfingen, Germany 25 G5 48 15N 9 1 E
Tailuko, Taiwan 59 E13 24 9N 121 37 E
Taimyr Peninsula = Taymyr, Poluostrov, Russia 51 B11 75 0N 100 0 E
Tain, U.K. 14 D4 57 49N 4 4W
T'ainan, Taiwan 59 F13 23 0N 120 10 E
Taínaron, Ákra, Greece 38 E4 36 22N 22 27 E
Taining, China 59 D11 26 54N 117 9 E
T'aipei, Taiwan 59 E13 25 2N 121 30 E
Taiping, China 59 B12 30 15N 118 6 E
Taiping, Malaysia 65 K3 4 51N 100 44 E
Taipingzhen, China 56 H6 33 35N 111 42 E
Tairbeart = Tarbert, U.K. 14 D2 57 54N 6 49W
Taishan, China 59 F9 22 14N 112 41 E
Taishun, China 59 D12 27 30N 119 42 E
Taita Hills, Kenya 86 C4 3 25 S 38 15 E
Taitao, Pen. de, Chile 122 H3 46 30 S 75 0W
T'aitung, Taiwan 59 F13 22 43N 121 4 E
Taivalkoski, Finland 8 D23 65 33N 28 12 E
Taiwan ■, Asia 59 F13 23 30N 121 0 E
Taiwan Strait, Asia 59 E12 24 40N 120 0 E
Taixing, China 59 A13 32 11N 120 0 E
Taiyara, Sudan 81 E3 12 36N 30 47 E
Taïyetos Óros, Greece 38 D4 37 0N 22 23 E
Taiyiba, Israel 75 C4 32 36N 35 27 E
Taiyuan, China 56 F7 37 52N 112 33 E
Taizhong = T'aichung, Taiwan 59 E13 24 9N 120 37 E
Taizhou, China 59 A12 32 28N 119 55 E
Taizhou Liedao, China 59 C13 28 30N 121 55 E
Ta'izz, Yemen 74 E3 13 35N 44 2 E
Tājābād, Iran 71 D7 30 2N 54 24 E
Tajikistan ■, Asia 50 F8 38 30N 70 0 E
Tajima, Japan 55 F9 37 12N 139 46 E
Tajo = Tejo →, Europe 35 F2 38 40N 9 24W
Tajrīsh, Iran 71 C6 35 48N 51 25 E
Tak, Thailand 64 D2 16 52N 99 8 E
Takāb, Iran 70 B5 36 24N 47 7 E
Takachiho, Japan 55 H5 32 42N 131 18 E
Takachu, Botswana 88 C3 22 37 S 21 58 E
Takada, Japan 55 F9 37 7N 138 15 E
Takahagi, Japan 55 F10 36 43N 140 45 E
Takaka, N.Z. 91 J4 40 51 S 172 50 E
Takamatsu, Japan 55 G7 34 20N 134 5 E
Takaoka, Japan 55 F8 36 47N 137 0 E
Takapuna, N.Z. 91 G5 36 47 S 174 47 E
Takasaki, Japan 55 F9 36 20N 139 0 E
Takatsuki, Japan 55 G7 34 51N 135 37 E
Takaungu, Kenya 86 C4 3 38 S 39 52 E
Takayama, Japan 55 F8 36 18N 137 11 E
Take-Shima, Japan 55 J5 30 49N 130 26 E
Takefu, Japan 55 G8 35 50N 136 10 E
Takengon, Indonesia 62 D1 4 45N 96 50 E
Takeo, Japan 55 H5 33 12N 130 1 E
Tåkern, Sweden 11 F8 58 22N 14 45 E
Tākestān, Iran 71 C6 36 0N 49 40 E
Taketa, Japan 55 H5 32 58N 131 24 E
Takev, Cambodia 65 G5 10 59N 104 47 E
Takh, India 69 C7 33 6N 77 32 E
Takht-Sulaiman, Pakistan 68 D3 31 40N 69 58 E
Takikawa, Japan 54 C10 43 33N 141 54 E
Takla L., Canada 104 B3 55 15N 125 45W
Takla Landing, Canada 104 B3 55 30N 125 50W
Takla Makan = Taklamakan Shamo, China 60 C3 38 0N 83 0 E
Taklamakan Shamo, China 60 C3 38 0N 83 0 E
Taku →, Canada 104 B2 58 30N 133 50W
Takum, Nigeria 83 D6 7 18N 9 36 E
Tal Halāl, Iran 71 D7 28 54N 55 1 E
Tala, Uruguay 127 C4 34 21 S 55 46W
Talachyn, Belarus 46 E5 54 25N 29 42 E
Talacogan, Phil. 61 G6 8 32N 125 39 E
Talagang, Pakistan 68 C5 32 55N 72 25 E
Talagante, Chile 126 C1 33 40 S 70 50W
Talak, Niger 83 B6 18 0N 5 0 E
Talamanca, Cordillera de, Cent. Amer. 120 E3 9 20N 83 20W
Talant, France 19 E11 47 19N 4 58 E
Talara, Peru 124 D2 4 38 S 81 18W
Talas, Kyrgyzstan 50 E8 42 30N 72 13 E
Talas, Turkey 72 C6 38 41N 35 33 E
Talâta, Egypt 75 E1 30 36N 32 20 E
Talata Mafara, Nigeria 83 C6 12 38N 6 4 E
Talaud, Kepulauan, Indonesia 63 D7 4 30N 126 50 E
Talaud Is. = Talaud, Kepulauan, Indonesia 63 D7 4 30N 126 50 E
Talavera de la Reina, Spain 34 F6 39 55N 4 46W
Talavera la Real, Spain 35 G4 38 53N 6 46W
Talayan, Phil. 61 H6 6 52N 124 24 E
Talayuela, Spain 34 F5 39 59N 5 36W
Talbandh, India 69 H12 22 3N 86 20 E
Talbert, Sillon de, France 18 D3 48 53N 3 5W
Talbot, C., Australia 92 B4 13 48 S 126 43 E
Talbragar →, Australia 95 E4 32 12 S 148 37 E
Talca, Chile 126 D1 35 28 S 71 40W
Talcahuano, Chile 126 D1 36 40 S 73 10W
Talcher, India 67 J14 21 0N 85 18 E
Talcho, Niger 83 C5 14 44N 3 28 E
Taldy Kurgan = Taldyqorghan, Kazakhstan 50 E8 45 10N 78 45 E
Taldyqorghan, Kazakhstan 50 E8 45 10N 78 45 E
Tālesh, Iran 71 B6 37 58N 48 58 E
Tālesh, Kūhhā-ye, Iran 71 B6 37 42N 48 55 E
Talguharai, Sudan 80 D4 18 19N 35 56 E
Tali Post, Sudan 81 F3 5 55N 30 44 E
Taliabu, Indonesia 63 E6 1 50 S 125 0 E
Talibon, Phil. 63 B6 10 9N 124 20 E
Talibong, Ko, Thailand 65 J2 7 15N 99 23 E
Talihina, U.S.A. 113 H7 34 45N 95 3W
Talisayan, Phil. 61 G6 9 0N 124 55 E
Taliwang, Indonesia 62 F5 8 50 S 116 55 E
Tall 'Afar, Iraq 70 B4 36 22N 42 27 E
Tall Kalakh, Syria 75 A5 34 41N 36 15 E
Talla, Egypt 80 B3 28 5N 30 43 E
Talladega, U.S.A. 109 J2 33 26N 86 6W
Tallahassee, U.S.A. 109 K3 30 27N 84 17W
Tallangatta, Australia 95 F4 36 15 S 147 19 E
Tallard, France 21 D10 44 28N 6 3 E
Tällberg, Sweden 10 D9 60 51N 15 2 E
Tallering Pk., Australia 93 E2 28 6 S 115 37 E
Talli, Pakistan 68 E3 29 32N 68 8 E
Tallinn, Estonia 9 G21 59 22N 24 48 E
Tallmadge, U.S.A. 110 E3 41 6N 81 27W
Tallulah, U.S.A. 113 J9 32 25N 91 11W
Tâlmaciu, Romania 43 E9 45 38N 24 19 E
Talmont-St-Hilaire, France 20 B2 46 27N 1 37W
Talne, Ukraine 47 H6 48 50N 30 44 E
Talnoye = Talne, Ukraine 47 H6 48 50N 30 44 E
Talodi, Sudan 81 E3 10 35N 30 22 E
Talovaya, Russia 48 E5 51 6N 40 45 E
Taloyoak, Canada 100 B10 69 32N 93 32W
Talpa de Allende, Mexico 118 C4 20 23N 104 51W
Talsi, Latvia 9 H20 57 10N 22 30 E
Talsi □, Latvia 44 A9 57 20N 22 40 E
Taltal, Chile 126 B1 25 23 S 70 33W
Taltson →, Canada 104 A6 61 24N 112 46W
Talurqjuak = Taloyoak, Canada 100 B10 69 32N 93 32W
Talwood, Australia 95 D4 28 29 S 149 29 E
Talyawalka Cr. →, Australia 95 E3 32 28 S 142 22 E
Tam Chau, Vietnam 65 G5 10 48N 105 12 E
Tam Ky, Vietnam 64 E7 15 34N 108 29 E
Tam Quan, Vietnam 64 E7 14 35N 109 3 E
Tama, U.S.A. 112 E8 41 58N 92 35W
Tamale, Ghana 83 D4 9 22N 0 50W
Taman, Russia 47 K9 45 14N 36 41 E
Tamani, Mali 82 C3 13 20N 6 50W
Tamano, Japan 55 G6 34 29N 133 59 E
Tamanrasset, Algeria 78 D7 22 50N 5 30 E
Tamaqua, U.S.A. 111 F9 40 48N 75 58W
Tamar →, U.K. 13 G3 50 27N 4 15W
Tamarinda, Spain 37 B10 39 55N 3 49 E
Tamarite de Litera, Spain 32 D5 41 52N 0 25 E
Tamashima, Japan 55 G6 34 32N 133 40 E
Tamási, Hungary 42 D3 46 40N 18 18 E
Tamaské, Niger 83 C6 14 49N 5 43 E
Tamaulipas □, Mexico 119 C5 24 0N 99 0W
Tamaulipas, Sierra de, Mexico 119 C5 23 30N 98 20W
Tamazula, Mexico 118 C3 24 55N 106 58W
Tamazunchale, Mexico 119 C5 21 16N 98 47W
Tamba-Dabatou, Guinea 82 C2 11 50N 10 40W
Tambacounda, Senegal 82 C2 13 45N 13 40W
Tambelan, Kepulauan, Indonesia 62 D3 1 0N 107 30 E
Tambellup, Australia 93 F2 34 4 S 117 37 E
Tambo, Australia 94 C4 24 54 S 146 14 E
Tambo de Mora, Peru 124 F3 13 30 S 76 8W
Tambohorano, Madag. 89 B7 17 30 S 43 58 E
Tambora, Indonesia 62 F5 8 12 S 118 5 E
Tambov, Russia 48 D5 52 45N 41 28 E
Tambre →, Spain 34 C2 42 49N 8 53W
Tambuku, Indonesia 63 G15 7 8 S 113 40 E
Tamburâ, Sudan 81 F2 5 40N 27 25 E
Tâmchekket, Mauritania 82 B2 17 25N 10 40W
Tâmega →, Portugal 34 D2 41 5N 8 21W
Tamenglong, India 67 G18 25 0N 93 35 E
Tamgué, Massif du, Guinea 82 C2 12 0N 12 18W
Tamiahua, L. de, Mexico 119 C5 21 30N 97 30W
Tamil Nadu □, India 66 P10 11 0N 77 0 E
Tamis →, Serbia, Yug. 42 F5 44 51N 20 39 E
Tamluk, India 69 H12 22 18N 87 58 E
Tammerfors = Tampere, Finland 9 F20 61 30N 23 50 E
Tammisaari, Finland 9 F20 60 0N 23 26 E
Tämnaren, Sweden 10 D11 60 10N 17 25 E
Tamo Abu, Pegunungan, Malaysia 62 D5 3 10N 115 5 E
Tampa, U.S.A. 109 M4 27 57N 82 27W
Tampa B., U.S.A. 109 M4 27 50N 82 30W
Tampere, Finland 9 F20 61 30N 23 50 E
Tampico, Mexico 119 C5 22 20N 97 50W
Tampin, Malaysia 65 L4 2 28N 102 13 E
Tamsweg, Austria 26 D6 47 7N 13 49 E
Tamu, Burma 67 G19 24 13N 94 12 E
Tamuja →, Spain 35 F4 39 38N 6 29W
Tamworth, Australia 95 E5 31 7 S 150 58 E
Tamworth, Canada 110 B8 44 29N 77 0W
Tamworth, U.K. 13 E6 52 39N 1 41W
Tamyang, S. Korea 57 G14 35 19N 126 59 E
Tan An, Vietnam 65 G6 10 32N 106 25 E
Tan-Tan, Morocco 78 C3 28 29N 11 1W
Tana →, Kenya 86 C5 2 32 S 40 31 E
Tana →, Norway 8 A23 70 30N 28 14 E
Tana, L., Ethiopia 81 E4 13 5N 37 30 E
Tana River, Kenya 86 C4 2 0 S 39 30 E
Tanabe, Japan 55 H7 33 44N 135 22 E
Tanafjorden, Norway 8 A23 70 45N 28 25 E
Tanaga, Pta., Canary Is. 37 G1 27 42N 18 10W
Tanahbala, Indonesia 62 E1 0 30 S 98 30 E
Tanahgrogot, Indonesia 62 E5 1 55 S 116 15 E
Tanahjampea, Indonesia 63 F6 7 10 S 120 35 E
Tanahmasa, Indonesia 62 E1 0 12 S 98 39 E
Tanahmerah, Indonesia 63 F10 6 5 S 140 16 E
Tanakpur, India 69 E9 29 5N 80 7 E
Tanakura, Japan 55 F10 37 10N 140 20 E
Tanami, Australia 92 C4 19 59 S 129 43 E
Tanami Desert, Australia 92 C5 18 50 S 132 0 E
Tanana →, U.S.A. 100 B4 65 10N 151 58W
Tananarive = Antananarivo, Madag. 89 B8 18 55 S 47 31 E
Tánaro →, Italy 28 D5 44 55N 8 40 E
Tancheng, China 57 G10 34 25N 118 20 E
Tanch'ŏn, N. Korea 57 D15 40 27N 128 54 E
Tanda, Ut. P., India 69 F10 26 33N 82 35 E
Tanda, Ut. P., India 69 E8 28 57N 78 56 E
Tanda, Ivory C. 82 D4 7 48N 3 10W
Tandag, Phil. 61 G7 9 4N 126 9 E
Tandaia, Tanzania 87 D3 9 25 S 34 15 E
Tăndărei, Romania 43 F12 44 39N 27 40 E
Tandaué, Angola 88 B2 16 58 S 18 5 E
Tandil, Argentina 126 D4 37 15 S 59 6W
Tandil, Sa. del, Argentina 126 D4 37 30 S 59 0W
Tandlianwala, Pakistan 68 D5 31 3N 73 9 E
Tando Adam, Pakistan 68 G3 25 45N 68 40 E
Tando Allahyar, Pakistan 68 G3 25 28N 68 43 E
Tando Bago, Pakistan 68 G3 24 47N 68 58 E
Tando Mohommed Khan, Pakistan 68 G3 25 8N 68 32 E
Tandou L., Australia 95 E3 32 40 S 142 5 E
Tandragee, U.K. 15 B5 54 21N 6 24W
Tandsjöborg, Sweden 10 C8 61 42N 14 43 E
Tane-ga-Shima, Japan 55 J5 30 30N 131 0 E
Taneatua, N.Z. 91 H6 38 4 S 177 1 E
Tanen Tong Dan = Dawna Ra., Burma 64 D2 16 30N 98 30 E
Tanew →, Poland 45 H9 50 29N 22 16 E
Tanezrouft, Algeria 78 D6 23 9N 0 11 E
Tang, Koh, Cambodia 65 G4 10 16N 103 7 E
Tang, Ra's-e, Iran 71 E8 25 21N 59 52 E
Tang Krasang, Cambodia 64 F5 12 34N 105 3 E
Tanga, Tanzania 86 D4 5 5 S 39 2 E
Tanga □, Tanzania 86 D4 5 20 S 38 0 E
Tanganyika, L., Africa 86 D3 6 40 S 30 0 E
Tangaza, Nigeria 83 C5 13 19N 4 55 E
Tanger, Morocco 78 A4 35 50N 5 49W
Tangerang, Indonesia 63 G12 6 11 S 106 37 E
Tangerhütte, Germany 24 C7 52 26N 11 48 E
Tangermünde, Germany 24 C7 52 33N 11 58 E
Tanggu, China 57 E9 39 2N 117 40 E
Tanggula Shan, China 60 C4 32 40N 92 10 E
Tanghe, China 56 H7 32 47N 112 50 E
Tangier = Tanger, Morocco 78 A4 35 50N 5 49W
Tangorin, Australia 94 C3 21 47 S 144 12 E
Tangorombohitr'i Makay, Madag. 89 C8 21 0 S 45 15 E
Tangshan, China 57 E10 39 38N 118 10 E
Tangtou, China 57 G10 35 28N 118 30 E
Tanguiéta, Benin 83 C5 10 35N 1 21 E
Tangxi, China 59 C12 29 3N 119 25 E
Tangyan He →, China 58 C7 28 54N 108 19 E
Tanimbar, Kepulauan, Indonesia 63 F8 7 30 S 131 30 E
Tanimbar Is. = Tanimbar, Kepulauan, Indonesia 63 F8 7 30 S 131 30 E
Taninthari = Tenasserim □, Burma 64 F2 14 0N 98 30 E
Tanjay, Phil. 61 G5 9 30N 123 5 E
Tanjong Malim, Malaysia 65 L3 3 42N 101 31 E
Tanjore = Thanjavur, India 66 P11 10 48N 79 12 E
Tanjung, Indonesia 62 E5 2 10 S 115 25 E
Tanjungbalai, Indonesia 62 D1 2 55N 99 44 E
Tanjungbatu, Indonesia 62 D5 2 23N 118 3 E
Tanjungkarang Telukbetung, Indonesia 62 F3 5 20 S 105 10 E
Tanjungpandan, Indonesia 62 E3 2 43 S 107 38 E
Tanjungpinang, Indonesia 62 D2 1 5N 104 30 E
Tanjungredeb, Indonesia 62 D5 2 9N 117 29 E
Tanjungselor, Indonesia 62 D5 2 55N 117 25 E
Tank, Pakistan 68 C4 32 14N 70 25 E
Tankhala, India 68 J5 21 58N 73 47 E
Tännäs, Sweden 10 B6 62 26N 12 42 E
Tannersville, U.S.A. 111 E9 41 3N 75 18W
Tannis Bugt, Denmark 11 G4 57 40N 10 15 E
Tannu-Ola, Russia 51 D10 51 0N 94 0 E
Tannum Sands, Australia 94 C5 23 57 S 151 22 E
Tano →, Ghana 82 D4 5 7N 2 56W
Tanon Str., Phil. 61 F5 10 20N 123 30 E
Tanout, Niger 83 C6 14 50N 8 55 E
Tanshui, Taiwan 59 E13 25 10N 121 28 E
Tansilla, Burkina Faso 82 C4 12 25N 4 23W
Tanta, Egypt 80 H7 30 45N 30 57 E
Tantoyuca, Mexico 119 C5 21 21N 98 10W
Tantung = Dandong, China 57 D13 40 10N 124 20 E
Tanumshede, Sweden 11 F5 58 42N 11 20 E
Tanunda, Australia 95 E2 34 30 S 139 0 E
Tanus, France 20 D6 44 8N 2 19 E
Tanzania ■, Africa 86 D3 6 0 S 34 0 E
Tanzilla →, Canada 104 B2 58 8N 130 43W
Tao, Ko, Thailand 65 G2 10 5N 99 52 E
Tao'an = Taonan, China 57 B12 45 22N 122 40 E
Tao'er He →, China 57 B13 45 45N 124 5 E
Taohua Dao, China 59 C14 29 50N 122 20 E
Taolanaro, Madag. 89 D8 25 2 S 47 0 E
Taole, China 56 E4 38 48N 106 40 E
Taonan, China 57 B12 45 22N 122 40 E
Taormina, Italy 31 E8 37 51N 15 17 E
Taos, U.S.A. 115 H11 36 24N 105 35W
Taoudenni, Mali 78 D5 22 40N 3 55W
Taoyuan, China 59 C8 28 55N 111 16 E
T'aoyüan, Taiwan 59 E13 25 0N 121 4 E
Tapa, Estonia 9 G21 59 15N 25 50 E
Tapa Shan = Daba Shan, China 58 B7 32 0N 109 0 E
Tapachula, Mexico 119 E6 14 54N 92 17W
Tapah, Malaysia 65 K3 4 12N 101 15 E
Tapajós →, Brazil 122 D5 2 24 S 54 41W
Tapaktuan, Indonesia 62 D1 3 15N 97 10 E
Tapanahoni →, Suriname 125 C8 4 20N 54 25W
Tapanui, N.Z. 91 L2 45 56 S 169 18 E
Tapauá →, Brazil 124 E6 5 40 S 64 21W
Tapes, Brazil 127 C5 30 40 S 51 23W
Tapeta, Liberia 82 D3 6 29N 8 52W
Taphan Hin, Thailand 64 D3 16 13N 100 26 E
Tapi →, India 66 J8 21 8N 72 41 E
Tapia de Casariego, Spain 34 B4 43 34N 6 56W
Tapirapecó, Serra, Venezuela 124 C6 1 10N 65 0W
Tapolca, Hungary 42 D2 46 53N 17 29 E
Tapuaenuku, Mt., N.Z. 91 K4 42 0 S 173 39 E
Tapul Group, Phil. 61 J4 5 35N 120 50 E
Tapurucuará, Brazil 124 D5 0 24 S 65 2W
Ţaqţaq, Iraq 70 C5 35 53N 44 35 E
Taquara, Brazil 127 B5 29 36 S 50 46W
Taquari →, Brazil 124 G7 19 15 S 57 17W
Tara, Australia 95 D5 27 17 S 150 31 E
Tara, Canada 110 B3 44 28N 81 9W
Tara, Russia 50 D8 56 55N 74 24 E
Tara, Zambia 87 F2 16 58 S 26 45 E
Tara →, Montenegro, Yug. 40 C2 43 21N 18 51 E
Taraba □, Nigeria 83 D7 8 0N 10 30 E
Taraba →, Nigeria 83 D7 8 30N 10 15 E
Tarabagatay, Khrebet, Kazakhstan 50 E9 48 0N 83 0 E
Tarābulus, Lebanon 75 A4 34 31N 35 50 E
Tarābulus, Libya 79 B8 32 49N 13 7 E
Taraclia, Moldova 43 D14 46 34N 29 7 E
Taraclia, Moldova 43 E13 45 54N 28 40 E
Taradehi, India 69 H8 23 18N 79 21 E
Tarajalejo, Canary Is. 37 F5 28 12N 14 7W
Tarakan, Indonesia 62 D5 3 20N 117 35 E
Tarakit, Mt., Kenya 86 B4 2 2N 35 10 E
Tarama-Jima, Japan 55 M2 24 39N 124 42 E
Taran, Mys, Russia 9 J18 54 56N 19 59 E
Taranagar, India 68 E6 28 43N 74 50 E
Taranaki □, N.Z. 91 H5 39 25 S 174 30 E
Taranaki, Mt., N.Z. 91 H5 39 17 S 174 5 E
Tarancón, Spain 32 E1 40 1N 3 1W
Taransay, U.K. 14 D1 57 54N 7 0W
Táranto, Italy 31 B10 40 28N 17 14 E
Táranto, G. di, Italy 31 B10 40 8N 17 20 E
Tarapacá, Colombia 124 D5 2 56 S 69 46W
Tarapacá □, Chile 126 A2 20 45 S 69 30W
Tarapoto, Peru 124 E3 6 30 S 76 20W
Tarare, France 21 C8 45 55N 4 26 E
Tararua Ra., N.Z. 91 J5 40 45 S 175 25 E
Tarascon, France 21 E8 43 48N 4 39 E
Tarascon-sur-Ariège, France 20 F5 42 50N 1 36 E
Tarashcha, Ukraine 47 H6 49 30N 30 31 E
Tarauacá, Brazil 124 E4 8 6 S 70 48W
Tarauacá →, Brazil 124 E5 6 42 S 69 48W
Taravo →, France 21 G12 41 42N 8 49 E
Tarawa, Kiribati 96 G9 1 30N 173 0 E
Tarawera, N.Z. 91 H6 39 2 S 176 36 E
Tarawera L., N.Z. 91 H6 38 13 S 176 27 E
Taraz, Kazakhstan 50 E8 42 54N 71 22 E
Tarazona, Spain 32 D3 41 55N 1 43W
Tarazona de la Mancha, Spain 33 F3 39 16N 1 55W
Tarbat Ness, U.K. 14 D5 57 52N 3 47W
Tarbela Dam, Pakistan 68 B5 34 8N 72 52 E
Tarbert, Arg. & Bute, U.K. 14 F3 55 52N 5 25W
Tarbert, W. Isles, U.K. 14 D2 57 54N 6 49W
Tarbes, France 20 E4 43 15N 0 3 E
Tarboro, U.S.A. 109 H7 35 54N 77 32W
Tărcău, Munţii, Romania 43 D11 46 39N 26 7 E
Tarcento, Italy 29 B10 46 13N 13 13 E
Tarcoola, Australia 95 E1 30 44 S 134 36 E
Tarcoon, Australia 95 E4 30 15 S 146 43 E
Tardets-Sorholus, France 20 E3 43 8N 0 52W
Tardoire →, France 20 C4 45 52N 0 14 E
Taree, Australia 95 E5 31 50 S 152 30 E
Tarfa, W. el →, Egypt 80 B3 28 25N 30 50 E
Tarfaya, Morocco 78 C3 27 55N 12 55W
Târgovişte, Romania 43 F10 44 55N 25 27 E
Târgu Bujor, Romania 43 E12 45 52N 27 54 E
Târgu Cărbuneşti, Romania 43 F8 44 57N 23 31 E
Târgu Frumos, Romania 43 C12 47 12N 27 2 E
Târgu-Jiu, Romania 43 E8 45 5N 23 19 E
Târgu Lăpuş, Romania 43 C8 47 27N 23 52 E
Târgu Mureş, Romania 43 D9 46 31N 24 38 E
Târgu Neamţ, Romania 43 C11 47 12N 26 25 E
Târgu Ocna, Romania 43 D11 46 16N 26 39 E
Târgu Secuiesc, Romania 43 E11 46 0N 26 10 E
Târguşor, Romania 43 F13 44 27N 28 25 E
Tărhăus, Vf., Romania 43 D11 46 40N 26 8 E
Ţarif, U.A.E. 71 E7 24 3N 53 46 E
Tarifa, Spain 35 J5 36 1N 5 36W
Tarija, Bolivia 126 A3 21 30 S 64 40W
Tarija □, Bolivia 126 A3 21 30 S 63 30W
Tariku →, Indonesia 63 E9 2 55 S 138 26 E
Tarim Basin = Tarim Pendi, China 60 C3 40 0N 84 0 E
Tarim He →, China 60 C3 39 30N 88 30 E
Tarim Pendi, China 60 C3 40 0N 84 0 E
Taritatu →, Indonesia 63 E9 2 54 S 138 27 E
Tarka →, S. Africa 88 E4 32 10 S 26 0 E
Tarkastad, S. Africa 88 E4 32 0 S 26 16 E
Tarkhankut, Mys, Ukraine 47 K7 45 25N 32 30 E
Tarko Sale, Russia 50 C8 64 55N 77 50 E
Tarkwa, Ghana 82 D4 5 20N 2 0W
Tarlac, Phil. 61 D4 15 29N 120 35 E
Tarm, Denmark 11 J2 55 56N 8 31 E
Tarma, Peru 124 F3 11 25 S 75 45W
Tarn □, France 20 E6 43 49N 2 8 E
Tarn →, France 20 D5 44 5N 1 6 E
Tarn-et-Garonne □, France 20 D5 44 8N 1 20 E
Tarna →, Hungary 42 C4 47 31N 19 59 E
Târnava Mare →, Romania 43 D8 46 10N 23 43 E
Târnava Mică →, Romania 43 D8 46 9N 23 55 E
Târnăveni, Romania 43 D9 46 19N 24 13 E
Tarnica, Poland 45 J9 49 4N 22 44 E
Tarnobrzeg, Poland 45 H8 50 35N 21 41 E
Tarnogród, Poland 45 H9 50 22N 22 45 E
Tarnos, France 20 E2 43 32N 1 28W
Târnova, Moldova 43 B12 48 10N 27 40 E
Târnova, Romania 42 E6 45 23N 21 59 E
Tarnów, Poland 45 H8 50 3N 21 0 E
Tarnowskie Góry, Poland 45 H5 50 27N 18 54 E
Tärnsjö, Sweden 10 D10 60 9N 16 56 E
Táro →, Italy 28 C7 45 2N 10 15 E
Ţārom, Iran 71 D7 28 11N 55 46 E
Taroom, Australia 95 D4 25 36 S 149 48 E
Taroudannt, Morocco 78 B4 30 30N 8 52W
Tarp, Germany 24 A5 54 39N 9 24 E
Tarpon Springs, U.S.A. 109 L4 28 9N 82 45W
Tarquínia, Italy 29 F8 42 15N 11 45 E
Tarragona, Spain 32 D6 41 5N 1 17 E
Tarragona □, Spain 32 D6 41 5N 1 0 E
Tarraleah, Australia 94 G4 42 17 S 146 26 E
Tarrasa = Terrassa, Spain 32 D7 41 34N 2 1 E
Tàrrega, Spain 32 D6 41 39N 1 9 E
Tarrytown, U.S.A. 111 E11 41 4N 73 52W
Tårs, Denmark 11 G4 57 23N 10 7 E
Tarshiha = Me'ona, Israel 75 B4 33 1N 35 15 E
Tarso Emissi, Chad 79 D9 21 27N 18 36 E
Tarsus, Turkey 70 B2 36 58N 34 55 E
Tartagal, Argentina 126 A3 22 30 S 63 50W
Tärtär, Azerbaijan 49 K8 40 20N 46 58 E
Tärtär →, Azerbaijan 49 K8 40 26N 47 20 E
Tartas, France 20 E3 43 50N 0 49W
Tartu, Estonia 9 G22 58 20N 26 44 E
Ţarţūs, Syria 70 C2 34 55N 35 55 E
Tarumizu, Japan 55 J5 31 29N 130 42 E
Tarussa, Russia 46 E9 54 44N 37 10 E
Tarutao, Ko, Thailand 65 J2 6 33N 99 40 E
Tarutung, Indonesia 62 D1 2 0N 98 54 E
Tarvísio, Italy 29 B10 46 30N 13 35 E
Taseko →, Canada 104 C4 52 8N 123 45W
Tash-Kömür, Kyrgyzstan 50 E8 41 40N 72 10 E
Tash-Kumyr = Tash-Kömür, Kyrgyzstan 50 E8 41 40N 72 10 E
Tashauz = Dashhowuz, Turkmenistan 50 E6 41 49N 59 58 E
Tashi Chho Dzong = Thimphu, Bhutan 67 F16 27 31N 89 45 E
Ţashk, Daryācheh-ye, Iran 71 D7 29 45N 53 35 E
Tashkent = Toshkent, Uzbekistan 50 E7 41 20N 69 10 E
Tashtagol, Russia 50 D9 52 47N 87 53 E
Tasiilaq, Greenland 4 C6 65 40N 37 20W
Tasikmalaya, Indonesia 63 G13 7 18 S 108 12 E
Tåsinge, Denmark 11 J4 55 0N 10 35 E
Tåsjön, Sweden 8 D16 64 15N 15 40 E
Taskan, Russia 51 C16 62 59N 150 20 E
Tasker, Niger 83 C7 15 8N 10 40 E
Taşköprü, Turkey 72 B6 41 30N 34 15 E
Taşlâc, Moldova 43 C14 47 4N 29 24 E
Tasman B., N.Z. 91 J4 40 59 S 173 25 E
Tasman Mts., N.Z. 91 J4 41 3 S 172 25 E
Tasman Pen., Australia 94 G4 43 10 S 148 0 E
Tasman Sea, Pac. Oc. 96 L8 36 0 S 160 0 E
Tasmania □, Australia 94 G4 42 0 S 146 30 E
Tăşnad, Romania 42 C7 47 30N 22 33 E
Tassili n'Ajjer, Algeria 78 C7 25 47N 8 1 E
Tassili Tin-Rerhoh, Algeria 83 A5 20 5N 3 55 E
Tata, Hungary 42 C3 47 37N 18 19 E
Tatabánya, Hungary 42 C3 47 32N 18 25 E
Tatahouine, Tunisia 79 B8 32 56N 10 27 E
Tatar Republic = Tatarstan □, Russia 48 C10 55 30N 51 30 E
Tatarbunary, Ukraine 47 K5 45 50N 29 39 E
Tatarsk, Russia 50 D8 55 14N 76 0 E
Tatarstan □, Russia 48 C10 55 30N 51 30 E
Tateyama, Japan 55 G9 35 0N 139 50 E
Tathlina L., Canada 104 A5 60 33N 117 39W
Tathra, Australia 95 F4 36 44 S 149 59 E
Tatinnai L., Canada 105 A9 60 55N 97 40W
Tatla L., Canada 104 C4 52 0N 124 20W
Tatlısu, Turkey 41 F11 40 24N 27 55 E
Tatnam, C., Canada 105 B10 57 16N 91 0W
Tatra = Tatry, Slovak Rep. 27 B13 49 20N 20 0 E
Tatry, Slovak Rep. 27 B13 49 20N 20 0 E
Tatshenshini →, Canada 104 B1 59 28N 137 45W
Tatsuno, Japan 55 G7 34 52N 134 33 E
Tatta, Pakistan 68 G2 24 42N 67 55 E
Tatuí, Brazil 127 A6 23 25 S 47 53W
Tatum, U.S.A. 113 J3 33 16N 103 19W
Tat'ung = Datong, China 56 D7 40 6N 113 18 E
Tatvan, Turkey 70 B4 38 31N 42 15 E
Taubaté, Brazil 127 A6 23 0 S 45 36W
Tauberbischofsheim, Germany 25 F5 49 37N 9 39 E
Taucha, Germany 24 D8 51 23N 12 29 E
Tauern-tunnel, Austria 26 D6 47 0N 13 12 E
Taufikia, Sudan 81 F3 9 24N 31 37 E
Taulé, France 18 D3 48 37N 3 55W
Taumarunui, N.Z. 91 H5 38 53 S 175 15 E
Taumaturgo, Brazil 124 E4 8 54 S 72 51W
Taung, S. Africa 88 D3 27 33 S 24 47 E
Taungdwingyi, Burma 67 J19 20 1N 95 40 E
Taunggyi, Burma 67 J20 20 50N 97 0 E
Taungup, Burma 67 K19 18 51N 94 14 E
Taungup Taunggya, Burma 67 K18 18 20N 93 40 E
Taunsa, Pakistan 68 D4 30 42N 70 39 E
Taunsa Barrage, Pakistan 68 D4 30 42N 70 50 E
Taunton, U.K. 13 F4 51 1N 3 5W
Taunton, U.S.A. 111 E13 41 54N 71 6W
Taunus, Germany 25 E4 50 13N 8 34 E
Taupo, N.Z. 91 H6 38 41 S 176 7 E
Taupo, L., N.Z. 91 H5 38 46 S 175 55 E
Tauragė, Lithuania 9 J20 55 14N 22 16 E
Tauragė □, Lithuania 44 C9 55 15N 22 17 E
Tauranga, N.Z. 91 G6 37 42 S 176 11 E
Tauranga Harb., N.Z. 91 G6 37 30 S 176 5 E
Taureau, Rés., Canada 102 C5 46 46N 73 50W
Taurianova, Italy 31 D9 38 21N 16 1 E
Taurus Mts. = Toros Dağları, Turkey 70 B2 37 0N 32 30 E
Tauste, Spain 32 D3 41 58N 1 18W
Tauz = Tovuz, Azerbaijan 49 K7 41 0N 45 40 E
Tavas, Turkey 39 D11 37 34N 29 4 E
Tavda, Russia 50 D7 58 7N 65 8 E
Tavda →, Russia 50 D7 57 47N 67 18 E
Tavernes de la Valldigna, Spain 33 F4 39 5N 0 13W
Taveta, Tanzania 86 C4 3 23 S 37 37 E
Taveuni, Fiji 91 C9 16 51 S 179 58W
Taviano, Italy 31 C11 39 59N 18 5 E
Tavignano →, France 21 F13 42 7N 9 33 E
Tavira, Portugal 35 H3 37 8N 7 40W
Tavistock, Canada 110 C4 43 19N 80 50W
Tavistock, U.K. 13 G3 50 33N 4 9W
Tavolara, Italy 30 B2 40 54N 9 42 E
Távora →, Portugal 34 D3 41 8N 7 35W
Tavoy = Dawei, Burma 64 E2 14 2N 98 12 E
Tavşanlı, Turkey 39 B11 39 32N 29 30 E
Taw →, U.K. 13 F3 51 4N 4 4W
Tawa →, India 68 H8 22 48N 77 48 E
Tawas City, U.S.A. 108 C4 44 16N 83 31W
Tawau, Malaysia 62 D5 4 20N 117 55 E
Taweisha, Sudan 81 E2 12 19N 26 40 E
Tawitawi, Phil. 63 B6 5 10N 120 0 E
Tawu, Taiwan 59 F13 22 30N 120 50 E
Taxco de Alarcón, Mexico 119 D5 18 33N 99 36W
Taxila, Pakistan 68 C5 33 42N 72 52 E

Tsyelyakhany

Topraisar, Romania 43 F13 44 1N 28 27 E
Topusko, Croatia 29 C12 45 18N 15 59 E
Torà, Spain 32 D6 41 49N 1 25 E
Tora Kit, Sudan 81 E3 11 2N 32 36 E
Toraka Vestale, Madag. 89 B7 16 20 S 43 58 E
Torata, Peru 124 G4 17 23 S 70 1W
Torbalı, Turkey 39 C9 38 10N 27 21 E
Torbat-e Heydārīyeh, Iran 71 C8 35 15N 59 12 E
Torbat-e Jām, Iran 71 C9 35 16N 60 35 E
Torbay, Canada 103 C9 47 40N 52 42W
Torbay □, U.K. 13 G4 50 26N 3 31W
Torbjörntorp, Sweden 11 F7 58 12N 13 36 E
Tordesillas, Spain 34 D6 41 30N 5 0W
Töreboda, Sweden 11 F8 58 41N 14 7 E
Torekov, Sweden 11 H6 56 26N 12 37 E
Torellò, Spain 32 C7 42 3N 2 16 E
Toreno, Spain 34 C4 42 42N 6 30W
Torfaen □, U.K. 13 F4 51 43N 3 3W
Torgau, Germany 24 D8 51 34N 13 0 E
Torgelow, Germany 24 B10 53 37N 14 1 E
Torhamn, Sweden 11 H9 56 6N 15 50 E
Torhout, Belgium 17 C3 51 5N 3 7 E
Tori, Ethiopia 81 F3 7 53N 33 35 E
Tori-Shima, Japan 55 J10 30 29N 140 19 E
Torigni-sur-Vire, France 18 C6 49 3N 0 58W
Torija, Spain 32 E1 40 44N 3 2W
Torin, Mexico 118 B2 27 33N 110 15W
Torino, Italy 28 C4 45 3N 7 40 E
Torit, Sudan 81 G3 4 27N 32 31 E
Torkamān, Iran 70 B5 37 35N 47 23 E
Torkovichi, Russia 46 C6 58 51N 30 21 E
Tormac, Romania 42 E6 45 30N 21 30 E
Tormes →, Spain 34 D4 41 18N 6 29W
Tornado Mt., Canada 104 D6 49 55N 114 40W
Tornal'a, Slovak Rep. 27 C13 48 25N 20 20 E
Torne älv →, Sweden 8 D21 65 50N 24 12 E
Torneå = Tornio, Finland 8 D21 65 50N 24 12 E
Torneträsk, Sweden 8 B18 68 24N 19 15 E
Tornio, Finland 8 D21 65 50N 24 12 E
Tornionjoki →, Finland 8 D21 65 50N 24 12 E
Tornquist, Argentina 126 D3 38 8 S 62 15W
Toro, Baleares, Spain 37 B11 39 59N 4 8 E
Toro, Zamora, Spain 34 D5 41 35N 5 24W
Torö, Sweden 11 F11 58 48N 17 50 E
Toro, Cerro del, Chile 126 B2 29 10 S 69 50W
Toro Pk., U.S.A. 117 M10 33 34N 116 24W
Törökszentmiklós, Hungary 42 C5 47 11N 20 27 E
Toronios Kólpos, Greece 40 F7 40 5N 23 30 E
Toronto, Canada 102 D4 43 39N 79 20W
Toronto, U.S.A. 110 F4 40 28N 80 36W
Toropets, Russia 46 D6 56 30N 31 40 E
Tororo, Uganda 86 B3 0 45N 34 12 E
Toros Dağları, Turkey 70 B2 37 0N 32 30 E
Torpa, India 69 H11 22 57N 85 6 E
Torquay, U.K. 13 G4 50 27N 3 32W
Torquemada, Spain 34 C6 42 2N 4 19W
Torrance, U.S.A. 117 M8 33 50N 118 19W
Torrão, Portugal 35 G2 38 16N 8 11W
Torre Annunziata, Italy 31 B7 40 45N 14 27 E
Torre de Moncorvo, Portugal 34 D3 41 12N 7 8W
Torre del Campo, Spain 35 H7 37 46N 3 53W
Torre del Greco, Italy 31 B7 40 47N 14 22 E
Torre del Mar, Spain 35 J6 36 44N 4 6W
Torre-Pacheco, Spain 33 H4 37 44N 0 57W
Torre Péllice, Italy 28 D4 44 49N 7 13 E
Torreblanca, Spain 32 E5 40 14N 0 12 E
Torrecampo, Spain 35 G6 38 29N 4 41W
Torrecilla en Cameros, Spain 32 C2 42 15N 2 38W
Torredembarra, Spain 32 D6 41 9N 1 24 E
Torredonjimeno, Spain 35 H7 37 46N 3 57W
Torrejón de Ardoz, Spain 34 E7 40 27N 3 29W
Torrejoncillo, Spain 34 F4 39 54N 6 28W
Torrelaguna, Spain 34 E7 40 50N 3 38W
Torrelavega, Spain 34 B6 43 20N 4 5W
Torremaggiore, Italy 29 G12 41 41N 15 17 E
Torremolinos, Spain 35 J6 36 38N 4 30W
Torrens, L., Australia 95 E2 31 0 S 137 50 E
Torrens Cr. →, Australia 94 C4 22 23 S 145 9 E
Torrens Creek, Australia 94 C4 20 48 S 145 3 E
Torrent, Spain 33 F4 39 27N 0 28W
Torrenueva, Spain 35 G7 38 38N 3 22W
Torreón, Mexico 118 B4 25 33N 103 26W
Torreperogil, Spain 35 G7 38 2N 3 17W
Torres, Brazil 127 B5 29 21 S 49 44W
Torres, Mexico 118 B2 28 46N 110 47W
Torres Novas, Portugal 35 F2 39 27N 8 33W
Torres Strait, Australia 96 H6 9 50 S 142 20 E
Torres Vedras, Portugal 35 F1 39 5N 9 15W
Torrevieja, Spain 33 H4 37 59N 0 42W
Torrey, U.S.A. 115 G8 38 18N 111 25W
Torridge →, U.K. 13 G3 51 0N 4 13W
Torridon, L., U.K. 14 D3 57 35N 5 50W
Torrijos, Spain 34 F6 39 59N 4 18W
Tørring, Denmark 11 J3 55 52N 9 29 E
Torrington, Conn., U.S.A. 111 E11 41 48N 73 7W
Torrington, Wyo., U.S.A. 112 D2 42 4N 104 11W
Torroella de Montgrì, Spain 32 C8 42 2N 3 8 E
Torrox, Spain 35 J7 36 46N 3 57W
Torsås, Sweden 11 H9 56 24N 16 0 E
Torsby, Sweden 10 D6 60 7N 13 0 E
Torshälla, Sweden 10 E10 59 25N 16 28 E
Tórshavn, Færoe Is. 8 E9 62 5N 6 56W
Torslanda, Sweden 11 G5 57 44N 11 45 E
Torsö, Sweden 11 F7 58 48N 13 45 E
Tortola, Br. Virgin Is. 121 C7 18 19N 64 45W
Tórtoles de Esgueva, Spain 34 D6 41 49N 4 2W
Tortoli, Italy 30 C2 39 55N 9 39 E
Tortona, Italy 28 D5 44 54N 8 52 E
Tortorici, Italy 31 D7 38 2N 14 49 E
Tortosa, Spain 32 E5 40 49N 0 31 E
Tortosa, C., Spain 32 E5 40 41N 0 52 E
Tortosendo, Portugal 34 E3 40 15N 7 31W
Tortue, I. de la, Haiti 121 B5 20 5N 72 57W
Tortum, Turkey 73 B9 40 19N 41 35 E
Torūd, Iran 71 C7 35 25N 55 5 E
Torul, Turkey 73 B8 40 34N 39 18 E
Toruń, Poland 45 E5 53 2N 18 39 E
Tory I., Ireland 15 A3 55 16N 8 14W
Torysa →, Slovak Rep. 27 C14 48 39N 21 21 E
Torzhok, Russia 46 D8 57 5N 34 55 E
Torzym, Poland 45 F2 52 19N 15 5 E
Tosa, Japan 55 H6 33 24N 133 23 E
Tosa-Shimizu, Japan 55 H6 32 52N 132 58 E
Tosa-Wan, Japan 55 H6 33 15N 133 30 E
Toscana □, Italy 28 E8 43 25N 11 0 E
Toscano, Arcipelago, Italy 28 F7 42 30N 10 30 E
Toshkent, Uzbekistan 50 E7 41 20N 69 10 E
Tosno, Russia 46 C6 59 38N 30 46 E
Tossa de Mar, Spain 32 D7 41 43N 2 56 E
Tösse, Sweden 11 F6 58 58N 12 39 E
Tostado, Argentina 126 B3 29 15 S 61 50W
Tostedt, Germany 24 B5 53 17N 9 42 E
Tostón, Pta. de, Canary Is. 37 F5 28 42N 14 2W
Tosu, Japan 55 H5 33 22N 130 31 E
Tosya, Turkey 72 B6 41 1N 34 2 E
Toszek, Poland 45 H5 50 27N 18 32 E
Totana, Spain 33 H3 37 45N 1 30W
Totebo, Sweden 11 G10 57 38N 16 12 E
Toteng, Botswana 88 C3 20 22 S 22 58 E
Tôtes, France 18 C8 49 41N 1 2 E
Tótkomlós, Hungary 42 D5 46 24N 20 45 E
Totma, Russia 50 C5 60 0N 42 40 E
Totnes, U.K. 13 G4 50 26N 3 42W
Totness, Suriname 125 B7 5 53N 56 19W
Toto, Nigeria 83 D6 8 26N 7 5 E
Totonicapán, Guatemala 120 D1 14 58N 91 12W
Totten Glacier, Antarctica 5 C8 66 45 S 116 10 E
Tottenham, Australia 95 E4 32 14 S 147 21 E
Tottenham, Canada 110 B5 44 1N 79 49W
Tottori, Japan 55 G7 35 30N 134 15 E
Tottori □, Japan 55 G7 35 30N 134 12 E
Touaret, Niger 83 A6 20 17N 7 8 E
Touba, Ivory C. 82 D3 8 22N 7 40W
Touba, Senegal 82 C1 14 50N 15 55W
Toubkal, Djebel, Morocco 78 B4 31 0N 8 0W
Toucy, France 19 E10 47 44N 3 15 E
Tougan, Burkina Faso 82 C4 13 11N 2 58W
Touggourt, Algeria 78 B7 33 6N 6 4 E
Tougouri, Burkina Faso 83 C4 13 20N 0 30W
Tougué, Guinea 82 C2 11 25N 11 50W
Toukoto, Mali 82 C3 13 27N 9 52W
Toul, France 19 D12 48 40N 5 53 E
Toulepleu, Ivory C. 82 D3 6 32N 8 24W
Toulon, France 21 E9 43 10N 5 55 E
Toulouse, France 20 E5 43 37N 1 27 E
Toummo, Niger 79 D8 22 45N 14 8 E
Toumodi, Ivory C. 82 D3 6 32N 5 4W
Tounan, Taiwan 59 F13 23 41N 120 28 E
Toungo, Nigeria 83 D7 8 20N 12 3 E
Toungoo, Burma 67 K20 19 0N 96 30 E
Touques →, France 18 C7 49 22N 0 8 E
Touraine, France 18 E7 47 20N 0 30 E
Tourane = Da Nang, Vietnam 64 D7 16 4N 108 13 E
Tourcoing, France 19 B10 50 42N 3 10 E
Touriñán, C., Spain 34 B1 43 3N 9 17W
Tournai, Belgium 17 D3 50 35N 3 25 E
Tournan-en-Brie, France 19 D9 48 44N 2 46 E
Tournay, France 20 E4 43 13N 0 13 E
Tournon-St-Martin, France 18 F7 46 45N 0 58 E
Tournon-sur-Rhône, France 21 C8 45 4N 4 50 E
Tournus, France 19 F11 46 35N 4 54 E
Tours, France 18 E7 47 22N 0 40 E
Toussora, Mt., C.A.R. 84 C4 9 7N 23 14 E
Touws →, S. Africa 88 E3 33 45 S 21 11 E
Touwsrivier, S. Africa 88 E3 33 20 S 20 2 E
Tovarkovskiy, Russia 46 F10 53 40N 38 14 E
Tovuz, Azerbaijan 49 K7 41 0N 45 40 E
Towada, Japan 54 D10 40 37N 141 13 E
Towada-Ko, Japan 54 D10 40 28N 140 55 E
Towanda, U.S.A. 111 E8 41 46N 76 27W
Towang, India 67 F17 27 37N 91 50 E
Tower, U.S.A. 112 B8 47 48N 92 17W
Towerhill Cr. →, Australia 94 C3 22 28 S 144 35 E
Towner, U.S.A. 112 A4 48 21N 100 25W
Townsend, U.S.A. 114 C8 46 19N 111 31W
Townshend I., Australia 94 C5 22 10 S 150 31 E
Townsville, Australia 94 B4 19 15 S 146 45 E
Towraghondi, Afghan. 66 B3 35 13N 62 16 E
Towson, U.S.A. 108 F7 39 24N 76 36W
Towuti, Danau, Indonesia 63 E6 2 45 S 121 32 E
Toya-Ko, Japan 54 C10 42 35N 140 51 E
Toyama, Japan 55 F8 36 40N 137 15 E
Toyama □, Japan 55 F8 36 45N 137 30 E
Toyama-Wan, Japan 55 F8 37 0N 137 30 E
Toyohashi, Japan 55 G8 34 45N 137 25 E
Toyokawa, Japan 55 G8 34 48N 137 27 E
Toyonaka, Japan 55 G7 34 50N 135 28 E
Toyooka, Japan 55 G7 35 35N 134 48 E
Toyota, Japan 55 G8 35 3N 137 7 E
Tozeur, Tunisia 78 B7 33 56N 8 8 E
Tqibuli, Georgia 49 J6 42 26N 43 0 E
Tqvarcheli, Georgia 49 J5 42 47N 41 42 E
Trá Li = Tralee, Ireland 15 D2 52 16N 9 42W
Tra On, Vietnam 65 H5 9 58N 105 55 E
Trabancos →, Spain 34 D5 41 36N 5 15W
Traben-Trarbach, Germany 25 F3 49 57N 7 7 E
Trabzon, Turkey 73 B8 41 0N 39 45 E
Tracadie, Canada 103 C7 47 30N 64 55W
Tracy, Calif., U.S.A. 116 H5 37 44N 121 26W
Tracy, Minn., U.S.A. 112 C7 44 14N 95 37W
Tradate, Italy 28 C5 45 43N 8 54 E
Trade Town, Liberia 82 D3 5 40N 9 50W
Trafalgar, C., Spain 35 J4 36 10N 6 2W
Traian, Brăila, Romania 43 E12 45 11N 27 44 E
Traian, Tulcea, Romania 43 E13 45 2N 28 15 E
Trail, Canada 104 D5 49 5N 117 40W
Trainor L., Canada 104 A4 60 24N 120 17W
Trákhonas, Cyprus 36 D12 35 12N 33 21 E
Tralee, Ireland 15 D2 52 16N 9 42W
Tralee B., Ireland 15 D2 52 17N 9 55W
Tramore, Ireland 15 D4 52 10N 7 10W
Tramore B., Ireland 15 D4 52 9N 7 10W
Tran Ninh, Cao Nguyen, Laos 64 C4 19 30N 103 10 E
Tranås, Sweden 11 F8 58 3N 14 59 E
Tranbjerg, Denmark 11 H4 56 6N 10 9 E
Trancas, Argentina 126 B2 26 11 S 65 20W
Trancoso, Portugal 34 E3 40 49N 7 21W
Tranebjerg, Denmark 11 J4 55 51N 10 36 E
Tranemo, Sweden 11 G7 57 30N 13 20 E
Trang, Thailand 65 J2 7 33N 99 38 E
Trangahy, Madag. 89 B7 19 7 S 44 31 E
Trangan, Indonesia 63 F8 6 40 S 134 20 E
Trangie, Australia 95 E4 32 4 S 148 0 E
Trångsviken, Sweden 10 A7 63 19N 13 59 E
Trani, Italy 31 A9 41 17N 16 25 E
Tranoroa, Madag. 89 C8 24 42 S 45 4 E
Tranqueras, Uruguay 127 C4 31 13 S 55 45W
Transantarctic Mts., Antarctica 5 E12 85 0 S 170 0W
Transilvania, Romania 43 D9 46 30N 24 0 E
Transilvanian Alps = Carpaţii Meridionali, Romania 43 E9 45 30N 25 0 E
Transtrand, Sweden 10 C7 61 6N 13 20 E
Transtrandsfjällen, Sweden 10 C6 61 8N 13 0 E
Transvaal, S. Africa 85 K5 25 0 S 29 0 E
Transylvania = Transilvania, Romania 43 D9 46 30N 24 0 E
Trápani, Italy 30 D5 38 1N 12 29 E
Trapper Pk., U.S.A. 114 D6 45 54N 114 18W
Traralgon, Australia 95 F4 38 12 S 146 34 E
Trarza, Mauritania 82 B2 17 30N 15 0W
Trasacco, Italy 29 G10 41 57N 13 32 E
Trăscău, Munţii, Romania 43 D8 46 14N 23 14 E
Trasimeno, L., Italy 29 E9 43 8N 12 6 E
Träslövsläge, Sweden 11 G6 57 4N 12 16 E
Trasvase Tajo-Segura, Canal de, Spain 32 E2 40 15N 2 55W
Trat, Thailand 65 F4 12 14N 102 33 E
Tratani →, Pakistan 68 E3 29 19N 68 20 E
Traun, Austria 26 C7 48 14N 14 15 E
Traunreut, Germany 25 H8 47 57N 12 36 E
Traunsee, Austria 26 D6 47 55N 13 50 E
Traunstein, Germany 25 H8 47 52N 12 37 E
Traveller's L., Australia 95 E3 33 20 S 142 0 E
Travemünde, Germany 24 B6 53 57N 10 52 E
Travers, Mt., N.Z. 91 K4 42 1 S 172 45 E
Traverse City, U.S.A. 108 C3 44 46N 85 38W
Travis, L., U.S.A. 113 K5 30 24N 97 55W
Travnik, Bos.-H. 42 F2 44 17N 17 39 E
Trbovlje, Slovenia 29 B12 46 12N 15 5 E
Trébbia →, Italy 28 C6 45 4N 9 41 E
Trebel →, Germany 24 B9 53 54N 13 2 E
Trébeurden, France 18 D3 48 46N 3 35W
Třebíč, Czech Rep. 26 B8 49 14N 15 55 E
Trebinje, Bos.-H. 40 D2 42 44N 18 22 E
Trebisacce, Italy 31 C9 39 52N 16 32 E
Trebišnjica →, Bos.-H. 40 D2 42 47N 18 8 E
Trebišov, Slovak Rep. 27 C14 48 38N 21 41 E
Trebižat →, Bos.-H. 29 E14 43 15N 17 30 E
Trebnje, Slovenia 29 C12 45 54N 15 1 E
Třeboň, Czech Rep. 26 B7 49 1N 14 48 E
Trebonne, Australia 94 B4 18 37 S 146 5 E
Trebujena, Spain 35 J4 36 52N 6 11W
Trecate, Italy 28 C5 45 26N 8 44 E
Tregaron, U.K. 13 E4 52 14N 3 56W
Tregnago, Italy 29 C8 45 31N 11 10 E
Tregrosse Is., Australia 94 B5 17 41 S 150 43 E
Tréguier, France 18 D3 48 47N 3 16W
Trégunc, France 18 E3 47 51N 3 51W
Treherne, Canada 105 D9 49 38N 98 42W
Tréia, Italy 29 E10 43 19N 13 19 E
Treignac, France 20 C5 45 32N 1 48 E
Treinta y Tres, Uruguay 127 C5 33 16 S 54 17W
Treis-karden, Germany 25 E3 50 10N 7 18 E
Treklyano, Bulgaria 40 D6 42 33N 22 36 E
Trelawney, Zimbabwe 89 B5 17 30 S 30 30 E
Trélazé, France 18 E6 47 26N 0 30W
Trelew, Argentina 128 E3 43 10 S 65 20W
Trélissac, France 20 C4 45 11N 0 47 E
Trelleborg, Sweden 11 J7 55 20N 13 10 E
Tremadog Bay, U.K. 12 E3 52 51N 4 18W
Trémiti, Italy 29 F12 42 8N 15 30 E
Tremonton, U.S.A. 114 F7 41 43N 112 10W
Tremp, Spain 32 C5 42 10N 0 52 E
Trenche →, Canada 102 C5 47 46N 72 53W
Trenčiansky □, Slovak Rep. 27 C11 48 45N 18 20 E
Trenčín, Slovak Rep. 27 C11 48 52N 18 4 E
Trenggalek, Indonesia 63 H14 8 3 S 111 43 E
Trenque Lauquen, Argentina 126 D3 36 5 S 62 45W
Trent →, Canada 110 B7 44 6N 77 34W
Trent →, U.K. 12 D7 53 41N 0 42W
Trentino-Alto Adige □, Italy 29 B8 46 30N 11 20 E
Trento, Italy 28 B8 46 4N 11 8 E
Trenton, Canada 102 D4 44 10N 77 34W
Trenton, Mo., U.S.A. 112 E8 40 5N 93 37W
Trenton, N.J., U.S.A. 111 F10 40 14N 74 46W
Trenton, Nebr., U.S.A. 112 E4 40 11N 101 1W
Trepassey, Canada 103 C9 46 43N 53 25W
Trepuzzi, Italy 31 B11 40 24N 18 4 E
Tres Arroyos, Argentina 126 D3 38 26 S 60 20W
Três Corações, Brazil 127 A6 21 44 S 45 15W
Três Lagoas, Brazil 125 H8 20 50 S 51 43W
Tres Lomas, Argentina 126 D3 36 27 S 62 51W
Tres Marías, Islas, Mexico 118 C3 21 25N 106 28W
Tres Montes, C., Chile 128 F1 46 50 S 75 30W
Tres Pinos, U.S.A. 116 J5 36 48N 121 19W
Três Pontas, Brazil 127 A6 21 23 S 45 29W
Tres Puentes, Chile 126 B1 27 50 S 70 15W
Tres Puntas, C., Argentina 128 F3 47 0 S 66 0W
Três Rios, Brazil 127 A7 22 6 S 43 15W
Tres Valles, Mexico 119 D5 18 15N 96 8W
Tresco, U.K. 13 H1 49 57N 6 20W
Treska →, Macedonia 40 E5 42 0N 21 20 E
Treskavica, Bos.-H. 42 G3 43 40N 18 20 E
Trespaderne, Spain 34 C7 42 47N 3 24W
Trets, France 21 E9 43 27N 5 41 E
Treuchtlingen, Germany 25 G6 48 58N 10 54 E
Treuenbrietzen, Germany 24 C8 52 5N 12 52 E
Trevi, Italy 29 F9 42 52N 12 45 E
Treviglio, Italy 28 C6 45 31N 9 35 E
Trevinca, Peña, Spain 34 C4 42 15N 6 46W
Treviso, Italy 29 C9 45 40N 12 15 E
Trévoux, France 21 C8 45 57N 4 47 E
Trgovište, Serbia, Yug. 40 D6 42 20N 22 10 E
Triabunna, Australia 94 G4 42 30 S 147 55 E
Triánda, Greece 36 C10 36 25N 28 10 E
Triangle, Zimbabwe 89 C5 21 2 S 31 28 E
Triaucourt-en-Argonne, France 19 D12 48 59N 5 2 E
Tribal Areas □, Pakistan 68 C4 33 0N 70 0 E
Tribsees, Germany 24 A8 54 5N 12 44 E
Tribulation, C., Australia 94 B4 16 5 S 145 29 E
Tribune, U.S.A. 112 F4 38 28N 101 45W
Tricárico, Italy 31 B9 40 37N 16 9 E
Tricase, Italy 31 C11 39 56N 18 22 E
Trichinopoly = Tiruchchirappalli, India 66 P11 10 45N 78 45 E
Trichur, India 66 P10 10 30N 76 18 E
Trida, Australia 95 E4 33 1 S 145 1 E
Trier, Germany 25 F2 49 45N 6 38 E
Trieste, Italy 29 C10 45 40N 13 46 E
Trieste, G. di, Italy 29 C10 45 40N 13 35 E
Trieux →, France 18 D3 48 43N 3 9W
Triggiano, Italy 31 A9 41 4N 16 55 E
Triglav, Slovenia 29 B10 46 21N 13 50 E
Trigno →, Italy 29 F11 42 4N 14 48 E
Trigueros, Spain 35 H4 37 24N 6 50W
Tríkeri, Greece 38 B5 39 6N 23 5 E
Trikhonis, Límni, Greece 38 C3 38 34N 21 30 E
Tríkkala, Greece 38 B3 39 34N 21 47 E
Tríkkala □, Greece 38 B3 39 41N 21 30 E
Trikomo, Cyprus 36 D12 35 17N 33 52 E
Trikora, Puncak, Indonesia 63 E9 4 15 S 138 45 E
Trilj, Croatia 29 E13 43 38N 16 42 E
Trillo, Spain 32 E2 40 42N 2 35W
Trim, Ireland 15 C5 53 33N 6 48W
Trincomalee, Sri Lanka 66 Q12 8 38N 81 15 E
Trindade, Brazil 125 G9 16 40 S 49 30W
Trindade, I., Atl. Oc. 2 F8 20 20 S 29 50W
Třinec, Czech Rep. 27 B11 49 41N 18 39 E
Trinidad, Bolivia 124 F6 14 46 S 64 50W
Trinidad, Cuba 120 B4 21 48N 80 0W
Trinidad, Trin. & Tob. 121 D7 10 30N 61 15W
Trinidad, Uruguay 126 C4 33 30 S 56 50W
Trinidad, U.S.A. 113 G2 37 10N 104 31W
Trinidad →, Mexico 119 D5 17 49N 95 9W
Trinidad & Tobago ■, W. Indies 121 D7 10 30N 61 20W
Trinitápoli, Italy 31 A9 41 21N 16 5 E
Trinity, Canada 103 C9 48 59N 53 55W
Trinity, U.S.A. 113 K7 30 57N 95 22W
Trinity →, Calif., U.S.A. 114 F2 41 11N 123 42W
Trinity →, Tex., U.S.A. 113 L7 29 45N 94 43W
Trinity B., Canada 103 C9 48 20N 53 10W
Trinity Is., U.S.A. 100 C4 56 33N 154 25W
Trinity Range, U.S.A. 114 F4 40 15N 118 45W
Trinkitat, Sudan 80 D4 18 45N 37 51 E
Trino, Italy 28 C5 45 12N 8 18 E
Trinway, U.S.A. 110 F2 40 9N 82 1W
Trionto, C., Italy 31 C9 39 37N 16 43 E
Triora, Italy 28 D4 44 1N 7 46 E
Tripoli = Tarābulus, Lebanon 75 A4 34 31N 35 50 E
Tripoli = Tarābulus, Libya 79 B8 32 49N 13 7 E
Trípolis, Greece 38 D4 37 31N 22 25 E
Tripolitania, N. Afr. 79 B8 31 0N 13 0 E
Tripura □, India 67 H18 24 0N 92 0 E
Tripylos, Cyprus 36 E11 34 59N 32 41 E
Trischen, Germany 24 A4 54 4N 8 40 E
Tristan da Cunha, Atl. Oc. 77 K2 37 6 S 12 20W
Trisul, India 69 D8 30 19N 79 47 E
Trivandrum, India 66 Q10 8 41N 77 0 E
Trivento, Italy 29 G11 41 47N 14 33 E
Trnava, Slovak Rep. 27 C10 48 23N 17 35 E
Trnavský □, Slovak Rep. 27 C10 48 30N 17 45 E
Troarn, France 18 C6 49 11N 0 11W
Trochu, Canada 104 C6 51 50N 113 13W
Trodely I., Canada 102 B4 52 15N 79 26W
Troezen, Greece 38 D5 37 25N 23 15 E
Trogir, Croatia 29 E13 43 32N 16 15 E
Troglav, Croatia 29 E13 43 56N 16 36 E
Tróia, Italy 31 A8 41 22N 15 18 E
Troilus, L., Canada 102 B5 50 50N 74 35W
Troina, Italy 31 E7 37 47N 14 36 E
Trois-Pistoles, Canada 103 C6 48 5N 69 10W
Trois-Rivières, Canada 102 C5 46 25N 72 34W
Troisdorf, Germany 24 E3 50 48N 7 11 E
Troitsk, Russia 50 D7 54 10N 61 35 E
Troitsko Pechorsk, Russia 50 C6 62 40N 56 10 E
Trölladyngja, Iceland 8 D5 64 54N 17 16W
Trollhättan, Sweden 11 F6 58 17N 12 20 E
Trollheimen, Norway 8 E13 62 46N 9 1 E
Trombetas →, Brazil 125 D7 1 55 S 55 35W
Tromsø, Norway 8 B18 69 40N 18 56 E
Trona, U.S.A. 117 K9 35 46N 117 23W
Tronador, Mte., Argentina 128 E2 41 10 S 71 50W
Trøndelag, Norway 8 D14 64 17N 11 50 E
Trondheim, Norway 8 E14 63 36N 10 25 E
Trondheimsfjorden, Norway 8 E14 63 35N 10 30 E
Trönninge, Sweden 11 H6 56 37N 12 51 E
Tronto →, Italy 29 F10 42 54N 13 55 E
Troodos, Cyprus 36 E11 34 55N 32 52 E
Troon, U.K. 14 F4 55 33N 4 39W
Tropea, Italy 31 D8 38 41N 15 54 E
Tropic, U.S.A. 115 H7 37 37N 112 5W
Tropojë, Albania 40 D4 42 23N 20 10 E
Trosa, Sweden 11 F11 58 54N 17 33 E
Trostan, U.K. 15 A5 55 3N 6 10W
Trostberg, Germany 25 G8 48 1N 12 33 E
Trostyanets, Ukraine 47 G8 50 33N 34 59 E
Trout →, Canada 104 A5 61 19N 119 51W
Trout L., N.W.T., Canada 104 A4 60 40N 121 14W
Trout L., Ont., Canada 105 C10 51 20N 93 15W
Trout Lake, Canada 104 B6 56 30N 114 32W
Trout Lake, U.S.A. 116 E5 46 0N 121 32W
Trout River, Canada 103 C8 49 29N 58 8W
Trout Run, U.S.A. 110 E7 41 23N 77 3W
Trouville-sur-Mer, France 18 C7 49 21N 0 5 E
Trowbridge, U.K. 13 F5 51 18N 2 12W
Troy, Turkey 39 B8 39 57N 26 12 E
Troy, Ala., U.S.A. 109 K3 31 48N 85 58W
Troy, Kans., U.S.A. 112 F7 39 47N 95 5W
Troy, Mo., U.S.A. 112 F9 38 59N 90 59W
Troy, Mont., U.S.A. 114 B6 48 28N 115 53W
Troy, N.Y., U.S.A. 111 D11 42 44N 73 41W
Troy, Ohio, U.S.A. 108 E3 40 2N 84 12W
Troy, Pa., U.S.A. 111 E8 41 47N 76 47W
Troyan, Bulgaria 41 D8 42 57N 24 43 E
Troyes, France 19 D11 48 19N 4 3 E
Trpanj, Croatia 29 E14 43 1N 17 15 E
Trstenik, Serbia, Yug. 40 C5 43 36N 21 0 E
Trubchevsk, Russia 47 F7 52 33N 33 47 E
Truchas Peak, U.S.A. 113 H2 35 58N 105 39W
Trucial States = United Arab Emirates ■, Asia 71 F7 23 50N 54 0 E
Truckee, U.S.A. 116 F6 39 20N 120 11W
Trudfront, Russia 49 H8 45 56N 47 40 E
Trudovoye, Russia 54 C6 43 17N 132 5 E
Trujillo, Honduras 120 C2 16 0N 86 0W
Trujillo, Peru 124 E3 8 6 S 79 0W
Trujillo, Spain 35 F5 39 28N 5 55W
Trujillo, U.S.A. 113 H2 35 32N 104 42W
Trujillo, Venezuela 124 B4 9 22N 70 38W
Truk, Micronesia 96 G7 7 25N 151 46 E
Trumann, U.S.A. 113 H9 35 41N 90 31W
Trumansburg, U.S.A. 111 D8 42 33N 76 40W
Trumbull, Mt., U.S.A. 115 H7 36 25N 113 8W
Trŭn, Bulgaria 40 D6 42 51N 22 38 E
Trun, France 18 D7 48 50N 0 2 E
Trundle, Australia 95 E4 32 53 S 147 35 E
Trung-Phan = Annam, Vietnam 64 E7 16 0N 108 0 E
Truro, Canada 103 C7 45 21N 63 14W
Truro, U.K. 13 G2 50 16N 5 4W
Truskavets, Ukraine 47 H2 49 17N 23 30 E
Trŭstenik, Bulgaria 41 C8 43 31N 24 28 E
Trustrup, Denmark 11 H4 56 20N 10 46 E
Trutch, Canada 104 B4 57 44N 122 57W
Truth or Consequences, U.S.A. 115 K10 33 8N 107 15W
Trutnov, Czech Rep. 26 A8 50 37N 15 54 E
Truxton, U.S.A. 111 D8 42 45N 76 2W
Truyère →, France 20 D6 44 38N 2 34 E
Tryavna, Bulgaria 41 D9 42 54N 25 25 E
Tryonville, U.S.A. 110 E5 41 42N 79 48W
Trzcianka, Poland 45 E3 53 3N 16 25 E
Trzciel, Poland 45 F2 52 23N 15 50 E
Trzcińsko Zdrój, Poland 45 F1 52 58N 14 35 E
Trzebiatów, Poland 44 D2 54 3N 15 18 E
Trzebiez, Poland 44 E1 53 38N 14 31 E
Trzebnica, Poland 45 G4 51 20N 17 1 E
Trzemeszno, Poland 45 F4 52 33N 17 48 E
Tržič, Slovenia 29 B11 46 22N 14 18 E
Tsagan Aman, Russia 49 G8 47 34N 46 43 E
Tsamandás, Greece 38 B2 39 46N 20 21 E
Tsandi, Namibia 88 B1 17 42 S 14 50 E
Tsaratanana, Madag. 89 B8 16 47 S 47 39 E
Tsaratanana, Mt. de, Madag. 89 A8 14 0 S 49 0 E
Tsarevo = Michurin, Bulgaria 41 D11 42 9N 27 51 E
Tsarevo, Bulgaria 41 D9 42 28N 25 52 E
Tsaritsáni, Greece 38 B4 39 53N 22 14 E
Tsau, Botswana 88 C3 20 8 S 22 22 E
Tsebrykove, Ukraine 47 J6 47 9N 30 10 E
Tselinograd = Astana, Kazakhstan 50 D8 51 10N 71 30 E
Tses, Namibia 88 D2 25 58 S 18 8 E
Tsetserleg, Mongolia 60 B5 47 36N 101 32 E
Tsévié, Togo 83 D5 6 25N 1 20 E
Tshabong, Botswana 88 D3 26 2 S 22 29 E
Tshane, Botswana 88 C3 24 5 S 21 54 E
Tshela, Dem. Rep. of the Congo 84 E2 4 57 S 13 4 E
Tshesebe, Botswana 89 C4 21 51 S 27 32 E
Tshibeke, Dem. Rep. of the Congo 86 C2 2 40 S 28 35 E
Tshibinda, Dem. Rep. of the Congo 86 C2 2 23 S 28 43 E
Tshikapa, Dem. Rep. of the Congo 84 F4 6 28 S 20 48 E
Tshilenge, Dem. Rep. of the Congo 86 D1 6 17 S 23 48 E
Tshinsenda, Dem. Rep. of the Congo 87 E2 12 20 S 28 0 E
Tshofa, Dem. Rep. of the Congo 86 D2 5 13 S 25 16 E
Tshwane, Botswana 88 C3 22 24 S 22 1 E
Tsigara, Botswana 88 C4 20 22 S 25 54 E
Tsihombe, Madag. 89 D8 25 10 S 45 41 E
Tsiigehtchic, Canada 100 B6 67 15N 134 0W
Tsimlyansk, Russia 49 G6 47 40N 42 6 E
Tsimlyansk Res. = Tsimlyanskoye Vdkhr., Russia 49 F6 48 0N 43 0 E
Tsimlyanskoye Vdkhr., Russia 49 F6 48 0N 43 0 E
Tsinan = Jinan, China 56 F9 36 38N 117 1 E
Tsineng, S. Africa 88 D3 27 5 S 23 5 E
Tsínga, Greece 41 E8 41 23N 24 44 E
Tsinghai = Qinghai □, China 60 C4 36 0N 98 0 E
Tsingtao = Qingdao, China 57 F11 36 5N 120 20 E
Tsinjoarivo, Madag. 89 B8 19 37 S 47 40 E
Tsinjomitondraka, Madag. 89 B8 15 40 S 47 8 E
Tsiroanomandidy, Madag. 89 B8 18 46 S 46 2 E
Tsiteli-Tsqaro, Georgia 49 K8 41 33N 46 0 E
Tsitondroina, Madag. 89 C8 21 19 S 46 0 E
Tsivilsk, Russia 48 C8 55 50N 47 25 E
Tsivory, Madag. 89 C8 24 4 S 46 5 E
Tskhinvali, Georgia 49 J7 42 14N 44 1 E
Tsna →, Russia 48 C6 54 55N 41 58 E
Tsnori, Georgia 49 K7 41 40N 45 57 E
Tso Moriri, L., India 69 C8 32 50N 78 20 E
Tsobis, Namibia 88 B2 19 27 S 17 30 E
Tsodilo Hill, Botswana 88 B3 18 49 S 21 43 E
Tsogttsetsiy = Baruunsuu, Mongolia 56 C3 43 43N 105 35 E
Tsolo, S. Africa 89 E4 31 18 S 28 37 E
Tsomo, S. Africa 89 E4 32 0 S 27 42 E
Tsu, Japan 55 G8 34 45N 136 25 E
Tsu L., Canada 104 A6 60 40N 111 52W
Tsuchiura, Japan 55 F10 36 5N 140 15 E
Tsuen Wan, H.K. 59 F10 22 22N 114 6 E
Tsugaru-Kaikyō, Japan 54 D10 41 35N 141 0 E
Tsumeb, Namibia 88 B2 19 9 S 17 44 E
Tsumis, Namibia 88 C2 23 39 S 17 29 E
Tsuruga, Japan 55 G8 35 45N 136 2 E
Tsurugi-San, Japan 55 H7 33 51N 134 6 E
Tsuruoka, Japan 54 E9 38 44N 139 50 E
Tsushima, Gifu, Japan 55 G8 35 10N 136 43 E
Tsushima, Nagasaki, Japan 55 G4 34 20N 129 20 E
Tsuyama, Japan 55 G7 35 3N 134 0 E
Tsvetkovo, Ukraine 47 H6 49 8N 31 33 E
Tsyelyakhany, Belarus 47 F3 52 30N 25 46 E

Tua →, *Portugal* **34 D3** 41 13N 7 26W
Tual, *Indonesia* **63 F8** 5 38 S 132 44 E
Tuam, *Ireland* **15 C3** 53 31N 8 51W
Tuamotu Arch. = Tuamotu Is., *Pac. Oc.* **97 J13** 17 0 S 144 0W
Tuamotu Is., *Pac. Oc.* **97 J13** 17 0 S 144 0W
Tuamotu Ridge, *Pac. Oc.* **97 K14** 20 0 S 138 0W
Tuanfeng, *China* **59 B10** 30 38N 114 52 E
Tuanxi, *China* **58 D6** 27 28N 107 8 E
Tuao, *Phil.* **61 C4** 17 55N 121 22 E
Tuapse, *Russia* **49 H4** 44 5N 39 10 E
Tuatapere, *N.Z.* **91 M1** 46 8 S 167 41 E
Tuba City, *U.S.A.* **115 H8** 36 8N 111 14W
Tuban, *Indonesia* **63 G15** 6 54 S 112 3 E
Tubani, *Botswana* **88 C3** 24 46 S 24 18 E
Tubarão, *Brazil* **127 B6** 28 30 S 49 0W
Tūbās, *West Bank* **75 C4** 32 20N 35 22 E
Tubas →, *Namibia* **88 C2** 22 54 S 14 35 E
Tübingen, *Germany* **25 G5** 48 31N 9 4 E
Tubruq, *Libya* **79 B10** 32 7N 23 55 E
Tubuai Is., *Pac. Oc.* **97 K13** 25 0 S 150 0W
Tuc Trung, *Vietnam* **65 G6** 11 1N 107 12 E
Tucacas, *Venezuela* **124 A5** 10 48N 68 19W
T'uch'ang, *Taiwan* **59 E13** 24 42N 121 25 E
Tuchodi →, *Canada* **104 B4** 58 17N 123 42W
Tuchola, *Poland* **44 E4** 53 33N 17 52 E
Tuchów, *Poland* **45 J8** 49 54N 21 1 E
Tuckanarra, *Australia* **93 E2** 27 7 S 118 5 E
Tucson, *U.S.A.* **115 K8** 32 13N 110 58W
Tucumán □, *Argentina* **126 B2** 26 48 S 66 2W
Tucumcari, *U.S.A.* **113 H3** 35 10N 103 44W
Tucupita, *Venezuela* **124 B6** 9 2N 62 3W
Tucuruí, *Brazil* **125 D9** 3 42 S 49 44W
Tucuruí, Reprêsa de, *Brazil* **125 D9** 4 0 S 49 30W
Tuczno, *Poland* **45 E3** 53 13N 16 10 E
Tudela, *Spain* **32 C3** 42 4N 1 39W
Tudmur, *Syria* **70 C3** 34 36N 38 15 E
Tudor, L., *Canada* **103 A6** 55 50N 65 25W
Tudora, *Romania* **43 C11** 47 31N 26 45 E
Tuella →, *Portugal* **34 D3** 41 30N 7 12W
Tugela →, *S. Africa* **89 D5** 29 14 S 31 30 E
Tuguegarao, *Phil.* **61 C4** 17 35N 121 42 E
Tugur, *Russia* **51 D14** 53 44N 136 45 E
Tui, *Spain* **34 C2** 42 3N 8 39W
Tuineje, *Canary Is.* **37 F5** 28 19N 14 3W
Tukangbesi, Kepulauan, *Indonesia* **63 F6** 6 0 S 124 0 E
Tukarak I., *Canada* **102 A4** 56 15N 78 45W
Tukayyid, *Iraq* **70 D5** 29 47N 45 36 E
Tûkh, *Egypt* **80 H7** 30 21N 31 12 E
Tukobo, *Ghana* **82 D4** 5 1N 2 47W
Tuktoyaktuk, *Canada* **100 B6** 69 27N 133 2W
Tukums, *Latvia* **9 H20** 56 58N 23 10 E
Tukums □, *Latvia* **44 B10** 56 55N 23 0 E
Tukuyu, *Tanzania* **87 D3** 9 17 S 33 35 E
Tula, *Hidalgo, Mexico* **119 C5** 20 5N 99 20W
Tula, *Tamaulipas, Mexico* **119 C5** 23 0N 99 40W
Tula, *Nigeria* **83 D7** 9 51N 11 27 E
Tula, *Russia* **46 E9** 54 13N 37 38 E
Tulancingo, *Mexico* **119 C5** 20 5N 99 22W
Tulare, *Serbia, Yug.* **40 D5** 42 48N 21 28 E
Tulare, *U.S.A.* **116 J7** 36 13N 119 21W
Tulare Lake Bed, *U.S.A.* **116 K7** 36 0N 119 48W
Tularosa, *U.S.A.* **115 K10** 33 5N 106 1W
Tulbagh, *S. Africa* **88 E2** 33 16 S 19 6 E
Tulcán, *Ecuador* **124 C3** 0 48N 77 43W
Tulcea, *Romania* **43 E13** 45 13N 28 46 E
Tulcea □, *Romania* **43 E13** 45 0N 28 30 E
Tulchyn, *Ukraine* **47 H5** 48 41N 28 49 E
Tūleh, *Iran* **71 C7** 34 35N 52 33 E
Tulemalu L., *Canada* **105 A9** 62 58N 99 25W
Tulgheş, *Romania* **43 D10** 46 58N 25 45 E
Tuli, *Zimbabwe* **87 G2** 21 58 S 29 13 E
Tulia, *U.S.A.* **113 H4** 34 32N 101 46W
Tuliszków, *Poland* **45 F5** 52 5N 18 18 E
Tulita, *Canada* **100 B7** 64 57N 125 30W
Ţūlkarm, *West Bank* **75 C4** 32 19N 35 2 E
Tulla, *Ireland* **15 D3** 52 53N 8 46W
Tullahoma, *U.S.A.* **109 H2** 35 22N 86 13W
Tullamore, *Australia* **95 E4** 32 39 S 147 36 E
Tullamore, *Ireland* **15 C4** 53 16N 7 31W
Tulle, *France* **20 C5** 45 16N 1 46 E
Tulln, *Austria* **26 C9** 48 20N 16 4 E
Tullow, *Ireland* **15 D5** 52 49N 6 45W
Tullus, *Sudan* **81 E1** 11 7N 24 31 E
Tully, *Australia* **94 B4** 17 56 S 145 55 E
Tully, *U.S.A.* **111 D8** 42 48N 76 7W
Tulnici, *Romania* **43 E11** 45 51N 26 38 E
Tulovo, *Bulgaria* **41 D9** 42 33N 25 32 E
Tulsa, *U.S.A.* **113 G7** 36 10N 95 55W
Tulsequah, *Canada* **104 B2** 58 39N 133 35W
Tulu Milki, *Ethiopia* **81 F4** 9 55N 38 20 E
Tulu Welel, *Ethiopia* **81 F3** 8 56N 34 47 E
Tulua, *Colombia* **124 C3** 4 6N 76 11W
Tuluceşti, *Romania* **43 E13** 45 34N 28 2 E
Tulun, *Russia* **51 D11** 54 32N 100 35 E
Tulungagung, *Indonesia* **63 H14** 8 5 S 111 54 E
Tuma, *Russia* **46 E11** 55 10N 40 30 E
Tuma →, *Nic.* **120 D3** 13 6N 84 35W
Tumaco, *Colombia* **124 C3** 1 50N 78 45W
Tumatumari, *Guyana* **124 B7** 5 20N 58 55W
Tumba, *Sweden* **10 E11** 59 12N 17 48 E
Tumba, L., *Dem. Rep. of the Congo* **84 E3** 0 50 S 18 0 E
Tumbarumba, *Australia* **95 F4** 35 44 S 148 0 E
Tumbaya, *Argentina* **126 A2** 23 50 S 65 26W
Tumbes, *Peru* **124 D2** 3 37 S 80 27W
Tumbur, *Sudan* **81 G3** 4 20N 31 34 E
Tumbwe, *Dem. Rep. of the Congo* **87 E2** 11 25 S 27 15 E
Tumby Bay, *Australia* **95 E2** 34 21 S 136 8 E
Tumd Youqi, *China* **56 D6** 40 30N 110 30 E
Tumen, *China* **57 C15** 43 0N 129 50 E
Tumen Jiang →, *China* **57 C16** 42 20N 130 35 E
Tumeremo, *Venezuela* **124 B6** 7 18N 61 30W
Tumkur, *India* **66 N10** 13 18N 77 6 E
Tump, *Pakistan* **66 F3** 26 7N 62 16 E
Tumpat, *Malaysia* **65 J4** 6 11N 102 10 E
Tumu, *Ghana* **82 C4** 10 56N 1 56W
Tumucumaque, Serra, *Brazil* **122 C5** 2 0N 55 0W
Tumut, *Australia* **95 F4** 35 16 S 148 13 E
Tumwater, *U.S.A.* **116 C4** 47 1N 122 54W
Tuna, *India* **68 H4** 22 59N 70 5 E
Tunadal, *Sweden* **10 B11** 62 26N 17 22 E
Tunas de Zaza, *Cuba* **120 B4** 21 39N 79 34W
Tunbridge Wells = Royal Tunbridge Wells, *U.K.* **13 F8** 51 7N 0 16 E
Tunçbilek, *Turkey* **39 B11** 39 37N 29 29 E
Tunceli, *Turkey* **73 C8** 39 6N 39 31 E
Tuncurry, *Australia* **95 E5** 32 17 S 152 29 E
Tundla, *India* **68 F8** 27 12N 78 17 E
Tundubai, *Sudan* **80 D2** 18 36N 28 35 E
Tunduru, *Tanzania* **87 E4** 11 8 S 37 25 E
Tundzha →, *Bulgaria* **41 E10** 41 40N 26 35 E
Tungabhadra →, *India* **66 M11** 15 57N 78 15 E
Tungaru, *Sudan* **81 E3** 10 9N 30 52 E
Tungla, *Nic.* **120 D3** 13 24N 84 21W
Tungsha Tao, *Taiwan* **59 G11** 20 45N 116 43 E
Tungshih, *Taiwan* **59 E13** 24 12N 120 43 E
Tungsten, *Canada* **104 A3** 61 57N 128 16W
Tunguska, Nizhnyaya →, *Russia* **51 C9** 65 48N 88 4 E
Tunguska, Podkamennaya →, *Russia* **51 C10** 61 50N 90 13 E
Tunica, *U.S.A.* **113 H9** 34 41N 90 23W
Tunis, *Tunisia* **78 A7** 36 50N 10 11 E
Tunisia ■, *Africa* **78 B6** 33 30N 9 10 E
Tunja, *Colombia* **124 B4** 5 33N 73 25W
Tunkhannock, *U.S.A.* **111 E9** 41 32N 75 57W
Tunliu, *China* **56 F7** 36 13N 112 52 E
Tunnsjøen, *Norway* **8 D15** 64 45N 13 25 E
Tunø, *Denmark* **11 J4** 55 57N 10 27 E
Tunungayualok I., *Canada* **103 A7** 56 0N 61 0W
Tununirusiq = Arctic Bay, *Canada* **101 A11** 73 1N 85 7W
Tunuyán, *Argentina* **126 C2** 33 35 S 69 0W
Tunuyán →, *Argentina* **126 C2** 33 33 S 67 30W
Tuo Jiang →, *China* **58 C5** 28 50N 105 35 E
Tuolumne, *U.S.A.* **116 H6** 37 58N 120 15W
Tuolumne →, *U.S.A.* **116 H5** 37 36N 121 13W
Tūp Āghāj, *Iran* **70 B5** 36 3N 47 50 E
Tupã, *Brazil* **127 A5** 21 57 S 50 28W
Tupelo, *U.S.A.* **109 H1** 34 16N 88 43W
Tupik, *Russia* **46 E7** 55 42N 33 22 E
Tupinambaranas, *Brazil* **124 D7** 3 0 S 58 0W
Tupiza, *Bolivia* **126 A2** 21 30 S 65 40W
Tupižnica, *Serbia, Yug.* **40 C6** 43 43N 22 10 E
Tupman, *U.S.A.* **117 K7** 35 18N 119 21W
Tupper, *Canada* **104 B4** 55 32N 120 1W
Tupper Lake, *U.S.A.* **111 B10** 44 14N 74 28W
Tupungato, Cerro, *S. Amer.* **126 C2** 33 15 S 69 50W
Tuquan, *China* **57 B11** 45 18N 121 38 E
Túquerres, *Colombia* **124 C3** 1 5N 77 37W
Tura, *Russia* **51 C11** 64 20N 100 17 E
Turabah, *Si. Arabia* **70 D4** 28 20N 43 15 E
Turabah, *Si. Arabia* **80 C5** 21 15N 41 34 E
Tūrān, *Iran* **71 C8** 35 39N 56 42 E
Turan, *Russia* **51 D10** 51 55N 95 0 E
Ţurayf, *Si. Arabia* **70 D3** 31 41N 38 39 E
Turbacz, *Poland* **45 J7** 49 30N 20 8 E
Turbe, *Bos.-H.* **42 F2** 44 15N 17 35 E
Turčianske Teplice, *Slovak Rep.* **27 C11** 48 52N 18 52 E
Turcoaia, *Romania* **43 E13** 45 7N 28 11 E
Turda, *Romania* **43 D8** 46 34N 23 47 E
Turek, *Poland* **45 F5** 52 3N 18 30 E
Turen, *Venezuela* **124 B5** 9 17N 69 6W
Turfan = Turpan, *China* **60 B3** 43 58N 89 10 E
Turfan Depression = Turpan Hami, *China* **52 E12** 42 40N 89 25 E
Turgeon →, *Canada* **102 C4** 50 0N 78 56W
Tŭrgovishte, *Bulgaria* **41 C10** 43 17N 26 38 E
Turgut, *Turkey* **39 D10** 37 22N 28 4 E
Turgutlu, *Turkey* **39 C9** 38 30N 27 43 E
Turgwe →, *Zimbabwe* **89 C5** 21 31 S 32 15 E
Turhal, *Turkey* **72 B7** 40 24N 36 5 E
Turia →, *Spain* **33 F4** 39 27N 0 19W
Turiaçu, *Brazil* **125 D9** 1 40 S 45 19W
Turiaçu →, *Brazil* **125 D9** 1 36 S 45 19W
Turiec →, *Slovak Rep.* **27 B11** 49 7N 18 55 E
Turin = Torino, *Italy* **28 C4** 45 3N 7 40 E
Turkana, L., *Africa* **86 B4** 3 30N 36 5 E
Türkeli, *Turkey* **41 F11** 40 30N 27 30 E
Turkestan = Türkistan, *Kazakhstan* **50 E7** 43 17N 68 16 E
Túrkeve, *Hungary* **42 C5** 47 6N 20 44 E
Turkey ■, *Eurasia* **72 C7** 39 0N 36 0 E
Turkey Creek, *Australia* **92 C4** 17 2 S 128 12 E
Turki, *Russia* **48 D6** 52 0N 43 15 E
Türkistan, *Kazakhstan* **50 E7** 43 17N 68 16 E
Türkmenbashi, *Turkmenistan* **50 E6** 40 5N 53 5 E
Turkmenistan ■, *Asia* **50 F6** 39 0N 59 0 E
Türkmenli, *Turkey* **39 B8** 39 45N 26 30 E
Türkoğlu, *Turkey* **72 D7** 37 23N 36 50 E
Turks & Caicos Is. ■, *W. Indies* **121 B5** 21 20N 71 20W
Turks Island Passage, *W. Indies* **121 B5** 21 30N 71 30W
Turku, *Finland* **9 F20** 60 30N 22 19 E
Turkwel →, *Kenya* **86 B4** 3 6N 36 6 E
Turlock, *U.S.A.* **116 H6** 37 30N 120 51W
Turnagain →, *Canada* **104 B3** 59 12N 127 35W
Turnagain, C., *N.Z.* **91 J6** 40 28 S 176 38 E
Turneffe Is., *Belize* **119 D7** 17 20N 87 50W
Turner, *U.S.A.* **114 B9** 48 51N 108 24W
Turner Pt., *Australia* **94 A1** 11 47 S 133 32 E
Turner Valley, *Canada* **104 C6** 50 40N 114 17W
Turners Falls, *U.S.A.* **111 D12** 42 36N 72 33W
Turnhout, *Belgium* **17 C4** 51 19N 4 57 E
Türnitz, *Austria* **26 D8** 47 55N 15 29 E
Turnor L., *Canada* **105 B7** 56 35N 108 35W
Turnov, *Czech Rep.* **26 A8** 50 34N 15 10 E
Tŭrnovo = Veliko Tŭrnovo, *Bulgaria* **41 C9** 43 5N 25 41 E
Turnu Măgurele, *Romania* **43 G9** 43 46N 24 56 E
Turnu Roşu, P., *Romania* **43 E9** 45 33N 24 17 E
Turobin, *Poland* **45 H9** 50 50N 22 44 E
Turpan, *China* **60 B3** 43 58N 89 10 E
Turpan Hami, *China* **52 E12** 42 40N 89 25 E
Turrës, Kala e, *Albania* **40 E3** 41 10N 19 28 E
Turriff, *U.K.* **14 D6** 57 32N 2 27W
Tursāq, *Iraq* **70 C5** 33 27N 45 47 E
Tursi, *Italy* **31 B9** 40 15N 16 28 E
Turtle Head I., *Australia* **94 A3** 10 56 S 142 37 E
Turtle Is., *S. Leone* **82 D2** 7 40N 13 0 E
Turtle L., *Canada* **105 C7** 53 36N 108 38W
Turtle Lake, *U.S.A.* **112 B4** 47 31N 100 53W
Turtleford, *Canada* **105 C7** 53 23N 108 57W
Turukhansk, *Russia* **51 C9** 65 21N 88 5 E
Turzovka, *Slovak Rep.* **27 B11** 49 25N 18 35 E
Tuscaloosa, *U.S.A.* **109 J2** 33 12N 87 34W
Tuscánia, *Italy* **29 F8** 42 25N 11 52 E
Tuscany = Toscana □, *Italy* **28 E8** 43 25N 11 0 E
Tuscarawas →, *U.S.A.* **110 F3** 40 24N 81 25W
Tuscarora Mt., *U.S.A.* **110 F7** 40 55N 77 55W
Tuscola, *Ill., U.S.A.* **108 F1** 39 48N 88 17W
Tuscola, *Tex., U.S.A.* **113 J5** 32 12N 99 48W
Tuscumbia, *U.S.A.* **109 H2** 34 44N 87 42W
Tuskegee, *U.S.A.* **109 J3** 32 25N 85 42W
Tustin, *U.S.A.* **117 M9** 33 44N 117 49W
Tuszyn, *Poland* **45 G6** 51 36N 19 33 E
Tutak, *Turkey* **73 C10** 39 31N 42 46 E
Tutayev, *Russia* **46 D10** 57 53N 39 32 E
Tuticorin, *India* **66 Q11** 8 50N 78 12 E
Tutin, *Serbia, Yug.* **40 D4** 42 58N 20 20 E
Tutóia, *Brazil* **125 D10** 2 45 S 42 20W
Tutong, *Brunei* **62 D4** 4 47N 114 40 E
Tutova →, *Romania* **43 D12** 46 7N 27 30 E
Tutrakan, *Bulgaria* **41 B10** 44 2N 26 40 E
Tuttle Creek L., *U.S.A.* **112 F6** 39 22N 96 40W
Tuttlingen, *Germany* **25 H4** 47 58N 8 48 E
Tutuala, *Indonesia* **63 F7** 8 25 S 127 15 E
Tutuila, *Amer. Samoa* **91 B13** 14 19 S 170 50W
Tutume, *Botswana* **85 J5** 20 30 S 27 5 E
Tutun, *Egypt* **80 J7** 29 9N 30 46 E
Tututepec, *Mexico* **119 D5** 16 9N 97 38W
Tuva □, *Russia* **51 D10** 51 30N 95 0 E
Tuvalu ■, *Pac. Oc.* **96 H9** 8 0 S 178 0 E
Tuxer Alpen, *Austria* **26 D4** 47 10N 11 45 E
Tuxpan, *Mexico* **119 C5** 20 58N 97 23W
Tuxtla Gutiérrez, *Mexico* **119 D6** 16 50N 93 10W
Tuy = Tui, *Spain* **34 C2** 42 3N 8 39W
Tuy An, *Vietnam* **64 F7** 13 17N 109 16 E
Tuy Duc, *Vietnam* **65 F6** 12 15N 107 27 E
Tuy Hoa, *Vietnam* **64 F7** 13 5N 109 10 E
Tuy Phong, *Vietnam* **65 G7** 11 14N 108 43 E
Tuya L., *Canada* **104 B2** 59 7N 130 35W
Tuyen Hoa, *Vietnam* **64 D6** 17 50N 106 10 E
Tuyen Quang, *Vietnam* **58 G5** 21 50N 105 10 E
Tūysarkān, *Iran* **71 C6** 34 33N 48 27 E
Tuz Gölü, *Turkey* **72 C5** 38 42N 33 18 E
Ţūz Khurmātū, *Iraq* **70 C5** 34 56N 44 38 E
Tuzi, *Montenegro, Yug.* **40 D3** 42 22N 19 20 E
Tuzla, *Bos.-H.* **42 F3** 44 34N 18 41 E
Tuzlov →, *Russia* **47 J10** 47 17N 39 57 E
Tuzluca, *Turkey* **73 B10** 40 3N 43 39 E
Tvååker, *Sweden* **11 G6** 57 4N 12 25 E
Tvardiţa, *Moldova* **43 D13** 46 9N 28 58 E
Tver, *Russia* **46 D8** 56 55N 35 55 E
Tvrdošín, *Slovak Rep.* **27 B12** 49 21N 19 35 E
Tvrdošovce, *Slovak Rep.* **27 C11** 48 6N 18 4 E
Tvŭrditsa, *Bulgaria* **41 D9** 42 42N 25 53 E
Twain, *U.S.A.* **116 E5** 40 1N 121 3W
Twain Harte, *U.S.A.* **116 G6** 38 2N 120 14W
Twardogóra, *Poland* **45 G4** 51 23N 17 28 E
Tweed, *Canada* **110 B7** 44 29N 77 19W
Tweed →, *U.K.* **14 F6** 55 45N 2 0W
Tweed Heads, *Australia* **95 D5** 28 10 S 153 31 E
Tweedsmuir Prov. Park, *Canada* **104 C3** 53 0N 126 20W
Twentynine Palms, *U.S.A.* **117 L10** 34 8N 116 3W
Twillingate, *Canada* **103 C9** 49 42N 54 45W
Twin Bridges, *U.S.A.* **114 D7** 45 33N 112 20W
Twin Falls, *Canada* **103 B7** 53 30N 64 32W
Twin Falls, *U.S.A.* **114 E6** 42 34N 114 28W
Twin Valley, *U.S.A.* **112 B6** 47 16N 96 16W
Twinsburg, *U.S.A.* **110 E3** 41 18N 81 26W
Twistringen, *Germany* **24 C4** 52 48N 8 37 E
Twitchell Reservoir, *U.S.A.* **117 L6** 34 59N 120 19W
Two Harbors, *U.S.A.* **112 B9** 47 2N 91 40W
Two Hills, *Canada* **104 C6** 53 43N 111 52W
Two Rivers, *U.S.A.* **108 C2** 44 9N 87 34W
Two Rocks, *Australia* **93 F2** 31 30 S 115 35 E
Twofold B., *Australia* **95 F4** 37 8 S 149 59 E
Tyachiv, *Ukraine* **47 H2** 48 1N 23 35 E
Tychy, *Poland* **45 H5** 50 9N 18 59 E
Tyczyn, *Poland* **45 J9** 49 58N 22 2 E
Tykocin, *Poland* **45 E9** 53 13N 22 46 E
Tyler, *Minn., U.S.A.* **112 C6** 44 18N 96 8W
Tyler, *Tex., U.S.A.* **113 J7** 32 21N 95 18W
Tyligul →, *Ukraine* **47 J6** 47 4N 30 57 E
Týn nad Vltavou, *Czech Rep.* **26 B7** 49 13N 14 26 E
Tynda, *Russia* **51 D13** 55 10N 124 43 E
Tyndall, *U.S.A.* **112 D6** 43 0N 97 50W
Tyne →, *U.K.* **12 C6** 54 59N 1 32W
Tyne & Wear □, *U.K.* **12 B6** 55 6N 1 17W
Týnec nad Sázavou, *Czech Rep.* **26 B7** 49 50N 14 36 E
Tynemouth, *U.K.* **12 B6** 55 1N 1 26W
Tyre = Sūr, *Lebanon* **75 B4** 33 19N 35 16 E
Tyrifjorden, *Norway* **9 F14** 60 2N 10 8 E
Tyringe, *Sweden* **11 H7** 56 9N 13 35 E
Tyrnyauz, *Russia* **49 J6** 43 21N 42 45 E
Tyrol = Tirol □, *Austria* **26 D3** 47 3N 10 43 E
Tyrone, *U.S.A.* **110 F6** 40 40N 78 14W
Tyrone □, *U.K.* **15 B4** 54 38N 7 11W
Tyrrell →, *Australia* **95 F3** 35 26 S 142 51 E
Tyrrell, L., *Australia* **95 F3** 35 20 S 142 50 E
Tyrrell L., *Canada* **105 A7** 63 7N 105 27W
Tyrrhenian Sea, *Medit. S.* **6 G8** 40 0N 12 30 E
Tysfjorden, *Norway* **8 B17** 68 7N 16 25 E
Tystberga, *Sweden* **11 F11** 58 51N 17 15 E
Tytuvėnai, *Lithuania* **44 C10** 55 36N 23 12 E
Tyub Karagan, Mys, *Kazakhstan* **49 H10** 44 40N 50 19 E
Tyuleni, Ostrova, *Kazakhstan* **49 H10** 45 2N 50 16 E
Tyuleniy, *Russia* **49 H8** 44 28N 47 30 E
Tyuleniy, Mys, *Azerbaijan* **49 K10** 40 12N 50 22 E
Tyumen, *Russia* **50 D7** 57 11N 65 29 E
Tywi →, *U.K.* **13 F3** 51 48N 4 21W
Tywyn, *U.K.* **13 E3** 52 35N 4 5W
Tzaneen, *S. Africa* **89 C5** 23 47 S 30 9 E
Tzermiádhes, *Greece* **36 D7** 35 12N 25 29 E
Tzoumérka, Óros, *Greece* **38 B3** 39 30N 21 26 E
Tzukong = Zigong, *China* **58 C5** 29 15N 104 48 E

U

U Taphao, *Thailand* **64 F3** 12 35N 101 0 E
U.S.A. = United States of America ■, *N. Amer.* **106 C7** 37 0N 96 0W
Uatumã →, *Brazil* **124 D7** 2 26 S 57 37W
Uaupés, *Brazil* **124 D5** 0 8 S 67 5W
Uaupés →, *Brazil* **124 C5** 0 2N 67 16W
Uaxactún, *Guatemala* **120 C2** 17 25N 89 29W
Ub, *Serbia, Yug.* **40 B4** 44 28N 20 6 E
Ubá, *Brazil* **127 A7** 21 8 S 43 0W
Uba, *Nigeria* **83 C7** 10 29N 13 13 E
Ubaitaba, *Brazil* **125 F11** 14 18 S 39 20W
Ubangi = Oubangi →, *Dem. Rep. of the Congo* **84 E3** 0 30 S 17 50 E
Ubauro, *Pakistan* **68 E3** 28 15N 69 45 E
Ubaye →, *France* **21 D10** 44 28N 6 18 E
Ubayyiḍ, W. al →, *Iraq* **70 C4** 32 34N 43 48 E
Ube, *Japan* **55 H5** 33 56N 131 15 E
Úbeda, *Spain* **35 G7** 38 3N 3 23W
Uberaba, *Brazil* **125 G9** 19 50 S 47 55W
Uberlândia, *Brazil* **125 G9** 19 0 S 48 20W
Überlingen, *Germany* **25 H5** 47 46N 9 10 E
Ubiaja, *Nigeria* **83 D6** 6 41N 6 22 E
Ubolratna Res., *Thailand* **64 D4** 16 45N 102 30 E
Ubombo, *S. Africa* **89 D5** 27 31 S 32 4 E
Ubon Ratchathani, *Thailand* **64 E5** 15 15N 104 50 E
Ubondo, *Dem. Rep. of the Congo* **86 C2** 0 55 S 25 42 E
Ubort →, *Belarus* **47 F5** 52 6N 28 30 E
Ubrique, *Spain* **35 J5** 36 41N 5 27W
Ubundu, *Dem. Rep. of the Congo* **86 C2** 0 22 S 25 30 E
Ucayali →, *Peru* **122 D3** 4 30 S 73 30W
Uchab, *Namibia* **88 B2** 19 47 S 17 42 E
Uchiura-Wan, *Japan* **54 C10** 42 25N 140 40 E
Uchquduq, *Uzbekistan* **50 E7** 41 50N 62 50 E
Uchte, *Germany* **24 C4** 52 30N 8 54 E
Uchur →, *Russia* **51 D14** 58 48N 130 35 E
Uckermark, *Germany* **24 B9** 53 5N 13 30 E
Ucluelet, *Canada* **104 D3** 48 57N 125 32W
Uda →, *Russia* **51 D14** 54 42N 135 14 E
Udagamandalam, *India* **66 P10** 11 30N 76 44 E
Udainagar, *India* **68 H7** 22 33N 76 13 E
Udaipur, *India* **68 G5** 24 36N 73 44 E
Udaipur Garhi, *Nepal* **69 F12** 27 0N 86 35 E
Udala, *India* **69 J12** 21 35N 86 34 E
Udbina, *Croatia* **29 D12** 44 31N 15 47 E
Uddeholm, *Sweden* **10 D7** 60 1N 13 38 E
Uddevalla, *Sweden* **11 F5** 58 21N 11 55 E
Uddjaur, *Sweden* **8 D17** 65 56N 17 49 E
Uden, *Neths.* **17 C5** 51 40N 5 37 E
Udgir, *India* **66 K10** 18 25N 77 5 E
Udhampur, *India* **69 C6** 33 0N 75 5 E
Udi, *Nigeria* **83 D6** 6 17N 7 21 E
Údine, *Italy* **29 B10** 46 3N 13 14 E
Udmurtia □, *Russia* **50 D6** 57 30N 52 30 E
Udon Thani, *Thailand* **64 D4** 17 29N 102 46 E
Udupi, *India* **66 N9** 13 25N 74 42 E
Udvoy Balkan, *Bulgaria* **41 D10** 42 50N 26 50 E
Udzungwa Range, *Tanzania* **87 D4** 9 30 S 35 10 E
Ueckermünde, *Germany* **24 B10** 53 44N 14 1 E
Ueda, *Japan* **55 F9** 36 24N 138 16 E
Uedineniya, Os., *Russia* **4 B12** 78 0N 85 0 E
Uele →, *Dem. Rep. of the Congo* **84 D4** 3 45N 24 45 E
Uelen, *Russia* **51 C19** 66 10N 170 0W
Uelzen, *Germany* **24 C6** 52 57N 10 32 E
Uetersen, *Germany* **24 B5** 53 40N 9 40 E
Uetze, *Germany* **24 C6** 52 28N 10 11 E
Ufa, *Russia* **50 D6** 54 45N 55 55 E
Uffenheim, *Germany* **25 F6** 49 33N 10 14 E
Ugab →, *Namibia* **88 C1** 20 55 S 13 30 E
Ugalla →, *Tanzania* **86 D3** 5 8 S 30 42 E
Uganda ■, *Africa* **86 B3** 2 0N 32 0 E
Ugento, *Italy* **31 C11** 39 56N 18 10 E
Ugep, *Nigeria* **83 D6** 5 53N 8 2 E
Ughelli, *Nigeria* **83 D6** 5 33N 6 0 E
Ugie, *S. Africa* **89 E4** 31 10 S 28 13 E
Ugíjar, *Spain* **35 J7** 36 58N 3 7W
Ugine, *France* **21 C10** 45 45N 6 25 E
Uglegorsk, *Russia* **51 E15** 49 5N 142 2 E
Uglich, *Russia* **46 D10** 57 33N 38 20 E
Ugljan, *Croatia* **29 D12** 44 12N 15 10 E
Ugljane, *Croatia* **29 E13** 43 35N 16 46 E
Ugra →, *Russia* **46 E9** 54 30N 36 7 E
Ugŭrchin, *Bulgaria* **41 C8** 43 6N 24 26 E
Uh →, *Slovak Rep.* **27 C15** 48 37N 22 0 E
Uherské Hradiště, *Czech Rep.* **27 B10** 49 4N 17 30 E
Uherský Brod, *Czech Rep.* **27 B10** 49 1N 17 40 E
Úhlava →, *Czech Rep.* **26 B6** 49 45N 13 24 E
Uhlenhorst, *Namibia* **88 C2** 23 45 S 17 55 E
Uhrichsville, *U.S.A.* **110 F3** 40 24N 81 21W
Uibhist a Deas = South Uist, *U.K.* **14 D1** 57 20N 7 15W
Uibhist a Tuath = North Uist, *U.K.* **14 D1** 57 40N 7 15W
Uig, *U.K.* **14 D2** 57 35N 6 21W
Uíge, *Angola* **84 F2** 7 30 S 14 40 E
Uijŏngbu, *S. Korea* **57 F14** 37 48N 127 0 E
Ŭiju, *N. Korea* **57 D13** 40 15N 124 35 E
Uinta Mts., *U.S.A.* **114 F8** 40 45N 110 30W
Uis, *Namibia* **88 B2** 21 8 S 14 49 E
Uitenhage, *S. Africa* **88 E4** 33 40 S 25 28 E
Uithuizen, *Neths.* **17 A6** 53 24N 6 41 E
Ujazd, *Poland* **45 H5** 50 23N 18 21 E
Újfehértó, *Hungary* **42 C6** 47 49N 21 41 E
Ujh →, *India* **68 C6** 32 10N 75 18 E
Ujhani, *India* **69 F8** 28 0N 79 6 E
Uji-guntō, *Japan* **55 J4** 31 15N 129 25 E
Ujjain, *India* **68 H6** 23 9N 75 43 E
Ujście, *Poland* **45 E3** 53 3N 16 45 E
Újszász, *Hungary* **42 C5** 47 19N 20 7 E
Ujung Pandang, *Indonesia* **63 F5** 5 10 S 119 20 E
Uka, *Russia* **51 D17** 57 50N 162 0 E
Ukara I., *Tanzania* **86 C3** 1 50 S 33 0 E
Uke-Shima, *Japan* **55 K4** 28 2N 129 14 E
Ukerewe I., *Tanzania* **86 C3** 2 0 S 33 0 E
Ukholovo, *Russia* **48 D5** 53 47N 40 30 E
Ukhrul, *India* **67 G19** 25 10N 94 25 E
Ukhta, *Russia* **50 C6** 63 34N 53 41 E
Ukiah, *U.S.A.* **116 F3** 39 9N 123 13W
Ukki Fort, *India* **69 C7** 33 28N 76 54 E
Ukmergė, *Lithuania* **9 J21** 55 15N 24 45 E
Ukraine ■, *Europe* **47 H7** 49 0N 32 0 E
Ukwi, *Botswana* **88 C3** 23 29 S 20 30 E
Ulaan-Uul, *Mongolia* **56 B6** 44 13N 111 10 E
Ulaanbaatar, *Mongolia* **51 E11** 47 55N 106 53 E
Ulaangom, *Mongolia* **60 A4** 50 5N 92 10 E
Ulaanjirem, *Mongolia* **56 B3** 45 5N 105 30 E
Ulamba, *Dem. Rep. of the Congo* **87 D1** 9 3 S 23 38 E
Ulan Bator = Ulaanbaatar, *Mongolia* **51 E11** 47 55N 106 53 E
Ulan Erge, *Russia* **49 G7** 46 19N 44 53 E
Ulan Khol, *Russia* **49 H8** 45 18N 47 4 E
Ulan Ude, *Russia* **51 D11** 51 45N 107 40 E
Ulanów, *Poland* **45 H9** 50 30N 22 16 E
Ulaş, *Sivas, Turkey* **72 C7** 39 26N 37 2 E
Ulaş, *Tekirdağ, Turkey* **41 E11** 41 14N 27 42 E
Ulaya, *Morogoro, Tanzania* **86 D4** 7 3 S 36 55 E
Ulaya, *Tabora, Tanzania* **86 C3** 4 25 S 33 30 E
Ulcinj, *Montenegro, Yug.* **40 E3** 41 58N 19 10 E
Ulco, *S. Africa* **88 D3** 28 21 S 24 15 E
Ulefoss, *Norway* **9 G13** 59 17N 9 16 E
Ulëz, *Albania* **40 E3** 41 46N 19 54 E
Ulfborg, *Denmark* **11 H2** 56 16N 8 20 E
Ulhasnagar, *India* **66 K8** 19 15N 73 10 E
Uliastay = Ulyasutay, *Mongolia* **60 B4** 47 56N 97 28 E
Ulithi Atoll, *Pac. Oc.* **63 B9** 10 0N 139 30 E
Uljma, *Serbia, Yug.* **42 E6** 45 2N 21 10 E
Ulla →, *Spain* **34 C2** 42 39N 8 44W
Ulladulla, *Australia* **95 F5** 35 21 S 150 29 E
Ullapool, *U.K.* **14 D3** 57 54N 5 9W
Ullared, *Sweden* **11 G6** 57 8N 12 42 E
Ulldecona, *Spain* **32 E5** 40 36N 0 20 E
Ullswater, *U.K.* **12 C5** 54 34N 2 52W
Ullŭng-do, *S. Korea* **55 F5** 37 30N 130 30 E
Ulm, *Germany* **25 G5** 48 23N 9 58 E
Ulmarra, *Australia* **95 D5** 29 37 S 153 4 E
Ulmeni, *Buzău, Romania* **43 E11** 45 4N 26 40 E
Ulmeni, *Maramureş, Romania* **43 C8** 47 28N 23 18 E
Ulonguè, *Mozam.* **87 E3** 14 37 S 34 19 E
Ulricehamn, *Sweden* **11 G7** 57 46N 13 26 E
Ulrika, *Sweden* **11 F9** 58 5N 15 23 E
Ulsan, *S. Korea* **57 G15** 35 20N 129 15 E
Ulsta, *U.K.* **14 A7** 60 30N 1 9W
Ulster □, *U.K.* **15 B5** 54 35N 6 30W
Ulstrem, *Bulgaria* **41 D10** 42 1N 26 27 E
Ulubat Gölü, *Turkey* **41 F12** 40 9N 28 35 E
Ulubey, *Turkey* **39 C11** 38 25N 29 18 E
Uluborlu, *Turkey* **39 C12** 38 4N 30 28 E
Uluçinar, *Turkey* **72 D6** 36 21N 35 57 E
Uludağ, *Turkey* **41 F13** 40 4N 29 13 E
Uludere, *Turkey* **73 D10** 37 28N 42 42 E
Uluguru Mts., *Tanzania* **86 D4** 7 15 S 37 40 E
Ulukışla, *Turkey* **72 D6** 37 33N 34 28 E
Ulungur He →, *China* **60 B3** 47 1N 87 24 E
Uluru = Ayers Rock, *Australia* **93 E5** 25 23 S 131 5 E
Uluru Nat. Park, *Australia* **93 E5** 25 15 S 131 20 E
Ulutau, *Kazakhstan* **50 E7** 48 39N 67 1 E
Ulva, *U.K.* **14 E2** 56 29N 6 13W
Ulverston, *U.K.* **12 C4** 54 13N 3 5W
Ulverstone, *Australia* **94 G4** 41 11 S 146 11 E
Ulya, *Russia* **51 D15** 59 10N 142 0 E
Ulyanovsk = Simbirsk, *Russia* **48 C9** 54 20N 48 25 E
Ulyasutay, *Mongolia* **60 B4** 47 56N 97 28 E
Ulysses, *U.S.A.* **113 G4** 37 35N 101 22W
Umag, *Croatia* **29 C10** 45 26N 13 31 E
Umala, *Bolivia* **124 G5** 17 25 S 68 5W
Uman, *Ukraine* **47 H6** 48 40N 30 12 E
Umaria, *India* **67 H12** 23 35N 80 50 E
Umarkot, *Pakistan* **66 G6** 25 15N 69 40 E
Umarpada, *India* **68 J5** 21 27N 73 30 E
Umatilla, *U.S.A.* **114 D4** 45 55N 119 21W
Umbagog L., *U.S.A.* **111 B13** 44 46N 71 3W
Umbakumba, *Australia* **94 A2** 13 47 S 136 50 E
Umbértide, *Italy* **29 E9** 43 18N 12 20 E
Umbrella Mts., *N.Z.* **91 L2** 45 35 S 169 5 E
Umbria □, *Italy* **29 F9** 42 53N 12 30 E
Ume älv →, *Sweden* **8 E19** 63 45N 20 20 E
Umeå, *Sweden* **8 E19** 63 45N 20 20 E
Umera, *Indonesia* **63 E7** 0 12 S 129 37 E
Umfuli →, *Zimbabwe* **87 F2** 17 30 S 29 23 E
Umgusa, *Zimbabwe* **87 F2** 19 29 S 27 52 E
Umim Urūmah, *Si. Arabia* **80 B4** 25 43N 36 35 E
Umka, *Serbia, Yug.* **40 B4** 44 40N 20 19 E
Umkomaas, *S. Africa* **89 E5** 30 13 S 30 48 E
Umlazi, *S. Africa* **85 L6** 29 59 S 30 54 E
Umm ad Daraj, J., *Jordan* **75 C4** 32 18N 35 48 E
Umm al Qaywayn, *U.A.E.* **71 E7** 25 30N 55 35 E
Umm al Qittayn, *Jordan* **75 C5** 32 18N 36 40 E
Umm Arda, *Sudan* **81 D3** 15 17N 32 31 E
Umm Bāb, *Qatar* **71 E6** 25 12N 50 48 E
Umm Badr, *Sudan* **81 E2** 14 13N 27 58 E
Umm Baiyud, *Sudan* **81 E3** 12 5N 31 40 E
Umm Bel, *Sudan* **81 E2** 13 35N 28 0 E
Umm Birkah, *Si. Arabia* **80 B4** 27 44N 36 31 E
Umm Boim, *Sudan* **81 E2** 11 43N 25 27 E
Umm Dam, *Sudan* **81 E3** 13 45N 30 59 E
Umm Debi, *Sudan* **81 E3** 14 37N 30 23 E
Umm Dubban, *Sudan* **81 D3** 15 23N 32 52 E
Umm el Fahm, *Israel* **75 C4** 32 31N 35 9 E
Umm Gafala, *Sudan* **81 E2** 13 22N 27 15 E
Umm Gimala, *Sudan* **81 E2** 11 27N 28 12 E
Umm Inderaba, *Sudan* **80 D3** 15 58N 30 41 E
Umm Keddada, *Sudan* **81 E2** 13 33N 26 35 E
Umm Koweika, *Sudan* **81 E3** 13 10N 32 16 E
Umm Lajj, *Si. Arabia* **70 E3** 25 0N 37 23 E
Umm Merwa, *Sudan* **80 D3** 18 4N 32 30 E
Umm Qantur, *Sudan* **81 E3** 14 17N 31 22 E
Umm Qurein, *Sudan* **81 F2** 9 58N 28 45 E
Umm Ruwaba, *Sudan* **81 E3** 12 50N 31 20 E
Umm Saiyala, *Sudan* **81 E3** 14 25N 31 10 E
Umm Shanqa, *Sudan* **81 E2** 13 14N 27 14 E
Umm Shutur, *Sudan* **81 F3** 7 17N 33 14 E
Umm Sidr, *Sudan* **81 E2** 14 29N 25 10 E
Umm Zehetir, *Egypt* **80 J8** 28 48N 32 31 E
Umnak I., *U.S.A.* **100 C3** 53 15N 168 20W
Umniati →, *Zimbabwe* **87 F2** 16 49 S 28 45 E
Umpqua →, *U.S.A.* **114 E1** 43 40N 124 12W
Umreth, *India* **68 H5** 22 41N 73 4 E
Umtata, *S. Africa* **89 E4** 31 36 S 28 49 E
Umuahia, *Nigeria* **83 D6** 5 31N 7 26 E
Umuarama, *Brazil* **127 A5** 23 45 S 53 20W
Umurbey, *Turkey* **41 F10** 40 13N 26 36 E
Umvukwe Ra., *Zimbabwe* **87 F3** 16 45 S 30 45 E
Umzimvubu, *S. Africa* **89 E4** 31 38 S 29 33 E
Umzingwane →, *Zimbabwe* **87 G2** 22 12 S 29 56 E

V

W

Wad Ban Naqa

Wad Ban Naqa, Sudan 81 D3 16 32N 33 9 E
Wad Banda, Sudan 81 E2 13 10N 27 56 E
Wad el Haddad, Sudan 81 E3 13 50N 33 30 E
Wad en Nau, Sudan 81 E3 14 10N 33 34 E
Wad Hamid, Sudan 81 D3 16 30N 32 45 E
Wad Medanî, Sudan 81 E3 14 28N 33 30 E
Wad Thana, Pakistan 68 F2 27 22N 66 23 E
Wadai, Africa 76 E5 12 0N 19 0 E
Wadayama, Japan 55 G7 35 19N 134 52 E
Waddeneilanden, Neths. 17 A5 53 20N 5 10 E
Waddenzee, Neths. 17 A5 53 6N 5 10 E
Waddington, U.S.A. 111 B9 44 52N 75 12W
Waddington, Mt., Canada 104 C3 51 23N 125 15W
Waddy Pt., Australia 95 C5 24 58 S 153 21 E
Wadebridge, U.K. 13 G3 50 31N 4 51W
Wadena, Canada 105 C8 51 57N 103 47W
Wadena, U.S.A. 112 B7 46 26N 95 8W
Wädenswil, Switz. 25 H4 47 14N 8 40 E
Wadern, Germany 25 F2 49 32N 6 53 E
Wadeye, Australia 92 B4 14 28 S 129 52 E
Wadhams, Canada 104 C3 51 30N 127 30W
Wādī as Sīr, Jordan 75 D4 31 56N 35 49 E
Wadi Gemâl, Egypt 80 C4 24 35N 35 10 E
Wadi Halfa, Sudan 80 C3 21 53N 31 19 E
Wadian, China 59 A9 32 42N 112 29 E
Wadlew, Poland 45 G6 51 31N 19 23 E
Wadowice, Poland 45 J6 49 52N 19 30 E
Wadsworth, Nev., U.S.A. 114 G4 39 38N 119 17W
Wadsworth, Ohio, U.S.A. 110 E3 41 2N 81 44W
Waegwan, S. Korea 57 G15 35 59N 128 23 E
Wafangdian, China 57 E11 39 38N 121 58 E
Wafrah, Si. Arabia 70 D5 28 33N 47 56 E
Wageningen, Neths. 17 C5 51 58N 5 40 E
Wager B., Canada 101 B11 65 26N 88 40W
Wagga Wagga, Australia 95 F4 35 7 S 147 24 E
Waghete, Indonesia 63 E9 4 10 S 135 50 E
Wagin, Australia 93 F2 33 17 S 117 25 E
Wagner, U.S.A. 112 D5 43 5N 98 18W
Wagon Mound, U.S.A. 113 G2 36 1N 104 42W
Wagoner, U.S.A. 113 H7 35 58N 95 22W
Wągrowiec, Poland 45 F4 52 48N 17 11 E
Wah, Pakistan 68 C5 33 45N 72 40 E
Wahai, Indonesia 63 E7 2 48 S 129 35 E
Wahiawa, U.S.A. 106 H15 21 30N 158 2W
Wâḥid, Egypt 75 E1 30 48N 32 21 E
Wahnai, Afghan. 68 C1 32 40N 65 50 E
Wahni, Ethiopia 81 E4 12 40N 36 39 E
Wahoo, U.S.A. 112 E6 41 13N 96 37W
Wahpeton, U.S.A. 112 B6 46 16N 96 36W
Waiau →, N.Z. 91 K4 42 47 S 173 22 E
Waibeem, Indonesia 63 E8 0 30 S 132 59 E
Waiblingen, Germany 25 G5 48 49N 9 18 E
Waidhofen an der Thaya, Austria 26 C8 48 49N 15 17 E
Waidhofen an der Ybbs, Austria 26 D7 47 57N 14 46 E
Waigeo, Indonesia 63 E8 0 20 S 130 40 E
Waihi, N.Z. 91 G5 37 23 S 175 52 E
Waihou →, N.Z. 91 G5 37 15 S 175 40 E
Waika, Dem. Rep. of the Congo 86 C2 2 22 S 25 42 E
Waikabubak, Indonesia 63 F5 9 45 S 119 25 E
Waikari, N.Z. 91 K4 42 58 S 172 41 E
Waikato →, N.Z. 91 G5 37 23 S 174 43 E
Waikerie, Australia 95 E3 34 9 S 140 0 E
Waikokopu, N.Z. 91 H6 39 3 S 177 52 E
Waikouaiti, N.Z. 91 L3 45 36 S 170 41 E
Wailuku, U.S.A. 106 H16 20 53N 156 30W
Waimakariri →, N.Z. 91 K4 43 24 S 172 42 E
Waimate, N.Z. 91 L3 44 45 S 171 3 E
Wainganga →, India 66 K11 18 50N 79 55 E
Waingapu, Indonesia 63 F6 9 35 S 120 11 E
Waini →, Guyana 124 B7 8 20N 59 50W
Wainwright, Canada 105 C6 52 50N 110 50W
Waiouru, N.Z. 91 H5 39 28 S 175 41 E
Waipara, N.Z. 91 K4 43 3 S 172 46 E
Waipawa, N.Z. 91 H6 39 56 S 176 38 E
Waipiro, N.Z. 91 H7 38 2 S 178 22 E
Waipu, N.Z. 91 F5 35 59 S 174 29 E
Waipukurau, N.Z. 91 J6 40 1 S 176 33 E
Wairakei, N.Z. 91 H6 38 37 S 176 6 E
Wairarapa, L., N.Z. 91 J5 41 14 S 175 15 E
Wairoa, N.Z. 91 H6 39 3 S 177 25 E
Waitaki →, N.Z. 91 L3 44 56 S 171 7 E
Waitara, N.Z. 91 H5 38 59 S 174 15 E
Waitsburg, U.S.A. 114 C5 46 16N 118 9W
Waiuku, N.Z. 91 G5 37 15 S 174 45 E
Wajima, Japan 55 F8 37 30N 137 0 E
Wajir, Kenya 86 B5 1 42N 40 5 E
Waka, Ethiopia 81 F4 7 2N 37 20 E
Wakasa, Japan 55 G7 35 20N 134 24 E
Wakasa-Wan, Japan 55 G7 35 40N 135 30 E
Wakatipu, L., N.Z. 91 L2 45 5 S 168 33 E
Wakaw, Canada 105 C7 52 39N 105 44W
Wakayama, Japan 55 G7 34 15N 135 15 E
Wakayama □, Japan 55 H7 33 50N 135 30 E
Wake Forest, U.S.A. 109 H6 35 59N 78 30W
Wake I., Pac. Oc. 96 F8 19 18N 166 36 E
WaKeeney, U.S.A. 112 F5 39 1N 99 53W
Wakefield, N.Z. 91 J4 41 24 S 173 5 E
Wakefield, U.K. 12 D6 53 41N 1 29W
Wakefield, Mass., U.S.A. 111 D13 42 30N 71 4W
Wakefield, Mich., U.S.A. 112 B10 46 29N 89 56W
Wakkanai, Japan 54 B10 45 28N 141 35 E
Wakkerstroom, S. Africa 89 D5 27 24 S 30 10 E
Wakool, Australia 95 F3 35 28 S 144 23 E
Wakool →, Australia 95 F3 35 5 S 143 33 E
Wakre, Indonesia 63 E8 0 19 S 131 5 E
Wakuach, L., Canada 103 A6 55 34N 67 32W
Walamba, Zambia 87 E2 13 30 S 28 42 E
Wałbrzych, Poland 45 H3 50 45N 16 18 E
Walbury Hill, U.K. 13 F6 51 21N 1 28W
Walcha, Australia 95 E5 30 55 S 151 31 E
Walcheren, Neths. 17 C3 51 30N 3 35 E
Walcott, U.S.A. 114 F10 41 46N 106 51W
Wałcz, Poland 45 E3 53 17N 16 27 E
Waldbröl, Germany 24 E3 50 52N 7 37 E
Waldburg Ra., Australia 93 D2 24 40 S 117 35 E
Waldeck, Germany 24 D5 51 12N 9 4 E
Walden, Colo., U.S.A. 114 F10 40 44N 106 17W
Walden, N.Y., U.S.A. 111 E10 41 34N 74 11W
Waldkirch, Germany 25 G3 48 5N 7 58 E
Waldkirchen, Germany 25 G9 48 43N 13 36 E
Waldkraiburg, Germany 25 G8 48 11N 12 24 E
Waldport, U.S.A. 114 D1 44 26N 124 4W
Waldron, U.S.A. 113 H7 34 54N 94 5W
Waldviertel, Austria 26 C8 48 30N 15 30 E
Walebing, Australia 93 F2 30 41 S 116 13 E
Walembele, Ghana 82 C4 10 30N 1 58W
Walensee, Switz. 25 H5 47 7N 9 13 E
Wales □, U.K. 13 E3 52 19N 4 43W
Walewale, Ghana 83 C4 10 21N 0 50W
Walgett, Australia 95 E4 30 0 S 148 5 E
Walgreen Coast, Antarctica 5 D15 75 15 S 105 0W
Walker, U.S.A. 112 B7 47 6N 94 35W
Walker, L., Canada 103 B6 50 20N 67 11W
Walker L., Canada 105 C9 54 42N 95 57W
Walker L., U.S.A. 114 G4 38 42N 118 43W
Walkerston, Australia 94 C4 21 11 S 149 8 E
Walkerton, Canada 102 D3 44 10N 81 10W
Wall, U.S.A. 112 D3 44 0N 102 8W
Walla Walla, U.S.A. 114 C4 46 4N 118 20W
Wallace, Idaho, U.S.A. 114 C6 47 28N 115 56W
Wallace, N.C., U.S.A. 109 H7 34 44N 77 59W
Wallaceburg, Canada 102 D3 42 34N 82 23W
Wallachia = Valahia, Romania 43 F9 44 35N 25 0 E
Wallal, Australia 95 D4 26 32 S 146 7 E
Wallam Cr. →, Australia 95 D4 28 40 S 147 20 E
Wallambin, L., Australia 93 F2 30 57 S 117 35 E
Wallangarra, Australia 95 D5 28 56 S 151 58 E
Wallaroo, Australia 95 E2 33 56 S 137 39 E
Walldürn, Germany 25 F5 49 34N 9 22 E
Wallenhorst, Germany 24 C4 52 21N 8 1 E
Wallenpaupack, L., U.S.A. 111 E9 41 25N 75 15W
Wallingford, U.S.A. 111 E12 41 27N 72 50W
Wallis & Futuna, Is., Pac. Oc. 96 J10 13 18 S 176 10W
Wallowa, U.S.A. 114 D5 45 34N 117 32W
Wallowa Mts., U.S.A. 114 D5 45 20N 117 30W
Walls, U.K. 14 A7 60 14N 1 33W
Wallula, U.S.A. 114 C4 46 5N 118 54W
Wallumbilla, Australia 95 D4 26 33 S 149 9 E
Walmsley, L., Canada 105 A7 63 25N 108 36W
Walney, I. of, U.K. 12 C4 54 6N 3 15W
Walnut Creek, U.S.A. 116 H4 37 54N 122 4W
Walnut Ridge, U.S.A. 113 G9 36 4N 90 57W
Walpole, Australia 93 F2 34 58 S 116 44 E
Walpole, U.S.A. 111 D13 42 9N 71 15W
Wals, Austria 26 D5 47 47N 12 58 E
Walsall, U.K. 13 E6 52 35N 1 58W
Walsenburg, U.S.A. 113 G2 37 38N 104 47W
Walsh, U.S.A. 113 G3 37 23N 102 17W
Walsh →, Australia 94 B3 16 31 S 143 42 E
Walsrode, Germany 24 C5 52 51N 9 35 E
Walterboro, U.S.A. 109 J5 32 55N 80 40W
Walters, U.S.A. 113 H5 34 22N 98 19W
Waltershausen, Germany 24 E6 50 54N 10 33 E
Waltham, U.S.A. 111 D13 42 23N 71 14W
Waltman, U.S.A. 114 E10 43 4N 107 12W
Walton, U.S.A. 111 D9 42 10N 75 8W
Walton-on-the-Naze, U.K. 13 F9 51 51N 1 17 E
Walvis Bay, Namibia 88 C1 23 0 S 14 28 E
Walvisbaai = Walvis Bay, Namibia 88 C1 23 0 S 14 28 E
Wamba, Dem. Rep. of the Congo 86 B2 2 10N 27 57 E
Wamba, Kenya 86 B4 0 58N 37 19 E
Wamba, Nigeria 83 D6 8 57N 8 42 E
Wamego, U.S.A. 112 F6 39 12N 96 18W
Wamena, Indonesia 63 E9 4 4 S 138 57 E
Wamsutter, U.S.A. 114 F9 41 40N 107 58W
Wamulan, Indonesia 63 E7 3 27 S 126 7 E
Wan Xian, China 56 E8 38 47N 115 7 E
Wana, Pakistan 68 C3 32 20N 69 32 E
Wanaaring, Australia 95 D3 29 38 S 144 9 E
Wanaka, N.Z. 91 L2 44 42 S 169 9 E
Wanaka L., N.Z. 91 L2 44 33 S 169 7 E
Wan'an, China 59 D10 26 26N 114 49 E
Wanapitei L., Canada 102 C3 46 45N 80 40W
Wandel Sea = McKinley Sea, Arctic 4 A7 82 0N 0 0W
Wandérama, Ivory C. 82 D4 8 37N 4 25W
Wanderer, Zimbabwe 87 F3 19 36 S 30 1 E
Wandhari, Pakistan 68 F2 27 42N 66 48 E
Wanding, China 58 E2 24 5N 98 4 E
Wandoan, Australia 95 D4 26 5 S 149 55 E
Wanfu, China 57 D12 40 8N 122 38 E
Wang →, Thailand 64 D2 17 8N 99 2 E
Wang Kai, Sudan 81 F2 9 3N 29 23 E
Wang Noi, Thailand 64 E3 14 13N 100 44 E
Wang Saphung, Thailand 64 D3 17 18N 101 46 E
Wang Thong, Thailand 64 D3 16 50N 100 26 E
Wanga, Dem. Rep. of the Congo 86 B2 2 58N 29 12 E
Wangal, Indonesia 63 F8 6 8 S 134 9 E
Wanganella, Australia 95 F3 35 6 S 144 49 E
Wanganui, N.Z. 91 H5 39 56 S 175 3 E
Wangaratta, Australia 95 F4 36 21 S 146 19 E
Wangary, Australia 95 E2 34 35 S 135 29 E
Wangcang, China 58 A6 32 18N 106 20 E
Wangcheng, China 59 C9 28 22N 112 49 E
Wangdu, China 56 E8 38 40N 115 7 E
Wangen, Germany 25 H5 47 41N 9 50 E
Wangerooge, Germany 24 B3 53 47N 7 54 E
Wangi, Kenya 86 C5 1 58 S 40 58 E
Wangiwangi, Indonesia 63 F6 5 22 S 123 37 E
Wangjiang, China 59 B11 30 10N 116 42 E
Wangmo, China 58 E6 25 11N 106 5 E
Wangolodougou, Ivory C. 82 D3 9 55N 5 10W
Wangqing, China 57 C15 43 12N 129 42 E
Wankaner, India 68 H4 22 35N 71 0 E
Wanless, Canada 105 C8 54 11N 101 21W
Wannian, China 59 C11 28 42N 117 4 E
Wanning, China 64 C8 18 48N 110 22 E
Wanon Niwat, Thailand 64 D4 17 38N 103 46 E
Wanquan, China 56 D8 40 50N 114 40 E
Wanrong, China 56 G6 35 25N 110 50 E
Wanshan, China 58 D7 27 30N 109 12 E
Wanshengchang, China 58 C6 28 57N 106 53 E
Wantage, U.K. 13 F6 51 35N 1 25W
Wanyuan, China 58 A7 32 4N 108 3 E
Wanzai, China 59 C10 28 7N 114 30 E
Wapakoneta, U.S.A. 108 E3 40 34N 84 12W
Wapato, U.S.A. 114 C3 46 27N 120 25W
Wapawekka L., Canada 105 C8 54 55N 104 40W
Wapikopa L., Canada 102 B2 52 56N 87 53W
Wapiti →, Canada 104 B5 55 5N 118 18W
Wappingers Falls, U.S.A. 111 E11 41 36N 73 55W
Wapsipinicon →, U.S.A. 112 E9 41 44N 90 19W
Warab □, Sudan 81 F2 7 30N 28 30 E
Warangal, India 66 L11 17 58N 79 35 E
Waraseoni, India 69 J9 21 45N 80 2 E
Waratah, Australia 94 G4 41 30 S 145 30 E
Waratah B., Australia 95 F4 38 54 S 146 5 E
Warburg, Germany 24 D5 51 28N 9 11 E
Warburton, Vic., Australia 95 F4 37 47 S 145 42 E
Warburton, W. Austral., Australia 93 E4 26 8 S 126 35 E
Warburton Ra., Australia 93 E4 25 55 S 126 28 E
Ward, N.Z. 91 J5 41 49 S 174 11 E
Ward →, Australia 95 D4 26 28 S 146 6 E
Ward Mt., U.S.A. 116 H8 37 12N 118 54W
Warden, S. Africa 89 D4 27 50 S 29 0 E
Wardha, India 66 J11 20 45N 78 39 E
Wardha →, India 66 K11 19 57N 79 11 E
Ware, Canada 104 B3 57 26N 125 41W
Ware, U.S.A. 111 D12 42 16N 72 14W
Waregem, Belgium 17 D3 50 53N 3 27 E
Wareham, U.S.A. 111 E14 41 46N 70 43W
Waremme, Belgium 17 D5 50 43N 5 15 E
Waren, Germany 24 B8 53 31N 12 40 E
Warendorf, Germany 24 D4 51 57N 8 1 E
Warialda, Australia 95 D5 29 29 S 150 33 E
Wariap, Indonesia 63 E8 1 30 S 134 5 E
Warin Chamrap, Thailand 64 E5 15 12N 104 53 E
Warka, Poland 45 G8 51 47N 21 12 E
Warkopi, Indonesia 63 E8 1 12 S 134 9 E
Warm Springs, U.S.A. 115 G5 38 10N 116 20W
Warman, Canada 105 C7 52 19N 106 30W
Warmbad, Namibia 88 D2 28 25 S 18 42 E
Warmbad, S. Africa 89 C4 24 51 S 28 19 E
Warmińsko-Mazurskie □, Poland 44 D8 54 0N 21 0 E
Warminster, U.K. 13 F5 51 12N 2 10W
Warminster, U.S.A. 111 F9 40 12N 75 6W
Warnemünde, Germany 24 A8 54 10N 12 4 E
Warner Mts., U.S.A. 114 F3 41 40N 120 15W
Warner Robins, U.S.A. 109 J4 32 37N 83 36W
Warnow →, Germany 24 A8 54 6N 12 9 E
Waroona, Australia 93 F2 32 50 S 115 58 E
Warracknabeal, Australia 95 F3 36 9 S 142 26 E
Warragul, Australia 95 F4 38 10 S 145 58 E
Warrego →, Australia 95 E4 30 24 S 145 21 E
Warrego Ra., Australia 94 C4 24 58 S 146 0 E
Warren, Australia 95 E4 31 42 S 147 51 E
Warren, Ark., U.S.A. 113 J8 33 37N 92 4W
Warren, Mich., U.S.A. 108 D4 42 30N 83 0W
Warren, Minn., U.S.A. 112 A6 48 12N 96 46W
Warren, Ohio, U.S.A. 110 E4 41 14N 80 49W
Warren, Pa., U.S.A. 110 E5 41 51N 79 9W
Warrenpoint, U.K. 15 B5 54 6N 6 15W
Warrensburg, Mo., U.S.A. 112 F8 38 46N 93 44W
Warrensburg, N.Y., U.S.A. 111 C11 43 29N 73 46W
Warrenton, S. Africa 88 D3 28 9 S 24 47 E
Warrenton, U.S.A. 116 D3 46 10N 123 56W
Warri, Nigeria 83 D6 5 30N 5 41 E
Warrina, Australia 95 D2 28 12 S 135 50 E
Warrington, U.K. 12 D5 53 24N 2 35W
Warrington, U.S.A. 109 K2 30 23N 87 17W
Warrington □, U.K. 12 D5 53 24N 2 35W
Warrnambool, Australia 95 F3 38 25 S 142 30 E
Warroad, U.S.A. 112 A7 48 54N 95 19W
Warruwi, Australia 94 A1 11 36 S 133 20 E
Warsa, Indonesia 63 E9 0 47 S 135 55 E
Warsak Dam, Pakistan 68 B4 34 11N 71 19 E
Warsaw = Warszawa, Poland 45 F8 52 13N 21 0 E
Warsaw, Ind., U.S.A. 108 E3 41 14N 85 51W
Warsaw, N.Y., U.S.A. 110 D6 42 45N 78 8W
Warsaw, Ohio, U.S.A. 110 F3 40 20N 82 0W
Warstein, Germany 24 D4 51 26N 8 22 E
Warszawa, Poland 45 F8 52 13N 21 0 E
Warta, Poland 45 G5 51 43N 18 38 E
Warta →, Poland 45 F1 52 35N 14 39 E
Warthe = Warta →, Poland 45 F1 52 35N 14 39 E
Waru, Indonesia 63 E8 3 30 S 130 36 E
Warwick, Australia 95 D5 28 10 S 152 1 E
Warwick, U.K. 13 E6 52 18N 1 35W
Warwick, N.Y., U.S.A. 111 E10 41 16N 74 22W
Warwick, R.I., U.S.A. 111 E13 41 42N 71 28W
Warwickshire □, U.K. 13 E6 52 14N 1 38W
Wasaga Beach, Canada 110 B4 44 31N 80 1W
Wasagaming, Canada 105 C9 50 39N 99 58W
Wasatch Ra., U.S.A. 114 F8 40 30N 111 15W
Wasbank, S. Africa 89 D5 28 15 S 30 9 E
Wasco, Calif., U.S.A. 117 K7 35 36N 119 20W
Wasco, Oreg., U.S.A. 114 D3 45 36N 120 42W
Wase, Nigeria 83 D6 9 4N 9 54 E
Waseca, U.S.A. 112 C8 44 5N 93 30W
Wasekamio L., Canada 105 B7 56 45N 108 45W
Wash, The, U.K. 12 E8 52 58N 0 20 E
Washago, Canada 110 B5 44 45N 79 20W
Washburn, N. Dak., U.S.A. 112 B4 47 17N 101 2W
Washburn, Wis., U.S.A. 112 B9 46 40N 90 54W
Washim, India 66 J10 20 3N 77 0 E
Washington, U.K. 12 C6 54 55N 1 30W
Washington, D.C., U.S.A. 108 F7 38 54N 77 2W
Washington, Ga., U.S.A. 109 J4 33 44N 82 44W
Washington, Ind., U.S.A. 108 F2 38 40N 87 10W
Washington, Iowa, U.S.A. 112 E9 41 18N 91 42W
Washington, Mo., U.S.A. 112 F9 38 33N 91 1W
Washington, N.C., U.S.A. 109 H7 35 33N 77 3W
Washington, N.J., U.S.A. 111 F10 40 46N 74 59W
Washington, Pa., U.S.A. 110 F4 40 10N 80 15W
Washington, Utah, U.S.A. 115 H7 37 8N 113 31W
Washington □, U.S.A. 114 C3 47 30N 120 30W
Washington, Mt., U.S.A. 111 B13 44 16N 71 18W
Washington Court House, U.S.A. 108 F4 39 32N 83 26W
Washington I., U.S.A. 108 C2 45 23N 86 54W
Washougal, U.S.A. 116 E4 45 35N 122 21W
Wasian, Indonesia 63 E8 1 47 S 133 19 E
Wasilków, Poland 45 E10 53 12N 23 13 E
Wasilla, U.S.A. 100 B5 61 35N 149 26W
Wasior, Indonesia 63 E8 2 43 S 134 30 E
Waskaganish, Canada 102 B4 51 30N 78 40W
Waskaiowaka, L., Canada 105 B9 56 33N 96 23W
Waskesiu Lake, Canada 105 C7 53 55N 106 5W
Wasserburg, Germany 25 G8 48 3N 12 14 E
Wasserkuppe, Germany 24 E5 50 29N 9 55 E
Wassy, France 19 D11 48 30N 4 58 E
Waswanipi, Canada 102 C4 49 40N 76 29W
Waswanipi, L., Canada 102 C4 49 35N 76 40W
Watampone, Indonesia 63 E6 4 29 S 120 25 E
Water Park Pt., Australia 94 C5 22 56 S 150 47 E
Water Valley, U.S.A. 113 H10 34 10N 89 38W
Waterberge, S. Africa 89 C4 24 10 S 28 0 E
Waterbury, Conn., U.S.A. 111 E11 41 33N 73 3W
Waterbury, Vt., U.S.A. 111 B12 44 20N 72 46W
Waterbury L., Canada 105 B8 58 10N 104 22W
Waterdown, Canada 110 C5 43 20N 79 53W
Waterford, Canada 110 D4 42 56N 80 17W
Waterford, Ireland 15 D4 52 15N 7 8W
Waterford, Calif., U.S.A. 116 H6 37 38N 120 46W
Waterford, Pa., U.S.A. 110 E5 41 57N 79 59W
Waterford □, Ireland 15 D4 52 10N 7 40W
Waterford Harbour, Ireland 15 D5 52 8N 6 58W
Waterhen L., Canada 105 C9 52 10N 99 40W
Waterloo, Belgium 17 D4 50 43N 4 25 E
Waterloo, Ont., Canada 102 D3 43 30N 80 32W
Waterloo, Qué., Canada 111 A12 45 22N 72 32W
Waterloo, S. Leone 82 D2 8 26N 13 8W
Waterloo, Ill., U.S.A. 112 F9 38 20N 90 9W
Waterloo, Iowa, U.S.A. 112 D8 42 30N 92 21W
Waterloo, N.Y., U.S.A. 110 D8 42 54N 76 52W
Watersmeet, U.S.A. 112 B10 46 16N 89 11W
Waterton Lakes Nat. Park, U.S.A. 114 B7 48 45N 115 0W
Watertown, Conn., U.S.A. 111 E11 41 36N 73 7W
Watertown, N.Y., U.S.A. 111 C9 43 59N 75 55W
Watertown, S. Dak., U.S.A. 112 C6 44 54N 97 7W
Watertown, Wis., U.S.A. 112 D10 43 12N 88 43W
Waterval-Boven, S. Africa 89 D5 25 40 S 30 18 E
Waterville, Canada 111 A13 45 16N 71 54W
Waterville, Maine, U.S.A. 109 C11 44 33N 69 38W
Waterville, N.Y., U.S.A. 111 D9 42 56N 75 23W
Waterville, Pa., U.S.A. 110 E7 41 19N 77 21W
Waterville, Wash., U.S.A. 114 C3 47 39N 120 4W
Watervliet, U.S.A. 111 D11 42 44N 73 42W
Wates, Indonesia 63 G14 7 51 S 110 10 E
Watford, Canada 110 D3 42 57N 81 53W
Watford, U.K. 13 F7 51 40N 0 24W
Watford City, U.S.A. 112 B3 47 48N 103 17W
Wathaman →, Canada 105 B8 57 16N 102 59W
Wathaman L., Canada 105 B8 58 10N 103 44W
Watheroo, Australia 93 F2 30 15 S 116 0 E
Wating, China 56 G4 35 40N 106 38 E
Watkins Glen, U.S.A. 110 D8 42 23N 76 52W
Watling I. = San Salvador I., Bahamas 121 B5 24 0N 74 40W
Watonga, U.S.A. 113 H5 35 51N 98 25W
Watrous, Canada 105 C7 51 40N 105 25W
Watrous, U.S.A. 113 H2 35 48N 104 59W
Watsa, Dem. Rep. of the Congo 86 B2 3 4N 29 30 E
Watseka, U.S.A. 108 E2 40 47N 87 44W
Watson, Australia 93 F5 30 29 S 131 31 E
Watson, Canada 105 C8 52 10N 104 30W
Watson Lake, Canada 104 A3 60 6N 128 49W
Watsontown, U.S.A. 110 E8 41 5N 76 52W
Watsonville, U.S.A. 116 J5 36 55N 121 45W
Wattiwarriganna Cr. →, Australia 95 D2 28 57 S 136 10 E
Wattwil, Switz. 25 H5 47 18N 9 6 E
Watuata = Batuata, Indonesia 63 F6 6 12 S 122 42 E
Watubela, Kepulauan, Indonesia 63 E8 4 28 S 131 35 E
Watubela Is. = Watubela, Kepulauan, Indonesia 63 E8 4 28 S 131 35 E
Wau = Wâw, Sudan 81 F2 7 45N 28 1 E
Waubamik, Canada 110 A4 45 27N 80 1W
Waubay, U.S.A. 112 C6 45 20N 97 18W
Wauchope, N.S.W., Australia 95 E5 31 28 S 152 45 E
Wauchope, N. Terr., Australia 94 C1 20 36 S 134 15 E
Wauchula, U.S.A. 109 M5 27 33N 81 49W
Waukarlycarly, L., Australia 92 D3 21 18 S 121 56 E
Waukegan, U.S.A. 108 D2 42 22N 87 50W
Waukesha, U.S.A. 108 D1 43 1N 88 14W
Waukon, U.S.A. 112 D9 43 16N 91 29W
Waupaca, U.S.A. 112 C10 44 21N 89 5W
Waupun, U.S.A. 112 D10 43 38N 88 44W
Waurika, U.S.A. 113 H6 34 10N 98 0W
Wausau, U.S.A. 112 C10 44 58N 89 38W
Wautoma, U.S.A. 112 C10 44 4N 89 18W
Wauwatosa, U.S.A. 108 D2 43 3N 88 0W
Waveney →, U.K. 13 E9 52 35N 1 39 E
Waverley, N.Z. 91 H5 39 46 S 174 37 E
Waverly, Iowa, U.S.A. 112 D8 42 44N 92 29W
Waverly, N.Y., U.S.A. 111 E8 42 1N 76 32W
Wavre, Belgium 17 D4 50 43N 4 38 E
Wâw, Sudan 81 F2 7 45N 28 1 E
Wāw al Kabīr, Libya 79 C9 25 20N 16 43 E
Wawa, Canada 102 C3 47 59N 84 47W
Wawa, Nigeria 83 D5 9 54N 4 27 E
Wawa, Sudan 80 C3 20 30N 30 22 E
Wawanesa, Canada 105 D9 49 36N 99 40W
Wawona, U.S.A. 116 H7 37 32N 119 39W
Waxahachie, U.S.A. 113 J6 32 24N 96 51W
Way, L., Australia 93 E3 26 45 S 120 16 E
Waycross, U.S.A. 109 K4 31 13N 82 21W
Wayi, Sudan 81 F3 5 8N 30 10 E
Wayland, U.S.A. 110 D7 42 34N 77 35W
Wayne, Nebr., U.S.A. 112 D6 42 14N 97 1W
Wayne, W. Va., U.S.A. 108 F4 38 13N 82 27W
Waynesboro, Ga., U.S.A. 109 J4 33 6N 82 1W
Waynesboro, Miss., U.S.A. 109 K1 31 40N 88 39W
Waynesboro, Pa., U.S.A. 108 F7 39 45N 77 35W
Waynesboro, Va., U.S.A. 108 F6 38 4N 78 53W
Waynesburg, U.S.A. 108 F5 39 54N 80 11W
Waynesville, U.S.A. 109 H4 35 28N 82 58W
Waynoka, U.S.A. 113 G5 36 35N 98 53W
Wazirabad, Pakistan 68 C6 32 30N 74 8 E
Wda →, Poland 44 E5 53 25N 18 29 E
We, Indonesia 62 C1 5 51N 95 18 E
Weald, The, U.K. 13 F8 51 4N 0 20 E
Wear →, U.K. 12 C6 54 55N 1 23W
Weatherford, Okla., U.S.A. 113 H5 35 32N 98 43W
Weatherford, Tex., U.S.A. 113 J6 32 46N 97 48W
Weaverville, U.S.A. 114 F2 40 44N 122 56W
Webb City, U.S.A. 113 G7 37 9N 94 28W
Webequie, Canada 102 B2 52 59N 87 21W
Webo = Nyaake, Liberia 82 E3 4 52N 7 37W
Webster, Mass., U.S.A. 111 D13 42 3N 71 53W
Webster, N.Y., U.S.A. 110 C7 43 13N 77 26W
Webster, S. Dak., U.S.A. 112 C6 45 20N 97 31W
Webster City, U.S.A. 112 D8 42 28N 93 49W
Webster Springs, U.S.A. 108 F5 38 29N 80 25W
Weda, Indonesia 63 D7 0 21N 127 50 E
Weda, Teluk, Indonesia 63 D7 0 20N 128 0 E
Weddell I., Falk. Is. 128 G4 51 50 S 61 0W
Weddell Sea, Antarctica 5 D1 72 30 S 40 0W
Wedderburn, Australia 95 F3 36 26 S 143 33 E
Wedel, Germany 24 B5 53 34N 9 42 E
Wedemark, Germany 24 C5 52 32N 9 43 E
Wedgeport, Canada 103 D6 43 44N 65 59W
Wedza, Zimbabwe 87 F3 18 40 S 31 33 E
Wee Waa, Australia 95 E4 30 11 S 149 26 E
Weed, U.S.A. 114 F2 41 25N 122 23W
Weed Heights, U.S.A. 116 G7 38 59N 119 13W
Weedsport, U.S.A. 111 C8 43 3N 76 35W
Weedville, U.S.A. 110 E6 41 17N 78 30W
Weenen, S. Africa 89 D5 28 48 S 30 7 E
Weener, Germany 24 B3 53 9N 7 20 E
Weert, Neths. 17 C5 51 15N 5 43 E
Węgierska-Górka, Poland 45 J6 49 36N 19 7 E
Węgliniec, Poland 45 G2 51 18N 15 10 E
Węgorzewo, Poland 44 D8 54 13N 21 43 E
Węgorzyno, Poland 44 E2 53 32N 15 33 E
Węgrów, Poland 45 F9 52 24N 22 0 E
Wehda □, Sudan 81 F3 8 30N 30 0 E
Wei He →, Hebei, China 56 F8 36 10N 115 45 E
Wei He →, Shaanxi, China 56 G6 34 38N 110 15 E
Weichang, China 57 D9 41 58N 117 49 E
Weichuan, China 56 G7 34 20N 113 59 E
Weida, Germany 24 E8 50 46N 12 2 E
Weiden, Germany 25 F8 49 41N 12 10 E
Weifang, China 57 F10 36 44N 119 7 E
Weihai, China 57 F12 37 30N 122 6 E
Weil, Germany 25 H3 47 35N 7 37 E
Weilburg, Germany 24 E4 50 28N 8 17 E
Weilheim, Germany 25 H7 47 50N 11 9 E
Weimar, Germany 24 E7 50 58N 11 19 E
Weinan, China 56 G5 34 31N 109 29 E
Weingarten, Germany 25 F4 49 3N 8 31 E
Weinheim, Germany 25 F4 49 32N 8 39 E
Weining, China 58 D5 26 50N 104 17 E
Weipa, Australia 94 A3 12 40 S 141 50 E
Weir →, Australia 95 D4 28 20 S 149 50 E
Weir →, Canada 105 B10 56 54N 93 21W
Weir River, Canada 105 B10 56 49N 94 6W
Weirton, U.S.A. 110 F4 40 24N 80 35W
Weiser, U.S.A. 114 D5 44 10N 117 0W
Weishan, Shandong, China 57 G9 34 47N 117 5 E
Weishan, Yunnan, China 58 E3 25 12N 100 20 E
Weissenburg, Germany 25 F6 49 2N 10 58 E
Weissenfels, Germany 24 D7 51 11N 12 0 E
Weisswasser, Germany 24 D10 51 30N 14 36 E
Wéitra, Austria 26 C7 48 41N 14 54 E
Weixi, China 58 D2 27 10N 99 10 E
Weixin, China 58 D5 27 48N 105 3 E
Weiyuan, China 56 G3 35 7N 104 10 E
Weiz, Austria 26 D8 47 13N 15 39 E
Weizhou Dao, China 58 G7 21 0N 109 5 E
Wejherowo, Poland 44 D5 54 35N 18 12 E
Wekusko L., Canada 105 C9 54 40N 99 50W
Welch, U.S.A. 108 G5 37 26N 81 35W
Weldya, Ethiopia 81 E4 11 50N 39 34 E
Welega □, Ethiopia 81 F3 9 25N 34 20 E
Welkite, Ethiopia 81 F4 8 15N 37 42 E
Welkom, S. Africa 88 D4 28 0 S 26 46 E
Welland, Canada 102 D4 43 0N 79 15W
Welland →, U.K. 13 E7 52 51N 0 5W
Wellesley Is., Australia 94 B2 16 42 S 139 30 E
Wellingborough, U.K. 13 E7 52 19N 0 41W
Wellington, Australia 95 E4 32 35 S 148 59 E
Wellington, Canada 110 C7 43 57N 77 20W
Wellington, N.Z. 91 J5 41 19 S 174 46 E
Wellington, S. Africa 88 E2 33 38 S 19 1 E
Wellington, Somst., U.K. 13 G4 50 58N 3 13W
Wellington, Telford & Wrekin, U.K. 13 E5 52 42N 2 30W
Wellington, Colo., U.S.A. 112 E2 40 42N 105 0W
Wellington, Kans., U.S.A. 113 G6 37 16N 97 24W
Wellington, Nev., U.S.A. 116 G7 38 45N 119 23W
Wellington, Ohio, U.S.A. 110 E2 41 10N 82 13W
Wellington, Tex., U.S.A. 113 H4 34 51N 100 13W
Wellington, I., Chile 122 H3 49 30 S 75 0W
Wellington, L., Australia 95 F4 38 6 S 147 20 E
Wells, U.K. 13 F5 51 13N 2 39W
Wells, Maine, U.S.A. 111 C14 43 20N 70 35W
Wells, N.Y., U.S.A. 111 C10 43 24N 74 17W
Wells, Nev., U.S.A. 114 F6 41 7N 114 58W
Wells, L., Australia 93 E3 26 44 S 123 15 E
Wells, Mt., Australia 92 C4 17 25 S 127 8 E
Wells Gray Prov. Park, Canada 104 C4 52 30N 120 15W
Wells-next-the-Sea, U.K. 12 E8 52 57N 0 51 E

Winschoten

Winschoten, *Neths.* **17 A7** 53 9N 7 3 E
Winsen, *Germany* **24 B6** 53 22N 10 13 E
Winsford, *U.K.* **12 D5** 53 12N 2 31W
Winslow, *Ariz., U.S.A.* **115 J8** 35 2N 110 42W
Winslow, *Wash., U.S.A.* **116 C4** 47 38N 122 31W
Winsted, *U.S.A.* **111 E11** 41 55N 73 4W
Winston-Salem, *U.S.A.* **109 G5** 36 6N 80 15W
Winter Garden, *U.S.A.* **109 L5** 28 34N 81 35W
Winter Haven, *U.S.A.* **109 M5** 28 1N 81 44W
Winter Park, *U.S.A.* **109 L5** 28 36N 81 20W
Winterberg, *Germany* **24 D4** 51 11N 8 33 E
Winterhaven, *U.S.A.* **117 N12** 32 47N 114 39W
Winters, *U.S.A.* **116 G5** 38 32N 121 58W
Wintersville, *U.S.A.* **110 F4** 40 23N 80 42W
Winterswijk, *Neths.* **17 C6** 51 58N 6 43 E
Winterthur, *Switz.* **25 H4** 47 30N 8 44 E
Winthrop, *U.S.A.* **114 B3** 48 28N 120 10W
Winton, *Australia* **94 C3** 22 24 S 143 3 E
Winton, *N.Z.* **91 M2** 46 8 S 168 20 E
Wipper →, *Germany* **24 D7** 51 16N 11 12 E
Wirrulla, *Australia* **95 E1** 32 24 S 134 31 E
Wisbech, *U.K.* **13 E8** 52 41N 0 9 E
Wisconsin □, *U.S.A.* **112 C10** 44 45N 89 30W
Wisconsin →, *U.S.A.* **112 D9** 43 0N 91 15W
Wisconsin Rapids, *U.S.A.* **112 C10** 44 23N 89 49W
Wisdom, *U.S.A.* **114 D7** 45 37N 113 27W
Wishaw, *U.K.* **14 F5** 55 46N 3 54W
Wishek, *U.S.A.* **112 B5** 46 16N 99 33W
Wisła, *Poland* **45 J5** 49 38N 18 53 E
Wisła →, *Poland* **44 D5** 54 22N 18 55 E
Wisłok →, *Poland* **45 H9** 50 13N 22 32 E
Wisłoka →, *Poland* **45 H8** 50 27N 21 23 E
Wismar, *Germany* **24 B7** 53 54N 11 29 E
Wisner, *U.S.A.* **112 E6** 41 59N 96 55W
Wissant, *France* **19 B8** 50 52N 1 40 E
Wissembourg, *France* **19 C14** 49 2N 7 57 E
Wisznice, *Poland* **45 G10** 51 48N 23 13 E
Witbank, *S. Africa* **89 D4** 25 51 S 29 14 E
Witdraai, *S. Africa* **88 D3** 26 58 S 20 48 E
Witham, *U.K.* **13 F8** 51 48N 0 40 E
Witham →, *U.K.* **12 E7** 52 59N 0 2W
Withernsea, *U.K.* **12 D8** 53 44N 0 1 E
Witkowo, *Poland* **45 F4** 52 26N 17 45 E
Witney, *U.K.* **13 F6** 51 48N 1 28W
Witnica, *Poland* **45 F1** 52 40N 14 54 E
Witnossob →, *Namibia* **88 D3** 23 55 S 18 45 E
Wittdün, *Germany* **24 A4** 54 38N 8 23 E
Witten, *Germany* **24 D3** 51 26N 7 20 E
Wittenberge, *Germany* **24 B7** 53 0N 11 45 E
Wittenburg, *Germany* **24 B7** 53 31N 11 4 E
Wittenheim, *France* **19 E14** 47 44N 7 20 E
Wittenoom, *Australia* **92 D2** 22 15 S 118 20 E
Wittingen, *Germany* **24 C6** 52 44N 10 44 E
Wittlich, *Germany* **25 F2** 49 59N 6 53 E
Wittmund, *Germany* **24 B3** 53 34N 7 46 E
Wittow, *Germany* **24 A9** 54 38N 13 20 E
Wittstock, *Germany* **24 B8** 53 10N 12 28 E
Witvlei, *Namibia* **88 C2** 22 23 S 18 32 E
Witzenhausen, *Germany* **24 D5** 51 20N 9 51 E
Wkra →, *Poland* **45 F7** 52 27N 20 44 E
Władysławowo, *Poland* **44 D5** 54 48N 18 25 E
Wleń, *Poland* **45 G2** 51 2N 15 39 E
Wlingi, *Indonesia* **63 H15** 8 5 S 112 25 E
Włocławek, *Poland* **45 F6** 52 40N 19 3 E
Włodawa, *Poland* **45 G10** 51 33N 23 31 E
Włoszczowa, *Poland* **45 H6** 50 50N 19 55 E
Woburn, *U.S.A.* **111 D13** 42 29N 71 9W
Wodian, *China* **56 H7** 32 50N 112 35 E
Wodonga = Albury-Wodonga, *Australia* **95 F4** 36 3 S 146 56 E
Wodzisław Śląski, *Poland* **45 H5** 50 1N 18 26 E
Wœrth, *France* **19 D14** 48 57N 7 45 E
Woinbogoin, *China* **58 A2** 32 51N 98 39 E
Woippy, *France* **19 C13** 49 10N 6 8 E
Wojcieszow, *Poland* **45 H2** 50 58N 15 55 E
Wokam, *Indonesia* **63 F8** 5 45 S 134 28 E
Woking, *U.K.* **13 F7** 51 19N 0 34W
Wokingham □, *U.K.* **13 F7** 51 25N 0 51W
Wolbrom, *Poland* **45 H6** 50 24N 19 45 E
Wołczyn, *Poland* **45 G5** 51 1N 18 3 E
Woldegk, *Germany* **24 B9** 53 27N 13 34 E
Wolf →, *Canada* **104 A2** 60 17N 132 33W
Wolf Creek, *U.S.A.* **114 C7** 47 0N 112 4W
Wolf L., *Canada* **104 A2** 60 24N 131 40W
Wolf Point, *U.S.A.* **112 A2** 48 5N 105 39W
Wolfe I., *Canada* **102 D4** 44 7N 76 20W
Wolfeboro, *U.S.A.* **111 C13** 43 35N 71 13W
Wolfen, *Germany* **24 D8** 51 39N 12 15 E
Wolfenbüttel, *Germany* **24 C6** 52 10N 10 33 E
Wolfratshausen, *Germany* **25 H7** 47 54N 11 24 E
Wolfsberg, *Austria* **26 E7** 46 50N 14 52 E
Wolfsburg, *Germany* **24 C6** 52 25N 10 48 E
Wolgast, *Germany* **24 A9** 54 3N 13 44 E
Wolhusen, *Switz.* **25 H4** 47 4N 8 4 E
Wolin, *Poland* **44 E1** 53 50N 14 37 E
Wollaston, Is., *Chile* **128 H3** 55 40 S 67 30W
Wollaston L., *Canada* **105 B8** 58 7N 103 10W
Wollaston Lake, *Canada* **105 B8** 58 3N 103 33W
Wollaston Pen., *Canada* **100 B8** 69 30N 115 0W
Wollongong, *Australia* **95 E5** 34 25 S 150 54 E
Wolmaransstad, *S. Africa* **88 D4** 27 12 S 25 59 E
Wolmirstedt, *Germany* **24 C7** 52 14N 11 37 E
Wołomin, *Poland* **45 F8** 52 19N 21 15 E
Wołów, *Poland* **45 G3** 51 20N 16 38 E
Wolseley, *S. Africa* **88 E2** 33 26 S 19 7 E
Wolsey, *U.S.A.* **112 C5** 44 24N 98 28W
Wolstenholme, C., *Canada* **98 C12** 62 35N 77 30W
Wolsztyn, *Poland* **45 F3** 52 8N 16 5 E
Wolvega, *Neths.* **17 B6** 52 52N 6 0 E
Wolverhampton, *U.K.* **13 E5** 52 35N 2 7W
Wondai, *Australia* **95 D5** 26 20 S 151 49 E
Wongalarroo L., *Australia* **95 E3** 31 32 S 144 0 E
Wongan Hills, *Australia* **93 F2** 30 51 S 116 37 E
Wŏnju, *S. Korea* **57 F14** 37 22N 127 58 E
Wonosari, *Indonesia* **63 G14** 7 58 S 110 36 E
Wonosobo, *Indonesia* **63 G13** 7 22 S 109 54 E
Wonowon, *Canada* **104 B4** 56 44N 121 48W
Wŏnsan, *N. Korea* **57 E14** 39 11N 127 27 E
Wonthaggi, *Australia* **95 F4** 38 37 S 145 37 E
Wood Buffalo Nat. Park, *Canada* **104 B6** 59 0N 113 41W
Wood Is., *Australia* **92 C3** 16 24 S 123 19 E
Wood L., *Canada* **105 B8** 55 17N 103 17W
Woodah I., *Australia* **94 A2** 13 27 S 136 10 E
Woodbourne, *U.S.A.* **111 E10** 41 46N 74 36W
Woodbridge, *Canada* **110 C5** 43 47N 79 36W
Woodbridge, *U.K.* **13 E9** 52 6N 1 20 E
Woodburn, *U.S.A.* **114 D2** 45 9N 122 51W
Woodenbong, *Australia* **95 D5** 28 24 S 152 39 E
Woodend, *Australia* **95 F3** 37 20 S 144 33 E
Woodford, *Australia* **95 D5** 26 58 S 152 47 E
Woodfords, *U.S.A.* **116 G7** 38 47N 119 50W
Woodlake, *U.S.A.* **116 J7** 36 25N 119 6W
Woodland, *Calif., U.S.A.* **116 G5** 38 41N 121 46W
Woodland, *Maine, U.S.A.* **109 C12** 45 9N 67 25W
Woodland, *Pa., U.S.A.* **110 F6** 40 59N 78 21W
Woodland, *Wash., U.S.A.* **116 E4** 45 54N 122 45W
Woodland Caribou Prov. Park, *Canada* **105 C10** 51 0N 94 45W
Woodridge, *Canada* **105 D9** 49 20N 96 9W
Woodroffe, Mt., *Australia* **93 E5** 26 20 S 131 45 E
Woods, L., *Australia* **94 B1** 17 50 S 133 30 E
Woods, L. of the, *Canada* **105 D10** 49 15N 94 45W
Woodstock, *Australia* **94 B4** 19 35 S 146 50 E
Woodstock, *N.B., Canada* **103 C6** 46 11N 67 37W
Woodstock, *Ont., Canada* **102 D3** 43 10N 80 45W
Woodstock, *U.K.* **13 F6** 51 51N 1 20W
Woodstock, *Ill., U.S.A.* **112 D10** 42 19N 88 27W
Woodstock, *Vt., U.S.A.* **111 C12** 43 37N 72 31W
Woodsville, *U.S.A.* **111 B13** 44 9N 72 2W
Woodville, *N.Z.* **91 J5** 40 20 S 175 53 E
Woodville, *Miss., U.S.A.* **113 K9** 31 6N 91 18W
Woodville, *Tex., U.S.A.* **113 K7** 30 47N 94 25W
Woodward, *U.S.A.* **113 G5** 36 26N 99 24W
Woody, *U.S.A.* **117 K8** 35 42N 118 50W
Woody →, *Canada* **105 C8** 52 31N 100 51W
Woolamai, C., *Australia* **95 F4** 38 30 S 145 23 E
Wooler, *U.K.* **12 B5** 55 33N 2 1W
Woolgoolga, *Australia* **95 E5** 30 6 S 153 11 E
Woomera, *Australia* **95 E2** 31 5 S 136 50 E
Woonsocket, *R.I., U.S.A.* **111 E13** 42 0N 71 31W
Woonsocket, *S. Dak., U.S.A.* **112 C5** 44 3N 98 17W
Wooramel →, *Australia* **93 E1** 25 47 S 114 10 E
Wooramel Roadhouse, *Australia* **93 E1** 25 45 S 114 17 E
Wooster, *U.S.A.* **110 F3** 40 48N 81 56W
Worcester, *S. Africa* **88 E2** 33 39 S 19 27 E
Worcester, *U.K.* **13 E5** 52 11N 2 12W
Worcester, *Mass., U.S.A.* **111 D13** 42 16N 71 48W
Worcester, *N.Y., U.S.A.* **111 D10** 42 36N 74 45W
Worcestershire □, *U.K.* **13 E5** 52 13N 2 10W
Wörgl, *Austria* **26 D5** 47 29N 12 3 E
Workington, *U.K.* **12 C4** 54 39N 3 33W
Worksop, *U.K.* **12 D6** 53 18N 1 7W
Workum, *Neths.* **17 B5** 52 59N 5 26 E
Worland, *U.S.A.* **114 D10** 44 1N 107 57W
Wormhout, *France* **19 B9** 50 52N 2 28 E
Worms, *Germany* **25 F4** 49 37N 8 21 E
Worsley, *Canada* **104 B5** 56 31N 119 8W
Wörth, *Germany* **25 F8** 49 1N 12 24 E
Wortham, *U.S.A.* **113 K6** 31 47N 96 28W
Wörther See, *Austria* **26 E7** 46 37N 14 10 E
Worthing, *U.K.* **13 G7** 50 49N 0 21W
Worthington, *Minn., U.S.A.* **112 D7** 43 37N 95 36W
Worthington, *Pa., U.S.A.* **110 F5** 40 50N 79 38W
Wosi, *Indonesia* **63 E7** 0 15 S 128 0 E
Wou-han = Wuhan, *China* **59 B10** 30 31N 114 18 E
Wousi = Wuxi, *China* **59 B13** 31 33N 120 18 E
Wowoni, *Indonesia* **63 E6** 4 5 S 123 5 E
Wrangel I. = Vrangelya, Ostrov, *Russia* **51 B19** 71 0N 180 0 E
Wrangell, *U.S.A.* **104 B2** 56 28N 132 23W
Wrangell Mts., *U.S.A.* **100 B5** 61 30N 142 0W
Wrath, C., *U.K.* **14 C3** 58 38N 5 1W
Wray, *U.S.A.* **112 E3** 40 5N 102 13W
Wrekin, The, *U.K.* **13 E5** 52 41N 2 32W
Wrens, *U.S.A.* **109 J4** 33 12N 82 23W
Wrexham, *U.K.* **12 D4** 53 3N 3 0W
Wrexham □, *U.K.* **12 D5** 53 1N 2 58W
Wriezen, *Germany* **24 C10** 52 42N 14 7 E
Wright = Paranas, *Phil.* **61 F6** 11 42N 125 2 E
Wright, *U.S.A.* **112 D2** 43 47N 105 30W
Wright Pt., *Canada* **110 C3** 43 48N 81 44W
Wrightson Mt., *U.S.A.* **115 L8** 31 42N 110 51W
Wrightwood, *U.S.A.* **117 L9** 34 21N 117 38W
Wrigley, *Canada* **100 B7** 63 16N 123 37W
Wrocław, *Poland* **45 G4** 51 5N 17 5 E
Wronki, *Poland* **45 F3** 52 41N 16 21 E
Września, *Poland* **45 F4** 52 21N 17 36 E
Wschowa, *Poland* **45 G3** 51 48N 16 20 E
Wu Jiang →, *China* **58 C6** 29 40N 107 20 E
Wu'an, *China* **56 F8** 36 40N 114 15 E
Wubin, *Australia* **93 F2** 30 6 S 116 37 E
Wubu, *China* **56 F6** 37 28N 110 42 E
Wuchang, *China* **57 B14** 44 55N 127 5 E
Wucheng, *China* **56 F9** 37 12N 116 20 E
Wuchuan, *Guangdong, China* **59 G8** 21 33N 110 43 E
Wuchuan, *Guizhou, China* **58 C7** 28 25N 108 3 E
Wuchuan, *Nei Monggol Zizhiqu, China* **56 D6** 41 5N 111 28 E
Wudi, *China* **57 F9** 37 40N 117 35 E
Wuding, *China* **58 E4** 25 24N 102 21 E
Wuding He →, *China* **56 F6** 37 2N 110 23 E
Wudinna, *Australia* **95 E2** 33 0 S 135 22 E
Wudu, *China* **56 H3** 33 22N 104 54 E
Wufeng, *China* **59 B8** 30 12N 110 42 E
Wugang, *China* **59 D8** 26 44N 110 35 E
Wugong Shan, *China* **59 D9** 27 30N 114 0 E
Wuhan, *China* **59 B10** 30 31N 114 18 E
Wuhe, *China* **57 H9** 33 10N 117 50 E
Wuhsi = Wuxi, *China* **59 B13** 31 33N 120 18 E
Wuhu, *China* **59 B12** 31 22N 118 21 E
Wujiang, *China* **59 B13** 31 10N 120 38 E
Wukari, *Nigeria* **83 D6** 7 51N 9 42 E
Wulajie, *China* **57 B14** 44 6N 126 33 E
Wulanbulang, *China* **56 D6** 41 5N 110 55 E
Wular L., *India* **69 B6** 34 20N 74 30 E
Wulehe, *Ghana* **83 D5** 8 39N 0 0W
Wulian, *China* **57 G10** 35 40N 119 12 E
Wuliang Shan, *China* **58 E3** 24 30N 100 40 E
Wuliaru, *Indonesia* **63 F8** 7 27 S 131 0 E
Wuling Shan, *China* **58 C7** 30 0N 110 0 E
Wulong, *China* **58 C6** 29 22N 107 43 E
Wulumuchi = Ürümqi, *China* **50 E9** 43 45N 87 45 E
Wum, *Cameroon* **83 D7** 6 24N 10 2 E
Wuming, *China* **58 F7** 23 12N 108 18 E
Wun Rog, *Sudan* **81 F2** 9 0N 28 20 E
Wundowie, *Australia* **93 F2** 31 47 S 116 23 E
Wuning, *China* **59 C10** 29 17N 115 5 E
Wunnummin L., *Canada* **102 B2** 52 55N 89 10W
Wunsiedel, *Germany* **25 E8** 50 2N 12 0 E
Wunstorf, *Germany* **24 C5** 52 25N 9 26 E
Wuntho, *Burma* **67 H19** 23 55N 95 45 E
Wuping, *China* **59 E11** 25 5N 116 5 E
Wuppertal, *Germany* **24 D3** 51 16N 7 12 E
Wuppertal, *S. Africa* **88 E2** 32 13 S 19 12 E
Wuqing, *China* **57 E9** 39 23N 117 4 E
Wurtsboro, *U.S.A.* **111 E10** 41 35N 74 29W
Würzburg, *Germany* **25 F5** 49 46N 9 55 E
Wurzen, *Germany* **24 D8** 51 22N 12 44 E
Wushan, *China* **56 G3** 34 43N 104 53 E
Wushishi, *Nigeria* **83 D6** 9 46N 6 7 E
Wusuli Jiang = Ussuri →, *Asia* **54 A7** 48 27N 135 0 E
Wutach →, *Germany* **25 H4** 47 37N 8 15 E
Wutai, *China* **56 E7** 38 40N 113 12 E
Wuting = Huimin, *China* **57 F9** 37 27N 117 28 E
Wutong, *China* **59 E8** 25 24N 110 4 E
Wutonghaolai, *China* **57 C11** 42 50N 120 5 E
Wutongqiao, *China* **58 C4** 29 22N 103 50 E
Wuwei, *Anhui, China* **59 B11** 31 18N 117 54 E
Wuwei, *Gansu, China* **60 C5** 37 57N 102 34 E
Wuxi, *Jiangsu, China* **59 B13** 31 33N 120 18 E
Wuxi, *Sichuan, China* **58 B7** 31 23N 109 35 E
Wuxiang, *China* **56 F7** 36 49N 112 50 E
Wuxuan, *China* **58 F7** 23 34N 109 38 E
Wuxue, *China* **59 C10** 29 52N 115 30 E
Wuyang, *China* **56 H7** 33 25N 113 35 E
Wuyi, *Hebei, China* **56 F8** 37 46N 115 56 E
Wuyi, *Zhejiang, China* **59 C12** 28 52N 119 50 E
Wuyi Shan, *China* **59 D11** 27 0N 117 0 E
Wuyishan, *China* **59 D12** 27 45N 118 0 E
Wuyo, *Nigeria* **83 C7** 10 23N 11 50 E
Wuyuan, *Jiangxi, China* **59 C11** 29 15N 117 50 E
Wuyuan, *Nei Monggol Zizhiqu, China* **56 D5** 41 2N 108 20 E
Wuzhai, *China* **56 E6** 38 54N 111 48 E
Wuzhi Shan, *China* **64 C7** 18 45N 109 45 E
Wuzhong, *China* **56 E4** 38 2N 106 12 E
Wuzhou, *China* **59 F8** 23 30N 111 18 E
Wyaaba Cr. →, *Australia* **94 B3** 16 27 S 141 35 E
Wyalkatchem, *Australia* **93 F2** 31 8 S 117 22 E
Wyalusing, *U.S.A.* **111 E8** 41 40N 76 16W
Wyandotte, *U.S.A.* **108 D4** 42 12N 83 9W
Wyandra, *Australia* **95 D4** 27 12 S 145 56 E
Wyangala, L., *Australia* **95 E4** 33 54 S 149 0 E
Wyara, L., *Australia* **95 D3** 28 42 S 144 14 E
Wycheproof, *Australia* **95 F3** 36 5 S 143 17 E
Wye →, *U.K.* **13 F5** 51 38N 2 40W
Wyemandoo, *Australia* **93 E2** 28 28 S 118 29 E
Wyk, *Germany* **24 A4** 54 41N 8 33 E
Wymondham, *U.K.* **13 E9** 52 35N 1 7 E
Wymore, *U.S.A.* **112 E6** 40 7N 96 40W
Wyndham, *Australia* **92 C4** 15 33 S 128 3 E
Wyndham, *N.Z.* **91 M2** 46 20 S 168 51 E
Wynne, *U.S.A.* **113 H9** 35 14N 90 47W
Wynyard, *Australia* **94 G4** 41 5 S 145 44 E
Wynyard, *Canada* **105 C8** 51 45N 104 10W
Wyola L., *Australia* **93 E5** 29 8 S 130 17 E
Wyoming, *Canada* **110 D2** 42 57N 82 7W
Wyoming □, *U.S.A.* **114 E10** 43 0N 107 30W
Wyomissing, *U.S.A.* **111 F9** 40 20N 75 59W
Wyong, *Australia* **95 E5** 33 14 S 151 24 E
Wyrzysk, *Poland* **45 E4** 53 10N 17 17 E
Wyśmierzyce, *Poland* **45 G7** 51 37N 20 50 E
Wysoka, *Poland* **45 E4** 53 13N 17 2 E
Wysokie, *Poland* **45 H9** 50 55N 22 40 E
Wysokie Mazowieckie, *Poland* **45 F9** 52 55N 22 30 E
Wyszków, *Poland* **45 F8** 52 36N 21 25 E
Wyszogród, *Poland* **45 F7** 52 23N 20 9 E
Wytheville, *U.S.A.* **108 G5** 36 57N 81 5W
Wyżyna Małopolska, *Poland* **45 H7** 50 45N 20 0 E

X

Xaçmaz, *Azerbaijan* **49 K9** 41 31N 48 42 E
Xai-Xai, *Mozam.* **89 D5** 25 6 S 33 31 E
Xainza, *China* **60 C3** 30 58N 88 35 E
Xangongo, *Angola* **88 B2** 16 45 S 15 5 E
Xankändi, *Azerbaijan* **70 B5** 39 52N 46 49 E
Xanlar, *Azerbaijan* **49 K8** 40 37N 46 12 E
Xanten, *Germany* **24 D2** 51 39N 6 26 E
Xánthi, *Greece* **41 E8** 41 10N 24 58 E
Xánthi □, *Greece* **41 E8** 41 10N 24 58 E
Xanthos, *Turkey* **39 E11** 36 19N 29 18 E
Xanxerê, *Brazil* **127 B5** 26 53 S 52 23W
Xapuri, *Brazil* **124 F5** 10 35 S 68 35W
Xar Moron He →, *China* **57 C11** 43 25N 120 35 E
Xarrë, *Albania* **40 G4** 39 44N 20 3 E
Xátiva, *Spain* **33 G4** 38 59N 0 32W
Xau, L., *Botswana* **88 C3** 21 15 S 24 44 E
Xavantina, *Brazil* **127 A5** 21 15 S 52 48W
Xenia, *U.S.A.* **108 F4** 39 41N 83 56W
Xeropotamos →, *Cyprus* **36 E11** 34 42N 32 33 E
Xertigny, *France* **19 D13** 48 3N 6 24 E
Xhora, *S. Africa* **89 E4** 31 55 S 28 38 E
Xhumo, *Botswana* **88 C3** 21 7 S 24 35 E
Xi Jiang →, *China* **59 F9** 22 5N 113 20 E
Xi Xian, *Henan, China* **59 A10** 32 20N 114 43 E
Xi Xian, *Shanxi, China* **56 F6** 36 41N 110 58 E
Xia Xian, *China* **56 G6** 35 8N 111 12 E
Xiachengzi, *China* **57 B16** 44 40N 130 18 E
Xiachuan Dao, *China* **59 G9** 21 40N 112 40 E
Xiaguan, *China* **60 D5** 25 32N 100 16 E
Xiajiang, *China* **59 D10** 27 30N 115 10 E
Xiajin, *China* **56 F9** 36 56N 116 0 E
Xiamen, *China* **59 E12** 24 25N 118 4 E
Xi'an, *China* **56 G5** 34 15N 109 0 E
Xian Xian, *China* **56 E9** 38 12N 116 6 E
Xianfeng, *China* **58 C7** 29 40N 109 8 E
Xiang Jiang →, *China* **59 C9** 28 55N 112 50 E
Xiangcheng, *Henan, China* **56 H8** 33 29N 114 52 E
Xiangcheng, *Henan, China* **56 H7** 33 50N 113 27 E
Xiangcheng, *Sichuan, China* **58 C2** 28 53N 99 47 E
Xiangdu, *China* **58 F6** 23 13N 106 58 E
Xiangfan, *China* **59 A9** 32 2N 112 8 E
Xianggang = Hong Kong □, *China* **59 F10** 22 11N 114 14 E
Xianghuang Qi, *China* **56 C7** 42 2N 113 50 E
Xiangning, *China* **56 G6** 35 58N 110 50 E
Xiangquan, *China* **56 F7** 36 30N 113 1 E
Xiangquan He = Sutlej →, *Pakistan* **68 E4** 29 23N 71 3 E
Xiangshan, *China* **59 C13** 29 29N 121 51 E
Xiangshui, *China* **57 G10** 34 12N 119 33 E
Xiangtan, *China* **59 D9** 27 51N 112 54 E
Xiangxiang, *China* **59 D9** 27 43N 112 28 E
Xiangyin, *China* **59 C9** 28 38N 112 54 E
Xiangyun, *China* **58 E3** 25 34N 100 35 E
Xiangzhou, *China* **58 F7** 23 58N 109 40 E
Xianju, *China* **59 C13** 28 51N 120 44 E
Xianning, *China* **59 C10** 29 51N 114 16 E
Xianshui He →, *China* **58 B3** 30 10N 100 59 E
Xiantao, *China* **59 B9** 30 25N 113 25 E
Xianyang, *China* **56 G5** 34 20N 108 40 E
Xianyou, *China* **59 E12** 25 22N 118 38 E
Xiao Hinggan Ling, *China* **60 B7** 49 0N 127 0 E
Xiao Xian, *China* **56 G9** 34 15N 116 55 E
Xiaofeng, *China* **59 B12** 30 35N 119 32 E
Xiaogan, *China* **59 B9** 30 52N 113 55 E
Xiaojin, *China* **58 B4** 30 59N 102 21 E
Xiaolan, *China* **59 F9** 22 38N 113 13 E
Xiaoshan, *China* **59 B13** 30 12N 120 18 E
Xiaoyi, *China* **56 F6** 37 8N 111 48 E
Xiapu, *China* **59 D12** 26 54N 119 59 E
Xiawa, *China* **57 C11** 42 35N 120 38 E
Xiayi, *China* **56 G9** 34 15N 116 10 E
Xichang, *China* **58 D4** 27 51N 102 19 E
Xichong, *China* **58 B5** 30 57N 105 54 E
Xichou, *China* **58 E5** 23 25N 104 42 E
Xichuan, *China* **56 H6** 33 0N 111 30 E
Xide, *China* **58 C4** 28 8N 102 19 E
Xiemahe, *China* **59 B8** 31 38N 111 12 E
Xieng Khouang, *Laos* **64 C4** 19 17N 103 25 E
Xifei He →, *China* **56 H9** 32 45N 116 40 E
Xifeng, *Gansu, China* **56 G4** 35 40N 107 40 E
Xifeng, *Guizhou, China* **58 D6** 27 7N 106 42 E
Xifeng, *Liaoning, China* **57 C13** 42 42N 124 45 E
Xifengzhen = Xifeng, *China* **56 G4** 35 40N 107 40 E
Xigazê, *China* **60 D3** 29 5N 88 45 E
Xihe, *China* **56 G3** 34 2N 105 20 E
Xihua, *China* **56 H8** 33 45N 114 30 E
Xilaganí, *Greece* **41 F9** 40 58N 25 28 E
Xiliao He →, *China* **57 C12** 43 32N 123 35 E
Xilin, *China* **58 E5** 24 30N 105 6 E
Xilókastron, *Greece* **38 C4** 38 5N 22 38 E
Xime, *Guinea-Biss.* **82 C2** 11 59N 14 57W
Ximeng, *China* **58 F2** 22 50N 99 27 E
Xin Jiang →, *China* **59 C11** 28 45N 116 35 E
Xin Xian = Xinzhou, *China* **56 E7** 38 22N 112 46 E
Xinavane, *Mozam.* **89 D5** 25 2 S 32 47 E
Xinbin, *China* **57 D13** 41 40N 125 2 E
Xincai, *China* **59 A10** 32 43N 114 58 E
Xinchang, *China* **59 C13** 29 28N 120 52 E
Xincheng, *Guangxi Zhuangzu, China* **58 E7** 24 5N 108 39 E
Xincheng, *Jiangxi, China* **59 D10** 26 48N 114 6 E
Xindu, *China* **58 B5** 30 50N 104 10 E
Xinfeng, *Guangdong, China* **59 E10** 24 5N 114 16 E
Xinfeng, *Jiangxi, China* **59 D11** 27 7N 116 11 E
Xinfeng, *Jiangxi, China* **59 E10** 25 27N 114 58 E
Xinfengjiang Skuiku, *China* **59 F10** 23 52N 114 30 E
Xing Xian, *China* **56 E6** 38 27N 111 7 E
Xing'an, *Guangxi Zhuangzu, China* **59 E8** 25 38N 110 40 E
Xingan, *Jiangxi, China* **59 D10** 27 46N 115 20 E
Xingcheng, *China* **57 D11** 40 40N 120 45 E
Xingguo, *China* **59 D10** 26 21N 115 21 E
Xinghe, *China* **56 D7** 40 55N 113 55 E
Xinghua, *China* **57 H10** 32 58N 119 48 E
Xinghua Wan, *China* **59 E12** 25 15N 119 20 E
Xinglong, *China* **57 D9** 40 25N 117 30 E
Xingning, *China* **59 E10** 24 3N 115 42 E
Xingping, *China* **56 G5** 34 20N 108 28 E
Xingren, *China* **58 E5** 25 24N 105 11 E
Xingshan, *China* **59 B8** 31 15N 110 45 E
Xingtai, *China* **56 F8** 37 3N 114 32 E
Xingu →, *Brazil* **122 D5** 1 30 S 51 53W
Xingwen, *China* **58 C5** 28 22N 104 50 E
Xingyang, *China* **56 G7** 34 45N 112 52 E
Xinhe, *China* **56 F8** 37 30N 115 15 E
Xinhua, *China* **59 D8** 27 42N 111 13 E
Xinhuang, *China* **58 D7** 27 21N 109 12 E
Xinhui, *China* **59 F9** 22 25N 113 0 E
Xining, *China* **60 C5** 36 34N 101 40 E
Xinjian, *China* **59 C10** 28 37N 115 46 E
Xinjiang, *China* **56 G6** 35 34N 111 11 E
Xinjiang Uygur Zizhiqu □, *China* **60 B3** 42 0N 86 0 E
Xinjie, *China* **58 D3** 26 48N 101 15 E
Xinjin = Pulandian, *China* **57 E11** 39 25N 121 58 E
Xinjin, *China* **58 B4** 30 24N 103 47 E
Xinkai He →, *China* **57 C12** 43 32N 123 35 E
Xinle, *China* **56 E8** 38 25N 114 40 E
Xinlitun, *China* **57 D12** 42 0N 122 8 E
Xinlong, *China* **58 B3** 30 57N 100 12 E
Xinmin, *China* **57 D12** 41 59N 122 50 E
Xinning, *China* **59 D8** 26 28N 110 50 E
Xinping, *China* **58 E3** 24 5N 101 59 E
Xinshao, *China* **59 D8** 27 21N 111 26 E
Xintai, *China* **57 G9** 35 55N 117 45 E
Xintian, *China* **59 E9** 25 55N 112 13 E
Xinxian, *China* **59 B10** 31 36N 113 51 E
Xinxiang, *China* **56 G7** 35 18N 113 50 E
Xinxing, *China* **59 F9** 22 35N 112 15 E
Xinyang, *China* **59 A10** 32 6N 114 3 E
Xinye, *China* **59 A9** 32 30N 112 21 E
Xinyi, *China* **59 F8** 22 25N 111 0 E
Xinyu, *China* **59 D10** 27 49N 114 58 E
Xinzhan, *China* **57 C14** 43 50N 127 18 E
Xinzheng, *China* **56 G7** 34 20N 113 45 E
Xinzhou, *Hubei, China* **59 B10** 30 50N 114 48 E
Xinzhou, *Shanxi, China* **56 E7** 38 22N 112 46 E
Xinzo de Limia, *Spain* **34 C3** 42 3N 7 47W
Xiongyuecheng, *China* **57 D12** 40 12N 122 5 E
Xiping, *Henan, China* **56 H8** 33 22N 114 5 E
Xiping, *Henan, China* **56 H6** 33 25N 111 8 E
Xiping, *Zhejiang, China* **59 C12** 28 16N 119 29 E
Xique-Xique, *Brazil* **125 F10** 10 50 S 42 40W
Xisha Qundao = Paracel Is., *S. China Sea* **62 A4** 15 50N 112 0 E
Xishui, *Guizhou, China* **58 C6** 28 19N 106 9 E
Xishui, *Hubei, China* **59 B10** 30 30N 115 15 E
Xitole, *Guinea-Biss.* **82 C2** 11 43N 14 50W
Xiu Shui →, *China* **59 C10** 29 13N 116 0 E
Xiuning, *China* **59 C12** 29 45N 118 10 E
Xiuren, *China* **59 E8** 24 27N 110 12 E
Xiushan, *China* **58 C7** 28 25N 108 57 E
Xiushui, *China* **59 C10** 29 2N 114 33 E
Xiuwen, *China* **58 D6** 26 49N 106 32 E
Xiuyan, *China* **57 D12** 40 18N 123 11 E
Xixabangma Feng, *China* **67 E14** 28 20N 85 40 E
Xixia, *China* **56 H6** 33 25N 111 29 E
Xixiang, *China* **56 H4** 33 0N 107 44 E
Xiyang, *China* **56 F7** 37 38N 113 38 E
Xizang Zizhiqu □, *China* **60 C3** 32 0N 88 0 E
Xlendi, *Malta* **36 C1** 36 1N 14 12 E
Xu Jiang →, *China* **59 D11** 28 0N 116 25 E
Xuan Loc, *Vietnam* **65 G6** 10 56N 107 14 E
Xuan'en, *China* **58 C7** 30 0N 109 30 E
Xuanhan, *China* **58 B6** 31 18N 107 38 E
Xuanhua, *China* **56 D8** 40 40N 115 2 E
Xuanwei, *China* **58 C5** 26 15N 103 59 E
Xuanzhou, *China* **59 B12** 30 56N 118 43 E
Xuchang, *China* **56 G7** 34 2N 113 48 E
Xudat, *Azerbaijan* **49 K9** 41 38N 48 41 E
Xuefeng Shan, *China* **59 D8** 27 5N 110 35 E
Xuejiaping, *China* **59 B8** 31 39N 110 16 E
Xun Jiang →, *China* **59 F8** 23 35N 111 30 E
Xun Xian, *China* **56 G8** 35 42N 114 33 E
Xundian, *China* **58 E4** 25 36N 103 15 E
Xunwu, *China* **59 E10** 24 54N 115 37 E
Xunyang, *China* **56 H5** 32 48N 109 22 E
Xunyi, *China* **56 G5** 35 8N 108 20 E
Xupu, *China* **59 D8** 27 53N 110 32 E
Xúquer →, *Spain* **33 F4** 39 5N 0 10W
Xushui, *China* **56 E8** 39 2N 115 40 E
Xuwen, *China* **59 G8** 20 20N 110 10 E
Xuyen Moc, *Vietnam* **65 G6** 10 34N 107 25 E
Xuyong, *China* **58 C5** 28 10N 105 22 E
Xuzhou, *China* **57 G9** 34 18N 117 10 E
Xylophagou, *Cyprus* **36 E12** 34 54N 33 51 E

Y

Ya Xian, *China* **64 C7** 18 14N 109 29 E
Yaamba, *Australia* **94 C5** 23 8 S 150 22 E
Ya'an, *China* **58 C4** 29 58N 103 5 E
Yaapeet, *Australia* **95 F3** 35 45 S 142 3 E
Yabassi, *Cameroon* **83 E6** 4 30N 9 57 E
Yabelo, *Ethiopia* **81 G4** 4 50N 38 8 E
Yablanitsa, *Bulgaria* **41 C8** 43 2N 24 5 E
Yablonovy Ra. = Yablonovyy Khrebet, *Russia* **51 D12** 53 0N 114 0 E
Yablonovyy Khrebet, *Russia* **51 D12** 53 0N 114 0 E
Yabrai Shan, *China* **56 E2** 39 40N 103 0 E
Yabrūd, *Syria* **75 B5** 33 58N 36 39 E
Yacheng, *China* **64 C7** 18 22N 109 6 E
Yacuiba, *Bolivia* **126 A3** 22 0 S 63 43W
Yacuma →, *Bolivia* **124 F5** 13 38 S 65 23W
Yadgir, *India* **66 L10** 16 45N 77 5 E
Yadkin →, *U.S.A.* **109 H5** 35 29N 80 9W
Yadrin, *Russia* **48 C8** 55 57N 46 12 E
Yaeyama-Rettō, *Japan* **55 M1** 24 30N 123 40 E
Yagaba, *Ghana* **83 C4** 10 14N 1 20W
Yağcılar, *Turkey* **39 B10** 39 25N 28 23 E
Yagodnoye, *Russia* **51 C15** 62 33N 149 40 E
Yahila, *Dem. Rep. of the Congo* **86 B1** 0 13N 24 28 E
Yahk, *Canada* **104 D5** 49 6N 116 10W
Yahotyn, *Ukraine* **47 G6** 50 17N 31 46 E
Yahuma, *Dem. Rep. of the Congo* **84 D4** 1 0N 23 10 E
Yahyalı, *Turkey* **72 C6** 38 5N 35 2 E
Yaita, *Japan* **55 F9** 36 48N 139 56 E
Yaiza, *Canary Is.* **37 F6** 28 57N 13 46W
Yajiang, *China* **58 B3** 30 2N 100 57 E
Yajua, *Nigeria* **83 C7** 11 27N 12 49 E
Yakima, *U.S.A.* **114 C3** 46 36N 120 31W
Yakima →, *U.S.A.* **114 C3** 47 0N 120 30W
Yako, *Burkina Faso* **82 C4** 12 59N 2 15W
Yakobi I., *U.S.A.* **104 B1** 58 0N 136 30W
Yakoruda, *Bulgaria* **40 D7** 42 1N 23 39 E
Yakovlevka, *Russia* **54 B6** 44 26N 133 28 E
Yaku-Shima, *Japan* **55 J5** 30 20N 130 30 E
Yakumo, *Japan* **54 C10** 42 15N 140 16 E
Yakutat, *U.S.A.* **100 C6** 59 33N 139 44W
Yakutia = Sakha □, *Russia* **51 C13** 66 0N 130 0 E
Yakutsk, *Russia* **51 C13** 62 5N 129 50 E
Yala, *Thailand* **65 J3** 6 33N 101 18 E
Yale, *U.S.A.* **110 C2** 43 8N 82 48W
Yalgoo, *Australia* **93 E2** 28 16 S 116 39 E
Yalinga, *C.A.R.* **84 C4** 6 33N 23 10 E
Yalkubul, Punta, *Mexico* **119 C7** 21 32N 88 37W
Yalleroi, *Australia* **94 C4** 24 3 S 145 42 E
Yalobusha →, *U.S.A.* **113 J9** 33 33N 90 10W
Yalong Jiang →, *China* **58 D3** 26 40N 101 55 E
Yalova, *Turkey* **41 F13** 40 41N 29 15 E
Yalta, *Ukraine* **47 K8** 44 30N 34 10 E
Yalu Jiang →, *China* **57 E13** 40 0N 124 22 E
Yalvaç, *Turkey* **72 C4** 38 17N 31 10 E
Yam Ha Melaḫ = Dead Sea, *Asia* **75 D4** 31 30N 35 30 E
Yam Kinneret, *Israel* **75 C4** 32 45N 35 35 E
Yamada, *Japan* **55 H5** 33 33N 130 49 E
Yamagata, *Japan* **54 E10** 38 15N 140 15 E
Yamagata □, *Japan* **54 E10** 38 30N 140 0 E
Yamaguchi, *Japan* **55 G5** 34 10N 131 32 E
Yamaguchi □, *Japan* **55 G5** 34 20N 131 40 E
Yamal, Poluostrov, *Russia* **50 B8** 71 0N 70 0 E
Yamal Pen. = Yamal, Poluostrov, *Russia* **50 B8** 71 0N 70 0 E
Yamanashi □, *Japan* **55 G9** 35 40N 138 40 E

Yuzha

Yamba, Australia 95 D5 29 26 S 153 23 E
Yambarran Ra., Australia 92 C5 15 10 S 130 25 E
Yambéring, Guinea 82 C2 11 50N 12 18 E
Yâmbiô, Sudan 81 G2 4 35N 28 16 E
Yambol, Bulgaria 41 D10 42 30N 26 30 E
Yamdena, Indonesia 63 F8 7 45 S 131 20 E
Yame, Japan 55 H5 33 13N 130 35 E
Yamethin, Burma 67 J20 20 29N 96 18 E
Yamma-Yamma, L., Australia 95 D3 26 16 S 141 20 E
Yamoussoukro, Ivory C. 82 D3 6 49N 5 17W
Yampa →, U.S.A. 114 F9 40 32N 108 59W
Yampi Sd., Australia 92 C3 16 8 S 123 38 E
Yampil, Moldova 47 H5 48 15N 28 15 E
Yampol = Yampil, Moldova 47 H5 48 15N 28 15 E
Yamrat, Nigeria 83 C6 10 11N 9 55 E
Yamrukchal = Botev, Bulgaria 41 D8 42 44N 24 52 E
Yamuna →, India 69 G9 25 30N 81 53 E
Yamunanagar, India 68 D7 30 7N 77 17 E
Yamzho Yumco, China 60 D4 28 48N 90 35 E
Yan, Nigeria 83 C7 10 5N 12 11 E
Yana →, Russia 51 B14 71 30N 136 0 E
Yanagawa, Japan 55 H5 33 10N 130 24 E
Yanai, Japan 55 H6 33 58N 132 7 E
Yan'an, China 56 F5 36 35N 109 26 E
Yanbian, China 58 D3 26 47N 101 31 E
Yanbu 'al Baḩr, Si. Arabia 70 F3 24 0N 38 5 E
Yanchang, China 56 F6 36 43N 110 1 E
Yancheng, Henan, China 56 H8 33 35N 114 0 E
Yancheng, Jiangsu, China 57 H11 33 23N 120 8 E
Yanchep Beach, Australia 93 F2 31 33 S 115 37 E
Yanchi, China 56 F4 37 48N 107 20 E
Yanchuan, China 56 F6 36 51N 110 10 E
Yanco Cr. →, Australia 95 F4 35 14 S 145 35 E
Yandoon, Burma 67 L19 17 0N 95 40 E
Yanfeng, China 58 E3 25 52N 101 8 E
Yanfolila, Mali 82 C3 11 11N 8 9W
Yang Xian, China 56 H4 33 15N 107 30 E
Yang-Yang, Senegal 82 B1 15 30N 15 20W
Yangambi, Dem. Rep. of the Congo 86 B1 0 47N 24 24 E
Yangbi, China 58 E2 25 41N 99 58 E
Yangcheng, China 56 G7 35 28N 112 22 E
Yangch'ü = Taiyuan, China 56 F7 37 52N 112 33 E
Yangchun, China 59 F8 22 11N 111 48 E
Yanggao, China 56 D7 40 21N 113 55 E
Yanggu, China 56 F8 36 8N 115 43 E
Yangjiang, China 59 G8 21 50N 111 59 E
Yangliuqing, China 57 E9 39 2N 117 5 E
Yangon = Rangoon, Burma 67 L20 16 45N 96 20 E
Yangping, China 59 B8 31 12N 111 25 E
Yangpingguan, China 56 H4 32 58N 106 5 E
Yangquan, China 56 F7 37 58N 113 31 E
Yangshan, China 59 E9 24 30N 112 40 E
Yangshuo, China 59 E8 24 48N 110 29 E
Yangtse = Chang Jiang →, China 59 B13 31 48N 121 10 E
Yangtze Kiang = Chang Jiang →, China 59 B13 31 48N 121 10 E
Yangxin, China 59 C10 29 50N 115 12 E
Yangyang, S. Korea 57 E15 38 4N 128 38 E
Yangyuan, China 56 D8 40 1N 114 10 E
Yangzhong, China 59 A12 32 22N 119 22 E
Yangzhou, China 59 A12 32 21N 119 26 E
Yanhe, China 58 C7 28 31N 108 29 E
Yanji, China 57 C15 42 59N 129 30 E
Yanjin, China 58 C5 28 5N 104 18 E
Yanjing, China 58 C2 29 7N 98 33 E
Yankton, U.S.A. 112 D6 42 53N 97 23W
Yanonge, Dem. Rep. of the Congo 86 B1 0 35N 24 38 E
Yanqi, China 60 B3 42 5N 86 35 E
Yanqing, China 56 D8 40 30N 115 58 E
Yanshan, Hebei, China 57 E9 38 4N 117 22 E
Yanshan, Jiangxi, China 59 C11 28 15N 117 41 E
Yanshan, Yunnan, China 58 F5 23 35N 104 20 E
Yanshou, China 57 B15 45 28N 128 22 E
Yantabulla, Australia 95 D4 29 21 S 145 0 E
Yantai, China 57 F11 37 34N 121 22 E
Yanting, China 58 B5 31 11N 105 24 E
Yantra →, Bulgaria 41 C9 43 40N 25 37 E
Yanwa, China 58 D2 27 35N 98 55 E
Yanyuan, China 58 D3 27 25N 101 30 E
Yanzhou, China 56 G9 35 35N 116 49 E
Yao Xian, China 56 G5 34 55N 108 59 E
Yao Yai, Ko, Thailand 65 J2 8 0N 98 35 E
Yao'an, China 58 E3 25 31N 101 18 E
Yaodu, China 58 A5 32 45N 105 22 E
Yaoundé, Cameroon 83 E7 3 50N 11 35 E
Yaowan, China 57 G10 34 15N 118 3 E
Yap I., Pac. Oc. 96 G5 9 30N 138 10 E
Yapen, Indonesia 63 E9 1 50 S 136 0 E
Yapen, Selat, Indonesia 63 E9 1 20 S 136 10 E
Yapero, Indonesia 63 E9 4 59 S 137 11 E
Yappar →, Australia 94 B3 18 22 S 141 16 E
Yaqui →, Mexico 118 B2 27 37N 110 39W
Yar-Sale, Russia 50 C8 66 50N 70 50 E
Yaraka, Australia 94 C3 24 53 S 144 3 E
Yaransk, Russia 48 B8 57 22N 47 49 E
Yarbasan, Turkey 39 C10 38 59N 28 49 E
Yardımcı Burnu, Turkey 39 E12 36 13N 30 25 E
Yare →, U.K. 13 E9 52 35N 1 38 E
Yaremcha, Ukraine 47 H3 48 27N 24 33 E
Yarensk, Russia 50 C5 62 11N 49 15 E
Yarfa, Si. Arabia 80 C4 24 37N 38 35 E
Yarí →, Colombia 124 D4 0 20 S 72 20W
Yarkand = Shache, China 60 C2 38 20N 77 10 E
Yarker, Canada 111 B8 44 23N 76 46W
Yarkhun →, Pakistan 69 A5 36 17N 72 30 E
Yarmouth, Canada 103 D6 43 50N 66 7W
Yarmūk →, Syria 75 C4 32 42N 35 40 E
Yaroslavl, Russia 46 D10 57 35N 39 55 E
Yarqa, W. →, Egypt 75 F2 30 0N 33 49 E
Yarra Yarra Lakes, Australia 93 E2 29 40 S 115 45 E
Yarram, Australia 95 F4 38 29 S 146 39 E
Yarraman, Australia 95 D5 26 50 S 152 0 E
Yarras, Australia 95 E5 31 25 S 152 20 E
Yartsevo, Sib., Russia 51 C10 60 20N 90 0 E
Yartsevo, Smolensk, Russia 46 E7 55 6N 32 43 E
Yarumal, Colombia 124 B3 6 58N 75 24W
Yasawa Group, Fiji 91 C7 17 0 S 177 23 E
Yaselda, Belarus 47 F4 52 7N 26 28 E
Yashi, Nigeria 83 C6 12 23N 7 54 E
Yashikera, Nigeria 83 D5 9 44N 3 29 E
Yashkul, Russia 49 G7 46 11N 45 21 E
Yasin, Pakistan 69 A5 36 24N 73 23 E
Yasinovataya, Ukraine 47 H9 48 7N 37 57 E
Yasinski, L., Canada 102 B4 53 16N 77 35W
Yasinya, Ukraine 47 H3 48 16N 24 21 E
Yasothon, Thailand 64 E5 15 50N 104 10 E
Yass, Australia 95 E4 34 49 S 148 54 E
Yāsūj, Iran 71 D6 30 31N 51 31 E
Yatağan, Turkey 39 D10 37 20N 28 10 E
Yatakala, Niger 83 C5 14 50N 0 22 E
Yates Center, U.S.A. 113 G7 37 53N 95 44W
Yathkyed L., Canada 105 A9 62 40N 98 0W
Yatsushiro, Japan 55 H5 32 30N 130 40 E
Yatta Plateau, Kenya 86 C4 2 0 S 38 0 E
Yavari →, Peru 124 D4 4 21 S 70 2W
Yávaros, Mexico 118 B3 26 42N 109 31W
Yavatmal, India 66 J11 20 20N 78 15 E
Yavne, Israel 75 D3 31 52N 34 45 E
Yavoriv, Ukraine 47 H2 49 55N 23 20 E
Yavorov = Yavoriv, Ukraine 47 H2 49 55N 23 20 E
Yavuzeli, Turkey 72 D7 37 18N 37 24 E
Yawatahama, Japan 55 H6 33 27N 132 24 E
Yawri B., S. Leone 82 D2 8 22N 13 0W
Yaxi, China 58 D6 27 33N 106 41 E
Yazd, Iran 71 D7 31 55N 54 27 E
Yazd □, Iran 71 D7 32 0N 55 0 E
Yazd-e Khvāst, Iran 71 D7 31 31N 52 7 E
Yazıköy, Turkey 39 E9 36 40N 27 20 E
Yazman, Pakistan 68 E4 29 8N 71 45 E
Yazoo →, U.S.A. 113 J9 32 22N 90 54W
Yazoo City, U.S.A. 113 J9 32 51N 90 25W
Ybbs, Austria 26 C8 48 12N 15 4 E
Yding Skovhøj, Denmark 11 J3 55 59N 9 46 E
Ye Xian = Laizhou, China 57 F10 37 8N 119 57 E
Ye Xian, China 56 H7 33 35N 113 25 E
Yebyu, Burma 64 E2 14 15N 98 13 E
Yechŏn, S. Korea 57 F15 36 39N 128 27 E
Yecla, Spain 33 G3 38 35N 1 5W
Yécora, Mexico 118 B3 28 20N 108 58W
Yedintsy = Edineţ, Moldova 43 B12 48 9N 27 18 E
Yedseram →, Nigeria 83 C7 12 30N 14 5 E
Yefremov, Russia 46 F10 53 8N 38 3 E
Yeghegnadzor, Armenia 73 C11 39 44N 45 19 E
Yegorlyk →, Russia 49 G5 46 35N 41 57 E
Yegorlykskaya, Russia 49 G5 46 35N 40 35 E
Yegoryevsk, Russia 46 E10 55 27N 38 55 E
Yegros, Paraguay 126 B4 26 20 S 56 25W
Yehuda, Midbar, Israel 75 D4 31 35N 35 15 E
Yei, Sudan 81 G3 4 9N 30 40 E
Yei, Nahr →, Sudan 81 F3 6 15N 30 13 E
Yejmiadzin, Armenia 49 K7 40 12N 44 19 E
Yekaterinburg, Russia 50 D7 56 50N 60 30 E
Yekaterinodar = Krasnodar, Russia 49 H4 45 5N 39 0 E
Yelabuga, Russia 48 C11 55 45N 52 4 E
Yelan, Russia 48 E6 50 55N 43 43 E
Yelarbon, Australia 95 D5 28 33 S 150 38 E
Yelatma, Russia 48 C5 55 0N 41 45 E
Yelets, Russia 47 F10 52 40N 38 30 E
Yélimané, Mali 82 B2 15 9N 10 34W
Yelizavetgrad = Kirovohrad, Ukraine 47 H7 48 35N 32 20 E
Yell, U.K. 14 A7 60 35N 1 5W
Yell Sd., U.K. 14 A7 60 33N 1 15W
Yellow Sea, China 57 G12 35 0N 123 0 E
Yellowhead Pass, Canada 104 C5 52 53N 118 25W
Yellowknife, Canada 104 A6 62 27N 114 29W
Yellowknife →, Canada 104 A6 62 31N 114 19W
Yellowstone →, U.S.A. 112 B3 47 59N 103 59W
Yellowstone L., U.S.A. 114 D8 44 27N 110 22W
Yellowstone National Park, U.S.A. 114 D9 44 40N 110 30W
Yelnya, Russia 46 E7 54 35N 33 15 E
Yelsk, Belarus 47 G5 51 50N 29 10 E
Yelwa, Nigeria 83 C5 10 49N 4 41 E
Yemen ■, Asia 74 E3 15 0N 44 0 E
Yen Bai, Vietnam 58 G5 21 42N 104 52 E
Yenagoa, Nigeria 83 E6 4 58N 6 16 E
Yenakiyeve, Ukraine 47 H10 48 15N 38 15 E
Yenakiyevo = Yenakiyeve, Ukraine 47 H10 48 15N 38 15 E
Yenangyaung, Burma 67 J19 20 30N 95 0 E
Yenbo = Yanbu 'al Baḩr, Si. Arabia 70 F3 24 0N 38 5 E
Yenda, Australia 95 E4 34 13 S 146 14 E
Yende Millimou, Guinea 82 D2 8 55N 10 10W
Yendéré, Burkina Faso 82 C4 10 12N 4 59W
Yendi, Ghana 83 D4 9 29N 0 1W
Yéni, Niger 83 C5 13 30N 3 1 E
Yenice, Ankara, Turkey 72 C5 39 14N 32 42 E
Yenice, Aydın, Turkey 39 D10 37 49N 28 35 E
Yenice, Çanakkale, Turkey 39 B9 39 55N 27 17 E
Yenice, Edirne, Turkey 41 F10 40 42N 26 9 E
Yenice →, Turkey 72 D6 37 37N 35 33 E
Yenifoça, Turkey 39 C8 38 44N 26 51 E
Yenihisar, Turkey 39 D9 37 22N 27 16 E
Yeniköy, Bursa, Turkey 41 F13 40 31N 29 22 E
Yeniköy, Çanakkale, Turkey 39 B8 39 55N 26 10 E
Yeniköy, Kütahya, Turkey 39 C11 38 52N 29 17 E
Yenipazar, Turkey 39 D10 37 49N 28 11 E
Yenisaía, Greece 41 E8 41 1N 24 57 E
Yenişehir, Turkey 41 F13 40 16N 29 38 E
Yenisey →, Russia 50 B9 71 50N 82 40 E
Yeniseysk, Russia 51 D10 58 27N 92 13 E
Yeniseyskiy Zaliv, Russia 50 B9 72 20N 81 0 E
Yennádhi, Greece 36 C9 36 2N 27 56 E
Yenne, France 21 C9 45 43N 5 44 E
Yenotayevka, Russia 49 G8 47 15N 47 0 E
Yenyuka, Russia 51 D13 57 57N 121 15 E
Yeo →, U.K. 13 G5 51 2N 2 49W
Yeo, L., Australia 93 E3 28 0 S 124 30 E
Yeo I., Canada 110 A3 45 24N 81 48W
Yeola, India 66 J9 20 2N 74 30 E
Yeoryioúpolis, Greece 36 D6 35 20N 24 15 E
Yeovil, U.K. 13 G5 50 57N 2 38W
Yepes, Spain 34 F7 39 55N 3 39W
Yeppoon, Australia 94 C5 23 5 S 150 47 E
Yeráki, Greece 38 D4 37 0N 22 42 E
Yerbent, Turkmenistan 50 F6 39 30N 58 50 E
Yerbogachen, Russia 51 C11 61 16N 108 0 E
Yerevan, Armenia 49 K7 40 10N 44 31 E
Yerington, U.S.A. 114 G4 38 59N 119 10W
Yerkesik, Turkey 39 D10 37 7N 28 19 E
Yerköy, Turkey 72 C6 39 38N 34 28 E
Yermak, Kazakhstan 50 D8 52 2N 76 55 E
Yermo, U.S.A. 117 L10 34 54N 116 50W
Yerólakkos, Cyprus 36 D12 35 11N 33 15 E
Yeropol, Russia 51 C17 65 15N 168 40 E
Yeropótamos →, Greece 36 D6 35 3N 24 50 E
Yeroskipos, Cyprus 36 E11 34 46N 32 28 E
Yershov, Russia 48 E9 51 23N 48 27 E
Yerushalayim = Jerusalem, Israel 75 D4 31 47N 35 10 E
Yerville, France 18 C7 49 40N 0 53 E
Yes Tor, U.K. 13 G4 50 41N 4 0W
Yesan, S. Korea 57 F14 36 41N 126 51 E
Yeşilhisar, Turkey 72 C6 38 20N 35 5 E
Yeşilırmak →, Turkey 72 B7 41 22N 36 37 E
Yeşilkent, Turkey 72 D7 36 57N 36 12 E
Yeşilköy, Turkey 41 F12 40 57N 28 49 E
Yeşilova, Turkey 39 D11 37 31N 29 46 E
Yeşilyurt, Manisa, Turkey 39 C10 38 22N 28 40 E
Yeşilyurt, Muğla, Turkey 39 D10 37 10N 28 20 E
Yesnogorsk, Russia 46 E9 54 32N 37 38 E
Yeso, U.S.A. 113 H2 34 26N 104 37W
Yessentuki, Russia 49 H6 44 5N 42 53 E
Yessey, Russia 51 C11 68 29N 102 10 E
Yeste, Spain 33 G2 38 22N 2 19W
Yetman, Australia 95 D5 28 56 S 150 48 E
Yeu, Î. d', France 18 F4 46 42N 2 20W
Yevlakh = Yevlax, Azerbaijan 49 K8 40 39N 47 7 E
Yevlax, Azerbaijan 49 K8 40 39N 47 7 E
Yevpatoriya, Ukraine 47 K7 45 15N 33 20 E
Yeya →, Russia 47 J10 46 40N 38 40 E
Yeysk, Russia 47 J10 46 40N 38 12 E
Yezd = Yazd, Iran 71 D7 31 55N 54 27 E
Yezerishche, Belarus 46 E5 55 50N 29 59 E
Yhati, Paraguay 126 B4 25 45 S 56 35W
Yhú, Paraguay 127 B4 25 0 S 56 0W
Yi →, Uruguay 126 C4 33 7 S 57 8W
Yi 'Allaq, G., Egypt 75 E2 30 22N 33 32 E
Yi He →, China 57 G10 34 10N 118 8 E
Yi Xian, Anhui, China 59 C11 29 55N 117 57 E
Yi Xian, Hebei, China 56 E8 39 20N 115 30 E
Yi Xian, Liaoning, China 57 D11 41 30N 121 22 E
Yialí, Greece 39 E9 36 41N 27 11 E
Yialiás →, Cyprus 36 D12 35 9N 33 44 E
Yi'allaq, G., Egypt 80 A3 30 21N 33 31 E
Yialousa, Cyprus 36 D13 35 32N 34 10 E
Yiáltra, Greece 38 C4 38 51N 22 59 E
Yianisádhes, Greece 36 D8 35 20N 26 10 E
Yiannitsa, Greece 40 F6 40 46N 22 24 E
Yibin, China 58 C5 28 45N 104 32 E
Yichang, China 59 B8 30 40N 111 20 E
Yicheng, Henan, China 59 B9 31 41N 112 12 E
Yicheng, Shanxi, China 56 G6 35 42N 111 40 E
Yichuan, China 56 F6 36 2N 110 10 E
Yichun, Heilongjiang, China 60 B7 47 44N 128 52 E
Yichun, Jiangxi, China 59 D10 27 48N 114 22 E
Yidu, China 57 F10 36 43N 118 28 E
Yidun, China 58 B2 30 22N 99 21 E
Yifag, Ethiopia 81 E4 12 4N 37 46 E
Yifeng, China 59 C10 28 22N 114 45 E
Yihuang, China 59 D11 27 30N 116 12 E
Yijun, China 56 G5 35 28N 109 8 E
Yıldız Dağları, Turkey 41 E11 41 48N 27 36 E
Yıldızeli, Turkey 72 C7 39 51N 36 36 E
Yiliang, Yunnan, China 58 D5 27 38N 104 2 E
Yiliang, Yunnan, China 58 E4 24 56N 103 11 E
Yilong, China 58 B6 31 34N 106 23 E
Yimen, China 58 E4 24 40N 102 10 E
Yimianpo, China 57 B15 45 7N 128 2 E
Yinchuan, China 56 E4 38 30N 106 15 E
Yindarlgooda, L., Australia 93 F3 30 40 S 121 52 E
Ying He →, China 56 H9 32 30N 116 30 E
Ying Xian, China 56 E7 39 32N 113 10 E
Yingcheng, China 59 B9 30 56N 113 35 E
Yingde, China 59 E9 24 10N 113 25 E
Yingjiang, China 58 E1 24 41N 97 55 E
Yingjing, China 58 C4 29 41N 102 52 E
Yingkou, China 57 D12 40 37N 122 18 E
Yingshan, Henan, China 59 B9 31 35N 113 50 E
Yingshan, Hubei, China 59 B10 30 41N 115 32 E
Yingshan, Sichuan, China 58 B6 31 4N 106 35 E
Yingshang, China 59 A11 32 38N 116 12 E
Yingtan, China 59 C11 28 12N 117 0 E
Yining, China 50 E9 43 58N 81 10 E
Yinjiang, China 58 C7 28 1N 108 21 E
Yinmabin, Burma 67 H19 22 10N 94 55 E
Yiofiros →, Greece 36 D7 35 20N 25 6 E
Yioúra, Nótios Aiyaíon, Greece 38 D6 37 32N 24 40 E
Yioúra, Thessalía, Greece 38 B6 39 23N 24 10 E
Yipinglang, China 58 E3 25 10N 101 52 E
Yirba Muda, Ethiopia 81 F4 6 12N 38 42 E
Yirga Alem, Ethiopia 81 F4 6 48N 38 22 E
Yirol, Sudan 81 F3 6 33N 30 30 E
Yirrkala, Australia 94 A2 12 14 S 136 56 E
Yishan, China 58 E7 24 28N 108 38 E
Yishui, China 57 G10 35 47N 118 30 E
Yíthion, Greece 38 E4 36 46N 22 34 E
Yitong, China 57 C13 43 13N 125 20 E
Yiwu, China 59 C13 29 20N 120 3 E
Yixing, China 59 B12 31 21N 119 48 E
Yiyang, Henan, China 56 G7 34 27N 112 10 E
Yiyang, Hunan, China 59 C9 28 35N 112 18 E
Yiyang, Jiangxi, China 59 C11 28 22N 117 20 E
Yizhang, China 59 E9 25 27N 112 57 E
Yizheng, China 59 A12 32 18N 119 10 E
Yli-Kitka, Finland 8 C23 66 8N 28 30 E
Ylitornio, Finland 8 C20 66 19N 23 39 E
Ylivieska, Finland 8 D21 64 4N 24 28 E
Yngaren, Sweden 11 F10 58 50N 16 35 E
Yoakum, U.S.A. 113 L6 29 17N 97 9W
Yobe □, Nigeria 83 C7 12 0N 11 30 E
Yog Pt., Phil. 63 B6 14 6N 124 12 E
Yogan, Togo 83 D5 6 23N 1 30 E
Yoğuntaş, Turkey 41 E11 41 50N 27 4 E
Yogyakarta, Indonesia 62 F4 7 49 S 110 22 E
Yoho Nat. Park, Canada 104 C5 51 25N 116 30W
Yojoa, L. de, Honduras 120 D2 14 53N 88 0W
Yŏju, S. Korea 57 F14 37 20N 127 35 E
Yokadouma, Cameroon 84 D2 3 26N 14 55 E
Yokkaichi, Japan 55 G8 34 55N 136 38 E
Yoko, Cameroon 83 D7 5 32N 12 20 E
Yokohama, Japan 55 G9 35 27N 139 28 E
Yokosuka, Japan 55 G9 35 20N 139 40 E
Yokote, Japan 54 E10 39 20N 140 30 E
Yola, Nigeria 83 D7 9 10N 12 29 E
Yolaina, Cordillera de, Nic. 120 D3 11 30N 84 0W
Yoloten, Turkmenistan 71 B9 37 18N 62 21 E
Yom →, Thailand 62 A2 15 35N 100 1 E
Yonago, Japan 55 G6 35 25N 133 19 E
Yonaguni-Jima, Japan 55 M1 24 27N 123 0 E
Yŏnan, N. Korea 57 F14 37 55N 126 11 E
Yonezawa, Japan 54 F10 37 57N 140 4 E
Yong Peng, Malaysia 65 L4 2 0N 103 3 E
Yong Sata, Thailand 65 J2 7 8N 99 41 E
Yongamp'o, N. Korea 57 E13 39 56N 124 23 E
Yong'an, China 59 E11 25 59N 117 25 E
Yongcheng, China 56 H9 33 55N 116 20 E
Yŏngch'ŏn, S. Korea 57 G15 35 58N 128 56 E
Yongchuan, China 58 C5 29 17N 105 55 E
Yongchun, China 59 E12 25 16N 118 20 E
Yongde, China 58 E2 24 5N 99 25 E
Yongdeng, China 56 F2 36 38N 103 25 E
Yongding, China 59 E11 24 43N 116 45 E
Yŏngdŏk, S. Korea 57 F15 36 24N 129 22 E
Yŏngdŭngpo, S. Korea 57 F14 37 31N 126 54 E
Yongfeng, China 59 D10 27 20N 115 22 E
Yongfu, China 58 E7 24 59N 109 59 E
Yonghe, China 56 F6 36 46N 110 38 E
Yŏnghŭng, N. Korea 57 E14 39 31N 127 18 E
Yongji, China 56 G6 34 52N 110 28 E
Yongjia, China 59 C13 28 10N 120 45 E
Yŏngju, S. Korea 57 F15 36 50N 128 40 E
Yongkang, Yunnan, China 58 E2 24 9N 99 20 E
Yongkang, Zhejiang, China 59 C13 28 55N 120 2 E
Yongnian, China 56 F8 36 47N 114 29 E
Yongning, Guangxi Zhuangzu, China 58 F7 22 44N 108 28 E
Yongning, Ningxia Huizu, China 56 E4 38 15N 106 14 E
Yongping, China 58 E2 25 27N 99 38 E
Yongqing, China 56 E9 39 25N 116 28 E
Yongren, China 58 D3 26 4N 101 40 E
Yongshan, China 58 C4 28 11N 103 35 E
Yongsheng, China 58 D3 26 38N 100 46 E
Yongshun, China 58 C7 29 2N 109 51 E
Yongtai, China 59 E12 25 49N 118 58 E
Yŏngwŏl, S. Korea 57 F15 37 11N 128 28 E
Yongxin = Jinggangshan, China 59 D10 26 58N 114 15 E
Yongxing, China 59 D9 26 9N 113 8 E
Yongxiu, China 59 C10 29 2N 115 42 E
Yongzhou, China 59 D8 26 17N 111 37 E
Yonibana, S. Leone 82 D2 8 30N 12 19W
Yonkers, U.S.A. 111 F11 40 56N 73 54W
Yonne □, France 19 E10 47 50N 3 40 E
Yonne →, France 19 D9 48 23N 2 58 E
York, Australia 93 F2 31 52 S 116 47 E
York, U.K. 12 D6 53 58N 1 6W
York, Ala., U.S.A. 113 J10 32 29N 88 18W
York, Nebr., U.S.A. 112 E6 40 52N 97 36W
York, Pa., U.S.A. 108 F7 39 58N 76 44W
York, C., Australia 94 A3 10 42 S 142 31 E
York, City of □, U.K. 12 D6 53 58N 1 6W
York, Kap, Greenland 4 B4 75 55N 66 25W
York, Vale of, U.K. 12 C6 54 15N 1 25W
York Haven, U.S.A. 110 F8 40 7N 76 46W
York Sd., Australia 92 C4 15 0 S 125 5 E
Yorke Pen., Australia 95 E2 34 50 S 137 40 E
Yorkshire Wolds, U.K. 12 C7 54 8N 0 31W
Yorkton, Canada 105 C8 51 11N 102 28W
Yorkville, U.S.A. 116 G3 38 52N 123 13W
Yoro, Honduras 120 C2 15 9N 87 7W
Yoron-Jima, Japan 55 L4 27 2N 128 26 E
Yorosso, Mali 82 C4 12 17N 4 55W
Yos Sudarso, Pulau = Dolak, Pulau, Indonesia 63 F9 8 0 S 138 30 E
Yosemite National Park, U.S.A. 116 H7 37 45N 119 40W
Yosemite Village, U.S.A. 116 H7 37 45N 119 35W
Yoshkar Ola, Russia 48 B8 56 38N 47 55 E
Yŏsu, S. Korea 57 G14 34 47N 127 45 E
Yotvata, Israel 75 F4 29 55N 35 2 E
You Jiang →, China 58 F6 22 50N 108 6 E
You Xian, China 59 D9 27 1N 113 17 E
Youbou, Canada 116 B2 48 53N 124 13W
Youghal, Ireland 15 E4 51 56N 7 52W
Youghal B., Ireland 15 E4 51 55N 7 49W
Youkounkoun, Guinea 82 C2 12 35N 13 11W
Young, Australia 95 E4 34 19 S 148 18 E
Young, Canada 105 C7 51 47N 105 45W
Young, Uruguay 126 C4 32 44 S 57 36W
Younghusband, L., Australia 95 E2 30 50 S 136 5 E
Younghusband Pen., Australia 95 F2 36 0 S 139 25 E
Youngstown, Canada 105 C6 51 35N 111 10W
Youngstown, N.Y., U.S.A. 110 C5 43 15N 79 3W
Youngstown, Ohio, U.S.A. 110 E4 41 6N 80 39W
Youngsville, U.S.A. 110 E5 41 51N 79 19W
Youngwood, U.S.A. 110 F5 40 14N 79 34W
Youxi, China 59 D12 26 10N 118 13 E
Youyang, China 58 C7 28 47N 108 42 E
Youyu, China 56 D7 40 10N 112 20 E
Yozgat, Turkey 72 C6 39 51N 34 47 E
Ypané →, Paraguay 126 A4 23 29 S 57 19W
Yport, France 18 C7 49 45N 0 15 E
Ypres = Ieper, Belgium 17 D2 50 51N 2 53 E
Yreka, U.S.A. 114 F2 41 44N 122 38W
Yssingeaux, France 21 C8 45 9N 4 8 E
Ystad, Sweden 11 J7 55 26N 13 50 E
Ysyk-Köl, Kyrgyzstan 50 E8 42 25N 77 15 E
Ythan →, U.K. 14 D7 57 19N 1 59W
Ytterhogdal, Sweden 10 B8 62 12N 14 56 E
Ytyk-Kyuyel, Russia 51 C14 62 30N 133 45 E
Yu Jiang →, China 58 F7 23 22N 110 3 E
Yu Xian = Yuzhou, China 56 G7 34 10N 113 28 E
Yu Xian, Hebei, China 56 E8 39 50N 114 35 E
Yu Xian, Shanxi, China 56 E7 38 5N 113 20 E
Yuan Jiang →, Hunan, China 59 C8 28 55N 111 50 E
Yuan Jiang →, Yunnan, China 58 F4 22 20N 103 59 E
Yuan'an, China 59 B8 31 3N 111 34 E
Yuanjiang, Hunan, China 59 C9 28 47N 112 21 E
Yuanjiang, Yunnan, China 58 F4 23 32N 102 0 E
Yüanli, Taiwan 59 E13 24 27N 120 39 E
Yüanlin, Taiwan 59 F13 23 58N 120 30 E
Yuanling, China 59 C8 28 29N 110 22 E
Yuanmou, China 58 E3 25 42N 101 53 E
Yuanqu, China 56 G6 35 18N 111 40 E
Yuanyang, Henan, China 56 G7 35 3N 113 58 E
Yuanyang, Yunnan, China 58 F4 23 10N 102 43 E
Yuba →, U.S.A. 116 F5 39 8N 121 36W
Yuba City, U.S.A. 116 F5 39 8N 121 37W
Yūbari, Japan 54 C10 43 4N 141 59 E
Yubdo, Ethiopia 81 F4 8 58N 35 24 E
Yūbetsu, Japan 54 B11 44 13N 143 50 E
Yubo, Sudan 81 F2 5 23N 27 25 E
Yucatán □, Mexico 119 C7 21 30N 86 30W
Yucatán, Canal de, Caribbean 120 B2 22 0N 86 30W
Yucatán, Península de, Mexico 98 H11 19 30N 89 0W
Yucatán Basin, Cent. Amer. 98 H11 19 0N 86 0W
Yucatan Str. = Yucatán, Canal de, Caribbean 120 B2 22 0N 86 30W
Yucca, U.S.A. 117 L12 34 52N 114 9W
Yucca Valley, U.S.A. 117 L10 34 8N 116 27W
Yucheng, China 56 F9 36 55N 116 32 E
Yuci, China 56 F7 37 42N 112 46 E
Yudu, China 59 E10 25 59N 115 30 E
Yuechi, China 58 B6 30 34N 106 25 E
Yuendumu, Australia 92 D5 22 16 S 131 49 E
Yueqing, China 59 C13 28 9N 120 59 E
Yueqing Wan, China 59 D13 28 5N 121 20 E
Yuexi, Anhui, China 59 B11 30 50N 116 20 E
Yuexi, Sichuan, China 58 C4 28 37N 102 26 E
Yueyang, China 59 C9 29 21N 113 5 E
Yugan, China 59 C11 28 43N 116 37 E
Yugoslavia ■, Europe 40 C4 43 20N 20 0 E
Yuhuan, China 59 C13 28 9N 121 12 E
Yuhuan Dao, China 59 C13 28 5N 121 15 E
Yujiang, China 59 C11 28 10N 116 43 E
Yukhnov, Russia 46 E8 54 44N 35 15 E
Yukon →, U.S.A. 100 B3 62 32N 163 54W
Yukon Territory □, Canada 100 B6 63 0N 135 0W
Yüksekova, Turkey 73 D11 37 34N 44 16 E
Yukta, Russia 51 C11 63 26N 105 42 E
Yukuhashi, Japan 55 H5 33 44N 130 59 E
Yulara, Australia 93 E5 25 10 S 130 55 E
Yule →, Australia 92 D2 20 41 S 118 17 E
Yuleba, Australia 95 D4 26 37 S 149 24 E
Yuli, Nigeria 83 D7 9 44N 10 12 E
Yuli, Taiwan 59 F13 23 20N 121 18 E
Yulin, Guangxi Zhuangzu, China 59 F8 22 40N 110 8 E
Yülin, Hainan, China 65 C7 18 10N 109 31 E
Yulin, Shaanxi, China 56 E5 38 20N 109 30 E
Yuma, Ariz., U.S.A. 117 N12 32 43N 114 37W
Yuma, Colo., U.S.A. 112 E3 40 8N 102 43W
Yuma, B. de, Dom. Rep. 121 C6 18 20N 68 35W
Yumbe, Uganda 86 B3 3 28N 31 15 E
Yumbi, Dem. Rep. of the Congo 86 C2 1 12 S 26 15 E
Yumen, China 60 C4 39 50N 97 30 E
Yumurtalık, Turkey 72 D6 36 45N 35 43 E
Yun Gui Gaoyuan, China 58 E3 26 0N 104 0 E
Yun Ho →, China 57 E9 39 10N 117 10 E
Yun Ling, China 58 D2 27 0N 99 20 E
Yun Xian, Hubei, China 59 A8 32 50N 110 46 E
Yun Xian, Yunnan, China 58 E3 24 27N 100 8 E
Yuna, Australia 93 E2 28 20 S 115 0 E
Yunak, Turkey 72 C4 38 49N 31 43 E
Yunan, China 59 F8 23 12N 111 30 E
Yuncheng, Henan, China 56 G8 35 36N 115 57 E
Yuncheng, Shanxi, China 56 G6 35 2N 111 0 E
Yunfu, China 59 F9 22 50N 112 5 E
Yungas, Bolivia 124 G5 17 0 S 66 0W
Yungay, Chile 126 D1 37 10 S 72 5W
Yunhe, China 59 C12 28 8N 119 33 E
Yunkai Dashan, China 59 F8 22 30N 111 0 E
Yunlin, Taiwan 59 F13 23 42N 120 30 E
Yunlong, China 58 E2 25 57N 99 13 E
Yunmeng, China 59 B9 31 2N 113 43 E
Yunnan □, China 58 E4 25 0N 102 0 E
Yunquera de Henares, Spain 32 E1 40 47N 3 11W
Yunt Dağı, Turkey 39 C9 38 56N 27 13 E
Yunta, Australia 95 E2 32 35 S 139 36 E
Yunxi, China 56 H6 33 0N 110 22 E
Yunxiao, China 59 F11 23 59N 117 18 E
Yuping, China 58 D7 27 13N 108 56 E
Yupyongdong, N. Korea 57 D15 41 49N 128 53 E
Yuqing, China 58 D6 27 13N 107 53 E
Yurga, Russia 50 D9 55 42N 84 51 E
Yurimaguas, Peru 124 E3 5 55 S 76 7W
Yuryev-Polskiy, Russia 46 D10 56 30N 39 40 E
Yuryevets, Russia 48 B6 57 25N 43 2 E
Yuscarán, Honduras 120 D2 13 58N 86 45W
Yushan, China 59 C12 28 42N 118 10 E
Yushanzhen, China 58 C7 29 28N 108 22 E
Yushe, China 56 F7 37 4N 112 58 E
Yushu, Jilin, China 57 B14 44 43N 126 38 E
Yushu, Qinghai, China 60 C4 33 5N 96 55 E
Yusufeli, Turkey 73 B9 40 50N 41 33 E
Yutai, China 56 G9 35 0N 116 45 E
Yutian, China 57 E9 39 53N 117 45 E
Yuxarı Qarabağ = Nagorno-Karabakh, Azerbaijan 70 B5 39 55N 46 45 E
Yuxi, China 58 E4 24 30N 102 35 E
Yuyao, China 59 B13 30 3N 121 10 E
Yuzawa, Japan 54 E10 39 10N 140 30 E
Yuzha, Russia 48 B6 56 34N 42 1 E

Yuzhno-Sakhalinsk

Yuzhno-Sakhalinsk, Russia 51 E15 46 58N 142 45 E
Yuzhou, China 56 G7 34 10N 113 28 E
Yvelines □, France 19 D8 48 40N 1 45 E
Yverdon-les-Bains, Switz. 25 J2 46 47N 6 39 E
Yvetot, France 18 C7 49 37N 0 44 E
Yzeure, France 19 F10 46 33N 3 22 E

Z

Zaanstad, Neths. 17 B4 52 27N 4 50 E
Zāb al Kabīr →, Iraq 70 C4 36 1N 43 24 E
Zāb aş Şagīr →, Iraq 70 C4 35 17N 43 29 E
Žabalj, Serbia, Yug. 42 E5 45 21N 20 5 E
Žabari, Serbia, Yug. 40 B5 44 22N 21 15 E
Zabarjad, Egypt 80 C4 23 40N 36 12 E
Zabaykalsk, Russia 51 E12 49 40N 117 25 E
Zabki, Poland 45 F8 52 17N 21 7 E
Ząbkowice Śląskie, Poland 45 H3 50 35N 16 50 E
Žabljak, Montenegro, Yug. 40 C3 43 18N 19 5 E
Zabłudów, Poland 45 F9 53 0N 23 19 E
Żabno, Poland 45 H7 50 9N 20 53 E
Zābol, Iran 71 D9 31 0N 61 32 E
Zābol □, Afghan. 66 D5 32 0N 67 0 E
Zābolī, Iran 71 E9 27 10N 61 35 E
Zabré, Burkina Faso 83 C4 11 12N 0 36W
Zábřeh, Czech Rep. 27 B9 49 53N 16 52 E
Zabrze, Poland 45 H5 50 18N 18 50 E
Zabzuga, Ghana 83 D5 9 20N 0 30 E
Zacapa, Guatemala 120 D2 14 59N 89 31W
Zacapu, Mexico 118 D4 19 50N 101 43W
Zacatecas, Mexico 118 C4 22 49N 102 34W
Zacatecas □, Mexico 118 C4 23 30N 103 0W
Zacatecoluca, El Salv. 120 D2 13 29N 88 51W
Zachary, U.S.A. 113 K9 30 39N 91 9W
Zachodnio-Pomorskie □, Poland 44 E2 53 40N 15 50 E
Zacoalco, Mexico 118 C4 20 14N 103 33W
Zacualtipán, Mexico 119 C5 20 39N 98 36W
Zadar, Croatia 29 D12 44 8N 15 14 E
Zadawa, Nigeria 83 C7 11 33N 10 19 E
Zadetkyi Kyun, Burma 65 G1 10 0N 98 25 E
Zadonsk, Russia 47 G10 52 25N 38 56 E
Zafarqand, Iran 71 C7 33 11N 52 29 E
Zafora, Greece 39 E8 36 5N 26 24 E
Zafra, Spain 35 G4 38 26N 6 30W
Żagań, Poland 45 G2 51 39N 15 22 E
Zagaoua, Chad 79 E10 15 30N 22 24 E
Žagarė, Lithuania 44 B10 56 21N 23 15 E
Zagazig, Egypt 80 H7 30 40N 31 30 E
Zāgheh, Iran 71 C6 33 30N 48 42 E
Zaglivérion, Greece 40 F7 40 36N 23 15 E
Zagnanado, Benin 83 D5 7 18N 2 28 E
Zagorá, Greece 38 B5 39 27N 23 6 E
Zagorje, Slovenia 29 B11 46 8N 15 0 E
Zagórów, Poland 45 F4 52 10N 17 54 E
Zagorsk = Sergiyev Posad, Russia 46 D10 56 20N 38 10 E
Zagórz, Poland 45 J9 49 30N 22 14 E
Zagreb, Croatia 29 C12 45 50N 15 58 E
Zāgros, Kūhhā-ye, Iran 71 C6 33 45N 48 5 E
Zagros Mts. = Zāgros, Kūhhā-ye, Iran 71 C6 33 45N 48 5 E
Žagubica, Serbia, Yug. 40 B5 44 15N 21 47 E
Zaguinaso, Ivory C. 82 C3 10 1N 6 14W
Zagyva →, Hungary 42 C5 47 5N 20 4 E
Zāhedān, Fārs, Iran 71 D7 28 46N 53 52 E
Zāhedān, Sīstān va Balūchestān, Iran 71 D9 29 30N 60 50 E
Zahlah, Lebanon 75 B4 33 52N 35 50 E
Zahna, Germany 24 D8 51 55N 12 49 E
Záhony, Hungary 42 B7 48 25N 22 11 E
Zainsk, Russia 48 C11 55 18N 52 4 E
Zaïre = Congo →, Africa 84 F2 6 4 S 12 24 E
Zaječar, Serbia, Yug. 40 C6 43 53N 22 18 E
Zaka, Zimbabwe 89 C5 20 20 S 31 29 E
Zakamensk, Russia 51 D11 50 23N 103 17 E
Zakataly = Zaqatala, Azerbaijan 49 K8 41 38N 46 35 E
Zakháro, Greece 38 D3 37 30N 21 39 E
Zakhodnaya Dzvina = Daugava →, Latvia 9 H21 57 4N 24 3 E
Zākhū, Iraq 70 B4 37 10N 42 50 E
Zákinthos, Greece 38 D2 37 47N 20 57 E
Zákinthos □, Greece 38 D2 37 47N 20 57 E
Zakopane, Poland 45 J6 49 18N 19 57 E
Zakroczym, Poland 45 F7 52 26N 20 38 E
Zákros, Greece 36 D8 35 6N 26 10 E
Zala, Ethiopia 81 F4 6 28N 37 13 E
Zala □, Hungary 42 D1 46 42N 16 50 E
Zala →, Hungary 42 D2 46 43N 17 16 E
Zalaegerszeg, Hungary 42 D1 46 53N 16 47 E
Zalakomár, Hungary 42 D2 46 33N 17 10 E
Zalalövő, Hungary 42 D1 46 51N 16 35 E
Zalamea de la Serena, Spain 35 G5 38 40N 5 38W
Zalamea la Real, Spain 35 H4 37 41N 6 38W
Zalău, Romania 42 C8 47 12N 23 3 E
Žalec, Slovenia 29 B12 46 16N 15 10 E
Zaleshchiki = Zalishchyky, Ukraine 47 H3 48 45N 25 45 E
Zalew Wiślany, Poland 44 D6 54 20N 19 50 E
Zalewo, Poland 44 E6 53 50N 19 41 E
Zalingei, Sudan 79 F10 12 51N 23 29 E
Zalishchyky, Ukraine 47 H3 48 45N 25 45 E
Zama L., Canada 104 B5 58 45N 119 5W
Zambeke, Dem. Rep. of the Congo 86 B2 2 8N 25 17 E
Zambeze →, Africa 87 F4 18 35 S 36 20 E
Zambezi = Zambeze →, Africa 87 F4 18 35 S 36 20 E
Zambezi, Zambia 85 G4 13 30 S 23 8 E
Zambezia □, Mozam. 87 F4 16 15 S 37 30 E
Zambia ■, Africa 87 F2 15 0 S 28 0 E
Zamboanga, Phil. 61 H5 6 59N 122 3 E
Zambrów, Poland 45 F9 52 59N 22 14 E
Zametchino, Russia 48 D6 53 30N 42 30 E
Zamfara □, Nigeria 83 C6 12 10N 6 0 E
Zamfara →, Nigeria 83 C5 12 5N 4 2 E
Zamora, Mexico 118 D4 20 0N 102 21W
Zamora, Spain 34 D5 41 30N 5 45W
Zamora □, Spain 34 D5 41 30N 5 46W
Zamość, Poland 45 H10 50 43N 23 15 E
Zamtang, China 58 A3 32 26N 101 6 E
Zan, Ghana 83 D4 9 26N 0 17W
Záncara →, Spain 33 F1 39 18N 3 18W
Zandvoort, Neths. 17 B4 52 22N 4 32 E
Zanesville, U.S.A. 110 G2 39 56N 82 1W
Zangābād, Iran 70 B5 38 26N 46 44 E
Zangue →, Mozam. 87 F4 17 50 S 35 21 E
Zanjān, Iran 71 B6 36 40N 48 35 E
Zanjān □, Iran 71 B6 37 20N 49 30 E
Zanjān →, Iran 71 B6 37 8N 47 47 E
Zannone, Italy 30 B6 40 58N 13 3 E
Zante = Zákinthos, Greece 38 D2 37 47N 20 57 E
Zanthus, Australia 93 F3 31 2 S 123 34 E
Zanzibar, Tanzania 86 D4 6 12 S 39 12 E
Zaouiet El-Kala = Bordj Omar Driss, Algeria 78 C7 28 10N 6 40 E
Zaouiet Reggâne, Algeria 78 C6 26 32N 0 3 E
Zaoyang, China 59 A9 32 10N 112 45 E
Zaozhuang, China 57 G9 34 50N 117 35 E
Zap Suyu = Zāb al Kabīr →, Iraq 70 C4 36 1N 43 24 E
Zapadna Morava →, Serbia, Yug. 40 C5 43 38N 21 30 E
Zapadnaya Dvina = Daugava →, Latvia 9 H21 57 4N 24 3 E
Zapadnaya Dvina, Russia 46 D7 56 15N 32 3 E
Západné Beskydy, Europe 27 B12 49 30N 19 0 E
Zapadni Rodopi, Bulgaria 40 E7 41 50N 24 0 E
Zapala, Argentina 128 D2 39 0 S 70 5W
Zapaleri, Cerro, Bolivia 126 A2 22 49 S 67 11W
Zapata, U.S.A. 113 M5 26 55N 99 16W
Zapatón →, Spain 35 F4 39 0N 6 49W
Zaporizhzhya, Ukraine 47 J8 47 50N 35 10 E
Zaporozhye = Zaporizhzhya, Ukraine 47 J8 47 50N 35 10 E
Zaqatala, Azerbaijan 49 K8 41 38N 46 35 E
Zara, Turkey 70 B3 39 58N 37 43 E
Zaragoza, Coahuila, Mexico 118 B4 28 30N 101 0W
Zaragoza, Nuevo León, Mexico 119 C5 24 0N 99 46W
Zaragoza, Spain 32 D4 41 39N 0 53W
Zaragoza □, Spain 32 D4 41 35N 1 0W
Zarand, Kermān, Iran 71 D8 30 46N 56 34 E
Zarand, Markazī, Iran 71 C6 35 18N 50 25 E
Zărandului, Munţii, Romania 42 D7 46 14N 22 7 E
Zaranj, Afghan. 66 D2 30 55N 61 55 E
Zarasai, Lithuania 9 J22 55 40N 26 20 E
Zárate, Argentina 126 C4 34 7 S 59 0W
Zarautz, Spain 32 B2 43 17N 2 10W
Zaraysk, Russia 46 E10 54 48N 38 53 E
Zard, Kūh-e, Iran 71 C6 32 22N 50 4 E
Zāreh, Iran 71 C6 35 7N 49 9 E
Zari, Nigeria 83 C7 13 4N 12 45 E
Zaria, Nigeria 83 C6 11 0N 7 40 E
Żarki, Poland 45 H6 50 38N 19 23 E
Zárkon, Greece 38 B4 39 38N 22 6 E
Zarneh, Iran 70 C5 33 55N 46 10 E
Zărneşti, Romania 43 E10 45 33N 25 18 E
Zarós, Greece 36 D6 35 8N 24 54 E
Żarów, Poland 45 H3 50 56N 16 29 E
Zarqā', Nahr az →, Jordan 75 C4 32 10N 35 37 E
Zarrīn, Iran 71 C7 32 46N 54 37 E
Zaruma, Ecuador 124 D3 3 40 S 79 38W
Żary, Poland 45 G2 51 37N 15 10 E
Zarza de Granadilla, Spain 34 E4 40 14N 6 3W
Zarzis, Tunisia 79 B8 33 31N 11 2 E
Zas, Spain 34 B2 43 4N 8 53W
Zaskar →, India 69 B7 34 13N 77 20 E
Zaskar Mts., India 69 C7 33 15N 77 30 E
Zastron, S. Africa 88 E4 30 18 S 27 7 E
Žatec, Czech Rep. 26 A6 50 20N 13 32 E
Zaterechnyy, Russia 49 H7 44 48N 45 11 E
Zator, Poland 45 J6 49 59N 19 28 E
Zavala, Bos.-H. 40 D1 42 50N 17 59 E
Zavāreh, Iran 71 C7 33 29N 52 28 E
Zave, Zimbabwe 89 B5 17 6 S 30 1 E
Zavetnoye, Russia 49 G6 47 13N 43 50 E
Zavidovići, Bos.-H. 42 F3 44 27N 18 10 E
Zavitinsk, Russia 51 D13 50 10N 129 20 E
Zavodovski, I., Antarctica 5 B1 56 0 S 27 45W
Zavolzhsk, Russia 48 B6 57 30N 42 0 E
Zavolzhye, Russia 48 B6 56 37N 43 26 E
Zawadzkie, Poland 45 H5 50 37N 18 28 E
Zawichost, Poland 45 H8 50 48N 21 51 E
Zawidów, Poland 45 G2 51 1N 15 1 E
Zawiercie, Poland 45 H6 50 30N 19 24 E
Zāwiyat al Bayḍā = Al Bayḍā, Libya 79 B10 32 50N 21 44 E
Zâwyet Shammas, Egypt 80 A2 31 30N 26 37 E
Zâwyet Um el Rakham, Egypt 80 A2 31 18N 27 1 E
Zâwyet Ungeîla, Egypt 80 A2 31 23N 26 42 E
Zāyā, Iraq 70 C5 33 33N 44 13 E
Zāyandeh →, Iran 71 C7 32 35N 52 0 E
Zaysan, Kazakhstan 50 E9 47 28N 84 52 E
Zaysan, Oz., Kazakhstan 50 E9 48 0N 83 0 E
Zayü, China 58 C1 28 48N 97 27 E
Zazafotsy, Madag. 89 C8 21 11 S 46 21 E
Zázrivá, Slovak Rep. 27 B12 49 16N 19 7 E
Zbarazh, Ukraine 47 H3 49 43N 25 44 E
Zbąszyń, Poland 45 F2 52 14N 15 56 E
Zbąszynek, Poland 45 F2 52 16N 15 51 E
Zblewo, Poland 44 E5 53 56N 18 19 E
Žďár nad Sázavou, Czech Rep. 26 B8 49 34N 15 57 E
Zdolbuniv, Ukraine 47 G4 50 30N 26 15 E
Ždrelo, Serbia, Yug. 40 B5 44 16N 21 28 E
Zduńska Wola, Poland 45 G5 51 37N 18 59 E
Zduny, Poland 45 G4 51 39N 17 21 E
Zeballos, Canada 104 D3 49 59N 126 50W
Zebediela, S. Africa 89 C4 24 20 S 29 17 E
Zebila, Ghana 83 C4 10 55N 0 30W
Zeebrugge, Belgium 17 C3 51 19N 3 12 E
Zeehan, Australia 94 G4 41 52 S 145 25 E
Zeeland □, Neths. 17 C3 51 30N 3 50 E
Zeerust, S. Africa 88 D4 25 31 S 26 4 E
Ẓefat, Israel 75 C4 32 58N 35 29 E
Zege, Ethiopia 81 E4 11 43N 37 18 E
Zeggerene, Iracher, Mali 83 B5 16 49N 2 16 E
Zégoua, Mali 82 C3 10 32N 5 35W
Zehdenick, Germany 24 C9 52 58N 13 20 E
Zeil, Mt., Australia 92 D5 23 30 S 132 23 E
Zeila, Somali Rep. 74 E3 11 21N 43 30 E
Zeist, Neths. 17 B5 52 5N 5 15 E
Zeitz, Germany 24 D8 51 2N 12 7 E
Żelechów, Poland 45 G8 51 49N 21 54 E
Zelengora, Bos.-H. 40 C2 43 22N 18 30 E
Zelenodolsk, Russia 48 C9 55 55N 48 30 E
Zelenogorsk, Russia 46 B5 60 12N 29 43 E
Zelenograd, Russia 46 D9 56 1N 37 12 E
Zelenogradsk, Russia 9 J19 54 53N 20 29 E
Zelenokumsk, Russia 49 H6 44 24N 44 0 E
Železná Ruda, Czech Rep. 26 B6 49 8N 13 15 E
Železnik, Serbia, Yug. 40 B4 44 43N 20 23 E
Zelienople, U.S.A. 110 F4 40 48N 80 8W
Želiezovce, Slovak Rep. 27 C11 48 3N 18 40 E
Zelina, Croatia 29 C13 45 57N 16 16 E
Zell, Baden-W., Germany 25 H3 47 42N 7 52 E
Zell, Rhld-Pfz., Germany 25 E3 50 1N 7 10 E
Zell am See, Austria 26 D5 47 19N 12 47 E
Zella-Mehlis, Germany 24 E6 50 39N 10 40 E
Zelów, Poland 45 G6 51 28N 19 14 E
Zeltweg, Austria 26 D7 47 11N 14 45 E
Zémio, C.A.R. 86 A2 5 2N 25 5 E
Zempléni-hegység, Hungary 42 B6 48 25N 21 25 E
Zemplínska šírava, Slovak Rep. 27 C15 48 48N 22 0 E
Zemun, Serbia, Yug. 40 B4 44 51N 20 25 E
Zengbé, Cameroon 83 D7 5 46N 13 4 E
Zengcheng, China 59 F9 23 13N 113 52 E
Zenica, Bos.-H. 42 F2 44 10N 17 57 E
Žepče, Bos.-H. 42 F3 44 28N 18 2 E
Zeraf, Bahr ez →, Sudan 81 F3 9 42N 30 52 E
Zerbst, Germany 24 D8 51 58N 12 5 E
Żerków, Poland 45 F4 52 4N 17 32 E
Zermatt, Switz. 25 J3 46 2N 7 46 E
Zernez, Switz. 25 J6 46 42N 10 7 E
Zernograd, Russia 49 G5 46 52N 40 19 E
Zerqan, Albania 40 E4 41 27N 20 20 E
Zestaponi, Georgia 49 J6 42 6N 43 0 E
Zetel, Germany 24 B3 53 25N 7 58 E
Zeulenroda, Germany 24 E7 50 39N 11 59 E
Zeven, Germany 24 B5 53 17N 9 16 E
Zevenaar, Neths. 17 C6 51 56N 6 5 E
Zévio, Italy 28 C8 45 22N 11 8 E
Zeya, Russia 51 D13 53 48N 127 14 E
Zeya →, Russia 51 D13 51 42N 128 53 E
Zeytinbaği, Turkey 41 F12 40 24N 28 47 E
Zeytindağ, Turkey 39 C9 38 58N 27 4 E
Zghartā, Lebanon 75 A4 34 21N 35 53 E
Zgierz, Poland 45 G6 51 50N 19 27 E
Zgorzelec, Poland 45 G2 51 10N 15 0 E
Zguriţa, Moldova 43 B13 48 8N 28 1 E
Zhabinka, Belarus 47 F3 52 13N 24 2 E
Zhailma, Kazakhstan 50 D7 51 37N 61 33 E
Zhambyl = Taraz, Kazakhstan 50 E8 42 54N 71 22 E
Zhangaly, Kazakhstan 49 G10 47 1N 50 37 E
Zhangaqazaly, Kazakhstan 50 E7 45 48N 62 6 E
Zhangbei, China 56 D8 41 10N 114 45 E
Zhangguangcai Ling, China 57 B15 45 0N 129 0 E
Zhangjiakou, China 56 D8 40 48N 114 55 E
Zhangping, China 59 E11 25 17N 117 23 E
Zhangpu, China 59 E11 24 8N 117 35 E
Zhangshu, China 59 C10 28 4N 115 29 E
Zhangwu, China 57 C12 42 43N 123 52 E
Zhangye, China 60 C5 38 50N 100 23 E
Zhangzhou, China 59 E11 24 30N 117 35 E
Zhanhua, China 57 F10 37 40N 118 8 E
Zhanjiang, China 59 G8 21 15N 110 20 E
Zhannetty, Ostrov, Russia 51 B16 76 43N 158 0 E
Zhanyi, China 58 E4 25 38N 103 48 E
Zhanyu, China 57 B12 44 30N 122 30 E
Zhao Xian, China 56 F8 37 43N 114 45 E
Zhao'an, China 59 F11 23 41N 117 10 E
Zhaocheng, China 56 F6 36 22N 111 38 E
Zhaojue, China 58 C4 28 1N 102 49 E
Zhaoping, China 59 E8 24 11N 110 48 E
Zhaoqing, China 59 F9 23 0N 112 20 E
Zhaotong, China 58 D4 27 20N 103 44 E
Zhaoyuan, Heilongjiang, China 57 B13 45 27N 125 0 E
Zhaoyuan, Shandong, China 57 F11 37 20N 120 23 E
Zharkovskiy, Russia 46 E7 55 56N 32 19 E
Zhashkiv, Ukraine 47 H6 49 15N 30 5 E
Zhashui, China 56 H5 33 40N 109 8 E
Zhayyq →, Kazakhstan 50 E6 47 0N 51 48 E
Zhdanov = Mariupol, Ukraine 47 J9 47 5N 37 31 E
Zhecheng, China 56 G8 34 7N 115 20 E
Zhegao, China 59 B11 31 46N 117 45 E
Zhejiang □, China 59 C13 29 0N 120 0 E
Zheleznogorsk, Russia 47 F8 52 22N 35 23 E
Zheleznogorsk-Ilimskiy, Russia 51 D11 56 34N 104 8 E
Zheltyye Vody = Zhovti Vody, Ukraine 47 H7 48 21N 33 31 E
Zhen'an, China 56 H5 33 27N 109 9 E
Zhenba, China 58 A6 32 34N 107 58 E
Zhenfeng, China 58 E5 25 22N 105 40 E
Zheng'an, China 58 C6 28 32N 107 27 E
Zhengding, China 56 E8 38 8N 114 32 E
Zhenghe, China 59 D12 27 20N 118 50 E
Zhengyang, China 59 A10 32 37N 114 22 E
Zhengyangguan, China 59 A11 32 30N 116 29 E
Zhengzhou, China 56 G7 34 45N 113 34 E
Zhenhai, China 59 C13 29 59N 121 42 E
Zhenjiang, China 59 A12 32 11N 119 26 E
Zhenkang, China 58 F2 23 58N 99 0 E
Zhenlai, China 57 B12 45 50N 123 5 E
Zhenning, China 58 D5 26 4N 105 45 E
Zhenping, Henan, China 56 H7 33 10N 112 16 E
Zhenping, Shaanxi, China 58 B7 31 59N 109 31 E
Zhenxiong, China 58 D5 27 27N 104 50 E
Zhenyuan, Gansu, China 56 G4 35 35N 107 30 E
Zhenyuan, Guizhou, China 58 D7 27 4N 108 21 E
Zherdevka, Russia 48 E5 51 56N 41 29 E
Zherong, China 59 D12 27 15N 119 52 E
Zhetiqara, Kazakhstan 50 D7 52 11N 61 12 E
Zhezqazghan, Kazakhstan 50 E7 47 44N 67 40 E
Zhicheng, China 59 B8 30 25N 111 27 E
Zhidan, China 56 F5 36 48N 108 48 E
Zhigansk, Russia 51 C13 66 48N 123 27 E
Zhigulevsk, Russia 48 D9 53 28N 49 30 E
Zhijiang, Hubei, China 59 B8 30 28N 111 45 E
Zhijiang, Hunan, China 58 D7 27 27N 109 42 E
Zhijin, China 58 D5 26 37N 105 45 E
Zhilinda, Russia 51 C12 70 0N 114 20 E
Zhirnovsk, Russia 48 E7 50 57N 44 49 E
Zhitomir = Zhytomyr, Ukraine 47 G5 50 20N 28 40 E
Zhizdra, Russia 46 F8 53 45N 34 40 E
Zhlobin, Belarus 47 F6 52 55N 30 0 E
Zhmerinka = Zhmerynka, Ukraine 47 H5 49 2N 28 2 E
Zhmerynka, Ukraine 47 H5 49 2N 28 2 E
Zhob, Pakistan 68 D3 31 20N 69 31 E
Zhob →, Pakistan 68 C3 32 4N 69 50 E
Zhodino = Zhodzina, Belarus 46 E5 54 5N 28 17 E
Zhodzina, Belarus 46 E5 54 5N 28 17 E
Zhokhova, Ostrov, Russia 51 B16 76 4N 152 40 E
Zhongdian, China 58 D2 27 48N 99 42 E
Zhongdong, China 58 F6 22 48N 107 47 E
Zhongdu, China 58 E7 24 40N 109 40 E
Zhongning, China 56 F3 37 29N 105 40 E
Zhongshan, Guangdong, China 59 F9 22 26N 113 20 E
Zhongshan, Guangxi Zhuangzu, China 59 E8 24 29N 111 18 E
Zhongtiao Shan, China 56 G6 35 0N 111 10 E
Zhongwei, China 56 F3 37 30N 105 12 E
Zhongxiang, China 59 B9 31 12N 112 34 E
Zhongyang, China 56 F6 37 20N 111 11 E
Zhoucun, China 57 F9 36 47N 117 48 E
Zhouning, China 59 D12 27 12N 119 20 E
Zhoushan, China 59 B14 30 1N 122 6 E
Zhoushan Dao, China 59 C14 30 5N 122 10 E
Zhouzhi, China 56 G5 34 10N 108 12 E
Zhovti Vody, Ukraine 47 H7 48 21N 33 31 E
Zhovtneve, Ukraine 47 J7 46 54N 32 3 E
Zhovtnevoye = Zhovtneve, Ukraine 47 J7 46 54N 32 3 E
Zhu Jiang →, China 59 F9 22 45N 113 37 E
Zhuanghe, China 57 E12 39 40N 123 0 E
Zhucheng, China 57 G10 36 0N 119 27 E
Zhugqu, China 56 H3 33 40N 104 30 E
Zhuhai, China 59 F9 22 15N 113 30 E
Zhuji, China 59 C13 29 40N 120 10 E
Zhukovka, Russia 46 F7 53 35N 33 50 E
Zhumadian, China 56 H8 32 59N 114 2 E
Zhuo Xian = Zhuozhou, China 56 E8 39 28N 115 58 E
Zhuolu, China 56 D8 40 20N 115 12 E
Zhuozhou, China 56 E8 39 28N 115 58 E
Zhuozi, China 56 D7 41 0N 112 25 E
Zhushan, China 59 A8 32 15N 110 13 E
Zhuxi, China 58 A7 32 25N 109 40 E
Zhuzhou, China 59 D9 27 49N 113 12 E
Zhytomyr, Ukraine 47 G5 50 20N 28 40 E
Zi Shui →, China 59 C9 28 40N 112 40 E
Žiar nad Hronom, Slovak Rep. 27 C11 48 35N 18 53 E
Zīārān, Iran 71 B6 36 7N 50 32 E
Ziarat, Pakistan 68 D2 30 25N 67 49 E
Zibo, China 57 F10 36 47N 118 3 E
Zichang, China 56 F5 37 18N 109 40 E
Zidarovo, Bulgaria 41 D11 42 20N 27 24 E
Ziębice, Poland 45 H4 50 37N 17 2 E
Zielona Góra, Poland 45 G2 51 57N 15 31 E
Zierikzee, Neths. 17 C3 51 40N 3 55 E
Ziesar, Germany 24 C8 52 16N 12 17 E
Zifta, Egypt 80 H7 30 43N 31 14 E
Zigey, Chad 79 F9 14 43N 15 50 E
Zigong, China 58 C5 29 15N 104 48 E
Ziguinchor, Senegal 82 C1 12 35N 16 20W
Zihuatanejo, Mexico 118 D4 17 38N 101 33W
Zijin, China 59 F10 23 33N 115 8 E
Zile, Turkey 72 B6 40 15N 35 52 E
Žilina, Slovak Rep. 27 B11 49 12N 18 42 E
Žilinský □, Slovak Rep. 27 B12 49 10N 19 0 E
Zillah, Libya 79 C9 28 30N 17 33 E
Zillertaler Alpen, Austria 26 D4 47 6N 11 45 E
Zima, Russia 51 D11 54 0N 102 5 E
Zimapán, Mexico 119 C5 20 54N 99 20W
Zimba, Zambia 87 F2 17 20 S 26 11 E
Zimbabwe, Zimbabwe 87 G3 20 16 S 30 54 E
Zimbabwe ■, Africa 87 F3 19 0 S 30 0 E
Zimi, S. Leone 82 D2 7 20N 11 20W
Zimnicea, Romania 43 G10 43 40N 25 22 E
Zimovniki, Russia 49 G6 47 10N 42 25 E
Zinder, Niger 83 C6 13 48N 9 0 E
Zinga, Tanzania 87 D4 9 16 S 38 49 E
Zingst, Germany 24 A8 54 26N 12 39 E
Ziniaré, Burkina Faso 83 C4 12 35N 1 18W
Zinnowitz, Germany 24 A9 54 4N 13 54 E
Zion National Park, U.S.A. 115 H7 37 15N 113 5W
Zirbitzkogel, Austria 26 D7 47 4N 14 34 E
Zirc, Hungary 42 C2 47 17N 17 52 E
Žiri, Slovenia 29 B11 46 5N 14 5 E
Žirje, Croatia 29 E12 43 39N 15 42 E
Zirl, Austria 26 D4 47 17N 11 14 E
Zirndorf, Germany 25 F6 49 27N 10 57 E
Ziros, Greece 36 D8 35 5N 26 8 E
Zirreh, Gowd-e, Afghan. 66 E3 29 45N 62 0 E
Zisterdorf, Austria 27 C9 48 33N 16 45 E
Zitácuaro, Mexico 118 D4 19 28N 100 21W
Žitava →, Slovak Rep. 27 C11 48 14N 18 21 E
Žitište, Serbia, Yug. 42 E5 45 30N 20 32 E
Zitong, China 58 B5 31 37N 105 10 E
Zítsa, Greece 38 B2 39 47N 20 40 E
Zittau, Germany 24 E10 50 53N 14 48 E
Zitundo, Mozam. 89 D5 26 48 S 32 47 E
Živinice, Bos.-H. 42 F3 44 27N 18 36 E
Ziwa Maghariba □, Tanzania 86 C3 2 0 S 31 30 E
Ziway, L., Ethiopia 81 F4 8 0N 38 50 E
Zixi, China 59 D11 27 45N 117 4 E
Zixing, China 59 E9 25 59N 113 21 E
Ziyang, Shaanxi, China 56 H5 32 32N 108 31 E
Ziyang, Sichuan, China 58 B5 30 6N 104 40 E
Ziyuan, China 59 D8 26 2N 110 40 E
Ziyun, China 58 E6 25 45N 106 5 E
Zizhong, China 58 C5 29 48N 104 47 E
Zlarin, Croatia 29 E12 43 42N 15 49 E
Zlatar, Croatia 29 B13 46 5N 16 3 E
Zlatar, Serbia, Yug. 40 C3 43 25N 19 47 E
Zlataritsa, Bulgaria 41 C9 43 2N 25 55 E
Zlaté Moravce, Slovak Rep. 27 C11 48 23N 18 24 E
Zlatibor, Serbia, Yug. 40 C3 43 45N 19 43 E
Zlatitsa, Bulgaria 41 D8 42 41N 24 7 E
Zlatna, Romania 43 D8 46 8N 23 11 E
Zlatna Panega, Bulgaria 41 C8 43 5N 24 9 E
Zlatni Pyasŭtsi, Bulgaria 41 C12 43 17N 28 3 E
Zlatograd, Bulgaria 41 E9 41 22N 25 7 E
Zlatoust, Russia 50 D6 55 10N 59 40 E
Zletovo, Macedonia 40 E6 41 59N 22 17 E
Zlín, Czech Rep. 27 B10 49 14N 17 40 E
Zlínský □, Czech Rep. 27 B10 49 20N 17 40 E
Złocieniec, Poland 44 E3 53 30N 16 1 E
Złoczew, Poland 45 G5 51 24N 18 35 E
Zlot, Serbia, Yug. 40 B5 44 1N 21 58 E
Złotoryja, Poland 45 G2 51 8N 15 55 E
Złotów, Poland 44 E4 53 22N 17 2 E
Zmeinogorsk, Kazakhstan 50 D9 51 10N 82 13 E
Żmigród, Poland 45 G3 51 28N 16 53 E
Zmiyev, Ukraine 47 H9 49 39N 36 27 E
Znamenka = Znamyanka, Ukraine 47 H7 48 45N 32 30 E
Znamyanka, Ukraine 47 H7 48 45N 32 30 E
Żnin, Poland 45 F4 52 51N 17 44 E
Znojmo, Czech Rep. 26 C9 48 50N 16 2 E
Zobeyrī, Iran 70 C5 34 10N 46 40 E
Zobia, Dem. Rep. of the Congo 86 B2 3 0N 25 59 E
Zoetermeer, Neths. 17 B4 52 3N 4 30 E
Zogang, China 58 C1 29 55N 97 42 E
Zogno, Italy 28 C6 45 48N 9 40 E
Zogqên, China 58 A2 32 13N 98 47 E
Zolochev = Zolochiv, Ukraine 47 H3 49 45N 24 51 E
Zolochiv, Ukraine 47 H3 49 45N 24 51 E
Zolotonosha, Ukraine 47 H7 49 39N 32 5 E
Zomba, Malawi 87 F4 15 22 S 35 19 E
Zongo, Dem. Rep. of the Congo 84 D3 4 20N 18 35 E
Zonguldak, Turkey 72 B4 41 28N 31 50 E
Zongyang, China 59 B11 30 42N 117 12 E
Zonqor Pt., Malta 36 D2 35 51N 14 34 E
Zonza, France 21 G13 41 45N 9 11 E
Zorgo, Burkina Faso 83 C4 12 15N 0 35W
Zorita, Spain 35 F5 39 17N 5 39W
Zorleni, Romania 43 D12 46 14N 27 44 E
Zornitsa, Bulgaria 41 D10 42 23N 26 58 E
Zorritos, Peru 124 D2 3 43 S 80 40W
Żory, Poland 45 H5 50 3N 18 44 E
Zorzor, Liberia 82 D3 7 46N 9 28W
Zossen, Germany 24 C9 52 13N 13 27 E
Zou Xiang, China 56 G9 35 30N 116 58 E
Zouan-Hounien, Ivory C. 82 D3 6 55N 8 15W
Zouar, Chad 79 D9 20 30N 16 32 E
Zouérate = Zouîrât, Mauritania 78 D3 22 44N 12 21W
Zouîrât, Mauritania 78 D3 22 44N 12 21W
Zourika, Niger 83 B6 19 15N 7 50 E
Zourma, Burkina Faso 83 C4 11 20N 0 50W
Zoushan Dao, China 59 B14 30 5N 122 10 E
Zoutkamp, Neths. 17 A6 53 20N 6 18 E
Zrenjanin, Serbia, Yug. 42 E5 45 22N 20 23 E
Zuarungu, Ghana 83 C4 10 49N 0 46W
Zuba, Nigeria 83 D6 9 11N 7 12 E
Zubayr, Yemen 81 D5 15 3N 42 10 E
Zubtsov, Russia 46 D8 56 10N 34 34 E
Zuénoula, Ivory C. 82 D3 7 34N 6 3W
Zuera, Spain 32 D4 41 51N 0 49W
Ẓufār, Oman 74 D5 17 40N 54 0 E
Zug □, Switz. 25 H4 47 9N 8 35 E
Zugdidi, Georgia 49 J5 42 30N 41 55 E
Zugersee, Switz. 25 H4 47 7N 8 35 E
Zugspitze, Germany 25 H6 47 25N 10 59 E
Zuid-Holland □, Neths. 17 C4 52 0N 4 35 E
Zuidbeveland, Neths. 17 C3 51 30N 3 50 E
Zuidhorn, Neths. 17 A6 53 15N 6 23 E
Zújar, Spain 35 H8 37 34N 2 50W
Zújar →, Spain 35 G5 39 1N 5 47W
Żukowo, Poland 44 D5 54 21N 18 22 E
Zula, Eritrea 81 D4 15 17N 39 40 E
Zülpich, Germany 24 E2 50 41N 6 39 E
Zumaia, Spain 32 B2 43 19N 2 15W
Zumárraga, Spain 32 B2 43 5N 2 19W
Zumbo, Mozam. 87 F3 15 35 S 30 26 E
Zummo, Nigeria 83 D7 9 51N 12 59 E
Zumpango, Mexico 119 D5 19 48N 99 6W
Zungeru, Nigeria 83 D6 9 48N 6 8 E
Zunhua, China 57 D9 40 18N 117 58 E
Zuni, U.S.A. 115 J9 35 4N 108 51W
Zunyi, China 58 D6 27 42N 106 53 E
Zuo Jiang →, China 58 F6 22 50N 108 6 E
Zuozhou, China 58 F6 22 42N 107 27 E
Županja, Croatia 42 E3 45 4N 18 43 E
Žur, Kosovo, Yug. 40 D4 42 13N 20 34 E
Zurbātīyah, Iraq 70 C5 33 9N 46 3 E
Zürich, Switz. 25 H4 47 22N 8 32 E
Zürich □, Switz. 25 H4 47 26N 8 40 E
Zürichsee, Switz. 25 H4 47 18N 8 40 E
Żuromin, Poland 45 E6 53 4N 19 51 E
Žut, Croatia 29 E12 43 52N 15 17 E
Zutphen, Neths. 17 B6 52 9N 6 12 E
Zuwārah, Libya 79 B8 32 58N 12 1 E
Zūzan, Iran 71 C8 34 22N 59 53 E
Žužemberk, Slovenia 29 C11 45 52N 14 56 E
Zvenigorodka = Zvenyhorodka, Ukraine 47 H6 49 4N 30 56 E
Zvenyhorodka, Ukraine 47 H6 49 4N 30 56 E
Zverinogolovskoye, Russia 50 D7 54 26N 64 50 E
Zvezdets, Bulgaria 41 D11 42 6N 27 26 E
Zvishavane, Zimbabwe 87 G3 20 17 S 30 2 E
Zvolen, Slovak Rep. 27 C12 48 33N 19 10 E
Zvonce, Serbia, Yug. 40 D6 42 57N 22 34 E
Zvornik, Bos.-H. 42 F4 44 26N 19 5 E
Zwedru = Tchien, Liberia 82 D3 5 59N 8 15W
Zweibrücken, Germany 25 F3 49 15N 7 21 E
Zwenkau, Germany 24 D8 51 13N 12 20 E
Zwettl, Austria 26 C8 48 35N 15 9 E
Zwickau, Germany 24 E8 50 44N 12 30 E
Zwierzyniec, Poland 45 H9 50 36N 22 58 E
Zwiesel, Germany 25 F9 49 1N 13 13 E
Zwoleń, Poland 45 G8 51 21N 21 36 E
Zwolle, Neths. 17 B6 52 31N 6 6 E
Zwolle, U.S.A. 113 K8 31 38N 93 39W
Żychlin, Poland 45 F6 52 15N 19 37 E
Żyrardów, Poland 45 F7 52 3N 20 28 E
Zyryan, Kazakhstan 50 E9 49 43N 84 20 E
Zyryanka, Russia 51 C16 65 45N 150 51 E
Zyryanovsk = Zyryan, Kazakhstan 50 E9 49 43N 84 20 E
Żywiec, Poland 45 J6 49 42N 19 10 E
Zyyi, Cyprus 36 E12 34 43N 33 20 E

AFGHANISTAN	ALBANIA	ALGERIA	ANDORRA	ANGOLA	ANTIGUA & BARBUDA	ARGENTINA
BARBADOS	BELARUS	BELGIUM	BELIZE	BENIN	BHUTAN	BOLIVIA
BURUNDI	CAMBODIA	CAMEROON	CANADA	CAPE VERDE	CENTRAL AFRICAN REP.	CHAD
CROATIA	CUBA	CYPRUS	CZECH REPUBLIC	DENMARK	DJIBOUTI	DOMINICA
ETHIOPIA	FAROE ISLANDS	FIJI	FINLAND	FRANCE	GABON	GAMBIA
GUINEA	GUINEA-BISSAU	GUYANA	HAITI	HONDURAS	HONG KONG	HUNGARY
ITALY	IVORY COAST	JAMAICA	JAPAN	JORDAN	KAZAKSTAN	KENYA
LEBANON	LESOTHO	LIBERIA	LIBYA	LIECHTENSTEIN	LITHUANIA	LUXEMBOURG
MALTA	MAURITANIA	MAURITIUS	MEXICO	MICRONESIA	MOLDOVA	MONACO
NEW ZEALAND	NICARAGUA	NIGER	NIGERIA	NORTHERN MARIANAS	NORWAY	OMAN
PORTUGAL	PUERTO RICO	QATAR	ROMANIA	RUSSIA	RWANDA	SAMOA
SLOVAK REPUBLIC	SLOVENIA	SOLOMON ISLANDS	SOMALIA	SOUTH AFRICA	SPAIN	SRI LANKA
SWITZERLAND	SYRIA	TAIWAN	TAJIKISTAN	TANZANIA	THAILAND	TOGO
UKRAINE	UNITED ARAB EMIRATES	UNITED KINGDOM	UNITED STATES	URUGUAY	UZBEKISTAN	VANUATU